The Oxford Dictionary of

Dance

Debra Craine has been Chief Dance Critic of *The Times* since 1994. She has studied ballet, modern dance, jazz, and dance notation. Debra has contributed to several leading reference books on dance including *The International Dictionary of Ballet* (1993) and has also worked as a theatre critic. She has been writing about dance for more than thirty years for publications in Great Britain and North America, and has appeared many times on radio as a dance critic.

Judith Mackrell has been Dance Critic of the *Guardian* since 1994. She studied English and Philosophy at the University of York and the University of Oxford. From 1981–86, she was a part-time lecturer in English and Dance at the University of Oxford, Oxford Polytechnic, and the Roehampton Institute, and has been a freelance dance writer and arts broadcaster since 1986, writing as dance critic of the *Independent* between 1986 and 1994. Judith was made an Honorary Fellow of the Laban Centre for Dance in 1995. Her previous books include *Out of Line* (1992), *Reading Dance* (1997), *Life in Dance: Darcey Bussell* (1998) and *Bloomsbury Ballerina: A Life of Lydia Lopokova* (2008).

⊕ SEE WEB LINKS

Many entries in this dictionary have recommended web links. When you see the above symbol at the end of an entry go to the dictionary's web page at www.oup.com/uk/reference/resources/dance, click on **Web links** in the Resources section and locate the entry in the alphabetical list, then click straight through to the relevant websites.

Oxford Paperback Reference

The most authoritative and up-to-date reference books for both students and the general reader.

forthcoming

The Oxford Dictionary of
Dance

SECOND EDITION

DEBRA CRAINE
JUDITH MACKRELL

OXFORD
UNIVERSITY PRESS

OXFORD
UNIVERSITY PRESS

Great Clarendon Street, Oxford OX2 6DP

Oxford University Press is a department of the University of Oxford.
It furthers the University's objective of excellence in research, scholarship,
and education by publishing worldwide in

Oxford New York

Auckland Cape Town Dar es Salaam Hong Kong Karachi
Kuala Lumpur Madrid Melbourne Mexico City Nairobi
New Delhi Shanghai Taipei Toronto

With offices in
Argentina Austria Brazil Chile Czech Republic France Greece
Guatemala Hungary Italy Japan Poland Portugal Singapore
South Korea Switzerland Thailand Turkey Ukraine Vietnam

Oxford is a registered trade mark of Oxford University Press
in the UK and in certain other countries

Published in the United States
by Oxford University Press Inc., New York

British Library Cataloguing in Publication Data

Data available

Library of Congress Cataloging in Publication Data

Data available

Library of Congress Control Number: 2010930321

ISBN-13: 978–0–19–956344–9

Typeset by SPI Publisher Services, Pondicherry, India
Printed in Great Britain by Clays Ltd., St Ives plc

Preface

This new edition of the *Oxford Dictionary of Dance* has been updated to reflect the rapid changes in dance during the past decade. Within classical ballet, new research and reconstruction continue to expand our knowledge of historic repertory even as new choreographers continue to find unexpected possibilities within the classical aesthetic. Modern dance, which has migrated far beyond its origins in North America and Europe, has been emerging as a dominant form in China, Africa and even the Middle East. Hip hop, for decades a dance of the inner city streets, has moved centre stage, its influence felt in jazz, contemporary, and classical dance. And the post modern legacy of mixing and merging dance cultures continues with ever surprising results—the Belgian-Moroccan choreographer Sidi Larbi Cherkaoui has collaborated with the monks of the Shaolin Temple; Austrian video artist Klaus Obermaier has worked with the dancer Julia Mach to create a 3D setting of Stravinsky's *Rite of Spring*.

One of the most significant changes, reflected in this new edition, is the emergence of the internet as a resource for dance. From rare footage of Anna Pavlova to the latest street dance virtuoso in Korea it is possible to see an astonishing range of performance and practice online. Many companies and individuals have websites that link to video footage of their work, and with new techniques of streaming live performance, dance can be experienced in ways that were undreamed of when we compiled our first edition of this dictionary.

Even so, the focus of the entries remains theatrical; and as with previous editions, limitations of space inevitably force us to highlight dancers, choreographers, and dance works that have been most prominent on the international stage. Certain areas beyond the mainstream—the anthropological as well as the most newly experimental—have been largely excluded.

Most entries have also been kept to a factual minimum, although major individuals, institutions, works, etc. receive a more discursive treatment, and we have included lengthy work lists for a very few artists. Pressure of space has limited the number of these, but reference books are included in our bibliography where comprehensive lists may be found. We have dropped bibliographies for individual entries, due to the unwieldy volume of material available, but leading magazines, biographies, and critical works are included in the bibliography, as well as all the standard reference works which we consulted in the writing of this dictionary. A significant new feature is the inclusion of web links to useful sites.

We have included a small number of themed entries on topics such as *shoes*, *film*, and *dance notation*, also on more diversionary topics such as *sport* and *fashion*. Although these do not aim to be comprehensive, we hope they offer interesting complementary background to the standard entries.

Ease of reading has been an important consideration, so we have kept abbreviations to a minimum. A list of those employed appears at the front of the book. Asterisks have been used (with discretion) to direct readers to other relevant entries. Names of companies, works, and artists have been anglicized except where this goes against conventional usage. In the controversial area of Russian transliteration we have adopted Oxford's own style but indicated variant spellings. In the equally controversial matter of Russian dates we have, where possible, adopted the new calendar. Many dance companies have complex histories, involving several changes of name (most notoriously the diaspora of Ballets Russes companies). We have aimed to clarify these changes and again indicated variant usage. In response to recent changes in the world map, we have generally opted to retain older place-names where appropriate to the period, updating only for recent entries. For certain entries, birth dates have proved unforthcoming. Dance is a youth-oriented profession and some artists remain sensitive about their age.

In compiling this dictionary we have been given more than generous help by David Leonard and all at Dance Books; also by Allen Robertson, Matt Wolf, Betsy Gregory, Donald Hutera, Mary Clarke, Elizabeth Souritz, George Dorris, and Leo Kersley; by the many company press offices around the world who have provided us with so much information; and by our editors and proofreaders at OUP. Thanks also are owed to Lisa C. Arkin for supplying information for some of the definitions. Responsibility for errors and omissions, of course, remains our own and we would be very grateful to any readers who can draw them to our attention.

Abbreviations

arr.	arranged by
attrib.	attributed to
chor.	choreographed by
des.	design(s) by
dir.	directed by
mus.	music by
orch.	orchestrated by
orig.	originally
perf.	performance by
prod.	produced by
Dan.	Danish
Eng.	English
Fr.	French
Ger.	German
Gk.	Greek
Heb.	Hebrew
Hung.	Hungarian
It.	Italian
Russ.	Russian
Sp.	Spanish
Sw.	Swedish

Abraxas Ballet in five scenes with choreography by Luipart, libretto and music by Werner Egk, and design by Wolfgang Znamenacek. Premiered 6 Jun. 1948 by the Bavarian State Opera, Prinzregenten Theatre, Munich, with Luipart, Irina Kladivova, and Schwarz. The plot is based on *Heine's libretto *Der Doctor Faust* (1847, written for Benjamin *Lumley but never staged) in which Faust makes a pact with a female devil, gaining youth and sexual gratification in exchange for his soul. His subsequent discovery of true love (with Marguerite) prompts him to tear up the pact, thereby causing both their deaths. The ballet was banned after five performances due to its 'satanic' content, but a second version re-choreographed by Charrat (1949) became one of the most popular ballets in the German repertoire. T. Schilling's staging (Dresden, 1957, revived Komische Oper) enjoyed similar success. (The title, *Abraxas*, refers to the central mystery of the Gnostics.)

abstract dance A term loosely used to describe dance works without plot or character, though it has been argued that no dance can be entirely abstract given that movement is performed by men and women and must evoke some human content. Many dance works with no ostensible storyline suggest powerful images to their viewers, for example, Cunningham's *Winterbranch* or Ashton's *Symphonic Variations*.

abstrakter Tanz Term used by *Schlemmer to describe the dance aesthetic he developed at the Bauhaus, Weimar, during the mid-1920s. Dancers dressed in elaborate, disguising costumes were choreographed to create the effect of colours and geometric forms moving in space, rather than to portray individuals or relationships.

academic dance A term loosely synonymous with classical ballet, i.e. the theatre dance which evolved from the court ballets of the 16th and 17th centuries and which was refined through the national schools of France, Italy, and Russia. Its steps, positions, and movements are codified in the danse d'école which is still taught in the daily class taken by all classical dancers.

Académie de Musique et de Poésie, L' Institution founded in Paris in 1570 by Charles IX to foster the love and study of arts.

Académie Royale de Danse, L' The first dance institution established in the Western world, founded in Paris in 1661 by Louis XIV. He gave thirteen dancing masters the task of establishing standards of perfection for the art of dance. This group met regularly (often at the tavern L'Epée de Bois) with the brief to codify existing court and character dances, as well as to subject private and public dance teachers to examination. Those who passed were given the diplomas necessary to practise their profession and appointed Académicien de l'Art de la Danse. Noverre attacked the Academy for having published no treatise on dance theory or technique, though he joined its ranks in 1775. After the fall of the monarchy in 1789 it was closed down, though was briefly revived (1856–66) under the title Société Académie de Professeurs-Artistes du Théâtre de l'Opéra, with the prime concern of teaching ballroom dances.

Académie Royale de Musique, L' The official name given to the Paris Opera in 1671. Its original name was L'Académie d'Opéra, given by its founders Abbé Perrin and the Marquis de Sourdéac in 1669. It was changed two years later with the first production of *Pomone* (19 Mar. 1671), a mixture of opera, ballet, and pastoral (mus. Robert Cambert, chor. Beauchamp). *Lully was director between 1672 and 1687 and the associated dance school, which still exists, was opened in 1713. The name of the institution has changed several times over the years and since 1871 has been called Théâtre National de l'Opéra. It is from this institution that French ballet has evolved rather than the Académie Royale de Danse.

academies of dance Several countries followed the model of the French academies of the 16th and 17th centuries by setting up institutions designed to maintain and perfect standards in the arts. One of the most famous dance academies is the Imperiale Regia Accademia di Ballo which was established in 1812 by Benedetto Ricci in Milan, attached to the Teatro alla Scala. London's Royal Academy of Dancing was opened in 1920.

Accademia Nazionale di Danza (National Academy of Dancing) School founded in Rome by Jia Ruskaia in 1948 for the training of teachers of dance.

Achcar, Dalal (*b* Rio de Janeiro *c.*1935) Brazilian dancer, choreographer, and ballet director, who pioneered the development of Brazilian ballet. She studied with Maria Makarova and with teachers in America and Europe before returning to *Brazil where, in 1960 she co-founded the Ballet Association of Rio de Janeiro with the aim of raising standards of ballet teaching and performance in the country. For her own short-lived but influential company she invited leading dancers to guest, including Fonteyn and Nureyev. She also organized seasons of visiting companies, including Paris Opera and the Royal Ballet. As a choreographer she made works that focused on Brazilian themes, using music and sets by Brazilian artists, as in *Floresta Amazonica* (*Forest of the Amazon*, 1975). She also staged the first Brazilian production of *The Nutcracker* in 1974. Her pas de deux *Something Special* (mus. Ernesto Nazareth, 1976) was danced by several companies around the world. In 1971 she founded the school that still bears her name. In 1983 she additionally began a long, if intermittent association with the ballet company at the Municipal Theatre in Rio de Janeiro. Appointed artistic director in 1983, 1987, and later in 1999, she was also director of the overall Foundation of the Municipal Theatre (1983–6 and 1991–4) during which time she oversaw a rise in technical standards and an expansion of the repertory, acquiring productions of *Giselle* and *Fille mal gardée* and also staging her own version of *Don Quixote*.

(((⊕))) SEE WEB LINKS
• Official website for Achcar

Acis and Galatea Ovid's story of the shepherd Acis and his love for the nymph Galatea (from *Metamorphoses*) has formed the basis of several ballet librettos, including Hilverding (Vienna, 1753), Noverre (mus. Aspelmayr, Vienna, 1722), O. Viganò (Venice, 1782), Ivanov (1896), and Fokine (mus. G. Kadletz, St Petersburg, 1905). Many choreographers have also been involved in stagings of the Handel opera, including *Wayne McGregor who paired a singer and a dancer for each role (Royal Opera and Ballet, 2009).

Acocella, Joan (*b* San Francisco, 13 Apr. 1945) US dance writer. She studied at Smith College and at the Universities of Padua, California (Berkeley), and Rutgers, becoming critic for *Dance Magazine* in 1982 and for the *New Yorker* in 1998. She has also written for other publications including *Wall Street Journal*; is author of *Mark Morris* (New York, 1993) and *Twenty-eight Artists and Two Saints* (2007) and editor of *André Levinson on Dance* (with Garafola, 1991) and *The Diary of Vaslav Nijinsky* (1999). She was awarded a Guggenheim Fellowship in 1993.

Acogny, Germaine (*b* Porto Novo, Benin, 1944) Sengalese dancer, choreographer teacher and director. She was introduced to traditional African dance through her grandmother, a Yoruba priestess, but she also trained in Western contemporary dance styles, in Paris, New York, and with *Béjart in Brussels. In 1968 she established a dance studio in Dakar, Senegal, and between 1977 and 1982 was director of Mudra Afrique International, a centre for African dance studies that she established with the help of Béjart. After the Mudra closed Acogny returned to Brussels to work further with Béjart, and toured as both performer and workshop leader throughout Europe and in Senegal.

In 1985 she founded a studio and company in Toulouse, France, and while continuing to perform as a soloist, for instance with musician Peter Gabriel, her reputation as a choreographer expanded as commissions from a range of companies including the City of São Paolo Ballet furthered her distinctive style, fusing classical and contemporary, African and European techniques. In 1995 she returned to Senegal where she founded L'École des Sables, a school that has subsequently become a world centre for African dance as well as her own company Jant-Bi. She has choreographed several works for that company starting with *Le coq est mort* (1999) but has continued to promote African dance in Europe becoming artistic director of dance in Department of African Creation, and director of the Choreographic Meetings of African Dance, both in Paris. Her success in raising the profile of her native dance led *Dance Magazine* to describe her as the 'first lady of modern African dance' in 1996.

She is recipient of several awards including Chevalier de L'Ordre de la Légion d'honneur and Knight of the National Order of the Lion of Senegal.

(((⊕))) SEE WEB LINKS
• Website for the company Jant-Bi

Acosta, Carlos (*b* Havana, 2 Jun. 1973) Cuban dancer and director. He studied at the National Ballet School of Cuba from 1983, then at Pinar del Rio. He worked with several companies in S. America and Italy, winning a gold medal at Lausanne in 1990, and in 1991 he joined English National Ballet as principal. In 1992 he joined National Ballet of Cuba and in 1993 moved to Houston Ballet where he created the role of Misgir in Stevenson's *The Snow Maiden* (1998). A classic product of Cuban training, with exceptional elevation, virtuoso pirouette technique, and an insouciant onstage charm Acosta rapidly became one of his generation's busiest and most popular male dancers, guesting with companies around the world. Since 1998 he has been most closely associated with the Royal Ballet, as principal and subsequently guest principal, and with that company has expanded his repertory of classical and modern roles, performing in many of the MacMillan ballets as well as creating roles in works by Page, Brandstrup, and Tuckett and performing Brighella in the company's revival of Tetley's *Pierrot Lunaire*. In 2007 Acosta danced Spartacus with the Bolshoi Ballet in both Moscow and London. In 2003 he choreographed his first work *Tocororo* and in 2006 directed the first of several programmes of ballet. His autobiography *No Way Home* was published in 2007.

(((●))) **SEE WEB LINKS**

• Website for Carlos Acosta

Acrobats of God Modern dance work in one act with choreography and costumes by Graham, music by Carlos Surinach, and set by Noguchi. Premiered 27 Apr. 1960 by Martha Graham Dance Company at 54th St. Theater, New York, with Graham, Ross McGehee, and Taylor. A lighthearted celebration of the art of dance and the discipline of the dancer's world.

adagio [It., slow; interchangeable with Fr. *adage*] Describes any slow dance movement (as opposed to fast, *allegro*). It is also used to designate the section of the classical ballet class in which exercises are focused on balance and line, plus the first section of the traditional four-part pas de deux in which the ballerina and her partner dance together.

Adagio Hammerklavier Ballet in one act with choreography by van Manen, music by Beethoven, and designs by Jean-Paul Vroom. Premiered 4 Oct. 1973 by the Dutch National Ballet at Stadsschouwburg, Amsterdam, with Radius, Ebbelaar, Sand, Juriens, Marchiolli, and Sinceretti. It is set to the Adagio from Beethoven's Piano Sonata in B flat (Op. 106, the *Hammerklavier*) as interpreted in the recording by Christoph Eschenbach. The music is played at an exceptionally slow tempo which is reflected in the slow pace of the movement for its six dancers. It has been revived for Berlin Opera Ballet (1975), the Royal Ballet (1976), and Houston Ballet (1978), among others.

Adam, Adolphe Charles (*b* Paris, 24 Jul. 1803; *d* Paris, 3 May 1856) French composer who wrote the scores for fourteen ballets, among them the most famous titles of the mid-19th century. They include *La Fille du Danube* (chor. F. Taglioni, Paris, 1836), *La Jolie Fille du Gand* (chor. Albert, Paris, 1842), *Le Diable à quatre* (chor. Mazilier, Paris, 1845), and *Le Corsaire* (chor. Mazilier, Paris, 1856). His masterpiece, though, was *Giselle* (chor. Coralli and Perrot, Paris, 1841) in which he developed the use of leitmotifs and atmo-

sphere to dramatically expressive and atmospheric effect.

Adams, Carolyn (*b* New York, 6 Aug. 1943) US dancer. She studied at Sarah Lawrence College, and performed with Waehner's Ballets Contemporains in Paris before joining the Paul Taylor Company in 1965. A dancer of great personality and charm, combining brilliant technique with dramatic presence, she became one of Taylor's most highly regarded soloists, creating roles in several of his works including *Public Domain* (1968), *Big Bertha* (1971), and *Esplanade* (1975). She retired from the company in 1982 and became active in dance education, and chair of Dance USA, a national service organization for professional dancers.

Adams, David (*b* Winnipeg, 16 Nov. 1928; *d* Stony Plain, Alberta, 24 Oct. 2007) Canadian dancer. He studied at the Winnipeg Ballet School, Sadler's Wells School, and with Volkova and Gontcharov, making his adult debut with the Royal Winnipeg Ballet in 1946. In the same year he joined Sadler's Wells Ballet then danced with various companies before becoming first soloist with National Ballet of Canada in 1951. An exceptionally athletic dancer he became Canada's first male ballet star. In 1961 he joined London Festival Ballet and in 1970 the Royal Ballet where he danced until 1976. He created roles in several works, including Taras's *Designs with Strings* (1948) and MacMillan's *Anastasia* (1971 version). He was director of Ballet for All from 1976 to 1977 and in 1978 returned to Canada to teach. With the Toronto-based Encore! Encore! dance reconstruction project he and his brother Lawrence Adams and sister-in-law Miriam Adams began reviving the heritage of Canadian ballet, including the reconstruction of Boris Volkoff's *The Red Ear of Corn* (1949, rev 1999).

Adams, Diana (*b* Stanton, Va., 29 Mar. 1926; *d* San Andreas, Calif., 10 Jan. 1993) US dancer and teacher. She studied with de Mille, Tudor, and others and made her debut in 1943 in *Oklahoma!* The same year she joined Ballet Theatre where she was promoted soloist in 1945, after which she danced with New York City Ballet as ballerina (1950–63). A dancer of unusually long limbs and graceful proportions she was originally considered a dramatic performer and created roles in de Mille's *Fall River Legend* (1948) and Tudor's *Undertow*, among others. Later she evolved into one of Balanchine's leading interpreters, creating roles in many of his works, such as *La Valse* (1951), *Opus 34* (1954), *Agon* (1957), and *Liebeslieder Walzer* (1960). She also created roles in Ashton's *Picnic at Tintagel* (1952) and Robbins's *Facsimile* (1946). Her film roles included Kelly's

Invitation to the Dance (1956). After retiring from the stage she taught at the School of American Ballet where she was also active in selecting Ford Scholarship students. It was she who recommended *Farrell to Balanchine.

Adams, John (*b* Worcester, Mass., 15 Feb. 1947) US composer. Dance plays an important role in two of his operas, *Nixon in China* (1987) and *The Death of Klinghoffer* (1991), where dancers (chor. Mark Morris) double up with singers for the main characters. The repeating, energetic rhythms and bright orchestral colours of his music have also lent themselves to pure dance works. He composed the score for Morris's *Joyride* (2008) and his concert scores have been used for, among others, Child's *Available Light* (New York, 1983), Varone's *Scribblings* (2008), and A. Page's *Fearful Symmetries* (London, 1994). That last score has also been used by P. Martins (New York, 1990), Doug Varone (*Rise*, New York, 1993), and Christopher d'Amboise (*Synchronicities*, Antwerp, 1999).

(⊕) SEE WEB LINKS
• Website for John Adams

Adventures in Motion Pictures British dance company. It was founded in 1987 by a group of students from London's Laban Centre and was originally a repertory ensemble performing a variety of small-scale works. M. *Bourne rapidly emerged as its main choreographer although the dancers, including Scott Ambler, remained significant collaborators. AMP's productions were noted for their wit, pastiche, and drama, for example *Spitfire* (1988) which parodied the manners of romantic ballet dancers through the posturing of male models, and *Town and Country* (1991), an affectionately satirical view of traditional English life. In 1993 the company was commissioned by Opera North to stage a new version of *The Nutcracker* which was to be the first of several re-writes of classical ballets—*Highland Fling* (1994, based on *La Sylphide*), *Swan Lake* (1995), *Cinderella* (1997), and *Car Man* (mus. Schredin-Bizet, arr. Terry Davies, 2000). In 2002 Bourne broke away to form New Adventures for whose debut he created *Play Without Words* (mus. Terry Davies, 2002). AMP, as a production company, retained the performing rights to some of Bourne's previous repertory.

Adzido British-African dance company. It operated between 1984 and 2005, originally founded by George *Dzikunu and Emmanuel Tagoe with the purpose of training students in African dance and drumming, but expanding into Europe's largest African dance company. Traditional African dance and music was showcased within theatrical productions, such as *In the Village of Africa* (1985), *Under African Skies* (1990), and *Siye Goli* (1991).

Africa Traditional dance culture has historically been centred around rural communities, and their collective rituals. Movement styles and music have varied widely from area to area and today many regions support professional dance companies to research and maintain local dance forms. Comparable companies have additionally been set up outside Africa, a seminal example being the now defunct *Adzido.

Over the centuries, the effects of the slave trade and enforced migrations have resulted in elements of African dance fusing with many other dance cultures around the world, creating hybrids such North-American tap and jazz.

In the 20th century, as Africa's population began to shift towards urban centres, dance practices changed. The earliest and most concentrated pockets of activity were in *South Africa. Pre-apartheid, these were dominated by ballet schools and companies that had been imported, initially, by white Europeans. Post-apartheid, the emergence of black modern-dance companies fundamentally shifted that balance.

Across the rest of the continent, modern dance developed fastest in the western regions, primarily through the influence of artists returning from Europe and North America. In 1968 Germaine *Acogny opened a dance studio in Senegal, teaching a mix of African and contemporary techniques. Her second school, L'École des Sables, was founded in 1995 and has since become base to her company Jant-Bi. Acogny has also been involved in the Adugna Community Dance Initiatives, launched in Ethiopia for the training of both traditional and contemporary dance. In Angola in 1995, the teacher and writer Alphonse Tierou launched a competition for African choreographers. Other important figures have included Koffi Koko from Bénin, who while developing his career abroad has frequently returned to Africa to teach, choreograph, and organize festivals; also the Kenyan choreographer and dancer Opiyo Okach. Partly based in France, his mixed-media productions, created with his Nairobi-based collective of dancers, musicians, and artists, have become a significant force in African dance theatre. Since the late 1980s hip-hop has developed a thriving scene, especially popular in Senegal and Nigeria. Generally there is no single aesthetic that typifies current dance practice in Africa, although much recent work can be seen as a direct response to the growing cultural mix of the cities, and to the changing political climate – for example the feminist collaborations of the Mali-based dancer and choreographer Kettly Noël, and South African-based Nelisiwe Xaba.

Afternoon of a Faun Ballet in one act with choreography by Robbins, music by Debussy, set and lighting by Rosenthal, and costumes by

Sharaff. Premiered 14 May 1953 by New York City Ballet at City Center, New York, with LeClercq and Moncion. It is set to the Debussy score *Prélude à l'après-midi d'un faune* to which Nijinsky created his famous 1912 work. Robbins's version portrays two dancers practising in a ballet studio in front of an imaginary mirror (the audience). The couple appear to be narcissistically absorbed in their own reflections, although in the kiss which concludes the ballet, there is a suggestion of the girl's sexual awakening. It has been revived by many companies including the Royal Ballet (1971), Australian Ballet (1978), Norwegian National Ballet (1991), the Bolshoi Ballet (2000), and San Francisco Ballet (2006).

After the Rain Ballet in one act with choreography by Christopher Wheeldon and music by Arvo Pärt. Premiered 22 Jan. 2005, by New York City Ballet at New York State Theatre with Wendy Whelan, Sofiane Sylve, Maria Kowroski, Jock Soto, Edwaard Liang, and Ask la Cour. The ballet is in two parts, the first for three couples, the second a pas de deux, evoking loss and reconciliation.

Agamemnon ballets There have been several dance works choreographed around the story of the mythological king of Mycenae (father of Iphigenia, Orestes, and Electra and murdered by his wife Clytemnestra on his return from Troy). These include Noverre's *Der gerächte Agamemnon* (mus. Aspelmayr, Vienna, 1772), Clerico's *Il ritorno d'Agamennone* (Florence, 1821), Laban's *Agamemnon's Tod* (1924), and Graham's *Clytemnestra* (mus. El-Dabh, 1958).

Age of Anxiety, The Ballet in one act with choreography by Robbins, music by Bernstein, sets by O. Smith, costumes by Sharaff, and lighting by Rosenthal. Premiered 26 Feb. 1950 by New York City Ballet, at City Center, New York, with LeClerq, Moncion, Bolender, and Robbins. It is set to Bernstein's 2nd Symphony, itself based on W. H. Auden's *The Age of Anxiety: A Baroque Eclogue* (1946) and portrays four characters losing their illusions in their attempt to penetrate the meaning of life. Neumeier created a version for Hamburg Ballet in 1979.

agitando Spanish term referring, in general, to the gypsy quality of a Spanish dance or dancer and, specifically, to the heel technique employed in non-flamenco Spanish dances.

Aglaë, ou l'Élève d'amour Ballet divertissement in one act with choreography by F. Taglioni and music by Johann Friedrich Keller. Premiered 22 Jan. 1841 in St Petersburg with M. Taglioni in the title role. It tells the story of the nymph Aglaë, her master Cupid, a faun, and a young man.

Aglië, Filippo d' (*b* Turin, 27 Mar. 1604; *d* Turin 19 Jul. 1667) Italian diplomat, poet, musician, and choreographer. He was one of the first choreographers of the Italian-French court ballet and staged many spectacular productions e.g. *Il tabacco* (Turin, 1650).

Agon Ballet in one act with choreography by Balanchine, music by Stravinsky, and lighting by Nananne Porcher. First performed at a benefit preview 27 Nov. 1957, and officially premiered 1 Dec. 1957, by New York City Ballet at City Center, New York, with Adams, Hayden, Mitchell, and Bolender. It is set to Stravinsky's specially commissioned score, the title of which is Greek for contest, and its twelve dancers, dressed in plain practice clothes, appear to compete for technical precedence in feats of balance, strength and co-ordination. In the pas de deux which concludes the second of the work's three major sections the traditional language of classical partnerwork is wittily and erotically inverted as the man and woman try to assert dominance over each other. Stravinsky's score, while astringently modernist in its serial compositional technique, refers back to the structure of court dances like saraband, galliarde, and branle, while Balanchine's athletic, stripped-down choreography retains echoes of those dances' characteristic steps and manners. The ballet is ranked as one of Balanchine's masterpieces. It has been revived for many other companies including Stuttgart Ballet (1970), Royal Ballet (1973), Paris Opera (1974), Berlin Opera Ballet (1977), Zurich Opera Ballet (1978), Birmingham Royal Ballet (1996), Bolshoi Ballet (1999), and Scottish Ballet (2006). Other choreographers who have used the same score include MacMillan (London, 1958) and T. Gsovsky (Berlin, 1958).

Ahn Ae-soon (*b* Seoul, 30 Apr. 1960) Korean dancer and choreographer. She studied at Ewha Women's University and with Yook Wan-soon. In 1983 she formed her own modern dance group as well as performing in Yook Wan-soon's company and in the same year choreographed *Guys and Dolls*, the first musical to be staged in Korea. In 1984 she joined the Korean Modern Dance Company, creating for it several works, such as *Sun, Moon, Breath* (mus. Nyman, 1994) which fused traditional Korean dance and rituals with the language of Western modern dance. Her most recent works for her own company include *11th Shadow* and *Circle – After the Other* (both 2005) and *Galapagos* (2008). Her company tours internationally.

(⊕) SEE WEB LINKS
• Website for Ahn Ae-soon

Ahonen, Leo (*b* Viipuri, 19 Jun. 1939) Finnish dancer, teacher, and ballet master. He studied at the ballet school of the Helsinki National Opera and at the Leningrad Ballet School and made his debut in 1954 with the Finnish National Opera Ballet. He subsequently guested with many other companies including the Kirov, the Bolshoi, Dutch National Ballet, Royal Winnipeg Ballet, and Houston Ballet. He founded and directed his own Texas Ballet Company and has also developed his own system of dance notation. He has become a celebrated teacher, frequently working with his wife and former dance partner Soili Arvola.

(((●))) SEE WEB LINKS

• Website for Ahonen and Arvola

ailes de pigeon (pistolet) [Fr., pigeon wings] A particularly demanding ballet step which most famously occurs in the Blue Bird variation in *Sleeping Beauty*. The dancer throws the left leg up, springing off the right which rises to beat beneath the left calf. He changes legs and beats, then changes again in order to land on the right foot, with the left leg stretched out into the air. It is performed en avant and en arrière.

Ailey, Alvin (*b* Rogers, Tex., 5 Jan. 1931; *d* New York, 1 Dec. 1989) US dancer, choreographer, and director. He studied in Los Angeles with Horton and later with Graham, Holm, and Weidman in New York, making his debut in Horton's company in 1950. In 1953, after Horton's death, he took over as director, then in 1954 went to New York to dance in the Broadway musical *House of Flowers*. In the same year he also appeared in the film *Carmen Jones*. A big, graceful dancer he gave his first New York concert in 1957 and in 1958 formed the Alvin Ailey American Dance Theater. In the company's first year he created *Blues Suite*, a work exploring the pain and anger of his own African-American heritage. It became one of his most popular works, defining his stylistic mix of modern, jazz, classical, and black dance as well as his unique ability to fuse powerful emotion with a flamboyant theatricality. In 1960 Ailey created the company's signature work *Revelations*, which was followed by numerous other works, including *Masekela Language* (mus. H. Masekela, 1969), *Cry* (a solo for Judith Jamison, mus. Alice Coltrane, 1971), and *Night Creature* (mus. Ellington, 1975) which has been taken into the repertoire of several other companies e.g. London Festival Ballet. He also choreographed works for the Robert Joffrey Ballet, including *Feast of Ashes* (mus. Carlos Surinach, 1962), and for American Ballet Theatre, including *River* (mus. Ellington, 1970), as well as for musical comedies and for Samuel Barber's opera *Antony and Cleopatra* (1966). Initially Ailey's company was perceived as an African-American ensemble but over the years it has recruited its dancers from a broad ethnic mix, and has become renowned for the highly individual personalities of its members.

In 1969 its associate school was founded and in 1974 its youth company, Alvin Ailey II. From 1964 the company began touring extensively overseas. In 1972 it changed its name to Alvin Ailey City Center Dance Theater when it became resident in that venue but reverted to its original name in 1976. In 1979 both the company and school moved to the Minskoff building. After Ailey's death Judith *Jamison took over as director, continuing his vision and his policies with marked success. In 2005 company and school moved into a purpose-built building in Manhattan, the Joan Weill Center for Dance, where it expanded its community and education projects. Under Jamison, Ailey's work continues to be key to the company's repertory, but it also features work by an eclectic range of other choreographers including Horton, McKayle, Talley Beatty, Lubovitch, Ulysses Dove, van Manen, Bill T. Jones, Jamison, Redha, Tharp, and Béjart.

(((●))) SEE WEB LINKS

• Website for the Ailey company

air, en l' [Fr., in the air] Refers to steps performed while jumping, also to those where the working leg (as opposed to the supporting leg) is positioned in the air rather than on the ground (par terre).

Airs Modern dance work in one act with choreography by P. Taylor, music by Handel, design by Gene Moore, and lighting by Tipton. Premiered 30 May 1978 at City Center, New York, by the Paul Taylor Dance Company. Its exuberant mix of classical and modern dance, combined with a courtly elegance of manner, brought it international popularity and it entered the repertory of many companies, including Rambert (1982).

Åkesson, Birgit (*b* Malmö, 1908; *d* Stockholm, 24 Mar. 2001) Swedish dancer and choreographer. She studied with Wigman and joined her company in 1931. In 1934 she made her solo debut in Paris after which she toured in Europe and America, developing her own style of modern dance. She created several ballets for the Royal Swedish Ballet in collaboration with Swedish composers, poets, and painters, including *Sisyphus* (mus. Blomdahl, 1957), *Rites* (mus. Lidholm, 1960), and *Icaros* (mus. Sven Erik Bäck, 1963). In 1964 she co-founded the Stockholm choreographic institute with Bengt Hager (now the State Dance School) where she was head of the choreography department until 1968. After her retirement she conducted research into traditional African dance.

Akimov, Boris (*b* Vienna, 25 Jun. 1946) Soviet dancer and director. He studied at the Moscow Ballet School and danced with the Bolshoi Ballet from 1965 to 1989, creating Rothbart in Grigorovich's *Swan Lake* (1969) and Prince Kurbsky in his *Ivan the Terrible* (1979). Since 1980 he has been a teacher in Russia and abroad, including with the Royal Ballet and La Scala. Between 2000 and 2003 he was director of the *Bolshoi Ballet.

A la recherche de… Ballet in three parts with choreography by Béjart, music by Webern in the first section and texts by Juan de la Cruz in the second. Premiered 26 Jul. 1968 by Ballet of the 20th Century in Avignon with Sifnios, Pinet, and Lanner in first section, M. Césares reciting in the second, and Bortoluzzi, Asakawa, Donn, Bari, Lommel, and Gielgud in the third. It moves from a display of pure neo-classical ballet to a symbolic tale of three men embarking on a quest and encountering the gods Rama, Krishna, and Shiva.

Albert, François Decombe (orig. François Decombe; *b* Bordeaux, 10 Apr. 1787 (some sources say 1789); *d* Fontainebleau, 19 Jul. 1865) French dancer and choreographer. He studied from the age of 10, with one short lapse, making his debut in Bordeaux in 1799. He became premier danseur at the Théâtre de la Gaité in Paris and in 1808 (some sources say 1803) moved to the Paris Opera where he was also ballet master (1829–42). He also worked in London at various times between 1821 and 1845, in Naples (1825), in Vienna (1830), and in Brussels (1838–40). At a time when male dance style was moving towards athletic technique Albert continued to exemplify the refined nobility of 18th-century ballet. He was considered the most handsome dancer in Europe. He created roles in Gardel's *Paul et Virginie* (1806), F. Taglioni's *Aglaë* (London version 1841), and his own *The Marble Maiden* (1845). He choreographed several other ballets, including *Cendrillon* (mus. A. Sor, Paris, 1823), *La Jolie Fille de Gand* (mus. Adam, Paris, 1842), and the ballet divertissements in Donizetti's opera *La Favorite* (Paris, 1841). As a teacher he developed systematic methods for improving the strength and stamina of his pupils, publishing a manual *L'Art de la danse à la ville et à la cour* (Paris, 1834).

Albertieri, Luigi (*b* Milan, 1860; *d* New York, 25 Aug. 1930) Italian dancer and ballet master. At the age of 10 he became the favourite pupil of Cecchetti who adopted him and they performed together in the London premiere of Manzotti's *Excelsior*. Between 1866 and 1902 he was premier danseur of the Empire Ballet in London, also working as choreographer at Covent Garden (1895–1902), and appearing in America in 1895. He was ballet master of Chicago Lyric Opera (1910–13) and between 1913 and 1927 was ballet master of the New York Metropolitan Opera House where he staged many ballets and operas. In 1915 he opened a school where Astaire was one of his most promising pupils. He wrote *The Art of Terpsichore* (New York, 1923).

Aldous, Lucette (*b* Auckland, NZ, 26 Sept. 1938) Australian dancer and teacher (she moved to Australia when she was four months old). She studied in Sydney then won a scholarship to Sadler's Wells Ballet School (1955–7). In 1957 she became soloist with Ballet Rambert, becoming ballerina, and remaining there till 1963. She danced with London Festival Ballet (1963–6), with the Royal Ballet (1966–70), then became principal ballerina with Australian Ballet (1971–7). A brilliant technician, her comic flair was displayed in roles like Swanilda and Kitri (which she danced in Nureyev's film of *Don Quixote*, 1973), though her lyrical gifts were also showcased in *La Sylphide*. In 1977 she danced in the film *The Turning Point*, partnered by Bujones. She married the dancer Alan Alder. After retiring from the stage she taught at the Australian Ballet School and at the West Australian Academy of Performing Arts.

Aldridge, Robert (*b c.*1738; *d* Edinburgh, 1793) Irish dancer and teacher. During the middle of the 18th century he ran a dance school in Dublin. He also choreographed some Irish ballets in London and went on to open a dance school in Edinburgh. He was the teacher of dancer Simon Slingsby.

alegrias Flamenco dance in 3/4 or 6/8 time which is characterized by its elegant style and opulent arm movements.

Aleksidze, Georgy (*b* Tbilisi, 7 Jan. 1941) Soviet-Georgian dancer and choreographer. He studied at Moscow Ballet School with A. Messerer and made his debut at the Tbilisi Opera in 1961. He then went to study at the Choreographers' Faculty of Leningrad Conservatory with F. Lopukhov and created his first ballet in 1966 for the newly created Chamber Ballet. Inspired by New York City Ballet's first visit to the Soviet Union in 1962 he was one of the first Soviet choreographers to create plotless ballets, though his output has also included several dramatic works. In 1968 he created *Oresteia* (mus. Falik) for the Kirov followed by *The Scythian Suite* (mus. Prokofiev, 1969). From 1967 he also taught at the Leningrad Conservatory and from 1972 to 1980 he was artistic director and chief choreographer of the Tbilisi Opera Ballet. His many works for the company included *Variations on a Theme by Mozart* (mus. Chopin), *Classical Symphony* (mus. Prokofiev), and *Berikoaba* (mus. Kvernadse, all 1973), *Coppélia* (1975), *Nutcracker* (1977), and *Medea* (mus. Gabichvadze, 1978). From 1980 to 1983 he was chief choreographer at Perm Theatre of Opera and Ballet, after which he worked at the opera studio of the Leningrad Conservatory (1983–5). In 1985 he returned to Tbilisi where he created several works including *Swan of Tuonela* (mus. Sibelius, 1988) and *Concerto Grosso* (mus.

Schnitke, 1989). In 1992 he founded a small company attached to the St Petersburg Cappella for which he choreographed many works.

Alexander Technique Body alignment technique developed by Frederic Matthias Alexander (1869–1955). With its emphasis on releasing unnecessary tension from the body and on re-discovering efficient ways of moving and positioning it has become widely respected among dancers both as a therapy and as a movement philosophy.

Alexandrova, Maria (*b* Moscow, 20 Jul. 1978) She trained at the Moscow Choreographic Academy from 1988, studying with Sofia Golovina and others. In 1997 she graduated into the Bolshoi, becoming soloist in 1999 and principal in 2004. A strong, intelligent dancer, with a versatile range she has created lead roles in Lacotte's *La Fille du Pharaon* (2000), Ratmansky's *The Bright Stream* (2003) and Juliet in Radu Poklitaru and Declan Donnellan's *Romeo and Juliet* (2003). Recipient of numerous awards including the Gold Mask, 2004.

Alhambra ballets The Alhambra Theatre in Leicester Square was one of London's leading music halls between 1864 and 1936, and featured ballet as one of its main attractions for many years. International star dancers appeared in the theatre, such as Legnani and Geltser, and while most of the ballets presented were little more than entertaining spectacle, some were choreographed by distinguished artists, including J. Hansen, Gorsky, and Berger. In 1919 Diaghilev's Ballets Russes premiered Massine's *La Boutique fantasque* and *Le Tricorne* here and in 1921 staged their opulent production of *The Sleeping Princess*.

Alice in Wonderland Several choreographers have used Lewis Carroll's book as a basis for ballet, including Charnley for London Festival Ballet (mus. Joseph Horovitz, 1953), E. Virginia Williams (Boston, 1972), Tetley for National Ballet of Canada (mus. D. Del Tredici, 1986), D. Deane for English National Ballet (mus. Tchaikovsky, arr. C. Davis, 1995), and Simon Dow for West Australian Ballet (mus. Shostakovich, 2007).

Allan, Maud(e) (*b* Canada, 27 Aug. 1873; *d* Los Angeles, 7 Oct. 1956) Canadian dancer. She studied music and fine art and became interested in movement through an enthusiasm for reviving the dance forms of ancient Greece. In 1903 she made her debut in Vienna in *The Vision of Salome* (mus. Marcel Rémy) in a daringly revealing costume, shocking many in the climax where she kissed John the Baptist's severed head. She danced mostly barefoot and toured around the world, finally settling in England where she taught in her own school (1928–40). She wrote *My Life and Dancing* (London and New York, 1908).

Allard, Marie (*b* Marseilles, 14 Aug. 1742 (some sources say 1738); *d* Paris, 14 Jan. 1802) French dancer. She is now famous for being the mother of Auguste Vestris (the result of a brief liaison with G. Vestris), but she was also a very popular dancer. Petite and piquant, she excelled in comic and character roles. She made her debut in Marseilles around 1752 and was prima ballerina at the Lyons Opera House (1754–6). She later danced at the Paris Opera (1761–81) where she appeared in many ballets, including the premiere of Mozart and Noverre's *Les Petits Riens* (1778). She is thought to have choreographed several of her own divertissements and entrées. She retired after several pregnancies had caused her to become too plump for public taste.

Allegri Diversi Ballet in one act with choreography by Bintley, music by Rossini, and design by Terry Bartlett. Premiered 15 Jan. 1987 by Sadler's Wells Royal Ballet, at Sadler's Wells, London, with Karen Donovon and Petter Jacobsson. A series of scintillating classical dance variations, set to Rossini's Variations for Clarinet and Small Orchestra and his Introduction, Theme, and Variations for Clarinet and Orchestra. It has been revived by Boston Ballet (1990) and Birmingham Royal Ballet (2004).

allegro [It., merry] General term to describe a quick and lively tempo, it also refers specifically to any combination of fast steps (as opposed to adagio) as well as to the section in a ballet class which follows adagio. Here dancers perform steps that are designed to improve their speed and attack, plus their ability to jump and turn.

Allegro, il penseroso ed il moderato, L' Modern dance work in two acts with choreography by Mark Morris, music by Handel, set by Adrianne Lobel, costumes by Christine Van Loon, and lighting by James F. Ingalls. Premiered 23 Nov. 1988 by the Mark Morris Dance Group at the Théâtre de la Monnaie, Brussels. Morris's setting of Handel's dramatic oratorio is ranked as one of his finest, most ambitious works. Structurally it follows Charles Jennens's text (based on Milton) and Handel's score in its alternation of sanguine and melancholic viewpoints. Visually it also draws on Blake's series of watercolour illustrations of Milton's poems. The movement contrasts pale, exquisite images of melancholy with extrovert, earthy humour, conjuring up a classical, pastoral world of goddesses, shepherds, artists, men, and beasts and concluding with a rousingly utopian vision of harmony.

Allegro Brillante Ballet in one act with choreography by Balanchine, music by Tchaikovsky, costumes by Karinska, and lighting by Rosenthal. Premiered 1 Mar. 1956 by New York City Ballet at

City Center, New York, with Maria Tallchief and Magallanes. This virtuoso setting of Tchaikovsky's 3rd Piano Concerto, Op. 75, is for one lead and four supporting couples, and has been taken into the repertory of many companies, including Sadler's Wells Royal Ballet (1973), San Francisco Ballet (1979), Royal New Zealand Ballet (2004), and Christopher Wheeldon's Morphoses (2007).

allemande [Fr. for German] Term applied to several dances or styles of movement popular between the 15th and 19th centuries, and denoting either a German origin or German characteristics. Arbeau records an allemande in duple time that was a simple processional dance. In the mid-18th century the term denoted lively turning dances in 3/4 time that came from Germany in which couples held each other in an unusually close embrace.

Alleyne, John (*b* Barbados, 25 Jan. 1960) Bajan-Canadian dancer, choreographer, and director. He trained at the National Ballet School, Toronto, and in 1978 joined Stuttgart Ballet as a dancer, creating several ballets for the company workshops. In 1984 he joined National Ballet of Canada as first soloist, dancing classical and modern principal roles, and becoming resident choreographer. His works for the company include *Blue-Eyed Trek* (1988) and *Interrogating Slam* (1991), created in a style which fuses an essentially classical idiom with modern power and stretch. During this period he also created several works for Ballet British Columbia, such as *Go Slow Walter* (1990). In 1992 he became artistic director of the company for which he has since created many works, including *The Don Juan Variations* (1995), *The Goldberg* (1998), *The Rite of Spring* (2005), and *A Streetcar Named Desire* (mus. Tobin Stokes, 2006) as well as choreographing for other companies, including New York City Ballet, San Francisco Ballet, Dance Theatre of Harlem, and Stuttgart Ballet.

allongé [Fr., lengthened] Designates an unusually elongated line in ballet. In an arabesque allongé the body is held almost parallel to the floor with the front arm and back leg extended.

All That Jazz Bob *Fosse's 1979 film about a workaholic film director which was based heavily on his own life. It features Airotica, one of his most aggressively erotic dance numbers.

Alma ou La Fille de feu Ballet in four acts with choreography by Cerrito and Perrot, music by G. Costa, libretto by André Jean-Jacques Deshayes, and design by W. Grieve. Premiered 23 Jun. 1842 at Her Majesty's Theatre, London. It tells the story of a beautiful statue who is brought to life by an evil demon, Belfegor, so that she might seduce and destroy men. When she herself falls in love, with the Moorish prince Emazor, she is turned back to stone. Cerrito as Alma had one of her greatest successes in this ballet, particularly in the pas de fascination where, accompanied by a tambourine, she was required to display her most bewitching qualities. Perrot also choreographed a substantial role for himself as Belfegor.

Alonso, Alberto (*b* Havana, 22 May 1917; *d* Gainsville, FL, 31 Dec. 2007) Cuban dancer and choreographer. Brother of Fernando Alonso, and brother-in-law of Alicia Alonso. He studied with several teachers including Preobrajenska and Idzikowski and danced with Ballets Russes de Colonel de Basil from 1935 to 1940. He subsequently danced with Ballet Theatre (1943–5), Ballet Alicia Alonso (1948–9) and, after 1966, with National Ballet of Cuba. From 1941 he also worked as ballet master and choreographer, creating several works including *Espacio y movimiento* (National Ballet of Cuba, mus. Stravinsky, 1966), which won the prize for best choreography at Varna in 1968, and *Carmen* (Bolshoi Ballet, mus. Bizet-Shchedrin, 1967, revived for many companies, including Ballet Argentino and Moscow Festival Ballet). In 1993 he settled in Florida where he became resident choreographer of Dance Theatre of Santa Fé, and staged his works for several American companies.

Alonso, Alicia (*née* Alicia Ernestina de la Caridad dei Cobre Martinez Hoyo; *b* Havana, 21 Dec. 1920) Cuban dancer and director. She studied in Havana, then in New York with Vilzak and at the School of American Ballet, and later with Volkova in London. She started her dancing career in Broadway musicals then in 1939 joined Ballet Caravan. In 1940 she moved to Ballet Theatre where she danced until 1960, though with some interruptions. Between 1941 and 1943 she performed with Havana's Pro-Arte company and in 1948 she returned to Havana to found Ballet Alicia Alonso and its associate school in 1950. Between 1955 and 1960 she also guested with various companies including Ballet Russe de Monte Carlo. For much of her career she performed with Youskevitch, their partnership regarded as one of the greatest of the 20th century. An intensely dramatic dancer as well as a pure classical technician, her most famous role was Giselle, but she also created roles in many new ballets including Tudor's *Undertow* (1945), Balanchine's *Theme and Variations* (1947), de Mille's *Fall River Legend* (1948) and most definitively, the title role in Alberto Alonso's *Carmen* (1967). Her own company became Ballet de Cuba in 1955, changing its name to National Ballet of Cuba after Fidel Castro came to power in 1959 and it became a state sponsored institution. As the company's director and prima ballerina Alonso became the dominant dance personality of Central America. She and the company have toured widely in the USSR, China, and Europe.

She has staged most of the standard classics, including *Giselle* (1945 for Pro-Arte and many times subsequently for different companies), *Swan Lake* (1954 for Ballet Alicia Alonso and 1976 for Teatro de Bellas Artes, Mexico), and *Sleeping Beauty* (1974 for Paris Opera and 1983 for La Scala), and has also choreographed several works. In 1975 she returned to dance the pas de deux from Act II of *Swan Lake* for a gala at American Ballet Theatre, and she continued to dance into old age, despite severely impaired eyesight. She was first married to the ballet director Fernando Alonso, then to Pedro Simon. She received the Decoration of Carlos Manuel de Cespedes in 1947 and was awarded the Médaille de la Ville de Paris and the Prix Pavlova in 1966.

Alonso, Fernando (*b* Havana, 27 Dec. 1914) Cuban dancer, teacher, and director. Brother of Alberto Alonso and first husband of Alicia Alonso. He studied in Havana and later New York with Mordkin and Vilzak and at the School of American Ballet. He made his debut with the Mordkin Ballet and also danced in musicals, with Ballet Caravan and with Ballet Theatre. Returning to Havana he became soloist with the Pro-Arte company and from 1948 to 1975 he was director of Alicia Alonso's company (subsequently National Ballet of Cuba). He later directed his own company, Ballet de Camagüey, for which he choreographed a version of *La Fille mal gardée*.

Alston, Richard (*b* Stoughton, 30 Oct. 1948) British dancer, choreographer, and director. He gave up art college to study dance, entering the London School of Contemporary Dance in 1967. In 1970 he joined London Contemporary Dance Theatre and in the same year began to create works for the company. In 1972 he formed *Strider, a small independent group performing works by him and other company members, and in 1975 he left for New York to study with Cunningham, returning to London in 1977 to form his own company. In 1980 he was made associate choreographer of Ballet Rambert and in 1982 he was co-founder of Second Stride, though he withdrew after two seasons. In 1986 he became Rambert's artistic director, and was responsible for changing the company's name to Rambert Dance Company and for shifting the repertoire from dramatic to more abstract dance, bringing in works from Cunningham, T. Brown, and Childs, as well as his own new creations. He left in 1993 and a year later formed the Richard Alston Dance Company based at The Place. Alston's early style reflected the influence of Cunningham in its clarity of line and fascination with pure dance, but it has also absorbed elements of English lyricism, notably the Ashton tradition, and in contrast to Cunningham has consistently drawn its inspiration from music. Much of the repertory has been set to contemporary scores, including *Wildlife* (mus.

Nigel Osborne, des. Richard Smith, 1984), *Soda Lake* (des. Nigel Hall, 1981), *Pulcinella* (mus. Stravinsky, des. Howard Hodgkin, 1987), *Hymnos* (mus. Peter Maxwell Davies, 1988), *Bach Measures* (mus. Harrison Birtwistle, 1996), *Red Run* (mus. Heiner Goebbels, 1998), and *Nigredo* (mus. Simon Holt, 2007) although Alston has also set works to classical composers, including Mozart, *Dealing with Shadows* (1990), Rameau, *Brisk Singing* (1997), and Ravel, *Shimmer* (2003). He has additionally created works for companies including Ballet Atlantique, the Royal Ballet, Ballet Theatre Munich, and Scottish Ballet, for whom Alston created *Carmen* (mus. Shchedrin-Bizet) in 2009.

(⊕) SEE WEB LINKS

• Website for the Place Theatre, with link to Alston's company

alta [Sp. and It., high] Term in use from the 14th century, which often designates dances performed by those of a high rank. Also refers to lively dance types featuring leaps, hops, and jumps.

Alton, Robert (*b* Bennington, Vt., 1902; *d* Hollywood, Calif., 12 Jun. 1957) US dancer and choreographer. He studied with Mordkin, becoming a dancer with his company, and during the 1930s and early 1940s he became a leading choreographer of Broadway musicals, including *Anything Goes, Ziegfeld Follies* (1938, 1940, and 1942), *Hellzapoppin'*, and *Pal Joey*. He was equally prominent in Hollywood, choreographing film musicals like *Ziegfeld Follies, Annie Get Your Gun, Show Boat, White Christmas, There's No Business like Show Business*, and *Daddy Long Legs*.

Amagatsu, Ushio (*b* Yokosuka City, 31 Dec. 1949) Japanese dancer, choreographer, and director. He studied classical and modern dance before going on to work with pupils of the *butoh master Hijikata. In 1972 he formed the seminal butoh collective Daira Kakudakan and in 1975 formed his own company *Sankai Juku, through which he evolved a more surreal, theatrical form of butoh. His many works include *Unetsu* (*The Egg Stands Out of Curiosity*) (1987), *Hibki* (1998), and *Toki* (2007). Between 1989 and 1990 he was also artistic director of Spiral Hall, Tokyo, where he created several works including *Apocalypse* (1989) in collaboration with Takashi Kako and Ismael Ivo. He has also directed operas, including *The Three Sisters* (mus. Peter Eötvös, 1998).

(⊕) SEE WEB LINKS

• Website for Sankai Juku

Amants magnifiques, Les Royal divertissement in which Louis XIV appeared as a dancer, probably for the last time in public. With a libretto by Molière, music by Lully, choreography by

Beauchamps, and stage machinery by Gasparo Virgarini, it was staged on 4 Feb. 1670 at St-Germain-en-Laye. It fulfilled the king's aim to include 'all that theatre might offer'. Dance and mime scenes linked by songs tell the story of two rival princes who, in a pastoral setting, compete to charm a young princess and her mother.

Amaya, Carmen (*b* Granada, 1913; *d* Bagùr, 19 Nov. 1963) Spanish dancer. Born into a dancing family she first performed in public at the age of 4, dancing in the waterfront bars of Barcelona. She began her international career in 1923 with Raquel Meller's company then went on to tour the world with her own company, many of whom were members of her family, gaining international fame for the fierce passion of her dancing and her unusual incorporation of male footwork into female dances. She was married to the guitarist Juan Antonio Aguero.

Amboise, Jacques d' (*b* Dedham, Mass., 28 July 1934) US dancer, choreographer, and teacher. He studied at the School of American Ballet and joined New York City Ballet in 1950, becoming principal (1953–84). He was initially a very American dancer, with an easy, natural charm, but developed into a superb classicist. Apollo was one of his finest roles, although he also created leading roles in many other Balanchine ballets, including *Western Symphony* (1954), *Ivesiana* (1954), *Episodes* (1959), *Raymonda Variations* (1961), *Movements for Piano and Orchestra* (1963), *Who Cares?* (1970), and *Davidsbündlertänze* (1980). He has also appeared in several films, including *Seven Brides for Seven Brothers* (1954) and *Carousel* (1956), also the 1962 television production of Stravinsky and Balanchine's *Noah and the Flood*. He has choreographed several ballets for NYCB including *The Chase* (mus. Mozart, 1963), *Tchaikovsky Suite* (mus. Tchaikovsky, 1969), and *Celebrations* (mus. Mendelssohn, 1982). From 1970 he taught at the School of American Ballet, and in 1976 he became founder-director of the National Dance Institute, a community dance project based in New York. He is father of the choreographer Christopher d'Amboise.

Ambrose, Kay (*b* Woking, 1914; *d* London, 1 Dec. 1971) British artist, writer and director. She illustrated Haskell's *Ballet* (Pelican, 1938) and collaborated with him on *Balletomane's Sketchbook* (1943) before publishing her own *Ballet Lover's Pocket Book* (1943), *Ballet Lover's Companion* (1948), and *Beginners, Please* (1953). In 1950 she became artistic director of Ram Gopal's company, in the same year publishing *Classic Dances and Costumes of India*, then in 1952 became artistic adviser of the National Ballet of Canada, designing around 30 productions for the company before retiring in 1961.

America *See* UNITED STATES, THE.

American Ballet, The Ballet company which emerged from the School of American Ballet. The SAB was founded by *Kirstein, *Balanchine, E. M. M. Warburg, and V. Dimitriev at the end of 1933 and opened in Jan. 1934. Its first student performance was given in Jun. 1934 in White Plains, New York, with a programme including Balanchine's *Serenade*. In Mar. 1935 the company gave a two-week season at the Adelphi Theater, New York, presenting seven ballets by Balanchine and with Dollar and Loring among the dancers. Though successful with the public, it was not well received by the critics. After a brief tour of NE America the company took up residence at the Metropolitan Opera House in autumn 1935 with Vilzak as premier danseur; the Christensen brothers and Erick Hawkins were also members. Balanchine created *The Bat* for the first season and in 1936 produced his controversial staging of Gluck's opera *Orpheus and Euridice* in which he placed the singers in the orchestra pit. In Apr. 1937 he mounted a Stravinsky Festival which featured *Baiser de la fée*, *The Card Game* (1st perf.), and *Apollon musagète* (all conducted by Stravinsky). In 1938 the company broke with the Met. over differences of artistic vision and remained inactive for three years, although during the period 1936–9 Kirstein organized the smaller group *Ballet Caravan as a showcase for American choreography, which involved some of AB's dancers. In 1941 the company was reassembled at the invitation of Nelson A. Rockefeller and amalgamated with Ballet Caravan under the title American Ballet Caravan for a five-month tour of S. America. Balanchine was artistic director and the dancers included Caccialanza, L. Christensen, Dollar, Bolender, Magallanes, and Taras. Its repertory featured *Ballet Imperial*, *Concerto Barocco*, *Billy the Kid*, *The Filling Station*, and *Apollon musagète*. The company was closed down after the tour but Kirstein and Balanchine went on to found Ballet Society in 1946, which in 1948 evolved into New York City Ballet.

American Ballet Center School founded by Robert Joffrey in Greenwich Village in 1953, which he co-directed with Arpino. It subsequently became known as the Joffrey Ballet School.

American Ballet Company Eliot Feld's New York-based company, originally known as the American Ballet Players. It gave its first performance on 27 Jun. 1969 at the 12th Festival of Two Worlds in Spoleto with a programme of three Feld ballets and a work by Herbert Ross. Its first New York season opened 21 Oct. 1969 but financial difficulties led to the company's closure in 1971. Feld and some of his dancers subsequently joined American Ballet Theatre, and in 1974 Feld founded a second company, the Eliot Feld Ballet.

American Ballet Theatre American ballet company. Originally known as Ballet Theatre, it was founded in 1940 by several ex-members of the Mordkin Ballet. With the financial backing of *Chase, who became co-director with *Smith in 1945 and under the initial direction of *Pleasant it had its debut on 11 Jan. 1940 at New York Radio City Center Theater, in a season which featured an impressive range of works from Fokine's *Les Sylphides* and Dolin's *Giselle* to Tudor's *Jardin aux lilas* and *Dark Elegies*, and six premieres including Loring's *The Great American Goof*. The company's aim was to preserve important works from the past as well as develop a strong new repertory and during the 1940s it was associated most closely with Fokine, Tudor, and de Mille. That decade saw the commissioning of many major ballets including Dolin's *Pas de quatre* (1941), Fokine's *Bluebeard* (1941), Tudor's *Pillar of Fire* (1942), *Romeo and Juliet*, *Dim Lustre* (1943), and *Undertow* (1945), Massine's *Aleko* and *Mam'zelle Angot* (1943), Robbins's *Fancy Free* (1944), Balanchine's *Theme and Variations* (1947), and de Mille's *Fall River Legend* (1948). It also nurtured a generation of American dancers including Kaye, D. Adams, and Kidd as well as producing its own classic ballerina in Alonso, though from the beginning it also relied on foreign artists as star principals, including Markova, Dolin, Baronova, Eglevsky, and Youskevitch. Lacking a permanent base in New York, touring played a major part in the company's existence both in the US and abroad (it first appeared in Europe in 1946) and in 1957 it changed its name to American Ballet Theatre.

After the creative push of the 1940s the company had less critical success during the 1950s. Fokine was dead and Tudor had left, though de Mille continued to choreograph new works for the repertory. In the 1960s it acquired Cullberg's *Lady from the Sea* (1960) and Robbins's critically acclaimed *Les Noces* (1965), and in 1967 staged its first full-length *Swan Lake*. In the same year Feld made an important debut as choreographer and dancer, with C. Gregory emerging as a star and ballerina. In 1970 Makarova joined the company and in 1974 staged a seminal production of Act II of *La Bayadère* which elicited a new classical authority from the dancers. The same year Baryshnikov joined and Tudor returned as associate director, creating *The Leaves are Fading* in 1975. Other important acquisitions of the 1970s were Tharp's *Push Comes to Shove* and Robbins's *Other Dances* (both 1976), and the company's new generation of dancers included Bujones, Kirkland, and van Hamel. In 1977 the company was granted an official home at New York's Met-

ropolitan Opera House and in 1980 Baryshnikov became artistic director. He strengthened the company's classical base, staging *Giselle* (1980) and *Swan Lake* (1988), among others, and acquiring MacMillan's *Romeo and Juliet* in 1985. At the same time he developed a new repertory of works by major modern dance choreographers, including Taylor, Cunningham, Tharp, and Mark Morris. During the 1980s Jaffe and L. Browne were among the new dancers to emerge as principals. In 1989 Jane Herman and Oliver Smith took over as co-directors, followed by ex-principal Kevin McKenzie in 1992. Financial uncertainties—always a problem for the company, despite Chase's injections of money—became acute during the 1990s, forcing the company to perform for only limited seasons each year. However, it maintained a strong roster of principals including Bocca, Carreno, A. Ferri, Herrera, R. and J. Kent, and E. Steifel, and in addition to expanding its repertoire of classics and full-length ballets, such as MacMillan's *Anastasia* in 1999, it also continued to premiere significant new works such as Tharp's, *Known by Heart* (mus. various, 1998). In the early years of the 21st century it consolidated a new generation of principals, including Angel Corella, Gillian Murphy, Xiomara Reyes, Marcelo Gomes, David Hallberg, and guest ballerina Diana Vishneva and continues to perform an annual seasons at New York's Metropolitan Opera House and City Center, as well as to tour both the US and abroad. Although its repertory is dominated by full-length classics it has also premiered new works by, among others, Jorma Elo, Morris, and Tharp. Its official school, the American Ballet Theatre School, was founded in 1972 with its own performing group but both were disbanded under Baryshnikov. A new junior ensemble, ABT Studio Company, was started in 1995 and the Jacqueline Kennedy Onassis School was founded in 2004.

 SEE WEB LINKS
• Website for American Ballet Theatre

American Dance Festival Annual programme of modern dance classes and performances founded by Martha Hill, which from 1948 was given annually at the end of the summer term of the Connecticut College School of Dance. Many major works were premiered there, including Graham's *Diversion of Angels* (as *Wilderness Star*, 1948), Limón's *The Moor's Pavane* (1949) and *A Choreographic Offering* (1964), Humphrey's *Night Spell* (1951) and *Ruins and Visions* (1953), Nikolais's *Kaleidoscope* (1956), Cunningham's *Antic Meet* (1958) and *Scramble* (1967), Lang's *Shirah* (1960), P. Taylor's *Insects and Heroes* (1961), and Tharp's *Medley* (1969). In 1978 the ADF was relocated to Durham, N. Carolina, and in 1984 it set up the International Choreographers Workshop. The increasingly international trend of the festival's programmes (which have introduced much new European and Japanese dance to the US) has also been reflected in the International Linkages Program, set up in the late 1980s to facilitate exchanges with foreign teachers. Since the 1980s it has also sponsored several historical projects, such as the Black Tradition in American Modern Dance Project, founded in 1987 under the direction of Gerald Myers to preserve classic works by African-American choreographers.

American Dance Machine New York-based school, research centre, and company dedicated to preserving dances from American musicals. It was founded in 1976, under the direction of Lee Theodore and the company made its official debut in Feb. 1978 at Ford's Theater, Washington, DC. Its activities dwindled after Theodore's death in 1987.

American Dance Theater Modern dance repertory company founded in 1964. Based in New York and under the direction of Limón, it made its debut 18 Nov. 1964 at New York State Theater, performing works by Limón, Humphrey, McKayle, and Sokolow. A second series of performances was given in Mar. 1965 at the same theatre, including works by Bettis, Cunningham, Draper, Hoving, Humphrey, Lang, Limón, Nikolais, and Sokolow. The company was then disbanded.

American Document Modern dance work in one act with choreography by Graham, music by Ray Green, set by Arch Lauterer, and costumes by Edythe Gilfond. Premiered 6 Aug. 1938 by the Martha Graham company, at Vermont State Armory, Bennington, with Graham, Hawkins, and Housely Stevens jun. as the Speaker. It is divided into six sections, which portray the course of American social history. Texts are spoken, including the Declaration of Independence, Jonathan Edwards's sermons, and lines from Walt Whitman. It was Graham's first work to feature a male soloist.

American Genesis Full-length dance pageant with choreography by Taylor, music by Bach, Haydn, Martinů, Gottschalk, and J. Faley. Its New York premiere (after preview performances on tour) was 14 Mar. 1974 by Paul Taylor Dance Company at Brooklyn Academy of Music with C. Adams, de Jong, and Taylor. It portrays the biblical Fall of Man within the context of the American dream.

American in Paris, An Gershwin's 1928 orchestral score has been choreographed several times by e.g. R. Page (Cincinnati, 1936) but the best-known dance version is in G. Kelly's 1951 film of the same title.

Amiel, Josette (*b* Vanves, 19 Nov. 1930) French dancer. She studied at the Conservatoire

Français and at Paris Opera Ballet School, making her debut at the Opéra Comique before joining the Paris Opera where she was promoted première danseuse in 1955 and étoile (1958–71). As well as dancing the classical ballerina roles she created new roles in Lifar's *Chemin de lumière* (1957) and Flindt's *La Leçon* (1963) and *Le Jeune Homme à marier* (1965), among others. After retiring from the stage she was active as a teacher and coach, for example staging Bourmeister's *Swan Lake* for Finnish National Ballet (1993) and Lander's *Études* for San Francisco Ballet in 1998. She taught at the Paris Opera Ballet School and was made Chevalier de la Légion d'honneur in 1975.

Amodio, Amedeo (*b* Milan, 14 Mar. 1940) Italian dancer and choreographer. He studied ballet at La Scala Ballet School and also Spanish dance with Antonio Marin in Madrid, making his debut at La Scala in 1958. He moved to Rome Opera House in 1966, becoming principal in 1968 and with his powerful technique and stage charisma soon became one of Italy's star dancers. He freelanced with several companies and also began choreographing in 1967 with *Escursioni* (mus. Berio) in Spoleto. Other works include *Oggetto amato* (mus. Bussotti, La Scala, 1976). In 1979 he became director of *Aterballetto raising its status from a small experimental group to an ambitious independent ballet company with a broad repertory of largely 20th-century works and well-known guests, including Terabust. He choreographed several ballets for it and also staged *Romeo and Juliet* (1987) and *The Nutcracker* (1989). He left in 1997 to become director of Teatro dell'Opera di Roma, then from 2003 was director of Teatro Massimo in Sicily. He continues to choreograph.

Amor Ballet spectacle in two parts with choreography and libretto by Manzotti, music by Romualdo Marenco, and design by A. Edel. Premiered 17 Feb. 1886 at La Scala, Milan, with Antonietta Bella, Ernestina Operti, and Cecchetti. Its action displays the progress of mankind from Chaos, through various historical scenes like the Triumph of Caesar and the Battle of Legnano, to an apotheosis in the Temple of Love. Its original cast featured hundreds of dancers, actors, children, and extras, also live animals including an elephant.

Amor brujo, El (Eng. title *Love, the Magician*) One-act ballet score by de Falla with a libretto by G. Martinez Sierra. Its first production was choreographed by Imperio and premiered 15 Apr. 1915 at Teatro Lara, Madrid, with Imperio. The story is set in an Andalusian village where a gypsy girl Candelas is haunted by her dead lover. When the latter tries to jinx her romance with another man, Carmelo, the two live lovers plan a ritual of exorcism. The ballet became famous in La

Argentinita's 1928 Paris version which toured internationally, and many versions have followed, including Lifar's for Paris Opera (1943), Antonio's (London, 1955), and P. Wright's for the Royal Ballet Touring Co. (Edinburgh, 1975).

Amour et son amour, L' Ballet in one act with choreography and libretto by Babilée, music by Franck, and design by Cocteau. Premiered 13 Dec. 1948 at the Théâtre des Champs-Elysées with Babilée and Philippart. It is set to Franck's 1888 tone poem *Psyché*, which portrays the mythological encounter between Eros and Psyche. A highly successful ballet using the same story (*Psyche et l'Amour*) with music by J. J. Rudolphe (Stuttgart) was choreographed by Noverre in 1762.

Ananiashvili, Nina (*b* Tbilisi, 19 Mar. 1964) Soviet-Georgian dancer. She was a champion ice skater aged 10 before entering the State Ballet School of Georgia (1973–7). She continued her training at the Moscow Ballet School from 1977 and made her debut in 1980 as Swanilda in a school production of *Coppélia*. In 1981 she graduated into the Bolshoi Ballet as a soloist. Her teachers in the company were Struchkova and Semenova, the former developing her dramatic powers, the latter the distinctive elegance of her classical technique. She has performed most of the standard ballerina roles as well as roles in several Grigorovich ballets. In 1988 she and Andris Liepa were guest artists with New York City Ballet, the first Soviet dancers to appear with the company. She was much applauded for her boldness in tackling the unfamiliar Balanchine style. One of the new generation of international Russian dancers, she subsequently guested with Boston Ballet, Royal Danish Ballet, Royal Ballet, Birmingham Royal Ballet, and others. Between 1993 and 2008 she was principal with American Ballet Theatre (while still performing with the Bolshoi) and in 1998 created the title role of Stevenson's *The Snow Maiden* for both Houston Ballet and ABT. In 1999 she joined Houston Ballet as principal. For several years she also performed intermittently with her own touring ensemble, Nina Ananiashvili and the Stars of the Bolshoi, and in 2004 became artistic director of the *State National Ballet of Georgia. She continued to dance with that company and has commissioned several works for it including ballets by *Ratmansky.

Anastasia Ballet in three acts with choreography and libretto by MacMillan, music by Tchaikovsky, Fritz Winckel, Rudiger Rufer, and Martinů, and design by B. Kay. Premiered 22 Jul. 1971 by Royal Ballet at Covent Garden, London, with Seymour, Beriosova, Rencher, Sibley, and Dowell. It was inspired by Anna Andersen's book *I Anastasia* in which she narrates her life-story as the youngest and only surviving daughter of Tsar Nicholas II. (At the time of the ballet's creation, it was uncertain whether Andersen's claims to be Anastasia were correct. Subsequent evidence has proved them to be fantasy.) In Act I, set to Tchaikovsky's 1st Symphony, A. and her family are seen at an idyllic picnic which is interrupted by news of the outbreak of the First World War. In Act II, set to Tchaikovsky's 3rd Symphony, a ball given for A. by the Tsar at the Winter Palace is disrupted by the outbreak of the October Revolution. Act III is presented in a radically different style. Set to electronic music and Martinů's *Fantaisies symphoniques*, it takes place in a Berlin hospital where Andersen is a patient. Events from Anastasia's past appear in dance and mime flashback, also in the form of old newsreel footage and Andersen's traumatized response to these memories/fantasies is conveyed in a rawly expressionist style of movement that is very different from the classical choreography of the first two acts. The ballet originally consisted of Act III alone and in this form was premiered 25 Jun. 1967 by the Berlin Opera Ballet with design by Kay, and Seymour as Andersen-Anastasia. This single-act version has since been revived for Stuttgart Ballet (with Haydée, 1976), American Ballet Theatre (1985), and English National Ballet (with Seymour, 1989). A revised version of the three-act ballet, overseen by Deborah MacMillan with new designs by Bob Crowley, was premiered by the Royal Ballet 2 May 1996 with Durante and revived by ABT in 1999.

Anastos, Peter (*b* Schenectady, NY, 1948) US dancer and choreographer. He studied in New York and Leningrad and began choreographing for various companies including Eglevsky's, and also Dallas and Pennsylvania Ballets. From 1974 he was director and star performer of the comic transvestite company Les Ballets Trockadero for which he choreographed many works. Between 1979 and 1981 he was resident choreographer of Garden State Ballet, in 1983 of Santa Fe Opera, then between 1994 and 1996 he was artistic director of Cincinnati Ballet. He continued to work extensively as a freelance choreographer, his works including *Cinderella* (with Baryshnikov for American Ballet Theatre, 1983), *The Lost World* (mus. Peter Golub, for Miami City Ballet, 1992), *Peter Pan* (for Ballet West and Cincinnati Ballet, 1994), and several works for the Santa Fe Festival Ballet, including *By Gershwin* (mus. Gershwin, 1999). He also choreographed for musicals and directed opera. In 2007 he was appointed director of Ballet Idaho.

 SEE WEB LINKS
• Website for Idaho Ballet

Anatomical & Mechanical Lectures upon Dancing John Weaver's 1721 treatise made a revolutionary attempt to describe human anatomy in relation to the demands of dance technique.

Anatomy Lesson, The (orig. Dutch title *De anatomische les*) Ballet in one act with choreography by Tetley, music by Marcel Landowsky, and design by Nicolaas Wijnberg. Premiered 28 Jan. 1964 by Nederlands Dans Theater at the Hague, with Flier. It is based on Rembrandt's painting *The Anatomy Lesson of Dr Tulp* and contrasts the inner life and passions of the man laid out on the table with the coldly scientific context in which he has been placed after death.

Anaya, Dulce (orig. Dulce Esperanza Wohner de Vega; *b* Rancho Boyeros, nr. Havana, 26 Dec. 1933) Cuban dancer. She studied at the Havana Sociedad Pro-Arte Musical School with the Alonsos and at the School of American Ballet, making her debut (as Dulce Wöhner) with Ballet Theatre in 1947. She subsequently joined Ballet de Cuba as ballerina, returned to Ballet Theatre (1951), was ballerina with Stuttgart (1957), with Munich State Opera (1958–63 and 1964–5), and with Ballet Concerto, Florida, from 1967. She founded Jacksonville Ballet Theatre in 1970, remaining there as director, and creating many works and continues to direct its associate school.

Ancient Voices of Children Modern dance work in one act with choreography by Bruce, music by G. Crumb, and design by Baylis. Premiered 7 Jul. 1975 by Ballet Rambert at Sadler's Wells Theatre, London. This setting of Crumb's song-cycle of poems by Lorca portrays a group of ragged children playing games of love and death. Other settings of Crumb's score include J. Stripling (Stuttgart, 1971), Butler (Ballet du Rhin, 1972), Tetley (Utah Repertory Theater, 1973), and Reiter-Soffer (in *Yerma*, Irish Ballet, 1976).

Andersen, Frank (*b* Copenhagen, 15 Apr. 1953) Danish dancer, teacher, and ballet director. From 1960 he studied at the Royal Danish Ballet School, also subsequently in New York and Leningrad, and made his stage debut in 1961 in child roles with the Royal Danish Ballet. In 1971 he graduated into the company, becoming solo (principal) dancer from 1977. He was a demi-caractère dancer of unusual vivacity and charm but also danced in the modern repertoire. In 1976 he co-founded Soloists of the Royal Danish Ballet, a touring group which performed internationally. During this time he was also an international guest artist performing in America, Europe, and Japan. He also taught and directed the Bournonville Summer Academy and from 1985 to 1994 was artistic director of the RDB where he concentrated on preserving the Bournonville inheritance as well as introducing works by Cranko, Balanchine, and Robbins, among others. He was director of the Royal Swedish Ballet (1995–9) and then returned to RDB as director between 2002 and 2008. He continues to work freelance, staging the works of Bournonville for companies around the world.

Andersen, Ib (*b* Copenhagen, 14 Dec. 1954) Danish dancer and choreographer. He studied at the Royal Danish Ballet School and graduated into the company in 1973, becoming solo (principal) dancer in 1975. He was an exemplary Bournonville stylist, with a brilliant allegro and flying elevation but also danced in many modern ballets, creating the role of the Boy in the RDB premiere of van Dantzig's *Monument for a Dead Boy* (1976). From 1980 to 1990 he was principal dancer with New York City Ballet where he created roles in Balanchine's *Davidsbündlertänze* (1980), Robbins's *Piano Pieces* (1981), Robbins and Tharp's *Brahms/Handel* (1984), and Martins's *Concerto for Two Solo Pianos* (1982), among others. He choreographed his first ballet in 1987: *1-2-3—1-2* (mus. Schoenberg, Royal Danish Ballet) and his first work for New York City Ballet in 1988, *Baroque Variations* (mus. Foss). In 1999 he staged a new production of *Giselle* for Les Grands Ballets Canadiens. After retiring from the stage he was ballet master at Pittsburg Ballet and as a member of the Balanchine Trust staged several of that choreographer's ballets worldwide. In 2000 he became director of Ballet Arizona, for which he has choreographed several works including *Play* (mus. several, 2007).

Andersen ballets Hans Christian Andersen (*b* Odense, 1805, *d* Copenhagen, 1875). The Danish poet and writer had a brief dancing career, making his debut in 1812 in C. Dahlén's *Armida*. He also became a close friend of August Bournonville and many of his fairy-tales have inspired dance librettos, including *The Red Shoes* (chor. Hassreiter, mus. Raoul Mader, Vienna, 1898, also filmed by Powell and Pressburger, 1948, chor. Massine and Helpmann), *The Little Mermaid* (chor. Beck, mus. Fini Henriques, Copenhagen, 1909), *Le Baiser de la fée* (after *The Ice Maiden*, chor. Nijinska, mus. Stravinsky, Paris, 1928, also many subsequent versions), *Les Cent Baisers* (after *The Swineherd*, chor. Nijinska, mus. Frédéric d'Erlanger, London, 1935, also as *The Swineherd*, chor. Lander, mus. Johann Hye-Knudsen, Copenhagen, 1936), *Le Roi nu* (after *The Emperor's New Clothes*, chor. Lifar, mus. Françaix, Paris, 1936), *The Steadfast Tin Soldier* (chor. Balanchine, mus. Bizet, 1975), and *The Snow Queen* (chor. Bintley mus. Tovey, after Mussorgsky, 1986 and chor. Corder, mus. Prokofiev, 2007). Petit choreographed the ballet sequences for the American film *Hans Christian Andersen*. Danish TV made a film of *The Swineherd* (chor. Flindt, 1969). In 2004 Brandstrup created *The Anatomy of a Storyteller*, a work based on Andersen's life and fiction.

Anderson, Jack (*b* Milwaukee, 15 Jun. 1935) US poet and dance critic. He was educated at Northwestern University, Indiana University, and University of California (Berkeley) and has written for several publications: *Dance Magazine*, *Ballet Review* (contributing editor), *Dancing Times* (New York Correspondent), and *New York Times*. In 1977 he co-founded *Dance Chronicle* (with G. Dorris) which he co-edited until 2008. He taught dance history and criticism at Connecticut College, New School for Social Research, and Long Beach State University, and has been author of several books including *Dance* (New York, 1974), *The Nutcracker Ballet* (New York, 1979), *The One and Only: The Ballet Russe de Monte Carlo* (London, 1981), *Ballet and Modern Dance: A Concise History* (Princeton, 1986, rev. 1992), *The American Dance Festival* (Duke Univ. Press, 1987), and *Art Without Boundaries: The World of Modern Dance* (Univ. of Iowa Press, 1997).

Anderson, Laurie (*b* Glen Ellyn, Illinois, 5 Jun. 1947) American composer and multi-media artist. She worked as a performance artist in New York before reaching international recognition with her 1981 record *O Superman*. Combining a resonant lyricism with an experimental use of new technology, Anderson's music has featured within film and other contexts. It has also been used widely in dance, including Trisha Brown's (*Set and Reset*, 1983 and *O Composite*, 2004), Bill T. Jones's (*About Five Rounds*, 1995), and Molissa Fenley's *Bridge of Dreams* (1994).

(⊕) SEE WEB LINKS
• Anderson's official website

Anderson, Lea (*b* London, 13 Jun. 1959) British dancer and choreographer. She studied at St Martins School of Art and Design then trained at the Laban Centre, graduating in 1984. She formed the all-female group the Cholmondeleys, choreographing its repertory. Her distinctive style married tiny, obsessive gestures with rhythmic group moves in works like *Baby Baby Baby* (mus. Nina Simone, 1985), *Flesh and Blood* (mus. Steve Blake, 1989), and *Cold Sweat* (mus. Steve Blake and Drosten Madden, 1990). In 1988 she founded the all-male group the Featherstonehaughs for which she created *Go Las Vegas* (mus. Blake, 1995), among others, and the two groups have joined to perform several productions including *Flag* (mus. Blake and Madden, 1988), and *Yippeee!!!* (mus. Blake 2006). She has made several works for television and choreographed Sam Mendes's production of *Cabaret* in 1995.

(⊕) SEE WEB LINKS
• Website for Cholmondeleys and Featherstonehaughs

Anderson, Reid (*b* New Westminster, BC, 1 Apr. 1949) Canadian dancer and director. He studied at the Dolores Kirkwood Academy and Royal Ballet School, joining Stuttgart Ballet in 1965. He was appointed soloist in 1972 and then principal (1974–85) creating roles in MacMillan's *Requiem* (1976) and *My Brother, My Sisters* (1978), Forsythe's *Urlicht* (1977) and *Orpheus* (1979), and Neumeier's *Lady of the Camellias* (1978), among others. In 1986 he was appointed artistic director of Ballet British Columbia, and from 1989 to 1996 was artistic director of National Ballet of Canada. In 1996 he moved to Stuttgart Ballet where as director he has focused on preserving the legacy of Cranko as well as encouraging a new generation of choreographers, for example Christian Spuck.

Anderson-Ivantzova, Elizabeth (*b* Moscow 21 Apr. 1890; *d* New York, 11 Nov. 1973) Russian-US dancer and teacher. She studied at the Imperial Theatre School, Moscow, graduating into the Bolshoi in 1906 where she was appointed ballerina in 1917. In 1918 she left Russia, and worked as choreographer for Nikita Baliev's Théâtre de Chauve-Souris in Paris (1920–1) as well as working in Berlin and Lisbon. In 1923 she moved to the US, staging Stravinsky's *Les Noces* at the New York Metropolitan Opera House in 1929. She also opened her own New York ballet studio where she taught from 1937 until her death, expounding her distinctive theories of placement in balance. Her pupils included Alicia Alonso.

Andersson, Gerd (*b* Stockholm, 11 Jun. 1932) Swedish dancer and actor. She studied at the Royal Swedish Ballet School and joined the company in 1948, becoming ballerina in 1958. She created roles in several ballets, such as Tudor's *Echoing of Trumpets*, and guested with several companies, including National Ballet of Canada and London Festival Ballet as well as acting in films. She retired from the stage in 1976 but continued to act, appearing in Ingmar Bergman's film *Fanny and Alexander* (1982).

Anderton, Elizabeth (*b* London, 28 May 1938) British dancer and director. She studied at Sadler's Wells School and in 1955 joined the Sadler's Wells Opera Ballet, moving to the Royal Ballet in 1957 where she danced until 1974, becoming soloist in 1958 and principal in 1961. She danced the standard ballerina roles as well as creating roles in several ballets, including Cranko's *Sweeney Todd* (1959), Ashton's *The Two Pigeons* (1961), Tudor's *Knight Errant* (1968), and Nureyev's *Romeo and Juliet* (1977). In 1976 she became teacher and guest dancer at London Festival Ballet, where she was assistant artistic director (1979–83 and 1984–90), and subsequently taught at the Royal Ballet.

Andreyanova, Elena (*b* St Petersburg, 13 Jul. 1819; *d* Paris, 26 Oct. 1857) Russian dancer. She studied at the Imperial Theatre School, St Petersburg, graduating into the Bolshoi Theatre, St Petersburg, in 1837 where she danced until 1855. An expressive mime, equally gifted in classical and character dances, she was the first Russian to dance Giselle (18 Dec. 1842). She attracted some criticism over the favouritism shown her by Aleksandr Gedeonov, director of the Imperial Theatres. But Petipa chose her as his partner in *Paquita* which he staged for his own debut in 1847 and she created roles in several ballets including Perrot's *La Filleule des fées* (1850), *The Naiad and the Fisherman* (1851), and *Gazelda* (1853). She was also one of the first Russian dancers to perform abroad, for example in Hamburg, London, Paris, and Milan in 1845, and in London again in 1852. She studied for a while with Blasis. Between 1852 and 1855 she toured Russia with a group of Imperial dancers. In 1855 she retired to Paris.

Angiolini, Gaspero (*b* Florence, 9 Feb. 1731; *d* Milan, 6 Feb. 1803) Italian dancer, choreographer, ballet master, and composer. He came from a theatrical family and had his first dance lessons from his father. Between 1747 and 1750 he danced in Venice with occasional guest performances around Italy and he created his first choreography in 1752 in Rome. In or around the same year he moved to Vienna to work under Hilverding. He danced in several of the latter's ballets and in 1758 became Hilverding's successor as ballet master in Vienna, remaining there until 1766 except for a period in St Petersburg. His ballets were strongly influenced by Hilverding's theories of the *ballet d'action though he developed his own choreographic idiom which attempted an unusually (for the time) close synthesis between music and dance. In 1761 he staged his pantomime ballet *Don Juan* to Gluck's music, in which he danced the title role. Audiences accustomed to the light-hearted dance divertissements of the age were moved and shocked by its tragic ending. He continued his fertile association with Gluck by choreographing the first performance of *Orpheus and Eurydice* (1762) and in 1765 set *Semiramide* (based on Voltaire's drama) to music by that composer. This work also shocked audiences with its brutal storyline but with it he established himself as a leading choreographer of ballet d'action. A brilliant dancer and mime himself, he demanded total expressiveness of face and gesture from his dancers as well as an impeccable technique. He composed his works almost in the form of classical Greek tragedies with a limited number of soloists and a chorus. Unlike Noverre whose own narrative ballets were accompanied by lengthy explanatory programme notes, he supplied only a bare outline of the plot, insisting that the dancers' 'silent speech' was sufficiently eloquent to convey the material.

In 1762 he left Vienna for a year to join Hilverding as assistant ballet master in St Petersburg and in 1766 succeeded him there as ballet master. He choreographed many works in Russia including *Les Chinoises en Europe* (to his own music) in 1767. Back in Italy between 1772 and 1773 he began making public attacks on Noverre whom he accused of plagiarizing Hilverding's ideas about the ballet d'action (*Lettere di Gaspero Angiolini a Mons. Noverre sopra i balli pantomimi*). He returned to Vienna (1774–6) where he created *L'Orphelin de la Chine* (1774), then moved back to St Petersburg for a second contract (1776–8). Between 1778 and 1782 he was again in Italy as ballet master at La Scala and elsewhere then returned to St Petersburg (1783–6) for the last time. Back in Italy he choreographed ballets for several theatres but was imprisoned for his republican activities in 1799. In 1801 he was released and returned to Milan. During his life he composed the music for many of his own ballets and also tried to develop a system of dance notation based on musical notation. He was married to his partner Maria Teresa Fogliazzi.

anglaise Term used in 18th-century France to distinguish the English style of contredanse (in which couples faced each other in rows) from the French (which was performed in a circle or square). Also used later to indicate dances of English origin.

Anglo-Polish Ballet Ballet company formed in London in 1940 by two dancers, Czeslow Konarski and Alicja Halama. In 1941 Jan Cobel became director and it gave a very successful tour of England, performing subsequent seasons in London until 1947. It also performed for the troops in Italy and India during the war. Gilmour, Kersley, and Rassine were among its dancers.

Animaux modèles, Les Ballet in one act with choreography and libretto by Lifar, music by Poulenc, and design by M. Brianchon. Premiered 8 Aug. 1942 at Paris Opera with Lifar, Schwarz, and Chauviré. It is based on six fables by La Fontaine.

Anisimova, Nina (*b* St Petersburg, 27 Jan. 1909; *d* Leningrad, 23 Sept. 1979) Russian dancer and choreographer. She studied at the Petrograd (later Leningrad) Ballet School with Romanova, Shiriaev, and Vagonova. In 1926 she graduated into the Maly Theatre of Opera and Ballet, then from 1927 to 1958 she danced with GATOB (later Kirov Ballet). In 1932 she created the role of Thérèse in Vainonen's *Flames of Paris* and in 1936 choreographed her first major ballet, *Andalusian Wedding* (mus. Chabrier) for Leningrad Ballet School. Her subsequent works include

Gayané (mus. Khachaturian, 1942) for the Kirov, Perm, *Songs of the Crane* (mus. Stepanov and Ismagilov, 1944) for Bashkir Opera, *The Magic Veil* (mus. Zaranek, 1947), and her own version of *Scheherazade* (mus. Rimsky-Korsakov, 1950), both for the Maly Theatre, Leningrad. In 1964 she staged *Swan Lake* for the Royal Danish Ballet. Between 1963 and 1974 she taught at the Choreographic Dept. of the Leningrad Conservatory.

Anna Karenina ballets Tolstoi's 1878 novel and its tragic heroine have been the basis for several ballets. Plisetskaya created a three-act version in 1972, in conjunction with Natalia Ryzhenko and Victor Smirnov-Golovanov. The libretto was by Boris Lvov-Anokhin, music by Shchedrin, and design by V. Leventhal (Plisetskaya's costumes by Pierre Cardin). Premiered 10 June by the Bolshoi Ballet, Moscow, with Plisetskaya, M. Liepa, Fadeyechev, and Y. Vladimirov. Full-length versions have been created by A. Prokovsky (mus. Tchaikovsky, 1979), Australian Ballet, and Ratmansky (mus. Shchedrin, Royal Danish Ballet, 2004; revived Finnish National Ballet, 2008).

Anouilh, Jean (*b* Bordeaux, 23 Jun. 1910; *d* Lausanne, 3 Oct. 1987) French playwright. His 1932 ballet for actors *Le Bal des voleurs* was rechoreographed by Massine (Nervi, 1960) and revived for Royal Ballet (London, 1963). He wrote several librettos for Petit including *Les Demoiselles de la nuit* (1948).

Ansermet, Ernest (*b* Vevey, 11 Nov. 1883; *d* Geneva, 20 Feb. 1969) Swiss conductor. He was hired by Diaghilev in 1915 and conducted premieres of Stravinsky's *L'Histoire du soldat* (1918), *Chant du rossignol* (1920), *Pulcinella* (1920), *Renard* (1922), and *Les Noces* (1923), also Satie's *Parade* (1917), de Falla's *Le Tricorne*, and Prokofiev's *Chout* (both 1923).

Anspannung–Abspannung Laban terminology for the contrasting actions of modern dance—the equivalent of Graham's *contraction and release.

Antheil, George (*b* Trenton, NJ, 8 Jul. 1900; *d* New York, 12 Feb. 1959) US composer. In 1923–4 he wrote the music for *Ballet mécanique*, a film planned with Fernand Léger and recently choreographed by Doug Varone (2001). The score, including doorbells and the sound of aeroplanes, was premiered in 1926. He also composed scores for Balanchine's *Dreams* (1935) and Loring's *Capital of the World* (1953).

Antigone Ballet in one act with choreography by Cranko, music by Theodorakis, and design by Rufino Tamayo. Premiered 19 Oct. 1959 by the Royal Ballet at Covent Garden, London, with Beriosova,

Burne, and MacLeary. This adaptation of Sophocles' tragedy was revived for Stuttgart Ballet in 1961. Other Antigone ballets include those by Gioia (Venice, 1790), G. Galzerani (Milan, 1825), and Sokolow (mus. Chávez, *c.*1940).

Antonio (orig. Antonio Ruiz Soler; *b* Seville, 4 Nov. 1922; *d* Madrid, 6 Feb. 1996) Spanish dancer, choreographer, and director. He studied, with his cousin Rosario, under Manuel Real (Realito) in Seville and made his debut with her in Liège in 1928. Their partnership was known as Los Chavalillos Sevillanos while they were children but they continued to dance with each other for the next twenty years appearing all over the world (US debut, 1940, London debut, 1951). Antonio in particular became the most famous Spanish dancer of his generation, with a charismatic personality and virtuoso footwork. The partnership split up in 1953 and he formed his own company, Antonio and the Ballets de Madrid. He choreographed many works for this, in a combination of Spanish and classical styles, and several were subsequently taken into the repertories of other companies.

Antonio, Juan (*b* Mexico City, 4 May 1945; *d* Toronto, 24 May 1990) Mexican dancer. He studied with Xavier Francis and Zaraspe, at the American Ballet Theatre School, and American Ballet Center, making his debut aged 18 at the Nuevo Teatro de la Danza Mexico. In 1964 he joined the Ballet Clásico de Mexico then subsequently danced with the companies of Lang, Sokolow, de Lavallade, Limón, and Tetley, and from 1967 with Louis Falco Dance Company, of which he became associate director.

Antony and Cleopatra ballets Antony and Cleopatra's historic love affair has inspired several ballets including Noverre's (Ludwigsburg, 1765), Aumer's (mus. Kreutzer, Paris, 1808), Igor Tchernichov's (mus. E. Lazarev, Leningrad, 1968), dell'Ara's (mus. Prokofiev, Milan, 1971), and B. Stevenson's (mus. Rimsky-Korsakov arr. Lanchbery, 2000).

Apache Dance A fast and racy dance routine that was popular in revues and music halls during the early years of the 20th century. It features a violent male (originally a Parisian gangster, the dance being named after the Apache gang) displaying his machismo in brutal, erotic partnership with a scantily clad girlfriend. It was first performed by Max Dearly and Mistinguette at Moulin Rouge on 27 July 1908 under the title *Valse chaloupée* using music by Offenbach. It became very popular in London and New York and was later adapted as a ballroom dance. Cole Porter included an 'Apache Dance' in his 1953 musical *Can-Can*.

Apollo Ballet in one act with choreography by Balanchine, music by Stravinsky, and design by André Bauchant. Premiered 12 Jun. 1928 by Diaghilev's Ballets Russes at Théâtre Sarah Bernhardt, Paris, with Lifar, Nikitina, Tchernicheva, and Doubrovska. It was performed under the title *Apollon musagète* until 1957 and follows the score in portraying Apollo's birth from his mother Leto, his education through (and flirtation with) the three Muses Terpsichore, Calliope, and Polyhymnia, and finally his ascent of Mt. Parnassus. The plot is subordinate to the choreography, however, which is widely regarded as the first example of neo-classical ballet. Balanchine not only stripped academic dance to a lean clarity but re-worked its vocabulary with a sharp and witty modernist twist. He subsequently revised and refined the ballet many times, cutting both music and dance and eventually omitting scenery. It is one of New York City Ballet's signature works and is also danced by companies all round the world. Other settings of the same score include Milloss's (Rome, 1951), T. Gsovsky's (Berlin, 1951), Lifar's (Milan, 1956) and M. Clark's (London, 1995).

Apollo ballets Several works have been inspired by the Greek god of music including Hilverding's *Apollon et Daphné* (1763), Noverre's *Apollon et les muses* (1782), Didelot's *Apollon et Daphné* (1802) and *Apollon et Persée* (1803), Nijinska's *Apollon et la belle* (1937), Bolm's *Apollon musagète* (1928), and Balanchine's **Apollo* (1928).

Apollon musagète Ballet in one act with choreography by Bolm, music by Stravinsky, and design by N. Remisoff. Premiered 27 Apr. 1928 at the Library of Congress, Washington, DC, with Bolm, Page, Berenice Holms, and Elise Reiman. It was the first setting of Stravinsky's score of the same title (commissioned by Elizabeth Sprague Coolidge) but has been superseded by Balanchine's version.

Appalachian Spring Modern dance work in one act with choreography by Graham, music by Copland, sets by Noguchi, and costumes by Edythe Gilfond. Premiered 30 Oct. 1944 at the Library of Congress, Washington, DC, with Graham, O'Donnell, Cunningham, and E. Hawkins. It portrays a young American bride and her husband taking possession of their land and their future life under the presiding gaze of a revivalist preacher and a pioneer woman. In its celebratory depiction of the pioneer ethos it represents the culmination of Graham's handling of American themes during the 1930s and 1940s.

Apparitions Ballet in one act with choreography by Ashton, libretto by Lambert, music by Liszt (orch. Gordon Jacob), and designs by Beaton. Premiered 11 Feb. 1936 by Vic-Wells Ballet at Sadler's Wells Theatre, London, with Helpmann,

Fonteyn, and Turner. It was inspired by Berlioz's *Symphonie fantastique* and its five scenes portray the quest of a romantic poet who, drugged with opium, searches for the perfect poetic expression of his love. Ashton's collaboration with Lambert and Beaton was seminal in the early development of English ballet, and this was also the first work in which he and Fonteyn established their special creative rapport. It was revived by London Festival Ballet in 1987 with Natalia Makarova.

Après-midi d'un faune, L' (Eng. title *The Afternoon of a Faun*) Ballet in one act with choreography by Nijinsky, music by Debussy, and design by Bakst. Premiered 19 May 1912 by Diaghilev's Ballets Russes, at the Théâtre du Chatelet, Paris, with Nijinsky as the Faun. It is set to Debussy's 1894 tone poem *Prélude à l'après-midi d'un faune* (itself inspired by Mallarmé's poem) and depicts a Faun who is spying on a group of nymphs going to bathe. He tries to embrace one of them but she flees, leaving her scarf behind. He seizes it and lies down on it, releasing his desire with an orgasmic pelvic thrust. It was Nijinsky's first work and its choreography (which required the dancers to move in flattened, profile positions with angled limbs and turned in feet) took over 100 rehearsals to perfect. Some critics were scandalized by the 'bestial' eroticism of the work, but its admirers, led by Rodin, were profoundly impressed by its novelty of expression. It was the only Nijinsky ballet to have been notated (Nijinsky wrote it down in his own idiosyncratic modification of the Stepanov system), and in 1989 Les Grands Ballets Canadiens premiered the first revival based on Nijinsky's score rather than on memories handed down by dancers. Debussy did not approve Nijinsky's interpretation but his music has been used several times since by, among others, Lifar (as a solo, 1935), Robbins (*Afternoon of a Faun*, 1953), and Elo (2002).

Ara, Ugo dell' (*b* Rome, 13 Apr. 1921) Italian dancer, choreographer, and ballet master. He studied at Rome Opera Ballet School and graduated into the company, where he became premier danseur, performing lead roles in works by Milloss. He then danced with La Scala (1946–50) though between 1949 and 1950 he toured in the musical *Carosello napoletano*, choreographed by himself. After 1950 he worked as a freelance choreographer, for example recreating the Ballet of the Nuns from Meyerbeer's *Robert le diable* (Palermo, 1966) and Manzotti's *Excelsior* (Florence, 1967).

arabesque [Fr., ornament] One of the basic positions of ballet. The dancer stands on one leg (either bent or straight), with the other extended behind with a straight knee and pointed foot. The arms are held in various positions that harmoniously extend the line of the arabesque. The body may be held vertically erect, or stretched forward parallel to the floor (in arabesque allongée) or inclined down towards the front foot, while still maintaining an extended line (in arabesque penchée). The position was known in the 18th century and was codified by Blasis.

Araiz, Oscar (*b* Bahía Blanca, 2 Dec. 1940) Argentinian dancer, choreographer, and director. He studied with Schottelius, Hoyer, and others and made his debut in 1958 at the Teatro Argentino in La Plata. From 1964 to 1967 he toured with the Hoy Ballet company which he co-directed with Susana Zimmermann and Ana Labat, and from 1968 to 1973 he was artistic director of the Ballet del Teatro San Martín in Buenos Aires, becoming one of S. America's most highly regarded choreographers. His first work was created in 1959, a duet based on a Gershwin prelude, and his many subsequent works include *El canto de Orfeo* (mus. Henry, 1964), *Orpheus* (mus. Stravinsky, 1964), *The Miraculous Mandarin* (mus. Bartók, 1967), and *Romeo and Juliet* (mus. Prokofiev, 1970). In 1970 he also choreographed the 'Dance Around the Golden Calf' for the Buenos Aires production of Schoenberg's *Moses and Aaron*. After 1977 he created works for Joffrey Ballet and in 1980 became director of Geneva Ballet, choreographing the full-length ballet *Tango* (mus. A. Stampone, 1981). Between 1990 and 1998 he returned to San Martín, re-staging several of his ballets as well as commissioning work from other Argentinian choreographers. He also began working as a theatre director but between 2005 and late 2006 was director of the Colón Ballet, for which he created several works including *La Rossignol* (mus. Stravinsky, 2005).

Araujo, Loipa (*b* Havana, *c.*1943) Cuban dancer and ballet mistress. She studied at Escuela de la Sociedad Pro-Arte Musical and also with the Alonsos, L. Fokine, and Parés, joining National Ballet of Cuba in 1959 where she became prima ballerina in 1967. She frequently guested abroad and in 1973 briefly joined Ballet de Marseille, where she created the lead role in Petit's *Les Intermittences du cœur* (1974). She returned to Cuba to become one of the company's most senior teachers but also teaches worldwide.

Arbeau, Thoinot (orig. Jehan Tabourot; *b* Dijon, 17 Mar. 1520 (some sources say 1519); *d* Langres, 21 Jul. 1595 (some sources say 1596)) French dance writer, author of the famous *L'Orchésographie*. Published in 1588, this treatise on 16th-century dancing, fencing, piping, and drumming was written in the form of a dialogue between Arbeau and his student Capriol. It supplies descriptions of numerous dances, plus musical

notation, with the steps and positions clearly defined, e.g. basse danse, pavane d'Espagne, galliarde, volte, courante, allemande, morisque, and 24 versions of the branle. Although Arbeau (a provincial writer) may not have accurately known how these dances were performed at court, his work provides insights into contemporary musical performance practice and also social convention (Capriol is instructed to 'spit and blow [his] nose sparingly' and to converse affably). It was translated into English by C. W. *Beaumont in 1925 and inspired Ashton's ballet *Capriol Suite* (mus. Warlock, 1930).

Arc Dance Company British modern dance company. It was founded in 1985 by Kim *Brandstrup and has been a showcase for his works, including *The Soldier's Tale* (mus. Stravinsky, 1986), *Antic* (mus. Ian Dearden, 1993), *Crime Fictions* (mus. Dearden, 1996), *The Return of Don Juan* (mus. Kim Helweg, 1999), *Brothers* (2000), *Hamlet* (2003), and *Anatomy of a Story Teller* (2004). The company has suspended operations at various points, due to financial difficulties and to Brandstrup's other freelance projects.

(⊕) SEE WEB LINKS
• Kim Brandstrup's website.

Archer, Kenneth (*b* London, 7 Feb. 1943) British designer and reconstructor of dance design. He trained in art history at the universities of Antioch and Essex and with his partner M. *Hodson he has been responsible for researching and reconstructing many early 20th-century ballets including Nijinsky's *Rite of Spring* (staged 1987) and *Jeux* (staged 1996), Börlin's *Skating Rink* (staged 1996), and Balanchine's *Cotillon* (staged 1988). His books include *Roerich East and West* (Bournemouth, 2000).

archives and museums Given the ephemeral nature of dance, archives and libraries are extremely important to students, historians, and lovers of the artform. Some of these are in private collections and difficult to access, but in the larger institutions, digitalization of material (i.e. the transfer of images and text to machine-readable format) is making some collections accessible via the internet.

The first major specialist archive, Les Archives Internationales de la Danse, was set up by Rolf de *Maré in 1931 in Paris. This not only housed a comprehensive library of books, magazines, programmes, models, designs, and scores but also presented lectures, demonstrations, and exhibitions. Between 1932 and 1936 it published a magazine and in 1932 it held its first choreographic competition which was won by Jooss with *The *Green Table*. In 1950 the AID was dissolved. Its books and engravings went to the Musée de l'Opéra in Paris and the rest to Stockholm's newly opened Dance Museum. This was the world's first dance museum with individual collections dealing in SE Asian dance, Diaghilev's Ballets Russes, Les Ballets Suédois, Jooss, and European modern dance.

The world's most inclusive archive is the Dance Collection in the Performing Arts Library at New York's Lincoln Center, which was formed in 1944. This contains millions of books, prints, photographs, programmes, manuscripts, and films and has special collections devoted to Isadora Duncan, Diaghilev, Denishawn, and Robbins. On receipt of Robbins's personal archive in 1998 the collection was re-named in his honour. More Diaghilev material is contained in the Lifar collection at the Wadsworth Atheneum, Hartford, Connecticut, and in the Stravinsky-Diaghilev Foundation which includes designs, posters, scores, and memorabilia. America also has important dance libraries in the Harvard University Theatre Collection and in the Universities of Florida and California.

In Paris the Musée de l'Opéra has extensive material relating to its dance history which dates back to the 17th century, including designs, paintings, and musical scores. It possesses Pavlova memorabilia and also *Kochno's collection which includes many Diaghilev photographs. The Theatre Collections at the Bibliothèque de l'Arsenal contain ballet material from the 17th and 18th centuries.

Milan's Museo Teatrale alla Scala and the Livia Sioni library contain extensive material on Italian ballet and in particular manuscripts by Blasis and Manzotti. The Dance Documentation Centre in Genzano, founded 1985, has a large collection of videos and books.

Germany's biggest research resource is the Dance Archive, based in Cologne, which is renowned for its 20th-century material, while the Dance Archive of the Academy of Arts in Leipzig, founded 1957, covers folk as well as stage dance.

In London, the London Archives of the Dance, previously held at the former Theatre Museum, has been taken over by the Victoria and Albert Museum. The collection holds press cuttings, scores, prints, photographs, and Diaghilev material as well as additional collections of books, journals, letters, programmes, designs, costumes etc. The Video Place at London's Place Theatre is developing an extensive video collection of new repertory and the National Resource Centre for Dance at the University of Surrey is another major centre of information. A museum relating to the history of the Royal Ballet and its school was opened at White Lodge in 2009, complementing the archive held at The Royal Opera House, that contains Royal Ballet material. Comparable collections are held by English National Ballet and Rambert Dance Company. The Royal Academy of Dancing and the Laban Centre also both have extensive collections.

Copenhagen's Theatre Museum houses much Bournonville material and extensive photographs and costumes.

In St Petersburg, major holdings of dance material include the State Institute of Theatre, Music, and Cinematography, the Mariinsky Theatre Museum, and the Vaganova School museum. In Moscow, the State Central Archive of Literature and Arts, founded 1941, holds considerable ballet material while the A. A. Bakhrushin State Central Theatrical Museum is the oldest Russian theatrical museum.

In India, most of the richest collections are in private libraries, one of the most noted palace collections being the Maharajah Serfoji Sarasvathi in Madras. Many schools are also home to collections including the Darpena Academy of Performing Arts in Ahmadabad.

In Japan, important collections include the Eiryo Ashihara collection at the National Diet Library in Tokyo, the Shochiku-Otani Library in Tokyo, and the Tsubouchi Memorial Theatre Museum at Waseda University.

Around the world, most opera houses and large dance companies have archives relating to their own work. The catalogues of many collections can now be accessed online.

(())) **SEE WEB LINKS**

- Website for Victoria and Albert Museum with link to the dance collection
- Website for Paris Opera with link to museum
- Website for Swedish Dance Museum
- Website for New York Public Library with link to performing arts archives
- Website for La Scala with link to museum
- Website for Goethe Institute with information on German archives
- Website for Surrey University with link to NRCD
- Website for Mariinsky with link to museum
- Website listing Russia's cultural museums and archives

Argentina During the 19th century there was only sporadic dance activity in the country's theatres, most based in Buenos Aires. In the 1830s a small company of dancers performed at the Teatro Coliseo and there were visits from Spanish dancers but it was not until the Teatro Colón opened in 1857 that classical European ballet was first performed, with Jean Rousset's company dancing *Giselle* and presenting other productions based on the works of Montplaisir and Perrot. Thierry's company appeared in 1860 and 1861, dancing versions of Romantic ballets such as *La Sylphide* and *Esmeralda*. Between 1861 and 1873 dances performed in programmes given by the Bouffes Parisiens were popular and in 1868 Josephine Lecerf had a personal success in *Robert le diable*. Buenos Aires' first ballet school was opened in 1879 by Giovanni Pratesi and in the same year a popular production of Manzotti's *Excelsior* was staged (a cigarette was named after the ballet and sold with pictures of the ballerinas). The first Argentinian production of *Coppélia* was danced in 1903.

In 1908 the new Teatro Colón was built, housing a small company of dancers and many more foreign artists began to appear. Preobrajenska came in 1912 (dancing in Dukas's opera *Ariane et Barbe-bleue*), Diaghilev's Ballets Russes came in 1913 and 1917, and Pavlova and Duncan in 1916. In 1925 the company at Teatro Colón was reorganized under the direction of Bolm. His soloists included R. Page and A. Ludmila and for the first time many Argentinian dancers were included in the company. During the following decades many guest choreographers were invited to mount their works in the company which became known as the Ballet Estable del Teatro Colón. These included Nijinska (during the 1920s and 1930s), Fokine (1931), Lifar (1934), and Balanchine (1942). In 1943 the Colón was the wartime base of de Basil's Original Ballet Russe. After the war the stream of guest choreographers continued with Lichine (1947), Massine (at various times between 1948 and 1953, also 1955), and Gsovsky, Tudor, Rosen, and Charrat during the 1950s. J. *Carter staged several ballets including his own versions of *Coppélia*, *Swan Lake*, and *Sleeping Beauty*, and in 1971 Nureyev staged and danced in his own *Nutcracker*, partnering the Colón's principal ballerina Olga *Ferri. In 1968 the company made its European debut at the International Dance Festival in Paris, but in 1971 it suffered the loss of nine principal dancers in an aircrash. Since then its directors have included Antonio Truyol, Ferri, Enrique Lommi, Bruno d'Astoli, Raquel Rosito, Ricardo Bustamente (appointed 1998), and *Araiz (appointed 2005). It continues to perform a varied repertory of classics and 20th-century works. The Colón's associated school, the Instituto Superior de Arte del Teatro Colón has produced many international star dancers, most recently *Bocca, Guerra, Nuñez; and *Herrera, who frequently return as guest with the company.

The first modern dance company in Argentina was founded in 1943 by a student of *Wigman, Miriam Winslow. This ran for only four years, however, and the next phase of activity was not until 1968 when the Balletto Contemporaneo de Ciudad de Buenos Aires, was founded at the Teatro San Martín under the direction of Araiz. In 1998 Araiz was succeeded by Maurice Wainrot and Kive Staiff. During the 1970s some independent modern dance groups (e.g. Nucleodanza) were established, but political conditions were not favourable to artistic experiment, and it was not until the restoration of democracy in 1983 that the rate of new activity significantly increased, with

the formation of groups including Brenda Angiel Aerial Dance Company, Tedancari, and Grupo Krapp. Argentinian companies which have gained the highest international profile, however, are those specializing in *tango.

Argentina, La (orig. Antonia Mercé; *b* Buenos Aires, 4 Sept. 1890 (some sources say 1888); *d* Bayonne, 18 Jul. 1936) Spanish dancer. Both her parents were professional dancers and she was trained in classical technique by her father, Manuel Mercé, who became ballet master at Madrid's Teatro Real. She made her debut aged 6 and was promoted to premiere danseuse of Madrid Opera at 11. At 14 she abandoned ballet to study Spanish dance with her mother and four years later began her first foreign tour. In 1929 she formed her own company, Ballets Espagnols d'Argentina, for which she choreographed several works, including *El amor brujo* (mus. de Falla). She recruited her corps de ballet from Paris Opera and her soloists, including Vicente Escudero, from Spain. But the company did not continue for long as solo performances were La Argentina's special forte. Among her world-wide public she was renowned for her dramatic presence, her exceptionally skilled castanet playing, and her revolutionary fusion of traditional forms with contemporary Spanish music. She was considered by many to be the greatest Spanish dancer of all time, the critic André Levinson claiming that she was responsible for the 20th-century renaissance of Spanish dance.

Argentinita, La (orig. Encarnacion López Julvez; *b* Buenos Aires, 1895; *d* New York, 24 Sept. 1945) Spanish dancer. Her Spanish parents brought her to Spain when she was a child and from a very young age she studied traditional Spanish dances, making her debut in Madrid when she was 6. She took her stage name as a tribute to La Argentina and her own foreign tours won her fame as a dancer of almost equal stature. In 1927 she founded the Ballet de Madrid with Federico García Lorca and in 1933 attempted the first large-scale theatrical presentation of flamenco in her ballet *Las Calles de Cadiz*. In 1939 she collaborated with Massine on *Capriccio espagnole*, and danced with American Ballet Theatre in 1945 in her own works *Bolero* (mus. Ravel) and *Goyescas* (mus. Granados). She was the sister of dancer Pilar *López.

Argyle, Pearl (orig. Pearl Wellman; *b* Johannesburg, 7 Nov. 1910; *d* Hollywood, Calif., 29 Jan. 1947) South African-British dancer. She studied with Rambert and Legat and made her debut in 1926 with Rambert's company, becoming ballerina with the Carmargo Society and also performing with Les Ballets 1933. She was then principal dancer with the Vic-Wells Ballet

(1935-8). She also danced in musicals and revues, including Cochran's 1932 production, *Magic Nights* (mus. various, chor. Bradley and Ashton). In 1938 she moved to the US where she performed in several Broadway musicals including *One Touch of Venus* (mus. Weill, chor. de Mille, 1943). Though never a strong technician she was noted for her outstanding beauty, especially her exquisite hands and arms. As an early muse to Ashton she created roles in his *Façade* and *Lady of Shalott* (both 1931); he wrote of her: 'she was an inspiration, one became drunk with her beauty.' She also created roles in de Valois's *Bar aux Folies-Bergère* and Howard's *Mermaid* (both 1934).

Ari, Carina (orig. Carina Janssen; *b* Stockholm, 14 Apr. 1897; *d* Buenos Aires, 24 Dec. 1970) Swedish dancer. She studied at the Royal Swedish Ballet School and with Fokine in Copenhagen and between 1920 and 1923 was ballerina with Les Ballets Suédois. She then embarked on a solo career but also choreographed several works for the Paris Opéra Comique and created the leading role in Lifar's *Le Cantique des cantiques* (Paris Opera, 1938). She also choreographed works for the Royal Swedish Ballet. She retired from the stage in 1939 and took up sculpting. In her will she endowed the Carina Ari Foundation to provide grants for young dancers as well as the Carina Ari Gold Medal for choreographers (recipients have included Ashton, Tudor, and Béjart).

Ariadne ballets The story of Ariadne, Theseus, and the Minotaur has inspired many choreographers including Deshayes (Paris, 1747), Hilverding (Vienna, 1754), Angiolini (Milan, 1773), Gallet (London, 1797), Reisinger (Moscow, 1875), Lifar (*Bacchus et Ariane*, mus. Roussel, Paris, 1931), Graham (*Errand into the Maze*, mus. Menotti, New York, 1947), John Taras (New York, 1947), and Ailey (mus. Jolivet, Harkness Ballet, 1965).

Armitage, Karole (*b* Madison, Wis., 3 Mar. 1954) US dancer and choreographer. She studied at the N. Carolina School of the Arts, the University of Utah, the School of American Ballet, and Harkness Ballet School. She made her debut with Geneva Opera Ballet (1972-5), then joined Cunningham's company in 1976 where she danced until 1980, creating roles in, among others, *Squaregame* (1976—a duet with Cunningham). She created her first work, a punk ballet called *Ne*, in 1978 (New York) then between 1979 and 1990 directed her own company, creating, for example, *The Watteau Duet* (1985). Her style is a fusion of modern and classical dance, frequently incorporating mixed-media elements and she has created works for many companies, including Paris Opera, American Ballet Theatre (*The Mollino Room*, 1986), New York City Ballet, White Oak,

Berlin Opera Ballet, Lyon Opera Ballet, Rambert Dance Company, and the Alvin Ailey company. During the early 1990s she focused on filmmaking, and choreographing for film and rock video, though she also made some work for ballet companies in Europe, such as *The Dog is Us* (Berlin Opera Ballet, 1994). Between 1996 and 1998 she was director of MaggioDanza, Florence, for which she choreographed several works, including *Apollo e Dafnè* (mus. Handel, 1997). In 1998 she returned to New York as a freelance dancer and choreographer, and subsequently founded her company Armitage Gone! Dance for which she has created several works including *Ligeti Essays* (mus. Ligeti, 2007).

(🌐) **SEE WEB LINKS**
• Website for the Karole Armitage company

Armitage, Merle (*b* Mason City, 1893; *d* 1975) US writer, designer, and impresario. He was in charge of the American publicity for Diaghilev's Ballets Russes and Anna Pavlova's company and promoted the early tours of Graham's group. He wrote the first book about her, *Martha Graham, Dancer* (1937).

Armour, Thomas (*b* Tarpon Springs, Fla., 7 Mar. 1909) US dancer, teacher, and director. He studied with Preobrajenska, Eglevsky, and others and danced with the companies of Rubinstein (1933-4), Nijinska (1934), Woizikowski (1935-8), Rio de Janeiro Opera House (1939), and Ballet Russe de Monte Carlo (1931-41). He founded his own school in Miami in 1949, became director of Miami Conservatory of Music and Dance, and in 1951 was founder-artistic director of Miami Ballet, named artistic director emeritus in 1995.

Arnold, (Sir) Malcolm (*b* Northampton, 21 Oct. 1921; *d* Norwich, 23 Sept. 2006) British composer who has written the scores for several ballets including Ashton's *Homage to the Queen* (1953) and Helpmann's *Elektra* (1963). MacMillan based his *Solitaire* (1956) on Arnold's *English Dances* and Bintley used his *Four Scottish Dances* for his *Flowers of the Forest* (1985). He was knighted in 1993.

Aroldingen, Karin von (*b* Berlin, 9 Sept. 1941) German-US dancer. She studied gymnastics in early childhood then ballet with T. Gsovsky in Berlin. In 1958 she made her debut with American Festival Ballet in Bremen, then was soloist with Frankfurt Ballet (1959-60). Here she danced the lead in Balanchine's *Seven Deadly Sins* which led to her joining New York City Ballet in 1962. Though she rose slowly through the company ranks (appointed soloist in 1967 and principal in 1972), her brilliant allegro technique made her a natural Balanchine dancer. She created roles in many of his ballets including *Who Cares?* (1970), *Violin Concerto* (1972), *Vienna Waltzes* (1977), *Kammermusik No. 2* (1978), and *Davidsbündlertänze* (1980) as well as in Robbins's *Goldberg Variations* (1972). In 1979 she joined the faculty of the School of American Ballet and retired from the stage in 1984. At his death Balanchine left her the rights to several of his ballets and she has gone on to stage his work for many other companies worldwide.

Arova, Sonia (*b* Sofia, 20 Jun. 1927; *d* California, 4 Feb. 2001) Bulgarian-British dancer and director. She studied with Preobrajenska, Lifar, and others and in 1942 joined the English International Ballet, moving to Ballet Rambert in 1946. In 1947 she moved to the Metropolitan Ballet and later guested with various companies around the world, frequently partnered by Nureyev and Bruhn. She was ballet director in Oslo (1966–70) where she helped to form the Norwegian National Ballet, then ballet director of the State Hamburg Opera (1970–1), after which she directed the San Diego Ballet. In 1976 she was appointed Director of Dance at the Alabama School of Fine Arts.

Arpino, Gerald (orig. Gennaro Peter Arpino; *b* Staten Island, NY, 14 Jan. 1928; *d* 29 Oct. 2008) US dancer, choreographer, and director. He began studying ballet at the age of 19 in Seattle with Mary Ann Wells and a year later moved to New York where he studied at the School of American Ballet, also with May O'Donnell and Gertrude Shurr. Between 1949 and 1953 he danced in O'Donnell's company, and in 1952 with the Nana Gollner/Peter Petroff company as well as occasionally performing on Broadway. In 1953 he co-founded a school with Robert *Joffrey (the *American Ballet Center in New York) and in 1956 they founded the Robert Joffrey Theatre Dancers (becoming the Robert Joffrey Ballet). He was principal dancer with the company and created his first work for them in 1961. In 1965 he became the company's assistant director, and sole director in 1988 after Joffrey's death. Nearly all of Arpino's ballets were made for that company. His choreography fuses classical and modern idioms, often taking dance to extremes of athleticism while at the same time dealing with political, sexual and spiritual themes. Among his best-known works are the all-male *Olympics* (mus. T. Mayuzumi, 1966), *The Clowns* (mus. Kay, 1968), the rock ballet *Trinity* (mus. Ralph Holdridge, 1970), which became the company's signature work, and the pure dance work *Suite Saint-Saëns* (1978). As director of Joffrey Ballet (since 1995 renamed Joffrey Ballet of Chicago) until his retirement in 2007 Arpino was committed to maintaining the company as a popular showcase for new American cho-

reography. He was responsible for mounting the box office hit *Billboards* in 1993, with music by Prince and choreography by L. Dean, Sappington, Moulton, and Pucci, and his later works included *Footnotes for R.J.* (mus. Teo Macero, Chicago, 1998). On retirement he was appointed Artistic Director Emeritus of the Joffrey company.

Arriaga, Guillermo (*b* Mexico City, 4 Jul. 1926) Mexican dancer, choreographer, and director. He studied at the National Ballet of Mexico and at the Mexican Dance Academy, later with Limón, Humphrey, Cunningham, Craske, Bolm, La Meri, and others. He danced with various companies including those of Lettie Carroll and Enrique Vela Quintero and in 1953 founded his own group, Contemporary Ballet. In 1956 he founded the Mexican Ballet and in 1958 the Popular Ballet of Mexico which he both directed and performed with until 1964. The company increasingly moved away from modern to folkloric dance and in 1964 Arriaga founded the Folkloric Ballet of Mexico which toured widely around the world. His most enduring work, *Zapata* (mus. Moncayo, 1953), was a celebration of Mexico's national hero, Emiliano Zapata. In 1983 he was appointed director of the Dance Department of the National Institute of Fine Arts where he founded the Dance Research, Documentation and Archives Centre and from 1985 to 1987 directed the National Dance Company.

arrière, en [Fr., backwards] Movements that travel, or are directed, backwards.

Artifact Ballet in four parts with choreography, scenery, and lighting by Forsythe, music by Eva Crossman-Hecht (pts. 1 and 4), Bach (pt. 2), and Forsythe (pt. 3). Premiered 5 Dec. 1984 at Frankfurt Opera House, by Frankfurt Ballet. Forsythe's third full-length work is essentially a pure dance work for a chorus of 36, two principal couples, and one lead woman, but two actors also move through the work declaiming interrogatory texts on the meaning of action, perception, and memory. At times the choreography deliberately courts chaos, at certain points Forsythe subverts theatrical convention, e.g. by having the curtain rise and fall at seemingly arbitrary points in the performance. The overall effect is of a large jigsaw puzzle of different theatrical elements, that eventually fall into place. It has been danced by Dutch National Ballet (since 1993) and, in a shortened version, by Scottish Ballet (2004) and San Francisco Ballet (2006).

Art of Movement Studio Teaching and research centre grounded in *Laban's theories of movement. It was founded in Manchester in 1946 and in 1953 it moved to Addlestone, Surrey, under the direction of Lisa Ullmann, offering courses in training professional dancers as well as effective ways of using dance in general education and therapy. It is now incorporated into the *Laban Centre for Movement and Dance in S. London.

Arts Educational School British school combining academic studies with specialist dance, music, and drama training. It was founded in 1945 in Tring Park.

Asafiev, Boris (pen-name: Igor Glyebov; *b* St Petersburg, 29 Jul. 1884; *d* Moscow, 27 Jan. 1949) Russian musicologist and composer. He was rehearsal pianist at the Mariinsky Ballet and in 1906 invited the student Nijinsky to choreograph his children's opera *Cendrillon*. He subsequently wrote the music for 28 ballets including Vainonen's *Flames of Paris* (1932), Zakharov's *Fountain of Bakhchisarai* (1934), and Lavrovsky's *Prisoner of the Caucasus* (1938). He wrote widely on ballet and music and was made People's Artist of the USSR.

Aschenbrödel Cinderella ballet in three acts with music by J. Strauss II. It was first choreographed by E. Graeb (Berlin Staatsoper, 2 May 1901) and later versions include J. Hassreiter's (Vienna, 4 Oct. 1908) and R. de Warren's (as *Cinderella*, Northern Ballet Theatre, Manchester, 17 Dec. 1979). *See also* CINDERELLA.

Aschengreen, Erik (*b* Copenhagen, 31 Aug. 1935) Danish dance critic. He was dance critic of *Berlingske Tidende* from 1964 and Danish correspondent of *Dance Magazine* and *Les Saisons de la danse*. His published works include *Études* (Copenhagen, 1970), he has lectured at the Royal Danish Ballet School and in the US and Canada, and until 2002 was Head of Dance Criticism and Aesthetics at the University of Copenhagen.

Ashley, Merrill (orig. Linda Michelle Merrill; *b* St Paul, Minn., 2 Dec. 1950) US dancer. She studied with Sybil de Neergaard and Phyllis Marmein and at the School of American Ballet, and in 1967 made her debut with New York City Ballet where she was appointed soloist in 1974 and principal in 1977. One of the last ballerinas to be trained directly by Balanchine her technique was considered exceptional in its dynamic allegro, precision, and musicality. She excelled in ballets like *Theme and Variations*, and Balanchine created two showcase roles for her in *Ballo della Regina* (1977) and *Ballade* (1980) as well as reviving *Four Temperaments* and *Square Dance* especially for her in 1976. Ashley's other created roles included the leads in Robbins's *Requiem Canticles* (1972), in Tharp and Robbins's *Brahms/Handel* (1984), and Martins's *Fearful Symmetries* (1990). She danced Petipa's *Paquita* and *Sleeping Beauty* as a guest artist with Sadler's Wells Royal Ballet in

1987. Between 1969 and 1973 she toured the US with a small company headed by d'Amboise and between 1980 and 1981 she was director and dancer with her own group, Merrill Ashley and Dancers, touring Hawaii. She retired from the stage in 1997, incidentally setting a record as the dancer with the longest career at NYCB, and has subsequently worked as a coach, also staging several works from the Balanchine repertory for companies worldwide. She has additionally directed the Dance Aspen Summer School, appeared several times on television, and is the author of *Dancing for Balanchine* (New York, 1984).

Ashton, (Sir) Frederick (*b* Guayaquil, Ecuador, 17 Sept. 1904; *d* Eye, 19 Aug. 1988) British dancer, choreographer, and director, regarded as one of the chief architects of 20th-century British classicism. He was inspired to dance after seeing Pavlova perform in Peru in 1917 and went to study with Massine in London in about 1923. Later he studied with Rambert, who sensed that his potential as a choreographer was greater than his dance talent and encouraged him to make his first ballet, *A Tragedy of Fashion* (mus. Goossens), in 1926. In 1928 he joined the Rubinstein Company in Paris, where he danced for both Massine and Nijinska, and in 1929 he returned to Rambert and created works both for her Ballet Club and for the Camargo Society. The most enduring of these, *Façade* (1931), is still in the repertory and displays much of the wit, fantasy, and elegance that informed his later style. He was invited to stage the Virgil Thomson/Gertrude Stein opera *Four Saints in Three Acts* in 1934 and during the 1930s he sharpened his craft in the commercial theatre, choreographing several numbers for revues and musical comedies.

In 1935 de Valois invited him to join the Vic-Wells Ballet as a dancer and choreographer and he remained with the company for the next 35 years (under its changing titles Sadler's Wells Ballet and Royal Ballet). Here he cemented a fertile musical relationship with conductor and composer Constant Lambert as well as an intense collaborative relationship with Margot Fonteyn which shaped both their careers. As both muse and star exponent of his style, Fonteyn created the leading roles in most of his ballets over the next 25 years. In works like *Les Patineurs* (1937) the distinguishing features of Ashton's style began to crystallize. Though profoundly influenced by the academic purity of Petipa, his own movement possessed a distinctive sensual plastique so that his fast, brilliant footwork was counterpointed by supple twists and curves in the body, and decorated with rippling arm movements and idiosyncratic angles of the head. Ashton always said that his dancers had to be unafraid 'of letting themselves go', though some of his greatest choreographic moments were characterized by profound simplicity and calm. *Symphonic Variations* (1946) was the first ballet he made when the company moved to the Royal Opera House and the luminous clarity of its dance images dominated the stage, demonstrating to British audiences that a ballet could stand alone without story or characters. In *Scènes de ballet* (1948) Ashton made another plotless masterpiece to Stravinsky's acerbic score. This emphasis on pure movement was also present in the many narrative works he went on to create—not only in their lyric dance interludes but in the musically inventive ways in which dance steps were shaped to create character. In *Cinderella* (1948), the first three-act British ballet, lyric dance was mixed with pantomime to create a distinctively British romantic comedy ballet (Ashton's own performance as the younger Ugly Sister in tow with Helpmann has become legendary). In *Ondine* (1958), described as a 'concerto for Fonteyn', he created a silvery dance language for the water-sprite heroine. He also created additional choreography for the Royal's staging of 19th-century classics such as *Sleeping Beauty* and *Swan Lake*. During the 1960s he began to make work for a younger generation of dancers. For Nadia Nerina and David Blair he created the fresh and funny lovers in *La Fille mal gardée* (1960) while *The Dream* (1964) launched the partnership of Antoinette Sibley and Anthony Dowell as Titania and Oberon. This also featured one of Ashton's greatest comic creations—Bottom—a figure of pathos as well as fun. Between 1963 and 1970 he was artistic director of the Royal Ballet (having been associate director from 1952) and this period is often viewed as the company's golden age, when its 'English' style was at its purest and the corps de ballet one of the finest in the world. His late ballets display a marked confidence and simplicity: in *Monotones* (1965 and 1966) the dancing is stripped to limpid essentials; in *Enigma Variations* (1968) character is distilled through a few gestures and steps; and in *Month in the Country* (1976) the whole of Turgenev's story is compressed into 45 minutes of poignant dance. He still liked to dazzle, though, and in 1980 created the virtuoso showstopper *Rhapsody* for Mikhail Baryshnikov and Lesley Collier.

Ashton choreographed most of his works for the Royal Ballet (he is now cited as its founder choreographer), though many are danced all over the world and he created several ballets for other companies, notably *Illuminations* (1950) for New York City Ballet (now in the Royal Ballet's repertory) and *Romeo and Juliet* (1955) for the Royal Danish Ballet (subsequently performed by English National Ballet). He was knighted in 1962 and received many other awards including Commander of the Order of Dannebrog, 1964; Companion of Honour, 1974; Hon. Doctor of Music,

London University, 1970, and Oxford University, 1976; and Order of Merit, 1977. Works include: *Capriol Suite* (mus. Warlock, 1930), *Façade* (mus. Walton, 1931), *Les Rendezvous* (mus. Auber-Lambert, 1933), *Mephisto Valse* (mus. Liszt, 1934), *Le Baiser de la fée* (mus. Stravinsky, 1935), *Apparitions* (mus. Liszt–Lambert, 1936), *Les Patineurs* (mus. Meyerbeer–Lambert, 1937), *A Wedding Bouquet* (mus. Lord Berners, 1937), *Dante Sonata* (mus. Liszt–Lambert, 1940), *The Wanderer* (mus. Schubert, 1941), *Symphonic Variations* (mus. Franck, 1946), *Valses nobles et sentimentales* (mus. Ravel, 1947), *Scènes de ballet* (mus. Stravinsky, 1948), *Cinderella* (mus. Prokofiev, 1948); *Illuminations* (mus. Britten, 1950), *Daphnis and Chloe* (mus. Ravel, 1951), *Picnic at Tintagel* (mus. Bax, 1952), *Sylvia* (mus. Delibes, 1952), *Homage to the Queen* (mus. Arnold, 1953), *Romeo and Juliet* (mus. Prokofiev, 1955), *Birthday Offering* (mus. Glazunov–Irving, 1956), *La Valse* (mus. Ravel, 1958), *Ondine* (mus. Henze, 1958), *La Fille mal gardée* (mus. Hérold–Lanchbery, 1960), *Two Pigeons* (mus. Messager–Lanchbery, 1961), *Perséphone* (mus. Stravinsky, 1961), *Marguerite and Armand* (mus. Liszt–Searle, 1963), *The Dream* (mus. Mendelssohn–Lanchbery, 1964), *Monotones* (mus. Satie, 1965 and 1966), *Sinfonietta* (mus. M. Williamson, 1967), *Jazz Calendar* (mus. R. R. Bennett, 1968), *Enigma Variations* (mus. Elgar, 1968), *Lament of the Waves* (mus. Masson, 1970), *Creatures of Prometheus* (mus. Beethoven, 1970), *Tales of Beatrix Potter* (film-ballet, dir. Reginald Mills, mus. Lanchbery, 1971), *Meditation from Thaïs* (mus. Massenet, 1971), *A Month in the Country* (mus. Chopin–Lanchbery, 1976), *Five Brahms Waltzes in the Manner of Isadora Duncan* (mus. Brahms, 1976), *Rhapsody* (mus. Rachmaninoff, 1980), and *La Chatte métamorphosée en femme* (mus. Offenbach, 1985). He also choreographed for several opera productions, including *The Fairy Queen* (mus. Purcell, 1946), *Orpheus and Euridice* (mus. Gluck, 1953), and *Death in Venice* (mus. Britten, 1973).

(()) SEE WEB LINKS

• Website listing all of Ashton's work

assemblé [Fr., assembled] A jump in which the dancer throws one leg up in the air and springs off the other foot, landing with both feet closed together. Variant assemblés (grands or petits) may travel in the direction of the raised leg or may be executed while turning or with a *beat.

Assembly Ball Ballet in one act with choreography and design by A. Howard, and music by Bizet. Premiered 8 Apr. 1946 by Sadler's Wells Opera Ballet at Sadler's Wells Theatre, London, with Brae, Kersley, and Newman. It is set to Bizet's Symphony in C and portrays the flirtatious encounters of several people at a ball.

Astafieva, Serafina (*b* St Petersburg, 1876; *d* London, 13 Sept. 1934) Russian dancer and teacher. She studied at St Petersburg Theatre School and graduated into the Mariinsky Ballet in 1895, a year later marrying the famous character dancer Jozef Kshessinsky (brother to the ballerina *Kshessinska). She subsequently danced with Diaghilev's Ballets Russes (1909–11) then opened a school in London where her pupils included Markova, Dolin, and Fonteyn.

Astaire, Fred (orig. Frederick Austerlitz; *b* Omaha, Nebr., 10 May 1899; *d* Los Angeles, 22 June 1987) US dancer and choreographer, considered to be one of the greatest tap dancers of the century. With very little formal training, he and his sister Adele began performing a vaudeville child act in 1906 which toured widely around the US. In 1917 they appeared in their first musical comedy (*Over the Top*) and subsequently starred in many musicals and revues in both London and New York—including the Gershwins' *Lady be Good* (1924) and *Funny Face* (1927). After Adele retired in 1932 he went to Hollywood where his appearance with Ginger Rogers in *Flying Down to Rio* (1933) created a sensation. They made 8 more films together in quick succession, including *The Gay Divorcee* (1934), *Top Hat* (1935), *Shall We Dance?* (1937), and *The Story of Vernon and Irene Castle* (1939). They made an ideally complementary couple, he slender, elegant, and dapper, she more earthy, pliant, and extrovert. Astaire subsequently made many films with other partners, including Eleanor Powell (*Broadway Melody of 1940*), Rita Hayworth (*You'll Never Get Rich*, 1941), Judy Garland and Ann Miller (*Easter Parade*, 1948), Leslie Caron (*Daddy Long Legs*, 1955), Audrey Hepburn (*Funny Face*, 1957), and Cyd Charisse (*Silk Stockings*, 1957). None of these partnerships displayed the unique chemistry of his work with Rogers, though their re-union in *The Barkleys of Broadway* (1947) proved to be disappointing. In the same year, however, Astaire received a special Academy Award for 'his unique artistry' which was presented to him by Rogers. Though he liked to pretend his dancing was effortless—'I just put my feet in the air and move them around'—he was in fact a notorious perfectionist both as choreographer and performer. From the late 1950s he concentrated on acting roles and television specials, though he did not give up dancing completely until his seventies. He received nine Emmy Awards and a *Dance Magazine* award in 1959. He wrote *Steps in Time* (New York, 1959).

Astarte Mixed-media ballet with choreography by Joffrey, music by Crome Syrcus, design and lighting by Thomas Skelton, and film by Gardner Compton. Premiered 20 Sept. 1967 by City Center Joffrey Ballet at City Center, New York, with Trinette Singleton and Maximiliano Zomosa. It is loosely based on the story of the Phoenician goddess Astarte and its fusion of rock music, strobe lighting, and film was regarded at the time as startlingly theatrical.

As Time Goes By Ballet in one act with choreography by Tharp, music by Haydn, costumes by Chester Weinberg, and lighting by J. Tipton. Premiered 10 Oct. 1973 at City Center, New York, with Beatriz Rodriguez and Larry Grenier. It is set to the last two movements of Haydn's 45th Symphony and though grounded in pure classical dance it reverses traditional male-female roles by presenting the ballerina as the assertive dancer and the man as the more vulnerable partner. This was Tharp's second work for the Joffrey Ballet.

Astrakan *See* LARRIEU, DANIEL.

Asylmuratova, Altynai (*b* Alma-Ata, 1 Jan. 1961) Russian dancer. She studied at the Leningrad (Vaganova) Ballet School under Inna Zubkovskaya and made her debut in the Kirov Ballet in 1978. She was appointed principal in 1982 and toured widely with the company, guesting with American Ballet Theatre in 1988, the Royal Ballet (various seasons from 1989), and Petit's Marseilles Ballet (1996–9). She became acknowledged as one of her generation's greatest ballerinas possessing a profound musicality and dramatic intelligence, and a range that extended from delicately drawn romanticism to witty charm. Though she excelled in the 19th-century ballerina roles she also showed her range in 20th-century ballets by MacMillan, Ashton, Balanchine, Petit, and Béjart. In 1999 she was appointed director of the Vaganova School, St Petersburg. In 1983 she was made Honoured Artist of the Russian Federation. She is married to the dancer Konstantin *Zaklinsky.

Atanassoff, Cyril (*b* Puteaux, 30 Jun. 1941) French dancer. He studied at Paris Opera Ballet School and made his debut with the company in 1957. He was appointed premier danseur in 1962 and étoile in 1964. A dancer of impeccably precise technique he was greatly admired by Balanchine whenever he danced in the latter's ballets. He also had a powerful dramatic talent which was revealed when Béjart created the role of the Young Man for him in *La Damnation de Faust* (1964). He also created roles in Petit's *Notre-Dame de Paris* (1965) and *Nana* (1976); in Butler's *Intégrales* and *Amériques* (both 1973); and in Spoerli's *La Fille mal gardée* (1981). He guested with companies throughout the world and after retiring from principal roles in 1986 he continued to work as a teacher and to dance occasional character roles.

Aterballetto Italian modern ballet company. It was founded in 1977 as an experimental ensemble based at Teatro Valli at Reggio Emilia, but its repertory was expanded when *Amodio took over direction in 1979 to include works by himself, Forsythe, Childs, Kylián, Petit, Balanchine, and others. It began to tour extensively in Italy, also to perform in the US, Russia, and much of Europe. By 1997 Amodio's own work had come to dominate the repertory and the company was perceived as stagnating. He was succeeded by Mauro *Bigonzetti, who introduced many of his own works into the repertory as well as acquisitions from Preljocaj and Kylián among others. Bigonzetti has remained the company's principal choreographer after being succeeded as director by Cristina Bozzolini in 2008.

 SEE WEB LINKS

• Website for Aterballetto

Atlanta Ballet US ballet company. It was founded in 1929 by Dorothy Alexander as the performing ensemble of her school. Initially called the Dorothy Alexander Concert Group, it was given its present name in 1967 and became a paradigm regional ballet company with a wide repertory of 19th- and 20th-century classics. Robert Barnett succeeded Alexander in 1963 followed by John McFall who was appointed director in 1994 and in 1996 opened the company's associate Centre for Dance Education.

SEE WEB LINKS

• Website for Atlanta Ballet

Atlas, Charles (*b* St Louis, Mo., 25 Mar. 1949) US film-maker, designer, and lighting specialist. He has made many films with Cunningham, such as *Walkaround Time* (1973), *Torse* (1977), *Channels/Inserts* (1981), *Coast Zone* (1984), and in 2000 the video dance *Melange* which formed part of a large television documentary about the choreographer. He has also collaborated on video and film projects with, among others, D. Dunn (*Secret of the Waterfall*, 1983), Michael Clark (*Hail the New Puritan*, 1986), Richard Move (various *Martha* performances in the late 1990s), and Rainer (*Variations*, 2002). He has also designed set and lighting for stage works by Clark and K. Armitage among others.

At Midnight Ballet in one act with choreography by Feld, music by Mahler, sets by Leonard Baskin, and costumes by Stanley Simmons. Premiered 1 Dec. 1967 by American Ballet Theatre at City Center, New York, with Marks, Sarry, Orr, and Gregory. It is set to Mahler's *Rückert Lieder* and portrays the romantic anguish of love. It is also in the repertories of Royal Swedish Ballet and Eliot Feld Ballet.

attack A particularly incisive accentuation of dance steps.

attitude Position in which the dancer stands on one leg with the other lifted in front or behind with the knee bent. Russian dancers generally hold the raised foot higher than the knee, so allowing the leg to be lifted higher. Other styles raise the knee higher than the foot. The position was originally inspired by Giovanni da Bologna's statue of Mercury and was codified by Blasis. It may be held as a balance or performed jumping or turning.

Auber, Daniel-François-Esprit (*b* Caen, 29 Jan. 1782; *d* Paris, 12 or 13 May 1871) French composer. He wrote no ballet scores but interludes and divertissements from his grand operas were important in the development of Romantic ballet, such as those from *Le Dieu et la bayadère* (chor. F. Taglioni, 1830), *Gustave* (chor. Taglioni, 1833), *L'Enfant prodigue* (chor. Saint-Léon, 1850), and *Le Cheval de bronze* (chor. L. Petipa, 1857). He spliced together the score for Mazilier's ballet *Marco Spada* (1857) from various of his own operas, and several choreographers have subsequently used his music for their ballets, including Ashton (*Les Rendezvous*, 1937), V. Gsovsky (*Grand Pas Classique*, 1949), and L. Christensen (*Divertissement d'Auber*, 1959).

Augusta, Mlle (orig. Caroline Augusta Josephine Thérèse Fuchs, Comtesse de Saint-James; *b* Munich, 17 Sept. 1806; *d* New York, 17 Feb. 1901) French dancer. She studied with F. Taglioni and Albert, making her debut in London's Drury Lane in 1833. She danced for a season at the Paris Opera in 1835, then travelled to the US where she enjoyed great personal success, dancing *La Bayadère* in 1836 and *La Sylphide* in 1938. She was New York's first Giselle (1846).

Augustyn, Frank (*b* Hamilton, Ont., 27 Jun. 1953) Canadian dancer. He studied at the National Ballet School and joined National Ballet of Canada in 1970 where he was appointed soloist in 1971 and principal in 1972. A dancer of compelling dramatic appeal and a skilled partner he became the company's leading danseur noble. He was also a frequent guest abroad, often partnering K. Kain. Between 1980 and 1981 he danced with Berlin Opera Ballet as principal and from 1984 to 1986 was guest artist with Boston Ballet. In 1989 he resigned from National Ballet of Canada and became artistic director of Ottawa Ballet. After that company disbanded in 1994 he became a teacher at the National Ballet School and guest ballet master with NBC. During the mid-1990s he hosted the twenty-part television series on ballet, *Footnotes*.

Auld, John (*b* Melbourne, 6 Jan. 1930) Australian dancer and director. He studied with several teachers including Borovansky, Preobrajenska, and Idzikowski and made his debut with the Borovansky Ballet in 1951. Between 1952 and 1953 he performed in musicals and revues in London, after which he was soloist with Borovansky Ballet (1954–8). Between 1960 and 1964 he danced with Ballet of Two Worlds and Festival Ballet, and was also artistic director of the latter company (1962–4). He was then appointed ballet master of the Gulbenkian Ballet (1965–7), after which he worked with the Royal Ballet touring company (1971–81) as assistant to the directors and as co-manager. In 1981 he moved to Sadler's Wells Royal Ballet as assistant director and character artist. He continued to work as occasional producer.

Aumer, Jean-Louis (*b* Strasbourg, 21 Apr. 1774 (some sources say 1776); *d* St-Martin-en-Bosc, Jul. 1833) French dancer and choreographer. He studied with Dauberval in Bordeaux and danced with his company in London (1791–2). In London he also danced with Noverre's company (1794) and at the King's Theatre (1795), going on to make his debut with the Paris Opera in 1798. He was then ballet master at the Paris Théâtre de la Porte St-Martin (1804–6) where he mounted several Dauberval works, including *La Fille mal gardée*, and also choreographed his own ballets, including the highly successful *Les Deux Créoles* (mus. Darondeau, 1806), based on the novel *Paul et Virginie*. His work closely followed Dauberval's principles of *ballet d'action, telling dramatic stories through expressive mime. In 1807 he became ballet master at Lyons then in 1808 was invited to create a work for the Paris Opera. *Les Amours d'Antoine et de Cléopâtre* (mus. R. Kreutzer) was highly successful and so impressed Jérome Napoleon, King of Westphalia, that he was engaged in 1809 as ballet master of the Kassel court theatre. In 1814 he moved to Lyons and then to Vienna where he choreographed numerous ballets and divertissements. In 1820 he returned to Paris as ballet master, amidst high expectations. But although he staged revivals of two Dauberval ballets and created many new works, including *La Belle au bois dormant* (mus. Hérold, 1829) and *Manon Lescaut* (mus. Halévy, 1830), he was not popular. His works were widely criticized for their excessive use of mime and their inability to create dance that furthered either character or plot. He retired in 1831.

Aureole Modern dance work in one act with choreography by Taylor, music by Handel, and lighting by T. Skelton. Premiered 4 Aug. 1962 at Connecticut College, New London, by the Paul Taylor Dance Company with Taylor, Elizabeth Walton, Wagoner, Sharon Kinney, and Renee Kim-

ball. A lyrical, buoyant dance which at the time marked Taylor's stylistic break from the American avant-garde. Its choreography fuses the blunt power of modern dance with the elevation of ballet, and at the time was seen as a rejection of the twin poles of modern dance then prevalent—the darkly dramatic and the abstractly cerebral. It has entered the repertories of many companies including Royal Danish Ballet (1968), Paris Opera Ballet (1974), and London Festival Ballet (1985).

Auric, Georges (*b* Lodève, 15 Feb. 1899; *d* Lodève, 23 Jul. 1983) French composer, who as a member of Les Six contributed to the ballet score *Les Mariés de la Tour Eiffel* (chor. Börlin, Paris 1921, Les Ballets Suédois). He also wrote the music for Nijinska's *Les Fâcheux* (1924), for Massine's *Les Matelots* (1925), *Le Peintre et son modèle* (1949), and *Bal de voleurs* (1960), for Balanchine's *La Pastorale* (1926) and *La Concurrence* (1932), for Lifar's *Phèdre* (1950), and for V. Gsovsky's *Chemin de lumière* (1952).

Aurora's Wedding (Fr. title *Le Mariage de la belle au bois dormant*) One-act divertissement of dance from Petipa's *Sleeping Beauty* with music by Tchaikovsky and additional choreography by Nijinska. Premiered by Diaghilev's Ballets Russes at the Paris Opera on 18 May 1922, with Trefilova and Vladimirov. Diaghilev had presented the full ballet in London in 1921 but had incurred huge debts in doing so. This shortened version was salvaged, and with scenery by Bakst and costumes by Goncharova (as well as costumes from *Pavilion d'Armide*) it proved very successful. It later entered the repertoire of de Basil's company and Dolin staged another production for American Ballet Theatre in 1941. After Vic-Wells Ballet staged the full-length *Sleeping Beauty* this version virtually disappeared.

Ausdruckstanz [Ger., expressive dance] The term dates from 1920s' Germany when it was used to describe new modern dance forms, distinguishing them from classical dance. It was, however, disdained by some of its most famous practitioners, e.g. *Wigman who preferred the term *Neue künstlerische Tanz* or 'new artistic dance'.

Australia Drama was much more popular than dance during the first half of the 19th century, though some incidental stage choreography is recorded from 1833 onwards and in 1840 Mme Velbein was appointed to oversee dance at Sydney's Royal Victoria Theatre, with Mme Rosine becoming ballet mistress at Melbourne's Royal Theatre in the same year. Dance performances became voguish around this time and the first European ballet companies began to visit. *La Sylphide* was danced in Melbourne during the 1840s and *La Fille mal gardée* in Sydney and Melbourne in 1855. In the same year, the visiting Lola *Montez attracted extraordinary audiences. In 1889 an Australian corps de ballet appeared in a Melbourne production of *Sinbad the Sailor* and was retained as the corps of the Royal Comic Opera Company with ballerina Mary Weir. New ballets arranged for the Royal Comic Opera and the Melba Opera Company at the beginning of the 20th century were critically well received, but ballet still remained a minority enthusiasm. In 1913, however, A. Genée performed in Melbourne with dancers from the Imperial Russian Ballet in performances of *Coppélia* and *Les Sylphides* and sparked widespread public interest in the art. This was rekindled in 1926 and 1927 when Pavlova toured the country. During the 1920s some distinguished dancers and teachers also settled in Australia including Mischa Burlakov, who with Louise Lightfoot founded the First Australian Ballet, which staged several Fokine ballets. In 1934 Victor Dandré presented the Levitoff Russian Ballet with Spessivtseva and Vilzak and in the same year Molly *Lake established an Australian branch of the Cecchetti Society. In 1938 the first Royal Academy of Dancing examiner was appointed and de Basil's Ballets Russes had a highly successful tour which they repeated in 1938 (under the name Covent Garden Russian Ballet) and in 1940 (as the Original Ballet Russe). It was on this tour that Lichine premiered his *Graduation Ball* in Sydney. Two important members of this company stayed on in Australia—Helene *Kirsova, who opened a studio in Sydney, followed by her own company, the Kirsova Ballet (1941–6), and *Borovansky, who opened a school in Melbourne in 1939. A company emerged from the school in 1940, becoming fully professional in 1944. Its repertoire was predominantly Russian but it also featured work by Australian choreographers Laurel Martyn and Dorothy Stevenson whose *Sea Legend* was the first all-Australian ballet. Premiered in 1943 in Melbourne it had music by Esther Rofe, and designs by Alan McCulloch and Jean Oberhansli. Though struggling with constant financial difficulties (it had to disband after every season) the company produced several fine dancers including Kathleen Gorham and Garth *Welch, and built up a solid audience for dance. Following Borovansky's death in 1959 the company's final season was directed by van Praagh. It was then absorbed into *Australian Ballet which she founded in 1962 with Government subsidy.

After the 1940s interest in ballet gathered momentum with the founding of many clubs, guilds, and new companies. Two Melbourne ballet groups were founded in 1940, West Australian Ballet was established in 1952 and Queensland Ballet (orig. Lisner Ballet) in 1960. Australia also became firmly established on the international touring circuit.

Modern dance activity dates back to 1938 with the opening of the Bodenwieser Studio in Sydney and the subsequent founding of the Bodenwieser Ballet, but it did not become prominent until the 1960s. In 1965 the educational modern dance group Ballet in a Nutshell was founded, becoming in 1971 the professionally run Dance Company (NSW). This was renamed the *Sydney Dance Company and its distinctive identity formed by choreographer-director Graeme *Murphy. The *Australian Dance Theatre was also founded in 1965 by Elizabeth *Dalman (with subsequent directors including *Meryl Tankard). Many other smaller companies have since emerged including: Dance North based in Townsville since 1973; Dance Exchange founded by Russell *Dumas and Nanette Hassall in 1976; the *Australian Choreographic Ensemble directed by Paul Mercurio in Sydney between 1992 and 1998; the Chrissie Parrott Dance Collective based in Perth; the physical theatre group, Desoxy Theatre, founded by Teresa Blake and Daniel Witton in Melbourne in 1990; Leigh Warren and Dancers founded in Adelaide in 1993; the street dance company Strange Fruit, set up in Melbourne in 1994; Chunky Move company set up in Melbourne in 1995 to present dance in relation with digital technology; and the Raw Metal tap dance company set up in Queensland in 1998. In recent years there has been a growing interest in aboriginal dance with the formation of *Bangarra Dance Theatre and the Aboriginal Islander Dance Theatre, while Asian influences are increasingly evident in the popularity of bharata natyam and butoh dance. In 1993 the first Green Mills Dance Project was held in Melbourne, a mixed festival of dance performances and classes that has rapidly acquired an international status. The country's main schools include the Australian Ballet School (Melbourne), the Scully Borovansky School (Sydney), and the Bodenwieser Dance Centre (Sydney).

((◉)) SEE WEB LINKS

• Website for Australia Dancing—a database for Australian dance institutions and personalities

Australian Ballet Australia's leading ballet company, based in Melbourne and, though not officially designated as such, the country's national company. It was founded by van *Praagh in 1962, with a government subsidy, using many dancers from the defunct company of *Borovansky (the latter is often called 'The Father of Ballet in Australia'). The company's first performance was *Swan Lake* with guest artists Sonia Arova and Eric Bruhn, and from the beginning it was closely connected to British ballet, via not only van Praagh but also Ray Powell, its first ballet master who was initially on leave from the Royal Ballet. The company's early repertoire included works by Ashton, Cranko, Balanchine, and Ray Powell. But van Praagh was keen to promote its Australian identity. In 1964 Helpmann choreographed his all-Australian ballet for the company, *The Display*, drawing an analogy between youthful sexuality and the mating dance of the lyre bird, and in 1965 he became co-artistic director. In the same year the company toured abroad, including performances at the 3rd International Festival of Dance in Paris. During this tour Nureyev staged his full-length *Raymonda* for the company, and subsequently retained close links as a guest artist and producer. Though very distant from the main centres of ballet activity the company rapidly attained high technical standards and a varied repertoire and continued to progress through new productions of the classics and works by 20th-century choreographers, from Fokine and Massine through to MacMillan, Cranko, Tetley, Moreland, and Kylián. More recently it has featured younger Australian choreographers like Tankard, Stephen Page, and S. Welch. In 1974 Helpmann took over as artistic director, succeeded by A. *Woolliams in 1976. In 1978 van Praagh returned for two years, followed by Marilyn Jones, then by Maina *Gielgud in 1983. Ross *Stretton was artistic director (1997–2001), succeeded by David McAllister from 2001. McAllister has encouraged the development of a new generation of Australian choreographers including Stephen Baynes, Natalie Weir, and Adrian Burnett, who was appointed resident choreographer in 2003; he has also commissioned works from an international range of choreographers, including McGregor and Ratmansky. In 1984 the company made its permanent theatrical base in the State Theatre, Victorian Arts Centre and in 1988 moved into its own purpose-built rehearsal and administrative premises, the Australia Ballet Centre. It tours extensively both in Australia and overseas and has gained a high international reputation for the unselfconscious vigour of its classical style. Its leading dancers have included Kelvin Coe, Lisa Pavane, and Steven Heathcote, and in recent years Madeleine Eastoe and Adam Bull. The company's school was opened in 1964 under the direction of Margaret Scott.

(⊕) SEE WEB LINKS
• Website for Australian Ballet

Australian Choreographic Ensemble Dance company founded by Paul Mercurio, former member of Sydney Dance Company and star of the film *Strictly Ballroom* (1992). It gave its first performance in Sydney in 1992 with Mercurio's own work *Contact* but was disbanded in 1998.

Australian Dance Theatre Adelaide-based modern dance company founded in 1965 by Elizabeth Dalman. Under the direction of Jonathan Taylor it was reorganized in 1977 to serve both Victoria and S. Australia. Its repertoire included works by Taylor and Norman Morrice. Leigh Warren took over as artistic director in 1985 and was succeeded by Meryl Tankard (1993–9), and by Garry *Stewart from 2000, whose works for the company include *Birdbrain* (2000), *The Age of Unbeauty* (2002), and *G* (2008), a modern critique of *Giselle*.

(⊕) SEE WEB LINKS
• Website for Australian Dance Theatre

Austria Ballets companies are attached to the opera houses of several Austrian cities: Baden bei Wien, Graz, Innsbruck, Klagenfurt, Linz, Salzburg, and St Pölten, though until recently their prime function has been performing in operas. Historically, the main centre of dance activity has been Vienna. During the 18th century some of the greatest ballet masters came to the Habsburg court including Hilverding, Angiolini, Noverre, and Viganò, instituting a lively tradition of dramatic ballets at the Kärntnertor Theater (the opera house). Dance was also popular at the city's Theater auf der Wieden with Friedrich Horschelt's fairy-tale ballets and *Vienna Children's Ballet drawing enthusiastic crowds, and at the Theater in der Leopoldstadt with Rainoldi's pantomimes. During the first half of the 19th century most of the great Romantic ballerinas performed in the city. In the 1820s Vienna's most renowned dancer, Elssler, came to fame while her rival Taglioni made her Viennese debut in 1822. Productions of many popular ballets were danced including *La Sylphide* (1836), *La Fille du Danube* (1839), *La Gitana* (1840), *Giselle* (1842), and *La Péri* (1844). After 1853 P. Taglioni made regular visits as guest choreographer and between 1855 and 1856 August Bournonville was ballet master, staging *Napoli* in 1856. In 1869 P. Taglioni's *Sardanapal* was the opening production of the Hofopertheater, the newly built Opera House. Karl Telle was in charge of the ballet company here until 1890, staging productions of *Coppélia* in 1876 and *Sylvia* in 1877, although ballet was by this time subservient to opera. He was succeeded by Josef Hassreiter whose first ballet *The Fairy Doll* (1888) achieved considerable success and is still in the repertory. He reigned until 1920 having choreographed 48 ballets, many to music by Josef Bayer. Between 1922 and 1928 Heinrich *Kröller was ballet master staging several ballets to music by Richard Strauss including *Couperin Suite* (1923), the latter being director of the State Opera. Margarete Wallmann, who had studied with Wigman, directed the Opera Ballet and its school from 1934 to 1939. Erika *Hanka was appointed in 1942 and choreographed many ballets based in European modern dance techniques, including *Homeric Symphony* (mus. T. Berger, 1950) and *Medusa* (mus. von Einem, 1957). She was, however, instrumental in re-introducing the classical repertoire with Gordon Hamilton's staging of *Giselle* opening the theatre on 29 Nov. 1955, after the re-opening of the Opera House (it had been destroyed in 1945). Standards rose but after Hanka's death in 1958 there was a disruptively rapid turnover of ballet masters and directors—Parlic (1958–61), Milloss (1961–6 and 1971–4), and Orlikowsky (1966–71). There were, however, two outstanding triumphs: Nureyev's 1964 production of *Swan Lake* and Grigorovich's 1973 production of *Nutcracker*. In 1976 Gerhard Brunner became director of the State Opera Ballet and its school and the repertoire expanded to include works by van Manen, Cranko, and Massine. A. *Woolliams took over the company's direction in 1994 (from Elena Tchernichova) and continued to expand the modern repertoire with new works by Renato Zernatto and Uwe Scholz. Subsequent directors have been Renato Zanella, appointed in 1995, and Gyula *Harangozo, appointed in 2005, and new works added to the repertory have included ballets by Jorma Elo. Other ballet performances take place at the Theater an der Wien and the Volksoper. In Salzburg the ballet company has also expanded its modern repertory under the direction of Peter Breuer whose own creations for the company include *Angels* (2007), while the company at Graz has works by Spoerli, Smok, and van Manen in its repertory. Modern dance groups are overshadowed by the opera house companies but a growing number of independent choreographers have begun working in the country during the past decade including Eva-Maria Lerchenberg-Thony, Willi Dorner, and Jochen Ulrich, their activity given focus by the biannual dance festival in Vienna and by the Austria Dances festival in Graz.

Austria's most important dance school is the State Opera Ballet School.

Autumn Leaves Ballet in one act with libretto and choreography by Pavlova, music by Chopin (various piano pieces), and design by Konstantin Korovin. Premiered in 1918 by the Anna Pavlova Ballet in Rio de Janeiro with Pavlova and Volinine. It portrays a chrysanthemum which has been carefully grown by a poet, but is destroyed by the harsh North wind.

Available Light Modern dance work in one act with choreography by Lucinda Childs, music by John Adams, stage design by architect Frank Gehry, and costumes by R. Shamask. Commissioned by Los Angeles Museum of Modern Art and premiered by Lucinda Childs Company in Los Angeles, Sept. 1983. In this setting of Adams's score, *Light Above Water*, the choreography's mathematically repeating moves are performed by dancers on a two-tiered stage. An open-air version was premiered at the Centre de Rencontres of Chateauvallon, July 1983, and the New York premiere was at the Opera House of the Brooklyn Academy of Music, Oct. 1983.

avant, en [Fr., forwards] All movements that either travel or are directed forwards.

Aveline, Albert (*b* Paris, 23 Dec. 1883; *d* Asnières, 3 Feb. 1968) French dancer, choreographer, teacher, and ballet master. He studied at the Paris Opera Ballet School from 1894 and joined the company after graduation, becoming étoile in 1908 and ballet master in 1917. He was a favourite partner of both Spessivtseva and Zambelli. He staged revivals of ballets by Mérante, Staats, and Clustine as well as choreographing several works including *La Grisi* (mus. O. Métra, 1935), *Jeux d'enfants* (mus. Bizet, 1941), *La Grande Jatte* (mus. Fred Barlow, 1950), and the prologue for *Les Indes galantes* (mus. Rameau, 1952).

awards In most countries distinguished dance artists are honoured by national awards and decorations. For example, in Britain Ashton was appointed to the Order of Merit in 1977 and in the USSR Ulanova was made Hero of Socialist Labour (both among the highest possible awards to be conferred on civilians). There are many specialist awards given to dance professionals by magazines, trusts, and institutions around the world, including the Pavlova and Nijinsky Prizes, the Bessie Awards, Capezio Awards, the *Dance Magazine* award and the Queen Elizabeth II Coronation Award (given by the Royal Academy of Dancing), as well as dance categories in arts and theatre awards such as the Olivier Awards.

Ayupova, Zhanna (*b* Petrozavodsk, 12 Oct. 1966) Russian dancer. She studied at the Leningrad (Vaganova) Ballet School under N. Kurgapkina, and graduated into the Kirov in 1984, becoming principal 1985–2007. She danced most of the classical and Soviet ballerina roles, also creating the lead in Alexei Ratmansky's *The Duet* (1998) and dancing one of the two ballerina roles in 'Emeralds' as part of the Kirov's company premiere of *Jewels*.

Babilée, Jean (orig. J. Gutmann; *b* Paris, 2 Feb. 1923) French dancer, choreographer, and actor. After studying at the Paris Opera Ballet School from 1936 (with Volinine and Gsovsky), he made his debut as a dancer in Cannes in 1940 with Marika Besobrasova's troupe. He joined the Paris Opera Ballet corps in 1943, although left shortly afterwards to join the French Resistance. After the war he became principal dancer of Roland Petit's Ballets des Champs-Elysées (1945–50) and when that company closed guested in Europe and America. He returned briefly to the Paris Opera in 1953, and to Petit's Ballets de Paris in 1954 before starting his own short-lived company, Les Ballets Jean Babilée (1955–9). A virtuoso dancer, possessed of exceptional elevation, he was celebrated for his Blue Bird and *Spectre de la rose*, although most closely identified with the lead role in *Le Jeune Homme et la mort*, which Petit choreographed for him in 1946. Other created roles included Charrat's *Jeu de cartes* (1945), Lichine's *Oedipe et le Sphinx* (1948), Massine's *Mario e il mago* (1956), and Lazzini's *Prodigal Son* (1967). He choreographed his first ballet in 1944, *Sérénité* (to Beethoven), for the Paris Soirées de la Danse and a list of his subsequent works includes *L'Amour et son amour* (mus. Franck, Ballets des Champs-Elysées, 1948), *Till Eulenspiegel* (Strauss, Ballets des Champs-Elysées, 1949), *Balance à trois* (mus. Damase, Monte Carlo Opera, 1955), and *Le Caméléopard* (mus. Sauguet, Les Ballets Jean Babilée, 1956). His stage career continued into middle age. Dancing the title role in Joseph Lazzini's *The Prodigal Son*, he was awarded the Gold Star for best dancer at the International Festival of Dance in Paris in 1967, Béjart created *Life* for him in New York in 1979, and in Paris in 1984, at the age of 61, he returned to his created role in Petit's *Le Jeune Homme et la mort* with the National Ballet of Marseilles. He briefly directed the Ballet du Rhin in Strasbourg (1972–3). Babilée also had a career in film, appearing in *La Ligne d'ombre* (1971) and *Duelle* (1975) and acted in stage productions of Tennessee Williams's *Orpheus Descending* and Jean Genet's *The Balcony*, as well as taking the lead in the dance drama *The Green Queen*, mounted by Béjart in 1963.

baby ballerinas The collective nickname given to Baronova (aged 13), Toumanova (14), and Riabouchinska (15) when they were members of the Ballets Russes de Monte Carlo in 1933. Now used to designate exceptionally precocious young women dancers.

Bacchanale A dance (or, in its wider context, a festival) in honour of Bacchus, the Roman god of wine. Used frequently in ballet as a divertissement of festive character dances staged to celebrate the autumn wine harvest.

Bacchanale Ballet in one act with choreography by Massine, music by Wagner, and designs by Dalí. Premiered 9 Nov. 1939 by the Ballet Russe de Monte Carlo at the Metropolitan Opera House, New York, with Krassovska, Theilade, Eglevsky, and Platoff. The work, set to the *Tannhäuser* ballet music, depicts the Wagner-inspired nightmares of Ludwig II of Bavaria. Ballets or divertissements with the same title have been produced by Mordkin, Fokine, and others.

Bach, Johann Sebastian (*b* Eisenach, 21 Mar. 1685; *d* Leipzig, 28 Jul. 1750) German composer. Although he wrote no ballet music, his work has been used by many choreographers. Signficant examples include Nijinska's *Étude* (Paris, 1931), Balanchine's *Concerto Barocco* (Concerto for 2 Violins in D minor, New York, 1941), Petit's *Le Jeune Homme et la mort* (Passacaglia in C minor, Paris, 1946), Cranko's *Brandenburgs 2 & 4* (London, 1966), Robbins's *The Goldberg Variations* (New York, 1971), Paul Taylor's *Esplanade* (various, New York, 1975), Béjart's *Notre Faust* (B minor Mass, Brussels, 1975), Neumeier's *St Matthew Passion* (Hamburg, 1981), Alain Platel's *Iets op Bach* (various, Les Ballets C de la B, 1998), Bigonzetti's *Homage to Bach* (various, Aterballetto, 2000).

Bagnolet International choreographic competition, held in the Paris suburb of Bagnolet. The Concours International de Chorégraphie: Le Ballet pour Demain was established in 1969, promoted by local and national governments. In the 1980s it became a key platform for young independent choreographers throughout Europe.

Bagouet, Dominique (*b* Angoulême, 9 Jul. 1951; *d* Montpellier, 9 Dec. 1992) French dancer and choreographer. He studied ballet at the Rosella Hightower School in Cannes (1965–9) and modern dance with C. Carlson in Paris (1974), moving to New York in 1975 where he also studied with Jennifer Muller, Lar Lubovitch, Maggie Black, and May O'Donnell. He danced with various companies including Alfonso Catá Ballet (1969), Béjart's Ballet of the 20th Century (1971–3), and Maguy Marin's Chandra Group (1973–4) before founding his own Bagouet Company in Paris in 1976. From 1980 he was artist in residence in Montpellier, director of the Montpellier National Choreographic Centre and founder of the Montpellier Dance Festival. In 1992, just months before his premature death from Aids, his company was invited to present *So schnell* at the Paris Opera. Bagouet's choreography was rigorously constructed, creating oblique narrative and character through a distinctive, detailed use of gesture. His works included *Under the Waning Light* (1980), *Elusives* (1982), *Love Deserts* (1984), *Assai* (1986), and *Basically Furnished* (1989).

Baiser de la fée, Le (Eng. title *The Fairy's Kiss*) Ballet in one act with choreography by Nijinska, music by Stravinsky (after Tchaikovsky), and designs by Benois. Premiered 27 Nov. 1928 by Ida Rubinstein's Company at the Paris Opera, with Rubinstein as the Fairy, Anatole Vilzak as the Young Man, and Ludmila Schollar as the Fiancée. Stravinsky based his libretto on the Hans Christian Andersen fairy-tale *The Ice Maiden*, in which a fairy steals a young man from his bride. The source material, and Stravinsky's score, have attracted numerous choreographers, among them Ashton (Sadler's Wells Ballet, 1935), Balanchine (American Ballet, 1937, the first of several stagings), MacMillan (Royal Ballet, 1960), Hynd (Dutch National Ballet, 1968, London Festival Ballet, 1974), Ratmansky (Kiev, 1994), Kudelka (Birmingham Royal Ballet, 1996), and Corder (Birmingham Royal Ballet, 2008). The 1935 British staging was notable for featuring the first major role created by Ashton for the young Fonteyn, who danced the Fiancée.

Baker, Josephine (*b* St Louis, Mo., 3 Jun. 1906; *d* Paris, 12 Apr. 1975) US-born dancer and singer who became a star of the Paris music halls. She began her career as a chorus girl in an African-American revue in Philadelphia and also appeared at the Cotton Club in Harlem. In the 1920s she was hired to work on the New York musical comedies *Shuffle Along* and *The Chocolate Dandies*, but her career break came when she went to Paris in 1925 in *La Revue nègre* at the Théâtre des Champs-Elysées. Paris was charmed; she posed for Picasso and Man Ray; André Levinson called her 'the black Venus'. For her debut at the Folies-Bergère, she wore a belt of bananas

and sang 'Yes, We Have No Bananas'. She subsequently made the French capital her home. As one of the first black international stars, she performed regularly at the Folies-Bergère and the Casino de Paris, as well as on numerous foreign tours. Her natural sexuality and scanty costumes, as well as her singing and dancing skills, guaranteed her audiences. She also studied ballet with Balanchine. She opened her first nightclub in 1926, Chez Joséphine, published her memoirs the following year and embarked on international touring in 1928. Her several film appearances included *Zouzou* (1934), co-starring Jean Gabin. During the Second World War Baker did volunteer work for the Red Cross and entertained French troops. Between 1954 and 1965 she adopted twelve children of various races, dubbing them her 'rainbow tribe'. She gave a series of farewell performances in the 1950s, largely to raise funds for her large family. On 8 Apr. 1975 she opened in *Joséphine*, a revue based on her life at the Bobino Music Hall in Paris, but died only four days later.

Baker's Dozen Modern dance in one act with choreography by Tharp, music by Willie 'The Lion' Smith, costumes by Santo Loquasto, and lighting by Jennifer Tipton. Premiered 15 Feb. 1979 by the Twyla Tharp company at the Opera House, Brooklyn Academy of Music, New York. It was one of the signature works of the Twyla Tharp company and in her autobiography, Tharp said it represented 'an ideal society'.

Bakst, Léon (orig. Lev Rosenberg; *b* Grodno, 10 May, 1866; *d* Paris, 27 Dec. 1924) Russian designer and painter. As part of Diaghilev's Ballets Russes, he revolutionized both theatrical design and contemporary fashion with the sensuality of his line and his exotic palette of colours. He first collaborated with Diaghilev in St Petersburg on the magazine *World of Art*, which he co-founded in 1899. His career as a designer began in 1900 with Petipa's *Le Cœur de la Marquise*, for the Hermitage Theatre in St Petersburg. In 1909 he went with Diaghilev to Paris, designing Fokine's *Cléopâtre*, and he remained with the Ballets Russes to design *Carnaval* and *Scheherazade* (1910), *Spectre de la rose* and *Narcisse* (1911), *Le Dieu bleu, Thamar, L'Après-midi d'un faune, Daphnis et Chloé* (1912), *Jeux* (1913), and *Les Femmes de bonne humeur* (1917). After a period of estrangement he returned to Diaghilev for his London staging of *The Sleeping Princess* (1921), for which he designed elaborate and extravagantly expensive sets and costumes. Bakst also worked with Ida Rubinstein and designed Pavlova's *The Sleeping Beauty* (New York, 1916), a production including real dogs, cats, and birds on stage. Although he worked in many styles, he is probably best remembered for his vibrant Orientalism, the most famous example being *Scheherazade*.

Bal, Le Ballet in one act with choreography by Balanchine, music by Rieti, and designs by de Chirico. Premiered 7 May 1929 by the Ballets Russes de Diaghilev in Monte Carlo, with Danilova, Dolin, Doubrovska, Lifar, and Balanchine. A young officer woos a beautiful woman at a masked ball. It was reconstructed by *Hodson for Rome Opera Ballet in 2005.

balancé Term used in classical ballet to denote a rocking step that transfers weight from one foot to the other, usually in 3/4 time.

Balanchine, George (orig. Georgi Balanchivadze; *b* St Petersburg, 22 Jan. 1904; *d* New York, 30 Apr. 1983) Russian-US dancer, choreographer and ballet director. Arguably the single most influential figure in 20th-century ballet and widely regarded as the chief architect of classical ballet in the US. He is most closely associated with *New York City Ballet which he founded with Lincoln *Kirstein. Balanchine trained at the Petrograd Ballet School (1914–21) and graduated into GATOB (as the Mariinsky company was then known) in 1921. He began choreographing in 1920 while still a student and, mentored by F. *Lopukhov, exhibited precocious signs of artistic independence. In 1924, while touring Germany with a company of Russian dancers and singers, he auditioned for, and was hired by, Diaghilev. Within a year he became chief choreographer of Diaghilev's Ballets Russes. It was here he met Stravinsky, who was to become his life-long collaborator. In 1928 Balanchine created *Apollo* (originally titled *Apollon musagète*, to Stravinsky's score) a work generally regarded as the world's first *neo-classical ballet; in 1929 he made the more expressionist *Prodigal Son*, to Prokofiev's score. After the death of Diaghilev in 1929, Balanchine spent several years working with companies in Europe, including a brief spell as artistic director of Les Ballets 1933, which he founded with Boris Kochno. Also in 1933 came Kirstein's invitation to go to America. There Balanchine founded the School of *American Ballet (1934) and out of it grew the American Ballet, which made its first appearance in New York in 1935. Balanchine's first ballet in the US, *Serenade* (1934), was made for his students; it has since become a signature work of New York City Ballet and been performed by many other companies around the world. The American Ballet was resident at the Metropolitan Opera House (1935–8), after which it was disbanded. For the next few years Balanchine worked in Hollywood and on Broadway musicals. The American Ballet was revived as American Ballet Caravan for a S. American tour in 1941.

In 1946 Balanchine and Kirstein founded *Ballet Society, which two years later became New York City Ballet, based at the City Center. In 1950 NYCB made its first European visit (to London); in 1962 it went to the USSR. In 1964 NYCB moved to the New York State Theater in Lincoln Center, which was built to Balanchine's specifications. His artistic leadership of NYCB turned it into one of the foremost companies in the world and the ballets he made for it are among the outstanding creations of the 20th century.

Although most of his time and energy was devoted to NYCB, Balanchine also worked with European companies and he helped to nurture regional ballet companies in the US. His great achievement was to take the classical ballet of his St Petersburg roots and redefine it in a new context. He experimented with several different styles (not all successful) and his attempts at narrative dance were generally mediocre. But his ability to honour the technical sophistication and sweeping elegance of 19th-century Russian classicism, while stripping it of its artifice, plot, and theatricality (even to the extent of eschewing sets and costumes) led to the development of neo-classicism, a form which married the essence of Russian ballet to the modernist sensibilities of mid-20th-century America. Works such as *The Four Temperaments*, *Theme and Variations*, *Symphony in C*, *Ballet Imperial*, *Agon*, and *Symphony in Three Movements* are now ranked high in the ballet canon. In his work he gave equal weight to ensemble and soloists alike, and he rejected (for the most part) the star system he had been brought up with.

At the heart of every Balanchine ballet is the basic belief: that dance is music brought to physical life. Balanchine's musical credentials were impeccable: he studied piano from the age of 5 and as a teenager continued his musical education by studying theory and piano at the Petrograd Conservatory of Music. His choice of scores was adventurous and ground-breaking from Bach to Xenakis. His output was also prolific. Balanchine created more than 200 ballets. For Diaghilev's Ballets Russes: *Le Chant du rossignol* (mus. Stravinsky, 1925), *Apollon musagète* (*Apollo*) (mus. Stravinsky, 1928), *Le Bal* (mus. Rieti, 1929), and *The Prodigal Son* (mus. Prokofiev, 1929); for Ballets Russes de Monte Carlo: *Cotillon* (mus. Chabrier, 1932) and *Le Bourgeois Gentilhomme* (mus. R. Strauss, 1932); for Les Ballets 1933: *Mozartiana* (mus. Tchaikovsky) and *The Seven Deadly Sins* (mus. Weill); for American Ballet: *Serenade* (mus. Tchaikovsky, 1934), *Le Baiser de la fée* (mus. Stravinsky, 1937), and *Jeu de cartes* (mus. Stravinsky, 1937); for American Ballet Caravan: *Concerto Barocco* (mus. Bach, 1941) and *Ballet Imperial* (mus. Tchaikovsky, 1941); for Ballet Russe de Monte Carlo: *Danses concertantes* (mus. Stravinsky, 1944); for Ballet Society: *The Four Temperaments* (mus. Hindemith, 1946) and *Orpheus* (mus. Stravinsky, 1948); for Paris Opera: *Le Palais de cristal* (later *Symphony in C*, mus. Bizet, 1947); for American Ballet Theatre: *Theme and Variations* (mus. Tchaikovsky, 1947).

For New York City Ballet: *Firebird* (mus. Stravinsky, 1949), *La Valse* (mus. Ravel, 1951), *Scotch Symphony* (mus. Mendelssohn, 1952), *Nutcracker* (mus. Tchaikovsky, 1954), *Western Symphony* (mus. Kay, 1954), *Pas de dix* (mus. Glazunov, 1955), *Allegro brillante* (mus. Tchaikovsky, 1956), *Divertimento No. 15* (mus. Mozart, 1956), *Agon* (mus. Stravinsky, 1957), *Square Dance* (mus. Vivaldi and Corelli, 1957), *Stars and Stripes* (mus. Sousa-Kay, 1958), *The Seven Deadly Sins* (mus. Weill, new version 1958), *Episodes* (mus. Webern, 1959), *Liebeslieder Walzer* (mus. Brahms, 1960), *A Midsummer Night's Dream* (mus. Mendelssohn, 1962), *Bugaku* (mus. Mayuzumi, 1963), *Movements for Piano and Orchestra* (mus. Stravinsky, 1963), *Don Quixote* (mus. Nabokov, 1965), *Variations* (mus. Stravinsky, 1966), *Jewels* (mus. Fauré, Stravinsky, and Tchaikovsky, 1967), *Slaughter on Tenth Avenue* (mus. R. Rodgers, 1968), *Who Cares?* (mus. Gershwin, 1970), *Symphony in Three Movements* (mus. Stravinsky, 1972), *Violin Concerto* (mus. Stravinsky, 1972), *Duo Concertant* (mus. Stravinsky, 1972), *Pulcinella* (with Robbins, mus. Stravinsky, 1972), *Coppélia* (with Danilova, mus. Delibes, 1974), *Vienna Waltzes* (mus. J. Strauss, Lehár, and R. Strauss, 1977), *Kammermusik No. 2* (mus. Hindemith, 1978), and *Davidsbündlertänze* (mus. Schumann, 1980).

For New York City Opera he choreographed *Le Bourgeois gentilhomme* (mus. R. Strauss, 1979) and *Dido and Aeneas* (mus. Purcell, 1979) while his Broadway musicals include *On Your Toes* (1936) and *The Boys from Syracuse* (1938).

Balanchine also choreographed for film including *The Goldwyn Follies* (1938), *On Your Toes* (1939), and *A Midsummer Night's Dream* (1966); and for television including Stravinsky's *Noah and the Flood* (1962). He was co-author (with F. Mason) of *Balanchine's Complete Stories of the Great Ballets* (1954, 1977). His awards include the Légion d'honneur (1975), Order of Dannebrog (1978), and US Medal of Freedom (1983). Balanchine married four of his ballerinas: Tamara Geva, Vera Zorina, Maria Tallchief, and Tanaquil LeClercq.

After his death the George Balanchine Foundation was established in 1983 to protect and expand his legacy through a variety of educational and research projects, including the Archive of Lost Choreography, which aims to retrieve Balanchine choreography no longer in the current repertoire. Also connected to the Foundation is the Balanchine Trust, founded in 1987 to oversee the staging of Balanchine choreography by companies around the world.

🌐 **SEE WEB LINKS**
• Balanchine Foundation
• Balanchine Trust

Balasaraswati (*b* Madras, 13 May 1918; *d* Madras, 9 Feb. 1984) Indian dancer. After making her debut at the age of 7 at the Ammanakshi Amman temple in Kanchipuram, she achieved fame throughout India as a classical S. Asian dancer. From 1961 she performed in Europe and the US, and taught widely in America. She choreographed more than 200 solos and several dance dramas. She was considered to be the premier interpreter of the Tanjore style of bharata natyam.

Bal de blanchisseuses, Le Ballet in one act with choreography by Petit, libretto by Kochno, music by V. Duke, and designs by Stanislav Lepri. Premiered 19 Dec. 1946 by the Ballets des Champs-Elysées, at the Théâtre des Champs-Elysées, Paris, with Danielle Darmance and Petit. It portrays a young apprentice flirting with a laundress and her co-workers in the streets of Paris.

Baldwin, Mark (*b* Fiji, 16 Jan. 1954) British-based dancer, choreographer and director. Born in Fiji, he was raised in New Zealand where he graduated with a Fine Arts degree from the Elam School of Fine Arts, University of Auckland. He was a founding member of Limbs Dance Company and danced with New Zealand Ballet and Australian Dance Theatre before moving to Britain where he joined Rambert Dance Company (1983–92). One of that company's key dancers for a decade, he also made his first important choreography there in 1991 (*Island to Island*). In 1992 he left Rambert and the following year started the Mark Baldwin Dance Company, which ran until 2001. During this time he additionally choreographed for Rambert, Modern Ballet of Argentina, Phoenix Dance Company, Cisne Negro, and the Turkish State Opera House. In 1996 he was also resident choreographer of Scottish Ballet, where he created *Haydn Pieces* and *Ae Fond Kiss*. In 1997 he created *Labyrinth* for the Berlin Staatsoper, in collaboration with the composer Hans Werner Henze and the sculptor Anish Kapoor. In 1998 he returned to Berlin to choreograph a full evening of works, including *Der Dämon* (mus. Hindemith) and *Die Josephslegende* (mus. R. Strauss). In 1999 he made his choreographic debut at the Royal Ballet with *Towards Poetry* (mus. Julian Anderson). In 2002 he was appointed artistic director of Rambert Dance Company where he encouraged the development of younger choreographers such as Rafael Bonachela as well as reviving past works, including a version of *Lady into Fox* (A. Howard with additional choreography by Baldwin, mus. Benjamin Pope, 2006). His own choreography has tended to avoid narrative but his works are expressive and often slyly humorous. In 1996 he put his work *Mirrors* onto the internet, inviting choreographic contributions from the public. Works created for his own company included *Dances from Cyberspace* (mus. Handel, 1995), *Concerto Grosso* (mus. Handel, 1995), *Vespri* (mus. Monteverdi, 1995), *Mirrors* (mus. Ravel, 1996), *Confessions* (mus. MacMillan, 1996), *A Collection of Moving Parts* (mus. Chopin, 1996). His recent works for Rambert have included *Constant Speed* (mus. Lehár, 2005), *Eternal Light* (mus. Howard Goodall, 2008), and *Comedy of Change* (mus. Julian Anderson, 2009). In 2006 he created *The Wedding* for Royal New Zealand Ballet.

(⊕) SEE WEB LINKS
• Website for Rambert with information on Baldwin

ballerina The term, which in Italian means female dancer, strictly refers to a principal female dancer in a ballet company. It is never correctly used in connection with any other form of dance.

ballet A form of Western academic theatre dance based on the danse d'école (classical school) and usually presented with elements of music and design to create a dramatic or lyric effect.

The history of ballet began with Renaissance spectacles which combined all the artforms in a single entertainment, and quickly moved to France where the foundations of classical ballet as we know it today were laid at the royal court. Louis XIV was a keen performer himself in his younger days, and featured in ballets by Lully and Beauchamps. Following his retirement, the Académie Royale de Musique was set up in 1671 and ballet became the province of professional performers instead of royal amateurs, while theatres replaced banquet halls as performance venues. By the early 19th century technique had been codified (*see* BLASIS, CARLO). Romantic ballet flowered in France during the first half of the 19th century, with ballets such as *Giselle*, but developed a more virtuosic, athletic style in Italy and Russia during the latter half of the 19th century, the era which saw the creation of the three Tchaikovsky ballets (*Swan Lake*, *The Sleeping Beauty*, and *The Nutcracker*) that form the core of the classical repertory. In 1909 Diaghilev brought Russian dance to the West, sparking an international ballet boom that eventually led to the creation of schools and companies throughout Europe and America (the founding of the Royal Ballet by de Valois, for example). Strictly speaking, the term ballet should only be applied to works based on the danse d'école and subsequent permutations of the academic form, but with the enormous cross-fertilization of dance

in the 20th century the term took on a much broader meaning and is now frequently used to describe a wide range of non-classically based theatrical dance.

Ballet Annual, The British yearbook, published between 1947 and 1963, and edited by Arnold Haskell.

ballet blanc A dance in which the women wear white tulle ballet dresses or romantic tutus, in the style seen in *La Sylphide* in 1832 and thereafter immortalized in many romantic lithographs. One of the most famous examples of ballet blanc is Act II of *Giselle*.

Ballet Boyz London-based dance company founded in 2001 by former Royal Ballet principals William Trevitt and Michael Nunn; originally also known as George Piper Dances. The company was noted for commissioning a wide range of contemporary choreographers, including Christopher Wheeldon, Michael Clark, and Russell Maliphant, and for Trevitt and Nunn's individual performances. In 2010 the 'second generation' Ballet Boyz was launched, with eight younger male dancers and Trevitt and Nunn as directors. The two have also become noted documentary makers. They directed and starred in Channel 4's landmark television series *Ballet Boyz* and won a 2008 International Emmy for their documentary *Strictly Bolshoi*.

(⊕) SEE WEB LINKS
• Company website for Ballet Boyz

Ballet Caravan A short-lived troupe founded by Lincoln Kirstein in 1936 as a platform for young choreographers in America. Among the talents it fostered were Lew Christensen (*Filling Station*), William Dollar, and Eugene Loring (*Billy the Kid*). Balanchine made two of his finest works for the company: *Ballet Imperial* (1941) and *Concerto Barocco* (1941). The company, which gave its first performance on 17 July 1936 at Bennington College in Vermont, was finally disbanded in 1941 after a less-than-successful tour (as American Ballet Caravan) to S. America.

Ballet Class Ballet in one act with choreography by A. Messerer, music by Liadov, Glazunov, Rubinstein, Liapunov, and Shostakovich. Premiered 6 May 1961, by the Ballet of the 20th Century, at the Théâtre Royal de la Monnaie in Brussels. A subsequent production was premiered 17 Sept. 1962, by the Bolshoi Ballet at the Metropolitan Opera House in New York, with Plisetskaya, Maximova, Fadeyechev, Vasiliev, and Lavrovsky under the new title *Class Concert*. The ballet, reminiscent of Harald Lander's *Études*, is a showcase of classical dancing which culminates in a series of dazzling virtuoso tricks. It has been revived by M. Messerer for the Royal Swedish Ballet, La Scala, and in 2007 for the Bolshoi.

Ballet comique de la reine, Le This production, performed 15 Oct. 1581, is widely acknowledged as the first ballet, although other court spectacles in a similar vein preceded it. It was performed at the Salle de Bourbon in the Louvre, a lavish marriage of music, song, and dance staged by Balthasar de Beaujoyeux (or Beaujoyeulx) on the occasion of the marriage of the Duc de Joyeuse and the Queen's sister, Mlle de Vaudemont. Running from 10 p.m. to 3.30 a.m., the ballet presented scenes from the legend of Circe. It was hugely successful and exorbitantly expensive and ensured its place in history with a lavishly illustrated book.

ballet d'action A ballet which is primarily designed to tell a story. One of the choreographers principally associated with the development of ballet as a narrative art form, rather than an ornamental spectacle, was Jean-Georges *Noverre, working in 18th-century France. Noverre believed that dance steps and gestures should be used to describe the characters' motives and advance the plotline rather than simply form pleasing patterns. In his work, the role of the corps de ballet was also enhanced, from decorative background to an integral part of the action. Noverre's reforms also required that music and costumes should be adapted to fit the dramatic imperative. Other choreographers to share Noverre's views were *Weaver, *Hilverding, and *Angiolini. *Fokine used Noverre as his model when arguing for similar reforms in early 20th-century Russia.

ballet de chevaux A ballet performed on horseback by knights, widely popular in the 17th century, especially in France, Italy, and Austria. The famed Lipizzaner stallions at the Spanish Riding School of Vienna can trace their roots back to these 17th-century entertainments.

ballet de cour A court ballet. Derived from the spectacles of the Italian Renaissance, which were designed as entertainment for the nobility, the ballet de cour was performed by aristocrats (usually enthusiastic amateurs under the guidance of a professional dancing master) from the royal courts of Europe and included elements of music and verse as well as dance. It enjoyed its greatest flowering in France, from the middle of the 16th century until the reign of Louis XIV a century later. The ballet de cour, with its lavish decor and costumes and elaborate special effects, was often used to mark an important event or to convey a political message. In the case of Louis XIV, who as a teenager appeared as the Sun in *Ballet de la Nuit*, the grand theatrical display was also used as a public assertion of power. The subject-matter of such ballets was usually mythological or allegorical. The *Ballet comique de la reine* (1581) is the earliest-known example of ballet de cour.

Ballet de la Nuit, Le A court ballet, one of the most famous examples of a ballet de cour, staged at the Salle du Petit-Bourbon in the Louvre, Paris, on 23 Feb. 1653. The ballet lasted twelve hours, beginning at sunset and ending with sunrise, and featured figures from mythology in various nocturnal episodes. One of the performers was Louis XIV, who was 14 at the time. He appeared as the Sun, a role which led to his being known as the Sun King.

Ballet der Lage Landen Dutch company founded in 1947 with Mascha Ter Weeme as artistic director. The company did important pioneering work in bringing ballet to the Dutch public. In 1959 it was absorbed into the Amsterdam Ballet, which in 1961 merged with the Netherlands Ballet to form Dutch National Ballet.

Ballet de Santiago See SANTIAGO BALLET.

ballet director The individual who heads a ballet company, usually a retired dancer or a choreographer. It is common nowadays for companies to divide management responsibilities between an artistic director, who decides on repertoire, casting, and general artistic policy, and an administrative director, who deals with budgets and other non-artistic matters.

Ballet du Grand Théâtre de Genève See SWITZERLAND.

Ballet du Nord French dance company founded in 1983 and based with its associate school at the National Choreographic Centre in Roubaix, in Northern France. Its founding director was Alfonso *Catá with subsequent directors including Jean-Paul Comelin from 1991 and C. *Carlson from 2004. The repertory includes works by Carlson herself as well as a broad range of French and international choreographers including Decouflé, Tero Saarinen, and Montalvo-Hervieu. The company frequently tours.

(●) SEE WEB LINKS
- Website for the National Choreographic Centre of Roubaix

Ballet du Rhin Ballet company founded in Strasbourg in 1972 with Jean Babilée as director. In 1973 Babilée left and in 1974 the company transferred to Mullhouse, with subsequent directors including Jean Seralli and Bertrand D'At. It has 36 dancers and performs a wide range of modern and classical repertory, with works by D'At, Childs, Forsythe, and others. It also performs reconstructions of baroque dance.

⊕ SEE WEB LINKS
- Website for the opera company with link to the Ballet du Rhin

Ballet Folklórico de México The national folklore company of Mexico. It was founded in 1952 by the dancer Amalia *Hernandez, who headed the company until 1998 and still acts as chief choreographer (with her daughter Norma Lopez as artistic director). A company of 75 dancers and musicians, it performs regularly throughout the US and Europe.

⊕ SEE WEB LINKS
- Website of the Ballet Folklórico de México

Ballet for All An offshoot of the Royal Ballet, founded in 1964 to bring ballet to new audiences in Britain. Its first director was Peter *Brinson, who created special ballet-plays that combined dance with narration in an effort to educate its audience. The company was disbanded in 1979.

Ballett Frankfurt *See* FRANKFURT BALLET.

Ballet Gulbenkian *See* GULBENKIAN BALLET.

Ballet Hispanico US dance company founded in 1970 by Tina Ramirez. The repertoire, which is inspired by Hispanic culture, showcases works by established and emerging Latino choreographers and fuses classical and contemporary forms. Under Ramirez it has included works by Alberto Alonso, David Rousseve Ann Reinking, and Alexandre Magno whose *The Red Guitar* (2005) is a Brazilian spin on the Orpheus and Eurydice myth. Under Eduardo Vilaro, who succeeded Ramirez as director in 2009, it also featured works by himself. Both the company and its associate school are based in New York.

⊕ SEE WEB LINKS
- Website for the Ballet Hispanico

Ballet Imperial Ballet in one act with choreography by Balanchine, music by Tchaikovsky, and designs by Doboujinsky. Premiered 29 May 1941, by American Ballet Caravan, at the Hunter College Playhouse, New York, with Marie-Jeanne, Gisella Caccialanza, William Dollar, and Nicholas Magallanes. A plotless ballet set to Tchaikovsky's 2nd Piano Concerto, this is Balanchine's tribute to Tsarist Russia, to the classical style of his roots in the Mariinsky (Imperial) Theatre in St Petersburg. It was revived for the Sadler's Wells Ballet in 1950 with new designs by Eugene Berman, and for New York City Ballet in 1964 (designs Ter-Arutunian), when the cast was led by Suzanne Farrell and Jacques d'Amboise. For a 1973 restaging at the New York State Theater, the choreographer changed the title to *Tchaikovsky Piano Concerto No. 2* after discarding the women's classical tutus and the men's princely tunics in favour of less formal costumes. The ballet has also been staged by the Ballet Russe de Monte Carlo (1944), Australian Ballet (1967), American Ballet Theatre (1988), and the Mariinsky (2004).

Ballet Internacional de Caracas Ballet company based in Venezuela, founded in 1975 by the Fundación Pro-Artes Coreograficas. It was directed by Vicente *Nebrada, who was also resident choreographer, with Zhandra Rodriguez its principal ballerina. In 1980 the company split and Nebrada formed the Ballet Nacional de Caracas (initially known as Ballet Fundación Teresa Carreño) and Rodriguez founded the Ballet Nuevo Mundo de Caracas with Dale Talley.

Ballet International *See* CUEVAS, MARQUIS GEORGE DE.

ballet master Originally a term describing the man at court who oversaw all dance aspects of a production, it now commonly refers to the individual who is responsible for setting the rehearsal schedule in a ballet company. Ballet masters are also in charge of ensuring the maintenance of performing standards and frequently coach dancers in new roles.

Ballet Nacional Chileno *See* CHILE.

Ballet Nacional Clásico *See* COMPAÑÍA NACIONAL DE DANZA; NATIONAL BALLET OF SPAIN.

Ballet Nacional de Cuba *See* NATIONAL BALLET OF CUBA.

Ballet Nacional de Mexico *See* BRAVO, GUILLERMINA.

Ballet Nacional Español *See* GADES, ANTONIO; SPAIN.

Ballet National de Marseilles French ballet company based in Marseilles. It was founded in 1972 by the choreographer Roland *Petit, who served as artistic director for 25 years and whose ballets dominated the repertoire; its associate school was founded in 1992. Between 1998 and 2004 Marie-Claude Pietragalla, an étoile of the Paris Opera Ballet, succeeded Petit as artistic director and widened the repertory to include works by Kylián, Claude Brumachon, and Pietragalla. Since 2004 the company and its school have been directed by F *Flamand who has brought to it his own repertory and his commitment to close creative collaboration with artists from other disciplines. He has additionally added works by Forsythe and others to the repertory, and encouraged younger choreographers such as Thierry Malandain, and Julien Lestel.

(⊕) SEE WEB LINKS
• Official website for Ballet National de Marseilles

Ballet of Flanders *See* ROYAL BALLET OF FLANDERS.

Ballet of the 20th Century (Ballet du XXᵉ Siècle) The Brussels-based company formed in 1960 with Maurice *Béjart as director. Attached to the Théâtre Royal de la Monnaie, its repertoire was a showcase for Béjart's own work, whose spectacular production values and highly coloured emotional content earned the company a high international profile through more than twenty years of touring. Productions included *Sacre du printemps* (mus. Stravinsky, 1959, which Béjart choreographed for Ballet-Théâtre de Paris, the ensemble which eventually became the Ballet of the 20th Century), *Bolero* (mus. Ravel, 1960), *Tales of Hoffmann* (mus. Offenbach, 1961), *A la recherche de Don Juan* (1962), *Les Noces* (mus. Stravinsky, 1961), *The Merry Widow* (mus. Lehár, 1963), *Ninth Symphony* (mus. Beethoven, 1964), *Mathilde* (mus. Wagner, 1965), *Romeo and Juliet* (mus. Berlioz, 1966), *Baudelaire* (1968), *The Firebird* (mus. Stravinsky, 1970), *Nijinsky, clown de Dieu* (music Henry-Tchaikovsky, 1971), *Stimmung* (mus. Stockhausen, 1972), *Le Marteau sans maître* (mus. Boulez, 1973), *Notre Faust* (mus. Bach, 1975), *Petrushka* (mus. Stravinsky, 1977), *Gaîté parisienne* (mus. Offenbach-Rosenthal, 1978), *Magic Flute* (mus. Mozart, 1981), *Wien, Wien nur du allein* (mus. Schoenberg, Beethoven, and others, 1982), *Messe pour le temps futur* (mus. Wagner, Beethoven, 1983), *Cinq nô modernes* (text Mishima, 1984), *Malraux; ou, La Métamorphose des dieux* (mus. Beethoven, Le Bars, traditional, 1986). The company attracted some major guest artists, among them Rudolf Nureyev, Suzanne Farrell, Judith Jamison, Maya Plisetskaya, Vladimir Vasiliev, Marcia Haydée, and Jean Babilée. In 1987 the company was disbanded when Béjart left the Théâtre de la Monnaie to found a new troupe in Lausanne.

balletomane A ballet enthusiast. The term was coined in the 19th century to describe the partisan fans of Russian ballet, so extreme in their support of a particular dancer that they occasionally became hysterical. Arnold Haskell introduced the term to the West in his 1934 book *Balletomania: The Story of an Obsession*. Today the term has less drastic connotations, and is more commonly used to refer to ballet lovers or experts.

ballet-opera A form of opera in which dance and music are equally important components in a production. Early examples include works by Campra, Lully, and Rameau. Although not strictly a ballet-opera, Gluck's *Orpheus and Eurydice* is often produced as one.

ballet-pantomime The term used to describe nearly all the ballets created at the Paris Opera during the Romantic period (*c*.1830–50), including such famous ballets as *Giselle* and *La Sylphide*. They were so called because they made extensive use of both dance and mime. Ballet-pantomime was the successor to the ballet d'action.

Ballet Rambert *See* RAMBERT DANCE COMPANY.

Ballet Review A non-profit-making US dance journal published by the Dance Research Foundation. It was founded in 1965 by Arlene Croce and continued for decades.

Ballet Russe There is much confusion regarding the use of the name Ballet Russe or Les Ballets Russes. The first company to use it was Serge Diaghilev's Ballets Russes (1909–29) but following his death various directors and impresarios, eager to capitalize on the Diaghilev phenomenon, used the title freely. The two most important successors to the Diaghilev company were the Ballet Russe de Monte Carlo (1938–62), which was in effect a US company based in New York (led by Denham and Massine), and Les Ballets Russes de Monte Carlo (1932–52), which was Colonel de Basil's (and initially also Blum's) touring enterprise and was variously known as Ballets Russes de Colonel W. de Basil, Covent Garden Russian Ballet, and Original Ballet Russe. Several choreographers worked with both subsequent companies, including Massine and Balanchine, who also worked with Diaghilev.

Ballet Russe de Monte Carlo A descendant of René Blum's Ballets de Monte Carlo, and part of the proliferation of companies which sprung up in the 1930s hoping to recapture the enormous popularity of Diaghilev's Ballets Russes. Although it eventually became an American company, it was founded when Massine, ballet master of the Ballets Russes de Monte Carlo, quarrelled with Colonel de Basil, who ran the Ballets Russes, and sought a company of his own. The opening season of the new Massine-directed troupe was at the Monte Carlo Opera in April 1938; with Massine choreographing *Gaîté parisienne* and *Seventh Symphony* for its debut. In June 1938 the company appeared at the Drury Lane Theatre in London. Just up the road, the rival Colonel de Basil Ballets Russes was performing at the Covent Garden Opera House. The two companies became engaged in a protracted lawsuit in pursuit of the performing rights to the Diaghilev repertoire (the battle was over Massine's ballets in particular); a legal compromise was eventually reached between Massine and de Basil. The London season of the Ballet Russe de Monte Carlo included the premiere of Massine's *Nobilissima visione*, considered one of his greatest creations. The following year, in Monte Carlo, Massine unveiled *Capriccio espagnol* and *Rouge et noir*. In 1939, with war looming in Europe, the company moved to the US with Massine still in charge (he resigned as director in 1942); based in New York the troupe never returned to Europe. During the Second World War the leading dancers included Danilova, Markova, Toumanova, Franklin, Platoff, Youskevitch, and, briefly, Lifar. With the move to America came a new American identity, both in terms of dancers and choreographers. Agnes de Mille made *Rodeo* for the company in 1942, while in 1944 Balanchine, who was resident choreographer, gave them *Danses concertantes* and *Le Bourgeois gentilhomme* (originally staged in 1932), as well as many other ballets, both new and revived. Sergei Denham became director in 1942. The troupe toured regional America but after the war came to rely more and more on the old European repertoire, and any new work was largely insignificant. In the early 1950s, following the departure of Danilova, the company was disbanded. It was revived as a touring outfit in 1954 with Maria Tallchief and Franklin as stars; the following season Alicia Alonso and Igor Youskevitch began an important association with the company. In the mid-1950s it toured exhaustively, giving 188 performances in 104 cities during one season alone. The Ballet Russe introduced many Americans to ballet and inspired many young Americans to take up the study of dance. In 1957 it appeared at the Metropolitan Opera, an engagement that broke box office records for a US company at that venue. However, with creativity stagnating and the repertoire shrinking, Denham finally closed the company at the end of the 1961–2 season. The last important work created for the company was probably Massine's *Harold in Italy* in 1954.

Ballets Africains, Les Dance company founded in the early 1950s in Paris by the Guinean Keita Fodeba. Originally an all-male folkloric troupe, it comprised musicians and dancers from several French colonies in Africa and the Caribbean. Following Guinean independence in 1958 the troupe became based in Guinea (Conakry) and took the name Les Ballets Africains of the Republic of Guinea. In 1969 Fodeba, heavily involved in politics (he held several posts in the country's new government), was imprisoned in Camp Boiro, and never seen again. The company, which tours extensively, was considered a pioneer in the development of African theatrical dance. It is currently directed by Hamidou Bangoura.

(⊕) SEE WEB LINKS
• Company website for Les Ballets Africains

Ballets de l'Étoile, Les *See* BÉJART, MAURICE.

Ballets de Monte Carlo, Les Ballet company, based at the Monte Carlo Opera, founded by René Blum in 1936 following his split from Colonel de Basil. Massine became artistic director in 1938, at which point the company's name was changed to *Ballet Russe de Monte Carlo. It continued to perform, erratically, until 1963 after which it was disbanded but in 1985 was revived as Les Ballets de Monte Carlo under the direction of Lacotte and Thesmar, and as the official ballet company of the Principality of Monaco. Its current director Jean-Christophe Maillot (appointed 1993) choreographs many of its ballets but the repertory also includes works by Balanchine, Childs, Forsythe, Duato, Kylián, and Cherkaoui, as well as revivals of ballets from the Diaghilev company. In 2000 it moved into a new base, L'Atelier, and a new home theatre, Le Salle des Princes.

(⊕) SEE WEB LINKS
• Company website for the Ballets de Monte Carlo

Ballets de Paris French company founded in 1948 by Roland Petit after his departure from the Ballets des Champs-Elysées. The first performance was at the Théâtre Marigny in Paris on 21 May 1948 with Charrat, Jeanmaire, Marchand, Petit, Skouratoff, Perrault, and Hamilton, with Fonteyn as a guest artist. Early repertoire included some of Petit's most important works: *Les Demoiselles de la nuit* (staged for Fonteyn in 1948), *Carmen* (1949), and *La Croqueuse de diamants* (1950). Guest choreographers included Charrat and Dollar. The company was officially disbanded in 1950 but Petit continued to revive it on an *ad hoc* basis throughout the 1950s and 1960s. For its 1953 Paris season Petit created *Le Loup*, *Deuil en 24 heures*, *Cine-Bijou*, and *Lady in the Ice* (with a libretto by Orson Welles). Later Petit works included *Cyrano de Bergerac* (1959) with Jeanmaire, Beaumont, Petit, Reich, and Ferran. The company's final appearance was on 9 Mar. 1966 at the Théâtre des Champs-Elysées.

Ballets des Champs-Elysées An influential French company which performed at the Théâtre des Champs-Elysées in Paris from 1945 to 1950 under the guidance of Roger Eudes, the theatre's director. It grew out of the Soirées de la Danse performances organized by the French critic Irène Lidova at the Sarah Bernhardt Theatre in Paris. These were designed to provide a forum for young choreographers rebelling against the tradition-bound Paris Opera. Roland Petit's first ballet, *Les Forains* (mus. Henri Sauguet, des. Christian Bérard), had been presented at one of these evenings, so impressing Eudes that he invited Petit to form a company at his theatre. Petit was joined by Lidova and the writer Boris Kochno, who had worked with Diaghilev. Petit and Charrat were among the first to make dances for the Champs-Elysées company. Dancers included Petit, Jeanmaire, Philippart, Perrault, and Vyroubova. The company was noted for its high artistic standards, its innovative choreography and elegant designs, its youthful dancers and distinguished collaborators, including several of Diaghilev's former associates—Cocteau, Kochno, and Bérard. Among its most significant creations were Charrat's *Jeu de cartes* (1945), Babilée's *L'Amour et son amour* (1948), Milloss's *Le Portrait de Don Quichotte* (1947), and Petit's *Déjeuner sur l'herbe*, *Le Rendez-vous*, *La Fiancée du diable* (1945), *Les Amours de Jupiter*, *Le Jeune Homme et la mort* (1946), and *Le Bal des blanchisseuses* and *Treize danses* (1947), the last bringing Violette Verdy and Leslie Caron to prominence. The company toured widely abroad, becoming a glamorous ambassador for post-war French dance. Petit left in 1947–8 (having fallen out with Kochno) to found Ballets de Paris. After his departure new works by Babilée and Lichine were added to the repertoire. Following the death of the designer Bérard and the loss of its leading ballerina Irene Skorik, the company lost its home at the Champs-Elysées Theatre in 1950 and disbanded shortly afterwards.

Ballets Jooss Company founded in 1933 by the German choreographer Kurt *Jooss. Forced to flee Nazi Germany, Jooss and members of the former Folkwang Tanzbühne Essen emigrated to England where they were offered a home first at Dartington Hall in Devon and then at the Jooss-Leeder school in Cambridge. The company toured extensively and during the Second World War performed for Britain's ENSA cultural programme. Jooss returned to Germany in 1949 and reorganized his company as Folkwang Tanztheater. It disbanded in 1953, after performing at Sadler's Wells Theatre in London. In the 1960s it was revived again as the *Folkwang Ballett Essen. The most famous work in the repertory was always Jooss's *The Green Table* (1932), although *The Big City* (1932), *Ball in Old Vienna* (1932), *The Prodigal Son* (1933), *Ballade* (1935), *Pandora* (1944), and *Dithyrambus* (1948) were also significant.

Ballets 1933, Les A Paris-based chamber ballet company which survived only one season, but was notable for having Balanchine as its sole choreographer. Specially commissioned scores were written by Milhaud and Weill, while Derain, Bérard, and Caspar Neher were the designers. Ballets performed at the Théâtre des Champs-Elysées in Paris and at the Savoy Theatre in London included *Fastes*, *Les Songes*, *L'Errante*, *Mozartiana*, and *The Seven Deadly Sins*. The company owed its existence to the patronage of a wealthy Englishman, Edward James, who was married to the Viennese dancer Tilly *Losch. She created leading roles in both *L'Errante* and *The Seven Deadly Sins*. One of the most significant meetings in ballet history, that of Balanchine and Lincoln Kirstein, took place during the company's appearance in London.

Ballet San Jose *See* CLEVELAND SAN JOSE BALLET.

Ballet Society Founded in 1946 by Lincoln *Kirstein and George *Balanchine, this was the precursor to *New York City Ballet. It was set up like a private club, performing new works before a subscription audience. Its productions included Balanchine's stagings of Ravel's *L'Enfant et les sortilèges*, Hindemith's *Four Temperaments*, and Stravinsky's *Orpheus*. In 1948 the company was invited to join the New York City Center of Music and Drama as New York City Ballet.

Ballet Sopianae Hungarian modern ballet troupe founded in 1960 by the dancer Imre *Eck and attached to the opera house in Pécs. During the first year of the company's existence Eck produced fourteen one-act ballets; he eventually choreographed more than a hundred. The Hungarian choreographer Sándor Tóth enjoyed a lasting success with his ballet *What Is Under Your Head?* (mus. Joszef Kincses, 1964) and went on to contribute many more works to the repertoire, including the full-length *Romeo and Juliet* (1980). In 1992 Istvan *Herczog became artistic director. It is now known as the Pécs Ballet. *See* HUNGARY.

Ballets Russes de Monte Carlo, Les Company founded in 1932 to succeed the Ballets Russes de Diaghilev. It was a fusion of the Ballets de l'Opéra de Monte Carlo and the Ballet de l'Opéra Russe à Paris, with Colonel de Basil as director and René Blum as artistic director. Many former members of the Diaghilev troupe joined the new Monte Carlo-based company, including Kochno (artistic adviser), Balanchine (who was appointed ballet master), and Massine. The addition of the three 'baby ballerinas', Baronova, Riabouchinska, and Toumanova, generated additional publicity. The company gave its first full season in Monte Carlo on 12 Apr. 1932 and went on to tour Europe with its repertoire of Diaghilev ballets, gaining considerable success in London. The following year it undertook its first US tour.

Additional dancers included Danilova, Eglevsky, and Lichine. In 1933 Balanchine left, having added *La Concurrence, Cotillon*, and *Le Bourgeois gentilhomme* to the repertoire. He was succeeded by Massine who created *Jeux d'enfants* (1932), *Beau Danube, Beach, Scuola di ballo, Les Présages*, and *Choreartium* (1933) for the company. The last two works were part of the new genre of *symphonic ballets; although the concept of choreographing to symphonic music caused considerable controversy at the time. Ballets by Nijinska were also mounted. The company began to falter in 1936 when de Basil and Blum quarrelled. The company lost its home at Blum's Monte Carlo theatre; Blum resigned and founded the Ballets de Monte Carlo (which was eventually absorbed into the Ballet Russe de Monte Carlo), while de Basil renamed his company Ballets Russes de Colonel W. de Basil. In 1938 the name was changed again, this time to Covent Garden Russian Ballet, and the following year it became the Original Ballet Russe. In 1938 the company was involved in the famous 'ballet war' in London, with de Basil's troupe at Covent Garden and Massine's rival Ballet Russe down the road at the Drury Lane Theatre. In 1937 Fokine was engaged as choreographer. The most important works of the middle years were Massine's *Symphonie fantastique* (1936), Lichine's *Francesca da Rimini* (1937), *Prodigal Son* (1938), and *Graduation Ball* (1940), and Fokine's *Cendrillon* and *Paganini* (1939). During the 1930s it was the world's most influential ballet company, giving regular seasons in Europe and America and touring extensively in Australia; one of its most important engagements was a regular summer season at Covent Garden. The company's four-year stay (1942-6) in S. America proved instrumental in the development of ballet in Brazil and Argentina. In the 1940s de Basil encountered a series of financial crises; in 1948 he disbanded the company, but he was planning to revive the enterprise when he died in 1951. His former associate, the designer George Kirsta, managed a brief revival with a company that performed in England in 1951, but within a year it, too, was gone.

Ballets Russes de Serge Diaghilev, Les

The company formed in 1909 by the Russian impresario Serge Diaghilev to bring Russian dance to the West. Its success in combining dance, music, and design to often radical effect and its electrifying roll call of dancers meant that its appearances in Europe before the First World War sparked an international ballet boom, while its dissolution two decades later prompted the establishment of schools and companies throughout Europe and N. America, many of them run by former Diaghilev dancers. Diaghilev had already brought Russian art, music and opera to the attention of Paris with

considerable success and in 1909 returned to the French capital with a programme of opera and ballet. On 19 May 1909 (the dress rehearsal on 18 May is often cited as the first night) his ballet company made its debut at the Théâtre du Chatelet, with *Le Pavillon d'Armide*, the Polovtsian Dances from *Prince Igor*, and *Le Festin*. The evening was a sensation. The company returned in 1910; in 1911 it was presented under Diaghilev's own name and made its debut in London. It eventually moved to Monte Carlo; following the October Revolution Diaghilev was forced to sever all ties with Russia. From then on it became a totally Western organization, dependent on private patronage and box-office earnings, although the company was frequently on the verge of bankruptcy and many of its seasons were salvaged only at the last minute. It continued to perform regularly in Paris, toured in Europe, and visited the US for the first time in 1916-17. It gave its last performance on 4 Aug. 1929 in Vichy. On 19 Aug. 1929 Diaghilev died, and the company was dissolved. By then its impact on European ballet was irreversible. The extraordinary confluence of talents gathered under Diaghilev's roof, with some of the leading composers and artists of the day collaborating on ballets, was never to be repeated.

During the twenty years of its existence the company's influence was enormous both on and off stage. Diaghilev's artistic policy, which placed as much emphasis on original music and design as on choreography, changed the way ballet was viewed in the West; while the vibrant and exotic Oriental look of some of its early productions set fashion trends in the streets of Europe's capitals. Its dancers were among the greatest names of the 20th century: Nijinsky, Pavlova, Karsavina, Fokine, Nijinska, and Bolm in 1909; Karsavina, Spessivtseva, Danilova, Tchernicheva, Doubrovska, Sokolova, Dolin, Lifar, Woizikowski, and Balanchine in 1929. In between came Rubinstein, Lopokova, Cecchetti, Massine, Rambert, and de Valois (the last two went on to found major companies of their own in Britain). Its chief choreographers were Fokine, Nijinsky, Massine, Nijinska, and Balanchine. The list of composers engaged by Diaghilev was equally impressive: Stravinsky, Ravel, Debussy, R. Strauss, Satie, de Falla, Respighi, Prokofiev, Poulenc, Auric, and Milhaud. Its designers were among the most important painters of the day: Benois, Bakst, Golovine, Roerich, Picasso, Derain, Goncharova, Matisse, Gris, Braque, Utrillo, Ernst, Miró, and de Chirico. The most significant productions are listed by choreographer. Fokine: *Le Pavillon d'Armide*, the Polovtsian Dances from *Prince Igor*, *Les Sylphides, Cléopâtre* (1909), *Le Carnaval, Scheherazade, Firebird* (1910), *Le Spectre de la rose, Narcisse, Petrushka* (1911), *Le Dieu bleu, Thamar, Daphnis and Chloe* (1912), and *Les Papillons, The Legend of Joseph* (1914). Nijinsky: *L'Après-midi d'un faune* (1912), *Jeux, Sacre du printemps* (1913) and *Till Eulenspiegal* (1916); Massine: *Las Meninas* (1916), *Les Femmes de bonne humeur, Parade* (1917), *La Boutique fantasque, The Three-Cornered Hat* (1919), *Le Chant du rossignol, Pulcinella* (1920), and *Les Matelots* (1925). Nijinska: *Renard* (1922), *Les Noces* (1923), *Les Biches, Les Fâcheux, The Night on Bare Mountain, Le Train bleu* (1924), and *Romeo et Juliette* (1926). Balanchine: *Barabau* (1925), *La Pastorale, Jack-in-the-Box, The Triumph of Neptune* (1926), *La Chatte* (1927), *Apollon musagète, The Gods Go a-Begging* (1928), and *Le Bal* and *Prodigal Son* (1929).

Ballets Suédois, Les Company founded in 1920 in Paris by Rolf de *Maré, a Swedish art patron and amateur ethnographer, who hoped to emulate the success of Diaghilev's Ballets Russes. The repertoire went to even greater extremes of experiment in style and subject matter, embracing African dance, Muslim traditions, roller-skating, feminism, and abstract art. The sole choreographer throughout the five years of its existence was the company's star performer Jean *Börlin, who had been a dancer with the Royal Swedish Ballet in Stockholm. Börlin's choreography was influenced by the Diaghilev repertoire, although he also created dances based on Swedish folklore and the folklore of other, non-European cultures. Like the Diaghilev troupe, the company was noted for its collaborations with avant-garde composers and painters, and Börlin often turned to poets like Claudel and Cocteau for his librettos. *L'Homme et son désir* placed its protagonist in a tropical rainforest; *La Création du monde*, subtitled *A Negro-Jazz Ballet*, was a marriage of African creation myths and American jazz; *Relâche* was a Dadaist multi-media spectacle which featured an appearance by Man Ray and a 'cinematographic entracte' which stands alone as a work of avant-garde cinema. The company made its debut on 25 Oct. 1920 at the Théâtre des Champs-Elysées in Paris, and toured extensively in Europe and the US until it was disbanded in 1925. Most of its dancers came from Scandinavia. The company was particularly associated with a group of composers known as Les Six; the score for *Les Mariés de la Tour Eiffel* (1921) was written by five of them (Auric, Milhaud, Poulenc, Tailleferre, and Honegger), and has the distinction of being the only orchestral work produced collectively by Les Six. Painters who collaborated with the company included Bonnard, Léger, and de Chirico. Unlike the Diaghilev repertoire, very few of the Ballets Suédois works have survived. In 1998 the Royal Swedish Ballet staged an evening of reconstructed works from the Ballets Suédois repertoire, including *Skating Rink* (originally reconstructed for the Zurich Ballet) and *Within the Quota*. Among Börlin's most important creations were *Maison de fous, Le Tombeau de*

Couperin, El Greco (1920), *L'Homme et son désir, Les Mariés de la Tour Eiffel* (1921), *Skating Rink* (1922), *La Création du monde* (1923), and *La Jarre* and *Relâche* (1924).

Ballets Trockadero de Monte Carlo, Les A company founded in 1974 in New York by a group of ballet enthusiasts 'for the purpose of presenting a playful, entertaining view of classical ballet in parody form and en travesti'. The all-male troupe, who first performed in late shows in Off-Off Broadway lofts, rapidly gained international popularity with their comic take on the classics. Their repertoire later broadened to take in 20th-century choreographers such as Balanchine, Cunningham, and Robbins. Far from being a pure comic act the company have acquired cult status among balletomanes for their respect for the traditional Russian repertoire, and their commitment to its classical style, even as they parody sylphs and swans in their man-sized tutus and pointe shoes. Currently directed by Tory Dobrin the cast of 'ballerinas' includes Maya Thickenthighya, Mikhail Mypansarov, Adam Baum, Ida Nevasayneva, Helen Highwaters, and Jacques D'Ambrosia. The company is more affectionately known as The Trocks.

(((●))) **SEE WEB LINKS**

• Company website for the Ballets Trockadero

Ballets: USA *See* ROBBINS, JEROME.

Ballett der Staatsoper Unter den Linden *See* GERMAN STATE OPERA BALLET; BERLIN STATE BALLET.

Ballet Theatre *See* AMERICAN BALLET THEATRE.

Ballet-Théâtre Contemporain A short-lived company established by the French Ministry of Culture in 1968 to create modern choreography in collaboration with modern musicians and painters. Originally based in Amiens (north of Paris), it moved to Angers where in 1978 it was absorbed into the Centre National de Danse Contemporaine. Choreographers who worked with the company included Joseph Lazzini, Jean Babilée, George Skibine, Brian Macdonald, John Butler, Jacques LeCog, Lar Lubovitch, John Neumeier, and Louis Falco. Jean-Albert Cartier, the founding artistic adviser, later moved to Nancy, where he helped to establish the Ballet Théâtre Français de Nancy.

Ballet-Théâtre de Paris *See* BALLET OF THE 20TH CENTURY.

Ballet West Regional US ballet company based in Salt Lake City, and founded in 1963 by Willam *Christensen. Initially Christensen choreographed much of the company's repertory but under subsequent directors Bruce Marks (1978–85) and

John Hart (1985–96) it expanded its repertory of 19th-century classics. Recent directors Jonas Käge (1997–2006) and Adam Sklute (appointed 2007) have added contemporary works by, among others, Bruce, Forsythe, Tharp, Morris, and S. Welch. Its official school is the Ballet West Academy.

(((( ))) SEE WEB LINKS

• Ballet West company website

Ballet Workshop A club based at the Mercury Theatre in London between 1951 and 1955, directed by David and Angela *Ellis. New works were presented on Sunday evenings. Choreographers included Jack Carter, Peter Darrell, and Walter Gore.

ballo Italian standard dances of the 15th and 16th centuries. The word ballet comes from its diminutive, balletto.

ballon A term commonly used to describe a dancer's proficiency in jumping. In strict classical usage, however, it designates a dancer's ability seemingly to hang suspended in the air during a jump.

Ballon, Claude (*b* Paris, 1671; *d* Versailles, 9 May 1744) French dancer, teacher, choreographer, and chancellor of the Académie Royale de Danse. He joined the Paris Opera in 1690, making his debut in *Cadmus et Hermione*, and rapidly became the most fashionable dancer of his day. In 1699 he performed in London. In 1712, or thereabouts, he retired from the Paris Opera to work at the Duchesse du Maine's court at Sceaux where in 1714 he performed (with great personal success) in *Apollon et les Muses*, a work widely considered to be a forerunner of the ballet d'action. In 1715 he became dancing master to the 5-year-old Louis XV; in 1719 he was appointed composer of the king's ballets. Also in 1719 he succeeded Pierre Beauchamps as head of the Académie Royale de Danse. In 1731 he was named Dancing Master to the Children of France. As a teacher, his private pupils included Marie Sallé. He is said to have been both handsome and charming, while exceptionally talented as a dancer. The roles pictured in his surviving portraits include those from *Amadis de Grèce* (1699) and *Le Carnaval et la Folie* (1704). Several of his duets with Marie Thérèse de Subligny were recorded in Feuillet notation, thus ensuring their survival. Often (but incorrectly) referred to as Jean Ballon (or Balon).

ballonné A jumping step in ballet in which one leg is stretched to either the front, the back, or the side. The dancer then jumps on the supporting leg, landing with the stretched leg bending at the

knee and the foot placed on the supporting ankle. A ballonné can be done in any direction.

ballotté A rocking step in ballet in which the body leans forward and backward during each transfer of weight.

ballroom dance Social dance usually performed by couples in dance halls or at social gatherings. During the 20th century these dances came to be performed widely in competitions, which flourished in Britain and America following the First World War. In 1929 the Official Board of Ballroom Dancing was founded and by the 1930s standardization of training and levels of expertise had been established. Today the annual Open British Championship ranks as the world's most important competition. Standard ballroom dances include the waltz, Viennese waltz, foxtrot, tango, lindy, charleston, and the quickstep. Latin American dances such as the rumba, samba, paso doble, and cha-cha-cha are also part of the ballroom repertoire. Recent television programmes including the competition *Strictly Come Dancing* have contributed to a mass revival of interest.

Banes, Sally (*b* Washington, DC, 9 Oct. 1950) US dance writer, critic, historian, and lecturer. Ph.D. from New York University (1980). She was a senior critic at *Dance Magazine*, dance editor at the *Soho Weekly News*, dance and performance art critic for *Village Voice*, and editor of *Dance Research Journal*. Currently Marian Hannah Winter Professor of Theatre and Dance Studies at the University of Wisconsin-Madison, where from 1992 to 1996 she was chair of the Dance Program. She has also taught at New York University, the School of Visual Arts, Florida State University, the State University of New York at Purchase, Wesleyan University, and Cornell University. One of America's leading writers on dance, her publications include *Terpsichore in Sneakers: Post-Modern Dance* (1980; rev. 1987), *Democracy's Body: Judson Dance Theater 1962–64* (1983, rev. 1993), *Greenwich Village 1963: Avant-garde Performance and the Effervescent Body* (1993), *Writing Dancing in the Age of Postmodernism* (1994), *Dancing Women: Female Bodies on Stage* (1998), *Subversive Expectations: Performance Art and Paratheater in New York 1976–85* (1998), and *Reinventing Dance in the 1960s* (with Baryshnikov and Andrea Harris, 2003). She has co-edited several collections of dance writing and photography and also worked on dance films and videos.

Bangarra Dance Theatre Australian contemporary dance company, founded by Carole Johnson in 1989, to showcase the dance and culture of the indigenous peoples of Australia. Since 1991, when Stephen *Page became principal choreographer and director, its repertory has been choreographed by Page (some material in collaboration with Frances Rings). While drawing inspiration from Aboriginal and Torres Strait Islander traditions the work also deals with issues facing the indigenous population in a modern urban environment. Productions include *Ochres* (1995), which explores the mystical significance of ochre, and *Fish* (1997), which celebrates the rivers and the seas. Both feature original scores by David Page, S. Page's brother. In 1997 Bangarra Dance Theatre collaborated with the Australian Ballet on *Rites*, a new version of Stravinsky's *Rite of Spring* choreographed by S. Page and revised in 2006. Bangarra performed at the Sydney Olympics in 2000 and tours internationally. Recent works include *Mathinna* (Page, 2008).

(((⊕))) SEE WEB LINKS
• Website for Bangarra Dance Theatre

Baras, Sara (*b* Cadiz, 25 Apr. 1971) Spanish dancer, director, and choreographer. She trained with her mother Concha Baras; then in Madrid with Merche Esmeralda, Antonio Canales, and others. From early on she possessed an exceptional technical range, her dancing embracing both classical and contemporary styles, and possessing a power and speed of footwork usually associated with men. During the 1990s Baras performed with several companies in Spain and featured in Mike Figgis's film documentary *Flamenco Women*. She formed her own company in 1998, presenting her own choreography in works such as *Suenos* (1999), *Sabores* (2005), and *Carmen* (2007) and distancing herself from more traditional flamenco companies by her use of contemporary choreographic forms and staging.

Bar aux Folies-Bergère Ballet in one act with choreography and libretto by Ninette de Valois, music by Chabrier, and designs by Chappell. Premiered 15 May 1934 by Ballet Rambert at the Mercury Theatre in London, with Markova, Argyle, Gould, and Ashton. The ballet is based on Manet's famous painting and was the only work ever choreographed by de Valois for the Rambert company.

Barber, Samuel (*b* West Chester, Pa., 9 Mar. 1910; *d* New York, 23 Jan. 1981) US composer. He wrote the music for Martha Graham's *Cave of the Heart* (1946). His scores have been used by many choreographers, including Bolender, Neumeier, MacMillan, Ailey, and Wheeldon.

Barberina, La (Barbarina) (orig. Barbara Campanini; *b* Parma, 1721; *d* Barschau, Silesia, 7 June 1799) Italian dancer. She was as famous for her love affairs off stage as for her brilliant technique on stage. She made her debut at the Paris

Opera in 1739, dancing in Rameau's *Les Fêtes d'Hébé*. Her success at the Paris Opera ultimately led to Sallé's retirement. Renowned for her pirouettes and entrechats huit, she made guest appearances in London and Dublin. When not dancing, she enjoyed liaisons with Prince de Carignan (director of the Paris Opera), Lord Arundel, the Marquis de Thébouville, and the Duke of Durfort. In 1744 she was hired by Frederick the Great of Prussia for an engagement in Berlin, but instead of honouring it she travelled with her lover, Lord Stuart Mackenzie, to Venice. The king then had her brought to Berlin by military guard. Once there, it seems she disarmed him with her beauty, for it is believed they became lovers. She danced at the Berlin Court Opera until 1748, when she fell out of favour with the Prussian king over her love affair with Charles-Louis de Cocceji, son of the king's chancellor. In 1749 she married Cocceji secretly against his family's wishes, accompanying him to exile in Silesia. They separated in 1759 and divorced in 1788. A year later, having purchased the Barschau estate in Silesia, she was given the title Countess von Barschau. She had her estates in Silesia turned into a charitable institution for impoverished noble ladies. Her colourful life was the subject of a 1935 ballet by Maudrik at the Berlin State Opera, entitled *Die Barberina*.

barn dance A rural American dance in 4/4 time which was introduced in the early 19th century. It is so named not because it was danced in a barn, but because it was performed to the song 'Dancing in the Barn'. It was originally called Military Schottische.

Barnes, Clive (*b* London, 13 May 1927; *d* New York 19 Nov. 2008) British-US dance critic. He was educated at Oxford University and started his career in Britain, writing for *The Times*, *New Statesman*, *Daily Express*, and *Spectator*. He was dance critic of the *New York Times* (1965–77) and additionally its drama critic (1967–77). In 1977 he became dance and drama critic of the *New York Post* and continued writing for it until a few weeks before his death He was also senior editor of *Dance Magazine* and a regular contributor since 1958.

Baron (Baron Nahum; *b* Manchester, 1906; *d* London, Sept. 1956) British ballet photographer. He was official photographer for the Sadler's Wells Ballet at Covent Garden. His photographs were published in several major editions: *Baron at the Ballet* (1950), *Baron Encore* (1952), and *Baron's Ballet Finale* (1958).

Baronova, Irina (*b* Petrograd, 28 Feb. 1919) Russian-born dancer, one of the three 'baby ballerinas'. Although she was born in Russia her entire career was in the West. She studied with Preobrajenska as a child in Paris, where her parents settled after emigrating from Russia. In 1932, at the age of 13, she was hired by Balanchine as one of three baby ballerinas for the Ballets Russes de Monte Carlo, the other two being Toumanova and Riabouchinska. She created roles in Massine's *Les Présages, Jeux d'enfants, Beau Danube* (1933), and Nijinska's *Les Cent Baisers* (1935). In 1939 she went to the US, appearing in the Hollywood film *Florian* (1939). When her husband (German Sevastianov) became managing director of (American) Ballet Theatre, she joined the company as prima ballerina (1941–42). She performed with various companies in the US throughout the 1940s, guesting with Denham's Ballet Russe de Monte Carlo and de Basil's Original Ballet Russe in New York and Cuba. She made a second film, *Yolanda* (Mexico, 1942), and appeared with Massine in the musical *A Bullet in the Ballet*. She retired from the ballet stage in 1946 and lived in England for many years. In 1986 she staged Fokine's *Les Sylphides* for Australian Ballet.

Barra, Ray (Raymond Martin Barallobre; *b* San Francisco, 3 Jan. 1930) US dancer, director and ballet master. He studied at San Francisco School of Ballet and American Ballet Theatre School and joined San Francisco Opera Ballet (1949). From 1953 to 1959 he danced with American Ballet Theatre. In 1959 he joined Stuttgart Ballet as a principal, where he remained until injury forced him to retire from the stage in 1966. He created roles in Cranko's *Romeo and Juliet* (1962), *Swan Lake* (1963), *Firebird* (1964), and *Onegin* (title role, 1965), and MacMillan's *Las Hermanas* (1963) and *Song of the Earth* (1965). He was ballet master of Berlin Opera Ballet (1966–70), Frankfurt Ballet (1970–73), and Hamburg Ballet (1973–76), associate director and guest choreographer of Madrid's Ballet Nacional Clásico in the late 1980s, and artistic director of Berlin Opera Ballet (1994–96). He has staged versions of the classics for the Bavarian State Ballet.

barre The wooden bar attached to the walls of a ballet studio at about waist height. It is used by dancers to aid balance during the exercises that constitute the first part of a daily class.

Bart, Patrice (*b* Paris, 30 Jul. 1945) French dancer, choreographer, and ballet master. He studied at the Paris Opera Ballet School and joined the company in 1959, becoming a member of the corps de ballet before his fifteenth birthday. He was promoted to danseur étoile in 1972. He excelled in demi-caractère roles, and was particularly noted for his Blue Bird. He became ballet master of the Paris Opera Ballet in 1986 (a position he still holds) and briefly acted as interim

ballet director. He retired from the stage in 1989. His first choreography was for the Berlin Staatsoper Ballet, a new staging of *Don Quixote*, in 1993, which was later taken into the repertoire of the Finnish National Ballet (1995). His other versions of the classics include *Coppélia* (Paris Opera, 1996), *Swan Lake* (Berlin Staatsoper, 1997), and *La Bayadère* (Bavarian State Ballet, 1998). In 2003 he choreographed *La Petite Danseuse de Degas* (mus. Denis Levaillant) for the Paris Opera. Gold medal, Moscow (1969).

Bartók, Béla (*b* Nagyszentmiklós, 25 Mar. 1881; *d* New York, 26 Sept. 1945) Hungarian composer. He wrote only two ballet scores: *The Wooden Prince* (1917), which was rejected by Diaghilev as 'false modernism', and *The Miraculous Mandarin* (1926), which was widely choreographed throughout the 20th century. Many of his concert works have also been used as ballet scores including the Sonata for 2 Pianos and Percussion (chor. by Béjart in *Sonate a trois*, 1957), the 2nd Violin Concerto (chor. By Henri Oguike in *In Broken Tendrils* 2002), the 4th String Quartet (chor. by M. Morris in *All Fours*, 2004 and de Keersmaeker in *Bartok Annotations* 1986, reprised in *Nacht* 2007), and the 3rd Piano Concert (by Wheeldon in *Even Fall* 2006). Other choreographers to have used his music include H. Holm, Stevenson, Juronics, Tomasson, S. Welch, and De Frutos.

Barton, Aszure (*b* Edmonton, Alberta, 16 Jul. 1975) Canadian choreographer. She trained at the National Ballet School in Toronto, the Royal Winnipeg Ballet, and the John Cranko Schule in Stuttgart, focusing on choreography early on in her career. Her style is grounded in the classical vocabulary, but is expanded through contemporary and collaborative techniques. She has created works for Mikhail Baryshnikov, Fang-Yi Sheu, American Ballet Theatre, Sydney Dance Company, the Martha Graham Company, Les Ballets Jazz de Montreal, and the National Ballet of Canada. From 2005 she was artist in residence at the Baryshnikov Arts Center in New York. Her works include: *Watch Her* (mus. Pergolesi, National Ballet of Canada 2009) and *One of Three* (mus. Ravel, American Ballet Theatre, 2009). Since 2002 she has directed her own company Aszure Barton & Artists.

Baryshnikov, Mikhail (*b* Riga, 27 Jan. 1948) Latvian-born Soviet-US dancer, choreographer and ballet director. One of the leading, international stars of 20th-century dance. He studied at the Leningrad Ballet School (the Vaganova) with Pushkin and joined the Kirov in 1967, where he rapidly rose to prominence. Jacobson choreographed the solo *Vestris* (1969) especially to showcase his technical brilliance, and Baryshnikov went on to create lead roles in Sergeyev's *Hamlet* (title role, 1970) and Kasatkina and Vasiliov's *Creation of the World* (Adam, 1971). In 1974, while on tour with a troupe of Soviet dancers, he defected in Toronto, following the example of his Kirov predecessors Nureyev and Makarova. He danced with many companies in the West, including the Royal Ballet and Paris Opera Ballet, but was most closely associated with American Ballet Theatre (1974–8, 1980–9), where he formed a partnership with Gelsey Kirkland. In addition to performing the classical repertoire, he actively sought the challenges of modern choreography, working with the Paul Taylor, Alvin Ailey, and Martha Graham companies, among others and enjoying enormous success with Twyla Tharp's crossover ballet *Push Comes to Shove* (1976), which became his signature piece. He joined New York City Ballet in 1978 for a season in order to work with Balanchine, although the choreographer was not able to create anything new for him. While at NYCB Baryshnikov did however create roles in two Robbins ballets, *The Seasons* and *Opus 19*. In 1980 he returned to ABT as principal dancer and artistic director, where he remained until 1989. His directorship met with mixed success; his stagings included *Giselle* (1980), *Cinderella* (1983), and *Swan Lake* (1988), but the last two were quickly withdrawn from the repertoire. As a pure classical dancer, he was possessed of a superlative technique and musicality as well as an exceptional ability to inhabit the characters he portrayed on stage.

Following his retirement from classical ballet, Baryshnkikov joined with Mark Morris to found the *White Oak Dance Project in 1990, using his celebrity and his still-compelling stage presence to bring modern dance to audiences around the world. For White Oak he commissioned new works from Taylor, Tharp, Lubovitch, and Robbins, among others, while reviving works by Holm, Graham, Limón, and Cunningham; he also oversaw the revivals of key works from Judson Dance Theatre. In 2002 White Oak was disbanded, but in 2005 Baryshnikov founded the Baryshnikov Arts Centre in New York, a creative base and performance space for artists from different disciplines. In 2006 under the auspices of the BAC he performed with Hell's Kitchen Dance, in a programme of works by BAC associates Aszure Barton and Benjamin Millepied. In 2007 he danced in Stockholm with Ana Laguna in M. Ek's *Place*.

The list of his created roles includes Neumeier's *Hamlet: Connotations* (1976), Ailey's *Pas de Duke* (1976), Petit's *Dame de pique* (1978), Robbins's *Other Dances* (1976), and *Opus 19* (1979), Ashton's *Rhapsody* (1980), MacMillan's *The Wild Boy* (1981), Tharp's *Push Comes to Shove* (1976), *The Little Ballet* (also called *Once Upon a Time*, 1983), and *Sinatra Suite* (1984), Armitage's *The Mollino*

Room (1986), and Morris's *Drink to Me Only with Thine Eyes* (1988) and *Wonderland* (1989).

He starred in several films, including *The Turning Point* (1977), *White Nights* (1985), *Dancers* (1987), and *The Cabinet of Dr Ramirez* (1991). He made his Broadway stage debut in 1989 in *Metamorphosis*, a play by Steven Berkoff based on Franz Kafka and went on to act in several productions including an evening of short Beckett plays, directed by JoAnne Akalaitis (2007). He has appeared frequently on television in America, featured in *Baryshnikov at the White House*, *Baryshnikov on Broadway*, and *Baryshnikov in Hollywood* as well as acting in the final series of *Sex and the City*. He made his debut as a choreographer with *Nutcracker* (American Ballet Theatre, 1976) followed by a new production of *Don Quixote* (ABT, 1978). He has been given honorary degrees at several universities and awarded many prizes, including Gold Medals at Varna, 1966, and Moscow, 1969. Nijinsky Prize, Paris, 1969. Emmy Award, 1979; Best Actor Award, Outer-Circle Drama Critics, 1989.

🕮 **SEE WEB LINKS**

● Website for the Baryshnikov dance foundation with link to the BAC

bas, en Indicates a low position in ballet, especially of the arms.

Basel Ballet Swiss municipal ballet company, based in Basel. The company was formed in 1955 when the Russian dancer and choreographer Vaslav Orlikovsky assumed the post of ballet master in Basel. He imported foreign dancers, built up the repertoire, and brought the company to international attention, using the classics as well as popular Soviet works to draw audiences. Orlikovsky also created two important ballets of his own: *Peer Gynt* (1956) and *The Prince of the Pagodas* (1961). The company fell into decline following his departure in 1967, but it was revitalized by Heinz Spoerli, who became resident choreographer (later company director) in 1973. He contributed many works to the repertoire, including a popular restaging of *Giselle*, and also invited outside choreographers such as Christopher Bruce, Forsythe, van Manen, and Cranko to create work. The company made its New York debut in 1983. Spoerli left the company in 1991. In 1996, following a decision by the theatre's management, the company was disbanded but it was subsequently revived and under the direction of Richard Wherlock (appointed 2001) operating as a mid-scale company and focusing on new works including *Orpheus and Persephone* (Cathy Marston, mus. Vasks, 2005).

Basil, Colonel de (Vassily Voskresensky; *b* Kaunas, 1888; *d* Paris, 27 Jul. 1951) Russian ballet impresario and co-director of the *Ballets Russes de Monte Carlo. Following service in the Russian Army during the First World War, the former Cossack officer began his theatrical career in Paris in 1925. He eventually became assistant to the exiled Georgian impresario Prince Zeretelli, who ran London and Paris seasons of Russian opera. In 1932 he founded the Ballets Russes de Monte Carlo with René Blum, running the business side of the company and organizing its tours. An unlikely advocate for Russian ballet, he nonetheless helped to bring it to a worldwide audience through the company's exhaustive international touring. After Massine left in 1938 (Blum having departed in 1936), he continued to direct the company under several names, the most commonly used being the Original Ballet Russe. The company disbanded in 1948.

basse danse A French term which refers to a group of 15th-century court dances. These were usually dignified walking dances, widely considered to be precursors of the minuet. Ashton's *Capriol Suite* features a basse danse.

Bat-Dor Dance Company Israeli dance company based in Tel Aviv, co-founded by Baroness Bethsabee de *Rothschild and the South African dancer Jeannette *Ordman. It made its debut in 1968 under the direction of Ordman, who was also its leading dancer. The company acquired a broad repertoire of modern works by choreographers including Tudor, van Dantzig, Lubovitch, Ailey, Jamison, and the Israeli choreographers Domy Reiter-Soffer, Igal Perry, and Ido Tadmor. After the death of Martha Graham it also acquired the performing rights to some of her works. However it was always in competition with *Batsheva Dance Company (also originally founded by Rothschild), and after Rothschild's death, Bat-Dor suffered extreme financial difficulties. It closed down in 2001, although Ordman continued to run its associate school.

Batsheva Dance Company Israeli dance company founded in 1964 and named after its sponsor, Baroness Bethsabee de Rothschild, *Martha Graham's wealthy benefactor. The foremost modern dance ensemble in Israel, it made its debut in Tel Aviv in 1964. From the beginning it took artistic advice from Martha Graham, and until 1970 it was directed by the ex-Graham dancer Jane Dudley. In the 1980s Robert Cohan, another Graham dancer, acted as artistic adviser. The repertoire featured works by Graham including *Errand into the Maze*, *Embattled Garden*, *Cave of the Heart*, and *Diversion of Angels*, plus *The Dream*, which Graham created for the company in 1974. In the mid-1970s, however, the special relationship between Batsheva and Graham was

severed when Linda Hodes (who had been joint artistic director) became a director of Graham's company in New York. Works by Robbins and Limón were added to Batsheva's repertoire and new works created. Guest choreographers included Tetley, Morrice, Butler, and Cranko and Israeli choreographers included Rena Gluck, Moshe Efrati, Ehud Ben-David, and Rina Schenfeld. In 1973 Bethsabee de Rothschild broke her ties with the company in order to devote her energies and financial support to Bat-Dor. Following her departure, the company received financial support from the Israeli Government. In the 1980s, under the joint directorship of Shelley Sheer and David Dvir, a younger generation of choreographers such as Mark Morris, Daniel Ezralow, and Ohad Naharin were brought in to make work. In 1990 *Naharin was appointed artistic director. He acquired works from Kylián, Vandekeybus, Preljocaj, and Forsythe; however in recent years his own works have increasingly dominated the repertory. The company tours internationally, and Naharin himself has become a major influence on younger Israeli choreographers.

(((●))) SEE WEB LINKS
• Website of Batsheva Dance Company

battement A ballet term which indicates a beating movement of a stretched or a bent leg.

batterie A ballet term which refers to movements in which the legs are beaten together in the air.

Baudelaire A dance spectacle in nine scenes based on the poems of Baudelaire, directed by Maurice Béjart, who adapted the text, created the choreography, and organized the musical montage. Premiered 9 Feb. 1968 by the Ballet of the 20th Century at Grenoble, with Michel Bringuies, Bortoluzzi, Donn, Lowski, Lommel, Albrecht, Bari, Gielgud, and Kerendi. Béjart incorporated songs by Debussy and excerpts from Wagner's *Tannhäuser* in this mammoth work, which draws a parallel between Baudelaire's paradise and the drug culture of the 1960s.

Bauhaus Dances Experimental dances by the painter Oskar *Schlemmer which sought to explore the relationship between a moving figure and space. His research into dance began after he joined the Bauhaus in 1920. In 1925 at Dessau he presented his so-called 'Bauhaustänze', which were essentially analytical studies of movement. *See also* TRIADIC BALLET.

Bausch, Pina (*b* Solingen, 27 Jul. 1940; *d* Wuppertal, 30 Jun. 2009) German dancer, choreographer, and company director. One of the most influential dance artists of the late 20th century.

She began her training at the age of 14 with Kurt *Jooss at the *Folkwang School in Essen and continued at the Juilliard School of Music in New York (1960–1) with Antony Tudor. Between 1961 and 1962 she danced with the New American Ballet at the Metropolitan Opera, a company then directed by Tudor, after which she returned to Germany as a soloist with Jooss's Folkwang Ballet. She began choreographing in 1968 and when Jooss retired in 1969 she became company director. In 1973 she was appointed director of Tanztheater Wuppertal, in Germany's industrial Ruhr Valley. Her debut work for Wuppertal was *Fritz* (mus. Wolfgang Hufschmidt, 1974) followed a year later by her landmark staging of Stravinsky's *Rite of Spring* (1975)—a work of primal power in which the dancers, divided tribally between the two sexes, performed on a stage covered with bare earth. With her 1976 production of *The Seven Deadly Sins* Bausch established her reputation as one of the most original and visionary creators of dance theatre.

A natural heir to the German expressionist dance tradition, Ausdruckstanz, Bausch's productions were not primarily about dance but about ideas and emotions (she herself said she was 'not interested in how people move, but in what moves them'); they were also created from an intensive collaborative process in which the dancers contributed their own biographical material as well as movement ideas. The resulting productions were not constructed by a linear narrative logic but by associative vignettes of dance, speech, and game playing. Props and costumes played a major role as did the stage sets, created with Bausch's two main designers, the late Rolf Borzik, followed by Peter Pabst. These were often masterpieces of theatrical imagination, and engineering: in *Arien* the stage was covered with water; in *Viktor* the action took place inside a huge earthwork grave; in *Nelken* the stage was carpeted with thousands of carnations. Her earlier works were dominated by darker emotions: alienation, anguish, frustration, and cruelty, hence Arlene *Croce's famously phrased criticism, 'the pornography of pain', however her later works were more overtly playful. A list of her productions includes *In the Wind of Time* (1969), *Actions for Dancers* (1971), *Tannhäuser-Bacchanale* (1972), *Fritz* (1974), *Iphigenia in Tauris* (1974), *Orpheus and Eurydice* (1975), *The Rite of Spring* (1975), *The Seven Deadly Sins* (mus. Weill, 1976), *Bluebeard* (1977), *Cafe Müller* (1978), *Kontakthof* (1978), *Arien* (1979), *Legend of Chastity* (1979), *Bandoneon* (1980), *Walzer* (1982), *Nelken* (1982), *On the Mountain a Cry Was Heard* (1984), *Two Cigarettes in the Dark* (1985), *Viktor* (1986), *Palermo, Palermo* (1989), *A Dreamplay* (1994), *Danzon* (1995), *Only You* (1996), *Masurca Fogo* (1998), *Agua* (2001), and *Follmond* (*Full Moon*, 2006).

Bausch also worked in film. In 1982 she collaborated with Fellini on *And the Ship Sails On*; she directed her own film, *The Lament of the Empress* (1989) and sequences of her choreography were incorporated in P. Almodóvar's *Talk to Her* (2002). She rarely worked outside her own company, although in 1997 she re-staged her *Rite of Spring* for the Paris Opera Ballet and the following year directed *Bluebeard's Castle* with Pierre Boulez (Aix-en-Provence). But this did not lessen her international impact. Her company toured worldwide and her productions have not only influenced many younger choreographers such as Vandekeybus, Platel, and Newson but many stage directors and designers.

(((🌐))) SEE WEB LINKS

• Website for the Wuppertal company

Bavarian State Ballet (Bayerische/s Staatsballett) Ballet company based in Munich, formerly known as the Munich State Opera Ballet or the Bavarian State Opera Ballet; also known as the Bavarian National Ballet. The company, which performs at the National Theatre, dates back to 1818 when the theatre opened. The Taglionis appeared as guest artists in 1825; Lucile Grahn was ballet mistress from 1869 to 1875 and under the control of Heinrich Kröller (1917–30) the company staged many important premieres, including R. Strauss's *Die Josephslegende* and Bartók's *The Wooden Prince*. Pia and Pino Mlakar ran the company from 1939 to 1944 (and again from 1952 to 1954), one of their most interesting acquisitions being a revival of F. Taglioni's 1826 ballet *Jocko, the Brazilian Ape*. Marcel Luipart (1945–8) was responsible for the world premiere of Werner Egk's *Abraxas* (1948) Subsequent directors included Victor Gsovsky (1950–2), Alan Carter (1954–9), Heinz Rosen (1959–68), Ronald Hynd (1970–3 and 1984–6), Lynn Seymour (1978–80), Konstanze Vernon (1989–98), and Ivan Liska (from 1998). In 1989 the company became independent of the opera and its name changed to Bavarian State Ballet. Since then its core repertoire has been based in the classics and in 20th-century heritage works by Cranko, Balanchine, and others; but the company has also honoured its tradition of presenting new or experimental works, acquiring repertory by Forsythe, Ek, Tharp, Childs, Teshigawara, and G. Murphy. In 2009 the company took part in Kylián's *Migratory Birds*, a multi-disciplinary installation that took place in many different spaces within the National Theatre.

(((🌐))) SEE WEB LINKS

• Website for the Bavarian State Ballet

Bayadère, La Ballet in four acts with choreography by Petipa, libretto by Sergei Khudekov and

Petipa, music by Minkus, and scenery and costumes by Ivan Andreyev, Mikhail Bocharov, Petr Lambin, Andrei Roller, Matvei Shishkov, and Heinrich Wagner. Premiered 4 Feb. 1877 at the Bolshoi Theatre, St Petersburg, with Vazem, Ivanov, Gorshenkova, and Johansson. The ballet is set in ancient India and its story based on Kalidasa's 5th-century Sanskrit masterpiece *Sakuntala*. It tells of the bayadère (temple dancer) Nikiya who loves the warrior Solor. Solor, although returning her love, is forced to become engaged to the Rajah's daughter Gamzatti. Gamzatti conspires to have her rival bitten by a snake, and Nikiya dies. In the famous Kingdom of the Shades scene, an opium-smoking Solor dreams of meeting his beloved again. In the final act, often omitted in later productions, the temple collapses during Solor and Gamzatti's wedding, burying them in the ruins. The Kingdom of the Shades, with its extraordinary opening procession of the corps de ballet moving slowly down a ramp, is considered one of Petipa's masterpieces. It was first seen in the West in 1961 performed by the Kirov; Nureyev then staged it for the Royal Ballet in 1963. Makarova mounted the first full-length *Bayadère* in the West (for American Ballet Theatre) in 1980; in 1992 Nureyev staged it for the Paris Opera and in 2002 the (Mariinsky) Kirov mounted an exhaustive period reconstruction. In 2006 Patrice Bart mounted a new version for the Bavarian State Ballet.

Bayanihan Philippine Dance Company
Philippine company founded in Manila in 1957 to preserve the traditions of Filipino folk dance and to present them on the international stage. Its first appearance in the West was at the Brussels World Fair of 1958. The company evolved from presenting simple folk dances to more stylized theatrical productions.

Bayerische/s Staatsballett *See* BAVARIAN STATE BALLET.

Baylis, Lilian (*b* London, 1874; *d* London, 1937) British theatre manager whose vision helped to create what eventually became the Royal Ballet. She began by running the Old Vic Theatre in 1912, and in 1926 she engaged de Valois to stage dances for the plays and operas she was presenting. When Sadler's Wells was rebuilt in 1931 Baylis took de Valois and her dancers with her to the new theatre, thus establishing a permanent home for both a national dance company and a school.

Baylis, Nadine (*b* London, 15 Jun. 1940) British designer. She studied at the Central School of Art and Design in London. She began an association with Ballet Rambert in 1965, designing Norman Morrice's *Realms of Choice*. She is most closely associated with the ballets of Glen Tetley, for whom she designed *Ziggurat* (Ballet Rambert,

1967), *Embrace Tiger and Return to Mountain* (Ballet Rambert, 1968), *Field Figures* (Royal Ballet, 1970), *Sacre du printemps* (Munich State Opera, 1974), *The Tempest* (Ballet Rambert, 1979), *Alice* (National Ballet of Canada, 1986), *Orpheus* (Australian Ballet, 1987), and *Oracle* (National Ballet of Canada, 1994). She also designed Michael Corder's *Romeo and Juliet* (1992) for the Norwegian National Ballet, London Contemporary Dance Theatre's *The Phantasmagoria* in 1987, and Ben Stevenson's *Alice in Wonderland* (1992) for Houston Ballet. An austere and stylish designer.

Baynes, Stephen (*b* Adelaide, South Australia, 1956) Australian dancer and choreographer. He trained at the Australian Ballet School and joined the company in 1976, where he was promoted to soloist in 1992. He additionally danced with Stuttgart Ballet between 1981 and 1984. In 1986 he created his first ballet, *Strauss Songs* (1986) and in 1995 was appointed resident choreographer of Australian Ballet, creating many more works for the company including *Beyond Bach* (1995), *1914* (mus. Graeme Koehne, 1998), *Molto Vivace* (mus. Handel, 2003), *Night Path* (mus. Richard Mills, 2008), and a new staging of *Raymonda* (2006).

He has also created works for La Scala Ballet, Sydney Dance Company, West Australian Ballet, and New York City Ballet's Diamond Project among others.

Beach Ballet in one act with choreography by Massine, music by Françaix, and designs by Dufy. Premiered 19 Apr. 1933 by the Ballets Russes de Monte Carlo, Monte Carlo, with Lichine, Riabouchinska, Baronova, and Massine. The gods of the sea take human form as bathers at a fashionable seaside resort.

Beach Birds Modern dance in one act with choreography by Cunningham, music by Cage, and costumes by Marsha Skinner. Premiered 20 Jun. 1991 by the Merce Cunningham Dance Company at Theater 11 in Zurich. An abstract, fluid work for eleven dancers, it was made using the LifeForms computer program. It was later revised for a film version called *Beach Birds for Camera*.

beat In ballet a term which means the beating of one leg against the other, or the beating of both legs together, often crossing one another, while in the air.

Beaton, (Sir) Cecil (*b* London, 14 Jan. 1904; *d* Salisbury, 18 Jan. 1980) British photographer, stage designer, and author. He was most closely associated with Ashton, designing sets and costumes for the latter's *Apparitions* (Vic-Wells Ballet, 1936), *Les Sirènes* (Sadler's Wells Ballet, 1946), *Les Patineurs* (Ballet Theatre, 1946), *Illuminations*

(New York City Ballet, 1950), *Picnic at Tintagel* (New York City Ballet, 1952), *Casse-Noisette* (Sadler's Wells Theatre Ballet, 1951), and *Marguerite and Armand* (Royal Ballet, 1963). He also designed Balanchine's *Swan Lake* for New York City Ballet in 1951, and the musical *My Fair Lady*. An elegant, romantic designer whose sets and costumes fused an instinct for contemporary fashion with an aura of timeless glamour. He won two Academy Awards, for *Gigi* (1958) and *My Fair Lady* (1964). Knighted in 1972.

Beatty, Patricia (*b* Toronto, 13 May 1936) Canadian dancer, choreographer, artistic director, and writer. She studied ballet with Gladys Forrester and Gweneth Lloyd in Toronto, and graduated from Bennington College in 1959. She studied modern dance at the Connecticut College Summer School, the José Limón School, and the Martha Graham School. She danced with Mary Anthony Dance Company (1959–60) and Pearl Lang Dance Company (1960–5). In 1965 she returned to Canada and opened a school. In 1967, drawing on the students she had trained, she founded the New Dance Group of Canada and in 1968 she co-founded (with David Earle and Peter Randazzo) Toronto Dance Theatre and its school. Most of her choreography has been for Toronto Dance Theatre. Her work is distinguished by its visual impact and the seriousness of its themes. Her later pieces are dedicated to exploring the power of the feminine in nature and the idea of the goddess in myth and religion. She retired from performing in 1983 and in 1993 gave up her position as resident choreographer of Toronto Dance Theatre. A list of her works includes *Against Sleep* (mus. Southam, 1968), *First Music* (mus. Ives, 1970), *Seastill* (mus. Southam, 1979), *Raptures and Ravings* (mus. Robert Daigneault, 1983), *Emerging Ground* (mus. Southam, 1983), *Mandala* (1992), *Gaia* (mus. Sharon Smith, 1993), *Garden of Origins* (mus. David Akal Jaggs, 1993), and *Assara* (mus. Sharon Smith, 1997).

Beatty, Talley (*b* Cedargrove, La., *c.*1923; *d* New York, 29 Apr. 1995) US dancer, choreographer, and company director. He trained with Katherine Dunham and made his professional debut in her company in 1940, undertaking additional later studies with Martha Graham. In 1946 he left Dunham to perform in musicals, including a revival of *Show Boat* (1946), as well as in Maya Deren's film, *A Study in Choreography for Camera* (1945). In 1949 he formed his own company, Tropicana, for which he created *Southern Landscape*, a work portraying the plight of African Americans in the South after the Civil War. In 1955 he disbanded his company, and focused on giving solo concerts and choreographing for others. His dances frequently highlighted social injustice, particularly for black Americans. A list of

his works includes *The Road of the Phoebe Snow* (1959), the full-length *Come and Get the Beauty of It Hot* (1960), *Powers of Six* (1964), and *Montgomery Variations* (1967). He also created *The Black District* (1968) and *The Stack Up* (1982) for the Alvin Ailey company; *Poème de l'extase* for Cullberg Dance Company in 1972, and *Cathedral of Heaven* for Batsheva Dance Company in 1973. Other companies with whom he worked include the Boston Ballet and Dance Theatre of Harlem and he also collaborated with Duke Ellington on two television specials: *A Drum Is a Woman* (NBC, 1956) and *Black, Brown and Beige* (CBS, 1974). His tribute to the composer, *Ellingtonia*, had its premiere at the American Dance Festival in 1993.

Beauchamps, Pierre (Beauchamp) (*b* Paris, 1631 (baptized 30 Oct.); *d* Paris, 1705) French dancer, choreographer, ballet master, and composer, who is credited with inventing the five classic positions of classical ballet. He trained as a violinist and dancer, making his debut as the latter in 1648, in the court ballet *Le Dérèglement des passions*. He subsequently appeared in many ballets de cour with Louis XIV, whom he taught. In 1661 he was appointed the first Intendant des Ballets du Roi, thus making him responsible for the staging of all ballets at court. As a choreographer he collaborated frequently with the composer Lully, the two of them sometimes contributing both music and steps to the same production (Lully had himself started his career as a dancer). Together they radically shaped the evolution of ballet, both at court and at the newly founded Paris Opera. As a composer Beauchamps also worked with Molière (who was in fact a relative) and contributed the score and choreography for the latter's 1661 comedy-ballet, *Les Fâcheux* (as well as conducting the orchestra). This was the first of many collaborations with Molière; later productions included *Le Mariage forcé* (1664) and *Le Bourgeois gentilhomme* (1670), both of which had music by Lully. On 19 Mar. 1671 Beauchamps choreographed *Pomone*, the first opera produced at the Paris Opera. In 1672 he joined the Paris Opera as ballet master, working in partnership with Lully until 1687, when Lully died and Beauchamps retired. In 1680 he was appointed chancellor of the Académie Royale de Danse. His most famous production was *Le Triomphe de l'amour* (1681), which was notable for featuring the first public appearance of professional female dancers. Following his retirement from the Paris Opera, he continued to work as court choreographer. As a dancer he was noted for his brilliant technique, and is said to have been one of the first to execute tours en l'air. He also designed his own system of notation, and in 1704 sued his rival notator Raoul-Auger Feuillet for plagiarism. Beauchamps lost. Rather than inventing the five classic ballet positions of arms and feet, he was probably the first to codify them. He is sometimes described as 'the father of all ballet masters'. He was also a noted art collector.

Beau Danube, Le (orig. title *Le Beau Danube bleu*) Ballet originally in two acts with choreography by Massine, music by Johann Strauss II and Josef Strauss arr. Roger Désormière, set by Vladimir and Elizabeth Polunin (after Constantin Guys), and costumes by É. de Beaumont. Premiered 17 May 1924, Soirées de Paris de Comte É. de Beaumont, Théâtre de la Cigale, Paris, with Lopokova and Massine. A comedy set in the Vienna Prater of the 1860s, and involving a love triangle between a hussar, his high-born fiancée, and his former mistress, a street dancer. This last role was particularly associated with Danilova, who performed it when Massine revived the ballet in its final one-act version in 1933 for the Ballets Russes de Monte Carlo. There have been many revivals, including London Festival Ballet in 1971 and the Joffrey Ballet in 1972.

Beaujoyeux, Balthasar de (Beaujoyeulx) (orig. Baldassare da Belgiojoso; *b* Paris, early 16th century; *d* Paris, *c*.1587) Italian-French violinist, composer, and choreographer. He was a personal servant to Catherine de Médicis and musical tutor to her sons. He took part in the masquerade *Défense du paradis* (1572), arranged the *Ballet aux ambassadeurs polonais* (1573), and choreographed the *Ballet comique de la reine* in 1581. The latter, a five-hour extravaganza celebrating the marriage of the Duc de Joyeuse to the Queen's sister, is widely considered to be the first ballet de cour. As such, he is regarded as the first French choreographer.

Beaumont, Comte Étienne de (*b* 8 Mar. 1883; *d* 1956) French designer and ballet patron. In 1924, in conjunction with Cocteau and Massine, he organized the Soirées de Paris at the Théâtre de la Cigale, which presented the first performances of many works by Massine, including *Salade*, *Mercure*, and *Le Beau Danube*.

Beaumont, Cyril William (*b* London, 1 Nov. 1891; *d* London, 24 May 1976) British critic, writer, bookseller, and publisher. One of the most important dance historians of the 20th century. He wrote more than 40 books on ballet, including the *Complete Book of Ballets*, and translated many early writings on the subject by Noverre, P. Rameau, and Gautier. He also recorded and preserved the Cecchetti system of training, and founded the Cecchetti Society to further the master's teaching methods. He became a ballet fan after seeing Pavlova perform in 1911 and the

following year saw Diaghilev's Ballets Russes, an event which prompted him to devote himself to chronicling the achievements of the Diaghilev era. In 1910 he opened a dance bookshop in Charing Cross Road in London which became world famous, and he kept it open for the next 55 years until his retirement in 1965. He was honoured by the French, Italian, and British governments. Author of *A Manual of the Theory and Practice of Classical Theatrical Dancing* (with Idzikowski, 1922), *A Bibliography of Dancing* (1929), *Michel Fokine and His Ballets* (1935), *The Complete Book of Ballets* (1937), *The Diaghilev Ballet in London* (1940), *Supplement to the Complete Book of Ballets* (1942), *The Ballet Called Giselle* (1944), *The Sadler's Wells Ballet* (1946), *Ballet Design: Past and Present* (1946), *Dancers Under My Lens* (1949), *The Ballet Called Swan Lake* (1952), *Ballets of Today* (1954), *Ballets Past and Present* (1955), and *A Bookseller at the Ballet*, his 1975 autobiography. Légion d'honneur (1950). Chairman of the Cecchetti Society from 1922 to 1970. Editor of *Dance Journal* (1924–39); dance critic of the *Sunday Times* (1950–9).

Beauty and the Beast 1. Ballet in one act with choreography by Cranko, music by Ravel, and designs by Margaret Kaye. Premiered 20 Dec. 1949, by Sadler's Wells Theatre Ballet, Sadler's Wells Theatre, London, with David Poole and Patricia Miller. A dance version of the fairy-tale; filmed for BBC Television in 1953. 2. Full-length ballet by Peter Darrell for Scottish Theatre Ballet, with libretto by Colin Graham, music by Thea Musgrave, and designs by Peter Minshall. Premiered 19 Nov. 1969 at Sadler's Wells Theatre, London. Other versions include Bintley's for Birmingham Royal Ballet (mus. Buhr, 2003).

Beck, Hans (*b* Haderslev, 31 May 1861; *d* Copenhagen, 9 Jun. 1952) Danish dancer, choreographer, and ballet master. His greatest achievement was the preservation of the Bournonville repertoire. He studied at the Royal Danish Ballet School and made his debut in 1871 (with Bournonville among the audience). He became a soloist in 1881 and performed all the leading male roles in the Bournonville repertoire. He was ballet master of the Royal Danish Ballet from 1894 to 1915 and ensured that the repertoire was dedicated to keeping alive the Bournonville legacy. It is his editions of Bournonville which continue to be performed in Copenhagen. He choreographed the solo variations for the last act of a new production of *Napoli*, and his production of *Coppélia* (1896) proved enduringly popular. Out of his own ballets, the best known was *The Little Mermaid* (1909), based on Hans Christian Andersen's fairy-tale and set to music by Fini Henriques. Ellen

Price, who danced the title role, was the inspiration behind the famous statue in Copenhagen's harbour.

Bedells, Phyllis (*b* Bristol, 9 Aug. 1893; *d* Henley on Thames, 2 May 1985) British dancer and teacher. She studied with Bolm, Cecchetti, and Pavlova, making her debut in 1906, at the age of 13, in *Alice in Wonderland* at the Prince of Wales Theatre in London. She danced regularly at the London Empire Theatre (1907–16), and from 1914 was prima ballerina there, the first British dancer to hold the post. She then danced in West End revues and in opera ballets at Covent Garden. In 1920 she was a founding member of the Royal Academy of Dancing, helping to draw up its first syllabus. She was also a member of the Camargo Society. In 1931 she appeared as a guest artist with the Vic-Wells Ballet. Following her retirement from the stage in 1935 she became active in teaching and as an examiner for the Royal Academy of Dancing. She published her autobiography, *My Dancing Days*, in 1954.

Beethoven, Ludwig van (*b* Bonn, prob. 16 Dec. 1770; *d* Vienna, 26 Mar. 1827) German composer. He wrote only two ballets: *Ritterballett* (chor. Habich, Bonn, 1791) and *The Creatures of Prometheus* (chor. S. Viganò, Vienna, 1801; new version by Ashton for Royal Ballet Touring Company, Bonn, 1970). His concert works however, have been used by many choreographers, most notably Massine (*Seventh Symphony*, Ballet Russe de Monte Carlo, 1938, *Moonlight Sonata*, American Ballet Theatre, 1944); Béjart (*Ninth Symphony*, Ballet of the 20th Century, 1964); Taylor (*Orbs*, Paul Taylor Company, 1966); van Manen (*Grosse Fuge* to String Quartet, Op. 133, Nederlands Dans Theater, 1971, and *Adagio Hammerklavier*, to Op. 106, Dutch National Ballet, 1973); Kudelka (*Pastorale*, National Ballet of Canada, 1990); de Keersmaeker (*Erts*, Brussels, 1992); and Tharp (Seventh Symphony, NYCB, 2000).

Behemoth Modern dance in one act with choreography by Mark Morris, performed in silence. Premiered 14 Apr. 1990, by the Mark Morris Dance Group at the Halles de Schaerbeek in Brussels. A ritualistic and emotionally introverted work. Joan Acocella, in her biography of Morris (1993), described it as 'the coldest, darkest dance Morris has ever made'.

Beijing Modern Dance Company Chinese contemporary dance company founded in 1995 under the auspices of the Beijing Municipal Bureau of Culture. In 1998 it became semi-independent of government and, under Zhang Changcheng's artistic direction, it developed a repertoire that blends East and West, traditional and modern. Its stylistic influences include folk

dance, martial arts, classical ballet, and Chinese opera, as well as contemporary dance techniques.

Béjart, Maurice (orig. M. Berger; *b* Marseilles, 1 Jan. 1927; *d* Lausanne, 22 Nov. 2007) French dancer, choreographer, and ballet director. A controversial and influential figure within 20th-century ballet whose works have ranged from pure dance to text-driven theatrical spectacle. The son of philosopher Gaston Berger, he studied dance in Marseilles, Paris (with Egorova), and London (with Volkova) and made his debut in 1945. From 1945 to 1947 he toured with Schwarz, Charrat, and Petit; in 1949–50 he performed with Mona Inglesby's International Ballet (where he was primarily cast as the Prince in *Swan Lake*) then from 1950 to 1952 he was with the Cullberg Ballet and the Royal Swedish Ballet. In 1953 he founded Les Ballets de l'Étoile (with the writer Jean Laurent), the precursor to the Ballet Théâtre de Paris de Maurice Béjart (1957). He choreographed several works for this troupe, including *Symphonie pour un homme seul* (1955), which was probably the first ballet ever choreographed to *musique concrète* (recorded sounds not made with musical instruments). In 1957 he created *Sonate à trois*, set to Bartók and based on Sartre's play *No Exit*. In 1959 he choreographed the hugely successful *Sacre du printemps* for the Brussels Opera, using a specially assembled company. This formed the nucleus of the Ballet of the 20th Century, set up the following year with Béjart as director. It was based at the Théâtre Royal de la Monnaie in Brussels and went on to achieve an exceptional international popularity, its repertoire of Béjart ballets bringing new, young audiences to dance. Flamboyant and ambitious productions like *Les 4 Fils Aymon*, 1961, and *The Merry Widow*, 1963, while firmly based in the classical technique, were staged with a modern sensibility, a seriousness of theme and a grandiose theatricality that divided Bejart's fans sharply from the many critics who deemed his work vulgar and pretentious. Béjart's speed in picking up on new trends led to him becoming one of the first choreographers to use electronic music and, in the late 1960s, to tap into the prevailing hippie zeitgeist, adding a veneer of mysticism and Eastern ideologies to his choreography (*Bakhti*, 1968, and *Nijinsky, clown de Dieu*, 1971, for example). He was also fascinated by Wagner, taking part in Wieland Wagner's 1961 Bayreuth production of *Tannhäuser*, choreographing *Venusberg* (1963), *Mathilde* (1965), *Baudelaire* (1968), and *Les Vainqueurs* (1969) to Wagner scores, and creating *Ring um den Ring* for the Berlin Opera Ballet in 1990. In 1970 he became head of the Mudra Centre in Brussels, an international training school for the performing arts.

In 1987, following a disagreement with the Monnaie management, Béjart moved to Lausanne, where his company was re-named Béjart Ballet Lausanne. In 1992 he founded the École-Atelier Rudra Béjart Lausanne, similar to the Mudra Centre. During the 1990s he collaborated several times with Sylvie *Guillem. Although he created several works for the Paris Opera Ballet (*Damnation of Faust*, 1964, *Renard*, 1965, and *Firebird*, 1970), most of his choreography was for his own company. A list of his other ballets includes *Symphony for a Lonely Man* (mus. Pierre Henry and P. Schaeffer, 1955), *Prométhée* (mus. Maurice Ohana, 1956), *Sonate à trois* (mus. Bartók, 1957), *Orphée* (mus. Henry, 1958), *Bolero* (mus. Ravel, 1960), *The Seven Deadly Sins* (mus. Weill, 1961), *Tales of Hoffmann* (opera by Offenbach, 1961), *Les 4 Fils Aymon* (with Charrat; mus. 15th and 16th century, 1961), *Les Noces* (mus. Stravinsky, 1962), *A la recherche de Don Juan* (revised version, mus. 16th century, 1962), *Suite viennoise* (mus. Schoenberg, Berg, and Webern, 1962), *Ninth Symphony* (mus. Beethoven, 1964), *L'Oiseau de feu* (second version; mus. Stravinsky, 1964), *Romeo and Juliet* (mus. Berlioz, 1966), *Messe pour le temps present, or Mass for Our Time* (1967), *A la recherche de . . .* (mus. various, 1968), *Serait-ce la mort?* (mus. R. Strauss, 1970), *Song of a Wayfarer* (mus. Mahler, 1971), *Nijinsky, clown de Dieu* (mus. Tchaikovsky and Pierre Henry, 1971), *Stimmung* (mus. Stockhausen, 1972), *Golestan—Garden of Roses* (1973), *Le Marteau sans maître* (mus. Boulez, 1973), *La traviata* (Verdi opera, 1973), *Seraphite* (mus. Mozart, 1974), *I trionfi* (mus. Berio, 1974), *Notre Faust* (mus. Bach, 1975), *Le Molière imaginaire* (mus. Rota, 1976), *Les Illuminations* (mus. Henry, oriental, 1979), *Eros-Thanatos* (mus. various, 1980), *La Flute enchantée* (mus. Mozart, 1981), *Wien, Wien nur du allein* (mus. Schoenberg, Beethoven, and others, 1982), *Messe pour le temps futur* (mus. Wagner, Beethoven, 1983), *Cinq nô modernes* (text Mishima, 1984), *The Contest* (mus. Le Bar and others, 1985), *Malraux, ou, La Métamorphose des dieux* (mus. Beethoven, Le Bars, traditional, 1986), *Le Martyre de Saint-Sébastien* (mus. Debussy, 1986), *Prélude à l'après-midi d'un faune* (mus. Debussy, 1987), *Piaf* (mus. Piaf, 1988), *1789 . . . et nous* (1989), *Tod in Wien* (mus. Mozart, 1991), *Le Mandarin merveilleux* (1992), *Lear-Prospero* (1994), *Journal* (1995), *Mutation X* (1998), *The Nutcracker* (1998), and *Mother Teresa and the children of the world* (2002). In 1997 in Lausanne he staged *Ballet for Life*, with music by Mozart and the rock group Queen and costumes by Versace; the work drew its inspiration from the lives of the singer Freddie Mercury and the dancer Jorge Donn, both of whom died of Aids. His company, under the direction of Gil Roman, continued to perform his work after his death.

He was the author of *Maurice Béjart: Un instant dans la vie d'autrui, Memoires* (Paris, 1979), and *Ballets par Béjart* (Paris, 1979). He also wrote the novel *Mathilde, ou le temps perdu* (1963) and the plays *La Reine verte* (1963) and *La Tentation de Saint-Antoine* (1967). Erasmus Prize (1974). Medal of the Order of the Rising Sun, Japan.

(🌐) **SEE WEB LINKS**

• Website for Béjart Ballet Lausanne

Belgium Dance came late to Belgium, and was restricted for the most part to Brussels and Ghent. As elsewhere in Europe, it took the form of a ballet company attached to the local opera house, and performances were usually limited to dancing in opera ballets. In 1816 a permanent corps de ballet was established at the Théâtre de la Monnaie in Brussels; in 1819 Jean-Antoine Petipa was hired as premier danseur and ballet master. In 1826 he founded the Conservatory of Dancing, the school where Marius Petipa and his brother Lucien began their dance studies. In 1841 the Royal Opera was founded in Ghent; a dance academy followed seven years later. Dance continued to be subordinate to opera, however, until well into the 20th century, and most of those working in Belgium were foreigners. After the First World War a resident ballet company was established at the Monnaie, and ballet productions began to proliferate. During the 1930s the first modern dance activity emerged Elsa Darciel, Lea Daan, and Isa Voos, most of it within the expressionist mid-European style. In 1947 the first independent ballet company in Belgium, Ballet Belges, was formed, although it was short-lived. In 1960 Béjart founded the Ballet of the 20th Century in Brussels, a company which achieved a huge following both at home and abroad, and was increasingly associated with a cross over of classical and contemporary styles. From this point dance in Belgium began to flourish, with both Flemish and French communities developing dance forms. In 1966 the Charleroi-based Ballet Royal de Wallonie was founded (renamed Charleroi/Danses-Centre Chorégraphique de la Communauté Française in 1991). In 1970 Antwerp launched its own Ballet of Flanders, later becoming Royal Ballet of Flanders. From the 1980s onwards a younger generation of Belgian choreographers began to set up their own independent companies, several of them including de *Keersmaeker, *Vandekeybus, *Platel, and *Cherkaoui achieving international reputations.

From 1988 to 1991 the US Mark *Morris Dance Company succeeded Béjart's as resident dance company at the Monnaie Opera House in Brussels; after which de Keersmaeker and her company Rosas were in residence. Although Rosas and its associate school P.A.R.T.S moved into their own building in 2007, they continued to be

supported by De Munt/Monnaie in partnership
with the Kaaitheater.

(((●))) **SEE WEB LINKS**
• Website for De Munt/Monnaie
• Website for Rosas and P.A.R.T.S.

Bell, Olivia (*b* Newcastle, NSW, 23 Jun. 1978)
Australian dancer. She studied locally, at the
Australian Ballet School and for a year at the
Paris Opera School, 1995. In the same year she
joined Australian Ballet, and despite taking two
years out (1997–9) was promoted to principal
in 2007. A commanding stage presence, with a
polished classical style, she has danced ballerina
roles across the repertory, including works by
Wheeldon, Robbins, Kylián, MacMillan, and Forsythe.

belly dancing *See* RAQS SHARQI.

Belsky, Igor (*b* Leningrad, 28 Mar. 1925; *d* St
Petersburg, 3 Jul. 1999) Soviet dancer, choreographer, and ballet director. He studied ballet at the
Leningrad (later Vaganova) Ballet School, graduating in 1943 into the Kirov and becoming one of
the company's leading character dancers (he additionally studied acting at the Leningrad Institute
for Theatre Arts, graduating in 1957). He created
roles in Jacobson's *Shurale* (1950) and *Spartacus*
(1956), Sergeyev's *Path of Thunder* (1958), Grigorovich's *The Stone Flower* (1957), and Boris
Fenster's *Taras Bulba* (1955) while his own choreography for the Kirov included *Coast of Hope*
(mus. A. Petrov, 1959), and *Leningrad Symphony*
(mus. Shostakovitch 1961). Both ballets were considered exemplary in their handling of Soviet
themes—patriotism, loyalty, and courage. He left
the Kirov in 1962 to become chief choreographer
and artistic director of the Leningrad Maly Theatre where he produced new versions of *The Little
Humpbacked Horse, Swan Lake*, and *Nutcracker*,
while creating *Eleventh Symphony* (mus. Shostakovich, 1966), and *Gadfly* (mus. Tchernov, 1967).
Between 1973 and 1977 he was back at the Kirov
as chief choreographer and artistic director, creating *Icarus* for the company in 1974. He was then
chief choreographer of the Leningrad Music Hall
(1979–92) and artistic director of the Vaganova
Ballet Academy (from 1992). As a teacher he additionally taught character dance in 1946 at the
Leningrad (Vaganova) School; and from 1966
taught choreography at the St Petersburg Conservatory. People's Artist RSFSR (1966).

Benesh, Rudolf and Joan British husband
and wife who devised the Benesh system of
*dance notation. Rudolf (*b* London, 16 Jan. 1916;
d London, 3 May 1975), an engineer, and Joan
(*née* Rothwell; *b* Liverpool, 24 Mar. 1920), a dancer, developed their system in 1955 and began

teaching it in 1956 at the Royal Academy of Dancing. In 1960 the Royal Ballet became the first
company to hire a professional choreologist. In
1962 Joan and Rudolf Benesh founded the Institute of Choreology, since renamed the Benesh
Institute (and incorporated into the Royal Academy of Dancing). The Benesh Institute is responsible for training choreologists and for preserving
notated scores. Benesh notators now work with
virtually every major ballet company in the Western world. Most new ballets are notated in the
Benesh system, while Labanotation continues to
be favoured by those working in non-classical
dance. Benesh Movement Notation uses a five-
line stave, similar to music, with symbols that
represent the various positions and movements
of a body.

Benjamin, Leanne (*b* Rockhampton, Australia, 13 Jul. 1964) British-Australian dancer. She
trained with Valerie Hansen in Queensland; then
at Royal Ballet School in London, winning the Prix
de Lausanne 1981. In 1983 she joined Sadler's
Wells Royal Ballet, where she created the role of
Gerda in Bintley's *The Snow Queen* (1986) and
was promoted to principal in 1987. She subsequently danced with London Festival Ballet
(1988–1990) and Deutsche Oper Ballet in Berlin
(1990) before joining the Royal Ballet in 1992. She
was made principal the following year and became one of the company's most versatile
ballerinas, dancing with a rare strength well into
her forties. She has been noted especially for
her interpretations of the MacMillan repertoire
and has created roles in many ballets including
Tharp's *Mr Worldly Wise*, Tetley's *Amores*,
McGregor's *Qualia*, and Wheeldon's *DGV*.

Bennett, Michael (*b* Buffalo, 8 Apr. 1943; *d*
Tucson, Ariz., 2 Jul. 1987) US dancer, choreographer and Broadway director. He studied tap, jazz,
and modern dance as a child and made his debut
in 1960 in a European touring production of *West
Side Story*. Returning to New York a year later, he
danced in the choruses of *Subways Are for Sleeping* (1961), *Nowhere to Go But Up* (1962), *Here's
Love* (1963), and *Bajour* (1964). On television he
danced for *The Ed Sullivan Show, Hollywood Palace*, and *The Dean Martin Show*. His first work as
a billed choreographer was for *A Joyful Noise*
(1966), which closed after only twelve performances on Broadway but still earned Bennett his
first Tony nomination for choreography. His first
Broadway hit was *Promises, Promises* (1968), a
musical based on Billy Wilder's 1960 film *The
Apartment. Coco* (1969) and *Company* (1970) followed. For *Follies* (1971) Bennett was hired as
co-director (with Harold Prince) and choreographer, gaining a Tony Award for each. In 1975 he
directed, choreographed, and wrote (winning a

Pulitzer Prize) *A Chorus Line*, the longest-running show on Broadway until it was overtaken by *Cats* in 1997. Other musicals on which he worked include *Ballroom* (1978) and *Dreamgirls* (1981), which ran for more than 1,500 performances on Broadway.

Bennetts, Kathryn (*b* Sydney, 30 Mar. 1954) Australian dancer and director. She studied at the Scully Borovansky and Australian Ballet Schools, joining Australian Ballet in 1973. Three years later she moved to Stuttgart Ballet, becoming soloist, and noted especially for her performances in the Forsythe repertory. When injury cut short her stage career in 1984 she retrained as a teacher and taught at the John Cranko School, National Ballet School, Canada, and also for numerous companies worldwide. In 1989 she became ballet mistress at Frankfurt Ballet, remaining there for 15 years and also staging Forsythe's ballets internationally. In 2005 she was appointed director of Royal Ballet of Flanders, where she has attempted to bridge the gap between its classical and modern repertories, and has acquired several Forsythe works including his full-length *Impressing the Czar*.

Bennington School of the Dance One of the major platforms for modern dance in the US during the 1930s. The summer dance courses, that were held between 1934 and 1942 at the Bennington College and Undergraduate Liberal Arts College for Women in Vermont, made a tradition of presenting works by leading choreographers including Graham, Humphrey, Holm, and Weidman. Among the works premiered there were Graham's *El Penitente* and *Letter to the World*, Humphrey's *New Dance*, *With My Red Fires*, and *Passacaglia in C minor*, and Holm's *Trend*. Younger choreographers such as Cunningham, Hawkins, and Limón also benefited from the Bennington platform. The college, which changed its name to Bennington School of the Arts in 1940, was the first to offer a degree in dance.

Benois, Alexandre (*b* St Petersburg, 4 May 1870; *d* Paris, 9 Feb. 1960) Russian painter and designer. One of the key figures of Diaghilev's Ballets Russes. Like Diaghilev he studied law at the University of St Petersburg and in 1899, along with Diaghilev, Bakst, and Nouvel, founded the art magazine *Mir Iskusstva* (The World of Art). The magazine led to Diaghilev curating Paris exhibitions of Russian art, whose success allowed him to branch out into Russian opera and, in 1909, ballet. Benois was the first artistic director of the Ballets Russes de Diaghilev, remaining with the company until 1911 when a quarrel led to his departure. He began designing for the ballet at the

Mariinsky Theatre in St Petersburg, where his productions included *Sylvia* (never staged), *Cupid's Revenge* (1902), and *Le Pavillon d'Armide* (1907). For the Ballets Russes he designed *Les Sylphides* and *Le Festin* (1909), *Giselle* (1910), *Petrushka* (1911), and *Song of the Nightingale* (1914). His career as a designer continued long after he parted from Diaghilev, and he subsequently worked with Ida Rubinstein's company (*Bolero*, *Le Baiser de la fée*, and *Nocturne*), the Ballets Russes de Monte Carlo (*Le Bourgeois gentilhomme*, 1932, *Graduation Ball* and *Nutcracker*, 1940, *Raymonda*, 1946), and London Festival Ballet (*Nutcracker* and *Graduation Ball*, 1957). His flair as a designer was for delicate and historically accurate stage settings, although he will be remembered most for the colourful folkloric designs of *Petrushka*. Author of *Reminiscences of the Russian Ballet* (London, 1941) and *Memoirs* (2 vols. London, 1960 and 1964).

Bérard, Christian (*b* Paris, 20 Aug. 1902; *d* Paris, 13 Feb. 1949) French painter and designer. One of the co-founders of the Ballets des Champs-Elysées (with Petit and Kochno, 1945). He designed Balanchine's *Cotillon* (Ballets Russes de Monte Carlo, 1932) and *Mozartiana* (Les Ballets 1933); Massine's *Symphonie fantastique* (Colonel de Basil's Ballets Russes, 1936), *Seventh Symphony* (Sergei Denham's Ballet Russe de Monte Carlo, 1938), and *Clock Symphony* (Sadler's Wells Ballet, 1948). For the Ballets des Champs-Elysées he designed Petit's *Les Forains* (1945) and Lichine's *La Rencontre* (1948).

Beretta, Caterina (*b* Milan, 8 Dec. 1839; *d* Milan, 1 Jan. 1911) Italian dancer and teacher. She danced in the first production of Verdi's opera *Les Vêpres siciliennes* in Paris in 1853, and was famous as a ballerina throughout Europe, appearing in London as well as in Italy. She was maîtresse de ballet at the Mariinsky Theatre in St Petersburg (1877), and also at La Scala (1905–8). Pavlova, Legnani, and Karsavina were among those she taught.

Berg, Alban (*b* Vienna, 9 Feb. 1885; *d* Vienna, 24 Dec. 1935) Austrian composer. Although he wrote no ballet music, his concert works have been used by choreographers, including Béjart (*Suite viennoise*, 1961), Tetley (*Threshold*, 1972), Robbins (*In Memory of . . .* , 1985), William Tuckett (*Enclosure*, 1990), and L. Childs *Opus One* (2003).

bergamasca (bergomask; bergamasco; bergamasque) An old Italian peasant dance, from the area around Bergamo in Lombardy. Believed to be a fast circular dance in duple time for men and women, although there are no extant records or notations. It originated in the mid-15th century.

Berger, Augustin (*b* Boskovice, 11 Aug. 1861; *d* Prague, 1 Jun. 1945) Czech dancer, choreographer, and ballet master. He danced at the opera houses in Dresden and Prague, and was a soloist at the Stavovské Theatre (1876–80). In 1883 he became a soloist at the Prague National Theatre. He eventually became ballet master of the Prague National Theatre (1912–23), where he helped to develop the national Czech ballet, and the court opera in Dresden (1900–10). He was artistic director of the Warsaw Ballet (1910–12), and staged *Carmen* at the Alhambra Theatre in London. He was ballet master of the Metropolitan Opera Ballet in New York (1926–32). He also choreographed the first non-Russian production of the second act of *Swan Lake* in 1888, an event attended by Tchaikovsky himself during a trip to Prague.

Bergsma, Deanne (*b* Pretoria, 1941) South African-born British dancer. She was a member of the Royal Ballet from 1958, becoming a principal in 1967. A tall, elegant dancer, she created the role of Lady Mary Lygon in Ashton's *Enigma Variations*. She retired from the company in 1974, although returned in 1988 to take the role of Berta in a revival of Ashton's *Ondine*.

Berio, Luciano (*b* Imperia, 24 Oct. 1925) Italian composer. He wrote the score for Béjart's *I trionfi* (Florence, 1974) and his concert music has been used by many choreographers including Tetley (*Circles*, Nederlands Dans Theater, 1968), van Manen (*Keep Going*, Düsseldorf, 1971), Morrice (*That Is the Show*, Ballet Rambert, 1971), van Dantzig (*Après visage*, Dutch National Ballet, 1972), Kylián (*Dream Dances*, Nederlands Dans Theater, 1979), Forsythe (*workwithinwork*, Frankfurt Ballet 1998), and Rafael Bonachela (*Voices*, London, 2006).

Beriosova, Svetlana (*b* Kaunas, 24 Sept. 1932; *d* London, 10 Nov. 1998) Lithuanian-born British dancer, teacher, and coach. Daughter of Nicholas *Beriozoff. She left Lithuania at the age of 3 and studied dance with her father in Paris. When the Second World War broke out the family moved to the US and she continued her studies at the Vilzak–Schollar school in New York, and later with Olga Preobrajenska in Paris and Vera Volkova in London. She made her debut in *The Nutcracker* with the Ottawa Ballet in 1947 aged 15 and danced briefly with the Grand Ballet du Marquis de Cuevas in Europe. In 1948–9 she was ballerina with the Metropolitan Ballet in England (where she created the role of 'heartbreak' girl in John Taras's *Designs with Strings*), before becoming a soloist with the Sadler's Wells Theatre Ballet in 1950. She transferred to the Sadler's Wells Ballet (later the Royal Ballet) in 1952, eventually becoming a ballerina in 1955. An aristocratic dancer, with expressive arms and back, she was noted for her interpretations of the classics, and was frequently hailed as the successor to Fonteyn. Like Fonteyn, she was particularly acclaimed for her Aurora and Odette-Odile, although she brought to these roles a 'Russian' quality unique in the Royal Ballet. Her performance as the Tsarevna in the 1954 revival of *The Firebird* was recorded on film. She created leading roles in Balanchine's *Trumpet Concerto* (1950), Cranko's *Prince of the Pagodas* (1957), and *Antigone* (1959), Ashton's *Birthday Offering* (1956), *Persephone* (1961, in which she also spoke the French text), and *Enigma Variations* (1968, the role of Lady Elgar), and MacMillan's *Baiser de la fée* (1960) and *Anastasia* (1971, the role of the Tsarina). She retired in 1975, although continued to coach.

Beriozoff, Nicholas (*b* Kaunas, 16 May 1906; *d* Zurich, 18 Feb. 1996) Lithuanian-British dancer, choreographer, and ballet master. He studied in Czechoslovakia at the National Ballet School in Prague and danced with the Prague Opera Ballet and with the Lithuanian National Ballet in Kaunas before joining René Blum's Ballets de Monte Carlo in 1936, where, as rehearsal assistant to Fokine, he learned the Fokine ballets that were to become his speciality as a producer. From 1938 to 1944 he danced with the Ballet Russe de Monte Carlo, decamping to the US with Massine. In 1944 a knee injury ended his career as a dancer, and it is as a ballet master that he is best remembered. He worked across Europe with many companies, including Ballet International (1944), Metropolitan Ballet (1948), La Scala, Milan (1950–1), London Festival Ballet (1951–4), and Grand Ballet du Marquis de Cuevas (1947, 1956, 1962). He also directed Stuttgart Ballet (where he was Cranko's predecessor, 1957–60), Finnish National Ballet, (1962–4), Zurich Ballet (1964–71), and Teatro San Carlo (1971–3). For London Festival Ballet he revived *Les Sylphides*, *Petrouchka*, *Scheherazade*, and the Polovtsian Dances from *Prince Igor*. His own choreography included *Le Baiser de la fée* (mus. Stravinsky, 1958), *Ondine* (mus. Henze, 1965), *Romeo and Juliet* (mus. Prokofiev, 1966), and *Cinderella* (mus. Prokofiev, 1967) as well as stagings of the 19th-century classics. Father of Svetlana *Beriosova.

Berkeley, Busby (*b* Los Angeles, 29 Nov. 1895; *d* Palm Desert, Calif., 14 Mar. 1976) US director, choreographer, and stager of extravagant Hollywood musicals in the 1930s. During the First World War he was an entertainment officer, staging elaborate drill routines and despite having no formal dance training he went on to act in, direct or produce 21 dance musicals on Broadway. In 1930 he went to Hollywood to work on the film *Whoopee* and for over a decade his spectacular dance sequences—often orchestrating complex geometric patterns from huge ensembles of dancers—featured in many of cinema's most successful musicals. His choreography took place on ambitious sets, operated by hydraulic lifts and revolving platforms, while his use of overhead camera angles allowed the full kaleidoscopic ingenuity of his choreography to be viewed. Daringly for the age, his dances were rich in sexual innuendo. As the most illustrious dance director in Hollywood history, he choreographed and/or directed more than 50 films, most of them musicals. These included *42nd Street* (1933), *Gold Diggers of 1933* (also *1935*, *1936*, and *1938*), *Footlight Parade* (1933), *Dames* (1934), *Fashions of 1934*, *Wonder Bar* (1934), *Varsity Show* (1937), *Hollywood Hotel* (1937), *Broadway Serenade* (1939), *Lady Be Good* (1941), *For Me and My Gal* (1942), *Ziegfeld Girl* (1943), *Girl Crazy* (1943), and *Jumbo* (1962). In January 1971 he supervised a Broadway revival of the 1925 stage musical *No, No Nanette*.

Berlin Opera Ballet The German ballet company based at the Opera House in the former West Berlin. Also known as the German Opera Ballet, or Deutsche Oper Berlin. It dates back to the opening of the Opera House in 1912, when dancers performed in ballets and opera-ballets, however the company did not become fully active until Rudolf Kolling's era as director between 1934 to 1945. After the Second World War, the company was moved out of the bomb-damaged Opera House to the Theater des Westens, not returning until 1961, but under the direction of Tatjana Gsovsky (1957–66) its repertory was expanded with her own new works including *Hamlet* and *The Moor of Venice*. Also in the repertory was Janine Charrat's staging of Egk's *Abraxas* in 1949 and Mary Wigman's controversial new version of *Sacre du printemps* in 1957. During the post-war period it was known as ballet company of the West Berlin Municipal Opera but in 1961 it became formally known as the Berlin Opera Ballet. When the British choreographer Kenneth MacMillan took over as director (1966–9) he created two new works for the company *Concerto* (1966) and *Anastasia* (1967) and built up its 19th-century repertory, with Antony Tudor's staging of *Giselle;* Nureyev's *Nutcracker*, and MacMillan's own stagings of *Swan Lake* and *The Sleeping Beauty*. Other foreign choreographers who have subsequently worked with the company include Balanchine, Cranko, van Manen, van Dantzig, Forsythe, and L. Childs, who choreographed the full-length *Light Explosion* in 1987. From 1972 to 1990 the company was directed by Gert Reinholm, followed by Peter Schaufuss, who staged the three Tchaikovsky ballets before departing in 1994. Richard Cragun succeeded him

as artistic director (1996–9). In 1999 Angelin Preljocaj was appointed artistic adviser while the future of the company, by now in serious decline, was re-examined. In 2004 it was amalgamated, along with the German State Opera Ballet, and the Komische Ballet into a single company, the Berlin State Ballet.

See BERLIN STATE BALLET.

Berlin Staatsoper Ballet *See* GERMAN STATE OPERA BALLET; BERLIN STATE BALLET.

Berlin State Ballet Ballet company amalgamated from the three historic Berlin companies, following the re-unification of Berlin: the two that were based at the former East Berlin opera houses, Staatsoper Unter den Linden (State Opera) and Komische Oper (Comic Opera); and the one based at the former West Berlin opera house, the Deutsch Oper (German Opera). The new company, Berlin State Ballet, was established in 2004 under the direction of Vladimir Malakhov, who had formerly been director of the Staatsoper company. Malakhov continued to dance with the new State Ballet, along with Bolshoi-trained Polina Semionova as principal ballerina, and guests such as Diana Vishneva. At its formation, most of the company's 80-plus dancers were drawn from the Staatsoper and Deutsch Oper companies as was its repertory, which alongside the 19th-century classics included works by Cranko, Balanchine, Forsythe, and Bigonzetti. It currently performs in both the Staatsoper and Deutsch Oper houses.

(((🌐))) SEE WEB LINKS

• Website for State Opera with link to the State Ballet

Berlioz, Hector (*b* Côte-Saint André, 11 Dec. 1803; *d* Paris, 8 Mar. 1869) French composer. Although he wrote nothing specifically for ballet (apart from divertissements within operas) his music has been used by many choreographers, notably Béjart (*Romeo and Juliet*, Ballet of the 20th Century, 1966 and *Damnation of Faust*, Paris Opera, 1964) and Massine (*Symphonie fantastique*, Ballets Russes de Monte Carlo, 1936 and *Harold in Italy*, Ballet Russe de Monte Carlo, 1954).

Berman, Eugene (*b* St Petersburg, 4 Nov. 1899; *d* Rome, 14 Dec. 1972) Russian-US painter and designer. One of the foremost ballet designers in America for more than thirty years. His productions included Ashton's *Devil's Holiday* (1939), Balanchine's *Concerto Barocco* (1941), *Danses concertantes* (1944), *Le Bourgeois gentilhomme* (1944), and *Pulcinella* (1972), Tudor's *Romeo and Juliet* (1943), and American Ballet Theatre's 1946 production of *Giselle*. He also designed the opulent setting for Balanchine's *Ballet*

Imperial when it was revived for Sadler's Wells Ballet in 1950.

Berners, Lord (Gerald Hugh Tyrwhitt-Wilson; *b* Bridgnorth, 18 Sept. 1883; *d* Berkshire, 19 Apr. 1950) British composer and designer most closely associated with Sadler's Wells Ballet. Self-taught as a composer, he wrote several ballet scores, including *The Triumph of Neptune* for Balanchine (1926) and *A Wedding Bouquet* (1937, which he also designed), *Cupid and Psyche* (1939), and *Les Sirènes* (1946), all for Ashton.

Bernstein, Leonard (*b* Lawrence, Mass., 25 Aug. 1918; *d* New York, 14 Oct. 1990) US composer and conductor. As a ballet composer, he worked mainly with the choreographer Jerome Robbins during the 1940s and 1950s, writing the music for Robbins's *Fancy Free* (1944), *Facsimile* (1946), and *Dybbuk Variations* (1974). For his part, Robbins choreographed all Bernstein's musicals, including *On the Town* (1944), *Wonderful Town* (1953), *Candide* (1956), and most successfully, *West Side Story* (1957). The latter, a collaboration between Bernstein, Robbins, Arthur Laurents (librettist), and Stephen Sondheim (lyricist), is regarded as one of the masterpieces of American musical theatre.

Bessies *See* SCHÖNBERG, BESSIE.

Bessmertnova, Natalia (*b* Moscow, 19 Jul. 1941; *d* Moscow, 19 Feb. 2008) Russian dancer. Star of the Bolshoi Ballet for three decades. She trained at the Moscow Bolshoi School from 1953 to 1961, and graduated into the company as one of the highest achievers in the school's history. Her repertoire included all the leading roles in the classical Russian repertoire (*Swan Lake*, *The Fountain of Bakhchisarai*, *Don Quixote*, and *Romeo and Juliet* in particular), and created the title role in Lavrovksy's production of *Giselle* at the Bolshoi Theatre in 1963. A dancer who uniquely combined Romantic delicacy and lyricism with extraordinary physical strength, she was equally well-suited to the robust theatrical works choreographed by her husband Yuri Grigorovich. She frequently danced in his *Legend of Love* (creating the role of Shirin in his Moscow version in 1965) and *Spartacus*, and created lead roles in many of his ballets including Anastasia in *Ivan the Terrible* (1975), the female lead in *Angara* (1976), Juliet in *Romeo and Juliet* (1979), Rita in *The Golden Age* (1982), and the title role in his staging of *Raymonda* (1984). She was recipient of numerous awards and honours including Gold Medal, Varna (1965), Anna Pavlova Prize (1970), People's Artist of the USSR (1976). In 1989 she was put on pension at the Bolshoi, and finally left the company in 1995.

Bessy, Claude (*b* Paris, 20 Oct. 1932) French dancer and ballet school director. After training at the Paris Opera Ballet School (from 1942), she joined the Paris Opera in 1945, and was promoted to étoile in 1956. She created leading roles in Lifar's *Snow White* (1951), *Noces fantastiques* (1955), and *Daphnis and Chloe* (1958), Cranko's *La Belle Hélène* (1955), and Skibine's *Daphnis and Chloe* (1959), while Gene Kelly created his *Pas de dieux* (1960) at the Paris Opera especially for her. She also made many television appearances and featured in Gene Kelly's film *Invitation to the Dance* (1956). From 1972 to 2004 she was director of the Paris Opera Ballet School. She also staged ballets for the Opéra Comique and the Comédie Française, and staged the dances for the musical *My Fair Lady* (1984). Published *Danseuse étoile* in 1961. Pavlova Prize (1961); Légion d'honneur (1972).

Bettis, Valerie (*b* Houston, 20 Dec. 1919; *d* New York, 26 Sept. 1982) US dancer, choreographer, company director, and educator. She studied with Hanya Holm in New York, and her later ballet studies were with Carmelita Maracci. She danced with Hanya Holm's company (1937–40) and appeared as a soloist (1941–8) performing her own work. In 1964 she founded the Dance Studio Foundation and the Valerie Bettis Dance/Theater Company, which she ran for several decades in New York. Many of the works she choreographed were solos for herself; her best-known was *The Desperate Heart* (1943), accompanied by a poem by John Malcolm Brinin. In 1947 she choreographed *Virginia Sampler* for the Ballet Russe de Monte Carlo, while her most successful ballet was *A Streetcar Named Desire* (mus. Alex North) which she choreographed for the Slavenska-Franklin Ballet in 1952. In 1954 it was taken into the repertoire of American Ballet Theatre, in 1974 by the National Ballet of Washington, and in 1986 by Dance Theatre of Harlem. She taught for many years at her New York studio, and was also considered a pioneer in television dance, making several programmes during the 1940s and 1950s. In the 1950s she went to Hollywood, appearing in several films as an actress. She choreographed Broadway shows and frequently appeared on stage as actress and singer.

Bewegungschor A term coined by Rudolf von Laban for his mass-movement choirs. He used them in such works as *The Rocking Temple* (1922), *Light Turn* (1923), *Agamemnon's Death* (1924), *Dusky Rhythms* (1925), and *Titan* (1927). For a time the use of Bewegungschor became popular in the German theatre, especially in opera productions.

bharata natyam A solo classical Indian dance form of religious origin performed traditionally by women. It is believed by some scholars to be more than 3,000 years old and was once performed by Hindu temple dancers, or devadasis. Today it is to be found mostly in southern India, in the Chennai region, although exponents have exported the artform to the West, particularly Britain, where it is popular with non-Asian audiences. Much of its traditional repertoire derives from the early part of the 19th century when four brothers, known as the Tanjore Quartet, codified its elements. Traditional performances can last up to three hours. The emphasis in the choreography is on the upper body, and the style is distinguished by its low centre of gravity, its rhythmic footwork, its straight spine, and its extensive vocabulary of hand gestures which carry dramatic meaning. The face is also used for expressive purposes, with the eyes, nose, and mouth all possessing their own specific choreographic language. The dance is in six parts, beginning with alarippu, which invokes the deity and greets the audience. The style incorporates the nirtta aspect of Indian dance (abstract, pure, and rhythmic) and nritya (expressive, rhythmic, and narrative). The performance ends with tillana, a purely rhythmic coda designed to showcase the dancer's mastery of complex rhythms. The female dancer wears a silk sari, usually decorated with gold, and her feet are bare, although bells are worn around the ankle. In Britain the Chennai-born choreographer Shobana *Jeyasingh is one of several to successfully blend bharata natyam and Western contemporary dance styles, while in India a new generation of choreographers is exploring other avenues of modernization, including abstraction, and extended ensemble work. *See* INDIA.

Biagi, Vittorio (*b* Viareggio, 24 May 1941) Italian dancer and choreographer. He studied at the La Scala ballet school and began his career with La Scala in Milan (1958–60) where he was a soloist. From 1961 to 1966 he was a member of Béjart's Ballet of the 20th Century in Brussels, where he created roles in Béjart's *Bacchanale de Tannhäuser*, *Divertimento*, and *Ninth Symphony*, in addition to starting his own choreography (*Jazz Impressions*, 1964; *L'Après-midi d'un faune*, 1965; *Walpurgis Night*, 1965). From 1966 to 1968 he was an étoile with the Paris Opéra Comique. His works from this period include *L'Enfant et les sortilèges* (1967) and *Platée* (1968). In 1969 he became ballet director at Lyon Opera. For Lyon he staged many ballets, including *Alexander Nevsky* (mus. Prokofiev), *Scythian Suite* (mus. Prokofiev), *Romeo and Juliet* (mus. Prokofiev), *Requiem* (mus. Berlioz, 1969), *Seventh Symphony* (mus. Beethoven), *Symphonie fantastique* (mus. Berlioz), and *Song of the Earth* (mus. Mahler). As a choreographer he created primarily narrative ballets, while as a dancer he was noted for his dramatic expression. He was founding artistic director of Aterballetto (1977–9) and in 1978 also founded his own company, Danza Prospettiva, in Italy, for which he created *Requiem senza parola* (1980) and *Don Juan* (1982). From 1982 to 1986 he was artistic director of the Teatro Massimo in Palermo. He subsequently directed and choreographed for New Ballet of Rome (1990–4), then in 2001 revived Danza Prospettiva, as well as choreographing for other Italian companies.

(((●))) **SEE WEB LINKS**
• Official website for Vittorio Biagi

Bias, Fanny (*b* Paris, 3 Jun. 1789; *d* Paris, 6 Sept. 1825) French dancer. After training at the Paris Opera Ballet School, she joined the company in 1807, eventually becoming a grand sujet (first-soloist). She danced in London in 1821, where the manager of the King's Theatre, John Ebers, described her 'beautiful little half steps, which, more than any other, correspond to the epithet twinkling'. She is remembered today for being one of the first dancers to be shown on pointe, a historic moment captured in a lithograph by Waldeck in 1821. Ill health forced her to retire and she died at the age of 36.

Biches, Les Ballet in one act with choreography by Nijinska, music by Poulenc, and designs by Marie Laurencin. Premiered 6 Jan. 1924, by the Ballets Russes de Diaghilev at the Théâtre de Monte Carlo, with Nijinska, Nemchinova, Tchernicheva, Sokolova, Vilzak, Woizikowski, and Zvereff. The title is a colloquial French term for 'the little darlings'. The ballet is set in the south of France in the 1920s at a chic house party where muscle-bound men and giggling girls flirt. A lesbian couple and a sexually ambiguous character dressed in blue add an erotic ambivalence to the proceedings. The choreography, reflecting the period, has a jazz inflection. It was revived by the Markova-Dolin Ballet in 1937, by the de Cuevas Ballet in 1947, and by the Royal Ballet in 1964.

Big Bertha Modern dance in one act with choreography by Paul Taylor, music from the collection of band machines in the St Louis Melody Museum. Premiered 9 Feb. 1971 by the Paul Taylor Company in New York. The ballet, influenced by the macabre cartoons of Charles Addams, shows an American family visiting a fair, where they become dangerously fascinated by Big Bertha, an animated doll on top of a musical box. A television version, which Taylor created as a duet, featured de Jong and Nureyev.

Big City, The Ballet in one act with choreography and libretto by Jooss, music by Alexander

Tansman, and designs by Heckroth. Premiered 21 Nov. 1932 by the Kurt Jooss company at the Folkwang Dance Stage in Cologne under the German title *Grossstadt 1926*. The ballet, a portrayal of urban angst, is widely regarded as the first to offer a serious critique of social issues. It was revived by Wuppertal Dance Theatre (1974), City Center Joffrey Ballet (1975), and Northern Ballet Theatre (1976).

Bigonzetti, Mauro (*b* Rome, 25 Feb. 1960) Italian dancer, choreographer, and company director. He trained at the Rome Opera Ballet School and danced with the Rome Opera Ballet as a soloist. In 1982 he joined Aterballetto, and danced with the company until 1993. He began to choreograph in 1990; his first work, *Sei in movimento* (mus. Bach), was taken into the repertoire of the Rome Opera Ballet. In the early 1990s he worked extensively with Italy's Balletto di Toscana, for whom he made *Turnpike* (mus. Bach, 1991), a piece inspired by America's highways, and *Mediterranea* (1993), a full-length ballet inspired by the cultural mix of people who live by the Mediterranean. The latter was so successful that it became Balletto di Toscana's signature work. Bigonzetti made his international debut as a choreographer with English National Ballet, for whom he choreographed *X. N. Tricities* (1994) and *Symphonic Dances* (mus. Rachmaninoff, 1995). His works tend to be abstract in approach and while grounded in the classical vocabulary can push their dancers to extreme physical limits. In 1997 he became artistic director of Aterballetto and during his first season he made six ballets, among them *Persephassa* (mus. Xenakis), *Furia Corporis* (mus. Beethoven), and *Comoedia*, the first part of a trilogy inspired by Dante's *Divine Comedy* (the final part of which was premiered in 2000). In 2008 he retired as director while remaining the company's resident choreographer. He has also made works for other companies, including the Stuttgart Ballet, the Berlin State Ballet (including *Caravaggio*, 2008), Ballet National de Marseilles, Ballet Argentino, and New York City Ballet (including *Oltramare*, mus. Bruno Moretti, 2008).

Bigottini, Émilie (*b* Toulouse, 16 Apr. 1784; *d* Paris, 28 Apr. 1858) French dancer. She studied at the Paris Opera Ballet School and joined the Paris Opera in 1801. She stayed there until 1823, creating numerous roles, including Nina in Milon's 1813 ballet *Nina, ou la folle par amour*. As a dramatic ballerina she won great praise; the Viennese described her as 'the ear of the deaf'. She was also acclaimed for her skills as a mime. Napoleon was one of her admirers, and among her many lovers was Napoleon's stepson, Eugène de Beauharnais.

Billboards Ballet in four sections with choreography by Laura Dean, Charles Moulton, Margot Sappington, and Peter Pucci, set to rock music by Prince. Premiered 27 Jan. 1993 at the University of Iowa in Iowa City. Choreographed to thirteen songs by the pop star Prince, the full-length rock ballet saved the Joffrey from financial disintegration. Although neither an artistic or critical success, *Billboards* earned millions of dollars at the box office during its first three years.

Billy the Kid Ballet in one act with choreography by Loring, libretto by Kirstein, music by Copland, and designs by Jared French. Premiered 16 Oct. 1938, by Ballet Caravan at the Chicago Opera House with Loring, Marie-Jeanne, L. Christensen, and Bolender. The first major US ballet about America, it was based on the Wild West tale of gunfighter William H. Bonney (Billy the Kid), who boasted that he had killed a man for every year of his life but whose career ended at the age of 21 when he was shot in an ambush by Pat Garrett, a sheriff who had been his friend. In 1940 it was taken into the repertoire of American Ballet Theatre. In 1988, on the occasion of its fiftieth anniversary, it was revived by Dance Theatre of Harlem and the Joffrey Ballet.

Bintley, David (*b* Huddersfield, 17 Sept. 1957) British dancer, choreographer, and ballet director. After training at the Royal Ballet Upper School, he joined Sadler's Wells Royal Ballet in 1976. He created roles in works by Seymour and MacMillan, but was noted for his superb character roles, especially in Ashton's ballets (Widow Simone in *La Fille mal gardée* and the little Stepsister in *Cinderella*). He began choreographing in 1978, becoming company choreographer in 1983. In 1985 he moved to Covent Garden where he became resident choreographer of the Royal Ballet. He had mixed success during this period, although *Still Life at the Penguin Café* (mus. Jeffes, Royal Ballet 1988) and *Hobson's Choice* (Sadler's Wells Royal Ballet, 1989, mus. Paul Reade) both became enduring additions to the repertory, and in 1993 he left Covent Garden to work freelance creating *Job* (mus. Vaughan Williams) for the San Francisco Ballet (1992) and *Edward II* for the Stuttgart Ballet (mus. John McCabe, 1995). In 1995 he became artistic director of Birmingham Royal Ballet, creating many ballets for the company including *Carmina Burana* (mus. Orff, 1995), *Nutcracker Sweeties* (mus. Ellington after Tchaikovsky, 1996), *The Protecting Veil* (mus. Tavener, 1998), *The Shakespeare Suite* (mus. Ellington, Strayhorn, 1999), *Arthur* (mus. McCabe, 2000), *Beauty and the Beast* (mus. Buhr, 2003), *Cyrano* (2nd version, mus. Carl Davis, 2007), and *Sylvia* (2nd version, mus. Delibes, 2009). A list of his other ballets includes *The Outsider* (mus. Bohác,

1978), *Take Five* (mus. Brubeck, 1978), *Meadow of Proverbs* (mus. Milhaud, 1979), *Adieu* (mus. Panufnik, 1980), *Night Moves* (mus. Britten, 1981), *The Swan of Tuonela* (mus. Sibelius, 1982), *Choros* (mus. Meyer, 1983), *Consort Lessons* (mus. Stravinsky, 1983), *Young Apollo* (mus. Britten, Crosse, 1984), *Flowers of the Forest* (mus. Britten and Arnold, 1985), *The Sons of Horus* (mus. McGowan, 1985), *The Snow Queen* (mus. Tovey after Mussorgsky, 1986), *Galanteries* (mus. Mozart, 1986), *Allegri Diversi* (mus. Rossini, 1987), *The Trial of Prometheus* (mus. Burgon, 1988), *The Spirit of Fugue* (mus. McGowan, 1988), *Brahms/Handel Variations* (mus. Brahms, 1990), and *Tombeaux* (mus. Walton, 1993).

In 2008 Bintley was appointed artistic adviser to the New National Theatre Ballet of Japan, becoming its part-time artistic director (in conjunction with his post at BRB) in 2010. He created his first ballet for the company in 2008, *Aladdin* (mus. Carl Davis).

BIPED Modern dance work with choreography by Cunningham, music by Gavin Bryars, digital décor by Shelley Eshkar and Paul Kaiser, costumes by Suzanne Gallo and lighting by Aaron Copp. Premiered 23 Apr. 1999 at University of California, Berkeley, US by the Cunningham company. One of Cunningham's larger and more lavish works, created for 13 dancers, this was also the choreographer's first experiment with digital imagery. It used *motion capture techniques to create a piece of virtual choreography that interacts with the live dancers on stage.

Birmingham Royal Ballet An offshoot of the Royal Ballet organization, now a fully autonomous company based in Birmingham, England. Until 1997, when it severed its links with the Royal Opera House, it was the touring company of the Royal Ballet. Its origins extend as far back as 1946 to the Sadler's Wells Opera Ballet, the company Ninette de Valois created for Sadler's Wells Theatre when the Sadler's Wells Ballet moved to Covent Garden. In 1947 it became Sadler's Wells Theatre Ballet, in 1957 the Royal Ballet Touring Company, and in 1976 Sadler's Wells Royal Ballet. In 1990 the company left Sadler's Wells and moved to Birmingham, thus confirming the distinctive identity it had already forged for itself. In the early years, as 'sister company' to the resident company at Covent Garden, it acted as a training ground for dancers and choreographers (most notably Cranko and MacMillan), and some of the most important British ballets were made for it, including Cranko's *Pineapple Poll* and *The Lady and the Fool*, MacMillan's *The Invitation*, and Ashton's *The Two Pigeons*. It has also been home to some of Britain's finest dancers, among them John Field, Doreen Wells, Peggy van Praagh,

David Blair, Margaret Barbieri, and Marion Tait. It was directed from 1975 to 1995 by Peter Wright, who gave the company fine productions of the classics, as well as reviving important early 20th-century works, such as Massine's *Choreartium* and Jooss's *The Green Table*. In 1995 David Bintley (another choreographer whose career had been nurtured here) became director, and created many new works for the company, among them *Carmina Burana*, *Far from the Madding Crowd*, *Nutcracker Sweeties*, and *Arthur*. In 2004 the Elmhurst Ballet School moved up to Birmingham to become the company's associate school.

*   BRB company website

Birthday Offering Ballet in one act with choreography by Ashton, music by Glazunov (arr. Irving), and designs by André Levasseur. Premiered 5 May 1956 by Sadler's Wells Ballet at Covent Garden, with Fonteyn, Grey, Elvin, Nerina, Jackson, Beriosova, Fifield, and Somes. A virtuosic classical display piece for seven ballerinas, it was created to celebrate the company's 25th birthday. In 1989 it was revived for American Ballet Theatre to celebrate that company's 50th anniversary in 1990.

Bissell, Patrick (*b* Corpus Christi, Tex., 1 Dec. 1957; *d* Hoboken, NJ, 28 Dec. 1987) US dancer. He studied at the School of American Ballet, joined the Boston Ballet in 1975 and American Ballet Theatre in 1977, where he became a principal in 1979. A tall, charismatic dancer, he was noted for his interpretations of Solor, Siegfried, and Romeo. He created lead roles in Tudor's *The Tiller in the Fields* (1978) and in Tetley's *Contredances* (1979). He left ABT in 1980 (dismissed by the management after failing to appear for a dress rehearsal) and briefly became a guest artist, working with the National Ballet of Canada, Scottish Ballet, and Pacific Northwest Ballet. He returned to ABT as a principal in 1981. He partnered many leading ballerinas including van Hamel, Gregory, Kirkland, Makarova, and Kain. He died at 30, the result of a drug overdose.

Bix Pieces, The Ballet in one act with choreography by Twyla Tharp, set to music by Bix Beiderbecke and *Abide With Me* by Thelonius Monk. Premiered 2 Nov. 1971 at the IX International Festival of Dance in Paris. Cast included Tharp, Sara Rudner, Rose Marie Wright, Isabel García-Lorca, and Kenneth Rinker. Inspired by Tharp's love of 1920s' and 1930s' jazz, the work combines classical ballet with popular dance styles like tap, ballroom, and baton-twirling.

Bjørn, Dinna (orig. D. B. Larsen; *b* Copenhagen, 14 Feb. 1947) Danish dancer, choreographer, and ballet director. The daughter of Niels Bjørn Larsen, she was admitted as an apprentice at the Royal Danish Ballet in 1964. In 1966 she made her debut as the Young Girl in Robbins's *Afternoon of a Faun*. As a principal dancer she performed both classical and contemporary works. Her most important roles included Masha (*Nutcracker*) and in *Sylphide*, *The Kermesse at Bruges*, and *Far from Denmark*. She also danced at the Tivoli Pantomime Theatre, where she created von Rosen's *Mam'zelle Nitouche* in 1970. She made her choreographic debut in 1970 with *8 plus 1* for the Royal Danish Ballet. In 1976, with Frank Andersen, she founded a company of soloists from the Royal Danish Ballet to perform Bournonville's works; the company continued for fourteen years and toured extensively. In 1987 she left the Royal Danish Ballet. She is one of the world's foremost experts on the Bournonville technique and has produced a number of Bournonville ballets for companies in Europe and the US, including *Napoli* and *Le Conservatoire* for the Danes, becoming advisor on Bournonville to the company from 1997. From 1990 to 2001 she was director of Norwegian National Ballet, moving on to direct the Finnish National Ballet. She remained with the Finnish Ballet until 2008, bringing in more contemporary works by Ek and Kylián among others and nurturing young Finnish choreographers such as Jorma Elo. After retiring as director she has worked freelance as a teacher, choreographer, and producer of the Bournonville repertoire.

Bjørnsson, Fredbjørn (*b* Copenhagen, 10 Sept. 1926; *d* Copenhagen, 19 Dec. 1993) Danish dancer, choreographer, and teacher. He trained at the Royal Danish Ballet School and joined the company in 1944, becoming a soloist in 1949. Early in his career his roles included Franz in *Coppélia* and the first Junior Cadet in *Graduation Ball*. He is best remembered as a character artist, particularly associated with the Bournonville repertoire: Eskimo in *Far from Denmark*, Carelis in *The Kermesse at Bruges*, Gennaro in *Napoli*, and Diderik in *A Folk Tale*. He was also much admired as Dr Coppelius, Petrushka, and the General in *Graduation Ball*. He choreographed several works, including *Behind the Curtain* (mus. Schmidt, 1954) and *Happiness on Journey* (mus. Sark, 1958) for the Royal Danish Ballet. He taught at the Royal Danish Ballet School and was an international guest teacher, and coach of the Bournonville repertoire. Knight of the Order of Dannebrog (1961). He was married to the dancer Kirsten Ralov.

Blache, Jean-Baptiste (*b* Berlin, 17 May 1765; *d* Toulouse, 24 Jan. 1834) French dancer and choreographer. He danced at the Paris Opera from 1781 to 1786 and then worked as a choreographer throughout France, including Montpellier, Bordeaux, Lyon, and Marseilles. His most popular ballets include *Les Meuniers*, *Daphnis*, *La Noce villageoise*, *La Fête indienne*, and *La Fille fugitive*, *ou La Laitière polonaise*, the first ballet to put dancers on roller skates. With Duport he made *Le Barbier de Séville* for the Paris Opera in 1806 and *Les Filets de Vulcain*, *ou Mars et Vénus* (mus. Schneitzhoeffer, 1826). His last major work was *Almaviva ou Rosine* for Lyon.

Black Crook, The A 19th-century theatrical extravaganza, which had an enormous impact on the development of American music hall and vaudeville. First produced on 12 Sept. 1866 at Niblo's Garden in New York, it was directed by David Costa who engaged a Great Parisienne Ballet Troupe from the Grand Opera, Paris. Marie Bonfanti and Rita Sangalli were the premières danseuses. The production, which used music, dance, and drama in a four-act spectacle, had a running time of five-and-a-half hours at its first performance. During the course of its sixteen-month run in New York and its subsequent touring versions hundreds of dancers were employed and its success helped to introduce ballet to Americans. The impresario William Wheatley used lavish sets and costumes imported from Europe and innovative stage effects that included calcine lights and sophisticated machinery. The plot involved an alchemist (the Black Crook of the title) who promised to deliver souls to Satan (represented by Zamiel, the Arch Fiend).

Black Swan The grand pas de deux in Act III of *Swan Lake*, in which the evil sorceress Odile seduces Prince Siegfried into believing she is his beloved Odette. Traditionally called the Black Swan because Odile is usually dressed in black, while the swan queen Odette is in white. The Petipa choreography is incisively virtuosic and includes the notorious 32 fouetté turns. The Black Swan is also a favourite showpiece for ballerinas and is often presented as an item on gala programmes.

Black Tights A 1960 French film showcasing ballets by Roland Petit. They include abbreviated versions of *La Croqueuse de diamants* (Jeanmaire, Dirk Sanders), *Cyrano de Bergerac* (Shearer, Petit), *Deuil en 24 heures* (Charisse, Petit), and *Carmen* (Jeanmaire, Petit, Kronstam).

Blair, David (orig. Butterfield; *b* Halifax, 27 Jul. 1932; *d* London, 1 Apr. 1976). British dancer and ballet master. After training at the Sadler's Wells Ballet School, he joined Sadler's Wells Theatre Ballet in 1947, and was promoted to soloist with Sadler's Wells Ballet at Covent Garden (the Royal Ballet) in 1953 and principal in 1955. He created roles in Cranko's *Pineapple Poll* (1951), *Harlequin* in April (1951), *Prince of the Pagodas* (title role, 1957), and *Antigone* (1959); Ashton's *La Fille mal gardée* (1960); and MacMillan's *Romeo and Juliet* (Mercutio, 1965). After the retirement of Michael Somes in 1961 Blair became Fonteyn's regular partner until Nureyev's arrival in the company. A brilliant, versatile dancer, he was particularly admired in demi-caractère roles, which showcased his flair for comedy. He was the first Colas, in Ashton's *La Fille mal gardée*, and it was in this role that he gave his farewell performance at Covent Garden in 1973. He was also a fine classical dancer, and staged productions of the classics in America: *Swan Lake* (1965) and *Sleeping Beauty* (1966) for the Atlanta Civic Ballet; *Swan Lake* (1967) and *Giselle* (1968) for American Ballet Theatre. After retiring he became a freelance teacher and coach. In 1976 he was appointed artistic director of Norwegian National Ballet but died of a heart attack, aged 43, before taking up the post.

Bland, Alexander Pseudonym for the husband-and-wife writing team of Nigel Gosling and the former dancer Maude *Lloyd. Gosling (*b* London, 29 Jan. 1909; *d* London, 21 May 1982), studied part-time at the Ballet Rambert School (1935–9) and started writing dance criticism in 1951 for *Ballet* magazine. 'Alexander Bland' was ballet critic of the *Observer* from 1955 to 1982, wrote *The Dancer's World* with M. Peto (1963), *A History of Ballet and Dance* (1976), and *The Royal Ballet—The First 50 Years* (1981), and edited *Nureyev, An Autobiography* (1962).

Blasis, Carlo (*b* Naples, 4 Nov. 1795 (some sources 1797); *d* Cernobbio, 15 Jan. 1878) Italian dancer, choreographer and codifier of classical technique who was arguably the most important ballet teacher of the 19th century. He studied with Dauberval in Bordeaux (where he learned the theories of Noverre) and Gardel in Paris. His first ballets were made for productions of operas by Gluck, Sacchini, and Mozart. From 1818 he danced at La Scala, Milan, and from 1826 to 1830 he was a soloist and choreographer at the King's Theatre in London; he also appeared in St Petersburg. In 1837, forced by injury to quit the stage, he became director of the school attached to La Scala, where his work helped to spread the influence of the Italian school, particularly to Russia. He was a guest teacher in several European cities, including Warsaw, Lisbon, and Paris. His students included Fanny Cerrito. His prime importance, though, is as a writer. His books on academic dance, its theories, and the codification of its technique, are among the most important published and the classical vocabulary still owes much to his work. Author of *Traité élémentaire, théoretique et pratique de l'art de la danse* (Milan, 1820, repr. New York, 1944, as *An Elementary Treatise upon the Theory and Practice of the Art of Dancing*); *The Code of Terpsichore* (London, 1828); *Notes Upon Dancing* (London, 1847); *L'uomo fisico, intellettuale e morale* (Milan, 1857); and *Dances in General, Ballet Celebrities, and National Dances* (Moscow, 1864).

Blaska, Félix (*b* Gomel, Belorussian Soviet Socialist Republic, 8 May 1941) French dancer, choreographer, and company director. He graduated from the Paris Conservatoire in 1960 and danced with the Marquis de Cuevas ballet, the Zizi Jeanmaire revue, and the Roland Petit company, where he started choreographing his own works (*Octandre*, 1966, and *Les Affinités electives*, 1967). In 1968 he created *Danses concertantes* (mus. Stravinsky) and *Équivalences* (mus. Jean-Claude Eloy) for the newly formed Ballet-Théâtre Contemporain in Amiens. He started his own troupe in 1969, Les Ballets de Félix Blaska, which moved to Grenoble in 1972 and for which he created many works including *En blanc et noir* (mus. Debussy), *Contre* (mus. Berio), *Electro Bach* (mus. Walter Carlos, 1969), *Ballet pour tam-tam et percussion* (mus. J. P. Drouet, 1970), *Sonate pour deux pianos et percussion* (mus. Bartók, 1971), *L'Homme aux loups* (mus. Marius Constant, 1974). During this period he also choreographed for the Marseilles Opera (*Deuxième concerto*, mus. Prokofiev, 1970), the Royal Danish Ballet, the Hamburg State Opera, and the Paris Opera (*La Poème électronique* and *Arcana*, 1973). After moving to the US he formed a new company, Crowsnest, with Martha Clarke in 1978 which made its debut at the American Dance Festival in 1979. He performed in and collaborated on several Clarke productions, including *The Garden of Earthly Delights* (1984) and *Vers la flamme* (1999). He also created a duet for himself and Martha Clarke for Pilobolus Dance Theatre in 1979 after which he continued to collaborate with Pilobolus. As a freelance choreographer his later works have included *Charlotte* (mus. Pärt, Ballet du Nord, 1990) and several productions for Circus Flora, featuring both animal and human performers. He has also worked in theatre, acting in *Kaos* (dir. Clarke, 2006).

((⊕)) SEE WEB LINKS
• Official website for Félix Blaska

Bliss, (Sir) Arthur (*b* London, 2 Aug. 1891; *d* London, 27 Mar. 1975) British composer. He was closely associated with the early years of Sadler's Wells Ballet, for which he wrote the music for de Valois's *Checkmate* (1937, also the libretto), Helpmann's *Miracle in the Gorbals* (1944), and *Adam Zero* (1946). He also wrote the score for Lew Christensen's *The Lady of Shalott* for San

Francisco Ballet in 1958. MacMillan used his *Music for Strings* in his 1961 ballet *Diversions* and Neumeier used his Quintet for Oboe and Strings for his 1969 work *Frontier*.

Blondy, Michel (*b* Paris, probably 1676 or 1677; *d* Paris, 6 Aug. 1739) French dancer, choreographer and teacher. He played an important role in the early development of dance in Paris. He was the nephew and pupil of Beauchamps and joined the Paris Opera in the 1690s, where he performed in ballets and operas by Lully and Campra. In 1729, already established as the leading danseur noble of his day, he became compositeur des ballets de l'Académie Royale de Musique (dance director of the Paris Opera). His best-known work was *Les Amours des déesses* (mus. Quinault, 1729). As a teacher, his students included Sallé and Camargo.

Blood Wedding Ballet in one act with choreography by Rodrigues, music by ApIvor, and designs by Isabel Lambert. Premiered 5 Jun. 1953 by Sadler's Wells Theatre Ballet at Sadler's Wells Theatre, London, with Fifield, Poole, and Trecu. The libretto, based on Lorca's 1933 play, is a violent portrait of jealousy and revenge in a Spanish village, as two men die for the love of the same woman. Other versions include Gades (mus. Emilio de Diego, 1974, filmed by Carlos Saura, 1981).

Bluebeard Ballet in four acts with choreography and libretto by Fokine, music by Offenbach, arr. Dorati, and designs by Marcel Vertes. Premiered 27 Oct. 1941 by Ballet Theatre at the Palacio de Bellas Artes, Mexico City, with Dolin, Markova, Baronova, and Ian Gibson. The ballet is based on Offenbach's famous 1866 opera *Barbe-bleu*, about the titular Count who kills his wives for their disobediance and curiosity. The first US performance was on 12 Nov. 1941 at the 44th Street Theatre in New York. Petipa also choreographed a version (with music by P. Schenk) for St Petersburg in 1896. In 1977 Pina Bausch choreographed *Bluebeard—While listening to a tape recording of Béla Bartók's opera Duke Bluebeard's Castle*, a postmodern version in which Bluebeard listens to a tape of Bartók's operatic interpretation of his own story.

Bluebell Girls The name given to the cabaret and nightclub dancers managed by Miss Bluebell, a.k.a. Margaret Kelly (*b* Dublin, 24 Jun. 1912; *d* 11 Sept. 2004), an Anglo-Irish dancer who ran the dance troupe at the Folies-Bergère in Paris. Similar to the Rockettes in America, the Bluebell Girls were a highly drilled ensemble, costumed in feathered head-dresses, G-strings, and high heels. They first appeared in the 1930s in Paris, and performed throughout Europe and America. In the 1950s they made their debut in Las Vegas,

which eventually became headquarters for the Bluebell Girls. Kelly retired at the age of 80, although the Bluebell Girls continued to stage their Las Vegas spectacles.

Blue Bird, The The famous pas de deux from the final act of Petipa's *The Sleeping Beauty*. It is a virtuoso display piece danced by Princess Florine and the Blue Bird as part of the wedding festivities for Aurora and the Prince, and is often to be found as a showpiece on gala programmes. Cecchetti performed the role of Blue Bird at the ballet's premiere in St Petersburg in 1890 (with Nikitina). The airborne choreography for the male is especially demanding with its series of *brisés volés.

Blues Suite Modern dance in one act with choreography by Ailey, set to traditional blues music, arranged and sung by Brother John Sellers. Premiered 30 Mar. 1958 by the Alvin Ailey Company at the 92nd Street YMHA in New York, with Thompson and Ailey. The dance, which takes place at night in a bordello, became one of the most popular works in the Ailey repertory.

Blum, René (*b* Paris, 13 Mar. 1878; *d* en route to Auschwitz, 28 Sept. 1942 (some sources say 28 Apr. 1942)) French ballet impresario. A former art critic, publisher, and theatre director, he was appointed ballet director of the Monte Carlo Opera after Diaghilev's death in 1929. In 1931 he joined forces with Colonel de Basil to found the Ballets Russes de Monte Carlo, with Blum contributing the artistic vision and de Basil the business acumen. Balanchine and Massine were hired, Diaghilev's old ballets were restaged, and the company's trio of *baby ballerinas fired the public's imagination. In 1934 Blum reduced his role from manager to artistic director and the following year left the company to form his own group. This, the René Blum Ballets de Monte-Carlo (with Fokine as ballet master), eventually became the Ballet Russe de Monte Carlo (co-directed by Massine), which enjoyed international success. Blum was probably the most important ballet impresario of the 1930s (and certainly one of the main conservators of the Diaghilev repertoire) but as a Jewish intellectual he was arrested by the Nazis in Paris, in 1941. After several months of detention in Compiègne and Drancy, he was deported to the Auschwitz concentration camp, dying during the journey.

Boal, Peter (*b* Bedford, NY, 1965) US dancer and director. He studied at the School of American Ballet and joined New York City Ballet in 1983; promoted to principal in 1989. Possessed of a superb technique and an aristocratic stage presence he performed lead roles in a wide repertoire, including Balanchine's *Agon, Apollo, A Midsummer Night's Dream, Prodigal Son*, and

Square Dance; Robbins's *Dances at a Gathering* and *Opus 19/The Dreamer*; and Martins's *The Sleeping Beauty*. He created roles in Robbins's *Brandenburg* and *Quiet City*; Martins's *Black and White*, *Eight Miniatures*, *Eight More*, *Les Gentilhommes*, *A Musical Offering*, *Les Petits Riens*, *Reliquary*, and *Stabat Mater*; Ulysses Dove's *Red Angels* and *Twilight*; and Sean Lavery's *Romeo and Juliet*. He also performed as a principal with Ballet du Nord in France and Birmingham Royal Ballet and between 1997 and 2005 taught at the School of American Ballet. In 2005 he retired from NYCB to become artistic director of Pacific Northwest Ballet.

Bocca, Julio (*b* Buenos Aires, 6 Mar. 1967) Argentinian dancer and company director. He first trained with his mother, a ballet teacher at the National Dance School in Buenos Aires, and with his father, who taught Argentine folk dancing, going on to study at the Instituto Superior de Arte de Teatro Colón in Buenos Aires from 1974 and later with Maggie Black and Wilhelm Burmann. In 1982 he joined Fundación Teresa Carreño de Venezuela, Caracas as principal, in the same year moving on to Ballet del Teatro Municipal de Rio de Janeiro. In 1985 he won the gold medal at Moscow's International Ballet Competition in Moscow, leading to invitations to guest with the Bolshoi and Novosibirsk Ballets in the same year. In 1986 he joined American Ballet Theatre as a principal where, despite his short stature, he danced most of the leading male roles in the classical repertoire. A fiercely dramatic dancer, he was particularly noted for his interpretations of Basil in *Don Quixote* and Romeo in MacMillan's *Romeo and Juliet*. He created lead roles in Morris's *Drink to Me Only with Thine Eyes* (1987) and Tharp's *Brief Fling* (1990). He also guested widely abroad with the Royal Ballet, Stuttgart Ballet, Paris Opera, La Scala Milan, Royal Danish Ballet, and English National Ballet, among others. In 1990, with Eleonora Cassano, he founded Ballet Argentino and its associate school to showcase and encourage young Argentinian dancers, becoming director in 2005. He was also noted for his performances of tango, dancing in the film *Tango* in 1998. He gave his farewell performance with ABT in 2006 and retired from the stage in 2007.

(((●))) SEE WEB LINKS

• Website for Ballet Argentino and the Julio Bocca Foundation

Bodenwieser, Gertrud (*b* Vienna, 3 Feb. 1890; *d* Sydney, 10 Nov. 1959) Austrian dancer, teacher, choreographer and company director. She taught mime and dance at the Vienna State Academy of Music and Dramatic Art, making her stage debut in 1919 and in 1923 starting her own company, which toured Europe and visited America. She was considered a leading exponent of *Ausdruckstanz. In 1939, after having been forced out of Austria by the Nazi annexation, she emigrated to Australia and re-formed her company as the Boldenwieser Ballet. This toured extensively in Australia, as well as travelling to South Africa and India in the 1950s. Through her teaching and choreography, Bodenwieser exerted a major influence on the development of modern dance in Australia.

Bogdanova, Nadezhda (*b* Moscow, 2 Sept. 1836; *d* St Petersburg, 5 Sept. (some sources 3 Sept.) 1897) Russian dancer. Dance was a family affair: she was trained by her father, Konstantin Bogdanov, dancing *La Sylphide* at the age of 12 with her father as James; her mother was the dancer Tatiana Karpakova; and the family toured together with its own troupe. In 1850 she moved to Paris with her family, eventually becoming principal dancer of the Paris Opera from 1851 to 1855 where she was especially celebrated in the title roles of *Giselle*, *La Sylphide*, and *Esmeralda*. She returned to Russia, dancing in St Petersburg and Moscow, and was much admired for her lyrical style. She took 42 curtain calls after her 1856 debut as Giselle at the Bolshoi Theatre in St Petersburg. She danced at the Bolshoi until 1864 when she fell out of favour with the ballet management. She spent the last three years of her career dancing in Warsaw, Vienna, Budapest, and Berlin. She retired prematurely in 1867.

Bojesen, Gudrun (*b* Copenhagen, 1976) Danish dancer. She studied at the Royal Danish Ballet School from 1984 and joined the company in 1992 as an apprentice, becoming soloist in 2000 and solo dancer (principal) in 2001. A pure Bournonville stylist with an intuitive dramatic gift she dances most of the 19th-century ballerina roles (Petipa and Bournonville) as well as the modern repertory of Forsythe, Ratmansky, Kylián, and others. She has toured widely with RDB and appeared as a guest with several companies, including Finnish National Ballet.

Bolender, Todd (*b* Canton, Ohio, 17 Feb. 1919; *d* Kansas City, Kansas, 12 Oct. 2006) US dancer, choreographer, and ballet director. After studying with Chester Hale, Vilzak, and at the School of American Ballet, he began his career in 1937 dancing with Ballet Caravan, the Littlefield Ballet, American Ballet Caravan, Ballet Theatre and Ballet Russe de Monte Carlo. While with Ballet Caravan, he created the role of the State Trooper in Lew Christensen's *Filling Station* (1938), Alias in Loring's *Billy the Kid* (1938), a Father in Loring's *City Portrait* (1939), and a leading role in Dollar's

A Thousand Times Neigh! (1940). In 1946 he joined Ballet Society, precursor to New York City Ballet, where during the next fifteen years he created many roles for Balanchine (Phlegmatic in *Four Temperaments*, *The Fox*, *Divertimento*, *Metamorphoses*, *Agon*, *Ivesiana*) and for Robbins (*Age of Anxiety*, *The Pied Piper*, *Fanfare*, *Quartet*, *The Concert*). His first choreographed ballet was *Mother Goose Suite* (mus. Ravel, 1943) which he made for American Concert Ballet, a group he co-founded with William Dollar and Mary Jane Shea. For NYCB he subsequently made several works including *The Miraculous Mandarin* (mus. Bartók, 1951), *Souvenirs* (mus. Barber, 1955), *The Still Point* (mus. Debussy, 1956), *Creation of the World* (mus. Milhaud, 1960), and *Piano Rag Music* (mus. Stravinsky, 1972). He was ballet director in Cologne (1963–6); and subsequently in Frankfurt (1966–9); then in 1975 he co-founded Pacific Northwest Ballet, which he ran until 1977. He was then director of the ballet company, Ataturk Opera House, Istanbul (1977–80) and between 1981 and 1995 was artistic director of Kansas City Ballet (which became the State Ballet of Missouri in 1986). He choreographed many works for that company, including *Classical Symphony* (mus. Prokofiev, 1982), *An American in Paris* (mus. Gershwin, 1987), and *Celebration* (mus. Gershwin, 1989). He also danced in and directed Broadway musicals.

bolero Spanish dance in triple time with the dancer also singing and playing castanets. Guitars and tambourine provide the instrumental accompaniment. It originated in the mid-18th century.

Bolero Ballet in one act with choreography by Nijinska, music by Ravel, and designs by Benois. Premiered 22 Nov. 1928 for the Ida Rubinstein Ballet at the Paris Opera, with Rubinstein, Vilzak. A gypsy dancing on a table in a Spanish tavern entices the onlookers. Several other versions have subsequently been choreographed, including J. Inger's (*Walking Mad*, Nederlands Dans Theater, 2001) and S. Welch's (Houston, 2004) but it is Béjart's brazenly seductive 1960 work that has achieved the most widespread success, with both male and female dancers taking the central role.

Bolger, Ray (*b* Dorchester, Mass., 10 Jan. 1904; *d* Los Angeles, 15 Jan. 1987) US dancer and actor. He appeared regularly in American films and television, as well as in revues and musicals, including Balanchine's ballet *Slaughter on Tenth Avenue* from the 1936 musical *On Your Toes*. His first Broadway appearance was in *The Passing Show* of 1926 and he won a Tony Award for his appearance in *Where's Charley?* (1948), which featured choreography by Balanchine. His most famous role was the Scarecrow in the 1939 film *The Wizard of Oz*.

Bolle, Roberto (*b* Casale Monferrato, 26 Mar. 1975.) Italian dancer. He trained locally and at La Scala Ballet School, dancing the role of Tadzio in Nureyev's *Death in Venice* while still a student. In 1994 he graduated into La Scala Ballet where he became principal in 1996, resident guest artist in 1998, and étoile in 2003. A dancer of exceptionally elegant proportions and technical fluency, Bolle has danced in both classical and contemporary ballets with La Scala and has also worked extensively abroad, guesting with the Royal Ballet, Paris Opera, Mariinsky Ballet, National Ballet of Canada, Stuttgart Ballet, Finnish National Ballet, and Staatsoper Berlin, among others. With English National Ballet he created roles in Derek Deane's stagings of *Swan Lake* (1997) and *Romeo and Juliet* (1998).

In 2006 he danced at the opening ceremony of the Turin Winter Olympics in a solo created for him by Enzo Cosimi.

Bolm, Adolph (*b* St Petersburg, 25 Sept. 1884; *d* Los Angeles, 16 Apr. 1951) Russian-US dancer and choreographer. He trained at the Imperial Ballet School in St Petersburg with Karsavin and Legat, graduating in 1903. He also studied later with Cecchetti. In 1904 he joined the Mariinsky company (later the Kirov Ballet) additionally dancing with Anna Pavlova on her first tours abroad and with Diaghilev's Ballets Russes from 1909 to 1917. He resigned from the Mariinsky in 1911. A superb character dancer, he created roles in Fokine's *Prince Igor* (Chief Warrior), *Le Carnaval* (Pierrot), *The Firebird* (Ivan Tsarevich), *Petrushka* (the Moor), *Thamar* (the slave to Karsavina), *Daphnis et Chloé* (Dorkon), *Le Coq d'or* (King Dodon), and *Midas* (title role). For Diaghilev he choreographed *Sadko* (mus. Rimsky-Korsakov, 1916). He toured the US with Diaghilev in 1916 and 1917, after which he remained in the US. He produced and choreographed operas and ballets at the New York Metropolitan Opera House, the Chicago Civic Opera, and the San Francisco Opera, where founded the ballet school. He choreographed the first production of Stravinsky's *Apollon musagète* in Washington in 1928 (two months ahead of Balanchine's Paris premiere) and staged some of Fokine's ballets at the Teatro Colón in Buenos Aires. For Ballet Theatre he choreographed Prokofiev's *Peter and the Wolf* in 1940, which became one of the most popular ballets in ABT's repertoire. In Hollywood, where he eventually settled, he was choreographer for several films (*The Mad Genius*, *The Men in Her Life*, and *Life of Cellini*) and in 1932 created *Ballet mécanique* set to the music of Aleksandr Mosolov's *The Iron Foundry*, which was performed at the Hollywood Bowl (under the title *The Spirit of the Factory*).

Bolshoi Ballet Russian ballet company with its own school, based in Moscow. It is customary to date the Bolshoi's origins back to 1776, when a private company of actors and dancers was founded by Prince Urusov and an Englishman called Michael Maddox. This eventually contributed to the ballet company of the Petrovsky Theatre, which was established in 1780 on the site of the present Bolshoi Theatre. The Petrovsky burned down in 1805, forcing the company to move to the Arbat (New Imperial) Theatre for the next twenty years. The present Bolshoi Theatre opened its doors on 19 Jan. 1825 (it was renovated after a fire in 1856). By 1850 the company comprised 155 dancers and among its most signficant stagings were the 1869 debut of Petipa and Minkus's *Don Quixote* and, in 1877, the first production of Reisinger and Tchaikovsky's *Swan Lake*. A unique Bolshoi style was forged from the ballets of early choreographers like Adam Glushkovsky, who ran the company from 1812 to 1839 and whose works made a feature of folk dancing, comedy, pantomime, and melodrama. However the main centre of ballet in 19th-century Russia was St Petersburg where the ballet company was directed by the prolific and powerful Petipa. By 1882 the size of the Bolshoi company had been cut by almost half, indicating its inferior status. This changed after the Russian Revolution, when the country's capital—and hence its artistic focus—moved to Moscow. The Bolshoi company had already begun its revitalization at the beginning of the 20th century under Gorsky's direction (1900–24), his many productions helping to develop its vividly dramatic style. The 1917 October Revolution led to the reorganization of the company, under the leadership of Gorsky and the dancers Geltser and Tikhomirov. The Communist regime, which after an initial hesitation, accepted ballet as a suitable entertainment for the people, encouraged choreographers to incorporate ideologically correct themes into their work, with ballets like Tikhomirov's *The Red Poppy* (1927) paving the way for the new genre of *Socialist Realism. The 1930s saw the arrival in Moscow of the Leningrad choreographers Vainonen (creator of *Gayané*) and Zakharov (creator of *Fountain of Bakhchisarai, Prisoner of the Caucasus, Taras Bulba*). During the Second World War the company was evacuated to Kuibyshev, but returned to its Moscow home in 1945 with the first production of Zakharov and Prokofiev's *Cinderella*.

The company entered a new era after the war with the transfer to Moscow of the Leningrad ballerina Ulanova and the choreographer Lavrovsky, who brought his *Romeo and Juliet* with him. In 1954 the Bolshoi premiered Lavrovsky's

and Prokofiev's *The Stone Flower*. The company could now boast a roster of stars including Plisetskaya, Struchkova, and Fadeyechev. In 1956 the company made its breakthrough visit to the West, astonishing audiences in London with Ulanova's Juliet and Lavrovsky's staging of *Giselle*; in 1959 it repeated its triumph in New York. In the following decades it established itself as the single most important cultural export of the Soviet Union. Important productions included Radunsky's *The Little Humpbacked Horse* (1960 with new music by Shchedrin); Kasatkina-Vasiliov's *Vanina Vanini* (1962); Goleizovsky's *Scriabiniana* (1962); Kasatkina-Vasiliov's *Heroic Poem* (1964); Vinogradov's *Asel* (1967); Plisetskaya's *Anna Karenina* (1972). Probably the most lasting of the one-act creations was Messerer's *Class Concert* (1962), which frequently toured abroad. In 1964 Grigorovich was appointed chief choreographer, later succeeding Lavrovsky as artistic director. Grigorovich stamped his own choreographic personality on the company with epic productions like *Spartacus* (1968), *Ivan the Terrible* (1975), and *The Golden Age* (1982), all exemplifying the name Bolshoi (Russian for big). These were the productions that were routinely performed on the company's lucrative foreign tours and sealed the international reputations of dancers like Bessmertnova, Maximova, Sorokina, Vasiliev, Liepa, Gordeyev, and Mukhamedov.

In the 1990s, forced to fend for itself in the capitalist marketplace, the Bolshoi underwent artistic as well as financial decline. Grigorovich, the effectiveness of his directorship waning, was ousted; standards of performance and production fell; the repertory appeared old-fashioned and threadbare in contrast to the Kirov (Mariinsky), which had already began to modernize while retaining its reputation for a collectively superb classical style. In 1995 Vladimir Vasiliev took over as director of the Bolshoi Theatre, with ultimate responsibility for both the ballet and opera companies. He staged new productions of *Swan Lake* and *Giselle*, as well as adding more international works to the repertoire and inviting new choreographers to make work for the company. This was still an uncertain period for the company however, with both financial and political issues affecting its running. In 1998 Vasiliev appointed Alexei *Fadeyechev as artistic director of the Bolshoi Ballet but in 2000 Vasiliev himself was sacked from his position as overall director and Fadeyechev was replaced by Boris *Akimov as director of the ballet. Akimov made some significant improvements, signing up the Kirov ballerina Svetlana Zakharova in 2003 and commissioning from Alexei Ratmansky the latter's internationally acclaimed re-creation of Lopukhov's 1935 ballet, *The Bright Stream*, but in 2004 Akimov was removed. His successor was Ratmansky and during the four years in which he was director he built on Akimov's achievements and was widely credited with bringing about an artistic renaissance. Ratmansky not only added several of his own ballets to the Bolshoi repertory, along with works by Western choreographers like Wheeldon and Tharp, he also oversaw an ambitious reconstruction of Petipa's *Le Corsaire* (2007) and continued to explore the legacy of the Soviet era with re-creations of Lopukhov's *The Bolt* (2005) and Vainonen's *Flames of Paris* (2008). A new generation of Bolshoi dancers gained international status, including Natalia Osipova, and for the first time in decades the company regained artistic parity with the Kirov. The internal politics of the Bolshoi remained troubled however and in 2008 Ratmansky retired as director to be replaced by Yuri Burlaka, with Grigorovich appointed ballet master in charge of his own repertory and Ratmansky retained as principal guest choreographer. Between 2005 and 2010 the company's home theatre underwent massive reconstruction and the ballet performed in the adjacent New Bolshoi Theatre. Most of the company's dancers are still drawn from its associate school, the Moscow State Academy of Choreography, which traces its origins back to dance classes held in a Moscow orphanage in 1773.

SEE WEB LINKS

• The Bolshoi Theatre website, with a link to the ballet company

Bolt, The Ballet in three acts with choreography by Lopukhov and music by Shostakovich. Premiered 8 Apr. 1931, by GATOB (later the Kirov Ballet), St Petersburg. It was the first example of a Soviet industrial ballet and satirized a group of drunken bourgeoisie who attempt, futilely, to sabotage the march of socialism by jamming a bolt into a machine. A new version was staged for the Bolshoi by *Ratmansky in 2005.

Bonachela, Rafael (*b* Barcelona, 1972) Spanish dancer, choreographer and director. He began his training in Spain, aged 15, then moved to the UK in 1991, training at the London Studio Centre and joining Rambert Dance Company in 1992. He began choreographing in 1999, creating nine works for Rambert including *21* and *Curious Conscience* (2005) and was made artistic associate of that company in 2003. In 2006 he formed his own company for which he has since created several works including *Voices* (mus. Berio, 2006), *Square Map of 4* (mus. Marius de Vries, 2008) and *The Land of Yes and the Land of No* (mus. Ezio Bosso, 2009). His style combines an aggressively physical dynamic with inventively expressive detail, focusing on human relationships and extreme states of emotion. In 2008 he was appointed artistic

director of Sydney Dance Company, running it in tandem with his own London-based company. Bonachela has also created works for companies including CandoCo and George Piper Dances and has choreographed for film, video, and stage including several collaborations with singer Kylie Minogue (e.g. the *Showgirl Tour*, 2005).

SEE WEB LINKS

• Website for the Bonachela company

Bonfanti, Marie (Maria; Marietta) (*b* Milan, 16 Feb. 1845; *d* New York, 25 Jan. 1921) Italian-US dancer and teacher. She studied with Blasis, both privately and at the La Scala school, and danced in Italy and London in the early 1860s. In 1866 she went to America as the prima ballerina assoluta (a billing she insisted upon in her contracts) starring in *The Black Crook* in New York. She toured the US and appeared in several musical revues, including *The White Fawn*, the follow-up to *The Black Crook*. She was prima ballerina of the Milan Italian Grand Opera Company, which toured the US, and also of the New York Metropolitan Opera House (1885–6). Following her retirement from the stage in 1892, she opened a school in New York, where she taught until 1916. One of her students was Ruth St Denis.

Bonnefoux, Jean-Pierre (*b* Bourg-en-Bresse, 25 Apr. 1943) French dancer. He studied at the Paris Opera Ballet School with Lorcia, Franchetti, and Mulys; joined the company in 1959 and was made an étoile in 1965. He created roles in ballets by Béjart (*Damnation of Faust*, 1964, *Webern Opus V*, 1966) and Petit (*Notre-Dame de Paris*, 1965). In 1970 he was invited to join New York City Ballet as a principal, dancing lead roles in many Balanchine ballets, including *Apollo*, *Orpheus*, *Agon*, *Who Cares?* and *Violin Concerto*, and creating roles in Robbins's *A Beethoven pas de deux* (1973) and *An Evening's Waltzes* (1973). He retired in 1980 to teach. With his wife, the former New York City Ballet star Patricia McBride, he directed the dance department at Indiana University. In 1996 he was appointed artistic director of the N. Carolina Dance Theater, with McBride as associate director, and has choreographed several works for the company, including versions of *Cinderella* and *Carmina Burana*. He and McBride also direct the annual Chautauqua Summer Dance programme. Nijinsky Prize (1965).

SEE WEB LINKS

• Website for the North Carolina Dance Theatre

Borchsenius, Valborg (*née* Jorgensen; *b* Copenhagen, 19 Nov. 1872; *d* Copenhagen, 5 Jan. 1949) Danish dancer and teacher. She entered the Royal Danish Ballet School in 1879 and while a student appeared as one of Nora's children in the first performance of Ibsen's *A Doll's House*. She made her official debut with the company in 1891, became a soloist in 1895, and danced with the Danish ballet until her retirement from the stage in 1918. She was frequently partnered by Hans Beck in the Bournonville ballets. During the 1930s and 1940s she helped Harald Lander to restage the Bournonville repertoire and became one of the leading Bournonville teachers in Denmark.

Börlin, Jean (*b* Haernosand, 13 Mar. 1893; *d* New York, 6 Dec. 1930) Swedish dancer and choreographer. He was responsible for the entire repertoire of the Paris-based *Ballets Suédois in the 1920s. He trained at the Royal Theatre in Stockholm and entered the corps de ballet in 1905. A protégé of Fokine, he left the company in 1918 to continue working with the Russian choreographer in Copenhagen. The Swedish patron Rolf de Maré financed a dance recital for him in Paris in 1920. When de Maré founded the Ballets Suédois in Paris that same year, Börlin became its star performer and sole choreographer. His many ballets revealed a wide-ranging and avant-garde choice of subject-matter and he worked with many of the leading composers (Milhaud, Honegger) and painters (Léger, Bonnard, de Chirico) in France in the 1920s. A list of his works includes *Iberia* (mus. Albéniz, 1920), *Les Vierges folles* (mus. Atterberg, 1920), *La Nuit de Saint Jean* (mus. Alfvén, 1920), *Jeux* (mus. Debussy, 1920), *L'Homme et son désir* (mus. Milhaud, 1921), *Les Mariés de la Tour Eiffel* (mus. Tailleferre, Auric, Honegger, Milhaud, Poulenc, 1921), *La Boite à joujoux* (mus. Debussy, 1921), *Skating Rink* (mus. Honegger, 1922), *La Création du monde* (mus. Milhaud, 1923), *Relâche* (mus. Satie, 1924), and *La Jarre* (mus. Casella, 1924). After the Ballets Suédois disbanded, Börlin gave recitals in South America and Paris before his premature death at the age of 37. He also appeared in two films directed by René Clair: *Entr'acte* (1924, part of *Relâche*) and *Le Voyage imaginaire* (1925).

Borodin, Alexander (*b* St Petersburg, 12 Nov. 1833; *d* St Petersburg, 27 Feb. 1887) Russian composer. Although he wrote no ballet music, the Polovtsian Dances from his opera *Prince Igor* was one of the most popular works in the repertoire of Diaghilev's Ballets Russes, choreographed by Fokine.

Borovansky, Edouard (*b* Prerov, 24 Feb. 1902; *d* Sydney, 18 Dec. 1959) Czech-Australian dancer, choreographer and director. He began his career in the corps de ballet at the National Theatre in Prague and joined Anna Pavlova's touring company in 1926, travelling to Australia in 1929.

He was a soloist with Colonel de Basil's Russian ballet companies (1932–9) and again toured Australia in 1938. When the Second World War broke out, he remained in Australia, opening a ballet school in Melbourne and founding the Borovansky Australian Ballet which made its debut in 1940. During the 1940s and 1950s the company toured Australia, attracting international guests such as Margot Fonteyn and Michael Somes. It was dissolved in 1961, two years after his death, but many of its dancers formed the nucleus of the Australian Ballet, founded by van Praagh in 1962.

Bortoluzzi, Paolo (*b* Genoa, 17 May 1938; *d* Brussels, 16 Oct. 1993) Italian dancer and ballet director. He studied with Ugo Dell'Ara, Victor Gsovsky, Asaf Messerer, and Béjart. He made his debut in 1957 at the Nervi Festival, briefly danced with Massine's Balletto Europeo in 1960, and in the same year joined Béjart's Ballet of the 20th Century, where he became one of the company's leading soloists, creating many roles in its repertory. After leaving Béjart in 1972 he continued to perform Béjart's choreography as a guest artist with various companies in Germany and America; he was a regular guest with American Ballet Theatre (1972–1). He opened a school in Turin in 1973, was ballet director of La Scala (1981–4), the German Opera on the Rhine, Düsseldorf (1984–90), and the Grand Theatre, Bordeaux (from 1990). His list of created roles in Béjart ballets includes *Boléro* (1960), *Ninth Symphony* (1964), *Les Oiseaux* (1965), *Romeo and Juliet* (1966), *Mass for Our Time* (1967), *Neither Flowers Nor Wreaths* (1968), *Baudelaire* (1968), *Bhakti* (1968), *Nomos Alpha* (1969), *Firebird* (1970), *Songs of a Wayfarer* (1971), *Nijinsky, clown de Dieu* (1971). Nijinsky Prize, Paris.

Boston Ballet US ballet company founded in 1964 by E. Virginia Williams, a local teacher and choreographer. It grew out of the New England Civic Ballet, a non-professional troupe fed by Williams's students. They were noticed by Balanchine, who recommended the company for a Ford Foundation grant, to allow it to become professional. Balanchine served as artistic adviser in the early days, thus allowing Boston to acquire a large number of his ballets. Other US choreographers represented in its early repertoire included Lang, Holder, de Mille, and Cunningham and its world premieres included Sokolow's *Time Plus Six* (mus. Teo Macero, 1966), Taras's *Dolly Suite* (mus. Fauré, 1971), Falco's *The Gamete Garden* (mus. Michael Kamen, 1971), and de Mille's *Summer* (mus. Schubert, 1975). From 1980 to 1984 Violette Verdy was joint artistic director, and in 1980 it became the first US company to visit China. Under the direction of Bruce Marks (1985–97) the company's international profile expanded and it moved into a permanent base in Boston. As well as securing the company's repertory of 19th-century classics Marks also made a point of commissioning work from contemporary choreographers including Bill T. Jones, Ralph Lemon, Susan Marshall, Mark Morris, and Twyla Tharp. The company has its own school, and a second company, Boston Ballet II. Subsequent directors have been Anna-Marie Holmes (from 1997) and Mikko Nissinen (from 2001). Jorma Elo was appointed resident choreographer in 2005, and his new version of *Rite of Spring* headed the company's centenary celebrations of Diaghilev in 2009.

(((⊕))) SEE WEB LINKS

• Boston Ballet website

Bouder, Ashley (*b* Carlisle, Pennsylvania, 10 Dec. 1983) American dancer. She trained at Central Pennsylvania Youth Ballet and at the School of American Ballet before joining New York City Ballet in 2000. A dancer of precocious strength and daring, she was promoted to principal in 2005 and has created roles in Martins's *Grazioso*, *Viva Verdi*, and *Octet*; Stroman's *Double Feature*; and Wheeldon's *Shambards*.

Boulez, Pierre (*b* Montbrison, 25 Mar. 1925) French composer. Although he has composed no music for the ballet, several of his concert pieces have been used by choreographers especially *Le Marteau sans maître* used by Paul Taylor in *Meridian* (1960), Béjart in *Pli selon pli* (1975) and Alston in *Le Marteau sans maître* (1992).

Bourgeois gentilhomme, Le 1. Comédie-ballet by Molière, with music by Lully and choreography by Beauchamps. Premiered 14 Oct. 1670 at Chambord. It was Molière's most famous comedy-ballet. A parody of 17th-century social climbers in which music, song and dance play equal parts in developing plot and characterization. 2. Ballet in one act with choreography by Balanchine, music by R. Strauss, and designs by Benois. Premiered 3 May 1932 by the Ballets Russes de Monte Carlo in Monte Carlo, with Lichine. It was revived in 1979 for Nureyev at New York City Opera.

Bourmeister, Vladimir (Burmeister) (*b* Vitebsk, Belarus, 15 Jul. 1904; *d* Moscow, 5 Mar. 1971) Soviet dancer, choreographer and ballet master. A distant relative of Tchaikovsky, he studied at Moscow's Lunacharsky Theatre Technicum (1925–9) and while still a student appeared with the Dramatic Ballet Workshop. In 1930 he joined the Moscow Art Ballet where he remained until his death, first as leading character dancer, then as chief choreographer and artistic director when the company became the Moscow Stanislavsky

and Nemirovich-Danchenko Musical Theatre (1941–60, 1963–71). He was a prolific choreographer, and his use of heroic themes, such as the bravery of Soviet youth during the Second World War, helped to define the genre of *Socialist Realism. The ballets he made in Moscow included *Straussiana* (1941), *The Merry Wives of Windsor* (mus. V. Oransky, 1942), *Lola* (mus. S. Vasilenko, 1943), *Scheherazade* (mus. Rimsky-Korsakov, 1944), *Carnaval* (mus. Schumann, 1946), *The Coast of Happiness* (mus. A. Spadavecchia, 1948), *La Esmeralda* (mus. Pugni, Glière, Vasilenko, 1950), *Jeanne d'Arc* (mus. N. Peiko, 1957), *Kalevipoeg* (mus. Eugen Kapp, 1961), *Bolero* (mus. Ravel, 1964), *Appassionata* (mus. Beethoven, 1970), and *A Lonely White Sail* (1970). For the Kirov Ballet he made *Tatiana* (mus. Aleksandr Krein, 1947). Today Bourmeister is best remembered for his 1953 production of *Swan Lake* which—controversially—used Tchaikovsky's score in its original sequence and restored cuts that had been made to the music. This production was introduced to the West when his company visited Paris in 1956; he then revived it for the Paris Opera in 1960. In 1961 he became the first Soviet choreographer permitted to work with a Western company when he was invited to choreograph *The Snow Maiden* (mus. Tchaikovsky) for London Festival Ballet. People's Artist of the USSR.

Bourne, Matthew (*b* London, 13 Jan. 1960) British dancer, choreographer, and company director. He studied at the Laban Centre for Movement and Dance, graduating in 1985 and joining Laban's Transitions Dance Company. Within two years he had co-founded Adventures in Motion Pictures (over which he later assumed sole control). He started making work for AMP in 1987, while continuing to perform; he was a founding member of Lea Anderson's all-male company, The Featherstonehaughs in 1988. His early pieces for AMP were witty, ironic, and wryly observant: *Spitfire* (1988) re-invented Jules Perrot's *Pas de quatre* with four male models; *The Infernal Galop* (1989) was a parody of French manners and culture. In 1992 he produced his first full-length work for AMP, *Deadly Serious*, a tribute to Alfred Hitchcock films. Bourne's natural gift for narrative generated invitations to choreograph for the dramatic and operatic stage and during the late 1980s and early 1990s he worked on productions for the Royal Shakespeare Company (*As You Like It*), the National Youth Theatre (*The Tempest*), and English National Opera (*A Midsummer Night's Dream*). He also became a sought-after choreographer for musicals, his West End credits including *Children of Eden* (1990) *Oliver!* (1994) and *Mary Poppins* (2004). For his own company he embarked on a series of extraordinarily successful re-imaginings of classic works, beginning with a new *Nutcracker* (1992) which was set in a Dickensian orphanage (Act 1) and a psychedelic Kingdom of the Sweeties (Act II). *Highland Fling* (1994) was an updated version of *La Sylphide* which featured the sylph as a New Age traveller and James as a lager lout while *Swan Lake* (1995) famously cast all of the swans, including the Odette-Odile role, as men, with Siegfried re-imagined as heir to the British throne, This production made Bourne one of the most internationally famous choreographers of his generation. After touring the UK the work enjoyed an exceptional West End run, followed by a long season on Broadway in 1998. It earned Bourne many awards including two Tonys, and since its premiere has toured internationally and been revived in the UK several times. Bourne's next classic productions were Prokofiev's *Cinderella* (1997) which was relocated to London during the Second World War and *The Car Man* (mus. Terry Davies and Shchedrin, after Bizet, 2000) which transferred the story of Carmen to 1960s small town America. He also created a version of *La Boutique Fantasque* for Images Dance Company in 1995, updating Massine's ballet to Carnaby Street in the 1960s. In 2002 Bourne broke from AMP to found the company New Adventures, for which he has since created the small-scale dance drama *Play Without Words* (mus. T. Davies); a dance version of the Tim Burton film *Edward Scissorhands* (mus. T. Davies based on themes by Danny Elfmann, 2005), and *Dorian Gray* (mus T. Davies, 2008). Bourne creates all of his work in close collaboration with his artistic team, especially designer Lez *Brotherston.

(⊕) SEE WEB LINKS

• Website for New Adventures

Bourne, Val (*b* Rangoon, 27 Dec. 1938) British dancer, arts administrator, and founder of Britain's Dance Umbrella festival. She trained at the Royal Ballet School, performed briefly with the Royal Ballet and danced with Sadler's Wells Opera Ballet for three years. In 1968 she began working as an arts administrator, first with London Festival Ballet and later with Ballet Rambert and in 1978 organized the first Dance Umbrella festival, which went on to become the largest festival of contemporary dance in the world. As its artistic director until 2006 she fostered the careers of dozens of British dance artists and introduced many international performers and companies to Britain. She has been recipient of numerous awards and honours including a 'Bessie'; an International Theatre Institute Award; CBE and Chevalier dans l'Ordre des Arts et Lettres.

Bournonville, Antoine (*b* Lyon, 19 May 1760; *d* Fredesborg, Denmark, 11 Jan. 1843) French dancer, choreographer, and ballet director. Father of August Bournonville. He studied with Noverre in Vienna and in Paris, where he danced at the Paris Opera. An invitation from King Gustav III of Sweden brought him to the Royal Swedish Opera in Stockholm, where he danced for ten years. In 1792 he travelled to Copenhagen but it was not until 1795 that Bournonville, having been distrusted as a known supporter of the French Revolution, was invited to join the Royal Danish Ballet. During his subsequent 24 years with the company he created leading roles in many ballets by Vicenzo Galeotti and eventually succeeded the latter as director of the Royal Danish Ballet (1816–23). One of Bournonville's best-known ballets was *Les Meuniers provençaux* (1785). In 1971 Mary Skeaping and Ivo Cramér reconstructed his 1789 ballet, *Fiskarena* (*The Fishermen*).

Bournonville, August (*b* Copenhagen, 21 Aug. 1805; *d* Copenhagen, 30 Nov. 1879) Danish dancer, choreographer, teacher, and ballet director. The most influential Danish choreographer of the 19th century. The son of Antoine Bournonville, he studied at the Royal Danish Ballet School, a pupil of both his father and Vincenzo Galeotti. He joined the company at the age of 15 and stayed three years (1820–3). The following year, still on salary in Copenhagen, he went to Paris to study with Vestris and joined the Paris Opera (1826–8). He frequently danced with Taglioni whom he considered an ideal ballerina and who he used as a model when training his own Danish dancers. In 1829 he returned to the Royal Theatre in Copenhagen as a guest artist but by the following year he had become not only a full member of the company but also its director. He was the Royal Danish Ballet's leading male soloist and chief choreographer and continued to perform with the company until retiring from the stage in 1848. Apart from working for one year at the Vienna Court Opera (1855–6) and three years at the Stockholm Opera (1861–4), he spent the rest of his career in Copenhagen. He retired in 1877, having built the Royal Danish Ballet into one of the world's leading companies; his numerous ballets forming the basis of a repertoire and style that are still recognized as uniquely Danish.

The Bournonville style was partly influenced by the choreographer's own qualities as a dancer—lightness, precision and grace—and it became celebrated for the detail and speed of its allegro, the buoyancy of its jumps, the open, easy carriage of the dancers' upper bodies, and the musical flow of their phrasing. Humanity and joie de vivre rather than simple technical brilliance characterized

Bournonville's conception of the classical Danish dancer.

In terms of their subject matter, Bournonville's ballets were influenced by his years in Paris and his contact with the emerging Romantic ballet. One of his earliest successes was a version of *La Sylphide* (1936) with a new score by H. Løvenskjold and a title role geared to his favourite Danish ballerina, L. *Grahn. In keeping with the Romantic interest in the exotic and his own fondness for travel Bournonville also created many ballets inspired by foreign cultures, the most famous of which remains *Napoli* (mus. H. S. Paulli, E. Helsted, N. W. Gade, and H. C. Lumbye, 1842)). His approach to Romantic subject matter, however, was more domestic and more dramatically realistic than that of his Paris-based contemporaries and his early interest in Nordic folklore and history inspired numerous ballets whose themes and characters were closer to home, most famously *A Folk Tale* (mus. Gade and J. P. E. Hartmann, 1854). A fuller list of his ballets includes, *Waldemar* (1835), *The Festival in Albano* (mus. J. F. Froehlich, 1839), *The Dancing School* (*Konservatoriet*, mus. Paulli, 1849), *The Kermesse in Bruges* (mus. Paulli, 1851), *La Ventana* (mus. Lumbye, 1854), *Flower Festival at Genzano* (mus. Helsted and Paulli, 1858), *Far from Denmark* (mus. Jos. Glaeser, L. Gottschalk, Lumbye, Eduart Dupuy, A. F. Lincke, 1860), *Valkyrien* (mus. Hartmann, 1861), and *The King's Lifeguards on Amager* (mus. W. Holm, Dupuy, and Lumbye, 1871). His last ballet was *From Siberia to Moscow*, which he made for the Royal Theatre in 1876, drawing on inspiration from a visit to Russia made two years earlier. As director of the opera at the Royal Theatre he also presented the Danish premieres of Wagner's *Lohengrin, Die Meistersinger*, and *Tannhäuser*. He published his memoirs *Mit Theaterliv* in three parts (1848, 1865, and 1877), which were translated into English as *My Theatre Life* (Middletown, Conn., 1979). After his death Bournonville's ballets continued to form the core of the Danish Ballet's repertory, and the preservation of his choreography and his style was undertaken by Beck in the early years of the 20th century. Beck's retirement brought about a temporary eclipsing of Bournonville but since 1950, regular ballet festivals in Copenhagen have showcased the repertory and a succession of scholars and ballet masters have led a revival of interest in the Bournonville heritage. His ballets are now performed worldwide. In 1979 Kirsten Ralov published *The Bournonville School*, a notated record of the daily classes that were the foundation of the Bournonville style.

bourrée 1. French folk dance performed either in 3/4 time or 2/2 time, with a strong rhythm and a skipping step. It was first recorded during the Renaissance. 2. A court dance popular in France during the 17th and 18th centuries. It was performed by couples, either on their own or with other couples. 3. In classical ballet, bourrées are usually tiny running steps in which the feet are kept close together. They are most often performed on pointe and can travel in any direction.

Bourrée fantasque Ballet in one act with choreography by Balanchine, music by Chabrier, and costumes by Barbara Karinska. Premiered 1 Dec. 1949 by New York City Ballet at City Center, New York, with LeClercq, Robbins, Maria Tallchief, Magallanes, Janet Reed, and Herbert Bliss. A light-hearted, plotless work in three movements. It was revived for London Festival Ballet in 1960, restaged by Balanchine for the Paris Opera Ballet in 1963, and revived by American Ballet Theatre in 1981.

Boutique fantasque, La (Eng. title *The Fantastic Toyshop*) Ballet in one act with choreography by Massine, decor and libretto by Derain, and music by Rossini (arr. Respighi). Premiered 5 Jun. 1919 by the Ballets Russes de Diaghilev at the Alhambra Theatre, London, with Cecchetti, Idzikowski, Lopokova, Massine, Sokolova, and Woizikowski. Set in the 1860s, the ballet tells the story of a toyshop in which the dolls come to life at night and prevent the management from selling off the can-can dancing dolls (originally danced by Lopokova and Massine) to separate customers. More subversive in conception than earlier toy ballets, such as *Coppélia*, it satirized various national types among the shop's customers, and used the personality quirks of its original cast to colour its comedic cameos. The ballet was revived many times, mostly by Massine, who staged it for Sadler's Wells Ballet in 1947. In 1995 Matthew Bourne created a new version for Images Dance Company, updating the action to Carnaby Street in 1960s London.

Boyarchikov, Nikolai (*b* Leningrad, 27 Sept. 1935) Soviet dancer, choreographer, and ballet director. He studied at the Leningrad Ballet School and graduated in 1954. He danced at the Maly Theatre in Leningrad from 1954 to 1971. From 1971 to 1977 he was artistic director of the ballet company at the Perm State Theatre. In 1977 he became chief choreographer and director of the Maly Theatre in Leningrad (later renamed the Mussorgsky Theatre, then the Mikhailovsky). A natural experimenter, he took advantage of relaxed relationships with the West to open up the Maly repertory to new influences. In 1989, following a visit to the American Dance Festival in Durham, N. Carolina, he invited Betty Jones to stage Limón's modern dance classic *There is a Time* at the Maly and also acquired works from the Balanchine and Diaghilev repertories. His own 1979 ballet *Orpheus and Eurydice* is credited as Russia's first rock ballet. Nevertheless many of his most popular works, created for the Maly and other companies, have had classic or Russian themes including *The Three Musketeers* (mus. V. Basner, Maly Theatre, 1964), *The Woodcut Prince* or *The Wooden Prince* (mus. Bartók, Maly Theatre, 1965), *The Queen of Spades* (mus. Prokofiev, Leningrad Chamber Ballet, 1968), *Romeo and Juliet* (mus. Prokofiev, Perm, 1972, also West Berlin German Opera, 1974), *The Miraculous Mandarin* (mus. Bartók, Perm, 1973), *Tsar Boris* (mus. Prokofiev, Perm Theatre, 1975), *Hercules* (1980), *The Robbers* (1983), *Macbeth* (1984), *The Marriage* (1986), *Quiet Flows the Don* (1988), *Petersburg* (1992). He retired from the Mikhailovsky in 2007.

Bozzacchi, Giuseppina (*b* Milan, 23 Nov. 1853; *d* Paris, 23 Nov. 1870) Italian dancer. Her promising career was the shortest on record. After training with the Milan prima ballerina Amina Boschetti, and studying with Mme Dominique in Paris she created the role of Swanilda in the first production of *Coppélia* in Paris in 1870. She danced it eighteen times before contracting a fever and died on her seventeenth birthday.

Brae, June (*b* Ringwood, Hampshire, 18 May 1917; *d* Bath, 3 Jan. 2000) British dancer. One of the principal stars of the Vic-Wells Ballet during the 1930s. She studied with George Goncharov in Shanghai (where she met Fonteyn), with Legat in London, and Kschessinska in Paris. She joined the Vic-Wells Ballet in 1935 and while additionally guesting with Ballet Rambert was promoted to principal with the Vic-Wells in 1936, creating the role of the Black Queen in de Valois's *Checkmate* (1937), the Rich Girl in Ashton's *Nocturne* (1936), and Josephine in his *A Wedding Bouquet* (1937). She also created roles in Ashton's *Les Patineurs* (1937), *Harlequin in the Street* (1937), and *Dante Sonata* (1940). She retired in 1942, but made a brief comeback in 1946, dancing with the Sadler's Wells Opera Ballet, where she created roles in Helpmann's *Adam Zero* and Howard's *Assembly Ball*. In 1981 she appeared at a gala marking the 50th anniversary of Sadler's Wells, performing in the orgy scene from de Valois's *The Rake's Progress*.

Brahms, Caryl (*b* Surrey, 1901; *d* London, 4 Dec. 1982) British writer and critic. She was best known as the author (with S. J. Simon) of the satirical novel *A Bullet in the Ballet* (1937). She was editor of *Footnotes to Ballet* (1936), and wrote *Robert Helpmann, Choreographer* (1943) and *A Seat at the Ballet* (1951). *A Bullet in the Ballet* was later turned into a musical starring Massine and Baronova.

Brahms, Johannes (*b* Hamburg, 7 May 1833; *d* Vienna, 3 Apr. 1897) German composer. Although he wrote no ballet music, his music has been used by many choreographers, most controversially Massine, who used his 4th Symphony for the 1933 ballet *Choreartium*. Other settings of his music include Nijinska's *Brahms Variations* (1944 set to *Variations on Themes by Handel and Paganini*): Balanchine's *Liebeslieder Walzer* (1960) and *Brahms-Schoenberg Quartet* (1966); Ashton's *Five Brahms Waltzes in the Manner of Isadora Duncan* (1976); Tharp's *Brahms' Paganini* (1980, set to the *Paganini Variations*); Tharp and Robbins's *Brahms/Handel* (1984, set to *Variation and Fugue on a Theme by Handel*), Tharp's *The Brahms-Haydn Variations* (2000, set to *Variations on a Theme by Haydn for Orchestra* and Mark Morris's *New Love Song Waltzes* (1982 set to *Neue Liebeslieder*) and *Love Song Waltzes* (1989, set to *Liebeslieder*).

Brandstrup, Kim (*b* Aarhus, 9 Jan. 1956) Danish-born, British-based choreographer. He studied film at the University of Copenhagen then moved to the UK where he studied with Nina Fonaroff at the London Contemporary Dance School. He choreographed several works for London Contemporary Dance Theatre, including *Orfeo*, which won an Olivier Award in 1989 and founded his own group, Arc Dance Company in 1985. His productions, many of them narrative based, are strongly influenced by the cinema, using striking visual imagery and the choreographic equivalents of cinematic montage and close-up to develop character and action. The early works were shaped by his training in modern dance but later works (several of them commissions for ballet companies) have since acquired more classical qualities of lightness and speed. Brandstrup's works for Arc have included *Peer Gynt* (1991), *Antic* (based on *Hamlet*, 1993), *Othello* (1994), *Saints and Shadows* (1994), *Les Noces* (1997), and *The Return of Don Juan* (1999). Other work includes *Sacre du printemps* (1991) for Geneva Ballet, Britten's *Death in Venice* (1992) for the Royal Opera and the Metropolitan Opera, *White Nights* for English National Ballet, *Mysteries* (1994), *Cupid and Psyche* (mus. Kim Helweg, 1997) and *Ghosts* for the Royal Danish Ballet, *Eidolon* (1996) and *Songs of a Wayfarer* (mus. Mahler, 2004) for Rambert Dance Company, *Sleeping Beauty* (1998) for the New Zealand Ballet, *Queen of Spades* (mus. Tchaikovsky, 2002) for Les Grands Ballets Canadiens, *Pulcinella* (2006) for Birmingham Royal Ballet, *Rushes* (mus. Prokofiev, 2008) for the Royal Ballet, and *Goldberg* (mus. Bach, 2009) in collaboration with Tamara Rojo.

(⊕) SEE WEB LINKS

• Official website for Kim Brandstrup

branle [Fr., swing, shake; can also be spelled bransle] The term for old French folk dances, frequently accompanied by singing. In modified form they found their way into the entertainments at the court of Louis XIV and hence later became connected with various ballets and pantomimes. In his *L'Orchésographie* (1588), Thoinot Arbeau described more than two dozen kinds of branles. In the 20th century the branle is featured in Balanchine and Stravinsky's *Agon*.

Braque, Georges (*b* Argenteuil, 13 May 1882; *d* Paris, 31 Aug. 1963) French painter and designer. Among his ballet designs were Nijinska's *Les Fâcheux* (1924), and Massine's *Salade* (1924) and *Zéphire et Flore* (1925).

Braunsweg, Julian (*b* Warsaw 1897; *d* London, 26 Mar. 1978) Polish-born British impresario and ballet director. His career began in Berlin in the 1920s with organizing theatre performances. He was manager of the Russian Romantic Ballet and acted as manager for several artists, including Karsavina and La Argentina, and several companies, Pavlova's and Nijinska's, the Metropolitan Ballet and the Original Ballet Russe among them. He founded London Festival Ballet (later English National Ballet) in 1950 and remained as its general director until 1965. Author of *Braunsweg's Ballet Scandals* (London, 1973).

Bravo, Guillermina (*b* Vera Cruz, 13 Nov. 1923) Mexican dancer, choreographer, director, and teacher, who is widely regarded as the most important figure in Mexican modern dance. She studied folk dance at the National School of Dance in Mexico City, music at the National Conservatory (1936) and ballet and modern dance with Estrella Morales (1938). Between 1940 and 1945 she performed with the Fine Arts Ballet and the Theater of the Arts Ballet and subsequently founded her own modern dance troupe, Ballet Waldeen, in 1946. In 1947 she co-founded the Academy of Mexican Dance, and the following year became the founding director of the National Ballet of Mexico. Initially based in Mexico City the company moved in 1991 to Queretaro, where Bravo also founded the National Center of Contemporary Dance (1991). Bravo continued dancing until 1960, and continued to direct the National Ballet of Mexico until its dissolution in 2006. Her teaching methods owed much to Martha Graham's technique, and to Feldenkrais, with whom she briefly studied. Her choreography, which featured in modern ballet, musical comedy, and drama productions, embraced a wide range of styles and subject matter, much of it with a strong Mexican theme.

Brazil Although there were visits by European dancers in the 19th century, ballet in Brazil did not become professionally active until 1927 when the former Pavlova dancer, Maria Oleneva, was invited to train a corps de ballet for the Teatro Municipal de Rio de Janeiro. Drawing her dancers from Brazil's ballet schools, Oleneva's troupe performed initially in opera and drama productions but after a few years was able to give complete ballet programmes. In 1934 the newly remodelled Teatro Municipal was reopened and a ballet season organized that included Lifar and three of his dancers, working with Oleneva's troupe. Five years later the company, the Municipal Ballet of Rio de Janeiro, gave its first official season, directed by guest choreographer Vaslav Veltchek. Veltchek returned to Rio in 1943 to mount a new all-Brazilian dance season, after which Yuco Lindenberg joined the company as choreographer and temporary director. In 1945, Lindenberg was succeeded by *Schwezoff and the company performed another major season featuring Brazilian-born ballerinas Edith Pudelko, Rosanova, Tamara Capeller, and Vilma Lemos Cunha. However during the years of Lindenberg's directorship in the late 1940s, the company barely survived and it was at a low artistic and financial ebb when Tatiana Leskova, a former ballerina with the Original Ballet Russe, was hired as ballet mistress, choreographer, and dancer in 1950. Under her direction the classics were staged and guest choreographers like Massine, Dollar, and H. Lander were brought in to work with the company. Leskova was succeeded by several short-term directors including Veltchek and Dalal *Achcar, although the latter returned for a second term in 1987. A constant influence on the Municipal Ballet company was Achcar who, during her several years as director of the Foundation of the Municipal Theatre (1983–6 and 1991–4) oversaw a rise in technical standards and an expansion of the repertory. During this period the company was built up to its present size of 100 dancers and acquired new works from Skibine and Araiz. The company continues to suffer from a rapid turnover of directors, including Jean-Yves Lameau (1995–9), Gustavo Mollajoli (1999–2002), Richard Cragun (2003–5) and Sergio Marshall (appointed 2006) but it continues to stage a wide repertory of classics, along with 20th-century works like Cranko's *Onegin* and new ballets by Brazilian choreographers such as Nebrada, Ivo, and Achcar.

Achcar's own influence on the Brazilian ballet scene dates back to 1960 when she co-founded the Ballet Association of Rio de Janeiro, and its associate company, with the mission of raising standards of ballet teaching and performance. She introduced the RAD syllabus into Brazil and established a professional teachers' course, while for her own short-lived but highly influential company she invited many of the world's leading dancers to guest, including Fonteyn and Nureyev.

She also organized seasons by visiting companies such as Paris Opera and the Royal Ballet.

A third company, the Ballet of the Fourth Centennial, was founded in São Paulo in 1953 under the direction of Milloss, and presented its first season of Brazilian ballets in Rio in 1954. Although it survived only a few years, its influence on the dance scene was significant due to its emphasis on Brazilian designers, composers, and themes.

Modern dance was largely introduced to Brazil by Chinita Ullman, who had studied with Wigman in Germany and returned to open a school in São Paulo. In 1954 Nina Verchinina, another veteran of the Original Ballet Russe, moved to Rio. As both a choreographer, working with the Municipal Ballet, and a teacher, who ran her own school for more than 30 years, she was a second major influence on the development of modern dance in the country. Several significant companies were established during the 1970s, including Ballet Stagium, founded in 1971 by Marika Gidali and Decio Otero; Grupo Corpo, founded in 1975 by members of the Pederneiras family in Belo Horizonte; and Cisne Negro, founded in 1977 in São Paulo by Hulda Bittencourt. These have acquired an international profile and Brazil's modern dance scene continues to be very active, with the Deborah Colker Dance Company, founded in 1993, and the hip-hop-influenced dance theatre troupe Membros, founded in Macáo in 1990 by Tais Vieira and Paulo Azevedo. Brazilian-born choreographers and performers such as Jean Abreu and *Ivo have acquired an international profile, and international interest has also grown in native Brazilian dance forms such as *capoeira.

(⊕) SEE WEB LINKS

- Website for the Teatro Municipal de Rio de Janeiro with link to the ballet company
- Website for Dalal Achcar

Brenaa, Hans (*b* Copenhagen, 9 Oct. 1910; *d* Copenhagen, 14 Apr. 1988) Danish dancer, teacher, and ballet director. He studied at the Royal Danish Ballet School from 1918 and joined the company in 1928; promoted to principal in 1945. He created roles in Balanchine's *Legend of Joseph* (1931) and in numerous ballets by Lander, including *Études* (1948). He produced *Aurora's Wedding* for the Royal Danish Ballet in 1950. After retiring from the stage in 1955 he became a producer, staging the Bournonville repertoire in Denmark and elsewhere. He also taught at the Royal Danish Ballet School in Copenhagen from 1942 and gave classes in the Bournonville style throughout Europe and America. Among the Bournonville productions he staged for the Royal Danish Ballet are *The Kermesse in Bruges* (1957 and 1978), *La Sylphide* (1967), *Konservatoriet* (1968),

The King's Volunteers on Amager (1970), *Far from Denmark* (1973), and *La Ventana* (1979).

Brianza, Carlotta (*b* Milan, 1867; *d* Paris, 1935 (some sources 1930)) Italian dancer. She was most famous for creating the role of Aurora in Petipa's *Sleeping Beauty*. She studied at the school of La Scala Ballet and graduated into the company, making her debut as prima ballerina in Manzotti's *Excelsior*. In 1883 she toured the US in the ballet, and in 1887 danced it in St Petersburg at the Arcadia Theatre. Her virtuoso, Italian technique thrilled audiences and she continued to be a popular guest artist in the Russian city and was eventually hired by the Mariinsky Theatre, where she made her company debut with Cecchetti in Ivanov's *The Tulip of Haarlem* in 1889. In 1890 Petipa chose her as his Aurora; in 1891 he used her again for the leading role in *Kalkabrino*. She returned to Europe shortly thereafter, where she continued to dance in Vienna, Italy, Paris, and London. After her retirement she taught in Paris. When Diaghilev staged *The Sleeping Princess* in London in 1921 he brought her out of retirement to assist Bronislava Nijinska in the staging and to dance Carabosse. Remarkably little is known about her later years; the date and circumstances of her death are also a mystery.

Bright Stream, The Ballet in three acts with choreography and libretto by Lopukhov, music by Shostakovich, and designs by V. Bobyshov. Premiered 4 Apr. 1935 by the Maly Theatre, Leningrad. The ballet, set on a collective farm, shows socialist morals prevailing over regressive behaviour when a married agronomist indulges in an extra-marital flirtation. It was intended to please the Soviet authorities, and as such is considered a seminal work of *Socialist Realism. However despite its initial success at the Maly, the ballet's music and movement vocabulary were criticized when it transferred to Moscow, as being inappropriate to their subject-matter. Lopukhov was dismissed from his post as ballet chief at the Maly Theatre, and his proposed appointment as director of the Bolshoi Ballet was cancelled. A new version was staged for the Bolshoi in 2003 by Ratmansky.

Bring in 'da Noise, Bring in 'da Funk US dance musical with choreography by Savion *Glover, music by Daryl Waters, Zane Mark, and Ann Duquesnay, book and lyrics by Reg E. Gaines. Conceived and directed by Savion Glover and George C. Wolfe. Premiered 15 Nov. 1995 at the Joseph Papp Public Theater in New York. It transferred to Broadway's Ambassador Theater in April 1996. The musical traces the history of black America through its dance forms, from the days of slave ships to the modern inner city, and it encompasses tap and hip-hop. It earned Glover the 1996 Tony Award for Choreography.

Brinson, Peter (*b* Llandudno, 6 Mar. 1923; *d* London, 7 Apr. 1995) British writer and dance educator. He was educated at Oxford University, graduating in 1948 to become scriptwriter and research director of the London Film Centre (1948–53). He wrote and produced the first stereoscopic ballet film, *The Black Swan*, in 1952; was editor of *Pavlova* (1954); and lectured on ballet at Oxford, Cambridge, and the University of London (1954–64). In 1964 he was founder-director of the Royal Ballet's Ballet for All; an initiative designed to introduce young people to theatrical dance. Briefly director of the Royal Academy of Dance (1968–9), his other posts included director of the British and Commonwealth Branch of the Gulbenkian Foundation (1971–82); head of research and community development at the Laban Centre, London (1982–7), and professor of dance at York University in Toronto. He chaired a national enquiry into the state of dance in education (1975–80) and wrote its concluding enquiry, *Dance Education and Training in Britain* (London, 1980). He was also author of *The Choreographic Art* (with van Praagh, London, 1963); *The Polite World* (with Joan Wildeblood, London, 1965); *Background to European Ballet* (London, 1966); *Ballet for All* (with Clement Crisp, London, 1970); *Dance as Education: Towards a National Dance Culture* (1991).

brisé In classical ballet, a travelling leap in which the legs are beaten rapidly in the air. The most famous example is the coda of the Blue Bird pas de deux in *The Sleeping Beauty*, which begins with a diagonal of 24 brisés volés.

Britain *See* GREAT BRITAIN.

Britten, Benjamin (*b* Lowestoft, 22 Nov. 1913; *d* Aldeburgh, 4 Dec. 1976) British composer. His only ballet score, *The Prince of the Pagodas*, was choreographed by Cranko in 1957 for the Royal Ballet and again by MacMillan in 1989, also for the Royal. His opera *Death in Venice* contains several ballet sequences, which were choreographed by Ashton at the work's premiere in 1973. His concert music has been used by many choreographers, including *Soirées musicales* (Tudor, 1938; Cranko in *Bouquet garni*, 1965), *Simple Symphony* (Gore, 1944; Dollar, 1961), *Variations on a Theme of Frank Bridge* (Ashton in *Le Rêve de Léonor*, 1949; Neumeier in *Stages and Reflections*, 1968; Bintley in *Night Moves*, 1981), *The Young Person's Guide to the Orchestra* (Robbins in *Fanfare*, 1953; Ashton in *Variations on a Theme of Purcell*, 1955), *Les Illuminations* (Ashton, 1950; Alston in *Rumours Visions*, 1996), and

Sinfonia da Requiem (Tetley in *Dances of Albion*, 1980; Kylián in *Forgotten Land*, 1981).

Broken Fall One-act modern dance, with choreography by Russell Maliphant, music by Barry Adamson, and lighting design by Michael Hulls. It was premiered on 9 Dec. 2003 at the Royal Opera House, with Sylvie Guillem, Michael Nunn, and William Trevitt all performing as guest artists with the Royal Ballet. A trio marked by fluid lifts and plunging falls, it represented a major step in Guillem's career away from classical and towards modern dance and also initiated her subsequent creative and performing partnership with Maliphant. The work additionally deepened Nunn and Trevitt's alliance with Maliphant, first seen in their performance of the latter's *Critical Mass* with their own company, George Piper Dances. It won an Olivier Award.

Bronze Horseman, The Ballet in three acts with choreography by Zakharov, music by Reinhold Glière, design by Mikhail Bobyshov, and libretto by Petr Abolimov, after the poem by Pushkin. Premiered 14 Mar. 1949 by the Kirov Ballet, St Petersburg, with Sergeyev and Dudinskaya. The ballet tells the story of the lovers Yevgeny and Parasha who are separated when the latter drowns in the St Petersburg flood of 1824. The Bronze Horseman is the famous statue of Peter the Great in St Petersburg which, in his grief-induced delirium, Yevgeny believes is pursuing him. The ballet was also staged at the Bolshoi Theatre in Moscow on 27 June 1949 with Yermolaev and Lepeshinskaya.

Brooklyn Academy of Music Theatre in the New York borough of Brooklyn, which is an important showcase for US contemporary dance.

Brotherston, Lez (*b* Liverpool, 6 Oct. 1961) British designer. He trained at Central School of Art and Design and while contributing designs to many opera and theatre productions is best known for his longstanding collaboration with choreographer Matthew *Bourne. This began with *Highland Fling* (1994) and continued with *Swan Lake, Cinderella, The Car Man, Play Without Words, Edward Scissorhands*, and *Dorian Gray*—his contributions going beyond design to co-developing the libretto and production concept. He also designed *Seven Deadly Sins* (2008) for the Royal Ballet; *Into the Woods* and *The Soldier's Tale* for Will *Tuckett; *Romeo and Juliet, Swan Lake, A Christmas Carol*, and *Dracula* for *Northern Ballet Theatre. He co-wrote and co-directed *Les Liaisons Dangereuses* (2005) with Adam *Cooper.

Brown, Carolyn (*b* Fitchburg, Mass., 26 Sept. 1927) US dancer and choreographer. She studied with her mother, Marion Rice, herself a student of the Denishawn school, and graduated in philosophy from Wheaton College in 1950. After attending a masterclass with Cunningham in Denver in 1951, she switched to full-time dance studies at the Juilliard School, and after further studies with Cunningham became one of the founding members of his company in 1953. During the next twenty years she was Cunningham's most important female dancer, the purity and articulation of her technique making her his ideal interpreter. She danced in 40 of his works, often collaborating with him and Cage in the creative process. She created a role in Cage's *Theatre Piece* (1960) and on pointe in Robert Rauschenberg's first dance work *Pelican* (1963). Her own choreography includes *Car Lot* (1968), *As I Remember It*, a solo in homage to Shawn (Jacob's Pillow, 1972), *Bunkered for a Bogey* (1973), *House Party* (1974), *Circles* (1975), and *Balloon II* (Ballet-Théâtre Contemporain, 1976). She retired from the stage in 1973 but continued to choreograph and teach and as artistic advisor to the Cunningham company was actively involved in re-staging his early works, not only for the company but for New York City Ballet, White Oak, and others. She has directed several films including *Dune Dance* and her autobiography *Chance and Circumstance: 20 years with Cage and Cunningham* was published in 2007.

Brown, Trisha (*b* Aberdeen, Wash., 25 Nov. 1936) US dancer, choreographer, and company director. One of the pioneering figures in postmodern American dance. She received a BA in Dance from Mills College in Oakland, California, and trained with Louis Horst, Anna Halprin, and Robert Dunn at the American Dance Festival. She was a founder member of Judson Dance Theatre in 1962 and also of the improvisational company, Grand Union, in 1970, before forming her own company in 1970. During the first years of her career, Brown stripped dance to a language of essentials, choreographing with a pared-down vocabulary of movement and frequently eschewing costumes, lighting, and music. *Falling Duet* (1968) consisted of two dancers taking turns falling and catching one another; while for the improvisational piece *Yellowbelly* (1969) Brown encouraged the audience to heckle the dancers. Fascinated by the process of making dance, she experimented with different performance sites. *Roof Piece* (1971) was danced on rooftops over twelve blocks in lower Manhattan, while *Walking on the Wall* (1971) featured dancers supported by ropes, pulleys, and mountain-climbing gear as they literally did as the title implied. In 1979 Brown began to collaborate with other artists, including Robert Rauschenberg; their *Glacial Decoy* (1979) marked a shift in her career towards

more theatrical staging and more elaborate choreography. She continued to work extensively in mixed-media presentations, but remained resolutely purist in her movement style, rejecting the glamour and artifice of classical ballet and the spectacle and storytelling of the Martha Graham school of modern dance. Late in her career she began choreographing to jazz and classical music, for example *M.O.* (1995), set to Bach's *Musical Offering*, and also to stage classical music productions. In 1998 she choreographed and directed Monteverdi's *L'Orfeo* at La Monnaie, in 2002 she staged *Winterreise*, with British singer Simon Keenlyside, and in 2006 she directed and choreographed a new chamber opera *Da Gelo a Gelo* to a score by Laurie Anderson. In 2004 she created her first work for classical dancers, *O zlozony O* (mus. L. Anderson, Paris Opera). A list of her other works includes *Trillium* (1962), *Lightfall* (1963), *Improvisation on a Chicken Coop Roof* (1963), *Rulegame 5* (1964), *Planes* (1968), *Man Walking Down the Side of the Building* (1970), *Accumulation* (1971), *Group Primary Accumulation* (1973), *Discs* (1973), *Drift* (1974), *Locus* (1975), *Water Motor* (1978), *Opal Loop* (1980), *Son of Gone Fishin'* (1981), *Set and Reset* (1983), *Lateral Pass* (1985), *Newark* (1987), *Astral Convertible* (1989), *Foray Forêt* (1990), *For M.G.: The Movie* (1991), *Twelve Ton Rose* (mus. Webern, 1996), *If You Couldn't See Me* (1994), a solo for Brown, *You Can See Us* (1995), a duet for herself and Mikhail Baryshnikov, and *Canto/Pianto* (mus. Monteverdi, 1997). Her work is in the repertory of several other companies including Scottish Ballet. Chevalier dans l'Ordre des Arts et des Lettres (1988).

(⊕) SEE WEB LINKS

• Website for the Trisha Brown company

Browne, Leslie (*b* New York, 29 Jun. 1958) US dancer. Born into a family of dancers, she studied with M. Craske, with her parents, Isabel Mirrow and Kelly Brown, and at the School of American Ballet (1972–4) before joining New York City Ballet in 1974. In 1976 she moved to American Ballet Theatre as a soloist becoming a principal in 1986. She excelled in dramatic roles, for example Hagar in Tudor's *Pillar of Fire*, and Kenneth MacMillan chose her for his first-cast Juliet when he staged *Romeo and Juliet* for ABT. In 1977 she danced and acted the juvenile lead in Herbert Ross's film *The Turning Point* and following that success appeared in two further Ross films, as Romola Nijinsky in *Nijinsky* (1980) and Nadine in *Dancers* (1987). Brown also toured with Baryshnikov and Company in 1985, 1986, and 1987 and after leaving ABT in the early 1990s she appeared in the 1993 Broadway musical version of *The Red Shoes*.

She currently teaches and choreographs for student dancers.

Bruce, Christopher (*b* Leicester, 3 Oct. 1945) British dancer, choreographer, and company director, whose career has been most closely associated with Rambert Dance Company. He studied in Scarborough and at the Rambert School, and joined Ballet Rambert in 1963. He became the company's leading male dancer after its re-formation in 1966, and was acclaimed for his performances in Nijinsky's *L'Après-midi d'un faune* and as Pierrot in Tetley's *Pierrot lunaire*. He created roles in Morrice's *The Realms of Choice* (1965), *Hazard* (1967), *Blind Sight* (1969), and *That is the Show* (1971), and in Tetley's *Embrace Tiger and Return to Mountain* (1968). He also created the role of the poet Lorca in *Cruel Garden*, which he co-choreographed with Lindsay Kemp for Rambert in 1977. He was associate director of Rambert (1975–9) and associate choreographer (1979–87). He was additionally associate choreographer of London Festival Ballet (now English National Ballet) between 1986 and 1991) and was appointed resident choreographer of the Houston Ballet in 1989. In 1994 he took over as artistic director of Rambert. A fluent and prolific choreographer, Bruce has been unusually successful in reaching a wide audience, works such as *Cruel Garden* (with Lindsay Kemp, mus. C. Miranda, 1977), *Ghost Dances* (mus. S. American folk-songs, 1981), *Swansong* (mus. Philip Chambon, London Festival Ballet, 1987), and *Rooster* (mus. The Rolling Stones, Geneva Ballet, 1991) gaining special popularity. His style embraces both classical and modern vocabularies and even when his works do not deal directly with narrative, they have a strongly expressive slant. Some, like *Swansong, are overtly political. A list of his other works includes *For Those who Die as Cattle* (no mus., 1972), *There Was a Time* (mus. Brian Hodgson, 1972), *Unfamiliar Playground* (mus. Anthony Hymas, Sadler's Wells Royal Ballet, 1974), *Ancient Voices of Children* (mus. G. Crumb, 1975), *Black Angels* (mus. G. Crumb, 1976), *Echoes of a Night Sky* (mus. G. Crumb, 1977), *Night with Waning Moon* (mus. G. Crumb, 1979), *Dancing Day* (mus. Holst, 1981), *Intimate Pages* (mus. Janáček, 1984), *Sergeant Early's Dream* (mus. folk-songs, 1984), *Remembered Dances* (mus. Janáček, 1985), *Silence is the End of Our Song* (Chilean poems, Royal Danish Ballet, 1985), *Land* (mus. Nordheim, London Festival Ballet, 1985), *The Dream is Over* (mus. John Lennon, the Cullberg Ballet, 1986), *Waiting* (mus. Errolyn Wallen, London Contemporary Dance Theatre, 1993), *Moonshine* (mus. Bob Dylan, Nederlands Dans Theater, 1993), *Crossing* (mus. Henryk Górecki, 1994), *Meeting Point* (mus. Michael Nyman, 1995),

Quicksilver (mus. Nyman, 1996), *God's Plenty* (mus. Dominic Muldowney, 1999), a full-length work based on Chaucer's *Canterbury Tales*. He retired from Rambert in 2002 but continued to choreograph, for example creating *Three Songs – Two Voices* (mus. Jimi Hendrix, arr. Nigel Kennedy) for the Royal Ballet in 2005 and *Hush* (mus. several) for Houston Ballet in 2006.

Bruhn, Erik (*b* Copenhagen, 3 Oct. 1928; *d* Toronto, 1 Apr. 1986) Danish dancer, choreographer, and ballet director. He studied at the Royal Danish Ballet School (from 1937) and joined the company in 1947, promoted to soloist in 1949. Although he remained closely associated with the Royal Danish Ballet for the next fifteen years, he performed extensively as a guest artist with the English Metropolitan Ballet, American Ballet Theatre, New York City Ballet, the National Ballet of Canada, the Royal Ballet, the Harkness Ballet, and the Ruth Page Ballet. At ABT he partnered Markova and Fracci. and his debut with the former in *Giselle* (Metropolitan Opera House, 1955) created a sensation. Bruhn was one of the finest male dancers of the 20th century, possessed of a pure classical technique and a striking nobility, his commitment to the drama and artistry of his roles never sacrificed to self-promoting virtuosity. As a foremost exponent of the Bournonville style, he was an outstanding James in *La Sylphide*. In later years he became a celebrated character artist, giving exceptionally detailed and moving interpretations of Madge and Dr Coppelius. He also excelled in more modern roles, including Jean in Cullberg's *Miss Julie* and Don José in Petit's *Carmen*. He created roles in Taras's *Designs with Strings* (1948), MacMillan's *Journey* (1957), Cullberg's *Lady from the Sea* (1960), Cranko's *Daphnis and Chloe* (1962), S. Hodes's *The Abyss* (1965), and in a pas de deux, choreographed specially for him and Makarova, in Ailey's *The River* (1971). He was director of the Royal Swedish Ballet (1967–71), resident producer of the National Ballet of Canada (1973–6), and director of the National Ballet of Canada from 1983 until his premature death three years later. He re-staged many of the classics for companies around the world, including the Royal Danish Ballet, the Royal Swedish Ballet, the Bavarian State Opera, the Harkness Ballet, and the National Ballet of Canada for whom he staged *La Sylphide* (1965), *Swan Lake* (1966), and *Coppélia* (1975). He won the Nijinsky Prize in 1963 and became a Knight of Dannebrog in 1963. Author (with Lillian Moore) of *Bournonville and Ballet Technique* (London, 1961).

Brumachon, Claude (*b* Rouen, 2 May 1959) French dancer, choreographer and director. He studied at the Fine Arts School and performed with Ballet de la Cité (1978–80), Christine Gérard (1980–1), and Karine Saporta (1982). His independent career as a choreographer dates back to the research group he founded with Benjamin Lamarche in 1981, which developed into a performing ensemble in 1984. From 1992 he was co-director of the Centre Chorégraphique National de Nantes, with Lamarche, where his company continues to be based. His style is athletic and occasionally physically punishing. His works, many created in collaboration with Lamarche, have often been performed in non-theatrical spaces including museums, castles, even on a submarine base (*Emigrants*, 1993). Recent works include *Icare* (mus. Bruno Billadon), *Rebelles* (2001), and *Phobos* (2007). His works for other companies include *Féline* for the Paris Opera (1989).

SEE WEB LINKS

• Website for CCN de Nantes and the Brumachon company

Buckle, Richard (*b* Warcop, 6 Aug. 1916; *d* 12 Oct. 2001) British dance writer and critic. Dance critic of the *Observer* from 1948 to 1955 and of the *Sunday Times* (1959–75), also founder of the influential magazine *Ballet* (1939–52). He organized the Diaghilev exhibition in Edinburgh in 1954, to commemorate the 25th anniversary of the impresario's death. Author of *Adventures of a Ballet Critic* (London, 1953), *In Search of Diaghilev* (London, 1955), *Modern Ballet Design* (London, 1955), *Nijinsky* (London, 1971), *Diaghilev* (London, 1979) and *Buckle at the Ballet* (London, 1980).

Bugaku Ballet in one act with choreography by Balanchine, music by Toshiro Mayuzumi, scenery and lighting by David Hays, and costumes by Barbara Karinska. Premiered 20 Mar. 1963 by New York City Ballet, City Center, New York, with Kent and Villella. The ballet, in three parts, enacts the ritualistic coupling of its leading dancers and was inspired by Japanese court dancers, whom Balanchine had seen in New York. Later performed by Dance Theatre of Harlem (1975) and Royal Ballet, Covent Garden (1988).

Buirge, Susan (*b* Minneapolis, 1940) US-French dancer, choreographer, and company director. She studied at the Juilliard School and with Alwin Nikolais and Murray Louis, dancing with Nikolais Dance Theater (1963–8) and Murray Louis Dance Company (1963–8). In 1968 she created the multi-media work *Televanilla* and in 1970 moved to France, where she became influential in the development of French New Dance. In 1975 she founded Dance Theater Susan Buirge, later renamed Susan Buirge Project, for which she created a series of conceptual and site specific works. She was additionally artistic consultant of the Aix Dance Festival (1980–6). After retiring

from the stage in 1990 she worked in Japan and was then artist in residence at the Arsenal Theatre in Metz, France, from 1997. Her recent work, including *Soli* (2005), has focused on Oriental themes and imagery.

Bujones, Fernando (*b* Miami, 9 Mar. 1955; *d* Miami, 10 Nov. 2005) US dancer. He studied with Alonso in Cuba and at the School of American Ballet (from 1967), making his debut with the Eglevsky Ballet in 1970 and joining American Ballet Theatre in 1972. He won the gold medal at Varna in 1974 (the first American to do so) and became a principal in 1974. He left ABT in 1985 (although returned in 1990 as a permanent guest artist) and pursued an internationally successful career as a guest artist. He appeared with companies in N. and S. America, Europe, and Japan as well as with the Bolshoi (1987) and was a regular guest with the Boston Ballet. He also appeared in the film *The Turning Point* (1978). A prodigiously talented dancer, he owed his stardom to his bravura technique and self-confidence. 'Baryshnikov has the publicity, I have the talent,' he was quoted as saying after winning Varna, although his rivalry with Baryshnikov at ABT eventually led to his departure from that company. He created roles in Tharp's *Bach Partita* (1984) and Béjart's *Trois études pour Alexandre* (1987). He published his autobiography, *Fernando Bujones*, in Rio de Janeiro in 1984. He made his final appearance with ABT in 1995; following his retirement from the stage he worked as a freelance teacher and choreographer, mainly in the US before being appointed director of Orlando Ballet in 2000, where he remained until his premature death.

bulerias A component of Spanish flamenco. It is usually danced at the end of flamenco performances. The dances are rapidly executed, with mime and elements of humour. Also called *chuflas* (boasting).

Bull, Adam (*b* Melbourne, 18 Aug. 1981) Australian dancer. He studied at the Australian Ballet School and graduated into the company in 2002, where he was promoted to principal in 2008. An elegant technician, and natural danseur noble, he went on to dance lead roles in most of the 19th-century classics, but also roles in works by Balanchine, Kylián, Murphy, Wheeldon, Stephen Baynes, and Stanton Welch.

Bull, Deborah (*b* Derby, 22 Mar. 1963) British dancer and director. She trained at the Royal Ballet School and won the 1980 Prix de Lausanne. She joined the Royal Ballet at Covent Garden in 1981, was promoted to principal in 1992 and became noted for her performances in ballets by MacMillan and Forsythe. After retiring from the Royal in 2001 she became artistic director of

ROH2, the organization supporting new and small-scale productions at the Royal Opera House. She has written several books, including *Dancing Away* (1998) and made numerous appearances on radio and television as a presenter of dance-related programmes.

Burgmüller, Friedrich (*b* Regensburg, 4 Dec. 1806; *d* Beaulieu, France, 13 Feb. 1874) German composer. He wrote *La Péri* for Coralli (1843), *Lady Henriette, ou la servante de Greenwich* for Mazilier (with F. von Flotow, 1844), and most famously the music for the Peasant pas de deux, in the first production of *Giselle* (1841).

Burlaka, Yuri (*b* Moscow, 1968) Russian dancer, choreographer, academic, and director. He studied at the Moscow Ballet School, graduating in 1986 into the Russian Ballet Company. Between 1993 and 1996, and in 2003, he additionally studied at the choreographic faculty of the Russian Academy of Theatre Arts, working as teacher and repetiteur until 2009 when he succeeded *Ratmansky as artistic director of the Bolshoi.

He has worked extensively on reconstructions of historic repertory, including works by Fokine (including dances from the opera *Ruslan and Ludmila*), Gorsky (*The Humpbacked Horse* and dances from *Samson et Dalila*), Petipa (*Harlequinade, Halte de Cavalerie, Naiade et le Pecheur, The Humpbacked Horse, Esmeralda*), and the Legat brothers (*The Fairy Doll*). He collaborated with Ratmansky on *Le Corsaire* (2007) for the Bolshoi and for the same company also staged *Paquita Grand Pas* (2008).

He is author of several books, including *the Ballet Repertoire of the 18th–20th Centuries* (2007).

Burra, Edward (*b* London, 1905; *d* Rye, 1976) British painter and ballet designer. He studied at the Chelsea School of Art and the Royal College of Art. Among the ballets he designed are *Rio Grande* (Ashton, 1932), *Don Juan* (Ashton, 1948), *Barabau* (de Valois, 1936), *Don Quixote* (de Valois, 1950), and *Miracle in the Gorbals* (Helpmann, 1944).

Burrow, The Ballet in one act with choreography and libretto by MacMillan, music by F. Martin, and designs by Georgiadis. Premiered 2 Jan. 1958, by the Royal Ballet, Covent Garden, with Heaton, Britton, Seymour, and MacLeary. The ballet deals with a group of people hiding in a small room from an unspecified threat. Parallels with *The Diary of Anne Frank* are often drawn, although MacMillan himself rejected the connection. It was the first ballet to bring the young Lynn Seymour to prominence.

Burrows, Jonathan (*b* Bishop Auckland, 23 Mar. 1960) British dancer, choreographer, and director. He studied at the Royal Ballet School

(from 1970) and danced with the Royal Ballet from 1979 to 1991, promoted to soloist in 1986. At Covent Garden he excelled in character roles. In 1988 he founded his own company, the Jonathan Burrows Group, which was initially supported by the Royal Ballet but after 1992 was fully independent. His early style was influenced by English folk dance which he taught at the Royal Ballet School (1979–84), his more recent work has involved a rigorous deconstruction of movement and rhythm, often to witty effect. Burrows's works for his own company included *Hymns* (1988), *dull morning, cloudy mild* (1989), *Stoics* (1991), *Very* (1992), *Our* (1994), and *The Stop Quartet* (1996). He also choreographed works for Sadler's Wells Royal Ballet (*Catch* and *The Winter Play*) and the Frankfurt Ballet (*Walking/music*, 1997). In 2000 he disbanded his company, since when he has collaborated with other performers, notably Matteo Fargion, with whom he has created three duets, *Both Sitting Duet* (2002), *Quiet Dance* (2005), and *Speaking Dance* (2006). He has taught widely including at de *Keersmaeker's school P.A.R.T.S. and Royal Holloway, University of London.

Bussell, Darcey (*b* London, 27 Apr. 1969) British dancer. She trained at the Royal Ballet School (1982–7), won the Prix de Lausanne in 1986, and joined Sadler's Wells Royal Ballet in 1987. The following year, still in the corps de ballet, she was famously chosen by Kenneth MacMillan to create the leading role in his full-length ballet, *The Prince of the Pagodas*. After its Covent Garden premiere, on 7 Dec. 1989 she was immediately promoted to principal. A tall, long-limbed dancer, Bussell broke the mould of the 'traditional' British ballerina with the athleticism and scale of her movement. Admired by audiences and critics alike, she became the first British ballerina since Fonteyn to achieve international stardom outside the dance world, thanks in part to her celebrity as a fashion model and her exposure on television. As a dancer, she was particularly acclaimed for her Aurora, Odette-Odile, and Cinderella, although she also excelled in the Balanchine repertoire and was invited several times to perform with New York City Ballet—a company considered by some to have been her natural home. In 1998 she guested with the Kirov Ballet, dancing *La Bayadère* with Igor Zelensky. She created roles in Bintley's *Spirit of Fugue* (1988), MacMillan's *Prince of the Pagodas* (1989) and *Winter Dreams* (1991), Page's *Bloodlines* (1990), Tharp's *Mr Worldly Wise* (1995), Christopher Wheeldon's *Pavane pour une infante défunte* (1996), *Tryst* (2002), and *DGV* (2006), and Tetley's *Amores* (1997), among others. In 2007 she retired from the Royal but continued to dance in occasional productions including *Viva La Diva*—a dance and music revue which she performed with singer Katherine Jenkins.

Butcher, Rosemary (*b* Bristol, 4 Feb. 1947) British choreographer, teacher and director. She studied dance at *Dartington College (1965–8) and at the University of Maryland (1968–9), after which further studies in New York with Elaine Summers and Yvonne Rainier (1970–2) brought her into contact with the Judson Church movement. She founded her own company in London in 1975 and was resident choreographer at London's Riverside Studios (1977–8). One of the leading minimalist choreographers of her generation her works have been informed by her interest in the visual arts and architecture, frequently performed in art galleries and utilizing art installations and film. A list of her works includes *Anchor Relay* (1977), *Traces* (1982), *The Site* (1983), *Flying Lines* (1985), *Touch the Earth* (1987), *Body as Site* (1993), *After the Last Sky* (1996), *Fractured Landscape, Fragmented Narratives* (1997), *White* (2004), *Woman and Memory* (2005). Butcher has taught widely including at Dartington College (1969–70, 1980–1), and the University of Surrey (1994–7). Visiting fellow of the Royal College of Art, London (1995–7).

Butler, John (*b* Greenwood, Miss., 29 Sept. 1918; *d* New York, 11 Sept. 1993) US dancer, choreographer, and director. He studied at the Graham School and at the School of American Ballet before dancing with the Martha Graham company (1945–55) and appearing in musicals and on television. In 1944 he appeared on Broadway dancing the lead role of Dream Curly in Agnes de Mille's *Oklahoma!* ballet. He founded his own company in 1955 (later renamed American Dance Theater), which toured Europe until it disbanded in 1961. He was one of the first dancemakers to marry classical ballet and modern dance and as well as creating works for his own company he choreographed for Broadway, New York City Opera, Alvin Ailey American Dance Theater, Australian Ballet, American Ballet Theatre, Batsheva Dance Company, Harkness Ballet, Metropolitan Opera, New York City Ballet, Nederlands Dans Theater, Paris Opera Ballet, Pennsylvania Ballet, and the Royal Winnipeg Ballet. His works include *The Unicorn, the Gorgon and the Manticore* (1956), created for Menotti and later taken into the repertoire of New York City Ballet, *Carmina Burana* (1959) for New York City Opera and revived for over 30 other companies, *After Eden* (mus. Lee Hoiby, 1967), for the Harkness Ballet, and *Portrait of Billie*, choreographed for Carmen de Lavallade and himself for the Newport Jazz Festival (1960) and taken into the repertoire of the Ailey company in 1974. At the Spoleto Festival in 1975 he choreographed *Medea* for Fracci and Baryshnikov, the first new work created for the Russian following his defection to the West and revived for ABT (1976). He was dance director for Menotti's annual Spoleto festival, and choreographed Menotti's television opera, *Amahl and the Night Visitors*, in 1951. He also choreographed for television and for ice shows. A noted teacher, he counted Lar Lubovitch and Glen Tetley among his pupils.

butoh An expressionist contemporary dance form which originated in Japan in the late 1950s. It was pioneered by choreographers such as Tatsumi Hijikata, Kazuo Ohno, and Kasai Akira. The first recorded butoh performance was Hijikata's *Kinjiki* in 1959. Although Hijikata stresses the spiritual imperative in butoh, the form is most readily identified by its physical appearance: the white painted faces, shaved heads, and nakedness of its performers and the distorted shapes of its slow-moving choreography. Companies such as Sankai Juku have added a designer sheen to butoh perfomances and attracted a new international audience.

Byrd, Donald (*b* New London, NC, 21 Jul. 1949) US dancer, choreographer and teacher. He was educated at Yale University (1967–8), Tufts University (1968–73), Cambridge School of Ballet (1969–73), London School of Contemporary Dance (1972), and the Alvin Ailey American Dance Center (1976). He danced with Twyla Tharp, Karole Armitage, and Gus Solomons junior before forming his own company, Donald Byrd/The Group, in 1978. Originally based in Los Angeles this moved to New York in 1983 and Byrd created more than 80 works for it including *Prodigal* (1991), *The Minstrel Show* (1991), *Drastic Cuts* (1992), *Bristle* (1993), *Life Situations: Daydreams on Giselle* (1995), *The Beast* (1996), *Still* (1996), and *Jazz Train* (1998). Many of his works deal with issues of racism, and in 1996 he choreographed *The Harlem Nutcracker*, set to David Berger's rearrangement (and expansion) of Duke Ellington and Billy Strayhorn's jazz version of Tchaikovsky's *Nutcracker Suite*. In 2002 he was forced to disband his company for financial reasons but in the same year was appointed choreographer and director for Spectrum Dance Theatre in Seattle for which he has since choreographed many works including *Bhangra Fever* (2007). He has also created works for many other companies including Alvin Ailey (*Shards*, 1988 and *Fin de siècle*, 1997), Pacific Northwest Ballet (*Capricious Night*, 1998 and *In the Courtyard*, 1999), and Ohio Ballet (*Ellington Phantasia*, 1999) while additionally choreographing for opera including John Adams's *I Was Looking at the Ceiling and Then I Saw the Sky* (1995); New York City Opera's *Carmina Burana* (1997); San Francisco Opera's *Aida* (1997), and Seattle Opera's *Julius Caesar*. In 2005 he choreographed the Broadway musical *The Color Purple*. Professor of Dance, California Institute for the Arts (1976–82).

cabriole In ballet a leaping step, usually performed by male dancers, in which stretched legs are beaten together in the air. The term derives from the Latin word *capra*, meaning goat; thus cabriole represents the leap of a goat. A well-known example occurs in the male variation in Act II of *Giselle*.

cachucha Spanish dance in 3/4 or 3/8 time, originally performed as a couple dance. In the mid-19th century the dance, in its solo form, was particularly associated with the Austrian ballerina Fanny Elssler, who in 1836 performed and choreographed her own arrangement of it in Coralli's *Le Diable boîteux*. This was notated by F. A. Zorn and recreated in 1967 for the Royal Ballet's Ballet for All group, danced by Philippa Heale. In 1981 it was filmed as *Fanny Elssler's Cachucha* with Margaret Barbieri.

Cage, John (*b* Los Angeles, 5 Sept. 1912; *d* New York, 12 Aug. 1992) US composer. He collaborated with Merce Cunningham over a period of 50 years and played a central role in the creative life of the latter's company. A radically experimental composer who rejected both harmony and traditional instrumentation, he began working with Cunningham in 1942, becoming music director of his company when it was formed in 1953. Cage wrote many scores for Cunningham, although in accordance with his, then, avant-garde principles, the music and choreography were created in isolation from one another, coming together only at the moment of performance and creating connections of phrasing, rhythm, and tone only by chance. A list of dance works which Cage composed for Cunningham, or for which Cunningham used his music, includes *Root of an Unfocus* (1944), *Four Walls* (1944), *The Seasons* (1947), *Sixteen Dances for Soloist and Company of Three* (1951), *Suite for Two* (1958), *Antic Meet* (1958), *Music with Dancers* (1960), *Aeon* (1961), *Field Dances* (1963), *Museum Event no. 1 and 2* (1964 marked the beginning of what became a series), *How to Pass, Kick, Fall and Run* (1965), *Second Hand* (1970), *Un jour ou deux* (Paris Opera, 1973), *Roaratorio* (1983), *Points in Space* (1986), and *Beach Birds* (1991). Other choreographers to use his scores include Preljocaj in

Empty Moves (set to the performance score *Empty Words*, 2004). Cage was author of *Silence* (Middletown, Conn., 1961), *A Year from Monday* (Middletown, Conn., 1967), *M* (Middletown, Conn., 1972), *Empty Words* (Middletown, Conn., 1980), and *For the Birds* (Boston, 1981).

Cage, The Ballet in one act with choreography and libretto by Robbins, music by Stravinsky (his Concerto in D), set and lighting by Rosenthal, and costumes by Ruth Sobotka. Premiered 14 Jun. 1951 by New York City Ballet at City Center, New York, with Kaye, Magallanes, Mounsey, and Maule. A group of predatory females castrate and kill two male intruders after mating with them. It has been revived by several companies including Birmingham Royal Ballet (1996), San Francisco Ballet (1998), and Australian Ballet (2008).

Cahusac, Louis de (*b* Montauban, 1700 (or 6 Apr. 1706); *d* Paris, 22 Jun. 1759) French ballet librettist, dance historian, and theorist on dance. He wrote the librettos for many opera ballets at the Académie Royale (the Paris Opera) from 1743 to 1759, collaborating with the composer Rameau on *Les Fêtes de Polymnie* (1745), *Les Fêtes de l'Hymen et de l'Amour* (1747), *Zaïs* (1748), *Naïs* (1749), *Zoroastre* (1749), and *La Naissance d'Osiris* (1754). In 1754 he published his three-volume treatise *La Danse ancienne et moderne, ou traité historique sur la danse*, in which he made the case for emphasizing dramatic structure and realism. In this he was a precursor of *Noverre.

cakewalk A syncopated, strutting male dance of African-American origin, popular in the US during the 19th century. It was widely performed by slaves for the entertainment of their owners, and derived its name from the fact that a piece of cake would be given as a reward to the dancer who performed with greatest virtuosity and imagination. At the end of the 19th century it was taken up by performers in minstrel shows and vaudeville. In 1951 New York City Ballet performed a work of the same name, choreographed by Ruthanna Boris, and with music by L. M. Gottschalk (arr. H. Kay), that was a parody of the old-fashioned minstrel show. Its finale was a cakewalk for the entire cast.

Calegari, Maria (*b* New York, 30 Mar. 1957) US dancer. She studied locally and from 1971 at the School of American Ballet, a pupil of Danilova. In 1974 she joined New York City Ballet becoming principal in 1983. A versatile dancer, she danced lead roles in numerous Balanchine and Robbins works, also creating roles in Martins's *Histoire du soldat* (1981); Robbins's *Piano Pieces* (1981), Gershwin *Concerto* (1982), *Glass Pieces* (1983), *Eight Lines* (1985), and *Ives Songs* (1988); in Tharp and Robbins's *Brahms/Handel* (1984); and in LaFosse's *Waltz Trilogy* (1991). She left the company in 1994, teaching at various institutions, including her own school in Connecticut between 2002 and 2004, and giving occasional performances, her last in 2004. She has also worked for the Balanchine Trust since 1996 and the Robbins Rights Trust since 2003, staging those two choreographers' ballets around the world.

She has made several television appearances and married to dancer Bart Cook.

Camargo, Marie (orig. Marie-Anne de Cupis de Camargo; baptized in Brussels, 15 Apr. 1710; *d* Paris, 28 Apr. 1770) French dancer of Spanish and Italian descent. One of the most celebrated and influential ballerinas in history. Born the daughter of Ferdinand Joseph de Cupis, the aristocratic Italian who was dancing master in Brussels, she made her debut in Brussels but continued her studies with Prévost and Blondy in Paris to become a member of the Paris Opera in 1726. Here she was the first ballerina to exhibit a virtuosity that rivalled male dancers and, on one occasion, famously executed an entirely improvised solo to cover for a male colleague's missed entrée. For eight years she enjoyed a fierce rivalry with the more graceful and poetic Sallé which ended when Camargo retired in 1734 to the country chateau of her lover, Louis de Bourbon, Comte de Clermont. In 1740 she returned to the stage to dance in 78 ballets, and reaffirm her position as queen of the Paris Opera. When she retired in 1751 she was granted the largest pension ever given to a dancer. She was possessed of a brilliant batterie and changed public perceptions about the way women should dance. Not only did she perform steps hitherto considered the exclusive province of the male—like cabrioles and entrechats—she also shortened the traditional skirt of the ballerina to just above the ankle to facilitate her movements, and ensure that the public could see her brilliant footwork. She was one of the stars of 18th-century ballet, who additionally influenced the fashions of the day, and inspired several culinary creations including Filet de Bœuf Camargo, Soufflé Camargo, and Bombe Camargo. Petipa choreographed *Camargo*, a ballet in her honour, in St Petersburg (1872). Enrico de Leva and Charles Lecocq wrote operas about her. In 1930 the Camargo Society was founded in London.

Camargo Society, The A group founded in London in 1930 to advance the development of British ballet by staging productions and nurturing the talents of UK dancers and choreographers. The brainchild of *Haskell and *Richardson, it provided a platform for such key British choreographers as Ashton, de Valois, and Tudor. Its first subscription performance was on 19 Oct. 1930 at the Cambridge Theatre. Ballets by de Valois (*Danse sacrée et danse profane*), and Ashton (*Pomona*) were included on the debut programme. Dancers were drawn from the schools of Rambert and de Valois, and the society recruited established stars such as Markova, Lopokova, Spessivtseva, and Dolin. Its subscribers included leading figures of British intellectual society. Like Diaghilev, the directors aimed to collaborate with contemporary painters and composers, commissioning designs from Duncan Grant and scores from Constant *Lambert among others. The society staged the first British productions of *Giselle* and *Swan Lake*, Act II. Among new British ballets to be premiered were de Valois's *Job* (1931), and *La Création du monde* (1931), Ashton's *Façade* (1931), and Tudor's *Adam and Eve* (1932). After two gala performances at Covent Garden, the society was dissolved in 1933. Many of its ballets were given to the Vic-Wells Ballet.

Campra, André (*b* Aix-en-Provence, baptized 4 Dec. 1660; *d* Versailles, 29 Jun. 1744) French composer. As chef d'orchestre royale et directeur des pages de musique, a post he took up in 1723, he wrote about 25 ballets and ballet operas for the Paris Opera, including *Les Ages* (1718) and *Les Amours de Mars et de Vénus* (1712). His 1699 ballet, *Le Carnaval de Venise*, was revived for the Aix-en-Provence Festival in 1975 with choreography by Schmucki.

Canada The first ballet company to be established in Canada was the *Royal Winnipeg Ballet, which gave its initial performances in 1939 on a semi-professional basis. The war disrupted further activity but from the late 1940s schools throughout the country sent troupes to perform in the Canadian Ballet Festival (1948–54) and in 1951 the *National Ballet of Canada, closely modelled on Sadler's Wells Ballet, was formed in Toronto by Celia *Franca. The following year Les *Grands Ballets Canadiens was established in Montreal. These three companies were to dominate Canadian ballet, with the Toronto-based company focused on a European and classical repertory and the Winnipeg and Montreal companies nurturing Canadian choreographers. Up until the 1970s Canadian ballet dancers like Lynn *Seymour and Jennifer *Penney found greater opportunities abroad, but a younger generation, led by Veronica *Tennant, Frank *Augustyn, and, especially, Karen *Kain, gave Canada its first home-based ballet stars, many of them trained at the National Ballet School, founded by Franca and Oliphant in 1959. Several regional ballet companies have been founded in the wake of the three main companies including Alberta Ballet, established in 1968, and Ballet British Columbia, established 1986.

Canada's thriving modern dance scene emerged in the 1960s, with the formation of Winnipeg Contemporary Dancers in 1964; La Groupe de la Place Royale in 1967; *Toronto Dance Theatre in 1968; and Anna Wyman Dance Theatre in Vancouver in 1971. Later companies were developed by Édouard *Lock, Robert Desrosiers, Margie *Gillis, Danny *Grossman, and Crystal *Pite. Through its international dance festival (Festival International de Nouvelle Danse), Montreal has become one of the most important centres for modern dance in the world as well as base to other companies like Ballets Jazz de Montreal (BJM) founded in 1972, O Vertigo, founded in 1984, and Compagnie Marie Chouinard (founded 1990).

Canada, National Ballet of *See* NATIONAL BALLET OF CANADA.

canary A jaunty toe-tapping dance in 3/4 or 6/8 time. It is similar to the jig and the gigue. It probably originated in the Canary Islands; hence its name. Its first recorded appearance in European dance history was in Fabritio Caroso's dance manual *Il ballarino* (1581). The first musical examples of canaries are found in the harpsichord suites of Couperin and de Chambonnières. The dance is mentioned in Shakespeare's *All's Well That Ends Well*: 'Make you dance Canary with sprightly fire and motion.'

can-can Famous for its licentious connotations, the dance nonetheless had its origins in the chahut, a decorous social dance invented by Monsieur Masarié in 1830. Within fifteen years it had moved into the French music halls where it emphasized such an immodest display of leg and undergarment that it was eventually banned by the authorities. An exhilarating, high-kicking dance in 2/4 time it was featured in Offenbach operas, most notably in *Orpheus in the Underworld*, and immortalized in Toulouse-Lautrec's drawings of dancers at the Moulin Rouge. In ballet, it can be found as the climax to two of Massine's best-known works, *Boutique fantasque* and *Gaîté parisienne*. It was also the subject of the 1953 Broadway musical *Can-Can*.

Canfield Modern dance with choreography by Cunningham, music by Pauline Oliveros, sets by Robert Morris, and costumes (uncredited) by Jasper Johns. Premiered 4 Mar. 1969 by the Merce Cunningham Dance Company, at Nazareth College in Rochester, New York, with Cunningham, C. Brown, Sandra Neels, Setterfield, Meg Harper, Susana Hayman-Chaffey, Jeff Slayton, Chase Robinson, and Mel Wong. The piece takes its title from the card game canfield, a type of solitaire named after Richard Canfield. A full-length, plotless work for nine dancers, which is divided into twenty-six sections, thirteen 'hands', and thirteen 'deals'.

Cao, Chi (*b* Shan Xi, 22 Mar. 1978) Chinese dancer. He trained at the Beijing Dance Academy and the Royal Ballet School, joining Birmingham Royal Ballet in 1995 and promoted to principal in 2002. He performs much of the 19th-century repertory, often partnering Nao Sakuma, but has also danced in works by Tharp, Ashton, MacMillan, Bintley, and others. His created roles include Bintley's *The Seasons* (2001) and *Concert Fantasy* (2002) and Oliver Hindle's *Bright Young Things* (1997). He starred as the Chinese dancer Li Cunxin in the 2009 film *Mao's Last Dancer*. He won the gold medal at Varna, 1998.

Cape Town City Ballet Ballet company based in Cape Town, South Africa. It originated from University of Cape Town Ballet Company, founded by Dulcie *Howes in 1934 with students from the UCT Ballet School performing with guest professionals. In 1963 this became CAPAB Ballet, a dramatically enlarged company funded by the Cape Performing Arts Board, and directed between 1967 and 1990 by David *Poole. Poole added many ballets of his own to the repertoire and for many years Phyllis *Spira was its leading ballerina. Frank Staff was also resident choreographer until his death in 1971. A classically based company, it also had ballets by Cranko, de Valois, Ashton, Bournonville, and Jooss in its repertoire. Guest artists who danced with the company include Fonteyn and Fracci. In 1991 Veronica *Paeper took over as artistic director, a prolific choreographer who made many original full-length works for the company and led it on several international tours. In 1997 CAPAB lost its state funding and changed its name to Cape Town City Ballet. Financial cutbacks required it to reduce dancer numbers to 24 and slim its repertory. In 2005 Paeper retired and was replaced by Keith Mackintosh as overall director. In 2008 the company's dancer and choreographer Robin van Wyk was promoted to artistic director alongside Mackintosh. The company continues to perform many works by Paeper, also new ballets by choreographers such as van Wyk and Sean Bovim.

SEE WEB LINKS
• Website for Cape Town City Ballet

capoeira A stylized martial-art dance originating from Brazilian slave culture, which is characterized by acrobatic fighting manœuvres and athletic dance steps. It has been designated as a national sport in Brazil, where it is taught in schools and performed, especially in festivals, as a contest between combatants. Once performed exclusively by men, it is now also danced by women and has exerted a considerable influence on modern dance in Europe and the US, where it was introduced in 1975.

Capriccio espagnol Ballet in one act with choreography by Massine in collaboration with Argentinita, libretto by Massine, music by Rimsky-Korsakov, and designs by Mariano Andreu. Premiered 4 May 1939 by the Ballet Russe de Monte Carlo, Monte Carlo, with Argentinita, Massine, Danilova, and Panaieff. A plotless Spanish-flavoured work involving five dances and four characters: a fortune-teller, a gypsy boy, a country girl, and a peasant. It was filmed in 1941 as *Spanish Fiesta*. Fokine choreographed a version for his own company in New York in 1924, *Olé Toro*.

Capriol Suite Ballet in one act with choreography by Ashton, music by Peter Warlock, and designs by William Chappell. Premiered 25 Feb. 1930 by Rambert Dancers at the Lyric Theatre, London, with Howard, Gould, Turner, Ashton, and Chappell. Although Warlock's music is taken from the airs in Arbeau's *Orchésographie*, Ashton gave the original French dances (including the pavane and the branle) an English Elizabethan setting. This was Ashton's first important ballet and was danced by Rambert for many years; later it was taken into the repertoire of the Vic-Wells Ballet (1938).

Capucilli, Terese (*b* Syracuse, NY, 1956) US dancer. She studied in Syracuse with Augustine and Boughton, gained a BA in Fine Arts at the State University of New York, and later studied at the Jacob's Pillow School in Massachusetts, and with Maggie Black in New York winning a scholarship to the Martha Graham School. After dancing with Kazuko Hirabayashi Dance Theater and Marcus Skulkind Dance Company she joined the Martha Graham company in 1979 where she remained until 2004 as its leading dancer and eventually its co-director. With her intense, heroically scaled stage presence Capucilli was the natural inheritor of Graham's own roles, taking over 25 of them as well as creating new roles in *The Rite of Spring* (The Chosen One, 1984), *Temptations of the Moon* (1986), and *Maple Leaf Rag* (Woman, 1990), and in the reconstructions of *Salem Shore*

(1992) and *Sketches from Chronicle* (1994). The 1937 solo *Deep Song* was reconstructed for her in 1988 and in 1993 Tharp choreographed a lead role for her in *Demeter and Persephone* (created for the Graham company). After Graham's death Capucilli became actively involved in the research and reconstruction of the choreographer's early works, however after the company's reorganization in 2004 she left and became a performer with the Buglisi Dance Company.

Caracalla Dance Theatre Lebanese company founded in 1970 by Abdel-Halim Caracalla. Surviving the on-going hostilities in the region it has managed to travel extensively in Europe and North America performing works by Caracalla such as *Taming of the Shrew* (1982), *Midsummer Night's Dream* (1990), and *Knights of the Moon* (2007) that have fused Western contemporary and traditional Middle Eastern dance.

Carlson, Carolyn (*b* Oakland, Calif., 7 Mar. 1943) US dancer, choreographer and director. She studied at Utah University, at the San Francisco Ballet School, and with Alwin Nikolais, with whom she danced (1965–71). She then moved to Paris, and performed and choreographed for companies in France, Germany, and Italy. From 1973 to 1980 she was danseuse étoile chorégraphique at the Paris Opera, where she founded the Groupe de Recherches Théâtrales de l'Opéra. For Paris she made *Densité, 21.5* (mus. Varèse), *L'Or des fous* (mus. G. Arrigo), and *Les Fous d'or* (mus. I. Wakhevitch, 1973), *Sablier prison* (mus. various), *Il y'a juste un instant* (mus. Barre Phillips, 1974), and *Wind, Water, Sand* (1976). She also created the leading role in Tetley's *Tristan* (Paris Opera, 1974). She directed her own group at the Teatro la Fenice in Venice (1980–5), where she played an important role in encouraging younger choreographers, then returned to Paris in the mid-1980s, where she similarly exerted a significant influence on the modern dance scene. She subsequently created work for the Folkwang Ballet in Essen, Nederlands Dans Theater and the Finnish National Ballet. Between 1993–5 she was artistic director of Cullberg Ballet, then worked largely as a solo artist, performing both choreographed and improvised material, while additionally creating work for other companies, including *Signes* (1997, Paris Opera Ballet). In 1999 she founded her own studio in Paris, as a centre for international teachers, then in 2005 was appointed director of the Choreographic Centre in Roubaix Nord Pas de Calais (*Ballet du Nord) for which she has since choreographed several works including *Full Moon* (2006). Between 1999 and 2002 she directed the Dance section of the Venice Biennale, during which time she founded the city's dance academy, Isola Danza.

Carmen Ballet in one act with choreography and libretto by Petit, music by Bizet, and designs by Antonio Clavé. Premiered 21 Feb. 1949 by the Ballet de Paris, Prince's Theatre (now Shaftesbury Theatre), London, with Jeanmaire, Petit, Perrault, and Hamilton. The ballet, based on the famous Bizet opera, caused a sensation at its debut, not least because of Petit's erotically charged choreography, especially the bedroom pas de deux he created for Jeanmaire and himself as Don José. Petit revived the ballet for several other companies, including the Royal Danish Ballet in 1960 and the Paris Opera in 1990. The ballet was captured on film, in *Black Tights* (1960). Other choreographers who have created versions of the story include Petipa (*Carmen et son torero*, Madrid, 1845), Goleizovsky (Moscow, 1931), R. Page (*Guns and Castanets*, Chicago, 1939), Alberto Alonso (*Carmen*, mus. Shchedrin after Bizet, Moscow, 1967), Cranko (mus. W. Fortner and W. Steinbrenner after Bizet, Stuttgart, 1971), Mats Ek (mus. Shchedrin–Bizet, Cullberg Ballet, 1992, filmed 1994), T. Brandsen (mus., Shchedrin–Bizet, W. Australia, 2000), M. Bourne (*Car Man*, mus. Shchedrin–Bizet, London, 2000), Elo (mus, Shchedrin–Bizet, Boston, 2006) and Alston (mus, Shchedrin–Bizet, Scottish Ballet, 2009). Antonio Gades choreographed a flamenco version in 1983, which was filmed by Carlos Saura.

Carmina Burana Carl Orff's famous musical setting of bawdy medieval songs has inspired many choreographers. The first production was 8 Jun. 1937 in Frankfurt with choreography by Inge Härtling. Its many successors have included versions by Lizzie Maudrik (Berlin State Opera, 1941), Hanka (La Scala, Milan, 1942–3), Wigman (Leipzig, 1943), H. Rosen (Bavarian State Opera, Munich, 1959), Butler (New York City Opera, 1959, revived Nederlands Dans Theater, 1962, Pennsylvania Ballet, 1966, Alvin Ailey, 1973), Nault (Les Grands Ballets Canadiens, 1967), Darrell (Berlin Opera Ballet, 1968), Bintley (Birmingham Royal Ballet, 1995), Natalie Weir (Australian Ballet, 2001), S Welch (American Ballet Theatre, 2003), and Septime Webre (Washington Ballet, 2007).

Carnaval, Le Ballet in one act with choreography and libretto by Fokine, music by Schumann, orchestrated by Glazunov, Rimsky-Korsakov, Liadov, Tcherepnin, and Arensky, and designs by Bakst. Premiered 5 Mar. 1910, at the Pavlov Hall, St Petersburg, with Karsavina, Leontiev, Schollar, Nijinska, Nijinsky, and Meyerhold. The ballet was first seen at a charity ball in which the masked dancers of the Mariinsky Imperial Ballet had to appear anonymously because of contract restrictions. It is a series of dances for commedia dell'arte characters including Columbine, Harlequin, and Pierrot. The designs were inspired by the Viennese Biedermeyer period of 1840. Widely considered to be one of Fokine's early masterpieces, it was taken into the repertory of Diaghilev's Ballets Russes (who premiered it 20 May 1910 in Berlin) and was often revived by Fokine. In 1911, with new designs by Bakst, it entered the Mariinsky repertoire. Karsavina and Lopokova were famous Columbines, Nijinsky frequently danced Harlequin. It was revived for several British companies.

Carnival of Animals, The Ballet in one act with choreography and designs by Andrée Howard, music by Saint-Saëns. Premiered 26 Mar. 1943 by Ballet Rambert, at the Mercury Theatre, London, with Elisabeth Schooling, Gilmour, Harrold, and Holmes. A Victorian child meets the various animals in the composer's Grand Zoological Fantasy, although *Le Cygne*, the most famous of them, is not included. Many choreographers have also used the score, including Siobhan Davies (1982 for Second Stride, revised for Rambert Dance Company in 2008); Ratmansky (2003 for San Francisco Ballet); and Wheeldon (2003 for New York City Ballet).

Caroline Mathilde Ballet in two acts with choreography by Flemming Flindt, music by Peter Maxwell Davies, and designs by Jens-Jacob Worsaae. Premiered 14 Mar. 1991 by the Royal Danish Ballet at the Royal Theatre, Copenhagen, with Rose Gad in the title role. It tells the story of the disastrous marriage between the 15-year-old English princess Caroline Mathilde and the 17-year-old Danish king, the epileptic and insane Christian VII. It was performed by the Royal Danish Ballet at Covent Garden in 1995.

Caron, Leslie (*b* Paris, 1 Jul. 1931) French-US dancer and actress. She studied at the Paris Conservatoire and made her debut in 1948 with the Ballets des Champs-Elysées. That same year she created the Sphinx in Lichine's *La Rencontre*. In 1951 she was hired by Gene Kelly for his film *An American in Paris*. Although she briefly returned to Petit's Ballet de Paris in 1954, dancing in his *La Belle au bois dormant* in London, she devoted the rest of her career to acting. Her Hollywood films include *Daddy Long Legs* (1954), opposite Fred Astaire, *Gigi* (1958), *Fanny* (1961), and *Father Goose* (1964). She also featured in the British film *The L-Shaped Room* (1963) and in Louis Malle's *Damage* (1992).

Carreño, Jose Manuel (*b* Havana, 25 May, 1968) Cuban dancer. He trained, from the age of 10, at the Provincial School of Ballet and the Cuban National Ballet School before graduating into the Cuban National Ballet. After winning competitions in America he moved to Britain, performing as principal dancer with English National Ballet (from 1990) and the Royal Ballet (from 1993). In 1995 he joined American Ballet Theatre where his technical virtuosity, classical style and exemplary partnering skills have been showcased in all of ABT's 19th-century repertory. He additionally dances in contemporary works including ballets by Robbins, Balanchine, Kylián, Tharp, and has created roles in several works including *Within You Without You* (chor. David Parsons, Ann Reinking, Natalie Weir, and Stanton Welch, 2002).

Carter, Alan (*b* London, 24 Dec. 1920) British dancer, choreographer, and ballet director. He studied with Astafieva and N. Legat and danced with the Vic-Wells Ballet (1937–41), where he created a principal role in Ashton's *Harlequin in the Street* (1938). He returned briefly to Sadler's Wells Theatre Ballet in 1946 after military service, when he choreographed his first ballet, *The Catch*. He also appeared in films, including *The Red Shoes*, *Tales of Hoffmann*, and *Invitation to the Dance*. He was director of several companies, including the St James Ballet, the London Empire Theatre Ballet, the Munich Ballet, Wuppertal, Bordeaux, Helsinki, and the Icelandic Ballet.

Carter, Jack (*b* Shrivenham, 8 Aug. 1923 (some sources say 1917); *d* London, 30 Dec. 1998) British dancer and choreographer. He studied at Sadler's Wells School and with Preobrajenska in Paris. He danced with Ballet Guild, Molly Lake's Continental Ballet, Original Ballet Russe, Ballet Rambert, and London Festival Ballet. As a choreographer he worked with Ballet der Lage Landen in Amsterdam (1954–7) for whom he made his most famous work, *The Witch Boy* (mus. L. Salzedo, 1956), additionally with other companies in Europe, S. America, and Japan. He was chief choreographer of London Festival Ballet (1965–70). A list of his works includes *Past Recalled* (mus. Bloch, 1953), *Love Knots* (mus. Hummel, arr. Salzedo, 1954), *The Life and Death of Lola Montez* (mus. Verdi, orch. Salzedo, 1954), *London Morning* (mus. Coward, 1959), *Agrionia* (mus. Salzedo, 1965), *Beatrix* (or *La Jolie Fille de Gand*, mus. Adam, Horovitz, 1966), *Cage of God* (mus. A. Rawsthorne, Western Theatre Ballet, 1967), *Pythoness Ascendant* (mus. Berio, 1973), *Three Dances to Japanese Music* (mus. Katada, Scottish Ballet, 1973), and *Lulu* (mus. Milhaud, Sadler's Wells Royal Ballet, 1976). He also staged versions of the classics including *Swan Lake* and *Coppélia*.

Casanova ballets Choreographers who have been inspired by the story of the famous 18th-century Italian adventurer Giacomo Girolamo Casanova include Laban (1923), Kröller (1929), Charrat

(*Casanova in London*, mus. W. Egk, Munich, 1969), and Preljocaj (*Casanova*, Paris Opera, 1998).

Castil-Blaze (orig. François-Henri-Joseph Blaze; *b* Cavaillon, 1 Dec. 1784; *d* Paris, 11 Dec. 1857) French ballet critic. From the early 1820s to 1832 his writings in the *Journal des débats* made him the leading ballet critic in Paris. Several of his works became standard reference works, among them *La Danse et le ballet depuis Bacchus jusqu'à Mlle Taglioni* (1832), *L'Académie Impériale de Musique . . . de 1645 à 1855* (published in three volumes, 1847–55); and *L'Opéra italien, 1548–1856* (Paris, 1856).

Castle, Irene and Vernon One of the most famous ballroom dancing couples in history. Vernon (*b* Norwich, UK, 2 May 1887; *d* Fort Benbrook, Tex., 15 Feb. 1918), Irene (*née* Foote, *b* New Rochelle, New York, 7 Apr. 1893; *d* Eureka Springs, Ark., 25 Jan. 1969). They married in 1911 and together performed in Europe and the US, especially renowned for their elegant interpretations of the Castle Walk, the Castle Polka, the Hesitation Waltz, and the Tango. Their joint career was cut short in 1918 when Vernon, an aerial photographer for the Royal Air Force, was killed in an air crash. Irene retired from dancing and wrote two books: *My Husband* (1919) and *Castles in the Air* (1958). In the 1939 film *The Story of Vernon and Irene Castle*, they were played by Fred Astaire and Ginger Rogers. Authors of *The Modern Dance* (1914).

Catá, Alfonso (*b* Havana, 3 Oct. 1937; *d* Tourcoing, France, 15 Sept. 1990) Cuban dancer, choreographer, and ballet director. He studied at the School of American Ballet in New York and went on to dance with many companies, including Petit, Joffrey, Grand Ballet du Marquis de Cuevas, Stuttgart Ballet, and New York City Ballet. He was director of the Geneva Ballet (1969–73), Frankfurt Ballet (1973–7), and the Baltimore Ballet (1980–1). In 1983 he became founding director of *Ballet du Nord and continued to direct the company until his death in 1990.

Catarina, ou La Fille du bandit Ballet in three acts with choreography and libretto by Perrot, music by Pugni, and designs by Charles Marshall. Premiered 3 Mar. 1846, at Her Majesty's Theatre, London, with Grahn, Gosselin, and Perrot. The ballet, said to be based on an incident in the life of the 17th-century Italian painter Salvatore Rosa, tells of Salvatore's love for Catarina, who is leader of a group of bandits. She, however, is also loved by her lieutenant, Diavolino. After several adventures, Catarina and Salvatore are happily united. Fanny Elssler enjoyed one of her biggest successes in the title role, in both Milan and St Petersburg.

Catherine Wheel, The A dance project destined for Broadway, with choreography by Twyla Tharp, music by David Byrne, sets and costumes by Santo Loquasto, and lighting by Jennifer Tipton. Premiered 22 Sept. 1981, by the Twyla Tharp Dance Company, at the Winter Garden Theater, New York. Described by Tharp, in her autobiography *When Push Comes to Shove*, as 'a full-length spectacle of the disintegration of family' the work was not a financial success and closed after a short Broadway run. However, the energetically charged final part, *The Golden Section*, survived as a one-act ballet in its own right and has been performed by several companies including Tharp's own (1983), Rambert Dance Company (1999), the Ailey company and Miami City Ballet (2006). Tharp adapted the entire ballet for television in 1983.

Cats Hit international musical based on the poems of T. S. Eliot (*Old Possum's Book of Practical Cats*) with music by Andrew Lloyd Webber, choreography by Gillian Lynne, and direction by Trevor Nunn. It opened in 1981 at the New London Theatre in London's West End and transferred to Broadway the following year, opening at the Winter Garden Theater on 7 Oct. 1982. On 19 June 1997 it became the longest-running show in Broadway history, and it was also the longest-running musical in London's West End, where it ran for 21 years.

Cavalry Halt, The One-act ballet with choreography by Marius Petipa and music by Johann Armsheirmer. Premiered in 1896 at the Mariinsky, St Petersburg with Legnani, M. Petipa, and P. Gerdt. A demi-caractère ballet, it tells the story of the comic and romantic shenanigans that occur when soldiers pause for rest and refreshment in a village. Later versions were by Clustine in 1898 and Shiryaev in 1919. It has recently been revived by the Mikhailovsky Ballet.

Cave of the Heart Modern dance in one act with choreography by Martha Graham, music by Samuel Barber, set by Isamu Noguchi, costumes by Edythe Gilfond, and lighting by Jean Rosenthal. Premiered 10 May 1946 by the Martha Graham company at the McMillin Theater, Columbia University, New York, with Graham, Hawkins, Yuriko, and O'Donnell. The choreography, rich in Jungian symbolism, is based on the legend of Medea and Jason. It was originally titled *Serpent Heart*, but became *Cave of the Heart* in 1947.

Cecchetti, Enrico (*b* Rome, 21 Jun. 1850; *d* Milan, 13 Nov. 1928) Italian dancer, choreographer, and ballet master. A renowned mime artist and one of the greatest teachers in the history of ballet, whose system of teaching, known as the Cecchetti method, is still used in schools around the world. He was born—in a theatre dressing-room—the son of two dancers and made his debut while only 5 years old in Genoa. He studied with Blasis' pupil Giovanni Lepri in Florence and made his La Scala debut in 1870 in *Gods from Valhalla*. He guested throughout Europe while still a dancer at La Scala (where he had been promoted to principal in 1885) and made his debut at the Mariinsky Theatre in St Petersburg in 1887 in Ivanov's *The Tulip of Haarlem*. A brilliant technician, he so impressed the Russians that he was appointed principal dancer and second ballet master to the Imperial Theatres. For a decade, from 1892, he taught at the school of the Imperial Theatres, where his pupils included Pavlova, Vaganova, Preobrajenska, Karsavina, Lopokova, Gorsky, Legat, Fokine, and Nijinsky. In 1902 he left to teach in Warsaw but returned to St Petersburg in 1906 to open a private school. In 1909 he was hired by Diaghilev as ballet master and character dancer for his new Ballets Russes company. Cecchetti remained with Diaghilev until 1918, creating several roles in ballets by Fokine and Massine. In 1918 he and his wife Giuseppina opened a ballet school in London, where his students included Rambert, de Valois, and Markova. He also ran the La Scala Ballet School in Milan (1925–8). In 1922 in London the Cecchetti Society was formed to preserve his system of teaching, and in 1924 it was incorporated into the Imperial Society of Teachers of Dancing. Among the roles he created were Carabosse and Blue Bird in *Sleeping Beauty* (1890), the Chief Eunuch in *Scheherazade* (1910), the Old Showman in *Petrushka* (1911), the Astrologer in *Le Coq d'or* (1914), the Shopkeeper in *La Boutique fantasque* (1919) and the Doctor in *Pulcinella* (1920). He made his last stage appearance in Milan in 1926, dancing the Old Showman. Although he choreographed some ballets, none have survived. He collaborated with Cyril Beaumont and Idzikowski on *A Manual of the Theory and Practice of Classical Theatrical Dancing: Cecchetti Method*, published in London in 1922.

Céleste, Madame (born Anastasie Céleste des Rousselles; *b* Marcilly-la-Campagne, 6 Aug. 1810; *d* Paris, 18 Feb. 1882) French dancer. She trained at the Paris Opera Ballet School and danced briefly with the Paris Opera. She toured the US extensively in the 1820s and 1830s and was much admired, presented to President Andrew Jackson in 1836 and credited with being the first ballerina to perform *La Sylphide* in America. Her fame rested more on her mime than her classical technique—in 1837 she was rejected by the Paris Opera—and one of her most successful roles was in the melodrama *The French Spy*. In 1843 she began a new career as a theatre manager, first at the Theatre Royal in Liverpool and then at the

Adelphi Theatre in London, which she co-managed with Benjamin Webster for fourteen years, presenting ballet burlesques. She subsequently managed the Lyceum Theatre in London. She made her farewell tour of the US in 1865-6 and retired from the stage in 1874 after appearing in *The Green Bushes*, another popular melodrama, in London.

Celis, Stijn (*b* 1964) Belgian dancer, choreographer, director, and set designer. He studied at the Stedelijk Ballet Institute in Antwerp and after completing military service in 1986 went on to dance with The Royal Ballet of Flanders, Zurich Ballet, Zurich Contemporary Dance, Geneva Ballet and Cullberg Ballet (1996-8). His first professional work *L'odeur de l'ombre* was choreographed in 1996 and taken into Cullberg's repertory in 1997, after which he created several more works for the company, including *Vertigo Maze* (2002) and *Sore Core* (2004). He has since choreographed for several companies including Ballet Gulbenkian, Les Grands Ballets Canadiens (*Les Noces*, 2002 and *The Lost Shoe*, 2007), Nederlands Dans Theater 2, Iceland Dance Theatre, also for Bern Ballet where he was artistic director (2004-2007). He has additionally trained as a set designer and created designs for dance (including works by Didy Veldman) as well as theatre and opera.

Cell Modern dance in one act with choreography by Robert Cohan, music by Ronald Lloyd, and designs by Norberto Chiesa. Premiered 11 Sept. 1969 at the Place Theatre, London. An abstract modern work for six dancers, it was created for the opening season of London Contemporary Dance Theatre. Its theme was society's suffocation of the individual and it became one of the most popular works in the LCDT repertoire.

Cendrillon See CINDERELLA.

Cent Baisers, Les (Eng. title *The Hundred Kisses*) Ballet in one act with choreography by Nijinska, libretto by Kochno, music by Frederic d'Erlanger, and set by J. Hugo. Premiered 18 Jul. 1935 by Colonel de Basil's Ballets Russes, at Covent Garden, London, with Baronova and Lichine. It is based on the Hans Christian Andersen fairytale about a swineherd, a princess, and a magic bowl.

Central Ballet of China See NATIONAL BALLET OF CHINA.

Cerrito, Fanny (*b* Naples, 11 May 1817; *d* Paris, 6 May 1909) Italian dancer. One of the most famous ballerinas of the Romantic era. She studied with Perrot, Blasis, and Saint-Léon, making her debut at the Teatro Regio in Naples in 1832. During the next twenty years she became a star throughout Europe, appearing in all the major capitals. In Vienna in 1841 she studied and performed with Arthur Saint-Léon, whom she married. A voluptuous, even erotic dancer, she was noted for her strength and fiery personality on stage. She created leading roles in *Alma ou La Fille de feu* (London, 1842), *Ondine* (London, 1843), *La Vivandière* (1844), and *Lalla Rookh* (London, 1846) and took part in the first productions of the *Pas de quatre* (London, 1845) and the *Le Jugement de Pâris* (London, 1846). Her marriage to Saint-Léon (who was also her dancing partner) broke up in 1851 when she became the mistress of the Marquis de Bedmar. From 1847 to 1854 she was at the Paris Opera, where she created title roles in Mazilier's *Orfa* (1852) and her own ballet *Gemma* (1854). In 1855 she appeared at Covent Garden and in 1856-7 at the Lyceum Theatre. In 1856 she took part in the celebrations in Moscow for Alexander II's coronation. While performing there she was struck by a piece of falling scenery, a fact which could have been instrumental in her decision to retire from the stage the following year. Ironically, for someone who had enjoyed such celebrity, her death in 1909 went unreported in the Paris press.

Chabukiani, Vakhtang (Chaboukiani) (*b* Tbilisi, 12 Mar. 1910; *d* Tbilisi, 5 Apr. 1992) Soviet dancer, choreographer, ballet master, and teacher. His early studies were with Maria Perrini in Tbilisi; then from 1926 he attended the Leningrad Ballet School. In 1929 he graduated into the *GATOB company (Kirov) and within two years became its leading soloist, a position he maintained until 1941. With his athletic, vigorous style, the Georgian-born dancer came to embody the Soviet ideal of heroic maleness, uninhibited and all-conquering. He created lead roles in many Soviet ballets, including Vainonen's, Jacobson's, and Chesnakov's *The Golden Age* (1930), Vainonen's *Flames of Paris* (1932) and *Partisans' Days* (1937), Zakharov's *Fountain of Bakhchisarài* (1934) and *Lost Illusions* (1936), and Lopukhov's *Taras Bulba* (1940). He also choreographed several of his own including *The Heart of the Hills* (mus. Andrei Balanchivadze, Kirov, 1938) and *Laurencia* (mus. A. Krein, 1939). In 1934 he toured the US, becoming, with Tatiana Vecheslova, the first Soviet dancer to do so. In 1941, after war forced the evacuation of many dancers from Leningrad, he returned to Tblisi, and for next 30 years he ran Tbilisi's Paliashvili opera house. There he choreographed and staged numerous works (many featuring powerful roles for himself), including *Othello* (mus. A. D. Matchavariani, 1957), *Poem-Ballet* (mus. Liszt and Gershwin, 1963), *Hamlet* (1971), and *The Demon* (mus. S. Sinadze, 1961), in which he took the title role at the age of 50. He retired from the stage in 1968. He did much to promote the cause of the male dancer in classical ballet, restaging the 19th-century repertoire in order to boost the function of the man beyond a mere partner. His 1947 production of *La Bayadère* for the Kirov (created with the help of his old teacher Ponamarev) completely redefined the part of Solor; indeed, the variations seen in most Russian productions now owe more to Chabukiani than to Petipa. His *Corsaire* is also part of the standard male repertoire. Chabukiani also featured prominently in Soviet ballet films, directing and dancing in *Masters of the Georgian Ballet* (1955) and *Othello* (1960), and appearing in *Stars of the Russian Ballet* (dancing in *Flames of Paris*, 1946). He taught extensively in the Soviet Union and abroad. People's Artist of the USSR, 1950; recipient Lenin Prize, 1958.

chaconne A dance in triple time, which probably originated in Spain (where it is known as the chacona). It began as a sensuous dance for a couple, but by the time it featured in the ballet de cour and the ballet operas of Lully and Rameau it had acquired a more modest refinement.

Chagall, Marc (*b* Vitebsk, 7 Jul. 1887; *d* St Paul de Vence, 28 Mar. 1985) Russian-French painter and designer. He designed Massine's *Aleko* (1942), Bolm's *The Firebird* (American Ballet Theatre, 1945) and Lifar's *Daphnis and Chloe* (1958). He also created the murals for the Metropolitan Opera House at Lincoln Center in New York. Légion d'honneur (1962).

chaîné [Fr., chained] A series of continuous turns on alternating feet in which the body rotates rapidly. The feet are kept as close together as possible.

Chalon, Alfred Édouard (*b* Geneva, 15 Feb. 1780; *d* London, 3 Oct. 1860) Swiss-British painter and illustrator. Much of what we know about the look of romantic ballet is owed to his lithographs and illustrations. He was Taglioni's portraitist and his 1845 lithograph of the *Pas de quatre*, with Carlotta Grisi, Marie Taglioni, Lucile Grahn, and Fanny Cerrito, is one of the most famous images in dance history.

Champion, Gower (*b* Geneva, Ill., 22 Jun. 1920 (some sources say 1919); *d* New York, 25 Aug. 1980) US dancer, choreographer, and director. Famed for his dance partnership with Marge Champion (also his wife), he choreographed his first musical in 1948 (*Lend an Ear*), which launched his career on Broadway and in Hollywood. His musical shows include *Bye Bye Birdie* (1960), *Carnival* (1961), *Hello Dolly* (1964), *I Do! I Do!* (1966), *The Happy Time* (1968), *Mack and Mabel* (1974), and *42nd Street* (1980). He was one of Broadway's leading director-choreographers.

Chandralekha (*b* Nadiad, Gujarat, 6 Dec. 1929; *d* Chennai, India, 30 Dec. 2006) Indian dancer, choreographer, designer, and writer. She was educated in Bombay and moved to Madras in 1949. She trained in bharata natyam with E. Pillai in Madras and made her debut in 1952. She enjoyed a career as a soloist in the late, 1950s and early 1960s. Disenchanted with the profession, however, she took up writing and designing and pursued radical feminist causes. In 1982 she was charged with sedition by the Indian government, although was later cleared. In 1984 she came out of retirement to present *Tillana*, originally made in 1960, at the East-West Dance Encounter in Bombay. In 1985 she returned to the stage with a groundbreaking production, *Angika*, which rejected the decoration and narrative of bharata natyam and offered new directions in Indian contemporary dance. Since then she produced work on a regular basis. She and her company toured internationally; in 1997 she collaborated with Toronto Dance Theater on *Namaskar*, the first time she had set her work on Western dancers. Author of the novel *The Street* and a collection of poems.

Chanel *See* FASHION.

changement de pieds [Fr., changing feet] A jump during which the position of the feet changes.

Chant du rossignol, Le (Eng. title *Song of the Nightingale*) Ballet in one act with choreography by Massine, music by Stravinsky, and designs by Matisse. Premiered 2 Feb. 1920 by the Ballets Russes de Diaghilev at the Paris Opera, with Karsavina, Sokolova, and Idzikowski. Based on the Hans Christian Andersen fairy-tale, the ballet tells the story of the Emperor of China who is saved from death by the song of the nightingale. The score is the symphonic poem which Stravinsky extracted from his opera *Le Rossignol*. In 1925 Diaghilev revived the ballet and commissioned the young Balanchine to choreograph it. It was Balanchine's first creation in the West. Later versions include Cranko (Munich, 1968) and Taras (New York City Ballet, 1972). In 1999 Kenneth Archer and Millicent Hodson staged a reconstruction of Balanchine's version for Les Ballets de Monte Carlo.

Chappell, William (*b* Wolverhampton, 27 Sept. 1908; *d* Rye, 1 Jan. 1994) British dancer and designer. An enormously versatile talent, he studied ballet with Rambert and art at the Chelsea Art School. A member of Ballet Rambert in its earliest days (1929–34), he also danced with the

Vic-Wells Ballet from 1934 to 1940. With the Camargo Society he created roles in de Valois's *Job* (1931) and Ashton's *Façade* (1931). At the Vic-Wells Ballet he created roles in de Valois's *The Haunted Ballroom* (1934), *The Rake's Progress* (1935), and *Checkmate* (1937). As a designer he worked for both Rambert and the Vic-Wells Ballet, designing Ashton's *Capriol Suite* (1930), *Les Rendezvous* (1933), and *Les Patineurs* (1937), de Valois's *Cephalus and Procris* (1931) and *Bar aux Folies-Bergère* (1934), and Tudor's *Lysistrata* (1932). He also designed productions of *Giselle* (1935) and *Coppélia* (1940) for Vic-Wells Ballet and in 1936 he designed Boris Romanov's *Nutcracker* staging for René Blum's Ballets Russes de Monte Carlo. He published *Studies in Ballet* in 1948, *Fonteyn: Impressions of a Ballerina* in 1951, and *Edward Burra: A Painter Remembered by his Friends* in 1982. From 1951 he worked as a producer of plays and revues. In 1980 he was reunited professionally with Frederick Ashton, designing his *Rhapsody* for the Royal Ballet. In 1985 he designed Ashton's *La Chatte metamorphosée en femme*.

character dance A wide ranging term, mostly used in ballet, to denote forms of dance which fall outside the category of classic-academic dance. It refers to the national dances that were prevalent in 19th-century ballets; also to folk, ethnic, and rustic dances. It is additionally used to describe choreography that specifically illustrates a character's function or occupation (sailor, farmer, shoemaker) or choreography that is performed by older dancers or by dancers portraying older figures. The latter are usually heavily reliant on mime. National dances (like Polish, Hungarian, Spanish, Italian, and Russian) are found in many 19th-century ballets where they are frequently performed as entertainments at court gatherings, and as such they provide a lively and exotic contrast to classical dancing. *Swan Lake* and *Raymonda* contain fine examples of national dancing which serve no overt narrative purpose but provide vivid diversion. Character dance associated with certain types of characters—such as jesters, buffoons, villains, magicians, and supernatural creatures—is rarely performed on pointe (a notable exception being the role of Bottom in Ashton's *The Dream*). In ballet, the demi-caractère dancer is often shorter in stature but possesses all the technical virtuosity of a leading artist. A famous example of the demi-caractère dancer is the Blue Bird in *The Sleeping Beauty*.

Charisse, Cyd (orig. Tula Ellice Finklea; *b* Amarillo, Tex., 8 Mar. 1922; *d* Los Angeles, 17 Jun. 2008) US dancer and actress. After studying with Bolm, Nico Charisse (her first husband), and Nijinska in California, she made her debut as a ballet dancer with Colonel de Basil's Ballets Russes in 1937. By 1946, however, she had moved on to commercial dance and in that world became one of the best-known dancers in the US, famous—like Betty Grable—for her long, elegant legs. She made several Hollywood films with Fred Astaire who once described her as 'beautiful dynamite'; and she also partnered Gene Kelly in *Singin' in the Rain* (1952). She appeared, either as dancer or actress, in many films, including *Mission to Moscow, Thousands Cheer, Ziegfeld Follies, The Harvey Girls, Till the Clouds Roll By, The Unfinished Dance, Fiesta, The Kissing Bandit, The Band Wagon, Brigadoon, It's Always Fair Weather, Meet Me in Las Vegas, Silk Stockings*, and in Petit's 1960 film *Black Tights*. She made her Broadway debut as the Russian ballerina in *Grand Hotel* in 1992.

charleston A fast-paced and strongly syncopated American social dance that was especially popular in the 1920s. It took its name from Charleston in South Carolina and was originally a solo dance performed by African-Americans. In 1926 it was accepted as a ballroom dance. Josephine Baker was one of its most celebrated performers.

Charlip, Remy (*b* Brooklyn, NY, 10 Jan. 1929) US dancer, choreographer, designer, writer, actor, artist, and teacher. He studied art at Straubenmuller Textile High School in New York and fine arts at Cooper Union in New York, graduating in 1949. He studied dance at the New Dance Group Studio and at the Juilliard School with Tudor and Craske. He began dancing and teaching in 1949 and from 1950 to 1961 was a member of the Merce Cunningham Dance Company, performing as well as designing costumes and posters. For Cunningham he created roles in *Suite for Five in Space and Time* (1956), *Antic Meet* (1958), and *Aeon* (1961). He also danced with Charles Weidman, Jean Erdman, and Donald McKayle. While with Cunningham, he also worked as director and performer with the Living Theater company and in 1958 co-founded the Paper Bag Players, a children's theatre in New York. From 1964 to 1970 he worked as choreographer, designer, performer, and director with the Judson Dance Theater after which he wrote and directed two plays, *Biography* (1970) and *Secrets* (1971), as director of the National Theater of the Deaf. In 1977 he founded his own company for which he created many works while additionally choreographing for London Contemporary Dance Theatre and the Joffrey Ballet among others. As a choreographer his work displays an unusual rhythmic sophistication and a highly developed sense of fun, with sign language frequently incorporated into the choreography. In 1972 Charlip initiated his 'air mail dances', a series in which he sent out sketches of 20–40 dance positions which he then invited contributors to link together in whatever way they chose. The resulting dances, performed by up to 250 people, were staged in Europe, S. America, Australia, and America. Charlip, a prolific author as well as choreographer, has illustrated and written more than two dozen books, some of them for children. His art works have been exhibited in France, Russia, Japan, and the US.

Charrat, Janine (*b* Grenoble, 24 Jul. 1924) French dancer, choreographer, and ballet director. She studied with Jeanne Ronsay, Egorova, and Volinine and made her debut in the film *La Mort du cygne* in 1937, playing the part of a 'petit rat' at the Paris Opera. By the age of 14 she was giving recitals in Paris, dancing solos created, precociously, by herself, which showcased her poetic qualities as a stage performer. From 1941 to 1944 she danced with Petit in a series of recitals which led to the creation of the Ballets des Champs-Elysées and in 1945 she choreographed a highly successful setting of Stravinsky's *Jeu de cartes* for the company. Still in her early twenties, Charrat was commissioned to make ballets for several other companies, including *Concerto No. 3* (mus. Prokofiev) for the Opéra Comique in 1947; '*Adame miroir* (mus. Milhaud) for Petit's Ballets de Paris in 1948; and *La Femme et son ombre* for the same company in 1949. *Abraxas* (mus. Werner Egk) created for the Berlin Municipal Opera in 1949, remains her most successful ballet. She founded her own company in 1951 (Les Ballets Janine Charrat, later renamed Ballet de France) and produced two successful works, *Le Massacre des Amazones* (mus. Y. Semenoff) and *Les Algues* (mus. Guy Bernard, 1953), in which she herself danced the role of the mad heroine. She also choreographed ballets for La Scala, Milan, Teatro Colón in Buenos Aires, the Monnaie, the Marquis de Cuevas company, the Geneva Ballet, the Vienna State Opera Ballet, and the Paris Opera. In 1961 she co-choreographed *Les 4 Fils Aymon* with Béjart in Brussels. During television filming of *Les Algues* in 1961 she was badly burned when her ballet skirt was set on fire by a lighted candelabra. After almost a year of recovery, she returned to the stage. From 1962 to 1964 she led the company at the Grand Theatre in Geneva and created several works there. In 1970 she opened a school in Paris. She was dance director at the Centre Pompidou (1980–9). She was awarded the Légion d'honneur in 1973.

Chase, Lucia (*b* Waterbury, Conn., 24 Mar. 1907; *d* New York, 9 Jan. 1986) US dancer and ballet director. Co-founder of *American Ballet Theatre. She studied drama and ballet at New York's Theater Guild School and then focused on ballet with Mordkin, Fokine, Tudor, Vilzak,

and Nijinska. She performed with the Mordkin Ballet from 1937 to 1939, and despite her late start performed the title roles in *The Sleeping Beauty* and *Giselle*. In 1940 she and Richard Pleasant founded Ballet Theatre (later American Ballet Theatre) with Chase as principal dancer (and prime financial backer). Here, however, she concentrated on dramatic and comedic roles, creating the role of Eldest Sister in Tudor's *Pillar of Fire* (1942) and the Greedy One in de Mille's *Three Virgins and a Devil* (1941). In 1945 she took over joint direction of American Ballet Theatre (with Oliver Smith) dedicating much of her energy and her personal fortune to the company's survival. Although she retired from the stage in 1960, she continued as company director until 1980 bringing in Tudor and Baryshnikov to ABT and encouraging US choreographers such as Robbins, Tetley, and Tharp. She retired in 1980 (when she was succeeded by Baryshnikov) and in the same year was awarded the US Medal of Freedom in 1980.

chassé [Fr., hunted] In ballet, a sliding step in which one foot appears to be chasing the other.

chat, pas de [Fr., step of the cat] In ballet, a cat-like leaping step, which moves sideways. It starts from a fifth position of the feet and ends in fifth position, with the dancer jumping off one foot and landing on the other.

Chatte, La Ballet in one act with choreography by Balanchine, libretto by Sobeka (alias Kochno), music by Sauguet, and designs by Naum Gabo and Antoine Pevsner. Premiered 30 Apr. 1927 by the Ballets Russes de Diaghilev in Monte Carlo, with Spessivtseva and Lifar. Balanchine based his ballet on Aesop's fable, in which a young man begs Aphrodite to change a cat into a young girl. The goddess grants him his wish, only for him to discover that the girl cannot reciprocate his love, whereupon the young man dies. The ballet's original constructivist decor featured transparent materials that dazzlingly reflected. Although the work had been intended as a showcase for Spessivtseva, it made a star of Lifar. Ronald Hynd choreographed a version using the same music for London Festival Ballet in 1978. *Hodson and Archer re-constructed Balanchine's version for Les Grands Ballets Canadiens in 1991.

Chauviré, Yvette (*b* Paris, 22 Apr. 1917) French dancer and teacher. Widely considered to be the finest French ballerina of her generation. She studied at the Paris Opera Ballet School and later with Boris Kniaseff and Victor Gsovsky, joining the Paris Opera Ballet in 1936 She was a favourite of Lifar who did much to promote her at the Opera by giving her major roles early on in her career. She created her first solo role in his *Le Roi nu* (1936) and appeared in the film *La Mort du* *cygne* a year later. In 1941, at the age of 24, she was promoted to étoile of the Paris Opera after stunning audiences with her eighteen-minute solo in Lifar's *Istar*. She remained almost exclusively with the company until her retirement in 1972, although when Lifar was forced to leave the Opera for political reasons in 1946, she joined him for a season at the Nouveau Ballet de Monte Carlo. On their return to Paris in 1947 Chauviré appeared in Lifar's ballet *Les Mirages*, in which she created the role of the Shadow, one of the parts most closely associated with her. She left the Opera again in 1949, and while returning in 1953, became a frequent guest with other companies, including the Royal Ballet and the Bolshoi. An elegantly classical dancer, possessed of exceptional personal glamour, she was especially renowned for her interpretation of *Giselle* (in which she made her farewell to the Paris Opera). She created roles in many of Lifar's ballets, including *David triomphant* (1937), *Alexandre le grand* (1937), *Le Chevalier et la demoiselle* (1941), *Istar* (1941), *Joan de Zarissa* (1942), *Suite en blanc* (1943), *Dramma per musica* (1946), *Chota Roustaveli* (1946), *Nautéos* (1947), *Mirages* (1947), *La Péri* (1957), and *Constellations* (1969). She also created a role in Cranko's *La Belle Hélène* in 1955, and the role of Marguérite in Gsovsky's *La Dame aux camélias*, first with the Berlin Ballet in 1957, then in an expanded version for Paris in 1960. She also created the female role in Gsovsky's famous *Grand pas classique* (1949), made for the Ballets des Champs-Elysées. From 1963 to 1968 she directed the Paris Opera Ballet School and from 1970 she directed the International Academy of the Dance in Paris. Although retired, she continued to make occasional stage appearances, including Lady Capulet in Nureyev's *Romeo and Juliet* in 1985. Chevalier de la Légion d'honneur (1964), Officier de la Légion d'honneur (1974), Commandeur de la Légion d'honneur (1988). Author of *Je suis ballerine* (Paris, 1960).

Checkmate Ballet in one act with prologue, with choreography by de Valois, libretto and music by Bliss, and designs by Edward McKnight Kauffer. Premiered 15 Jun. 1937, by the Vic-Wells Ballet at the Théâtre des Champs-Elysées in Paris, with Brae, May, Helpmann, and Turner. The pieces from a chess game enact a story of love and death, in which the Black Queen seduces, then murders the Red Knight, and humiliates the enfeebled Red King. The work's London premiere was on 15 Oct. 1937 at Sadler's Wells Theatre. The ballet remains, along with *The Rake's Progress*, among de Valois's most significant work.

Cherkaoui, Sidi Larbi (*b* Antwerp, 10 Mar. 1976) Belgian-Moroccan dancer, choreographer, and director. He taught himself to dance by watching music videos then taking classes in a variety of styles including ballet, tap, jazz and flamenco. A natural talent, with exceptional flexibility and control, he performed with the Gang Bang Hip Hop crew and on television, before finally embarking on full-time dance training at P.A.R.T.S., the school directed by de *Keersmaeker. In 1998 he was invited by Alain *Platel to join the collective, Les Ballets C de la B. As well as performing with that company he created for it *Rien de Rien* (2000) and *Foi* (2003). His language reflects his eclectic dance background and his works nearly always feature a powerful dramatic or thematic dynamic (sometimes developed in relationship with dramaturge Guy Cools). In 2006 Cherkaoui's own group became based at the Toneelhuis in Antwerp, since when he has created several works including *Myth* (2007), *Origin* (2008), and *Babel* (2010). He has also collaborated with Akram *Khan in their loosely autobiographical duet *Zero Degrees* (mus. Nitin Sawhney, des. Antony Gormley, 2005) and with the monks of the Shaolin Temple in *Sutra* (mus. Szymon Brzóska, des. Gormley). He has additionally made works for other companies, including *In Memoriam* (2004) and *Mea Culpa* (2006) for Les Ballets de Monte Carlo; *End* (2006) for Cullberg Ballet; *The Wood Man* (2007) for Royal Danish Ballet; and *Loin* (mus. Biber, 2008) for Geneva.

Children of Theatre Street A Soviet-US film (1978) portraying the daily life of the famous St Petersburg Ballet School, then known as the Vaganova Institute. The film was directed by Robert Dornhelm, with English commentary spoken by Princess Grace of Monaco. It featured as its climax a graduation performance by students.

Childs, Lucinda (*b* New York, 26 Jun. 1940) US dancer and choreographer. She graduated as a dance major from Sarah Lawrence College in 1962 (where her teachers included Bessie Schönberg) and then studied at the Cunningham studio, becoming a member of the *Judson collective in 1963. In 1973 she formed the Lucinda Childs Dance Company, from which she became established as one of America's leading modern dance choreographers. Her early works were conceptual pieces like *Carnation* (1964), a solo which she danced with props such as hair rollers and a blue plastic bag, or *Street Dance* (1964) during which she offered her audience, seated in the windows of a loft, an architectural tour of a New York block. She became best known, however, as a choreographer of minimalist works, deploying a rigorously spare movement vocabulary to create complex patterns and perspectives. From the late 1970s Childs began to work in a more theatrically expansive style. *Dance* (1979) was not only her first full-length work, it was also the first time

Opera which date back to the late 18th century. Western theatrical dance dates back only to the middle of the 20th century, when teachers from the Bolshoi helped establish the Beijing Dance Academy in 1954 and those from the Kirov helped establish the Shanghai Dance School in 1960. China's first ballet company was the Experimental Ballet Troupe, set up within the Beijing Academy in 1959 and staging its first full-length ballet, *Swan Lake*, under the guidance of the Russian ballet master Petr Gusev; this production also marked the founding of the fully professional *National Ballet of China. In 1962 the Beijing Ballet (as it was then known) made its foreign debut, in Burma and in 1964 the British ballerina Beryl Grey went to China to work with the company. However, with the arrival of the Cultural Revolution in the mid-1960s Western ballet was banned as decadent. With relations between the Soviet Union and China also severed, Chinese ballet developed its own teachers and its own aesthetic, focusing on national revolutionary subject-matter. The *Red Detachment of Women* (created in 1964 just before the Cultural Revolution) and *The White-Haired Girl* (staged by the Shanghai School of Dance) were both personally supervised by Mao Zedong's wife and were performed to the exclusion of all other repertory until the end of the Revolution. The style of these new ballets blended the classical academic vocabulary with traditional Chinese acrobatics and mime. Western classical ballet was reintroduced into China in the 1970s. Today the leading company is the Beijing-based *National Ballet of China, which draws its dancers from the Beijing Dance Academy. Under the direction of Zhao *Ruheng it successfully expanded its repertory while maintaining a distinctive Chinese identity, most successfully in *Raise the Red Lantern* (2001), a stage adaptation of Zhang Yimou's award-winning film. The Shanghai Ballet, directed by Ha Muti, is the country's second company and several smaller classical companies are based in other provinces including the Liaoning Ballet, founded 1980.

Modern dance in the country dates back to the work of individual pioneers like Wu Xiaobang who studied Western dance while in Japan and founded the Tianna Dance Art Studio in 1960 as a centre for modern dance teaching and choreography. This was closed down during the years of the Cultural Revolution however and modern dance was effectively banned from China until 1980. It returned to the region after Willy Tsao, a choreographer who had trained in the US, founded the City Contemporary Dance Company in Hong Kong. As soon as state-sponsored modern dance training had been instituted in mainland China, in Guangdong Province in 1987 and in Beijing in 1991, Tsao was invited to help set up the two companies formed from their students,

the *Guangdong Modern Dance Company and the *Beijing Modern Dance Company. Both troupes have nurtured a new generation of Chinese dancers and choreographers, such as Shen Wey, Sang Jijia, Wang Mei, and Zhou Niannian who have fused Western idioms with a Chinese aesthetic. Both troupes tour internationally. Other companies to emerge have been the Beijing LDTX Modern Dance Company and Wen Hui's Living Dance Studio; however independent modern dance activity struggles to survive.

The country still maintains its folk and acrobatic dance traditions to a very high standard through state-sponsored companies like the Central National Song and Dance Troupe. The Guangdong Acrobatic Troupe's production of *Swan Lake* (2005) toured internationally to considerable acclaim.

Chiriaeff, Ludmilla (*b* Riga, 24 Jan. 1924; *d* Montreal, 22 Sept. 1996) Latvian-Canadian dancer and ballet director. Founder of the Montreal-based company Les *Grands Ballets Canadiens. She studied in Berlin with Alexandra Nikolaeva, and after dancing with Colonel de Basil's Ballets Russes (1936) as an apprentice, she performed with Fokine, Massine and at the Berlin Opera Ballet (1940-1). During the Second World War she was sent to a Nazi labour camp, but escaped to Switzerland, and in 1949 founded Les Ballets du Théâtre des Arts in Geneva. In 1952 she moved to Canada and became one of the most influential figures in Montreal's emerging dance scene. As well as opening her own school she began choreographing for Canadian television (1952-7), creating dozens of ballets for the small screen with her own troupe, Les Ballets Chiriaeff. In 1955 her company also began to perform in theatres and in 1957 became known as Les *Grands Ballets Canadiens. Chiriaeff choreographed many works for its repertoire, which mixed new and populist works with the classics. Her 1962 staging of *Cendrillon* (mus. Mozart) was Canada's first original full-length ballet. She also encouraged Canadian designers, composers, and choreographers to work with the company, in order to create a genuine French-Canadian identity for it. The company made its US debut in 1959. One of Chiriaeff's most significant productions was Stravinsky's *Les Noces*, which she choreographed in 1956 and then remounted in 1973. She retired as director in 1974 but continued to run the company's two schools. Companion of the Order of Canada (1984). Nijinsky Medal (1992).

Chirico, Giorgio di (*b* Volos, 10 Jul. 1888; *d* Rome, 20 Nov. 1978) Greek-Italian painter and set designer. He designed Börlin's *The Jar* (*La giara*) for the Ballets Suédois (1924), Balanchine's *Le Bal* for Diaghilev's Ballets Russes (1929), *Bacchus and Ariadne* (Lifar, 1931), *Protée* (Lichine, 1938),

Amphion (Milloss, 1944), *Dances from Galanta* (Milloss, 1945), *The Legend of Joseph* (Wallmann, 1951), and *Apollon musagète* (Lifar, 1956). His surrealist architectural visions are among the most striking dance sets in the repertory.

Chopin, Fryderyk Frantizek (*b* Zelazowa Wola, 1 Mar. 1810; *d* Paris, 17 Oct. 1849) Polish composer. Although he wrote no music for ballet, his works for piano have been frequently used as ballet scores, many of them in orchestral arrangements. The most famous example is Fokine's for *Chopiniana* (1907, restaged 1909 as *Les Sylphides*). Robbins was also drawn to Chopin, using his music for *The Concert* (1956), *Dances at a Gathering* (1969), and *In the Night* (1970). Ashton chose Chopin for *A Month in the Country* (1976) and Neumeier for *Lady of the Camellias* (1978). Nijinska's *Chopin Concerto* (1937) and *In Memoriam* (1949) are also set to his music.

Chopiniana The original title of *Les *Sylphides*.

Choreartium Ballet in four movements, with choreography by Massine, music by Brahms, and designs by Constantine Terechkovich and Eugène Lourié. Premiered 24 Oct. 1933 by Ballets Russes de Monte Carlo, at the Alhambra Theatre, London, with Baronova, Danilova, Riabouchinska, Verchinina, Zorina, Jasinski, Lichine, Petrov, and Shabelevski. An abstract choreographic response to Brahms's 4th Symphony, it was the second of Massine's 'symphonic' ballets, and considered by the musical establishment to be sacrilegious in its appropriation, for dance, of a classic score. Massine revived it in Buenos Aires in 1959 and again in Edinburgh in 1960. Birmingham Royal Ballet mounted a major revival in 1991, staged by Tatiana Leskova after Massine.

choreographer One who makes dances. The person responsible for creating and arranging the steps and patterns of a dance work.

choreography Derived from the Greek for dance and writing. Although the term originally referred to the actual writing down of the steps of a dance (which today is called dance notation), ever since the late 18th century it has meant the art of composing dance.

choreology Derived from the Greek, its literal translation is 'the science of dance'. The term is most closely associated with the system of dance notation invented by Rudolf and Joan *Benesh, who defined the term in their 1977 book *Reading Dance* as 'the scientific and aesthetic study of all forms of human movement made possible by Benesh Movement Notation'. It was first used in the 1920s by Rudolf Laban. Today, those trained in the Benesh system are known as choreologists.

Most of the world's major ballet companies have a choreologist on their staff, and most new ballets are now notated by a choreologist.

Chorus Line, A A long-running Broadway musical, directed and choreographed by Michael Bennett with music by Marvin Hamlisch, book by James Kirkwood, and lyrics by Ed Kleban. Premiered 21 May 1975 at the New York Shakespeare Festival Public Theater, it transferred to Broadway's Shubert Theater on 25 Jul. 1975 where it ran until 1990. The musical depicts an audition for a job in a Broadway chorus line. It won nine Tony Awards and the Pulitzer Prize for Best Musical Play of the 1975–6 season, and successfully raised the profile of the director-choreographer on Broadway.

Christensen, Aage Thordal See THORDAL-CHRISTENSEN, AAGE.

Christensen, Lew (*b* Brigham City, Utah, 9 May (some sources 6 May) 1909; *d* California, 9 Oct. 1984) US dancer, choreographer, and ballet director. The youngest of the three dancing Christensen brothers. Like his siblings he trained with his uncle Lars Peter Christensen in Salt Lake City and continued his studies with Stefano Mascagno and L. Albertieri in New York and at Balanchine's School of American Ballet. After touring the vaudeville circuit with his brothers, he joined the American Ballet in 1936, becoming one of the most important of the early Balanchine dancers. In 1937 he was Balanchine's first American Apollo, which prompted Kirstein to write of his 'suave and monumental elegance' in the role. Tall, blond, and handsome, and possessed of a strong technique, he was America's first danseur noble of the 20th century. As a choreographer, he distinguished himself from the start by making works on American themes with *Pocahontas* (mus. E. Carter, 1936) and *Filling Station* (mus. V. Thomson, 1938), both for Ballet Caravan. In 1946 he joined the faculty of the School of American Ballet, and also became ballet master of Ballet Society and later New York City Ballet. In 1951 he moved to California to take over direction of the San Francisco Ballet from his brother Willam. He choreographed over 70 ballets and operas for San Francisco, including *Con amore* (mus. Rossini, 1953), *Nutcracker* (1954), *Beauty and the Beast* (mus. Tchaikovsky, 1958), *Divertissement d'Auber* (1959), *Jest of Cards* (mus. Krenek, 1962), and *Life: A Do It Yourself Disaster* ('A Pop Art Ballet', mus. Ives, 1965).

Christensen, Willam (orig. William Christensen; *b* Brigham City, Utah, 27 Aug. 1902; *d* 14 Oct. 2001) US dancer, choreographer, teacher, and ballet director. He studied with his uncle Lars Peter Christensen in Salt Lake City, with Stefano

Mascagno and L. Albertieri in New York and with Fokine, in whose company he later danced. Between 1927 to 1932 he toured the vaudeville circuit with his brothers *Lew and Harold, then opened a school in Portland, Oregon, out of which grew the Portland Ballet. From 1937 he danced with the San Francisco Opera Ballet, becoming ballet master and choreographer in 1938. When the opera disbanded its ballet company during the Second World War, he and his brother Harold bought the opera's ballet school and established the independent San Francisco Ballet. He choreographed the first American full-length versions of *Coppélia* (1939), *Swan Lake* (1940), and *Nutcracker* (1944). He left San Francisco Ballet in 1951 to become Professor of Dance at the University of Utah. In 1952 he founded the Utah Ballet, later Ballet West (1968).

Chroma One-act ballet with choreography by Wayne McGregor, music by Joby Talbot (based on songs by the White Stripes), designs by John Pawson and lighting by Lucy Carter. Premiered 17 Nov. 2006 by the Royal Ballet at Covent Garden, with Cojocaru, Watson, Rojo, Bonelli, and Lamb. An abstract but intensely atmospheric work for ten dancers, its success resulted in McGregor's appointment as resident choreographer of the Royal Ballet.

Chronicle Modern dance in five sections with choreography by Graham, music by Wallingford Riegger, designs by Isamu Noguchi, and costumes and lighting by Graham. Premiered 20 Dec. 1936 by the Martha Graham company at the Guild Theater in New York. '*Chronicle* does not attempt to show the actualities of war; rather, by evoking war's images, it sets forth the fateful prelude to war, portrays the devastation of spirit which it leaves in its wake, and suggests an answer' (Graham). Although the original work in its entirety has been lost, three sections have been reconstructed from film clips by the Martha Graham company: 'Spectre-1914', 'Steps in the Street' (reconstructed by Graham herself in 1989), and 'Prelude to Action'.

Chujoy, Anatole (*b* Riga, 1894; *d* New York, 24 Feb. 1969) Latvian-US writer, editor, and critic. A graduate in law from the University of St Petersburg, he was also a committed balletomane and after emigrating to the US in the early 1920s cofounded the influential *Dance Magazine* in 1936, which he edited until 1941. He founded *Dance News* in 1942, remaining as editor and publisher until his death. He wrote, edited, and translated many books on dance, including the groundbreaking *Dance Encyclopedia* (New York, 1949; second edition, with P. W. Manchester, 1967), and *The New York City Ballet* (New York, 1953).

He also translated the first English edition of Vaganova's *Fundamentals of the Classical Ballet* (New York, 1946, later published as *Basic Principles of Classical Ballet*) and edited Fokine's *Memoirs of a Ballet Master* (London, 1961).

Ciceri, Pierre (*b* Paris, 17 or 18 Aug. 1782; *d* Saint-Chéron, 22 Aug. 1868) French designer and chief decorator of the Paris Opera. He designed the sets for Taglioni's *La Sylphide* (1832), Coralli's *Giselle* (1841), and Mazilier's *Le Diable à quatre* (1845). He was the first to use gas lighting to illuminate the stage.

Cieplinski, Jan (*b* Warsaw, 10 May 1900; *d* New York, 17 Apr. 1972) Polish dancer, choreographer, teacher, and writer. He trained at the ballet school at Warsaw's Wielki Theater and performed there (1917–21). He was briefly a member of Anna Pavlova's company and then directed his own troupe (1922–5). From 1925 to 1927 he danced with Diaghilev's Ballets Russes. He was then ballet director in Stockholm (1927–31) and in Budapest (1931–4), then between 1938–9 was choreographer for the Polish Ballet, creating among other works *The Highlanders* (mus. Szymanowski, 1938). During the Second World War he worked in Warsaw and Budapest and in 1948 moved to London, where he worked with the Anglo-Polish Ballet, Legat Ballet, and the Mercury Theatre. From 1959 he lived in New York, working as a teacher and writer. Author of *Outline of Polish Ballet History* (1956).

Cincinnati Ballet US regional dance company founded in 1962 with an associate school attached to the University of Cincinnati College-Conservatory of Music. Its first artistic director was David McLain but after 1980 he was succeeded by a number of short-term directors, until Victoria Morgan (appointed 1997) re-introduced stability. Morgan introduced works by Balanchine and Massine into the repertory along with new ballets from S. Welch, Trey McIntyre, and Morgan herself.

(⊕) SEE WEB LINKS
• Website for the Cincinnati Ballet

Cinderella Perrault's fairy-tale has been frequently adapted for ballet, starting with a version by Duport in Vienna in 1813. In 1822 François Decombe (widely known as Monsieur Albert) choreographed *Cendrillon* with music by Fernando Sor for the King's Theatre in London and re-staged it for the Paris Opera the following year. In 1893 the Mariinsky Theatre staged a version with choreography by Ivanov, Cecchetti, and M. Petipa to music by Boris Schell or Schel, which featured Legnani making her Mariinsky debut (and stunning audiences with her celebrated feat of 32 consecutive fouettés). Fokine staged *Cendrillon* (mus. Frederic d'Erlanger, designs Goncharova) for the Original Ballet Russe (de Basil) at Covent Garden on 19 Jul. 1938. Andrée Howard choreographed a version (mus. Carl Maria von Weber) for Ballet Rambert in 1935, with Pearl Argyle in the title role and Frederick Ashton as the Prince. But it was not until Prokofiev's 1944 score that the fairy tale acquired the status of a ballet classic. The first Prokofiev staging was at the Bolshoi Theatre on 21 Nov. 1945 (its Russian title was *Zolushka*), with choreography by Zakharov, designs by Pyotr Williams, and featuring Olga Lepeshinskaya as Cinderella. On 8 Apr. 1946 Sergeyev staged *Zolushka* (sets by Boris Erdman) for the Kirov with Natalia Dudinskaya as Cinderella and himself as the Prince. Ashton's historic version for Sadler's Wells Ballet (again using the Prokofiev score, although eliminating the extended Act III divertissement) was premiered at the Royal Opera House on 23 Dec. 1948, the first full-length British ballet. Scenery and costumes were by Jean-Denis Malclès; the cast included Shearer, Somes, Ashton, and Helpmann. The Royal Ballet revived it on 23 Dec. 1965 with new sets and costumes by Henry Bardon and David Walker, with Fonteyn, Blair, Ashton, and Helpmann. It entered the repertoire of the Australian Ballet in 1972. Subsequent versions of this score include Rodrigues's for La Scala, Milan (1956), Celia Franca's for National Ballet of Canada (Toronto, 1968), Stevenson's for National Ballet of Washington (1970), Maguy Marin's bleak expressionist version for Lyon Opera Ballet (1985), Nureyev's Hollywood-inspired *Cendrillon* (starring Sylvie Guillem, Paris Opera Ballet, 1986), Vasiliev's for the Ballet Theatre of the Kremlin (1991), Michael Corder's (English National Ballet (1996), Matthew Bourne's World War II version (1997), and Stijn Celis's, as *The Lost Shoe*, for Les Grands Ballets Canadiens (2007). Stagings to other scores include de Warren for Northern Ballet Theatre (mus. J. Strauss II, 1979), Darrell for Scottish Ballet (mus. Rossini, 1979).

Cintolesi, Ottavio (*b* Santiago, 14 Apr. 1924) Chilean dancer, choreographer, and director. He studied at the Dance Conservatory of the University of Chile with Uthoff, Jooss, and V. Sulima. In 1946 he joined the National Ballet of Chile, where he became principal dancer and choreographer in 1948 and ballet master in 1950. In 1958 he became founder-director and chief choreographer of the Santiago Ballet, a position he held until 1966. After working mostly in Europe in the 1970s he returned to the Santiago Ballet (1979–82).

Circe Modern dance in one act with choreography and libretto by Graham, music by Hovhaness, set by Noguchi, and lighting by Rosenthal. Premiered 6 Sept. 1963 by the Martha Graham company at the Prince of Wales Theatre in London, with Hinkson, Ross, and Clive Thompson. Graham's adaptation of the myth of Circe was created as a homage to Robin Howard, founder of London Contemporary Dance School and Theatre.

Circus Polka A 'ballet for elephants' choreographed by Balanchine to a commissioned score by Stravinsky and performed by the Ringling Brothers, Barnum and Bailey Circus at Madison Square Garden in New York in the spring of 1942. Properly titled *Fifty Elephants and Fifty Beautiful Girls*, at the first performances it starred Vera Zorina. It was an enormous success, and was performed 425 times. In 1972 Jerome Robbins choreographed *Circus Polka* for the Stravinsky Festival using female students from the School of American Ballet and casting himself as ringmaster. At its premiere (New York State Theater, 23 June 1972) it was so well received it was immediately repeated.

Clark, Michael (*b* Aberdeen, 2 Jun. 1962) British dancer, choreographer, and company director. He trained in ballet and traditional Scottish dance then studied at the Royal Ballet School with Richard Glasstone (1975–9). In 1979 he joined Ballet Rambert, creating roles in works by Richard Alston, but left in 1981 to work as a freelance dancer with Ian Spink and Karole Armitage. He was resident choreographer at London's Riverside Studios (1983) and founded his own company in 1984. As a dancer he was admired for his startling grace and controlled technique but his early works as a choreographer established his reputation as a flamboyant iconoclast, using camp or obscene visual imagery and assaulting his audience with post-punk rock music. For many years he was branded the 'enfant terrible' of British dance, with works like *I Am Curious Orange* (mus. The Fall, 1988) overturning the precepts of classical dance. In 1989 he and his then lover, the US choreographer Stephen Petronio, appeared together in bed in a London art gallery performing a fifteen-minute duet with an explicit sexual agenda. But Clark's notoriety did not eclipse his considerable talent for making dances. In 1992 his version of *Rite of Spring*, titled *Mmm*, or *Michael's Modern Masterpiece*, with additional music by the Sex Pistols and Sondheim, showed his ability to tackle classic scores while *O* (1994), set to Stravinsky's *Apollo* featured the most luminous dance invention of his career. In 1998 he returned to the stage after a long absence with *current/SEE*, which revealed a fresh interest in the fundamentals of dance composition and in 2005 embarked on the *Stravinsky Project*, revising and expanding *Mmm* and *O* and in 2007 premiering a new setting of *Les Noces*, titled *I Do*. In 2009 he premiered *Come, Been and Gone* (mus. David Bowie, Lou Reed, and others) for his own company. Clark has also created works for several other companies including Paris Opera Ballet (*Angel Food*, 1985), Scottish Ballet (*Hail the Classical*, 1985), London Festival Ballet (*Drop Your Pearls and Hog it, Girl*, 1986), Ballet Rambert (*Swamp*, mus. Bruce Gilbert, 1986), George Piper Dances (*Satie Stud*, 2003), and Baryshnikov (*Rattle Your Jewellery*, 2003, revised version 2004). A list of his other works includes, *Hail the New Puritans* (1984), *No Fire Escape in Hell* (1986), and *Because We Must* (1987). He danced the role of Caliban in Peter Greenaway's film *Prospero's Books* (1991) and has also collaborated with the film-maker Charles Atlas.

(⊕) SEE WEB LINKS

• Website for the Michael Clark company

Clarke, Martha (*b* Baltimore, 3 Jun. 1944) US dancer, choreographer, and theatre director, renowned for her multi-disciplinary approach. She studied at the Peabody Conservatory and at the Juilliard School with Tudor and Sokolow. She danced with Anna Sokolow's company (1963–1966) and Pilobolus Dance Theater (1971–8) then in 1978 she co-founded Crowsnest Dance Company with the French choreographer Félix *Blaska and the Pilobolus dancer Robby Barnett. As a choreographer she became best known as the creator of full-length works which blurred the distinctions between dance and theatre, the most famous of which was *The Garden of Earthly Delights* (mus. Richard Peaslee). Inspired by the paintings of the Dutch painter Hieronymus Bosch it combined dance with acrobatics and spectacular stage effects. Later works have included *Vienna: Lusthaus*, (1986); *The Hunger Artist* (1987) based on stories by Kafka, *Miracolo d'amore* (1988) inspired by drawings by Tiepolo, and *Vers la flamme* (mus. Scriabin, 1999). Clarke's works are in the repertory of several other companies, including Rambert, Joffrey, American Ballet Theatre, and Nederlands Dans Theater 3, for which she choreographed *An Uncertain Hour* (mus. Berg, Wolf, Schumann, and Webern, 1995). Clarke has also worked extensively in the theatre and opera. In 1982 she collaborated with actor Linda Hunt on *A Metamorphosis in Miniature*, which won an Obie award for best American new play, and her subsequent productions include *A Midsummer Night's Dream* which she directed for American Repertory Theatre in 2004. In 1996 she choreographed and directed Tan Dun's *Marco Polo* for the Munich Biennale and in 1997 directed *Orpheus and Eurydice* for English National Opera and New York City Opera.

Clarke, Mary (*b* London, 23 Aug. 1923) British writer on dance and between 1963 and 2008 editor of *Dancing Times*, Britain's oldest dance magazine. During her long career as one of Britain's leading critics and dance historians she was also London correspondent of *Dance Magazine*, New York (1943–55); assistant editor and contributor to *Ballet Annual* (1952–63); dance critic of the *Guardian* (1977–94) and the author of many books, including *The Sadler's Wells Ballet: A History and an Appreciation* (London 1955); *Six Great Dancers* (1957); *Dancers of Mercury: The Story of Ballet Rambert* (London 1962); *Ballet, an Illustrated History* (with Clement Crisp, London, 1973, second edition 1992); *Making a Ballet* (with Crisp, 1974); *Introducing Ballet* (with Crisp, 1976); *The Encyclopedia of Dance and Ballet* (editor, with David Vaughan, 1977); *Design for Ballet* (with Crisp, 1978); *Ballet in Art* (with Crisp, 1978); *The History of Dance* (with Crisp, 1981); *Dancer: Men in Dance* (with Crisp, 1984); *Ballerina* (with Crisp, 1987). Queen Elizabeth II Coronation Award, Royal Academy of Dancing (1990). Nijinsky Medal, Poland, 1996. Knight of the Order of Dannebrog, Denmark (1992).

Class Concert *See* BALLET CLASS.

classical ballet A form of theatrical dance that has evolved over the past 300 years from its origins in France. It is highly academic in its training and technically demanding in performance. It differs from most other forms of dance in its fundamental requirement of turnout, in which the legs rotate 90 degrees in the hip socket to allow greater freedom of movement. This gives ballet its distinctive line. Pointework is another defining feature.

Clauss, Heinz (*b* Esslingen, 17 Feb. 1935) German dancer and ballet school director. He studied in Stuttgart and with Nora Kiss and Preobrajenska in Paris and joined the Stuttgart Ballet in 1951 while still a student. Between 1957 and 1959 he danced with Zurich Ballet as a soloist, then between 1959 and 1967 was with the Hamburg State Opera Ballet. In 1967 he returned to Stuttgart as a principal, where he created leading roles in many Cranko ballets, among them *Onegin* (new version 1967), *Présence* (1968), *Taming of the Shrew* (1969), and *Brouillards* (1970). He was also famous for his interpretation of Balanchine's *Apollo*, which he danced in Hamburg under the choreographer's direction. He subsequently staged many Balanchine and Cranko works for companies in Europe and America. He was director of the John Cranko Ballet School in Stuttgart from 1976 to 1990. One of the outstanding German dancers of the 20th century.

Cléopâtre Ballet in one act with choreography and libretto by Fokine, music by Arensky, set by O. Allegri, costumes by M. Zandin. Premiered 21 Mar. 1908 at the Mariinsky Theatre, St Petersburg, with Pavlova, Gerdt, Preobrajenska, Nijinsky, Fokine, and Karsavina. A dance telling of the doomed romance between Cleopatra and the slave Amoûn. The Diaghilev company presented an extended version on 2 June 1909 with additional music (by Glinka, Glazunov, Rimsky-Korsakov, and Taneyev) and new designs by Bakst at the Théâtre du Châtelet in Paris, with Rubinstein, Pavlova, Fokine, Karsavina, and Nijinsky.

Cleveland-San Jose Ballet US regional ballet company. It was founded in 1976 as Cleveland Ballet by Ian Horvath and Dennis *Nahat, changing its name in 1986 when it acquired a second home in San Jose, California. Nahat's original works and his stagings of the classics formed the backbone of its repertory. It was disbanded in 2000 but reformed as Ballet San Jose, with Nahat as director and choreographer.

clog dance A percussive folk dance performed in wooden-soled shoes which originated in northern England. Its most famous appearance in ballet is in Ashton's *La Fille mal gardée*, where it is performed by Widow Simone.

Cloud Gate Dance Theatre Taiwan-based dance company founded by Lin *Hwai-min in 1973. Its style blends traditional Chinese Opera movements and martial arts with Western contemporary dance techniques. It draws on Asian myths, folklore, religion, and history for its subject-matter. It was the first modern dance company to be founded in the Republic of China on Taiwan and with its current international touring schedule, it has become the country's most celebrated cultural export.

Clustine, Ivan (*b* Moscow, 10 Aug. 1862; *d* Nice, 21 Nov. 1941) Russian dancer, ballet master, and choreographer. He trained at the Moscow Theatre School and graduated into the Bolshoi Ballet in 1882. He was promoted to premier danseur in 1886 and ballet master in 1898. Among the ballets he made for the Bolshoi were *Stars* (1898), *Magic Dreams* (1898), and *The Magic Slipper* (1899). In 1903 he left the Bolshoi and Russia, opening a ballet school in Paris and becoming ballet master of the Paris Opera (1909–14). At the Opera he choreographed *Rusalka* (1911), *Les Bacchantes* (1912), and *Suite de danses* (1913), among others. He was then ballet master of Anna Pavlova's company from 1914 until her death in 1931 and choreographed some of the most popular ballets in her repertoire, including *The Fairy Doll*, *Gavotte Pavlova*, and an abridged version of *The Sleeping Beauty*.

Clytemnestra Modern dance in two acts with prologue and epilogue, with choreography and libretto by Martha Graham, music by Halim El-Dabh, sets by Noguchi, costumes by Graham and Helen McGehee, and lighting by Rosenthal. Premiered 1 Apr. 1958 by the Martha Graham company at the Adelphi Theater, New York, with Graham, Bertram Ross, Paul Taylor, McGehee, and Yuriko. In the Underworld a guilt-ridden Clytemnestra reviews her life of treachery and murder while she waits for the gods to decide her fate. Based on Aeschylus' *Oresteia*, it was Graham's only full-length work and considered by many to be her masterwork.

Cocteau, Jean (*b* Maison-Lafitte, nr. Paris, 5 Jul. 1889; *d* Milly-le-Forêt, 11 Oct. 1963) French writer, artist, designer, and film director. Part of Diaghilev's circle from the first Paris season in 1909, he wrote the scenarios for several of the ballets as well as designing company posters. He wrote the librettos for Fokine's *Le Dieu bleu* (1912), Massine's *Parade* (1917), and Nijinska's *Le Train bleu* (1924). He also worked with Börlin and the Ballets Suédois in the 1920s, writing *Les Mariés de la Tour Eiffel* (1921), and with Roland Petit, writing *Le Jeune Homme et la mort* (1946). He wrote *L'Amour et son amour* for Babilée in 1948 and *Phèdre* for Lifar in 1950, a ballet he also designed. He wrote numerous articles and essays on dance, and made many sketches and caricatures of the Diaghilev circle.

Code of Terpsichore Book by Blasis considered to be the leading reference work on classic-academic dance technique in the 19th century. First published in London in 1828, it was republished in Paris in 1830 under the title *Manuel complet de la danse*.

Cohan, Robert (*b* New York, 27 Mar. 1925) US dancer, choreographer, teacher, and company director. One of the most influential figures in the development of modern dance in Britain through his directorship of *London Contemporary Dance Theatre, the first *Graham-based company in Europe. Following service in the US Navy during the Second World War, he studied dance with Martha Graham and joined her company in 1946, staying for ten years and becoming one of her regular partners, as well as teaching at the Graham school. He also worked in the theatre, on Broadway, and in films, and ran his own company (1958–62). In 1962 he returned to the Graham company and in 1966 he became co-director. He additionally worked as choreographer for the Batsheva Dance Company (1964–5). In 1967 he left New York to run the newly established London School of Contemporary Dance, which led to the creation in 1969 of London

Contemporary Dance Theatre. For the next twenty years he made numerous works for LCDT, among them *Cell* (mus. Ronald Lloyd, 1969), *Stages* (mus. A. Nordheim and B. Downes, 1971), *People Alone* (mus. Downes, 1972), *Mass* (mus. Vladimir Rodzianko, 1973, revived 1977 with mus. J. Weir), *Waterless Method of Swimming Instruction* (mus. Downes, 1974), *Stabat Mater* (mus. Vivaldi, 1975, revived by Rambert Dance Company, 1995), *Class* (mus. John Keliehor, 1975), *Forest* (mus. Brian Hodgson, 1977), *Songs, Lamentations and Praises* (mus. G. Burgon, 1979), *Field* (mus. Hodgson, 1980), *Dances of Love and Death* (mus. Carl Davis and Conlon Nancarrow, 1981), *The Phantasmagoria* (mus. Barrington Pheloung, 1987), *In Memory* (mus. Henze, 1989), and *Metamorphosis* (mus. Britten, 1989). His choreography, much influenced by Graham, was noted for its theatrical imagination and visual flair. After stepping down from LCDT in 1988 (although he returned in an advisory capacity 1992–4) Cohan worked with Scottish Ballet, for whom he choreographed *A Midsummer Night's Dream* (mus. Pheloung, Mendelssohn, 1993) *The Four Seasons* (mus. Vivaldi, 1996) and *Aladdin* (mus. C. Davis, 2000). He has taught extensively in the US and also worked as a lighting designer, using the name of Charter.

Cojocaru, Alina (*b* Bucharest, 27 May 1981) Romanian dancer. She studied at the Kiev Ballet School and briefly at the Royal Ballet School (1998), before joining the Kiev Ballet as principal (1998). The following year she joined the Royal Ballet where she was promoted to soloist in 2000 and principal in 2001. A dancer of exceptional lightness, musicality and classical style she excels in roles like Giselle and Aurora, but she also possesses a wide stylistic and expressive range. In MacMillan works such as *Manon, Mayerling,* and *Romeo and Juliet*, she has revealed a powerful dramatic intelligence while in the modern repertory she has created roles in many works including Page's *This House Will Burn* (2001), Bintley's *Les Saisons* (2003), and McGregor's *Chroma* (2006). She has guested with the Kirov, American Ballet Theatre, Royal Danish Ballet, and others, most frequently partnered by Johan Kobborg.

Cole, Jack (*b* New Brunswick, NJ, 27 Apr. 1911; *d* Los Angeles, 17 Feb. 1974) US dancer and choreographer. He studied with St Denis and Ted Shawn in New York and performed with Shawn's Men Dancers in 1933, and later with the Humphrey-Weidman company. In 1936–7 he toured with his own group on the nightclub circuit and he continued to dance in clubs for more than 30 years. He created *Hindu Serenade* for the Ziegfeld Follies of 1942 and choreographed several Broadway musicals, including *Kismet* (1953), (1957),

while he directed and choreographed *Donnybrook!* and *Kean* in 1961. He choreographed the original Broadway productions of *A Funny Thing Happened on the Way to the Forum* (1962) and *Man of La Mancha* (1965). In Hollywood he trained dancers for screen musicals, and also choreographed the film *On the Riviera* (1951). Among the stars he coached were Rita Hayworth, Betty Grable, and Marilyn Monroe. He choreographed *Requiem for Jimmy Dean* (1968) for the Harkness Ballet.

Collier, Lesley (*b* Orpington, 13 Mar. 1947) British dancer. She studied with Irene Ayres and at the Royal Ballet School, where she danced the leading role in *The Two Pigeons* at her graduation performance. She joined the Royal Ballet in 1965 and was promoted to principal in 1972. During her three decades with the Royal Ballet she danced all the ballerina roles in the repertoire, celebrated for the authority and musicality of her interpretations. She was particularly associated with Lise in Ashton's *La Fille mal gardée*, a role which showcased her flair for comedy, and with Giselle. She also created roles in MacMillan's *Elite Syncopations* (1974) and *Four Seasons* (1975), van Manen's *Four Schumann Pieces* (1975), Ashton's *Rhapsody* (with Baryshnikov, 1980), Tetley's *Dances of Albion* (1980), and Miranda in Nureyev's *The Tempest* (1982). For David Bintley she created roles in *Consort Lessons* (1983), *Galanteries* (1986), and Roxane in *Cyrano* (1991). Following her retirement from the stage in 1995, she taught at the Royal Ballet School and was ballet mistress with the Royal.

comédie-ballet A kind of comedic entertainment which included a large element of ballet; most popular in the 17th and 18th centuries in France. Its most famous exponents were Molière and Lully.

commedia dell'arte Italian improvised comic theatre popular from the 16th to 18th centuries, whose stock characters, such as Harlequin and Columbine, became familiar to audiences all over Europe. The form, which incorporated many dance-related elements such as acrobatics and pantomime, has provided the inspiration for many ballets, from Petipa's *Les Millions de Harlequin* (1900), to Fokine's *Carnaval* (1910), Massine's *Pulcinella* (1920), and Tetley's *Pierrot lunaire* (1962).

Communauté Society of French dancing masters and violinists founded by Louis XIV in 1659. It led, in 1661, to the formation of the *Académie Royale de Danse.

Compan, Le Sieur One of the earliest writers on the subject of dance, he published his treatise in Paris in 1787, with the grand title of *Diction-naire de danse, contenant l'histoire, les règles et les principes de cet art.*

Compañía Nacional de Danza State-run Spanish dance company which grew out of the company founded by Victor *Ullate in 1979; previously known as Ballet Nacional Clásico and Ballet del Teatro Lírico Nacional. In 1990, when the company was reorganized and the current name adopted, Nacho *Duato was appointed artistic director. Duato, a prolific choreographer fusing modern and classical idioms, lent the company a unique style and repertory until he left in 2010. Since 1992 it has toured internationally.

((())) SEE WEB LINKS

• Website for Compañía Nacional de Danza

Company B Ballet in one act with choreography by Paul Taylor and music by the Andrews Sisters. Premiered 20 Jun. 1991 by the Houston Ballet at the Kennedy Center in Washington. A poignant, nostalgic piece inspired by the popular culture of the Second World War era, it looks at the men who went to war and the women they left behind. It is one of Taylor's most popular works and has been re-staged for many companies, including the Royal Swedish Ballet, San Francisco Ballet, South Africa's State Theatre Ballet (formerly PACT Ballet), and Taylor's own.

competitions Although the dance world has fewer competitions than classical music there are a number of high-profile events designed to launch the careers of young artists. Varna in Bulgaria hosts one of the most prestigious, while the Moscow competition is also important. Others include the New York International Ballet Competition, the Erik Bruhn competition, staged by the National Ballet of Canada, and the annual Prix de Lausanne, which is for students aged 16–19. The Paris suburb of *Bagnolet hosts a choreographic competition for creators of modern dance, as does The Place in London.

computer dance In the 1980s choreographers began using computers as an aid to making work. For some it was simply an economic and efficient way to sort out their movement ideas before going into the studio but for others, such as Merce Cunningham, who pioneered the use of the Life Forms software programme, it became a radically creative tool. Manipulating dance figures on the computer screen allowed Cunningham to explore new possibilities of movement and co-ordination, and resulted in his works acquiring an even denser complexity of choreographic construction. More recent developments include Wayne McGregor's work with cognitive scientists, developing a software programme capable of making its own

choreographic decisions. This would be unlikely ever to match the sophistication of human choreographers; the immediate goal would be to create a tool for jolting the choreographer's creative processes out of existing patterns and habits. Choreographers have also developed interactive dance programs that have allowed their audience to play an active role, via computer installations or home computers, in determining the action on screen.

Comus Ballet in two scenes, with choreography by Helpmann, music by Purcell, and designs by Oliver Messel. Premiered 14 Jan. 1942 by Sadler's Wells Ballet at the New Theatre, London, with Helpmann, Fonteyn, J. Hart, and Paltenghi. Based on Milton's masque, its largely mimed action tells the story of the magician Comus, son of Bacchus and Circe, whose attempts to seduce a Lady are thwarted by her chastity.

Concert, The Ballet in one act with choreography by Robbins, music by Chopin (partly orchestrated by Hershy Kay), and costumes by Irene Sharaff. Premiered 6 Mar. 1956 by New York City Ballet, City Center, New York, with LeClercq, Mounsey, Curley, and Bolender. One of the funniest ballets in the classical repertory, combining musical puns, sight gags, and slapstick, it features a group of over-imaginative music lovers and the fantasies inspired in them by a piano recital of Chopin music. Its subtitle, *The Perils of Everybody*, echoes the famous Perils of Pauline serials of the silent films era. Revived for the Spoleto Festival in 1958 with new scenery by Saul Steinberg. The Royal Ballet revived it in 1975 for Covent Garden with new scenery by Edward Gorey.

Concerto Ballet in one act with choreography by MacMillan, music by Shostakovich, and designs by Jürgen Rose. Premiered 30 Nov. 1966 by the Berlin Opera Ballet, with Carli, Kapuste, Seymour, Holz, and Kesselheim. A plotless ballet set to Shostakovich's 2nd Piano Concerto, Op. 102, it was MacMillan's first creation as director of the Berlin company. It was subsequently revived for American Ballet Theatre and the Royal Ballet touring company in 1967. It has entered the repertory of several other companies, including Pacific Northwest Ballet, Australian Ballet, and San Francisco Ballet.

Concerto Barocco Ballet in one act with choreography by Balanchine, music by Bach, designs by Eugene Berman. Premiered 29 May 1941 by the American Ballet Caravan at Hunter College Playhouse in New York, with Marie-Jeanne, Mary Jane Shea, and William Dollar. A plotless ballet set to Bach's Concerto in D minor for Two Violins, it epitomizes Balanchine's genius for creating a danced dialogue with music. It had its first official performance (New York being considered a preview) on 27 Jun. 1941 at the Teatro Municipal in Rio de Janeiro, part of the American Ballet Caravan's S. American tour. It entered the repertoire of New York City Ballet on 11 Oct. 1948 and has subsequently been revived for many companies around the world. While the original costumes were highly decorated it is now generally performed without decor and with the dancers in practice clothes.

Conservatory, The, or A Proposal of Marriage Through a Newspaper (orig. Dan. title *Konservatoriet*) Ballet in two acts with choreography by Bournonville and music by Holger Paulli. Premiered 6 May 1849 by the Royal Danish Ballet in Copenhagen. In its original staging, the ballet featured a dancing class of the Paris Conservatory set against a background of complicated romantic intrigues. In 1941 in Copenhagen H. Lander and V. Borchsenius revised the ballet using the classroom scene only. This latter staging was taken into the repertoires of the Joffrey Ballet (1969) and London Festival Ballet (1973), the Royal Swedish Ballet (1973), Paris Opera Ballet (1976), the Royal Ballet (1982), and the Bolshoi Ballet (1989). The two-act version was revived by the Royal Danish Ballet in 1995. The ballet showcases a typical Bournonville class in which the great Danish choreographer pays tribute to his illustrious teacher Auguste Vestris.

Contact Improvisation The term given to a system of improvised movement which is based on the relationship between two moving bodies and the effect that the laws of gravity, momentum, friction, and inertia have on their movement. The system was devised by Steve *Paxton in New York in 1972. It has since had a significant influence on many contemporary choreographers.

contraction and release Key elements in the Martha Graham technique of modern dance. They refer to the action of the body at the moment of the exhalation of breath (the contraction) and the moment of inhalation (the release).

Cook, Bart (*b* Ogden, Utah, 7 Jun. 1949) US dancer. He studied with W. Christensen and at the School of American Ballet (from 1970) and joined New York City Ballet in 1971, becoming a principal in 1979. Dancing with the company until 1993 he created leading roles in Robbins's *Scherzo fantastique* (1972), *An Evening's Waltzes* (1973), *Dybbuk Variations* (1974), and *The Four Seasons* (1979), and in Balanchine's *Vienna Waltzes* (1977). In 1981 he became assistant ballet master and following his retirement from the stage he worked for the Balanchine Trust, staging Balanchine's ballets. Chairman of the dance faculty at

the Richmond Ballet Center for Dance in Virginia (1997).

Cooper, Adam (*b* London, 22 Jul. 1971) British dancer, actor and choreographer. He studied at the Arts Educational School and at the Royal Ballet School, joining the Royal Ballet in 1989, where he was promoted to principal in 1994. Although not a purely classical dancer, he performed many leading roles in both the 19th- and 20th-century repertoires. He also created roles in MacMillan's *Winter Dreams* and *The Judas Tree*, in Bintley's *Tombeaux* and Page's *Bloodlines*, *Renard*, and *Ebony Concerto*. In 1995 he was chosen by the choreographer Matthew Bourne to star in his production of *Swan Lake* in which Cooper portrayed the Male Swan. This radical staging, which enjoyed huge success in the West End and on Broadway, brought Cooper international fame as did his subsequent performances in Bourne's 1997 version of *Cinderella*. In 1997 he officially left the Royal Ballet to work freelance. He also began a career as a choreographer, creating works for Scottish Ballet and the K Ballet in Japan, the full-length ballet *Les Liaisons Dangereuses* (2005), and a dance tribute to the music of Richard Rodgers *Shall We Dance* (2009). He has also worked in musicals, choreographing and dancing in *On Your Toes* (2002) and *Singin' in the Rain* (2004) among others. As a dancer, actor, and singer he has appeared in many other productions, including *Guys and Dolls* (2006), *Zorro* and *Wizard of Oz* (both 2008). He is married to the dancer Sarah Wildor.

(((⊕))) SEE WEB LINKS
• Adam Cooper website

Cope, Jonathan (*b* Crediton, 20 Dec. 1962) British dancer. He trained at the Royal Ballet School and joined the Covent Garden company in 1982, where he was promoted to soloist in 1985, and principal in 1986. Although briefly abandoning the stage for personal reasons, he was otherwise one of the Royal's most impressive male dancers. Tall and classically good-looking, with a finely proportioned physique, he was a natural danseur noble and frequently cast as Siegfried, Solor, Albrecht, and Florimund. He was partner to Darcey Bussell and Sylvie Guillem with whom he was especially acclaimed in *Manon*, *Romeo and Juliet*, and *A Month in the Country*. He created roles in many ballets including MacMillan's *Different Drummer* and *Prince of the Pagodas*; Bintley's *Galanteries*; Page's *A Broken Set of Rules* and *Fearful Symmetries*; and Wheeldon's *Tryst*. After retiring from the stage in 2004 he became a ballet master with the Royal.

Copland, Aaron (*b* Brooklyn, NY, 14 Nov. 1900; *d* North Tarrytown, NY, 2 Dec. 1990) US composer.

He was one of the key figures in the development of an American musical style, incorporating folksongs, cowboy melodies, square dance tunes, and traditional hymns into his music. He wrote the scores for several dance works including Ruth Page's *Hear Ye! Hear Ye!* (1934), Eugene Loring's *Billy the Kid* (1938), Agnes de Mille's *Rodeo* (1942), Martha Graham's *Appalachian Spring* (1944), and Heinz Rosen's *Dance Panels, Ballet in Seven Movements* (1963). Other ballets using his music include Tudor's *Time Table* (1941), Humphrey's *El Salon Mexico* (1943), Robbins's *The Pied Piper* (1951), and Neumeier's *Hamlet: Connotations* (1976).

Coppélia (*La Fille aux yeux d'émail*) Ballet in three acts with choreography by Saint-Léon, libretto by Charles Nuitter and Saint-Léon, music by Delibes, scenery by Cambon, Despléchin, and Lavastre (or Levastre), and costumes by Alfred Albert. Premiered 25 May 1870 at the Paris Opera with Bozzacchi as Swanilda and Eugénie Fiocre as Franz. The ballet is based on E. T. A. Hoffmann's story *Der Sandmann* (although it is much more light-hearted than the macabre original) and weaves the romance of Swanilda and Franz into a tale of the old toy maker Dr Coppelius, who dreams of bringing one of his mechanical doll to life. Franz falls in love with the doctor's creation, Coppélia, believing her to be human, but returns to Swanilda at the end when all indiscretions are forgotten in the final grand divertissement. The ballet was noted for its ingenious integration of classical and folk dance material and remains one of the most popular works in the international repertoire, although little remains of the original Saint-Léon choreography. In its original staging, the role of Franz was danced by a woman. The Paris Opera continued the traditional en travestie casting as late as 1958. The first production in London was a one-act version at the Empire Theatre on 8 Nov. 1884. A full-length staging was premiered on the same stage on 14 May 1906 with Adeline Genée as Swanilda. The first New York production was on 11 Mar. 1887, given by the American Opera at the Metropolitan Opera House with Marie Giuri and Felicita Carozzi. Petipa staged his own version in St Petersburg in 1884, which cast Franz as a male dancer. This was the production brought to the West by Sergeyev who mounted a two-act version (after Petipa and Cecchetti) for the Vic-Wells Ballet with Lydia Lopokova as Swanilda and Stanley Judson as Franz on 21 Mar. 1933. A three-act version for the Sadler's Wells Ballet followed on 15 Apr. 1940 with Mary Honer as Swanilda and Robert Helpmann as Franz. On 2 Mar. 1954 de Valois staged the full-length ballet at Covent Garden with new designs by Osbert Lancaster, a production which was revived by the Royal Ballet in

2000. The work has received countless new stagings, including Pierre Lacotte's reconstruction of the original Saint-Léon for the Paris Opera in 1973, Balanchine and Danilova's for New York City Ballet in 1974, Roland Petit's for Marseilles in 1975 with Karen Kain as Swanilda, Peter Wright's for Sadler's Wells Royal Ballet (1976) and for Birmingham Royal Ballet (1995), and Sergei Vikharev's for the Bolshoi (2009).

Coq d'or, Le (Eng. title *The Golden Cockerel*, orig. Russ. title *Zolotoi petushok*) Opera in three acts with music by Rimsky-Korsakov and libretto by V. Belsky after Pushkin's poem. Although written as an opera, it was as a ballet that the work earned its international reputation. Fokine staged it for Diaghilev's Ballets Russes on 24 May 1914 at the Paris Opera, with all the roles performed by dancers, leaving the singers to sing the action from the side of the stage. Each singer was paired with a dancer; only the Golden Cockerel did not appear on stage. The designs, based on Russian folk art, were by Goncharova. Fokine's cast included Karsavina, Bulgakov, and Cecchetti. Fokine restaged his work for de Basil's Ballets Russes in 1937 as a one-act ballet without using singers, starring Baronova and Riabouchinska. This was the version revived by Beriozoff for London Festival Ballet in 1976. The humorous ballet recounts the folk tale of the Golden Cockerel, which rewards those who keep their promises.

Coralli, Jean (orig. Giovanni Coralli Peracini; *b* Paris, 15 Jan. 1779; *d* Paris, 1 May 1854) Italian-French dancer and choreographer. Best known as the co-choreographer of *Giselle*. He studied at the Paris Opera Ballet School and made his debut as a dancer there in 1802. As a choreographer he made early work for Vienna, Milan, Lisbon, and Marseilles, and was ballet master of the Théâtre de la Porte-Saint-Martin (1825–9). But he is best remembered for his work at the Paris Opera where he went as ballet master in 1831 (remaining until 1850). A list of his ballets there includes *L'Orgie* (mus. M. E. Carafa, 1831), *La Tempête, ou L'île des génies* (mus. Schneitzhoeffer, 1834), *Le Diable boiteux* (mus. C. Gide, 1836), *La Chatte métamorphosée en femme* (mus. A. de Montfort, 1837), *La Tarentule* (mus. Gide, 1839), *Giselle* (in collaboration with Perrot, mus. Adam, 1841), *La Péri* (mus. Burgmüller, 1843), *Eucharis* (mus. E. Deldevez, 1844), and *Ozai, ou L'Insulaire* (mus. Gide, 1847). As one of the most famous choreographers of the Romantic era, he created four ballets for Fanny Elssler and one for Carlotta Grisi. His enduring legacy, *Giselle*, was not typical of his work. He preferred the spectacle of more exotic subject-matter and was praised for his ability to create magical stage effects. It is however his choreography for the Wilis in Act II, with its air of poetic mystery, which remains one of the most resonant images of Romantic ballet.

Corder, Michael (*b* London, 17 Mar. 1955) British dancer and choreographer. He studied at the Royal Ballet School and joined the Royal Ballet in 1973. In 1978–9 he was with Dutch National Ballet, between 1979 and 1981 he was with Sadler's Wells Royal Ballet as a soloist, and from 1981 he was with the Joffrey Ballet. He created his first work in 1974 for the Royal Ballet Choreographic Group and his first professional production was *Rhyme nor Reason* (mus. Stravinsky) for Sadler's Wells Royal Ballet in 1978. As a choreographer he rapidly established a reputation for the fluency and classical finesse of his dance invention, one of the few of his generation to remain within the language of the danse d'ecole. He made several more works for the Sadler's Wells company including *Day into Night* (mus. Martinů, 1980), *Three Pictures* (mus. Bartók, 1981), *The Wand of Youth* (1985), and *Gloriana* (1987) while for the Royal Ballet he made *L'Invitation au voyage* (1982), *Party Game* (1984), *Number Three* (1985), *Masquerade* (mus. Stravinsky, 1999), and the 'Water' choreography for the revised version of Ashton's *Homage to the Queen* (2006). For English National Ballet he made *Cinderella* (mus. Prokofiev, 1996), which was taken into the repertoire of the Boston Ballet, *Melody on the Move* (mus. various, 2003), and *The Snow Queen* (mus. Prokofiev, 2007). He has also choreographed *Romeo and Juliet* (mus. Prokofiev, 1992) for the Norwegian National Ballet and Stravinsky's *Le Baiser de la fée* for Birmingham Royal Ballet (2008) along with works for the Hong Kong Ballet, the Royal Danish Ballet, and the Kobayashi Ballet Theater in Tokyo.

Corella, Angel (*b* Madrid, Nov 8, 1975) Spanish dancer and company director. He studied with Victor Ullate in Madrid and joined American Ballet Theatre in 1995, where he was promoted to principal the following year. An extrovert, virtuoso dancer, he performs most of the leading roles in the repertoire, and is especially noted for his Romeo, Solor, and Don Basilio. In 2008 he founded the Corella Ballet, the first new classical ballet company in Spain in 20 years.

Cornejo, Herman (*b* San Luis, Argentina, 13 May 1981) Argentinian dancer. He trained at the Superior Institute of Art at the Colón Theatre in Buenos Aires and at the School of American Ballet in New York, at 16 becoming the youngest ever Gold Medallist in the International Dance Competition in Moscow (1997). He danced with Ballet Argentino before joining American Ballet Theatre in 1999, where he was promoted to principal in 2003. An exceptionally stylish, technically

accomplished dancer, he has created roles in Tharp's *Rabbit and Rogue* and *I Dig Love* (in *Within You Without You: A Tribute to George Harrison*).

corps de ballet The term originally referred to the entire body of dancers within a ballet company, although nowadays it refers to the dancers who regularly perform together as a group, as opposed to soloists, principals, or character artists. On stage the dancers of the corps de ballet may act as a frame for the soloists but some of the greatest classical choreography is for the corps de ballet alone, as the complex patterns created by two or three dozen dancers create their own visual, musical, and dramatic poetry. Famous examples include the hallucinatory Kingdom of the Shades scene in *La Bayadère*, in which the dancers of the corps enter the stage one by one, repeating the same phrase of movement until the stage is filled with their massed presence; also Acts II and IV of *Swan Lake* and Act II of *Giselle*.

Corsaire, Le Ballet in three acts, with choreography by Mazilier, libretto by Henri Vernoy de Saint-Georges and Mazilier, music by Adam, sets by Martin, Despléchin, Cambon, and Thierry, costumes by Albert, and machinery by Sacré. Premiered 23 Jan. 1856 at the Paris Opera, with Carolina Rosati and Domenico Segarelli. The story is very loosely based on Byron's poem, *The Corsair* and tells of a young Greek woman, Medora, who is sold as a slave girl to the lecherous Ottoman Pasha Seyd and through a series of dramatically staged rescues and lucky escapes (including a shipwreck) ends up safely in the embrace of the dashing pirate Conrad. An earlier version of the ballet, choreographed by F. D. Albert to music by Robert Bochsa, was premiered at the King's Theatre in London in 1837, but it was eclipsed by the popularity of Mazilier's staging. Perrot staged a version (after Mazilier) with additional music by Pugni at the Bolshoi Theatre in St Petersburg in 1858 that featured Petipa as Conrad; with Petipa contributing a pas d'esclave with music by Prince Peter von Oldenburg. Petipa revived it in 1868 in a new version for his wife, Marie Petipa, which included the Le Jardin Animé scene to music by Delibes. The ballet's most significant staging occurred in 1899 when Petipa completely reworked it for the Mariinsky (with additional music by Drigo and Minkus) with Pierina Legnani as Medora. This is the production which formed the basis for subsequent Russian stagings during the 20th century, including Gorsky's (Bolshoi, 1912) that gave Conrad and Medora a new love duet, Gusev's (Maly, 1955) and K. Sergeyev's 1973. In 2007 Ratmansky staged a reconstructed version of the 1899 production for the Bolshoi, which reinstated Petipa's original mass choreography for the Jardin Animé scene. In the West the ballet has most often been represented by the *Corsaire* pas de deux (originally conceived as a pas de trois), whose extrovertly virtuoso choreography has made it a gala favourite. However Boston Ballet staged a full-length version of the ballet, based on K. Sergeyev's staging, in 1992 and American Ballet Theatre presented a revised production of this in 1998. In 2007 the Bavarian State Ballet mounted a version based on Petipa's 1899 staging.

coryphée [Fr., derived from the Greek for leader of the chorus] In the hierarchy of classical ballet, as set out by the French and Russian traditions, the term is applied to a minor soloist.

Cote, Guillaume (*b* Lac-Saint-Jean, Quebec, 17 Sept 1981) Canadian dancer. He studied at the National Ballet School of Canada and graduated into the National Ballet of Canada in 1999; appointed principal in 2004. An elegantly classical dancer and intelligent actor he dances most of the principal repertory and has created a number of lead roles in ballets by James Kudelka, including Ferdinand in *An Italian Straw Hat*, Prince Charming in *Cinderella*, and Will in *The Contract* (*The Pied Piper*). He has also guested with several companies, including American Ballet Theatre, English National Ballet, and Staatsoper Berlin, and as a freelance composer has written the music for several dance and theatre productions.

cotillon A popular ballroom dance dating back to the late 18th century. It was usually danced as the finale to a ball and featured a leading couple, with a continual changing of partners throughout. It is danced in the second act of Tchaikovsky's opera *Eugene Onegin*.

Cotillon Ballet in one act with choreography by Balanchine, libretto by Kochno, music by Chabrier, and designs by Christian Bérard. Premiered 12 Apr. 1932 by the Ballets Russes de Monte Carlo in Monte Carlo, with Toumanova, Lichine, and Woizikowski. The action, which unfolds in a ballroom, is secondary to the development of atmosphere. Hodson and Archer reconstructed the ballet for the Joffrey Ballet in New York on 26 Oct. 1989.

Coton, A. V. (orig. Edward Haddakin; *b* York, 1906; *d* Blackheath, 7 Jul. 1969) British dance critic and writer. He worked as a merchant seaman and policeman before taking up ballet criticism in 1935 and helping Tudor to form the London Ballet in 1938. He was ballet critic of the *Daily Telegraph* (1954–69). Author of *A Prejudice for Ballet* (London, 1938), *The New Ballet: Kurt Jooss and his Work* (London, 1946), and *Writings on Dance 1938–68* (ed. posthumously; London, 1975).

cou-de-pied Sur le cou-de-pied describes the position that places the working foot on the ankle of the supporting leg.

Coulon A famous family of French dancers who performed at the Paris Opera in the 18th and 19th centuries. They include Anne-Jacqueline (who danced at the Opera from 1778 to 1802); her brother Jean-François (1764–1836), who taught Taglioni; and his son Antoine-Louis (1796–1849). The latter's son Eugene was a popular ballroom dancing teacher in England.

coupé [Fr., cut] An intermediary step in which one foot takes the place of the other foot.

courante [Fr., running dance] A 16th-century French court dance.

Covent Garden (The Royal Opera House) London's premier opera house and home of the *Royal Ballet since 1946. It opened in 1732 as a dramatic theatre but was destroyed by fire in 1809 and rebuilt the following year. It became the Royal Italian Opera in 1847 but was again destroyed by fire in 1856. The present opera house was rebuilt in 1858. In 1946, after the Second World War, it became the permanent home of the Royal Ballet (then known as the Covent Garden Opera) and the Royal Ballet which, as the Sadler's Wells Ballet, transferred to Covent Garden from its home at Sadler's Wells. In 1997 the Royal Opera House closed for a two-year redevelopment, forcing the Royal Ballet and Opera to tour during the closure period. It reopened in December 1999.

Cragun, Richard (*b* Sacramento, Calif., 5 Oct. 1944) US dancer. He studied tap and ballet locally, then trained at the Banff School of Fine Arts in Canada, with Gweneth Lloyd and Betty Farrally, at the Royal Ballet School in London, and with Vera Volkova in Copenhagen. In 1962 he joined the Stuttgart Ballet, where he was promoted to principal in 1965. Although guesting frequently with other companies he remained at Stuttgart until 1996, forming his celebrated 30-year partnership with the ballerina Marcia Haydée. A virtuoso dancer, with a robustly masculine stage presence, he was one of the leading male artists of the latter half of the 20th century. He was noted for his interpretations of Romeo and Onegin in Cranko's stagings and created roles in many other Cranko ballets, including *L'estro armonico* (1963), *Opus 1* (1965), *Mozart Concerto* (1966), *Présence* (1968), *Taming of the Shrew* (1969, the role of Petruchio), *Brouillards* (1970), *Poème de l'extase* (1970), *Carmen* (1971), *Initials R.B.M.E.* (1972), and *Traces* (1973). He also created roles in Peter Wright's *The Mirror Walkers* (1963), MacMillan's *Song of the Earth* (1965), *Requiem* (1977), and *My*

Brother, My Sisters (1978), Tetley's *Voluntaries* (1973) and *Daphnis and Chloe* (1975), Neumeier's *Lady of the Camellias* (1978) and *A Streetcar Named Desire* (1983), which showcased his continuing partnership with Haydée, Forsythe's *Orpheus* (1979), Kylián's *Forgotten Land* (1981), and several works by Béjart, including *La Danse* (1983) and *Operette* (1985). In 1990 he revived his childhood tap skills, starring in the Stuttgart revival of the Broadway musical *On Your Toes*. He retired from the stage in 1996 and was appointed artistic director of the Berlin Opera Ballet. He left Berlin in 1999 and in 2001 became founding director of the DeAnima company, near Rio de Janeiro. With choreographer Roberto de Oliveira and William Forsythe as artistic consultant, this company has built up a repertory of contemporary ballet works and also runs community projects for disadvantaged young people. Cragun is also a cartoonist, and has mounted several exhibitions of his work.

⊕ SEE WEB LINKS

• Website for the DeAnima company

Cramér, Ivo (*b* Gothenburg, 5 Mar. 1921) Swedish dancer, choreographer, and ballet director. He studied with Cullberg, Volkova, and Sigurd Leeder, dancing in 1944 with the Cullberg Group and touring Sweden with a troupe of his own in 1945. From 1946 to 1947 he was co-director with Cullberg of Swedish Dance Theatre and from 1948 to 1949 director of the Verde Gaio folk dance company in Lisbon. He worked extensively as a freelance choreographer and operetta director in Scandinavia, most notably with the Royal Swedish Ballet, for whom he choreographed the folkloric version of *The Prodigal Son* (mus. H. Alfvén, 1957), which is considered his masterwork. He founded the Cramér Ballet in Stockholm with his wife Tyyne Talvo in 1967, and made many ballets for the company, including *Good Evening, Beautiful Mask* (1971), about the assassination of King Gustav III (founder of the Royal Swedish Ballet), and *Peasant Gospel* (1972). He ran the company until 1975—when he became director of the Royal Swedish Ballet—but returned to it five years later and continued to direct it until 1986. A choreographer much interested in Nordic folk art and religious themes, he was also a pioneering producer of early ballets and worked on many historical reconstructions, especially works from the 18th century (often in collaboration with Mary Skeaping). His 1989 reconstruction of Dauberval's *La Fille mal gardée* for Nantes Opera Ballet was a particular success. In 1992 he staged a Noverre ballet, *Medée et Jason*, for the Ballet du Rhin.

Cranko, John (*b* Rustenburg, 15 Aug. 1927; *d* en route from Philadelphia to Stuttgart, 26 Jun. 1973) South African dancer, choreographer, and director. Architect of the Stuttgart Ballet. He studied at the Cape Town University Ballet School and after choreographing his first ballet there in 1945, the suite from Stravinsky's *The Soldier's Tale*, he gained popular success with his setting of Johan Strauss's polka *Tritsch-Tratsch* (1946). In 1946 he went to England to study at Sadler's Wells School and subsequently joined Sadler's Wells Theatre Ballet, and Sadler's Wells Ballet at Covent Garden. He never worked again in S. Africa. In Britain he retired from the stage at 23 to focus on choreography, and created numerous works for Sadler's Wells (later the Royal) Ballet including *Children's Corner* (mus. Debussy, 1947), *Sea Change* (mus. Sibelius, 1949), *Beauty and the Beast* (mus. Ravel, 1949), *Pineapple Poll* (mus. Sullivan, arr. Mackerras, 1951), *Harlequin in April* (mus. Richard Arnell, 1951), *Bonne-Bouche* (mus. Arthur Oldham, 1952), *The Shadow* (mus. E. von Dohnányi, 1953), *The Lady and the Fool* (mus. Verdi, arr. Mackerras, 1954), *The Prince of the Pagodas* (mus. Britten, 1957), and *Antigone* (mus. Theodorakis, 1959/60). At the same time he also worked extensively as a guest choreographer: for New York City Ballet he choreographed *The Witch* (mus. Ravel, 1950); for Ballet Rambert, *Variations on a Theme* (mus. Britten, 1954) and *La Reja* (mus. Scarlatti, 1959); for Paris Opera, *La Belle Hélène* (mus. Offenbach–Rosenthal, 1955); and for La Scala, Milan, *Romeo and Juliet* (mus. Prokofiev, 1958). He additionally directed and choreographed the London revues *Cranks* (1955) and *New Cranks* (1960) and also directed the first production of Britten's opera *A Midsummer Night's Dream* at Aldeburgh in 1960. In 1961, after the failure of his *Antigone* for Covent Garden and a musical, *Keep Your Hair On*, Cranko accepted the invitation to direct the Stuttgart Ballet. He went on to turn the provincial German company into one of the world's leading ensembles, developing a team of superb dancers—such as Haydée, Barra, and Cragun—and choreographing many new ballets for them. His early death from a heart attack, while flying home from a US tour, was a loss to the international ballet world, as well as to Stuttgart. As a choreographer he had an exceptional gift for creating full-length story ballets, combining detailed characterization with a dramatic sweep and theatrical flair. His productions of *Romeo and Juliet*, *Onegin*, and *Taming of the Shrew* have all entered the international repertoire. A list of the works he created for Stuttgart includes *The Catalyst* (mus. Shostakovich, 1961), *Daphnis and Chloe* (mus. Ravel, 1962), *Romeo and Juliet* (Stuttgart staging, mus. Prokofiev, 1962), *L'estro armonico* (mus. Vivaldi, 1963), *Swan*

Lake (producer, 1963), *Jeu de cartes* (mus. Stravinsky, 1965), *Onegin* (mus. Tchaikovsky–Stolze, 1965), *Opus 1* (mus. Webern, 1965), *Mozart Concerto* (1966), *The Nutcracker* (1966), *The Interrogation* (mus. B. A. Zimmermann, 1967), *Quatre images* (mus. Ravel, 1967–8), *Présence* (mus. Zimmermann, 1968), *Taming of the Shrew* (mus. Scarlatti–Stolze, 1969), *Brouillards* (mus. Debussy, 1970), *Poème de l'extase* (mus. Scriabin, 1970), *Carmen* (mus. Bizet–Fortner–Steinbrenner, 1971), *Initials R.B.M.E.* (mus. Brahms, 1972), and *Traces* (mus. Mahler, 1973).

Craske, Margaret (*b* Norfolk, 26 Nov. 1892; *d* Myrtle Beach, SC, 18 Feb. 1990) British dancer and teacher. She danced briefly with Diaghilev (her career was cut short by injury), and as former pupil of Cecchetti, she was chosen by him to carry on his teachings when he left England in 1923 to retire to his native Italy. In 1924 she opened her own school in London and among her pupils were Ashton, Dolin, Tudor, van Praagh, and Fonteyn. From 1939 to 1946 she settled in India, becoming a disciple to the guru Meher Baba, but in 1946 moved to the US where she re-established her reputation as a superb teacher and a leading authority on the Cecchetti method. She was initially ballet mistress of American Ballet Theatre, then from 1950 to 1968 taught at the Metropolitan Opera Ballet School, after which she ran her own Manhattan School of Dance (1968–83). Paul Taylor, Agnes de Mille, Glen Tetley, Viola Farber, and Carolyn Brown were among those who were influenced by her teaching. Craske was also co-author (with C. W. Beaumont) of *The Theory and Practice of Allegro in Classical Ballet (Cecchetti Method)* (1930) and (with F. Derra de Moroda) *Practice of Advanced Allegro in Classical Ballet (Cecchetti Method)* (1956).

Creation of the World, The (orig. Fr. title *La Création du monde*) Ballet in one act with choreography by Börlin, libretto by Blaise Cendrars, music by Milhaud, and designs by Léger. Premiered 25 Oct. 1923 by the Ballets Suédois at the Théâtre des Champs-Elysées, Paris, with Börlin and Ebon Strandin. It retells the story of the Creation through the imagination of a black African. Other versions are by de Valois (Camargo Society, 1931), MacMillan (Royal Ballet, 1964), and Bolender (New York City Ballet, 1964). A ballet of the same title using music by Andrei Petrov was choreographed for the Kirov by Natalia Kastakina and Vladimir Vasiliov with a created role for Baryshnikov.

Creatures of Prometheus, The Heroic-allegorical ballet in two acts with choreography by S. Viganò and music by Beethoven. Premiered 28 Mar. 1801 at the Burg Theatre, Vienna, with Cesari, Mme Brendi, Cassentini, and Viganò. One of only two ballet scores by Beethoven, it was subsequently used by several other choreographers, including Lifar for the Paris Opera in 1929, Milloss (Augsburg, 1933), de Valois for Vic-Wells Ballet in 1936, and Ashton for the Royal Ballet Touring Group in Bonn in 1970. Viganò choreographed a new version for La Scala in Milan in 1813 using music by different composers. The ballet portrays Prometheus as the creator of mankind.

Crickmay, Anthony (*b* Woking, 20 May 1937) British ballet and theatre photographer. He has worked mainly with the Royal Ballet, although also with companies in Europe and N. America. Noted for the glamour and polish of his dance photography.

Crisp, Clement (*b* Romford, 21 Sept. 1931) British dance critic and writer. He was educated at Bordeaux and Oxford Universities, becoming ballet critic of the *Spectator* (1966–70) and dance critic of the *Financial Times* since 1970. As one of Britain's pre-eminent critics he has additionally published numerous books including *Ballet for All* (with P. Brinson, London, 1970, revised edition, 1980); *Ballet: An Illustrated History* (with M. Clarke, London, 1973, revised edition, 1992); *Making a Ballet* (with Clarke, London, 1974); *Ballet in Art* (with Clarke, 1976); *Design for Ballet* (with Clarke, London, 1978); *Introducing Ballet* (with Clarke, 1978); *History of Dance* (with Clarke, London, 1981); *The Balletgoer's Guide* (with Clarke, 1981); *Dancer* (with Clarke, 1984); and *Ballerina* (with Clarke, 1987). He was also librarian and archivist of the Royal Academy of Dancing (1963–85) and archivist from 1985. His honours include Queen Elizabeth II Coronation Award, Royal Academy of Dancing, 1992. Knight of the Order of Dannebrog, Denmark, 1992.

Croce, Arlene (*b* Providence, RI, 5 May 1934) US critic and writer on dance. She founded *Ballet Review* in 1965, continuing as editor until 1978, and through her column in the *New Yorker* (1974–98) became one of America's foremost and most influential dance critics. She was author of *The Fred Astaire and Ginger Rogers Book* (New York, 1972) and her collected reviews were published in four volumes: *Afterimages* (1978), *Going to the Dance* (1982), *Sight Lines* (1987), and *Writing in the Dark* (2000). She also worked in television, as a writer for the *Dance in America* series.

croisée [Fr., crossed] A position in classical ballet in which the body is presented at a sideways angle to the audience and in which the working leg crosses the line of the body.

Cruel Garden Modern dance in two acts with choreography by Christopher Bruce, direction by Lindsay Kemp, music by Carlos Miranda, sets by Ralph Koltai, and costumes by Kemp. Premiered 5 Jul. 1977 by Ballet Rambert at the Roundhouse in London, with Bruce, John Tsakiris, Michael Ho, and John Chesworth. A surreal fantasy based on the life and writings of the murdered Spanish poet Federico García Lorca.

Crumb, George (*b* Charleston, W. Va., 24 Oct. 1929) US composer. His score *Ancient Voices of Children* has been used by many choreographers, including J. Stripling (Stuttgart, 1971), Butler (in *La Voix*, Ballet du Rhin, 1972), and, most notably, Christopher Bruce for Ballet Rambert in 1975. Bruce also used his music for *Black Angels* (Rambert, 1976), *Echoes in Autumn for Stationary Flying* (Utah Repertory Dance Theatre, 1973), *Echoes of a Night Sky* (Rambert, 1977), and *Night with Waning Moon* (Rambert, 1979).

Cry Solo modern dance with choreography by Ailey, music by Alice Coltrane, Laura Nyro, and Voices of East Harlem, and lighting by Chenault Spence. Premiered 4 May 1971 by the Alvin Ailey company at City Center, New York, with Judith Jamison. This life-affirming solo, created specially for Jamison, became her most famous role. The choreographer dedicated it to 'black women everywhere—especially our mothers'.

csardas (czardas) A Hungarian dance for couples. It first appeared in Hungarian ballrooms in the mid-19th century. The dance is in two parts: the first slow and melancholy, the second fast and high-spirited. There are several famous examples in classical ballet, including the ballroom act in *Swan Lake* and the divertissement in *Raymonda*.

Cuba One of the first significant performances of European classical ballet in Cuba was Fanny Elssler's 1841 appearance in *La Sylphide* at the Tacón Theatre in Havana. During subsequent decades some touring companies visited, notably Pavlova's, which performed in Cuba in 1915, 1917, and 1918, but indigenous Cuban ballet activity did not emerge until the early 1930s when ballet evenings were presented by the Sociedad Pro-Arte Musical. The first director of this school was the Russian Nikolai Yavorsky (1931–8); one of its first graduates was Alberto Alonso, who was hired by de Basil's Ballets Russes in 1935. A subsequent graduate was Alicia *Alonso, hired by Ballet Caravan in 1939. In 1948 she started her own company in Havana, drawing on the resources of the SPAM, and in 1950 added her own school. In 1955 her company was renamed Ballet de Cuba, and following the Revolution of 1959 it was reorganized as the *National Ballet of Cuba, with full state support.

On its first S. American tour that year it was led by Alonso and Igor Youskevitch. The company soon attracted international attention, partly because of its active touring and partly because its dancers were so successful in competitions like Varna. It still ranks as the pre-eminent Cuban dance company, with a large repertoire of both classical and modern works by Cuban choreographers. Cuba's active policy of developing young dance talent has produced many fine dancers, especially men, although several, including Jose Manuel *Carreño and Carlos *Acosta, have made their careers abroad. In 1967 the Cuban choreographer Alberto Alonso was invited to the Bolshoi Ballet to create a new ballet for Maya Plisetskaya. The work, *Carmen*, which had its debut on 28 Apr. 1967, marked the first time that a foreign choreographer had been invited to work with the Bolshoi. The Danza Contemporánea de Cuba, founded in 1959 by Ramiro Guerra with generous support from the state, is the country's leading modern dance ensemble and in recent years has opened up its repertory to outside choreographers including Rafael *Bonachela and Mats *Ek. Other smaller companies have emerged since the 1990s. *Salsa, Cuba's national dance form, has achieved enormous international popularity both on stage and in classes and dancehalls.

Cuevas, Marquis George de (orig. Marquis de Peidrablanca de Guana de Cuevas; *b* Santiago, 26 May 1885; *d* Cannes, 22 Feb. 1961) Chilean-American patron and director of his own company, *Grand Ballet du Marquis de Cuevas. A passionate balletomane, he was married to Margaret Strong, granddaughter of John D. Rockefeller, and it was her personal fortune that allowed de Cuevas to run his own company from his base in Paris. He founded his first company, Ballet International, in 1944. In 1947 he took over the Nouveau Ballet de Monte Carlo, renaming it first the Grand Ballet de Monte Carlo and then the Grand Ballet du Marquis de Cuevas. In 1947 he hired Bronislava Nijinska as his ballet mistress. Unusually for a European company, his had a strong line-up of American dancers, among them Rosella Hightower, Marjorie Tallchief, William Dollar, and George Skibine. He also took ballets by US choreographers into the repertoire. His company toured exhaustively between 1947 and 1960. He hired some of the biggest names in dance, including Markova, Toumanova, Massine, Lichine, and Bruhn. The company continued briefly after his death, under the directorship of his nephew Raymundo de Larrain, but was dissolved in 1962. The Marquis was a flamboyant figure, much loved by the French public, and he was a frequent giver of elaborate balls. At one such event, the so-called 'Ball of the Century', he appeared dressed as the Sun King while his corps de ballet performed Act II of *Swan Lake* on a raft in the middle of a lake. His last production was *The Sleeping Beauty*, begun by Nijinska and finished by Robert Helpmann, and it was in this that Nureyev made his debut in the West after defecting from the Kirov in 1961.

Cullberg, Birgit (*b* Nyköping, 3 Aug. 1908; *d* Stockholm, 8 Sept. 1999) Swedish dancer, choreographer, and ballet director. Despite early training in both classical and modern dance, she decided to become a professional at the late age of 27 after seeing a performance of Kurt Jooss's *The Green Table* in Stockholm. She studied with Jooss and Sigurd Leeder at *Dartington Hall in England (1935–9), and later with Graham in New York. She founded her first group in 1939 and in 1942 gave her first solo recital in Stockholm. With Ivo Cramér (her pupil) she founded the Swedish Dance Theatre in 1946, which toured Europe. Her breakthrough came in 1950 with *Miss Julie*, based on the Strindberg play (she had been a literature student at Stockholm University and frequently used literary sources for her ballets). Its success brought her to the attention of the Royal Swedish Ballet, where from 1952 to 1956 she was resident choreographer. She then pursued a freelance career, choreographing for the Royal Danish Ballet (*The Moon Reindeer* in 1957) and American Ballet Theatre (*Lady from the Sea*, 1960). In 1967 she returned to Sweden to found her own government-backed company, the Cullberg Ballet, which she directed until 1985. She made her last appearance as a dancer at the age of 68, performing in her son Mats Ek's ballet *Soweto*. A pioneer in the field of television dance, she made many ballets for the small screen; *The Evil Queen* won her the Prix d'Italia in 1961. Her ballets, strongly influenced by Jooss were known for their psychological depth and strong drama, although she was also known for her satiric humour. Her best-known works include *Miss Julie* (mus. T. Rangström, 1950), *Medea* (mus. Bartók–Sandberg, 1950), *Romeo and Juliet* (mus. Prokofiev, 1955, second version), *The Moon Reindeer* (mus. K. Riisager, 1957), *Lady from the Sea* (mus. Riisager, 1960), *Eden* (mus. H. Rosenberg, 1961), *I Am Not You* (mus. B. Brustad, 1966), *Romeo and Juliet* (mus. Prokofiev, 1969, third version), *Bellman* (mus. Beethoven, 1971), *Revolt* (mus. Bartók, 1973), and *War Dances* (mus. A. Petterson or Petersson, 1979). Two of her sons, Niklas and Mats *Ek, also became dancers.

Cullberg Ballet, The Stockholm-based company founded by the Swedish Government in 1967 to provide a platform for the choreography of Birgit Cullberg. It was directed by Cullberg until 1985, and by her son, the choreographer Mats *Ek,

from 1985 to 1993. As well as works by Cullberg and Ek, the repertoire features choreography by Ulf Gadd, Elsa Marianne von Rosen, Flindt, Cunningham, Ailey, Jooss, Béjart, Bruce, Kylián, and more recently by Sidi Larbi Cherkaoui, Johan Inger, and Crystal Pite. Carolyn Carlson succeeded Ek as artistic director (1993–5) and was succeeded by Lene Wennergren-Juras (1995–2003) and Johan Inger (2003–08) whose works for the company have included *Point of Eclipse* (2007) and *Position of Elsewhere* (2009). After two years of being run by a temporary artistic director Anna Grip was appointed to the post in 2010 with a policy of expanding the company's performance activities into gallery installation and film. Ek continues to be Cullberg's principal guest choreographer.

((⊕)) SEE WEB LINKS

• Website for the Cullberg Ballet

Cuni, Diana (*b* Copenhagen, 1975) Danish dancer. She studied at the Royal Danish Ballet School and joined the company as an apprentice in 1991, becoming soloist in 2001. A dancer of exceptional fluency, her command of the Bournonville technique combines speed, precision and a rare feel for plastique. Cuni's ballerina repertoire includes Teresina in *Napoli* and Kitri in *Don Quixote*, as well as roles in the contemporary repertory, including Forsythe's *In the middle....*

Cunningham, Merce (*b* Centralia, Wash., 16 Apr. 1919; *d* New York, 26 Jul. 2009) US dancer, choreographer, and company director. One of the towering figures of 20th-century modern dance. He studied tap, folk, and ballroom dancing locally, followed by training in modern dance at the Cornish School of Fine Arts in Seattle, at Mills College, Oakland, California, and at the Bennington Summer School of Dance. In 1939 he joined the Martha Graham company and for the next six years was one of her leading performers. A lithe, witty dancer with a fine elevation he created roles in many of her works, including *Every Soul is a Circus* (1939), *El Penitente* (1940), *Letter to the World* (1940), *Punch and Judy* (1941), *Deaths and Entrances* (1943), and *Appalachian Spring* (1944). During this time he also studied ballet at the School of American Ballet. In 1942 he gave a recital of his own choreography at *Bennington College using music by John *Cage and in 1944 he and Cage gave a joint concert at the Humphrey-Weidman Studio Theater in New York. Cage, Cunningham's life partner, was also to become his musical collaborator and adviser until his death. After leaving Graham's company in 1945 Cunningham became an independent choreographer developing a style that combined aspects of ballet (fast rhythmic footwork and high leg extensions) with the free, mobile torso and blunt thrust of modern dance. His works also made a point of eschewing narrative, character, or theme. One of his early commissions was *The Seasons* (mus. Cage) for Ballet Society, which was danced at its premiere on 18 May 1947 by Tanaquil LeClercq and Cunningham. He set up his own company in the summer of 1953, with dancers including Carolyn Brown, Viola Farber, Remy Charlip, and Paul Taylor and John Cage and David Tudor as resident musicians. The company gave its New York debut on 29 Dec. 1953 at the Theater de Lys in Greenwich Village, touring the US in 1955, and making its first international tour in 1964. As an increasingly central figure in the American avant-garde, Cunningham worked with leading figures from the art world including Robert Rauschenberg (resident designer 1954–64), Andy Warhol, Frank Stella, and Jasper Johns. However a defining feature of these collaborations was Cunningham's insistence upon the creative independence of design, dance, and music in each work. With the exception of his earliest choreography these three elements usually came together for the first time in performance, and the only commonality between them was that they happened within the same time frame and within the same space. Cunningham also began to create his dances through chance procedures, allowing decisions about the order or trajectory of the movement or the number of dancers to be made by the toss of a coin, for example, or the roll of the *I Ching*. Throughout his long career Cunningham continued to experiment with new creative methods. He was the first major choreographer to use computer technology, creating movement sequences on screen before setting them on his dancers, and thus facilitating an increasing complexity of action and stage patterning. In 1991 he helped develop the choreographic computer software Life Forms. His 1999 work *BIPED* was his first digital dance, in which computer-generated images, including dancing figures, were projected onto the stage to create a perspective-altering interaction with the live performers. Apart from a few exceptions including *Septet* (1953, set to music by Satie) most of the scores accompanying Cunningham's work were specially composed for him and were electronic rather than orchestral or acoustic. He favoured a select group of composers although exceptions from this included rock groups Radiohead and Sigur Ros who provided the score for *Split Sides* (2003).

Cunningham also experimented with the staging of his works, initiating the concept of the Event in 1964. Events were performances of excerpts from the repertory which were arranged into a single evening without interval and often danced in non-theatrical spaces, such as gyms and art galleries.

Several of his works entered the repertoires of ballet and modern dance companies around the world, and his company toured internationally. His influence on other choreographers was monumental, both in terms of his movement style (which, like Graham, is now ranked as one of the major schools of modern dance) and the boldness of his experimental imagination. He continued working until a few weeks before his death—his last work was *Nearly Ninety* (2009). Cunningham was a guest teacher at universities throughout America and opened his own New York studio in 1959. A selection of his works includes *The Seasons* (mus. Cage, 1947), *Septet* (mus. Satie, 1953), *Minutiae* (mus. Cage, 1954), *Suite for Five* (mus. Cage, 1956), *Nocturnes* (mus. Satie, 1956), *Antic Meet* (mus. Cage, 1958), *Summerspace* (mus. Morton Feldman, 1958), *Rune* (mus. Wolff, 1959), *Crises* (mus. Nancarrow, 1960), *Aeon* (mus. Cage, 1961), *Story* (mus. Ichiyanagi, 1963), *Field Dances* (mus. Cage, 1963), *Winterbranch* (mus. LaMonte Young, 1964), *How to Pass, Kick, Fall and Run* (mus. Cage, 1965), *Scramble* (mus. Ichiyanagi, 1967), *RainForest* (mus. D. Tudor, 1968), *Walkaround Time* (mus. D. Behrman, 1968), *Canfield* (mus. P. Oliveros, 1969), *Tread* (mus. Wolff, 1970), *Signals* (mus. Tudor, Mumma, Cage, 1970), *Landrover* (mus. Cage, 1972), *Un jour ou deux* (mus. Cage, Paris Opera, 1973), *Sounddance* (mus. Tudor, 1975), *Changing Steps* (mus. Cage, 1975), *Rebus* (mus. Behrman, 1975), *Squaregame* (mus. Kosugi, 1976), *Locale* (mus. Kosugi, for video, 1979), *Roadrunners* (mus. Tone, 1979), *Duets* (mus. Cage, 1980), *Fielding Sixes* (mus. Cage, 1980), *Quartet* (mus. Tudor, 1982), *Roaratorio* (mus. Cage, 1983), *Pictures* (mus. Behrman, 1984), *Points in Space* (mus. Cage, for video, 1986), *Fabrications* (mus. Pimenta, 1987), *Field and Figures* (mus. Tcherepnin, 1989), *Inventions* (mus. Cage, 1989), *Beach Birds* (mus. Cage, 1991), *Trackers* (mus. Pimenta, 1991), *Change of Address* (mus. Zimmerman, 1992), *CRWDSPCR* (mus. John King, 1993), *Ocean* (mus. David Tudor and Andrew Culver, 1994), *Signals* (mus. Cage, 1994), *Ground Level Overlay* (mus. Stuart Dempster, 1995), *Rondo* (mus. Cage, 1996), *Pond Way* (mus. Brian Eno, 1998), *BIPED* (mus. Gavin Bryars, 1999), *Way Station* (mus. Takehisi Kosygi, 2001), *eyeSpace* (mus. Mikel Rouse, 2006), and *Nearly Ninety* (mus. various, 2009). He collaborated with directors Charles Atlas and Elliot Caplan, choreographing works especially for the camera like *Points in Space*, which have explored and expanded the possibilities of dance on screen. In 2009 the Cunningham Foundation announced its Legacy Plan, which laid out plans for the archiving and posthumous performance of Cunningham's work. He was author of *Changes:*

Notes on Choreography (New York, 1968) and recipient of numerous awards including L'Ordre des Arts et des Lettres, 1983, National Medal of Arts, US, 1990, named as 'Living Legend' by Library of Congress, 2000, Officier de la Légion d'honneur, 2004.

SEE WEB LINKS

• Website for the Cunningham company and foundation

Currier, Ruth (*née* Miller, *b* Ashland, Ohio, 1926) US dancer, choreographer, teacher, and ballet director. She studied with Humphrey and Limón and joined the latter's company in 1949. She created roles in several Limón works, including *There is a Time* (1956) and *Missa Brevis* (1958). She served as Humphrey's assistant (1952–8) and completed *Brandenburg Concerto No. 4* after Humphrey's death in 1958. She formed Ruth Currier and Dancers in 1961. After Limón's death in 1972 she was artistic director of his company for five years.

Curry, John (*b* Birmingham, 9 Sept. 1949; *d* Binton, 15 Apr. 1994) British ice skater, choreographer, and creator of Dance Theatre of Skating.

A virtuoso skater, he was much admired for the musicality and artistry of his competitive skating. He won both the Olympic Gold Medal and the World Championship in 1976. That same year he started his Theatre of Skating (later called Ice Dancing) troupe in London. He engaged choreographers such as Kenneth MacMillan, Peter Martins, and Twyla Tharp and later worked with Laura Dean, Eliot Feld, and Lar Lubovitch. He died prematurely from an Aids-related illness.

Cyrano de Bergerac Ballet in three acts, with choreography and libretto by Petit, music by Constant, sets by Basarte, and costumes by Saint-Laurent. Premiered 17 Apr. 1959 by the Ballets de Paris at the Alhambra Theatre in Paris, with Petit, Jeanmaire, and Reich. The ballet is based on Rostand's 1897 heroic comedy about Cyrano, the poet with the unfortunate nose who is forced to woo the woman he loves on behalf of another man. It was revived for the Royal Danish Ballet in 1961. David Bintley choreographed a full-length version for Covent Garden in 1991 using a commissioned score by Wilfred Josephs, followed by a second version for Birmingham Royal Ballet, in 2007 with a new score by C. Davis.

D

Dafora, Asadata (*b* John Warner Dafora Horton, Freetown, Sierra Leone, 1890; *d* New York, 4 Mar. 1965) West African singer, dancer, composer, choreographer, and writer. He studied singing in Milan and in 1912 joined a touring ensemble of African dancers. In 1929 he moved to the US where he presented dance dramas based on African legends, using authentic African dance and music, the most successful of which was *Kykunkor* (1934). These popular productions pioneered the appreciation of African traditions and inspired artists like P. Lang.

Dai Ailian (*b* Trinidad, 10 May 1916; *d* Beijing, 9 Feb. 2006) Chinese dancer, choreographer, director, and pioneer in the development of ballet in China. She trained locally and in 1931 moved to London where she studied ballet with Dolin, Craske, and others, also modern dance with Borrows-Goossens and with Laban and Jooss at Dartington. She returned to China in 1940 where she studied indigenous dance forms and taught modern dance as well as performing in various solo and group recitals. A committed popularizer of dance, she was appointed director of the Central Song and Dance Ensemble (1949–54) after which she was principal of the Beijing Ballet Academy (1956–64), director of the *Central Ballet (1963–4), and vice-director of the Central Opera and Ballet Theatre (1964–6). During the Cultural Revolution (1966–76) she was marginalized but in 1978 was reinstated as artistic adviser of the Central Ballet. In 1989 she founded the London-based Chinese Dance and Mime Theatre Company, choreographing new works in both London and China and continuing her research into local Chinese dance forms.

Dakin, Christine (*b* New Haven, 25 Aug. 1949) US dancer, choreographer, and teacher. She studied at the Martha Graham School and performed with various companies, including Lang's, before joining the Graham company as principal dancer from 1976. In 1988 she recreated, with Graham, the speaking part in *Letter to the World* and in 1993 created the lead role in Tharp's *Demeter and Persephone*. She has taught internationally as well as at the Graham, Ailey, and Juilliard schools and in 1997 was appointed associate artistic director

of the Graham company becoming joint director (with Terese Capucilli) in 2007.

Dalcroze *See* JAQUES-DALCROZE, ÉMILE.

Dale, Margaret (*b* Newcastle upon Tyne, 30 Dec. 1922; *d* London, 28 Jan. 2010) British dancer, choreographer, and television director. She studied with Nellie Potts and from 1937 at the Sadler's Wells School, joining Vic-Wells Ballet in 1938 where she became soloist in 1942. She created roles in de Valois's *The Prospect Before Us* (1940) and Helpmann's *Comus* (1942) as well as dancing many character roles. In 1953 she choreographed *The Great Detective* for Sadler's Wells Theatre Ballet and between 1951 and 1955 created six ballets for BBC TV. In 1954 she left the Royal Ballet to work with the BBC where she produced and directed many dance programmes until leaving in 1976 to become associate professor and chairman of the Dance Department at York University, Canada, remaining in those posts for one year.

Dalí, Salvador (*b* Figueras, 11 Mar. 1904; *d* Figueras, 23 Jan. 1989) Spanish surrealist painter who designed several ballets including Massine's *Bacchanale* (1939), *Labyrinth* (1941), and *Mad Tristan* (1944), Argentinita's *Café de Chinitas* (1944), and Béjart's *Gala* (1961).

Dallas Ballet US ballet company. It was founded in 1957 as an educational organization called the Dallas Civic Ballet, but in 1969 expanded its professional scope with the appointment of G. Skibine and Marjorie Tallchief as director and associate director respectively. The company's associated school was opened in 1971 and the repertoire grew to include many Skibine ballets as well as works by Balanchine and Taras. After Skibine's death F. Flindt was appointed artistic director (1981–9). The company was then dissolved and in 1993 the Fort Worth Ballet was renamed Fort Worth-Dallas Ballet, incorporating works by S. Welch and Kevin O'Day into its repertory.

Dalman, Elizabeth (*b* Adelaide, 23 Jan. 1934) Australian dancer, teacher, choreographer, and director. She studied classical ballet locally and modern dance both at the Folkwang School, Essen, and with Nikolais, before dancing with the Ballet der Lage Landen (1958–9) then in the Dutch and Australian productions of *My Fair Lady*. In 1964 she opened her own school in Adelaide, from which developed the *Australian Dance Theatre in 1965. She was director and choreographer of the company until 1975 after which she taught extensively in New York, the Netherlands, and Australia. In 1990 she founded Mirramu Creative Arts Centre in New South Wales, for which she created several site-specific works including a dance drama event on the shores of Lake George, Canberra in 1999.

d'Amboise, Jacques *See* AMBOISE, JACQUES D'.

Dame aux camélias, La The younger Dumas's 1848 novel has inspired many ballets including Taras's *Camille* (mus. Schubert-Rieti, Original Ballet Russe, 1946), Tudor's *Lady of the Camellias* (mus. Verdi, New York City Ballet, 1951), T. Gsovsky's *La Dame aux camélias* (Berlin Festival, mus. Berlioz, 1964), Ashton's *Marguerite and Armand* (mus. Liszt-Searle, Royal Ballet, 1963), and Neumeier's *Lady of the Camellias* (mus. Chopin, Stuttgart, 1978.)

Dance and Dancers British monthly dance magazine, dealing with all forms of theatre dance. It was first published in 1950 with Peter Williams as editor. He was succeeded by John Percival who was editor from 1981 until the magazine folded in 1995.

Dance Books Dance bookshop in London's Cecil Court, founded in 1964 as Ballet Bookshop, becoming Dance Books in 1974, under the co-direction of David Leonard and John O'Brien. It relocated to Hampshire in 2001 but continues to retail on line and by mail order. It also publishes a significant list of British and foreign dance books and between 1992 and 2008 it published the magazine *Dance Now*.

(⊕) SEE WEB LINKS
• Official website for Dance Books

Dance Chronicle US dance journal, noted for its academic authority. It was founded by George Dorris and Jack Anderson in 1977 and was edited by them until 2008 when they were succeeded by Joellen Meglin and Lynne Brooks. It is published three times a year.

Dance Europe British monthly dance magazine, covering all aspects of dance performance in Europe, with some coverage of America and Asia. It was founded in 1995 by Emma Manning and Naresh Kaul.

Dance Index Historic series of scholarly dance writings which was first published in 1942 by Dance Index, Ballet Caravan Inc. under the editorship of Baird Hastings, Lincoln Kirstein, and Paul Magriel and which ceased publication in 1948.

Dance Magazine American monthly magazine devoted to all forms of theatre dance. It was first published in 1927 under Ruth Eleanor Howard under the title *The American Dancer*. Between 1938 and 1941 it ceased publication but it is now one of the world's major dance publications. In 1954 it presented the first of its *Dance Magazine* Awards, its recipients including many of the major names in 20th-century dance. Long-standing editor Richard Philp stood down in 1999 and the current editor Wendy Perron was appointed in 2004. The magazine has offices in New York and California.

(⊕) SEE WEB LINKS
• Official website for *Dance Magazine*

Dancemakers Toronto-based modern dance company. It was founded in 1974 as a co-operative, by a group of dancers and choreographers that included Andrea Ciel Smith and Marcy Radly. Initially it performed to local audiences with a repertory featuring Canadian choreographers such as Kudelka and C. House as well as works by Lubovitch, P. Taylor, Cohan, and others. During the late 1980s it suffered a loss of direction and Serge Bennathan was appointed director and resident choreographer in 1990 to focus its identity and raise its international profile. Bennathan created many works for the company including the full-length *C'est beau ça, la vie* (mus. collage, Michael J. Baker, 1998). His successor as director and resident choreographer was Michael Trent, appointed in 2006.

(⊕) SEE WEB LINKS
• Official website for Dancemakers

Dance Masters of America A professional association for dance teachers founded in 1848 (although its present name dates from 1926). It currently has separate divisions for Ballroom, Performing Arts, and Business Administration.

Dance Museum Stockholm's Dansmuseet, opened in 1953 to display Rolf de Maré's large collection of Asian dance costumes, masks, and instruments. It expanded to include other areas of dance including comprehensive documentation of Les *Ballets Suédois. Originally housed at the Royal Theatre, it now has its own building.

dance notation Dance only acquired a fully comprehensive system of notation during the 20th century, which means that many ballets

Groups of signs, such as those for movements of the head and body or for contact and support, combine to provide the means to describe all human movement. While the body actions are plotted in the stave, details of rhythm, phrasing and dynamics are written immediately above the stave, while those concerning direction, location and travel are written below.

This short sequence is composed of a 'starting position' and a four count movement phrase in which the first movement is performed very strongly (ff) and the last is phrased over two counts (ɸ identifies the 'missing' beat and the curved line above indicates continuity of movement). The change of direction over two counts is shown below the stave. The recording also contains details of head, body, wrist and ankle actions.

Photographs by Chris Cheetham

Benesh Movement Notation © Royal Academy of Dance 1991

prior to this date were either lost or handed down in partial form. The fact that movement requires both spatial and temporal notation makes it hard to record accurately on paper although attempts to do so date back to the late 15th century. In early notation, letters were used to denote various steps, e.g. R for reverence, s for single, d for double. This method was used in two surviving manuscripts: Margherita d'Austria's *Livre des Basses Danses* (*c*.1460) and *L'Art et instruction de bien danser* (*c*.1488). More elaborate descriptions of the manner in which dances should be performed were published in books by the leading dancing masters of the 16th and 17th centuries, the most famous of these being Arbeau's *L'Orchésographie* (Langres, 1588). The first sophisticated attempt at a system was published by *Feuillet in his *Chorégraphie ou L'Art de décrire la danse par caractères, figures et signes demonstratifs* (Paris, 1700), which was based on ideas originated by *Beauchamps. This became popular all round Europe as a means of recording and teaching dances. It depicted the floor patterns of the dances, adding signs for the direction of each step as well as for turns, beats, and other details of footwork. The problem of notating body and arm positions was addressed in the 19th century by *Saint-Léon in his *Sténochorégraphie* (Paris, 1852) and by the dancing master Albert Zorn in his *Grammatik der Tanzkunst* (Leipzig, 1887), both of whom used stylized stick figures to record whole body movement. The idea of writing down dance in a manner similar to music was first developed by B. Klemm in 1855 and further developed by the Russian dancer *Stepanov. In his *Alphabet des mouvements du corps humain* (Paris, 1892) he placed movement symbols on a special stave while recording the floor patterns above it. This system was taught at the Imperial Ballet and was used by *Sergeyev to notate the Petipa and Ivanov ballets which he later mounted in the West. During the 20th century the necessity for recording styles of movement other than ballet led to attempts at more rigorous and complete notation based on abstract symbols. The most famous of these was originated by *Laban and first published in 1926 in his *Choreographie*. Now widely referred to as *Labanotation this system uses a vertical staff to represent the body and has symbols that indicate not only the position but also the direction, duration, and the quality of any movement. The system has since been refined and elaborated by many scholars and is so accurate that any dance can be protected by the laws of copyright. Hitherto any dancer or choreographer could stage someone else's work with few restrictions, hence the number of 19th-century productions around Europe and America of ballets originally created by Taglioni, Perrot, etc. Another widely used system is that developed by R. and J. *Benesh. This began as a shorthand for notating ballets and was first published as *An Introduction to Benesh Dance Notation* (London, 1956). Now termed 'choreology', the Benesh system uses a five-line musical stave running horizontally across the page with abstract stick figures indicating the position of the body and special symbols indicating timing, direction, etc. Though most widely used in ballet companies, choreology has subsequently evolved to deal with non-classical movement also, and together with Labanotation is the most internationally used system. Other systems have been less widely adopted, for example N. *Eshkol and A. Wachman's, published in *Movement Notation* (London, 1958), which is based on a mathematical record of the degree of rotation made by each of the moving parts of the body. Recently the availability of simple and inexpensive video equipment has provided another means of recording dances.

🌐 SEE WEB LINKS

- Website for information about dance notation

Dance Notation Bureau A centre for the analysis of movement, primarily concerned with Labanotation, which was founded in New York in 1940. It offers a research library and training programmes as well as aid to dance professionals in the notation and reconstruction of dance works. Currently it is in the process of developing an extensive database and digitizing its collection of dance scores by e.g. Forsythe and Balanchine.

Dance Now Quarterly British dance magazine published by Dance Books covering most areas of theatre dance. It was founded in 1992 with David Leonard and Ann Nugent (later Allen Robertson) as editors and ceased publication in 2008.

Dance Observer Magazine founded by *Horst in 1934 to expound the theories and publicize the development of modern dance. It ceased publication when Horst died in 1964.

Dance Perspectives A series of quarterly critical monologues, which was published in New York from 1958 to 1976.

Dancer's World, A A historic television documentary made in 1957 about Graham and her company which featured Graham as commentator, explaining her dance philosophy and technique. It was screened in many countries.

Dances at a Gathering Ballet in one act with choreography by Robbins, music by Chopin, costumes by J. Eula, and lighting by T. Skelton. Premiered 22 May 1969 (gala benefit preview, 8 May) by New York City Ballet at the State

Theater, New York, with McBride, Villella, A. Kent, Leland, Mazzo, Verdy, A Blum, J. Clifford, Maiorano, and Prinz. It was first conceived as a pas de deux for McBride and Villella but grew as Robbins enlarged his chosen music to include a selection of études, waltzes, mazurkas, a nocturne, and a scherzo. In its final form, five couples dance in response to the music and to the changes in landscape and mood evoked by the lighting. It was dedicated to Jean Rosenthal (who died 1 May 1969) and has been revived for Royal Ballet (1970) and Paris Opera Ballet (1991), both in stagings by Robbins himself, also by San Francisco Ballet in 2002.

Dance Symphony, The Greatness of Creation (also *The Magnificence of the Universe*; orig. Russ. title *Tants simfoniya—Velichiye myrozdaniya*) Ballet in one act with choreography by Lopukhov, music by Beethoven, and costumes by Pavel Goncharov. Premiered 7 Mar. 1923 by GATOB in Leningrad with Balanchine (then still Balanchivadze), Gusev, Lavrovsky, Mikhailov, and Danilova. This setting of Beethoven's 4th Symphony was one of the first and most ambitious attempts at a symphonic ballet. Its four themes are monumentally titled: 'Birth of Light', 'Triumph of Life over Death', 'Awakening of Nature in the Sun of Spring', and 'The Cosmogonic Spiral', and its choreography (for eighteen dancers) runs a gamut of forms from strict classicism to free invention. Although performed only once (it was fiercely criticized—partly on the grounds of obscenity), the ballet exerted considerable influence on other choreographers. In 2000, Natalia Voskresenskaya reconstructed the work for NBA Ballet, Tokyo.

Dance Theater Workshop New York-based performance space. It was founded by Jeff Duncan, Jack Moore, and Art Bauman in 1965 for the presentation of new dance work and in 1975 it moved to Robbins's American Theater Laboratory where, under the artistic direction of David White, it began to present regular seasons. It has subsequently aided the early careers of several major choreographers including Mark Morris and Bill T. Jones. In the early 1980s it founded its *Bessie Award scheme, designed to honour artists outside the dance mainstream.

Dance Theatre Journal British dance magazine published by the *Laban Centre. Originally titled *Laban News* it changed its name in 1983 under its founding editors Chris de Marigny and Alastair Macaulay. With an emphasis primarily on modern and post-modern dance it has been especially successful in nurturing new generations of dance writers. Its current editor is Martin Hargreaves.

(⊕) SEE WEB LINKS
• Website for Laban Centre with link to *DTJ*.

Dance Theatre of Harlem The first major ballet company to prioritize black dancers. It was founded by Arthur *Mitchell, who was himself a principal dancer with New York City Ballet during the 1950s and 1960s and who, after the assassination of Martin Luther King in 1968, felt impelled to fight for the position of black dancers in the world of ballet. In order to counter prejudice against them and to nurture their talent he founded a school in Harlem, which opened in 1969 with K. Shook as artistic adviser and after its first summer attracted over 400 pupils. Two years later Mitchell formed a company which gave its first performance on 8 Jan. 1971 at the Guggenheim Museum in New York, presenting three chamber ballets by Mitchell. Other works in its first season were by Balanchine and Robbins, and the company's unique energy and charm won them widespread acclaim. In the same year it gave its European debut at the Spoleto Festival and in 1981 it became the first black company to appear at Covent Garden. Mitchell subsequently nurtured many impressive dancers including the ballerina V. Johnson and male principals P. Russell, J. Cippola, and D. Williams. The company's repertoire not only boasted a wide range of 20th-century classics, including works by Nijinska, de Mille, and Balanchine but also a distinctive black classicism. Works by choreographers like *Holder and Vincent Mantsoe drew on the company's African and African-American heritage while Mitchell and Franklin's 1984 staging of *Giselle* famously re-located the ballet to a Creole setting, drawing on issues of American race and class conflict. In 1992 the company toured to S. Africa and to celebrate its 30th anniversary in 1999 it gave the New York premiere of an expanded version of *South African Suite* (mus. various, chor. Mitchell and others). While suffering periodic financial stresses, Dance Theatre of Harlem retained its position as one of the world's leading companies, until it was forced to suspend operations in 2004. The school continues to function.

Dance Umbrella British annual dance festival, based in London, and presenting modern and post-modern dance. Its first programme was organized by V. *Bourne in 1978, at the request of the Arts Council, and its success led to a rapid expansion. The London management team went on to organize similar festivals in other towns (e.g. Woking and Newcastle) and promoted national tours by visiting artists. Bourne remained director until 2007, when she was succeeded by Betsy Gregory. Boston (US) also ran an annual Dance Umbrella festival between 1980 and 1999.

Danceworks Australian modern dance company based in Victoria between 1983 and 2006. Founded by Nanette Hassall it was vigorous in the promotion of new Australian choreography.

Dancing Times The oldest monthly dance magazine in current publication. It was founded in London in 1894 as the house magazine of the Cavendish Rooms, but was bought by P. J. S. *Richardson and T. M. Middleton in 1910 and turned into a national periodical covering all forms of social and theatrical dance. It played an important role in the founding of the Royal Academy of Dancing. Richardson was editor until 1957 when he was succeeded by A. H. Franks, then by Mary Clarke in 1963. In 1956 the ballroom and social dance sections were moved to the *Ballroom Dancing Times*. In 1992 the company attained newspaper trust status and in 2008 Clarke was succeeded by Jonathan Gray.

(●) SEE WEB LINKS

• Website for *Dancing Times*

Dandré, Victor E. (*b* 1870; *d* London, 1944) Russian ballet impresario, and probable husband of Pavlova. A wealthy landowner with a passion for ballet, he became involved with Pavlova in 1914, acting as her manager throughout her career. Following Pavlova's death in 1931 he assembled a company which toured to Europe, S. America, India, and Australia and in 1938 he managed the Ballets Russes de Colonel de Basil, renaming the company Royal Covent Garden Russian Ballet and later the Original Ballet Russe. He wrote *Anna Pavlova in Art and Life* (London, 1932).

Danielian, Leon (*b* New York, 31 Oct. 1920; *d* Canaan, Conn., 8 Mar. 1997) US dancer, choreographer, and teacher. He studied with Mordkin, at the School of American Ballet, and with Fokine, Dolin, and Tudor, making his debut in 1937 in the corps of the Mordkin Ballet. In 1938 danced on Broadway in *I Married an Angel* (mus. Rodgers, chor. Balanchine), after which he was a soloist with the newly formed Ballet Theatre (1939–41) and dancer with de Basil's Original Ballet Russe (1941–2). He was then principal dancer with Ballet Russe de Monte Carlo (1943–57, continuing as guest artist until 1961) where he danced roles in the Balanchine and Massine repertoire. During a period when most top male dancers were Russian or English he was a rare example of American male talent (he was the first American to perform an *entrechat huit). He was considered an exemplary classicist with exceptional speed, elevation, and elegance of line. During his career he also appeared as principal guest artist with various companies including Ballets des Champs Elysées and San Francisco Ballet, as well as dancing in

various opera productions. From 1956 he was choreographer with Ballet Russe de Monte Carlo and in 1960 he became director and choreographer of his own ballet group. An eloquent and dedicated teacher, he became director of American Ballet Theatre School (1968–80). In 1980 he was appointed Assistant Dean of Dance at Purchase State University of New York, and from 1982 to 1991 he was Professor of Dance at the University of Texas.

Daniels, Pauline (*b* 1951) Dutch dancer and choreographer. She studied at the Theaterschool in Amsterdam and at the London School of Contemporary Dance, later with Cunningham and Farber in New York. She was a dancer with Rotterdam Danscentrum (1971–5) then in 1977 was co-founder of Stichting Dansproduktie where she was both dancer and choreographer. She left the company to pursue a solo career and also to teach at the Amsterdam Theaterschool.

Danilova, Alexandra (*b* Peterhof, 11 Nov. 1903; *d* New York, 13 Jul. 1997) Russian-US dancer and teacher. She studied at the Petrograd Theatre School where her teachers included Vaganova and Preobrajenska and graduated in 1920. In 1921 she joined GATOB becoming soloist in 1922. In 1924 she left Russia with Balanchine and a small group calling themselves the Soviet State Dancers and was engaged by Diaghilev to dance with his Ballets Russes (1924–9) becoming ballerina in 1927. In 1925 and again from 1929 to 1930 she danced with Monte Carlo Opera Ballet, after which she starred in the musical *Waltzes from Vienna* (mus. A Rasch, London, 1931–2). She was then ballerina of de Basil's Ballets Russes (1933–8) and prima ballerina of the Ballet Russe de Monte Carlo (1938–52). She was also guest ballerina with several companies including Sadler's Wells Ballet (1949) and London Festival Ballet (1951). Between 1954 and 1956 she toured with her own group, Great Moments of Ballet, and gave her farewell performance in 1957 as a guest artist with Ballet Russe de Monte Carlo at the New York Met. She was one of the most popular dancers of her era—technically versatile with enormous charm, elegance, and wit. Massine said her performance of the Street Dancer in his ballet *Beau Danube* was like 'champagne on the stage'. She danced all the major ballerina roles, most famously Odette and Swanilda, and created principal roles in several Balanchine works including *The Triumph of Neptune* (1926), *Le Bal* (1928), *Danses concertantes* (1944), and *La sonnambula* (1946). She staged and choreographed ballets for opera as well as for several ballet companies including *Coppélia* for New York City Ballet (1974). Between 1964 and 1989 she was a teacher at the School of American Ballet. In 1986 she was awarded the Handel Medallion, New York, and in 1989 a Kennedy Center Award. Her autobiography, *Choura*, was published in New York in 1986.

Danilova, Maria (*b* St Petersburg, 1793; *d* St Petersburg, 20 Jan. 1810) Russian dancer. She studied at the Imperial Theatre School in St Petersburg where she was considered exceptionally talented particularly by Didelot who cast her in several of his ballets while she was still at school. She danced partly on *pointe and at 15 she scored a notable triumph in *Les Amours de Vénus et d'Adonis ou La vengeance de Mars*, partnered by Duport with whom she had an unhappy love affair. This was considered to have undermined her delicate constitution, since she died of consumption aged 17.

Danina, or Jocko the Brazilian Ape Ballet in four acts with choreography and libretto by F. Taglioni and music by Peter von Lindpaintner. Premiered 12 Mar. 1826 in Stuttgart with M. Taglioni, Anton Stuhlmüller, and Jean Briol. This popular ballet was based on a French melodrama about a Brazilian woman, Danina, who saves an ape, Jocko, from being bitten by a snake. The ape later repays her kindness by preventing her son from being kidnapped. The ballet was given 33 performances during its first two seasons alone and was staged in many European cities. It was reconstructed by Pia and Pino Mlaker for Bavarian State Ballet (1940).

Danovschi, Oleg (*b* Vosnesensk, Ukraine, 9 Feb. 1917; *d* 21 Oct. 1996) Romanian dancer and choreographer. He studied with Kniaseff and others and made his debut with the company of Ivan Dubrovin. From 1938 to 1970 he was with Bucharest Opera as principal dancer, becoming ballet master, choreographer, and director of that company. As well as staging the classics he created many works in an epic dramatic style. In 1979 he founded and directed Fantasio, the first independent Romanian ballet company.

danse d'école [Fr., school dance] Term which refers to the pure academic style of classical ballet founded on the principles laid down by *Beauchamps, *Blasis, and subsequent teachers.

danse macabre The image of Death as a dancer, urging mankind forward in its heedless dance to destruction extends far back to ancient art and ritual but was particularly widespread during the 14th and 15th centuries. A 20th-century adaptation of this concept can be seen in Jooss's *Green Table* (1932).

Danses concertantes Ballet in one act with choreography by Balanchine, music by Stravinsky and design by Eugene Berman. Premiered 10

Sept. 1944 (two years after the concert premiere of the score) by Ballet Russe de Monte Carlo at City Center, New York, with Danilova and Danielian. An exuberant witty setting of Stravinsky's score of the same title it was subsequently reworked for New York City Ballet's Stravinsky Festival in 1972. Other versions include MacMillan (London, 1955), Blaska (Amiens, 1968), and Taras (Berlin, 1971).

danseur, danseuse [Fr., (male and female) dancer] These terms are no longer in popular English-speaking usage, though they are still used when designating types of dancer, e.g. danseur noble, a dancer who performs princely classical roles, or danseur caractère, a character dancer.

Danseuses Viennoises Viennese-based troupe of small girls, which toured Europe and the US (1845–8) under the direction of Josephine Weiss. They were very popular, appealing to a public taste for diminutive dancers which had previously been gratified in troupes like the one appearing in the Horschelt *Vienna Children's Ballet. This latter ensemble performed in Vienna between 1815 and 1817 and nurtured several stars possibly including Elssler though she denied any connection with it. Weiss's company was finally closed down due to moral objections.

Dansomanie, La Comedy ballet with choreography by Gardel and music by E. N. Méhul. Premiered 14 Jun. 1800 at Paris Opera, with Gardel. It was the first new work to be premiered at the Opera after the revolution and tells the story of a gentleman who is so fanatical about dance that he insists on his entire household being able to dance—including his daughter's suitors. Contemporary critics worried that Gardel was parodying the artform and playing with trivial subject-matter, but the ballet was very popular with audiences and was revived several times for example in Paris (1811, 1819, and 1824), Sweden (1804), and Vienna (1805). Reconstructions have been performed at Drottningholm (chor. Cramér and Skeaping after Gardel, 1976) and Paris (chor. Cramér after Gardel, 1986).

Dansproduktie Amsterdam-based modern dance company. It was founded as a co-operative in 1977 but from 1983 was run by Bianca van Dillen, staging mixed-media works like *George* (chor. van Dillen, A. Linseen, and D. Louwerse, mus. G. Antheil, 1987). It folded in 1993.

Dante Sonata Ballet in one act with choreography by Ashton, music by Liszt, and design by Fedorovitch. Premiered 23 Jan. 1940 by Vic-Wells Ballet, Sadler's Wells, London, with Fonteyn, Brae, Somes, and Helpmann. Ashton's powerful response to the fall of Poland in 1939 was choreographed in a style untypically close to modern dance and performed barefoot. It was revived by Birmingham Royal Ballet in 2000.

Dantzig, Rudi van (*b* Amsterdam, 4 Aug. 1933) Dutch dancer, choreographer, and director. He studied with Gaskell and made his debut with her Ballet Recital in 1952, dancing full time with it (1954–9) after it became Netherlands Ballet. In 1959 he became a founder member of Nederlands Dans Theater but in 1960 returned to Gaskell's company (which became Dutch National Ballet in 1961) becoming co-director in 1969 and sole director in 1971. He retired in 1991 but continued as resident choreographer until 1994 when he left to pursue a career as a writer. He created many works for Dutch National Ballet but also worked as guest choreographer for many companies including Ballet Rambert, Royal Ballet, Royal Danish Ballet, American Ballet Theatre, and the Bat-Dor Company. Gaskell commissioned his first ballet, *Night Island*, in 1955 (mus. Debussy, revived Ballet Rambert, 1966) but his first work to achieve international fame was *Monument for a Dead Boy* (mus. Jan Boerman, 1965) which was subsequently revived for several companies including Harkness Ballet (1960) and American Ballet Theatre (1973). The ballet's probing psychological approach became a characteristic of his subsequent works, many of which were made in collaboration with van *Schayk as both dancer (initially) and designer. Van Dantzig's style combined academic classicism with a Graham-based modern vocabulary, and he frequently used 20th-century music as in *Moments* (mus. Webern, 1968), *Epitaph* (mus. Ligeti, 1969), *The Ropes of Time* (mus. Boerman, created for Nureyev and the Royal Ballet, 1970), *Painted/Coloured Birds* (mus. Castiglioni and J. S. Bach which used film images as well as dance), *Four Last Songs* (mus. R. Strauss, 1977), and *Bend or Break* (mus. Meijering, 1987). He also choreographed his own versions of *Romeo and Juliet* (1967) and *Swan Lake* (1988) and his last work for DNB was *Pleisterplaats* (1994). In 1991 he was appointed Officer of the Order of Oranje Nassau.

Daphnis and Chloe (orig. Fr. title *Daphnis et Chloé*) Ballet in one act with choreography and libretto by Fokine, music by Ravel, and design by Bakst. Premiered 8 Jun. 1912 at the Théâtre du Châtelet, Paris, with Karsavina, Nijinsky, and Bolm. It is set to Ravel's score of the same title and is based on the pastoral by Longus which tells of the love of a young shepherd, Daphnis, for Chloe. She is captured by pirates but is restored to him by the intervention of Pan. Fokine originally wrote the libretto in 1904 in the first flush of his enthusiasm for ancient Greek themes but it

was turned down by the management of the Imperial Theatres. He ultimately choreographed the ballet for Diaghilev's Ballets Russes. Its reception was overshadowed by the premiere of Nijinsky's *L'*Après-midi d'un faune*, given less than three weeks earlier. A more successful version was Ashton's for Sadler's Wells Ballet, premiered in London on 5 Apr. 1951 with Fonteyn, Somes, Elvin, Field, and Grant. This followed Fokine's libretto fairly closely but John Craxton's designs gave it a more contemporary feel. Other versions include Lifar (design by Chagall, Paris, 1958), Cranko (design by Georgiadis, Stuttgart, 1962), van Manen (2nd suite only, design by Vroom, Dutch National Ballet, 1972), Tetley (Stuttgart, 1975), Taras (design by J. Elula, New York City Ballet, 1975), Graeme Murphy for Sydney Dance Company (1980), Lucinda Childs for Grand Ballet of Geneva (2003), and Spoerli for Zurich in 2004).

Dark Elegies Ballet in one act with choreography and libretto by Tudor, music by Mahler, and design by Nadia Benois. Premiered 19 Feb. 1937 by Ballet Rambert at Duchess Theatre, London, with Lloyd, van Praagh, de Mille, Gore, and Laing. This setting of Mahler's *Kindertotenlieder* was Tudor's own favourite work and is considered by many to be his greatest. Following Mahler's song-cycle it portrays members of a community mourning the loss of their children after some unspecified tragedy and gradually moving from anguish to acceptance. The baritone sings on stage and the dancers, moving in a fusion of classical and expressionist styles, parallel his words with their own potent though often unspecific images. It has been revived by many other companies, including Ballet Theatre (in a re-staging by Tudor, New York, 1940), National Ballet of Canada (1955), Dutch National Ballet (1972), Royal Ballet (1980), Paris Opera Ballet (1985), San Francisco Ballet (1991), Joffrey Ballet Company (2008), and by the Limón Company (1999) in a version without pointework.

Dark Meadow Modern dance work in one act with choreography by Graham, music by Chavez, costumes by Edythe Gilfond, lighting by Rosenthal, and set by Noguchi. Premiered 23 Jan. 1946 by the Graham company at the Plymouth Theater, New York, with Hawkins and Graham. It is one of Graham's most densely symbolic representations of the human psyche, influenced by the writings of Jung, and was described by her as a 're-enactment of the Mysteries which attend the eternal adventure of seeking'.

Darrell, Peter (orig. Skinner; *b* Richmond, 16 Sept. 1929; *d* Glasgow, 2 Dec. 1987) British dancer, choreographer, and director. He studied at Sadler's Wells Ballet School and danced with

Sadler's Wells Ballet (1944–6) and then Sadler's Wells Theatre Ballet (1946–7). He left to dance in musicals and with various companies including London Festival Ballet, and choreographed his first work *Midsummer Watch* for Ballet Workshop in 1951. In 1957 he founded Western Theatre Ballet with Elizabeth West and when she died in 1962 he became its sole director, moving with the company to Glasgow in 1969 where it became Scottish Theatre Ballet (now Scottish Ballet). From the beginning Darrell's choreography shaped his company's unique image. *Prisoners* (mus. Bartók, 1957) established his commitment to exploring social issues in dance while *Mods and Rockers* (mus. The Beatles, 1963) demonstrated his swiftness in responding to contemporary material and attracting young audiences. His theatrical instincts were displayed in works as various as *Jeux* (mus. Debussy, 1963) which turned Nijinsky's original libretto into a mystery ballet; *Home* (mus. Bartók, 1965) about a young woman in a mental hospital; and the ambitious 1966 piece *Sun into Darkness* (mus. Malcolm Williamson) about barbaric ritual in a Cornish village. When the company moved to Scotland Darrell was obliged to widen his range to cater for a larger audience, as in *Tales of Hoffmann* (mus. Offenbach, arr. Lanchbery, 1972) and *Cinderella* (mus. Rossini, 1979) and to stage productions of the classics such as *Giselle* (1971) and *Swan Lake* (1977). He also made works for several other companies, such as *La Péri* (mus. Dukas, London Festival Ballet, 1973), but it was with Scottish Ballet that he made his international reputation, nurturing a company of versatile dancers with a wide-ranging repertoire of experimental and classical work.

Darsonval, Lycette (orig. Alice Perron; *b* Coutances, 12 Feb. 1912; *d* St Lô, 1 Nov. 1996) French dancer, choreographer, and teacher. She studied at Paris Opera Ballet School and joined the Paris company in 1930. She left in 1933 to guest abroad, with Lifar among others, returned in 1936, and was promoted étoile in 1940. She remained with the company until 1960, although she spent some time guesting and also touring with her own small group in France and abroad. A virtuoso, expressive dancer, she performed the major ballerina roles as well as creating leading roles in several ballets, including Lifar's *David triomphant* (1937), *Sylvia* (1941), and *Suite en blanc* (1943) and Balanchine's *Le Palais de cristal* (1947). She also choreographed two works for the Opera (one of the few women ever to do so) and successfully re-worked *Sylvia* for the company in 1979 (staging it also for Central Ballet of Peking in 1980). She gave her farewell performance in *Giselle* in 1959 by which time she was already director of the Opera Ballet School (1957–9, the

first woman appointed to the position). Between 1963 and 1964 she was maîtresse de ballet at Nice Opera Ballet and between 1971 and 1976 professor of dance at Nice Conservatory. In 1975 she returned to the Paris Opera School as teacher. Her many honours include Commandeur de l'Ordre National du Mérite and Chevalier des Arts et des Lettres.

Dartington College Devon-based arts college. The premises was used as a base by Laban, Jooss, and others during and just after the Second World War, and from 1963 the college ran a teacher-training course in Graham-based modern dance. After being taken over by Mary Fulkerson in 1973 it became a focus for post-modern dance studies and training. In 2008 the college merged with University College Falmouth and offers a choreography degree.

Dauberval, Jean (orig. Jean Bercher; *b* Montpellier, 19 Aug. 1742; *d* Tours, 14 Feb. 1806) French dancer, choreographer, and ballet master. He studied at the Paris Opera Ballet School with Noverre and danced in Bordeaux and Lyons before joining the Paris company in 1761. Between 1762 and 1764 he danced under Noverre in Stuttgart as well as working at London's King's Theatre as dancer and choreographer (1763–4) and dancing in Paris where he was promoted premier danseur demi-caractère in 1763 and premier danseur noble in 1773. In the same year he was also appointed assistant ballet master, first to Vestris and later M. Gardel, resigning following differences with the latter in 1783. He was renowned as a dramatically expressive dancer but is now best remembered as a choreographer. He created his first work in 1759 during a season at Turin but his most famous ballet, *La Fille mal gardée*, was created in Bordeaux where he was ballet master (1785–90). Influenced by Noverre's theories of the *ballet d'action, Dauberval was one of the first choreographers to create ballets about ordinary people—handling both serious and comic subjects and weaving together dance and mime with unusual subtlety. His other works included *Le Déserteur* (1784) and *Le Page inconstant* (after Beaumarchais's *Le Mariage de Figaro*, 1787). His pupils included Didelot, Aumer, and S. Viganò and he was married to the dancer Mlle Théodore.

Davidsbündlertänze Ballet in one act with choreography by Balanchine, music by Schumann, and design by Ter-Arutunian. Premiered 19 Jun. 1980 (gala preview 12 Jun.) by New York City Ballet at New York State Theater, New York, with Farrell, von Aroldingen, Watts, Mazzo, d'Amboise, Luders, Martins, and I. Andersen. This setting of Schumann's 1837 piano cycle Op. 6 was created three years before Balanchine's death and surprised critics with its mysterious, Romantic quality. The stage is set as a melancholy ballroom, peopled by four emotionally fraught couples. There are some glancing references to Schumann's own life but the work's meaning seems ultimately held in the anguished and hesitant style of the dancing.

Davies, (Sir) Peter Maxwell (*b* Manchester, 8 Sept. 1934) British composer. He has written dance scores for W. Louther's *Vesalii Icones* (London, 1970) and for F. Flindt's *Salome* (Copenhagen, 1978) and *Caroline Mathilde* (Copenhagen, 1991). His concert music has also been used by others, including B. Moreland in *Journey to Avalon* (London Festival Ballet, 1980) and R. Alston in *Bell High* (1980) and *Hymnos* (1988—both for Ballet Rambert).

Davies, Siobhan (*b* London, 18 Sept. 1950) British dancer and choreographer. She studied art before enrolling at the London School of Contemporary Dance in 1967 and performed as a founder member of London Contemporary Dance Theatre in 1969 while still a student. She became one of its leading dancers, also performing with Ballet for All in 1971, and in 1974 was appointed associate choreographer with London Contemporary Dance Theatre. Her many works for the company included *Relay* (mus. C. Wood and B. Watson, 1972), *The Calm* (mus. G. Burgon, 1974), *Sphinx* (mus. Barrington Pheloung, 1977), and *Something to Tell* (mus. Britten, 1980). In 1981 she left to form her own group for which she choreographed, for example, *Plain Song* (mus. Satie), and in 1982 she was co-founder of Second Stride (with Spink and Alston). She created many works for that company—her rangy, fluid style revealing a basic debt to Cunningham but also displaying her own delicate nuances of characterization and humour, as shown in *Silent Partners* (1984). She also continued to make work for London Contemporary Dance Theatre, such as *New Galileo* (1984), and in 1988 re-formed her own company. Her works from this date have evinced a range of styles (from the intimately gestural to the sharply percussive), often in response to her choice of music, including *White Man Sleeps* (mus. Kevin Volans, 1988), *Different Trains* (mus. Reich, 1990), *Art of Touch* (mus. Matteo Fargion, 1995), and *Trespass* (mus. G. Barry, 1996). She has also choreographed works for Rambert Dance Company, including *Winnsboro' Cotton Mill Blues* (1992, revived for Siobhan Davies Dance Company, 1998), for English National Ballet, *Dancing Ledge* (1990), and, for Royal Ballet, *A Stranger's Taste* (1999). In recent years her choreography has been created for a variety of smaller spaces, e.g. *Birdsong* (mus. Andy Pink, 2004) and has focused on increasingly

subtle detail of movement and expression. In 2006 her company moved into its own base in South London.

Davis, Carl (*b* New York, 1936) US composer. He has written the scores for several ballets including *A Simple Man* (chor. Lynne, Northern Ballet Theatre, 1987), *The Picture of Dorian Gray* (chor. D. Deane, Sadler's Wells Royal Ballet, 1987), *A Christmas Carol* (chor. Massimo Moricone, Northern Ballet Theatre, 1992), *Aladdin* (chor. Robert Cohan, Scottish Ballet, 2000), and *Cyrano de Bergerac* (new production, chor. Bintley, Birmingham Royal Ballet, 2007), and arranged music by Tchaikovsky for the score of D. Deane's *Alice* (1995).

Davis, Chuck (*b* Raleigh, NC, 1 Jan. 1937) US dancer, choreographer, and director. He studied with Owen Dodson and danced with several companies before founding his own Chuck Davis Dance Company in 1967. He specialized in presenting traditional African-American dances but has also choreographed his own works including *Odun De* (mus. Saleem, 1986) and *Waterwheel* (1995). He has been active in raising the profile of African-American dance, founding the annual festival DanceAfrica in 1977, and the performance and educational organization African American Dance Ensemble in 1994.

(🌐) **SEE WEB LINKS**

• Website for the African American Dance Ensemble

Dawson, David (*b* London, 1972) British dancer and choreographer. He trained at the Royal Ballet School, graduating into Birmingham Royal Ballet in 1991, moving to English National Ballet as soloist in 1994, and joining Dutch National Ballet the following year, where he created roles in works by Eagling, Brandsen, Gallili, and d'Amboise among others. Between 2000 and 2002 he danced with Ballett Frankfurt as principal, before focusing on choreography. His first ballets, based in the classical vocabulary but with a distinctive sensuousness and freedom of movement, were created for workshop performances at DNB and were followed by *Psychic Whack* (1999), *A Million Kisses to my Skin* (mus. Bach, 2000), and *Grey Area* (mus. Niels Lanz, 2002). In 2004 he became resident choreographer for Dutch National Ballet, creating *Morning Ground* (mus. Chopin 2004) and *The Gentle Chapters* (mus. Thom Willems, 2006) among others.

In 2006 he was appointed resident choreographer of Dresden SemperOper Ballett for which he has since created *The Disappeared* (mus Pärt 2006), *Giselle* (2008), and *The World According to Us* (mus. Willems 2009).

Dawson has also created works for other companies including *Reverence* (mus. Bryars, 2005) for the Mariinsky (making him the first British choreographer to create a work for that company); *A Sweet Spell of Oblivion* (mus. Bach, 2007) for Royal Ballet of Flanders; and *Faun(e)* (mus. Debussy, 2009) for English National Ballet.

His works are in the repertoires of many companies worldwide and he is the recipient of numerous awards including the Prix Professional, Lausanne, The Golden Mask, the Choo San Goh Choreography Award, and Benois de la Danse Choreography Award.

Daydé, Bernard (*b* Paris, 3 Feb. 1921) French designer. His many designs for dance include Béjart's *L'Etranger* (1957), Lander's *Études* (London Festival Ballet, 1956), Flindt's *La Leçon* (1964), and Paris Opera's *Hommages à Varèse* (1973).

Daydé, Liane (*b* Paris, 27 Feb. 1932) French dancer. She studied at the Paris Opera Ballet School and graduated into its company at the age of 13, becoming étoile in 1950. A tiny, charming, and brilliant dancer, her almost childlike appearance was exploited by Lifar when he created the role of Snow White for her in *Blanche-Neige* (1951). She left the Opera in 1960 to work as an international guest artist. In 1961 she danced with the Grand Ballet du Marquis de Cuevas and after 1962 with the Grand Ballet Classique de France, a touring company directed by her husband, Claude Giraud. She danced most of the classical ballerina roles as well as creating leading parts in Lifar's *Romeo and Juliet* (1955), Lander's *Printemps à Vienne* (1954), and Rosen's *Dance Panels in Seven Movements* (1963). After retiring from the stage she became a teacher, subsequently directing the dance department of the Regional Conservatory of the City of Paris.

Day on Earth Modern dance work in one act with choreography by Humphrey and music by Copland. Premiered 10 May 1947 at Beaver County Day School, Massachusetts, by José Limón Dance Company with Limón. Set to Copland's 1941 Piano Sonata, it evokes the human cycle of work, love, marriage, death, and birth.

Dead Dreams of Monochrome Men Full-length dance theatre work, directed by Lloyd Newson. Premiered 5 Oct. 1988 by DV8 Physical Theatre at the Third Eye Centre, Glasgow. It is based on the story of the mass murderer Dennis Nilsen and, through movement that fuses raw expression with physical risk-taking, four dancers explore issues of male loneliness, desire, and trust.

Dean, Christopher (*b* Nottingham, 27 Jul. 1958) British ice dancer and choreographer. He formed his renowned ice-dance partnership with Jayne Torvill in 1975, winning four consecutive world championships from 1981 to 1984. In 1984 the pair won the gold medal in the Sarajevo Olympics, performing a free dance interpretation of Ravel's *Bolero* which set new standards for musicality and expression within the sport. Between 1985 and 1990 they toured the world with their own company also starring in the television special *Fire and Ice* in which Dean danced without skates. In 1990 they returned to amateur competitions, winning the gold medal at the World Championships in 1994, then continued to stage a number of spectacular ice dance shows. Dean retired from performing in 1998 but returned in 2007 to appear in the UK television show *Dancing on* Ice. In 1996 Dean choreographed his first stage ballet for English National Ballet, *Encounters* (mus. Paul Simon). *See also* TORVILL AND DEAN.

Dean, Laura (*b* Staten Island, NY, 3 Dec. 1945) US dancer and choreographer. She studied at the High School of Performing Arts, at the School of American Ballet and also with Hoving, Sansardo, and Cunningham. She made her debut with the Paul Taylor Dance Company in 1965 and also danced with Sanasardo, Monk, K. King, and Robert Wilson. She began choreographing in 1967 and formed the Laura Dean Dance Company in 1971. Her work was strictly minimalist in style, featuring repetitive, often spinning movements, performed in geometric patterns and on a steady pulse. She frequently collaborated with Steve Reich notably in *Drumming* (1975) and *Song* (1976), in which the performers vocalized as they danced. In 1976 she changed the name of her company to Laura Dean Musicians and Dancers, reflecting the use of her own musical compositions in her dances, for example *Tympani* (1980) and *Fire* (1982, revived 1989). In 1980 she also began to create works for other companies including *Night* (mus. Dean, City Center Joffrey Ballet, 1980), *Space* (mus. Reich, New York City Ballet, 1988), and the first section of *Billboards* (mus. Prince, Joffrey Ballet, 1993). She additionally created several works for ice dance companies, including *Reflections* (1993). The last work she created for her own company was *View over Atlantis* (mus. Jon. Scoville, 2000) after which it was disbanded. The Dean Dance and Music Foundation, established in 1972 and then merged into her company, was disbanded in 2007. Dean has taught widely, in institutions including the Universities of Texas and Rhode Island.

Deane, Derek (*b* Cornwall, *c.*1954) British dancer, choreographer, and director. He studied at the Royal Ballet Upper School and joined the company in 1972, becoming principal in 1978 and creating roles in several ballets including *Mayerling* and *Valley of Shadows*. He also choreographed several works including *Fleeting Figures* (1984) and *The Picture of Dorian Gray* (mus. C. Davis, 1987) for Sadler's Wells Royal Ballet. In 1989 he left the Royal Ballet, becoming deputy artistic director and resident choreographer at Teatro dell'Opera in Rome (1990–2) and working freelance. Between 1993 and 2001 he was artistic director of English National Ballet for which he staged new productions of *Giselle* (1994), *Swan Lake* and *Nutcracker* (1997), *Romeo and Juliet* (1998), and *Sleeping Beauty* (2000) among others. He also choreographed the full-length ballet *Alice in Wonderland* (mus. Tchaikovsky, arr. Davis, 1995) and *Strictly Gershwin* (mus. Gershwin, 2008), both for English National Ballet.

Death and the Maiden Ballet in one act with choreography and costumes by A. Howard and music by Schubert. Premiered 23 Feb. 1937 by Ballet Rambert at the Duchess Theatre, London, with Howard. It is set to the Andante con moto from Schubert's String Quartet in D minor and portrays a young girl being overcome by Death. It was revived by Ballet Theatre in 1940 and Northern Dance Theatre in 1969. Other choreographers who have used Schubert's quartet include Walter (Wuppertal, 1964), R. North (Ballet Rambert, 1984), and Elo (Norwegian Ballet, 2008).

Deaths and Entrances Modern dance work in one act with choreography by Graham, music by Hunter Johnson, set by Arch Lauterer, costumes by Edythe Gilford, and lighting by Rosenthal. Premiered 26 Dec. 1943 by Martha Graham and Company at 46th St. Theater, New York with Graham, Dudley, Maslow, Hawkins, and Cunningham. It is based on the lives of the Brontë sisters, but rather than narrating their stories it focuses on the relationships within the family, and on the workings of memory and the imagination. A preview performance was given on 18 Jul. at Bennington College Theater. Other Brontë ballets include Hynd's *Charlotte Brontë* (mus. D. Young, Royal Ballet Touring Company, 1974) and G. Lynne's *The Brontës* (mus. D. Muldowney, Northern Ballet Theatre, 1995).

deboulé [Fr., suddenly running away] A fast sequence of half turns performed by stepping onto one leg, and completing the turn by stepping onto the other, the dancers stepping high on the toes and with the legs held very close together. These can be performed in a circle (en manège) or a straight line (chaîné).

Debussy, Claude (*b* St Germain-en Laye, 22 Aug. 1862; *d* Paris, 26 Mar. 1918) French composer. He wrote several commissioned scores for ballet and dance theatre including *Le Martyre de Saint-Sébastien* (chor. Fokine, 1911, also by Béjart, 1986) and most famously *Jeux* for Nijinsky (1913), though he remained notoriously aloof from the choreographic process. His concert music has also been used by many choreographers, such as the lush tone poem *Prélude à l'après-midi d'un faune* in Nijinsky's ballet, *L'Après-midi d'un faune*, 1912 and in Robbins's *Afternoon of a Faun* (1953); *La Mer* in Schilling's 1968 and Lifar's 1984 ballets of the same title; several piano preludes in Cranko's *Brouillards* (1970); *Clair de Lune* in Béjart's ballet of the same title (1977); and music from *Pelléas et Mélisande* in Petit's 1984 ballet.

Decouflé, Philippe (*b* Paris, 1961) French dancer, choreographer, and director. He danced with the companies of Régine Chopinot, Karole Armitage, and Nikolais and in 1983 founded his company, DCA. His work creates arresting stage images and optical illusions out of dance, video imagery, lighting effects, mirrors, stage machinery, and elaborate costumes, and his productions include *Codex* (1986), *Petites pièces montées* (1993), *Decodex* (1995), *Shazam* (1998), *Tricodex* (2003, for Lyon Opera Ballet), and *Sombrero* (2007). He has also directed the opening and closing ceremonies of the 1992 Winter Olympics, the 2007 Rugby World Cup parade in Paris, and the Japanese musical *DORA, the cat who lived a million times* (1996) as well as directing several short films and commercials.

⊕ SEE WEB LINKS
• Website for company DCA

dedans [Fr., inside] Term indicating that a movement travels or is turned in towards the body rather than away from it (en dehors).

défilé [Fr., march past] A spectacular parade, often used in continental opera houses to mark the opening or closing of the season, in which the entire ballet company is presented to the audience on stage. It starts with the most junior dancers and progresses through the company hierarchy to the stars.

dégagé [Fr., disengaged] A movement in which one foot is freed to move forward, backward or to the side, along the floor.

Degas, Edgar Hilaire Germain (*b* Paris, 19 July 1834; *d* Paris, 26 Sept. 1917) French painter. He drew, painted, and modelled many studies of dancers which focused on real rather than idealized qualities, for example their peculiar musculature and their attitudes of exhaustion as well as of beauty. He also exaggerated more abstract compositional elements such as the play of light and shade over their bodies. These studies have inspired several ballets including Ashton's *Foyer* *de la danse* (1932) and Lifar's *Entre deux rondes* (1940).

D'Egville, James Harvey (*b* c.1770; *d* c.1836) British dancer and choreographer. He was the son of Pierre D'Egville (ballet master at Drury Lane and Sadler's Wells Theatres), and as a child danced at the King's Theatre (1783). Between 1784 and 1785 he performed at the Paris Opera and was much admired by Dauberval. After 1793 he was back in London, working with Noverre, and between 1799 and 1809 he was choreographer at the King's Theatre, creating such works as *Achille et Déidamie* (1804). He composed the music for many of his ballets and also founded an academy of dance—responding to the non-availability of foreign dancers during the Napoleonic Wars and the need to train English replacements. After the war ended, however, the demand for English dancers decreased, and interest in developing English talent waned.

De Hesse, Jean–Baptiste François (Des-Haies; Dezaics; Deshayes) (*b* The Hague, Sept. 1705; *d* Paris, 22 May 1779) French dancer, choreographer, and ballet master, possibly related to the famous Deshayes family. He was trained by his French parents, both actors, and toured with them performing mostly comic, grotesque, and character parts. He began choreographing his own dances and was ballet master of Le Théâtre des Petits Appartements at Versailles (1747–51) where he worked with children and groups of both professional and non-professional artists. He went on to the Paris Opéra Comique from which he retired in 1768. His works, considered to be seminal in the developing trend of the *ballet d'ac-tion, included *Le Pédant* (1748) and *Divertissement pantomime, la Guingette* (1750).

dehors [Fr., outwards] Term indicating that a movement turns or travels away from the body as opposed to inwards (en dedans).

De Jong, Bettie *See* JONG, BETTIE DE.

Delibes, Clément Philibert Léo (*b* St-Germain-du-Val, 21 Feb. 1836; *d* Paris, 16 Jan. 1891) French composer. He studied under Adam and was commissioned to write part of the score for Saint-Léon's *La Source* (Paris Opera, 1866). Delibes composed Act II and the first scene of Act III; Minkus composed the rest. In 1867 he contributed to the score for *Le Corsaire* and in 1870 was commissioned to compose *Coppélia* (chor. Saint-Léon, Paris Opera, 1870). Influenced by Adam, this score made extensive use of leitmotifs for character and mood but its vivid scene painting was surpassed in his score for *Sylvia* (chor. Mérante, Paris Opera, 1876) which is renowned for its brilliant and varied orchestration. Tchaikovsky

both admired and was influenced by Delibes's ballet music.

Deller, Florian (orig. Drosendorf; baptized 2 May 1729; *d* Munich, 19 Apr. 1773) Austrian violinist and composer. A member of the Stuttgart court orchestra, he later became one of Noverre's closest collaborators, writing the music for the latter's *Orfeo ed Euridice* (1763), *Der Sieg des Neptun* (1763), and *La Morte di Licomede* (1764).

Dello Joio, Norman (*b* New York, 24 Jan. 1913; *d* New York, 24 Jul. 2008) US composer. Noted for his melodic gifts, he wrote the music for Loring's *Prairie* (1942), Kidd's *On Stage!* (1945), Graham's *Diversion of Angels* (1948), *Seraphic Dialogue* (orig. *Triumph of St. Joan*, 1951), and *A Time of Snow* (1968), and Limón's *There is a Time* (1956).

Delsarte, François (*b* Solesmes, 11 Nov. 1811; *d* Paris, 20 Jul. 1871) French music teacher. He developed a system known as the Delsarte method by which performers were taught to develop the expressiveness of their bodies. He divided human movement into three categories (eccentric, concentric, and normal) and three zones (head, torso, and limbs) in his attempt to develop his pupils' physical control. His adherents, including Jaques-Dalcroze and Shawn, made use of his methods in evolving modern dance techniques.

demi [Fr., half] Designates any movement or position executed in half measure, e.g. a demi-plié in which the legs are not bent as fully as they can be, or a demi-retiré where the pointed foot crosses the supporting leg at calf rather than knee height. Demi-caractère is a type of dancer or style of dancing in which academic technique is coloured by a more dramatic or comic element of character.

Demoiselles de la nuit, Les Ballet in one act with choreography by Petit, libretto by Anouilh, music by J. Françaix, and design (including the ballet's fantastic cat masks) by Fini. Premiered 22 May 1948 by Ballets de Paris at the Théâtre Marigny, Paris, with Fonteyn, Petit, and Hamilton. It tells the story of a musician who falls in love with his beautiful cat Agathe, who has assumed semi-human form. Agathe tries to be faithful to her human lover but is lured away by the sound of tomcats and the call of freedom. She leaps off the rooftops and the musician falls to his death as he tries to grab hold of her. She falls after him and they are united in death. It was revived by American Ballet Theatre in 1951.

Denard, Michaël (*b* Dresden, 5 Nov. 1944) French dancer. He did not begin serious training until the age of 17 when he studied with Golovine, Franchetti, and others. He made his debut at Capitole de Toulouse in 1963, then went on to dance with many companies including those of Lorca, Massine, and Pierre Lacotte until joining Paris Opera Ballet in 1966. He was appointed premier danseur in 1969 and étoile in 1971. His technical elegance, expressive stage presence, and adroit partnering equipped him both for the classics and also for the 20th-century repertoire. He created the role of Iskander in Lifar's 1969 revival of *Istar* and leading roles in Petit's *Shéhérazade* (1974) and *Symphonie fantastique* (1975). He was also admired by Béjart who created lead roles for him in *Comme la Princesse Salome est belle ce soir* and *Oiseau de feu* (both 1970) in which he was able to express his full dramatic range. He also appeared in many Balanchine ballets and in Cunningham's *Un jour ou deux* (1973) and his interest in new work was also given an outlet in his many appearances with the Opera's Groupe de Recherche Chorégraphique. He guested with many other companies including American Ballet Theatre (where between 1972 and 1975 he was Gregory's frequent partner) and with Ballet of the 20th Century. After retiring from the Opera in 1989 he turned increasingly to acting, for example taking the role of the narrator in Béjart's *Ring um den Ring* (1989) but also performing character dance roles, for example Widow Simone in Paris Opera's *La Fille mal gardée* (2007). He was also artistic director of the Berlin Staatsoper Ballet (1992-6).

Denby, Edwin (*b* Tientsin, China, 1903; *d* Searsport, Me., 12 Jul. 1983) US writer and critic. He studied at Harvard University, in Vienna, and at Hellerau-Laxenburg, and during the 1930s danced with the Darmstadt company. He was then appointed dance critic of *Modern Music* (1936-42) and the *New York Herald Tribune* (1942-5). He also contributed to many dance magazines. His reviews were collected together in two volumes: *Looking at Dance* (London, 1944 and New York, 1949) and *Dancers, Buildings and People in the Streets* (New York, 1965), and in the collected edition *Dance Writings*, ed. Cornfield and Mackay (London, 1986 and New York, 1987).

Denham, Sergei (orig. Dokuchayev *b* Moscow, 1897; *d* New York, 30 Jan. 1970) Russian-US impresario. As a ballet enthusiast he became vice-president of the American corporation which took over the running of the Ballet Russe de Monte Carlo in 1938, following the departure of Massine. He directed the company for 24 years and founded the Ballet Russe School in New York in 1954.

Denishawn The school and company of Ruth St Denis and Ted Shawn, from which most American modern dance descends. The school was founded in 1915 in Los Angeles, teaching many forms of dance including oriental, primitive, and German modern dance, and further studios rapidly spread throughout the US. Many of the early modern dance pioneers were taught at Denishawn including Graham, Humphrey, Shurr, Weidman, and Cole, and its musical director was Horst. Dancers from the school, performing with its founders, formed the Denishawn company which toured widely until 1931 when the couple separated and disbanded both it and the school.

Denmark Ballets were performed at the court in Copenhagen from the second half of the 16th century and were heavily influenced by French taste. In 1722 the Lille Grønnegade Theatre was built to stage Danish work, with dance playing a popular role in many of its productions and in 1748 the Theatre Royal (built to accommodate ballet, opera, and theatre) became home to the Royal Danish Ballet. This company has dominated Danish dance ever since. At first it was run by a series of French and Italian ballet masters, most outstandingly *Galeotti, who radically improved its standards. Between 1775 and 1811 Galeotti produced a repertoire of over 50 ballets and divertissements, one of which, *The Whims of Cupid* (1786), is still performed today. Under Antoine Bournonville's direction (1816-23) ballet declined but the advent of his son August turned the company into a major artistic force. August *Bournonville was not only a performer of inspiring virtuosity but proved to be the greatest choreographer the country has ever produced, creating over 50 ballets many of which still form the basis of the company's repertoire today. He also reorganized the education of dancers and during his years as director (1829-75) he tightly controlled both school and company to ensure strict standards, so much so that while ballet suffered a marked decline in both quality and popularity in the rest of Europe, it enjoyed a renaissance in Denmark. After Bournonville's death the company deteriorated, though Beck and Borchsenius tried to preserve some of the former's works, but it revived dramatically under Harald *Lander's direction (1932-51) and under subsequent directors ithas established a world-wide reputation performing not only its Bournonville heritage but also a wide 20th- to 21st-century repertoire (*see also* ROYAL DANISH BALLET). Other dance activity in the country received relatively little encouragement until the 1980s when the New Danish Dance Theatre was established in 1981 under the direction of Randi Patterson, producing contemporary-classical crossover work. It was directed by Warren Spears from 1987 to 1999 and is currently directed by Tim Rushton. Other small contemporary companies include Granhoj Dans, founded in Aahus in 1993 by Palle Granhoj. In 1997 the city of Holstebro invited Peter *Schaufuss to establish a new company, the Peter Schaufuss Ballet Company, to serve the Jutland area.

The country's leading school is the Royal Danish Ballet School, but the Danish National School of Theatre has a contemporary dance section, admitting just 20 students each year, and the Dansens Hus in Copenhagen is a dedicated facility for contemporary dance offering space for rehearsals and classes.

Denvers, Robert (orig. Nennertheim; *b* Antwerp, 9 Mar. 1942) Belgian dancer, teacher, and director. He trained at the Strasbourg Ballet with Jean Combes and at the Studio Wacker with Nora Kiss and Victor Gsovsky, making his debut with the Grand Ballet du Marquis de Cuevas in 1961. He was a soloist with Béjart's Ballet of the 20th Century (1963–73), after which he was soloist with National Ballet of Canada. In 1977 he went to New York to study, and between 1977 and 1979 was teacher and assistant director of Béjart's company. In 1979 he established his own studio in New York and until 1987 also worked as guest teacher with many companies, including New York City Ballet and Paris Opera. Between 1987 and 2005 he was artistic director of the Royal Ballet of Flanders where he not only added many full-length ballets to the repertoire but also focused on new commissions from, among others, Mauricio Wainrot and resident choreographer Danny Rousseel. In 1999 he married the company's principal ballerina, Aysem Sunal.

Derain, André (*b* Chatou, 10 Jun. 1880; *d* Chambourcy, 8 Sept. 1954) French painter. One of the Fauves group he was commissioned by Diaghilev to design Massine's *La Boutique fantasque* (1919). He proved himself a brilliant colourist and went on to design many other ballets including Balanchine's *La Concurrence* (1932) and *Les Songes* (1933), also Lifar's *Salade* (1935), Fokine's *L'épreuve d'amour* (1936), Ashton's *Harlequin in the Street* (1938), Petit's *Que le diable l'emporte* (1948), and other Massine ballets including *Mam'zelle Angot* (1947), *Les Femmes de bonne humeur* (prod. of Grand Ballet de Marquis de Cuevas, 1949), and *La Valse* (1950).

Derman, Vergie (*b* Johannesburg, 18 Sept. 1942) South African-British dancer. She studied at the Royal Ballet School and made her debut with the company in 1962. After a year with the Berlin Opera Berlin (1966–7) she returned and was promoted soloist in 1968 and principal in 1972. She was a favourite dancer of MacMillan and created roles in several of his ballets including *Anastasia* (extended version, 1971), *Manon* and *Elite Syncopations* (1974), and *Four Seasons* (1975) as well as Ashton's *The Dream* (1964) and *Jazz Calendar* (1968).

Derra de Moroda, Friderica (*b* Pozsony (Bratislava), Hungary, 2 Jun. 1897; *d* Salzburg, 19 Jun. 1978) Greek-British dancer, teacher, ballet mistress, and writer. She studied in Munich and toured parts of Europe as a recital dancer before coming to London in 1913 to dance in music hall and pantomimes. She studied with Cecchetti, becoming co-founder of the Cecchetti Society and revising the Cecchetti *Manual* in 1932 with Craske and Beaumont. She arranged dances for Glyndebourne and Sadler's Wells Operas and in Berlin founded and directed the KDF Ballet (1940–4). After the war she founded a school in Salzburg where she taught until 1967. She was an international authority on 18th-century dance notation and Cecchetti.

derrière [Fr., behind] Indicates that a movement is directed backwards from the dancer's body.

Descombey, Michel (*b* Bois-Colombe, 28 Oct. 1930) French dancer, choreographer, and director. He studied with Egorova and at the Paris Opera Ballet School making his debut in the company in 1947. He was appointed premier danseur in 1959 and became ballet master in 1963. Between 1971 and 1973 he was ballet director at Zurich then in 1975 moved to Mexico where he became chief choreographer and associate director of the Ballet Teatro del Espacio de Mexico in 1977. He began choreographing in 1958 for the Opéra Comique (Paris) and his subsequent works, which often made use of contemporary music and design, included *L'Enfant et les sortilèges* (mus. Ravel, 1960), *Sarracenia* (mus. Bartók, 1964), *Coppélia* (mus. Delibes, 1966), *Spectacle Berio* (1970), *Mandala* (mus. Toshiro Mayuzumi, 1970), and *ES, le 8ème jour* (mus. Stockhausen, 1973). After 1977 most of his works were created for Ballet Teatro del Espacio, including *Pavana para un amor muerto* (1985) and *La Silla* (mus. Webern, 1999).

Deshayes, André Jean-Jacques (*b* Paris, 24 Jan. 1777; *d* Batignolles, 9 Dec. 1846) French dancer and choreographer. The son of a celebrated dance teacher he also descended from a famous French theatrical family. He trained at the Paris Opera school and in 1794 made his debut with the company, working under Gardel. Ambitious and restless he also guested abroad, in Lisbon (1799) and London (1800), and finally left the opera in 1802. After this he danced in Milan, Naples, Germany, and Vienna and was principal dancer at London's King's Theatre (later Her

Majesty's) for long periods between 1800 and 1842. Here he was much admired not only for the strength and elegance of his technique but also for his expressiveness. He was also the theatre's official choreographer during this time where he created over a dozen ballets including *Masaniello* (mus. Auber, 1829), *Kenilworth* (mus. Costa, 1831), and *Faust* (mus. Adam, 1837). His works were characterized by strong story lines, imaginative local colour, and extensive mime. In 1842 he joined forces with Perrot to stage the first London production of *Giselle* and also that year wrote the libretto for *Alma ou la Fille de feu* which he staged with dances by Perrot and Cerrito. He married Élisabeth Duchemin who as Mme Deshayes became one of the most distinguished female dancers on the London stage.

design Dance is a visual artform and the design of the stage and of the dancers' costumes naturally plays a major role in establishing the style and tone of any work. Narrative works may depend heavily on scenery and costumes to identify the characters and the action, a plotless ballet may take its mood from an abstract set, lighting, backdrop, or costumes. In any work, what the dancers wear will influence greatly how we look at their movement.

In the court ballets of the 15th–17th centuries artists, architects, and artisans were employed as stage designers. These ballets were often elaborate spectacles, intended to display the status of the nobility or monarchs who had commissioned them. Scenery often involved complex stage machinery designed to create magical effects while the dancers' costumes, often fantastical versions of court dress, were extremely opulent, involving highly ornamented clothes and huge wigs. When dance moved onto the stage, specialist theatre designers began to emerge and by the early 19th century some regarded themselves as poets of the theatre. As the highly formalized classical settings of the 18th century gave way to *Romanticism, designers created mysterious moonlit forests for sylphs and wilis to inhabit or colourful exotic settings for gypsies and adventuresses. The invention of gas lighting made it possible to create evocative shadows, to suggest woodland glades or starry nights through which dancers flew using flying wires and harnesses. At the same time the dancers' costumes became much simpler. Ornamental wigs were out of fashion, the women's dresses featured shorter, more lightweight skirts. The men no longer wore the stiff skirt or tonnelet of the 18th century but simple tights, trunks, and tunics which gave them more freedom to move. Costumes aimed to reflect the ballet's dramatic setting, for example drifting white skirts for sylphs or versions of national or peasant costume for exotic ballets.

Towards the middle and end of the 19th century taste shifted back towards more ornamental design. Extravagantly detailed scenery reflected the period's love of spectacle, with ballets taking place in rajahs' palaces, temples, or even on storm-tossed seas. The dancers retained freedom of movement in their costumes, with the women's skirts gradually shortened to form the first version of the now familiar *tutu, but authenticity was not considered essential. Ballerinas wore tutus whatever the historical or geographical setting of their role, and frequently adorned themselves with their personal jewellery. When *Fokine started crusading for artistic reform in ballet (from 1904) one of his concerns was that design should more faithfully reflect subject-matter. In his own ancient Greek ballet *Eunice* (1907) he fought, unsuccessfully, for his dancers to perform bare-legged and with bare feet. (The Imperial Theatre's management forced him to put his dancers in flesh-coloured tights with knees and toes painted on.) But once Fokine had joined *Diaghilev (who shared his belief in ballet as fully integrated theatre) he was allowed to pursue his vision of a new realism, and easel painters like *Benois, *Bakst, and *Golovine were commissioned to create carefully researched but poetic settings for ballets like *Petrushka, *Scheherazade, and The *Firebird. Some of these painters also began to experiment with colour and pattern as a means of defining a mood or style, such as Bakst's dappled stage canvas for Nijinsky's *L'*Après-midi d'un faune* (1912). When the *Ballets Russes entered its more radically modernist phase Diaghilev began to commission avant-garde painters whose designs brought new aesthetics from the art world onto the stage—Cubism, Fauvism, and Surrealism—sometimes even dominating the ballet, as in Picasso's Cubist ballet *Parade* (1917). Design by modernist painters also determined the look of many works performed by Les *Ballets Suédois (1920–5) and influenced the aesthetic of choreographer Oskar *Schlemmer who, aiming for a purely abstract form of dance, clothed his dancers in sculpted costumes that virtually concealed their human form. By contrast as *Balanchine pursued his own version of neo-classical purity he often stripped his stages down to a bare minimum, in ballets like The *Four Temperaments* (revised version, 1951) and *Agon* (1957) putting his dancers in practice costumes on an empty stage so that the choreography would be free of visual distraction. In modern dance *Graham began by working on bare stages and with her dancers wearing simple jersey dresses which revealed the uncompromising bluntness of the choreography's lines. When she began to use sets she frequently worked with the sculptor *Noguchi whose free-standing sets amplified the symbolism and setting of the piece as well as providing a physical architecture on and around which the dancers could move. *Cunningham, by contrast, frequently collaborated with artists whose designs were created separately from the choreography and thus had a more contingent relationship with the dance, for example Andy Warhol's helium-filled balloons which bobbed unpredictably through *RainForest* (1968), or Jasper Johns's free-standing set for *Walkaround Time* (1968) which squeezed the dancers into sometimes confined spaces. Such designs did not aim to define meanings within the choreography but to create an independent visual place within which the dance moved. Many of Cunningham's works have also been shown on bare stages and he tended to clothe his dancers in unitards so that their movement can be plainly seen.

During the second half of the 20th century, building materials and stage machinery became increasingly sophisticated, making it possible to build more complex sets. In Maria Bjørnson's controversial designs for the Royal Ballet's 1994 production of *Sleeping Beauty* the scenery was changed with a speed that looked like the closing and opening of a giant's eye and in Act II the cobwebs surrounding the sleeping Aurora magically ripped apart at the Prince's kiss. Realism, surrealism, and abstraction were now considered equal options for any dance designer.

In some dances the set is central to the entire conception and execution of the piece. Japanese choreographer and designer Saburo *Teshigawara created works like *Bones in Pages* (1991) which took place in a kind of art installation and with which the choreography was created specifically to interact. *DV8's *Strange Fish* (des. Peter Davison, 1992) had a set constructed with numerous cubbyholes, doors, and footholds which allowed the dancers to make abrupt entrances and exits from all round the stage, as well as a false water tank beneath the floor in which dancers were briefly immersed. Lighting also became far more sophisticated with the advent of computer-operated systems. Artists like *Rosenthal established lighting as a major design force in the 1940s and 1950s, not only cueing day- or night-time and basic mood but also defining the stage space. In Dana *Reitz and Sara *Rudner's 1993 work *Necessary Weather* lighting designer *Tipton was actually listed as co-choreographer, creating pools and columns of light within and around which the dancers moved, casting them into silhouette or colour that altered the apparent dynamic of the movement.

In the new millennium the most significant new developments in design have come from the advent of digital technology. Projected images and video footage frequently take over from physical stage settings; virtual dancers or avatars may appear among the live dancers, the use of 3D imagery completely re-drawing the stage space. In some cases these digital effects are interactive, with light, images, and sound triggered by the actual movements of the dancers.

By the late 20th century almost all costume options became available to dance, from historically realistic costumes to tutus, jeans, designer clothes, and nudity. Most costumes still aim to flatter the dancers and give them freedom to move—although many choreographers, such as Jiri *Kylián, Michael *Clark, and Philippe *Decouflé, may also use constricting or distorting costumes for surreal or dramatic effect.

Designs with Strings (*Design for Strings; Dessins pour Six; Variationer*) Ballet in one act with choreography by Taras, music by Tchaikovsky, and design by George Krista. Premiered 6 Feb. 1948 by the Metropolitan Ballet in Edinburgh with Beriosova, Arova, Franca, Delysia Blake, Bruhn, and David Adams. Taras's setting of the second movement of Tchaikovsky's Trio in A major was an early example of the plotless ballet and has been revived for several companies including Ballet Theatre (1950), Royal Danish Ballet (1952), Berlin Opera Ballet (1964), and Dance Theatre of Harlem (1974).

Desoxy Theatre Australian dance, theatre, and music group. It was founded in 1990 by Teresa Blake and Daniel Witton, performing mixed-media events. It makes frequent appearances at international festivals.

Desrosiers Dance Theatre Toronto-based dance company of ten dancers directed by Robert Desrosiers (*b* Montreal, 1953) between 1980 and 1999. Desrosiers choreographed all of the company's repertory, his works, such as *Jeux* (mus. E. Cadesky and J. Lang, 1992), fusing dance with acrobatics, mime, and theatrical effects. The company toured Canada, the US, and Europe. Desrosiers also choreographed for other companies including National Ballet of Canada (*Blue Snake*, 1989). In 2004, he appeared as himself in Robert Altman's film *The Company*.

dessous [Fr., under] Indicates that a step (e.g. a jeté or assemblé) is executed with the working foot starting in front of the supporting foot and ending up behind it.

dessus [Fr., over] Indicates that a step (e.g. a jeté or assemblé) is executed with the working foot starting behind the supporting foot and ending up in front of it.

Deuce Coupe Ballet in one act with choreography by Tharp, music by the Beach Boys, and design by New York graffiti artists. Premiered 1 Mar. 1973 by City Center Joffrey Ballet with Tharp and her dancers. This was Tharp's first work for a classical company and was a literal bringing together of dance worlds, featuring Tharp's own modern dancers as well as the classical dancers of the Joffrey Ballet. At its centre a classical soloist performs academic steps, in alphabetical order, while around her the other dancers execute much freer, pop-inflected dances. The revised version *Deuce Coupe II* for Joffrey dancers only and with new design by James Rosenquist was premiered 1975.

Deutsche Oper, Berlin *See under* BERLIN OPERA BALLET.

deutscher A dance for individual couples in 3/4 or 3/8 time, also called the ländler, popular during the 18th and early 19th centuries.

Deux Pigeons, Les (Eng. title *The Two Pigeons*) Ballet in three acts with choreography by Mérante, libretto by Mérante and Henry Régnier, music by Messager (his first ballet score), sets by Rubé, Chaperon, and J. B. Lavastre, and costumes by Bianchini. Premiered 18 Oct. 1886 at the Paris Opera with Marie Sanlaville and Rosita Mauri. The story is based on La Fontaine's fable of the two pigeons, in which the hero Pepino (originally a travesti role) fantasizes about a life of pleasure with the gypsies and abandons his fiancée Gourouli. Disguised as a gypsy she follows him to the gypsy camp where she sees him being robbed. Chastened he returns home to her and is forgiven. A one-act version was choreographed by Aveline at the Opera in 1919 (possibly 1923) with Zambelli as Gourouli (she had learnt the original role from Mauri) and it was not until 1942 that the role of Pepino was finally danced by a man. Ashton's two-act version, set to John Lanchbery's arrangement of Messager's music and with designs by Jacques Dupont, was premiered on 14 Feb. 1961 by the Royal Ballet Touring company at London's Covent Garden with Seymour and Gable.

de Valois, Ninette *See* VALOIS, NINETTE DE.

devant [Fr., in front] A movement that is executed in front of the dancer's body.

developpé [Fr., developed] A movement where the dancer draws one foot up the side of the supporting leg and then slowly unfolds the working leg into the air, where it is held. Modern ballerinas have become famous for being able to achieve the 'half past twelve position' where the working foot is lifted almost as high as the dancer's ear. Developpés can be performed to the front and back as well as to the side.

Devi, Ritha (*b* Baroda, 12 Jun. 1934) Indian dancer and teacher. She studied many forms of Indian dance including bharata natyam, kathakali, and odissi with some of India's most acclaimed gurus and from 1958 toured internationally as a solo dancer. She retired to teach Indian dance technique at New York University.

Devil in the Village, The (orig. Croatian title *Davo u selu*) Ballet in three acts with choreography and libretto by Pia and Pino Mlakar, music by F. Lhotka, and design by Roman Clemens. Premiered 18 Feb. 1935 in Zurich with the Mlakars, Mischa Panajew, and Maja Küblera. It tells the story of Mirko, a young man who is seduced by the devil to tread the slippery downward path to hell. His good heart finally wins out against the latter's cunning and he returns just in time to save his beloved Jela from being married to a wealthy fool. A very popular ballet, it was revived in this and other versions in many middle European countries.

Devil's Violin, The *See* VIOLON DU DIABLE, LE.

Diable à quatre, Le (Eng. title *The Devil to Pay* or *The Wives Metamorphosed*) Ballet in three acts with choreography by Mazilier, libretto by Adolphe de Leuven, music by Adam, sets by P. L. C. Ciceri, E. D. J. Despléchin, and C. Séchan, and costumes by P. Lormier. Premiered 11 Aug. 1845 at the Paris Opera with Grisi, L. Petipa, Mazilier, and Maria Jacob. The plot is based on an English farce of the same title and contrasts the lives of two Polish women, a spoilt Countess and Mazourka, a sweet-tempered woman who is married to a brutal basket-maker called Mazourki. The two women encounter a magician disguised as a blind fiddler. The Countess behaves offensively but Mazourka is kind and in return he causes them to change places for a day. Mazourka astonishes everybody at the Countess's castle with her unexpected kindness while the Countess has to suffer Mazourki's rough treatment. Chastened, she promises to behave more humanely when returned to her real life, while Mazourki promises never to beat his wife again. The ballet's simple comic realism, rare during the *Romantic era, was warmly praised, and gave Grisi the opportunity to display a sparkling wit, rather than her usual poetic lyricism. The first London production was at the Drury Lane Theatre (1845) and the first in New York at Broadway Theater (1848).

Diable boîteux, Le (Eng. title *The Devil on Two Sticks*) Ballet in three acts with choreography by Coralli, libretto by Butat de Gurguy and A Nourrit, music by Casimir Gide, sets by Feuchères, C. Séchan, J.-P.-M. Diéterle, C. A. Cambon, and H.-R. Philastre, and costumes by E. Lami. Premiered 1 Jun. 1836 at the Paris Opera, with Elssler and Mazilier. The plot is based on Le Sage's novel of the same title and tells the story of a Spanish student, Cléophas, who helps a demon to escape from a bottle and is rewarded by an introduction to three beautiful women, the dancer Florinda, the rich woman Dorotea, and the penniless Paquita. His attempts to pursue the first two are thwarted by other admirers and he also loses his money gambling. Finally he realizes it is Paquita he loves, and with a purse of gold given to them by Florinda they decide to marry. The ballet became famous for the *cachucha which Elssler danced as Florinda. Based on a traditional Spanish rhythm, this dance is characterized by intricate stamping and tapping footwork, coquettish glances, and a supple, swaying torso. It became the most talked-about ballet in Paris and in the first London production of 1836 at the Drury Lane Theatre Pauline Duvernay scored a personal triumph.

Diaghilev, Serge (b Novgorod, 31 Mar. 1872; d Venice, 19 Aug. 1929) Russian impresario, who played a major role in re-creating ballet for the 20th century. He studied law (and, briefly, musical composition) in St Petersburg where he also joined the circle of artists surrounding *Benois and *Bakst. With this group he was co-founder of the art review Mir iskusstva (The World of Art) in 1899 which ran till 1904. Between 1899 and 1901 he was also Assistant to the Director of Imperial Theatres where he oversaw the publication of the theatre annual, though disagreements over his supervision of a production of *Sylvia led to his dismissal. In 1905 he mounted an exhibition of historical portraiture at the Tarud Palace and in 1906 took a lavish exhibition of Russian painting to Paris. In 1907 he presented five concerts of Russian music at the Paris Opera and in 1908 returned with a production of Boris Godunov with Chaliapin. This led to an invitation to bring a season of Russian opera and ballet in May and Jun. 1909. With a company that included Russia's finest young dancers, Pavlova, Karsavina, Nijinsky, and Bolm and a repertoire that featured the radical new choreography of *Fokine he scored a huge triumph. Repeated visits led to the formation of a full company, Les *Ballets Russes, which became permanent when Nijinsky resigned from the Mariinsky Theatre in 1911 and he and Diaghilev left Russia for good. For the next eighteen years the company toured widely in Europe and N. and S. America, and though often close to bankruptcy was regarded as one of the most inspired and experimental troupes in the world. Its success was primarily due to Diaghilev's genius for spotting new talent and setting up collaborations between artists. He believed that ballet should be a complete theatrical art and that music, design, and choreography should equally break new ground. His ballets reflected, and were

sometimes even catalysts for, new artistic trends. Most of his designers were painters, creating vibrant imagery, patterns, and colours for the stage. The exotic palette of Bakst's designs for the early Fokine ballets influenced not only other stage designers but also fashion and interior decoration. Picasso's Cubist costumes for *Parade were typical of the way that Diaghilev's artist-designers (e.g. Matisse, Braque, di Chirico, and Miró) enlivened the possibilities of stage design with their own unique aesthetic. Diaghilev also encouraged leading new composers to write scores for him, many of which revolutionized both the genre of ballet music and also the principles of musical composition, e.g. Stravinsky's Petrushka and The Rite of Spring, Satie's Parade, and Debussy's Jeux. Diaghilev also nurtured the talents of some of the 20th century's greatest choreographers, including Fokine, Nijinsky, Massine, Nijinska, and Balanchine, through he quarrelled with them all and his taste often followed his heart—both Nijinsky and Massine were Diaghilev's lovers and both fell out of favour when they fell in love with women. Finally, throughout its twenty years of existence his company attracted some of the era's greatest dancers, not only émigrés from Russia like Spessivtseva and Danilova but also dancers like the English ballerina Markova who had no national ballet company with which to perform. In 1921 an opulent production of The *Sleeping Princess in London nearly brought Diaghilev to financial ruin, but he was saved by securing a permanent base for his company at the Monte Carlo Casino. After his death in 1929 many of the ballets in his repertoire survived in the companies of *Blum and de *Basil and are still performed today. Many of his commissioned scores, too, have become classics of the 20th-century concert repertoire, while his company's designs are treasured in museum collections. But it was perhaps through his dancers and choreographers, e.g. Balanchine, Fokine, Lifar, Markova, Massine, Danilova, de Valois, and Rambert, many of whom went on to found schools and companies throughout the world, that Diaghilev's influence has been most widespread.

Diana ballets Diana, or Artemis, the goddess of hunting, chastity, and the moon has been the subject of several ballets including Noverre's Diane et Endymion (mus. Starzer, Vienna, 1772), Onorato Viganò's Diana sorpresa (Venice, 1774), and Nijinska's Aubade (mus. Poulenc, 1929). Heine published a ballet libretto Die Göttin Diana in 1854 which does not seem to have been produced. The famous pas de deux, Diana and Actaeon, often performed as a gala divertissement, is based on a pas de deux from Petipa's Esmeralda.

Didelot, Charles-Louis (*b* Stockholm, 1767; *d* Kiev, 7 Nov. 1837) French dancer, choreographer, and teacher. He studied with Louis Frossard and his father at the Royal Theatre in Stockholm and later in Paris with Dauberval, Lany, Deshayes, Noverre, and both G. and A. Vestris. As a student he danced at the Paris Opera in 1783 then in 1786 returned to Stockholm to dance in opera productions where he also created his first choreography. Between 1787 and 1789 he was in London, as leading dancer under Noverre at the King's Theatre, then after dancing with Dauberval in Bordeaux (1789–90) he was appointed leading dancer under Noverre at Paris Opera (from 1791), where he danced with Guimard. In 1796 he moved back to London where he staged his most famous ballet *Zephyr and Flora* (mus. Bossi) at the King's Theatre on 7 Jul. 1796. Here he introduced dancing from wires, or flying ballet. Other innovations with which he is credited include the wearing of flesh-coloured tights and simplified costumes and, in his later ballets, some rudimentary dancing on pointe. Between 1801 and 1811 he was choreographer for the Imperial Ballet in St Petersburg where he reorganized the whole system of teaching, introducing the finest points of French technique as well as insisting on expressive acting. In doing so he established the essential principles of the great St Petersburg style. Between 1811 and 1816 he worked in London and Paris, reviving several of his ballets, then returned to Russia where he continued his reforms. Differences with Emperor Nicholas I led to his official dismissal in 1830, although he actually retired in 1834. He created over 50 ballets in a style heavily influenced by the *ballet d'action of Noverre and Dauberval—Pushkin remarked that there was more poetry in his ballets than in the entire French literature of the time. These included *Apollo and Daphne* (1802), *Cupid and Psyche* (mus. C. Cavos, 1810), and *The Prisoner of the Caucasus* (mus. C. Cavos, 1823). He was also in charge of the first Russian production of Dauberval's *La Fille mal gardée*. His second wife was Rose Colinette, a popular dancer of the time.

Dido and Aeneas Modern dance setting of Purcell's opera, with choreography by Mark Morris, set by Robert Bordo, and costumes by Christine Van Loon. Premiered 11 Nov. 1989 by the Mark Morris Dance Company at Théâtre Varia, Brussels. The action is presented by the dancers, while the singers are seated with the orchestra. Dido is a male role, created for Morris, who originally conceived the whole work as a solo for himself. The role still doubles up with that of the Sorceress, thus linking the two characters as mirror images of each other. Other choreographed settings of the opera include Henri Oguike's

(2003), Sasha Waltz's (2005), and *McGregor, La Scala Opera (2006, revived Royal Ballet, 2009).

Dienes, Valéria (*b* Szekszárd, 25 May 1879; *d* Budapest, 8 Jun. 1978) Hungarian teacher, choreographer, and dance theoretician. She studied at Budapest University then with Henri Bergson at the Paris Collège de France. After seeing Isadora *Duncan perform and taking lessons with Raymond Duncan she developed her own system of teaching and choreographing which she called the *Orchestric School*. This analysed basic elements of human movement—space, time, power, and meaning—in choreographic terms of sculpture, rhythm, dynamics, and symbolism. She taught and published widely and in 1917 began to give performances. During the 1920s and 1930s she produced several large-scale movement dramas often involving the musical collaboration of Lajos Bárdos. These included *The Eight Beatitudes* (1926), *The Children's Road* (1935), and *The Mother* (1937). Her collected works were published in 1996 and the Orchestrics Foundation was created in Hungary in 1991 for reviving the Duncan–Dienes movement method.

Dieu bleu, Le Ballet in one act with choreography by Fokine, libretto by Cocteau and F. de Madrazo, music by R. Hahn, and design by Bakst. Premiered 13 May 1912 by Ballets Russes de Diaghilev at Théâtre du Châtelet, Paris. Nijinsky originally starred as the Indian god who succeeds in reuniting two lovers.

Dieu et la bayadère, Le Ballet divertissement from Auber's opera, based on Goethe's ballad *Der Gott und die Bajadere* with choreography by F. Taglioni. Premiered 13 Oct. 1830 at the Paris Opera with M. Taglioni. The role of Zoloé the bayadère was one of M. Taglioni's most successful creations, and the story is similar to that of Petipa's *La Bayadère* (St Petersburg, 1877).

Diversion of Angels Modern dance work in one act with choreography by Graham, music by Dello Joio, set by Noguchi (abandoned after the first performance), costumes by Graham, and lighting by Rosenthal. Premiered 13 Aug. 1948 by Martha Graham Dance Co. at Connecticut College, New London, with O'Donnell, Lang, McGehee, Hawkins, and Cohan. It is one of Graham's few purely lyric works. It tells no story but celebrates the passions of youth, love, and dancing. Its original title, *Wilderness Stair: Diversion of Angels*, was taken from a poem by Ben Belitt. It was revived by American Ballet Theatre in 1999.

Diversions Welsh modern dance company. It was founded in 1983 under the direction of Roy Campbell-Moore to perform a wide-ranging repertoire including works by Campbell-Moore,

Dorfman, Bill T. Jones, and Stijin Celis. In 2004, as the National Dance Company of Wales, it moved into its new base at the Wales Millennium Centre, Cardiff.

(⊕) SEE WEB LINKS

• Website for Diversions

Divertimento No. 15 Ballet in one act with choreography by Balanchine, music by Mozart, set by Morcom and costumes by Karinska. Premiered 31 May 1956 by New York City Ballet at the American Shakespeare Festival Theater, Stratford, Connecticut. Its New York premiere was 19 Dec. 1956 at the New York State Theater with D. Adams, Hayden, Mounsey, Wilde, Millberg, Magallanes, Tobias, and Jonathan Watts. Balanchine's setting of Mozart's Divertimento in B flat major, K. 287, is choreographed for five ballerinas, three men and eight corps de ballet, the movement luminously reflecting the mood and structure of each of the score's five movements. Although it has no plot its dance imagery can partly be viewed as a celebration of love. A first version of the ballet was premiered under the title *Caracole* in 1952 at City Center, New York, and a later version with sets by Hays was premiered 27 Apr. 1966 at New York State Theater. It has entered the repertory of many companies including Dutch National Ballet (1971), Royal Danish Ballet (1978), Paris Opera Ballet (1978), San Francisco Ballet (1979), Birmingham Royal Ballet (1989), and Suzanne Farrell Ballet (2003).

divertissement [Fr., entertainment] A term originally given to the songs and dances which featured in 18th-century stage spectacles, either as inter-act diversions or as episodes loosely connected with the plot. It is also used to describe (1) the ballet interludes which featured in many 18th-century French operas, such as Rameau's *Platée* and Gluck's *Iphigénie en Aulide* and (2) the suite of dances which often dominated the final acts of late 19th-century ballets (e.g. the dances performed by fairy-tale characters in *The Sleeping Beauty*). The term is also given to concert programmes of varied solos, duets, and small group dances.

Docherty, Peter (*b* Blackpool, 21 Jun. 1944) British designer. He trained at Regent Street Polytechnic, Central School of Art and Design, and the Slade. His ballet designs include Peter Darrell's *Ephemeron* (Western Theatre Ballet, 1968), *Tales of Hoffmann* (American Ballet Theatre production, 1973), and *Mary, Queen of Scots* (Scottish Ballet, 1976), and many works by Hynd, including *In a Summer Garden* (Royal Ballet, 1972), *The Sanguine Fan* and *Nutcracker* (both London Festival Ballet, 1976), *Rosalinda* (PACT Ballet, 1977, London Festival Ballet, 1979, and Berlin Opera Ballet, 1998), *Les Valses* (Grands Ballets Canadiens, 1980), *Hunchback of Notre Dame* (Houston Ballet, 1988), and *Sleeping Beauty* (new production, English National Ballet, 1993); also W. Dollar's *Francesca da Rimini* (Asami Maki Ballet, 1978) and Louther's *Cages of Love* (Dance Theatre Corporation, 1988). He has lectured on Theatre Design at Wimbledon School of Art and at St Martins Central School of Art and Design where he has been professor since 1996. His publications include *Design for Performance—from Diaghilev to the Pet Shop Boys* (1996).

Dolan, Michael Keegan (*b* Dublin, 4 Jan. 1969) Irish choreographer and founder of Fabulous Beast Dance Theatre. He trained at the Central School of Ballet in London and choreographed for theatre, opera, and film before founding Fabulous Beast in 1997. He has written and choreographed a number of innovative dance-theatre productions, including *The Flowerbed* (2000), loosely based on *Romeo and Juliet*; *Giselle* (2003), a retelling of the 19th-century ballet; *The Bull* (2005), based on an ancient Irish epic *The Táin*; and *James Son of James* (2007), a satire of a society in transition. In 2009 he choreographed a version of *Rite of Spring*, commissioned by English National Opera.

Dolgushin, Nikita (*b* Leningrad, 8 Nov. 1938) Russian dancer, choreographer, and teacher. He studied at the Leningrad (Vaganova) Ballet School, and graduated into the Kirov Ballet in 1959. Between 1961 and 1966 he was principal dancer with Novosibirsk Ballet (dir. Gusev) except for a season with Australian Ballet in 1963, and he then joined Moiseyev's State Concert Ensemble (1966–8). In 1969 he became a principal with the Maly Theatre Ballet where he danced until 1983. He has also guested regularly with the Kirov (partnering Makarova in 1968) and abroad, making several appearances in film and on television. Tall and elegant with an unusually refined technique (he was often described as an intellectual dancer), he danced lead roles in the classics as well as creating many new roles including Colin in Vinogradov's versions of *La Fille mal gardée* (1971), Franz in his version of *Coppélia* (1973), and Prince Igor in his *Yaroslavna*. He began choreographing in 1967 and his works include *Concert in White* (mus. Tchaikovsky, Maly Theatre Ballet, 1969), *Romeo and Juliet* (mus. Tchaikovsky, Maly Theatre Ballet, 1971, new production Leningrad Conservatory Student Ballet, 1980), *King Lear* (with Aleksidze, Leningrad Conservatory Student Ballet, 1990), and *The Cinderella Suite* (mus. Prokofiev, Towson State University, 1991). After retiring from the stage he became professor of the Choreographer's Faculty of Leningrad Conservatory and artistic director of the Student

Ballet. In 2007 he developed the latter into an independent company, performing repertory by himself as well as reconstructions of ballets from the early 20th century, for example Fokine's *Le Pavillon d'Armide*. From 1989 he was also guest instructor for the International Ballet Symposium at Towson State University. He was made People's Artist of the USSR in 1976.

Dolin, (Sir) Anton (orig. Sydney Francis Patrick Chippendall Healey-Kay; *b* Slinfold, 27 Jul. 1904; *d* Paris, 25 Nov. 1983) British dancer, choreographer, and director. He studied in Brighton, then later with Astafieva, Nijinska, and Cecchetti, appearing as a child actor and dancing as a page (as Patrikieff) in Diaghilev's 1921 production of *The Sleeping Princess*. In 1924 he joined Diaghilev's Ballets Russes as a soloist, creating roles in Nijinska's *Le Train bleu* (1924) and Balanchine's *The Prodigal Son* and *Le Bal* (both 1929). He also appeared in revues, and from 1927 to 1928 ran his own company with Nemchinova, choreographing ballets to Gershwin's *Rhapsody in Blue* and Chopin's 'Revolutionary' Étude. In 1930 he became a founder member and dancer of the Camargo Society. He created the role of Satan in de Valois's *Job* in 1931, and was then principal guest artist with the Vic-Wells Ballet (1931–5). In 1933 he also danced with de Basil's Ballets Russes and in 1935 he founded the Markova-Dolin Ballet with Markova, which toured widely in the UK until 1938. In 1939 he danced with the Original Ballet Russe in Australia and in 1940 joined New York's newly formed Ballet Theatre, not only dancing principal roles but also staging several classics and choreographing his version of *Pas de quatre* (mus. Pugni, 1941), which he subsequently staged all over the world. He also created the title role in Fokine's *Bluebeard* (1941). Between 1944 and 1945 he appeared with New York's *Seven Lively Arts* revue for which he choreographed the first production of Stravinsky's *Scènes de ballet*. He then toured with the reformed Markova-Dolin Ballet (1945–8) after which he guested with the Original Ballet Russe, Sadler's Wells Ballet, and Ballet Russe de Monte Carlo. In 1950 he and Markova formed Festival Ballet (becoming London Festival Ballet) which he directed and danced with until 1961. He then directed Rome Opera Ballet (1961–4), after which he freelanced as teacher, ballet master, and choreographer all around the world. As the first British male dancer to win world acclaim in the 20th century he was a vital role model within the emerging British ballet scene. He was noted as an exemplary partner, though his critics complained that his technique was marred by flashy effects, and by too many excursions into commercial theatre. He acted in several plays and films including the role of Cecchetti in Herbert Ross's 1980 film *Nijinsky* and was author of several books includ-

ing *Divertissement* (London, 1931), *Alicia Markova* (London, 1953), *Autobiography* (London, 1960), and *The Sleeping Ballerina—The Story of Olga Spessivtzeva* (London, 1966). He was knighted in 1981.

Dollar, William (*b* St. Louis, Mo., 20 Apr. 1907; *d* Flourtown, Pa., 28 Feb. 1986) US dancer, choreographer, director, and teacher. He studied with Fokine, Mordkin, Balanchine, Vladimirov, and Volinine and made his debut with the Municipal Opera St Louis in 1930. He danced with Philadelphia Opera Ballet (1933–5), becoming principal with American Ballet (1935–7) then principal with Ballet Theatre in 1940. In 1941 he danced with American Ballet Caravan and in 1942 with New Opera Company, subsequently guesting with American Ballet Theatre, Ballet International (1944), and Grand Ballet du Marquis de Cuevas. He also performed in musicals and films including *The Goldwyn Follies* (dir. Marshall, chor. Balanchine, 1938). As one of the first American classical male dancers he created roles in many Balanchine ballets including *Le Baiser de la fée* (1937) and *Four Temperaments* (1946). He began choreographing in 1936, his first ballet *Concerto* (mus. Chopin, Ballet Caravan) was created with Balanchine who was a major influence on his style. His other works include a recreation of Nijinsky's *Jeux* (mus. Debussy, Ballet Theatre, 1950) and *Le Combat*, renamed *The Duel* (mus. de Banfield, Petit's Ballet de Paris, 1949). After arthritis forced his early retirement he worked as a teacher and ballet master in Europe, N. and S. America, and Iran.

Domenico da Piacenza (D. da Ferrara) (*b* Piacenza, *c.*1400; *d* Ferrara, *c.*1476) Italian dancer and teacher. Little is known about his life except that he was probably teaching in Piacenza from around the 1440s and arranged and performed dances for court festivities and weddings. He worked at the court in Ferrara where he assembled his theories about the art of dance in his treatise *De arte saltandi et choreas ducendi* in a period some time between 1450 and 1460. This is now in the Paris National Library. Written in the third person, it analyses the qualities necessary for a good dancer and its illustrative comments frequently illuminate the spirit of the era's dance. He gives instructions for eighteen balli (usually in mixed rhythm) and four bassedanze (in 6/8 time). Descriptions of his dances suggest he was drawn to dramatic mime and to small numbers of dancers whom he deployed in elaborate floor patterns.

Donizetti, Gaetano (*b* Bergamo, 29 Nov. 1797; *d* Bergamo, 8 Apr. 1848) Italian composer. He wrote no ballet scores but some of his operas contained ballet divertissements, e.g. *Les Martyrs* (chor. Coralli, 1840) and *La Favorite* (chor. Albert, 1840). The music for some of these has later been used by e.g. Howard in *Veneziana* (1953), Balanchine in *Donizetti Variations* (1960), and Harkarvy in *La Favorita* (1969).

Donizetti Variations Ballet in one act with choreography by Balanchine, music by Donizetti, costumes by Karinska, and lighting by Hays. Premiered 16 Nov. 1960 by New York City Ballet at City Center, New York, with Hayden and Watts. This setting of music from Donizetti's opera *Dom Sébastien de Portugal* was originally titled 'Variations from *Don Sebastian*' and is choreographed for a principal couple and a corps of six women and three men. It has been revived by several companies including Hamburg State Opera (1967) and American Ballet Theatre (1984).

Don Juan ou Le Festin de pierre Ballet pantomime in three acts with choreography by Angiolini, libretto by Angiolini and Raniero di Calzabigi (based on Molière's 1665 play), music by Gluck, and designs by Giovanni Maria Quaglio. Premiered 17 Oct. 1761 at the Burg Theatre, Vienna. It was the first dance work to tell the story of the legendary philanderer, and was a classic example of the *ballet d'action as developed by Noverre. Its simple, dramatic narrative and (for that era) surprisingly tragic ending made it very popular with audiences and it was kept in the repertory for more than 40 years. Some later 18th-century productions followed Angiolini's, including Galeotti's for Milan, 1766, and LePicq's for the King's Theatre, London, 1785 (as *Il convitato di pietra*). New versions set to Gluck's score include Kröller (Vienna State Opera Ballet, Vienna, 1924), Fokine (Ballets de Monte Carlo, London, 1936), Massine (as *Don Giovanni*, Teatro alla Scala, Milan, 1959), and Neumeier (Frankfurt Ballet with additional music by de Victoria, Frankfurt, 1972, revived National Ballet of Canada, 1974). Other dance treatments of the story include those by O. Viganò (Venice, 1787), T. Gsovsky (mus. R. Strauss, Berlin, 1938), Ashton (mus. R. Strauss, London, 1948), and L. Christensen (mus. Rodrigo, San Francisco, 1973).

Donn, Jorge (*b* Buenos Aires, 28 Feb. 1947; *d* Lausanne, 1 Dec. 1992) Argentinian dancer. He studied at the Teatro Colón Ballet School and in 1963 joined Béjart's Ballet of the 20th Century where he rapidly became a principal. A dancer with a magnetic stage presence, capable of great power as well as fluid lyricism, he created lead roles in many of Béjart's works, including *Ninth Symphony* (1964), *Romeo and Juliet* (1966), *Nijinsky, clown de Dieu* (1971), *Notre Faust* (1975), *Dichterliebe* (1978), and *Magic Flute*

(1981). He also guested abroad with various companies including the Bolshoi. In 1976 he was appointed artistic director of the Yantra Company and in 1980 joint artistic director of Ballet of the 20th Century. In 1989 he briefly took over direction of the Vichy Company, then returned to Béjart's company, under its new name Béjart Ballet Lausanne. He appeared in several films and television productions including *Le Danseur* (Béjart, 1968) and *La Vie d'un danseur* (French television, 1968).

Don Quixote The hero of Cervantes' novel has been the subject of many ballets but most surviving productions are based on Petipa's. This has a complex history. Petipa's first version was a four-act comedy ballet, with music by Minkus and design by Isakov, Shenian, and Shagin. Premiered at Moscow's Bolshoi Theatre on 26 Dec. 1869 with Sobeshanskaya, Sokolov, and Geltser. His second version was extended to five acts using the same music and designs but with many choreographic revisions, including the addition of numerous classical ensembles. This was premiered 21 Nov. 1871 in St Petersburg. Its plot centres on the love affair between Kitri and Basilio (described in the second volume of the novel), and their attempts to escape Kitri's arranged marriage to the foppish Gamache. Don Quixote and his servant Sancho Panza are almost incidental characters whose adventures link the plot together, for example the famous tilting at windmills scene and the Don's dream of his ideal woman, Dulcinea, which provides the ballet with its lyrical vision scene. In 1900 Gorsky mounted a drastically revised production for Moscow's Bolshoi Theatre, retaining some of Petipa's choreography but controversially introducing much more comic realism in the mime and characterization. This version was also shown in St Petersburg in 1902 with a cast including Kschessinska and N. Legat and it remained in the repertoire of both the Bolshoi and Kirov companies forming the basis of subsequent productions, such as those of Lopukhov (Leningrad, 1923) and Zakharov (Moscow, 1940). It was also the basis for the first complete production of the ballet in the West staged by Witold Borkowski for Ballet Rambert (London, 1962). Other subsequent productions based on the Petipa/Gorsky version have been Nureyev's for Vienna State Opera Ballet (Vienna, 1966, revived for Australian Ballet, 1970) and Baryshnikov's for American Ballet Theatre (Washington, 1978, revived for Royal Ballet, 1993). One of the most robust and varied of the extant classics, its mixture of Spanish dance, pure classicism, and comic farce has sustained its popular appeal. Several early ballets were choreographed on the subject of Cervantes' hero including Hilverding (Vienna, 1740), Noverre (Vienna, 1768), Didelot (St Petersburg,

1808), and Bournonville (Copenhagen, 1837). Twentieth-century versions of the same story include those of de Valois (mus. R. Gerhard, London, 1950), Lifar (as *Le Chevalier errant*, mus. Ibert, Paris, 1950), and Spoerli (Zurich, 2006). Balanchine's version (New York City Ballet, 1965) is set to music by Nabakov, and created in homage to its original Dulcinea, Suzanne *Farrell. It is now also in the repertory of Farrell's company. In 2010 Ratmansky created a new version for Dutch National Ballet based on Petipa's 1869 original.

Dorati, Antal (*b* Budapest, 9 Apr. 1906; *d* Gerzensee, nr. Berne, 13 Nov. 1988) Hungarian-US conductor who was second conductor for the Ballet Russe de Monte Carlo (1935–7), conductor for the Original Ballet Russe (1938–41), and music director of Ballet Theatre (1941–5). He also arranged the music for several ballets including Lichine's *Graduation Ball* (after J. Strauss, 1940) and Fokine's *Bluebeard* (after Offenbach, 1941). In the 1950s he conducted the first complete recordings of Tchaikovsky's ballet scores. His autobiography *Notes of Seven Decades* was published London, 1979.

Dorfman, David (*b* Chicago, 7 Nov. 1961) US dancer, choreographer, and director. He trained with Nagrin and at Connecticut College and danced with various companies including Kei Takei's Moving Earth and Susan Marshall. He founded his own company in 1985 for which he has choreographed many works, including *Desired Effect* (mus. Froot, 1990), *A Cure for Gravity* (mus. Joe Jackson, 1997), *See Level* (mus. Chris Peck, 2003), and *Underground* (mus. Jonathan Bepter, 2006). His style is fast, acrobatic, and imagistic, sometimes combining text with dance as in *Sleep Story* (1987) and *Gone Right Back* (mus. Elaine Buckholtz, Shannon McGuire, and Dorfman, 1997). The company tours extensively in N. and S. America and Europe. He has also created work for other companies, including Diversions Dance Company, Balletethnic Dance Company, and Uppercut Dance Theatre and has directed community dance projects.

((⊕)) SEE WEB LINKS
• Website for David Dorfman company

Dorris, George (*b* Eugene, Ore., 3 Aug. 1930) US teacher, writer, and editor. He studied at the University of Oregon and Northwestern University. He was associate editor of *Ballet Review* (1967–78), and contributor to *Ballet Today, Dance Now*, and *Dancing Times*. In 1977 he was founder (with J. Anderson) of *Dance Chronicle* which he continued to co-edit until 2008. He was also associate editor of the *International Encyclopedia of Dance* (New York, 1998) and editor of *The Royal*

Swedish Ballet (London, 1999). He has also lectured widely on dance history.

Doubrovska, Felia (orig. Felizata Dluzhnevska; *b* St Petersburg, 1896; *d* New York, 18 Sept. 1981) Russian-US dancer and teacher. She studied at the Imperial Theatre School in St Petersburg and in 1913 graduated into the Mariinsky Theatre, where she became a soloist. In 1920 she left Russia for Paris to become ballerina with Diaghilev's Ballets Russes where she danced until 1929. An unusually tall and technically adventurous dancer, she created the role of the Bride in Nijinska's *Les Noces* (1923), Polyhymnia in Balanchine's *Apollo musagète* (1928), and the Siren in his *Prodigal Son* (1929). Between 1929 and 1931 she danced with Pavlova then subsequently with various companies including Ballets Russes de Monte Carlo (1932), Nijinska's company (1934), de Basil's Ballets Russes, London (1937), and Metropolitan Opera Ballet in New York where she was prima ballerina (1938–9). After retiring she became a much respected teacher at the School of American Ballet (1949–80). She was married to the dancer Pierre *Vladimirov.

Dougill, David (*b* Blackpool, 10 Jan. 1944) British dance critic. He was research assistant to Richard Buckle between 1968 and 1975 and has been critic of the *Sunday Times* since 1975.

Douvilier, Suzanne Theodore (*née* Vallande; *b* Dole; *d* New Orleans, 30 Aug. 1826) French dancer and choreographer. It is thought she studied at Paris Opera Ballet School and in 1792 came to New York with her partner, Alexandre Placide. They toured America before making a base in Charleston where she danced in ballets by Gardel and Noverre and also choreographed her own *Echo and Narcissus* (1796). She married the singer Louis Douvilier after he fought a duel with Placide and settled with him in New Orleans where she continued to perform as well as choreograph many ballets, for which she also designed and painted the scenery.

Dove, Ulysses (*b* Columbia, SC, 17 Jan. 1947; *d* New York, 11 Jun. 1996) US dancer and choreographer. He studied dance locally and at Bennington College, making his debut with Mary Anthony and Lang. Between 1970 and 1973 he danced with Cunningham and between 1973 and 1980 with Ailey's company where he became a principal. He created his first work for Ailey in 1979 and in 1980 was appointed assistant director of the Choreographic Research Group of the Paris Opera. His style was characterized by an urgent athleticism and was driven by vigorous if abstract emotion. He created works for many companies including American Ballet Theatre (*Serious Pleasures*, 1992, inspired by Kazantzakis's novel *The*

Last Temptation of Christ), Royal Swedish Ballet (*Dancing on the Front Porch of Heaven*, 1993), and New York City Ballet (*Red Angels*, 1994, and *Twilight*, 1996).

Dowell, (Sir) Anthony (*b* London, 16 Feb. 1943) British dancer and director. He studied with June Hampshire and from 1953 at Sadler's Wells Ballet School, becoming the Royal Ballet School. In 1960 he joined Covent Garden Opera Ballet and in 1961 the Royal Ballet where he was promoted principal in 1966. With his unforced technical facility, elegant classical line, and natural poise he rapidly became the leading danseur noble of his generation, performing all the major classical roles. In 1964 Ashton paired him with Antoinette Sibley in *The Dream*, and in doing so initiated one of the era's great partnerships, the dancers' slender bodies and classical line achieving a startling correspondence with each other. The role of Oberon drew out a quality of magical glamour from Dowell, while the experience of working with Tudor on the leading role in *Shadowplay* (1967) considerably deepened his dramatic expression. He also created roles in many other ballets including Ashton's *Monotones* (1965), *Jazz Calendar* (1968), *Enigma Variations* (1968), *Meditation from Thaïs* (1971), and *A Month in the Country* (1976), and MacMillan's *Anastasia* (1971 version) and *Manon* (1974). Between 1978 and 1980 he took leave of absence to dance with American Ballet Theatre where he partnered Makarova and experienced the technical challenge of a new repertoire. He continued to make occasional dance appearances into his fifties, creating roles in MacMillan's *Winter Dreams* (1991) and Wright's revised version of *The Nutcracker* (1999). In 1984 he was appointed assistant to Norman Morrice, the Royal Ballet's director; a year later he was made associate director, and in 1986 was appointed artistic director, retiring in 2001. He succeeded in checking falling technical standards in the company and nurtured important new talent, notably Bussell. He staged new productions of Petipa and Ivanov's *Swan Lake* (1987) and Petipa's *Sleeping Beauty* (1994). He was knighted in 1995. He continues to work with the Royal as guest coach and to stage individual Ashton ballets for other companies.

Doyle, Desmond (*b* Cape Town, 16 Jan. 1932; *d* Marica, Brazil, Jul. 1991) South African dancer and ballet master. He studied with Dulcie Howes, danced with University Ballet of Cape Town, and joined Sadler's Wells Ballet in 1951, becoming soloist in 1953. He created roles in several ballets including Ashton's *Jazz Calendar* (1968) and *Enigma Variations* (1968), Cranko's *Lady and the Fool* (1955), and MacMillan's *The Invitation* (1960) and

Romeo and Juliet (1965). He was ballet master of the Royal Ballet (1970–5).

Dracula ballets The legend of the vampires became extremely popular among choreographers in the late 20th century, inspiring well over twenty works within two decades. Bram Stoker's novel *Dracula* has been the direct basis of several versions, including Stuart Sebastian (mus. various, Royal Ballet of Flanders, 1991), Gable and Pink (mus. P. Feeney, Northern Ballet Theatre, 1996 and revived for Royal New Zealand Ballet, Norwegian National Ballet, Atlanta and Colorado Ballets among others), and Mark Godden (mus. Mahler, Royal Winnipeg Ballet, 1998). Other looser interpretations include Kudelka's *Dracula* (mus. Baker, Grands Ballets Canadiens, 1985, revised as *Love, Dracula*, 1989), Ezralow's *Irma Vep* (mus. Bartók, London Contemporary Dance Theatre, 1987), Mark Morris's *One Charming Night* (mus. Purcell, 1985), Stevenson's *Dracula* (mus. Liszt, arr. Lanchbery, Houston Ballet, 1997), and David Nixon's *Dracula* (Northern Ballet Theatre, mus. several, 2005). Mark Godden's version for Royal Winnipeg Ballet (mus. Mahler, 1998) formed the basis of Guy Maddin's award-winning film in 2001.

Draper, Paul (*b* Florence, 25 Oct. 1909; *d* 20 Sept. 1996) US tap dancer and choreographer. He studied locally and at the School of American Ballet and during the late 1920s taught ballroom dance and appeared in clubs and revues. In 1933 he teamed up with Jack Albertson to found Paul Draper and Company, then as a soloist he began to combine tap with classical music, attempting to create a classical artform. He became widely respected in the American dance community and between 1940 and 1949 appeared with Larry Adler, the concert harmonica player, performing both classical and jazz numbers. Both artists were blacklisted in 1951 and Draper's career suffered, though he continued to choreograph and perform, often very experimental works like *Name-Who? Number-What?...* (1966) at the American Dance Festival.

Dream, The Ballet in one act with choreography and libretto by Ashton, music by Mendelssohn (arr. Lanchbery), scenery by Henry Bardon, and costumes by David Walker. Premiered 2 Apr. 1964 by the Royal Ballet at Covent Garden, London, with Sibley, Dowell, K. Martin, and A. Grant. It was created to mark Shakespeare's quatercentenary and broadly follows the plot of his *A Midsummer Night's Dream*. However, its central characters are effectively Oberon and Titania, the roles which launched the partnership of Sibley and Dowell. It has been revived by several companies including Royal Ballet Touring

Company (designs by Peter Farmer, 1966), also by Australian Ballet (1969), Joffrey Ballet (1973), Royal Swedish Ballet (1975), National Ballet of Canada (1978), Ballet West (1985), and American Ballet Theatre (2002). Other treatments of the same story include Petipa (St Petersburg, 1877), Fokine (St Petersburg, 1906), Balanchine (New York, 1962), Neumeier (Hamburg, 1977), and de Warren (Manchester, 1981).

Drew, David (*b* London, 12 Mar. 1938) British dancer and choreographer. He studied in Bristol and at Sadler's Wells School and joined Sadler's Wells Ballet in 1955. After returning from national service he was promoted to soloist in 1961 and principal in 1974. He created roles in several ballets including Ashton's *The Dream* (1964), Tudor's *Shadowplay* (1967), and MacMillan's *Manon* (1974), *Mayerling* (1978), and *Isadora* (1981). He choreographed his first ballet, *Intrusion*, in 1969 (mus. Schubert, Royal Ballet). After retiring from principal roles he became a senior character artist and teacher at the Royal Ballet School.

Drigo, Riccardo (*b* Padua, 30 Jun. 1846; *d* Padua, 1 Oct. 1930) Italian composer and conductor. He was conductor at the Mariinsky Theatre, St Petersburg (1886–1917) where he led the premieres of *Sleeping Beauty* (1890), *Nutcracker* (1892), and his re-orchestration of *Swan Lake* (1895). He composed scores for several ballets, including Petipa's *The Talisman* (1889) and *The Pearl* (1896) and Ivanov's *The Magic Flute* (1893). He also edited and amended scores for older ballets, such as *Le Corsaire*.

Drink to Me Only with Thine Eyes Ballet in one act with choreography by Mark Morris, music by Virgil Thomson, and costumes by Santo Loquasto. Premiered 31 May 1988 by American Ballet Theatre at Metropolitan Opera House, New York, with Baryshnikov, Bocca, Jaffe, and van Hamel. This setting of Thomson's thirteen piano études takes its name from the famous 17th-century song and was Morris's third work for a classical company (commissioned by Baryshnikov). The dancers, dressed in simple white costumes, perform deceptively plain-looking ballet steps set in increasingly resonant patterns. It has entered the repertories of the Royal New Zealand Ballet, English National Ballet, Washington Ballet, and San Francisco Ballet (1996).

Driver, Senta (*b* Greenwich, Conn., 5 Sept. 1942) US dancer and choreographer. She studied at Ohio State University and danced with the Paul Taylor Company (1967–73) before founding her own company, Harry, which she directed until 1991. Her works experimented with all aspects of dance performance, including sound (and silence), the roles of male and female dancers,

and the use of weight and body mass. After retiring from dance she trained as a nurse.

Dror, Liat (*b* Kibbutz Lochamei-Hagentot, Jul. 1960) Israeli dancer and choreographer. She studied at the Rubin Music and Dance Academy in Jerusalem and with the Dance Workship of the Kibbutz Dance company and created her first work in 1986. In 1987 she and her partner Nir Ben-Gal (*b* Jul. 1959) began working as a choreographic and performance duo, creating *Two Room Apartment* (1987) and *Equus Asinus* (1988), among others. In 1992 they expanded into a company (still under their joint names) developing their imagistic, often brutal style of dance theatre in works like *Anta Oumri* (1994), *The Enquiry* (1996), and *The Dance of Nothing* (1998). They occasionally choreographed for other companies, e.g. Batsheva and London Contemporary Dance Theatre and in 1999 founded a dance centre and base in the Negev desert, South Israel.

(())) SEE WEB LINKS
• Website for the Dror and Ben-Gal company

Drottningholm Swedish court theatre which was built in 1766 near the castle of Drottningholm. Opera and ballet used to be performed there every summer until the shooting of King Gustaf III in 1792. After a long period of neglect the stage machinery and about 30 18th-century sets were found to be still intact and the theatre was restored in 1921 for the performance of small-scale and period works.

Drumming Modern dance work in one act with choreography by Laura Dean and music by Steve Reich. Premiered 3 Apr. 1975 by the Laura Dean Dance Company at the Brooklyn Academy of Music, New York. Its vocabulary of simple repetitive steps mirrors the trance-like power of the music. Also de Keersmaeker (1998).

Drummond, (Sir) John (*b* London, 1934; *d* 6 Sept. 2006) British writer, television producer, administrator, and dance activist. He was writer, editor, and producer at the BBC (1958–78) during which time he created two seminal documentaries on artists associated with Diaghilev, whose interviews are recorded in *Speaking of Diaghilev* (London, 1997). As director of the Edinburgh Festival (1978–83) he was responsible for enlarging its dance programme and in his various roles as Director of the BBC Proms and Controller of Music for Radio 3 was responsible for raising the profile of dance on radio. He was active on many dance committees, also governor of both the Royal and Birmingham Royal Ballets.

Drzwiecki, Conrad (*b* Poznán, 14 Oct. 1926; *d* 25 Aug. 2007) Polish dancer, choreographer, and director. He studied with Mikolaj Kopinsky, Woizikowski, and others and made his debut in 1946 with Kopinsky's company in Kraków. He danced with Poznán Opera Ballet (1947 and 1950–6) and between 1956 and 1963 worked abroad, for example with Grand Ballet du Marquis de Cuevas. He was ballet master and choreographer of Poznán Opera (1963–73) after which he was founder, artistic director, and choreographer of the Poznán-based Polish Dance Theatre. His works include versions of *The Miraculous Mandarin* (1970) and *Les Biches* (1973). He also created works for other companies including Berlin Opera Ballet (*The Moor of Venice*, 1975, and *Epitaph for Don Juan*, 1980) and La Scala (*The Childhood of Jesus*, 1980).

Duato, Nacho (*b* Valencia, 8 Jan. 1957) Spanish dancer, choreographer, and director. He trained at the Rambert School, Béjart's Mudra School, and at the Alvin Ailey American Dance Center making his debut with Cullberg Ballet in 1980. In 1981 he joined Nederlands Dans Theater where he was appointed Resident Choreographer in 1988. He has created works for many companies including Cullberg, Nederlands Dans Theater, Berlin Opera Ballet, Australian Ballet, Hubbard Street Dance, and Stuttgart Ballet. His versatile style fuses the physical lyricism of Kylián with his own distinctive theatrical imagination. Between 1990 and 2010 he was artistic director of *Compañia Nacional de Danza for which he created many works including *Tabulae* (mus. A. Iglesias, 1994), *Por vos muero* (mus. 15th- and 16th-century Spanish music, 1996), *Romeo y Julieta* (mus. Prokofiev, 1997), *Multiplicity* (mus. Bach, 1999), and *Alas* (mus. several, 2006).

(()) SEE WEB LINKS

• Website for the Compañia Nacional de Danza

Dublin *See* IRELAND.

Dubrovska, Felia *See* DOUBROVSKA, FELIA.

Dudinskaya, Natalia (*b* Kharkov, 21 Aug. 1912; *d* 29 Jan. 2003) Ukranian-Soviet dancer and teacher. She studied with her mother and then at the Petrograd Ballet School under Vaganova. She made her debut as Princess Florine before graduating in 1931, and six months after joining GATOB (Kirov) she danced Odette-Odile. A brilliantly virtuoso dancer with a powerful jump she danced all the major classical roles but also created many roles in new ballets including the title role (her most famous creation) in Chabukiani's *Laurencia* (1939); also K. Sergeyev's *Cinderella* (1946), Zakharov's *The Bronze Horseman* (1949), Jacobson's *Shuraleh* (1950), and Fenster's *Taras Bulba* (1955). Though lacking the expres-

sive acting talent of dancers like Ulanova, she dominated the company for much of her career, only retiring from principal roles when she was 52. She taught the Class of Perfection at the Kirov (1951–70) and in addition taught at the Leningrad Ballet School (from 1964) and was repetiteur at the Kirov (1963–78). She frequently appeared in film and television and was made People's Artist of the USSR in 1957 and appointed to the order of the Red Banner in 1973. She was married to the dancer and choreographer Konstantin Sergeyev.

Dudley, Jane (*b* New York, 3 Apr. 1912; *d* 19 Sept. 2001) US dancer, choreographer, teacher, and director. She studied at the Wigman School (1931–5) under Holm and was a soloist with Graham's company (1936–46). In 1938 she created her signature work *Harmonica Breakdown* (mus. Terry and McGhee) and in 1942 she formed the Dance Trio with Sophie Maslow and William Bales, for which she choreographed several works including *The Lonely Ones* (1946) and with which she toured the US until 1952. With the Trio she was also a charter member of the New London Summer School of Dance (1948–52). She taught at Bennington College (1966–8) and was then artistic director of the Batsheva Dance Company (1968–70). In 1970 she was appointed vice-principal and director of dance studies at London School of Contemporary Dance, where she continued to teach. She also continued to choreograph and even to perform in her eighties, creating *Proverbs* (mus. Klezmer, 1990).

Duets Modern dance work in one act with choreography by Cunningham, design by Mark Lancaster, and music by Cage (*Improvisation III*). Premiered 26 Feb. 1980 by Merce Cunningham Dance Company at City Center, New York. A dance elegantly constructed around six duets, it was revived for American Ballet Theatre in 1982.

Dukas, Paul (*b* Paris, 1 Oct. 1865; *d* Paris, 17 May 1935) French composer. His dance poem *La Péri* (1911) was first choreographed by Clustine in Paris in 1912 and has since been used by many other choreographers. He also composed the symphonic poem *L'Apprenti sorcier* (1897) which was choreographed by Fokine in Petrograd in 1916.

Duke, Vernon (orig. Vladimir Dukelsky; *b* Pskov, 10 Oct. 1903; *d* Santa Monica, Calif., 1969) Russian-US composer. He wrote the music for several ballets including Massine's *Zéphire et Flore* (1924), Petit's *Le Bal des blanchisseuses* (1946), and L. Christensen's *Emperor Norton* (1957). He also composed ballet music for several musicals, including *Ziegfeld Follies* (1935) and *Cabin in the Sky* (1940), and for the film *Goldwyn*

Follies (1938) all of which were choreographed by Balanchine.

Dumas, Russell (*b* Brisbane, 17 Oct. 1946) Australian dancer, choreographer and director. He studied ballet and modern dance and danced with many companies including Ballet Rambert and the groups of Trisha Brown and Tharp, before becoming co-director of the Sydney-based company Dance Exchange (1976) which he continues to direct. His created works for it include *Surround* (1993) and *The Oaks Café* (ongoing 1997–2000). In 1985 he established the Dancelink programme, bringing international teachers and performers into Australia.

Dumoulin, David (dates unknown) French dancer, the youngest of four famous dancing brothers (the eldest, a half-brother, Henri; François and Pierre). He danced at the Paris Opera (1705–51) and frequently partnered Camargo, Prévost, and Sallé.

Duncan, Irma (orig. Irma Dorette Henriette Ehrich-Grimme; *b* Schleswig-Holstein, 26 Feb. 1897; *d* Santa Barbara, Calif., 20 Sept. 1977) German-US dancer and teacher; adopted daughter of Isadora Duncan. She was one of the first pupils to join Isadora's Grünewald school and made her debut at the Berlin Kroll Opera in 1905. She toured with the children's group, then in 1911 became a teacher at the Elizabeth Duncan school (run by Isadora's sister) in Darmstadt. In 1914 she went to teach in Isadora's school in Bellevue-sur-Seine and between 1918 and 1920 she performed as one of the six Duncan girls in New York. She then danced with Isadora in Paris and in 1921 founded the Moscow school with her. After Isadora's death in 1927 she became director of the school and toured the US and China with her pupils. In 1930 she settled in the US and gave her last performance in New York, *Ode to Peace*, set to the last movement from Beethoven's 9th Symphony. She was author of *Isadora Duncan's Russian Days* (with A. Ross Macdougall, New York, 1929), *The Technique of Isadora Duncan* (New York, 1937), and *Duncan Dancer* (Middletown, Conn., 1966).

Duncan, Isadora (*b* San Francisco, 26 May 1877; *d* Nice, 14 Sept. 1927) US dancer and teacher who pioneered the free dance movement. She took a few classes in ballet but then rebelled against what she considered its unnatural contortions and constrictions. Her own dance style, inspired by the movements of waves and trees, by ancient Greek sculpture, and by the writings of Nietzsche and Havelock Ellis, was based on simple flowing movements of the body which for her expressed the rhythms of nature and the nobler emotions of man. She believed that the solar plexus was the source of all movement, and her dancing, unlike ballet, acknowledged gravity and the body's weight. Her vocabulary was composed of simple runs, skips, and jumps; large, expressive gestures and playful mime. She danced bare-legged and with bare feet in loose, filmy tunics, and, rebelling against the prevailing view that great classical music was inappropriate for dance, she used the scores of Beethoven, Chopin, Mendelssohn, and Schubert, among others. Her professional career began as an actress in the troupe of Augustin Daly, then in 1897 she moved with her family to London where she studied ancient Greek art and consolidated her ideas on dance. She began to give recitals in private homes and art galleries, and in 1902 Loie Fuller sponsored her concerts in Vienna and Budapest. She made her first professional appearance in Paris at the Théâtre Sarah Bernhardt in 1903 though French audiences did not seriously appreciate her until 1909 when she performed at the same time as Diaghilev's Ballets Russes. In 1903 she visited Greece with her family, where they built a house and in 1904 she toured Russia where she possibly influenced Fokine in his own choreographic innovations. In 1905 she opened a school for 40 children in Grünewald, near Berlin, with her sister Elizabeth, which she moved to Paris in 1908. She left most of the teaching to others but supported the school financially from her own performances which she gave all over Europe to rapturous acclaim. Her dances were fuelled by her fierce libertarian beliefs and by the passions and tragedies of her own life. She had several affairs, in bold defiance of social convention, with, among others, the stage designer E. Gordon Craig, the sewing machine millionaire Paris Singer, and the poet Sergei Esenin (who went mad and committed suicide in 1925). She tragically lost her two children in a drowning accident in 1913 and her two famous dances of this period, the *Marseillaise* (1915) and the *Marche Slave* (1916), portrayed the resilience of human spirit in the face of adversity.

Though her performances were carefully prepared they were given in an improvisatory spirit and their effect relied heavily on her considerable charisma and her profound emotional response to music. She never created a technique that could be passed on to others, though she had a huge influence on many who saw her, including Ashton, who much admired the flow and plastique of her movement. America never responded very enthusiastically to her work though she performed there on several visits. She was, however, very popular in Russia. She expressed fervent sympathy for the new Soviet state and opened a school in Moscow in 1921. She also composed two dances for Lenin's funeral and toured the Ukraine, donating her earnings to the poor. In

1924 she left Russia in poverty and in 1925 settled in Nice where she gave a few performances. She gave her last recital in Paris in July 1927 and was killed soon afterwards when her scarf became entangled in the wheel of her open car. Her autobiography *My Life* was published in New York, 1927, and London, 1928 (with some posthumous editorial tampering). Though the 'Isadorables' (six of her pupils who staged Duncan-style recitals) continued to teach her ideas and her movement after her death, no one could replicate the magic of her own performances. Interest in Duncan waned after the 1940s, though the 1980s saw a revival. Impressions of her dancing can be drawn from many contemporary drawings and photographs, from the television documentary by Ken Russell (1966), from Karel Reisz's film *Isadora* (1969), and from Ashton's dance homage, *Five Brahms Waltzes in the Manner of Isadora Duncan*, created for Lynn Seymour. The first version, with only one waltz, was premiered at a gala in Hamburg (1975), the complete version was premiered by Ballet Rambert (London, 1976). Béjart choreographed a solo, *Isadora*, for Plisetskaya (Brussels, 1976) and MacMillan a two-act *Isadora* for the Royal Ballet (London, 1981, revised version 2009). The Isadora Duncan International Institute was founded in 1977 to preserve her legacy, while dancer and choreographer Lori Belilove, who has reconstructed several of Duncan's works, now also runs the Isadora Duncan Dance Foundation.

(⊕) SEE WEB LINKS
• Website for the Isadora Duncan Dance Foundation
• Website for the Isadora Duncan Institute

Dunham, Katherine (*b* Chicago, 22 Jun. 1912; *d* New York, 21 May 2006) US dancer, teacher, choreographer, and director who helped establish African-American dance as an international theatre form. She studied anthropology, specializing in dance at the University of Chicago, and took dance classes locally, making her major professional debut in Page's *La Guillablesse* in 1933. After a period of dance research in the West Indies (1937–8) she returned to Chicago to work for the Federal Theatre Project, and was then appointed director of dance for the New York Labor Stage in 1939, choreographing movement for plays and musicals. In 1940 she presented her own programme of work, *Tropics and Le Jazz Hot—from Haiti to Harlem*, with a specially assembled company. This launched her career as a choreographer. In the same year she and her company danced in the Broadway musical *Cabin in the Sky* (chor. Balanchine), after which she moved to Hollywood to dance and choreograph for various films including *Carnival of Rhythm* (1942) and *Stormy Weather* (1943). She

developed her own style of black revues, designed by her husband John Pratt, with which she toured the US. These productions, such as *Carib Song*, *Bal Negère*, and later *Bamboche*, included full-scale ballets that were based on her anthropological research, including *Rites de Passage* (1943) and *Chôros* (1943, revived Alvin Ailey Dance Theater, 1972) as well as numbers based on popular dance forms. The combination of theatrical dance, vivid costumes, and traditional music won a huge audience for African-American dance while the school she opened in 1945 in New York, which taught ballet, modern, and Afro-Cuban dance, trained a generation of black dancers to follow her. In 1963 she choreographed the New York Metropolitan Opera House production of *Aida*, and between 1965 and 1966 was technical cultural adviser to the President and the Minister of Cultural Affairs in Senegal. She was subsequently appointed director of the Performing Arts Training Center at Southern Illinois University, East St Louis. She was author of *Katherine Dunham's Journey to Accompong* (New York, 1946) and the autobiographical *A Touch of Innocence* (London, 1959). In 1987 the Alvin Ailey Dance Theater staged fourteen of her works in a programme titled *The Magic of Katherine Dunham*.

Dunn, Douglas (*b* Palo Alto, Calif., 19 Oct. 1942) US dancer and choreographer. He studied with members of Princeton Regional Ballet Co. (1962–4), then took courses at various places, including the Martha Graham Summer School, the Joffrey School, and Margaret Jenkins Studio. In 1968 he moved to New York where he began working with Yvonne Rainer and studying with Cunningham. He danced with Cunningham's company (1969–73) and was also a member of the avant-garde improvisational group, Grand Union (1970–6), forming his own group in 1978. A puckish, idiosyncratic performer, his minimalist choreographic structures have often incorporated text, props, and a humorous play of gesture. Some have been largely improvised, others conceived around specific sites. In his 1974 work *101* he lay motionless for several hours a day on top of a maze which he had built in his SoHo loft and through which the audience were free to wander. In *Disappearances* (1994) his dancers performed amidst the lunchtime crowds in Wall Street, New York. His other works include *Four for Nothing* (1974), *Gestures in Red* (1975), *Lazy Madge* (1976), *Pulcinella* (mus. Stravinsky, Paris Opera, 1980), *Cycles* (mus. Steve Lacey, Groupe de Recherche Chorégraphique, 1981), *Landing* (mus. Lacey, 1992), *Spell for Opening the Mouth of N.* (mus. Joshua Fried, 1996), *Muscle Shoals* (mus. Lacey, 2002), and *The Higgs Field* (2004).

Dunning, Jennifer (*b* New York, 4 Feb. 1942) US dance writer. She studied ballet and modern dance and in 1977 became critic and reporter for the *New York Times*. Her publications include *But First a School: The First Fifty Years of the School of American Ballet* (New York, 1985) and *Alvin Ailey, a Life in Dance* (New York, 1996).

Duo Concertant Ballet in one act with choreography by Balanchine, music by Stravinsky, and lighting by Ronald Bates. Premiered 22 Jun. 1972 by New York City Ballet at State Theater New York, with Mazzo and Martins. In this setting of Stravinsky's five-part duo for violin and piano the two dancers periodically engage with the musicians who play on stage. It has been revived by many companies, including the Royal Ballet (1995).

Dupond, Patrick (*b* Paris, 14 Mar. 1959) French dancer and director. He studied at Paris Opera School and graduated into the Paris company in 1975, becoming premier danseur in 1979 and étoile in 1980. His precocious talent won him the Varna Gold Medal, with a special citation for excellence at the age of 17. From the beginning of his career his flamboyantly virtuoso technique and charismatic charm attracted the interest of contemporary choreographers and although he danced the classical repertory he was best known for his created roles in, for example, Neumeier's *Vaslav* (orig. chor. in Hamburg, 1979, but soon after taken into the Paris Opera repertory), Petit's *Le Fantôme de l'Opéra* (1980), Ailey's *Au bord de précipice* (1983), Nureyev's *Romeo and Juliet* (1984), Béjart's *Salomé* (1985), and Tharp's *Grand Pas: Rhythm of the Saints* (1991). His handsome looks and theatrical flair brought him international star status and from 1980 he danced widely as a guest artist with, among others, Ballet du Rhin, American Ballet Theatre, Ballet of the 20th Century, and Twyla Tharp. In 1985 he founded his own group, Patrick Dupond and Stars, appearing also as principal guest artist with Paris Opera, and in 1988 he became artistic director of Ballet de Nancy. Between 1990 and 1995 he was director of the Paris Opera where he brought in works by Tharp, Robbins, Graham and others. After leaving he continued to dance there as étoile until 1997, also appearing in television and film. In 1999 he starred in a dance and equestrian spectacle (with the equestrian Ballet du Cadre Noir de Saumur), choreographed by J.-H. Tanto, but a serious accident the following year curtailed his activities. He was made Commandeur des arts et lettres in 1988.

Dupont, Aurélie (*b* Paris, 15 Jan. 1973) French dancer. She studied at the Paris Opera Ballet School from the age of 10 and graduated into the company in 1989, promoted to first dancer in 1996 and named étoile in 1998 after her performance as Kitri in Nureyev's production of *Don Quixote*. A classically elegant, Parisian dancer, she has been especially renowned for her dramatic interpretations in both classical and contemporary repertories and has created roles in works by Brown, Preljocaj, Millepied, and Petit (*Rythme de valses*, 1994). In 2002 she guested with the Kirov in their production of *Romeo and Juliet*. She was gold medallist at Varna in 1992.

Duport, Louis Antoine (*b* Paris, 1781; *d* Paris, 19 Oct. 1853) French dancer, choreographer, and ballet master. He made his debut at the Paris Opera in 1797 where he rapidly became one of the most successful dancers of his time, rivalling even the legendary Vestris. (In 1804 they agreed to appear on stage together in an unofficial competition of prowess. A contemporary wrote: 'It would take a Virgil to describe this contest.') Especially admired for the speed of his pirouettes and the vivacity of his dancing, he also began choreographing ballets, including *Acis et Galathée* (mus. Darondeau, 1805), with the ambition of unseating the reigning ballet master Gardel. As he sought more and more power at the Opera the authorities, including Napoleon himself, were forced to try to curb his demands. Thwarted, he fled Paris in 1808 disguised as a woman in the company of a former mistress of Napoleon. He went first to Vienna where he produced *Figaro or the Barber of Seville*, then to St Petersburg where he enjoyed spectacular popularity (he is mentioned in Tolstoy's *War and Peace*). His outrageous ego infuriated Didelot who was ballet master there until 1811, and in 1812 Duport finally left for Vienna. Here he choreographed many ballets for the Kärntnertor Theater including *La Fille mal gardée* (after Dauberval, 1814), though according to Elssler 'he never gives the public anything new'. He also danced in Naples (1817 and 1820) and at London's King's Theatre (1819), before returning to co-direct the Kärntnertor Theatre with the impresario-producer D. Barbaia. In 1836 he retired to Paris.

A talented child dancer of the same name performed in America during the first half of the 1790s though it is not established whether he had any connection with his famous namesake.

Dupré, Louis (*b* c.1690; *d* Dec. 1774) French dancer, choreographer, and ballet master. He studied at the Paris Opera school and may have appeared in the company as a child before making his official adult debut in 1714. Known as Le Grand Dupré and admired for his elegant physique and noble dancing, he did not retire from his position as premier danseur until 1751 and continued dancing into his sixties. For a few years he also lived and worked in London; he presented a group of students at Lincoln's Inn Fields and also at theatres in Dresden and Warsaw. He staged several works for the Paris Opera and for the Opéra Comique and until 1743 was director of the Opera's ballet school where Vestris and Noverre were among his pupils. Casanova admired his dancing in his *Mémoires*.

Dupuy, Dominique and Françoise (Dominique, *b* Paris, 31 Oct. 1930; Françoise, *née* Michand, *b* Lyon, 6 Feb. 1925) French dancers and choreographers. Françoise trained with Zvereff, Cunningham, and others, Dominique with Preobrajenska, Cunningham, and others and they both danced with Ballet des Arts. In 1951 they married and in the same year formed Ballets Modernes de Paris, the first important professional modern dance company in France, which lasted until 1979. They both choreographed works for the company, separately and together, including *The Miraculous Mandarin* (mus. Bartók, 1965), as well as for other ensembles. They have both taught widely. In 1990 she was appointed director of dance at the Institut de Formation à l'Enseignement de la Danse et de la Musique (later the Centre National de la Danse) and from 1991 to 1995 he was director of the dance department of the Institut de Pédagogie Musicale et Chorégraphique.

Durang, John (*b* York, Pa., 6 Jan. 1768; *d* Philadelphia, 1822) US dancer and choreographer, the first American-born dance artist to become widely famous. He had no formal dance training but was fascinated by the theatre and at 15 left home to learn the craft. He appeared with the Old American Company of Lewis Hallam (1785–96) in both Philadelphia and New York, learning dance and mime skills from several performers, then became director of pantomimes for Ricketts circus troupe, before moving to the Chestnut Theatre (1800–19) where he taught and staged many ballets. As a dancer he was particularly famous for his hornpipes and Harlequinades. His children were all trained as dancers, including his son Charles (1794–1870) who became a performer, ballet master, stage manager, critic, and writer.

Durante, Viviana (*b* Rome, 8 May 1967) Italian dancer. She studied in Italy then at the Royal Ballet School, London, graduating into the company in 1984, where she was promoted principal in 1989. A dancer of classical elegance and polish, she came to prominence in 1987 when she replaced an injured Odette mid-performance, having never actually learnt the role. The rest of the standard classical ballerina roles quickly followed, and she grew rapidly in authority, although she was sometimes criticized for the coolness of her interpretations. It was dancing in the MacMillan repertoire, particularly *Manon* (1991, with Mukhamedov) that broke through her reserve, revealing a powerful acting talent. She went on to create the role of Irina in MacMillan's *Winter Dreams* (1991), the only female role in his *Judas Tree* (1992), and to dance the title role in the revival of his full-length *Anastasia* (1996). She has also created roles in ballets by Bintley, including *Cyrano* (1991), and Page, including *Now langorous, now wild…* (1996). From 1996 she worked with the Royal as a guest artist, also appearing with American Ballet Theatre, K Ballet, and Ballet Boyz. In 2008 she appeared as The Ballerina in Tony Harrison's play *Fram* (London).

Dutch National Ballet (Dutch: Het Nationale Ballet) The Netherlands' national ballet company. Based in Amsterdam, it was formed in 1961 through an amalgamation of Sonia Gaskell's Netherlands Ballet and the two-year-old Amsterdam Ballet, directed by Mascha ter Weeme. The two women ran it jointly for one season then Gaskell was sole director until 1965, when Rudi van Dantzig and Robert Kaesen joined her as co-directors. Van Dantzig created his seminal *Monument for a Dead Boy* for the company in the same year. Gaskell left in 1969, followed two years later by Kaesen. Harkarvy took the latter's place for one season after which van Dantzig remained as sole director until 1991. During its early years the company had an almost unmanageably large repertoire of 19th-century classics, major 20th-century ballets, and new works. The dancers were also expected to perform in Opera productions. Under van Dantzig there was a greater focus on work by its trio of resident choreographers—himself, Toer van Schayk, and Hans van Manen (who created *Adagio Hammerklavier* for the company in 1973)—thereby giving the company a more distinct identity. However, it retained its commitment to both classicism and the 20th-century canon, particularly Balanchine. (In 1996 it presented a two-week Balanchine festival, performing nine of his ballets.) In 1986 the company moved to the newly built Muziektheater and in 1987 van Manen left, but works from a new generation, including Maguy Marin and Édouard Lock, continued the company's commitment to new choreography. In 1991 van Dantzig was succeeded by Wayne Eagling who maintained the balance between old and new in the repertoire, introducing works by several European choreographers including himself, and also reviving classics of modern dance such as Graham's *Errand into the Maze*. In 2003 Ted Brandsen was appointed as Eagling's successor bringing in new repertory by Morris, Ratmansky, and by the company's resident choreographers, Brandsen himself, van Manen, Krzysztof Pastor and, from 2004, David Dawson. The company tours extensively in the Netherlands and abroad.

 SEE WEB LINKS

• Website for the Dutch National Ballet

Duvernay, Pauline (*b* Paris, 1813; *d* Norfolk, 1894) French dancer. She studied with F. Taglioni and Vestris at the Paris Opera school making her debut in *Mars et Vénus* in 1831. She made her London debut in Aumer's *La Belle au bois dormant* in the same year. In 1836 she scored a huge personal success as Florinda in Coralli's *Le Diable boiteux* (revived as *The Devil on Two Sticks*) at Drury Lane. She was generally a great favourite with audiences due to her delicate beauty and elegant technique, but her career was adversely affected by a disastrous love affair and she retired in 1837, marrying an English banker in 1845.

DV8 Physical Theatre British dance theatre company. It was founded by Lloyd Newson in 1986 and, influenced by the work of Pina Bausch and European dance theatre, it has committed itself to work which reflects issues in the real world rather than abstract dance concerns. It makes a practice of involving all performers in the creation of the work, drawing on their personal experiences as well as their choreographic ideas. Its first major work, *My Sex, Our Dance* (1987), was a duet for Newson and Charnock in which physical risk-taking mirrored the emotional challenges of a male relationship. In *My Body, Your Body* (1987) eight male and female dancers explored sexual stereotyping while *Dead Dreams of Monochrome Men* (1988) tackled issues of male alienation and desire. The work was filmed for television, as were several of the company's subsequent productions, including *Strange Fish* (1994), and *Enter Achilles* (1995), which won the Prix d'Italia award in 1996. Recent works include *Cost of Living* (2003, filmed 2004) and *To Be Straight with You* (2008). The company tours internationally.

 SEE WEB LINKS

• DV8 Website

Dvořák, Antonín (*b* Nehalozeves, 8 Sept. 1841; *d* Prague, 1 May 1904) Czech composer. He wrote no ballet scores but several of his compositions have been used for dance, including *Symphonic Variations* (chor. Hynd, London Festival Ballet, 1970) and several pieces for Tudor's *The Leaves are Fading* (American Ballet Theatre, 1975).

Dybbuk Variations Ballet in one act with choreography by Robbins, music by Bernstein, sets by Ter-Arutunian, and costumes by Patricia Zipprodt. Premiered 16 May 1974 by New York City Ballet at New York's State Theater, with McBride and Tomasson. It is based on the play by Ansky about a Jewish girl who is possessed by the soul of her lover, and evokes the story's atmosphere and relationships via a series of dance episodes. Other versions of the same story include P. Lang's (mus. Meyer Kupferman and Joel Spiegelman, New York, 1975) and K. Brandstrup's (mus. Ian Dearden, London, 1988).

Dying Swan, The (orig. Russ. title *Umirayushchy lebed*; Fr. title *Le Cygne*) Solo ballet in one act with choreography by Fokine and music by Saint-Saëns. Premiered at a gala on 22 Dec. 1907 at the Hall of Noblemen, St Petersburg, with Pavlova. This setting of Saint-Saëns's music from *Le Carnaval des animaux* was created for Pavlova. Its poignant fluttering movements not only convey the struggles of the dying bird, but also evoke the art of the ballerina, performer of an ephemeral art which 'dies' after every show. A film of Pavlova dancing it still survives and it remains 'her' ballet (she became known as the Immortal Swan). Other celebrated performances have been by Markova, Ulanova, and Plisetskaya. Les Ballets Trockadero perform a notorious comic, 'moulting' version and de Frutos also created his own solo to the music in 1990.

Dzikunu, George Kwame Ghanaian dancer and director. He was born into a family of Master Drummers from the Anlo tribe and performed with the African Theatre Troupe and Ghana National Dance Ensemble where he also studied choreography. He formed the Sankofa Dance Company which came to UK in 1974. He remained in London and in 1984 founded *Adzido Pan African Dance Ensemble for which he choreographed and directed many works, including *Sye Goli* (1992).

Eagling, Wayne (*b* Montreal, 27 Nov. 1950) Canadian dancer, choreographer, and director. He studied with Patricia Ramsay and at the Royal Ballet School, joining the company in 1969 where he was promoted soloist in 1972 and principal in 1975. A strong and supple dancer, he performed the major classical roles but was best known for his interpretations of the 20th-century repertory. He created roles in MacMillan's *Triad* (1972), *Elite Syncopations* (1974), *Gloria* (1980), and *Different Drummer* (1984), van Manen's *Four Schumann Pieces* (1975), and Bintley's *Consort Lessons* (1983), among others. He began choreographing in the 1980s with works such as *Frankenstein, the Modern Prometheus* (mus. Vangelis, Royal Ballet, London, 1984), *Beauty and the Beast* (mus. Vangelis, Royal Ballet, London, 1986), *Byron* (mus. Tchaikovsky, La Scala Ballet, Italy, 1988), *Nijinsky* (mus. Debussy, Ballet of Naples, Naples, 1989), and *The Last Emperor* (Hong Kong, 1997). Between 1991 and 2003 he was director of the Dutch National Ballet where he not only maintained the classical and neo-classical repertory but also commissioned new works by, for example, Ashley Page and David Dawson. He collaborated with van Schayk on new versions of *The Nutcracker* (1996) and *The Magic Flute* (1999) both for Dutch National Ballet. In 2005 he was appointed director of English National Ballet, creating his first work for the company in 2008, *Resolution* (mus. Mahler).

Earle, David (*b* Toronto, 17 Sept. 1939) Canadian dancer, choreographer and director. He studied locally and at the National Ballet School of Canada, later with Graham, Limón, and others in New York. He danced with the Limón company (1965–6) then worked as dancer, choreographer, and assistant artistic director at London Contemporary Dance Theatre (1966–8) before returning to Canada where he co-founded Toronto Dance Theatre (Canada's first major modern dance company) and its school. He remained director until 1994, assuming the role of resident choreographer (1994–6), and created many works for the company, including *El amor brujo* (mus. de Falla), *Dreamsend* (mus. Webern), *Sunrise* (mus. Brahms), and *Untitled Monument* (mus. Takemitsu, 1992). In 1997 he founded the Dance Foundation David Earle and Dancetheatre David Earle in Ontario for which he has created works such as *The Heart at Night* (mus. Shostakovich, 2005). He continues to teach widely in Canada.

(🌐) SEE WEB LINKS
• Website for Toronto Dance Theatre

Early, Fergus (*b* Worthing, 4 Aug. 1946) British dancer, choreographer, and director. He studied at the Royal Ballet School and danced with Royal Ballet (1964–8). He was then assistant ballet master and choreographer with Ballet for All, leaving in 1971 to work freelance, including teaching at London School of Contemporary Dance, and in 1976 to become co-founder of the X6 dance collective, a London-based focus of independent dance activity. He choreographed several works during this period including *Naples* (mus. Paulli, Helsted, and Gade, 1978 for X6, revived 1982 for Extemporary Dance Theatre) then in 1987 founded the community dance group Green Candle for which he has since choreographed and directed many works.

Eaters of Darkness (orig. Ger. title *Die im Schatten leben*) Ballet in one act with choreography by Gore, music by Britten, and design by H. Heckroth. Premiered 29 Jan. 1958 by Frankfurt Ballet, Frankfurt, with Hinton, Paul Herbinger, and Wolfgang Winter. This setting of Britten's *Variations on a Theme of Frank Bridge* is one of Gore's most powerful ballets with an especially dramatic ballerina role. It tells the story of a young bride who is falsely committed to an asylum by her husband, and there becomes genuinely mad. It was revived by several companies including Harkness Ballet (1970, a version filmed for German television) and Northern Ballet Theatre (1976).

Ebony Concerto Stravinsky's 1945 concerto for jazz clarinet which has been choreographed by, among others, Taras (New York City Ballet, 1960), Cranko (Munich, 1970), van Manen (Dutch National Ballet, 1976), Woetzel (New York City Ballet, 1994), and Ashley Page (Royal Ballet, 1995).

Ebreo, Guglielmo (Guillaume le Juif; William the Jew of Pesaro) (*b* c.1420; *d* c.1481) Italian dancing master. He studied with Domenico da Piacenza in the 1440s and travelled extensively between major Italian courts including Naples, Urbino, Milan, and Ferrara (where he was dancing master to Isabella d'Este), teaching, performing, and choreographing court festivities. In 1480 he was recommended as the finest dancer in Italy. He was also author of *Guglielmi Hebraei pisauriensis de pratica seu arte tripudii vulgari opusculum* (1463), a treatise in which he defended the nobility of the art of dance, emphasizing the important role of music, describing the qualities necessary for dancers (memory, style, posture, musicality, etc.), and recording dances by himself and his contemporaries.

ecarté [Fr., wide apart] Any position in ballet where the leg is raised at an oblique angle to the body and where the body itself is placed at an oblique angle to the audience.

echappé [Fr., escaped] A jump in which the feet spring apart from a closed to an open position.

Echoing of Trumpets (orig. Sw. title *Ekon av Trumpeter*) Ballet in one act with choreography by Tudor, music by Martinů, and design by Birger Bergling. Premiered 28 Sept. 1963 by Royal Swedish Ballet in Stockholm with Gerd Andersson, Svante Lindberg, Anette Wiedersheim-Paul, and Mario Mengarelli. This setting of Martinů's *Fantaisies symphoniques* is a brutal portrait of village women victimized by an occupying army. Though it has been associated with specific Nazi attacks in the Second World War Tudor himself claimed it was more broadly concerned with people's sadistic compulsion to dominate each other. 'The soldiers…torment [the women] until they make the women feel degraded and, in so doing, they degrade themselves.' It has been revived by Metropolitan Opera Ballet (as *Echoes of Trumpets*, New York, 1966), American Ballet Theatre (Michigan, 1967), and London Festival Ballet (1973).

Eck, Imre (*b* Budapest, 2 Dec. 1930; *d* 1999) Hungarian dancer, choreographer, and director. He studied with Nádasi, and danced with Budapest State Opera Ballet (1946–60) where he was promoted character solo dancer in 1950. He began choreographing in the 1950s, creating his first major work for BSOB in 1958—*Csongor and Tünde* (mus. L. Weiner), then in 1960 he founded the Ballet Sopianae, based in Pécs, which he directed until 1968 but continued with as chief choreographer until 1993. Though Eck began his career in isolation from modern developments in Western ballet he created a repertory that was, for Hungary, avant-garde. His early ballets were centred around strong, even sensational themes

while his style mixed classical vocabulary with jazz, acrobatics, and expressionist dance. Many of his ballets were set to music by Bartók and other Hungarian composers, including the first production of W. Bukovy's *Hiroshima* (1962). Other works for Ballet Sopianae included *The Wooden Prince* (mus. Bartók) and *The Miraculous Mandarin* (mus. Bartók, both 1965), *Lulu* (mus. Berg, 1967), *Salome* (mus. Petrovics, 1979), and *Carmina Burana* (mus. Orff, 1989). His works for BSOB included *Le Sacre du printemps* (mus. Stravinsky, 1963) and *Ondine* (mus. Henze, 1969). He also choreographed for Finnish National Ballet, for example *Tempest* (mus. Sibelius, 1974) and *Swan of Tuonela* (mus. Sibelius, 1988).

École de Danse de l'Opéra de Paris, L'
The ballet school of the Paris Opera which dates back to 1713 and supplies nearly all of the company's dancers. Girls enter at the age of 8–12 and boys at 13. It is considered to be one of the finest schools in the world and teaches an academic curriculum alongside ballet training. Claude Bessy was director between 1981 and 2004 and was succeeded by Élisabeth Platel.

ecossaise Contredanse originating either from France or Germany, performed by four or more couples in 2/4 time. It was based on genuine or imitated Scottish airs and was popular in Europe during the first two decades of the 19th century.

Education of the Girl Child Mixed-media work with choreography by Meredith Monk. The original solo version was premiered 22 Apr. 1972, at the House Loft, New York, and the final version 8 Nov. 1973, at 70 Grand St., New York. It incorporated music, movement, text, and visual imagery, with Part 1 showing Monk and six other women 'taking a walk through life' and Part 2 showing Monk as an old woman, reliving her life backwards.

Edur, Thomas (*b* Tallinn, 20 Jan. 1969) Estonian dancer. He studied at the State Ballet School and joined Estonian State Opera Ballet. With his partner Agnes *Oaks he joined English National Ballet in 1990 as principal. Noted for his elegant classical style and exemplary partnering skills, he appeared in most of the classics as well as the 20th-century repertory, creating roles in Roriz's *Seven Silences of Salome* (1993) and McGregor's *2Human* (2003), among others. Between 1996 and 1997 he and Oaks danced with Birmingham Royal Ballet, then worked freelance, re-establishing their links with English National Ballet as principal guest artists. In 2009 Oaks retired from the stage and Edur was appointed director of the Estonian Ballet.

Edward II Ballet in two acts with libretto and choreography by Bintley, music by John McCabe, sets by Peter J. Davison, and costumes by Jasper Conran. Premiered by Stuttgart Ballet, Stuttgart, with Wolfgang Stollwitzer and Sabrina Lenzi. It is based on Marlowe's play and highlights the contrast between the King's private passions and the violence of the Barons. In 1997 it was revived for Birmingham Royal Ballet with the same two principals.

Edwards, Leslie (*b* Teddington, 6 Aug. 1916; *d* 8 Feb. 2001) British dancer and ballet master. He studied with Rambert and at Sadler's Wells Ballet School making his debut with the Vic-Wells Ballet (later Sadler's Wells and Royal Ballet) in 1933. Apart from two seasons with Ballet Rambert (1935–7) he stayed with the company until retiring in 1993. He was one of its finest character dancers, and created roles in, for example, de Valois's *The Rake's Progress* (1935), Ashton's *Enigma Variations* (1968), *Tales of Beatrice Potter* (1971), and *La Fille mal gardée* (1975), Helpmann's *Miracle in the Gorbals* (1944), Massine's *Donald of the Burthens* (1951), MacMillan's *Noctambules* (1956), and Cranko's *Prince of the Pagodas* (1957) and *Antigone* (1959). From 1958 he was teacher at Royal Ballet School and ballet master for Royal Opera and from 1967 was director of the Royal Ballet Choreographic Group. In 1962 he was guest director of Washington Ballet.

effacé [Fr., obscured] A position in ballet where the body is at an oblique angle to the audience and thus only partly seen.

Eglevsky, André (*b* Moscow, 21 Dec. 1917; *d* Elmira, NY, 4 Dec. 1977) Russian-US dancer and teacher. He studied with Egorova, Kshessinska, Volonine, N. Legat, and at the School of American Ballet, joining de Basil's Ballets Russes de Monte Carlo in 1931 (possibly 1932). He subsequently danced with Woizikowski's company (1935), R. Blum's Ballets de Monte Carlo (1936–7), American Ballet (1937–8), Ballet Russe de Monte Carlo (1939–42), Ballet Theatre (1942–3 and 1945–6), Marquis de Cuevas' Ballet International (1944), Massine's Ballet Russe Highlights (1945), de Basil's Original Ballet Russe (1947), de Cuevas's Grand Ballet de Monte Carlo (1947–50), and New York City Ballet (1951–8). The first great male dancer of the post-Diaghilev era, he was renowned for his grace and virtuosity (especially his ability to perform over a dozen pirouettes). He was also a fine actor and excelled in Fokine's ballets, creating roles in his *L'Épreuve d'amour* (1936), *Don Juan* (1936), and *Les Éléments* (1937). He created roles in many other works, too, including Massine's *Choreartium* (1933) and *Mam'zelle Angot* (1943) and Balanchine's *Capriccio brillant*

(1951), *Swan Lake* (1951), *Scotch Symphony* (1952), *Western Symphony* (1954), and *Waltz-Scherzo* (1958). He also appeared at Radio City Music Hall and in Chaplin's film *Limelight* (1952). From 1958 he taught at School of American Ballet and in 1961 founded the Eglevsky School in New York. He was co-author (with John Gregory) of *The Heritage of a Ballet Master, Nicolas Legat* (New York, 1977).

Egorova, Lubov (became Princess Nikita Troubetzkoy; *b* St Petersburg, 8 Aug. 1880; *d* Paris, 18 Aug. 1972) Russian dancer and teacher. She studied at the Imperial Theatre School, St Petersburg, with Cecchetti and graduated into the Mariinsky Theatre in 1898. Her qualities of simplicity and lyricism did not immediately win her admirers in an era dominated by extrovert virtuosos and she was not promoted ballerina until 1914. She did, however, become renowned for her interpretations of both Odette and Giselle. In 1917/18 she moved to Paris where she danced with Diaghilev's Ballets Russes (1921–2) and in 1923 opened her own school, founding Les Ballets de la Jeunesse in 1937. Among her pupils were S. Schwarz, Charrat, Lifar, and Dolin. She was married to Prince Troubetzkoy and was awarded Chevalier de l'Ordre des arts et lettres (1964).

Egypt The country is rich in indigenous dance forms, but during the late 19th and 20th centuries it became largely identified with the bastardized cabaret form of belly dance. In 1959 Mahmoud Reda formed the Firqat Reda troupe in order to research disappearing folk dances and re-stage them in theatrical forms, and in 1963 the Ministry of Culture founded a second folkloric ensemble, the National Folkloric Troupe. Both companies are now maintained by the Folk Art section of the Ministry of Culture and tour widely both at home and abroad. Recent research has revealed more about the ritual origins of many of these dances especially *Raqs sharqi, the Egyptian solo dance form, which has become popular outside the country and is both taught and performed widely. Ballet was introduced in 1958 via the government-sponsored Ballet Institute which was modelled on the Soviet training system and directed by A. Zhukov. This is now part of Cairo's Academy of Arts. Cairo Ballet Company evolved out of the Institute and gave its first performance in 1966 with *The Fountain of Bakhchisarai*, directed by Lavrovsky. Its repertory includes the classics and some Egyptian works such as *The Difficult Days* (inspired by events of the 1967 Arab–Israeli war; chor. Abd el Monein Kamel, mus. Mukhtar Ashrafi). The company first toured E. Europe and the USSR during the 1970s, and Japan in 1977. In 1988 Cairo Opera Ballet was founded at the newly rebuilt Opera House, directed by Kamel, with

Russian and Ukrainian dancers in its ranks and in 1999 was integrated into the National Cultural Center, under the direction of Kamel. Contemporary works by Kamel and Béjart among others are combined with a repertory of 19th-century classics. Modern dance has been slow to come to Egypt though the Cairo Opera Dance Theatre was established in 1993 under the direction of Walid Awni and now tours internationally.

(⊕) SEE WEB LINKS
• Website for Cairo Opera Ballet

Eidos: Telos Modern dance work in three parts, with choreography by Forsythe, text by Dana Caspersen, music by Thom Willems, costumes by Stephen Galoway and Naoki Takizawa, and video production by Richard Caon. Premiered 28 Jan. 1995 by Frankfurt Ballet, Frankfurt. This densely wrought mix of dance, spoken text, and theatrical imagery was made in close collaboration with its cast and its sections are linked by the concepts of time and death. The first section, 'Self Meant to Govern', is often performed as a separate work.

Eifman, Boris (b Rubtsovsk, 22 Jul. 1946) Soviet dancer, choreographer, and director. He studied at Kishinev Ballet School, graduating in 1964, then at the choreographic faculty of Leningrad Conservatory with Aleksidze, graduating in 1972. He joined Kishinev Opera and Ballet Theatre in 1964 where he was appointed soloist, and was then appointed ballet master at Leningrad Ballet School (1972–7). In 1977 he became founding artistic director of Leningrad Theatre of Contemporary Ballet, also known as New Ballet (1977–8), Leningrad Ballet Ensemble (1978–80), and Leningrad (later St Petersburg) Boris Eifman Ballet Theatre (from 1990). After creating his first work in 1970 Eifman rapidly came to represent the vanguard of Soviet modern ballet. Though based in classical technique, his style possessed an acrobatic attack and expressive freedom, and his highly theatrical approach embraced a wide range of material including rock ballets, ballet buffo, fairytales, and works based on literary themes. He has since created around 50 ballets, many of them full length, including *Gayané* (mus. Khachaturian, Maly Theatre, Leningrad, 1972), *Firebird* (mus. Stravinsky, Kirov, Leningrad, 1975, and New Ballet, Leningrad, 1978), *Bivocality* (mus. Pink Floyd, New Ballet, Leningrad, 1977), *The Legend* (mus. Kogan, Leningrad Theatre of Contemporary Ballet, Leningrad, 1982), *The Master and Margarita* (mus. Petrov, Leningrad Theatre of Contemporary Ballet, Leningrad, 1987), *Thérèse Raquin* (mus. Bach, Boris Eifman Ballet Theatre, Paris, 1990), *The Murderers* (mus. Bach, Mahler, and Schnitke, BEBT, 1991), *The Karamazovs* (mus.

Rachmaninoff, Mussorgsky, and Wagner, BEBT, 1995), *Red Giselle* (1997), *My Jerusalem* (mus. various, BEBT, 1998), *Russian Hamlet* (mus. Beethoven and Mahler, BEBT, 1999) *Don Juan* (mus. Mozart and Berlioz, 2001) and *Onegin* (mus. Tchaikovsky and others, 2009). His company first appeared in Paris in 1988, London in 1992, and New York in 1998. In 2004 he choreographed *Musagète* (mus. several) for New York City Ballet as part of its Balanchine Centenary programme. Eifman has also choreographed for various films. In 1988 he was made Honoured Artist of the Russian Federation.

(⊕) SEE WEB LINKS
• Website with link to Eifman

Eight Jelly Rolls Modern dance work in one act with choreography by Tharp, music by Jelly Roll Morton and The Red Hot Peppers, design by Kermit Love, and lighting by Tipton. Premiered 22 Jan. 1971 at Oberlin College, Ohio, with Tharp, Rudner, R. M. Wright, I. García Lorca, D. Reitz, and others. This was Tharp's first major work to be choreographed to music, also marking her shift from austere minimalism to popular dance. A revised version was performed in New York, Sept. 1971.

Eiko and Koma (Eiko Otake, b Tokyo, 14 Feb. 1952; Koma Otake, b Niigata, 27 Sept. 1948) Japanese-US dancers and choreographers. They studied law and political science but in 1971 joined the Tatsumi Hijikata Butoh company in Tokyo. In 1972 they performed their first work together and in the same year also began studying with *Ohno. In 1972 they moved to Germany and studied with Manja Chmiell, a follower of Wigman (1972–3) and toured in Europe before settling in the US in 1976. While inspired by *butoh forms, their work is attuned to natural, elemental themes, expressed through austere, distorted but also serenely beautiful movement, as in *Grain* (mus. trad., 1983), *Thirst* (silent, 1985), *Land* (mus. Robert Mirabal, 1991), *Wind* (mus. Mirabal, Eiko, and Koma, 1993), *Breath* (1998), *Be With* (2001, with Halprin), *Death Poem* (2004), and *Mourning* (2007). They have also choreographed work for CoDanceCo and Dance Alloy. In 1996 they were jointly awarded a MacArthur Fellowship.

(⊕) SEE WEB LINKS
• Website for Eiko and Koma

Einstein on the Beach Opera in four acts directed by Robert Wilson, with music by Philip Glass, libretto ('spoken texts') by C. Knowles, L. Childs, and S. M. Johnson, and choreography by Andy de Groat and Childs. Premiered in Avignon in 1976, it has been revived for Next Wave Festival, Brooklyn Academy of Music (1984), among others.

Ek, Mats (*b* Malmö, 18 Apr. 1945) Swedish dancer and choreographer, son of Birgit Cullberg and actor Anders Ek; brother of dancer Niklas Ek. He started his career as an actor then studied dance at Stockholm Ballet Academy from 1972. He danced with Cullberg Ballet (1973–4) and Düsseldorf Ballet (1974–5), then returned to Cullberg Ballet which subsequently became the Mats Ek/Cullberg Ballet. He began choreographing in 1976 with *The Officer's Servant* and his later works for the Cullberg include *Soweto* (mus. collage of contemporary scores, 1977), *The Four Seasons* (mus. Vivaldi, 1978) and *Carmen* (1992). He achieved international acclaim with his re-workings of *Giselle*, *Swan Lake* (1987), and *Sleeping Beauty* in which his elemental dance style, fusing classical ballet, folk, and modern dance, was put in the service of radical re-interpretations of the original libretti. (He is quoted as saying 'a fairy-tale is like a pretty little cottage but there's a sign on the door saying *Mined Area*'.) In *Giselle* (1982) the heroine is presented as a simple peasant, living in a rural world which revolves often brutally around the twin poles of sexuality and death. When Giselle's naïvety turns to madness she is dispatched to a lunatic asylum. In his *Sleeping Beauty* (Hamburg Ballet, 1996) the heroine rebels against her parents, turns drug addict, and heads a stubborn course towards disillusionment. His other works also bear narrative traces, in their attention to psychological detail, their strong, even surreal imagery, and mixture of humour and pain. Ek left Cullberg in 1993 to work freelance, but continued to maintain a close association with the company. His subsequent works include the dance theatre piece *Dance with your Neighbour* (1994), with both dance and text by Ek, *She was Black* (mus. Górecki, Cullberg Ballet, 1995), *A Sort Of* (mus. Górecki, Nederlands Dans Theater, 1997), *Appartement* (Paris Opera Ballet, mus. Flesh Quartet, 2000), *Aluminium* (Compañia Nacional de Danza, mus. Adams, 2005) and *Place* (for Baryshnikov, mus. Flesh Quartet, 2007). He has created many ballets for television, including *Smoke* (1995) and directed opera, including *Orphée* (Stockholm, 2007).

Ek, Niklas (*b* Stockholm, 16 Jun. 1943) Swedish dancer. He is the son of Birgit Cullberg and actor Anders Ek; brother of choreographer Mats Ek. He studied with Donya Feuer in Stockholm and in New York with Graham and Cunningham. After dancing briefly with Cunningham's company he worked with Cullberg Ballet (1967–72), then Ballet of the 20th Century (1972–5), then again with Cullberg. A versatile dancer with an extremely powerful personality he continued performing in his fifties, dancing with Nederlands Dans Theater 3 and partnering Guillem in M. Ek's film dance

Smoke (1995). From the 1990s he also pursued an acting career in film, television, and theatre.

Electric Boogaloos (orig. Electronic Boogaloo Lockers) Funk and street dance group founded in 1977 by Boogaloo Sam and Nate 'Slide' Johnson in Fresno, California. The group's characteristic style, known as locking, is a fluid variant of *popping, in which small, sharp moves (including flexions of the limbs and rolls of the head, shoulder and hip) pass in quick succession through the body. Locking was widely popularized through the group's appearance on the television series *Soul Train*. Boogaloo Sam still performs with the group along with a later generation of performers including Poppin' Pete.

(⊕) SEE WEB LINKS
• Website for the Electric Boogaloos

Elektra Ballet in one act with choreography by Helpmann, music by Arnold, and design by A. Boyd. Premiered 26 Mar. 1963 by the Royal Ballet at Covent Garden, London, with Nerina, Blair, Mason, and Rencher. It tells the myth of Electra in colourfully dramatic dance imagery. Other versions of the story include Charrat's *Electre* (mus. Pousseur, Brussels, 1960) and Taubert's *Electra—Study about Hysteria* (mus. Stockhausen, Brunswick, 1972).

Éléments, Les 1. Ballet in one act with choreography by Perrot, music by Bajetti, and design by C. Marshall. Premiered 26 Jun. 1847 at Her Majesty's Theatre, London. It was conceived as a showcase for the talents of Grisi (Fire), Rosati (Water), and Cerrito (Air) in an attempt to repeat the huge success of *Pas de quatre* (1845). After an opening ensemble dance representing the earth the three ballerinas competed to assert the dominance of their particular element. 2 A one-act ballet by Fokine, with music by Bach and design by Bouchene, which was probably premiered 1 Apr. 1937 by R. Blum's Ballets de Monte Carlo at Alhambra Theatre, London, with Theilade and Eglevsky. This setting of Bach's Overture in B minor featured ensemble numbers for Water, Flowers, Air, and Flames, and solos for Flora, Zephyr, Vulcan, and the Tritons.

élévation [Fr., height] Dance movements which are performed in the air, in contrast to those (terre à terre) which hardly leave the floor.

Elgar, (Sir) Edward (*b* Broadheath, 2 Jun. 1857; *d* Worcester, 23 Feb. 1934) British composer. He wrote only one ballet score, *The Sanguine Fan*, which was originally performed as a mimed play at London's Chelsea Palace (1917) for charity. Its first ballet production was R. Hynd's *L'Éventail* (1976), for London Festival Ballet, which was premiered at Monte Carlo's International Arts Festival (at subsequent performances the English title was restored). The score *Enigma Variations* was first choreographed by Frank Staff (Cambridge, 1940) and more famously by Ashton for his work of the same title (Royal Ballet, 1968). Other ballets to Elgar's music include Tom Ruud's *Introduction and Allegro* (San Francisco Ballet, 1980), Paul Taylor's *Sunset* (set to the Serenade for Strings and Elegy for Strings, 1983) and Doug Varone's *Victorious* (set to the Cello Concerto in E minor, 2007).

Eliasen, Johnny (*b* Copenhagen, 1949) Danish dancer. He studied at the Royal Danish Ballet School and danced with Scandinavian Ballet as a soloist (1964–5), then with RDB from 1966 where he was promoted soloist in 1972. A versatile, dramatic performer, he created leading roles in Flindt's *Felix Luna* and *Trio* (both 1973), and *Triumph of Death* (1971). In 1987 he became ballet master of London Festival Ballet, in 1990 was appointed deputy artistic director of the Berlin Opera Ballet, and between 1994 and 1997 was with RDB as assistant artistic director, and temporary director. Since 1997 he has taught internationally and has staged the Bournonville repertory.

Elite Syncopations Ballet in one act with choreography by MacMillan, music by Scott Joplin and others, and design by Ian Spurling. Premiered 7 Oct. 1974 by Royal Ballet at Covent Garden, London, with Derman, Mason, Park, Penney, Coleman, Eagling, MacLeary, Sleep, and Wall. This ragtime ballet is set in a dance hall and accompanied by a twelve-piece band seated at the back of the stage. Its flamboyantly dressed dancers perform a series of burlesque and virtuoso routines. It has been revived by Sadler's Wells Royal Ballet (1978), National Ballet of Canada (1978), Houston Ballet (1990), and San Francisco Ballet (2003), and was filmed by the BBC in 1975.

Elkins, Doug (*b* New York, 1960) US dancer and choreographer. He did not begin formal training until he was 19, but taught himself to dance at clubs, his style an eclectic mix of hip-hop, martial arts, ballet, and modern dance. Between 1988 and 2004 he directed his own company for which he choreographed many works including *BipolarbearNOS* (mus. Evren Celimi, 1998). He continues to teach widely and has also created works for other groups, such as Union Dance and CandoCo. In 2008 he presented *Fraulein Maria* (mus. Rodgers and Hammerstein) for a temporary ensemble Doug Elkins and Friends.

(()) SEE WEB LINKS
• Official website for Doug Elkins

Ellis, Angela and David (Angela, *née* Dukes, *b* London, 5 Nov. 1920; *d* London, 21 Dec. 2006; David, *b* London, 1921) Daughter and son-in-law of M. Rambert, both of them British dancers and teachers. She studied with Rambert, Volkova, V. Gsovsky, and Craske. He studied with Rambert, Volkova, and V. Gsovsky. Both danced with Ballet Rambert (she 1943–7 and he from 1946) and he was its associate director until 1966. They formed London Ballet Workshop together in 1951 to give choreographers, composers, and designers opportunities to experiment together. She went on to direct Rambert School, he became director of the Mercury Theatre Trust until he returned to medical research.

Elmhurst Ballet School English stage school. It was founded in 1922 and in 2004 became the associate school of Birmingham Royal Ballet. Past pupils include M. Park. Desmond *Kelly was appointed artistic director in 2008.

Elo, Jorma (*b* Helsinki, 30 Aug. 1961) Finnish dancer, choreographer, and designer. He studied modern dance before embarking on formal ballet training at the Finnish National Ballet School, with a subsequent year at the Vaganova Academy in 1979. In 1978 he graduated into the Finnish National Ballet, moving to the Cullberg Ballet in 1984 and to Nederlands Dans Theater in 1990. Here he choreographed his first ballets for workshops and went on to make several works for the company including *Plan to A* (mus. Biber, 2004). His style is based in the classical vocabulary but also reflects the wide repertory he performed as a dancer, displaying a facility for combining the influences of Kylián, Forsythe, Ek, and others to surprising and virtuoso effect. In 2005 he was appointed resident choreographer for Boston Ballet, having already created two works for that company, *Sharp Side of Dark* (mus. Bach, 2002) and *Plan to B* (mus. Biber, 2004). At Boston he has since gone on to create *Carmen* (mus. Bizet-Shchedrin, 2006), *Brake the Eyes* (mus. Mozart and various, 2007) among others. A prolific choreographer, Elo has additionally made works for many other companies including Alberta Ballet, *L'Aprés-midi d'un faune* (mus. Debussy) and *Spectre de la Rose* (mus. Weber) both 2002; Finnish National Ballet, *Twisted Shadow* (mus. Sibelius, 2002) among others; American Ballet Theatre, *Glow—Stop* (mus. Mozart and Glass, 2006) and *C. to C.* (mus. Glass, 2007); Hubbard Street Dance Chicago, *From All Sides* (mus. Turnage, 2007); Norwegian National Ballet, *Death and the Maiden* (mus. Schubert, 2008); Royal Danish Ballet, *Lost on SLOW* (mus. Vivaldi, 2008); San Francisco Ballet, *Double Evil* (mus. Glass and Martinov, 2008); New York City Ballet, *Slice to Sharp* (mus. Biber and Vivaldi, 2009).

He additionally designs the costumes, lighting, and video effects for his ballets.

El Penitente *See* PENITENTE, EL.

Elssler, Fanny (orig. Franziska Elssler; *b* Gumpendorf, 23 Jun. 1810; *d* Vienna, 27 Nov. 1884) Austrian dancer and choreographer who was considered to exemplify more of the sensual than the ethereal qualities of Romantic ballet. She studied with her sister Therese E. (1808–78) at Horschelt's ballet school at the Theater an der Wien, possibly dancing with Horschelt's notorious *Vienna Children's Ballet. In 1818 both sisters joined the Kärntnertor Theater where their older sister Anna E. (1804–63) was already performing. Here Fanny performed in ballets by F. Taglioni, A. Vestris, and others. Between 1825 and 1827 she danced in Naples, returning to Vienna (1827–30) then making her debut in Berlin (1830), London (1833), and Paris (1834). For this she was coached by A. *Vestris and created the role of Alcine in Coralli's *La Tempête*. She remained at the Opera until 1840 where the dramatic intensity and sensuousness of her performances ensured that her popularity soon rivalled Taglioni's. The contrast between their styles was identified by Gautier as pagan and Christian respectively. Among her most successful created roles were Florinda in Coralli's *Le Diable boiteux* (1836) for which she choreographed her famously exotic solo, the cachucha; Sarah in Mazilier's *La Gypsy* (1839), and Lauretta in Coralli's *La Tarentule* (1839). In 1840 she went to America and toured as far south as Havana. Though she earned a fortune she had to pay Paris Opera a large sum for breach of contract by staying away so long. In 1842 she returned to Europe, dancing in Vienna, Berlin, Brussels, Dublin, and Hamburg, also dancing her first Giselle in London (1843) which was highly acclaimed, particularly the mad scene. In 1844 she danced at La Scala (where the political climate undermined her success), followed by triumphant performances in *La Esmeralda* in Budapest and London. She returned to Italy (1846–8) and in 1848 made her Russian debut in St Petersburg and in Moscow where she was received with tumultuous enthusiasm. One of her finest roles was Lise in Dauberval's *La Fille mal gardée*. In 1851 she gave twelve farewell performances at Vienna's Kärntnertor Theater, mostly in *La Esmeralda*, *Catarina*, and *Faust*. Her final appearance was on 21 June 1851. Her sister Therese, who had created much of the choreography for her early ballets, often appeared with her in en travestie roles, though in certain quarters she was mocked for her unusual height.

Elvin, Violetta (*née* Violetta Prokhorova; *b* Moscow, 3 Nov. 1925) Soviet-British dancer. She studied at Bolshoi Ballet School with Gerdt, Kozhukova, and others and in 1942 graduated into the Bolshoi Ballet as a soloist. In 1943 she danced as ballerina with State Theatre Tashkent and in 1944 re-joined the Bolshoi at its wartime location in Kuibyshev. After returning to Moscow with the company (1945–6) she left for London with her English husband and joined Sadler's Wells Ballet where she remained as principal dancer until 1956. A dancer with an exotic glamour and attack rare in the UK, she also represented Britain's first close acquaintance with the Soviet style. She danced most of the ballerina roles as well as creating roles in Ashton's *Cinderella* (Summer Fairy, 1948), *Daphnis and Chloe* (Lykanion, 1951), *Homage to the Queen* (1953), and *Birthday Offering* (1956), and Petit's *Ballabile* (1950). She also guested with various companies including La Scala, Milan, and retired from the stage in 1956. Between 1985 and 1986 she was ballet director at Teatro San Carlo, Naples.

emboîté [Fr., boxed in] A series of steps where alternate legs are swung a little out to the side, then closed in front. Resembles the movement of plaiting.

Embrace Tiger and Return to Mountain Ballet in one act with choreography by Tetley, music by Morton Subotnick, and design by Baylis. Premiered 21 Nov. 1968 by Ballet Rambert at J. Cochrane Theatre, London, with Craig, Bruce, Taylor, and Willis. This setting of Subotnick's score *Silver Apples of the Moon* was inspired by the focused calm of the Chinese martial art T'ai Chi. It has been revived by Nederlands Dans Theater, Royal Swedish Ballet, and the Feld Ballet.

Empire ballets The Empire Theatre was, along with the Alhambra Theatre, London's main platform for ballet at the end of the nineteenth century. Between 1887 and 1914 it drew large crowds to performances by some of the era's finest dancers, including Cecchetti (one of its first premier danseurs), Genée (who was prima ballerina there, 1897–1907), and also Kyasht, Bedells, and Bolm. Katti Lanner was ballet mistress there from 1887 to 1897.

enchaînement [Fr., linking] A combination of several steps or movements.

Enfant et les sortilèges, L' (Eng. title *The Spellbound Child*) Lyric fantasy in two parts with choreography by Balanchine, libretto by Colette, and music by Ravel. Premiered 21 Mar. 1925 at Monte Carlo. It tells the story of a destructive child who is attacked by the toys, animals, and wildlife he has abused. Balanchine created choreography for the entire opera in 1946, again in 1975 in New York, and in 1981 for National Education

Television. Descombey staged it in Paris, 1960, and Charrat in Vienna, 1964. Kylián choreographed a dance of the same title to Ravel's score in 1984.

English Folk Dance and Song Society, The

Society founded by Cecil Sharp in London in 1911, with the aim of preserving English folk dance and music. The two Dance and Music societies were originally separate but merged in 1932.

⊕ SEE WEB LINKS

• Website for The English Folk Dance and Song Society

English National Ballet

(formerly London Festival Ballet) British ballet company based in London. It has its origins in the *Markova-*Dolin company which toured Britain (1935–7) and was re-formed as Gala Performances of Ballet in 1949. The two stars were anxious to drop their names from the company in order to avoid having to dance at every performance and when it was again re-formed in 1950 it took its title from the approaching Festival of Britain (1951). It gave its first performance as Festival Ballet in 1950, under the management of impresario Julian Braunsweg and the artistic direction of Dolin, first in Bournemouth, then at the Stoll Theatre, London. In 1951 it took the title London's Festival Ballet, establishing regular seasons at London's Royal Festival Hall from 1952, and at London's Coliseum from 1969. In the same year it changed its name to London Festival Ballet. It was renamed English National Ballet in 1989 to emphasize the company's status both nationally and internationally, and in 1997 finally severed its links with the Festival Hall, using the Coliseum as its London base. It has always toured widely both at home and abroad and from the start its aim has been to present ballet to the widest possible audience. Its repertory has ranged from 19th-century classics such as Dolin's 1950s' staging of *Giselle*, to works from the Diaghilev and subsequent Ballets Russes repertoires, to more recent work, such as Lander's *Études* (1954), Carter's *Witch Boy* (1957), and Dolin's *Variations for Four* (1957). Later acquisitions have included Bourmeister's *The Snow Maiden* (1961), Nureyev's *Sleeping Beauty* (1975), P. Schaufuss's *La Sylphide* (1979), and Michael Corder's *Cinderella* (1996) and *Snow Queen* (2007). From the beginning the company has drawn its dancers from around the world and featured international guest artists, including Danilova, Toumanova, T. Lander, Flindt, Evdokimova, Ruanne, Terabust, Maximova, and Asylmuratova. Markova was the company ballerina until 1952 and continued to guest until her retirement in 1964. She also staged the company's production of *Les Sylphides* (1976). Dolin retired

as artistic director in 1960 but continued to make guest appearances as Drosselmeyer in *The Nutcracker* until 1980. Braunsweg left in 1965. Subsequent directors were Donald Albery (1965–8), Beryl Grey (1968–79), and John Field (1979–84), under whose direction the repertory focused more heavily on the classics. When *Schaufuss took over in 1984 however he introduced a more adventurous policy, bringing in new works by, among others, M. Clark, S. Davies, and C. Bruce (*Swansong*, 1987). He also introduced Ashton's *Romeo and Juliet* into the repertory. He was succeeded in 1990 by Ivan *Nagy and in 1993 by Derek *Deane. Deane pursued an increasingly populist policy, with his own full-length *Alice in Wonderland* (1995), for example, and productions of *Swan Lake* (1997), *Romeo and Juliet* (1998), and *Sleeping Beauty* (2000) designed for a mass audience in London's Royal Albert Hall. Matz Skoog was director between 2001 and 2005, adding works by McGregor and Hampson, among others, to the repertory. He was succeeded by Wayne *Eagling whose additions to the repertory have included works by MacMillan, Corder, and himself. The company's official school, based at Markova House, London, was founded in 1988.

⊕ SEE WEB LINKS

• Website for English National Ballet

Englund, Sorella

(b Helsinki, 1945) Finnish dancer. She studied with E. Sylverston and joined the State Opera Ballet, moving to the Royal Danish Ballet in 1967 where she was promoted soloist in 1970. She created roles in Flindt's *Triumph of Death* (1971) and Holm's *The Firebird* (1972), among other works. Her stage career was cut short by illness, which she has since publicly discussed in symposiums on anorexia, but she has continued to perform character roles and to be active in staging Bournonville productions, including *La Sylphide* for Scottish Ballet and *Abdallah* for National Ballet of Canada (1997). She has also taught widely, for example at Boston Ballet (1996–9) and at the New Danish Dance Theatre.

Enigma Variations

Ballet in one act with choreography by Ashton, music by Elgar, and design by Julia Trevelyan Oman. Premiered 25 Oct. 1968 by Royal Ballet, Covent Garden, London, with Rencher, Beriosova, and Doyle. Unlike F. Staff's abstract setting of 1940, Ashton's version follows the composer in creating a set of vividly delineated character studies based on Elgar and his friends. Though Oman's designs place the ballet very precisely in 'Worcestershire, 1898', it evokes qualities of pathos, tenderness, loyalty, and nostalgia, and an image of the artist's solitariness, which possess a universal resonance. The choreography is classically based but deeply interwoven with naturalistic gesture. It was filmed in 1969 and has been revived by Birmingham Royal Ballet.

Enters, Angna (*b* New York, 28 Apr. 1907; *d* Tenafly, NJ, 25 Feb. 1989) US dancer, painter, and writer. She studied ballet in Milwaukee, and also danced with Michio Ito, in 1922, performing as his partner in a series of recitals in 1923. The same year she created her first piece, *Ecclesiastique*, which later became known as *Moyen Age*, and the following year presented her first solo programme. For the next 36 years she choreographed, designed, and performed her own dance works. Numbering over 300, these fusions of art, dance, and theatre were early examples of mixed media work, and had an international following. She also exhibited as a painter and sculptor and illustrated the several books she wrote on her life and work. After retiring from the stage in 1960 she taught at several US universities.

entrechat [Fr., caper] A jump in which the dancer's legs cross rapidly in front and behind each other while still in the air. They range from an entrechat deux, where the legs are crossed once, to an entrechat dix. Even-numbered entrechats are finished by landing on both feet, odd-numbered with the dancer landing on one foot. Camargo is said to be the first to perform an entrechat quatre on stage and shortened her skirt in order to do so.

entrée [Fr., entrance] An entrance or opening dance. Also an individual dance within a larger segment of performance. The 17th- and 18th-century court ballets were composed of several entrées of four or more dancers and a closing Grand Ballet that featured all the dancers. In 19th-century ballets, individual acts were divided into several entrées, each one advancing the plot or theme, and performed by one or more principals with members of the corps de ballet.

épaulement [Fr., shoulder] The slight twist in the torso, from the waist upwards, which tilts one or other shoulder slightly forwards, thus giving an extra three-dimensional quality to a pose.

Episodes Ballet in two parts with choreography by Graham and Balanchine, music by Webern, set and lighting by David Hays, and costumes by Karinska. Premiered 14 May 1959 by the Martha Graham Dance Company and New York City Ballet at City Center, New York, with Graham, Ross, McGehee, Winter, S. Wilson, Verdy, Watts, D. Adams, d'Amboise, Kent, Magallanes, Hayden, Moncion, and P. Taylor. It was first planned as a close collaboration between the choreographers but developed into two separate sections. Part 1 by Graham was set to Webern's Passacaglia, Op. 1, plus Six Pieces for Orchestra, Op. 6, and it portrayed Mary Stuart (danced by Graham) recalling events from her life as she awaits her execution. Part 2, by Balanchine, was a series of plotless dances set to Webern's Symphony, Op. 21 (an ensemble dance), Five Pieces for Orchestra, Op. 10 (a pas de deux), Concerto, Op. 24 (pas de deux with female quartet), Variations for Orchestra, Op. 30 (solo for Paul Taylor), and Ricercar for Six Voices from Bach's *Musical Offering* (an ensemble dance). Graham's part was soon dropped as was Taylor's solo, so in its current form the ballet now consists of the remaining four Balanchine sections. This version has been revived by Berlin Opera Ballet (1969), Dutch National Ballet (1973) and Scottish Ballet (2005).

Epitaph Ballet in one act with choreography by van Dantzig, music by Ligeti, and design by van Schayk. Premiered 26 Jun. 1969 by Dutch National Ballet at Stadsschouwburg, Amsterdam, with G. Wijnoogst, van Schayk, and C. Geldorp. This setting of Ligeti's *Atmosphères* and *Volumina* deals with failures of communication in modern urban society. It has been revived for Munich Ballet (1972).

Épreuve d'amour, L' Ballet in one act with choreography by Fokine, music by various composers, and design by Derain (who was also co-librettist with Fokine). Premiered 4 Apr. 1936 by R. Blum's Ballets Russes de Monte Carlo, at Monte Carlo, with Nemchinova, Eglevsky, Yazvinsky, Oboukhov, and Kirsova. Based on a Korean fairy-tale, this light and witty piece of chinoiserie tells the story of a Mandarin's daughter who is engaged to a rich Ambassador but loves an impoverished youth. The latter disguises himself as a dragon and steals all the Ambassador's gold so that the Mandarin loses interest in the marriage and allows his daughter to marry her beloved. The ballet's score was initially attributed to Mozart when first discovered (in Graz, 1928) but it is now believed to be a collection of pieces written by various composers for Effisio Catte's *Der Rekrut* (*The Recruit*)—a divertissement first performed at the Vienna Kärntnertor Theater in 1838. After its discovery, the score was first choreographed by H. J. Fürstenau in Karlsruhe (1930). The Fokine version was revived by G. Gé (Finnish National Ballet, 1956) and by Beriozoff (Indiana University, 1980).

Erdman, Jean (*b* Honolulu, 20 Feb. 1917) US dancer, choreographer, and teacher. She studied with Graham at Bennington Summer School and at School of American Ballet as well as with various teachers of Eastern dance. Between 1938 and 1944 she performed with Graham where she danced major roles, including the One who Speaks in *Letter to the World*. She returned later to guest. Her own first works were made in collaboration with Cunningham and in 1944 she formed her own group for which she choreographed extensively. Her work increasingly shifted towards mixed-media, as in *The Coach with the Six Insides* (1962), based on Joyce's *Finnegans Wake*, which toured both the US and Europe. In the 1970s she founded the Theatre of the Open Eye where she produced plays by Yeats and her own work such as *Gauguin in Tahiti* (1976) and *The Shining Hour* (1980). She also taught, including at Columbia University.

Errand into the Maze Modern dance work in one act with choreography by Graham, music by Menotti, set by Noguchi, and costumes by Edythe Gilfond. Premiered 28 Feb. 1947 by Martha Graham Dance Company at Ziegfeld Theater, New York, with Graham and M. Ryder. Based on the legend of Theseus and the Minotaur, it symbolizes the struggle between the self and its most secret terrors. It has been revived by Batsheva Dance Company and by Dutch National Ballet (1999).

Escuardo, Vicente (*b* Valladolid, 27 Oct. 1892; *d* Barcelona, 4 Dec. 1980) Spanish dancer. Though born into a middle-class family he learnt flamenco from gypsies and at fairs. He then studied in Paris, evolving his own more refined style, and with his partner Carmita García travelled the world, gaining a reputation as the most patrician of all Spanish dancers. He retired from the stage in 1961.

Eshkol, Noa (*b* Safad, 28 Feb. 1924; *d* 2007) Israeli dance notator. She founded the Chamber Dance Group in 1954, choreographing many works for it and also developing the Eshkol-Wachman notation system, in collaboration with one of her first students Abraham Wachman, which was an anatomical and mathematical mapping of the spatial coordinates of movement. Her books include *Movement Notation* (London, 1958).

Esmeralda, La Ballet in three acts with choreography and libretto by Perrot, music by Pugni, sets by W. Grieve, and costumes by Mme Copère. Premiered 9 Mar. 1844 at Her Majesty's Theatre, London, with Grisi, Perrot, Saint-Léon, and A. L. Coulon. It is based on Hugo's novel *Notre-Dame de Paris* (1831) and tells the story of the deaf and hunchbacked Quasimodo who is hopelessly in love with the gypsy girl Esmeralda, who, in turn, loves Captain Phoebus. The priest Frollo is also infatuated with Esmeralda and stabs Phoebus out of jealousy. Esmeralda is then accused of Phoebus's murder but Quasimodo exposes Frollo's crime. Elssler scored an exceptional triumph in this ballet when she danced it in St Petersburg in 1849 and the work's unusually vivid characterization and tight

dramatic structure ensured its enduring popular appeal. Petipa choreographed a new version in 1886 in St Petersburg for which Drigo composed several new numbers, including the Diana and Actaeon pas de deux which is still performed today (though in choreography based on the 1935 Vaganova staging). A completely new version with a tragic ending was choreographed by Bourmeister in 1950. With a libretto by himself and Tikhomirov and music by Glière and S. Vasilenko it was premiered 14 Oct. at the Moscow Stanislavsky and Nemirovich-Danchenko Lyric Theatre. A third version was choreographed by Beriozoff in 1954 for London Festival Ballet to music arranged by G. Corbett. Other treatments of the same story include Gorsky's *Gudule's Daughter* (Moscow, 1902), Petit's *Notre-Dame de Paris* (Paris Opera, 1965), B. Wells's *The Hunchback of Notre Dame* (Australian Ballet, 1981), and C. Gable and M. Pink's *The Hunchback of Notre Dame* (mus. P. Feeney, Northern Ballet Theatre, 1998). A much earlier version was by Antonio Monticioni at La Scala, Milan, in 1839.

Espinosa Renowned family of dancers and teachers, originally of Spanish extraction. Léon E. (1825–1904) studied at the Paris Opera school, danced at the Théâtre de la Porte-Saint-Martin, then toured the US (where he was reputedly captured by Indians in 1850) before joining the Bolshoi Ballet in Moscow as premier danseur de contrast (a category specially invented for him as he was so short). He finally settled in London in 1872 where he opened a school. His wife and daughter (Lea) both taught tap dance as well as ballet. His son Édouard (1871–1950) was a dancer and producer of spectacular entertainments as well as being a renowned teacher and author of several books. De Valois was one of his pupils. He was one of the founders of the Royal Academy of Dancing in 1920 and of the British Ballet Organisation in 1930. After his death the latter was directed by his son Edward Kelly-Espinosa (*d* 13 Oct. 1991) and daughter Yvette E. (*d* 5 May 1992). The wife of Édouard's nephew Geoffrey, Bridget E. (*née* Kelly; *b* 1928) danced with Embassy Ballet (1947) and International Ballet (1948) and was artistic director of Elmhurst Ballet School from 1966.

Esquivel, Jorge (*b* Havana, 1950) Cuban dancer. He studied with F. Alonso, Joaquín Banegas, Anna Leontieva, Michel Gurov, and Plisetski, graduating in 1968 to become a member of National Ballet of Cuba (with which he had already danced part-time). He was promoted to principal in 1972 and created roles in A. Mendez's *La Dame aux camélias* (1971) and Albert Alonso's *Viet Nam: la lección* (1973), among others. He became celebrated as one of Cuba's finest male dancers, and his departure from the island in 1992 was considered a major defection. He joined San Francisco Ballet as principal dancer, eventually becoming senior character dancer and teacher.

Estonia Professional dance in Estonia dates back to the beginning of the 20th century, with the small troupe based at the Tallinn opera house from 1918. It gave its first full-length performance in 1922, *Coppélia*, staged by Kriger. Between 1925 and 1944 it was directed by Rahel Olbrei, and between 1944 and 1951 by Anna Ekston, who also founded the Tallinn Ballet School. Subsequent directors have included Enn Suvi (1967–73) and Mai Murdmaa (1974–2001) who choreographed many works for its repertory including *Crime and Punishment* (mus. Pärt, 1994) and *Catulli Carmina* (mus. Orff, 1994). The uncertain financial situation of Estonia during the last years of the 20th century hindered the development of the company and many of its finest dancers left, including Thomas Edur and Agnes Oaks, who joined English National Ballet in 1990. The situation has improved in recent years with Tiit Härm's appointment as artistic director (2001–9) resulting in a stronger balance between classics and new repertory, including work by himself, Elo, and Bigonzetti, and Thomas *Edur returning in 2009 as his successor. A smaller company has also been based at Tartu's Vanemuine Theatre since 1939. It was founded by Ida Udel and currently has a repertory dominated by popular classics such as *Carmina Burana* (mus. Orff, chor. Mare Tommingas, 1992) and *Peter Pan* (chor. Oksana Titova, 2008). Modern dance emerged in Estonia during the 1930s with the foundation of several studios in Tallinn influenced by Duncan and Laban. It was repressed during the Soviet occupation but re-emerged during the 1990s with Dance Theatre Nordstar founded by Saima Kranig in 1991; Fine 5 founded in 1991 with choreographer René Nõmmik, and the establishment of the contemporary dance base, Kanuti Gildi Saal in Tallin in 2002.

(⊕) SEE WEB LINKS
• Website for the Estonian Ballet

étoile [Fr., star] The highest rank of dancer at the Paris Opera.

Étude Ballet in six movements with choreography by Nijinska and music by Bach. It has been revised several times. The first version was titled *Holy Études* and was premiered 3 Aug. 1925 by Theatre Chorégraphique Nijinska at Margate, England. The second, *Un estudio religioso*, was premiered 27 Aug. 1926 at Teatro Colón, Buenos Aires, and the best-known was the 1931 version *Étude* created for Opera Russe de Paris with Nijinska and Lichine.

Études (original Dan. title *Étude*) Ballet in one act with choreography by H. Lander, music by

Riisager (after Czerny), and design by Erik Nordgren. Premiered 15 Jan. 1948 by Royal Danish Ballet in Copenhagen with M. Lander, Brenaa, and Jensen. This virtuoso staging of a ballet class has become a showcase for dancers around the world. It opens with the dancers at the barre then progresses through increasingly difficult exercises in adagio, petit and grand allegro. A revised version was created in 1951 with T. Pils (later Lander), Bruhn, and Jensen and a third version for Paris Opera 19 Nov. 1952. Always extremely popular with audiences, the ballet has been revived (with some revisions) by many companies including London Festival Ballet (for whom it has become a signature work, London, 1955), American Ballet Theatre (New York, 1961), and San Francisco Ballet (1998). It was revised for Danish television in 1969.

eurythmics (also Fr., *eurythmie*) From the Greek *eurhythmia*, meaning rhythmic order and graceful motion. The term was used during the Renaissance to designate unity between parts and harmonious proportion of part to whole. At the beginning of the 20th century it was used specifically to designate the movement theories and practice developed by *Jaques-Dalcroze which were influenced by Delsarte and the new modern dance. Exercises in breathing, rhythmic awareness, group movements, and plastic gesture were used to explore and extend the body's response to music. These became a seminal influence in the teaching of dance and music in Europe and the US.

Evans, Albert (*b* Atlanta, Georgia, 29 Dec. 1968) American dancer. He trained at Terpsichore Expressions in Atlanta and at the School of American Ballet, joined New York City Ballet in 1988 where he was promoted to principal in 1995. A strong, charismatic dancer in the Balanchine repertoire, he has also created roles in many ballets, including Dove's *Red Angels* and *Twilight*, Ratmansky's *Russian Seasons*, Stroman's *Double Feature*, and Wheeldon's *Klavier*. He retired from NYCB in 2010.

Evdokimova, Eva (*b* Geneva, 1 Dec. 1948; *d* New York, 2 Apr. 2009) US dancer. She studied at the Munich State Opera Ballet School and at the Royal Ballet School as well as with M. Fay (London), Volkova (Copenhagen), and Dudinskaya (Leningrad). In 1966 she joined Royal Danish Ballet then in 1969 moved to the Berlin Opera Ballet where she was prima ballerina (1973–85). She was particularly renowned for her interpretations of romantic roles, bringing an exceptional delicacy, refinement, and musicality to *Giselle*, among other works. Her repertory favoured the major Bournonville and Petipa roles but she also danced in ballets by Cranko and Tetley and created roles in Luipart's *Scarecrows* (1970) and

Hynd's *Nutcracker* (1976) and *Coppélia* (1985), among others. From 1971 she also guested internationally appearing with London Festival Ballet, as well as the Kirov, American Ballet Theatre, and National Ballet of Canada. She gave her last public performances in 1990 after which she worked internationally as teacher and coach.

Éventail de Jeanne, L' Ballet in one act with choreography by Yvonne Franck and Alice Bourgat, music by various composers, sets by P. Legrain and R. Moulaert, and costumes by Laurencin. Premiered privately on 16 Jun. 1928 in the Paris studio of the ballet mistress Jeanne Dubost. Dubost had herself conceived the ballet as a musical caprice and had given the ten leaves of her fan to ten different composers asking each of them to compose a single dance number. They were: Ravel (Fanfare), Ferroud (March), Ibert (Valse), Roland-Manuel (Canarie), Delannoy (Bourrée), Roussel (Sarabande), Milhaud (Polka), Poulenc (Pastourelle), F. Schmitt (Finale), and Auric. The resulting ballet was so well received it was taken into the repertory of the Paris Opera where it was premiered by Toumanova (then a virtuoso 10-year-old) and other *petits rats from the Opera school on 4 Mar. 1929.

Events Performance devised by Cunningham in which extracts from various works (old and new) are performed as a continuous whole and in an order determined by chance. They were originally conceived as a way of allowing Cunningham's company to perform in non-theatrical spaces, hence the first was called *Museum Event 1* (performed in Vienna, 1964) and a later series in 1968 were called Gymnasium Events. Cunningham also subsequently staged them in conventional theatres, with the intention of opening up fresh views of his choreography.

Every Soul is a Circus Modern dance work in one act with choreography by Graham, music by Paul Nordhoff, set by Philip Stapp, and costumes by Edythe Gilfond. Premiered 27 Dec. 1939 by Martha Graham Dance Company at St James' Theater, New York, with Graham, Hawkins, and Cunningham (his first role with the company). It is based on a poem by Vachel Lindsay which humorously dissects the split personality of a woman. The central female character observes the reactions of her various partners as she flirts with a mischievous acrobat and a bullish ringmaster.

Excelsior Ballet in six parts with choreography by Manzotti, music by Romualdo Marenco, and design by Alfredo Edel. Premiered on 11 Jan. 1881 at Teatro alla Scala, Milan, with Bice Vergani, Carlo Montanara, and Rosina Viale. This spectacular ballet, celebrating the progress of human civilization, was conceived at a time when the public's taste for ballet had declined into hunger for lavish entertainment but also when Italian national optimism was at a peak. In many ways it prefigured the epics of Hollywood. It traced human progress in terms of a tumultuous struggle between the Spirits of Light and Darkness, dramatizing such landmarks as the invention of the steamship, the iron bridge, telegraphy, and the building of the Suez Canal and the Mont Cenis tunnel. The final defeat of Darkness is marked by a Grand Festival of the Nations and an apotheosis of light and peace. The choreography for the original production was arranged for several hundred of dancers and was lavishly staged. It was extremely popular and was revived all over Europe albeit in frequently reduced versions. In Vienna it was in the repertory from 1885 to 1914, receiving 329 performances. It was re-staged by dell'Ara for the Teatro Communale, Florence (1967), and for La Scala (1974).

Extemporary Dance Theatre British modern dance company. It was established in 1976 by students of the London School of Contemporary Dance with G. Powell as director. Under E. Claid (director between 1981 and 1990) it became a successful repertory company performing works by M. Clark, D. Gordon, V. Farber, and others. L. Newson danced with it from 1981 to 1985. It was disbanded in 1991.

extension Dancers are said to have good extension if they are able to raise their leg high into the air and sustain the position. A trend among modern female dancers—exemplified by Sylvie Guillem—has been to aim for the half-past-midnight extension, i.e. with the lifted leg raised so high that it virtually brushes the dancer's ear.

Ezralow, Daniel (*b* Los Angeles, *c.*1957) US dancer and choreographer. He trained locally and at the University of California (Berkeley) before going to New York in 1976 where he studied with the Ailey and Joffrey companies. He made his debut with Bruce Becker and Jane Kosminski's 5 × 2 Plus Dance Company (1976–9), going on to dance with the companies of Lubovitch (1978), P. Taylor (1979–83), and Pilobolus. In 1983 he formed Momix with other ex-members of Pilobolus and went on to co-create many works for both companies. A prolific choreographer he also created work for Batsheva, London Contemporary Dance Theatre, Berlin Opera Ballet, as well as working extensively in film, television, musicals, and music videos. In 1994, he began performing solo work, for example *Mandala* (1997), and subsequently founded the Daniel Ezralow Dance Company for which his works include *Why Be Extraordinary When You Can Be Yourself* (2007).

Fables for Our Time Modern dance work in four parts with choreography by Weidman and music by Freda Miller. Premiered 11 Jul. 1947 by the Charles Weidman Dance Theater Company at Jacob's Pillow Dance Festival with Weidman and Betty Osgood. It was based on four comic fables by James Thurber and became Weidman's most popular work. The New York premiere was 18 Apr. 1948.

Fabre, Jan (*b* Antwerp, 14 Dec. 1958) Belgian choreographer, performance artist, and theatre director. He studied visual arts and presented a series of solo performance works (1976–82) exploring the dynamics of ordinary human movement within the context of theatrical ritual. In 1980 he began creating group works for dance, opera, and theatre, including *The Sound of One Hand Clapping* (mus. Knapik, 1990) for Frankfurt Ballet. He introduced classical movement into his vocabulary in *The Power of Theatrical Madness* (1984), a production that featured a dancer repeating a slow phrase of movement for thirteen minutes with her back to the audience. In 2002 he choreographed and directed a controversial version of *Swan Lake* for the Royal Flanders Ballet, which featured a live owl in its cast. Recent works include *Angel of Death* (2003) and *Another Sleepy Dusty Delta Day* (2008).

Fabulous Beast Dance Theatre Irish contemporary dance company founded in 1997 by Michael Keegan-Dolan. Internationally acclaimed for its strong theatricality and caustic social commentary, its productions include *The Flowerbed* (2000), loosely based on *Romeo and Juliet*; *Giselle* (2003), a retelling of the 19th-century ballet; *The Bull* (2005), based on the ancient Irish epic *The Táin*; *James Son of James* (2007), a satire of a society in transition; and *Rite of Spring* (2009, in collaboration with English National Opera).

(((●))) **SEE WEB LINKS**
• Company website for FBDT

Façade Ballet in one act with choreography by Ashton, music by Walton, and design by John Armstrong. Premiered 26 Apr. 1931 by the Camargo Society at the Cambridge Theatre, London, with Lopokova, Ashton, and Markova. Walton's score was originally composed as a setting for Edith Sitwell's witty poems but is here used on its own to accompany Ashton's series of choreographic satires on popular dance forms and their dancers (*Scotch Rhapsody, Yodelling Song, Polka, Foxtrot, Waltz, Popular Song, Tango, Tarantella*). With its mix of succinct observation and absurdity the ballet was an immediate hit, and was taken into the repertories of Ballet Rambert and later the Vic-Wells Ballet. It is still danced by both the Royal and Birmingham Royal Ballets though some consider that its comedy has coarsened over the years. It has also been revived by several other companies, including City Center Joffrey Ballet (1969), Australian Ballet (1972), and Teatro Regio Ballet (1992). An earlier version was choreographed by Gunter Hess in Hagen, Germany.

face, en [Fr., facing] Any position in which the dancer's body is squarely facing the audience.

Fâcheux, Les 1. Seminal comédie-ballet with music and choreography by Beauchamps and libretto by Molière. Premiered 17 Aug. 1661 in front of Louis XIV at Vaux. Text and dance were combined to tell the story of a man thwarted from meeting his beloved by a string of eccentrics and bores. The ballet was a direct forerunner of Noverre's *ballet d'action. 2. Ballet in one act based on Molière, with libretto by Kochno, choreography by Nijinska, music by Auric, and design by Braque. Premiered 19 Jan. 1924 by Diaghilev's Ballets Russes at Monte Carlo with Tchernicheva, Vilzak, and Dolin. Despite the latter's novelty pointe work and the excellence of Braque's designs this ballet was not a success. Massine choreographed a new version for the same company, premiered in Monte Carlo on 3 May 1927 and danced in it himself, but with no greater success.

Facsimile Ballet in one act with choreography by Robbins, music by Bernstein, set by Oliver Smith, and costumes by Sharaff. Premiered 24 Oct. 1946 by Ballet Theater at Broadway Theater, New York, with Kaye, Robbins, and Kriza. This study of social mores is centred around a love triangle between a woman and two men on a beach.

Fadeyechev, Alexei (*b* Moscow, 16 Aug. 1960) Russian dancer and director. He studied at the Bolshoi Ballet School with Alexander Prokofiev, and graduated into the Bolshoi Ballet in 1978 as a principal dancer, holding that position for twenty years. Under the coaching of his father Nikolai he developed a refined classical style and a dramatic stage presence and he performed most of the major roles in the repertory. He also guested with many companies, including the Royal Ballet, Kirov, Royal Danish Ballet, Birmingham Royal Ballet, Boston Ballet, and Tokyo Ballet. Between 1998 and 2000 he was artistic director of the Bolshoi Ballet, mounting a critically acclaimed revival of Gorsky's 1900 version of *Don Quixote* in 1999. Since 2004 he was worked with Ananiashvili, as assistant director of the State Ballet of Georgia, staging several of the classics for the company.

Fadeyechev, Nikolai (*b* Moscow, 27 Jan. 1933) Soviet dancer and teacher; father of Alexei Fadeyechev. He studied at the Bolshoi Ballet School (1943–52) with Rudenko and graduated into the Bolshoi Ballet. He was promoted soloist in 1953 and his combination of technical ease, dramatic talent, and exceptional partnering skills led to him dancing most of the principal roles in the classical and modern repertories. He was the favourite partner of Plisetskaya and also created roles in Vinogradov's *Asel* (1967), Alonso's *Carmen Suite* (1967), Grigorovich's *Swan Lake* (1969), and Plisetskaya's *Anna Karenina* (1972). In 1961 he was principal guest artist with Paris Opera and he also danced Albrecht in the BBC's 1958 film of *Giselle*. He was made People's Artist of the USSR in 1976 and a year later retired to become teacher and rehearsal director with the Bolshoi. In 1993 he became associated with the Renaissance Ballet in Moscow. He is married to dancer Irina Holina.

fado Portugese folk-song of a melancholic, nostalgic nature, often linked to Spanish flamenco music and dance. (*Fado* means fate.)

Fagan, Garth (*b* Kingston, 3 May 1940) Jamaican-US dancer and choreographer. He studied African-Caribbean dance with Pearl Primus and Lavinia Williams and took master classes with Cunningham, Limón, Graham, and Ailey. As a teenager he toured with the Jamaican National Dance Company and while studying in Detroit (1960–70) also performed with various companies, including Dance Theater of Detroit. In 1970 he began teaching at the State University of New York at Brockport and formed a company out of enthusiastic but untrained adult dancers. The Bottom of the Bucket But…Dance Theater formed the basis of his Bucket Dance Theater which within a decade became a highly trained

ensemble, performing Fagan's eclectic mix of jazz, modern, and African-Caribbean dance. His many works include *Prelude* (1981), *Easter Freeway Processional* (mus. Glass, 1983), *Griot New York* (mus. Wynton Marsalis, 1991), *Drafts of Shadows* (1993), *Trips and Trysts* (mus. Marsalis, 2000), and *Senku* (mus. several, 2006). He has also choreographed for Dance Theatre of Harlem, including *Footprints Dressed in Red* (mus. J. Adams, 1986), for the José Limón Company, *Never No Lament* (mus. Kronos Quartet, 1994), for the Broadway musical, *The Lion King* (1997) for which he won a Tony award, and for New York City Ballet, *Ellington Elation*, the middle section of *Duke!* (mus. Ellington, 1999).

(((●))) **SEE WEB LINKS**

• The Fagan company website

failli [Fr., failed] The dancer springs into the air, landing on the front foot with the back foot raised. The back foot then slides through to the front. During the spring the body is turned slightly inwards towards the front foot with the face turned away.

Fairy Doll, The (orig. Ger. title *Die Puppenfee*) Pantomime-divertissement in one act with choreography by Hassreiter, libretto by F. Gaul and Hassreiter, music by Joseph Bayer, and designs by A. Brioschi. Premiered 4 Oct. 1888 at the Court Opera, Vienna, with C. Pagliero. It is set in a toy shop and portrays a group of dolls coming to life after their owner has shut up for the night. They dance with each other under the leadership of the Fairy Doll, to whom they pay homage in their final procession. The title role was mimed in the original version. The ballet has remained in the Vienna State Opera's repertoire (receiving its 750th performance in 1973) and different versions have been staged all over the world, most famously N. and S. Legat's (St Petersburg, 1903) and I. Clustine's for the Bolshoi (Moscow, 1901) which was re-staged for Pavlova in 1914 and became one of the most famous items in her repertory. Massine's *La Boutique fantasque* (1919) offered a lively, satirical spin on a similar concept.

Fairy's Kiss, The See BAISER DE LA FÉE, LE.

Falco, Louis (*b* New York, 2 Aug. 1942; *d* 26 Mar. 1993) US dancer, choreographer, and director. He studied at the American Ballet Theatre School, American Ballet Center, and with Limón, Weidman, and Graham, making his debut with the Limón Dance Company in 1960. In 1967 he formed his own group for which he choreographed many works, including *Caviar* (1970), *Escargot* (1978), and *Kate's Rag* (1980), the majority of which were set to music by Burt Alcantara. Many of his early dances tended towards lyrical abstraction but after

1971 he increasingly incorporated text and props. He also made works for Nederlands Dans Theater (*Eclipse*, 1974), for Ballet Rambert (*Tutti Frutti*, 1973), and La Scala Ballet (*The Eagle's Nest*, 1980). In 1980 he choreographed the film *Fame*.

Falla, Manuel de (*b* Cadiz, 23 Nov. 1876; *d* Alta Gracia, Argentina, 14 Nov. 1946) Spanish composer who wrote two ballet scores: *El amor brujo* (chor. Pastora Imperio, 1915; new version chor. Peter Wright for Royal Ballet Touring Company, 1975) and *Le Tricorne* (chor. Massine, 1919). His posthumous opera *Atlantida* features several dance numbers (prod. M. Wallmann, La Scala, Milan, 1962).

fall–recovery The dynamic opposition of movement, which forms the basis of Humphrey's system of modern dance and corresponds to Graham's contraction–release and Laban's Anspannung–Abspannung.

Fall River Legend Ballet in one act with choreography by de Mille, music by Morton Gould, sets by Oliver Smith, and costumes by Miles White. Premiered 22 Apr. 1948 by Ballet Theatre at the Metropolitan Opera House, New York, with A. Alonso, D. Adams, Kriza, and Bentley. It is based on the real-life murder case of Lizzie Borden who was accused of killing her parents with an axe in 1892. It is not a historical record but explores the frustrations and loneliness of a spinster in a small American town, and her resort to violence as a means of release. Lizzie later became one of Nora Kaye's most celebrated roles. The ballet has been revived for several companies including Dance Theatre of Harlem (1983) and Birmingham Royal Ballet (1994). Frank Staff also choreographed a ballet on the same story (S. Africa, 1975).

Fancy Free Ballet in one act with choreography by Robbins, music by Bernstein, set by Oliver Smith, and costumes by Kermit Love. Premiered 19 Apr. 1944 by Ballet Theatre at the Metropolitan Opera House, New York, with Lang, Kriza, Robbins, Bentley, and Reed. This seminal all-American ballet portrays three sailors on leave in New York, who meet two girls on a hot summer night. It was Robbins's first ballet, and an instant hit. With its cast of brash and lively modern characters, its mix of classical and vernacular dance, it influenced not only American ballet but also theatre and cinema and was turned into the musical *On the Town* (mus. Bernstein, chor. Robbins, dir. George Abbott, 1944) and later a film of the same title (1949). Robbins revived the ballet for New York City Ballet in 1980 and it has since entered the repertories of many companies including Dance Theatre of Harlem (1985), San Francisco Ballet (2001), Birmingham Royal Ballet (2002),

and Pacific Northwest Ballet (2006). New versions have been choreographed by F. Marteny (Graz, 1969, and Ballet of Marseilles, 1971) and T. Schilling (E. Berlin 1971).

fandango A Spanish dance, believed to originate from S. America, in 3/4 or 6/8 time. It is accompanied by guitars and castanets and one of its distinctive features is that the dancers periodically speed up then come to a sudden stop. One of its first appearances in ballet was in Angiolini and Gluck's *Don Juan* (1761) and it also features in Mozart's *Le nozze di Figaro* (1786). Tudor created a ballet of the same name for National Ballet of Canada (mus. Padre Soler, 1972).

Fanfare Ballet in one act with choreography by Robbins, music by Britten, and design by I. Sharaff. Premiered 2 Jun. 1953 at City Center, New York, by New York City Ballet with Mounsey, Larsson, Jillana, d'Amboise, Bolender, Bliss, and Hobi. It mirrors the logic of its music, Britten's *Young Person's Guide to the Orchestra* (*Purcell Variations*), by portraying the qualities of individual instruments through dance. It was revived for Royal Danish Ballet in 1956.

Fantasia Disney's seminal 1940 cartoon contains some masterpieces of animated choreography. Fairies, fish, and mushrooms dance to sections of Tchaikovsky's *Nutcracker* while Ponchielli's *Dance of the Hours* becomes a ballet for ostriches, hippos, and alligators. Disney's team made extensive drawings of real dancers including Baranova, Riabouchinska, and Lichine to ensure the comic accuracy of the movement.

farandole A lively old Provençal dance in 6/8 time which was originally performed by couples holding hands as they danced through the streets. It appears at the beginning of the Vision Scene in *Sleeping Beauty* and in *Flames of Paris*.

Farber, Viola (*b* Heidelberg, 25 Feb. 1931; *d* Bronxville, NY, 24 Dec. 1998) US dancer, choreographer, and teacher. She studied with Craske, and Cunningham, joining the latter's company when it was founded in 1953. She stayed with Cunningham until 1965, as well as dancing with P. Taylor, after which she began choreographing for her own company which from 1968 toured widely in N. America and Europe. Her style was characterized by dense, demanding movement, a wry sense of humour, and an allusive dramatic quality. Her works include *Survey* (mus. David Tudor, 1971) and *Dune* (mus. Alvin Lucier, 1972). Between 1981 and 1983 she was artistic director of the Centre Nationale de Danse Contemporaine in Angers, and after working as a freelance choreographer and teacher throughout

Europe and the US she was appointed director of dance at Sarah Lawrence College, New York in 1988. In 1995 she performed the *Three Step* (*Shipwreck*) with her ex-pupil Ralph Lemon.

Farmer, Peter (*b* Luton, 3 Nov. 1941) British designer. His first ballet designs were for Jack Carter's *Agrionia* (1964), and he has since designed for most of the major ballet companies, including Stuttgart Ballet (Peter Wright's *Giselle*), Royal Ballet Touring Company (Ashton's *The Dream*), London Festival Ballet (Carter's *Coppélia*), Australian Ballet (Prokovsky's *The Three Musketeers*), Royal Ballet (MacMillan's *Winter Dreams* and *Sleeping Beauty*, 2006), Vienna State Opera (MacMillan's *Manon*), Birmingham Royal Ballet (Peter Wright's *Coppélia*) and Perm Ballet (Makarova's *Swan Lake*).

Farrell, Suzanne (orig. Roberta Sue Ficker; *b* Cincinnati, 16 Aug. 1945) US dancer. She studied locally and at the School of American Ballet, making her debut with New York City Ballet in 1961. A tall, almost regal dancer, with a lyrical musicality and a capacity to push her technique to seemingly precarious limits, she became Balanchine's last muse—the instrument with which he conducted his final experiments in neo-classical dance (he used to refer to her as his Stradivarius). In 1965 she was promoted to principal and as well as dancing the standard Balanchine repertory she created several new roles, for example in *Movements for Piano and Orchestra* (1963), *Don Quixote* (which was almost a love-letter from choreographer to dancer, 1965), *Variations* (1966), *Jewels* (in which her classical qualities were crystallized in the 'Diamonds' pas de deux, 1967), and *Slaughter on Tenth Avenue* (New York City Ballet staging, in which the extravagant scale of her technique was exploited to raunchy effect in the role of Strip-tease Girl, 1969). In 1969 she married the dancer Paul Mejia which strained relations with the possessive Balanchine to breaking-point. A year later she left to dance with Béjart's Ballet of the 20th Century, where as the company's new star she created roles in several of his works, including *Sonate* (1970), *Nijinsky*, *clown de Dieu* (1971), and *I trionfi* (1974). In 1975 she returned to NYCB where, dancing with an even greater technical authority she assumed many of her old roles as well as creating several new ones, for example in Robbins's *Piano Concerto in G* (1975) and Balanchine's *Union Jack* (1976), *Vienna Waltzes* (1977), *Davidsbündlertänze* (1980), and a new version of *Mozartiana* (1981). During this time she also performed as an international guest star, for example with the Royal Danish Ballet (1976), and appeared in many television dance films. Since retiring from the stage in 1989 she has taught at the School of

American Ballet, staged several Balanchine works including *Scotch Symphony* for the Kirov Ballet in 1988 and in 1999 founded her own company, Suzanne Farrell Ballet, based at the Kennedy Center, Washington and performing an extensive repertory of Balanchine works. Her autobiography *Holding on to the Air*, written with Toni Bentley, was published New York, 1990.

(⊕) SEE WEB LINKS
• Home website for the Kennedy Center with link to the Suzanne Farrell Ballet

Farron, Julia (*b* London, 22 Jul. 1922) British dancer and teacher. She studied at the Cone-Ripman school and became the first scholarship pupil to attend the Sadler's Wells Ballet School in 1931. When she joined the Vic-Wells Ballet in 1936 she was its most junior member. A crisp, elegant dancer with strong dramatic talents she created roles in several ballets, most notably Princess Belle Épine in Cranko's *Prince of the Pagodas* (1957), but while remaining with the company until 1961 she failed to join its top rank of ballerinas. After retiring as a dancer she continued to perform some mime roles, e.g. Lady Capulet in MacMillan's *Romeo and Juliet* which she created in 1965. She also taught at the Royal Ballet School and between 1983 and 1989 was artistic director, then director, of the Royal Academy of Dancing. She married the choreographer Alfred Rodrigues.

farruca An expressive, virile dance, of gypsy origin, from Andalusia. It is performed by the Miller in Massine's *Le Tricorne*.

Farruquito (orig. Juan Manuel Fernandez Montoya; *b* Seville 1982) Spanish dancer. As descendent of a long line of gypsy flamenco dancers (his mother was the dancer Farruca, his grandfather the dancer Farruco) he trained at the family school and made his stage debut aged 5 in the Broadway run of *Flamenco Puro*. At the age of 11 he appeared in Carlos Saura's film *Flamenco* and at the age of 15, after the death of his grandfather, he assumed the role as head of the family dynasty. A dancer of exceptional fluidity, beauty, and speed he positioned himself as one of the leading exponents of traditional (puro) flamenco and as the star of his own family-based troupe achieved international acclaim. (In 2003 the US magazine *People* placed him in their list of the 'World's Most Beautiful People'.) His involvement in a fatal traffic incident, and subsequent criminal charges kept him off stage between 2004 and 2008, after which he returned in the production *Puro*.

fashion Throughout history the costumes worn by dancers have been influenced by contemporary fashions in their cut and fabric—even when they have been specially adapted to stage use.

During the 20th century fashion designers also began to be directly commissioned to create costumes for dance—sometimes to create a particular look for the dancers, sometimes to bring in the added cachet of a voguish name. Diaghilev was one of the first directors to collaborate with a major fashion talent, commissioning Chanel to design the costumes for *Le Train bleu* (chor. Nijinska, 1924) with its cast of chic young people. (The work of his own designers, especially Bakst, also, conversely, had a profound influence on contemporary fashion designers, e.g. Poiret.) Later haute couture designers who have worked for dance include Halston, who designed nearly all of Graham's costumes between 1975 and 1988 (controversially, since some felt his costumes added an inappropriate sleekness and glamour to the choreography), Calvin Klein for Graham (*Maple Leaf Rag*, 1990), Versace for Béjart (ten works including *Le Presbytère*, 1997), Katherine Hamnett for Rambert Dance Company (Alston's *Strong Language*, 1987), Isaac Mizrahi for American Ballet Theatre (Twyla Tharp's *Brief Fling*, 1990) and for Mark Morris (several works including *I Don't Want to Love*, 1996), Oscar de la Renta for Twyla Tharp (*Sinatra Suite*, 1984), Lacroix for American Ballet Theatre (*Gaîté parisienne* and *Swan Lake*, both 1988) and for Paris Opera (*Jewels*, 2001), Jasper Conran for Royal Ballet (Bintley's *Tombeaux*, 1993), Scottish Ballet (*Sleeping Beauty*, 1994), and *Swan Lake*, 1995), Stuttgart Ballet (Bintley's *Edward II*, 1995), and Birmingham Royal Ballet (Bintley's *Brahms Handel Variations*, 1994, *Nutcracker Sweeties*, 1996, and *Arthur*, 2000), Rei Kawabuko for Cunningham (*Scenario*, 1997), Hussein Chalayan for Michael Clark (*current\SEE*, 1998), Julian Macdonald for Alston (*Shimmer*, 2004).

Fateyev, Yuri (*b* Leningrad, 1964) Russian dancer, teacher, and director. He trained at the Vaganova Choreographic School, graduating into the Mariinsky (Kirov) Ballet in 1982. He danced many leading classical roles but became best known as a character dancer, excelling as the Jester in *Swan Lake*. In 2003 he was appointed repetiteur for the company, with particular care of the Balanchine repertory. He was additionally guest teacher at companies including the Royal Ballet, Bolshoi Ballet, Swedish Royal Ballet, Pacific Northwest Ballet (USA), and he also mounted the St Petersburg production of *Le Corsaire* for the Royal Danish Ballet. In 2008 he was appointed acting artistic director of the Mariinsky, where he attempted to maintain the momentum of modernizing the company's repertory, encouraging new choreographers from within the ranks and inviting in guests such as Wheeldon and McGregor.

Fauré, Gabriel (*b* Pamiers, 12 May 1845; *d* Paris, 4 Nov. 1924) French composer. He wrote no ballet scores but his concert music has often been used for dance, most notably *Pelléas et Mélisande* (chor. J. J. Etcheverry, Brussels, 1953, and Balanchine in the Emeralds section of *Jewels*, New York, 1967. The latter also incorporates Fauré's *Shylock* Overture). Other choreographed scores include *Pavane* (chor. MacMillan, London, 1973 and Wheeldon, London, 1996 among others), *Requiem* (chor. MacMillan, Stuttgart, 1976, and also G. Casado and J. Russillo, 1976), and the various piano pieces and songs used in A. Howard's *La Fête étrange* (London, 1940).

Faust ballets The legend of Faust has been a recurringly popular theme in dance. In 1723 John Rich presented his ballet pantomime *The Necromancer or the History of Dr Faustus* at the Lincolns Inn Fields Theatre in London and during the 19th century there was a rash of *Faust*-inspired ballets, including Bournonville's *Faust* (mus. P. L. Keck, Royal Danish Ballet, 1832), Deshayes's *Faust* (mus. Adam, London's King's Theatre, 1833), Perrot's *Faust* (mus. Panizza, Milan, with Elssler as Gretchen, 1848), P. Taglioni's *Satanella oder Metamorphosen* (mus. Hertel, based on Jaques Cazotte's *Diable amoureux*, Berlin, 1852), Reisinger's *Mephistophelia* (mus. Kredler, Hamburg, 1856), and Lanner's *Faust* (mus. M. Lutz and E. Ford, London's Empire Theatre, 1895). Remislav Remislavsky's *Faust* (mus. František Skvor, Prague National Theatre, 1926) was based on the libretto *Der Doktor Faust*, written by Heinrich Heine in 1847 but not staged at that date. Heine's libretto also inspired Kirsanova's *Faust* (mus. Henry Krips, Australian National Ballet, 1941) and Heiner Luipart's **Abraxas* (mus. W. Egk, Munich, 1948). There have been several dance stagings of Berlioz's *La Damnation de Faust* including Béjart's (Paris Opera, 1964). Béjart also choreographed *Notre Faust* to Bach's B minor Mass (Brussels, 1975).

Fearful Symmetries Ballet in one act with choreography by P. Martins and music by John Adams. Premiered 3 May 1990 by New York City Ballet at New York State Theater, New York. It is set to Adams's 1988 score of the same title. Other versions include Doug Varone (*Rise*, 1993), A. Page (Royal Ballet, 1994), and C. d'Amboise (*Synchronicities*, Royal Ballet of Flanders, 1999).

Fedicheva, Kaleria (*b* Ust-Ijory, 20 Jul. 1936; *d* 13 Sept. 1994) Soviet dancer. She studied at the Leningrad Choreographic School, graduating in 1955 into the Kirov Ballet. She was best known for her modern repertory and created roles in several ballets, including Belsky's *Leningrad Symphony* (second premiere, 1961), K. Sergeyev's *The*

Distant Planet (1963), and *Hamlet* (1970), and Vinogradov's *Prince of the Pagodas* (1972). In 1975 she left the USSR to join her American husband, dancer Martin Freedman, and in the same year staged the pas d'action from Act II of *La Bayadère* for US Terpsichore.

Fedorova, Sophia (*b* Moscow, 28 Sept. 1879; *d* Neuilly, 3 Jan. 1963) Russian dancer. She studied at the Moscow Theatre School under V. Tikhomirov and graduated into the Bolshoi in 1899. A dancer of outstanding dramatic talent she performed both character and classical roles with a rare intensity. She created roles in several Gorsky ballets, including Mercedes in *Don Quixote* (1900), Esmeralda in *Gudule's Daughter* (1902), and during various seasons with Diaghilev's Ballets Russes (1909–13 and 1928) she also created roles in Fokine's Polovtsian Dances from *Prince Igor* (1909) and *Scheherazade* (1910). In 1913 her debut performance of Giselle unnerved viewers with its almost nightmarish realism and the same year marked her increasing mental fragility. She was forced to leave the Moscow stage in 1917 and in 1922 sought treatment in Paris. She danced with Pavlova's company between 1925 and 1926 and again with Diaghilev, but in 1930 she suffered a nervous collapse.

Fedorovitch, Sophie (*b* Minsk, 15 Dec. 1893; *d* London, 25 Jan. 1953) Russian-British stage designer who played a seminal role in the development of British ballet. She studied painting in Moscow and at the St Petersburg Academy but after the Revolution settled in London in 1920. During the next decade she lived in various European cities, exhibiting her paintings but from 1932 worked almost exclusively in stage design. Her first professional commission came from Rambert, to design Ashton's first ballet *A Tragedy of Fashion* (1926). She and Ashton became close friends and collaborators and she designed many of his works including *Le Baiser de la fée* (1935), *Symphonic Variations* (1946), and *Valses nobles et sentimentales* (1947), the sophisticated economy of her design having an important influence on his choreography. She designed for several other British choreographers including de Valois, Tudor, and Howard as well as for opera and theatre. Between 1951 and 1953 she was a member of the artistic advisory panel of Sadler's Wells Ballet—a role she had unofficially undertaken for many years.

Feeney, Philip (*b* 1954) British composer. He studied at Cambridge, and at the Accademia di Santa Cecilia in Rome and composed his first dance score in 1987, Michael Pink's *Mémoire Imaginaire*, for Northern Ballet Theatre. His kaleidoscopic range of styles, coupled with his capacity to produce vivid narrative atmosphere has made him popular with choreographers, especially those of story ballets. He has formed a long association with NBT, his scores for that company including *Cinderella* (Christopher Gable, 1993), *Dracula* (Gable and Pink, 1996), *The Hunchback of Notre Dame* (Pink, 1997), *A Streetcar Named Desire* (Didy Veldman, 2001), and *Hamlet* (David Nixon, 2008).

He has also written the music for many of Michael Keegan-Dolan's works including *Giselle* (2004) and *The Bull* (2006), Adam Cooper's *Les Liaisons Dangereuses* (2005), Didy Veldman's *Greymatter* (Rambert Dance Company, 1997), and Patrick Lewis's *Manoeuvre* (English National Ballet, 2002).

Feld, Eliot (*b* Brooklyn, NY, 5 Jul. 1942) US dancer, choreographer, and director. He studied at the High School of Performing Arts, at the School of American Ballet, and with Richard Thomas, making his professional debut aged 12 in off-Broadway shows. In 1958 he danced in Robbins's *West Side Story* and also performed with the companies of Lang, Maslow, and McKayle. He then danced with American Ballet Theatre (1963–8, 1971–2) and in 1967 choreographed his first ballet for the company, *Harbinger* (mus. Prokofiev), to critical acclaim. A year later he created *Meadowlark* (mus. Haydn) for Royal Winnipeg Ballet. Between 1969 and 1971 he was director and choreographer of his own group, the American Ballet Company, creating *Early Songs* (R. Strauss, 1970) and *The Gods Amused* (mus. Debussy, 1971), among others. Between 1971 and 1972 he was again with ABT then from 1972 to 1974 he was a freelance choreographer, for example for City Center Joffrey Ballet, creating *Jive* (mus. Gould, 1973). In 1974 he founded the Eliot Feld Ballet (becoming Feld Ballet *c.*1980, Feld Ballets/NY in 1990, and Feld Ballet Tech in 1997) for which he has since choreographed most of his works. He is a highly prolific choreographer whose vocabulary draws freely on modern and classical vocabularies and, despite criticisms of gimmickery, his work has retained its populist appeal. He makes use of an unusually eclectic range of music, though he has made several works to scores by Reich, including *Grand Canyon* (1985), *Kore* (1988), *Clave* (1992), *Tongue and Groove* (1995), and *Isis in Transit* (2008). In 1997 Feld choreographed a revival of Bernstein's musical *On the Town* (New York Shakespeare Festival). He is additionally an energetic dance activist, becoming founder and director of the New Ballet School, New York in 1978 (which gave free tuition to inner-city children) and in 1982 becoming instrumental in the founding of the Joyce Theater which functions both as home for his company and a venue for middle-scale dance. In 2003 his company was disbanded but in 2004 became active again.

(⊕) SEE WEB LINKS
- Website for the Feld company

Felix (orig. Felix Fernandez García; *b* c.1896; *d* Epsom, 1941) Spanish dancer who was Massine's assistant for *Le Tricorne*. He was spotted by Diaghilev dancing in Seville and engaged to help Massine with the Spanish choreography of his 1919 ballet. He believed that he would also be dancing the role of the Miller, and his disappointment at not being cast apparently exacerbated his unstable mental condition. He was found dancing on the altar of a London church and committed to an asylum.

feminist ballets Classical ballet has not been noted for the vigour of its sexual politics though Filippo Taglioni's *La Révolte au sérail* (1833) is sometimes viewed as an early feminist ballet, with its heroine Zulma and her fellow harem inmates banding together with working women to protest against the tyranny of men. Later and more serious contenders for the genre are Nijinska's *Les Biches* with its wry analysis of male and female roles both on and off the stage (see Lynn *Garafola's study of the ballet in *Diaghilev's Ballets Russes*, New York, 1989), *Les Noces*, with its harrowing suggestions of bridal sacrifice, and Page's *An American Pattern* (1937). Some Soviet ballets have also taken a markedly feminist line in their presentation of powerful heroines, for example in Kasatkina and Vasiliov's *Heroic Poem* (*The Geologists*), 1964. Generally, however, the most overtly feminist attitudes to feature in dance have appeared in modern choreography. Isadora *Duncan's vision of dance was bound up with her desire for female emancipation and she claimed that her art was 'symbolic of the freedom of woman and her emancipation from the hidebound conventions that are the warp and woof of New England Puritanism'. She and later performers like *Graham, *Humphrey, and *Wigman moved with a strength and freedom atypical of classical ballerinas, and also presented women in powerful roles. Duncan's prediction in 1902 that future dancers would 'dance not in the form of a nymph nor fairy nor coquette but in the form of a woman in her greatest and purest expression' was borne out by the complex and assertive dance heroines created by Graham and others. Significantly, many of the early modern companies were all-female and, even more importantly, were directed and choreographed by women. (In ballet women have exercised power as teachers and ballet mistresses much more than as directors and choreographers.) Later in the century the blurring of distinction between male and female dancers became evident in the choreography of both sexes. *Cunningham and some later *postmodern choreographers often created works where men and women were given identical movements to perform, while the duet form *Contact Improvisation, pioneered by Steve *Paxton in the 1970s, became one way of enabling women to master a more active (and traditionally male) role in partnering. Works that directly addressed issues of sexual politics included Jacky Lansley's feminist re-write of *Giselle* as *I Giselle* (London, 1981) and the repertories of *DV8 and *Urban Bush Women. In recent years it has become common for modern dance and some classical ballet to reflect looser social attitudes towards sexuality and gender in their presentation of movement, character, etc. Feminism has become a mainstream part of dance scholarship, reflected in the writings of Susan Foster, among many; seminal publications include *Dance Gender and Culture* (ed. Helen Thomas, London, 1993) and Sally *Banes's *Dancing Women* (New York, 1998). A parallel development has been the development of male and gay dance studies, reflected in Ramsay Burt's *The Male Dancer* (London, 1995) and Peter Stoneley's *A Queer History of the Ballet* (London, 2007).

Femmes de bonne humeur, Les See GOOD-HUMOURED LADIES, THE.

Fenley, Molissa (*b* Las Vegas, Nev., 15 Nov. 1954) US dancer and choreographer. She studied dance at Mills College, California (1971–5) and in 1978 made her New York choreographic and performance debut at the Cunningham studio with *Planets*. Her performing style was unusually fast and energetic, its exhaustive repetitions of movement made possible by Fenley's intensively athletic training programme. Her own stamina was particularly tested in extended solo works such as *Eureka* (1982) and *State of Darkness* (1988, a solo version of Stravinsky's *Rite of Spring*), *Sita* (mus. Glass, 1995), and *Trace* (mus. Hart Makwaia, text Jesurun, 1997). More recently she has created group works, such as *Hemispheres* (mus. Anthony Davis, 1983) and *Desert Sea* (mus. Harrison, 2005) for her own ensemble, as well as *A Descent into the Maelstrom* (mus. P. Glass, 1986) for Australian Dance Theatre and *Bridge of Dreams* (1994) for Berlin Opera Ballet.

(⊕) SEE WEB LINKS
- Link to Fenley's website

Fenster, Boris (*b* Petrograd, 17 Apr. 1916; *d* Leningrad, 29 Dec. 1960) Soviet dancer, choreographer, and ballet master. He studied at the Leningrad Ballet School and after graduating in 1936 joined the Maly Ballet. He was later appointed chief choreographer (1945–53) after which he was moved to the Kirov. His early ballets tended to be highly dramatic and based on literary themes, including *The False Bridegroom* (mus.

Chulaki, 1946) and *Youth* (mus. Chulaki, 1949), but in later works like *Taras Bulba* (mus. Solovyov-Sedoy, 1955) he began to explore the possibilities of more abstract dance imagery. He died at the premiere of his final ballet, *Masquerade* (mus. Laputin, 1960).

fermé [Fr., closed] Refers to positions where the dancer's feet are touching rather than being apart (ouvert).

Ferri, Alessandra (*b* Milan, 6 May 1963) Italian dancer. She studied at the ballet school of Teatro La Scala (1974–8) and at the Royal Ballet School (1979–80). In 1980 she joined the Royal Ballet, becoming principal in 1983. An instinctively dramatic dancer with a tiny, flexible physique she excelled in the MacMillan repertoire, creating roles in his *Valley of Shadows* (1983), *The Seven Deadly Sins* (television version, 1983), and *A Different Drummer* (1984). In 1985, she starred in Zeffirelli's production of *Swan Lake* in Milan and in the same year joined American Ballet Theatre as principal where apart from a leave of absence (1995–7) she remained until retiring from the stage in 2007. She danced both the classical and modern repertories and also guested abroad with National Ballet of Canada, Balletto Argentino, and, most regularly, at La Scala where she was named prima ballerina assoluta. She created roles in Petit's *Le Diable amoureux* (Ballet National de Marseille, 1989), Maillot's *In Flight* (American Ballet Theatre, 1997) among others and also appeared on television and in film, notably *Dancers* (dir. Ross, 1987).

Ferri, Olga (*b* Buenos Aires, 20 Sept. 1928) Argentinian dancer, choreographer, and director. She studied with A. Bulnes, then in Paris with V. Gsovsky and Zvereff, and later in the US. In 1959 she danced with Les Ballets de l'étoile in Paris, with Berlin Opera Ballet, and with Munich State Opera Ballet, then during the 1960s danced with London Festival Ballet. Between 1971 and 1976 she danced at Teatro Colón, with Washington Ballet, and Eglevsky Ballet, then from 1976 to 1977 returned to Teatro Colón as guest prima ballerina and artistic director. She was considered to be one of the great Giselles of her era. In 1980 she became artistic adviser to the Argentine Classical Ballet Foundation.

Festin de l'araignée, Le (Eng. title *The Spider's Banquet*) Ballet pantomime in one act with choreography by Staats, libretto by G. de Voisins, music by Roussel, and design by Maxime Dethomas. Premiered 3 Apr. 1913 at Théâtre des Arts, Paris, with Sarah Djeli. It tells a cautionary tale about a spider and its prey. Later versions by Aveline (Paris Opera, 1940), Howard (Sadler's Wells Ballet, 1944), and Bintley (Royal Ballet School, 1997).

Fête étrange, La Ballet in one act with choreography by A. Howard, libretto by Ronald Crichton, music by Fauré, and design by Fedorovitch. Premiered 23 May 1940 by London Ballet at the Arts Theatre, London, with Lloyd, Staff, and Paltenghi. It is based on Alain-Fournier's novel *Le Grand Meaulnes* and portrays the experience of a young boy who stumbles upon an engagement party in a mysterious chateau, and by falling in love with the young châtelaine unintentionally causes her estrangement from her fiancé. With its sensitive, understated treatment of the central characters this ballet was widely considered Howard's greatest achievement. In 1957 it was revived for Royal Ballet and in 1971 for Scottish Theatre Ballet.

Fêtes chinoises, Les Noverre's first ballet success. Its date is uncertain, possibly premiered in Paris in 1749 or in Marseilles or Strasbourg. It was later performed in Lyons, Paris, and London, sometimes under the title *Les Métamorphoses chinoises*.

Feuillet, Raoul-Auger (*b* c.1660; *d* 14 Jun. 1710) French dancing master, choreographer, author, and reputed inventor of the Feuillet system of dance notation. He taught ballroom dances from his studio in Paris and in 1700 published his *Chorégraphie ou L'Art de décrire la danse par caractères, figures et signes demonstratifs*, the first known method for using symbols to notate dance. In 1704 he was unsuccessfully sued for plagiarism by Beauchamps who claimed to have invented the system himself 22 years earlier. Feuillet had in fact failed to acknowledge his considerable debt to the latter but had also expanded and improved on Beauchamps's system in his own publication. He continued to embellish and refine it in later publications and also published collections of his own dances. The highly influential *Chorégraphie* was translated into several languages: P. Siris's English translation, *The Art of Dancing Demonstrated in Characters and Figures*, appeared in 1706.

Field, John (orig. John Greenfield; *b* Doncaster, 22 Oct. 1921; *d* Esher, 3 Aug. 1991) British dancer and director. He studied in Liverpool with Edna Slocombe and Shelagh Elliott-Clarke and made his debut with the Liverpool Ballet Club in 1938 before moving to London. Here he studied briefly at Sadler's Wells School and joined the Vic-Wells Ballet in 1939. He danced for two years before serving in the Second World War and on his return became one of the company's leading male principals, partnering Grey, Beriosova, and Elvin in the classics. In 1956 he was appointed director of Sadler's Wells Theatre Ballet (later the Royal Ballet Touring Company) and there developed an impressive roster of dance and choreographic talent. In 1970 he was made co-director of the Royal Ballet with MacMillan but resigned a year later to become director at La Scala, Milan (1971–4). He was subsequently director of the Royal Academy of Dancing (1975–8), of London Festival Ballet (1979–84), and of the British Ballet Organisation (1984–91).

Field Figures Ballet in one act with choreography by Tetley, music by Stockhausen, and design by Baylis. Premiered 9 Nov. 1970 by Royal Ballet at Theatre Royal, Nottingham, with Bergsma, Kelly, Derman, O'Conaire, Clarke, Johnson, and O'Brien. It is constructed around a central pas de deux which is repeatedly disrupted by five other dancers. Nureyev danced part of the ballet in his film *I am a Dancer* (1972).

Fifield, Elaine (*b* Sydney, 28 Oct. 1930; *d* Perth, 11 May 1999) Australian dancer. She studied with Elizabeth Scully and at Sadler's Wells School, joining Sadler's Wells Theatre Ballet in 1947, becoming principal dancer and creating the title role in Cranko's *Pineapple Poll* (1951). Between 1954 and 1957 she was ballerina with Sadler's Wells Ballet (later Royal Ballet) and created a role in Ashton's *Birthday Offering* (1956). She also danced with the Borovansky Ballet (1956–8) and then danced for periods with the Australian Ballet (1964–6 and 1969). She was married to the conductor John Lanchbery, and wrote *In My Shoes* (London, 1967).

Fille de marbre, La Ballet in two acts with choreography and libretto by Saint-Léon, music by Pugni, sets by C. A. Cambon and J. Thierry, and costumes by P. Lormier. Premiered 20 Oct. 1847 at Paris Opera with Cerrito, Saint-Léon, and Desplaches. It tells the story of a sculptor who falls in love with his beautiful marble statue. The devil agrees to bring the marble girl to life on condition that she herself does not fall in love. When she fails to comply, she is returned to stone.

Fille du Danube, La Ballet in two acts with choreography and libretto by F. Taglioni, music by Adam, sets by Ciceri, Despléchin, Diéterle, Feuchères, and Séchan, and costumes by H. d'Orschwiller. Premiered 21 Sept. 1836 at the Paris Opera with M. Taglioni, Legallois, Leroux, and Mazilier. It tells the story of an orphaned girl (found as a child on a river bank) who falls in love with a nobleman's son. When her lover's father seeks to marry her instead, she throws herself into the river. Her lover follows her and after enduring several trials of their strength and courage they are allowed to return to earth. A reconstruction of

the ballet was staged by Fracci and Gillian Whittingham for Rome Opera Ballet, 2007.

Fille du Pharaon, La (orig. Russ. title *Doch faraona*) Ballet in three acts with choreography by Petipa, libretto by Vernoy de Saint-Georges and Petipa, music by Pugni, sets by A. Roller and Wagner, and costumes by Kelwer and Stolyarov. Premiered 30 Jan. 1862 at St Petersburg's Bolshoi Theatre with Rosati, Goltz, Petipa, and Ivanov. It was inspired by Gautier's *Le Roman de la momie* and tells the story of an English lord who, under the influence of opium, dreams that the beautiful (dead) Princess Aspicia comes to life and that, in his wooing of her, he turns into an Egyptian, Ta-Hor. Typical of the opulence of the Tsar's productions it was nearly four hours long and had a cast of 400. Its huge success led to Petipa's appointment as assistant ballet master. In 2000 it was reconstructed for the Bolshoi by *Lacotte and again became a popular favourite.

Fille mal gardée, La (Eng. title *Vain Precautions*, also *The Unchaperoned Daughter*) Ballet in two acts with choreography and libretto by Dauberval, set to various popular French songs. Premiered 1 Jul. 1789 at Bordeaux's Grand Theatre with Mlle Théodore (Dauberval's wife) as Lise. This seminal work was one of the first ballets to deal with everyday characters and their lives. It tells the story of Lise and her lover Colas, and their attempts to outwit her mother's plans to marry her to Alain, the simple-witted son of a rich landowner. Its original title was *Le Ballet de la paille* but it gained its present title when staged at London's Pantheon Theatre in 1791. Highly popular, it was performed all around Europe, although not at the Paris Opera until 1803. In 1828 Dauberval's pupil Aumer revived it for the Opera with a new musical arrangement by Hérold, which included Rossini melodies and some of his own music. Elssler danced Lise to much acclaim in 1837 and the ballet remained in the Paris repertory until 1854. In St Petersburg it was first produced in 1818 by Didelot (who had danced Colas under Dauberval's coaching in 1791) followed by another production in 1828, and in 1850 Elssler danced in the Moscow production. P. Taglioni produced a new version to music by Hertel for Berlin in 1864 and when Petipa and Ivanov staged their own new production in St Petersburg (1885) with Zucchi and P. Gerdt they used the same score. This was the basis of many subsequent productions, including those of Gorsky (Moscow, 1901), Lavrovsky (Leningrad, 1937), Nijinska (Ballet Theatre, 1940, incorporating elements from Mordkin's 1938 production for the Mordkin Ballet), and Balashova (Nouveau Ballet de Monte Carlo, 1946, later taken into the repertory of the Grand Ballet du

Marquis de Cuevas). Vinogradov's 1971 version for the Maly Theatre, Leningrad, returned to the Hérold score and in 1989 the Dauberval original was reconstructed by Ivo Cramér for Nantes Opera Ballet, using traditional airs arranged by Farncombe. H. Spoerli choreographed a new version for Paris Opera in 1981 using music adapted by J.-M. Damase but the most popular version seen today is Ashton's two-act version. Set to Lanchbery's arrangement of the Hérold music and with designs by Osbert Lancaster, it was premiered 28 Jan. 1960 by the Royal Ballet at Covent Garden, London, with Nerina, Blair, Grant, and Holden. This recaptured the innocence and humour of the Dauberval original but also exploited the advanced virtuosity of 20th-century dancers (the choreography for Colas included some of the most dazzling dance Ashton wrote for a man). It is acknowledged as one of his most perfectly constructed ballets, with its seamless mix of humour and tenderness, classical dance, and mime (Karsavina taught Ashton mime sequences that date back to Zucchi's acclaimed performances) and it is loved for its vivid characterizations, especially the high-spirited lovers, the sharp but tender Widow Simone, and the daft, dreamy Alain. It has since been revived for many companies, including Royal Danish Ballet (1964), Australian Ballet (1967), Budapest State Opera Ballet (1971), PACT Ballet (1969), Munich State Opera Ballet (1971), Royal Swedish Ballet (1972), State Ballet of Turkey (1973), San Francisco Ballet (1978), Joffrey Ballet (1986), Houston Ballet (1992), and Paris Opera (2007).

Filleule de fées, La Ballet in three acts with choreography by Perrot, libretto by V. de Saint-Georges, music by Adam and H. F. de Saint-Julien, sets by Cambon, Thierry, and Despléchin, and costumes by P. Lormier and H. d'Orschwiller. Premiered 8 Oct. 1849 at Paris Opera with Grisi, L. Petipa, and Perrot. It tells the story of Ysaure who is in love with Hugues but whose marriage may not be celebrated in the palace of the fairies until Hugues submits to various trials. It famously featured an airy, fleet-footed performance from Grisi as well as Victor Sacré's sensational stage effects.

Filling Station Ballet in one act with choreography by L. Christensen, libretto by Kerstein, music by V. Thomson, and design by Paul Cadmus. Premiered 6 Jan. 1938 by Ballet Caravan at the Avery Memorial Theater, Hartford, Connecticut, with Christensen, Marie-Jeanne, Hawkins, Kidd, and Bolender. It was one of the first all-American ballets and its cast of contemporary cartoon-style characters includes Mac the filling station attendant, some truck drivers, a motorist, a drunk couple, and a gangster who shoots a girl—who miraculously survives. In 1951 it was revived by San Francisco Ballet and in 1953 by New York City Ballet.

film As a performing art, dance has existed primarily in the theatre, but during the 20th century the art of dancers and choreographers was also, increasingly, recorded by the camera. At the beginning of the century most film was taken by amateurs and only snippets remain of great dancers such as Pavlova, Spessivtseva, and Wigman alongside erratic records of early works by choreographers such as Fokine, Balanchine, and Graham. However, as filming techniques became both cheaper and simpler many companies and institutions started to preserve dance on film in order to complement notated records of choreography. Soviet companies did this quite routinely from the 1950s onwards (also preserving productions of some Western companies for their archives); Massine built up a collection of silent films of his works (which are used as aids in revivals); Graham's repertory was put on film in the mid-1960s, and Cunningham had his repertory videotaped in the early 1970s. In the 1960s the Dance Collection of New York's Public Library began a systematic effort to collect film records of classical and modern works, and since the advent of cheap video equipment even the smallest companies, theatres, and collections now preserve dance on videotape.

These films were for the purposes of record (though video is now also widely used as a rehearsal tool) rather than for public performance. However, since the 1930s choreographers and directors have also explored the potential of dance film as an alternative to live theatre. Early examples were the 1934 film of Humphrey's *Air for the G String* and *La Mort du cygne* (1938), choreographed by Lifar and featuring Slavenska, Chauviré, and Charrat. In 1941 Massine's *Capriccio espagnol* and *Gaîté parisienne* were both filmed in Hollywood, making use of sophisticated cinematic techniques to compensate for the loss of live performance. It was in the 1950s, however, that film versions of dance works started to become common. Paul Czinner produced two feature-length films of the Bolshoi and Royal Ballet, and Soviet film-makers also began making similar films, for example of Ulanova in Lavrovsky's *Romeo and Juliet*. Graham had *Appalachian Spring* filmed, and created the popular film *A Dancer's World*. Once television entered the world's sitting-rooms dance was filmed with increasing regularity, allowing a much larger audience access to both modern and classical repertory—as well as the chance to see star performances. Documentaries, too, gave the public a view of the working lives of dancers and choreographers which normally take place behind studio doors. Now that so much dance has been transferred to video and DVD it is possible for the public to own filmed versions of dances the way they own books, music CDs, or reproductions of paintings.

However, television exemplifies the shortcomings of transferring dance from stage to screen. First, the latter is a two-dimensional medium, so the spatial element of dance is flattened. Secondly, the camera and the editor pre-determine most of the ways in which viewers will see the choreography, giving audiences less freedom to scan the dancers as they do in the theatre. Thirdly, on the small screen the dancers lose much of their live impact and their detail. When a whole corps de ballet is squeezed onto a television screen the dance is reduced to a set of pin figures; if dancers are shown in close-up they are inevitably detached from the surrounding choreography. Some of these issues may be avoided where the choreography has either been adapted for the camera or created specially for it, rather than transferred from the stage.

Original dance sequences have played an important role in cinema from the era of the silent movies when directors like D. W. Griffith used dancers to enhance the emotional impact of scenes, such as the Babylon scenes in *Intolerance*, or alternatively as a tasteful image of eroticism as in Valentino's tango in *The Four Horsemen of the Apocalypse*. But it was with the advent of the film musical that dance came into its own. Busby *Berkeley used a barrage of cinematic effects in the filming and editing of his specially choreographed choral dances, transforming his dancers into kaleidoscopic patterns in films like *42nd Street* or *Gold Diggers of 1933* (both 1933). Fred *Astaire, by contrast, used few special effects but concentrated on making his dances look fluent and natural for the camera. Though his sequences were often highly virtuosic, they were woven into the storyline and the developing characters. Gene *Kelly focused on the dancing body in an even more intimate fashion, with elaborate camera movements presenting the choreography in angled close-ups as well as in plain view (see Beth Genné's writings on *Singin' in the Rain*). He did, however, use more lavish special effects in *On the Town* where the dances were filmed on location all round Manhattan. During the 1950s film adaptations of stage musicals generally underwent a decline in the sensitivity and care with which dance sequences were handled, though the choreography for *West Side Story* (chor. Robbins, 1961) retained a raw, visceral, and musical impact. Some of the most successful dance sequences for the camera have actually featured in films about dancers and dance, such as The *Red Shoes* (chor. Helpmann and Massine, 1948), and the *Turning Point* (1977), *Nijinsky* (1980), *Fame* (1980), and Robert Altman's *The Company* (2003). Ashton's *Tales of Beatrix Potter* (1971) was an entire ballet

created specially for the cinema—which then proved to work less well when transferred to the stage in 1992. Mark Godden's 1998 ballet *Dracula* (mus. Mahler, Royal Winnipeg Ballet) was however arguably more successful when it became the basis of Guy Maddin's award-winning film in 2001.

Outside the mainstream cinema, several experimental film-makers have worked with dance, for example the American poet and film-maker Maya Deren, whose *Choreography for the Camera* (1945) utilized stylized editing techniques, reverse, slow, and fast motion, to capture the movement quality of dancer Talley Beatty, and Shirley Clarke whose *Moment in Love* (1957) was made in collaboration with *Sokolow. Since the 1950s the most innovative filming of dance has mostly occurred within the less expensive and smaller-scale medium of television. M. *Dale and F. *Flindt were among the first choreographers to make works especially for television, although technological innovations like hand-held cameras, computer editing, and graphics give today's choreographers and directors far greater range in the creation of uniquely televisual dance, for example Cunningham's *Points in Space* (dir. E. Caplan, 1986, later adapted for stage), DV8's *Strange Fish* (stage version 1992, television version dir. D. Hinton, 1993), and Tharp's *Catherine Wheel* (stage version, 1981, television version, 1983). Such a large body of work has been made or adapted for the camera that television is now established as a genre with its own awards, e.g. IMZ Dance Screen.

See also under TELEVISION.

Finland Ballet in Finland dates back to the opening of the Alexander Theatre in Helsinki in 1879 where a group of dancers was employed to perform in opera and in occasional ballet performances (for which soloists were imported from St Petersburg). After the country gained its independence from Russia a full-size ballet company, the Finnish Opera Ballet (later becoming Finnish National Ballet) was formed with George Gé (from St Petersburg) as ballet master (1921–34). He staged the first Finnish *Swan Lake* in 1922. The first Finnish choreographer was Irja Koskinen who staged Sibelius's *Scaramouche* in 1955, and gradually the company built up its own native dance talent (though still importing many guest stars from Leningrad). After the late 1950s the company began to tour abroad, for example to the Edinburgh Festival in 1959 and London in 1979. Modern dance emerged in Finland during the 1920s. Duncan had toured the country in 1908 and during the following decade the influence of German modern dance was felt in the founding of several small studios. A resurgence of activity in the 1960s led to the foundation of Dance Theatre Raatikkoin 1972 by Marjo Kuusela, and to the consolidation of many other companies from the 1980s onwards, including Dance Theatre Eri founded in 1989 and directed by Tiina Lindfors, Lassi Sairela, and Eeva Soini; the Tero *Saarinen company (originally named Company Toothpick) which was founded in 1996 and is now resident in Helsinki's Alexander Theatre; and *Helsinki City Theatre which was directed by Uotinen between 1982 and 1991, and now tours widely abroad. Dance festivals in Finland, notably the International Dance Festival of Kuopio, bring in increasing numbers of foreign companies. Rimpparemmi, the country's main folk dance troupe, was formed 25 years ago and tours widely.

Finnish National Ballet Finland's national ballet company. It was founded (as the Finnish Opera Ballet) in 1921 under the direction of Edvard Fazer who imported George Gé from St Petersburg Imperial Ballet as ballet master. Gé staged *Swan Lake* in 1922 followed by other 19th-century classics as well as works by Fokine. In 1934 Gé was succeeded by Alexander Saxelin, a Russian character dancer, but he returned to the company as ballet master from 1955 to 1962. After Gé's death Beriozoff was appointed to the post, staging *Esmeralda* for the ballerina Maj-Lis Rajala, his own version of *Sleeping Beauty*, and a new staging of *Sacre du printemps*. In 1970 the Finnish choreographer Elsa Sylvestersson became ballet mistress, followed by Konstantin Damianov, with Juhani Raiskinen as director from 1974. The repertory expanded to include Soviet ballets such as *Fountain of Bakhchisarai* and *Stone Flower*, as well as works by European and native Finnish choreographers. Doris Laine was made prima ballerina in 1956 and other principal dancers included Leo Ahonen and Matti Tikkanen. Laine was director from 1984 to 1992 and was replaced by Jorma Uotinen, under whose direction the company's repertory expanded to embrace a wide range of modern ballet including works by himself, Carlson, Forsythe, Preljocaj, Naharin, as well as a new staging of *Giselle* by Guillem (1998), her first major production for the stage. In 2001 Dinna Bjorn became director, adding new works by Elo, Ek, and Kylián to the repertory, and in 2008 was succeeded by Kenneth Greve.

((⊕)) SEE WEB LINKS

• Website for the Finnish Opera House with link to the Finnish National Ballet

Fiocre, Eugénie (*b* Paris, 2 Jul. 1845; *d* 1908) French dancer. She was a principal at Paris Opera (1864 and 1875) where she was renowned for her beauty and for her dancing in travesti roles. She created Franz in *Coppélia* (1870), and Degas painted her in Saint-Léon's ballet *La Source*.

Firebird (orig. Russ. title *Zhar-ptitsa*; Fr. title *L'Oiseau de feu*) Ballet in one act with choreography and libretto by Fokine, music by Stravinsky, design by Golovin (sets and costumes) and Bakst (costumes). Premiered 25 Jun. 1910 by Diaghilev's Ballets Russes at the Paris Opera with Karsavina, Fokine, and Fokina. The story is based on various Russian fairy-tales and tells of Prince Ivan who captures a magical Firebird while out hunting. She trades one of her feathers for her freedom. Later, Ivan encounters a group of beautiful young women and falls in love with their leader, the Tsarevna, but is then surrounded by monsters, slaves of the evil Kostchei who holds the women captive. He summons the Firebird with her feather, and she kills Kostchei, freeing the Tsarevna to marry Ivan. One of Diaghilev's early Russian productions, it featured Stravinsky's first commissioned ballet score. It has been revived several times: Diaghilev, with new designs by Goncharova (1926), Sadler's Wells Ballet (1954), Maly Theatre Ballet (1962), Bolshoi Ballet (1964), and Kirov (1993). New versions include Bolm (des. Chagall, Ballet Theatre, 1945), Balanchine (same Chagall des., New York City Ballet, 1949), and a later version with Robbins (1970), Lifar (Paris Opera, 1954), Cranko (Stuttgart, 1964), Béjart (all-male version, set to the concert suite, Ballet of the 20th Century, 1964), Neumeier (sci-fi version, Frankfurt Ballet, 1970), Tetley (Royal Danish Ballet, 1981), Taras (Caribbean version, Dance Theatre of Harlem, 1982), Scholz (Stuttgart, 1998), Wheeldon (Boston Ballet, 1999), Krzysztof *Pastor (West Australian Ballet, 1999), and Yuri Possukhov (Oregon Ballet Theatre, 2004 and San Francisco Ballet, 2007).

fish dive Dramatic pose executed in classical pas de deux where the woman is held almost upside-down by her partner, with her ankles crossed, her back arched, and her head lifted up and away from the floor.

Fitzjames, Louise and Nathalie French dancing sisters. Louise (*b* Paris, 10 Dec. 1809) danced at Paris Opera (1832–46) where her greatest success was as the Abbess in *Robert le diable*, a role she danced over 230 times. She was reviled by Gautier for her emaciated appearance but also danced Taglioni's role in *Le Dieu et la bayadère* and appeared in Albert's *La Jolie Fille de Gand* in 1842. Nathalie (*b* 1819) danced at Paris Opera (1837–42) where she created the peasant pas de deux in *Giselle* with Mabillé in 1841. She later toured Italy and America. She also performed as a singer, once appearing as singer, mime, and dancer during a single performance at Versailles in 1842.

***Five Brahms Waltzes in the Manner of
Isadora Duncan*** Ballet in one act with choreography by Ashton and music by Brahms. It originated as a short gala piece for Lynn Seymour,
premiered 22 Jun. 1975 at the State Opera House,
Hamburg, using only one Brahms Waltz, Op. 39,
No. 15. In this impressionistic recall of Duncan,
Seymour was dressed in a near-transparent shift
like that worn by Duncan and though the movement was not an authentic reconstruction it
evoked the visionary lyricism of her performances.
The final version, with Waltzes Nos. 1, 2, 8, 10, and
13 added, was premiered by Seymour for Ballet
Rambert's 50th anniversary gala at Sadler's Wells
on 15 Jun. 1976. It has been revived by American
Ballet Theatre, Rambert Dance Company, and
Birmingham Royal Ballet.

five positions The standard positions of the
feet in ballet date back to Beauchamps's identifi-
cation at the end of the 17th century. In all five the
legs and feet are turned out: 1st position: the heels
touch with the feet ideally aiming to form a
straight line; 2nd position: the feet are placed
apart with the distance between the heels slightly
less than hip-width; 3rd position: the feet cross so
that the heel of the front foot fits the hollow of the
instep of the back foot; 4th position: one foot is
placed a small distance in front of the other (in
4th croisé the front heel is placed opposite the toe
of the back foot, in 4th ouvert the front heel is
opposite the heel of the back foot); 5th position:
the feet are fully crossed and just touching each
other so that the front heel fits against the base of
the big toe of the back foot. Lifar attempted to
introduce a 6th position where the feet are placed
parallel side by side and the legs turned in; and a
7th, also parallel, where one foot is placed slightly
forward of the other.

5 Tangos Ballet in one act with choreography by
van Manen, music by Piazolla, and design by
Vroom. Premiered 3 Nov. 1977 by Dutch National
Ballet at Stadsschouwburg, Amsterdam, with
S. Marchiolli and C. Farha. It is set to Piazolla's *5
Tangos for Bandoneon* and is danced by seven
couples. It has been revived by several companies, including Berlin Opera Ballet (1979), Stuttgart Ballet (1981), Sadler's Wells Royal Ballet
(1982), Birmingham Royal Ballet (1991), and
Houston Ballet (2008).

Flamand, Frédéric (*b* Brussels 1946) Belgian
choreographer and artistic director. He studied
theatre and visual arts before founding the
multi-disciplinary company Plan K in 1973.
A study of representations of the human body
developed his interest in choreography and he
went on to create dance works for the company
such as *Scan Lines* (1984). Between 1989 and 1994

he collaborated with the artist Fabrizio Plessi on a
trilogy about the history of technology, beginning
with *La Chute d'Icare* (mus. Michael Nyman,
1989), set in the Renaissance and concluding
with *Ex Machina* (1994) set in the present day.
In 1991 he was appointed artistic director of the
Ballet Royal de Wallonie, which he renamed
Charleroi/Danses. His work there focused on
relationships between dance and architecture, as
in *Metapolis* (2000), created with architect Zaha
Hadid. In 2004 Flamand was appointed director
of the Ballet National de Marseille (with Eric Vu
An as his assistant from 2005) and has since created several works for the company, including
Metamorphoses (2007), which have merged the
dancers' classical training with his own more contemporary idiom. In 2003 he was artistic director
of the Venice Biennale dance festival and in 2004
was appointed to the faculty of University of
Architecture in Venice, running interdisciplinary
workshops centred on dance.

(🌐) **SEE WEB LINKS**

• Website for Ballet National de Marseille

flamenco The traditional gypsy dance and
music of S. Spain, in whose undulating vocals,
supple arm movements, and stamping footwork
(*zapateado*) can be discerned powerful Moorish
and Arabic influences. The basic dance forms are
named after the styles or *palos* of the songs which
they have traditionally accompanied and are
variously distinguished by their mood, rhythmic
pattern, or geographical origin. They include
alegrías, a dance of consolation; sevillanas (a
form of *seguidillas), a fiesta dance of non-gypsy
origin in 3/4 or 6/8 time; bulerías, a fast dance,
whose irregular 12-beat patterns allow great freedom for improvisation; and soleá, an intense,
typically female dance, in 12 beats, characterized
by spiralling movements of the arms and hips. It is
argued that originally these were danced to the
accompaniment of singing and clapping only,
with guitars and castanets added later. Individual
performances are distinguished by the inventive-
ness with which dancers play with the rhythms of
each dance and by their intensity of expression—
great flamenco dancers are known for their *duen-
de*, a quality which expresses both their soul and
their ability to translate themselves into pure
states of emotion. Flamenco was originally
danced in streets and cafés but in the 20th century
it became increasingly popular in the theatre (*see*
SPAIN). Flamenco enjoyed a major international
revival in the 1980s with A. *Gades and Carlos
Saura's flamenco films *Carmen* and *Blood Wedding*; also with world tours of traditional flamenco
shows like Cumbre Flamenca and with dancers
like Joaquin Cortes reaching new audiences with
his high-tech 'flamenco fusion' shows. It has

continued to expand in the 21st century, with dancers like *Farruquito maintaining a purity of technique and presentation and others like Sara *Baras developing a more modern idiom.

Flames of Paris, The (orig. Russ. title *Plamya Parizha*) Ballet in four acts with choreography by Vainonen, libretto by N. Volkov and V. Dmitriev, music by Asafiev, and design by V. Dmitriev. Premiered 7 Nov. 1932 by GATOB, Leningrad, with Chabukiani, Jordan, Anisimova, Dudinskaya, and K. Sergeyev. It is set in the third year of the French Revolution (1792) and its action contrasts the political fervour of the oppressed people of Marseilles with the Court decadence at Versailles as the former march to Paris and storm the Tuileries. Even though originally tailored to serve the State's demand for politically correct ballet it was a rich theatrical spectacle, with choreography ranging from vigorous folk dancing to court dances and pure classical numbers (including exceptionally virtuoso variations for the men). The fourth-act pas de deux has often been performed as a gala piece. Asafiev's score drew on similarly eclectic sources, including popular songs and baroque music, while Dmitriev's designs were on an epic scale. It was staged in Moscow in 1933, with an abbreviated version filmed for the Soviet film *Trio Ballet* (1953) and in 2008 a revised version was staged by *Ratmansky for the Bolshoi.

Flatley, Michael (*b* Chicago, 16 Jul. 1958) Irish-US dancer and choreographer. He began to study step dancing locally at the age of 11 and at 16 established a world record by tapping 28 times per second. At the age of 17 he became the first American to win the World Irish Dancing Championships and in 1993 starred in the Irish dance and music special *Mayo 5000* with his partner Jean Butler. He then appeared in the *Riverdance* entertainment which featured in the 1994 Eurovision Song Contest. From this emerged the hit show *Riverdance* which he helped to choreograph and in which he starred for two years. In 1995 he left to create and star in his own equally successful show *Lord of the Dance*, which was followed by a second showcase *Feet of Flames* (1998). He retired from international touring in 2001 but in 2005 created a new production *Celtic Tiger* and despite injury has continued to dance occasional performances, including on television.

Flick und Flocks Abenteuer (Eng. title *Flik and Flok*) Comedy ballet in three acts with choreography by P. Taglioni and music by Hertel. Premiered 20 Sept. 1858 at the Court Opera Berlin. This colourful tale of two friends' magical adventures was hugely popular, receiving over 400 performances in Berlin between 1858 and 1885. It was revived for Milan (1862) and Vienna (1865).

Flier, Jaap (*b* Scheveningen, 27 Feb. 1934) Dutch dancer, choreographer, and director. He studied with Gaskell and made his debut in 1950 with Ballet Recital before moving to Netherlands Ballet. Here he danced the classical repertory as well as creating his first ballet, *The Trial* (1955). In 1959 he became a founder member of Nederlands Dans Theater and as one of its principal dancers created many roles including the lead in Tetley's *The Anatomy Lesson* (1964). He also choreographed several ballets including *Nouvelles aventures* (mus. Ligeti, 1968) and *Hikyo* (mus. Kazuo Fukushima, 1971). Between 1973 and 1975 he was director of Australian Dance Theatre and between 1975 and 1976 he directed Sydney Dance Company. He subsequently returned to the Netherlands to teach, choreograph and give occasional performances. He was made Knight of the Order of Orange Nassau, in 1968.

Flindt, Flemming (*b* Copenhagen, 30 Jun. 1936; *d* Sarasota, Florida 3 Mar. 2009) Danish dancer, choreographer, and director. He studied at the Royal Danish Ballet and Paris Opera Schools, graduating into the RDB in 1955 as a soloist (principal). He rapidly developed a career as an international guest artist performing with many companies including London Festival Ballet (1955), Ballet Rambert (1960), Royal Ballet (1963), and Bolshoi Ballet (1968). In 1961 he was made an étoile at the Paris Opera. A dancer who excelled in the standard classics and Bournonville repertory he was also admired in modern works, for example those of Lander, Cullberg, and Petit, and when he was artistic director of RDB (1966–78) he brought in work by many modern choreographers including Taylor, Robbins, Tetley, and Field. He choreographed his first ballet, *The Lesson* (mus. Delerue), in 1963. This adaptation of Ionesco's *La Leçon* was specially made for Danish television and later adapted for the stage, premiered by RDB, Paris, 1964. His many other works for the company include *The Miraculous Mandarin* (mus. Bartók, 1967), *The Triumph of Death*, a television ballet in which the whole cast controversially danced naked (mus. Koppel, 1971, staged RDB, 1972), *The Nutcracker* (mus. Tchaikovsky, 1971), *Jeux* (mus. Debussy, 1973), and *Dreamland* (mus. Koppel, 1974). Flindt introduced a new public to dance although he was criticized for threatening the purity of the Danish style and for the flamboyance of his Bournonville stagings and in 1978 he resigned to form his own company, for which he choreographed *Salome* (mus. P. M. Davies, 1978). In 1981 he was appointed director of the Dallas Ballet and from 1989 worked freelance, reviving some of his past ballets as well as creating new ones. He additionally formed a close connection to Cleveland Ballet (now Ballet San Jose), for which he created several works including *Phaedre* (mus. Glass, 1987). He returned to RDB to create *Caroline Mathilde* (mus. P. M. Davies, 1991) and *Legs of Fire* (mus. E. Norby, 1998) and remained active, staging his ballets until shortly before his death. He was made Knight of Dannebrog in 1974 and awarded the Carina Ari Medal in 1975. He was married to the dancer Vivi Gelker (*see* FLINDT, VIVI).

Flindt, Vivi (*née* Gelker; *b* Copenhagen, 22 Feb. 1943) Danish dancer. She studied at Royal Danish Ballet School and graduated into the company, making her debut as Miss Julie in 1965 and becoming soloist in 1967. She married the dancer Flemming Flindt in 1970. As well as dancing the Bournonville repertory she created roles in several of her husband's ballets, including *The Miraculous Mandarin* (1967), *Sacre du printemps* (1968), *Triumph of Death* (1971), *Felix Luna* (1973), and *Salome* (1978).

Flore et Zéphire Ballet divertissement in one act with choreography and libretto by Didelot, music by Cesare Bossi, and design by Liparotti. Premiered at the King's Theatre, London, on 7 Jul. 1796 with Collinet (Mme Didelot), Hilligsberg, and Didelot. In many ways the work prefigured 19th-century Romanticism. Its plot is based on the Greek myth in which Zéphire, God of the Wind, falls in love with the nymph Flore, is then distracted by another beauty, but finally sweeps his true love up with him into the sky. By exploiting the advanced stage machinery of the King's Theatre, Didelot was able to fly his dancers through the air on wires and also aid his ballerinas in their efforts to hover on the tips of their toes. His choreography exaggerated differences between male and female dancing, and by experimenting with a more fluid and natural style of mime it created a dance language both more realistic and poetic than the current style. The ballet was very popular and performed all around Europe, thus establishing Didelot's reputation. Taglioni made her London debut in it in 1830. Massine created a ballet on the same subject, *Zephyr et Flore* (mus. Dukelsky, 1925).

Flores Canelo, Raúl (orig. R. F. González; *b* Coahuila, 19 Apr. 1929; *d* Mexico City, 3 Feb. 1992) Mexican dancer, choreographer, designer, and director. He studied at the Mexican Dance Academy, then in 1951 joined the National Ballet of Mexico, moving to Fine Arts Ballet in 1959 as dancer and designer. After a year studying modern dance in the US, he founded the Independent Ballet of Mexico in 1966, for which he choreographed and designed many works including *La espera* (mus. Revueltas, 1973), *Terpsicore en México* (mus. various, 1987), and *Poeta* (mus. Schubert and others, 1988). His eclectic style displayed a distinctive wit and irreverence.

Florestan and his Sisters Pas de trois introduced by Diaghilev into *Aurora's Wedding* (1923) using the Act III music from *Sleeping Beauty* which originally accompanied the Diamond, Gold, Silver, and Sapphire Fairy variations.

Flower Festival in Genzano (orig. Dan. title *Blomsterfesten i Genzano*) Ballet in one act with choreography by Bournonville and music by E. Helsted and H. S. Paulli. Premiered 19 Dec. 1858 by the Royal Danish Ballet in Copenhagen. It tells the story of two 19th-century lovers, Rosa and Paolo and while no longer performed in full a pas de deux from one of the ensemble dances has become a popular gala piece—a brilliant showcase for the Bournonville style.

Flowers Full-length dance, mime, and theatre piece with choreography, libretto, and design by Lindsay Kemp and music by Joji Hirota. Premiered Dec. 1973 at Bush Theatre, London, by Lindsay Kemp and Company. It is based freely on the life and writings of Genet and when Kemp first appeared as its tragic heroine Divine he became established as one of the leading performers and directors of the 1970s avant-garde.

Fokina, Vera (*née* Antonova; *b* 3 Aug. 1886; *d* New York, 29 Jul. 1958) Russian dancer. She studied at the Imperial Theatre School, St Petersburg, graduating into the Mariinsky in 1904. In 1905 she married Mikhail Fokine and danced in many of his ballets both with Diaghilev's Ballets Russes and in the US. She created roles in *Carnaval* and *Firebird* (both 1910).

Fokine, Mikhail (in the West he called himself Michel Fokine; *b* St Petersburg, 5 May 1880; *d* New York, 22 Aug. 1942) Russian dancer, choreographer, teacher, director, and pioneering influence in 20th-century ballet. He studied at the Imperial Theatre School, St Petersburg, graduating in 1898 into the Mariinsky Theatre. He began teaching at the Theatre School in 1902 and was promoted first soloist in the company in 1904, partnering Karsavina and Pavlova. However, his interests lay primarily with choreography and ballet reform. He created his first ballet for the Theatre School graduation performance in 1905 and two years later created his first major ballet for the Mariinsky Theatre, *Le Pavillon d'Armide* (mus. N. Tcherepnin, 1907). Both works were made in accordance with his ambition to transform ballet into a serious and integrated artform, rather than the formulaic entertainment to which he felt it had descended.

His aims were based on five principles, which he later formulated in a letter to *The Times* (6 Jul. 1914):

(1) Individual ballets should be choreographed in styles which were appropriate to their subjects, rather than in a uniform classical language. Fokine himself choreographed *Chopiniana* (1907, later *Les Sylphides*) in a lyrical, Romantic style, *Eunice* (1907) in the style of ancient Greece, and *Petrushka* (1911) in a style of folk and character dancing appropriate to a Russian street fair.

(2) Dance and mime should have no place in a ballet unless they were dramatically expressive.

(3) Expressive mime should be incorporated into dance, involving, where appropriate, the whole body rather than being restricted to conventional hand gestures.

(4) Group ensembles should be used to convey dramatic atmosphere rather than be used for purely decorative purposes.

(5) Dance music and design should be equal partners in ballet, each reflecting the dance's subject-matter, setting, and historical period.

These crusading ideas met with hostility from the conservative Mariinsky directorate and Fokine accepted Diaghilev's invitation to join the Ballets Russes and put his reforms into practice. During his period with that company (1909–14) he produced his most successful body of work including *Les Sylphides* (mus. Chopin, 1909), the Polovtsian Dances from *Prince Igor* (mus. Borodin, 1909), *Cléopâtre* (mus. Arensky and others, 1909), *Carnaval* (mus. Schumann, 1910), *Scheherazade* (mus. Rimsky-Korsakov, 1910), *Firebird* (mus. Stravinsky, 1910), *Le Spectre de la rose* (mus. Weber, 1911), *Petrushka* (mus. Stravinsky, 1911), *Le Dieu bleu* (mus. Hahn, 1912), *Daphnis and Chloe* (mus. Ravel, 1912), *Papillon* (mus. Schumann, 1912), and *The Legend of Joseph* (mus. R. Strauss, 1914). He continued to work occasionally for the Imperial Theatres and returned to St Petersburg in 1914 after falling out with Diaghilev (due to the latter's promotion of Nijinsky as a rival choreographer). In 1918 Fokine left Russia for good and worked mainly in Scandinavia, performing, teaching, and staging his ballets with his wife Vera. In 1920 he began working in the US, occasionally with his own company which was called the Fokine Ballet in 1922, then between 1924 and 1925 the

American Ballet or the Fokine Dancers. Otherwise, he was freelance working with, among others, Metropolitan Opera House and Ziegfeld Follies in the US, and abroad with Paris Opera (1921), His Majesty's Theatre, London (1923), Teatro Colón (1931), Ida Rubinstein's Co., Paris (1934–5), and La Scala, Milan (1936). He was chief choreographer for R. Blum's Ballets de Monte Carlo (1936–8) and for Ballet Theatre (1941–2). His ballets during this period include *The Sorcerer's Apprentice* (mus. Dukas, Petrograd, 1916), *Bolero* (mus. Ravel, Paris, 1935), *L'Épreuve d'amour* (mus. various, Monte Carlo, 1936), *Don Juan* (mus. Gluck, London, 1937), *Bluebeard* (mus. Offenbach-Dorati, Mexico City, 1941). He also founded a school in New York in 1921. He was married to the dancer Vera Fokina, their son Vitale Fokine was a ballet teacher in New York, and their granddaughter Isabelle Fokine danced with the Pittsburgh Ballet and staged several of his works for the Kirov and other companies.

folk dance Term denoting any kind of dance which has been developed within a traditional community, rather than being created by a choreographer or teacher. Steps and patterns are passed on from one generation to another, gradually undergoing change. Many folk dances have their origins in ritual—fertility, marriage, religious, or war—and express the character of the community who dance them. The term was coined in the 18th century to distinguish 'peasant' dance forms from those of the upper classes, but the distinction itself dates back to the 15th century when ballroom dances first began to emerge as separate forms. In the past folk dances have exerted a strong influence on social and theatre dance, particularly during the Romantic period when they were considered to add both local and expressive colour. They have also influenced the styles of some 20th- and 21st-century choreographers such as Ek, Kylián, and Morris who was himself a performer with a Balkan folk dance troupe in the US. However, with urbanization and demographic change many of the original dances have been lost, even though many Western countries, during the 20th century, attempted to re-discover and preserve these dances, often through specialist troupes of folk dancers. Even where they have survived, however, they are mostly staged as theatre or as tourist attractions rather than being performed as genuine community events.

Folk Tale, A (orig. Dan. title *Et folkesagn*) Ballet in three acts with choreography and libretto by Bournonville, music by N. Gade and J. P. Hartmann, and design by Christensen, Lund, and Lehmann. Premiered 20 Mar. 1854 by the Royal Danish Ballet, Copenhagen, with J. Price. It is based on a

Danish fairy story about a girl, Hilda, who lives with the trolls and saves a young nobleman Ove from their power, echoing the supernatural focus of *Giselle*, created thirteen years earlier. It has been revived in major productions by Lander and Borchsenius (1941), Brenaa (1969), and K. Ralov (1979), the controversially modern designs of the latter production replaced by the more traditional staging of 1991, directed by F. Andersen and A. M. Vessel Schlüter and designed by HM Queen Margrethe II. Other productions include Berlin Opera Ballet (staged P. Schaufuss after Bournonville, Berlin, 1983) and London Festival Ballet (extracts, staged P. Schaufuss, 1988).

Folkwang Ballett Essen German dance company originating from the theatrical training school founded by the city of Essen in 1927. *Jooss was the school's director of dance, and was joined there by F. Leeder and others, who together formed a company (Folkwang Tanztheater-Studio) in 1928. In 1929 this was amalgamated into the Essen opera house and under the name Folkwang-Tanzbühne presented many ballets by Jooss, notably *The Green Table* (1932). Under threat of Nazi persecution the company (now called Ballets Jooss) moved to Dartington in the UK in 1933. Jooss returned to Essen in 1949 and the Folkwang Tanztheater was revived for several tours until 1951. During the 1960s it became active again as the Folkwang Ballett, and between 1968 and 1973 was directed by Bausch. She was succeeded by Susanne Linke and Reinhild Hoffmann who ran the organization under its new title Folkwang Tanzstudio between 1975 and 1977; however Bausch resumed her connection in 1983 and from 1999 it was co-directed by her and Henrietta Horn, the latter choreographing much of its repertory.

((⊕)) SEE WEB LINKS
• Website for the Folkwang Ballett Essen company and school

fondu [Fr., melted] A step where the dancer bends the supporting leg, also a soft melting quality of movement.

Fonteyn, (Dame) Margot (orig. Peggy Hookham; *b* Reigate, 18 May 1919; *d* Panama City, 21 Feb. 1991) British ballerina who became the most internationally famous dancer of her age. She studied with H. Bosustov in Ealing, with G. Goncharov in Shanghai, and with N. Legat and Astafieva in London before being accepted at Sadler's Wells School in 1934. In the same year she made her debut with the Vic-Wells Ballet as a Snowflake in *The Nutcracker* and after Markova's departure from the company in 1935 she began to dance ballerina roles, including Markova's role in *Rio Grande* and Odette in *Swan Lake*, as well as creating her first major role, the Fiancée in Ash-

ton's *Le Baiser de la fée*. By 1939 she had danced Giselle and Aurora as well as becoming established as Ashton's muse, creating roles in *Apparitions* (1936), *Les Patineurs* (1937), and *A Wedding Bouquet* (1937). During the war she toured widely with the company and afterwards matured into the supreme exponent of the British ballet style. Although she was not a brilliant virtuoso, the exceptional beauty of her dancing was produced by a combination of qualities—great musicality, an apparently instinctive purity of line, lyrical expressiveness, and the rare intimacy which she established with audiences. She continued to create many new roles in, for example, Ashton's *Symphonic Variations* (1946), *Scènes de Ballet* (1948), *Daphnis and Chloe* (1951), and *Ondine* (1958) as well as Petit's *Les Demoiselles de la nuit* (1948). After the war she was international guest artist with various companies including Ballets de Paris (1948) and in 1959 she loosened her ties with the Royal Ballet to become a guest artist. In 1961 she danced with Nureyev for the first time in a charity gala and their ensuing partnership brought her a new artistic lease of life which lasted for a decade-and-a-half. His flamboyant Russian technique complemented her more English reserve to create the most famous partnership in ballet history. They appeared in the premiere of MacMillan's *Romeo and Juliet* (1965) and created the title roles in Ashton's *Marguerite and Armand* (1963). In 1979 she presented the television series *The Magic of Dance* and in the same year was awarded the title prima ballerina assoluta of the Royal Ballet, one among many distinctions which also included Dame Commander of the Order of the British Empire in 1956, Order of the Finnish Lion in 1960, and several honorary doctorates. Many of her performances have been filmed for television. In 1955 she married Panamanian politician Roberto Arias who ten years later was paralysed by the bullets of a would-be assassin. Her autobiography *Margot Fonteyn* was published in London, 1975 and New York, 1976.

Foregger, Nikolai (*b* 18 Apr. 1892; *d* Kuibyshev, 8 Jun. 1939) Russian drama director and ballet master. He invented and taught his own system of physical movement, and as director of his own ensemble (1921–5) created his highly controversial work *Dance of Machines* in which he demonstrated his vision of a modernist dance which would incorporate 'dances of the pavement, of rushing motor cars...the grandeur of skyscrapers'. He was chief regisseur in Kharkov (1929–34), in Kiev (1934–6), and in Kuibyshev (1938–9).

Fornaroli, Cia (*b* Milan, 16 Oct. 1888; *d* New York, 16 Aug. 1954) Italian dancer and teacher. She studied at the La Scala Ballet School and with Cecchetti, and after performing minor roles in the ballets of Manzotti became prima ballerina at New York's Metropolitan Opera Ballet (1910–14). Between 1914 and 1916 she guested in Barcelona, Madrid, and Teatro Colón, Buenos Aires, then moved to Teatro Costanzi in Rome (1916–20). She was appointed prima ballerina assoluta at La Scala, Milan (1921–33), her musically expressive dancing making her the most highly regarded Italian ballerina of her generation. She also guested in various European theatres and danced with Pavlova's company as well as appearing in Italian silent films. In 1929 she succeeded Cecchetti as director of the La Scala School and in 1933 began to create her own ballets. Due to Fascist attacks on her husband, Dr Walter Toscanini, she was forced to leave Italy for New York where she became ballet mistress at Ballet Theatre in 1940 and ran her own school (1944–66). After her death her husband handed over their collection of dance memorabilia to the Dance Collection of the New York Public Library.

Forsythe, William (*b* New York, 30 Dec. 1949) US dancer, choreographer, and director. He studied with Jonathan Watts, Maggie Black, and Finis Jhung at the Joffrey Ballet School from 1969 and danced with the company (1971–3) before moving to Stuttgart Ballet (1973–81). He choreographed his first ballet *Urlicht* in 1976 (mus. Mahler, Noverre Society, staged Stuttgart Ballet, 1976) and became the company's resident choreographer until 1981, also creating there his highly popular work *Love Songs* (mus. Aretha Franklin and Dionne Warwick, 1979). After freelancing in Europe he was appointed choreographer of the Frankfurt Ballet in 1982, becoming its director and chief choreographer in 1984. Almost from the beginning his work was a conscious assault on the 'gracious rhetoric' of classical ballet. His dancers moved with a force that sent them almost off balance, their bodies stretched and tilted at drastic angles and their movements slamming from one position to another. In duets they often appeared combative rather than mutually supportive. Some works were created without obvious plot or character—simply deconstructing the theatrical language of ballet—while others placed dance within surreal theatrical contexts. In *France/Dance* (1983) papier-maché animals, figures, and buildings were dotted around the stage as an actor recited a fragmented text; in *Interrogation of Robert Scott* (1986) a television screen showed a man apparently under interrogation while several voices (live and recorded) posed questions and answers. Both his choreographic style and his stage concepts have exercised a profound influence on younger choreographers. Other works from his early to middle period include *Steptext* (mus. J. S. Bach, Aterballetto, 1984, staged Frankfurt Ballet, 1985, and Royal

Ballet, 1995), *The Loss of Small Detail* (mus. Willems, Frankfurt Ballet, 1987), *Impressing the Czar* (including *In the middle somewhat elevated*, mus. Willems, Beethoven, Stuck, Crossman-Hecht, Frankfurt Ballet, 1988, one-act version Paris Opera, 1988, also staged Royal Ballet, 1992), *Herman Schmerman* (mus. Willems, New York City Ballet, 1992, also staged Royal Ballet, 1993), *Limb's Theorem* (mus. Willems, Frankfurt Ballet, 1990), and *Quintett* (mus. Bryars, Frankfurt Ballet, 1993). In his more recent works he has choreographed in increasingly close collaboration with his dancers, and productions like *Kammer/Kammer* (mus. various, 2000) for Frankfurt Ballet have made a point of emphasizing the creative process involved in assembling the movement along with its accompanying sound, images, and text. In 2004 he left Frankfurt Ballet to form his own smaller company, aiming to explore in greater depth the process of collaboration and experiment with different modes of performance. Works for the Forsythe Company include *Three Atmospheric Studies* (2005).

(((●))) **SEE WEB LINKS**

• Website for the Forsythe company

Forti, Simone (*b* Florence, 1935) Italian-US dancer and choreographer. She studied with Anna Halprin, Robert Dunn, Graham, and Cunningham and began performing in 1960 with her first husband, the painter and dancer Robert Morris. Her choreography eschewed formal dance elements in favour of an ongoing exploration of the natural movement of animals and people. She also performed in improvised events with her second husband Robert Whitman.

Fort Worth/Dallas Ballet *See* TEXAS BALLET THEATRE.

Fosse, Bob (*b* Chicago, 23 Jun. 1927; *d* Washington, DC, 23 Sept. 1987) US dancer, choreographer, and producer. The son of vaudeville performers he danced in burlesque from the age of 13 and performed as the opening act of striptease shows at 17. In 1940 he formed a night-club team with Charles Gross called the Riff Brothers and began choreographing for amateur productions. He made his debut as a Broadway dancer in 1950 and established himself as a professional choreographer with the musical *The Pajama Game* (1953, filmed 1957). With his provocative jazzy style, and unsentimental, even acid tone, he became one of the most sought-after choreographers of musicals and films and a profound influence on succeeding generations of theatre choreographers. In his later works he was director and choreographer, including *Sweet Charity* (1966), *Cabaret* (the film, 1971), *Chicago* (1975), and *Dancin'* (1978). His film *All that Jazz* (1979) was a frankly autobiographical portrayal of a workaholic Broadway director with a heart problem and it featured his most aggressively erotic dance number *Airotica*. In 1986 he wrote, staged, and choreographed his final musical, *Big Deal*. A compilation of his greatest dance numbers was presented in the Broadway show *Fosse* (dir. Tod Haimes, 1999).

fouetté [Fr., whipped] A whipping movement. It has various applications, the most popularly known being the virtuoso *fouetté rond de jambe en tournant en dehors*, in which the dancer throws the working leg out to the side and whips the foot in as she turns. The 32 *fouetté* turns performed in the coda of the Act III pas de deux of *Swan Lake* (first executed by Legnani) are one of the most famous challenges in the classical ballerina's repertory.

Fountain of Bakhchisarai, The (orig. Russ. title *Bakhchisaraisky fontan*) Ballet in four acts with choreography by Zakharov, libretto by N. Volkov, music by Asafiev, and design by Khodasevich. Premiered 28 Sept. 1934 by GATOB in Leningrad with Ulanova, Vecheslova, and Mikhail Dudko. It is based on Pushkin's poem of the same title and tells the story of Maria, a Polish princess who is abducted by Khan Girei. Though she does not return his love she still arouses the jealousy of his chief wife Zarema who stabs her. In his grief the Khan builds a fountain of tears to Maria's memory. It was Zakharov's first and most successful ballet and a seminal work in the evolution of Soviet dramatic ballets, both in its use of literary sources and in its application of Stanislavsky's theatrical methods to the creation of realistic dance characterization. It was subsequently staged at the Stanislavsky Nemirovich-Danchenko Theatre in Moscow, Apr. 1936 and at the Bolshoi Theatre in June 1936, and has been revived by many East European and Russian companies. Nijinsky's father, Foma Nijinsky, choreographed a ballet on the same subject in 1892.

Four Last Songs (orig. Dutch-Ger. title *Vier letzte Lieder*) Ballet in one act with choreography by van Dantzig, music by R. Strauss, and design by van Schayk. Premiered 16 May 1977 by Dutch National Ballet at Stadsschouwburg, Amsterdam, with Farha, Sand, Sinceretti, Marchiolli, Jurriëns, Radius, and Ebbelaar. It is performed to Karajan's recording of Strauss's score with singer Gundula Janowitz and presents Death as a soothing rather than ominous presence. It was revived for Vienna State Opera Ballet in 1979. Other choreographers who have used the same music include Béjart (*Serait-ce la mort?* 1970) and Ben Stevenson (1999).

Four Saints in Three Acts Opera by Virgil Thomson, with choreography by Ashton, libretto by Gertrude Stein, and designs by Kate Drain Lawson. Premiered 7 Feb. 1934 at Wadsworth Atheneum, Hartford, Connecticut, with A. Hines. A. Dorsey, E. Matthews, B. Robinson Wayne, B. Howard, E. Bowner, and B. Fitzhugh Baker (singers) and C. L. Baker, E. Dickerson, M. Hart, F. Miller, M. Baird, and B. Smith (dancers). A shortened version of the score was choreographed by Morris in 2000.

Four Schumann Pieces Ballet in one act with choreography by van Manen, music by Schumann and design by Jean-Paul Vroom. Premiered 31 Jan. 1975 by the Royal Ballet at Covent Garden, London, with Dowell, Penney, Collier, and Eagling. A plotless setting of Schumann's String Quartet in A major, Op. 41, No. 3. It was revived for Dutch National Ballet and National Ballet of Canada in 1976.

Four Seasons, The Ballet in one act. (Version 1) With choreography by MacMillan, music by Verdi, and design by Peter Rice. Premiered 5 Mar. 1975 by the Royal Ballet at Covent Garden, London, with Derman, Parkinson, MacLeary, Collier, Coleman, Ashmole, Eagling, Mason, Wall, Dowell, Penney, and Sleep. This lighthearted setting of ballet music composed by Verdi for the first Paris production of *Les Vêpres siciliennes* (chor. L. Petipa, 1855) also incorporates ballet music from Verdi's *Jérusalem* and *Don Carlos*. It was revived with new designs by Barry Kay for Paris Opera (1978). (Version 2) With choreography by Robbins, music by Verdi, and design by Santo Loquasto (costumes). Premiered 18 Jan. 1979 by New York City Ballet at the State Theater, New York, with K. Nichols, Duell, S. Saland, B. Cook, J.-P. Frohlich, McBride, and Baryshnikov. This suite of classical dances portraying the changing seasons is set to Verdi's ballet music for *Les Vêpres siciliennes* and also incorporates his ballet music from *I Lombardi* and *Il trovatore*.

Other settings of the *Vêpres* music include those by J. Carter (Ambassador Ballet, 1950) and Prokovsky (New London Ballet, 1973), and other ballets portraying the seasons include those by Hilverding (Vienna *c*.1750), Perrot (mus. Pugni, London, 1848), Petipa (*Les *Saisons* mus. Glazunov, St Petersburg, 1900), plus several settings of the famous Vivaldi violin concertos including Walter (Düsseldorf, 1970), Cohen (Scottish Ballet, Glasgow 1996), Kudelka (National Ballet of Canada, 1997), and S. Welch (Houston, 2007).

Four Temperaments, The Ballet in one act with choreography by Balanchine, music by Hindemith, design by Kurt Seligmann, and lighting by Rosenthal. Premiered 20 Nov. 1946 by Ballet Society at the Central High School of Needle Trades, New York, with Dollar, Moylan, Danieli,

Bolender, and LeClercq. Set to Hindemith's commissioned score *Theme with Four Variations* (*According to the Four Temperaments*), the dance is a series of variations based on the four humours—melancholic, sanguinic, phlegmatic, and choleric. It contains some of the most intricately composed and vividly suggestive images in Balanchine's choreography. In 1951 it was re-staged and revised by Balanchine for New York City Ballet with no decor and with the dancers in practice clothes. It is one of Balanchine's most frequently performed ballets and has been revived by dozens of companies including Royal Swedish Ballet (1960), La Scala Ballet (1962), Royal Danish Ballet (1963), Paris Opera (1963), National Ballet of Canada (1969), Berlin Opera Ballet (1970), Pacific Northwest Ballet (1970), Royal Ballet (1973), San Francisco Ballet (1974), Sadler's Wells Ballet (1976), Dance Theatre of Harlem (1979), Royal Flanders Ballet (1990), Ballet National de Marseilles (2003), and Scottish Ballet (2004).

Fourth Symphony, The Ballet in one act with choreography by Neumeier, music by Mahler, and design by Marco Arturo Marelli. Premiered 31 Mar. 1977 by the Royal Ballet at Covent Garden, London, with Sleep, Seymour, Wall, and Coleman. It is set to Mahler's 4th Symphony and its four parts ('Beginning', 'Shadows', 'Evening', and 'Epilogue: The Lost Paradise') portray a boy's rite of passage into adulthood. It was revived for Hamburg Ballet in 1977. Araiz used the same music for *Eternity is Now* choreographed for the Royal Winnipeg Ballet.

foxtrot Popular ballroom dance of American origin danced to a march-like ragtime (slow or fast). From 1913 it was widely danced around the world.

Foyer de la danse Studio behind the stage at the Paris Opera which is now used as a rehearsal stage and a reception venue but which was notorious in the 19th century (during the reign of Dr Véron) as the salon where members of the Jockey Club could meet dancers. Ashton's *Foyer de danse* (mus. Berners, Ballet Club, 1932) was based on Degas's studies of Paris dancers and portrayed an encounter between a dancer (orig. Markova) and her lascivious admirers.

Fracci, Carla (*b* Milan, 20 Aug. 1936) Italian dancer and director. She studied at the La Scala Ballet School from 1946 with V. Volkova and others, graduating into the company in 1954. In 1956 she was promoted soloist and in 1958 principal, becoming established as Italy's leading ballerina but also as the first Italian dancer to win an international reputation in the 20th century. Among the roles she created at La Scala were Juliet in Cranko's *Romeo and Juliet* (1958) and

Elvira in Massine's *Don Giovanni* (1959). She also guested widely around Italy and appeared with many companies abroad, including London Festival Ballet (1959 and 1962), Royal Ballet (1963), Stuttgart Ballet (1965), and Royal Swedish Ballet (1969), and from 1967 was also a principal guest artist with American Ballet Theatre. Her greatest role was Giselle which she danced with many partners including Nureyev, Vasiliev, Kronstam, Baryshnikov, and above all Bruhn with whom she filmed the work in 1969. She was also renowned for her interpretation of other romantic roles, in which she was compared to Taglioni. In 1964 she married the theatre director Beppe Menegatti with whom she formed the occasional touring company Carla Fracci and Dancers. Menegatti also produced many ballets with and for her, collaborating with choreographer Loris Gai in *The Seagull* (after Chekhov, 1968), *Macbeth* (1969), and *The Stone Flower* (1973), among others. In 1990 she danced a reconstruction of Duncan's solo *Fate's Warning* (chor. M. Hodson). She was director of ballet in Naples (1990–1) then in Verona (1995–7) where in 1996 she danced Karsavina's role in Hodson and Archer's reconstruction of Nijinsky's *Jeux*. In 2000 she was appointed director of La Scala Ballet, appearing with that company in Dec. 1999 in a revival of Manzotti's *Excelsior*, but shortly afterwards became director of the Rome Opera Ballet, consolidating that company's classical repertory and performing as occasional character dancer. She appeared as Karsavina in Ross's 1980 film *Nijinsky* and her television film, *An Hour with Carla Fracci*, won the Goldon Rose of Montreux in 1973. She was a recipient of the Leopardo d'oro in 1959.

Franca, Celia (*b* London, 25 Jun. 1921; *d* Ottawa, 19 Feb. 2007) British-Canadian dancer, choreographer, and ballet director. She studied at the Guildhall School of Music and at the Royal Academy of Dancing with Rambert, Tudor, and Idzikowski. She made her debut in 1936 in the revue *Spread it Abroad* (chor. Gore) and in the same year joined Ballet Rambert where she stayed until 1939 creating the role of the Dope Fiend in Gore's *Paris Soir* (1939). Still in London, she danced with Ballet des Trois Arts (1939), the Arts Theatre (1940), and International Ballet (1941), then between 1941 and 1946 she danced with Sadler's Wells Ballet creating roles in, among others, Helpmann's *Hamlet* (1942) and *Miracle in the Gorbals* (1944). Between 1947 and 1949 she danced with Metropolitan Ballet and between 1949 and 1951 with Ballet Workshop (both in London) as well as guesting with Ballet Rambert in 1950. She choreographed her first ballet for Ballet Rambert, *Constanza's Lament* (mus. Beethoven, 1938), and went on to create two works for Sadler's Wells

Theatre Ballet, including *Khadra* (mus. Sibelius) as well as ballets for television. In 1951 she moved to Canada where she founded the National Ballet of Canada and later its associate school. She was dancer with the company (1951–9), director (1951–74), and also choreographer of several works including her own versions of *The Nutracker* (1964) and *Cinderella* (1968). After retiring from the company she was a guest teacher in Canada and abroad. She published *The National Ballet of Canada* (with Ken Bell, Toronto, 1979).

France Ballet in France originated from early entertainments at court which were composed of music, dance, and poetry. The seminal production **Ballet comique de la reine* (commissioned by Catherine de Médicis in Paris, 1581) set an example from which later examples of *ballet de cour evolved. Most of the greatest dancers and ballet masters of the 16th and 17th centuries were associated with court ballet in Paris and in the late 17th century a systematic attempt to raise standards of dance was instituted, first with the founding of the *Académie Royale de Danse in 1661 and secondly with the opening of a dancing school attached to the *Académie Royale de Musique in 1672. In the same year *Lully was appointed director of the Académie Royale de Musique and, working in close collaboration with *Beauchamps, rapidly raised the status of dance. In his ballet *Triomphe de l'amour* (1681) Mlle de *Lafontaine became the first female professional dancer to appear at the Palais Royal. During the 18th century travelling ballet masters like Noverre and Dauberval encouraged the spread of ballet to the provinces. Noverre's *Caprices de Galatée* (1758), remarkable for being the first ballet to be performed without any spoken text, was danced in Lyons while Dauberval's *La Fille mal gardée* (1789), the first notable ballet about everyday life and ordinary people, was premiered in Bordeaux. Ballet reached a pitch of popularity during the first half of the 19th century with Romantic classics like *La Sylphide* (F. Taglioni, 1832) and Coralli-Perrot's *Giselle* (1841). This was the great age of the ballerina and Taglioni, Elssler, Grisi, and Cerrito were starry rivals for the public's devotion and the critics' favour. This golden era ended with the death of Emma *Livry, Taglioni's natural successor, and though fine dancers were still produced by the school, new ballets tended to be stale repetitions of old formulas. The public's enthusiasm was transferred to opera and Paris was no longer regarded as the ballet capital of the world. Saint-Léon's *Coppélia* (1870) and the premiere of Mérante's *Sylvia* at the opening of the opulent Palais Garnier theatre in 1876 were only temporary pauses in the decline of the art, the French having lost their greatest native choreographer, Marius *Petipa, to Russia. It was from Russia, though, that Paris received its next injection of energy, with the regular seasons given by Diaghilev's Ballets Russes between 1909 and 1929. Many French composers, painters, and writers collaborated with Diaghilev on new work, and ballet again became a highly fashionable art form. Jacques Rouché, director of the Paris Opera from 1914, was stimulated by the Russian competition and commissioned new ballet scores from composers like Dukas and Ravel as well as inviting Fokine, Pavlova, Spessivtseva, and others to work in his theatre. When *Lifar took over direction of the Opera Ballet in 1929 he revitalized the company and enthused a new public (though he alienated the less disinterested balletomanes by closing the *Foyer de la danse to the public—hence ending liaisons between dancers and their admirers at the Opera). After 1945 many new, small, adventurous companies emerged both within and outside Paris, such as *Ballets des Champs-Elysées, the de *Cuevas Ballet, the companies of *Petit, *Charrat, *Babilée, and a few years later those of *Béjart and *Miskovitch. Lifar was recalled to the Opera in 1947 (after having left in 1944 for political reasons), and worked there until 1959. He was succeeded by a rapid turnover of directors and the Opera went into an artistic decline. During the 1970s it began to look to a younger audience by bringing in work by modern choreographers such as Cunningham and Carlson and between 1983 and 1989 entered a new, if controversial, period under the direction of Nureyev. He brought forward young stars like Guillem, Platel, Hilaire, and Jude and widened the repertoire with works by Forsythe, Tharp, and others. Dupond and his successor Brigitte Lefèvre also continued this trend bringing in works by younger choreographers like Angelin *Preljocaj. Outside Paris the proliferation of dance activity continued under the government's policy of decentralization. In 1966 André Malraux set up the first of the state Maisons de la Culture which provided important bases for all the arts, and the *Ballet-Théâtre Contemporain, based first in Amiens (1968–72) and then in Angers (1972–8), led the way in developing an experimental new edge in ballet. *Ballet du Rhin was founded in 1972 and in 1972 Petit took over *Ballet National de Marseilles. Other regional ballet companies include *Ballet du Nord and Ballet-Théâtre Français de Nancy. Although Béjart, France's most prolific contemporary choreographer, left to work in Brussels and later Switzerland, he continued to maintain a strong presence in his native country. During the 1980s a large number of modern dance choreographers (several profiting from generous funding in regional choreographic centres) emerged, including Dominic Baguouet, Maguy Marin, Angelin Preljocaj, Jean Claude Gallotta, Daniel Larrieu, and Claude Brumachon. Together these have created a powerful international reputation for new French dance. Numerous festivals including those at Avignon, Paris, and Lyons as well as adventurous programming by venues like Paris's Théâtre de la Ville have ensured that a very wide range of international companies are seen in the country every year.

Franck, César (*b* Liège, 10 Dec. 1822; *d* Paris, 8 Nov. 1890) Belgian composer. He wrote no ballet scores but his concert music has been used for dance, for example in Isadora Duncan's *Redemption* (Paris, 1915), Ashton's *Symphonic Variations* (London, 1946), Babilée's *Psyché* (Paris, 1948), and in Doug Varone's *Heaven* (Jacob's Pillow, 2003).

Frankfurt Ballet (Ballett Frankfurt) Ballet performances were given at the Frankfurt National Theatre (opened 1782) and at the Frankfurt Opera (opened 1880) but an independent ballet company at the Opera did not emerge until after the Second World War. There was a fast turnover of directors during this period, including Lutz (1948–51), Gore (1957–9), T. Gsovsky (1959–66), Neumeier (1969–73), and Catá (1973–6), until William Forsythe's appointment in 1984. The company became a showcase for Forsythe's choreography, with 35 dancers performing on the opera and playhouse stages in Frankfurt's main theatrical complex. In 1996 it also acquired the performing space of TAT, a converted tramway depot. Forsythe left the company in 2004 to found his own troupe after which the company was disbanded.

Frankie and Johnny Ballet in one act with choreography by R. Page and Stone, libretto by Michael Blandford and Jerome Moross (also music), and design by Paul Dupont. Premiered 19 Jun. 1938 by the Page-Stone Ballet at Great Northern Theatre, Chicago, with Page and Stone. It is based on the popular American ballad about a prostitute who shoots her faithless pimp. It has been revived by several companies, including Ballet Russe de Monte Carlo (1945), Pittsburgh Ballet (1976), Dance Theatre of Harlem (1981), and Joffrey Ballet (1999).

Franklin, Frederic (*b* Liverpool, 13 Jun. 1914) British-US dancer, choreographer, teacher, and director. He studied with Shelagh Elliott-Clarke in Liverpool then with Kyasht, N. Legat, and Egorova. He made his amateur stage debut as a tap dancer and his professional debut with Josephine Baker and Mistinguette in the cabaret at Casino de Paris, 1931. From 1933 he danced in London cabarets, musicals, and operetta becoming soloist in the Markova-Dolin company (1935–7). In 1938

he was appointed principal dancer with Ballet Russe de Monte Carlo, becoming ballet master in 1944. A dynamic, dramatically gifted dancer, he created roles in many ballets including Massine's *Gaîté parisienne* (1938), *Seventh Symphony* (1938), and *Rouge et noir* (1939), Ashton's *The Devil's Holiday* (1939), and de Mille's *Rodeo* (1942). In 1949 he and Danilova (his regular partner) were guest stars with Sadler's Wells Ballet and in 1952 he founded the Slavenska-Franklin ballet with Mia Slavenska, touring the US and the Far East. He returned to Ballet Russe de Monte Carlo (1954–6), after which he worked as director or adviser with many companies including American Ballet Theatre (1961), National Ballet, Washington, DC, and its associated school (1962–74), where he also choreographed several works; Pittsburgh Ballet Theatre (1974–7); and Cincinnati Ballet, where he was resident choreographer from 1978, creating his lyrical *Sylvia pas de deux* (mus. Delibes, 1978). He also continued to perform character roles. His legendary memory has enabled him to stage classics and the Ballet Russe repertoire for La Scala, Milan (1961), New York City Ballet (1964), and for many American companies, such as Dance Theatre of Harlem for whom he staged their Creole version of *Giselle* (1984); Tulsa Ballet, for whom he staged his *Coppélia* (1995); and American Ballet Theatre, with whom he formed a permanent association in 1996, staging ballets and also performing character roles such as Madge in *La Sylphide* and the Friar in *Romeo and Juliet*.

Freefall Ballet in one act with choreography and design by Tetley and music by Max Schubel. Premiered 13 Apr. 1967 by the Repertory Dance Theatre at the University of Utah. It is set to Schubel's Concerto for 5 Instruments (*Insected Surfaces*) and its choreography parallels the free association of images and ideas. It was revived for Ballet Rambert, 13 Nov. 1967, and again, with new designs by N. Baylis, in 1975.

Fridericia, Allan *See* ROSEN, ELSA-MARIANNE VON.

Froman, Margarita (*b* Moscow, 8 Nov. 1890; *d* Boston, 24 Mar. 1970) Russian-Yugoslav dancer, choreographer, teacher, and ballet mistress. She studied at the Imperial Theatre School, Moscow, graduating into the Bolshoi Theatre in 1909. Between 1914 and 1916 she danced with Diaghilev's Ballets Russes then in 1917 returned to the Bolshoi as ballerina for a year, leaving in 1918 to dance with Mordkin. In 1921 she and her three brothers emigrated to Yugoslavia where they worked at the Zagreb Opera Ballet. As ballerina and choreographer she initiated the revival of ballet in Yugoslavia, staging the classics and the

Ballets Russes repertoire (alone and in collaboration with her brothers) as well as creating several works including *The Gingerbread Man* (mus. Baranovič, 1923). In 1937 she worked as choreographer at the State Opera Ballet Belgrade, creating works such as *The Legend of Ochrid* (mus. Hristić, 1947) as well as founding and directing various schools (her pupils included Mia Slavenska). In the early 1950s she moved to the US where she taught at her own school in Connecticut.

Frontier Modern dance in one act, with choreography by Graham, music by Horst, set by Noguchi, and costumes by Graham. Premiered 28 Apr. 1935 at the Guild Theater, New York, with Graham and her company. It portrays the determination and energy of the early pioneers. It was originally danced as part of a larger work, *Perspectives Nos. 1 and 2*, but the group section in this work, 'Marching Song', was subsequently dropped.

Frutos, Javier De (*b* Caracas, 15 May 1963) Venezuelan dancer and choreographer. He trained in Venezuela, at the London School of Contemporary Dance, at the Cunningham studios, and with Sara Rudner and others in New York, making his debut in Danza Teatro de Abelardo Gameche in 1983. He also performed with several other companies including Laura Dean Dancers (1989–92). His first work, *The Dying Swan* (mus. Saint-Saëns), was choreographed in 1990, after which he created and performed a string of solo works including *Sweetie J* (mus. Bartók, 1995). He subsequently founded his own company for which he created works like *Grass*, set to music from Puccini's *Madam Butterfly* (1997) as well as creating works for other companies including *Elsa Canasta* (mus. Cole Porter, 2003) for Rambert Dance Company and *Milagros* (mus. Stravinsky, 2006) for Royal New Zealand Ballet. Meticulously crafted, his works often feature an explicit even confrontational treatment of sex and violence. Between 2006 and 2008 he was director of Phoenix Dance Theatre where in addition to reviving classic modern dance repertory for the company, including Limon's *Chaconne*, he created several new works including *Paseillo* (mus. Mozart, 2006) and *Blue Roses* (2008). He subsequently worked as a freelance choreographer, his works including *Eternal Damnation to Sancho and Sanchez* (mus. Ravel, 2009). He has also choreographed for musicals including *Carousel* (2006) for Chichester Festival.

Fuller, Loie (*b* Fullersburg, Ill., 22 Jan. 1862; *d* Paris, 21 Jan. 1928) US dancer, choreographer, designer, and director. She had no formal dance education but gained her experience on stage as an actress, playwright, singer, dancer, and producer between 1865 and 1891. In 1891 a chance manœuvre dealing with an over-long skirt gave her the idea of *The Serpentine Dance* (1891), a solo whose effects were created by manipulating long trains of silk. Her subsequent dances gained her a world-wide audience, particularly in Europe where she made her debut in 1892. Embraced as a fellow revolutionary by the Symbolists, Impressionists, and Art Nouveau movements she was painted and sculpted by many artists. Her works employed light, thrown on lengths of diaphanous silk which she then manipulated with her own body movements and with long sticks to create an exotic range of forms, as in *The Butterfly* (1892), *Clouds* (1893), and *Fire Dance* (1895). From 1900 she began creating group works and using more complex costumes and light effects. She formed her own school in 1908 and in the same year published her autobiography, *Quinze ans de ma vie* (English translation, London, 1913). She continued performing until 1925 during which time she made significant contributions to the arts of stage costume and lighting.

Fuoco, Sofia (orig. Maria Brambilla; *b* Milan, 16 Jan. 1830; *d* Carate Lario, 4 Jun. 1916) Italian dancer. She studied with Blasis at the school of La Scala, Milan, from *c*.1837 becoming one of his special group of 'Pleiades'. She made her debut at La Scala in 1839 and was precociously appointed prima ballerina assoluta in 1843, in the same year dancing the first Giselle there. A lively dancer (*fuoco* signifies fire and passion in Italian), she acquired something of a cult following, though she was renowned more for her impressive technique than her acting ability. In 1846 she created one of the roles in F. Taglioni's staging of Perrot's *Pas de quatre*. Between 1846 and 1850 she danced various seasons at the Paris Opera where she was known as La Pointue due to her brilliance on pointe; she appeared in London in 1847 and 1848, and during the last decade of her career divided her time between Italy, France, and Spain. She retired in the late 1850s.

Fuzelier, Louis (*b* 1677; *d* 1752) French writer who wrote the libretti for several ballets, including *Les Indes galantes* (1727).

G

Gable, Christopher (*b* London, 13 Mar. 1940; *d* Halifax, 23 Oct. 1998) British dancer, actor, and ballet director. He studied at the Royal Ballet School and joined the touring section of the Royal Ballet in 1957, promoted to soloist in 1959 and principal in 1961 Early on he was paired with Lynn Seymour; their mutual flair for dramatic interpretation making theirs one of the most acclaimed partnerships in British ballet. A glamorous stage presence, Gable was also fine danseur noble material, but after transferring to Covent Garden in 1963 he stayed for only four years, before pursuing a career in acting. He created roles in MacMillan's *The Invitation* (1960) and *Images of Love* (1964), and Ashton's *The Two Pigeons* (1961). MacMillan additionally created *Romeo and Juliet* (1965) for him and Seymour, although its premiere was danced by Fonteyn and Nureyev, a snub that soured Gable's subsequent relationship with the Covent Garden management. His acting career was relatively successful, including the title role in Ken Russell's film *The Boy Friend* (1972) and Lysander in Peter Brook's 1970 staging of *A Midsummer Night's Dream*. In 1982 he opened the Central School of Ballet in London, which he continued to direct until his death. In 1987 he was appointed artistic director of Northern Ballet Theatre leading the campaign to save the company from potential closure following a threat to its public funding. He created the role of L. S. Lowry in Gillian Lynne's *A Simple Man* for Northern Ballet Theatre in 1987, also the role of Don Quixote in his own production, *The Amazing Adventures of Don Quixote*, for the same company in 1989. He staged many productions for NBT, including *Giselle* (1990, 1997), *Romeo and Juliet* (1991), *Swan Lake* (1992), *A Christmas Carol* (1992), *Cinderella* (1993), *The Brontës* (with Gillian Lynne, 1995), *Dracula* (1996), and *The Hunchback of Notre Dame* (with Michael Pink, 1998).

Gabovich, Mikhail (*b* Velikiye Gulyaki, Ukraine, 7 Dec. 1905; *d* Moscow, 12 Jul. 1965) Russian dancer and teacher. He studied at the Bolshoi Ballet School (Moscow Theatre School), a pupil of Alexander Gorsky and Vasily Tikhomirov, and graduated into the company in 1924 where he continued as a soloist until his retirement in 1952. One of the most acclaimed of the Bolshoi's leading dancers, he excelled in both the traditional repertoire and in modern works such as *Fountain of Bakhchisarai* and *The Bronze Horseman*. His partnership with Ulanova was much admired. He created roles in several ballets, including Antoine in Vainonen's Moscow staging of *The Flames of Paris* (1934), Vladimir in Zakharov's *The Prisoner of the Caucasus* (1938), Andrei in Zakharov's *Taras Bulba* (1941), the Prince in Zakharov's *Cinderella* (1945), and Romeo in Lavrovsky's 1946 Moscow version of *Romeo and Juliet*. He was director of the Bolshoi Ballet School (1954–8), and continued to teach there until his death. Father of the Bolshoi dancer Mikhail Mikhailovich Gabovich. Also a writer about dance, including ballet theory and criticism. Author of *The Ballet School of the Bolshoi Theatre* (Moscow, 1957).

Gad, Rose (*b* Copenhagen, 20 Sept. 1968) Danish dancer. She studied at the Royal Danish Ballet School from 1978 and after joining the company as an apprentice in 1985 was promoted to principal in 1991. She danced her first major role aged just 15, Cupid in Grigorovich's production of *Don Quixote*. A delicately formed, elegant dancer, she was ideally suited to the Bournonville repertoire but also danced much of the 20th-century repertory including Robbins's *Afternoon of a Faun* and *The Concert*, Balanchine's *Theme and Variations*, *Tchaikovsky Pas de deux*, *Apollo*, and *Serenade*, and MacMillan's *Manon*, the latter showcasing her powerful dramatic presence. She also danced the leading ballerina roles in *Giselle*, *The Sleeping Beauty*, and *Swan Lake*. In 1991 she created the title role in Flindt's full-length *Caroline Mathilde*. In 1997 she was appointed principal dancer at the Hamburg Ballet but returned to the Royal Danish Ballet in 1999. She was the first recipient of the Erik Bruhn Prize (1988). She retired in 2010.

Gadd, Ulf (*b* Gothenburg, 8 Mar. 1943; *d* Bali, 9 Jun. 2008) Swedish dancer, choreographer, and ballet master. He studied at the Royal Swedish Ballet School, joining the Royal Swedish Ballet in 1960. He became a soloist in 1965. In 1968 he danced with the Harkness Ballet in the US, before returning to Sweden. In 1969 he made his choreographic debut in Gothenburg with *Ebb and Flood* (mus. Telemann), which he later staged for London Festival Ballet. In 1970 he created a very successful version of *The Miraculous Mandarin*, which he went on to stage for the Royal Swedish Ballet, American Ballet Theatre, and the Berlin Opera Ballet. A natural popularizer, impatient with the academic conventions of ballet, he co-founded the New Swedish Ballet (Les Nouveaux Ballets Suédois) in 1970, which toured Europe. Between 1972 and 1988 he was with Gothenberg Ballet as ballet master, principal dancer, and artistic director (appointed 1976). A list of his works includes *Choreographic Études* (mus. Ohana, Cullberg Ballet, 1973), *Maison de fous* (mus. Viking Dahl, 1973), *Sleeping Beauty* (with B. Holmgren, Royal Swedish Ballet, 1974), *Kalevala* (mus. Sibelius, Gothenburg, 1975), *Queen Kristina* (1978), *Coppélia* (mus. Delibes, 1979), *Diaghilev's Russian Ballet* (1980), *The Rite of Spring* (1982), *The Ring* (mus. Wagner, 1983), and *Tango Buenos Aires 1907* (mus. Argentinian tango, 1985). In 1988 he went to Bali to study its dance and music. Between 1996 and 1999 he returned to Sweden as ballet director in Gothenburg but then went back to Bali where he had converted to Hinduism.

Gades, Antonio (*b* Alicante, 14 Nov. 1936; *d* 20 Jul. 2004), Spanish flamenco dancer and company director. He studied dance in Madrid and performed with Pilar López's company from 1952 to 1961. His first works as a choreographer were created in Italy but in 1963 he returned to Spain to form his own company. Its early success in Barcelona resulted in an invitation to the New York World's Fair in 1964, followed by extensive international touring and in 1978 he was invited by the Spanish Ministry of Culture to form the *National Ballet of Spain (Ballet Nacional Español). In 1974 he created *Blood Wedding*, inspired by Lorca's play and set to music by Emilio de Diego, which was filmed in 1981 by Carlos Saura and starred him and his partner Cristina *Hoyos. Staged in a rehearsal hall, without sets or costumes it was hugely successful, raising the profile of flamenco worldwide and leading to further collaborations between Saura and Gades (*Carmen*, and *El amor brujo*, created for both stage and film). During the 1980s and 1990s Gades formed several companies including Ballet Antonio Gades con Cristina Hoyos, which toured internationally.

Gaîté parisienne Ballet in one act with choreography by Massine, libretto and designs by Comte Étienne de Beaumont, and music by Offenbach arranged by Manuel Rosenthal. Premiered 5 Apr. 1938 by the Ballet Russe de Monte Carlo in Monte Carlo with Tarakanova, Eugénie Delarova, Massine, Jeanette Lauret, Franklin, and Youskevitch. A humorous divertissement set in

a Paris night-club, the ballet portrays the flirtatious interaction between characters from Offenbach's *La Vie parisienne*—a wealthy Peruvian, a Glove-Seller, a Flower Girl, and an Officer. It was Massine's first work for the newly created Ballet Russe de Monte Carlo and in 1941 it was filmed by Warner Brothers and released as *The Gay Parisian*. It was also revived for several companies, including the Royal Swedish Ballet (1956), American Ballet Theatre (1970), London Festival Ballet (1973), and Les Ballets de Monte Carlo (1989). American Ballet Theatre remounted it in 1988 with controversial new costumes by Christian Lacroix.

Gala Performance Ballet in one act with choreography and libretto by Tudor, music by Prokofiev, and designs by Hugh Stevenson. Premiered 5 Dec. 1938 by the London Ballet at Toynbee Hall Theatre, London, with van Praagh, Maude Lloyd, Gerd Larsen, Tudor, and Laing. A wicked parody of ballet conventions, set to Prokofiev's 3rd Piano Concerto and his Classical Symphony, it shows preparations for a gala followed by the gala itself. Three rival ballerinas, La Reine de la danse from Moscow, La Déesse de la danse from Milan, and La Fille de Terpsichore from Paris, compete for the audience's approval. It was revived for several companies including Ballet Rambert (1940), Ballet Theatre (1941), the National Ballet of Canada (1953), Berlin Opera Ballet (1963), Royal Danish Ballet (1970), and Australian Ballet (1990). Although Tudor himself grew to dislike this ballet, it remains one of his most popular creations.

Galeotti, Vincenzo (orig. Vincenzo Tomazelli or Tomasselli; *b* Florence, 5 Mar. 1733; *d* Copenhagen, 16 Dec. 1816) Italian-Danish dancer, choreographer, teacher, and ballet master. Generally considered to be the father of Danish ballet. After studying in Italy with Gaspero Angiolini, he danced with many European companies before settling in Venice, where between 1765 and 1769 he choreographed opera ballets and divertissements. After time spent dancing at London's King's Theatre (1769–71), where he staged several works including Gluck's *Orfeo*, he returned to Venice as ballet master of the San Moise Theatre (1771–5). From there he was invited to Copenhagen in 1775 as ballet master, solo dancer, and teacher at the Royal Theatre. He spent the remainder of his life there, laying the foundations of the Royal Danish Ballet. He continued to dance until the age of 77 and made his last appearance on stage as Friar Laurence in *Romeo and Juliet*. He was responsible for creating a repertoire of more than 30 ballets for Copenhagen. A list of his works includes *Dido Abandoned* (1777), *Don Juan* (1781), *Semiramis* (1787), *Telemachus on the Isle of Calypso* (1792), *Annette and Lubin* (1797),

Lagertha (mus. Claus Schall, 1801, the first ballet dealing with a Nordic theme), *Inez de Castro* (1804), *Romeo and Juliet* (1811), and *Macbeth* (1816). His most popular work was a comedy, *The Whims of Cupid and the Ballet Master* (mus. Jens Lolle, 1786), which is the world's oldest surviving ballet, still performed in Denmark.

Galili, Itzik (*b* Tel Aviv, 1961) Israeli dancer, choreographer and director. He started training late, taking classes in folk, classical, and contemporary dance before performing with Bat-Dor Company and then with Batsheva. He began choreographing in 1990 (*Double Time*) and in 1991 moved to the Netherlands to create works on his own group of dancers including *The Butterfly Effect* (1992). In 1997 he founded a permanent, publicly funded company NND/Galili Dance, based in Groningen. Here he created numerous works, including *Beautiful You* (1999), *For Heaven's Sake* (2001), *Mono Lisa* (2003), *Hikarrizatto* (2004), *Exile Within* (2006), and *Heads or Tales* (2007). In 2009 he joined Krisztina de Châtel to form a new company, Dansgroep Amsterdam, its repertory created by themselves, their dancers, and invited choreographers, including Mark Baldwin.

Galili's fluid, rhythmically exact style incorporates influences from various forms, including hip-hop, samba, classical, and contemporary dance, as well as elements from film and theatre. His evocations of human relationships are frequently filtered through a wry sense of the absurd. A prolific choreographer, his works are in the repertory of many companies including Stuttgart Ballet, Ballets de Monte Carlo, Batsheva, Les Grands Ballets Canadiens, Royal Finnish Ballet, Royal Winnipeg Ballet, Rambert Dance Company, and Dutch National Ballet. He has also choreographed for television including *A Sense of Gravity* (2002).

galliard (**gaillard**) A light-hearted vigorous court dance performed in triple time, mainly after a pavane. It is thought to have originated in Lombardy. It was particularly popular at the court of England's Elizabeth I, where a variant known as the volta was much loved by the Queen.

galop A spirited North German round dance in 2/4 time. It was first popular during the 1820s and eventually spread from Germany to France and England, where it was absorbed into the quadrille. It is characterized by a change of step or hop at the end of each musical phrase. The galop was also popular on the stage of the Paris Opera in the Romantic period, being danced in both operas and ballet-pantomimes.

Garafola, Lynn (*b* New York, 12 Dec. 1946) US critic and writer on dance. She studied Comparative Literature at City University of New York and from 1985 has been a freelance critic, feature writer, and contributing editor of *Dance Magazine*; series editor of Studies in Dance History (1992–8); one of America's leading dance historians. She is the author and editor of many books on dance including *Diaghilev's Ballets Russes* (1989, reprinted 1998), *André Levinson on Dance: Writings from Paris in the Twenties* (editor, with Joan Acocella, 1991), *Rethinking the Sylph: Essays on the Romantic Ballet* (editor, 1997), *José Limón: An Unfinished Memoir* (editor, 1998), *Dance for a City: Fifty Years of the New York City Ballet* (editor, with Eric Foner, 1999), *The Ballets Russes and Its World* (editor, with Nancy Van Norman Baer, 1999), and *Legacies of Twentieth-Century Dance* (2005). She has also translated *The Diaries of Marius Petipa* (1992). She is Professor of Dance Studies at Barnard and in 2005 was elected Fellow to the American Academy of Arts and Sciences.

García Lorca, Federico *See* LORCA, FEDERICO GARCÍA.

Gardel, Maximilien (*b* Mannheim, 18 Dec. 1741; *d* Paris, 11 Mar. 1787) French dancer, choreographer, and ballet master. He was born the son of a ballet master at the court of King Stanislas of Poland and studied at the Paris Opera School (Académie Royale de Musique) from 1755, making his official debut at the Paris Opera in 1759. In 1772 he became the first dancer to appear without a mask or a wig when he performed Apollo in Rameau's *Castor et Pollux*, possibly making this bold move in order to distinguish himself from Gaetano Vestris, who had originally been scheduled to take the role. In 1773 he was appointed ballet master, along with Dauberval, at the Paris Opera. In 1781 he became ballet master, succeeding Noverre. He was a keen exponent of Noverre's revolutionary concept of the *ballet d'action, promoting dance as a dramatic art rather than decorative entertainment. He often drew on the comic operas of the period for his stories. In 1787 he suffered a minor cut to his foot which became infected, and he died. He was succeeded by his younger brother Pierre Gardel. A list of his works for the Paris Opera includes *Ninette à la cour* (1778), *Mirza et Lindor* (mus. Gossec, 1779), *La Rosière* (1783), *Le Premier Navigateur* (mus. Grétry, 1785), *Le Coq du village* (mus. Favart, 1787), and *Le Déserteur* (1788).

Gardel, Pierre (*b* Nancy, 4 Feb. 1758; *d* Paris, 18 Oct. 1840) French dancer, choreographer, teacher, and ballet master. He was taught by his elder brother, Maximilien, at the Paris Opera School from 1771 and became premier danseur noble of the Paris Opera in 1780. In 1780–1 he was a leading dancer with Noverre's company at the King's Theatre in London. In 1787 he succeeded his brother as chief ballet master of the Paris Opera. A prolific choreographer, he often shocked audiences with his choice of subject-matter, which included biblical stories, but won wide popularity with the vivid spectacle of his productions. Unlike his contemporaries, he often chose to commission original music for his ballets. He retired in 1829. A list of his works includes *Télémaque* (mus. Müller, 1790), *Psyché* (mus. Müller, 1790), *Le Jugement de Pâris* (1793), *La Dansomanie* (mus. Méhul, 1800), *Achille à Scyros* (mus. Cherubini, 1804), *Paul et Virginie* (mus. Kreutzer, 1806), *La Fête de Mars* (mus. Kreutzer, 1809), *Persée et Andromède* (mus. Méhul, 1810), *Proserpine* (mus. Schneitzhoeffer, 1818), and *La Servante justifiée* (mus. Kreutzer, 1818). He also composed the dances for Mozart's *Don Giovanni* at its Paris Opera debut in 1805. From 1799 to 1815 he was director of the Paris Opera Ballet School, where one of his pupils was Blasis. He was married to the ballerina Marie Gardel, who performed in his ballets.

Garden of Earthly Delights, The Full-length dance theatre production with choreography by Martha Clarke, music by Richard Peaslee, lighting by Paul Gallo, costumes by Jane Greenwood, libretto by Peter Beagle. Premiered by the Crowsnest company at St Clement's Church in New York in Nov. 1984. A large-scale work inspired by the paintings of Hieronymus Bosch, its fusion of dance with acrobatics and spectacle was one of the pioneering mixed-media productions. It was revived by Rambert Dance Company in 1994.

Garnier *See* PALAIS GARNIER.

Gaskell, Sonia (*b* Vilkaviskis, 14 Apr. 1904; *d* Paris, 9 Jul. 1974) Lithuanian-Dutch dancer, teacher, choreographer, and ballet director. One of the most important figures in the development of Dutch ballet. She studied in Kharkov in the Ukraine but fled to Palestine in 1921 to avoid the pogroms against Jews in Russia. She arrived in Paris in 1925 where she trained with Lubov Egorova and Léo Staats. She began her career as a cabaret dancer, touring Europe in the 1930s, then became founder and choreographer of Les Ballets de Paris (1936–9) before going to Amsterdam in 1939 as a teacher with her Dutch husband. During the Second World War she went into hiding, although managed to continue giving ballet lessons, and afterwards ran several companies, Ballet Studio '45, Ballet Recital, and the Netherlands Ballet. She also founded the Netherlands Ballet Academy in The Hague. In 1961 she became artistic director of the newly formed Dutch National Ballet, a position she held until 1968. Although she choreographed many ballets for her various companies, it was as a teacher and director that Gaskell made her greatest contribution. She gave the Netherlands a ballet company capable of performing the 19th-century classics, and promoted new choreographers from within her ranks, notably van Dantzig.

GATOB The abbreviation for Gosudarstvenny Akademichesky Teatre Opery i Baleta, or State Academic Theatre for Opera and Ballet. It was the name given to St Petersburg's Mariinsky Theatre, home of the *Kirov Ballet, between 1917 and 1935.

Gautier, Théophile (*b* Tarbes, 30 Aug. (some sources say 31 Aug.) 1811; *d* Neuilly, 23 Oct. 1872) French poet, writer, ballet critic, and librettist. As art and drama critic of *La Presse* from 1836 to 1855 he wielded considerable influence on the development of French romantic ballet during the 1830s and 1840s. He also wrote as a critic for *Le Moniteur universel* (1855–68). He was Carlotta Grisi's greatest admirer (and married her sister) and, in collaboration with Vernoy de Saint-Georges, wrote the libretto of *Giselle* for her in 1841. He also wrote the librettos for *La Péri* (1843), *Pâquerette* (1851), *Gemma* (1854), and *Sacountala* (1858). *Le Spectre de la rose* (1911) is based on one of his poems while *Le Pavillon d'Armide* (1907) is based on one of his stories. Some of his copious writings on dance were collected by C. W. Beaumont and published as *The Romantic Ballet as Seen by Théophile Gautier* (London, 1932, reprinted London, 1973). Ivor Guest's 1986 collection entitled *Gautier on Dance* is considered the best English edition of Gautier's dance writings.

gavotte A dance in 4/4 time and steady rhythm which originated in the Pays de Gap region of France (where the residents were known as Gavots). It started in the 14th century as a simple peasant dance but became a fashionable court dance under Marie Antoinette. In its more complex form, it was performed by professional dancers.

Gayané Ballet in four acts with choreography by Nina Anisimova, libretto by Konstantin Derzhavin, music by Khachaturian, sets by Natan Altman, and costumes by Tatyana Bruni. Premiered 9 Dec. 1942 by the Kirov Ballet in Perm, with Dudinskaya, Zubkovsky, Konstantin Sergeyev, Tatayna Vecheslova, and Boris Shavrov. The ballet, set in an Armenian cotton collective, tells the story of the cotton picker Gayané and her lover Armen, set against a background of political and military intrigue. The ballet, firmly within the Soviet school of *Socialist Realism, celebrates the virtues of collective labour and incorporates Armenian folk dance into the choreography. The ballet includes the famous Sabre Dance, often performed on its own as a showpiece. Anisimova re-staged the ballet twice for the Kirov in St Petersburg, in 1945 and 1952. Vainonen choreographed a new version for the Bolshoi in Moscow in 1957, while Anisimova restaged her version for the Bolshoi in 1961. Boris Eifman choreographed yet another new staging for the Maly Theatre in St Petersburg in 1972.

Gé, George (orig. George Grönfeldt; *b* St Petersburg, 1893; *d* Helsinki, 19 Nov. 1962) Finnish dancer, choreographer, and ballet master. One of the pioneers of ballet in Finland. He studied with Legat and was engaged as the first Finnish ballet master of the Helsinki Suomalainen Opera (1921–35), the beginnings of the Finnish National Ballet. His first production was *Swan Lake* (1922). In 1935 he relocated to France where he worked with Fokine and the Ballets Russes de Monte Carlo, also in Paris at the Folies-Bergère. From 1939 to 1945 he was ballet master of the Royal Swedish Ballet. He returned to Helsinki in 1955 to become ballet master of the Finnish National Ballet for a second time, a post he held until his death. One of his most noted achievements was the reconstruction of Fokine's *L'Épreuve d'amour*.

Geltser, Ekaterina (Geltzer) (*b* Moscow, 14 Nov. 1876; *d* Moscow, 12 Dec. 1962) Russian-Soviet dancer who is generally regarded as the first 'Soviet' ballerina. She was the daughter of Vasily Geltser, mime artist and ballet master at the Bolshoi Ballet (who also co-wrote the original libretto for *Swan Lake*) and studied at the Bolshoi School from 1884, graduating into the company in 1894. She took further studies with Christian Johansson and Petipa in St Petersburg. In 1896 she went to St Petersburg to dance with the Mariinsky for two years, then returned to the Bolshoi where she was promoted to first ballerina in 1901. A stocky dancer with a robust, even heroic style, Geltser was the definitive Bolshoi ballerina in the early part of the 20th century, her forceful stage personality showcased especially in the dramatic roles of Gorsky. She created the role of Swanilda in Gorsky's new staging of *Coppélia* (1905), Colombine in his *Harlequinade* (1907), the title role in his *Salammbô* (1910), Medora in his 1912 staging of *Le Corsaire*, and Tsar-Maiden in his *Little Humpbacked Horse* (1914). She also danced the traditional ballerina repertory, excelling most in the demi-caractère roles of Kitri and Esmeralda. She appeared with Diaghilev's Ballets Russes in Paris in 1910; the following year at the Alhambra Theatre in London with dancers from the Bolshoi. She also appeared at the Metropolitan Opera House in New York with Mordkin's All-Star Imperial Russian Ballet, dancing Odette-Odile in the first complete *Swan Lake* ever seen in America

(1911). One of her most significant creations was the role of Tao-Hoa in the groundbreaking Soviet ballet *The Red Poppy* (1927), choreographed by her husband and stage partner Vassily *Tikhomirov. She retired from the Bolshoi in 1935, although continued to tour extensively in Russia. She was one of the first ballerinas to be awarded the title of People's Artist of the USSR (1925).

Genée, (Dame) Adeline (orig. Anina Jensen; *b* Hinnerup, Århus, 6 Jan. 1878; *d* Esher, 23 Apr. 1970) Danish-British dancer. She studied with her aunt and uncle in Denmark, making her debut in Christiania, Oslo, at the age of 10 in their touring company. In 1893 she joined the Centralhallen Theatre in Stettin, moving to the Berlin Court Opera in 1896, and shortly afterwards to the Munich Court Opera. In 1897 she moved to London, beginning her ten-year reign as lead ballerina at the Empire Theatre, and introducing ballet to a wide public at a time when there were no British ballet companies. The first of many US tours followed. She made her New York debut in 1908 in Ziegfeld's *The Soul Kiss* and went on to enjoy great success in America in musicals. From 1912 she also danced at the Coliseum and the Alhambra in London, and managed tours of Australia and New Zealand in between. A natural soubrette her most famous role was Swanilda in *Coppélia*, which was perfectly suited to the vivacity of her personality and the brilliance of her technique. She retired from the stage in 1917. Today she is most widely remembered as the founder and president of the *Royal Academy of Dancing (previously known as the London Association of Operatic Dancing) from 1920 to 1954. She was also a founder-member of the Camargo Society. The Adeline Genée Gold Medal is the highest award given to a dancer by the RAD. Dame Commander of the British Empire, 1950.

Georgi, Yvonne (*b* Leipzig, 29 Oct. 1903; *d* Hanover, 25 Jan. 1975) German dancer, choreographer, ballet director, and teacher. An important figure in the German dance renaissance of the 1950s and 1960s. She studied in Leipzig, at the Dalcroze Institute in Hellerau (1920) and from 1921 at the Wigman School in Dresden, where she performed with the Wigman group. Although trained in the Wigman aesthetic, and with no significant classical influences in her background, she maintained an interest in ballet and eventually became closely associated with it. She made her Leipzig debut in 1923, and toured as a solo recitalist throughout Europe and North America; additionally presenting duet evenings with Harald Kreutzberg. In 1924 she joined Kurt Jooss's company in Münster. She was ballet mistress in Gera (1925) and in Hanover (1926–31, 1933–6), where she also opened a school. She additionally worked in the Netherlands, where in 1931 she founded a dance school and a performing group in Amsterdam, which eventually became the Ballets Yvonne Georgi. In 1941 the group became the resident company of the Amsterdam Opera House and Georgi remained in Holland during the course of the war. Afterwards she was in Paris, choreographing Berger's 1950 film *Ballerina*, and in Germany where she moved in 1951, as ballet mistress of the Abraxas company and then Düsseldorf Opera Ballet (1951–4). She was ballet director in Hanover (1954–70) and director of the dance department at Hanover's Academy of Music until 1973. Although a minor choreographer, she staged ballets throughout Germany and her 1962 ballet *Metamorphosen* is considered one of the outstanding German ballets of the period.

Georgiadis, Nicholas (*b* Athens, 14 Sept. 1923; *d* 10 Mar. 2001) Greek theatre designer. His career was launched by Kenneth MacMillan who commissioned him to design his first professional ballet, *Danses concertantes*, in 1955, while Georgiadis was still a student at London's Slade School of Art. He subsequently designed MacMillan's *House of Birds* (1955), *Noctambules* (1956), *The Burrow* (1958), *Agon* (1958), *The Invitation* (1960), *Las Hermanas* (1963), *Romeo and Juliet* (1965), *Swan Lake* (Berlin, 1969), *Manon* (1974), *Mayerling* (1978), and *The Prince of the Pagodas* (1989). He also designed Cranko's *Daphnis and Chloe* (Stuttgart, 1962) and Nureyev's *Swan Lake* (Vienna, 1964), *Sleeping Beauty* (Milan, 1966, National Ballet of Canada, 1972, London Festival Ballet, 1975), *Nutcracker* (London, 1968), and *Raymonda* (Zurich, 1972). He was ranked among the leading ballet designers of the latter half of the 20th century.

Gerdt, Pavel (orig. Paul Friedrich Gerdt; *b* Volinkino, nr. St Petersburg, 4 Dec. 1844; *d* Vamaljoki, Finland, 12 Aug. 1917) Russian dancer and teacher, who was the leading male dancer in late 19th-century Russia. He studied at the Imperial Theatre School in St Petersburg with Petipa and Johansson and joined the Imperial Ballet in 1860, four years prior to his graduation in 1864. During the next 56 years he danced at both the Bolshoi and Mariinsky Theatres in St Petersburg. He had more than 100 roles in his repertoire, most of them in ballets by Petipa. His career was extended due to his ability to make the transition from premier danseur to character artist, and to his particular talent as a mime. He created the role of Prince Désiré in *The Sleeping Beauty* in 1890 when he was 46 years old, and the role of Prince Siegfried in Petipa's 1895 St Petersburg staging of *Swan Lake* when he was 50. He also created leading roles in Petipa's *La Camargo* (1872), *Paquita* (1881), *Coppélia* (1884), *The Talisman* (1889), *Kalkabrino* (1891), *Cinderella* (Prince Charming, 1893), *Raymonda* (1898), and in Ivanov's *Nutcracker* (1892). He also excelled as Conrad in *Le Corsaire*, Solor in *La Bayadère*, and Albrecht in *Giselle*. He gave his farewell performance as Don Gamache in *Don Quixote* in 1916. From 1880 to 1904 he taught at the Imperial Theatre School and he counted among his students Pavlova, Karsavina, Fokine, and Vaganova. He created a ballet for Anna Pavlova's graduation performance and collaborated with Ivanov on Delibes's *Sylvia* in 1901.

German Opera Ballet *See* BERLIN OPERA BALLET.

German State Opera Ballet The ballet company attached to the Staatsoper Unter den Linden in the former East Berlin. Also called Ballett der Staatsoper Unter den Linden, or the Staatsoper Ballet. Under the direction of Tatjana *Gsovsky (1945–52), it became the model for ballet companies throughout the former East Germany with its associated school strongly influenced by Soviet teaching methods. Gsovsky's successor Daisy Spies (1952–5) staged more contemporary works such as *The Lord's Law* and *The Converted Philistine* which were tailored to meet the strict artistic criteria of the Communist authorities and under Lilo Gruber's direction (until 1970) the company continued as an important centre for Soviet-style dance. Following German reunification in 1989 the company broadened its repertoire to include works by Balanchine, Cranko, and Nureyev. Michaël Denard, a former star of the Paris Opera Ballet, took over as director in 1992; in 1993 Maurice *Béjart was appointed chief guest choreographer. Denard resigned at the end of the 1995–6 season and in 2004 the company was merged with the Berlin Opera Ballet and the Komische Ballet to become the new *Berlin State Ballet, directed by Vladimir Malakhov. This currently performs on the stages of both the Unter den Linden and Deutsch Opera Houses.

(((⊕))) SEE WEB LINKS
• Website for State Opera with link to the State Ballet

Germany As elsewhere in Europe, ballet in Germany began with productions at court, one of the earliest being Darmstadt's *Die Befreiung des Friedens* (*The Liberation of Peace*) in 1600, which was in effect a 'sung ballet'. In 1717 in Leipzig, Gottfried Taubert published his *Der rechtschaffene Tantzmeister*, the first important German dance treatise. Stuttgart was put on the ballet map when Noverre worked there from 1760 to 1767, developing his controversial reforms while acting as ballet master. Stuttgart also attracted Filippo Taglioni and his daughter Marie, who both worked in the city from 1824 to 1828. There they created

Danina, oder Jocko der Brasilianische Affe (1826), one of the most popular ballets of the day. Thirty years later Berlin played host to Paul Taglioni, Marie's brother, when he took charge of the Berlin Court Opera Ballet (1856–83). After the First World War, and the dissolution of the Empire regular ballet performances were staged at the State Opera (Staatsoper), whose ballet directors included Heinrich Kröller (1921–3) and Rudolf von *Laban (1930–4). After the Second World War the company, renamed the German State Opera Ballet (also known as the Staatsoper Ballet), continued in what was now East Berlin. In 1955 the company moved back to its rebuilt house, Unter den Linden. Berlin's second opera house, the Charlottenburg, which opened in 1912 in the Western part of the city, became the German Opera House, home to the *Berlin Opera Ballet.

The Second World War, and the Nazi regime, halted the development of ballet in the country. During the 1950s, as ballet in East Germany came under the influence of the Soviet school, the two main companies in East Berlin became dominated by the aesthetics and politics of *Socialist Realism. In West Germany, meanwhile, ballet enjoyed a renaissance, with every opera house maintaining a company. Most of these were classically based and from the 1960s onwards, several came under British and American influence, due to the influx of directors and choreographers like John Cranko in Stuttgart, Kenneth MacMillan in Berlin, William Forsythe in Frankfurt, and John Neumeier in Hamburg. These four companies in particular attained an international profile for their innovation and excellence, although in 2004 Ballet Frankfurt was dissolved as Forsythe reformed his own smaller scaled company. Other leading regional companies included *Bavarian State Ballet in Munich, Ballet of the German Opera on the Rhine in Dusseldof. In Eastern Germany, the Leipzig Ballet (under Uwe Scholz's direction) came to symbolize the rebirth of dance following the collapse of Communism. In 2004 the Berlin Opera Ballet, the German State Opera Ballet (the Staatsoper Ballet), and the Komische Ballet were amalgamated into a single company, the *Berlin State Ballet.

Modern dance in Germany dates back to visits by Isadora Duncan and Ruth St Denis in the early 1900s, and as interest in classical dance began to wane at this time it was overtaken by the new expressive dance, or *Ausdruckstanz. In 1911 Jaques-Dalcroze opened his institute for applied rhythm in the Dresden suburb of Hellerau. The leading figures in German modern dance after the First World War were Rudolf von Laban (who had set up his school in Munich in 1910) and Mary *Wigman, both of whom ran influential schools. The most significant work to emerge from this period was Kurt Jooss's *The Green Table*, which

was premiered by the Essen *Folkwang Ballet in Paris in 1932. The Folkwang Ballet continued after the war, although developments in classical ballet outstripped those in modern dance. The balance shifted in the 1970s as Pina *Bausch's company in Wuppertal emerged as one of the most dominant troupes not only in Germany but the world. The scale of Bausch's reputation overshadowed other modern dance activity in the country, as did that of William Forsythe when the latter's work with Frankfurt became increasingly radical in its experimentation. However Dance Forum Cologne, founded in 1971 and largely under the direction of Jochen *Ulrich, also played a pioneering role in establishing the post-war modern dance scene, presenting the works of guest choreographers such as Christopher Bruce and van Manen, as well as Ulrich's own repertory. Despite the success of the company it folded in 1997. By this time other smaller modern dance groups were emerging as well as two significant companies *Sasha Waltz and Guests, founded by Waltz and Jochen Sandig in Berlin in 1993, and Amanda Miller's Pretty Ugly Dance Company, founded in 1992 (and between 1997 and 2004 attached to the Freiburg Theatre where it was known as Freiburg Pretty Ugly Dance Company). Both these troupes received significant funding and have gone on to gain international reputations.

Gershwin, George (*b* Brooklyn, NY, 26 Sept. 1898; *d* Hollywood, Calif., 11 Jul. 1937) US composer. Although he wrote no ballet scores his songs and concert music have been widely choreographed. *Rhapsody in Blue* has been used by Dolin and Milloss, among others, Piano Concerto in F has been used by Gene Kelly for *Pas de dieux* (Paris Opera 1960), Robbins for *The Gershwin Concerto* (New York City Ballet, 1982), and S. Welch (Houston, 2008). Songs from *An American in Paris* were choreographed by Wheeldon, (New York City Ballet, 2005). Balanchine also used Gershwin songs for his 1970 work *Who Cares*?

Geva, Tamara (orig. Tamara Gevergeyeva; *b* St Petersburg, 17 Mar. 1906; *d* New York, 9 Dec. 1997) Russian-US dancer and actress. She studied in St Petersburg and joined GATOB (as the Kirov was known in those days). She married Balanchine when she was 16 (he was 18) and went with him to the West in 1924, travelling in a troupe known as the Soviet State Dancers, all of whom were subsequently hired by Diaghilev. She left the Diaghilev company and danced with Ballets Russes de Monte Carlo. Eventually she ended up in America where she appeared in the *Ziegfeld Follies*. She starred on Broadway in *On Your Toes* in 1936, dancing Balanchine's famous ballet *Slaughter on Tenth Avenue*. She enjoyed a career as an actress in musicals, plays, and films and, with Haila Stoddard, wrote a musical comedy, *Come Play With Me* (mus. Dana Suesse). Author of the autobiography *Split Seconds*.

Ghost Dances Modern dance in one act with choreography by Christopher Bruce set to S. American folk music arranged by Nicholas Mojsiejenko, sets by Bruce, costumes by Belinda Scarlett, and lighting by Nick Chelton. Premiered 3 Jul. 1981 by Ballet Rambert at the Bristol Old Vic. Bruce's tribute to victims of political oppression in S. America became one of the most popular works in the Rambert repertoire. It has also been danced and filmed by Houston Ballet.

Gielgud, Maina (*b* London, 14 Jan. 1945) British dancer and ballet director. The niece of the actor John Gielgud. She studied at the Hampshire School in London and later with a succession of individual teachers including Karsavina, Idzikowski, V. Gsovsky, Egorova, and Rosella Hightower. She made her debut in 1961 with Petit's Ballets de Paris then moved to the Grand Ballet du Marquis de Cuevas in 1962 and to the Grand Ballet Classique de France (1963–6) before joining the Ballet of the 20th Century (1967–71). Here she created roles in several Béjart ballets, *Ni Fleurs, ni couronnes*, *Baudelaire*, *Bhakti* (all 1968), *Les 4 Fils Aymon II* (1969), and *Serait-ce la mort?* (1970). In 1971 she moved to Berlin Opera Ballet and the following year to London Festival Ballet where she remained until 1975. As a freelance guest artist she appeared with many companies, including Sadler's Wells Royal Ballet. From 1978 she toured with her own theatre production, *Steps, Notes and Squeaks*, which took audiences on a backstage tour of the ballet. Her first choreography was *The Soldier's Tale* in 1980. In 1983 she was appointed artistic director of the Australian Ballet and during her thirteen-year tenure revived the company's international profile. She resumed overseas touring, produced several stagings of the classics, introduced works by outside choreographers such as Béjart, Forsythe, and Duato, and developed new Australian choreographers. From 1997 to 1999 she was artistic director of the Royal Danish Ballet after which she has worked freelance, teaching internationally and also reviving productions from the classic and Béjart repertories.

(()) SEE WEB LINKS
• Maina Gielgud's website

gigue A spirited dance in 6/8 or 12/8 time, popular in France in the early 1700s. Somewhat similar to the Irish jig.

Gillis, Margie (*b* Montreal, 9 Jul. 1953) Canadian dancer and choreographer. She studied locally, and with May O'Donnell and others in New York before launching her career as a solo artist in Vancouver in 1975. She also performed as a guest artist with several companies including Les Grands Ballets Canadiens, the Paul Taylor company, Momix, and with Martha Clarke appearing in the latter's *The Garden of Earthly Delights* in 1984 and *Vers la flamme* in 1999. In 1982 Taylor made *Duet* for Gillis and her brother Christopher, a long-time member of the Taylor company. In 1981 she founded her own company but also continued her solo career, choreographing and performing over 80 works for herself—many with a strong political slant. She has additionally choreographed for other companies, including Cirque du Soleil, and taught widely, an advocate of her own method of 'active kinesthesis'. Order of Canada 1988.

(()) SEE WEB LINKS
• Website for Margie Gillis

Gillot, Marie-Agnes (*b* Caen, 7 Sep. 1975) French dancer. She studied at the Paris Opera Ballet School from 1985 and graduated into the company in 1990 when she was just 15. She was promoted to étoile in 2004. A tall and lyrical dancer, she excels in the traditional ballerina repertoire but is also acclaimed for her versatility in the modern repertoire, especially in ballets by Ek, Carlson, and Lock.

Gilmour, Sally (*b* Malaya, 2 Nov. 1921; *d* 23 May 2004) British dancer. She studied with Karsavina in London (1930–3) and at the Rambert school before joining Ballet Rambert in 1937. As the company's leading ballerina for over a decade she created roles in Howard's *Lady into Fox* (1939), *The Fugitive* (1944), *Sailor's Return* (1947), and *Orlando's Silver Wedding* (1951), Staff's *Peter and the Wolf* (1940), and Gore's *Confessional* (1941), *Simple Symphony* (1944), *Mr Punch* (1946), *Concerto Burlesco* (1947), and *Winter Night* (1948). She retired from Rambert in 1953, although returned to help revive some of the early works in the company's repertoire. She appeared as Louise in the musical *Carousel* in the West End in 1950.

Gilpin, John (*b* Southsea, 10 Feb. 1930; *d* London, 5 Sept. 1983) British dancer. A successful child actor, he studied dance from 1940 at the Cone-Ripman and Rambert schools. In 1943 he won the Adeline Genée Gold Medal, the youngest person ever to do so. He joined Ballet Rambert in 1945, becoming a principal. During the 1949 season he danced with Roland Petit's company, and in 1950 with Le Grand Ballet du Marquis de Cuevas. Later in 1950 he returned to London and joined London Festival Ballet, first becoming its premier danseur and then its artistic director (1965–7). Widely considered to be one of the most brilliant male dancers Britain had produced, he also guested with the Royal Ballet and American

Ballet Theatre among many others. He created roles in Howard's *The Sailor's Return* (1947), Ashton's *Le Rêve de Léonor* (1949), Beriozoff's *Esmeralda* (1954), and Dolin's *Variations for Four* (1957). As a ballet master and teacher he worked in Copenhagen, Ankara, and Tokyo. He appeared in Maxim Mazumdar's play *Invitation to the Dance*, which was based on his own life, and starred as Oberon in Lindsay Kemp's *Midsummer Night's Dream* in Italy in 1981. He won the Nijinsky Prize in Paris in 1957. Published his autobiography, *A Dance With Life*, in London in 1982.

g

Gingerbread Heart, The Ballet in three acts with choreography by Froman, music by K. Baranovic, sets by A. Augustinic, and costumes by Inges Kostincer-Bregovac. Premiered 17 Jun. 1924 in Zagreb. It tells the story of a young man who gives a gingerbread heart to his fiancée and features a dream sequence in which gingerbread figures are brought to life. At the time it was one of Yugoslavia's most popular ballets.

Ginner, Ruby (*b* Cannes, 8 May 1886; *d* Newbury, 13 Feb. 1978) British dance teacher and expert on ancient Greek dance. She studied ballet before researching Greek dance and founding her London-based ensemble, the Grecian Dancers, in 1913. During the First World War she established the Ruby Ginner School of Dance (later the Ginner-Mawer School of Dance and Drama) and in 1923 founded the Association of Teachers of the Revived Greek Dance. This evolved into the Greek Dance Association, which was ultimately absorbed into the Imperial Society of Teachers of Dancing. She wrote *The Revived Greek Dance* (London, 1933) and *Gateway to Dance* (1960).

Gipsy, La See GYPSY, LA.

Giselle Ballet in two acts with choreography by Coralli and Perrot, libretto by Vernoy de Saint-Georges, Gautier, and Coralli, music by Adam, sets by Pierre Ciceri, and costumes by Paul Lormier. Premiered 28 Jun. 1841 at the Paris Opera, with Grisi (Giselle), Lucien Petipa (Albrecht), Adèle Dumilâtre (Myrtha). The most famous of all Romantic ballets, it is now in the repertoire of virtually every classical company in the world. Set in Germany's Rhine Valley, it was inspired by a story by Heinrich Heine, and tells the tragedy of the innocent peasant girl Giselle in love with the philandering Count Albrecht, who is betrothed to Bathilde, herself the daughter of a Duke. Albrecht's pursuit of Giselle provokes the jealous gamekeeper Hilarion to expose the former's true identity, an act which drives Giselle to madness and, eventually, death. The second act takes place within the moonlit domain of the Wilis, vengeful spirits of brides who died before

their wedding day. Led by their queen, Myrtha, the Wilis seek to kill all men who wander into their world. Hilarion is their first prey, but Albrecht is saved from death by the intervention of Giselle who, even after death, remains faithful to him. When dawn breaks the Wilis return to their graves and Albrecht is left alone with the knowledge that he has lost his true love. With its evocation of the supernatural, its portrait of eternal love, and its exploration of the duality of the body and the spirit, *Giselle* is often considered the quintessential Romantic ballet. Following its Paris premiere productions of the ballet were rapidly staged elsewhere: London, St Petersburg, and Vienna (1942), Berlin and Milan (1843), and Boston (1846). The title role became the testing ground for leading ballerinas, from Carlotta Grisi, who originated the role in Paris, to Fanny Elssler who danced it in London, to Alicia Alonso, Carla Fracci, Alicia Markova, and Galina Ulanova more than a century later. The original Paris production survived until 1868; but almost all subsequent stagings have been based on Petipa's St Petersburg productions (the last of which was in 1884). Diaghilev's Ballets Russes reintroduced *Giselle* into western Europe in 1910 with a new staging by Fokine starring Karsavina but during the next 100 years alongside many traditional productions of *Giselle* the ballet has also attracted radical reinterpretation. Some versions, like the Dance Theatre of Harlem's, have relocated the libretto and choreography to a new time and setting—here the Louisiana swamps. Others have entirely re-written the material, like Mats Ek's production for the Cullberg Ballet, set in a lunatic asylum and Michael Keegan-Dolan's modern Irish version for Fabulous Beast Dance Theatre.

Gitana, La Ballet in three acts with prologue, with choreography and libretto by Filippo Taglioni, and music by Hermann Schmidt and Daniel Auber. Premiered 5 Dec. 1838 at the Bolshoi Theatre in St Petersburg with Marie Taglioni and Nikolai Osipovich Glotz. Lauretta, the daughter of a Duke, is kidnapped as a child and raised by a tribe of gypsies. She falls in love with Ivan, son of the Governor of Nishni Novgorod. The title role was particularly associated with Taglioni. Not to be confused with Mazilier's ballet *La *Gypsy* or *La Gipsy* (1839).

Glass, Philip (*b* Baltimore, 31 Jan. 1937) US composer. His music has frequently been used by choreographers, most notably Robbins in *Glass Pieces* (New York City Ballet, 1983) and Lucinda Childs in *Dance* (New York, 1979), *Mad Rush* (Paris, 1981), and *Field Dances* (New York, 1984). Glass composed the score for Tharp's 1986 ballet *In the Upper Room* and for her 1996 ballet *Heroes*.

Glazunov, Alexander (*b* St Petersburg, 10 Aug. 1865; *d* Paris, 21 Mar. 1936) Russian composer. He wrote the music for three Petipa ballets: *Raymonda* (1898)—the work for which he is best known—*Les Ruses d'amour* (1900), and *Les Saisons* (1900). Balanchine used music from *Raymonda* for his *Pas de dix* (1955), *Raymonda Variations* (1961), and *Cortège hongrois* (1973). Ashton used selections from Glazunov's music for his *Birthday Offering* (1956). Gorsky choreographed his 5th Symphony in 1916, one of the world's first symphonic ballets. Tharp used Glazunov's *Scènes de ballet* for *The Little Ballet* in 1984.

Glière, Reinhold (*b* Kiev, 11 Jan. 1875; *d* Moscow, 23 Jun. 1975) Russian composer. He wrote the scores for several ballets, including *The Red Poppy* (1927), and *The Bronze Horseman* (1949).

glissade [Fr., glide] A gliding movement, which can be executed either forward, backward, or to the side. It is used mostly as a linking step.

Gloria 1. Ballet in one act with choreography by MacMillan, music by Poulenc, and designs by Andy Klunder. Premiered 13 Mar. 1980 by the Royal Ballet at Covent Garden with Eagling, Penney, Hosking, and Ellis. The ballet is inspired by Vera Brittain's *Testament of Youth* and is set to Poulenc's *Gloria*. It is a heartfelt evocation of the tragic waste of young life in the trenches of the First World War. 2. Ballet in one act with choreography by Mark Morris and music by Vivaldi. Premiered 12 Dec. 1981 by the Mark Morris Dance Group, at the Bessie Schönberg Theater, Dance Theater Workshop, New York. A work partly inspired by the sentiments of the Roman Catholic Mass.

Glover, Savion (*b* Newark, NJ, 19 Nov. 1973) US dancer and choreographer. He made his Broadway debut as the title character in *The Tap Dance Kid* when he was 10 and went on to star in *Black and Blue* (1989), *Jelly's Last Jam* (1992), and **Bring in 'da Noise, Bring in 'da Funk* (1995) for which he also won a Tony award for Best Choreography. He made his film debut in 1988 co-starring with Gregory Hines and Sammy Davis Jr. in *Tap*, and went on to feature in Spike Lee's *Bamboozled* (2000) and *Happy Feet* (in which he was the motion capture dancer, providing the blueprint for the film's animated penguin hero). Glover, a brilliant exponent of rhythm tap (as opposed to the more polished school of stage tap exemplified by Astaire), is widely considered to be the most important voice in contemporary American tap. Although his style is influenced by the heavy beats of hip-hop he also dances to live jazz and classical music, his rhythmically elaborate performances making him figure on stage as part of the musicians' ensemble as well as a dancer.

⊕ SEE WEB LINKS
• Website for Savion Glover

Gluck, Christoph Willibald von (*b* Erasbach, 2 Jul. 1714; *d* Vienna, 15 Nov. 1787) German composer. He wrote the music for Angiolini's *Don Juan* (1761), *Alessandro* (1765), and *Semiramis* (1765). His operas *Orpheus and Eurydice* (1762) and *Iphigenia in Aulis* (1774) contain ballet sections and in certain productions have been staged entirely by choreographers including Balanchine (Metropolitan Opera House, New York, 1963), Pina Bausch (1975), and Mark Morris (Edinburgh Festival 1996 and Metropolitan Opera House, 2007).

Glushkovsky, Adam (*b* St Petersburg, 1793; *d* Oct. 1870) Russian dancer, teacher, and choreographer. He studied at the Imperial Theatre School in St Petersburg, a student of Didelot, who was also his guardian, and graduated in 1809; he later studied with Louis Duport. After dancing in St Petersburg for several years, he moved to Moscow where he became chief choreographer of the Bolshoi Theatre, its leading demi-caractère dancer and director of the Bolshoi Ballet School in 1812. He stayed with the Bolshoi until 1839, retiring from performing in 1831. He revived all of Didelot's most important ballets, including *Zéphire et Flore*, and was the first to choreograph a ballet based on a poem by Pushkin when he staged his *Ruslan and Lyudmila* in 1821 at the Bolshoi. At the school he set rigorous training standards, thus helping to establish its reputation as a leading institution. He also ensured its survival when, in 1812, he saved the school from potential destruction by evacuating it just days before Napoleon's army invaded Moscow. Author of *Memoirs of a Ballet Master*, first published in 1856.

Goddard, Jonathan (*b* Chertsey, Surrey, 12 Dec. 1979) British dancer. He trained at Rambert School and danced with Scottish Dance Theatre from 1999, the Richard Alston Company from 2002, and Rambert Dance Company from 2008. A dancer of exceptional clarity of line and musical intelligence, Goddard became the first contemporary dancer to win the Critic's Circle Best Male Dancer award in 2007. He has created roles in numerous works, including Alston's *Gypsy Mixture* (2005) and danced the 2008 revival of Alston's *Dutiful Ducks*.

Godden, Mark (*b* Dallas, 1958) American dancer and choreographer. He studied drama before taking up ballet at the age of 20, training at the Royal Winnipeg Ballet School and graduating into the company in 1984 where he was promoted to soloist in 1989. Apart from a brief period with Nederlands Dans Theater he remained with the company as dancer and also created his first works there. He was appointed resident choreographer from 1990 to 1994, creating *Myth* (mus. Barber, 1990), *La Princesse et le Soldat* (mus. Stravinsky, 1991), and *Angels in the Architecture* (mus. Copland, 1993) among others, and developing a style that fused the classical vocabulary with contemporary cultural references and dance forms. He also forged a relationship with Les Grands Ballets Canadiens, choreographing *Chambre* (mus. Christopher Rouse, 1993) and *Open Blue* (mus. Michael Torke, 1994) and has continued to make works for both Canadian companies including *Miroirs* (mus. Ravel 1995), *Dracula* (mus. Mahler, 1998), and *Magic Flute* (mus. Mozart, 2003) for Winnipeg—the last two works both adapted for film.

He has choreographed for other companies including Boston Ballet and Harid Dance Conservatory where Godden has been permanent guest choreographer since 1995.

Gods Go a-Begging, The (*Les Dieux mendiants*) Ballet in one act with choreography by Balanchine, libretto by Kochno (using the pen name Sobeka), music by Handel arranged by Beecham, sets by Bakst, and costumes by J. Gris. Premiered 16 Jul. 1928 by the Ballets Russes de Diaghilev at Her Majesty's Theatre in London with Danilova and Woizikowski. A young shepherd falls in love with a maid at an aristocrats' picnic. When the lovers are mocked by the others, they reveal themselves to be gods. De Valois staged a version for Vic-Wells Ballet in 1936 (excerpts of which were revived by the Royal Ballet at the Barbican Theatre in 1998 to mark the de Valois centenary), while Lichine did a version for Ballets Russes de Monte Carlo in 1937.

Godunov, Alexander (*b* Sakhalin Island, 28 Nov. 1949; *d* Los Angeles, 18 May 1995) Soviet dancer. He studied locally and at the Bolshoi Ballet School in Moscow, graduating into the company in 1966. As a soloist he created the role of Karenin in Plisetskaya's *Anna Karenina* (1972) and the leading role in Boccadora's *Love for Love* (1976). He won the Gold Medal at the Moscow competition in 1973. In 1979, while the Bolshoi was on tour in America, he defected, an act which led to a political confrontation between the US and the Soviet Union. He joined American Ballet Theatre, where he stayed until 1982. After leaving ABT, he took up an acting career, appearing in films such as *Witness*, *Die Hard*, and *The Money Pit*.

Goh, Choo-San (*b* Singapore, 1948; *d* New York, 28 Nov. 1987) Chinese dancer, teacher, choreographer and ballet director. He studied in Singapore at the Singapore Ballet Academy and obtained a degree in biochemistry at the University of Singapore. In 1970 he left to join Dutch National Ballet, where he spent five years as a dancer and began to choreograph. In 1976 he became resident choreographer of the Washington Ballet and in 1984 was named associate artistic director. His ballets were taken into the repertoires of many companies, including Alvin Ailey American Dance Theater, American Ballet Theatre, Australian Ballet, Boston Ballet, Royal Danish Ballet, Dance Theatre of Harlem, Houston Ballet, Joffrey Ballet, Paris Opera Ballet, and Royal Swedish Ballet. His best-known work was *Configurations* (mus. Barber), commissioned by Baryshnikov for American Ballet Theatre in 1981. He died prematurely of an Aids-related illness.

Goldberg Variations, The Ballet in two parts with choreography by Robbins, music by Bach, and costumes by Joe Eula. Premiered 27 May 1971 by New York City Ballet at the State Theater in New York with Kirkland, Leland, Clifford, Maiorano, von Aroldingen, Blum, McBride, Tomasson, and Martins. A plotless ballet set to the theme and 30 variations of Bach's great keyboard score.

Golden Age, The Ballet in three acts with choreography by Vasily Vainonen (with Vasily Chesnakov and Leonid Jacobson), libretto by Alexander Ivanovsky, music by Shostakovich, and designs by Vera Khodasevich. Premiered 26 Oct. 1930 at the GATOB (later the Kirov) in Leningrad with Ulanova, Olga Iordan, and Boris Shavrov. Set in an unnamed capitalist city in the West, the ballet portrays a touring Soviet football team outwitting the bullying, cheating tactics of their opponents and ending with them joining with capitalist workers in a dance of solidarity. The ballet, following the principles of the *Socialist Realist school was the prize-winning entry in a competition for new ballet librettos, but after one season its score, by a young, provocative Shostakovich was deemed 'ideologically destructive' and the ballet disappeared from the repertoire. 50 years later Grigorovich choreographed an entirely new ballet to Shostakovich's score for the Bolshoi in 1982 with designs by Simon Virsaladze. A new libretto, by Ivan Glikman and Grigorovich, only partly drew on the original. It retained the political sentiments of the original but set the action in the post-revolutionary Soviet state in 1923 where the Golden Age is the name of a decadent nightclub. In a small Soviet resort on the Black Sea the idealistic young fisherman Boris falls in love with the cabaret dancer Rita, and tries to rescue her from her boyfriend, the gang leader Jashka. The first performance, on 4 Nov. 1982, starred Irek Mukhamedov as Boris, Natalia Bessmertnova as Rita, and Geminas (or Gediminas) Taranda as

Jashka. It became one of the most popular ballets in the Bolshoi's repertoire, frequently performed on foreign tours. The Mariinsky (Kirov) premiered its own, much less successful new version in 2006. Choreographed by Noah Gelber it portrayed two retired Soviet athletes, recalling their impassioned courtship during the 1920s.

Goleizovsky, Kasyan (b Moscow, 5 Mar. 1892; d Moscow, 4 May 1970) Russian dancer and choreographer. Pioneering member of the Moscow avant-garde during the 1920s. He studied first in Moscow and then (1902–9) in St Petersburg, where he was a pupil of Fokine. He graduated in 1909 and danced with the Bolshoi (1909–18). In 1916 he established his own Moscow studio, called the Quest, and made numerous concert miniatures for it. He also began to stage small productions at theatres outside the Bolshoi, especially in cabaret theatres such as the Bat or the Mamonovsky Theatre of Miniatures where his work acquired a popular following. In 1918 he was invited to head the studio of the Bolshoi Theatre School and in 1922 he formed his own company, the Moscow Chamber Ballet, for which he made some of his most innovative works, including *Faun* (mus. Debussy) and *Salomé* (mus. Strauss), daring in its portrayal of eroticism on stage. His boldly experimentalist stance was an influence and an inspiration to other young Russian choreographers, most notably George Balanchine. His most significant ballet was *Joseph the Beautiful* (mus. Vasilenko, 1925) which was created for the Bolshoi's Experimental Theatre troupe, but whose depiction of the individual's struggle for freedom proved too controversial for the traditionalists, led by Tikhomirov, and it was dropped from the repertoire. His later works also met with opposition. *Lola*, created for the Bolshoi in 1925 was cancelled by the management; *The Whirlwind* (1927) was performed by the Bolshoi only once. With his works now dropped from the Bolshoi repertoire, Goleizovsky increasingly turned to concert programmes and music halls for his livelihood, although in 1933–4 he made a brief return to the Bolshoi, and again in the 1960s when the post-Stalinist era was opening up new opportunities for choreographers. He additionally researched and choreographed folkloric material. During the late 1930s he worked in various Soviet regions arranging folk dances and during the Second World War choreographed for the Song and Dance Ensemble of the Ministry of the Interior. His researches were published in *Forms of Russian National Choreography* or *Images of Russian Folk Choreography* (Moscow, 1964).

A list of his other ballets includes Polovtsian Dances from *Prince Igor* (Moscow, 1934), *Sleeping Beauty* (Kharkhov, 1935), *Fountain of Bakhchisarai* (Minsk, 1939), *Two Roses* (mus. A. Lensky,

Moscow, 1941), *Scriabiniana* (Bolshoi Theatre, Moscow, 1962), and *Leili and Medzhnun* (mus. S. Balasanian, Moscow, 1964).

Golovin, Alexander (b Moscow, 1 Mar. 1863; d Pushkin, or Detskoye Selo, 17 Apr. 1930) Russian painter and designer. He designed both opera and ballet for the Imperial Theatres in St Petersburg and Moscow, although his most famous commissions were for Diaghilev's Ballets Russes: Fokine's *Firebird* (1910) and the Act II *Swan Lake* production (with Konstantin Korovin) in 1911. He also designed Fokine's *Jota Aragonesa* (1916) and Lopukhov's *Solveig* (1927).

Golovine, Serge (b Monte Carlo, 20 Nov. 1924; d Paris, 31 Jul. 1998) French dancer and teacher. He studied with Julie Sedova in Nice (from 1935) and with Gustave Ricaux in Monaco, later with Preobrajenska and Volinine in Paris. He performed with the Opera Ballet of Monte Carlo during the Second World War and in 1947 he joined the Paris Opera Ballet, where he eventually became a soloist, but it was with the Grand Ballet du Marquis de Cuevas (1949–61), that he achieved international fame. Particularly renowned for his elevation, and batterie, he excelled in the *Blue Bird pas de deux* and *Spectre de la rose*; but was also acclaimed for his Petrushka. He created the role of the Man in Lifar's *L'Amour et son destin* (1957). In 1962 he founded his own troupe, Les Compagnons de la Danse, for whom he made several works; from 1964 to 1969 he was artistic director and principal dancer of the Geneva Opera Ballet. He retired from the stage in 1976 but continued to teach, at his own school, which he founded in Geneva in 1969, and later at the Paris Opera Ballet School (from 1981). Légion d'honneur (1998).

Goncharova, Natalia (b Ladyzhino, 4 Jun. 1881; d Paris, 17 Oct. 1962) Russian painter and designer. Most closely associated with the Diaghilev company, she designed several of its key works, including Fokine's *Le Coq d'or* (1914), Nijinska's *Renard* (with her husband Larionov, 1922), *Les Noces* (1923), and *Une nuit sur le mont chauve* (1924) and the 1926 revival of Fokine's *Firebird*. She also designed Fokine's *Ygrouchka* (New York, 1921) and *Cendrillon* (London, 1938), Lifar's *Sur le Borsythène* (with Larionov, Paris, 1932) and Massine's *Bogatyri* (New York, 1938), as well as the 1954 Sadler's Wells Ballet production of *Firebird*. Her designs, which often drew inspiration from Russian folk art and Orthodox religious symbolism, were noted for their strong use of colour.

Good-Humoured Ladies, The (orig. Fr. title *Les Femmes de bonne humeur*) Ballet in one act, with choreography and libretto by Massine, music by Domenico Scarlatti arranged by Vincenzo Tommasini, and designs by Bakst. Premiered

12 Apr. 1917 by the Ballets Russes de Diaghilev at the Teatro Costanzi in Rome, with Lopokova, Tchernicheva, Massine, Cecchetti, Idzikowski, and Woizikowski. Massine based his ballet on Goldoni's comedy, *Le donne di buon umore*, about the deceptions and flirtations engineered by Costanza and her maid Mariuccia, but he also drew inspiration from Futurist art and modern cinema. He revived it for several companies, including the Royal Ballet in 1962, a production that was not a success.

gopak A spirited dance in duple time originating in the Ukraine. It was originally danced only by men. A famous example occurs in Zakharov's ballet *Taras Bulba*.

Gopal, Ram (*b* Bangalore, 20 Nov. 1917; *d* 12 Oct. 2003) Indian dancer, choreographer, and teacher. A pioneering ambassador for classical Indian dance around the world. He studied katha-kali with Kunju Kunrup, bharata natyam with Sundaram, kathak with Misra, and manipuri with Nabakumar. He first came to Europe in 1938 and brought his own company to London in 1939, embarking on the foreign tours that would help raise the international profile of Indian dance. He opened the Academy for Indian Dance and Music in London in 1962 and wrote several books including *Dances of India, Legend of the Taj Mahal*, and his autobiography *Rhythm in the Heavens* (London, 1957).

Gordeyev, Viacheslav (*b* Moscow, 3 Aug. 1948) Russian dancer and ballet director. He studied at the Bolshoi Ballet School in Moscow, graduating in 1968. He joined the Bolshoi Ballet where he danced all the leading male roles in the standard repertory. In 1973 he won the Gold Medal at the Moscow competition. He started to choreograph in 1981 and in 1983 became artistic director of the Moscow-based Russian State Ballet (formerly the Russian Ballet Company of Moscow), for whom he choreographed most of his ballets. Director of the Bolshoi Ballet (1995–7).

Gordon, David (*b* New York, 14 Jul. 1936) US dancer and choreographer. He began dancing with James Waring while studying art at Brooklyn College, and had further dance studies with Cunningham, Louis Horst, and Robert Dunn. He was at the centre of the post-modern movement in New York, performing with *Judson Dance Theater during the 1960s, also with Yvonne *Rainier (1966–70), and with *Grand Union from 1970. He also collaborated with Douglas Dunn and frequently worked with his wife, the dancer Velda Setterfield. In 1971 he formed his own company, the Pick Up Performance Company for which he created many works. A highly analytical choreographer, his productions also had a strong

theatrical quality, incorporating speech and making frequent reference to film and popular music. A list of his work for his own company includes *Random Breakfast* (1963), *Walks and Digressions* (1966), *One Part of the Matter* (1972), *What Happened* (1978), *T.V. Reel* (1982), *Trying Times* (1982), *Framework* (1983), and *United States* (1989). He also choreographed for several other companies including American Ballet Theatre (*Field, Chair and Mountain*, 1985 and *Murder*, 1986); Dance Theatre of Harlem (*Piano Movers*, 1984); Paris Opera (*Punch and Judy*, 1992), and the White Oak Dance Project. He choreographed Philip Glass and Robert Coe's opera *The Photographer* (1983). Gordon has also had a distinguished career in the theatre, writing and directing plays such as *The Mysteries* and *What's So Funny?* (1991), *The Family Business* (1994), and *Aristophanes in Birdonia* (2006). In 1994 he directed *Schlemiel the First*, a klezmer musical based on stories by Isaac Bashevis Singer and in 1995 he directed Max Frisch's *The Firebugs* for the Guthrie Theater in Minneapolis. He has collaborated with his playwright son Ain on several works including *Silent Movie* (1997). Although his choreographic activity has waned, his recent works include *Dancing Henry Five* (2004) incorporating music and text from Olivier's film of the Shakespeare play.

Gore, Walter (*b* Waterside, Scotland, 8 Oct. 1910; *d* Pamplona, Spain, 16 Apr. 1979) British dancer, choreographer, and company director. One of Rambert's early choreographers. He studied acting at the Italia Conti School (from 1924) and dance with Massine and Rambert, joining the latter's company in 1930. Between 1935 and 1937 he worked briefly with the Vic-Wells Ballet, where he created the title role in de Valois's *The Rake's Progress*, and then in West End musicals as dancer and choreographer. After returning to Ballet Rambert as a soloist, he created his first ballet for the company in 1938, *Valse finale* (mus. Ravel). Service in the Royal Navy during the Second World War interrupted his choreographic career, but on his return to Rambert he created *Simple Symphony* (mus. Britten, 1944), *Mr Punch* (mus. Oldham, 1946), *Concerto burlesco* (mus. Bartók, 1946), *Winter Night* (mus. Rachmaninoff, 1948), and *Antonia* (mus. Sibelius, 1949). He left Rambert in 1950 to work freelance, for example choreographing *La Damnée* (1951) for Ballets des Champs-Elysées and *Carte blanche* (mus. J. Addison, 1953) for Sadler's Wells Theatre Ballet. In 1953 he formed the Walter Gore Ballet which toured Australia. He subsequently worked in America, Amsterdam, and Frankfurt, where he was director of the Frankfurt Ballet (1957–9) and choreographed *Eaters of Darkness* (mus. Britten, 1958), then becoming founder and director of

*London Ballet (1961–3) and ballet master of the Gulbenkian Ballet in Lisbon (1965–9). His later works included *Night and Silence* (mus. Bach, arr. Mackerras, Edinburgh Festival, 1958), *Sweet Dancer* (mus. F. Martin, Ballet Rambert, 1964), and *Embers of Glencoe* (mus. Tom Wilson, Scottish Theatre Ballet, 1973). Although he choreographed more than 80 ballets, few survived in the repertoire.

Górecki, Henryk (*b* Czernice, 1933) Polish composer. During the 1990s his concert music became very popular with choreographers including Nacho Duato (*Lament*, 1990), Christopher Bruce (*Crossing*, 1994), and Mats Ek (*She Was Black*, 1995 and *A Sort of*, 1997).

Gormley, Antony (*b* London, Aug. 30, 1950) British sculptor and stage designer. He studied at Cambridge then at the Central School of Art, Goldsmiths, and the Slade, developing an interest in the human figure. His major works for dance have been his collaboration with Akram Khan and Sidi Larbi Cherkaoui on *Zero Degrees* (2005), providing life-size mannequins which were manipulated by the performers; and his collaboration with Cherkaoui and the monks from China's Shaolin Temple on *Sutra* (2008), designing a set of large boxes that were arranged to resemble a variety of objects, from coffins to lotus flowers to castle walls. Also designed *Babel* (2010).

Gorsky, Alexander (*b* St Petersburg, 18 Aug. 1871; *d* Moscow, 20 Oct. 1924) Russian dancer, choreographer, ballet master, and teacher. A pioneer in the development of dramatic ballet in Russia. He entered the Imperial Theatre School in St Petersburg in 1880, where he studied with Petipa, and graduated in 1889 into the Mariinsky Theatre where he was appointed soloist in 1895. He began teaching at the school in 1896 and was responsible for ensuring that the *Stepanov system of notation was introduced into its syllabus. In 1899 he was sent to Moscow to mount *Sleeping Beauty* at the Bolshoi, using the notated score of Petipa's St Petersburg staging. In 1900 he moved full time to Moscow where he became premier danseur and regisseur of the Bolshoi Ballet; in 1902 he was appointed director, a position he held until his death in 1924. During this period he revitalized the company, modernizing its productions to give them greater dramatic relevance and creating new ballets. Shortly after arriving in Moscow, he produced his own version of *Don Quixote*, and in 1901 staged revised versions of *Swan Lake* and *The Little Humpbacked Horse*, which have remained extant. In 1902 he choreographed his first completely original work *Gudule's Daughter* (mus. Anton Simon and based on the story of *The Hunchback of Notre-Dame*).

A list of his other works includes *The Magic Mirror* (mus. Arseny Koreshenko, 1905), *Pharaoh's Daughter* (mus. Pugni, 1905), *Coppélia* (1905), *Raymonda* (1908), *Études* (mus. Rubinstein, 1908), *Salammbô* (mus. Arends, 1910), *Giselle* (1907), *Le Corsaire* (mus. Adam, 1912), *Love is Quick* (mus. Grieg, 1913), *Eunice and Petronius* (mus. Chopin, 1915), *Fifth Symphony* (mus. Glazunov, 1916), *La Bayadère* (1917), *Stenka Razin* (mus. Glazunov, 1918), *Nutcracker* (1919, the first Moscow staging), *Swan Lake* (new version, 1920), *Salome's Dance* (mus. R. Strauss, 1921), *Les Petits Riens* (mus. Mozart, 1922), *Giselle* (1922), and *The Venus Grotto* (mus. Wagner, 1923). In 1911, for the coronation of George V, he staged *The Dance Dream* at the Alhambra Theatre in London. The victim of deteriorating mental health in his later life, he died in a mental hospital.

Goslar, Lotte (*b* Dresden, 27 Feb. 1906; *d* Great Barrington, Mass., 16 Oct. 1997) German-US dancer and mime artist. She studied with Wigman and appeared in cabaret in Berlin before leaving Germany in 1933. As part of Erika Mann's cabaret The Peppermill, she visited the US in 1937 and subsequently worked in Hollwood, choreographing for her own company and for film. She also taught a highly individual form of dance-mime, her pupils including Marilyn Monroe.

Gosling, Nigel *See* BLAND, ALEXANDER.

Gothenburg Ballet Swedish company which dates back to 1920 when the local Stora Teater became a full-time opera house with a resident ballet company. As in most European opera houses, the ballet was usually to be found in opera productions and evenings devoted to ballet were initially rare. However Ivo Cramér, Cullberg, and Massine worked with the company in the 1950s, and Cullberg and Lifar staged several productions there during the 1960s. In 1967 Conny Borg's appointment as ballet director created a new era for the company, as Borg attempted to build up a repertory of new and contemporary ballets with guest choreographers such as Cullberg, Cramér, Gore, Lander, and Petit. In 1970 Borg was succeeded by E. M. von Rosen, who added a more classical focus to the repertory with stagings of *Napoli*, *La Sylphide*, *Swan Lake*, and *Romeo and Juliet*. But Ulf Gadd (artistic director 1976–88) and Flemming Flindt also contributed new works as did US choreographer Robert North, who was artistic director from 1991 to 1996, and created *The Snowman* (mus. Howard Blake) for the 1993–4 season. In 1996 Ulf Gadd returned as artistic director; succeeded by Anders Hellström in 1999 and by Johannes Öhman in 2007.

Gould, Diana (*b* London, 12 Nov. 1912; *d* 25 Jan. 2003) British dancer. She studied with

Rambert in London and Egorova in Paris, dancing with Diaghilev's Ballets Russes at the age of 13 and later with Pavlova. She was one of the leading soloists in the early days of Ballet Rambert where she created roles in Ashton's *Leda and the Swan* (1928) and *Capriol Suite* (1930), in Tudor's *The Planets* (1934), and in de Valois's *Bar aux Folies-Bergère* (1934). She also danced with Balanchine's Les Ballets 1933. After leaving Rambert in 1935 she danced briefly with de Basil's Ballets Russes, with the Markova-Dolin company (1935-7), and with the Arts Theatre Ballet (1940-1). She also appeared as an actress and was in a touring production of *The Merry Widow* (1944-6). She retired from the stage after marrying the violinist Yehudi Menuhin in 1947.

Gould, Morton (*b* Richmond Hill, 10 Dec. 1913; *d* Orlando, Fla., 21 Feb. 1996) US composer. He composed the score for Agnes de Mille's *Fall River Legend* (1948) and E. Martinez's *Fiesta* (1957). His concert music was used by Robbins (*Interplay*, 1945), Balanchine (*Clarinade*, 1964), and Eliot Feld (*Jive*, 1973). In 1952 he composed Tap Dance Concerto—for tap dancer and symphony orchestra.

Graduation Ball Ballet in one act with choreography and libretto by Lichine, music by Johann Strauss, arranged by Antal Dorati, and designs by Benois. Premiered 28 Feb. 1940 by the Original Ballet Russe at the Theatre Royal, Sydney, with Riabouchinska, Lichine, Orlov, and Runanine. The ballet, set in 1840s Vienna, is a comic-romantic depiction of a group of young military cadets visiting a girls' boarding school for their graduation ball. A perennial favourite, it was revived for many companies, including the Royal Danish Ballet (1952) and London Festival Ballet (1957).

Graham, Martha (*b* Allegheny, Pa., 11 May 1894; *d* New York, 1 Apr. 1991) US dancer, choreographer, teacher, and company director. The towering figure of 20th-century American modern dance, she was its single most important influence. The technique she developed, antithetical to classical ballet in every sense, spread throughout North America and Europe, while her intensely personal choreography opened up the art form to new forms of dramatic expression. She began studying at the Denishawn school in 1916; at the comparatively late age of 22, and joined the Denishawn company, where she remained until 1923. She then performed with the musical revue *Greenwich Village Follies* (1923-5) and taught at the Eastman School of Music in Rochester, New York. On 18 Apr. 1926 she gave her first solo recital in New York at the 48th Street Theater. A year later she founded the Martha Graham School of Contemporary Dance, which

became the leading school of its kind in the world. Her system of teaching stressed the importance of the lower back and pelvis in generating movement, and also the importance of breathing, the stylized method of which became known as the principle of *contraction and release. Her choreography, with its earthbound dynamic and angular shaping, was revolutionary, although later her style softened into a more fluid and lyrical line. Her company was born out of her school giving its first performance in 1929 and touring internationally from the 1950s. Initially it was an all-women ensemble, but from 1944 Graham included men. She called her productions ballet, although they were nothing like the fairy tales of classical repertory. Her narrative works drew their inspiration from Greek mythology (Medea in *Cave of the Heart*, Jocasta in *Night Journey*, Clytemnestra), Native American folklore (*El Penitente*), real-life historical figures (Emily Dickinson in *Letter to the World*, the Brontë sisters in *Deaths and Entrances*, Joan of Arc in *Seraphic Dialogue*) and were characterized by an intense exploration of the interior worlds of their characters, particularly the female ones. In *Lamentation* (mus. Kodály, 1930), she explored the dynamics of grief; in *Frontier* (mus. Horst, 1935) she celebrated the pioneer women who settled in the American West, a theme she returned to again, most notably in *Appalachian Spring* (1944). Graham was not purely serious, *Every Soul is a Circus* (1939) and *Acrobats of God*, were both humorous works while *Diversion of Angels* was a work of unusual lyricism. Graham the choreographer was inextricably linked to Graham the dancer, and she continued to perform until 1969; when she was 74.

She worked closely with her collaborators, including the music adviser Louis *Horst and the designer Isamu *Noguchi. Among those she taught, and later danced with, were the choreographers Bertram Ross, Erick Hawkins, Merce Cunningham, Paul Taylor, and Robert Cohan. In the 1957 film *A Dancer's World* she explained her artistic philosophy and illustrated her system of teaching. In 1975 she choreographed *Lucifer* for Margot Fonteyn and Rudolf Nureyev, a work which also marked her first collaboration with the fashion designer Halston. She created 181 works in total. Author of *The Notebooks of Martha Graham* (New York, 1973) and her autobiography *Blood Memory* (New York, 1991). In 1976 she received the Medal of Freedom, the highest civilian honour in the US. A list of her works includes *Primitive Mysteries* (mus. Horst, 1931), *American Document* (mus. Ray Green, 1938), *El Penitente* (mus. Horst, 1940), *Letter to the World* (mus. Hunter Johnson, 1940), *Deaths and Entrances* (mus. Hunter Johnson, 1943), *Herodiade* (mus. Hindemith, 1944), *Appalachian Spring* (mus. Copland, 1944), *Cave of the Heart* (mus. Barber,

1946), *Errand into the Maze* (mus. Menotti, 1947), *Night Journey* (mus. William Schuman, 1947), *Diversion of Angels* (mus. Dello Joio, 1948), *Seraphic Dialogue* (mus. Dello Joio, 1955), *Clytemnestra* (mus. Halim El-Dabh, 1958), *Episodes: Part 1* (mus. Webern, 1959), *Acrobats of God* (mus. Surinach, 1960), *Phaedra* (mus. Robert Starer, 1962), *Circe* (mus. Hovhaness, 1963), *The Witch of Endor* (mus. Schuman, 1965), *Cortege of Eagles* (mus. Eugene Lester, 1967), *A Time of Snow* (mus. Dello Joio, 1968), *The Lady of the House of Sleep* (mus. Starer, 1968), *The Archaic Hours* (mus. Lester, 1969), *Mendicants of Evening* (mus. David Walker, 1973), *Myth of a Voyage* (mus. Hovhaness, 1973), *Lucifer* (mus. El-Dabh, 1975), *Frescoes* (mus. S. Barber, 1978 or 1979), *Acts of Light* (mus. C. Nielsen, 1981), *The Rite of Spring* (mus. Stravinsky, 1984), *Persephone* (mus. Stravinsky, 1987), *Night Chant* (mus. Carlos Nakai, 1988), *American Document* (mus. John Corigliano, 1989), *Steps in the Street* (reconstruction, mus. Wallingford Riegger, 1989), and *Maple Leaf Rag* (mus. Joplin, 1990). Following her death the Martha Graham Dance Company continued under the direction of Ronald Protas, who set up the Martha Graham Trust to license her work to dance companies and schools. Graham's works are now in the repertoires of several major ballet companies, including Dutch National Ballet and American Ballet Theatre. In 2000 the company suspended operations due to financial problems; in 2003 it resumed under new direction. It is primarily devoted to the preservation and performance of the Graham repertory although it has some commissioned works in the repertory by Tharp, Stroman, Childs, and Robert Wilson among others.

(((●))) SEE WEB LINKS

● Website for the Martha Graham company and school

Grahn, Lucile (*b* Copenhagen, 30 Jun. 1819; *d* Munich, 4 Apr. 1907) Danish dancer. The most important Danish dancer of her day, and the first to achieve stardom outside Denmark. She studied with Bournonville at the Royal Danish Theatre School in Copenhagen; later with Jean-Baptiste Barrez in Paris and made her debut at the age of 7 in Copenhagen, in the role of Cupid. She became a favourite of Bournonville, creating the role of Astrid in his *Valdemar* in 1835, a year after her official debut and in 1836 dancing the title role in his staging of *La Sylphide*, a ballet that was to bring her fame outside Denmark. Quitteria in his *Don Quixote* followed in 1837, the year she was appointed principal. But shortly afterwards she left Copenhagen to launch herself on an international career. It was widely believed her departure was caused by Bournonville making sexual advances, although it may have been his dictato-

rial style of leadership that she fled. She made her Paris Opera debut in *Le Carnaval de Venise* in 1838 and joined the Paris Opera in 1839, where she became Elssler's rival. In 1843 she made her first appearance in St Petersburg. She was one of the four original ballerinas in Perrot's *Pas de quatre*, made in London in 1845. Also at Her Majesty's Theatre in London, she created the title role in Perrot's *Eoline* (1845) and in his *Catarina, ou La Fille du bandit* (1846). She guested frequently on all the main stages of Europe and her break with Denmark was sealed when she supported Germany in the war with Denmark in 1848. She resigned as a dancer in 1856, but worked as a ballet mistress in Leipzig (1858–61) and at the Munich Court Opera (1869–75) where she helped Wagner to stage *Das Rheingold* and *Die Meistersinger von Nürnberg*.

Grand Ballet du Marquis de Cuevas Ballet company founded by Marquis George de *Cuevas in 1947. It was initially known as the Grand Ballet de Monte Carlo and was supported by the principality of Monaco. Its stars included Rosella Hightower, Marjorie Tallchief, George Skibine, and William Dollar. In 1950 the company became autonomous, left Monte Carlo for France, and was renamed Le Grand Ballet du Marquis de Cuevas. It had regular Paris seasons and toured throughout France with its repertoire based on the classics. It was with this troupe, in 1961, that Rudolf Nureyev made his first appearance with a Western company, dancing in its new production of *The Sleeping Beauty*. When de Cuevas died in 1961 the company was dissolved.

Grand Duo Modern dance in one act with choreography by Mark Morris, music by Lou Harrison, and costumes by Susan Ruddie. Premiered 16 Feb. 1993 by the Mark Morris Dance Group, at the Fine Arts Center at the University of Massachusetts in Amherst. A powerful and primitivist abstract work set to four of the five movements of Harrison's *Grand Duo for Violin and Piano*, it offers a potent vision of Morris's darker side as choreographer.

grand pas Found only in classical ballet, it consists of an entrée for ballerina, premier danseur, and corps de ballet, followed by an adagio, variations, and a coda. Both *Paquita* and *Raymonda* feature grand pas. It is also performed as a concert number, especially the Grand Pas from *Paquita*.

Grand Pas Classique Pas de deux choreographed by Victor Gsovsky with music by Auber. Premiered 12 Nov. 1949 at the Théâtre des Champs-Elysées in Paris with Chauviré and Skouratoff. Distinguished by its dazzling display of classical virtuosity, it has remained popular with dancers everywhere.

Grands Ballets Canadiens de Montréal, Les The Montreal-based company founded by Ludmilla *Chiriaeff in 1957. Despite her Russian origins, Chiriaeff strove to give the company a Canadian identity, using Canadian composers, encouraging Canadian choreographers, and drawing inspiration from French-Canadian folklore. The company has toured widely ever since visiting the US for the first time in 1959 and Europe in 1969. The repertoire mixes the 19th-century classics with landmark works from the 20th century, such as Nijinsky's *L'Après-midi d'un faune* and Kurt Jooss's *The Green Table* but it has also pursued a successful policy of showcasing contemporary choreographers. Paul Taylor, Mark Morris, James Kudelka, Édouard Lock, Nacho Duato, William Forsythe, and Jiří Kylián all have works in the repertory and one of the company's most popular works was Fernand Nault's 1970 staging of the rock opera *Tommy*. Directors succeeding Chiriaeff have included *Nault (1965–74), Brian *Macdonald (1974–7), Lawrence Rhodes (1989–99), and Gradimir Pankov, who was appointed in 1999. In recent years the company has been active in reviving the Diaghilev repertoire and continues to encourage new repertory, with commissioned works by Kim Brandstrup, Shen Wei, and Stijn Celis among others. The company has an associated school.

(⊕) SEE WEB LINKS
• Website for Les Grands Ballets Canadiens de Montréal

Grand Union, The US improvisatory dance collective founded in 1970 by a group of post-modern choreographers in New York City. Its membership included Trisha Brown, David Gordon, Yvonne Rainier, and Steve Paxton. It broke up in 1976.

Grant, Alexander (*b* Wellington, 22 Feb. 1925) New Zealand dancer and ballet director. He studied with Kathleen O'Brien and Jean Horne and (from 1946) at Sadler's Wells Ballet School, making his debut while still a student. During the Second World War he performed as a song and dance man entertaining the troops in the Pacific then joined Sadler's Wells Ballet (later the Royal Ballet). His first major role was the Barber in Massine's 1947 Covent Garden revival of *Mam'zelle Angot* and two years later he was promoted to soloist. He became the Royal Ballet's leading character dancer, indeed one of the 20th century's finest character artists, and created roles in many ballets. He was especially associated with the works of Ashton, for whom he created roles in *Cinderella* (1948), *Daphnis and Chloe* (1951), *Sylvia* (1952), *Birthday Offering* (1956), *Ondine* (1958), *La Fille mal gardée* (1960), *Persephone* (1961), *The Dream* (1964), *Jazz Calendar* (1968), *Enigma Variations* (1968), and *A Month in the Country* (1976). He was also acclaimed as Petrushka and created the role of Drosselmeyer in the Joffrey Ballet's 1987 production of *The Nutcracker*. He was a principal with the Royal Ballet from 1950 to 1976. From 1971 to 1975 he ran the Royal Ballet's Ballet for All group. He was artistic director of the National Ballet of Canada (1976–83). He also worked as dancer and coach with London Festival Ballet (1985–9).

GRCOP Groupe de Recherche Chorégraphique de l'Opéra de Paris. The experimental wing of the Paris Opera Ballet. It was founded in 1981 and was active throughout the 1980s.

Great Britain Theatrical dance in Great Britain dates back to the beginning of the 18th century with works like John Weaver's comic ballet d'action *The Tavern Bilkers* (1702) and his serious ballet d'action *The Loves of Mars and Venus* (1717). Handel included a substantial dance element in several of his operas of the 1730s (*Il pastor fido*, *Ariodante*, and *Alcina*). Didelot's most famous ballet, *Zéphyre et Flore*, was premiered in London in 1796, while Blasis published his *Code of Terpsichore* there in 1828. Romantic ballet flourished in the 1840s, thanks mainly to the productions of Perrot (*Ondine, La Esmeralda, Pas de quatre*). Late in the 19th century two London theatres, the Alhambra and the Empire, housed most of the important dance events in the country. Diaghilev's Ballets Russes came to Covent Garden in 1911, inspiring a new generation of dance lovers with its vibrant modernist repertoire; its fateful production of the *The Sleeping Princess* was premiered at the Alhambra Theatre in 1921. Modern British ballet owes its roots to two early 20th-century pioneers, Marie *Rambert and Ninette de *Valois, both of whom had danced with Diaghilev. Rambert opened a school in London in 1920 and her students began performing as a company in 1926. Her troupe, which eventually became Ballet Rambert and later *Rambert Dance Company, was the birthplace of two of the most important British choreographers, Ashton and Tudor. In 1966, when it moved away from classical dance and established itself as the leading modern dance company in the country, its formative repertory was created by choreographers such as Tetley and the young Christopher Bruce. De Valois, meanwhile, opened her school in 1926, her company, the Vic-Wells Ballet, made its debut in 1931 and was based at Sadler's Wells Theatre for fifteen years until it moved to Covent Garden in 1946. In 1949 the Sadler's Wells Ballet, with Fonteyn as its star, made its first appearance in the US, a triumphant visit that established its international reputation. In 1956 it received a royal charter, becoming the *Royal Ballet. A second company, which remained at Sadler's Wells, was set up as a sister organization and this was the group which, in 1990, became *Birmingham Royal Ballet. The Royal Ballet had the enormous advantage of two defining choreographers—Ashton and MacMillan—who helped to create a new national style recognized around the world, although de Valois was always careful to emphasize the importance of the Russian tradition through her stagings of the 19th-century classics. In 1950 Markova and Dolin started London Festival Ballet, which eventually became *English National Ballet, the country's second largest company after the Royal. Today it is Britain's premier touring organization. *Scottish Ballet, which grew out of the Bristol-based Western Theatre Ballet, was founded in 1969, *Northern Ballet Theatre (based in Leeds) grew out of Laverne Meyer's Northern Dance Theatre, set up in Manchester in 1969. Modern dance in Britain was initially inspired by Martha Graham, whose company had visited London in the 1950s. In 1969 *London Contemporary Dance Theatre was founded by Robin Howard with Robert Cohan as artistic director. It drew its performers from the school Howard had founded two years earlier to train students in the Graham technique. Although disbanded in the 1990s, LCDT was the most important forum for new contemporary choreography and spawned many independent choreographers (led by Richard Alston and Siobhan Davies) who set up their own companies. In 1978 Val *Bourne, a former dancer, founded *Dance Umbrella, still the country's pre-eminent showcase for new choreography. Its annual London festivals feature international as well as British artists and companies. In the 21st century modern dance continues to flourish, fed partly by the meshing of different vocabularies, such as hip-hop and Indian dance; by the crossing of boundaries between dance, physical theatre, visual art, and new technologies and by the choice of many non-British choreographers to base their careers in the UK. The refurbished Sadler's Wells theatre in London ranks as one of the major dance houses in the world.

Greco, Emio (*b* Brindisi, 6 Nov. 1965) Italian dancer, director, and choreographer. He trained at the Rosella Hightower Centre in Cannes and danced in cabaret before joining the Ballet Antibes of Patrick Tridon. In 1987 he moved to Paris and between 1992 and 1996 performed with the company of Jan Fabre, additionally working with Sabura Teshigawara. In 1995 he met theatre director Pieter C. Scholten and the following year moved to Amsterdam to found their joint company Emio Greco|PC. Their investigations into new forms of dance language have involved intensive scrutiny of the body's relationship with space, light, sound, and text; evolving a style of detailed precision and extreme physicality that has been

displayed in productions such as the *Double Points* series (five works created between 1996 and 2002) and *Hell* (2005). Many of their works have been created in collaboration with visual artists, and they have additionally directed and choreographed theatre and opera, including *Orfeo ed Euridice* (2004).

(((●))) SEE WEB LINKS
• Website with link to Emio Greco|PC

Greco, José (*b* Montorio-nei-Frentani, Italy, 23 Dec. 1919; *d* 26 Dec. 2000) Spanish-Italian dancer. One of the most important figures in Spanish dance in the 20th century. He was raised in New York, where he studied Spanish dance with Helen Veola; later studied with La Argentinita and La Quica. He danced in nightclubs until 1942 when La Argentinita chose him as her partner. After her death in 1945 he danced with her sister, Pilar López. In the late 1940s he formed his own company, which took Spanish dance around the world. His productions were large in scale and played to audiences of up to ten thousand. Through his appearances on television and in films such as *Around the World in Eighty Days* (1955) and *Ship of Fools* (1964) he helped to popularize Spanish dance in America. Following his retirement from the José Greco company in the mid-1990s he settled in Lancaster, Pennsylvania, where he taught. His son José Greco II formed his own flamenco company.

Green Table, The Ballet, or 'dance of death in eight scenes', with choreography and libretto by Jooss, music by Frederick Cohen, and designs by Hein Heckroth. Premiered 3 Jul. 1932 by the Folkwang Tanzbühne at the Théâtre des Champs-Elysées in Paris, with Jooss, Uthoff, Elsa Kahl, Lisa Czobel, and Karl Bergeest. The ballet, which begins with a group of black-suited diplomats arguing around a green table, makes a powerful attack on the futility of war and its horrific consequences for the general population. It won first prize at the inaugural choreographic competition organized by Rolf de Maré and Les Archives Internationales de la Danse in Paris. The ballet became Jooss's signature work and he staged it many times over the years, including a production for the Joffrey Ballet in 1967. His daughter, Anna Markard, staged it for Les Grands Ballets Canadiens in 1991 and for Birmingham Royal Ballet in 1992.

Gregory, Betsy (*b* 1 Jan. 1952, Massachusetts) British-American dancer and director. She trained at London Contemporary Dance School (1973–76) and in 1982 became a founder member of *Second Stride. After retiring from the stage she was associate director of The *Place (1994–97) then worked under Val *Bourne at *Dance Umbrella, Britain's largest festival of contemporary dance, becoming artistic director in 2007.

Gregory, Cynthia (*b* Los Angeles, 8 Jul. 1946) US dancer. She studied ballet with Carmelita Maracci, Michel Panaieff, and Robert Rossellat. In 1961 she joined San Francisco Ballet where she created leading roles in several works by Lew Christensen. In 1965 she joined American Ballet Theatre where she was quickly promoted to principal, dancing classical ballerina roles as well as excelling in works by Balanchine and Tudor. She made her debut as Odette-Odile in 1967, a role that remained closely associated with her. With ABT she created roles in Feld's *At Midnight* (1967), Smuin's *The Eternal Idol* (1969), Nahat's *Brahms Quintet* (1969), Ailey's *The River* (1970), the title role in Nureyev's 1975 staging of *Raymonda*, and Tharp's *Bach Partita* (1984). In 1974 she became the first American to dance in Cuba. A consummate technician, her statuesque physique and dramatic presence made her a very distinctive personality on stage. She retired from ABT in 1991, dancing her farewell performance as Odette-Odile with Fernando Bujones although for a short while she continued to guest with other companies including Cleveland San Jose Ballet. She now stages the classical repertory and coaches for companies around the world.

Greve, Kenneth (*b* Copenhagen, 1969) Danish dancer, choreographer, and director. He trained at the Royal Danish Ballet School, and then at the School of American Ballet, graduating into New York City Ballet in 1986 then moving to American Ballet Theatre in 1988 and to Paris Opera Ballet in 1989 where Nureyev promoted him to étoile. He additionally danced with Stuttgart Ballet in 1990 and the Vienna State Opera Ballet in 1991, finally returning to Denmark, as principal dancer, in 1992. An exceptionally tall dancer with a commanding dramatic presence, Greve danced lead roles in both the classical and 20th-century repertories and also guested widely, partnering *Ya-nowsky in performances with the Royal Ballet. He has choreographed several ballets for students and workshops, also *Hamlet* (2003) for the South African Ballet and *Nutcracker* (2007) for the Royal Danish Ballet.

In 2008 he retired from the stage to become director of the National Ballet of Finland. He is married to the dancer Marie-Pierre Greve.

Grey, (Dame) Beryl (orig. Beryl Groom; *b* London, 11 Jun. 1927) British dancer and ballet director. She studied with Madeline Sharp and at Sadler's Wells Ballet School where she was a pupil of de Valois, Sergeyev, and Volkova; later studies with Anna Northcote and Andrey de Vos. She joined Sadler's Wells Ballet (later the Royal Ballet)

in 1941 when she was just 14, a unique British version of the famous Russian 'baby ballerinas'. On her fifteenth birthday she danced her first Odette-Odile, and soon afterwards added *Giselle* and *The Sleeping Beauty* to her repertory. An exceptionally tall and elegant dancer, she was an outstanding Lilac Fairy and Queen of the Wilis and danced the former role at the historic re-opening of the Royal Opera House in 1946. Her list of created roles is comparatively small: Ashton's *The Quest* (1943), *Les Sirènes* (1946), *Cinderella* (Winter Fairy, 1948), *Homage to the Queen* (1953), and *Birthday Offering* (1956); de Valois's *Promenade* (1943); Massine's *Donald of the Burthens* (1951); and Cranko's *Lady and the Fool* (1955). In 1952 she made the first stereoscopic ballet film, *The Black Swan*, with John Field. In 1957, after sixteen years with the Royal Ballet, she loosened her ties with the company to dance as an international guest artist. She was the first Western dancer to guest at the Bolshoi (1957–8) and subsequently danced in Leningrad, Kiev, and Tbilisi. She wrote about her experiences in the Soviet Union in *Red Curtain Up* (London, 1958). In 1964 she danced in China, performing with the Peking and Shanghai Ballet companies, and narrating her experiences in *Through the Bamboo Curtain* (London, 1965). From 1968 to 1979 she was artistic director of London Festival Ballet (later English National Ballet) and also served as Chairman (from 1984) and President (from 1991) of the Imperial Society of Teachers of Dancing. In 1984 she staged *Giselle* for the West Australian Ballet, in 1986 *The Sleeping Beauty* for the Royal Swedish Ballet. She continues to coach her former repertory. Dame of the Order of the British Empire 1988.

Grigoriev, Serge (*b* Tichvin or Tikhvin, 5 Oct. 1883, *d* London, 28 Jun. 1968) Russian dancer and ballet master. He was regisseur for the Diaghilev company for twenty years, responsible for its day-to-day running. He trained at the Imperial Theatre School in St Petersburg, graduating in 1900 into the Mariinsky Theatre company. In 1909 he was hired by Diaghilev as business manager and rehearsal director for the Ballets Russes Paris season; he stayed with the company until Diaghilev's death, the only member of the impresario's entourage to do so. As a dancer he created the role of Shah Shariar in Fokine's *Scheherazade* (1910), Guidone in Fokine's *Le Coq d'or* (1914), and the Russian Merchant in Massine's *La Boutique fantasque* (1919). When the Ballets Russes folded in 1929 he joined de Basil's Ballets Russes de Monte Carlo as chief regisseur, staying with that company until it, too, disbanded in 1948. Working with his wife, the dancer Lubov Tchernicheva, he produced several Fokine revivals for Sadler's Wells/Royal Ballet: *Firebird* (1954), *Les Sylphides* (1955),

Petrushka (1957), and the Polovtsian Dances from *Prince Igor* (1965). For London Festival Ballet they staged *Scheherazade* (1956). Author of *The Diaghilev Ballet* (London, 1953).

Grigorovich, Yuri (*b* Leningrad, 2 Jan. 1927) Soviet dancer, choreographer, and ballet director. The most important Russian choreographer of the latter half of the 20th century, he ran the Bolshoi Ballet for 30 years. He studied at the Leningrad Ballet School (later the Vaganova) with Vladimir Ponomarev and Alexander Pushkin, and graduated in 1946. From 1946 to 1964 he was a soloist with the Kirov, mostly cast in demi-caractère roles, and among the ballets in which he created roles were Zakharov's *The Bronze Horseman* (1949), Vainonen's *Nutcracker* (1954), Fenster's *Taras Bulba* (1955), and Sergeyev's *The Path of Thunder* (1957). His choreographic career was launched in 1957 when he choreographed Prokofiev's *The Stone Flower* for the Kirov, a revolutionary ballet which proved so successful he was invited to stage it for the Bolshoi Ballet in Moscow in 1959. His next important work was Melikov's *Legend of Love*, which he made for the Kirov in 1961 (and later restaged for the Bolshoi in 1965). In 1961 he was appointed ballet master in Leningrad. In 1964, however, he moved to Moscow as chief choreographer and artistic director of the Bolshoi Ballet, and during the next 30 years his repertory came to dominate the company's style and image. His stagings of the classics (*Sleeping Beauty*, *Nutcracker*, *Swan Lake*, *Raymonda*, and *Giselle*) were often criticized for their simplistic editing but his own ballets were a triumph of theatrical energy and emotional thrust. He proved to be a master of larger-than-life dramatic statement and intense lyrical expression; he was particularly adept at choreography en masse, often filling the stage with a thrilling display for the ensemble. His production of Khachaturian's *Spartacus* in 1968 became his most popular ballet, featuring some of the most explosive choreography ever written for the male dancer. However *Ivan the Terrible* (mus. Prokofiev, 1975), *Romeo and Juliet* (mus. Prokofiev, 1979), and *The Golden Age* (mus. Shostakovich, 1982) were also extremely successful. He formed his own company in 1990 and after leaving the Bolshoi continued to stage his productions around the world. In 2008 he was invited back to the Bolshoi, as ballet master in charge of his own repertory. People's Artist of the RSFSR 1966, Lenin Prize 1970. He married the ballerina Natalia *Bessmertnova.

Grisi, Carlotta (*b* Visinada, Jun. 1819; *d* St Jean, Switzerland, 20 May 1899) Italian dancer. One of the great ballerinas of the Romantic era, she earned her place in history by creating the title role in *Giselle*. She studied at the La Scala

ballet school in Milan with Claude Guillet and joined the La Scala corps de ballet in 1829 while still a child. In 1834, while on tour in Italy, the 14-year-old Grisi met Jules Perrot, who was to become the most important influence in her career. He choreographed most of his important ballets for her; she became both his pupil and his mistress and in 1836 took the name of Madame Perrot, although they never married. In 1836 and 1837 she danced in Paris, London, and Vienna, although did not really come to the public's attention until 1840 when she appeared with Perrot in the character dances of the opera *Zingaro* in Paris. The following year she joined the Paris Opera; her first roles were ballet divertissements in operas, among them Donizetti's *La Favorite*. Then came the title role in *Giselle* in the summer of 1841, choreographed by Coralli and Perrot. Other ballerina roles followed: in Albert's *La Jolie Fille de Gand* (1842), Coralli's *La Péri* (1843), Perrot's *La Esmeralda* (London, 1844), *Pas de quatre* (London, 1845), *Les Quatres saisons* (London, 1848), *La Filleule de fées* (Paris, 1849), *The Naiad and the Fisherman* (St Petersburg, 1851), and *Gazelda* (St Petersburg, 1853), Mazilier's *Le Diable à quatre* (Paris, 1845), *Paquita* (Paris, 1846), and *Grisélidis* (Rome, 1848), and P. Taglioni's *Métamorphoses* (London, 1850). Grisi regularly appeared in London throughout the 1840s, and was ballerina with the Imperial Theatres in St Petersburg (1850–3). She retired in 1854, barely 34 years old, to Switzerland. Gautier, who wrote the librettos of *Giselle* and *La Péri* for her, wrote of Grisi that 'she is nature and artlessness personified'.

Grosse Fuge Ballet in one act with choreography and costumes by van Manen, music by Beethoven, sets by Jean Paul Vroom. Premiered 8 Apr. 1971 by Nederlands Dans Theater in Scheveningen, with Sarstädt, Benoit, Venema, Vervenne, Westerdijk, Christe, Waterbolk, and Koning. Set to two Beethoven scores (Op. 133, 130), this sensuous work explores the relationships between four male–female couples. It has been revived for many companies including the Royal Ballet, Birmingham Royal Ballet, Houston Ballet, San Francisco Ballet, and Lyon Opera Ballet.

Grossman, Danny (orig. Daniel Williams; *b* San Francisco, 13 Sept. 1942) US dancer, teacher, choreographer, and director based in Canada. He studied with Gertrude Shurr, May O'Donnell, Wishmary Hunt, and Don Farnworth. He danced with the Paul Taylor Company from 1963 to 1973, then moved to Canada having been invited to perform with Toronto Dance Theatre. He maintained a long association with that company but in 1978 founded his own Toronto-based company, Danny Grossman Dance Company, for which he has since made many works. His choreography, athletic and entertaining in style, often explores social and political themes. His works are in the repertoire of several companies including the Paris Opera Ballet, Les Grands Ballets Canadiens, and the National Ballet of Canada. During the 1990s Grossman's company began to stage revivals of modern dance classics, including works by Charles Weidman, Paul Taylor, Anna Sokolow, and Robert Desrosiers and from 2005 began to manage the staging and teaching of Grossman's own repertory worldwide.

🌐 SEE WEB LINKS
• Website for Danny Grossman Dance Company

grossvatertanz (grandfather dance) A 17th-century German dance in polonaise style usually performed at wedding parties. A famous theatrical example is to be found in the first act of Tchaikovsky's *Nutcracker*.

Groupe de la Place Royale, Le Canadian experimental dance company founded in 1966 by Jeanne Renaud in Montreal. Renaud choreographed more than 40 works for the troupe before being succeeded by Peter Boneham and Jean-Pierre Perreault. In 1977 the company moved to Ottawa and from 1988 onwards re-created itself as a choreographic base and laboratory for Canadian choreographers until its closure in 2009.

Gsovsky, Tatjana (orig. T. Isatchenko; *b* Moscow, 18 Mar. 1901, *d* Berlin, 29 Sept. 1993) Russian-German dancer, ballet director, choreographer, and teacher. One of the most important influences on German ballet in the 20th century, and the leading German choreographer of the 1940s and 1950s. She studied at the Duncan studio in St Petersburg (Petrograd) and later with Laurent Novikov, Vera Kirsanova, Preobrajenska, and at the Dalcroze school in Dresden-Hellerau. After the October Revolution she became ballet mistress in Krasnodar, where she met Victor Gsovsky, the dancer and teacher whom she married. She left Russia in 1925 ending up in Berlin where she and her husband started a school in 1928. She worked as a choreographer in German variety theatres and at the opera houses in Essen, Leipzig, and Dresden. From 1945 to 1952 she was ballet director of the German State Opera in East Berlin, where she choreographed many works. After a short time with the Teatro Colón in Buenos Aires (1952–3), she returned to Germany and joined the Municipal Opera in West Berlin (later the Berlin Opera Ballet) where she remained from 1954 to 1966. In 1955 she founded the pioneering chamber group, the Berlin Ballet, which toured widely and in 1961 became the touring section of the Berlin Opera Ballet. She

was also ballet director in Frankfurt (1959–66). She created numerous ballets, most of them for the companies in East and West Berlin. She choreographed the first productions of Henze's *Der Idiot* (*The Idiot*, Berlin, 1952), Orff's *Trionfo di Afrodite* (Milan, 1953), Egk's *Die chinesische Nachtigall* (Munich, 1953), Nono's *Der rote Mantel* (*The Red Cloak*, Berlin, 1954), Sauguet's *Die Kameliendame* (Berlin, 1957), Klebe's *Menagerie* (Berlin, 1958), Gassmann's *Paean* (Berlin, 1960), and Blacher's *Tristan* (Berlin, 1965). She choreographed the first German production of Prokofiev's *Romeo and Juliet* (Berlin, 1948) and Weill's *The Seven Deadly Sins* (Frankfurt, 1960). Author of *Ballett in Deutschland* (Berlin, 1954).

Gsovsky, Victor (*b* St Petersburg, 12 Jan. 1902, *d* Hamburg, 14 Mar. 1974) Russian dancer, teacher, choreographer, and ballet director. He studied with Eugenie (Evgenia) Sokolova in St Petersburg and started teaching while still very young. He married Tatjana Isatchenko, whom he met in Krasnodar, and went with her to Berlin in 1925. He was appointed ballet master at the German State Opera, where he remained for three years; with his wife he opened a school in Berlin in 1928. From 1930 to 1933 he worked as a choreographer for the German UFA Film Company. After that he worked and travelled widely. From 1937 he was ballet master of the Markova-Dolin company; in 1938 he began teaching in Paris and in 1945 was appointed ballet master of the Paris Opera. In 1946–7 he was ballet master with the Ballets des Champs-Elysées and again in 1948 and 1953 with the Metropolitan Ballet in London in 1947. From 1950 to 1952 he was ballet director of the Munich State Opera. After leaving Munich he worked as a choreographer and ballet master in several European locations. He was ballet master in Düsseldorf (1964–7) and at the Hamburg State Opera (1967–70). He staged the first post-war production of *La Sylphide* for the Ballets des Champs-Elysées in 1946. His best-known work by far is the *Grand Pas Classique* (mus. Auber, 1949), which is still performed in galas around the world. An influential teacher, his students included Yvette Chauviré, Violette Verdy, and Vera Zorina.

Guangdong Modern Dance Company Mainland China's first professional modern dance company. It was founded in 1992 under the auspices of the Guangdong Province Department of Culture and with Willy *Tsao as artistic director. From the start the company aimed to develop its own distinctly Chinese aesthetic and its own choreographers, who have included *Shen Wei, Xing Liang, Sang Ji-jia, and Liu Qi. In 2008 the company collaborated with San Franciscan choreographer Margaret Jenkins on *Other Suns*. Tsao, who left the post of artistic director in 1998, returned to it in 2004. The company tours widely in China and abroad and since 2004 has hosted the annual Guangdong Modern Dance Festival.

(((●))) SEE WEB LINKS

• Website for the Guangdong company

Guérin, Isabelle (*b* Rosny sous Bois, 6 May 1961) French dancer. She studied at the Paris Conservatoire and the Paris Opera Ballet School, and joined the Paris Opera Ballet in 1978, becoming an étoile in 1985. She created roles in Armitage's *GV 10* (1984), Nils Christe's *Before Nightfall* (1985), Nureyev's *Cinderella* (1986), Forsythe's *In the middle somewhat elevated* (1987), Tharp's *Rules of the Game* (1989), and Preljocaj's *Le Parc* (1994). A glamorous and versatile dancer, she was equally acclaimed in the classical and modern repertories. She retired from the Paris Opera in 2001. Pavlova Prize (1988).

Guest, Ivor (*b* Chislehurst, 14 Apr. 1920) British dance historian. A solicitor by profession, he became one of the leading authorities on 18th- and 19th-century dance and author of many books on dance. A list of his titles includes *The Ballet of the Second Empire 1858–70* (London, 1953), *The Romantic Ballet in England* (London, 1954), *The Ballet of the Second Empire 1847–1858* (London, 1955), *Adeline Genée* (London, 1958), *The Alhambra Ballet* (New York, 1959), *The Dancer's Heritage* (London, 1960), *The Empire Ballet* (London, 1962), *The Romantic Ballet in Paris* (London, 1966, revised 2008), *Two Coppélias* (London, 1970), *Fanny Elssler* (London, 1970), *Le Ballet de l'Opéra de Paris* (Paris, 1976, London 2006), *Gautier on Dance* (1986), *The Ballet of the Enlightenment* (London, 1996), and *The Divine Virginia: A Biography of Virginia Zucchi* (London, 2008). Also author of *Adventures of a Ballet Historian: An Unfinished Memoir* (1982). He discovered Hérold's original score for *La Fille mal gardée*.

Guglielmo Ebreo *See* EBREO, GUGLIELMO.

Guillem, Sylvie (*b* Paris, 23 Feb. 1965) French dancer. The most internationally famous ballerina of her generation, for whom the term superballerina was coined. After early training as a gymnast she studied at the Paris Opera Ballet School (1977–80) and joined the Paris Opera Ballet in 1981. A protégée of Nureyev, possessed of an extraordinarily powerful and supple body and uniquely glamorous stage presence, she quickly came to prominence and created leading roles in a number of ballets, Forsythe's *France/Dance* (1984), van Dantzig's *No Man's Land* (1984), Armitage's *GV 10* (1984), Child's *Premier Orage* (1984), Christe's *Before Nightfall* (1985), and Béjart's *Mouvement-Rythme-Étude* (1985). She

was promoted to étoile in 1984 after her first performance of *Swan Lake*. In 1986 she created the leading role in Nureyev's Hollywood-era *Cinderella* and a principal role in Béjart's *Arepo*; in 1987 she created a leading role in Forsythe's *In the middle somewhat elevated* and in Neumeier's *Magnificat*. In 1989, following a disagreement with Nureyev, she moved to London's Royal Ballet, where she became a principal guest artist. Her repertoire with the Royal Ballet included the leading roles in *Giselle, La Bayadère, Sleeping Beauty, Cinderella, Swan Lake, Romeo and Juliet, Month in the Country, Manon, Don Quixote, Symphony in C, Grand Pas Classique, Herman Schmerman*, and *In the middle somewhat elevated*. In 2000 she also inherited Fonteyn's role in the first revival of Ashton's *Marguerite and Armand* thereby sealing her development from dazzling technician to a dance actress of subtlety and power. In 2002 she took the title role in the Royal Ballet's staging of Mats Ek's *Carmen*. As a classical ballerina Guillem guested worldwide, but while still at the peak of her international fame she followed the example of Baryishnikov by exploring other forms of dance. Her collaboration with the modern choreographer Russell Maliphant resulted in two award-winning creations, *Broken Fall* (2003) and *Push* (2005); she also worked with Maliphant and Robert Lepage on *Eonnagata* (2009). In 2006 she collaborated with Akram Khan on the duet *Sacred Monsters*. In 1998 she staged *Giselle* for the Finnish National Ballet. Gold medal Varna 1983. Pavlova Prize (1989).

(((●))) SEE WEB LINKS

• Sylvie Guillem's website

Guimard, Marie-Madeleine (baptized Paris, 27 Dec. 1743; *d* Paris, 4 May 1816) French dancer. A celebrated ballerina with the Paris Opera whose notorious love life ensured her celebrity off stage as well as on. She began her stage career at the age of 10 when she danced in the corps de ballet of the Comédie-Française, making her official debut in 1756 (or 1758). In 1762 she moved to the Paris Opera where in 1766 she was promoted to première danseuse de demi-caractère. One of her earliest roles was as Terpsichore in *Les Fêtes grècques et romaines*, and throughout her career she was often associated with the muse of dance (an image committed to canvas by Fragonard in a painting the ballerina hung in her Paris villa). During her 27 years with the Paris Opera she appeared in more than 100 ballets by Laval, Noverre, and Maximilien and Pierre Gardel, and in operas by Mozart, Rameau, and Gluck. She often danced for the court at Versailles and Fontainebleau. She was considered a great dramatic artist and was admired for her terre-à-terre dancing. Ironically she was famous for portraying naïvety and innocence on stage, qualities far removed from her real-life personality. Behind the scenes, she agitated for parity with the male stars of the Paris Opera and for a say in how the company was managed. She also enjoyed a love life to rival that of any courtesan, counting bishops and princes among her lovers. In 1772 she built a new home in Paris where she staged pornographic ballets and plays in her own private theatre. In 1789 she followed Noverre to London and appeared at the King's Theatre and at Covent Garden, finding another adoring public among the British. Later in 1789 she married the dancer and poet Jean-Étienne Despréaux and retired from public life.

Gulbenkian Ballet Company founded by the Portuguese Gulbenkian Foundation in Lisbon in 1965. It had its own studios and theatre housed in the foundation's building, which opened in 1970. Its founding ballet master was Walter Gore and it nurtured Portuguese dancers and choreographers, notably Rui *Horta. It was disbanded in 2005.

Gusev, Pyotr (Petr) (*b* St Petersburg, 29 Dec. 1904; *d* St Petersburg, 30 Mar. 1987) Soviet dancer, teacher, and ballet master. Although little known in the West, his impact on 20th-century Soviet ballet was considerable, while he was also the most influential figure in the development of classical dance in China. He studied at the Imperial Theatre School with Ponomarev and Shiriaev. At school he was friendly with Balanchine and joined his Young Ballet group. After graduating in 1922, Gusev joined GATOB (later the Kirov) where he remained until 1935. He and his wife Olga Mungalova were popular performers on the Mariinsky stage, famous for their acrobatic brilliance. In 1935 he moved to the Bolshoi in Moscow, where he was a soloist for the next ten years. When his stage career ended he was appointed artistic director at the Kirov (1945–50), then at Leningrad's Maly Theatre (1960-2), and Novosibirsk Theatre (1963-6). He often worked abroad as a teacher and ballet master, especially in China (1958–62) where he was instrumental in creating the school of Chinese classical dance. He was responsible for the first ballet academies in Beijing, Shanghai, and Guangzhou and taught the first generation of Chinese dancers and choreographers. In Russia he taught extensively at the Bolshoi Ballet School and in Leningrad. He also served several times as ballet master of the Moscow Stanislavsky and Nemirovich-Danchenko Music Theatre. He mounted numerous productions of the 19th-century Russian repertoire. His created roles include: Asak in *The Ice Maiden* (Lopukhov, 1927), title role in *The Nutcracker* (Lopukhov, 1929), and Jerome in *The Flames of Paris* (Vainonen, 1932). His own choreography includes his 1951 production of *The Seven Beauties* (mus. Karaev) for Baku and his 1966 production of *The Three Musketeers* (mus. Basner) for Novosibirsk. He also wrote extensively about dance theory.

Gymnopédies Satie's three piano pieces, composed in 1888, have been used by several choreographers as ballet scores, including Ashton for *Monotones* (Royal Ballet, 1965) and van Manen for *Squares* (Nederlands Dans Theater, 1969).

Györ Ballet Hungarian ballet company based in the city of Györ. It was founded in 1979 by Iván *Markó and until he left the company in 1991 the repertoire was dominated by his works. He was succeeded as director by János Kiss who has since introduced a range of other choreographers into the repertoire including Maguy Marin, Robert North, and Robert Cohan as well as encouraging new choreographers such as Barbara Bombicz and Ottó Demcsák.

⊕ SEE WEB LINKS
• Website for the Györ Ballet

Gypsy, La Ballet in three acts with choreography by Mazilier, libretto by Vernoy de Saint-Georges and Mazilier, music by Benoist, Ambroise Thomas, and Marliani, sets by Philastre and Cambon, and costumes by Paul Lormier. Premiered 28 Jan. 1839 at the Paris Opera with Elssler and Mazilier. The ballet, set in the time of England's Charles II, is based on Cervantes' *Novelas exemplares*, which tells of the abduction of Sarah, daughter of a Scottish lord, who is taken from her home in a castle and forced to live among the gypsies. Twelve years later, having grown up as a gypsy, she is the victim of a love triangle which sees her beloved Stenio murdered by her rival Mab, queen of the gypsies. In a fit of revenge, Sarah takes a dagger to Mab. It was Mazilier's first ballet. Not to be confused with *La *Gitana*, a ballet by F. Taglioni which starred Marie Taglioni and was performed at the same time in St Petersburg.

H.Art.Chaos All-female Japanese dance company. It was founded in 1989 by choreographer Sakiko Oshima and dancer Naoko Shirakawa, with a repertory featuring Oshima's original work, as well as brutally theatrical deconstructions of ballet classics such as *Rite of Spring* and *Sleeping Beauty*. The company also presents work in collaboration with Singapore Dance Theatre, and tours widely.

⊕ SEE WEB LINKS
• Official company website

habanera A slow Cuban dance, in 2/4 time with dotted rhythms. It may have originated in Africa: it came to Spain in the late 19th century via Havana (Habana = Havana). There is a famous example in Bizet's *Carmen* which is an adaptation of Yradier's popular song, *La Paloma*.

Häger, Bengt (*b* Malmö, 27 Apr. 1916) Swedish museum director and author. He worked with several companies as impresario and in 1950 founded the Stockholm Dance Museum which he directed until 1989. In 1963 he also became founder director of the Swedish State Dance School, leaving in 1971. He served on numerous committees and boards including the Carina Ari Memorial Foundation and was author of several books and articles on dance including *Les Ballets Suédois* (Paris, 1989).

Hallberg, David (*b* Rapid City, South Dakota 18 May 1982) American dancer. He studied jazz and tap before beginning formal ballet training at the Arizona Ballet School aged 13. In 1999 he transferred to the Paris Opera Ballet School while additionally attending American Ballet Theatre's summer courses. In 2000 he joined ABT's Studio Company, becoming a full company member in 2001, after which he was promoted soloist in 2004 and principal in 2005. Possessed of exceptional suppleness, precision, and fluency of phrasing, Hallberg is a natural danseur noble; he additionally dances lead roles in many 20th- and 21st-century works including ballets by Jooss, Balanchine, Tudor, Kylián, Tharp, and Forsythe. His international guest appearances include performances with the Bolshoi.

Halprin, Anna (*née* A. Shumann; *b* Winnetka, Ill., 13 Jul. 1920) US dancer, choreographer, and teacher. She studied with Margaret H'Doubler at the Univ. of Wisconsin and made her debut in Weidman's *Sing out Sweet Land* (1945). In 1948 she set up a studio in San Francisco with Welland Lathrop where she taught until 1955, at which point she founded Dancers Workshop, a group where dancers could collaborate with artists from other disciplines. She presented the first of her Summer Workshops in 1959, in which groups of avant-garde artists including Terry Riley, LaMonte Young, Yvonne Rainer, and Meredith Monk collaborated on works like *Birds of America* (1959). While based on the West Coast Halprin had a seminal influence on the New York experimental dance scene and during the early 1960s her works appeared in avant-garde festivals in Europe. A warrant for her arrest was issued in 1967 after New York performances of *Parades and Changes* (1965) because the event featured nude performers. Many of her works, including *Cement Spirit* and *Imitations and Transformations* (both 1971), were created communally within her inter-racial, multi-disciplinary workshops and her interest subsequently shifted from professional to community dance work. In 1995 she created and directed *Planetary Dance: A Prayer for Peace*, a work performed by hundreds of participants in Berlin, to commemorate the 50th anniversary of the end of the Second World War. In June 1999, aged 79, she performed two solos combining speech and dance and in 2001 created *Be With* with Eiko and Koma. She continued to revive her past works.

Hamburg Ballet Ballet company based at Hamburg Opera House. Its origins date back to ballet performances given during the 17th century by dancers associated with the opera company and by visiting companies and artists. During the 1830s and 1840s the great Romantic ballerinas, including Taglioni, Elssler, and Grahn, danced there and during the 1880s Katti Lanner choreographed her first ballets for the company. During the 20th century there was little notable activity until 1959 when Peter van Dyk became director of ballet at the opera and a close connection was forged with Balanchine who revived many of his ballets for the company and also directed some opera productions. In 1973 John *Neumeier was appointed director and virtually re-created the company in his own image. Though some works by other choreographers (Cranko, Béjart, Kylián) have been brought into the repertory, it has been dominated by the 60-plus ballets made by Neumeier, including *St Matthew Passion* (1980), *Nijinsky* (2000), and *Parzival—Episodes and Echo* (2006). Their ambitious scale, theatricality, and variety have showcased the company's fine dancers and brought it an international reputation to rival *Stuttgart's. It frequently tours abroad, in Europe, the US, S. America, and Israel. Since 1978 a school has been attached to the company and since 1989 both it and the company have been housed in Ballettzentrum Hamburg.

Hamel, Martine van (*b* Brussels, 16 Nov. 1945) Dutch-US dancer, choreographer, and director. The daughter of a diplomat, she studied in Copenhagen, Java, The Hague, Caracas, and with Betty Oliphant at the National Ballet School of Canada (1958–62). She made her debut with the National Ballet of Canada in 1963, becoming principal in 1965. She danced many ballerina roles but after moving to America in 1970 joined the Joffrey Ballet as a soloist, and then joined the corps of American Ballet Theatre in 1971, becoming principal in 1973. A tall, strong dancer with a technique that embraced both a muscular power and a delicate expressiveness, she became established as one of the leading classical ballerinas in America. She also danced the modern repertoire, creating roles in, among others, Tharp's *Push Comes to Shove* (1976), in which she was a definitively witty vamp, and Morris's *Drink to Me Only with Thine Eyes* (1988). After leaving ABT in 1991 she guested with various companies, primarily Nederlands Dans Theater 3 (1992–7). She also choreographed several works and from 1984 directed her occasional company New Amsterdam Ballet. Since 2004 she has returned to ABT, teaching at the school and performing character roles.

Hamlet Ballet in one act with choreography and libretto by Helpmann, music by Tchaikovsky, and design by Leslie Hurry. Premiered 19 May 1942 by Sadler's Wells Ballet at New Theatre, London, with Helpmann, Fonteyn, Franca, and Paltenghi. It is set to Tchaikovsky's *Fantasy Overture* and though based on Shakespeare's tragedy it does not re-tell the plot, but portrays the dying Hamlet reliving crucial moments of his life. It was revived for the Royal Ballet in 1964 and 1981 and for Australian Ballet in 1970. Other choreographic treatments of the play include Francesco Clerico

(own mus., Venice, 1788), Louis Henry (mus. Gallenberg, Vienna, 1822), Nijinska (mus. Liszt, Paris, 1934), V. Gsovsky (mus. Blacher, Munich, 1950), Chabukiani (mus. Ravaz Gabichvadze, Tbilisi, 1971), Neumeier (*Hamlet: Connotations*, mus. Copland, New York, 1976), MacMillan (*Sea of Troubles*, mus. Martinů and Webern, Dance Advance, London, 1988), Kim Brandstrup (*Antic*, mus. Ian Dearden, 1993), P. Schaufuss (mus. Sort Sol/Black Sun and Rued Langgaard, Elsinore, 1996), and Wheeldon (*Elsinore*, mus. Pärt, Moscow, 2007).

Hampson, Christopher (*b* Manchester, 31 Mar. 1973) He trained at the Royal Ballet School and graduated into English National Ballet in 1992, becoming soloist in 1996. He began creating workshop ballets in 1992 and created his work for ENB in 1997. In the same year he left to first become a freelance choreographer. His works include *The Nutcracker* (2002) and *Trapeze* (mus. Prokofiev, 2003) for ENB, *Romeo and Juliet* (mus. Prokofiev, 2003) and *Cinderella* (2007) both for Royal New Zealand Ballet, and *Giselle* (2007) for National Theatre of Prague.

Handel, George Frideric (orig. Georg Friedrich Händel; *b* Halle, 23 Feb. 1685; *d* London, 14 Apr. 1759) German-British composer. He wrote no full ballet scores though several of his operas contained ballet divertissements, such as *Almira* (1705), and dance played an important role in operas like *Il pastor fido* (1734) which had a Terpsichore prologue choreographed and danced by Sallé, and *Alcina* (1735) in which the dance role of Cupid was also created by her. Many dance pieces have been set to his concert works including P. Taylor's *Aureole* (1962), Cranko's *Concerti Grossi* (1964), and Morris's *L'Allegro, il penseroso ed il moderato* (1988).

Hanka, Erika (*b* Vincovci, Croatia, 18 Jun. 1905; *d* Vienna, 15 May 1958) Austrian dancer, choreographer, and director. She studied modern dance under Bodenwieser (1923–4) and ballet with Irmgard Thomas, making her debut with Fritz Kaiserfeld in Graz, 1927. The same year she founded a school of dance and gymnastics in Vienna. Between 1929 and 1935 she danced at the Düsseldorf Opera House where she was also assistant to the ballet director (1931–5), after which she joined Ballets Jooss in exile in England (1935–8). She returned to Germany to work as choreographer and ballet director at Apollo Theatre Cologne (1938–9), then at Essen Opera House (1939–40), Hamburg State Opera House (1940–2), and finally, after the success of her ballet *Joan von Zarissa* (mus. Egk, 1940, revived

1941 in Vienna), she took over direction of the Vienna State Opera Ballet (1942–58). The company was struggling with low standards and morale but during the war and post-war years she succeeded in building up a strong repertory of works—many choreographed by herself—in the modern *Ausdruckstanz idiom. Her best-known work is probably *The Moor of Venice* (mus. Blacher, 1955). As the public's taste for ballet revived in the late 1940s she began to focus on more classical training and repertory. The last premiere she oversaw was of a Balanchine work, marking the company's return to an international status.

Hansen, Emil (*b* 1843; *d* 1927) Danish dancer and ballet master. He studied with August Bournonville and became one of the great danseurs nobles of the Royal Danish Ballet. Between 1881 and 1893 he was also the company's ballet master and choreographed several ballets, including *Aditi* (mus. Rung). He also developed his own system of dance notation in which he recorded the original choreography of several ballets including Bournonville's *Napoli*.

Harangozó, Gyula (*b* Budapest, 19 Apr. 1908; *d* Budapest, 30 Oct. 1974) Hungarian dancer, choreographer, and ballet master. He studied at the Budapest State Opera Ballet School and in 1926 joined the company, becoming soloist in 1928. He was noted for his comic gifts and interpretations of character roles and from 1936 to 1974 (apart from two years as ballet master at La Scala Milan, 1939–41) he was the company's chief choreographer—effectively dominating Hungarian ballet for four decades. His style was a blend of classical and folk dance and his best-known ballets include *The Wooden Prince* (1939, revised 1958) and *The Miraculous Mandarin* (1945, revised 1956), both to Bartók's music. He also worked in a wide variety of genres, including versions of the Polovtsian Dances from *Prince Igor* (mus. Borodin, 1938, revised 1961), *Romeo and Juliet* (mus. Tchaikovsky, 1939), *Le Tricorne* (mus. de Falla, 1947), *Coppélia* (mus. Delibes, 1953), and *Scheherazade* (mus. Rimsky-Korsakov, 1959), and also choreographed extensively for film and television. He was made Eminent Artist of the Hungarian Republic, 1957, and awarded Gold Medal of Socialist Labour, 1966. His son, also named Gyula Harangozó followed him as a dancer and director.

Harangozó, Gyula, jun. (*b* Budapest, 1956) Hungarian dancer and director. He trained at the National Ballet Institute in Budapest and at the Moscow Choreographic Institute, graduating into the Hungarian State Opera Ballet in 1976 and becoming soloist in 1978. In 1982 he moved to the Vienna State Opera Ballet, becoming principal in 1985 and guesting internationally. From 1996 he was ballet director of the Hungarian State Opera and in 2005 became director of the Vienna State Opera Ballet.

Hard Nut, The Modern dance work in two acts with choreography by Mark Morris, music by Tchaikovsky, set by Adrianne Lobel, and costumes by Martin Pakledinaz. Premiered 1 Dec. 1991 by the Mark Morris Dance Group at Théâtre Royale de la Monnaie, Brussels, with C. Marshall, R. Besserer, and W. Wagner. This dark, ironic, and highly comic version of *The Nutcracker* is inspired by the work of cartoonist Charles Burns. It is set in a suburban American household where the Stahlbaums' guests wear 1960s bell-bottoms and Afro wigs.

Harkarvy, Benjamin (*b* New York, 16 Dec. 1930; *d* New York, 30 Mar. 2002) US dancer, choreographer, and ballet master. He studied with Chaffee and Caton, at the School of American Ballet and with Tudor, Craske, and others, making his debut with the Brooklyn Lyric Opera (1949–50). After dancing with various concert groups he taught at the Fokine School (1951–5) and in 1955 founded his own school in New York, establishing his reputation as an outstanding, if unorthodox, teacher. In 1957 he was appointed director of the Royal Winnipeg Ballet; in 1958 he became ballet master of Netherlands Ballet and in 1959 formed his own company, Nederlands Dans Theater, with the intention of marrying classical tradition with experiment. He was artistic co-director until 1969 and choreographed many works for the company including *Septet* (mus. Saint-Saëns, 1959), *Madrigalesco* (mus. Vivaldi, 1963), and *Recital for Cello and Eight Dancers* (mus. Bach, 1964). In 1969 he moved to Harkness Ballet as artistic joint director, then in 1970 became co-director of Dutch National Ballet. He resigned after a year and moved to Pennsylvania Ballet as associate director, becoming artistic director (1973–82). He created several ballets there including *Time Passed Summer* (mus. Tchaikovsky, 1973). After leaving he worked as a freelance choreographer and teacher, and taught at the Juilliard School from 1990, becoming director of the Dance Division in 1992.

Harkness, Rebekah (*b* St Louis, 17 Apr. 1915; *d* New York, 17 Jun. 1982) US composer, director, and president of the Harkness foundation. She studied music with Nadia Boulanger and dance with L. Fokine, and in 1961 established the Harkness Foundation which sponsored Robbins's Ballet USA (1961) and the Joffrey Ballet (1962–4). She set up her own *Harkness Ballet in 1964, the Harkness House for Ballet Arts in New York in 1965, and opened the Harkness Theater on Broadway in 1974. The Foundation continued to support dance projects including the 92nd Street Y Harkness Dance Center.

Harkness Ballet US ballet company named after its founder Rebekah Harkness. It was established in 1964 and gave its debut performance in Cannes in 1965 under the direction of Skibine, with Marjorie Tallchief as ballerina and a repertory featuring work by Ailey, Skibine, Bruhn, Brian Macdonald, and S. Hodes. It toured widely, giving its New York debut in 1967. The same year Macdonald was also appointed director but was succeeded by Lawrence Rhodes (1968), who was then joined by Harkarvy in 1969. These changes undermined the company's identity and in 1970 Harkness amalgamated it with the Harkness Youth Ballet (founded 1969) under the direction of Ben Stevenson who was succeeded by Vicente Nebrada. In 1972 she purchased the Harkness Theater which opened with a brief season by the company in 1974. Though the vitality of the dancers was widely admired, the repertory failed to establish a distinct personality and the company was soon disbanded. Its school, Harkness House for Ballet Arts (founded in 1965), continued to operate.

Harlem, Dance Theatre of *See* DANCE THEATRE OF HARLEM.

Harlequinade English commedia dell'arte, a pantomime.

Harlequinade Commedia dell'arte ballet in two acts with choreography by Balanchine, music by Drigo, and design by Ter-Arutunian. Premiered 4 Feb. 1965 by New York City Ballet at New York State Theater with McBride and Villella. This is a re-working of Petipa's *Les Millions d'Arlequin* (1900), set to Drigo's original score. It tells the story of how Harlequin is given gold by a Good Fairy so that he can free Columbine from the power of her wealthy father. An extended production was premiered 14 Jan. 1973. Other versions of the score include Lichine (1950), Brenaa (after Petipa, 1958), and Dolin (after Petipa, 1960).

Härm, Tiit (*b* Tallinn, 1946) Estonian dancer and choreographer. He studied in St Petersburg and made his debut as a soloist with the ballet of the Estonia Theatre in 1966. Betweeen 1967 and 1968 he was first soloist with Young Ballet of Moscow then from 1971 to 1990 étoile with the Estonian National Ballet, where he performed both the modern and classical repertories. He began creating ballets while still a dancer, including *Confession* (mus. Edison Denisov, Estonia, 1984). He was appointed director of the Estonian Ballet (1990–2) then became ballet master at La Scala (1992–4), at Rome Opera Ballet (1995–7), then again at La Scala before returning to

Estonian Ballet as director 2001–9). He created several works for the company including new versions of *Romeo and Juliet* and *Swan Lake* as well as bringing in works by choreographers such as Elo and Bigonzetti.

Harper, Meg (*b* Evanston, Ill., 1944) US dancer, teacher, and choreographer. She studied at the University of Illinois and with Joan Skinner and Cunningham, joining the latter's company in 1967. She remained there for ten years, also teaching at the Cunningham Studio (1968–91). From 1979 to 1990 she was dancer and assistant rehearsal director with the Lucinda Childs Company. She created her first work, *Long-Distance*, for the Cunningham Dance Studio in 1978. She now freelances as a teacher and choreographer.

Harrington, Rex (*b* Peterborough, Ont., 30 Oct. 1962) Canadian dancer. He trained at the National Ballet School, Toronto, and joined National Ballet of Canada in 1983, becoming principal in 1988. Possessed of a powerful technique and charismatic dramatic presence he performed in both the classical and modern repertories, and created many roles, for example in Tetley's *Alice* (1986), *La Ronde* (1987), and *Tagore* (1989), in Kudelka's *The Actress* (1994), *Nutcracker* (1995), *The Four Seasons* (1997), and *Swan Lake* (1999), and in Alleyne's *Blue-Eyed Trek* (1988). He partnered many celebrated ballerinas, including Maximova, Fracci, Kain, and Hart and guested with companies around the world, including La Scala (1993), Australian Ballet (1993), San Francisco Ballet (1994), CAPAB Ballet (1996), and Royal Winnipeg Ballet (many seasons from 1988). He retired from ballet in 2004 to pursue an acting career.

Harrison, Lou (*b* Portland. Ore., 1917; *d* 2 Feb. 2003) US composer. During the Second World War, while collaborating with John Cage on percussion recitals, he also worked as a dancer and dance critic. He wrote several scores for dance including *Changing World* (1936) and *Rhymes with Silver* (1997). Morris commissioned the latter score as well as choreographing works to Harrison's *Grand Duo* (1993) and *World Power* (1995).

Hart, Evelyn (*b* Toronto, 4 Apr. 1956) Canadian dancer. She studied at the National Ballet School (1971–2) then at Royal Winnipeg Ballet School from 1973, making her debut with the company while still a student in 1974. Though initially having to combat her own insecurity as a dancer, she won a devoted public through her passionately emotional interpretations and unusually lyrical style, and was promoted soloist in 1978 and principal in 1979. She danced both the classical and modern repertory, creating leading roles in Nebrada's *The Firebird* (1982) and Duse's *Cinderella*

(Bavarian State Ballet, 1990), and guested abroad with Dutch National Ballet (1982), Sadler's Wells Royal Ballet (1984), and Bavarian State Opera Ballet (from 1990). After leaving Royal Winnipeg Ballet in 2005 she guested occasionally with the Pro Arte Danza, among others, finally retiring in 2006. She was made Officer of the Order of Canada in 1983.

Hart, John (*b* London, 4 Jul. 1921) British dancer and director. He studied with Judith Espinosa and at the Royal Academy of Dancing, joining the Vic-Wells Ballet in 1938 where he was rapidly promoted to principal. He was dancing lead classical roles before the age of 21 as well as creating roles in, for example, de Valois's *The Prospect Before Us* (1940). After war service (1942–6) he returned to the company as principal, creating roles in Ashton's *Sylvia* (1952) and *Homage to the Queen* (1953). In 1955 he was appointed ballet master, becoming assistant director of the Royal Ballet (1962–70). He was then director of ballet at the US International University of Performing Arts in San Diego, California (1970–4), and also artistic director of PACT Ballet Johannesburg (1971–5) where he staged several Ashton ballets. Between 1975 and 1977 he worked as administrator of the Royal Ballet, then in 1980 was appointed artistic director of San Diego Ballet. During 1985 he was dance director of San Diego Opera then subsequently artistic director of Ballet West, Utah (1985–97). He has published two books of dance photographs including *Ballet and Camera* (London, 1956).

Harvey, Cynthia (*b* San Rafael, Calif., 17 May 1957) US dancer. She studied at the Novato School of Ballet in California then at the National Ballet of Canada School, the San Francisco Ballet School, the School of American Ballet, and American Ballet Theatre School. In 1974 she joined ABT, becoming soloist in 1978 and principal (1982–6). With her strong, crisp technique and stylistic versatility she danced both classical and modern repertories, creating leading roles in McFall's *Interludes* (1983) and Baryshnikov's *Cinderella* (1984). In 1986 she moved to the Royal Ballet as a principal guest artist where she extended her range, performing in the classics and several Ashton ballets. She also created a role in Bintley's *Still Life at the Penguin Café* (1987). In 1988 she returned to ABT (while continuing to guest with the Royal until 1990) where she created a role in Tharp's *Quartet* (1988). She has also guested with Baryshnikov and Company (various seasons 1980–6), with Nureyev and Friends, Northern Ballet Theatre (1982), and Sadler's Wells Royal Ballet (various seasons 1987–90). She gave her last performance at a gala performance of *Die Fledermaus* with San Francisco Opera. Since

retiring she has taught for ABT, the Royal Ballet, and Norwegian National Ballet, and assisted Makarova in staging her production of *Bayadère*.

Haskell, Arnold Lionel (*b* London, 19 Jul. 1903; *d* Bath, 14 Nov. 1980) British ballet writer, educator, and enthusiast. He studied at Cambridge and in 1930 was one of the co-founders of the Camargo Society. He also helped in the founding of Sadler's Wells Ballet School. In 1935 he became ballet critic for the *Daily Telegraph*, and subsequently for other newspapers. Between 1947 and 1965 he was director of the Sadler's Wells, later Royal Ballet School (overseeing its expansion to include an academic education), and from 1956 was a governor of the Royal Ballet. From 1947 to 1963 he edited *Ballet Annual*. He was best known for *Ballet* (1938) his popular introduction to dance appreciation, which helped break down many British prejudices against the art, but he wrote several other books, including *Balletomania* (London, 1934), *Diaghileff* (London, 1935, the first detailed biography), *In His True Centre* (London, 1951), and *Balletomane at Large* (London, 1972).

Hassreiter, Joseph (*b* Vienna, 30 Dec. 1845; *d* Vienna, 8 Feb. 1940) Austrian dancer, choreographer, teacher, and ballet master. He began his formal training aged 9 and probably made his debut while still a child at the Kärntnertor Theater. In 1864 he was appointed to the Munich Court Theatre, becoming principal in 1866, then moved to Württemberg Court Theatre as principal (1868–9). In 1870 he joined the Vienna Court Opera Ballet as a soloist. He stayed with the company until 1920 having been subsequently promoted to ballet master, head of the school, and teacher of soloists. His first and most popular ballet, *The Fairy Doll* (1888), is still in the repertory of the State Opera but he created over 40 others including *Rouge et noir* (1894). He was admired as a craftsmanlike entertainer, though some critics complained of the slightness of his subject-matter.

haut, en [Fr., high up] Position of the arms where one or both are raised above the head.

Hawkins, Erick (*b* Trinidad, Col., 23 Apr. 1909; *d* New York, 23 Nov. 1994) US dancer and choreographer. He studied at the School of American Ballet and with Kreutzberg, making his debut with American Ballet in 1935. He danced with the company for two years as well as performing with Ballet Caravan (1936–9). In 1938 he joined Martha Graham's company as her first male dancer, and remained there until 1951 creating roles in *American Document* (1938), *Every Soul is a Circus* (1939), *Letter to the World* (1940), *Punch and Judy* (1941), *Deaths and Entrances* (1943), *Appalachian Spring* (1944), *Dark Meadow* (1946),

Cave of the Heart (1946), Night Journey (1947), and Diversion of Angels (1948). He married Graham in 1948 but they were separated in 1950 and divorced in 1954. He formed his own company and after creating some early dramatic works began evolving the abstract style for which he is best known. Influenced by Greek and oriental art his choreography stressed natural, unforced movement. Some critics remained unimpressed by what they saw as the naïvety of his style, others saw in it a kind of innocent sensuality. He worked in close collaboration with his wife, composer Lucia Dlugoszewski, who accompanied his dances using prepared instruments, and with sculptor Ralph Dorazio. He created many works including Here and Now with Watchers (1957), Early Floating (1962), Naked Leopard (1965), Angels of the Inmost Heaven (1971), Plains Daybreak (1983), Avanti (1984), New Moon (1989), and Many Thanks (1994). He taught his Normative Theory of Movement at his New York studio and gave his first London season in 1980. His company continued to perform after his death and in 1999 premiered two works choreographed by Dlugoszewski, Radical Ardent and Taking Time to be Vulnerable. In 2001 Katherine Duke was appointed artistic director, overseeing both the teaching of Hawkins's technique and the preservation of his repertory.

(((⊕))) SEE WEB LINKS

• Official company website for Erick Hawkins Dance

hay (hey) A country dance dating back to the 1520s, or earlier, and featuring a serpentine formation in which two lines of dancers thread through each other. This movement is featured in other dances, including the *farandole.

Hay, Deborah (*b* New York, 18 Dec. 1941) US dancer and choreographer. She studied at Henry St. Playhouse and with Cunningham, performing with the companies of Limón and Cunningham until she became absorbed in the avant-garde dance collective, Judson Church. Her work here was influenced by the movement rituals of T'ai Chi and focused on the individual qualities of performers, leading on to works where she presented non-trained dancers in non-theatrical spaces like gyms and parks. Her pieces have included Victory 14 (1964), 20 Permutations of 2 Sets of 3 Equal parts in a Linear Order (1969), The Grand Dance (ongoing 1977–9), and The Genius of the Heart (1980). During the 1990s she focused on creating and performing solo works including The Other Side of O (1998) but has recently returned to working with larger ensembles, including the Forsythe Company. Her books include Moving Through the Universe in Bare Feet—Ten Circle Dances for Everybody (together with Donna

Jean Rogers, New York, 1974) and My Body, the Buddhist (2004).

(((⊕))) SEE WEB LINKS

• Official website for the Deborah Hay Dance Company

Haydée, Marcia (*née* M. H. Salaverry Pereira de Silva; *b* Niteroi, 18 Apr. 1939) Brazilian dancer and director. She studied in Rio de Janeiro with Vaslav Veltchek and in 1951 danced with the corps de ballet of Rio's Teatro Municipal before going to Sadler's Wells School for further training. She later studied with Egorova and Preobrajenska, joining the Grand Ballet du Marquis de Cuevas in 1957 then moving to Stuttgart Ballet in 1961 where she was promoted prima ballerina in 1962. Though not a brilliant technician she established herself as one of the great dance actresses of her generation and as well as performing most of the classic ballerina roles she created roles in many Cranko ballets including Romeo and Juliet (1962), Onegin (1965), The Taming of the Shrew (1969), Carmen (1971), and Initials R.B.M.E. (1972). She also created roles in MacMillan's Song of the Earth (1965), Miss Julie (1970), and Requiem (1977), in Tetley's Voluntaries (1973), and Neumeier's Hamlet: Connotations (1976), a range that encompassed comedy and tragedy as well as pure dance. Her frequent partner was Richard Cragun and between them they helped establish Stuttgart as a world centre for dance. She also guested widely with, among others, National Ballet of Canada, American Ballet Theatre, and English National Ballet. In 1976 she was appointed artistic director of Stuttgart Ballet where she introduced ballets by guest choreographers such as Kylián and van Manen as well as encouraging choreographic talent from within the company and creating some works of her own. In 1993 she also took over direction of Santiago Ballet, finally retiring from both companies in 1995. In 1999 she created the role of Blanche in Jean Christoph Blavier's setting of Balzac's novel Le Lys dans la vallée, for Stuttgart Ballet, with Vladimir Malakhov dancing her young lover, Félix. She continues to perform character roles, including Lady Capulet and in 2001 she performed the specially created duet Tristan and Isolde with choreographer Ismael Ivo (Hong Kong). She was awarded German Honour of Merit: First Prize in 1981.

Hayden, Melissa (orig. Mildred Herman; *b* Toronto, 25 Apr. 1923; *d* Winston-Salem, NC, 9 Aug. 2006) Canadian-US dancer and teacher. She studied with B. Volkov, Vilzak, and Schollar and made her debut in 1945 at Radio City Music Hall before joining Ballet Theatre the same year. After a season touring with the Alicia Alonso ballet in 1949 she joined New York City Ballet as a soloist in 1950, becoming principal in 1955 after a brief return to ABT (1953–4). She danced with NYCB until 1973, apart from guest engagements with the Royal Ballet and the National Ballet of Canada in 1963. A bravura dancer, renowned for her unusual stamina and insouciant wit, she created roles in many ballets including Robbins's *Age of Anxiety* (1950) and *The Pied Piper* (1951), Ashton's *Illuminations* (1950), Bolender's *The Miraculous Mandarin* (1951), and Balanchine's *Caracole* (1952), *Divertimento No. 15* (1956), *Agon* (1957), *Stars and Stripes* (1958), *Liebeslieder Walzer* (1960), *A Midsummer Night's Dream* (1962), *Brahms-Schoenberg Quartet* (1966) and *Cortège hongrois*, which was created for her as a farewell tribute in 1973. She also performed the ballerina role in Chaplin's film *Limelight* (1953). In 1973 she was appointed artist-in-residence at Skidmore College, New York; in 1974 she opened her own school in Saratoga, New York, and in 1976 was appointed artistic director of Pacific Northwest Dance in Seattle. In 1983 she joined the faculty of the North Carolina School of the Arts and coached dancers for the Balanchine Foundation's Interpreters Archive. She wrote *Off Stage and On* (New York, 1963) and *Dancer to Dancer* (Garden City, NY, 1981) and was awarded the Handel Medallion of the City of New York in 1973.

Haydn, Franz Joseph (*b* Rohrau, probably 31 Mar. 1732; *d* Vienna, 31 May 1809) Austrian composer. He wrote no ballet scores but many dance works have been set to his concert music including Viganò's Milan production of *The Creatures of Prometheus* (1813), Massine's *Clock Symphony* (Sadler's Wells Ballet, 1948), Balanchine's *Trumpet Concerto* (Sadler's Wells Ballet, 1950), Taras's *Haydn Concerto* (New York City Ballet, 1968), Tharp's *As Time Goes By* (Joffrey Ballet, 1973) and *Push Comes to Shove* (American Ballet Theatre, 1976), and Kylián's *Symphony in D* (Nederlands Dans Theater, 1976, revised 1977).

Hays, David (*b* New York, 1930) American designer who designed the sets for many New York City Ballet productions including Balanchine's *Stars and Stripes* (1958), *Episodes* (1959), *Liebeslieder Walzer* (1960), *A Midsummer Night's Dream* (1962), *Bugaku* (1963), and the 1966 version of *Divertimento No. 15*. In 1967 he changed careers to found the National Theatre of the Deaf, based in Washington.

Heart of the Hills, The (orig. Russ. title *Serdtse gor*) Ballet in three acts with choreography by Chabukiani, libretto by G. Leonidze and N. Volkov, design by Simon Virsaladze, and music by A. Balanchivadze (brother of Balanchine). Premiered 28 Jun. 1938 by the Kirov, Leningrad, with Chabukiani, Vecheslova, and Koren. This was Chabukiani's first work, and it closely conformed to the political demands of Soviet art in its portrayal of a peasant uprising in Georgia, led by the youthful Djardje in protest against heavy taxes imposed by their overlord. Using dance imagery rather than mime to present the drama, Chabukiani incorporated Georgian dance idiom with classical ballet. An earlier version, titled *Sunny Youth*, was shown at Tbilisi Theatre of Opera and Ballet in 1936.

Heathcote, Stephen (*b* Wagin, W. Australia, 16 Oct. 1964) Australian dancer. He studied with Kira Boulsoff and Shelley Rae in Perth and at the Australian Ballet School, joining the company in 1983. Though not a conventionally classical dancer he was a charismatic stage presence, and was promoted principal in 1987. He was especially distinguished in the modern repertory, creating roles in Tetley's *Orpheus* (1987), and Kudelka's *The Book of Alleged Dances* (1999), among others but he also danced most major classical roles, performing Albrecht with the Kirov Ballet in 1989. He danced for a season with American Ballet Theatre in 1992 and also guested with several other companies including the Royal Danish Ballet and Birmingham Royal Ballet. After retiring in 2007 he worked as a coach, also performing character roles. He received the Order of Australia in 1991.

Heaton, Anne (*b* Rawalpindi, 19 Nov. 1930) British dancer and teacher. She studied at Sadler's Wells School, making her debut in 1945 with Sadler's Wells Opera. In 1946 she joined Sadler's Wells Theatre Ballet creating roles in Ashton's *Valses nobles et sentimentales* (1947) among others, then in 1948 moved to Sadler's Wells Ballet where she became a principal, excelling in Romantic ballets like *Giselle* but also creating roles in MacMillan's *The Burrow* (1958) and *The Invitation* (1960). Her career was curtailed by injury, and she danced only as a guest artist between 1959 and 1962. After retiring she taught at the Arts Educational School and also staged some ballets, including *Giselle* for Iranian National Ballet in 1971. She married John Field.

Heeley, Desmond (*b* 1932) British designer. He began designing for the stage in 1947 and though largely based in the US he has designed for ballet companies around the world, including Royal Ballet, English National Ballet, La Scala, Stuttgart, and Houston. His earliest ballet designs include MacMillan's *Solitaire* (Sadler's Wells Theatre Ballet, 1956—though these were initially intended for another ballet, possibly *The Angels*) and Cranko's *Prince of the Pagodas* (Royal Ballet, 1957). He designed several productions for Bruhn, including *Swan Lake* (National Ballet of Canada, 1967) and *La Sylphide* (American Ballet

Theatre, 1983), also for Hynd including *Merry Widow* (Australian Ballet, 1975) and *Coppélia* (English National Ballet, 1985). In 1998 he designed Stevenson's *The Snow Maiden* for Houston Ballet and American Ballet Theatre. He has also worked extensively in theatre, opera, musicals, and film.

Heine, Heinrich (*b* Düsseldorf, 13 Dec. 1797; *d* Paris, 17 Feb. 1856) German poet and writer, whose story of the Wilis (contained in *Geschichte der neuren schönen Literatur in Deutschland*, 1833, French version *De l'Allemagne*, Paris, 1835) provided Gautier with the inspiration for his *Giselle* libretto (1841). Heine also wrote two of his own ballet librettos. *Die Göttin Diana* (1846) was offered to Lumley at Her Majesty's Theatre, while *Der Doctor Faust* (1847) was actually commissioned by Lumley. Neither project was realized, though some later *Faust ballets made use of his libretto.

Heinel, Anna Fredrike (*b* Bayreuth, 4 Oct. 1753; *d* Paris, 17 Mar. 1808) German dancer. She studied with Lépy and later with Noverre in Stuttgart but made her debut in 1767 at the Paris Opera. A dancer of unusual virtuosity (she is credited with inventing the pirouette à la seconde) she was dubbed 'La Reine de la danse'. This aroused the jealousy of G. *Vestris and in 1771 she left to become principal dancer at the King's Theatre, London. She performed there frequently until 1773 when she returned to the Paris Opera and became a leading interpreter of Noverre's ballets, such as *Jason et Medée*, and appeared in the first Paris productions of Gluck's *Orphée et Euridice* (1774) and *Iphigénie en Tauride* (1778). She retired in 1782 and she and Vestris made up their quarrel. She gave birth to his son Adolphe in 1791 and in 1792 they were married.

Helliwell, Rosemary (*b* London, 28 Jul. 1955) British dancer and choreographer. She studied at the Doreen Bird School and the John Cranko Ballet School, becoming a dancer with Stuttgart Ballet in 1976 and resident choreographer in 1977, creating *Hedda Gabler* (mus. J. Skrowaczewski, 1981), among others. She has also been guest choreographer with many companies including Hong Kong Ballet. In 1984 she was appointed professor of dance at the Akademie des Tanzes, Heidelberg-Mannheim, and in 1998 assistant director.

Hellstrom, Anders (*b* Stockholm, 1962) Swedish dancer and director. He studied at the Royal Swedish Ballet School and graduated to the company in 1980. In 1984 he moved to Hamburg Ballet and in 1993 to Ballett Frankfurt. He was director of Gothenburg Ballet (1999–2002) during which time he raised the company's inter-

national profile, acquiring works by Forsythe, Duato, and McGregor among others. He was appointed director of Nederlands Dans Theater in 2004.

Helpmann, (Sir) Robert (*b* Mount Gambier, 9 Apr. 1909; *d* Sydney, 28 Sept. 1986) Australian dancer, choreographer, director, and actor. He studied locally as a child then with Pavlova's company while it was touring Australia. After performing in musicals and revues he came to London in 1933 and was accepted into the Vic-Wells (later Sadler's Wells) Ballet where he was promoted principal in 1934. In 1935 he danced with Weidman and in the revue *Stop Press* but otherwise remained with Sadler's Wells Ballet until 1950 (and as occasional guest artist thereafter). Although he lacked a powerful technique, his vivid dramatic talent, musicality, and stage presence allowed him to portray convincingly elegant classical princes as well as to create memorable interpretations of contemporary roles. His celebrated partnership with Fonteyn played a major part in the development of Sadler's Wells Ballet and in the popularization of dance in Britain. He created many leading roles in, among others, de Valois's *The Haunted Ballroom* (1934), *Checkmate* (1937), *The Prospect Before Us* (1940), and *Don Quixote* (1950), and Ashton's *Apparitions* (1936), *A Wedding Bouquet* (1937), *Dante Sonata* (1940), *Don Juan*, and *Cinderella* (both 1948). He created his first workshop ballet, *La Valse* (mus. Ravel) in 1939 for the Royal Academy of Dancing and his first professional ballet in 1942, *Comus* (mus. Purcell–Lambert) for Sadler's Wells Ballet. This was followed by *Hamlet* (mus. Tchaikovsky, 1942), *Miracle in the Gorbals* (mus. Bliss, 1944), and *Adam Zero* (mus. Bliss, 1946). Though his choreographic ideas were not original he had an instinct for inventive staging and narrative and created the leading roles in all these works. During this period he also worked occasionally as an actor and opera producer, appearing notably in the films *The Red Shoes* (1948) and *Tales of Hoffmann* (1951). In 1955 he went to Australia with the Old Vic Company, starring with Katharine Hepburn in *The Merchant of Venice*, *Measure for Measure*, and *The Taming of the Shrew*. In 1960 he collaborated with Nijinska on the de Cuevas production of *Sleeping Beauty* and in 1963 worked with Ashton on the Royal Ballet production of *Swan Lake*. In the same year he also choreographed *Elektra* (mus. Arnold) for the Royal Ballet. In 1965 he was appointed joint director (with van Praagh) of Australian Ballet, having choreographed a ballet for the company in 1964, *The Display* (mus. M. Williamson). He subsequently created *Yugen* (mus. Y. Toyama, 1965), *Sun Music* (mus. P. Sculthorpe, 1968), and *Perisynthyon* (mus. Williamson, 1974) for the company. Between 1975 and 1976 he was sole director of Australian Ballet, during which time he produced R. Hynd's ballet *The Merry Widow*, which became the biggest hit in its repertoire. In 1973 he directed and performed the title role in Nureyev's film *Don Quixote*. Though he retired from Australian Ballet in 1976 he continued making occasional stage appearances until his death. He was knighted in 1968.

Helsinki Dance Company Finnish modern dance company. Founded in 1973, its major artistic growth began in 1982 when Jorma Uotinen took over as director and choreographer. He created sixteen works, the best known of which, *Kalevala* (1985), toured Europe extensively. Between 1991 and 1996 the company had various directors until Kenneth Kvarnstrom took over, creating new works such as *no-no* (1996). He was succeeded by Nigel Charnock (2003–05) whose works for the company included *Baby* (2004) then by Ville Sormunen in 2006 who encouraged visiting choreographers to expand its stylistic range.

(((●))) SEE WEB LINKS

• Link to official Helsinki Dance Company website

Hendel, Henriette (*née* Johanne H. Rosine Schüler; *b* Döbeln, 13 Feb. 1772; *d* Köslin, 4 Mar. 1849) German dancer, mime, and actress. The daughter of travelling players she was trained by ballet masters at various theatres. Though she began her career as an actress she increasingly specialized in performances of expressive mime and sculpted poses (rather in the manner of an 18th-century Isadora Duncan) taking her subjects from ancient mythology and Renaissance art. She toured Germany, Scandinavia, and Russia for over a decade, and Goethe and Schiller were among her admirers.

Henie, Sonja (*b* Oslo, 8 Apr. 1912; *d* en route to Oslo, 12 Oct. 1969) Norwegian figure skater. She was advised to learn ballet by Pavlova and studied with Karsavina, beginning her skating training aged 5. In 1923 she was Norwegian champion, between 1927 and 1936 she held ten consecutive world champion titles, and between 1928 and 1936 she won three consecutive Olympic gold medals. Her skating style was strongly influenced by her ballet training and she performed an ice version of *The Dying Swan*. In 1938 she began to work in Hollywood, in, among others, the film *Sun Valley Serenade* (1941). She died of leukaemia on a plane flight to Oslo.

Henry, Louis-Xavier-Stanislas (*b* Versailles, 7 Mar. 1784; *d* Naples, 4 Nov. 1836) French dancer and choreographer. He studied at the Paris Opera School with Deshayes, Gardel, and Coulon, making his debut with the company in 1803. A dancer admired for the nobility of his style he also strove to equal the new athleticism of Auguste Vestris and Duport. He began choreographing in 1805 with *L'Amour à Cythère* (mus. Gaveaux, Paris) and in 1807 went to Milan where he danced at La Scala, and, under the influence of Viganò's pantomime dramas, developed a highly successful choreographic career. He had equal success in Naples and Vienna, returning to France in 1816 to become ballet master at Théâtre de la Porte-St-Martin. He choreographed over 125 ballets, and was renowned for his heroic, tragic mode of Romanticism as well as for the unusually disciplined moves of his corps de ballet. His works included *Otello* (mus. Gallenberg, Naples, 1808), *Hamlet* (mus. Gallenberg, Théâtre de la Porte-St-Martin, 1816), *La silfide* (mus. Carlini, Milan, 1828), and *William Tell* (mus. Pugni, Rossini, and others, Milan, 1833). In 1835 he moved to Paris Opera as ballet master choreographing *L'île des pirates* (mus. Gide, Carlini, and others) for Fanny Elssler. But his pantomimic style was not to French taste by this period and he returned to Naples.

Henry Street Settlement Playhouse New York theatre which was originally founded as an actor's school in 1915 and was taken over by Nikolais's Dance Theater from 1948 to 1970, becoming a major platform for experimental dance.

Henze, Hans Werner (*b* Gutersloh, 1 Jul. 1926) German composer. A prolific writer for the theatre, fascinated by the challenge of creating new music for theatre, many of his works have featured such closely integrated vocal, dance, and mime elements that they can barely be put in a separate category from pure ballet scores. He wrote several of the latter, however, including *Pas d'action* (chor. V. Gsovsky, Munich, 1954, revised as *Tancredi*, chor. Nureyev, Vienna, 1966), *Ondine* (chor. Ashton, London, 1958), and *Orpheus* (chor. Forsythe, Stuttgart, 1979). Among the other ballets created to his scores are *Fragmente* (Cranko, 1968), *Gemini* (Tetley, 1973), *Einhorn* (Neumeier, 1985), and *Labyrinth* (M. Baldwin, Schwetzingen, 1997).

Herczog, István (*b* Budapest, 1943) Hungarian-German dancer, choreographer, and director. He studied at the State Ballet Institute in Budapest, graduating in 1962, and between 1966 and 1991 he danced in various German companies including Stuttgart Ballet, Bavarian State Opera Ballet, and Düsseldorf Ballet. He created his first ballet, *6th Symphony*, set to Shostakovich's score, in 1980, and between 1988 and 1991 was ballet director and chief choreographer for Dortmund Opera, creating his own versions of *Romeo and Juliet* and *Coppélia*. Between 1992 and 2002 he was director and chief choreographer of the Pécs Ballet in Hungary, creating works such as *Carmina Burana* (1998), several of which remain current in the repertory.

Hering, Doris (*b* New York, 11 Apr. 1920) US dance writer and administrator. Between 1950 and 1970 she was associate editor and principal critic of *Dance Magazine*, thereafter becoming its critic-at-large as well as teaching dance history in several schools and universities. She was also active in development of the American Regional Ballet movement becoming Executive Director of the National Association for Regional Ballet. She is the author and editor of several books including *25 Years of American Dance* (1950) and *Dance in America* (1985).

Heritage Repertory Term loosely used to denote ballets (mostly created in the 20th century) that have gained permanent positions with the repertory of a company. While distinct from the 19th-century classical canon, they are nonetheless perceived as having 'classic' status. Ballets by choreographers such as Tudor, Ashton, de Mille, Nijinska, Balanchine, and MacMillan come into this category.

Hermanas, Las Ballet in one act with choreography and libretto by MacMillan, design by Georgiadis, and music by F. Martin. Premiered 13 Jul. 1963 by Stuttgart Ballet, Stuttgart, with Papendick, Haydée, Keil, and Barra. It is set to Martin's Concerto for Harpsichord and Small Orchestra and is based on Federico García Lorca's *The House of Bernarda Alba*. Reproducing the claustrophobic atmosphere of Lorca's play, MacMillan's tautly expressive movement tells the story of five sisters raised in a repressive household. The eldest is engaged to be married, but her fiancé is seduced by the youngest sister and the pair are betrayed by the jealous middle sister. The ballet ends with the eldest sister resigned to lonely spinsterhood, and the youngest hanging herself in shame. It was revived for Western Theatre Ballet (1966), American Ballet Theatre (1967), Australian Ballet (1979), Dance Theatre of Harlem (1996), and Sarasota Ballet (2007). Other versions of the same story include those by Ailey (*Feast of Ashes*, mus. Surinach, 1962), Sertic (*Las apasionadas*, mus. Kelemen, 1964), and Pomare (*Las desenamoradas*, mus. M. Coltrane, 1967).

Herman Schmerman Ballet in one act with choreography by Forsythe, music by Thom Willems, and costumes by Gianni Versace. Premiered by New York City Ballet on 28 May 1992. A piece for five dancers which deconstructs the formal hierarchies of classical ballet, particularly the pas de deux. It was staged by the Frankfurt Ballet on 26 Sept. in the same year and by the Royal Ballet

in 1993. It is now in the repertory of many other companies, including Compagñia Nacional de Danza (1996).

Hernandez, Amalia (*b* Mexico City 1917; *d* 4 Nov. 2000) Mexican dancer, choreographer, teacher, and ballet director. She studied with Sybine (from Pavlova's company), with Argentinita and with Waldeen and founded her own folk dance troupe in 1952. This developed into the state-subsidized Ballet Folklórico de México, resident at the Bellas Artes theatre, with its own school and two companies, one resident, one touring. She remained director until 1998 when she was succeeded by her daughter and grandson, Norma and Salvador Lopez.

(🌐) **SEE WEB LINKS**

• Official website of the Ballet Folklórico de México

Herodiade Modern dance work in one act with choreography by Graham, music by Hindemith, set by Noguchi, and costumes by Edythe Gilfond. Premiered under the title *Mirror Before Me* on 28 Oct. 1944 at Library of Congress, Washington, DC, with Graham and O'Donnell. It is based on Mallarmé's poem and portrays Herodias, mother of Salome, as she looks into a mirror and, seeing images of her past and future life, struggles to come to terms with the prospect of age and death. Its New York premiere was on 15 May 1945 at the National Theater. Darrell choreographed a ballet on the same story, *Herodias*, for Scottish Theatre Ballet, 1970.

Heroic Poem (The Geologists) See FEMINIST BALLETS.

Hérold, Louis-Joseph-Ferdinand (*b* Paris, 28 Jan. 1791; *d* Paris, 19 Jan. 1833) French composer. While working as repetiteur at the Paris Opera he composed several ballet scores, all of which were choreographed by Aumer, including *La Somnambule* (1827), a new version of *La Fille mal gardée* (1828), and *La Belle au bois dormant* (1829).

Herrera, Paloma (*b* Buenos Aires, 21 Dec. 1975) Argentinian dancer. She studied with Olga Ferri and at Minsk Ballet School making her debut as Cupid in *Don Quixote* at the Teatro Colón. In 1991 she joined American Ballet Theatre, becoming soloist in 1993 and principal in 1995. Her rapid promotion in the company was driven by an unusually precocious talent and she has since created several leading roles in ballets including Kudelka's *Cruel World* (1994), Duato's *Without Words* (1998), and Tharp's *The Brahms-Haydn Variations* (2000).

High School of Performing Arts Performing arts school. It was established in 1948 as part of New York's Metropolitan Vocational High School, becoming amalgamated with the High School of Music and Arts in 1961 and in 1984 amalgamated again with the Fiorello H. LaGuardia High School of Music, Arts and Performing Arts. The dance department highlights modern dance training alongside academic studies and it has produced many leading US dancers. Its teachers have included G. Shurr, Joffrey, A Hutchinson, and Malinka. The school was showcased in the 1980 film *Fame*.

Hightower, Rosella (*b* Ardmore, Okla., 10 Jan. 1920; *d* Cannes, 4 Nov. 2008) US dancer, director, and teacher. She studied with Fokine, Vilzak, and Vladimirov in New York and in 1938 joined Ballet Russe de Monte Carlo, moving to Ballet Theatre as a soloist in 1941. Between 1945 and 1946 she danced variously with Massine's Ballet Russe Highlights, de Basil's Original Ballet Russe, and the Markova-Dolin company, after which she danced with Nouveau Ballet de Monte Carlo (later the Grand Ballet du Marquis de Cuevas, 1947–62) where she became its star ballerina and one of the most popular dancers in Europe. During this period she also guested with other companies (including with Bruhn and Nureyev) and continued to do so until 1977. Her virtuoso technique gave her an unusually wide range, embracing both classical and contemporary repertories and she created roles in many works including Massine's *Mam'zelle Angot* (1943), H. Lander's *La Sylphide* (Cuevas production, 1953), and Béjart's *Variations* (1969). In 1962 she founded the Centre de Danse Classique in Cannes which became a major centre for ballet in S. France, after which she was appointed director of the Nouveau Ballet Opera de Marseille (1969–72), then of Ballet de Nancy (1975–8). She was also guest teacher with several companies, most regularly Ballet of the 20th Century (where her daughter Dominique Robier was a dancer) and in 1976 founded her own company in Cannes. In 1981 she became the first American director of Paris Opera, where she was responsible for commissioning experimental works such as Dunn's *Pulcinella* (1981). She left in 1983 and was then ballet director of La Scala, (1985–6). She continued to teach, also returning to the stage to dance in François Verret and Denise Luccioni's modern dance work *L. et eux, la nuit* (Festival de Chateauvallon, 1991). She was made Officier de la Légion d'honneur in 1988.

Hijikata, Tatsumi (*b* Akita, 9 Mar. 1928; *d* 21 Jan. 1986) Japanese performer and choreographer who created the form *butoh dance. He studied at the Ando Mitsuko Modern Dance Institute and joined Ando's company in 1953. In 1959 he created his first work *Kinjiki* (Forbidden Colours),

based on the work of Genet. It is commonly regarded as the first example of butoh, although Hijikata did not coin the term ankoku butoh until 1961. His early works, influenced by the novelist Mishima, frequently centred on homoerotic sadism and subversive political imagery. In his middle period, termed Hijikata butoh, his works began to feature female as well as male performers and expanded to larger-scale productions whose imagery reflected the natural world and Japanese traditions. In his final period he began to incorporate elements from *kabuki.

Hilaire, Laurent (*b* Paris, 8 Nov. 1962) French dancer. He studied at Paris Opera Ballet School and graduated into the company in 1980, becoming étoile in 1985 (he was promoted by Nureyev, unusually without having first been named premier danseur). A tall dancer with a handsome, elegant technique, he was particularly suited to the classical repertory but also created roles in many new works including Forsythe's *In the middle somewhat elevated* (1987). A regular partner of Guillem, both while she was at the Opera and abroad, he also guested with Alessandra Ferri in Italy, Kain in Canada, and Morishita in Vienna. He retired from the stage in 2007 to become ballet master at the Paris Opera.

Hill, Martha (*b* E. Palestine, Ohio, *c*.1901; *d* New York, 19 Nov. 1995) US dance educator and administrator. She studied at the Kellog School of Physical Education, Michigan, and later studied various techniques including Graham's, with whose company she performed (1929–31). Her commitment was to teaching rather than performance, however, and during her long career she taught at many institutions including the universities of Oregon and Columbia, Bennington College, and the Juilliard School where she was director of the dance department (1951–85). She also founded summer programmes at Bennington, Mills College, University of California, and Connecticut College. Her leadership in the field of education had a profound influence on the development of US dance, as did her contribution to many advisory panels. When she retired from the Juilliard she was named artistic director emerita.

Hill, Robert (*b* W. Babylon, NY, 5 Feb. 1961) US dancer, director, and choreographer. He began training aged 17 in Florida Hill and won a scholarship to the School of American Ballet. After a further year's study at the Philadelphia College of Performing Arts he made his debut with Atlantic Contemporary Ballet before joining American Ballet Theatre in 1982. He was appointed soloist in 1986, but then performed with New York City Ballet (1989–90), Royal Ballet (1990–2), and with

La Scala, Scottish Ballet, and San Francisco Ballet, before returning to ABT as principal in 1994. He danced both the classical and 20th-century repertories, although an injury which kept him off the stage (1992–4) limited his range. He created several roles including Morris's *Drink to Me Only with Thine Eyes* (1988) and Kudelka's *Cruel World* (1994) and retired from the company in 2002. He created his first ballet for ABT in 1999, *Baroque Game* (mus. Dmitry Polischuk) followed by *Concerto No. 1 for Piano and Orchestra* (mus. Lowell Liebermann) among others. Between 2003 and 2007 he was artistic director of Ballet de Monterrey, after which he founded his own company Robert Hill Dance. His choreography is in the repertory of several other companies including Kansas Ballet.

(♦) SEE WEB LINKS

• Official website for the Robert Hill company

Hilverding (van Wewen), Franz (Hilferdin; Hilferding; Helwerding; Helferting) (baptized Vienna, 17 Nov. 1710; *d* Vienna, 29 May 1768) Austrian dancer, choreographer, ballet master, and teacher. He was born into a family of famous comedians and his father Johann Baptist H. was also a theatre director. He probably studied at the Imperial Court Dance School in Vienna and later with Michel Blondy in Paris (*c.*1734–6). From *c.*1737 he was a court dancer in Vienna and from *c.*1740 a choreographer, arranging dances, ballets, and pantomimes for court operas there. In 1742 he was appointed ballet master at the Kärntnertor Theater and from 1752 he also worked as ballet master for the Burgtheater, creating more than 30 ballets, including *Le Turc généreux* (mus. Rameau, 1758). In these he pioneered the principles of *ballet d'action—integrating pantomime with dance, creating large-scale expressive effects with the corps de ballet and aiming for theatrical realism. One of his pupils, Angiolini, attacked Noverre for claiming these ideas as his own. In 1758 Hilverding went to Russia as ballet master and choreographer of the Imperial Theatres of St Petersburg and Moscow where he created many more works including *La Victoire de Flore sur Borée* (mus. Starzer, 1760). In 1764 he returned to Vienna and in 1766 took over the lease of Kärntnertor Theater in an attempt to revive Austrian ballet. He is said to have died a bankrupt.

Hindemith, Paul (*b* Hanau, 16 Nov. 1895; *d* Frankfurt, 28 Dec. 1958) German composer who wrote the scores for several ballets including Massine's *Nobilissima visione* (London, 1938), Graham's *Herodiade* (Washington, 1944), and Balanchine's *The Four Temperaments* (New York, 1946, concert premiere, 1940). He also wrote the music for mechanical organ for Schlemmer's *Triadic Ballet* (Donaueschingen, 1926.) His concert music has also been used for dance in Balanchine's *Metamorphoses* (New York, 1952), van Manen's *Five Sketches* (Five pieces for String Orchestra, Op. 44, The Hague, 1966), Harkarvy's *Aswingto* (Concert Music for String Orchestra and Woodwind, Op. 50, The Hague, 1969), Balanchine's *Kammermusik No. 2* (New York, 1978), and van Manen's *Opening* (Amsterdam, 1986), among others.

Hines, Gregory (*b* New York, 14 Feb. 1946; *d* 9 Aug. 2003) US tap dancer, singer, actor, and director. He started training when he was 3 with Henry LeTang and at 5 made his professional debut with his brother Maurice as The Hines Kids, appearing in nightclubs. He danced in several Broadway musicals, including *Sophisticated Ladies* (1981) and performed and choreographed the tap sequences for *Jelly's Last Jam* (1993). His close-to-the-floor rhythm work and his incorporation of Afro-Caribbean moves into tap were credited with re-vitalizing a form which during the 1980s seemed in serious decline.

Hinkson, Mary (*b* Philadelphia, 16 Mar. 1930) US dancer and teacher. She studied with Graham, Horst, Schwezoff, and others, joining Graham's company in 1952. Here she became a leading soloist creating roles in, among others, *Seraphic Dialogue* (1955), *Acrobats of God* (1960), and *Circe* (1963). She also guested with various companies, including Butler's and McKayle's (she created the female role in *Rainbow 'Round my Shoulder*, 1959). In 1951 she began teaching at Graham's school, subsequently teaching freelance and at the Juilliard School. In 1971 she became member of staff of the Cologne Summer Academy. She was also director of dance at Britain's National Choreographic Summer School and worked for the John Butler Foundation, staging Butler's ballets.

Hinton, Paula (*b* Ilford, 1 Jun. 1924; *d* Birkenhead, 5 Nov. 1996) British dancer. She studied with H. Delamere-Wright in Liverpool, joining Ballet Rambert in 1944 where her exceptional dramatic gift was quickly recognized. She then danced with Gore (whom she married) and also with Ballets des Champs-Elysées, Original Ballet Russe, London Festival Ballet, and P. López. She was ballerina with Frankfurt Municipal Stages (1956–8), Edinburgh Festival Ballet, and Gore's London Ballet (1961) and Gulbenkian Ballet (1965–9), as well as guesting with Western Theatre Ballet (1965), Harkness Ballet (1970), and Northern Dance Theatre (1971–2 and 1976). She created roles in many of Gore's ballets, such as *Antonia* (1949). She was considered an exceptionally fine Giselle.

hip-hop Hip-hop dance originated in New York among young Hispanic and African-American men during the late 1960s as part of the hip-hop culture of rap, scratch music, and graffiti art. The dance is always changing but essentially embraces the two styles of break dance and body popping. The former is an athletic solo form in which the performer enters the dance arena in a sideways motion then dives or breaks to the floor, spins around on his head, shoulders, or buttocks and ends with a freeze position. Body *popping involves a series of fast, sharp actions that travel through the body in a robotic-looking alternation of move and freeze with variants of the style also including *locking and *krumping. After the dance and its music became internationally current from the late 1970s they were occasionally incorporated into theatre dance, by *Doug Elkins, among others but since the turn of the century there has been a rapid expansion of activity with dance crews competing in international hip-hop competitions and raising the level of virtuosity. Choreographers like *Rennie Harris from Pure-Movement company in America and Kate Prince from ZooNation in Britain have increasingly developed hip-hop as a sophisticated language for dance theatre as have Bruno Beltrão (Grupo de Rua de Niteroi) and the Membros company from Brazil.

Hiroshima (orig. Czech title *A paráncs*) Ballet in five scenes with choreography by I. Eck, libretto by V. Vašut, and music by V. Bukový. Premiered 21 Dec. 1962 at Pécs with B. Veöreös and G. Stimácz. It portrays the internal struggles of the US pilot who dropped the atom bomb on Hiroshima and during the 1960s was performed in several versions around eastern Europe, including Němeček's for Prague National Theatre, 1964.

Histoire du soldat *See* SOLDIER'S TALE, THE.

Hitchins, Aubrey (*b* Cheltenham, 1906; *d* New York, 16 Dec. 1969) British dancer and teacher. He studied with Cecchetti, N. Legat, and Egorova and went on to partner Pavlova (1925–30). He then danced with Le Chauve-Souris and with Nemchinova and Oboukhoff. In 1943 he founded his own company and from 1947 taught in New York.

Hobson's Choice Ballet in three acts with choreography by Bintley, music by Paul Reade, and design by H. Griffen. Premiered 13 Feb. 1989 by Sadler's Wells Royal Ballet at Covent Garden, London, with Karen Donovon and Michael O'Hare. It is based on Harold Brighouse's play of the same title, telling the story of Maggie, daughter of the drunken boot-shop proprietor Hobson, and her love for Will Mossop the lowly boot-hand. Dedicated to de Valois: For Madam an 'English ballet', Bintley's realistic evocation of life in the North of England is paralleled by the naturalistic detail of both design and score.

Hodes, Linda (*née* L. Margolies; *b* New York, 3 Jun. 1933) US dancer, teacher, and choreographer. She began studying at Graham's school aged 9 and joined her company in 1953. Here she created roles in *Seraphic Dialogue* (1955), *Clytemnestra* (1958), *Acrobats of God* (1960), and *Phaedra* (1962) as well as dancing with P. Taylor and Tetley and on Broadway. In 1964 she taught Graham technique at Batsheva Dance Company, for which she choreographed *The Act* (mus. B. Page and B. Johnson, 1967) and of which she was co-artistic director (1972–5). She was then co-artistic director of the Martha Graham company (1979–91), director of the Paul Taylor School and of Taylor 2 (1992–8) and from 1998 began work editing the Taylor Foundation's Repertory Preservation Project. She was married to American dancer Stuart Hodes (*b* 1924) who performed with Graham (1947–58) and also danced on Broadway.

Hodson, Millicent (*b* Indianapolis, 31 Jul. 1945) US choreographer and dance reconstructionist. She studied literature at the universities of Indiana and California, Berkeley, and dance in California and New York, receiving her Ph.D. in 1985 in the history of dance and the visual arts. In 1987 the Joffrey Ballet premiered her reconstruction of Nijinsky's *Sacre du printemps* and with her collaborator Kenneth *Archer she has subsequently reconstructed Nijinsky's *Till Eulenspiegel* (Paris, 1994), *Jeux* (Verona, 1996), Börlin's *Skating Rink* (Zurich, 1996), Balanchine's *Cotillon* (Joffrey Ballet 1988), *Le Bal* (Rome, 2005), and Massine and Prokofiev's *Pas D'Acier* (Princeton, 2005) among others. She has lectured widely in England and the US.

Hoffmann, Ernst Theodor Amadeus (*b* Konigsberg, 24 Jan. 1776; *d* Berlin, 25 June 1822) German writer and composer whose stories have been the basis of several ballets, most famously *Der Sandmann* for *Coppélia* (chor. Saint-Léon, Paris, 1870) and *Der Nussknacker und der Mäusekönig* for *The Nutcracker* (chor. Ivanov, St Petersburg, 1892). Ashton and Massine choreographed dances for Powell's 1951 film based on the opera *Tales of Hoffmann*, and Béjart choreographed a dance version of the opera in 1961 for his Ballet of the 20th Century as did Darrell for Scottish Theatre Ballet in 1972.

Holden, Stanley (*b* London, 27 Jan. 1928; *d* Thousand Oaks, CA, 11 May 2007) British dancer and teacher. He studied at the Bush-Davies School and Sadler's Wells School, joining Sadler's Wells Ballet in 1944. In 1948, after military service he joined Sadler's Wells Theatre Ballet where he created Pierrot in Cranko's *Harlequin in April* (1951). After teaching in S. Africa (1954–7) he returned to Touring Royal Ballet, becoming a soloist with the Royal Ballet (1958–60) and then principal (1960–9). An exuberant dancer but with a capacity for almost Chaplinesque pathos, he was best known for character roles especially Widow Simone in Ashton's *La Fille mal gardée* which he created in 1960. In 1970 he became director of the Dance Academy of the Performing Arts Council in Los Angeles, and in 1972 opened his own school, Holden Dance Center. This closed in 1997, after which Holden taught in Culver City.

Holder, Geoffrey (*b* Port-of-Spain, 1 Aug. 1930) British-US dancer, choreographer, and designer. He studied traditional dances in the W. Indies and gave his first performances in the company of his brother Bosco. In 1953 he went to New York where he taught at the Dunham school and danced in various Broadway shows, at the Metropolitan Opera House, with John Butler's company, and with his own group. He choreographed, composed, and designed *Prodigal Prince* for Ailey's company in 1971, choreographed *Dougla* (1974) and *Banda* (1982) for Dance Theatre of Harlem and designed Taras's *Firebird* (1982) for that company. He also directed and designed *The Wiz* on Broadway (1975) and has continued to exhibit his own paintings. He married the dancer Carmen de Lavallade.

Holger, Hilde (*b* 1905; *d* 22 Sept. 2001) Austrian dancer, choreographer, and teacher. She studied with Bodenwieser and in 1926 opened her School of Art, Movement, and Expression, developing her own style of expressionist movement. She was forced to leave Austria by the Nazis and moved to Bombay where she continued to perform and teach. In 1949 she left and settled in London where she taught and directed, including a seminal production for people with learning difficulties, *Towards the Light* (1969). Her pupils have included Lindsay Kemp.

Holland *See* NETHERLANDS.

Holm, Hanya (*née* Johanna Eckert; *b* Worms, 3 Mar. 1893; *d* New York, 3 Nov. 1992) German-US dancer, teacher, choreographer, and one of the formative influences of American modern dance. She studied at the Dalcroze School in Hellerau and joined Wigman in 1921 both as company dancer and as teacher in Wigman's school. She performed in the premieres of Wigman's *Feier* (1928) and *Totenmal* (1930) and in 1931 went to New York to open an American branch of the Wigman school. This evolved into her own Hanya Holm Studio which was one of the city's most important dance schools between 1936 and its closure in 1967, with Tetley and Nikolais among its pupils. In 1936 she also formed her own group with which she choreographed her epic work of social criticism, *Trend* (mus. Varèse, 1937), also *Metropolitan Day* (mus. G. Tucker, 1938) and *Tragic Exodus* (mus V. Fine, 1939). In 1941 she established her Center of the Dance in Colorado Springs at which she taught annual summer courses and further developed her method of teaching by creative exploration rather than set technique. Despite the strong political bias of her work she was both humorist and populist, and created award-winning choreography for the hit musicals *Kiss Me, Kate* (1948), *My Fair Lady* (1956), and *Camelot* (1960). In 1961 she was appointed head of the dance department of New York Musical Theater Academy. She continued teaching at various schools until 1985 and in the same year premiered a new work, *Capers*, for the Don Redlich Dance Company, which performs much of her work.

Homage to the Queen Pièce d'occasion in one act for Elizabeth II's coronation with choreography by Ashton, music by M. Arnold, and design by Messel. Premiered 2 Jun. 1953 by Sadler's Wells Ballet at Covent Garden, London, with Fonteyn, Somes, Nerina, Rassine, Elvin, Hart, Grey, and Field as the four couples portraying the four elements. A new version was staged by the Royal Ballet in 2006 with Ashton's original *Air* section supplemented by Bintley's choreography for *Earth*, Corder's for *Water*, and Wheeldon's for *Fire*.

Honegger, Arthur (*b* Le Havre, 10 Mar. 1892; *d* Paris, 27 Nov. 1955) Swiss composer who wrote the music for several ballets including Börlin's *Les Mariés de la Tour Eiffel* (together with the other members of 'Les Six', 1921) and *Skating Rink* (1922), Nijinska's *Les Noces de l'amour et de Psyché* (after Bach, 1938), Massine's *Amphion* (1934), Fokine's *Semiramis* (1934), Lifar's *Cantique des cantiques* (1938) and *Chota Roustaveli* (with Tcherepnin and Harsanyi, 1946), and Peretti's *L'Appel de la montagne* (1945). Other works using his music include T. Shawn's *Pacific 231* (1933), Howard's *Lady into Fox* (1939), Neumeier's *Von Unschuld und Erfahrung* (1967), and van Manen's *Brainstorm* (1982).

Hong Kong Under British rule, the region's modern and classical dance scene began to flourish in the late 1970s. The City Contemporary Dance Company in Kowloon was established under the direction of *Willy Tsao (performing works by Tsao, Helen Lai, and others); and the Hong Kong Academy for Performing Arts Ensemble was founded in Wanchai under the artistic direction of Margaret Carlson. Both companies made a feature of showcasing Asian and Western dancers in repertory that fused Chinese and Western dance influences. The Hong Kong Ballet was founded in Happy Valley in 1979, under the direction of Garry Trinder and went on to perform the standard Western classical repertoire as well as new works by Trinder, Choo-San Goh, Dony Retier-Soffer, Bengt Jorgen, and Bintley. Stephen Jefferies was appointed director in 1995. In 1981 the City Council were also responsible for founding the Hong Kong Dance Company in order to promote more indigenous Chinese dance forms, and the company continues to tour widely within the region. After Hong Kong was restored to Chinese rule in 1997 artists feared that their activities might be censored in line with mainland Chinese cultural policy, and a new level of social and political concern became evident in the work of younger choreographers such as Helen Lai, Danny Yung (co-founder of Zuni Icosehedron), and Jacky Yu (founder of E-Side Dance Company). Dance has continued to thrive however. In 1999, Rosalind Newman, who taught at the Hong Kong Academy of Performing Arts from 1989, founded her own company Dance HK/NY, while a generation of new choreographers such as Sang Jijia has been nurtured by the City Contemporary Dance Company, which also acquired its own base for rehearsal and education in 2007. John Meehan took over direction of the Hong Kong Ballet in 2006, acquiring new works from choreographers including Eagling, S. Welch, and Natalie Weir. In 2000 the region hosted a European Union festival of modern dance.

(⊕) SEE WEB LINKS

- Official website for the Hong Kong Ballet
- Official website for the CCDC

Hopi dance The Hopi people of N. Arizona have traditionally believed that it is their duty to provide rain, and dance has played a major part in the ritual ceremonies by which they have sought to bring this about. These ceremonial dances have become internationally celebrated for their rhythmic intricacy and complex orchestration of groups as well as their use of elaborate costumes and masks.

Hopps, Stuart (*b* London, 2 Dec. 1942) British dancer, teacher, and choreographer. He studied at the London School of Contemporary Dance and with Cunningham, and danced with several companies including Hettie Loman's (1962–5). In 1970 he began to choreograph for Scottish Theatre Ballet, becoming founder director of its modern dance group, Movable Workshop (1974–5). He has since choreographed extensively in opera, theatre, and film as well as dance.

hornpipe English step dance originally accompanied by a wooden hornpipe (now obsolete). In the mid-18th century it became widely associated with sailors and around the same time it changed from triple to duple time.

Horosko, Marian (*b* Cleveland, 4 Aug. 1927) US dancer and writer. She studied at the Juilliard School and School of American Ballet and made her debut with Ballet Russe de Monte Carlo aged 12. She later danced with Metropolitan Ballet (1951–4) and with New York City Ballet (1954–62). She also performed in films and on Broadway. During the 1960s she was film curator of the Lincoln Center Dance Collection and from 1963 to 1980 worked as television and radio producer, writing and co-producing the *Dance in America* series (1971–4). She has written several books, including *Martha Graham: Evolution of her Dance Theory and Training* (1991) and *Sleeping Beauty: The Ballet* (1994).

Horschelt, Friedrich (*b* Cologne, 13 Apr. 1793; *d* Munich, 9 Dec. 1876) German dancer, choreographer, and ballet master. Between 1815 and 1821 he was ballet master at the Theater an der Wien where his Children's Ballet (6–12-year-olds, possibly once including Fanny Elssler) became so notorious for impropriety that it was disbanded by Imperial decree. He moved to Munich where he choreographed for many operas until 1848. He was a member of the famous Horschelt family, his father Franz, sisters Karoline and Barbara, and son August also being professional dancers.

Horst, Louis (*b* Kansas City, 12 Jan. 1884; *d* New York, 23 Jan. 1964) US pianist, composer, teacher, writer, and formative influence on American modern dance. He studied in San Francisco and Vienna and between 1915 and 1925 was musical director for St Denis. In 1926 he began collaborating with Graham, becoming musical director of her company and also composing several scores for her, including *Primitive Mysteries* (1931), *Frontier* (1935), and *El Penitente* (1940). Until he left the company in 1948 he not only helped form Graham's musical taste but was her closest adviser on artistic and choreographic issues. He also taught dance composition at the Neighborhood Playhouse School of Theater in New York (1928–64) at the summer courses of Bennington College (1935–45), at Connecticut College Summer School (1948–63), and at Juilliard School (1958–63). In 1934 he founded the magazine *Dance Observer* which he edited until his death. He was author of *Pre-Classic Dance Forms* (1937) and *Modern Dance Forms* (1960). When in 1963 he was made doctor *honoris causa* of Wayne State University he was described as 'the illustrious dean of American dance'.

Horta, Rui (*b* Lisbon, 20 Apr. 1957) Portuguese-German dancer and choreographer. He studied with the Gulbenkian Ballet and in the US with Alvin Ailey American Dance Theater and on his return to Portugal directed Lisbon Dance Company, becoming founder director of the Frankfurt-based S.O.A.P. Dance Theatre in 1991. His works have been driven as much by ideas as pure dance, for example *Object Constant* (1994) which offers a witty deconstruction of the conventions of post-modern performance. He has also choreographed works for several other companies, including Gulbenkian Ballet (1997, 1999), Cullberg Ballet (1998), Nederlands Dans Theater 2 (1999), Phoenix Dance Theatre (2003), and Malmö Opera. After disbanding S.O.A.P. he created works for a company of dancers based in Munich, including *Zeitraum* (1999) then in 2000 returned to Portugal where he founded a multi-disciplinary arts centre The Space of Time as his base. He continues to work freelance and with his own dancers, his most recent works including *Setup* (2005) and *Pure* (2008).

SEE WEB LINKS
• Website for Space of Time

Horton, Lester (*b* Indianapolis, 23 Jan. 1906; *d* Los Angeles, 2 Nov. 1953) US dancer, choreographer, and teacher. He studied with Bolm in Chicago but his most formative influences were the Japanese dance actor Michio Ito and the dance of Native American Indians. In 1928 he choreographed the pageant *The Song of Hiawatha* and moved with the production to California, where he was based for most of his career. In 1934 he formed his own company, Lester Horton Dancers, with which he danced and for which he choreographed many works. Although based on the West Coast the company also appeared in New York and Jacob's Pillow. A neck injury forced him to retire from performing in 1944 but he continued to choreograph, and design, dances for his company and also for film and nightclubs. His distinctive dance style emphasized a powerful stillness in the torso from which radiated asymmetrical movements of the limbs. In 1948 he opened his own theatre in Los Angeles. His best-known work, *The Beloved*, has been performed by many companies including Ailey's and Dance Theatre of Harlem. Other works include *Salome* (percussion accompaniment, 1934), *Conquest* (mus. Lou Harrison, 1938), and *Totem Incantation* (mus. Judith Hamilton, 1948). He was an influential teacher, his pupils including de Lavallade, Lewitsky, Trisler, and Ailey.

House, Christopher (*b* Newfoundland, 30 May 1955) Canadian dancer, choreographer, and director. He began his training at the late age of 21 in Ottawa and at York University, Toronto, then in 1979 joined Toronto Dance Theatre. After creating two works for the company, including *Schola Cantorum* (mus. Satie, 1981) he was appointed resident choreographer, becoming director in 1994. His early style was formal and technically complex, although in works like *Encarnado* (mus. Viver, 1993) he also began to experiment with narrative. During this period he also created works for Les Grands Ballets Canadiens, including *Agitato* (mus. Roger Sessions, 1992), for the National Ballet of Canada, including *Café Dances* (mus. various, 1991), and for Ballet British Columbia. His more recent works have tended to be full-length, multi-disciplinary productions, including *Timecode Break* (2006) and *Chiasmata* (2007).

Houston Ballet US ballet company based in Houston, Texas. In 1955 the Houston Ballet Foundation was formed and established a ballet academy with T. Semenova as its director. Its pupils gave occasional performances and in 1967 it staged *Giselle* under the direction of Nina Popova. The production's success prompted the Foundation to establish a fully professional company with Popova as artistic director. The Houston Ballet gave its first performance in 1968 with sixteen dancers and five ballets in its repertoire. In 1975 Popova was succeeded by James Clouser but the following year was replaced by Ben Stevenson, who directed the company for the next 27 years, expanding it to its present size of around 60 dancers. Stevenson created much of the repertory, including *Cinderella*, *Peer Gynt*, and *The Snow Maiden* as well as presenting 19th-century classics, such as P. Wright's production of *Giselle*. Other additions included Ashton's *Two Pigeons*, Cranko's *The Lady and the Fool*, and Lynne's *Café soiré*. Kenneth MacMillan was the company's artistic associate (1989–92), and Christopher Bruce its resident choreographer from 1989. In 2003 Stanton Welch was appointed director introducing works into the repertory from Forsythe, Wheeldon, and others, as well as choreographing his own ballets, including *Marie* (mus. Shostakovich, 2009). The company maintains close links with the Houston Ballet Academy.

SEE WEB LINKS
• Website for Houston Ballet

Hoving, Lucas (orig. Hovinga; *b* Groningen, 5 Sept. 1912; *d* San Francisco, 5 Jan. 2000) Dutch-US dancer, choreographer, and teacher. He studied with Georgi in Holland and Jooss at Dartington, performing with Ballets Jooss before moving to the US in the mid-1940s where he danced in the companies of Graham, Bettis, and Limón. With the last he created roles in Limón's *Le Malinche* (1949), *The Moor's Pavane* (1949), and *Emperor Jones* (1956), also in Humphrey's *Night*

Spell (1951) and *Ruins and Visions* (1953). His performance as the Friend, or Iago, in *The Moor's Pavane* conveyed a malevolence which many think has never been surpassed. In the early 1960s he formed his own company for which he choreographed several works, notably *Icarus* (mus. Shin-Ichi Matsushita, 1963) which has been revived by Ailey and other companies. He taught at various institutions including Juilliard School, Essen Folkwang School, and Swedish State Dance School and was director of Rotterdam Dance Academy (1971–8). He continued to teach and to choreograph, including *Pits and Thumbs* (mus. Xenakis, Lucas Hoving Performance Group, 1984) and *Rush Hour* (Dance Company Reflex, Netherlands, 1990), and in 1984 founded the Dancelab in San Francisco which became the Lucas Hoving Performance Group in 1985. In 1984 he returned to the stage in an autobiographical solo created for him by Remy Charlip, *Growing up in Public*.

Howard, Alan (*b* Chicago, 7 Aug. 1930; *d* Chicago, 6 Mar. 2003) US dancer and teacher. He studied with E. McRae and in 1949 joined Ballet Russe de Monte Carlo where he remained until 1960, becoming premier danseur. He also danced with the Slavenska Ballet, New York City Ballet, and Radio City Music Hall. He founded the Pacific Ballet Academy in San Francisco which produced the Pacific Ballet and choreographed several works for the company.

Howard, Andrée (*b* London, 3 Oct. 1910; *d* London, 18 Mar. 1968) British dancer, choreographer, and designer. She studied with Rambert, Egorova, Preobrajenska, Trefilova, and Kshessinska and was a founder member of Ballet Club in 1930. In 1933 she moved to de Basil's Ballets Russes but illness curtailed her dancing activities and in the same year she turned to choreography. Her first work, created for Ballet Club, was *Our Lady's Juggler*, a re-working of Susan Salaman's 1930 ballet of the same name set to music by Respighi. This was followed by others, including *Mermaid* (with Salaman, mus. Ravel, 1934), *Cinderella* (mus. Weber, 1935), *Death and the Maiden* (mus. Schubert, 1937), and *Lady into Fox* (mus. Honegger, 1939), all for Ballet Club (later Ballet Rambert). When in 1939 she was invited to New York for American Ballet Theatre's inaugural season, she staged and danced in the last two ballets. In 1940 she created *La Fête étrange* (mus. Fauré) for London Ballet, which went into the repertory of Ballet Rambert and was later revived by the Royal Ballet (1957) and Scottish Theatre Ballet (1971). Its economical but intensely atmospheric creation of mood typified Howard's poetic gifts, also her ability to create drama through pure dance. As a freelance choreographer she created several more

works for Ballet Rambert including *Carnival of Animals* (mus. Saint-Saëns, 1943) and *The Sailor's Return* (mus. Oldham, 1947) which was the first British two-act ballet. Other works include *Twelfth Night* (mus. Grieg, International Ballet, 1942), *Assembly Ball* (mus. Bizet, Sadler's Wells Theatre Ballet, 1946), *Mardi gras* (mus. Salzedo, SWTB, 1946), *Selina* (mus. Rossini, SWTB, 1948), *A Mirror for Witches* (mus. Aplvor, Sadler's Wells Ballet, 1952), *La Belle Dame sans merci* (mus. A. Goehr, Edinburgh Festival Ballet, 1958), and *Les Baricades mystérieuses* (mus. Couperin, Turkish State Ballet, 1963). She designed many of her own ballets, also collaborating with Sophie Fedorovitch. In later years she concentrated on painting.

Howard, Robin (*b* London, 17 May 1924; *d* 12 Jun. 1989) British dance benefactor and founder of London Contemporary Dance Theatre. After seeing Graham's company in London in 1954 he became an ardent enthusiast of her work and in 1963 arranged her London and Edinburgh seasons. In the same year he also set up a trust to fund British dancers travelling to New York to study her technique. In 1965 he arranged for Graham teachers to give classes in London and from that base he founded the London School of Contemporary Dance in 1966. In the same year he set up the Contemporary Ballet Trust (from 1970 the Contemporary Dance Trust) to further develop modern dance in Britain and in 1967 London Contemporary Dance Theatre gave its first performances (as Contemporary Dance Group). In 1969 he acquired The Place which became headquarters to both school and company and with which he retained close links until his death.

Howes, Dulcie (*b* Cape Province, 1908) South African dancer, teacher, and pioneer of dance in S. Africa. She studied with Helen Webb and then moved to London where she studied ballet and mime with Craske and Karsavina and Spanish dancing with Elsa Brunelleschi. She toured with Pavlova's company and returned to S. Africa in 1930 where she founded the University of Cape Town School of Ballet in 1934. Its performing group became the University of Cape Town Ballet for which she choreographed many ballets. In 1965 it achieved fully professional status as the CAPAB Ballet (*See* CAPE TOWN CITY BALLET). As teacher and director she nurtured many artists including Cranko, Poole, and Rodrigues. She retired from the company in 1969 and from the UCT School of Ballet in 1973.

Hoyer, Dore (*b* Dresden, 12 Dec. 1911; *d* Berlin, 31 Dec. 1967) German dancer and choreographer. She studied at the Gret Palucca School and began choreographing and performing professional solo work in 1933. She was also a member of Wigman's company (1935–6) and performed at the Deutsche Tanzbühne (1940–1), the Theater des Volkes, in Dresden (1941–3), and the theatre at Graz (1943–4). She ran her own school in Dresden (1946–8) and directed the ballet company at Hamburg Staatsoper (1949–51), attempting, unsuccessfully to transform it into a modern dance ensemble. She continued to perform her own solo works until 1966, winning special acclaim in S. America during the 1950s.

Hoyos, Cristina (*b* Seville, 13 Jul. 1946) Spanish dancer. She made her debut aged 12 in the children's production 'Galas Juveniles' and began choreographing her own work. From the age of 16 she began specializing in flamenco and worked in 'tablaos' (flamenco clubs). A dancer of fierce power and uncompromising personality she joined Gades's company in 1969 as his partner, creating the role of the Bride in *Blood Wedding* (1974). In 1975 she toured and danced in her own show, and with Gades formed the company which appeared in the film version of *Blood Wedding* (dir. Saura). She also danced in Saura's film *Carmen* and won particular acclaim for her performance of Candelas in his film *El amor brujo* (1986). She and Gades directed and danced in Ballet Antonio Gades con Cristina Hoyos (1983–8), then in 1989 she founded her own Ballet Cristina Hoyos, now Ballet Flamenco Andalucia which tours internationally and was the first flamenco company to perform at the Palais Garnier. Injury has recently curtailed her range as a dancer but she continues to choreograph and perform in works with her company, including *Romancero Gitano* (2008). She was closely involved in setting up the Museo del Baile Flamenco in Seville.

Hubbard Street Dance Chicago Chicago-based modern dance company. It was founded in 1977 by Lou Conte, originally as a showcase for his own choreography, then subsequently as a repertory company, featuring work by Daniel Ezralow and Tharp and, more recently, European choreographers like Kylián and Duato. In 1998, it moved into a purpose-designed base, Hubbard Street Dance Center, alongside Conte's dance school (founded in 1974) and the junior company HSDC2. In 2000 Conte was succeeded by Jim Vincent, who widened the repertory with works by Naharin, Forsythe, and others while commissioning new works from Lubovitch, Elo, HSDC's associate director Lucas Crandall, and Vincent himself. The company has forged a close relationship with the Chicago Symphony Orchestra—making it one of the few US modern dance companies to perform regularly to live music. It tours widely both in America and abroad.

 SEE WEB LINKS

• Hubbard Street Dance Chicago website

Hübbe, Nikolaj (*b* Copenhagen, 30 Oct. 1967) Danish dancer. He studied at the Royal Danish School and later in Paris and the US joining the Royal Danish Ballet in 1986 where he was promoted soloist (principal) in 1988. A powerful dancer whose height did not compromise his swiftness, he not only excelled in the Bournonville repertory but also in neo-classical ballets and in dramatic roles like Onegin, in which he was a memorably complex, compelling figure. In 1992 he moved to New York City Ballet where he made his debut in Martins's *Zakoussi* (a duet made specially for him). At his peak, the completeness of his range was compared by some critics to the young Baryshnikov's. He retired from the stage in 2008 to become director of the Royal Danish Ballet, staging a controversial new, updated version of *Napoli* for the company in 2009.

Hulls, Michael (*b* Warminster, 9 Mar. 1959) British lighting designer. He trained in dance and theatre at *Dartington College, and studied lighting design with Jennifer *Tipton in 1992. Considered a choreographer or sculptor of light, his designs frequently overlay a patterned or sculpted effect onto the dance material. He has created over 20 works with choreographer Russell *Maliphant, beginning with *Unspoken* (1995) and subsequently including *Critical Mass* (1999), *Broken Fall* (2003), *Push* (2005), and *Eonnagata* (with Sylvie Guillem and Robert Lepage, 2009), for which he received the 2009 Knight of Illumination award. Hulls has also designed the lighting for Jonathan Burrows (*The Stop Quartet*), Akram Khan (*Rush*), Laurie Booth, Javier De Frutos, and Dutch National Ballet, among others as well as lighting for contemporary music concerts and the theatre.

His works with Maliphant have received numerous awards including an Olivier and South Bank Show Dance Award. Channel 4 commissioned the 2006 documentary *Light and Dance* about the men's unique working relationship.

Humpbacked Horse, The *See* THE LITTLE HUMPBACKED HORSE.

Humphrey, Doris (*b* Oak Park, Ill., 17 Oct. 1895; *d* New York, 29 Dec. 1958) US dancer, choreographer, teacher, and one of the major formative influences on US modern dance. She studied at the Francis W. Parker School in Chicago and in 1913 began teaching ballroom dance. In 1917 she attended the Denishawn school in Los Angeles and was taken into the company where she danced until 1928, when she left to found a school and company in New York with Weidman. Her own choreography was stripped bare of spectacle and virtuosity and was based on the principle of 'dancing from the inside out', i.e. devising movement specially to express specific emotional and physical states. While Graham's technique was based on the opposition of contraction and release, Humphrey's was based on the concepts of *fall and recovery. She believed that dance existed in 'the arc between two deaths', i.e. between the two static positions of standing and lying prone. Drama and kinetic excitement occurred when the body moved off balance and grappled with the force of gravity. Unlike Graham, she did not choreograph primarily around her own personality but created group dances of complex, contrapuntal design. Some of these were abstract, such as *Drama of Motion* (no mus., 1930) though several of her early works were inspired by nature, including *Water Study* (no mus., 1928) and *Life of the Bee* (no mus. in first production, later addition of mus. by Hindemith, 1929), and the majority of her works had a dramatic element, such as *The Shakers* (mus. trad., 1931), which portrayed an early American religious community; the trilogy *New Dance* (*Theater Piece*, *With My Red Fires*, and *New Dance*, mus. W. Riegger, 1935–6) which evoked a social utopia, and *Passacaglia in C minor* (mus. J. S. Bach, 1938) which celebrated the human spirit in dance of grand architectural design. In 1944 severe arthritis forced her to retire as a dancer but she continued to work as teacher, choreographer, and artistic director for Limón's dance company. Her works from this period include *Lament for Ignacio Sánchez Mejías* (mus. Lloyd, 1946), based on the poetry of Lorca; *Day on Earth* (mus. Copland, 1947), a semi-abstract, semi-dramatic portrayal of the cyclical nature of human joy and sorrow; *Ritmo Jondo* (mus. Surinach, 1953); *Ruins and Visions* (mus. Britten, 1953); and a rare mixed-media work, *Theatre Piece No. 2* (mus. Luening, 1956). In 1934 she joined the staff of Bennington School of Dance and she continued to teach there and at the Juilliard School until her death. Her last, unfinished work, *Brandenburg Concerto No. 4* (mus. Bach) was produced posthumously in 1959. She was author of *The Art of Making Dances* (New York, 1959) and 'New Dance' (*Dance Perspectives*, no. 25). Several of her works entered the repertories of dance companies around the world, while the Limón Dance Company has continued to perform her work. Mino Nicolas also formed the Doris Humphrey Repertory Dance Company in the early 1980s to focus on revivals and performances of the Humphrey repertory while also becoming executive director of the Doris Humphrey Institute.

(((⊕))) SEE WEB LINKS

• Website for the Doris Humphrey Institute

• Website for the Doris Humphrey Society

Hungarian National Ballet (Hungarian State Opera Ballet; Budapest Ballet). Hungary's leading ballet company which performs in Budapest's State Opera House and also in the city's Erkel Theatre. Its origins date back to ballet performances held at the Ofen Court Theatre and the National Theatre, but in its current form it was established in 1884 with the opening of the State Opera House. At first it was subordinate to the opera company and its early, rather parochial style evolved via the influences of Hungarian folk dancing and Russian ballet. Demands for higher standards led to the engagement of the Italian ballet master Nicola Guerra. He not only raised the company's technical and artistic levels but also choreographed nineteen works for the company between 1902 and 1915, including *Adventures of Love* (mus. Mader, 1902), *Hungarian Dance Suite* (mus. Liszt and Szikla, 1907), *Prometheus* (mus. Beethoven, 1913), and *Games of Amor* (mus. Mozart, 1913). After Guerra the company declined (although Polish choreographer Jan Cieplinski created some notable ballets) until 1937 when Ferenc Nádasi was engaged as ballet master. Under his regime standards rose sharply (among the dancers he trained were Melinda Ottrubay and Ernö Vashegyi) and he also established a school within the Opera. Equally important was the emergence of Gyula *Harangozó as a choreographer. *Scene in the Czárdas* (mus. J. Hubay and J. Kenessey, 1936) was his first ballet on a national theme and he became internationally renowned for the ballets he created to music by Bartók, such as *The Miraculous Mandarin*. (*See* HARANGOZÓ) After the Second World War a new generation of dancers emerged such as N. Kovács and I. Rab, and in 1948 Charrat mounted Stravinsky's *Jeu de cartes*. In 1950 the Ballet State Choreographic Institute, now the Hungarian Dance Academy, was founded from the merger of the Opera school and a private school run by Nádasi and during the rest of the decade many Soviet ballet masters were brought into the company to teach the Russian repertory, including Messerer, Zakharov, Lavrovsky, and Chabukiani. At first native artists like Nádasi and Harangozó were pushed aside, but they were reinstated once their quality was acknowledged by the Soviet authorities. During the 1960s and 1970s a new generation of Hungarian choreographers emerged including Imre *Eck and László *Seregi. The latter created many works for the company during the 1970s, some like *Spartacus* in the Soviet mould, others like *The Cedar Tree* more distinctively individual. Antal Fodor also created works for the company, introducing neo-classical and modern influences into its style, and during the

1970s the repertory also opened up to include foreign works by, among others, Ashton, Béjart, Balanchine, and Ailey. Since the 1960s the 120-strong company has toured regularly in Europe. Seregi was artistic director from 1977, Gabor Keveházi from 1990, and Gyorgy Szakály from 1992 and Gyula Harangozó (jun.) from 1999 to 2005. Under their influence a new generation of Hungarian choreographers has emerged, such as Lilla Pártay who created *Anna Karenina* (mus. Tchaikovsky, 1991), and Péter László who choreographed *Derby* (mus. Gyorgy Vukán, 1989). Political changes during the early 1990s affected the funding of the ballet, which drove it to stage productions in cooperation with the Opera company and with private funds. But under the recent direction of Harangozó and Keveházi, who returned in 2005, the repertory has been widened with the acquisition of works by MacMillan, Cranko, Kylián, Balanchine, and Forsythe, and new creations including Pártay's *Gone with the Wind* (mus. Dvorak, 2007) and Keveházi's setting of Beethoven's 9th Symphony (created with Iván Markó, 2006). The company still takes most of its dancers from its associate Hungary Dance Academy.

(((⊕))) SEE WEB LINKS

- Official website of the Hungarian Opera with link to the ballet company

Hungary Ballet was first performed in Hungary in the mid-18th century at the court of Prince Esterházy but the popularity it gained after visits by Noverre's Vienna dancers in 1772 and by Viganò in the 1790s was eclipsed during the early 19th century by pantomimes, Harlequinades, etc. During this period, however, Hungarian folk dance societies toured Europe with much success. In 1837 the National Theatre was opened in Pest, presenting its first ballet production, *La Fille mal gardée* (chor. János Kolosánszky, mus. Ferenc Kaczér), in 1839. In 1846 Cerrito and Saint-Léon danced *Ondine*, *Giselle* was staged in 1847, and Grahn and Taglioni were among the ballerinas who danced there during the 1850s. The first and greatest Hungarian prima ballerina of the 19th century was Emilia Aranyváry (active 1852–9), but otherwise local ballet activity was mediocre, the resident company being headed by the lacklustre choreographer Frigyes Campilli who mounted versions of romantic ballets (incl. *Esmeralda*, 1856) between 1846 and 1886.

In 1884 the State Opera House was opened in Budapest with its own ballet company attached. This became the national ballet ensemble and as the *Hungarian National Ballet dominated dance activity in the country. During the 20th century, though, other companies emerged. In 1946 the first professional provincial company was established in Szeged, performing a repertory largely

borrowed from Budapest. During the 1950s it was directed by Zoltán *Imre who choreographed much of the repertory and after Imre left Hungary it closed down. In 1986 it re-opened under the direction of impresario R. Bokor, who commissioned works from various guests (including Imre who returned as artistic consultant, then director between 1986 and 1993) as well as staging older works such as Jooss's *The Green Table*. Since 1993 the company has been under the direction of Andras Pataki and Tamás Joronics. Re-named Szeged Contemporary Ballet and oriented towards contemporary dance theatre it performs a wide repertory of Hungarian and international work including modern versions of *Carmina Burana* and *The Miraculous Mandarin*.

In 1960 Imre Eck founded the *Ballet Sopianae at the National Theatre at Pécs, creating a repertory of youth-oriented political ballets. His was one of the first attempts at a modern style of choreography in Hungary, created largely without access to Western ideas. One of the company's young dancers, Sándor Tóth, emerged as a choreographic talent in *What is under your hat?* (mus. Jószef Kinczes, 1964), among others, and took over direction of the company in 1968 with Eck as artistic director. Their experimental approach was very popular and the company, which became known as the Pécs Ballet, toured widely in Hungary as well as in Europe and America. Between 1992 and 2001 it was directed by István *Herczog, who acquired works by M. Ek and Smok for the repertory, and from 2001 to 2005 it was directed by Gábor Keveházi who added works by younger choreographers such as Jorma Elo. Since 2005 it has been directed by Balázs Vincze. It has close links with the Pécs Arts Vocational Secondary School.

The Győr Ballet, founded in 1979 by Iván Markó, is Hungary's only classical company to be financially independent of a theatre, though it performs extensively at the Kisafuldy. Initially its repertoire was dominated by Markó's own full-length narrative works, but after its direction was taken over by János Kiss in 1991, new works entered the repertory from North, Cohan, Gunter Pick, and Kiss. It now tours internationally and maintains close links with the Győr Dance and Visual Arts School.

The emerging modern dance scene, influenced by Central European teachers and choreographers, was banned after the Soviet occupation in 1948, but was re-activated from the mid-1980s. Among the most prominent groups to emerge were Artus, founded by Gábor Goda in 1985 to perform mixed-media works fusing poetry, dance and acrobatics; TranzDanz, founded by Péter Gerzson-Kovács in 1991, combining jazz, folk dance, and text; the Sarbo Company, founded in 1990, and strongly influenced by de Keersmaeker;

and the Bozsik company based at the Katona József Theatre and led by Yvette Bozsik whose works, such as *The Miraculous Mandarin* (1995), have drawn on folk dance and the styles of Wigman and Bausch. More recent groups include The OFF Dance Company, founded in 1995 by Adrienn Hód and others, and presenting mixed-media works such as *Arboretum* (mus. Tibor Szemző, 2005) and the 1 More Movement Theatre, founded by Mark Fenyves and Istvan Palosi in 1997 (and re-named Hungarian Art of Movement company in 2006) to re-create traditions of modern dance from the pre-war era. The Budapest Dance School, Hungary's first school for contemporary dance, was founded in 1983 and the Hungarian Contemporary Dance Festival, established in 1992, runs every two years. This partly takes place at The National Dance Theatre, which was opened in Budapest in 2001 and has become a major venue for all forms of dance, presenting classical, contemporary, and folk companies from Hungary, plus an increasingly wide range of foreign companies.

Folk dance remains central to the country's dance culture. The Hungarian State Folk Ensemble was founded in 1949 under the direction of Miklós *Rábai, as a combined choir, orchestra, and dance troupe. Originally it presented elaborate Soviet-style stagings of folk music and dance numbers, but from the 1980s, under the direction of Sándor Tímár, it began to present more authentic and more intimate stagings of folk material, drawing on older traditions. It has toured worldwide.

(⊕) SEE WEB LINKS

- Official website for the Pécs Ballet
- Official website for the Györ Ballet
- Database for Hungarian dance activity

Hurok, Solomon (*b* Pogar, 9 Apr. 1888; *d* New York, 5 Mar. 1974) Russian-US impresario. He emigrated to the US in 1906 and began presenting concerts for labour organizations and workers' groups. His prime interest was music but from 1916 he began presenting dance and among his outstanding clients were Pavlova, Duncan, Wigman, Argentinita, Graham, Ballet Russe de Monte Carlo, Original Ballet Russe, Ballet Theatre, Sadler's Wells and Royal Ballet, Bolshoi Ballet, Kirov Ballet, National Ballet of Canada, and Stuttgart Ballet. He wrote *Impresario* (New York, 1947) and *Solomon Hurok Presents* (New York, 1955).

Hus family Family of dancers who were widely active in Europe through the 18th and 19th centuries. Auguste H. (*b* 1735; *d* after 1781) was a dancer with Paris Opera (1756-60), had ballets staged at the Théâtre de la Foire, and was choreographer at the Comédie-Française (1759-60). He may also be the Jean Baptiste H. who danced and choreographed in Lyon and Turin for various seasons between 1761 and 1781. His adopted son was Eugene H. (orig. Pierre-Louis Stapleton, *b* Brussels, 1758; *d* Brussels, 1823) who danced in Lyon; Paris, and Bordeaux and became founder director of the ballet company at Brussels' Théâtre de la Monnaie in 1815. Auguste's brother Pierre H., also known as Pietro, was director of the ballet school and choreographer at the Teatro San Carlo in Naples. Pierre's son Auguste (1820-50) danced widely in Italy and Vienna and directed the ballet school at La Scala.

Hutchinson, Ann (*b* New York, 3 Nov. 1918) US dancer and dance notator. She studied with Jooss and Leeder at Dartington (1936-9) then moved to New York where she continued her training with Graham, Limón, Tudor, and others. She appeared in modern dance concerts and on Broadway, then concentrated on research into dance notation, specializing in Labanotation and working closely with Laban when she returned to England in 1947. She was co-founder and president of the New York Dance Notation Bureau (1940-61) and co-founder of the International Council of Kinetography Laban in 1961. During her long career she has notated many major works and taught notation at New York School of Performing Arts, at Juilliard School, and in London where she has lived since 1962. She is author of *Labanotation* (New York, 1954, revised edition, 1970) and in 1987 she started the Language of Dance series, which has published major new scores such as *Nijinsky's 'Faune' Restored*, and several books on notation and issues surrounding its practice. She is married to dance writer Ivor Guest.

Hyltin, Sterling (*b* Amarillo, Texas, 8 Jul. 1985) American dancer. She trained at the Dallas Metropolitan Ballet and the School of American Ballet, joining New York City Ballet in 2003 where she was promoted to principal in 2007. A light elegant dancer with powerful legs and feet, she performs the Balanchine and Robbins repertories as well as creating leading roles in Wheeldon's *Rococo Variations* and in Martins's *Romeo and Juliet* (Juliet) and *The Red Violin*.

Hynd, Ronald (orig. Ronald Hens; *b* London, 22 Apr. 1931) British dancer, choreographer, and ballet director. He studied with Rambert and danced with Ballet Rambert (1949-52) before moving to Sadler's Wells (later Royal Ballet, 1952-70). Although never a top-rank classical dancer he was a highly versatile performer and after being appointed soloist in 1954 created roles in many ballets, including Cranko's *Prince of the Pagodas* (1957) and *Antigone* (1960), and danced with Margot Fonteyn's World Tour (1963). He choreographed his first work in 1968, Stravinsky's *Le Baiser de la fée* for Dutch National Ballet (revived London Festival Ballet, 1974) and from 1970 to 1973 and 1984 to 1986 was ballet director for the Bavarian State Opera Ballet, Munich. Otherwise he worked as a freelance choreographer with LFB (later English National Ballet) for various seasons between 1970 and 1993 as well as for Houston Ballet and others. A fluent choreographer with a light, popular touch, his ballets sprang from a wide range of score and subjects, and include *Dvořák Variations* (mus Dvořák, LFB, 1970), *Charlotte Brontë* (mus. Young, Royal Ballet New Group, 1974), *The Merry Widow* (mus. Lehár, arr. Lanchbery, Australian Ballet, 1975), *The Sanguine Fan* (mus. Elgar) and *The Nutcracker* (mus. Tchaikovsky; both for LFB, 1976), *Rosalinda* (mus. J. Strauss, PACT Ballet, 1978, rev. LFB, 1979), *Papillon* (mus. Offenbach, Houston Ballet, 1979, rev. Sadler's Wells Royal Ballet, 1980), *The Hunchback of Notre Dame* (mus. Berlioz, arr. Lanchbery, Houston Ballet, 1988), *Les Liaisons amoureuses* (mus. Offenbach, arr. Davis, Northern Ballet Theatre, 1989), and *The Sleeping Beauty* (mus. Tchaikovsky, ENB, 1993). He married the former dancer Annette Page.

Ibert, Jacques (*b* Paris, 15 Aug. 1890; *d* Paris, 6 Feb. 1960) French composer who wrote several scores for dance including Nijinska's *Les Rencontres* (Paris, 1925), R. Page's *Gold Standard* (Chicago, 1934), Fokine's *Diane de Poitiers* (Paris, 1934), Petit's *Les Amours de Jupiter* (Paris, 1934), and Lifar's *Escales* (Paris, 1948), and *Le Chevalier errant* (Paris, 1950). He also wrote the music for the 'Circus' number in Gene Kelly's film **Invitation to the Dance* (1952). Various choreographers have set dances to his *Divertissement*, including W. Gore (in *Street Games*, New Ballet Co., 1952), M. Pink (London Festival Ballet, 1981), and M. Morris (in *Lucky Charms* 1994). P. Wright choreographed his *Quintet* for woodwind (Stuttgart, 1963).

Icare Ballet in one act with choreography and rhythms by Lifar, instrumentation by G. Szyfer, and design by P. Larthes. Premiered 9 Jul. 1935 at Paris Opera with Lifar. Lifar's re-telling of the Icarus myth is essentially a solo danced against the choral movement of a group. It shows Icarus' attempts to fly and his tragic fall after he flies too close to the sun. Lifar's rhythm score (performed by a range of percussion instruments) was an attempt to free dance from the dictates of music. It was revived in 1962 with new designs by Picasso. Other dance treatments of the myth include L. Hoving (mus. Shin-Ichi Matsushita, 1963), V. Vasiliev (mus. S. Slonimsky, Bolshoi Ballet, 1971), Arpino (in *The Relativity of Icarus*, mus. G. Samuel, New York, 1974), and Flamand (*The Fall of Icarus*, mus. Nyman, 1989).

ice dancing The speed, rhythm, and fluency of skating are all qualities associated with dance, and dancing on ice, either solo or in couples, has a long social history (Samuel Pepys is recorded as dancing with Nell Gwyn on the Thames during the Great Frost of 1683). The modern form of ice dance, i.e. skating based on ballroom dances, was introduced in Vienna in 1868 by the US skater Jackson Haines, and for decades vied for prominence with the figure-based skating popular in Britain. Since the Second World War ice dance has been established world-wide as a professional sport and performance art, with the first World Championships being held in 1952.

Competitions include compulsory dances, in which specific ballroom dances are performed with the dancers also tracing a set pattern on the ice, and original dances. These have incorporated an increasing range of elements from ballroom dance, disco, and classical dance. Ice dancers are judged on the same qualities of grace, line, co-ordination, and invention that are expected from floor-bound dancers, although in some competition events there can be a tension between the aesthetic content of the work and the need to display the appropriate range of skating techniques. It has been individual dancers rather than choreographers who have tended to advance the form most radically, for example the Russians Oleg and Lyudmila Protopopov who took the World Championships by storm in 1962 with their (then) startling use of classical adage and big Soviet-style lifts. In 1976 John *Curry won the European, World, and Olympic titles with performances heavily based on the idiom of classical ballet. His choreography was a serious interpretation of the music and within the limits imposed by ice and skating boots he introduced a range of classical jumps, turns, batterie, and ports de bras. He was equally successful in the theatre. Tharp choreographed the performances he gave at Madison Square Garden, New York (Nov. 1976), and Darrell and MacMillan both choreographed solos for his Theatre of Skating which was premiered on 27 Dec. 1976 at Cambridge Theatre, London. In 1984 Torvill and Dean's Olympic-winning duet *Bolero* (mus. Ravel) took ice dance to new levels of dramatic expression, although some of Dean's innovations, such as guiding his partner by her leg or skate were deemed illegal in subsequent amateur competitions. Professional competitions which became popular during the 1980s allowed for much freer styles of choreography. During the 1990s ice dance versions of films and musicals became very successful, for example *The Phantom of the Opera* and *Beauty and the Beast*, while from 2000 classical ballets like *Sleeping Beauty* and *Swan Lake* became popular material for adaptation.

While ice dancing has been influenced by the theatre, choreographers have in turn exploited the poetry of ice dance for the stage, as in Ashton's *Les Patineurs* (1937), which mimics the swooping flight of skaters and their fluent turns as well as mining the comic potential for falls. In 1996 Christopher Dean choreographed *Encounters* for English National Ballet, a work which did not take skating as its subject, but which did draw choreographically on Dean's own ice dance style.

Iceland Due to the country's relative geographic isolation, ballet did not arrive until the 1930s when Asta Nordmann returned from overseas study to set up a school. Productions choreographed by herself and danced by her students were performed in Reykjavik. The National Theatre was opened in 1950 and a ballet school founded in 1952. Helgi *Tomasson was trained there. The professional Icelandic Dance Company was founded by Alan Carter in 1973, with ten dancers trained in ballet, folk, and modern dance. In 1975 they staged *Coppélia*. Carter was succeeded in 1975 by Natalia Conus who introduced stylistic elements from the Bolshoi. Later choreographers to work with the company have included Yuri Chatal, *Dolin, Jochen *Ulrich, and Nanna Ólafsdóttir, who staged her own version of *Daphnis and Chloe* in 1985, the first full-length ballet by an Icelander. In 1996 the company was taken over by Katrin Hall, who re-named it Iceland Dance Theatre and altered its focus to contemporary styles, with works by Horta, Kylián, Jorma Uotinin, and others added to the repertory as well as works by Icelandic choreographers such as Hall herself. The company has also produced new works in collaboration with the Norwegian company Carte Blanche, for example Ina Christel Johannessen's *Ambra* (mus. several, 2008). It toured the US for the first time in 2007.

(((🌐))) SEE WEB LINKS
- Official website for the Iceland Dance Theatre

Ice Maiden, The (orig. Russ. title *Ledyanaya deva*) Ballet in three acts with choreography by Lopukhov, music by Grieg (mostly from *Peer Gynt*, arr. Asafiev), and design by Golovin. Premiered 27 Apr. 1927 by GATOB (later the Kirov) in Leningrad, with Mungalova and Gusev. It tells the story of an ice maiden, who, disguised as a beautiful woman, lures men to their deaths. Its style was considered seminal in its mix of classical ballet, authentic folk dance, and bold acrobatics. An earlier, less successful version, *Solveig*, was choreographed by P. N. Petrov using the same music and design (GATOB, 1922) and a later version (after Lopukhov) by Gusev (Novosibirsk, 1964).

Idzikowski, Stanislas (also spelled Idzikowsky; *b* Warsaw, 1894; *d* London, 12 Feb. 1977) Polish-British dancer and teacher. He studied with Cecchetti and made his debut with London Empire Theatre Ballet in 1911 in the musical *New York*. In 1912 he danced with Pavlova's company, in 1913 with the Imperial Russian Ballet of T. and A. Kosloff, and in 1914 he joined Diaghilev's Ballets Russes. Though unusually short, he was a dazzling virtuoso with an extraordinary jump and took over many of Nijinsky's roles as well as creating roles in Massine's *The Good-Humoured Ladies* (1917), *Les Contes russes* (1917), *La Boutique fantasque* (1919), *Le Tricorne* (1919), and *Pulcinella* (1920), also in Balanchine's *Jack in the Box* (1926) and the Blue Bird in the 1921 production of *The Sleeping Princess*. He left the company in 1924 to dance with Lopokova at the Coliseum and with Comte de Beaumont's 'Soirées de Paris', then rejoined Diaghilev (1925–9). He directed his own company from 1929 to 1930 and was then guest artist with Vic-Wells Ballet (1933–4). From 1933 he also taught in London and was author (with C. W. Beaumont) of *A Manual of Classical Theatrical Dancing* (London, 1922).

Illuminations Ballet in one act with choreography by Ashton, music by Britten, and design by Beaton. Premiered 2 Mar. 1950 by New York City Ballet at City Center, New York, with Magallanes, Hayden, and LeClercq. It is set to Britten's *Les Illuminations*, itself a setting of poems by Rimbaud, and is constructed as a series of quasi-surreal dance-vignettes portraying aspects of the poet's life, loves, and imagination. It was commissioned by Balanchine and was Ashton's first ballet for a US company. It was revived for Joffrey Ballet (1980) and for Royal Ballet (1981). Other choreographers who have used the same music include T. Gsovsky (Berlin Opera Ballet, 1961), Norman Walker (Berlin Opera Ballet, 1969), and Alston (in *Rumours, Visions*, Richard Alston Dance Co., 1996).

Imperial Ballets *See* BOLSHOI BALLET; KIROV BALLET.

Imperiale Accademia di Ballo The ballet school attached to La Scala di Milano. Founded by B. Ricci in 1812, it was reformed by Blasis when he became director in 1837 and became one of Europe's foremost schools, producing Grisi, Cerrito, Legnani, and Zucchi, among others. Cecchetti was also a pupil and was director from 1928 to 1933. *See* SCALA BALLET, LA.

Imperial Society of Teachers of Dancing Society founded in 1904 to supervise teachers of ballroom and other types of dance from around the (then) British empire. It conducts its own examinations and issues diplomas to teachers (either Member or Fellow of ISTD) in over 40 countries world-wide. The Cecchetti Society was incorporated in 1924 and the Greek Dance

Association in 1951, and it now has ten faculties each specializing in different forms of theatrical, recreational, and social dance.

Impressing the Czar See IN THE MIDDLE SOMEWHAT ELEVATED.

Imre, Zoltán (*b* Jánoshalma, 1943; *d* Budapest, 30 Jun. 1997) Hungarian dancer, choreographer, and director. He studied at the Hungarian State Ballet Institute and danced with Szeged National Theatre (1961–8), choreographing his first work for the company, *Composition* (mus. Bach), in 1966. He was then soloist with Tanzforum Köln (1971–4) after which he moved to Ballet Rambert where he was soloist, choreographer, and company assistant (1974–8). He choreographed two works for the company, including *The Accident* (mus. Imre and Crosby, 1977). In 1986 he returned as choreographer and artistic consultant to the newly reformed Szeged Ballet company creating *Stabat Mater* (mus. Pergolesi, 1988) and *Dream About Kafka* (1992), among other works. He was also artistic director of the company from 1990 to 1993.

Inbal [Heb., clapper of a bell] The National Ballet and Dance Theatre of Israel, founded by Sara Levi Tanai in 1949. Its aim was originally to preserve Yemenite songs and dances, with *The Yemenite Wedding* as one of Levi-Tanai's most popular productions, but later elements from other folk traditions were incorporated. It made its London debut in 1957 and New York in 1958. In 1992 Levi-Tanai was retired from the company and replaced by Rena Sharett, then in 1994 by Margalit Oved. In 1996 the company's status changed to that of a multicultural folk arts centre, which has subsequently presented reconstructions of Levi-Tanai works.

Inbal Pinto Dance Company Israeli modern dance company founded by Inbal Pinto and Avshalom Pollock in 1992 to perform their choreography. Its productions, often inspired by cinema and highly visual in style, are created in collaboration with artists from other disciplines—for example *Trout* (2008) which was made in collaboration with experimental music ensemble Kitchen Orchestra, and has the dancers performing in a shallow pool of water. Other recent works include *Wrapped* (1998) and *Boobies* (2002).

(⊕) SEE WEB LINKS
• Website for the Inbal Pinto company

Indes galantes, Les Opera ballet, originally performed with prologue, two entrées, and epilogue (its third entrée was added two days after the first performance and its fourth entrée added a year later), with choreography by M. Blondy (probably), music by Rameau, design by Servandoni, and libretto by Louis Fuzelier. Premiered 23 Aug. 1735 at Paris Opera. It tells four love stories, each from a different part of the world: 'Le Turc généreux', 'Les Incas du Pérou', 'Les Fleurs', and 'Les Sauvages'. Sallé had a personal triumph in the third entrée (which she probably also choreographed) but though the work enjoyed a popular success it was dropped from the repertory in 1771. It was revived in 1952 in a spectacular production mounted by Maurice Lehmann. The prologue, 'Le Palais d'Hébé', was choreographed by Aveline with design by Dupont, and the subsequent entrées were 'Le Turc généreux' (chor. Aveline, des. Wakhevitch), 'Les Incas' (chor. Lifar, des. Carzou), 'Les Fleurs' (chor. H. Lander, des. Fost and Moulène), and 'Les Sauvages' (chor. Lifar, des. Chapelain-Midy). It was premiered 18 June at Paris Opera with Vyroubova, Darsonval, Daydé, Lifar, Kalioujny, and Renault.

India See SOUTH ASIA.

Indonesia The diverse ethnic population of the nation is reflected in the rich variety of its traditional dance forms. These range from the stylized refinement of Javanese court dances to animal- and nature-inspired rituals. The best-known dance traditions originate from Bali and Central Java, and reflect Hindu/Buddhist influences from India. In Balinese dance forms, both theatrical and ceremonial, the dancer's stylized facial expressions and articulate gestures are reminiscent of Indian dance, although they adopt a more fixed posture of the body. In the many dance theatre forms, like topéng and barong, masks are a dominant feature. Literary sources for Balinese dance theatre draw on many aspects of S. and S.E. Asian tradition.

In Javanese court dances hand movements are unusually harmonious and delicate and the dancers' phrasing is extremely smooth, lacking stamping or percussive rhythms. Javanese dance theatre embraces many different genres, including wayang wong, which features the use of puppets, wayang topéng which uses masks, and langendria which is a form of dance opera. Performers are beginning to incorporate modern influences into classical styles, for example at the Yogyakarta Centre of Performing Arts, in Java.

Indrani, Rehman (*b* Chennai, 19 Sept. 1930; *d* 5 Feb. 1999) Indian dancer. She studied with her mother, Ragini Devi, and made her debut in Devi's company. Later in her career she developed her knowledge of less-well-known styles of Indian dance such as Odissi, and her international tours helped to win worldwide understanding and respect for the range of Indian dance.

Inger, Johan (*b* Stockholm, 1967) Swedish dancer, choreographer, and director. He trained at the schools of the Royal Swedish Ballet and National Ballet of Canada, joining RSB in 1985 and becoming soloist in 1989. In 1990 he joined *Nederlands Dans Theater where he choreographed his first major work, *Mellantid* (for NDT 2) in 1995. He went on to choreograph many more works for NDT1, 2, and 3 including *Dream Play* (mus. Stravinsky, 2000), *Walking Mad* (mus. Ravel and Pärt, 2001), and *Out of Breath* (mus. Jacob ter Veldhuis, 2002). In 2003 Inger was appointed artistic director of Cullberg Ballet, his works for that company including *Phases* (mus. Reich, 2003), *Within Now* (mus. Reich, 2004), *Point of Eclipse* (mus. Jean-Louis Huhta, 2007) and *Position of Elsewhere* (mus. Huhta and Bach). He retired as director in 2008.

Inglesby, Mona (orig. Vredenburg; *b* London, 1918; *d* East Sussex, 6 Oct. 2006) British-born dancer, choreographer and director. She studied with Rambert, Craske, and Egorova and danced with Ballet Club, Ballet Rambert, and Dandré's Russian Ballet in 1939. In 1940 she founded her own International Ballet, which toured widely in the UK and Europe, contributing significantly to the popularization of ballet in the country. She was the company's director, choreographer, and principal ballerina, excelling in demi-caractère roles like Swanilda. She staged several productions of the 19th-century classics, using the notations of *Sergeyev which she subsequently sold to the Harvard Collection. Her own works included *Endymion* (mus. Moszkowski, 1941) and the choreography for Leslie French's production, *Everyman* (mus. R. Strauss, 1943). She retired in 1953, also disbanding her company.

Initials R.B.M.E Ballet in one act with choreography by Cranko, music by Brahms, and design by Rose. Premiered 18 Jan. 1972 by Stuttgart Ballet, Stuttgart. This plotless setting of Brahms 2nd Piano Concerto is named after the four leading dancers at Stuttgart who danced its principal roles—Richard Cragun, Birgit Keil, Marcia Haydée, and Egon Madsen.

In Memory of . . . Ballet in one act with choreography by Robbins and music by Berg. Premiered 13 Jun. 1985 by New York City Ballet at New York State Theater. It is set to Berg's Violin Concerto, an elegy on the death of Manon Gropius. It contains the last major role created for Farrell.

Intermezzo Ballet in one act with choreography by Feld, music by Brahms, and design by Stanley Simmons. Premiered 29 Jun. 1969 by American Ballet Company in Spoleto with Sarry, Lee, Stirling, Sowinski, Figueroa, and Coll. This plotless

setting of Brahms's piano music Opp. 39, 117, No. 3 and 118, No. 3 is danced by three couples with the pianist as part of the action. It has been revived for several companies including National Ballet of Canada and American Ballet Theatre (both 1972), Stuttgart Ballet (1975), and New York City Ballet (2006).

International Ballet British ballet company. It was founded by M. *Inglesby in 1940 and gave its first performance 19 May 1941 in Glasgow. It appeared in London every year and toured widely in the UK and Europe. Inglesby was chief choreographer, but the repertory also included ballets by Fokine (*Les Sylphides* and *Carnaval*), Howard, and Turner, as well as productions of classics like *Swan Lake*, *Sleeping Beauty*, and *Coppélia* in productions mounted by N. *Sergeyev and based on the notations he took with him from St Petersburg. Turner, Shearer, Franca, and Arova were among its dancers. It closed in 1953.

International Dance Council Institution founded in Paris in 1973 under the auspices of UNESCO as a forum for the exchange of ideas and developments in dance, and to protect the rights of choreographers. Membership includes artists and organizations from over 150 countries.

(((●))) SEE WEB LINKS
• Official website for the International Dance Council

Interplay Ballet in one act with choreography by Robbins, music by M. Gould, and design by Carl Kent. Premiered 1 Jun. 1945 as part of Billy Rose's *Concert Varieties* review at Ziegfeld Theatre, New York, with Kriza, Reed, Kidd, and Robbins. This setting of Gould's *American Concertette* was Robbins's second ballet. It is a celebration of carefree youth, and its four movements are titled Free Play, Horseplay, Byplay, and Teamplay. It was taken into the repertory of Ballet Theatre, with new designs by Oliver Smith, and it has been revived for New York City Ballet (1952), Joffrey Ballet (1972), Royal Danish Ballet (1977), and San Francisco Ballet (1990), among others.

In the middle somewhat elevated Ballet in one act with choreography and design by Forsythe and music by Thom Willems. Premiered 30 May 1987 by Paris Opera, Paris, with Guillem and Hilaire. It is a virtuoso piece of plotless dance in which classical lines are flamboyantly distorted and classical decorum yields to a mood of aggressive cool. In 1988 it was performed by Ballett Frankfurt, in Frankfurt as the centrepiece of a larger work, *Impressing the Czar*, with design by Michael Simon and Férial Münich and additional music by Leslie Stuck, Eva Crossman-Hecht, and Beethoven. The additional three sections are a series of surreal, theatrical meditations on the rise and fall of Western culture. In *Potemkin's Signature* (part 1) the stage is partially covered by a giant chessboard chequered by miniature towers around which the dancers reference great art works from the past; in *La Maison de Mezzo-Prezzo* (part 3) the art is sold off by auction, while in *Bongo Bongo Nageela* (part 4) a bacchanale of schoolgirls dance St Sebastian to death. The full version was subsequently revived for the Royal Ballet of Flanders in 2006. The one-act version has entered the repertory of many companies, including the Royal Ballet and the Mariinsky Ballet.

In the Night Ballet in one act with choreography by Robbins, music by Chopin, design by Joe Eula, and lighting by Thomas Skelton. Premiered 29 Jan. 1970 by New York City Ballet at State Theater, New York, with Mazzo, Verdy, McBride, Blum, Martins, and Moncion and pianist G. Boelzner. Robbins's setting of Chopin's piano nocturnes (Opp. 27, No. 1, 55, Nos. 1 and 2, and 9, No. 2) portrays the relationships of three couples, suggesting light and shades of emotion before all six dancers are united for a final ensemble. It is often considered as an extension to *Dances at a Gathering*, made the previous year. It has been revived for many companies including Royal Ballet (1973), National Ballet of Cuba (1978), San Francisco Ballet (1985), Australian Ballet (1985), Houston Ballet (1986), Paris Opera (1989), Bavarian State Ballet (2001), and Mariinsky Ballet (2009).

In the Upper Room Ballet in one act with choreography by Tharp, music by Glass, design by Norma Kamali, and lighting by Tipton. Premiered 28 Aug. 1986 at the Ravinia Festival, Illinois, with Tharp, Washington, and Bishton. It is one of Tharp's most popular works, contrasting the power and energy of modern dance with the speed and aerial dexterity of ballet. It has been revived by several companies including American Ballet Theatre (1989), Birmingham Royal Ballet (1999), and the Bolshoi Ballet (2007).

Intimate Letters Janáček's 2nd String Quartet, to which several choreographers have set works, including P. Smok (1968), H. King (Scottish Ballet, 1978), L. Seymour (Sadler's Wells Royal Ballet, 1978), Kylián (Royal Swedish Ballet, 1980), and Mark Baldwin (London, 1997).

Invitation, The Ballet in one act with choreography and libretto by MacMillan, music by Matyas Seiber, and design by Georgiadis. Premiered 10 Nov. 1960 by the Touring Royal Ballet, New Theatre, Oxford, with Seymour, Gable, Heaton, and Doyle. It is inspired by B. Guido's *The House of the Angel* and Colette's *Le Blé en herbe* and with sometimes shocking realism portrays a young couple's sexual initiation by an older married couple, ending with the older man's rape of the girl. Its graphic style and stark emotional material represented a seminal departure from the decorative fantasies that then prevailed among ballet librettos. It has been revived for Royal Ballet (1962) and Berlin Opera Ballet (1966).

Invitation to the Dance Ballet film by G. Kelly which was produced in 1952 but not released until 1956. Its three parts are titled 'Circus' (mus. Ibert, with Sombart, Kelly, and Youskevitch), 'Ring around the Rosy' (mus. A. Previn, with Paltenghi, Dale, Youskevitch, Bessy, D. Adams, and Toumanova), and 'Sinbad the Sailor' (mus. Rimsky-Korsakov's *Scheherazade* adapted by R. Eden, a mix of cartoon and live dance with Kelly and D. Kasady).

Iran Western dance took root in Iran during the 1950s. In the early 1950s the American Nila Cram-Cook formed a small company which danced in Persian style but used Western music. During the same period Nejad Ahmadzadeh founded the company's national folk dance and music troupe. In 1956, Ahmadzadeh and his wife Aida also founded a ballet academy at the request of the Minister for Culture. From this a company developed rapidly under Ahmadzadeh's direction, helped by Dollar and de Valois who sent Ann Cock, M. Zolan, S. Vane, and Marion English to teach and stage ballet productions. This became known as the *Iranian National Ballet. In 1971 its ballet master Robert de *Warren left to study the folk traditions of the country and, under the sponsorship of the Empress Farah, formed the Mahalli Dancers of Iran company which preserved and performed native Iranian dances. Both companies were dissolved after the revolution of 1979.

Iranian National Ballet The resident dance company of Roudaki Hall Opera House in Teheran. It was founded in 1958 and sponsored in part by the Iranian Ministry of Culture and Arts, under the artistic direction of Nejad Ahmadzadeh, with his wife Aida as leading ballerina. It began with a dozen dancers and by 1978 had expanded to 46, one-third being Iranian. The repertory had works by Ailey and Cullberg as well as several classics. Heaton staged *Giselle* in 1970 and *Coppélia* in 1971 and Chabukiani mounted *Swan Lake* in 1970–1. Ahmadzadeh was succeeded in 1977 by Ali Pourfarrokh. It was dissolved after the revolution of 1979; however in 2007 Nima Kiann founded the Swedish-based company Les Ballet Persans, also known as the New Iranian National Ballet, which attempted to resurrect the spirit of the defunct company, with material mixing Western fantasies and Iranian cultural traditions.

Ireland Ireland's most famous dance personality remains Ninette de Valois. Although she spent most of her working life in England, she formed an eight-year collaboration with the Abbey Theatre (1926–34) in which she notably staged some plays by Yeats and also set up the short-lived Abbey School of Ballet. In 1945 Joan Denise Moriarty set up a ballet school in Cork, from which emerged the semi-professional Cork Ballet Company. It gave its first performance at the Cork Opera House in Jun. 1947 and had annual seasons there, often with guest artists. During the 1960s there were two unsuccessful attempts to found permanent professional ballet companies but both failed due to lack of funds. In 1974 Moriarty founded the state-funded fully professional Irish Ballet Company, which became the Irish National Ballet in 1983. She created several works for it including *The Playboy of the Western World* (mus. Sean O'Riada, 1978). Domi Reiter-Stoffer was artistic adviser from 1974 to 1989 and created several works for the company including *Lady of the Camellias* (mus. Saint-Saëns, 1984). In 1986 Vourenjuuri-Robinson took over as director but in 1989 the Irish Arts Council withdrew funding from it, as well as from Dublin Contemporary Dance Theatre, and both companies folded. In 1997 Anne Maher and Günther Falusey founded Ballet Ireland in Dublin, to re-establish classical ballet in the city and with funding from the Arts Council it currently tours a wide repertory of narrative ballets. Cork City Ballet, under the direction of Alan Foley, performs a small repertory of classical excerpts and some modern ballets by Bigonzetti, Foley, and others. There are several modern dance groups based in North and South Ireland, but *Fabulous Beast Dance Theatre, Dance Theatre Ireland, and CoisCéim are among the few to have attained a high profile. The country's best-known dance activity remains Irish step dance which acquired international popularity during the 1990s through the hit show *Riverdance* and its various stage spin-offs.

(((●))) SEE WEB LINKS
- Website for Cork City Ballet
- Website for Ballet Ireland

Irving, Robert (*b* Winchester, 28 Aug. 1913; *d* Winchester, 13 Sept. 1991) British ballet conductor. He was musical director of Sadler's Wells and the Royal Ballet from 1949 to 1958 before moving to New York City Ballet. He was considered to be one of the world's finest modern ballet conductors, and also conducted for Graham's company.

Isadora Ballet in two acts with choreography by MacMillan, libretto by Gillian Freeman, music by Richard Rodney Bennett, and design by B. Kay. Premiered 30 Apr. 1981 by the Royal Ballet, Covent Garden, London, with M. Park/ Mary Miller, L. Connor, J. Hosking, D. Rencher, R. MacGibbon, and S. Jefferies. In this ballet based on the life of Isadora Duncan, the title role is divided between a dancer and an actress who speaks a text based on quotations from Duncan's memoirs. It is considered one of MacMillan's less successful full-length ballets and rarely performed, although Deborah MacMillan attempted a revised version for the Royal Ballet in 2009.

Israel Ballet performances date back to the 1920s when Rina Nikova, a Russian émigrée dancer, founded her own company in Jerusalem and staged classically based works with biblical themes. During the 1930s settlers from central Europe like Gertrud *Kraus and Tilla Rossler established some modern dance activity via various studios and solo performances and vigorously opposed the establishment of classical dance as being out of sympathy with the country's character. The 1930s also saw the origins of a folk dance movement, by Rivka Sturman, Gurit Kadman, and others, who drew on Arab and Druze steps as well as their own choreographic invention to create dances that symbolized the link between the new Jewish settlers and the land. The most successful use of indigenous dance forms was that of Sara Levi-Tanai who founded the *Inbal Dance Theatre in 1949. At the beginning she fused modern ballet technique with the softer, grounded style of Yemenite dance but later drew on a wider range of folk traditions. After the late 1940s American modern dance became a major influence with the arrival of some US dancers in Israel and trips by Israeli dancers to study at New York's Juilliard School and with Graham. Kraus and Talley Beatty formed the short-lived Israel Ballet Theatre in 1951 and Anna Sokolow staged several works for the Lyrical Theatre (1962–4). Most of the latter's dancers joined the *Batsheva Dance Company which was founded by Bethsabee de *Rothschild in 1964, and was the first permanent professional modern dance company in Israel. Its style was grounded in Graham technique and it featured works by Graham, Sokolow, Cranko, Tetley, Robbins, Cohan, Butler, and Morrice in its repertory. In 1974 it was given state funding, confirming Batsheva as Israel's leading dance company. After Ohad *Naharin became director in 1990 Batsheva loosened its links with the Graham legacy as Naharin's own distinctively theatrical choreography dominated the repertory and also exercised a profound influence on a younger generation of Israeli dancers and choreographers. After Graham's death the rights to her repertory were transferred to the *Bat-Dor Dance Company, which had been founded by Rothschild in 1968, with Jeannette Ordman as its artistic director. Competition between the two companies was often acrimonious and Bat-Dor got into financial difficulty, folding in 1999 and now primarily operating as a dance centre.

Ballet activity in Israel became more focused in 1967 with the forming of the Classical Ballet Company, now The *Israel Ballet, by B. Yampolsky and Hillel Markman. Classical dance was also encouraged by the introduction of the English RAD syllabus into dance teaching and the opening of the Russian-oriented Haifa dance centre in 1969 by Lisa Schubert. Schubert also founded the Piccolo Ballet in 1975. Modern dance remains dominant however and a number of small companies have emerged despite the disruptions caused to arts activity by ongoing hostilities with the Arab neighbours. The Tel-Aviv based Kibbutz Contemporary Dance Company was founded by Yehudit Arnon in 1970 as a repertory company but now largely performs work by its resident choreographer Rami Be'er (who succeeded Arnon as director in 1996), including the full-length *Black Angels* made in 1992 to commemorate the 500th anniversary of the expulsion of the Jews from Spain. KCDC-2, the company's children's ensemble, was formed in 1994. The company tours internationally and in 1993 became the first Israeli group to dance in Beijing. Other leading companies include Koldemema (Voice of Silence) founded in 1975 by ex-Batsheva dancer and choreographer Moshe Efrat and the ensemble of Liat *Dror and Nir Ben-Gal, established in 1992 and gaining an international reputation for its European style of hard-edged risk-taking choreography. Prominent among the younger generation is Yasmeen Godder whose works are typified by their topical, political focus. Some of the country's most successful choreographers have chosen to make their careers abroad including Jasmin Vardimon and Hofesh *Shechter in the UK and Emmanuel Gat in France; however the dance scene remains diverse enough to sustain the annual Karmiel Dance Festival, established in 1987.

(⊕) SEE WEB LINKS

• Website for Kibbutz Contemporary Dance Company

Israel Ballet, The Tel Aviv-based ballet company. It was founded as a small chamber group in 1967, under the direction of Berta Yampolsky and Hillel Markman, who had previously danced with Ballet Russe de Monte Carlo. In 1973 it expanded dramatically with the incorporation of fifteen Jewish-American dancers and its 30-plus dancers now perform a repertoire that ranges from productions of the classics to Balanchine, Charrat, Spoerli, Lubovitch, Krzysztof Pastor, and work by Israeli choreographers such as Yampolsky and Domi Reiter-Stoffer. In 2004 the company moved into a new purpose-built base with its associate school The Classical Ballet Centre. It regularly tours abroad.

(⊕) SEE WEB LINKS

• Website for The Israel Ballet

Istomina, Avdotia (*b* St Petersburg, 17 Jan. 1799; *d* St Petersburg, 8 Jul. 1848) Russian dancer. She studied with Didelot at the Imperial Theatre School, St Petersburg and made her debut as Galatée (a role she created) in his *Acis and Galatea* (1816). A dancer with an outstanding technique for her time, famed for her speed, elevation, and pirouettes, she was also a fine actress and created leading roles in several of Didelot's ballets, including *Cora and Alonso* (1820), *Alcestis* (1821), and *The Prisoner of the Caucasus* (1823). She was also renowned for her performances in *Zéphire et Flore*. Pushkin described her glowingly in the opening chapter of *Eugene Onegin* and also wrote the ballet libretto *Les Deux Danseuses* with her in mind. She also frequently appeared in vaudeville and drama, retiring from the stage in 1836. She died of cholera.

Italy Considered to be the birthplace of ballet. From the early 15th century most Italian courts employed a dancing master and the first dance treatises were also published in Italy, including *De arte saltandi et choreas ducendi* by *Domenico da Piacenza, c.1450–60. The lavish court entertainments choreographed by these dancing masters often became famous, such as Bergonzio di Botta's 'dinner ballet' staged at Tortona in 1489, and were the inspiration for the *ballet de cour which subsequently flourished in France. This new form of spectacle overshadowed Italian activity (even though some of its most important artists were Italians working in France, such as Balthasar de Beaujoyeux who staged Le *Ballet comique de la reine* in 1581). When ballet moved from the courts into the theatre, Milan emerged as the main centre with the opening of the Scala Theatre in 1778 and particularly with the engagement of *Viganò as ballet master (from 1812 until his death). The Imperial Academy of Dancing was established in 1813 and when *Blasis became director in 1837 it became one of the finest schools in the world, producing ballerinas of the stature of Cerrito, Fuoco, Ferraris, Rosati, and Legnani. During the 1830s and 1840s La Scala became one of the world centres of Romantic ballet. Cerrito, Elssler, Taglioni, and Grisi often appeared there; Luigi Henry's *La silfide* was seen in 1828 (four years earlier than Taglioni's in Paris); A. Cortesi choreographed a *Giselle* with new music by Bajetti in 1843; M. Taglioni staged her version of Perrot's *Pas de quatre* in 1846; and Perrot choreographed his *Faust* in 1848. But this activity was not confined to Milan. In Naples ballet performances dated back to 1737 with the opening of the Teatro San Carlo. Here the public was sufficiently enthusiastic to fight over rival dancers Beccari and Sabatini and during the first years of the 19th century were presented with over 40 new ballets created by Gaetano Gioia. Standards were raised by the opening of a ballet school attached to the San Carlo in 1812 under the direction of P. *Hus. S. *Taglioni was later director and was also an acclaimed choreographer, and Grisi began her career at the theatre in 1835. In Rome there was little significant ballet activity during the 18th century but during the Romantic period it, too, attracted visits from ballerinas like Cerrito, Grisi, Elssler, Taglioni, and Grahn, and in other cities like Venice, Turin, and Florence, visiting ballerinas and ballet masters worked for occasional seasons. During the second half of the century, however, ballet declined as it became overshadowed by opera. In Milan many well-known ballet masters were engaged at La Scala, including P. *Taglioni and H. Monplaisir as were many star ballerinas such as Zucchi and Legnani, but the latter worked mostly abroad due to the lack of creative energy and enthusiasm left in Italy. *Manzotti's spectacular productions, such as *Excelsior* (1881), revived some enthusiasm as did Brianza's appearance in her own production of *The Sleeping Beauty*, but these did not halt the decline. In Rome, too, there were brief revivals of interest with productions of *Excelsior* in 1883 and Saint-Léon's *Coppélia* in 1885, but there was no continuity of performance tradition and this trend continued throughout Italy into the 20th century. Diaghilev's Ballets Russes visited Rome in 1911 and 1917 but were not widely appreciated and although *Cecchetti was appointed director of the La Scala school he did not have any lasting influence. At La Scala Ballet there was a rapid turnover of ballet masters and choreographers but none stayed long enough to establish a clear identity for the company—especially as the dancers (as in all Italian opera houses) also had to serve opera productions. In Rome the ballet school of the Teatro dell'Opera was founded in 1928 and between 1934 and 1960 the company, under the alternating direction of R. Romanov and *Milloss, staged several productions of the classics. Since then, however, few directors have lasted longer than one or two seasons and at Naples and Florence (where recent directors have included *Armitage and David Bombana) activity is similarly sporadic. Italy has produced only a few internationally known choreographers, such as Massimo Moricone, *Bigonzetti, and Virgilio Sieni. One of the country's most influential figures in recent years has been *Fracci, via her own performances and also her attempts, with Menegatti and Gai, to run touring companies.

Other major features of the Italian scene have been the international festivals such as Nervi-Genoa, Verona, Spoleto, and Castiglioncello which at various times have strongly promoted dance, also the smaller independent ballet companies which have succeeded in challenging the more stagnant opera house companies. These include *Aterballetto which is resident at Teatro Valli, Balletto di Toscana, the Milan Ballet (founded 1997), and MaggioDanza, which began as a corps de ballet attached to the Florence Opera in 1969 but has since developed a strong repertory of classical and modern works.

Modern dance has not flourished in Italy in comparison with other European countries. In 1980 Carolyn Carlson was invited to direct and choreograph a group of dancers at the Teatro la Fenice and had some success in nurturing emerging choreographers such as Luisa Casiraghi, Rafeaella Giordano, and Giorgio Rossi, but after her departure in 1985 the momentum slipped. Small groups have tended to come and go in different areas of the country, finding little official support, such as the short-lived Olympic Dance Company formed in 1996, under the direction of Gillian Whittingham and including dancers Alessandro Molin and Gheorghe Iancu, which attempted an ambitious fusion of modern and classical repertory with works by Wayne McGregor and others. Other companies active in Italy include Enzo Cosimi's group, founded in 1982; Movimento Danza Company, founded by choreographer Gabriella Stazio in 1984; Danzaricera, a Rome-based organization encouraging choreographic experimentation and research; Spellbound Dance Theatre founded by Mauro Astofi in 1994; Balletto Civile, a dance theatre and choral ensemble directed by Michela Lucenti; and Pneuma, founded by Mauro de Candion in 2006. Most recently a company was launched in 2009 by the National Dance Academy of Rome, with initial artistic advice from Pina Bausch, direction by Margherita Parilla, and a mixed repertory of international work, including choreography by Bausch. An important new stimulus to the modern dance scene has been the Dance Section of the Venice Biennale, which became known as the Venice International Festival of Contemporary Dance. It was established in 1999 and under the direction of choreographers such as Carlson, Armitage, Flamand, and Ivo has programmed a wide range of Italian and international work.

Ito, Michio (*b* Tokyo, 13 Apr. 1892; *d* Tokyo, 6 Nov. 1961) Japanese dancer and choreographer. He studied art in Europe and after seeing Nijinsky and Duncan perform in 1911, he went to Hellerau-Dresden to study with Dalcroze and later to London. He made his debut at the Coliseum in 1915 and in 1916 went to New York where he worked until 1929 after which he was in Los Angeles until 1942 and then in Tokyo. His musical, impressionistic works were described by him as dance poems, and early on in his career he collaborated with both W. B. Yeats and Ezra Pound.

Ivanov, Lev (*b* Moscow, 2 Mar. 1834; *d* St Petersburg, 11 Dec. 1901) Russian dancer, ballet master, choreographer, and teacher. He studied in Moscow and then at the Imperial Theatre School, St Petersburg, making his debut with the Imperial Theatre while still a student in 1850 (he graduated in 1852). A hard-working dancer with a prodigious memory and unusual musicality, he was given leading parts from 1858 and finally promoted premier danseur in 1869, performing classical and character roles. He began teaching in 1858 at the lower school of the Imperial Theatre School, and was appointed regisseur in 1882, then second ballet master under Petipa in 1885. His first ballet was choreographed in 1885—a new version of Hertel's *La Fille mal gardée*—and this was followed by *Tulip of Haarlem* (mus. Schel, 1887) and various small pieces including the Polovtsian Dances for Borodin's opera *Prince Igor* (1890). (These so impressed Fokine that he incorporated them into his own later version.) In 1892 he choreographed *The Nutcracker*, taking over its detailed scenario from Petipa who had become ill. Though his handling of the ballet was controversial, the lyrical choreography for the Snowflakes prefigures his contribution to *Swan Lake*. A year later he choreographed *The Magic Flute* (mus. Drigo) and *Cinderella* (with Petipa and Cecchetti, mus. Fitinhof–Schel). In 1894 he choreographed Act II of *Swan Lake* for a Tchaikovsky memorial matinée and this was so successful that Petipa decided to stage the whole ballet (which had been produced in Moscow in 1877 and 1882 but then dropped). For the new 1895 version Ivanov choreographed the two lakeside acts (II and IV) which remain his greatest contribution to ballet, eloquently musical, and rich in compositional invention and dramatic imagery (though a few writers have, controversially, attempted to contest his authorship, attributing the entire ballet to Petipa). His other works included *Awakening of Flora* (mus. Drigo, 1894, chor. in collaboration with Petipa), *Acis and Galathea* (mus. A. Kadletz, 1896), *The Daughter of the Mikado* (mus. Vrangel, 1897), and new versions of Perrot's *Marcobomba* and Saint-Léon's *Graziella* (both 1899). He died while collaborating with P. Gerdt on Delibes's *Sylvia*.

Ivan the Terrible (orig. Russ. title *Ivan Grozny*) Ballet in two acts with choreography by

Grigorovich, music by Prokofiev (taken from Eisenstein's film of the same title, with excerpts from his 3rd Symphony and *Alexander Nevsky*, arr. by M. Chulaki), and design by Simon Virsaladze. Premiered by the Bolshoi Ballet, Moscow 20 Feb. 1975 with Vladimirov, Bessmertnova, and B. Akimov. It is essentially a portrait of the controversial personality of Ivan IV and, via a series of danced tableaux, shows how Ivan sinks into sadistic cruelty after the poisoning of his beloved wife Anastasia. It has been revived by Paris Opera, 1976.

Ives, Charles (*b* Danbury, Conn., 20 Oct. 1874; *d* New York, 19 May 1954) US composer. He wrote no ballet scores but his concert music has been used several times for dance, such as Balanchine's *Ivesiana* (New York City Ballet, 1954), H. Spoerli's *Flowing Landscapes* (Basel, 1975), and P. Martins's *Calcium Light Night* (Spokane, Washington, 1977).

Ivesiana Ballet in one act with choreograhy by Balanchine, music by Ives, and lighting by Rosenthal. Premiered 14 Sept. 1954 by New York City Ballet at City Center, New York, with Reed, Moncion, Wilde, d'Amboise, Kent, Bolender, D. Adams, Bliss, and LeClercq. Its six original sections were titled 'Central Park in the Dark', 'Hallowe'en', 'The Unanswered Question', 'Over the Pavements', 'In the Inn', and 'In the Night'. In a subsequent revision (premiered 16 Mar. 1961) Balanchine dropped the 2nd and 4th sections. It has been revived for Dutch National Ballet (1968) and Berlin Opera (1971). 'The Unanswered Question' section is sometimes performed alone, for example by the Suzanne Farrell Ballet.

Ivo, Ismael (*b* São Paulo) Afro-Brazilian dancer. He studied drama and dance in Brazil and performed there as a solo dancer, before being invited to New York by Ailey in 1983. Here he continued creating and performing solo works such as *Phoenix* (1985) and *Delirium of a Childhood* (mus. Mahler, 1989), in which the charismatic intensity, and sculptural power of his style brought him an international reputation. From the early 1990s he based his own group Compagnie Ismael Ivo in Stuttgart, presenting works like *Othello* (jointly chor. with Johann Kresnik, 1995). In 2001 he co-created an award-winning production of *The Maids* with Kofi Koko and also created and performed the duet *Tristan and Isolde* with M. *Haydee in Hong Kong. He was appointed director of Venice Dance Festival in 2005.

Jacobson, Leonid (Yakobson) (*b* St Petersburg, 15 Jan. 1904; *d* Moscow, 17 Oct. 1975) Soviet dancer, choreographer, and ballet master. He began his studies at the late age of 16, taking evening classes at the Leningrad Ballet School. His rapid progress, however, admitted him to day classes and he graduated in 1926 into GATOB (later the Kirov). He specialized in character roles, although he also began to choreograph early on in his career. His first notable achievement was his collaboration with Kaplan, Vainonen, and Tchesnakov in the first production of Shostakovich's *The Golden Age* in 1930 but his more daring innovations of style and approach ran foul of the Soviet authorities, and he was once banned from working for six years. He continued to dance with the Kirov until 1970, although for periods he worked elsewhere, for example at the Bolshoi Ballet (1933 to 1942) as dancer and choreographer, and as a choreographer with the Isadora Duncan studio in Moscow in 1948. His major ballets included *Shurale* (mus. Yarullin, Kirov, 1950), *Solveig* (mus. Grieg, Maly Theatre, 1952), and *Spartacus* (Kirov, 1956), which was the first setting of Khatchaturian's score. He created several ballets for the Kirov in the 1960s, including *The Bedbug* (1962), for which he cast a young Natalia Makarova in the lead, *New Love* (1963), and *Land of Miracles* (1967). His unusually acrobatic dance skills also made him a popular concert artist, and he choreographed more than 100 concert pieces. It was Jacobson who made *Vestris*, the solo Baryshnikov danced when he won the International Ballet Competition in Moscow in 1969. One of Jacobson's miniatures was *Rodin*, with music by Debussy and inspired by Rodin sculptures at the Hermitage. In 1990 it entered the repertoire of San Francisco Ballet. He formed his own company, Choreographic Miniatures, in St Petersburg in 1970, although it appeared abroad as the Jacobson Ballet. After his death it became the State Ballet of Leningrad.

Jacob's Pillow Home of the international Jacob's Pillow Dance festival in Becket, Massachusetts. It was started by Ted Shawn who bought an 18th-century farm named Jacob's Pillow in 1930 and turned it into a summer theatre.

Originally the residence of his Men Dancers company, it soon offered summer dance courses and rehearsal facilities. In 1933 it held its first public performance; in 1941 a festival was established there, the first dance festival in the USA. Shawn continued to direct the festival until his death in 1972. Its theatre is named after him. Among the works created there is Tudor's *Pillar of Fire* (1941). The name Jacob's Pillow refers to a large pillow-shaped boulder on the property.

(⊕) SEE WEB LINKS

• Website for the Jacob's Pillow theatre and festival

Jacobsson, Petter (*b* Stockholm, 1963) Swedish dancer, choreographer, and director. He studied at the Royal Swedish Ballet School (1971–81) and the Vaganova School in St Petersburg (1981–2) before joining the Royal Swedish Ballet (1982–3). He was then soloist with London Festival Ballet (1983) becoming principal with Sadler's Wells Royal Ballet (later Birmingham Royal Ballet) from 1985 to 1990, continuing as guest artist with the company until 1994 and making his choreographic debut with the company with *Someone* (1992). In 1994 he moved to New York where he danced with Tharp among others and between 1999 and 2002 he was artistic director of the Royal Swedish Ballet, creating several works for the company but also bringing in guest contemporary choreographers such as Mathilde Monnier. In 1997 he formed a choreographic partnership with Thomas Caley, called Scentrifug, which specialized in a fusion of dance, visual arts, and film. A list of his recent works includes *La Verage* (1996), *Twinsoul* (1997), *The Secret Double* (1998), *Under the Surface* (1999), *Nightlife* (2002), and *Paradise?* (2006).

Jaffe, Susan (*b* Washington, DC, 22 May 1962) US dancer. She studied at the Maryland School of Ballet, the School of American Ballet, and the American Ballet Theatre School, dancing with American Ballet Theatre II from 1978 and joining American Ballet Theatre in 1980, where she was promoted to principal in 1983. She remained with the company until retiring in 2002, dancing the ballerina repertory and creating roles in works such as Tharp's *Known by Heart* (1998) and *Brahms/Haydn Variations* (2000), Dove's *Serious Pleasures* (1992), and Morris's *Drink To Me Only with Thine Eyes* (1988) and *Gong* (2001). She also appeared frequently as a guest artist. A dancer of great classical authority, she was especially admired for her performances in *Swan Lake* and *Giselle*. She retired from dancing in 2002 after which she founded her own school in Princeton and was appointed to the faculty of ABT's school.

Jamaica National Dance Theater Company Company founded in 1962 at the time of Jamaica's independence from Great Britain. In 1967 Rex Nettleford, one of the company's founders, was appointed artistic director and principal choreographer. The company's style blends traditional Caribbean dance drama and ritual with contemporary modern dance and ballet. Works deal with social issues, religious themes, and folklore while abstract dance is also represented in the repertoire. The company tours internationally, and has a very active educational programme.

Jamison, Judith (*b* Philadelphia, 10 May 1943) US dancer, choreographer, and director. She studied at the Judimar School of Dance, at the Philadelphia Dance Academy, where she was discovered by Agnes de Mille, and later with Tudor and Maria Swoboda. She made her New York debut as a guest artist with American Ballet Theatre, dancing in de Mille's *The Four Marys* in 1965. Later in 1965 she joined the Alvin Ailey company where she became one of its leading dancers. Inspired by her dramatic, statuesque stage presence Ailey choreographed many roles for her, including the solo *Cry* (1971) which established her international reputation. Other choreographers who also created for her included Neumeier (*Legend of Joseph*, Vienna, 1977) and Béjart (*Le Spectre de la rose*, 1979). In 1980 she left the Ailey company to work as a freelance dancer and choreographer, starring in the Broadway musical *Sophisticated Ladies* in 1981 and briefly running her own company, the Jamison Project. After Ailey's death in 1989 she was appointed artistic director of the Alvin Ailey American Dance Theater. She widened the company's repertoire by adding creations of her own and by bringing in works by Lar Lubovitch and Jawole Willa Jo Zollar among others. She also oversaw the company's move to its purpose-built home in New York. A list of her own choreography includes *Divining* (Ailey company, 1984), *Just Call Me Dance* (for Béjart's company, 1984), *Time Out* (for Washington Ballet, 1986), *Time In* (1986), *Into the Life* (1987), *Tease* (1988), *Forgotten Time* (1989), *Rift* (1991), *Hymn* (1993), *Riverside* (1995), and *Sweet Release* (1996).

Janáček, Leoš (*b* Hukvaldy, 3 Jul. 1854; *d* Ostrava, 12 Aug. 1928) Czech composer. Although he wrote no music for the ballet, his concert music has been used by many choreographers. Tudor choreographed his First String Quartet for the Juilliard School in 1971; Lynn Seymour his *Intimate Letters* for Sadler's Wells Royal Ballet in 1968. Kylián has frequently used his music, including *Intimate Letters* for Swedish television in 1980, *Glagolitic Mass* for Nederlands Dans Theater (1979), *Sinfonietta* for NDT (1978), and various piano pieces for *Return to a Strange Land* (Stuttgart Ballet 1975, revived Royal Ballet 1984).

Janet Smith and Dancers *See* SCOTTISH DANCE THEATRE.

Japan Traditional dance has flourished in Japan for centuries within highly stylized forms of dance drama. Bugaku, which is a semi-religious dance, originated in the 7th century but until the latter half of the 20th century it was performed exclusively at the imperial court or in certain shrines. *Kabuki, which developed at the end of the 16th century, was the first popular dance theatre for commoners. In its early days it was performed by female prostitutes and some of its manifestations were considered so immoral that the women were banned from performing it by the authorities. Male dancers then adopted the kabuki style, taking on the female roles themselves. Being an *onnagata* (female impersonator) became an honoured profession. Today kabuki is seen throughout the world. Western theatrical dance arrived in Japan in the 20th century. Visits by the Pavlova company, the Denishawn Dancers, and the Ruth Page company in the 1920s sparked public interest and by the 1930s ballet had taken hold. The first schools were established, out of which grew new classical companies, including the *Komaki Ballet, founded 1946. Training, style, and repertoire were greatly influenced by the Soviet model. For many years the most important of the Japanese companies was the *Tokyo Ballet, founded in 1964, although it came to be associated with an increasingly contemporary repertory. In 1997 the newly built New National Theatre of Tokyo launched its own ballet company, under the direction of Maki Asami, to perform both classical and neo-classical ballet. Today Japanese ballet audiences are among the most enthusiastic in the world. Companies like the Royal Ballet and the Kirov are regular visitors, and Western stars like Sylvie Guillem and Evelyn Hart have been idolized there. In recent years Japanese-born dancers have found great success in the West. Tetsuya *Kumakawa and Miyako *Yoshida led a new generation of fine Japanese classical dancers trained and performing abroad, although Kumakawa returned home to popular acclaim when he founded his touring company K Ballet, based in Japan, in 1998. Independent Japanese choreographers, such as Saburo *Teshigawara, have been very active in the field of postmodern dance. *Butoh, an expressionist dance form which originated in Japan in the 1950s, is seen around the world performed by Japanese companies.

Jaques-Dalcroze, Émile (b Vienna, 6 Jul. 1865; d Geneva, 1 Jul. 1950) Swiss music teacher and theoretician. He was responsible for developing a system of training music students to understand rhythm by translating sounds into physical movements. It was a principle that could be applied to dance as well as to music and it had a significant influence on several early choreographers, Nijinsky among them. Jaques-Dalcroze called his system 'rhythmic gymnastics', although it is popularly known as *eurythmics. He established his Institute for Applied Rhythm in Hellerau-Dresden in 1910, which trained several modern dance pioneers in Germany, including Wigman and Georgi. After the First World War the school was moved to Vienna, but was forced to close when the Nazis invaded Austria in 1938. Jaques-Dalcroze established another school in Geneva in 1915, where he taught until he died. Author of *Rhythm, Music and Education* (1921) and *Eurythmics, Art and Education* (1930).

Jardin aux lilas See LILAC GARDEN.

Jazz Calendar Ballet in one act with choreography by Ashton, music by Richard Rodney Bennett, and designs by Derek Jarman. Premiered 9 Jan. 1968 by the Royal Ballet at Covent Garden with Derman, Park, Lorrayne, Grant, Sibley, Nureyev, Doyle, and Trounson. Ashton's uncertain attempt at a jazz ballet, based on the English children's rhyme that begins 'Monday's child is fair of face, | Tuesday's child is full of grace,' etc. was given credibility by Jarman's designs, which were stylishly in turn with the spirit of 1960s 'swinging London'

Jazz dance Dance form developed by African-Americans in the US in the early part of the 20th century. It drew on African rhythms and techniques which isolated different parts of the body in movement. The name was first used during the First World War, and by the 1920s jazz had been taken up by white society. Its absorption into show business, through films, television, and Broadway, brought it an enormous international audience. In 1936 Balanchine choreographed the jazz ballet *Slaughter on Tenth Avenue*, as the climax to the Broadway musical *On Your Toes* and jazz continued to influence the ballet stage, for example in works by Robbins and Tharp. Leading jazz choreographers have included Katherine *Dunham and Bob *Fosse.

Jeanmaire, Renée (Zizi) (b Paris, 29 Apr. 1924) French dancer, singer, and music hall star. She studied at the Paris Opera School from 1933 and entered the company in 1939, where she remained until 1944. Although possessing a brilliant classical technique, she never fitted the ballerina mould and found her greatest success in the chic and exuberant choreography of Roland Petit, whom she married in 1954. Before working with Petit she appeared in the Soirées de la Danse in Paris (1944), and danced with the Nouveau Ballet de Monte Carlo (1946), where she created principal roles in several ballets by Lifar, and with de Basil's Ballets Russes for its final London season in 1947. In 1948 she joined Petit's Ballets de Paris, creating leading roles in many of his ballets, including—famously—*Carmen* (1949), which transformed her overnight from classical dancer to long-legged, short-haired gamine. *La Croqueuse de diamants* (1950) revealed that she had a husky and attractive singing voice. Although she created the role of Roxane in Petit's *Cyrano de Bergerac* in 1959, by the 1950s her career was focused on cabaret and film and it was here that she achieved her greatest fame. Her many film appearances included *Hans Christian Andersen* (1951) with Danny Kaye; also *Black Tights* (1960), *Anything Goes* (1956), *Charmants Garçons* (1957), and *Folies-Bergère* (1960), all of them choreographed by Petit. Her significant Broadway success was starring in *The Girl in Pink Tights* (1953). In 1970 she and Petit bought the Casino de Paris, where she starred in *La Revue*, which Petit choreographed and directed. A second revue, *Zizi, je t'aime*, followed in 1972. She made her comeback at the Paris Opera in Petit's *Symphonie fantastique* in 1975. In 1990 she created the role of Carabosse in her husband's Ballet de Marseilles staging of *The Sleeping Beauty*, a role she performed on pointe. In 1996 she returned to the stage for a show dedicated to the French singer Serge Gainsbourg. She was made Chevalier de la Légion d'honneur in 1974.

Jefferies, Stephen (b Reintelm, West Germany, 24 Jun. 1951) British dancer and ballet director. He studied at the Royal Ballet School (1967–9) and joined the Royal Ballet Touring Company in 1969. In 1976 he danced with the National Ballet of Canada as principal, returning to the Royal's main company in 1977, again as a principal. He was widely regarded as one of the finest dance-actors of his generation, especially acclaimed in the MacMillan repertoire. He created roles in MacMillan's *Ballade* (1972), *The Poltroon* (1972), *Isadora* (1981), and *Different Drummer* (1984); Bruce's *Unfamiliar Playground*

(1974); Peter Wright's *El amor brujo* (1975); Tetley's *Dances of Albion* (1980); Bintley's *Adieu* (1980), *Consort Lessons* (1983), *The Songs of Horus* (1985), *Still Life at the Penguin Café* (1988), *The Planets* (1990), and *Cyrano* (title role, 1991); Corder's *L'Invitation au voyage* (1982); and Eagling's *Frankenstein, the Modern Prometheus* (1985). While in Canada he created the role of Morris in Kudelka's *Washington Square* (1977). He also appeared in Minoru Miki's opera *An Actor's Revenge* at the Old Vic in 1979 (a non singing role) and in the Lloyd Webber musical *Song and Dance* at London's Palace Theatre in 1982. In 1995 he left the Royal Ballet and the following year became director of the Hong Kong Ballet. During his 10-year tenure he raised technical standards and revitalized the repertory with his own stagings of the classics and with new works, many of them with Chinese themes. He created several of these himself including the full-length *The Legend of the Great Archer* (mus. Kuan Nai-Chun, 2004).

Jenkins, Margaret (*b* San Francisco, Calif., 1942) US dancer and choreographer. She trained at the Juilliard School in New York, with Graham, Limón, and Tudor, and attended the University of California in Los Angeles, dancing with Al Huang. In 1965 she returned to New York and joined the Tharp company; also danced with Viola Farber, James Cunningham, and Gus Solomons jun. From 1964 to 1970 she taught at the Merce Cunningham Studio and helped to stage his works in Europe. She started choreographing in the late 1960s and in 1973 founded her own San Francisco-based company, Margaret Jenkins Dance Company, for which she has created numerous works. Many have a strong political theme, and some of the most recent have been site specific works, for example *Danger Orange* (2004) which addressed issues around US national security and was performed in San Francisco's Justin Herman Plaza. Her works are also in the repertoire of the Cullberg Ballet, the Oakland Ballet, and San Francisco Ballet and she has recently collaborated with the Indian company Tanusree Shankar on *A Slipping Glimpse* (2006) and with Guangdong Modern Dance Company on the trilogy *Other Suns* (2007–9).

(((●))) SEE WEB LINKS

• Website for the Margaret Jenkins company

Jeppesen, Lis (*b* Copenhagen, 5 Apr. 1956) Danish dancer. She studied at the Royal Danish Ballet School from 1963, and made her debut while still a student, taking the role of the White Girl in van Dantzig's *Monument for a Dead Boy* in 1973. She joined the Royal Danish Ballet full time in 1974, promoted to principal in 1980 and continuing with the company as character dancer

from 1997. She was considered one of the finest Bournonville dancers of her day but also excelled in the Romantic repertory and additionally created roles in new works such as Flindt's *Dreamland* (1974) and Andersen's *Fête galante* (1989). She won the Pavlova Prize in 1979.

jeté [Fr., thrown] A jump that takes off on one leg and lands on the other. The step can travel in any direction, forwards, backwards, and sideways, and has many manifestations, including a small, springing version (petit jeté) and a large leaping version (grand jeté).

Jeu de cartes (*The Card Game*) Ballet in three 'deals' with choreography by Balanchine, libretto and music by Stravinsky, and designs by Irene Sharaff. Premiered 27 Apr. 1937 by the American Ballet at the Metropolitan Opera House in New York, with Dollar. Each scene represents a separate poker hand, the dancers giving dramatic life and personality to the individual 'cards'. It was the first collaboration between Stravinsky and Balanchine in the US. The ballet was revived by the Ballet Russe de Monte Carlo (New York, 1940) with Frederic Franklin as the joker. A different version using the Stravinsky score was choreographed by Janine Charrat in 1945 for the Ballets des Champs-Elysées in Paris with Babilée as the joker. Cranko also did a version for Stuttgart in 1965, which was revived for the Royal Ballet in 1966 and for Birmingham Royal Ballet in 2008.

Jeune Homme et la mort, Le Ballet in one act, with choreography by Petit, music by J. S. Bach, libretto and costumes by Cocteau, and sets by Georges Wakhevitch. Premiered 25 Jun. 1946 by the Ballets des Champs-Elysées at the Théâtre des Champs-Elysées in Paris with Babilée and Philippart. A young Parisian painter waits in his attic for the young woman he desperately desires. When she arrives she rejects him, and he eventually hangs himself. The woman places a death-mask on his face and takes him away, out onto the neon-lit rooftops of Paris. The music, in stark contrast to the violence of the drama, is an orchestrated version of Bach's serene Passacaglia in C minor, performed without the Fugue. An influential work in French post-war ballet, it was seen at the time as shockingly erotic. It also provided Babilée with his most famous role. Petit restaged it for American Ballet Theatre in 1951; ABT revived it for Baryshnikov in 1975. Petit also restaged it for the Paris Opera Ballet in 1990. Other stagings include Ballet National de Marseilles (1984), Berlin Opera Ballet (1985), and the Boston Ballet (1998).

Jeux Ballet in one act with choreography and libretto by Nijinsky, music by Debussy, and designs by Bakst. Premiered 15 May 1913 by the Ballets Russes de Diaghilev at the Théâtre des Champs-Elysées in Paris with Nijinsky, Karsavina, and Schollar. Nijinsky's second ballet for Diaghilev, it was the first in the company's repertoire to deal with a contemporary subject. The ballet, set to a commissioned score by Debussy, portrays the sexually ambiguous flirtations between two women and a young man playing tennis. Nijinsky wrote in his diary that '*Jeux* is the life of which Diaghilev dreamed. He wanted to have two boys as lovers. He often told me so, but I refused. In the ballet, the two girls represent the two boys and the young man is Diaghilev. I changed the characters as love between three men could not be represented on stage.' Nijinsky's 'experiment in stylized gesture' was not a success and was dropped after just five performances. In 1996 it was reconstructed by Millicent Hodson and Kenneth Archer for Verona. Börlin made a version for the Ballets Suédois in 1920, Dollar for Ballet Theatre in 1950, Darrell for Western Theatre Ballet in 1963, Taras for New York City Ballet in 1966, Flindt for Paris Opera Ballet in 1973, and Van Schayk for Dutch National Ballet in 1977.

Jeux d'enfants Ballet in one act with choreography by Massine, libretto by Kochno, music by Bizet, and designs by Joan Miró. Premiered 14 Apr. 1932 by Colonel de Basil's Ballets Russes in Monte Carlo, with Riabouchinska, Toumanova, and Lichine. A girl playing with her toys at night in the nursery falls in love with one of them, the Traveller, when he comes to life. Balanchine did a version for New York City Ballet in 1955 which was revised in 1959, and a second production, as *The Steadfast Tin Soldier*, in 1975, while Petit did a version for Ballet National de Marseilles in 1974.

Jewels Ballet in three parts with choreography by Balanchine, music by Fauré, Stravinsky, and Tchaikovsky, costumes by Barbara Karinska, sets by Peter Harvey, and lighting by R. Bates. Premiered 13 Apr. 1967 by New York City Ballet, at the State Theater in New York, with Verdy, Ludlow, Paul, Moncion, McBride, Villella, P. Neary, Farrell, and d'Amboise. Inspired by jewellery in the collection of Van Cleef and Arpels in New York, it is made up of three plotless works united into an evening-length ballet. The first, 'Emeralds', is set to Fauré's *Pelléas et Mélisande* and *Shylock*; the second, 'Rubies', to Stravinsky's Capriccio for Piano and Orchestra; the third, 'Diamonds', to Tchaikovsky's 3rd Symphony (without the first movement). The 'Rubies' section was taken into the repertoires of several companies including the Paris Opera Ballet (1974), Dutch National Ballet (1977), and the Royal Ballet (1989). The full-length ballet has been revived

for the Kirov, the Paris Opera, the National Ballet of Canada, and the Royal Ballet.

Jeyasingh, Shobana (*b* Chennai, 26 Mar. 1957) Indian-born British-based choreographer and company director. She studied at the University of Sussex in England, gaining an MA in Renaissance studies, and trained as a dancer in bharata natyam, the classical dance of South Asia. During the 1980s she toured Britain as a solo bharata natyam performer and in 1989 founded the Shobana Jeyasingh Dance Company. Becoming one of the leading modern dance choreographers in Britain, Jeyasingh experimented with elements of the bharata natyam style, re-imagining it for her ensemble and extending it into the language of post-modern dance. She has collaborated with some of Britain's leading composers, including Michael Nyman, Glyn Perrin, and Graham Fitkin. A list of work for her own company includes *Configurations* (mus. Nyman, 1989), *Correspondences* (mus. Volans, 1990), *Making of Maps* (mus. Alistair McDonald, 1992), *Romance . . . with Footnotes* (mus. Glyn Perrin, Karaikudi Krishnamurthy, 1993), *Duets with Automobiles* (for video, mus. Orlando Gough, 1994), *Raid* (mus. Glyn Perrin, Haiyaraaja, 1995), *Palimpsest* (mus. Graham Fitkin, 1996), *Memory and Other Props* (mus. Alistair McDonald, 1998), *Fine Frenzy* (mus. Django Bates, 1999), *Phantasmaton* (mus. Jocelyn Pooks, 2002), *Exit No Exit* (mus. Nyman, 2006), and *Faultline* (mus. Errollyn Wallen, 2007). She has also created work for City Contemporary Dance Company (Hong Kong) and Ballet Black among others.

(((⊕))) **SEE WEB LINKS**
• Website for the Shobana Jeyasingh company

jig An old British folk dance. It may have derived from either the French gigue or the Italian giga. A fast solo dance, it is usually performed in 6/8 or 12/8 time and is characterized by its lively footwork.

Jin Xing (*b* Shenyang, Lianoning Province, 13 Aug. 1967) Chinese dancer, choreographer, actor, and director. Jin was born a boy to ethnic Korean parents and at the age of 9 joined the local military song and dance academy. Three years later he was moved to Beijing to study at the People's Army Dance Institute, reaching the military status of Colonel aged 17 as well as the highest rank of dancer. He graduated in 1984, and danced with the National Dance Company before studying modern dance in Guangdong in 1987. Between 1988 and 1991 he was allowed a period of study in New York, training at the studios of Graham and Cunningham, and between 1991 and 1993 he additionally worked in Rome and Brussels, performing, teaching, and choreographing. In 1993 he returned to China to organize a training course for choreographers and in 1996 to become artistic director for the Beijing Modern Dance Company. In the same year he underwent surgery to become a woman. Jin's works for BMDC, a fusion of Eastern and Western contemporary styles, included *Sun Flower* 1996 and *Red and Black* (1998). In 1999 she formed her own company (which operated without state funding and was eventually based in Shanghai) and since then has created the multi-media work *Cross Border* (2002, with pianist Joanna MacGregor), *Shanghai Tango* (2003), and *Shanghai Beauty* (with Jutta Hall and Dieter Baumann, 2005).

Joan of Arc Ballet in three acts with choreography by Bourmeister, libretto by V. Pletneva, music by N. Peiko, and designs by V. Ryndin. Premiered 29 Dec. 1957 by the Stanislavsky and Nemirovich-Danchenko Music Theatre in Moscow with Bovt and Kuzmin. The ballet tells the story of Joan of Arc. Other choreographers who have based ballets on her life include S. Viganò (Milan, 1821) and Martha Graham (*Seraphic Dialogue*, New York, 1955).

Job A 'masque for dancing' in eight scenes, with choreography by de Valois, libretto by Geoffrey Keynes, music by Vaughan Williams, designs by Gwendolen Raverat, and wigs and masks by Hedley Briggs. Premiered 5 Jul. 1931 by the Camargo Society at the Cambridge Theatre in London, with Dolin and Stanley Judson. The ballet, which relies heavily on mime and staged tableaux to narrate its story, is based on William Blake's illustrations to *The Book of Job*. At the composer's request it was described as 'a masque for dancing', and it was Vaughan Williams himself who insisted that pointework should not be used. It tells of Job's absolute belief in God and the challenges set in his path to question his faith. Drawing inspiration as it did from Blake and Vaughan Williams, it was considered the first truly English ballet. It was revived for the Vic-Wells Ballet in 1931, for Sadler's Wells Ballet in 1948, for the Royal Ballet Touring Company in 1970, and for Birmingham Royal Ballet in 1993. Ted Shawn also choreographed a different version of the story in 1931 for the Denishawn Dancers in New York. In 1992 David Bintley choreographed a new version for the San Francisco Ballet.

Joffrey, Robert (orig. Abdulla Jaffa Anver Bey Khan; *b* Seattle, 24 Dec. 1930; *d* New York, 25 Mar. 1988) US dancer, choreographer, and ballet director. Founder of the Joffrey Ballet. He studied ballet locally and at the School of American Ballet. He also studied modern dance at the High School of the Performing Arts in New York, where he taught from 1950. He danced with Petit's Ballets de Paris (1949–50), and with May O'Donnell and Company (1951–3) but began to choreograph his own work early in his career. His first ballets were for his own solo recital in Seattle in 1948 followed by *Persephone* (mus. R. Silverman) which he made for a workshop programme in New York in 1952. He also staged pieces for Ballet Rambert in London (1955) and worked in musicals and operas. He formed his first company, Robert Joffrey Ballet Concert, in 1954; its first programme featured *Pas de déesses* (mus. J. Field) and *Le Bal masqué* (mus. Poulenc). Subsequent works included *Harpsichord Concerto* (mus. de Falla) and *Pierrot Lunaire* (mus. Schoenberg). In 1956 he founded the Robert Joffrey Theatre Ballet with Arpino, which became known as the *Harkness Ballet after Joffrey fell out with his patron, Rebekah Harkness in 1964. The following year he started another company, named the City Center Joffrey Ballet from 1966 onwards, and from 1977 the Joffrey Ballet. Joffrey's works for his two companies included *Gamelan* (mus. Lou Harrison, 1963), which drew on Balinese movement; *Astarte* (mus. Crome Syrcus, 1967), a highly controversial multi-media rock ballet; also *Remembrances* (mus. Wagner, 1973) and *Postcards* (mus. Satie, 1980). As a company director he also promoted the development of young American dancers and encouraged the creation of experimental American choreography, commissioning Ailey, Tetley, Tharp, Morris, Dean, and Forsythe. He also staged important revivals of 20th-century ballets, by Ashton (at one point his company had ten Ashton ballets in its repertoire), Balanchine, Cranko, Fokine, de Mille, Robbins, and Tudor, and was responsible for starting the Jooss and Massine revivals. He was particularly interested in the Diaghilev legacy; when he died he was planning an evening of ballets by Nijinsky and Nijinska. He founded the American Ballet Center, later the Joffrey Ballet School.

Joffrey Ballet US ballet company founded in New York but now based in Chicago. It grew out of the Robert Joffrey Ballet Concert, which first performed at the New York YM-YWHA in 1954. A chamber ensemble, it drew its dancers from the American Ballet Center, which was directed by Joffrey and Gerald *Arpino. In 1956 the company started to tour, initially as Robert Joffrey Theatre Ballet. In 1960 it became the Robert Joffrey Ballet. At that time the repertoire featured ballets by Joffrey and Arpino; its mandate was to be specifically American. The commissioning policy was adventurous: when Alvin *Ailey was invited to make a work, it was a pioneering example of a ballet company turning to the world of modern dance. Ten years later the Joffrey invited Twyla

Tharp to make her first work for a ballet company and the resulting commission, *Deuce Coupe*, was one of the biggest hits in its history. Rebekah Harkness was an important early benefactor, and among the developments she made possible was extensive foreign touring, including the company's first trip to the Soviet Union in 1963. But in 1964 she and Joffrey fell out, and most of the repertoire and the dancers were taken into the newly founded *Harkness Ballet. Joffrey started all over again, building up a new company which made its debut in 1965 as the Robert Joffrey Ballet. Following a successful season at the New York City Center in 1966 it was invited to become the theatre's resident ballet company with Joffrey as artistic director and Arpino as chief choreographer. The 1960s and 1970s were a golden era for the company with Arpino's successful rock ballet *Trinity* (1970), Joffrey's revival of Kurt Jooss's *The Green Table* (1967) and revivals of other early 20th-century classics like Ashton's *Façade*, Cranko's *Pineapple Poll*, Fokine's *Petrushka*, and Massine's *Le Tricorne*, *Le Beau Danube*, and *Parade*. In 1973 Tharp made her second work, *As Time Goes By*, for the Joffrey. The company continued as City Center Joffrey Ballet until 1977. From 1977 it performed as the Joffrey Ballet, with a second home established in Los Angeles from 1982. During the 1980s ballets by Forsythe, Kylián, Kudelka, Morris, and Dean entered the repertoire. In 1987 Joffrey's most important piece of dance archaeology took place when he directed a revival of Nijinsky's 1913 ballet *Le Sacre du printemps*, reconstructed by Millicent Hodson and Kenneth Archer. Following Joffrey's death in 1988 Arpino took over and despite one temporary falling out with the company board he continued Joffrey's policies. As well as bringing new choreographers into the company, Arpino acquired a revival of Massine's *Les Présages* in 1992. Also in 1992, with his eye firmly on the box office, he commissioned four choreographers, Laura Dean, Charles Moulton, Margot Sappington, and Peter Pucci, to make a new populist work for the company. The resulting ballet, *Billboards*, set to music by the rock star Prince, earned the company millions but the shallowness of its choreography and designs also generated much damaging criticism. In 1995 the Joffrey was suffering a financial crisis and had to relocate from New York to Chicago. In 2007 Ashley Wheater was appointed Arpino's successor, re-focusing the company with revivals of its *heritage repertory while bringing in works by Wheeldon, Helgi Tomasson, and others. In 2003 Robert Altman's film *The Company* used the Joffrey for its fictional portrait of the daily life of a ballet company.

(●) SEE WEB LINKS

• Website for the Joffrey Ballet and Academy

Johansson, Christian (*b* Stockholm, 20 May 1817; *d* St Petersburg, 25 Dec. 1903) Swedish dancer and teacher. Although Swedish, he spent most of his career in Russia. He studied at the Royal Swedish Ballet School from 1829 and with Bournonville in Copenhagen. In 1837 he was appointed premier danseur in Stockholm where he partnered M. Taglioni but in 1841 moved to St Petersburg where, after a successful debut in *La Gitana*, he was made premier danseur. He remained at the Imperial Theatres until 1869, creating roles in several ballets by Perrot. It is as a teacher, however, that he achieved lasting fame. After retiring from the stage he became chief teacher at the Imperial Theatre School, where his pupils included Kshessinska, Preobrajenska, P. Gerdt, Nikolai Legat, Vaganova, Pavlova, and Karsavina. He became one of the most important figures in the development of the Russian school of dancing, credited with introducing greater use of ballon (influenced by his Bournonville training), precision batterie, and a variety of virtuoso pirouettes. So inventive was his teaching it is said that he never repeated an enchaînement. He also accompanied his own classes playing a violin.

Johns, Jasper (*b* Augusta, Ga., 15 May 1930) US painter and designer. One of the leading painters of the latter half of the 20th century, he collaborated with Merce Cunningham, and was artistic adviser to the Cunningham company. He worked with Cunningham on *Suite de danses* (a dance for television, costumes 1961), *RainForest* (uncredited, costumes 1968), *Walkaround Time* (set and costumes, 1968), *Canfield* (costumes, 1969), *Second Hand* (costumes, 1970), *Landrover* (costumes, 1972), *TV ReRun* (set and costumes, 1972), *Un jour ou deux* (set and costumes, Paris Opera Ballet, 1973), and *Exchange* (set and costumes, 1978).

Johnson, Virginia (*b* Washington, DC, 25 Jan. 1950) US dancer. She studied at the Washington DC School of Ballet from 1953, a pupil of Mary Day, and later with Arthur Mitchell and Karel Shook in New York. In 1969 she became associated with the fledgling *Dance Theatre of Harlem performing in its first season and eventually becoming its leading ballerina, possibly the first black dancer in history to be ranked seriously as a classical ballerina. She created roles in many Mitchell ballets, including *Holberg Suite* (1970), *Tones* (1970), *Rhythmetron* (1971), *Fête noire* (1972), and his groundbreaking 'Creole' production of *Giselle* (1984). She also created roles in works by Raines (*Haiku*, 1973, and *After Corinth*, 1975); Fagan (*Footprints Dressed in Red*, 1986); and Tetley (*Dialogues*, 1991). A tall and supremely elegant dancer, Johnson possessed an unusually versatile range. Romantically lyrical in *Giselle*, she also excelled in 20th-century dramatic works like de Mille's *Fall River Legend*, Limón's *The Moor's Pavane*, and Bettis's *A Streetcar Named Desire*. She additionally danced key Balanchine ballets including *Agon*, *Concerto Barocco*, *Allegro Brillante*, *Serenade*, *Tchaikovsky Pas de deux*, and *The Four Temperaments*. Although spending most of her career with DTH she also guested with other companies including Washington Ballet and the Royal Ballet. After retiring from the stage in 1997 she taught and became editor-in-chief of *Pointe* magazine. She choreographed the television film *Ancient Voices of Children*, in which she also danced.

Jones, Betty (*b* Meadville, Pa., 1926) US dancer and educator. She studied with Evelyn Blevins and at Jacob's Pillow with Ted Shawn and Alicia Markova in the 1940s; studied ballet with Maggie Black, Margaret Craske, and Tudor, and modern dance with Hanya Holm, Louis Horst, Humphrey, and Limón. She made her professional debut in a USO tour of the musical *Oklahoma!* in the South Pacific in 1945 and toured (1946–7) in de Mille's *Bloomer Girl*. She danced with José Limón's company from 1947 to 1972, where she created her most famous role, Desdemona in his *The Moor's Pavane* (1949), when she was just 22. She was considered the foremost exponent of the Limón style and created roles in many of his works. She founded her own company, Dances We Dance, with Fritz Ludin, in 1964. She taught extensively in the US and Europe and additionally staged reconstructions of the Humphrey–Limón repertoire.

Jones, Bill T. (*b* Bunnell, Fla., 15 Feb. 1952) US dancer, choreographer, and company director. He discovered dance while in college on a sports scholarship (State University of New York at Binghamton) and there met Arnie *Zane, a photographer who was to become his partner and collaborator. Together they studied dance and became co-founders of American Dance Asylum, based in Binghamton in 1973. Jones was tall, black, and graceful, Zane was short, white, and pugnacious, and on stage they formed a dramatically arresting partnership. Their early works together included *Monkey Run Road*, *Blauvelt Mountain* (both 1979), and *Valley Cottage* (1980). In 1982 they formed Bill T. Jones/Arnie Zane Dance Company for which they created many works, including *Secret Pastures* (1984), which had settings by the graffiti artist Keith Haring. In 1983 Jones was commissioned by the *Ailey company to make *Fever Swamp*; Jones and Zane collaborated on a second Ailey work, *Ritual Ruckus* (*How to Walk an Elephant*), in 1985. Following Zane's death from Aids in 1988, Jones (who openly acknowledges being HIV-positive, too) has continued to run the company and

to deepen his reputation as a provocative and controversial choreographer. His work deals with issues such as homosexuality, racism, and death. His 1994 full-length production *Still/Here*, which explored the experience of coping with terminal illness, generated a heated debate in the dance world after the critic Arlene Croce branded it 'victim art'. *Blind Date* (2005) dealt with issues of patriotism in a world dominated by the war on terror and Iraq. Jones has also choreographed works for several other companies including Lyon Opera Ballet, Berlin Opera Ballet, and Boston Ballet and was associate choreographer of Lyon (1994–6). He has also worked with opera companies, choreographing Tippett's *New Year* in 1990 for Houston Grand Opera and Glyndebourne Festival Opera; he also conceived, co-directed, and choreographed *Mother of Three Sons* for the Munich Biennale, New York City Opera, and Houston Grand Opera. As a stage director, he directed Derek Walcott's *Dream on Monkey Mountain* for the Guthrie Theater in Minneapolis in 1994 while his choreography for the Broadway musical *Spring Awakening* won a Tony award in 2007. In 2009 he directed and choreographed the Broadway musical *Fela!*

For his own company Jones has choreographed well over 100 works, which include *Soon* (mus. Weill, Bessie Smith, 1988), *D-Man in the Waters* (mus. Mendelssohn, 1989), *Last Supper at Uncle Tom's Cabin/The Promised Land* (mus. Jules Hemphill, 1990), *History of Collage Revisited* (mus. Charles Amirkhanian and 'Blue' Gene Tyranny, 1990), *Broken Wedding* (mus. Klezmer Conservatory Band, 1992), *Die Offnung* (mus. John Oswald, 1992), *Love Defined* (mus. Daniel Johnston, 1992), *Last Night on Earth* (mus. Kurt Weill, Bessie Smith, 1992), *War Between the States* (mus. Ives, 1993), *Bill and Laurie: About Five Rounds* (with Laurie Anderson, 1996), *Sur la place* (mus. Brel, 1996), *We Set Out Early . . . Visibility Was Poor* (mus. Stravinsky, Cage, Vasks, 1997), *How! Do! We! Do!* (with the singer Jessye Norman, 1999), *Black Suzanne* (mus. Shostakovich, 2002), *Phantom Project* (2003), *Reading, Mercy and the Artificial Nigger* (mus. Daniel Bernard Roumain, 2004), and *Another Evening I Bow Down* (mus. Roumain, 2006). Author of autobiography, *Last Night on Earth* (New York, 1995).

(((⊕))) SEE WEB LINKS

- Website for the Bill T. Jones/Arnie Zane Dance Company

Jones, Marilyn (*b* Newcastle, NSW, Feb. 1940) Australian dancer, choreographer, teacher, and ballet director. She studied with Lorraine Norton and van Praagh in Australia and at the Royal Ballet School in London (1956). In 1957 she danced briefly with the Royal Ballet; in 1958 she toured Australia with the Beth Dean company and with Robert Pomie's Ballet Français. She danced with the Borovansky Ballet as a soloist (1959–61) and in Europe with the Grand Ballet du Marquis de Cuevas as prima ballerina (1961–2). She returned to Australia in 1962 to join the newly founded Australian Ballet and spent the next ten years as the company's prima ballerina. After a two-year break, she returned to the Australian Ballet as resident principal (1974–8), adding Tatiana in Cranko's *Onegin* and Juliet in his *Romeo and Juliet* to her considerable repertoire. She produced *Sylvia* for Ballet Theatre of Queensland (1974). From 1979 to 1982 she was artistic director of the Australian Ballet. Following her retirement she taught and in 1990 founded the Australian Institute of Classical Dance with the aim of establishing an Australian dance syllabus. Mother of the choreographer Stanton *Welch.

Jong, Bettie De (*b* Sumatra, Indonesia, 5 May 1933) Dutch-US dancer, teacher, and ballet mistress. She studied with Max Dooyes, Jan Bronk, Graham, and Limón. She danced with several US modern dance companies, including those of Graham, Lang, Hoving, and Butler. In 1962 she joined the Paul Taylor Company, creating roles in many of his works. One of her most memorable roles was the automaton in *Big Bertha* in which her powerful, chilling presence defined the nightmarish horror of the work. In 1973 she became the company's ballet mistress. She also taught in London at the London Contemporary Dance School and the Rambert School.

Jooss, Kurt (*b* Wasseralfingen, 12 Jan. 1901; *d* Heilbronn, 22 May 1979) German dancer, choreographer, teacher, and ballet director. He attended the Stuttgart Academy of Music, where he studied dance with Laban; in 1922–3 they worked together in Mannheim and Hamburg with Jooss dancing in Laban's ballets and acting as his assistant. Jooss was appointed ballet master in Münster in 1924 and founded the Neue Tanzbühne with the Estonian dancer Aino Siimola (later his wife), Sigurd Leeder, and Hein Heckroth. Among the works he made for this company were *Ein persisches Märchen* (mus. Egon Wellesz, 1924), *Der Dämon* (mus. Hindemith, 1925), and *Die Brautfahrt* (mus. Rameau and Couperin, 1925). In 1926 he and Leeder went to Paris to study ballet with Lubov Egorova and the following year Jooss was appointed director of the dance department at the Essen Folkwang School. This launched the *Folkwang Tanztheater in 1928. In 1930, when Jooss was appointed ballet master of the Essen Municipal Theatre, his company became the Folkwang Tanzbühne. He created *Le Bal* (mus. Rieti, 1930), Polovtsian Dances from *Prince Igor* (mus. Borodin, 1930), *Coppélia*

(1931), *Prodigal Son* (mus. Prokofiev, 1931), *Pulcinella* (mus. Stravinsky, 1932), and—his most famous work—*The Green Table* (mus. Cohen, 1932). It was *Green Table*, a scathing anti-war piece based on the medieval Dance of Death, which drew him to international attention when the work won first prize at the first choreographic competition organized by Rolf de Maré and Les Archives Internationales de la Danse in Paris. Here Jooss's synthesis of classical and modern dance was at its most theatrically effective. Two other important works were created at this time: *Big City* (mus. Tansman) and *Ball in Old Vienna* (mus. Lanner, both 1932). In 1933, with the Nazis taking power in Germany, Jooss and his company were forced to flee. They found a new home in *Dartington, England, then in Cambridge. From their English base they toured the world as the *Ballets Jooss. In 1947 the company was disbanded and Jooss went to Santiago de Chile. In 1949 he returned to Essen and re-established the Folkwang School and the Folkwang Tanztheater. The company was later disbanded due to lack of local government support, but the school continued. In 1962 he re-formed the company as Folkwang Tanzstudio, with Pina Bausch. He retired as head of the dance school in 1968. His daughter, Anna Markard, has supervised productions of *The Green Table* around the world. A list of Jooss's other ballets includes *Drosselbart* (mus. Mozart, 1929), *Pavane* (mus. Ravel, 1929), *Petrushka* (mus. Stravinsky, 1930), *Seven Heroes* (mus. Purcell-Cohen, 1933), *The Prodigal Son* (mus. Cohen, 1933), *Ballade* (mus. J. Colman, 1935), *The Mirror* (mus. Cohen, 1935), *Johann Strauss, Tonight* (1935), *Company at the Manor* (mus. Beethoven-Cook, 1943), and *Pandora* (mus. R. Gerhard, 1944).

Joplin, Scott (*b* Texarkana, Tex., 24 Nov. 1868; *d* New York, 1 Apr. 1917) US ragtime pianist and composer. The resurgence of interest in ragtime music in the 1970s resulted in a number of ballets set to Joplin's music, the best known of which is MacMillan's *Elite Syncopations* (Royal Ballet, 1974). Other Joplin ballets include J. Waring's *Eternity Bounce* (1973), A. Cata's *Ragtime* (1973), G. Veredon's *The Ragtime Dance Company* (1974), and B. Moreland's *Prodigal Son in Ragtime* (London Festival Ballet, 1974).

Jordan, Stephanie (*b* Karachi, Pakistan, 21 Jan. 1951) British dance writer. She studied music at the Universities of Birmingham, and California, Los Angeles and dance with various teachers, including Alston. She has lectured in music and dance studies at several colleges and universities, and was appointed Research Professor in Dance at the University of Surrey, Roehampton in 2000. She is author and editor of numerous publications including *Striding Out: Aspects of Contemporary and New Dance in Britain* (1992), *Moving Music: Dialogues with Music in 20th-Century Ballet* (2000), and *Stravinsky Dances: Re-Visions across a Century* (2007).

Joseph the Beautiful Ballet in two acts with choreography by Kasyan Goleizovsky, music by Sergei Vasilenko, and designs by Boris Erdman. Premiered 3 Mar. 1925, by the Bolshoi Ballet at the Experimental Theatre in Moscow with Lubov Bank, Vasily Efimov, and Aleksei Bulgakov. The biblical story of Joseph was choreographed by Goleizovsky with such explicit eroticism and with such daringly innovative choreography (many of the movements were performed with the dancers lying down) that the Soviet authorities tried to ban it. Changes to both choreography and to the dancers' revealing costumes were demanded. But while the choreographer remounted the ballet in Odessa and Kharkov in the following years it was never again produced at the Bolshoi.

jota A quick dance from northern Spain performed in 3/8 time. A dance for couples who play castanets, it is accompanied by someone who sings and plays the guitar. A notable theatrical example of the jota can be found in Massine's and de Falla's *Three-Cornered Hat*.

jour ou deux, Un *See* UN JOUR OU DEUX.

Jowitt, Deborah (*b* Los Angeles, 8 Feb. 1934) US dancer, choreographer, teacher, and dance writer. She studied with Graham, Limón, and at the American Ballet Center making her stage debut in 1953 and presenting her own choreography from 1962. During the 1960s she both performed and choreographed with New York's Dance Theater Workshop. In 1967 she began to write a regular dance column for *The Village Voice*, becoming chief dance critic for the magazine until 2008. Her articles on dance have appeared in numerous publications and have been collected in *Dance Beat* (1977) and *The Dance in Mind* (1985). She has also published *Time and the Dancing Image*, (1988), *Jerome Robbins: His Life, His Theater, His Dance* (2004), and edited *Meredith Monk* (1997). A founding member of the Dance Critics' Association, she served at various times as its treasurer, newsletter editor, and cochairman. In addition to lecturing and conducting workshops both in the US and abroad, she teaches and choreographs in the Dance Department of New York University's Tisch School of the Arts.

Joyce Theater Theatre located in lower Manhattan which regularly programmes dance. It is one of the world's most important modern dance venues.

Judas Tree, The Ballet in one act with choreography by MacMillan, music by Brian Elias, and designs by Jock McFadyen. Premiered 19 Mar. 1992 by the Royal Ballet at Covent Garden with Irek Mukhamedov, Viviana Durante, and Michael Nunn. A quasi-religious story of betrayal set on a modern building site, it was MacMillan's last work for Covent Garden. It won the Olivier Award in 1992, while the television version, directed by Ross MacGibbon, won the 1998 International Emmy Award for Performing Arts.

Jude, Charles (*b* Mytho, South Vietnam, 25 Jul. 1953) French dancer. He studied with A. Kalioujny and S. Peretti and at the Nice Conservatory (1968–72). In 1972 he joined the Paris Opera Ballet; he was promoted to danseur étoile in 1977. He danced all the leading male roles in the classical repertoire, as well as in ballets by Fokine, Nijinska, Lifar, Tudor, Robbins, Balanchine, and Grigorovich (*Ivan the Terrible*). He created leading roles in Nureyev's *Raymonda* (1983), *Washington Square* (1985), and *Cinderella* (1986), and in Neumeier's *Magnificat* (1987). He took part in the touring ensemble, Nureyev and Friends (1980–92), and danced with the Royal Ballet, the Vienna Opera Ballet, La Scala, Milan, and the Royal Danish Ballet. In 1996 he was appointed artistic director of the Bordeaux Opera Ballet, where he continued to perform Romeo, probably his most successful role and the Faun, in his company's revival of Nijinsky's ballet. He choreographed a new version of *Nutcracker* for Bordeaux in 1997. Chevalier de la Légion d'honneur (1996).

Judgment of Paris, The Ballet in one act with choreography by Tudor, libretto and designs by Hugh Laing, and music by Kurt Weill. Premiered 15 Jun. 1938 by the London Ballet at the Westminster Theatre, London, with Langfield, de Mille, Bidmead, Tudor, and Laing. The Greek myth of three goddesses competing for the golden apple is re-told as social satire. The action takes place in a sordid bar in Paris around 1900; the three goddesses are a trio of ageing prostitutes (Juno, Minerva, and Venus); and the judge (Paris in the original) is here turned into a drunken patron. The ballet is set to Weill's Suite from *The Threepenny Opera*. Tudor re-staged it for Ballet Rambert in 1940 and for American Ballet Theatre (also 1940).

Judson Dance Theater A ground-breaking collective of choreographers working in New York in the 1960s whose avant-garde work gave birth to the movement eventually known as *postmodern dance. The first Judson performance was given on 6 Jul. 1962 at Judson Memorial Church on Washington Square in New York's Greenwich

Village. The choreographers were united in their rejection of traditional form and technique, of narrative and overt theatricality, although they chose different ways of expressing their radicalism. Founding members included Lucinda Childs, Yvonne Rainer, Steve Paxton, David Gordon, and Trisha Brown; later came Twyla Tharp. One of the most important features of Judson Dance Theater was the collaboration of visual artists (such as Robert Rauschenberg) and composers who also made choreography.

Jugement de Pâris, Le Ballet divertissement in one act with choreography by Perrot, music by Pugni, and design by Charles Marshall. Premiered 23 Jul. 1846 at Her Majesty's Theatre in London, with M. Taglioni, Grahn, Cerrito, and Saint-Léon.

In an effort to capitalize on the huge success of the *Pas de quatre* (1845), Perrot staged this divertissement on a classical Greek theme, the centrepiece of which features three goddesses competing for the favours of the shepherd Paris (diplomatic to the end, he chooses none). Taglioni gave her farewell performance in this ballet on 21 Aug. 1847. Perrot re-staged it, as *Le Soucis du maître de ballet*, in St Petersburg in 1851.

Juilliard School of Music, Dance Department One of the leading dance schools, established in 1952 at the Juilliard in New York. Teachers have included de Mille, Graham, Humphrey, Limón, Robbins, and Tudor. Since 1964 it has been based at Lincoln Center in New York.

j

kabuki Japanese form of dance theatre dating back to the 16th century. Kabuki means song, dance, and acting, although the term originally meant shocking or strange, in reference to the form's unusual style. It originated in performances given by O-Kuni, a dancer and lay priestess from the Izmumo region who created a fusion of prayer dance, folk dance, comic mime, and erotic dance for herself and her all-female troupe. Her shows were very popular in Kyoto and evolved into dance dramas whose vernacular style contrasted with the refined and aristocratic noh theatre. Part of their popularity derived from their overtly erotic content however and this eventually led to a ban on women appearing in kabuki performances (from 1629) and on boys (from 1652). Adult male dancers thus took over the kabuki style, creating the profession of female impersonator or *onnagata*. This became an honoured calling for which boys, often from kabuki dynasties, would be trained from childhood. Kabuki evolved through four basic stages, the first theatrical stage that took its inspiration from historical sagas, the second that focused more on pure dance content, the third that drew its stories from folk material, and the fourth that aimed for more contemporary narratives. In its classic form kabuki became an integrated mix of dance, gesture, music, costume, make-up, and dramatic stage effects. Performances are long by Western standards and slow moving, but are rich in imagery and emotion. Two famous works are *Chushingura* (*The Forty-Seven Loyal Samurai*), a historical tale of honour and revenge, and *Sumidagawa* (*The Sumida River*), the story of a mad woman's search for her lost son. Kabuki dance troupes (as distinct from kabuki theatre troupes) also now give independent performances, with both male and female artists taking part. The form remains popular in Japan, especially with the stage and film star Ichikawa Ebizo gaining cult status among the young, and it enjoys a loyal international following.

Kain, Karen (*b* Hamilton, Ont., 28 Mar. 1951) Canadian dancer. She studied at the National Ballet of Canada School and joined the National Ballet of Canada in 1969. A versatile dancer whose powerful classical technique was linked with unusual dramatic intensity, she was appointed principal in 1970, dancing the classical and 20th-century repertories with equal success. Though she was guest artist with Ballet National de Marseilles for several seasons (1974–82) and also danced with many other companies, she was the first Canadian ballerina to make her international reputation without permanently leaving her native country. She created roles in many ballets including Petit's *Nana* (Paris Opera, 1976), and Tetley's *Alice* and *La Ronde* (both 1987). She frequently partnered Nureyev at home and abroad and appeared several times on television. During her forties she relinquished most of the ballerina roles but continued to perform less-demanding roles, creating the lead in Kudelka's *The Actress* (1994). In 1998 she was invited to become artistic associate with the National Ballet of Canada and in 2005 became its director, overseeing revivals of the classics (including Nureyev's staging of *Sleeping Beauty*) and bringing in works by new choreographers including Dominique Dumain and Davide Bombano. In 2004 she was appointed Chair of Canada's Council for the Arts.

She was recipient of the Order of Canada in 1976.

Kammermusik No. 2 Ballet in one act with choreography by Balanchine, music by Hindemith, and costumes by Ben Benson. Premiered 26 Jan. 1978 by New York City Ballet at the State Theater, New York, with von Aroldingen, C. Neary, Luders, and Lavery. A setting of Hindemith's Op. 36, No. 1 for piano and twelve solo instruments that evokes the emotional and erotic undercurrents between its two principal couples and a chorus of eight men.

Karalli, Vera (Coralli; Koralli) (*b* Moscow, 8 Aug. 1889; *d* Baden, nr. Vienna, 16 Nov. 1972) Russian dancer. She studied with Gorsky at the Imperial Theatre School, Moscow and joined the Bolshoi in 1906 where she was promoted ballerina in 1914. In 1909 and again between 1919 and 1920 she also danced with Diaghilev's company, performing in *Pavillon d'Armide*, *Thamar*, and *Prince Igor*. One of her most celebrated stage roles was Giselle. Though never a great technician, her charismatic stage presence brought her considerable fame and she became one of Russia's first film stars. She was ballet mistress in Bucharest (1930–7) then had a studio in Paris (1938–41), after which she taught in Vienna.

Karinska, Barbara (orig. Varvara Zhmoudska; *b* Kharkhov, 3 Oct. 1886; *d* New York, 18 Oct. 1983) Russian-US designer and costume maker. She left Russia in 1928 and worked as a seamstress in Paris, executing designs by Dalí, Matisse, Beaton, and others. In 1930 she went to the US, working in Hollywood and in New York, then in 1949 designing her first ballet costumes for Balanchine's *Bourrée fantasque*. She became New York City Ballet's pre-eminent costume designer and maker, and, while her taste was not universally admired, some regarded her cutting skills and designs as exemplary, with Walter Terry calling her 'ballet's most cherished sorceress'.

Karsavina, Tamara (*b* St Petersburg, 9 Mar. 1885; *d* Beaconsfield, 26 May 1978) Russian-British dancer, the most famous of Diaghilev's ballerinas. She was the daughter of the Mariinsky dancer and teacher Platon Karsavin and studied at the Imperial Theatre School with Cecchetti, Gerdt, and Johansson, also with C. Beretta in Milan. In 1902 she graduated into the Mariinsky as soloist, becoming ballerina in 1909. Although she stayed with the company until 1918 she also danced extensively with Diaghilev's Ballets Russes from 1909, creating roles in many ballets including Fokine's *Les Sylphides* (1st version, 1908), *Cléopâtre* (1909), *Carnaval* and *Firebird* (both 1910), *Spectre de la rose*, *Narcisse*, and *Petrushka* (all 1911), *Le Dieu bleu*, *Thamar*, *Papillon*, and *Daphnis and Chloe* (all 1912), and *Le Coq d'or* (1914), Nijinsky's *Jeux* (1913), and Massine's *Le Tricorne* (1919) and *Pulcinella* (1920). A dancer revered not only for the versatility of her technique but for the poetic expression and intelligence of her interpretations, she was also renowned in classical ballerina roles. She left Russia in 1918 with her second husband, the British diplomat Henry J. Bruce, and settled in London. She continued to guest with Diaghilev's company for various seasons in London, Paris, and Monte Carlo (1919–29), then from 1930 to 1931 she danced with Ballet Rambert, helping to stage several ballets including some by Fokine. After retiring from the stage she remained a major influence on British ballet, acting as Vice-President of the Royal Academy of Dancing between 1946 and 1955, giving lecture-demonstrations in ballet mime and advising the Royal Ballet in the staging of various Diaghilev ballets as well as *The Nutcracker*, *Giselle*, and *La Fille mal gardée*. (She coached Fonteyn in several of her own former roles, and it is said other dancers might also have profited from her advice had she been consulted more frequently.) Her autobiography, *Theatre Street*, was published in London (1930) and her textbook *Classical Ballet: The Flow of Movement* in London (1962). The toasts for her ninetieth birthday were proposed by Ashton and John Gielgud.

Kasatkina, Natalia (*b* Moscow, 7 Jun. 1934) Soviet dancer and choreographer. She graduated from the Moscow Ballet School into the Bolshoi Ballet in 1954 where she became one of the company's leading character dancers. Later she began to choreograph with her husband V. Vasiliov, creating their first joint ballet *Vanina Vanini* (mus. Karetnikov) in 1962. Other works by them include *Heroic Poem* (*The Geologists*) (mus. Karetnikov, 1964), *Le Sacre du printemps* (mus. Stravinsky, 1965, a version set in the second millennium BC), *Preludes and Fugues* (mus. Bach, 1968), and *Romeo and Juliet* (mus. Prokofiev, 1972). They also created *The Creation of the World* (mus. A. Petrov, 1971) for the Kirov. She and Vasiliov subsequently became directors of the Moscow Classical Ballet, an internationally touring company for which they have created many works including *Mowgli* (2007), set to music by the young composing prodigy Alex Prior.

Kastl, Sonja (*b* Zagreb, 14 Jul. 1929) Yugoslavian dancer, choreographer, and director. She studied with Froman, Preobrajenska, Skeaping, and others and joined Zagreb National Ballet in 1945, becoming prima ballerina and then, in 1965, ballet mistress. She choreographed numerous ballets, often in association with Nevanka Bidjin, in which she explored contemporary Yugoslavian music, including *Symphony of a Dead Soldier* (mus. Branimir Sakač, 1959) and *Symphony in D* (mus. Luka Sorkočević, 1965).

kathak Dance from the former N. India. Its name derives from *katha* meaning story and its performance originates from the *kathaks* or storytellers who used to give religious and moral instruction in narrative form. Music, mime, and dance became important features of their technique and when this mingled with the decorative dance styles introduced by the Moguls (14th–17th centuries) kathak became a complex movement form capable of dealing with the themes of Hindu myth as well as more human stories. Subsequently its narrative content became highly refined (that which remained dealing primarily with the stories of Radha and Krishna) and dancers focused on music and rhythm. Kathak performers are noted for their virtuosic fast turns and stamping footwork, whose rhythms, exaggerated by ankle bells, develop into highly complex metrical sequences. Today's dancers may be pure classicists or, like British-based Akram *Khan develop the language into a more contemporary style of dance.

kathakali Indian dance-drama form from Kerala in SW India. Its name has the same derivation as *kathak but as a dance form it is far more vividly theatrical in style. The stories in its repertory are taken from the ancient Indian epics *Ramayana* and *Mahabharata* as well as from folk tales. Its dancer-actors (who are traditionally male, due to the strenuousness of performances) employ vigorous, highly stylized gestures to reflect the words sung by the musicians standing behind them as well as to evoke the atmosphere and setting of each scene. Costumes and headdresses are elaborate and the make-up (which can take four hours to apply) symbolizes the moral nature of the characters, with different colours depicting good, evil, male, or female qualities. Performances often begin at dusk and may last for sixteen hours.

Kay, Hershy (*b* Philadelphia, 17 Nov. 1919; *d* Danbury, Conn., 2 Dec. 1981) US composer. He wrote and arranged the music for several ballets including Balanchine's *Western Symphony* (1954), *Who Cares?* (orchestration of Gershwin, 1970), and *Union Jack* (1976), also Robbins's *The Concert* (arr. of Chopin, 1956).

Kaye, Nora (orig. Nova Koreff; *b* New York, 17 Jan. 1920; *d* Santa Monica, Calif., 28 Feb. 1987) US dancer and director. She studied at the Metropolitan Opera Ballet School with Fokine, Vilzak, and Schollar and at the School of American Ballet, making her debut in children's ballets at the Metropolitan Opera House. In 1935 she joined American Ballet and in 1939 became one of the founding dancers of Ballet Theatre (later American Ballet Theatre), having danced in several Broadway musicals. She was promoted to ballerina in 1942 and remained with the company until 1959 (except for a period with New York City Ballet, 1951–4), where she became renowned as its greatest dramatic artist. A dance-actress of sometimes shocking intensity she created many roles, most memorably those of Hagar in Tudor's *Pillar of Fire* (1942) and Lizzie Borden in de Mille's *Fall River Legend* (1948—though illness prevented her from dancing on the opening night). She also danced classic roles, such as *Giselle*. At NYCB she created roles in Robbins's *The Cage* (1951) and Tudor's *La Gloire* (1952), and on her return to ABT went on to create roles in MacMillan's *Winter's Eve* and H. Ross's *Paean* (both 1957), among others. She married Ross in 1959 and with him founded Ballet of Two Worlds in 1960. As its prima ballerina she created roles in several of Ross's ballets, including *Rashomon Suite* and *The Dybbuk* (both 1960/1). She retired from the stage in 1961 though she continued to work as a producer for some of Ross's films, such as *The Turning Point* (1977) and *Dancers* (1987).

She was on ABT's board of directors from 1977 to 1983 and continued to advise the company until her death.

Kchessinska, Mathilda *See* KSHESSINSKA, MATHILDA.

Keeler, Ruby (*b* Halifax, NS, 25 Aug. 1909; *d* Los Angeles, 28 Feb. 1993) US dancer and actress. She studied with Helen Guest and later with Jack Blue, giving some of her earliest performances with the Eastside Sextette in 1920. After working in various clubs and on Broadway she became a star attraction of the Ziegfeld productions. In 1933 she went to Hollywood to star in Busby Berkeley's *42nd Street* and subsequently worked with Berkeley on many other films. During the mid-1960s there was a revival of interest in Berkeley's work and Keeler appeared frequently with him at screenings of their films. In 1971 she made a triumphant return to the stage in his 1971 Broadway revival of *No, No, Nanette*. She was married to Al Jolson (1929–39).

Keersmaeker, Anne Teresa de (*b* Mechelen, 11 Jun. 1960) Belgian dancer, choreographer, and director. She studied for two years at the Mudra school where she created her first work *Asch* in 1980. After a year at the New York University's School of the Arts she returned to Belgium to complete the four-part duet *Fase* (mus. Reich) and in 1983 launched her all-woman company Rosas in *Rosas Danst Rosas* (mus. de Mey and Vermeersch). Her original influences were minimalists like L. Dean and Childs but in *Bartók/Aantekeningen* a more theatrically expressionist vein emerged, developed through text and film. During the 1980s she was supported by the Kaaitheater in Brussels, but in 1992 became resident choreographer at the city's Monnaie Opera House with an expanded company of men and women and in 1995 founded the school P.A.R.T.S. Most of her works have been created for herself and her company, including *Ottone, Ottone* (1988), *Un moto di gioia*, (mus. Mozart, 1992), *Verklärte Nacht* (mus. Schoenberg, 1995), *Amor constante más allá de la muerte* (mus. Thierry de Mey, 1995), *Just Before* (mus. several, 1997), *Drumming* (mus. Reich, 1998), *I Said I* (1999), *Rain* (mus. Reich 2001), *Desh* (2004, revised 2005), and *Sister* (2007), although she has recently collaborated with members of the theatrical collective Stan. In 1998 she made her debut in opera, directing Bartók's *Duke Bluebeard's Castle* at the Monnaie. Peter Greenaway directed the film *Rosas* of her work in 1991.

(((●))) SEE WEB LINKS
- Website for Rosas

Kehlet, Niels (*b* Copenhagen, 6 Sept. 1938) Danish dancer. He studied at the Royal Danish Ballet School and graduated into the company in 1957 where he was promoted to soloist (principal) in 1961. A demi-caractère virtuoso, gifted with a strong classical technique, extrovert stage presence, and dramatic versatility, his wide repertory extended from James in *La Sylphide* to Mercutio in Neumeier's *Romeo and Juliet*, Franz in *Coppélia*, and Colas in Ashton's *La Fille mal gardée*. He also danced modern works, creating roles in several ballets such as Flindt's *The Three Musketeers* (1965) and *The Miraculous Mandarin* (1967) and von Rosen's *Don Juan* (1967). He frequently guested abroad, with the Fracci-Menegatti-Gai company in Italy, for example, and made many television appearances. In 1991 he directed Stars and Soloists of the Royal Danish Ballet and since retiring from principal roles has worked as teacher and mime artist with the RDB.

Keil, Birgit (*b* Kowarschen, 22 Sept. 1944) German dancer. She studied at the schools of both the Stuttgart Ballet and the Royal Ballet, joining Stuttgart Ballet in 1961. In 1964 she was promoted soloist and rapidly became one of its leading ballerinas. A tall, elegant, almost ethereal dancer with a pure classical technique, she performed much of the standard ballerina repertory but also created roles in many works, including MacMillan's *Las Hermanas* (1963), *Song of the Earth* (1965), *Miss Julie* (1970), and *My Brother, My Sisters* (1978); Cranko's *Opus 1* (1965), *Salade* (1968), *Orpheus* (1970), and *Initials R.B.M.E.*; Tetley's *Voluntaries* (1973) and *Greening* (1975); Kylián's *Return to the Strange Land* (1974) and *Forgotten Land* (1981); and van Manen's *Shaker Loops* (1987). She guested with many companies around the world including American Ballet Theatre, Royal Ballet, and Paris Opera and appeared on television in MacMillan's *The Seven Deadly Sins* (1984), among others. After retiring from the stage in 1995 she set up the Birgit Keil Foundation in Stuttgart and in 1997 became professor, then director of the Dance Academy in Mannheim. In 2003 she also took over direction of the ballet company at the Badisches Staatstheater in Karlsruhe. She was recipient of the Order of Merit, First Class, of the German Federal Republic (1982).

Kelly, Desmond (*b* Penhalonga, S. Rhodesia, 13 Jan. 1942) British dancer. He studied with Ruth French in London and joined London Festival Ballet in 1959 where he was appointed principal in 1963. After guesting with New Zealand Ballet, Washington National Ballet, and Zurich Ballet with his wife, dancer Denise LeComte, he joined Royal Ballet in 1970 as principal. Although not a virtuoso he was a fine partner and actor and created roles in several ballets, including Tetley's *Field Figures* (1970), J. Carter's *Shukumei* (1957), and MacMillan's *Playground* (1979). He was a favoured partner of Fonteyn and a renowned Albrecht. In 1976 he joined Sadler's Wells Royal Ballet where he became ballet master (1978) and assistant director (1990) and continued to perform some character roles. In 2008 he was appointed artistic director of *Elmhurst Ballet School.

Kelly, Gene (*b* Pittsburgh, 3 Aug. 1912; *d* Beverly Hills, Calif., 2 Feb. 1996) US actor, dancer, choreographer, and film director. He studied dance as a child, and while still pursuing his academic education (at Pittsburgh University) was staging his own shows and running a dance school. In 1939 he went to New York where he performed in musicals, including the lead role in *Pal Joey* (1940). His dance style was a fusion of tap, soft shoe, ballet, modern, jazz, and folk, and was executed with an unusual gymnastic attack. He also possessed a strong cinematic personality and became involved in directing the films in which he performed (often in collaboration with Stanley Donen), including *On the Town* (1949), *An American in Paris* (1951, with Vincente Minnelli), and *Singin' in the Rain* (1952). In all these films Kelly sought new ways of integrating dance into film. However, his most ambitious ballet film, *Invitation to the Dance* (1952, released 1956), was his least successful. He created the ballet *Pas de dieux* (mus. Gershwin) for Paris Opera in 1960 and was recipient of the Légion d'honneur in the same year.

Kemp, Lindsay (*b* Isle of Lewis, *c*.1939) British mime, actor, dancer, and director. He studied at Bradford Art College and Rambert Ballet School and first performed at the Edinburgh Festival in 1964, appearing subsequently in cabaret, musicals, and film (including Ken Russell's *Savage Messiah*, 1972). In the early 1970s he produced David Bowie's Ziggy Stardust concerts and achieved his own first hit with *Flowers* in 1973, a mime, dance, and music spectacle based on Genet's writings in which Kemp played Divine, the first of his exotically larger-than-life creations. Later shows have included *Salome* (1977), *A Midsummer Night's Dream* (1979), *Cinderella* (1995), and *Dreamdances* (2002). Kemp has also created two works for Ballet Rambert, *The Parade's Gone By* (mus. Miranda, 1975) and *Cruel Garden* (with C. Bruce, mus. Miranda, 1977, revived English National Ballet, 1988). His work has always enjoyed greater popularity in Europe and Japan than in the UK, where Kemp's harshest critics have dismissed his flamboyance and excess as indulgent. He has made appearances in several films including Derek Jarman's *Jubilee* (1977) and Todd Haynes's *The*

Velvet Goldmine (1998) and in 2007 directed a production of Offenbach's *Tales of Hoffmann* (Calabria Festival). He is now based in Italy.

Kemp, William Sixteenth-century British actor and dancer who was listed as 'head master of Morrice dancers' in Shakespeare's company. He was said to have danced from London to Norwich in 1599.

Kent, Allegra (*b* Santa Monica, Calif., 11 Aug. 1938) US dancer and teacher. She studied with Bronislava and Irina Nijinska, with Carmelita Maracci, and at the School of American Ballet. In 1953 she joined New York City Ballet where she was promoted to principal in 1957. An exceptionally lyrical dancer, who projected an aura of poetic mystery on stage, she created roles in several Balanchine ballets, including 'The Unanswered Question' section of *Ivesiana* (1954), *Agon* (1957), *Bugaku* (1963), and *Brahms-Schoenberg Quartet* (1966). She also created roles in Robbins's *Dances at a Gathering* (1969) and *Dumbarton Oaks* (1972), as well as dancing in the Broadway musical *Shinbone Alley* (1957) and guesting occasionally abroad. After retiring in mid-1981 she worked as a freelance teacher and in 1990 was dancer and associate director with John Cliffords Ballet of Los Angeles. She continues to teach and to coach the Balanchine repertory and in 1997 published her autobiography *Once a Dancer*.

Kent, Julie (*b* Bethesda, Md., 11 Jul. 1969) US dancer. She trained at the Academy of the Maryland Youth Ballet and the School of American Ballet, joining American Ballet Theatre in 1985 as apprentice and becoming full-time member in 1986, soloist in 1990, and principal in 1993. She has danced leading roles in the classical and 20th-century repertories and created roles in several works, including Kudelka's *Cruel World* (1994), Tharp's *Known By Heart* (1998), and *The Brahms-Haydn Variations* (2000), and Duato's *Without Words* (2004). In 1987 she starred in the film *Dancers* (dir. H. Ross).

Kerensky, Oleg (*b* London, 9 Jan. 1930; *d* New York, 9 Jul. 1993) British critic. He wrote for the *Daily Mail* (1957–71), *New Statesman* (1968–78), and *International Herald Tribune* (1971–8), contributed to *Encyclopaedia Britannica* (1974), and wrote *Ballet Scene* (London, 1970), *Anna Pavlova* (London, 1973), and *The Guinness Guide to Ballet* (London, 1981).

Kermesse in Bruges, The (orig. Danish title *Kermessen i Brugge*) Ballet in three acts with choreography and libretto by Bournonville, music by Paulli, sets by C. F. Christensen, and costumes by E. Lehmann. Premiered 4 Apr. 1851 by the Royal Danish Ballet in Copenhagen with J. Price.

G. Brodersen, F. Hoppensach, and F. Hoppe. It is inspired by the bourgeois Flemish painting style of the 17th century and takes place at a Holy Fair in 17th-century Bruges, telling the comic story of three brothers who receive three magic gifts. One of the most popular of Bournonville's ballets, it is still in the repertory. Subsequent productions include Royal Swedish Ballet (staged S. Lund, 1858), Royal Danish Ballet (staged H. Lander and Borchsenius, 1943, and by H. Brenaa in two acts, 1979, and by Jan Maargaad and D. Bjørn, 2000), also stagings of the Act I pas de deux for New York City Ballet (S. Williams after Bournonville, 1977) and Bolshoi Ballet (J. Graff and K. Ralov after Bournonville, 1986), among others.

Kersley, Leo (*b* Watford, 1920) British dancer and teacher. He studied with Idzikowski and Rambert and danced with Ballet Rambert (1936–9 and 1940–1). In 1941 he joined Sadler's Wells Ballet then danced with the Anglo-Polish Ballet (1942–3) and with Sadler's Wells Theatre Ballet (1946–51). He taught in Europe and the US and in 1959 opened a school in Essex with his wife, Janet Sinclair. They were co-authors of *A Dictionary of Ballet Terms* (London, 1952).

Kevázi, Gábor (*b* Budapest, 25 Feb. 1953) Hungarian dancer, choreographer, and director. He studied at the Hungarian State Dance Academy and at the Vaganova School and graduated into the Hungarian National Ballet in 1972, where he continued dancing as principal until 1992 and also guested around the world. He was artistic director of Hungarian State Ballet 1988–92, returning to the post from 2005 and was also artistic director of Pécs Ballet between 2001 and 2005. His first works were created for students of the Hungarian Ballet Academy, followed by creations for Pécs and the National Ballet. A list of his works includes *Cristoforo* (mus. Szackcsi, 1992, in which Nureyev danced his last performance) and *Hymn to Man* (chor. with Markó, mus Beethoven, 2006). He is recipient of numerous awards and prizes including silver medal at Varna.

Khachaturian, Aram Ilyich (*b* Tbilisi, 6 Jun. 1903; *d* Moscow, 1 May 1978) Soviet composer. He wrote the ballet music for *Happiness* (chor. I. Arbatov, Yerevan, 1939) which was rewritten to become the score for *Gayané* (chor. Anisomova, Kirov Ballet, 1942) and for *Spartacus* (many productions, including Jacobson, Kirov Ballet, 1956, and Grigorovich, Bolshoi Ballet, 1968).

Khan, Akram (*b* London, 29 Jul. 1974) British dancer and choreographer. He studied kathak with Pratap Pawar, and modern dance at De Montfort University and at Northern School of Contemporary Dance. Between 1987 and 1989 he toured with Peter Brook's *Mahabarata* and began performing his own choreography as a student. While continuing to dance classical kathak recitals (in which his technical power and grace have been widely acclaimed) Khan's work as a choreographer has evolved through a fusion of Indian and Western idioms. In 2002 he launched his own company for which he has created several works including *Related Rocks* (mus. Magnus Linberg, 2001) and *Kaash* (mus. Nitin Sawhney, des. Anish Kapoor, 2002). He has also embarked on a sequence of high-profile collaborations with performers from very different traditions, creating the duet *Zero Degrees* with Sidi Larbi Cherkaoui (des. Antony Gormley, mus. Sawhney, 2005), *Sacred Monsters* with Sylvie Guillem (mus. Philip Shepherd, additional chor. Lin Hwai Min and Gauri Sharma Tripathi, 2006), and *In-I* with Juliette Binoche (2008). These duets have featured a mix of dance and spoken text. In 2008 Khan created *bahok* (mus. Sawhney) with dancers from his own company and members of the National Ballet of China and in 2010 premiered *Gnosis* created in collaboration with Tripathi and performed with Yoshie Sunahata.

(((●))) SEE WEB LINKS

• Website for the Akram Khan company

Kidd, Michael (*b* Brooklyn, NY, 12 Aug. 1919; *d* Los Angeles, 23 Dec. 2007) US dancer, choreographer, and director. He studied at the School of American Ballet with Vilzak and Schollar and made his debut in the musical *The Eternal Road* (1937). He danced with American Ballet and Ballet Caravan (1937–40), with Loring's Dance Players (1941–2) and finally with Ballet Theatre (1942–7) where he created a role in Robbins's *Interplay* (1945) and also choreographed the ballet *On Stage!* (mus. Dello Joio, 1945). After retiring from ballet he became a successful choreographer for Broadway and Hollywood, working on *Finian's Rainbow* (1947), *Guys and Dolls* (1951), *Seven Brides for Seven Brothers* (1954), *Destry Rides Again* (1959), and *Hello Dolly!* (1969 film version) among others. He also choreographed the television special *Baryshnikov in Hollywood* (1982).

Kim Wha-suk (*b* Kwangju, S. Korea, 2 Dec. 1949) Korean dancer, choreographer, and director. She studied at Ewha Women's University, joining the Yook Wan-soon Dance Company (1969–76) and in 1971 co-founding her own company with Kim Bock-hee. Working in a fusion of Korean and Western idioms they co-choreographed many works, including *For My Friend in the Sky* (mus. Milhaud, 1984). In 1985 she also founded the SAPPHO Modern Dance Company. She has taught at several universities

and in 1989 founded the Korean Dance Education Society for which she has subsequently acted as president.

kinesiology The study of human movement, from the point of view of both mechanical action and anatomical structure.

Kinetic Molpai Modern dance work in eleven sections with choreography by Ted Shawn and music by Jess Meeker. Premiered 5 Oct. 1935 by Ted Shawn and his Men Dancers at Goshen, New York. Shawn's choreography is a paean to male power and energy and was revived by the Alvin Ailey City Center Dance Theater in 1972.

Kinetographie Official name of Laban's system of dance notation, which is generally referred to in English as Labanotation.

King, Kenneth (*b* Freeport, NY, 25 Aug. 1948) US dancer and choreographer. He took up dance while studying philosophy at Antioch College and later trained with Cunningham and Forti. During the 1960s he performed with Meredith Monk. His own dances have typically combined rapid, repetitive movement with spoken monologues on scientific and philosophical issues, such as his solo *Upper Atmospheric Disturbances* (1995) and the duet (with Frances Alenikoff) *www//alenikoffking.com* (1997). He is author of several articles and the book *Writing in Motion* (2003).

King's Theatre Built in the Haymarket, 1704–5, as London's principal ballet and opera theatre. When it burned down in 1789 a new theatre was built on the same site in 1793. Under the direction of Lumley it presented many of the great Romantic ballerinas. In 1837 its name changed to Her Majesty's Theatre. It features as the background in de Valois's ballet *The Prospect Before Us.*

King's Volunteers on Amager, The See LIFE GUARDS ON AMAGER, THE.

Kirkland, Gelsey (*b* Bethlehem, Pa., 29 Dec. 1952) US dancer. She studied at the School of American Ballet and joined New York City Ballet in 1968 where her extraordinary gifts led to her rapid promotion, as soloist in 1969 and principal in 1972. A dancer of rare speed, lightness, and strength, she was compared to a humming-bird by Balanchine who created his new production of *Firebird* for her in 1970, and in the same year *Suite No. 3*. Robbins created roles for her in *The Goldberg Variations* (1971), *Scherzo fantastique* (1972), and *An Evening's Waltzes* (1973) but she became dissatisfied with the lack of dramatic content in NYCB's repertory and left for American Ballet Theatre in 1974, often dancing with Baryshnikov and Nureyev. Here she created roles in Tudor's *The Leaves are Fading* and Neumeier's *Hamlet:*

Connotations (both 1976) as well as dancing many of the classic ballerina roles. However, personal problems and illness frequently interrupted her career and she left the company for good in 1984. Though she guested to much acclaim with the Royal Ballet in 1980 and 1986 it was felt that she had not achieved her potential to become one of the truly great ballerinas of the century. Her own somewhat sensational account of her early life and career appeared in *Dancing on my Grave: An Autobiography*, written with her first husband, Greg Lawrence (New York, 1986), and its sequel, *The Shape of Love* (New York, 1990). After retiring from the stage she moved to Australia but has continued to coach in the US and in Europe and in 2007 returned to ABT to assist with the staging of its new production of *Sleeping Beauty*, in which she also made her debut as Carabosse.

Kirov Ballet *See* MARIINSKY BALLET.

Kirsova, Helene (orig. Ellen Wittrup Hansen; *b* Denmark, *c*.1911; *d* London, 22 Feb. 1962) Danish dancer, teacher, choreographer, and director. She studied with Staats at Paris Opera and danced with Le Ballet Franco Russe and Rubinstein's company before becoming a founding member of de Basil's Ballets Russes de Monte Carlo in 1932, where she was leading dancer until 1937. In 1940 she opened a dance school in Sydney and in 1941 a company which became known as the Kirsova Ballet and was Australia's first professional ballet company. She staged several classics as well as choreographing her own works, including *Faust* (mus. H. Krips, 1941, based on Heine's libretto). The company disbanded in 1944 and she retired from teaching in 1947. She wrote *Ballet in Moscow Today* (London, 1956).

Kirstein, Lincoln (*b* Rochester, NY, 4 May 1907; *d* New York, 5 Jan. 1996) US director, writer, and patron who helped shape the course of 20th-century American ballet. He was educated at Harvard University and, developing a keen interest in ballet, used some of his personal wealth to bring Balanchine to America with the promise of his own company and school. In 1934 the two men co-founded (with E. M. M. Warburg) the School of American Ballet of which Kirstein was president until 1989. In 1935 they co-founded the American Ballet and in 1936 Ballet Caravan which Kirstein directed until 1941. In 1946 he was co-founder and secretary of Ballet Society, becoming general director of its successor, New York City Ballet, from 1948 to 1989. He also founded the Dance Archives of New York's Museum of Modern Art in 1940, was founder and editor of the series Dance Index (New York, 1942–8), and the sponsor of Japanese theatre tours to the US, including the Grand Kabuki (1960). He was ghostwriter of

part of Romola Nijinsky's biography of Nijinsky (1932–3) and was sole author of many other books including *Dance* (New York, 1935), *Blast at Ballet, a Corrective for the American Audience* (New York, 1938), *Movement and Metaphor* (New York, 1970), *The New York City Ballet* (New York, 1972), and *Nijinsky Dancing* (New York, 1975). In 1987 he was awarded the Handel Medallion.

Kisselgoff, Anna (*b* Paris, 12 Jan. 1938) US dance writer. She studied ballet with V. Belova and J. Yazvinsky and was educated at Bryn Mawr College, the Sorbonne, and Columbia University. She became dance critic and reporter for the *New York Times* in 1968 and between 1977 and 2005 was its principal critic. She taught at Yale and Barnard College and was appointed Knight of the Dannebrog (1986) and Chevalier des Arts et Lettres (1990).

Kistler, Darci (*b* Riverside, Calif., 4 Jun. 1964) US dancer. She studied with Irina Kosmovska in Los Angeles and then at the School of American Ballet. In 1979 her precocious success in the School's Workshop performance led to her becoming an apprentice with New York City Ballet, promoted to full company member in 1980, soloist in 1981, and principal in 1983. Even as a teenager Kistler performed with a ballerina's assurance, her ability to project emotional and musical nuance in combination with the grand scale of her dancing causing many to consider her the successor of Suzanne Farrell. She danced most of the leading roles in the Balanchine repertory and also created roles in numerous works including Robbins's *Gershwin Concerto* (1982), and *Piccolo Balletto* (1986), and Martins's *Histoire du soldat* (1981), *Echo* (1989), *Sleeping Beauty* (1991), and *Stabat Mater* (1998). Injury interrupted her career between 1983 and 1985 and again in 1998 and 1999, but Kistler continued dancing with NYCB until 2010, the last ballerina of the Balanchine era. She additionally guested with the Princeton Ballet, among others, and appeared on US television as well as teaching at the School of American Ballet from 1994 onwards. In 1991 she married Peter *Martins.

Klamt, Jutta (*b* Striegau, 23 Feb. 1890; *d* Aarau, Switzerland, 26 May 1970) German dancer and teacher. Self-taught, she gave her debut recital in Berlin, in 1919 and, after founding a school and later a company, became one of the key figures of German modern dance. Unlike Wigman and others she and her husband Gustav Vischer were willing to compromise their style to the aesthetic and political dogma of the Nazis.

Kniaseff, Boris (*b* St Petersburg, 1 Jul. 1900; *d* Paris, 7 Oct. 1975) Russian-French dancer, choreographer, and teacher. He studied with Mordkin and others in Moscow and with Sokolova in St Petersburg and made his debut at Voronezh Opera in 1916. In the same year he became dancer and ballet master at Kharkov Opera. In 1917 he went to Constantinople where in 1918 he created his first ballet and was dancer and ballet master at Sofia Opera (1919–20). After this he danced with many companies including his own Les Ballet Stylisés (1926–8) and Ballets Russes de Boris Kniaseff (1930). He created several ballets for both companies. In 1928 he was dancer and choreographer at Théâtre des Champs-Elysées where he partnered his then wife Spessivtseva, and from 1932 to 1934 he was dancer and ballet master at Paris's Opéra Comique. In 1937 he opened his studio in Paris where his pupils included Chauviré. He also taught in Lausanne, Geneva, Rome, Athens, and Buenos Aires, using his famous 'barre par terre' system in which pupils performed classical exercises lying on the floor.

Kobborg, Johan (*b* Odense, 5 Jun. 1972) Danish dancer, producer, and director. He trained at Funen Ballet Academy then at the Royal Danish Ballet School, entering the company in 1989 as an apprentice and promoted to principal in 1994, after making his debut as James in *La Sylphide*. A dancer gracefully shaped by his Bournonville schooling Kobborg also proved to be an arresting actor, and when he joined the Royal Ballet in 1999 he excelled in dramatic ballets such as *Mayerling*, *Romeo and Juliet*, *Manon*, as well as classics like *Giselle*. He has created roles in works by Wheeldon, Page, Brandstrup, and many others and has formed a regular partnership with Alina Cojocaru. The two perform in galas around the world and have guested with numerous companies including the Bolshoi, the Kirov, and Morphoses. As director, choreographer, and producer Kobborg has organized several programmes of ballet, including *Out of Denmark* for London's Queen Elizabeth Hall; staged productions of *Napoli* (Act III) (2007), and *La Sylphide* (2005), the latter originally for the Royal Ballet but also in the repertories of the Bolshoi, Zurich Ballet, and Kobayashi Ballet Tokyo, and created work for the Royal Ballet's New Choreography showcase (2009). Recipient of many awards including Best Male Dancer, Critics Circle (2001).

(((⊕))) SEE WEB LINKS
• Website for Johan Kobborg

Kobler family Austro-German family of dancers who performed together as a ballet company. They toured around Europe from the mid-18th century to the beginning of the 19th (when they appeared in Amsterdam in 1812 they were billed at 'Les Grotesques') and only occasionally employed outsiders.

Kochno, Boris (*b* Moscow, 3 Jan. 1904; *d* Paris, 8 Dec. 1990) Russian-French ballet librettist and dance writer. In 1920 he became Diaghilev's secretary and advised him closely on many ballets. He wrote several librettos for Les Ballets Russes including *Les Fâcheux* (1924), *Zéphire et Flore* (1925), *La Chatte* (1927), *The Gods Go a-Begging* (1928), and *Prodigal Son* (1929). After Diaghilev's death he became artistic adviser of Ballets Russes de Monte Carlo where he wrote librettos for *Cotillon* and *Jeux d'enfants* (both 1932) and then in 1933 was co-founder with Balanchine of Les Ballets 1933. From 1934 to 1937 he was back with the Monte Carlo company then in 1945 he wrote the libretto for *Les Forains* whose success led to the founding, with Petit, of Les Ballets des Champs-Elysées. He was co-director of the company until 1951 and his several librettos for Petit included *Les Amours de Jupiter* and *Le Bal des blanchisseuses* (both 1946). He was author of *Le Ballet* (Paris, 1954) and *Diaghilev et Les Ballets Russes* (Paris, 1970). Some of his librettos were published under the pen name Sobeka.

Kodály, Zoltán (*b* Kecskemét, 16 Dec. 1882; *d* Budapest, 6 Mar. 1967) Hungarian composer. He wrote no ballet scores but his concert music has often been used for dance in, for example, Graham's *Lamentations* (New York, 1930), Limón's *Missa Brevis in tempore belli* (New York, 1958), and Eck's *Peacock Variations* (Ballet Sopianae, 1971).

Koegler, Horst (*b* Neuruppin, 22 Mar. 1927) German dance writer. He was educated at Kiel University and Halle/Saale Academy of Theatre. Between 1957 and 1959 he was ballet critic of *Die Welt*, then moved to *Stuttgart Zeitung*, becoming music editor (1977–92) then continuing freelance. He has also been German correspondent of various magazines including *Dance Magazine*, *Dance and Dancers*, and *Dance Now* and editor of the German annual *Ballett* from 1965. His books include *Ballett International* (Berlin, 1960), *Balanchine und das moderne Ballett* (Velber, 1964), *Reclams Ballettlexikon* (Stuttgart, 1984), and *Kleines Wörterbuch* (Stuttgart, 1999). He also edited *The Concise Oxford Dictionary of Ballet* (London, 1977).

Kolb, Igor (*b* Pinsk, Belarus, 6 Jun. 1977) Belarus/Russian dancer. He studied at the Byelorussian State Ballet School and danced with the Minsk Ballet while still a student. After seven auditions he joined the Mariinsky Ballet in 1996, where he was appointed principal in 2003. An elegant dancer, his dramatic sensitivity coupled with his bravura technique has been showcased in the company's classical repertory but he is also a versatile stylist performing in more recent works by MacMillan, Forsythe, and Ratmansky. He has guested with the Teatro dell'Opera, Rome and the Vienna State Ballet.

Kolosova, Evgenia (*b* St Petersburg, 15 Dec. 1780; *d* St Petersburg, 30 Mar. 1869) Russian dancer and teacher. As a student at the Imperial Ballet School she performed many children's roles and was a favoured pupil of Valberg. She subsequently became a favourite of Didelot, creating roles in, among others, *Raoul de Créquis* (1819) and also directing the school during his absence (an exceptional status for a woman during that period). An unusually dramatic dancer, she also appeared as an actress.

Kolpakova, Irina (*b* Leningrad, 22 May 1933) Soviet dancer. She studied at Leningrad Ballet School with Vaganova and graduated into the Kirov Ballet in 1951. A dancer of exceptionally pure classical style she became one of the company's leading ballerinas, her particular lightness and elegance especially suited to *Sleeping Beauty*, *Giselle*, *Raymonda*, and *The Nutcracker*. She also performed the 20th-century repertory, however, creating roles in, among others, Grigorovich's *The Stone Flower* (1957) and *Legend of Love* (1961), Belsky's *Coast of Hope* (1959), Kasatkina and Vasiliov's *Creation of the World* (1971), and Vinogradov's *The Fairy of the Rond Mountains* (1980). She retired in 1987 becoming teacher and repetiteur with the company and in 1990 was appointed ballet mistress with American Ballet Theatre. She was made People's Artist of the USSR in 1965 and Hero of Socialist Labour in 1983. Her husband Vladilen Semyonov was her frequent stage partner.

Kolpin, Alexander (*b* Copenhagen, 1 Jun. 1965) Danish dancer. He studied at the Royal Danish Ballet School and became apprentice to the company in 1981, becoming principal from 1988. A dancer whose clean-cut precision was balanced by buoyant energy, he excelled in Bournonville ballets but also danced a wide modern repertory, creating roles in Flindt's *Caroline Mathilde* (1991), among others. He guested with several companies, including Australian Ballet, though injury forced him to take long absences from the stage and an early retirement. In 1991 he was appointed artistic director of the touring company Soloists and Principals of the RDB and founded the International Ballet of Copenhagen, a company that gathers together guest dancers from companies worldwide to perform both the Bournonville repertory and newly commissioned ballets.

Komaki Ballet Japanese ballet company. It was founded by Masahide Komaki in 1946 as the Tokyo Ballet Company (a totally separate organization from today's Tokyo Ballet Company) and as well as being the first Japanese company to perform *Swan Lake* it helped foster a nationwide interest in ballet. It toured widely in Japan with Momoko Tani and later Sakiko Hirose as ballerina until 1949.

Komar, Chris (*b* Milwaukee, 30 Oct. 1947; *d* New York, 17 Jul. 1996) US dancer. He studied at the University of Wisconsin and in 1969 became a founder member of the Milwaukee Ballet Company. In 1971 he went to New York to study with Cunningham and joined his company in 1972. Here he created many roles and later took over several of Cunningham's own roles in, for example, *Winterbranch* and *Signals*. In 1973 he also became a teacher at the Merce Cunningham Studio and went on to stage numerous Cunningham works in Europe and America. In 1992 he became assistant artistic director of the company.

Koner, Pauline (*b* New York, 26 Jun. 1912; *d* New York, 8 Feb. 2001) US dancer, choreographer, and teacher. She studied ballet with Fokine, Spanish dance with Cansino, and Oriental dance with Michio Ito. In 1926 she made her debut with Fokine's company and toured the US with Ito (1928–9). She started her solo career in 1930 and toured extensively until joining Limón's company in 1946. She became principal dancer and stayed with the company until 1960 creating roles in Limón's *The Moor's Pavane* (1949) and Humphrey's *Ruins and Visions* (1953), among others. In 1947 she additionally founded her own company with which she toured internationally until 1963, later forming the Pauline Koner Dance Consort (1976–82). Her most famous solo was *Farewell* (1962), set to the last movement of Mahler's *Song of the Earth*. She also choreographed *Poeme* (1969) for the Ailey company. She lectured widely in America, Europe, and Japan, and in 1986 was appointed teacher at the Juilliard School. In 1989 she published her autobiography, *Solitary Song* (Duke Univ. Press). She was married to conductor Fritz Mahler.

Konservatoriet *See* CONSERVATORY, THE, OR A PROPOSAL OF MARRIAGE THROUGH A NEWSPAPER.

Korea The sophisticated traditional dances of Korea are distinguished from most other Asian dance forms by their predominantly triple, rather than duple, rhythms. Historically they have been influenced both by religious imagery (a combination of Shamanism, Taoism, Confucianism, and Buddhism) and by the displays given by *keesaengs*, cultivated courtesans like Japanese geishas who specialized in exquisite, delicately nostalgic dance and poetry. In 1976 the Chang Mu Dance Company was founded in Seoul (S. Korea) to perform traditionally based work by Korean choreographers but Western influences were promoted in the country in 1984 with the founding of the Universal Ballet Company, also in Seoul. Initially the company was designed to marry elements from traditional dance with Western ballet but it grew increasingly Westernized in focus after the appointment of Roy Tobias as artistic director in 1988. Many of the standard classics as well as works by Tobias, Dollar, Fokine, and Balanchine were introduced into the repertory and this policy was continued when Bruce Steivel became director in 1995, creating his own versions of popular classics such as *Cinderella*, He was succeeded by Vinogradov in 1998. The company, made up of both Korean and non-Korean dancers, has toured to Europe and Japan and made its US debut in 1999. It has an associated school in Washington DC.

Modern dance activity in Korea has emanated largely from the Graham-based dance department at Ewha University, directed by Yook Wansoon, and several companies have been founded by her pupils, including *Kim Wha-suk and Kim Bock-hee. There is also a very lively hip-hop scene, led by internationally award-winning crews like Rivers and Gamblers, who receive state support. In 2008 Seoul hosted the first of its International Dance Festivals.

Korrigane, La Ballet in two acts with choreography by Mérante, libretto by François Coppé and Mérante, music by C. M. Widor, sets by Lavastre, Rubé, and Chaperon, and costumes by Lacoste. Premiered 1 Dec. 1880 at Paris Opera with Mauri, Sanlaville, and Mérante. It is set in 17th-century Brittany and tells the story of Yvonette who is bewitched by the Queen of the Korriganes. In the second act (reminiscent of *Giselle*) Yvonette's lover Lilez comes to find her among the ghostly korriganes. The lovers dance together until the korriganes finally scatter at dawn. An enormously popular ballet, it received over 100 performances at the Opera.

Kovak, Iztok (*b* Trbovlje, 7 Aug. 1962) Slovenian dancer and choreographer. He studied various dance forms including jazz, classical, and modern dance in Slovenia and in workshops abroad, creating his award-winning solo, *How I Caught a Falcon*, in 1991. In 1993 he formed his group EnKnap presenting mixed-media work often with artists and/or musicians among the dancers, such as *Codes of Cobra* (1997). Though based in Slovenia, the company's work has been produced in collaboration with European producers and has toured widely.

Kowroski, Maria (*b* Michigan, 1976) US dancer. She studied locally and at the School of American Ballet, joining New York City Ballet in 1995.

An unusually tall, slender, and supple dancer with a huge extension and lyrical line, she was given principal roles even while a member of the corps de ballet. In 1999 she was officially promoted principal, and in the same year created a role in *Blossom Got Kissed*, Susan Stroman's contribution to the Ellington ballet *Duke!* In addition to dancing the standard Balanchine and Robbins repertory she has also created roles in works by several other choreographers including Martins, Bigonzetti, Elo, Wheeldon, and Eifmann. She has guested with the Kirov and Munich Ballet.

Kozlov, Leonid and Valentina (*b* 1947 and 1955 respectively) Soviet dancers. As husband and wife they were soloists with the Bolshoi Ballet until defecting during the company's 1979 US tour. They performed with various companies before joining New York City Ballet as principals in 1983. They subsequently divorced.

krakowiak [Fr. cracovienne] An energetic dance in 2/4 time from the Krakow district in Poland, performed both by couples or by larger numbers of dancers. Characterized by syncopated rhythms, stamping footwork, and clicked heels it was very popular in Romantic ballets, and was danced by Elssler in *La Gypsy* (1839).

Krassovska, Nathalie (orig. Natasha Leslie; *b* Petrograd, 3 Jun. 1919; *d* Dallas 8 Feb. 2005) Soviet-US dancer and teacher. The daughter of Diaghilev dancer Lydia Krassovska, she studied in Russia then with Preobrajenska, Legat, and at the School of American Ballet. She danced with various companies including Les Ballets 1933, Ballets Russes de Monte Carlo (as ballerina 1936–50), and London Festival Ballet (1950–9). After retiring she taught in Dallas, Texas.

Krassovska, Vera (*b* Petrograd, 19 Aug. 1915; *d* St Petersburg, 15 Aug. 1999) Soviet ballet critic and historian. She studied with Vaganova at the Leningrad Choreographic School and graduated into the Kirov in 1933. In 1941 she left and in the same year published her first press article, becoming a faculty member of the Leningrad Theatre Institute in 1951. Her many publications include detailed histories of Russian and Western ballet, as well as critical biographies including *V. Chabukiani* (1956), *Nijinsky* (1974), and *Agrippina Iakovlevna Vaganova* (1989).

Kraus, Gertrud (*b* Vienna, 6 May 1903; *d* Tel Aviv, 22 Nov. 1977) Austrian-Israeli dancer, choreographer, and teacher. She studied at the Vienna State Academy and between 1928 and 1950 performed recitals of her own expressionist choreography, touring in Europe and Israel, both alone and with her group. In 1935 she founded the Gertrud Kraus Dance Company in Israel, and additionally ran her own school, based in Tel Aviv (1935–73). Many of the country's best-known dancers trained with her. In later years she was also active as a painter and sculptor.

Kresnik, Johann (*b* Carinthia, 12 Dec. 1939) Austrian dancer, choreographer, and director. He studied at the ballet school of Graz Theatre, and joined the company in 1959, moving to Bremen (1960) and then Cologne (1962). From 1968 to 1979 he was ballet master at the Bremen theatre and created numerous works, many with powerful, anti-establishment messages, including *PIGasUS* (1970). He was then in Heidelberg (1980–89), back in Bremen as director of his own company (1989–94), and finally in Berlin. He has also worked freelance as choreographer and theatre director.

Kreutzberg, Harald (*b* Liberec (Reichenberg), 11 Dec. 1902; *d* Muri, Switzerland, 25 Apr. 1968) German dancer, choreographer, and teacher. He studied with Wigman, joined Hanover Ballet in 1922 and Berlin State Opera (1924–1926), then from 1928 to 1931 gave recitals in America and Europe with Yvonne Georgi, his partner becoming Ruth Page in 1931. Renowned for his theatricality and humour, as well as for his inventive use of costumes and masks, he became his generation's leading male exponent of German modern dance. He continued working under the Nazis and resumed international touring after the war, retiring in 1959. He opened his own school in Bern in 1955.

Kriger, Viktorina (Krieger) (*b* St Petersburg, 9 Apr. 1893; *d* Moscow, 23 Dec. 1978) Russian/ Soviet dancer, director, and writer. She studied at the Imperial Theatre School, Moscow with Tikhomirov and graduated into the Bolshoi Ballet in 1910. With her virtuoso technique and dramatic gifts she became one of Gorsky's leading ballerinas, outstanding in roles such as Swanilda and Kitri. In 1921 she danced with Pavlova's company but was considered too powerful a rival and left, dancing with Mordkin in Moscow in 1923. In 1925 she rejoined the Bolshoi where she remained until 1948. At the same time she toured widely giving concert performances and in 1929 founded the Moscow Art Ballet which performed chamber versions of popular ballets. She attempted to employ Stanislavsky's teaching methods in her productions and in 1939 the company became part of the Stanislavsky and Nemirovich-Danchenko Theatre. She created roles in several ballets including the stepmother in Zakharov's *Cinderella* (1945). In 1926 she began writing on ballet and was an active journalist until the end of her life. She was author of *My Notes* (Moscow,

1930) and director of Bolshoi Theatre Museum from 1955 to 1963. She was made Honoured Arts Worker of the Russian Federation in 1951.

Kriza, John (*b* Berwyn, Ill., 15 Jan. 1919; *d* Naples, Fla., 18 Aug. 1975) US dancer who was the first US-born and trained male principal of a major American company. He studied at the Stone-Camryn School and with Dolin and Tudor at the School of American Ballet, dancing with the Page-Stone Ballet (1939–40), then in 1940 became a founding member of Ballet Theatre (later American Ballet Theatre). With his casual, all-American image he was very popular with audiences and was rapidly promoted to principal. Though the title role of Loring's *Billy the Kid* was not made on him it became his own and he also famously created the role of the sentimental sailor in Robbins's *Fancy Free* (1944). Other created roles were in Robbins's *Interplay* (1945), Kidd's *On Stage!* (1945), and de Mille's *Fall River Legend* (1948). He guested with Ballet Caravan and New York City Ballet as well as dancing in several musicals. When he retired in 1966 he became assistant to the directors of ABT.

Kröller, Heinrich (*b* Munich, 25 Jul. 1880; *d* Würzburg, 25 Jul. 1930) German dancer, choreographer, and ballet master. He studied at Munich Opera Ballet School and with Zambelli and Staats in Paris. He was soloist at Munich Court Opera Ballet in 1903, first soloist in 1906 and then principal dancer in Dresden from 1907. In 1917 he returned to Munich as ballet master, also working at Berlin State Opera as director, then at Vienna State Opera. He choreographed many ballets including the first German production of Strauss's *Legend of Joseph* (Berlin, 1921). He stopped dancing in 1925 but continued as ballet master in Munich where he made a large body of modern ballets as well as directing opera.

Kronstam, Henning (*b* Copenhagen, 29 Jun. 1934; *d* Copenhagen, 28 May 1995) Danish dancer, teacher, and artistic director. He studied at Royal Danish Ballet School and graduated into the company in 1952, becoming solo dancer (principal) in 1956. An outstanding romantic dancer with a brilliant technique, he performed many of the great Petipa and Bournonville roles but also created roles in Ashton's *Romeo and Juliet* (1955), Flindt's *The Three Musketeers* (1966), and von Rosen's *Don Juan* (1967) as well as winning acclaim as Balanchine's Apollo and as Iago in Limón's *The Moor's Pavane*. He guested widely abroad and in 1978 was appointed artistic director of the RDB while continuing to perform character roles. After resigning as director in 1985 he became ballet master with the company until

1993. He was appointed Knight of Dannebrog in 1964.

krumping A style of hip-hop that originated in California, drawing on elements of clowning (face painting, comic expressiveness), popping, and African dance. It is characterized by inventive, free style movement, often focusing on the chest and arms, and often involving some physical contact between the dancers suggestive of a ritual battle. It has become more aggressive in tone than its clowning origins.

Kshessinska, Mathilda (Kschessinskaya) (*b* Ligova, 31 Aug. 1872; *d* Paris, 6 Dec. 1971) Russian dancer and teacher. Daughter of the popular Polish character dancer Felix Krzesinski she studied at the Imperial Theatre School, St Petersburg with Ivanov, Johansson, and Cecchetti, graduating into the Mariinsky Theatre in 1890. She was appointed ballerina in 1892, prima ballerina in 1893, and prima ballerina assoluta in 1895 (the only ballerina other than Legnani to have been officially granted the title). Her meteoric rise was partly fuelled by her brilliant virtuosity—she was the first Russian ballerina to execute 32 fouettées—and also by her lively glamour. She danced the great Petipa ballerina roles, created roles in his *Le Réveil de Flore* (1894) and *Les Saisons* (1900), as well as creating Kitri in Gorsky's 1902 production of *Don Quixote*. Her career also owed much to her close links with the Royal family. She was mistress of the Tsarevich Nikolai (later Tsar Nikolai II), and then of the Grand Duke Andrei whom she married in 1921, and she wielded huge social influence. After 1904 she reduced her performances at the Mariinsky to those of guest ballerina and also performed at Paris Opera (1909) and with Diaghilev's Ballets Russes (1911–12). She left Russia for the Cote d'Azur in 1920 and in 1929 opened a school in Paris where her pupils included Eglevsky, Riabouchinska, Chauviré, and Fonteyn. Her last stage appearance was at a charity gala in London in 1936. She was author of *Souvenirs de la Kschessinska* (Paris, 1970); English version *Dancing in St Petersburg* (London, 1970).

kuchipudi Traditional Indian dance-drama performed by male dancers of the brahman caste. It dates back to the 16th century, and originates from the village of the same name.

Kudelka, James (*b* Newmarket, Ont., 10 Sept. 1955) Canadian dancer and choreographer. He studied at the National Ballet School and joined the National Ballet of Canada in 1972, becoming soloist in 1976 and principal in 1981. Though a gifted demi-caractère dancer his interest rapidly focused on choreography and in 1973 he created his first work for the company *Sonata* (mus.

Franck). Developing a succinctly expressive style that fused classical and modern idioms he created several more ballets including *A Party* (mus. Britten, 1976), *Washington Square* (mus. Baker, 1977), and *Playhouse* (mus. Shostakovich, 1980) and was then officially designated company choreographer (1980–2). In 1981 he joined Les Grands Ballets Canadiens as a principal dancer, becoming resident choreographer in 1984. He created many works for the company, including *In paradisum* (mus. Baker, 1983) and *Diversion* (mus. Britten, 1985), as well as choreographing for several other companies including Joffrey Ballet, San Francisco Ballet, and National Ballet of Canada for which he created *Pastorale* (1990) to Beethoven's 6th Symphony. Between 1990 and 1992 he worked freelance after which he was appointed artist in residence at National Ballet of Canada, creating *Actress* (1994), a new version of *The Nutcracker* (1995), and *The Four Seasons* (mus. Vivaldi, 1997). He continued to create works for other companies, including *Le Baiser de la fée* (mus. Stravinsky, 1996, for Birmingham Royal Ballet), *Cinderella* (mus. Prokofiev, 2005 for Boston Ballet), and *Little Dancer* (mus. Glass, 2008, for Houston Ballet). Between 1996 and 2005 he was artistic director of National Ballet of Canada after which he stepped down to become resident choreographer.

Kuhn, Hans Peter (*b* Kiel, 1952) German sound artist and composer. As a pioneering specialist in sound environments and installations (frequently mixing found noise with music) he began his career-long collaboration with Robert Wilson in 1978. In the dance world he has worked closely with Laurie Booth creating the sound for several productions including *Completely Birdland* (for Rambert Dance Company, 1991), and also with Dana Reitz (*Suspect Terrain*, 1990). His recent works for dance include *Frankenstein* for Alias Dance Theatre (2007).

Kumakawa, Tetsuya (*b* Hokkaido, 5 Mar. 1972) Japanese-British dancer. He studied locally, then at the Royal Ballet School, graduating into the company in 1989 when he was also promoted soloist, becoming principal (1993–1998). A charismatic demi-caractère dancer with outstanding aerial virtuosity and an extravagant pirouette technique, he dances a wide repertory of classical and modern roles. He has been one of the few dancers permitted to dance the Baryshnikov role in Tharp's *Push Comes to Shove* and he has created roles in MacMillan's *Prince of the Pagodas* (1989) and Tharp's *Mr Worldly Wise* (1995), among others. In 1998 he left the Royal to lead and star in his own company, K Ballet. Based in Tokyo, but touring internationally, the company performs the classical repertory with a few works by Ashton, MacMillan, and Balanchine and some newly commissioned work. It opened its associate school in 2004, Kumakawa enjoys cult status in Japan, though in 2007 injury forced him off the stage for long periods.

SEE WEB LINKS

• Website for the K Ballet and its school

Kun, Zsuzsa (*b* Budapest, 9 Dec. 1934) Hungarian dancer and teacher. She studied at Budapest State Opera Ballet School and in Moscow with Semenova, E. Gerdt, and Messerer. In 1949 she joined the Budapest State Opera Ballet becoming one of the company's most popular ballerinas until she retired in 1977. A musical and dramatic dancer, she performed both classical and Soviet ballerina roles as well as creating roles, including the title role in Seregi's *Sylvia* (1972). She guested widely, including with the Bolshoi Ballet and London Festival Ballet and was director of the Hungarian State Ballet Institute (1972–9).

Kyasht, Lydia (Kyaksht) (*b* St Petersburg, 25 Mar. 1885; *d* London, 11 Jan. 1959) Russian-British dancer and teacher. She studied at the St Petersburg Imperial Ballet School with Gerdt and graduated into the Mariinsky Theatre in 1902, dancing there until 1908. She was also a soloist with the Bolshoi (1903–4) and performed in various concert recitals. She claimed to be the first to dance Fokine's *Dying Swan* in 1905. In 1908 she went to London where she succeeded Genée as prima ballerina at the Empire Theatre, performing there for several seasons until 1913. In 1912 she also danced with Diaghilev's Ballets Russes (and again in 1919), and made her New York debut in 1914. After returning to Russia to dance concert performances (1914–17) she settled in London and founded her own school (which moved to Cirencester in 1948) while also dancing in cabaret and the theatre. In 1939 she founded her own company, Ballet de la Jeunesse Anglaise, which toured England (1939) and Europe (1944) and in 1940 also ran the Lydia Kyasht Ballet. From 1953 she taught at the Legat School. She was author of *Romantic Recollections* (London, 1929) and was sister of Georgi Kyasht (1873–1936), a soloist at the Mariinsky Theatre and later ballet master at Buenos Aires, Vienna State Opera, and elsewhere.

Kylián, Jiří (*b* Prague, 21 Mar. 1947) Czech dancer, choreographer, and director. He studied at the Prague conservatory and at the Royal Ballet School, joining Stuttgart Ballet in 1968, where he became a soloist. In 1970 he choreographed the first of his many ballets for the company, *Kommen und Gehen* (mus. Bartók), and was recognized by Cranko as a major talent. In 1973 he made his first work for Nederlands Dans Theater, *Viewers* (mus. Martin), and in 1975 was appointed co-artistic director of NDT, becoming artistic director and choreographer in 1977. In 1995 he was named Officer in the Ordre van Oranje Nassau. In 1999 he resigned as director of NDT, succeeded by Marian Sarstädt, but retained his post as resident choreographer and artistic adviser until 2009. From the outset his style fused the fleetness and precision of classical ballet with the weight and muscularity of modern dance, and early works like *Symphony of Psalms* (mus. Stravinsky, 1978) exemplified the special fluency of his movement. Movements unfurled in a seamless connection with the music, and individual dancers were knit into large eloquent groups or into the lyrically sculpted duets and pas de trois which characterize one of his best-known works, *Return to the Strange Land* (mus. Janáček, 1975). Though these works were not overtly narrative they encompassed a wide emotional range from the exuberance of *Sinfonietta* (mus. Janáček, 1978) to the darker emotions of *Field Mass* (mus. Martinů, 1980) and *Heart's Labyrinth 1* (mus. Schoenberg, Webern, Dvořák, 1984) or the athleticism of his Aboriginal-based *Stamping Ground* (mus. Chavez, 1983). In recent years his fluency has been deliberately disrupted by more angular movement and abrupt gestures, and he has introduced surreal theatrical elements to express complex ideas as in *Bella Figura* (mus. various, 1995). Though Kylián has choreographed almost exclusively for NDT and its sister companies (NDT 2 and 3), creating over 100 works for the organization, his works have been taken into the repertories of many companies around the world. His other works include *Transfigured Night* (mus. Schoenberg, NDT 1975), *Nuages* (mus. Debussy, Stuttgart Ballet, 1976), *Symphony in D* (mus. Haydn, NDT, two-part version 1976, three-part version 1977, and four-part version 1981), *November Steps* (mus. Takemitsu, NDT, 1977), *Rainbow Snake* (mus. Norby, NDT, 1978), *Dream Dances* (mus. Berio, NDT, 1979), *Forgotten Land* (mus. Britten, Stuttgart Ballet, 1981), *Les Noces* (mus. Stravinsky, NDT, 1982), *Dreamtime* (mus. Takemitsu, NDT, 1983), *L'Enfant et les sortilèges* (mus. Ravel, NDT, 1984), *Silent Cries* (mus. Debussy, NDT, 1986), *L'Histoire du Soldat* (mus. Stravinsky, NDT, 1986), *Hearts Labyrinth* (new version, mus. Schoenberg, Webern, and Dvořák, NDT, 1987), *No More Play* (mus. Webern, NDT, 1988), *Falling Angels* (mus. Reich, 1989), *Sweet Dreams* (mus. Webern, NDT, 1990), *Sarabande* (mus. Bach, NDT, 1990), *Un Ballo* (mus. Ravel, NDT2, 1991), *Petite Mort* (mus. Mozart, NDT, 1991), *Obscure Temptations* (mus. Cage, NDT3, 1991), *Whereabouts Unknown* (mus. Pärt, Reich, Ives, and de Roo, NDT, 1993), *Arcimboldo* (mus. various, 1995, revised for NDT1, 2 and 3, 2000), *Wings of Wax* (mus. von

k

Biber, Cage, Glass, and Bach, NDT, 1997), *Indigo Rose* (mus. various, NDT2, 1999), *Tar and Feathers* (mus. based on Mozart, NDT, 2005), and *Gods and Dogs* (mus. Beethoven, NDT 2, 2008). He retired from his official post as resident choreographer for NDT in 2009 but continues to have a close association with the company.

k

Laast, Anthony van (*b* Bognor Regis, 31 May 1951) British dancer and choreographer. He studied at the London School of Contemporary Dance (1968–70) and performed with London Contemporary Dance Theatre (1971–80), after which he became one of the UK's leading choreographers for musical theatre, working on *Song and Dance* (1981), *Candide* (1987), *Joseph and the Amazing Technicolor Dreamcoat* (1991), *Jesus Christ Superstar* (1998), *Mama Mia!* (1999), and *Bombay Dreams* (2002), among others. He has also choreographed for theatre and opera, including *The Mikado* (English National Opera, 1985) and in 2010 directed the street dance spectacle *Blaze*.

Laban, Rudolf von (orig. R. L. de Varalja; *b* Pozsony (now Bratislava), 15 Dec. 1879; *d* Weybridge, 1 Jul. 1958) Hungarian dancer, choreographer, ballet master, and dance theorist. He studied painting, dancing, and acting in Paris and Munich and toured N. Africa with a revue troupe. Between 1907 and 1910 he performed in Germany and Austria and in 1910 founded a school in Munich, where Wigman was one of his pupils. After the First World War he taught in Nuremberg, Mannheim, and Stuttgart (where Jooss was one of his pupils) and in 1925 established an Institute of Choreography in Würzburg. He was then ballet director of the Berlin Staatsoper (1930–4), also staging large productions for amateur mass-movement choirs around Germany. In 1938 he went to England and worked with Jooss at Dartington Hall, after which he founded the Art of Movement Studio with Lisa Ullmann in Manchester. Although not a choreographer of lasting significance Laban became the leader of the pre-war Central European school of modern dance by virtue of his teaching and the theories by which he and his pupils analysed the laws of dynamics and expression in human movement. Most important was his development of a new system of dance notation, Kinetographie Laban which was first published in 1926 and later codified as Labanotation. In England he applied his theories to dance education and also to designing corrective physical exercises for factory workers. He wrote several books including *Ein Leben für den Tanz* (*A Life for the Dance*, Dresden 1935, London 1975), *Modern Educational Dance* (London, 1948), *Principles of Dance and Movement Notation* (London, 1956), and *Choreutics* (London, 1966).

Laban Centre London-based college specializing in modern dance training, also providing degree courses for dance and related studies. It originated from Laban's Art of Movement Studio which was opened in Manchester in 1948, then moved to Adleston, Surrey in 1953. In 1973, under the direction of Marion North, it moved to New Cross in London, and to Deptford in 2003. It pioneered the first British BA Honours Degree in Dance Theatre (1976) and the first MA in Dance Studies (1980) and now offers several other degree courses. Its advanced performing company, Transitions, was set up in 1983.

Labanotation The English-American term for Kinetographie Laban, Rudolf von *Laban's system of dance notation. The Kinetographic Institute at the Essen Folkwang School and the Dance Notation Bureau in New York are the two main centres of study. Ann Hutchinson's *Labanotation: The System of Analysing and Recording Movement* (New York 1954, 1970) is the best-known English annotation.

Labyrinth Ballet in one act with choreography by Massine, music by Schubert, and libretto and design by Dalí. Premiered 8 Oct. 1941 by Ballet Russe de Monte Carlo at Metropolitan Opera House, New York, with Eglevsky, Toumanova, and Franklin. This setting of Schubert's 7th Symphony portrays classicism as the thread of Ariadne, leading art through the confusing labyrinth of romanticism.

Lacarra, Lucia (*b* San Sebastian, 24 Mar. 1975) Spanish dancer. She studied at the Victor Ullate School and made her debut with his company aged 15. In 1994 she moved to National Ballet of Marseilles as principal dancer, creating roles in Petit's *Bolero* (1997), among others. In 1997 she moved to San Francisco Ballet, where she created the title role in Tomasson's staging of *Giselle* (1999) and in 2002 moved to the Bavarian State Ballet in Munich. She has guested with several other companies, including English National

Ballet and La Scala and is regularly partnered by *Malakhov.

Lac des cygnes *See* SWAN LAKE.

Lacotte, Pierre (*b* Chatou, 4 Apr. 1932) French dancer, teacher, choreographer, and director. He studied at the Paris Opera School under Gustave Ricaux and others (1942–6), graduating into the Paris Opera where he created a major role in Lifar's *Septuor* (1950) and was promoted premier danseur in 1952. In 1955, ambitious to choreograph his own work, he founded the Ballet de la Tour Eiffel for which he created several ballets including *Solstice* (mus. Wayenberg, 1955). He toured widely with the company until 1960 (also dancing as principal at New York's Metropolitan Opera Ballet, 1956–7) and was then director of the Ballet National Jeunesses Musicales de France (1963–8) with his wife Ghislaine Thesmar as ballerina. He created many works for the company including *Hamlet* (mus. Walton, 1964) and *La Voix* (mus. Leveillée, 1965) and also worked as guest choreographer for Ballet Rambert in 1966, creating *Intermede* (mus. Vivaldi) and other ballets. In 1972 he staged Taglioni's original *La Sylphide* for French television which was staged by the Paris Opera in the same year, followed by *Coppélia*, 1973. He has re-created many 19th-century ballets, based on research into original documentation, including Taglioni's *Nathalie* (Moscow Classical Ballet, 1980), Mazilier's *Marco Spada* (Rome Opera Ballet, 1981), a new production of Perrot and Coralli's *Giselle* (Ballet National de Nancy, 1991, orig. staged for Ballet du Rhin, 1978), and *Paquita* (Paris Opera, 2001)—though certain historians have contested their accuracy. Between 1985 and 1988 he was choreographer and associate director of Ballets de Monte Carlo creating *L'Apprenti sorcier* (mus. Dukas, 1985) and between 1991 and 1999 he was artistic director of the Ballet de Nancy, reconstructing Taglioni's *L'Ombre* for the company in 1993. His later reconstructions include a version of *Pharaoh's Daughter* for the Bolshoi in 2000 and a full-length *Paquita* for Paris Opera in 2003.

Lady and the Fool, The Ballet in one act with libretto and choreography by Cranko, music by Verdi (arr. Mackerras), and design by Richard Beer. Premiered 25 Feb. 1954 at New Theatre, Oxford, by Sadler's Wells Theatre Ballet with P. Miller, MacMillan, and Mosaval. It is set to a selection of music from Verdi's lesser-known operas and tells the humorously sentimental story of a society beauty, La Capricciosa, who rejects her aristocratic suitors in favour of two tramp figures, Moondog and Bootface. A revised version was performed by Sadler's Wells Ballet in 1955 and it has been revived for several companies including

Stuttgart (1961), Berlin Opera Ballet (1965), Royal Danish Ballet (1971), and Houston Ballet (1978).

Lady from the Sea, The Ballet in one act with libretto and choreography by Cullberg, music by K. Riisager, and designs by Kerstin Hedeby. Premiered 21 Apr. 1960 by American Ballet Theatre at Metropolitan Opera House, New York, with Serrano, Bruhn, and Tetley. It is based on Ibsen's play of the same title and tells the story of Ellida who is trapped in a loveless marriage and longs for her real love, a sailor who has returned to the sea. It was revived for the Royal Swedish Ballet in 1961. An earlier version of the same story was choreographed by E. Leese for National Ballet of Canada (mus. S. Honigman, 1955).

Lady into Fox Ballet in one act with libretto and choreography by A. Howard, music by Honegger (arr. Charles Lynch), and design by Nadia Benois. Premiered 15 May 1939 at Mercury Theatre, London, by Ballet Rambert with Gilmour and Boyd. It is set to various orchestrated piano pieces by Honegger and, inspired by David Garnett's novel of the same title, it tells the story of an elegant woman who is really a vixen. Torn between her natural instincts and her love for her husband she finally escapes civilization to rejoin the wild. It was revived for Ballet Theatre in 1940 and a partly reconstructed version, with additional choreography by Mark Baldwin and a new score by Benjamin Pope, was premiered by Rambert Dance Company in 2006.

Lady of the Camellias (orig. Ger. title *Die Kameliendame*) Ballet in three acts with libretto and choreography by Neumeier, music by Chopin, and design by J. Rose. Premiered 4 Nov. 1978 by the Stuttgart Ballet at Württembergisches Staatstheater with Haydée, Madsen, Keil, Cragun, and R. Anderson. It is set to original concert music by Chopin, including the complete 2nd Piano Concerto, and is based on the novel *La Dame aux camélias* by Dumas *fils* (1848). Starting with the auction scene—performed almost like a scene in a play—the ballet then follows the plot of the novel closely except that it also integrates the characters of Manon Lescaut and des Grieux as mirror images of the main lovers. It was revived for Hamburg Ballet in 1980. Other choreographic treatments of Dumas's novel and play include F. Termanini's *Rita Gauthier* (mus. Verdi, Turin, 1857), Taras's *Camille* (mus. Schubert-Rieti, Orig. Ballet Russe, 1946), Tudor's *Lady of the Camellias* (mus. Verdi, New York City Ballet, 1951), Page's *Camille* (mus. Verdi, Chicago, 1957), T. Gsovsky's *Die Kameliendame* (mus. Sauguet, Berlin, 1957), Ashton's *Marguerite and Armand* (mus. Liszt, arr. Searle, Royal Ballet, 1963), Alberto Mendez's *Nous nous verrons hier soir* (mus. Sauguet, National

Ballet of Cuba, 1971), J. Lefèbre's *Dame aux camé-lias* (mus. Verdi, Charleroi, 1980), and Domi Re-iter-Stoffer's *Lady of the Camellias* (mus. Saint-Saëns, 1984).

Lafontaine, Mlle de (La Fontaine) (*b* c.1655; *d* Paris c.1738) Often regarded as the first profes-sional female dancer. She was born in France and little is known about her early life until she made her debut in 1681 at the Paris Opera in Lully's *Le Triomphe de l'amour*. She also created the leading roles in several other Lully ballets, including *Pha-éton* (chor. Beauchamps, 1683) and *Acis et Gala-tée* (chor. Beauchamps, 1686). Much admired for her elegance, she was leading ballerina in at least eighteen ballets and operas between 1681 and 1693. She retired into a convent.

La Fosse, Robert (*b* Beaumont, Tex., 1960) US dancer and choreographer. He studied at the Marsha Woody Academy and at Harkness House, joining American Ballet Theatre in 1977, and becoming principal in 1983. In 1985 he danced Romeo in MacMillan's staging of *Romeo and Juliet* for ABT, and in 1986 moved to New York City Ballet, creating roles in Robbins's *Quiet Lady* and *West Side Story Suite*, Tharp's *Octet* and *Septet*, and Martins's *A Fool for You* and *Tea Rose*, among others. He also appeared for three months in the musical *Jerome Robbins' Broadway*. He guested with Twyla Tharp during 1992 and direct-ed the touring company, Stars of American Ballet, through many seasons. He choreographed his first ballet, a pas de deux *Rappacini's Daughter*, for Baryshnikov's temporary company in 1985 and developed a parallel career as a choreogra-pher. In 1988 he created *Woodland Sketches* for the American Music Festival and following that several works for NYCB including *Danses de cour* (mus. R. Strauss, 1994), *Concerto in Five Move-ments* (mus. Prokofiev, 1997), and a section of the Ellington ballet *Duke!* (1999). He has also choreo-graphed for Les Ballets Trockadero de Monte Carlo, including *Stars & Stripes Forever* (1996) and in 1997 created a *Nutcracker* for the Russian Ballet Theatre of Delaware. He has additionally choreographed for opera. In 2002 he retired from NYCB but continued to make work for the com-pany, including *Land of Nod* (mus. Richard Rod-gers, 2003), as well as to teach and choreograph freelance. He published his autobiography *Noth-ing to Hide* in 1987 and has made numerous appearances on television.

Laine, Doris (*b* Helsinki, 15 Feb. 1931) Finnish dancer. She studied in Helsinki, Moscow, and with A. Northcote and joined the Finnish National Ballet in 1947, becoming prima ballerina in 1956. A frequent guest artist abroad, she was director of the Finnish National Ballet from 1984 to 1992 after

which she became director of the Finnish arts council.

Laing, Hugh (orig. Skinner; *b* Barbados, 6 Jun. 1911; *d* New York, 11 May 1988) British dancer. He studied with Craske and Rambert in London and with Preobrajenska in Paris, joining London Ballet Club (later Ballet Rambert) in 1932. Al-though never a brilliant technician his personal magnetism and dramatic gifts made him one of the great dance actors of his generation and he created roles in many early Tudor ballets, such as *Jardin aux lilas* (1936) and *Dark Elegies* (1937), as well as dancing the title role in Nijinsky's *L'Après-midi d'un faune* (1936). During 1937 he danced in recitals with de Mille and in 1938 performed with (Tudor's) London Ballet in which he created roles in *Judgment of Paris*, *Gala Performance*, and *Soirée musicale* (all 1938). In 1939 he left with Tudor for the US where he was principal dancer with Ballet Theatre (later American Ballet The-atre) between 1940 and 1950 and created roles in Fokine's *Bluebeard* (1941), Massine's *Aleko* (1942), and de Mille's *Tally Ho* (1944), and several more Tudor ballets including *Pillar of Fire* (1942), *Romeo and Juliet* and *Dim Lustre* (both 1943), *Undertow* (1945), and *Nimbus* (1950). In 1950 he moved to New York City Ballet where he created several more roles in, for example, Tudor's *Lady of the Camellias* (1951) and Balanchine's *Bayou* (1952). He also danced in Balanchine's *Tyl Ulen-spiegel* and *Prodigal Son* in which he was much acclaimed. Between 1954 and 1956 he again danced with ABT, and appeared in musicals in London and on Broadway. He retired from the stage to become a commercial photographer, also assisting Tudor in many restagings of his ballets. He was married to dancer Diana Adams between 1947 and 1953.

Lake, Molly (*b* Cornwall, 3 Jun. 1900; *d* London, 2 Oct. 1986) British dancer and teacher. She stud-ied with Astafieva and Cecchetti and danced in the companies of Pavlova and Markova-Dolin. In 1945 she co-founded the Embassy Ballet (subse-quently Continental Ballet) with her husband, Travis Kemp, and M. Honer. In 1954 she was appointed director of the Ankara Conservatoire and remained there for twenty years, returning to London to teach at the London School of Con-temporary Dance and at her own school.

La La La Human Steps Montreal-based mod-ern dance company. It specializes in high-tech staging and in a style of fast, athletic dance chor-eographed by Édouard Lock and for many years embodied in the virtuoso performances of its lead-ing female dancer, Louise Lecavalier. It emerged out of Lock's company Lock-Danseurs (formed 1980) and in 1981 won Canada's prestigious Jean

A. Chalmers choreographic award for the production *Oranges*, followed by a Bessie for *Human Sex* in 1985. With *New Demons* (1987) the company established an international reputation, which was expanded by worldwide broadcasts of their performance with rock star David Bowie in 1990 and by European concert appearances with Frank Zappa (1992). Later productions have included *2* (mus. various, 1995), *Amelia* (mus. David Lang, 2002), and *Amjad* (mus. Gavin Bryars and others, 2007).

Lamb, Sarah (*b* Boston, 17 Oct, 1980) American dancer. She trained at Boston Ballet School (1994–98), and joined the company in 1998, promoted to principal in 2003. She then moved to the Royal Ballet as first soloist and was promoted to principal in 2006. A dancer whose delicate proportions belie her powerful technique and dramatic attack, she dances a wide range of repertory, and has created roles in Alastair Marriott's *Tanglewood* (2005), Wheeldon's *Fire* (part of *Homage to The Queen*, 2006) and *Electric Counterpoint* (2008), and McGregor's *Chroma* (2006).

Lambada Latin American dance in 4/4 time. Originating from Brazil, it evolved into a fast, sensual couple dance, performed in close physical contact and fusing elements of the samba and rumba. It acquired international popularity in the 1980s. A modern variant is Zouk, slightly less acrobatic but with an emphasis on turns.

Lambert, Constant (*b* London, 23 Aug. 1905; *d* London, 21 Aug. 1951) British conductor and composer who played a seminal role in the development of English ballet. He studied at the Royal College of Music and wrote his first ballet score, *Romeo and Juliet*, for Diaghilev (chor. Nijinska, 1926). In 1930 he became conductor of the Camargo Society and between 1931 and 1947 was music director of the Vic-Wells Ballet (becoming Sadler's Wells Ballet) where, with his commitment to the Diaghilevian ideal of unity between dance, music, and design, he exercised a major influence on the artistic as well as musical direction of the company. His close association with Ashton began with *Pomona* (1930), using the score he had originally written for Nijinska in 1927, and continued with his scores for *Rio Grande* (1932), *Horoscope* (1938), and *Tiresias* (1951). He additionally arranged the scores for several other Ashton ballets including *Les Rendezvous* (mus. Auber, 1933) and *Les Patineurs* (mus. Meyerbeer, 1937), as well as writing the libretto and selecting Liszt's music for *Apparitions* (1936). Other arrangements included those for de Valois's *The Prospect Before Us* (mus. W. Boyce, 1940) and Helpmann's *Comus* (mus. Purcell, 1942). During the war he played the piano for the company's

performances and after resigning his post in 1947 was re-appointed music director of Sadler's Wells Ballet in 1948, conducting their first New York performance in 1949. He was author of *Music Ho! A Study of Music in Decline* (London, 1934). His wife Isabel designed Ashton's *Tiresias* and *Madame Chrysanthème*.

Lambranzi, Gregorio Eighteenth-century Venetian choreographer and ballet master. His book *Neue und Curieuse Theatralische Tantz-Schul* (Nuremberg, 1716) contains written descriptions, drawings, and melodies for 50 contemporary dances including sarabande, bourrée, and rigaudon as well as military, sport, and trading dances. The English translation was published in 1928 (by F. Derra de Moroda) and a facsimile edition by Dance Horizons (New York, 1972).

Lamentation Modern dance work in one act with choreography and costume by Graham and music by Kodály. Premiered 8 Jan. 1930 at Maxine Elliott's Theater, New York, with Graham. It is set to Kodály's Piano Piece, Op. 3, No. 2 and features a single dancer who remains seated throughout the work. Swathed in a tube of jersey material her swaying, keening movements are a distillation of profound grief. It became one of Graham's signature pieces and was filmed in 1943.

La Meri (orig. Russell Meriwether Hughes; *b* Louisville, 13 May 1899; *d* San Antonio, Tex., 7 Jan. 1988) US dancer, teacher, and writer. She studied various ethnic dance forms in the US and the Far East and performed them on extensive tours. In 1938 she founded the New York School of Natya with St Denis (later Ethnological Dance Center) and its performing ensemble Exotic Ballet. She taught and lectured widely and wrote many books, including *Principles of the Dance Art* (1933) and *Gesture Language of the Hindu Dance* (New York, 1941).

Lamhut, Phyllis (*b* New York, 14 Nov. 1933) US dancer and choreographer. She studied with Nikolais and Lewis and became a leading dancer with Nikolais's company. She began creating her own works in 1950, which were performed in recitals at the Henry Street Playhouse, and subsequently by the Limón company. Between 1970 and 1996 she directed her own company, for which she choreographed many works and after 1996 she taught choreography and improvisation for the New York University Tisch School of the Arts.

Lancaster, Sir Osbert (*b* 1908; *d* London, 27 Jul. 1986) British painter, cartoonist, author, and ballet designer. He created the designs for Cranko's *Pineapple Poll* (1951) and *Bonne-Bouche* (1952), de Valois's *Coppélia* (1954), Ashton's *La*

Fille mal gardée (1960), and Lander's *Napoli* (London Festival Ballet production, 1954). He was knighted in 1975.

Lanchbery, John (*b* London, 15 May 1923; *d* 27 Feb. 2003) British conductor and composer. He was musical director of the Metropolitan Ballet (1947-9) and in 1951 joined Sadler's Wells Theatre Ballet, becoming principal conductor of the Royal Ballet in 1960. Between 1972 and 1978 he was musical director of Australian Ballet, after which he moved to American Ballet Theatre (1978-80). He then worked freelance, as musical arranger and conductor for ballet companies world-wide. His musical arrangements include the scores for MacMillan's *Mayerling* (1978), Ashton's *La Fille mal gardée* (1960), *The Dream* (1964), and *A Month in the Country* (1976)—all for the Royal Ballet; Nureyev's *Don Quixote* (Australian Ballet, 1966) and *La Bayadère* (Paris Opera, 1991), Hynd's *The Merry Widow* (Australian Ballet, 1975), and *The Hunchback of Notre Dame* (Houston Ballet, 1988), and Stevenson's *The Snow Maiden* (Houston Ballet and American Ballet Theatre, 1998). He composed the scores for several films, including Ross's *The Turning Point* (1977).

Landé, Jean-Baptiste (*b* date unknown; *d* St Petersburg, 26 Feb. 1748) French dancer and ballet master. He danced in Paris, Dresden, and Stockholm where he was also royal dancing master (1721-7). In 1734 he was invited to St Petersburg to arrange a performance at a dancing school for young aristocrats. His success inspired the foundation of a much larger school in 1738 under his direction, which became the basis of the St Petersburg Imperial Ballet School.

Lander, Harald (orig. Alfred Bernhardt Stevnsborg; *b* Copenhagen, 25 Feb. 1905; *d* Copenhagen, 14 Sept. 1971) Danish-French dancer, choreographer, director, and teacher. He studied at the Royal Danish Ballet School under Beck from 1913, joining the company in 1923. Later he studied Russian folk dance in the USSR (1926-7) and then went to the US to study ballet with Fokine, Tarasoff, and Bolm (1927-9). In 1929 he returned to RDB as a solo dancer (principal) and created his first ballet, *Gaucho* (mus. Ressen), for the company in 1931. Between 1932 and 1951 he was its artistic director and oversaw a period of creative revitalization. He raised technical standards among the dancers, introduced new ballets from Europe, initiated the renaissance of the Bournonville repertoire and himself choreographed about 30 ballets, working with a variety of styles and subject matter. These included *Football* (mus. Poulenc, 1933), *Bolero* (mus. Ravel, 1934), *The Little Mermaid* (mus. Henriques, 1936),

The Seven Deadly Sins (mus. Weill, 1936), *The Sorcerer's Apprentice* (mus. Dukas, 1940), and *Étude* (Czerny, arr. Riisager, 1948). After a disagreement with the directors of the Royal Theatre he moved to Paris in 1951 to become resident choreographer at the Paris Opera (taking French citizenship in 1956). Here he created *Printemps à Vienne* (mus. Schubert, 1954) and *Concerto aux étoiles* (mus. Bartók, 1956) and mounted revivals of Galeotti's *The Whims of Cupid* and the flowers act from *Les Indes galantes*. He also re-staged *Étude* for the company as *Études* in 1952. He directed the Opera school (1956-7 and 1959-63) and also worked widely abroad staging his own works and mounting the ballets of Galeotti and Bournonville for companies including the Grand Ballet du Marquis de Cuevas, London Festival Ballet, American Ballet Theatre, and La Scala Milan. In 1962 he returned to Copenhagen to choreograph *Les Victoires de l'amour* (mus. Lully, 1962) and reinstate some of his old works. He was married to the dancers Margot Lander (1932-50), Toni Lander (1950-65), and then to Lise Lander. He was made Knight of the Dannebrog in 1951 and awarded the Medal of Honour of the City of Paris.

Lander, Margot (*née* M. Florentz-Gerhardt; *b* Copenhagen, 2 Aug. 1910; *d* Copenhagen, 19 Jul. 1961) The most important Danish ballerina of the first half of the 20th century. She studied at the Royal Danish Ballet School from 1917 and joined the company in 1928, becoming solo dancer (principal) in 1933 and first solo dancer (prima ballerina) in 1942 (the first to be given the title in Denmark). Although not an outstanding technician she had exceptional personality and grace, and created roles in many of Lander's ballets (she was married to Lander from 1932 to 1950), as well as dancing works from the Bournonville repertory. She was also much admired in *Coppélia* and *Swan Lake*. She retired in 1950.

Lander, Toni (*née* T. Pihl Petersen; *b* Copenhagen, 19 Jul. 1931; *d* Salt Lake City, 19 May 1985) Danish dancer and teacher. She studied at Royal Danish Ballet School from 1939 and joined the company in 1948, becoming solo dancer (principal) in 1950. Her powerful technique and long, strong lines were given their perfect showcase in Lander's *Études* (which she inherited, after a few early performances, from Margot Lander), and in 1950 she and Lander were married. In 1951 she moved with him to Paris where she continued her studies with Egorova and Preobrajenska. Between 1951 and 1952 she was guest ballerina with Original Ballet Russe and between 1951 and 1954 with Paris Opera Ballet. She also made regular appearances as principal with London Festival Ballet (1954-9), Ballet Théâtre Français (1958), and

American Ballet Theatre (1961–71). In 1971 she returned to the Royal Danish Ballet as soloist and teacher, retiring from the stage in 1976. After divorce from Harald L. she married dancer Bruce Marks (1966). She was made Knight of the Dannebrog in 1957.

ländler A turning couple dance from Austria in 3/4 or 3/8 time which was very popular during the late 18th and early 19th centuries. It was a forerunner of the waltz.

Lane, Maryon (orig. Patricia Miller, *b* Zululand, 15 Feb. 1931; *d* 13 Jun. 2008) S. African dancer and teacher. She studied in Johannesburg and at Sadler's Wells School, joining Sadler's Wells Theatre Ballet in 1947, becoming principal in 1948, then moved to the Royal Ballet as soloist (1955–68). A petite, musical dancer and gifted actor she created roles in several MacMillan ballets including *Somnambulism* (1953), *Laiderette* (1954), *Danses concertantes* (1955), and *Diversions* (1961). She also created roles in Ashton's *Valses nobles et sentimentales* (1947) and *Ondine* (1958) and Cranko's *Prince of the Pagodas* (1957). In 1966 she danced with Ballet Rambert and after retiring from the stage taught at the Royal Ballet School before moving to Cyprus where she opened her own school in Kyrenia. She was married to dancer David Blair.

Lang, Pearl (*b* Chicago, 29 May 1922) US dancer, choreographer, and teacher. She studied with Graham, Horst, M. Stuart, and others and danced with Page in Chicago before joining Graham's company in 1941. As soloist (1942–52, and occasional guest after 1952) she created roles in *Diversion of Angels* (1948), *Canticle for Innocent Comedians* (1952), and *Ardent Song* (1954), and danced many other major roles, to which she brought a powerful lyricism and moral force. In 1952 she formed her own company for which she created many works including *Rites* (1953), *Shirah* (1960), and *The Possessed* (1975), as well as solos for herself including *Moonsong* and *Birdsong* (both 1952). She also appeared in several musicals and worked as a guest choreographer with various companies including Dutch National Ballet and Batsheva Dance Company. She taught and lectured widely.

Lanner, Katti (orig. Katherina Lanner; *b* Vienna, 14 Sept. 1829; *d* London, 15 Nov. 1908) Austrian dancer, choreographer, ballet mistress, and teacher; daughter of composer Joseph Lanner. She studied at the Vienna Court Opera School and made her debut in *Angelica* at the Kärntnertor Theater in 1845, where she continued to dance until 1856, appearing with Elssler and Cerrito. After the death of her father in 1856 she began travelling, dancing in Berlin, Munich, and Dresden, then touring Scandinavia and Russia. She was ballerina and ballet mistress at the State Theatre, Hamburg (1862–3), where, becoming the first woman to make a career as a regular choreographer, she created ten ballets. She then founded her own troupe, the Viennese Ballet Company, with which she danced in Europe and America (1869–72), and then, with a second troupe, the Kathi (*sic*) Lanner Choreographic Connection, she toured the US (1873–5). In 1876 she moved to London where she was ballet mistress at Her Majesty's Theatre (1877–81), choreographing divertissements for the Italian opera seasons, and then ballet mistress (1887–97) at the Empire Theatre. She turned this into London's most popular ballet venue, not only engaging Genée as ballerina in 1896 but also choreographing 34 ballets for the theatre. Her many works included *The Sports of England* (mus. Hervé, 1887), *Cleopatra* (mus. Hervé, 1889), *Orfeo* (mus. Wenzel, 1891), *On Brighton Pier* (mus. Ford, 1894), *Faust* (mus. Lutz, Ford, 1895), and *Sir Roger de Coverley* (mus. Carr, 1907). From 1876 she was also director and teacher of London's National Training School of Dancing and in her work here as well as in the theatre she was largely responsible for sustaining the English ballet scene during one of its least active periods.

Lany, Jean-Barthélemy (*b* Paris, 24 Mar. 1718; *d* Paris, 29 Mar. 1786) French dancer, choreographer, and ballet master. He was son of the ballet master Jean Lany and became solo dancer at the Paris Opera in 1740. In 1743 he went to Berlin where he choreographed several ballets in which Noverre danced. In 1747 he returned to Paris Opera as dancer then ballet master, and choreographed the first productions of several Rameau operas including *Platée* and *Zoroastre* (both 1749) and *Les Paladins* (1760). Noverre wrote admiringly of the musicality and vivacity of Lany's dancing, but he was considered to lack originality as a choreographer. In 1773 and 1775 he worked in Turin and London, then became a teacher in Paris where his pupils included Gardel and Dauberval. He was brother of Louise-Madeleine Lany.

Lany, Louise-Madeleine (*b* Paris, 1733; *d* Paris, 1777) French dancer, daughter of ballet master Jean Lany and sister of dancer and teacher Jean-Barthélemy Lany. She studied with her brother and made her debut at the Opéra Comique in 1743, appearing at the Paris Opera in 1747 where she remained until 1767 as one of its most brilliant virtuosos. She is said to have been the first female dancer to execute an entrechat six and huit. But although Noverre reckoned her 'the leading dancer in the world' by virtue of her 'beauty, precision, and daring' her reputation has since been eclipsed by *Sallé's.

Larionov, Mikhail (*b* Tiraspol, 22 May 1881; *d* Fontenay-aux-Roses, 10 May 1964) Russian painter and designer. He studied at the Moscow Institute of Painting, Sculpture, and Architecture where in 1900 he met his future wife, the artist *Goncharova. At Diaghilev's invitation he exhibited in the Union of Russian Artists section at the Salon d'Automne, Paris, in 1906 and then in 1914 settled in the city where he designed several Ballets Russes productions including Massine's *Soleil de nuit* (1915) and Nijinska's *Renard* (1922). His work was always based in popular Russian art though he was alert to contemporary trends, including the Futurists and played a strong role in guiding Diaghilev's artistic taste.

Larrieu, Daniel (*b* Marseilles, 23 Nov. 1957) French dancer and choreographer. He initially trained in horticulture, but became interested in dance and began performing in 1978 with Wes Howard's Quatuor de Danse, joining Régine Chopinot in 1982 and in the same year forming his own group, Astrakan. His piece, *Un sucre ou deux* (1982), based on a series of naturalistic gestures and accompanied by Prokofiev's *Romeo and Juliet*, won the Bagnolet choreographic competition of that year. A choreographer with an ironic, often surreal sense of humour, his most internationally famous work, *Waterproof* (1986, commissioned by the Centre National de Danse Contemporaine at Angers), was staged in a number of Olympic-sized swimming pools, with large video screens projecting underwater images to a collage of musical extracts. It was filmed for television and is still performed. Astrakan was based in Marne la Vallée (1990–2) and was re-named Compagnie Daniel Larrieu in 1993 when Larrieu was appointed director of the Centre Chorégraphique National de Tours. His later works for the company include *Un geste ou deux* (mus. various, 1995), *Delta* (mus. Scanner, Robin Rimbaud, 1996), *Cenizas* (mus. various, 2001), *Red et Noir* (2002), *Siamois d'Or* (mus. various 2004), and *Voyage en drakéole* (2008). He has also choreographed for several other companies, such as *Attentat poétique* for Paris Opera (1992) and for opera, including *Salomé* for Lyon (1990).

(((●))) **SEE WEB LINKS**

• Website for the Daniel Larrieu company

Larsen, Gerd (*b* Oslo, 20 Feb. 1921; *d* London, 4 Oct. 2001) Norwegian-British dancer. She studied with Craske and Tudor and made her debut with Tudor's London Ballet in 1938, where she created the role of the French ballerina in his *Gala Performance* (1938). She then danced with Ballet Rambert, International Ballet, and Sadler's Wells Ballet (from 1944), becoming soloist there in 1954. While a graceful classical dancer, she became best known as one of the Royal Ballet's mimes, outstanding in roles like the mother in *Giselle*. She was a senior teacher with the company and was married to the dancer Harold Turner.

Larsen, Niels Bjørn (*b* Copenhagen, 5 Oct. 1913; *d* 13 Mar. 2003) Danish dancer, choreographer, and ballet master. He studied at the Royal Danish Ballet School from 1920 and made his debut with the company in *Coppélia* when still a child. His official debut with RDB was in 1933 and after dancing various guest seasons with the Trudi Schoop Comic Ballet (1935–9) he was appointed solo dancer (principal) with RDB in 1942, becoming the company's most distinguished mime. During his performing career he created a wide variety of characters though he was most famous for his mysterious but touching Dr Coppelius. In 1940 he formed his own company with which he toured Scandinavia until 1946, then in 1951 he was appointed temporary artistic director of RDB, taking on the role officially between 1953 and 1956 and again between 1958 and 1965. He was also artistic director of Copenhagen's Tivoli Theatre (1956–80). From 1946 he taught at the RDB School and from 1947 taught with the company as well as choreographing extensively for ballet, opera, film, plays, and musicals, including *Peter and the Wolf* (mus. Prokofiev, RDB, 1960) and *The Little Mermaid* (mus. Henriques, Tivoli Theatre, 1977). His official farewell performance was as Madge in *La Sylphide* with RDB (1986) but he continued to work even into his eighties, teaching mime, performing character roles, and guesting with other companies. In 1995 he reconstructed *Konservatoriet*. He was father of the dancer Dinna Bjørn, and made Knight of the Dannebrog.

Last, Brenda (*b* London, 17 Apr. 1938) British dancer and ballet mistress. She studied with Volkova and at the Royal Ballet School and joined Western Theatre Ballet in 1957 creating roles in Darrell's *A Wedding Present* (1962), among others. In 1963 she joined the Touring Company of the Royal Ballet, becoming principal in 1965. A tiny, quick, extrovert dancer she created roles in several ballets including Ashton's *Creatures of Prometheus* (1970) and P. Wright's *Arpège* (1975). She was appointed ballet mistress of the Royal Ballet's New Group in 1974, while still dancing principal roles, notably Swanilda. She remained with Sadler's Wells Royal Ballet until 1977, then became director of Norwegian National Ballet (1977–80), after which she returned to teach in London.

Latvia Ballet in Latvia dates back to 1911 and the performance of opera divertissements at the Riga Opera House. In 1921 the first full-length ballet was performed in Riga, *La Fille mal gardée*, staged by N. Sergeyev from the Mariinsky Theatre. In 1932 a ballet school was founded in Riga and the ballerina Alexandra Fedorova became a major force in the city teaching, choreographing, and staging many ballets from the Russian classical repertoire (1925–37). Her work was aided by a succession of guest ballet masters including Fokine (1929) and Tikhomirov (1933). During the post-war period Elena Tangiyeva-Birzniece was ballerina and chief choreographer in Riga, creating the first Latvian-Soviet ballet, *Laima* (mus. Anatole Lepin, 1947). Evgeny Changa also choreographed many works between 1950 and 1961, including a version of *Spartacus* in 1960 and there has subsequently been a strong tradition of nurturing native choreographers including Irene Strode, Alexander Lembergs, and most recently Aivan Leimaris. There was also a ballet company at the Liepaja Opera House from the early 1920s to 1950 and a company is still active at the Riga Operetta Theatre. Modern dance is less active than ballet in Latvia but there are companies such as that led by Olga Zitluhina (who also teaches choreography at the Latvian Academy of Culture) and Dzirnas, led by Angris Danlevics. The Baltic Ballet Festival founded by Lita Beiris in 1995 showcases Baltic and international dance companies each year. Latvia has a flourishing folk dance scene headed by the company Daile, which was founded in 1968.

Laubin, Reginald and Gladys (Gladys Laubin, *née* Tortoiseshell; *b* Paterson, NJ; *d* 1996; Reginald Laubin, *b* Detroit; *d* Urbana, Ill., 5 Apr. 2000) US dancers, choreographers, and researchers. They lived on Native American Indian reservations for over twenty years, researching and giving concerts of indigenous dances. They published *Indian Dances of North America* (Oklahoma, 1975).

Laurencia Ballet in three acts with choreography by Chabukiani, libretto by E. Mandelberg, music by A. Krein, and design by S. Virsaladze. Premiered 22 Mar. 1939 by the Kirov Theatre, Leningrad, with Dudinskaya and Chabukiani. It is based on the 17th-century play *Fuente ovejuna* (The Sheep Well) by Lope de Vega and tells the story of a peasant uprising in a Castilian village, led by Laurencia and her fiancé, Frondoso. Created at the height of Soviet demands for 'choreodrama', Chabukiani's fusion of Spanish folk and classical dance created vivid character and local colour. It was very popular and was revived many times in Russia and E. Europe. The pas de six from Act I was staged by Nureyev for the Royal Ballet in 1965. Alexander Chekrygin's ballet on the same theme, *Comedians* (mus. Glière, Bolshoi, 1931), was later revised by Alexei Tchitchinadze as

A Daughter of Castile and premiered at the Stanislavsky and Nemirovich-Danchenko Music Theatre, Moscow, in 1955. Mikhail Messerer staged a new production of *Laurencia* for the Mikhailovsky Ballet in 2010, the first time the ballet had been revived in half a century.

Lausanne, Prix de *See* COMPETITIONS.

Lauterer, Arch (*b* 1904; *d* Oakland, Calif., 1957) US set and lighting designer. He based his principles of design on Appia's writings, using light and architectural forms to create a fluid, uncluttered space for dance. He taught at Bennington College (1933–43) and collaborated with many choreographers, including Graham, Humphrey, Holm, and Weidman.

Lavallade, Carmen de (*b* Los Angeles, 6 Mar. 1931) US dancer. She studied with Melissa Blake and C. Maracci and became a leading dancer with Horton's company in 1950. She was a celebrated beauty and also appeared in films, such as *Carmen Jones* (1954), and on Broadway. In 1956 she began working with J. Butler, creating roles in several of his ballets, including *Carmina Burana* (1959) and *Portrait of Billy* (1960). She also danced with the companies of Ailey, Tetley, and McKayle, New York City Opera, and American Ballet Theatre. Her husband, Geoffrey Holder, choreographed several works for her including her trademark solos *Three Songs for One* (1963) and *Come Sunday* (1968). In 1970 she was appointed to the Yale Drama faculty to teach movement to actors, and also worked as an actress but she continued to dance and to choreograph her own work, including productions at the Metropolitan Opera and also *Bitter Sweet Love* for the Ailey company in 2000. In 1999 she celebrated 50 years of her career in a performance with her stage partners, Gus Solomons jun. and Dudley Williams. She has continued to teach and lecture widely including at Adelphi University.

Lavery, Sean (*b* Harrisburg, Pa., 16 Aug. 1956) US dancer. He studied with R. Thomas and B. Fallis and in 1972 joined San Francisco Ballet. In 1974 he moved to Frankfurt Ballet, danced as guest artist with U.S. Terpsichore in 1976, and in 1977 joined New York City Ballet where he was promoted principal dancer in 1978. He danced both the classic and the Balanchine repertories and created roles in several ballets including Martins's *Symphony No. 1*. (1981). After retiring from the stage in 1986 he continued as ballet master with the company, also creating ballets, notably for Florida Ballet, such as *Classical Symphony* (mus. Prokofiev, 1998) and staging the Balanchine repertory for the Trust. In 2003 he joined the faculty of the School of American Ballet.

Lavrovsky, Leonid (*b* St Petersburg, 18 Jun. 1905; *d* Paris, 27 Nov. 1967) Soviet dancer, choreographer, director, and teacher. He studied at the Petrograd (later Leningrad) Ballet School, graduating into GATOB (later the Kirov) in 1922. He remained there until 1935, dancing principal roles as well as appearing with Evenings of Young Ballet (dir. Balanchine and V. Dmitriev) with which he created a role in Lopukhov's *Dance Symphony* (1923). He began to teach in 1922 and created his first ballet for the Leningrad Ballet School in 1928. In 1934 he choreographed the full-length *Fadetta* (mus. from Delibes's *Sylvia*, later staged by the Maly Theatre, 1936, and by the Bolshoi Ballet, 1952) and in 1935 *Katerina* (mus. Rubinstein and Adam, later staged by the Kirov, 1936). In 1935 he was made director of the Maly Theatre and in 1938 director of the Kirov where he remained until 1944. His commitment to narrative ballet, using an expanded classical vocabulary and powerfully stylized mime, was exemplified in works like *Prisoner of the Caucasus* (mus. Asafiev, 1938) and *Romeo and Juliet* (mus. Prokofiev, 1940). Between 1942 and 1943 he worked at the Spendiarov Theatre in Yerevan then in 1944 he became chief choreographer at the Bolshoi Ballet, remaining there until 1956 and returning again from 1960 to 1964. Here his most important productions included stagings of *Giselle* (1944) and *Raymonda* (1945) and new ballets such as *The Red Poppy* (mus. Glière, 1949), *The Legend of the Stone Flower* (mus. Prokofiev, 1954), *Paganini* (mus. Rachmaninoff, 1960), and *Night City* (set to Bartók's music for *The Miraculous Mandarin*, 1961), his later ballets showing a trend towards more abstract dance. He also mounted the definitive version of his *Romeo and Juliet* in 1946. Between 1959 and 1964 he also worked for Moscow's Ballet on Ice Company creating *A Winter Fantasy* (1959), among other works, and in 1964 he was appointed director of the Bolshoi Ballet School. He was also teacher at the Choreographer's Faculty of the Institute of Theatrical Art (1948–67), becoming professor in 1952. He was married to the dancer Yelena Chikvaidze and was father of the dancer Mikhail Lavrovsky. He was made People's Artist of the USSR in 1965.

Lavrovsky, Mikhail (*b* Tbilisi, 29 Oct. 1941) Soviet-Georgian dancer, choreographer, and director. The son of Leonid Lavrovsky, he studied at the Moscow Ballet School and graduated in 1961 into the Bolshoi Ballet. He became a principal, partnering such ballerinas as Bessmertnova and Semenyaka and excelling in the ballets of Grigorovich until finally retiring in 1988. After 1977 he was additionally guest principal dancer and guest choreographer for several seasons with Tbilisi Ballet, becoming its artistic director (1983–5). He made several works for that company including

Mziri (mus. Toradze, 1977), *Porgy and Bess* (mus. Gershwin, 1983), and *The Dreamer* (mus. Gershwin, 1989), but from the late 1980s has been based in Moscow as ballet master of the Bolshoi and subsequently as director of his own school. He has created works for the Moscow Chamber Ballet, *More Powerful than Gold and Death* (mus. Wagner, 1996) and the Bolshoi, *Fantasy on the Theme of Casanova* (mus. Mozart, 1993,) and *Matador* (2001). He has also choreographed for some Western companies, including Atlanta Ballet (1989). He was made People's Artist of the USSR in 1976.

Lawrence, Ashley (*b* Hamilton, NZ, 5 Jun. 1934; *d* Tokyo, 7 May 1990) British conductor. He studied at the Royal College of Music and became conductor of Touring Royal Ballet Company (1962–6). In 1966 he moved to Berlin Opera Ballet as conductor, then in 1970 to Stuttgart, rejoining the Royal Ballet in 1972, where he was music director from 1973 to 1987. He subsequently worked freelance, guesting with various companies including Paris Opera, Sadler's Wells Royal Ballet, and Royal New Zealand Ballet.

Lawson, Joan (*b* London, 1907; *d* 18 Feb. 2002) British dancer, teacher, and writer. She studied with Margaret Morris and Astafieva and danced in opera, revues, and with the Nemchinova-Dolin company, going on to teach at the Royal Ballet School (1963–71). She contributed to dance magazines as well as writing several books including *European Folk Dance* (London, 1953), *Classical Ballet, its Theory and Technique* (London, 1960), and *A History of Ballet and its Makers* (London, 1964). In two important manuals, *Teaching of Classical Ballet: Common Faults in Young Dancers* (London, 1973) and *Teaching Young Dancers: Muscular Coordination in Classical Ballet* (New York, 1975), she outlined her anatomical approach to the teaching of ballet.

Leaves are Fading, The Ballet in one act with choreography by Tudor, music by Dvořák, set by Ming Cho Lee, and costumes by P. Zipprodt. Premiered 17 Jul. 1975 by American Ballet Theatre at New York State Theater, New York, with Tcherkassky, Kirkland, Tippet, C. Ward, and Kage. Set to a selection of Dvořák's music (including the String Quartets, Opp. 77 and 80), it is a series of wistful romantic duets for seven couples which seem to embody a woman's nostalgic memories. Unusually for Tudor, it is a near-plotless work. It is in the repertory of several companies, including the Royal Ballet, the Kirov, Paris Opera, and Ballet West.

LeBlanc, Tina (*b* Erie, Pa., 17 Oct. 1966) US dancer. She trained locally and at the School of American Ballet, School of American Ballet

Theatre, and School of Pennsylvania Ballet and danced with Central Pennsylvania Ballet (1975–82), Joffrey II, and Joffrey Ballet (1982–92) before joining San Francisco Ballet as principal from 1992 to 2009. A very versatile dancer, her repertory ranged from Lise in Ashton's *La Fille mal gardée* to Balanchine's *Rubies* and she created roles in many works, including Bintley's *The Dance House* (1994), Morris's *Pacific* (1995), Tomasson's *Criss-Cross* (1997), and Wheeldon's *Quaternary* (2005).

Leclair, André (*b* Brussels, 29 Jan. 1930) Belgian dancer, choreographer, and director. He studied with M. Querida and V. Gsovsky and in 1947 danced with Ballets des Champs-Elysées, becoming dancer with Béjart's Ballet of the 20th Century, where he created roles in *Symphonie No. 9* (1966), among others. In 1956 he choreographed his first ballet and in 1966 was appointed ballet master of the Royal Opera Antwerp, becoming ballet director in 1968. In 1970 he was appointed chief choreographer of Ballet of Flanders. He created over 50 works, most of them showcases for virtuoso classical dance, including *Ritus Paganus* (mus. F. Glorieux, 1972).

LeClercq, Tanaquil (*b* Paris, 2 Oct. 1929; *d* New York, 31 Dec. 2000) US dancer and teacher. She studied with Mordkin and at the School of American Ballet, making her debut at Jacob's Pillow Festival in 1945. She joined Ballet Society (later New York City Ballet) as a soloist in 1946 becoming principal dancer in 1948. With her sophisticated, stylish technique and sharp intelligence she excelled in a wide repertory, creating roles in over 25 of Balanchine's ballets including *Four Temperaments* (1946), *Divertimento* (1947), *Bourrée fantasque* (1949), *La Valse* (1951), *Western Symphony*, and *Ivesiana* (both 1954), as well as roles in Ashton's *Illuminations* (1950) and Robbins's *Age of Anxiety* (1950), *Afternoon of a Faun* (1953), and *The Concert* (1956). Her career was cut short when she contracted polio on tour in Copenhagen in 1956, though she subsequently taught at Dance Theatre of Harlem (1974–82) and published two books, *Mourka, the Autobiography of a Cat* (New York, 1964) and *Ballet Cookbook* (New York, 1967). She was married to Balanchine (1952–69).

Lee, Mary Ann (*b* Philadelphia, Jul. 1824 (some sources say 1823); *d* Philadelphia, 25 Jan. 1899) US dancer and teacher, who was also the first US ballerina to gain local renown. She studied with Paul Hazard in Philadelphia and made her debut as a child actress *c*.1832. In 1837 she first appeared as a professional dancer in Philadelphia dancing in *The Maid of Kashmir* (an English version of *La Bayadère*), then became leading dancer at the Walnut Street Theatre, Phi-

ladelphia (1838–9). She made her New York debut in 1839, appearing in *La Bayadère* and *The Sisters*, and also danced some of Elssler's famous pieces which she learned from her partner James Sylvain, such as *La Cachucha*. In Boston in 1842 she danced the title role of Taglioni's *La Sylphide* in her own staging and in 1844 she went to study at Paris Opera with Coralli. On her return to the US she staged several major European ballets, including *Giselle* (Boston, 1946). She herself danced the title role, the first American to do so. She retired early in 1847, owing to illness, though she returned for occasional performances, and opened a school in Philadelphia in 1860.

Leeder, Sigurd (*b* Hamburg, 14 Aug. 1902; *d* Herisau, 20 Jun. 1981) German dancer, choreographer, ballet master, and teacher. His early interest in dance was developed by Sarah Norden, a student of Laban in Hamburg and in 1920 he made his debut at the Hamburger Kammerspiele, after which he founded his own group. In 1924 he joined Jooss's Neue Tanzbühne, moving with him to Essen in 1928 where they founded the Folkwang Tanz Theatre and co-directed the dance department of the Folkwang School. With Jooss he also emigrated to *Dartington, England, in 1934 where they co-directed the Jooss-Leeder School and in 1935 the Jooss Ballet. They moved to Cambridge in 1940, with Leeder becoming ballet master of the company until 1947 and choreographing *Sailor's Fancy* (mus. Martin Penny). After the company disbanded he opened his own school in London. Between 1955 and 1964 he was teaching in Santiago at the University of Chile, after which he moved his school to Herisau, Switzerland, where he remained until his death.

Lefèvre, Brigitte (*b* Moulins en Gilbert, 15 Nov. 1944) French dancer, choreographer, and director. She studied at the Paris Opera Ballet School from the age of 8 and entered the company aged 16, but continued her studies in other areas of modern dance and jazz, creating her first work, *Mikrokosmos* (mus. Bartók) for the Avignon Festival in 1970. In 1972 she left the POB to co-found the Théâtre du Silence with Jacques Garnier, which was based in La Rochelle (1974–85). Alongside their own work she and Garnier presented works by international choreographers, including Cunningham and Lubovitch. In 1985 she was appointed principal inspector of dance at the Ministry of Culture, in 1992 she became general director of the Paris Opera House and in 1994 deputy director of the Opera House and director of the ballet. From 1995 her duties were focused on artistic direction of the Paris Opera Ballet, and while maintaining the classical repertory she also pursued a policy of bringing in more modern repertory including works by Bausch and

Forsythe, and commissions from Ek, Preljocaj, Teshigawara, and others. She was made Chevalier of the Legion d'honneur in 2007.

Legat, Nicolai (*b* St Petersburg, 27 Dec. 1869; *d* London, 24 Jan. 1937) Russian dancer, ballet master, choreographer, and teacher. He studied with his father Gustav and at the Imperial Theatre School with Gerdt, Johansson, and others. He made his debut while still a student and in 1888 graduated into the Mariinsky Theatre, becoming principal and favoured partner to ballerinas like Legnani, Pavlova, Kshessinska, and Trefilova. Although too stocky to be considered an ideal danseur noble he was a brilliant technician, dancing in over 70 ballets during his career and creating roles in Petipa's *Kalkabrino* (1891) and Ivanov's *Nutcracker* (1892), among others. In 1902 he became assistant ballet master at the Mariinsky with his brother, Sergei, becoming chief ballet master from 1910. While he choreographed a few ballets (most famously *The Fairy Doll*, with his brother, mus. Bayer and others, 1903), he concentrated on teaching, taking over the Mariinsky's *classe de perfection* from Johansson in 1905. Among his pupils were Egorova, Preobrajenska, Vaganova, Karsavina, Fokine, Nijinsky, and Bolm. After a disagreement with the Mariinsky he left in 1914, teaching in various private schools, touring music halls in Paris and London with his wife Nadine Nicolayeva, and staging ballets for the popular theatre. In 1922 he left Russia for good, unable to find a place in the emerging Soviet ballet. He took over from Cecchetti as ballet master of Diaghilev's company (1925–6) then settled in London where he taught at his own studio. His pupils included Danilova, Lopokova, de Valois, Markova, Dolin, Eglevsky, and Fonteyn. After his death the school continued in his name, later moving to Sussex. He was also a clever caricaturist, publishing *Russian Ballet in Caricature* (St Petersburg, 1903, English edition, 1939).

Legat, Sergei (*b* St Petersburg, 27 Sep. 1875; *d* St Petersburg, 1 Nov. 1905) Russian dancer; younger brother of Nicolai Legat. He studied at the Imperial Theatre School with Johansson and Gerdt, graduating in 1894 into the Mariinsky Theatre. Though six years his brother's junior he soon outshone him and by 1903 was appointed premier danseur. He also taught at the school (Nijinsky was one of his pupils) and worked as repetiteur at the Mariinsky. He committed suicide, apparently unbalanced by his unhappy relations with Maria Petipa (Petipa's daughter), his common-law wife, and by his anguish over the divisions caused by the dancers' strike of 1905.

Legend of Joseph (orig. Ger. title. *Die Josephslegende*; title of Paris first production *La Légende de Joseph*) Ballet in one act with choreography by Fokine, libretto by H. G. Kessler and H. von Hofmannsthal, music by R. Strauss, set by J. M. Sert, and costumes by Bakst. Premiered 14 May 1914 by Diaghilev's Ballets Russes at the Paris Opera with Kousnetzova and Massine—the latter's debut performance with the company. It is set to Strauss's ballet score of the same title and based on the biblical story in which Joseph virtuously rejects the lascivious advances of Potiphar's wife. However, its setting was updated to the court of a 16th-century Venetian doge and the ballet concluded with Potiphar's wife strangling herself with her rope of pearls. Later versions include Kröller (Berlin Staatsoper, 1921), Balanchine (Royal Danish Ballet, Copenhagen, 1931), Tudor (Teatro Colón, 1958), Neumeier (Vienna, 1977, the first purely dance version of the work), B. R. Beinert (Zurich), and Spoerli (Düsseldorf), both 1992.

Legend of Judith Modern dance work in one act with choreography by Graham, music by Mordecai Seter, and design by Dani Karavan. Premiered 25 Oct. 1962 by the M. Graham Dance Company at Habima Theatre, Tel Aviv, with Graham, L. Hodes, Ross, and Yuriko. It is an intimate, psychological portrait of the biblical character, focusing on her memories, visions, and moral conflicts.

Legend of Love (orig. Russ. title *Legenda o liubvi*) Ballet in three acts with choreography by Grigorovich, libretto by Nazim Hikmet, music by Arif Melikov, and design by Simon Virsaladze. Premiered 23 Mar. 1961 by the Kirov, Leningrad, with Kolpakova, Moisseyeva, Gribov, and Gridin. It is based on a play by the Turkish writer N. Hikmet and explores the conflict between love and duty through the story of its heroine, Queen Mekhmene-Banu. She sacrifices her beauty to save the life of her ailing sister Shirien, but regrets her action when Shirien falls in love with her own lover, the painter Ferkhad. On her orders, he sacrifices his love for Shirien to go and build a waterway through the Iron Mountain to bring water to his thirsty people. Unusually for its era, the work eschewed the mime-orientated narrative of much Soviet ballet, relying on pure dance to tell the story. It was re-staged for the Bolshoi (by Grigorovich) in 1965 and was frequently performed in E. Europe.

Léger, Fernand (*b* Argentan, 4 Feb. 1881; *d* Gif-sur-Yvette, 17 Aug. 1955) French painter and designer, best-known for the monumental forms of his 'machine aesthetic'. He created the designs for Börlin's *Skating Rink* and *La Création du monde* (both 1923), Lifar's *David triomphant* (1937), and Charrat's *Léonard de Vinci* (1952).

Legnani, Pierina (*b* Milan, 30 Sept. 1868; *d* Milan, 15 Nov. 1930) Italian ballerina. She studied with Beretta in Milan and in 1890 appeared as prima ballerina at London's Alhambra Theatre in Casati's ballet *Salandra*. In 1892 she was appointed prima ballerina at La Scala then moved to St Petersburg in 1893 where she was prima ballerina at the Mariinsky Theatre until 1901. Here she created numerous roles for Petipa including the title role of *Cinderella* (1893), Odette-Odile in *Swan Lake* (1895), and the title roles in *Raymonda* (1898) and *Camargo* (1901). A dancer of unusual technical brilliance and refinement, her most celebrated feat was executing 32 continuous fouetté turns, which she first performed in *Aladdin* at the Alhambra in 1892. She was appointed prima ballerina assoluta at the Mariinsky (the only official holder of this title apart from Kshessinska) and spurred Russian dancers to emulate her virtuosity. After retiring from the stage she lived in Italy and served on the examining board of La Scala Ballet School until four months before her death.

Legris, Manuel (*b* Paris, 19 Oct. 1964) French dancer. He studied at the Paris Opera Ballet School and entered the company in 1980, when he was promoted étoile in 1986. A stylist of considerable wit and subtlety he remained with the company until 2009, dancing both the classical and modern repertoires and creating roles in several ballets, including *France/Dance* (Forsythe, 1983), *Magnificat* (Neumeier, 1987), and *Sylvia* (Neumeier, 1997). He also guested with other companies including performances of *Onegin* with Stuttgart. In 1996 he founded his own occasional touring group, giving opportunities to younger dancers and in 2010 became artistic director of the Vienna State Opera Ballet and its associate school.

(((⊕))) **SEE WEB LINKS**
• Website for Manuel Legris

Leibovitz, Annie (*b* Westbury, Conn., 2 Oct. 1949) US photographer. She studied at San Francisco Art Institute and became a freelance professional photographer in 1970, working for the Rolling Stones and for *Vanity Fair*, among others. She has created highly personalized images of many dancers and choreographers including Mark Morris, Mikhail Baryshnikov, Merce Cunningham, and Bill T. Jones.

Lemon, Ralph (*b* Minnesota, 1953) US dancer and choreographer. He studied at the University of Minnesota and with Nancy Hauser, dancing with her company (1977–9). He moved to New York and danced with various companies including Meredith Monk's (1979–81) and in 1981 presented his first concert of work. He founded his

own company in 1985 for which he has choreographed many works including *Persephone* (mus. Davis, 1991). His works have also been performed by other companies, including the Alvin Ailey Repertory Ensemble (*Folkdance*, 1998) and Lyon Opera Ballet (*My Tears Have Been My Meat Night and Day*, 1994). In 1995 he disbanded his dance company to form the multi-disciplinary ensemble Cross Performance, working with dance, theatre, film and visual arts. His projects for this have included the trilogy *Geography* (1997–2005).

Leningrad *See* ST PETERSBURG.

Leningrad Ballet School *See* MARIINSKY BALLET; VAGANOVA, AGRIPPINA.

Leningrad Symphony (orig. Russ. title *Sedmaya simfoniya*) Ballet in one act with libretto and choreography by Belsky, music by Shostakovich, and design by Mikhail Gordon. Premiered 14 Apr. 1961 by the Kirov, Leningrad, with Sisova and Soloviev. It is set to the first movement of Shostakovich's 7th Symphony ('Leningrad'), and portrays the city's heroic resistance to the German siege of 1942. There are other versions by Massine (Ballet Russe Highlights, New York, 1945) and L. Ogoun (Brno, 1962).

leotard A close-fitting garment, like a bathing suit, with or without sleeves, made in supple stretch fabric. It was invented by the French acrobat Jules Léotard (1830–70) and is now commonly worn by dancers on stage and in rehearsal, as well as by sportsmen and women and keep-fit enthusiasts.

Lepeshinskaya, Olga (*b* Kiev, 28 Sept. 1916; *d* Moscow, 20 Dec. 2008) Soviet ballerina and teacher. She studied at the Moscow Ballet School and graduated into the Bolshoi in 1933 where she was ballerina until 1963. A model Soviet ballerina she was a joyful, impetuous dancer with a powerful, almost masculine, technique and a high flying jump. Celebrated in comedy roles like Lise in Gorsky's version of *La Fille mal gardée* (her debut role) and Kitri in *Don Quixote*, she also created roles in several ballets including Zakharov's *Taras Bulba* (1941), *Cinderella* (1945), and the Moscow version of Zakharov's *The Bronze Horseman* (1949). She made frequent international tours in a programme of concert pieces and taught widely after her retirement, also writing ballet reviews during the 1970s and 1980s. She was made People's Artist of the USSR in 1947.

LePicq, Charles (Lepic; Pick; Lepij) (*b* Naples, 1744 (some sources say Strasbourg 1749); *d* St Petersburg, 1806) French dancer and choreographer. He studied with Noverre in Stuttgart and danced with his company from 1761 becoming danseur sérieux in 1763. After 1764 he danced in many European cities with his wife, dancer Anna Binetti, and was celebrated for his elegant, courtly style. He also staged Noverre's ballets and from 1770 choreographed his own. He was at Paris Opera (1776–81) but the jealous intrigues of Vestris and Gardel prompted him to leave, first for Naples, then in 1782 to London's King's Theatre where he danced under Noverre, becoming ballet master himself in 1783. He then moved to St Petersburg where he was ballet master (1786–98) and married prima ballerina Gertruda Rossi. He staged ballets by Dauberval, Gardel, and Noverre there and also choreographed several of his own, including *Bergère* (1790), *Didon abandonnée* (1795), and *Tancrède* (1798). Throughout his career he remained a loyal supporter of Noverre, his works closely adhering to the latter's principles of *ballet d'action.

Le Riche, Nicolas (*b* Sartrouville, 29 Jan. 1972) French dancer. He studied at the Paris Opera Ballet School and graduated into the company in 1988, becoming étoile in 1993. The last of Nureyev's protégés in the company, he combined a virtuoso technique with a charismatic dramatic presence and was successful in both the classical and modern repertories. He created roles in several works, including Petit's *Camera Obscura* (1994), *Le Guépard* (with Ballet de Marseilles, 1995), Preljocaj's *Casanova* (1998), and Forsythe's *Pas/parts* (2000) and guested with several companies, most notably partnering Sylvie Guillem at the Royal Ballet, in *Romeo and Juliet* and *Marguerite and Armand* (the first to dance Nureyev's role since the ballet was created). He began choreographing his own works in 2001, including *Caligula* (mus. Vivaldi, 2005).

Leskova, Tatiana (*b* Paris, 1922) French-Brazilian dancer, choreographer, and ballet mistress. She studied with Egorova and others and made her debut at Paris Opera Comique in 1937. In 1938 she danced with Ballet de la Jeunesse, then from 1939 with Original Ballet Russe as a principal. She left for Rio de Janeiro in 1945 and appeared with various companies before becoming ballet mistress, dancer, and choreographer with the city's Teatro Municipal in 1950. Here she created many works and re-staged the classics, becoming artistic director (with Jorge García) in the late 1970s. She also founded her own school in the city. She subsequently worked as freelance ballet mistress, reviving Massine's *Les Présages* for Paris Opera (1989), Joffrey Ballet (1992), and Australian Ballet (2007) and his *Choreartium* for Birmingham National Ballet (1991).

Leslie, Natasha *See* KRASSOVSKA, NATHALIE.

Lesson, The (orig. Dan. title *Enetime*; often under French title, *La Leçon*) Television ballet in one act with choreography by Flindt, music by G. Delerue, and design by Daydé. Premiered on Danish television 16 Sept. 1963 with Flindt, Amiel, and T. Chelton. It is inspired by Ionesco's play of the same title but takes the original school-room scenario into the ballet studio. Here it shows a teacher becoming so crazily incensed by a female pupil's work that he kills her, the action suggesting that exactly the same scenario will be repeated the next day, with a different pupil. It was Flindt's first ballet and his most successful, receiving the Prix Italia and subsequently transferring to the stage. The first production was at Paris Opéra Comique, 6 Apr. 1964, with Flindt, Amiel, and L. Garden and it has since been revived by several companies, including Royal Danish Ballet (1964), Western Theatre Ballet (1967), City Center Joffrey Ballet (1968), San Francisco Ballet (1998), by Johan Kobborg (London, 2003), and the Royal Ballet (2005).

Lester, Keith (*b* Guildford, 9 Apr. 1904; *d* London, 8 Jun. 1993) British dancer, choreographer, and teacher. He studied with Dolin, Astafieva, N. Legat, and Fokine and made his debut in the latter's dances for *Hassan* in London, 1923. He danced in several concert tours, his partners including Kyasht (1924–6), Karsavina (1927–30), and Spessivtseva (1931). He also danced with various companies including Rubinstein's (Paris, 1934) and Markova-Dolin Ballet (1935–7) for which he also choreographed several works including *David* (mus. Jacobson, 1935) and *Pas de quatre* (mus. Pugni, 1936). In 1939 he danced with Tudor's London Ballet (also choreographing *Pas de déesses* to music by Pugni). In 1940 he founded Arts Theatre Ballet with H. Turner for which he created *Sylvia* (mus. Delibes, 1940), among others. From 1945 to 1960 he worked at London's Windmill Theatre as principal dancer and choreographer, staging over 150 shows and created the Windmill's famous fan dances. He was appointed principal teacher of London's Royal Academy of Dancing in 1964 and was made Fellow of the RAD in 1975.

Letestu, Agnès (*b* Paris, 1971) French dancer. She studied at the Paris Opera Ballet School from 1983 and graduated into the company in 1987 where she was promoted to premiere danseuse in 1993 and named étoile in 1997, after her performance in Nureyev's production of *Swan Lake*. A tall slender, aristocratic dancer with a natural gift for communicating emotion on stage, she has been equally successful in classical and modern repertories and has guested widely, including with National Ballet of Cuba, Dutch National Ballet, Tokyo Ballet, English National Ballet, and the Mariinsky.

Letter to the World Modern dance work in one act with choreography by Graham, music by H. Johnson, costumes by E. Gilford, and set by A. Lauterer. Premiered 11 Aug. 1940 by the Martha Graham Dance Company at Bennington College Theater, Vermont, with Graham, Dudley, Hawkins, and M. Cunningham. It is a psychological portrait of the poet Emily Dickinson, with extracts of her work spoken by an actress.

Levasseur, André (*b* Paris, 18 Aug. 1927) French designer. Known for the elaborate but chic style of his costumes, he created the designs for Ashton's *Birthday Offering* (1956), *La Péri* (1957), *La Valse* (1958), and *Raymonda pas de deux* (1962), Balanchine's *La Somnambule* (Cuevas production, 1957) and *Theme and Variations* (American Ballet Theatre, 1958), Taras's *Piège de lumière* (New York City Ballet production, 1964), and Lazzini's *Coppélia* (1965).

Levinson, André (*b* St Petersburg, 1 Jan. 1887; *d* Paris, 3 Dec. 1933) Russian critic and dance writer. While still a professor of Romance languages at St Petersburg University he was a vigorous writer of dance criticism, displaying in his articles a staunch defence of academic dance principles and attacking the reforms of Fokine and Diaghilev (though he became a champion of Isadora Duncan). In 1918 he left Russia for Paris where he taught at the Sorbonne and became one of the most influential critics in France. He published articles on a wide range of dance subjects and wrote many books including *Ballet romantique* (1919), *L'Œuvre de Léon Bakst* (1921), *La Danse au théâtre* (1924), *La Vie de Noverre* (1925), *Paul Valéry, philosophe de la danse* (1927), *La Argentina, Anna Pavlova* (both 1928), *Marie Taglioni, La Danse d'aujourd'hui* (both 1929), *Les visages de la danse* (1933), and *Serge Lifar* (1934).

Levi-Tanai, Sara (*b* Jerusalem, 1911; *d* Ramat Gam, 3 Oct. 2005) Israeli dancer, choreographer, and ballet director. She taught herself and in 1949 founded the *Inbal Dance Theatre, creating for it over 40 dances. including *Story of Ruth* (mus. Tuvia, 1961) and *Jacob* (mus. Mar-Haim, 1973).

Lewitzky, Bella (*b* Los Angeles, 13 Jan. 1916; *d* San Francisco, 16 Jul. 2004) US dancer, choreographer, and teacher. She studied with Horton, and as a dancer in his company was a major influence on his evolving style, creating leading roles in his *Sacre du printemps* (1937) and *Salome* (1938). With Horton William Bowne and her husband Newell Reynolds she formed the Dance Theatre, but by 1951 left to form her own school, Dance Associates. In 1966 she founded the Bella Lewitzky Dance Company with which she not only performed but for which she created many works in a pure dance vein, including *Kinaesonata* (1970). As choreographer, performer, and teacher she became one of the major exponents of modern dance on the West Coast. The group disbanded in 1995 but Lewitzky remained an active force in dance.

Liat Dror and Nir Ben-Gal Dance Company See DROR, LIAT.

Lichine, David (orig. David Lichtenstein; *b* Rostov-on-Don, 25 Oct. 1910; *d* Los Angeles, 26 Jun. 1972) Russian-US dancer, choreographer, and teacher. He studied with Egorova and Nijinska in Paris, making his debut there with Rubinstein's company in 1928 then going on to dance with Pavlova's company (1930), Nijinska's company, and Ballet de l'Opéra Russe à Paris (1931–2), and La Scala, Milan (1932). A versatile and engaging demi-caractère dancer, he was appointed principal dancer with Ballets Russes de Monte Carlo in 1932, staying with the company until 1941 during its subsequent reincarnations as de Basil's Ballets Russes and Original Ballet Russe, and creating roles in many ballets, including Balanchine's *Cotillon* and *Le Bourgeois gentilhomme* (both 1932), Massine's *Jeux d'enfants* (1932), *Choreartium* and *Les Présages* (both 1933), and *Union Pacific* (1934). He began to choreograph his own works for the company in 1933, his many ballets including *Francesca da Rimini* (mus. Tchaikovsky, 1937), *Prodigal Son* (mus. Prokofiev, 1938), and his most popular work, *Graduation Ball* (mus. Strauss, arr. Dorati, 1940). In 1941 he joined Ballet Theatre with his second wife Riabouchinska where he also choreographed one ballet and completed Fokine's *Helen of Troy* (mus. Offenbach, 1942). He returned for various seasons to the Original Ballet Russe (1946–8) and in 1947 worked at the Teatro Colón as principal dancer and choreographer. In 1948 he was choreographer with Ballets des Champs-Elysées creating *La Création* which was, unusually for that era, danced in silence. He then settled in Los Angeles, where he choreographed for film and commercial theatre and also worked as a freelance choreographer in Europe creating numerous ballets for London Festival Ballet, La Scala, and Berlin Opera Ballet, among others. After 1959 he concentrated on directing (with his wife) the Los Angeles Ballet Theatre and its school.

Lido, Serge (orig. Serge Lidoff; *b* Moscow, 28 Jan. 1906; *d* Paris, 6 Mar. 1984) Russian-French photographer. Though based in Paris he gained an international reputation for his dance photos, which were published in magazines and also collected in book form, such as *Danse* (1947) and *Les Étoiles de la danse dans le monde* (1975).

Liebeslieder Walzer Ballet in one act with choreography by Balanchine, music by Brahms, set by David Hays, and costumes by Karinska. Premiered 22 Nov. 1960 by New York City Ballet at New York's City Center with D. Adams, Hayden, Jillana, Verdy, B. Carter, Ludlow, Magallanes, and Watts. In this setting of Brahms waltzes (Opp. 52 and 65) for piano duet and four singers, Balanchine said he had meditated on the 'changing aspects of love'. The musicians perform from the left-hand side of the stage on which four couples dance variations on the waltz. During the first half the dancers are in ballroom dress but for the second the women have changed into tutus and pointe shoes and the dancing becomes more abstractly classical. It has since been revived by many companies including Vienna State Opera Ballet, Royal Ballet, Zurich Ballet, Pacific Northwest Ballet, Boston Ballet, and San Francisco Ballet. In the NYCB revival of 1984 at the State Theater it had a new set by David Mitchell and was danced by Farrell, McBride, Saland, Nichols, Lavery, Cook, I. Andersen, and Duell. Other settings of the same music include M. Morris's *New Love Song Waltzes* (1982) and *Love Song Waltzes* (1989) and Alston's *Waltzes in Disorder* (1998).

Lied von der Erde, Das See SONG OF THE EARTH.

Liepa, Andris (*b* Moscow, 6 Jan. 1962) Soviet-Russian dancer; son of Maris Liepa. He studied at the Moscow Ballet School (1971–81) and graduated into the Bolshoi Ballet. His lyrical, handsome style directed him towards the major classical roles and he was promoted soloist, then principal in 1983. In 1988 he and his partner Ananiashvili became the first Soviets to gain official permission to guest with an American company, dancing works from the Balanchine repertory with New York City Ballet. Later that year he was also given permission to dance with American Ballet Theatre where he remained until 1989. On his return he was appointed principal dancer with the Kirov, creating the title role in the second version of Vinogradov's *Petrushka* (1990), and he subsequently guested with Béjart in Lausanne, with Paris Opera, La Scala, Bolshoi, and Ballet Theatre of the Kremlin Palace of Congresses, Moscow. In 1993 he began collaborating with Isabelle Fokine on restoring some of Fokine's ballets for the Russian stage and has subsequently staged them worldwide. Since retiring from dancing he has worked as a freelance choreographer, producer, and director in areas including ballet galas, theatre, and video. He was made Honoured Artist of the Russian Federation in 1986.

(⊕) SEE WEB LINKS
• Website for Andris Liepa

Liepa, Maris (*b* Riga, 27 Jul. 1936; *d* Moscow, 26 Mar. 1989) Soviet dancer. He studied at the Ballet Schools of Riga (1947–50) and Moscow (1953–5) and made his debut with Riga's Latvian Theatre of Opera and Ballet in 1955. In 1956 he moved to the Stanislavsky and Nemirovich-Danchenko Music Theatre in Moscow as soloist, then in 1960 was appointed principal dancer with the Bolshoi where he remained until 1977. A passionate and charismatic performer, his most memorable creations were Farkhad in the Moscow version of *Legend of Love* (1965), Crassus in Grigorovich's *Spartacus* (1968), and Vronsky in *Anna Karenina* (Plisetskaya and others, 1972). After much research he revived Fokine's *Spectre de la rose* for himself and Bessmertnova in 1967. Between 1963 and 1980 he taught at the Moscow Ballet School, in 1983 he was appointed choreographer at the Sofia Opera House in Bulgaria, and was finally artistic director of Moscow's Theatre of Contemporary Musical Drama (1987–9). His first wife was Maya Plisetskaya. He was made Honoured Artist of the USSR in 1976.

Lifar, Serge (*b* Kiev, 2 Apr. 1905; *d* Lausanne, 15 Dec. 1986) Russian-French dancer, choreographer, director, and writer, who was largely responsible for the re-birth of 20th-century French ballet. He studied with Nijinska in Kiev (1921–3) and made his debut with Diaghilev's Ballets Russes in 1923 while continuing studies with N. Legat, Cecchetti, and Vladimirov. With his strikingly exotic looks, dramatic versatility, and ruthless dedication to the artform he emerged as the outstanding European male dancer of his generation, becoming soloist (1924) and premier danseur (1925). He created roles in many of Diaghilev's ballets including Nijinska's *Les Fâcheux* and *Le Train bleu* (both 1924), Massine's *Zéphire et Flore* (1935) and *Ode* (1928), and Balanchine's *La Chatte* (1927), *Apollon musagète* (1928), and *Prodigal Son* (1929). His first piece of choreography was a new version of Stravinsky's *Renard* (1929). After Diaghilev's death he was invited to Paris Opera, initially as premier danseur and as choreographer of *Creatures of Prometheus* (mus. Beethoven, 1929), but subsequently becoming étoile, choreographer, and director. On the strength of his personal prestige and irresistible enthusiasm he was able to revive the near moribund company, improving technical standards (particularly among the men) and reviving the classics such as *Giselle*, in which he himself danced a memorable Albrecht. He also choreographed many ballets—mostly with himself in the leading male role. These tended to be narrative, with the exception of the popular abstract ballet, *Suite en blanc* (mus. Lalo, 1943), and included *Bacchus et Ariane* (mus. Roussel, 1931), *Salade* (mus. Milhaud) and *Icare* (mus. Szyfer), both 1935, *David* *triomphant* (mus. Rieti) and *Alexander le grand* (mus. Gaubert), both 1937, *Sylvia* (mus. Delibes), *Le Chevalier et la damoiselle* (mus. Gaubert), *Istar* (mus. d'Indy), and *Bolero* (mus. Ravel), all 1941. Between 1938 and 1939 he was guest artist with Denham's Ballet Russe de Monte Carlo. In 1944 he left Paris after accusations of collaboration with the Germans and formed Nouveau Ballet de Monte Carlo for which he choreographed several works including *Aubade* (mus. Bach), *La Péri* (mus. Dukas), and *A Night on the Bare Mountain* (mus. Mussorgsky), all 1946. In 1947 he returned to Paris Opera where he remained until 1958, as choreographer, dancer, and director, creating, among other ballets, *Le Chevalier errant* (mus. Ibert) and *Phèdre* (mus. Auric), both 1950, *Blanche-Neige* (mus. Yvain, 1951), *Fourberies* (mus. Rossini, 1952), and *Romeo and Juliet* (mus. Prokofiev, 1955). He guested with other companies and from 1958 worked entirely freelance with Netherlands Ballet, London Festival Ballet, and Grand Ballet du Marquis de Cuevas, among others. Despite his prolific output few of his works are regularly performed today. As well as creating ballets he founded the Paris Institut Chorégraphique in 1947 which became Université de la Danse in 1957, and he wrote over 25 books, including the controversial *Traité de danse académique* (Paris, 1949) and *Traité de chorégraphie* (Paris, 1952), defending the principles of classical dance; also *Vestris, dieu de la danse* (Paris, 1950) and his autobiography, *Ma vie* (1965, Eng. trans., New York, 1970).

Lifeguards on Amager, The (orig. Dan. title *Livjaegerne pa Amager*, alternative English title *The King's Volunteers on Amager*) Ballet in two acts with choreography by Bournonville and music by W. Holm. Premiered 19 Feb. 1871 by the Royal Danish Ballet in Copenhagen. It portrays the Kings Volunteers flirting with local peasant girls as they stand guard against the British navy. The principal character was based on the musician Édouard du Puy, a notorious rake.

Life of the Bee Modern dance work in one act with choreography by Humphrey and music by Hindemith. Premiered 31 Mar. 1929 by the Humphrey-Weidman Group at the Guild Theater, New York. It depicts the birth and death of a queen bee, using a vocabulary of distorted movements and exaggerations of scale and speed. At its original performances it was accompanied by off-stage humming, later by Hindemith's Kammermusik No. 1.

Ligeti, György (orig Sándor; *b* Dicsöszentmárron, 1923) Hungarian composer. He wrote no ballet scores but his concert music has been used by several choreographers, including Wheeldon

in *Polyphonia* (several piano scores, 2001), *Morphoses* (String Quartet No. 1, 2002), and *Continuum* (2002), Armitage in *Ligeti Essays* (various pieces, 2007), de Keersmaeker in *Achterland* (piano études, 1990) and Alston in *Volumina* (2006).

Lightfoot, Paul (*b* Kingsley, 31 Aug. 1966) British dancer and choreographer. He studied at the Royal Ballet School and joined the Junior Group of Nederlands Dans Theater (now NDT2) in 1985. In 1987 he joined NDT1 as dancer and in 1989 created his first professional work, *The Bard of Avon*, for NDT2. In 1991 he formed a choreographic partnership with Sol Léon, with whom he has since created over 30 works, developing a strikingly imagistic style. Their first work for NDT1 was *Seconds* (1992) followed by *Solitaire* (mus. Bach, 1994), which won the Lucas Hoving Prize, and *Start to Finish* (mus. Purcell, Tollet, Albinoni, Handel, and The Cranberries, 1996). In 2002 Lightfoot and Léon were appointed joint resident choreographers of NDT and in 2003 artistic advisers to the company. Their recent works together include *Shutters Shut* (2001), *Shoot the Moon* (mus. Glass, 2006), and *Same Difference* (mus. Glass, 2007).

🌐 **SEE WEB LINKS**

• Website for Nederlands Dans Theater

Lilac Garden Ballet in one act with choreography and libretto by Tudor, music by Ernest Chausson, and designs by Hugh Stevenson (who also collaborated on the libretto). Premiered 26 Jan. 1936 by Ballet Rambert at the Mercury Theatre, London, with Maude Lloyd, Laing, Tudor, and van Praagh. Set to Chausson's *Poème*, it is one of *Tudor's first great psychological ballets exploring the secret emotional lives of a quartet of Edwardian lovers. On the eve of her marriage Caroline encounters the man she really loves, along with the woman who, unknown to her, is her fiancé's discarded mistress. The ballet has been revived for many companies, including American Ballet Theatre (1940), New York City Ballet (1951), National Ballet of Canada (1953), Royal Ballet (1968), Royal Danish Ballet (1970), Les Grands Ballets Canadiens (1980), Royal Swedish Ballet (1985), Paris Opera Ballet (1985), National Ballet of Cuba (1986), and the Kirov Ballet (1991).

Limón, José (*b* Culiacán, 12 Jan. 1908; *d* Flemington, NJ, 2 Dec. 1972) Mexican-US dancer, choreographer, and teacher. Though originally intending to be a painter he studied dance with Humphrey and Weidman and developed into a performer of magnificent intensity. He danced with their company from 1930 to 1940, as well as appearing in Broadway musicals and touring with M. O'Donnell. In 1942 he married costume designer P. Lawrence and after serving in the Second World War he formed his own company (1946), with Humphrey as artistic director and himself, Kroner, Currier, B. Jones, and Hoving as soloists. Its repertory featured works by Humphrey and Limón himself including his most famous piece, *The Moor's Pavane* (mus. Purcell, 1949). During the 1950s the company expanded to present larger ensemble works. A choreographer of deep moral sensibility, Limón's other dances included *The Traitor*, based on Judas' betrayal of Christ (mus. G. Schuller, 1954), *There is a Time*, inspired by the great Ecclesiastes passage (mus. Dello Joio, 1956), *Missa Brevis*, portraying the survival of faith in Communist Europe (mus. Kodály, 1958), and *The Unsung* (1970), a work danced in silence, honouring Native American warriors. He taught at the Juilliard School and various colleges and after his death the company continued to function in New York with the aim of preserving his and Humphrey's work. Under the direction of Carla Maxwell (appointed 1978) the Limón Dance Company has also been committed to commissioning and staging new work. Some of Limón's dances have been revived by other companies, for example *Missa Brevis* by Ailey's company and *The Moor's Pavane* by American Ballet Theatre, National Ballet of Canada, Royal Swedish Ballet, and Nureyev and Friends (UK), among others, and *Chaconne* by Phoenix.

(( )) SEE WEB LINKS
• Website for the Limón Dance Company

Linden, Anya (*née* Eltenton; *b* Manchester, 3 Jan. 1933) British dancer. She studied with Koslov in Hollywood and at the Sadler's Wells School, joining Sadler's Wells Ballet in 1951. She was promoted to soloist in 1954 then principal in 1958 and created roles in several ballets, including MacMillan's *Noctambules* (1956) and *Agon* (1958) and Cranko's *Prince of the Pagodas* (1957). She retired in 1965 but as Lady Sainsbury became an influential force in British ballet. She was co-editor (with Crisp and Brinson) of *Ballet Rambert: 50 Years and On* (London, 1981).

lindyhop American jazz couple dance, danced to Swing music. It first appeared at Harlem's Savoy Ballroom in the 1920s where black dancers embellished the choppy steps of the Charleston with increasingly flamboyant improvised moves—fast spins, cartwheels, throws, and jumps where the woman leaped with her legs straddling her partner's waist or shoulders. After it became popular with white dancers it was known as the jitterbug. It enjoyed a major revival in Britain and the US during the 1980s and 1990s, led by veteran performers such as Frank *Manning and Norma Mill-

er and companies such as the London-based Jiving Lindy Hoppers.

Lin Hwai-min (*b* Taiwan, 19 Feb. 1947) Taiwanese choreographer and director. He studied Chinese opera movement in Taiwan, classical court dance in Japan and Korea and modern dance in New York, founding *Cloud Gate Dance Theatre in 1973. Some of his works, such as *Songs of the Wanderers* (1994), have drawn on Asian literary sources while his choreography has developed a distinctive blend of traditional Eastern theatre styles with Western dance techniques. The visual imagery of his work is central to many of his productions, with the use of mirrors, lighting, and painted surfaces amplifying the choreography of works such as *Moonwater* (mus. Bach 1998) and *Wild Cursive* (mus. several, 2005) His works, which tour internationally, are in the repertories of some foreign companies including *Smoke* (2002) for Zurich Ballet. In 1983 Lin founded the dance department at Taiwan's National Institute of the Arts, and in 2000 he became artistic director of the Novel Dance Series, bringing experimental dance artists to Taiwan. He has also directed opera, including *Rashomon* at Graz (1996) and *Tosca* in Taiwan (2002). He contributed choreography to Guillem's solo in *Sacred Monsters* (2006). He is recipient of the Raman Magsaysay award, among many others.

(( )) SEE WEB LINKS
• Website for Cloud Gate Dance Theatre

Linke, Suzanne (*b* Lüneburg, 19 Jun. 1944) German dancer and choreographer. She studied at the Mary Wigman Studio, Berlin (1964–7), and at the Folkwang School in Essen (1967–70), dancing with Folkwang Dance Studio (1970–3) and collaborating with P. Bausch and others. She then became choreographer with the Rotterdam Dance Centre from 1970, then at the Folkwang Dance Studio (1975–85), creating works such as *Satie* (1977) and *Ballet of Woman* (medieval music, 1981) and developing the contemporary expressionist style with which she has subsequently handled her distinctively political and autobiographical concerns. From 1985 she worked freelance, creating works on herself and her own group, such as *Affekte* (*Emotions*, mus. Pierre Henry, 1990), as well as for other companies, such as *?Tristan und Isolde?* (mus. Ludger Brümmer, 1992) for Nederlands Dans Theater. In 1994 she was appointed co-director (with Urs Dietrich) of the Bremer Tanztheater for which he choreographed, among others, *Hamletszenen* (mus. Ronald Steckel, 1996), and in 1996 was also appointed artistic director of the Choreographic Centre NRW in Essen. Between 2000 and 2001 she was artistic director of the choreographic centre

Zollverein, in Essen. She continues to perform, often reworking her own solos for other dancers.

Liszt, Ferenc (Franz) (*b* Raiding, 22 Oct. 1811; *d* Bayreuth, 31 Jul. 1886) Hungarian composer. He wrote no ballet scores but his concert music has frequently been used for dance by, among others, Fokine (*Les Préludes*, 1913, also chor. by St Denis in 1928), Nijinska (*Hamlet*, 1934), T. Gsovsky (*Orphée*, 1955, also chor. by Milloss, 1966), P. Darrell (*Othello*, the first movement of *Faust Symphony*, 1973), and A. Page (. . . *now langorous, now wild* . . . set to *Hungarian Rhapsodies* Nos. 6, 15, and 17, 1996). Arrangements of Liszt's music have been used for Nijinska's *Le Bien-aimé* (1928), Ashton's *Mephisto Waltz* (1934), *Apparitions* (1936), *Dante Sonata* (1940), and *Marguerite and Armand* (1963), for MacMillan's *Mayerling* (1978), and Stevenson's *Dracula* (1997), among others.

Littlefield, Catherine (*b* Philadelphia, 1905 (some sources say 1908); *d* Chicago, 19 Nov. 1951) US dancer, choreographer, teacher, director, and pioneering force in American ballet. She studied with her mother, Caroline Littlefield, later with Albertieri in New York and with Staats and Egorova in Paris, making her debut on Broadway in 1921. From 1926 she appeared in local performances of the Grand Opera Company and in 1934 formed her own Catherine Littlefield Ballet Company, which two years later became the Philadelphia Ballet (the first ballet company of exclusively US dancers). Here she was dancer and choreographer, creating *Barn Dance* (trad. US music, 1937), and also staging the first US full-length production of *Sleeping Beauty* (1937). The company performed in Europe in 1937, and from 1939 until it was disbanded in 1942 (due to the war) was the resident ballet company of Chicago Civic Opera. During the 1940s she choreographed for Broadway musicals and made pioneering contributions to the artistry of ice dance, choreographing notably for Sonja Henje's revues (1942–8). She continued to teach, and her pupils included D. Krupska, Z. Solov, and E. Caton.

Little Humpbacked Horse, The (orig. Russ. title *Konyok-gorbunok*) Ballet in four acts with choreography and libretto by Saint-Léon and music by Pugni. Premiered 15 Dec. 1864 at the Bolshoi Theatre, St Petersburg, with Marfa Muravieva and Nikolai Troitzky. It is based on the popular Russian fairy-tale by Pyotr Yershov and tells the story of Ivanushka, a young man who destroys the power of the wicked Khan and wins the hand of the Tsar-Maiden by accomplishing various spectacular feats with the help of the little Humpbacked Horse. It concludes with a grand divertissement celebrating the different nations of Russia, as Saint-Léon, con-

sciously trying to appeal to Russian taste, was eager to include (his versions of) Russian national dance. In 1895 it was revived by Petipa at the Mariinsky Theatre, St Petersburg, with a new prologue and apotheosis and some additional dances. Gorsky choreographed two later versions in 1901 and 1914 and though little remained of the original it became established as a major national ballet and a popular vehicle for ballerinas. Radunsky choreographed his own version to a new score by Shchedrin for the Bolshoi Theatre, Moscow, in 1960 and Belsky created his version to the same score for the Maly Theatre in Leningrad in 1963 as did Ratmansky in his new version for the Mariinsky (2009). The Radunsky version was filmed in 1961 with Plisetskaya and Vasiliev. The underwater scene from the Gorsky version is danced by Les Ballets Trockadero de Monte Carlo.

Little Stork, The (orig. Russ. title *Aistynok*, alternative English title *The Baby Stork*) Ballet in three acts with choreography by Radunsky, Lev Pospekhin, and Popko, music by D. Klebanov, and design by R. Makarov, T. Diakova, and V. Zimin. Premiered 6 Jun. 1937 at a graduation performance of the Bolshoi Ballet School at the Bolshoi Filial Theatre with Struchkova. It tells the story of a lost stork rescued by children whose good fortune is paralleled by that of a small black African boy who escapes oppression by finding shelter in the USSR. Other versions include Grigorovich's (Leningrad, 1948).

Livry, Emma (orig. Emma-Marie Emarot; *b* Paris, 24 Sept. 1842; *d* Neuilly, 26 Jul. 1863) French dancer. She studied at the Paris Opera School and later with Taglioni, making her debut with the Paris Opera aged 16 in the title role of *La Sylphide*. She was appointed to premiere danseuse the same year. A dancer of an unusually light poetic quality, she created roles in three works, including M. Taglioni's *Le Papillon* (1860), before the tragic accident which ended her life. During the dress rehearsal for *La Muette de Portici* in 1862 her dress was set alight by the theatre's gas lamps, and she died eight months later from the resulting burns.

Lloyd, Gweneth (*b* Eccles, 1901; *d* 1 Jan. 1993) British-Canadian teacher and choreographer. She studied at the Ginner-Mawar Dance School in London and after moving to Canada founded (with B. Farrally) the Winnipeg Ballet Club in 1938, which subsequently became the Royal Winnipeg Ballet and School. She choreographed many works for the company including the first all-Canadian ballet, *Shadow on the Prairie*, until she left it in 1958. She also established a school in Toronto in 1950.

Lloyd, Margaret (*b* South Braintree, Mass., 1887; *d* Brookline, Mass., 29 Feb. 1960) US critic and writer. She wrote dance criticism for the *Christian Science Monitor* (1936–60) and was also author of the classic *Borzoi Book of Modern Dance* (1949).

Lloyd, Maude (*b* Cape Town, 16 Aug. 1908; *d* London, 27 Nov. 2004) South African-British dancer and critic. She studied with H. Webb in Cape Town and with Rambert from 1927, becoming one of the first dancers in Rambert's company. A dancer of particular clarity and intelligence she became a leading dancer, inheriting many of Markova's roles and also creating leading roles in, among others, Tudor's *Lilac Garden* (1936) and *Dark Elegies* (1937). In 1938 she moved to Tudor's London Ballet as dancer (becoming co-director in 1939), creating one of the ballerina roles in *Gala Performance* (1938). She also danced briefly with the Markova-Dolin Ballet but in 1941, two years after marrying art critic Nigel Gosling, she retired from the stage. In 1951 she and Gosling began contributing joint ballet reviews to the magazine *Ballet* under the pseudonym Alexander Bland. In 1955 Bland became dance critic of the *Observer* and, until Gosling's death in 1982, published several books including *The Nureyev Image* (London, 1976) and *A History of Ballet and Dance* (London, 1976).

Lock, Édouard (*b* Casablanca, 3 Mar. 1954) Canadian dancer and choreographer. He studied film at Concordia University and dance with Le Groupe Nouvelle Aire, which he subsequently joined. In 1979 he was invited by Les Grands Ballets Canadiens to choreograph a workshop production and in 1980 he formed his own company, Lock-Danseurs which became La La La Human Steps in 1985. His 1981 work, *Orange*, was awarded a Jean A. Chalmers award, and *Human Sex* (1985) a Bessie. Recent works for his own company include *Étude* (mus. Gavin Bryars, 1996), and *Salt* (mus. various, 1998) and *Amelia* (mus. David Lang, 2002). In 2002 he created *André Auria* for Paris Opera. His strenuously athletic movement language and his exploration of multi-media (video, song, text, rock music) have also made him a natural collaborator with rock artists like David Bowie.

(((●))) SEE WEB LINKS

• Website for La La La Human Steps

Locking *See* ELECTRIC BOOGALOOS.

London The first London ballet performances were given by French and Italians during the 17th and 18th centuries, though two English men, John *Weaver (dancer, choreographer, teacher, and writer) and John *Rich (impresario and mime artist) were also influential personalities within the dance scene. Rich presented M. Sallé and her brother in London in 1725 and London's taste for ballet was further whetted by A. Vestris and Noverre performing seasons at the King's Theatre and Drury Lane, as well as by Didelot's work at the King's Theatre (1796–80). However, efforts to establish an English academy of dancing by the English ballet master James Harvey *D'Egville were unsuccessful and the domination of foreigners continued with *Blasis's appointment as ballet master at the King's Theatre (1830–40), M. *Taglioni's debut in 1830, and *Perrot's appointment as ballet master at Her Majesty's Theatre (1842–8) under the direction of B. *Lumley. Here Perrot created *Pas de quatre* (1845) for Taglioni, Cerrito, Grisi, and Grahn and London became briefly one of the most active ballet centres in the world. After Lumley's resignation, however, ballet was allowed to slide at Her Majesty's and performances continued largely in the programmes of music halls, such as the Alhambra and Empire where K. *Lanner and *Genée were the dominant dance personalities. The arrival of Russian-based companies at the beginning of the 20th century and regular seasons by Diaghilev's *Ballets Russes provided an important new stimulus to British ballet, and during the 1920s and 1930s London saw the establishment of seminal schools and companies by *Rambert and de *Valois, as well as the foundation of the *Camargo Society and various short-lived companies like the *Markova-Dolin company and Tudor's *London Ballet. Between these, the first solid generation of English dancers and choreographers was nurtured. After the war de Valois's *Sadler's Wells Ballet moved to Covent Garden, to become the Royal Ballet in 1956. In the late 1960s the foundation of the *London Contemporary Dance School and Theatre, and Ballet Rambert's switch to a modern repertoire, opened up a new modern dance scene. With the founding of international festivals, such as London's *Dance Umbrella in 1978, the proliferation of small- and middle-scale companies, and the emergence of venues capable of programming a wide range of styles, notably Sadler's Wells Theatre, London has become one of the most diverse and cosmopolitan dance cities in the world.

London Ballet British ballet company founded by Walter Gore in 1961. With Hinton as its ballerina and a repertory consisting of Gore's ballets, including *The Night and the Silence*, *Light Fantastic*, *Peepshow*, and *Rencontre*, and selected classics, such as *Giselle* and Act II of *Swan Lake*, it gave its first performance in Jul. 1961 at Hindlesham Hall near Ipswich. It appeared at the Edinburgh Festival that year and toured extensively in Britain and abroad but ceased operations in 1963.

London Ballet, The British ballet company formed by Antony Tudor and Agnes de Mille in 1938. It first performed under the name Dance Theatre at Oxford Playhouse, becoming the London Ballet in Dec. 1938 when it performed at its London base, Toynbee Hall. Its repertory consisted of works which Tudor had created for Ballet Rambert, such as *Lilac Garden* and *Dark Elegies*, plus new ballets, including *Judgment of Paris*, *Soirée musicale*, and *Gala Performance*. Among its dancers were P. Clayden, G. Larsen, M. Lloyd, van Praagh, and Laing. After Tudor and Laing went to New York, Lloyd and van Praagh became co-directors, expanding the repertory with Howard's *La Fête étrange*, among others. In June 1940 it was subsumed into Ballet Rambert.

London Contemporary Dance School Modern dance school founded by Robin *Howard in 1966, the first European school authorized to teach the Graham technique. Based at The Place, N. London, it was directed by Robert *Cohan and though its main teaching style was grounded in Graham it also offered classes in other techniques, including classical ballet, Cunningham, and Limón. Many of the first generation of British modern choreographers, including Richard *Alston and Siobhan *Davies, studied there. It has subsequently evolved a more formal curriculum which embraces dance history and criticism as well as performance and choreography. Veronica Lewis has been director since 1998.

London Contemporary Dance Theatre British modern dance company. It made its debut as the Contemporary Dance Group in 1967, with students from London Contemporary Dance School, and gave its first full season as LCDT in 1969 at the Place Theatre. Under the direction of Robert *Cohan its early repertory featured works by Graham, Ailey, Taylor, Sokolow, and increasingly Cohan himself, but American works were soon replaced by company choreography by, among others, Alston, R. North, and S. Davies (the last two becoming associate choreographers in 1974). As the company expanded (to about twenty dancers) it played a key role in developing a British audience for modern dance, touring extensively round the UK as well as abroad (its US debut was at the American Dance Festival, 1974). By the mid-1980s it began to lose its artistic edge and in 1989 Dan *Wagoner took over as director. He introduced new European and American works (including his own) as well as choreography by company members, including Jonathan Lunn and Darshan Singh Bhuller, but as a more varied repertory company it failed to secure a new popular image. After a succession of short-term directorships it was disbanded in 1996 and the newly formed Richard *Alston

Dance Company took over as resident dance company of The Place.

London Festival Ballet *See* ENGLISH NATIONAL BALLET.

Lopatkina, Uliana (*b* Kerch, 23 Oct. 1973) Russian-Ukrainian dancer. She studied at the Vaganova Academy under Dudinskaya, and graduated into the Kirov (later Mariinsky) in 1991, where she was rapidly promoted to principal. A dancer whose extreme pliancy and slenderness facilitates an apparently boneless fluidity, she has been outstanding in the Romantic roles such as Giselle and Odette. However, she has also danced ballerina roles in the rest of the classical and Soviet repertory, and performs some of the modern repertory such as *Symphony in C*, *Jewels*, *In the Night*, and *Le Jeune Homme et la mort*. She has toured with the Mariinsky throughout the world .

López, Pilar (*b* San Sebastian, 4 Jun. 1912 (some sources say 1906); *d* Madrid, 25 Mar. 2008) Spanish dancer, choreographer, and sister of legendary dancer La Argentinita. She studied with J. Castelão in Madrid and danced with her sister's company until La Argentinita's death in 1945. In 1946 she formed her own company, Ballet Español, which trained many of Spain's leading male dancers, including J. Greco, M. Vargas, and A. Gades who all subsequently formed their own companies. She herself was a dancer of great elegance, energy, and style, and also choreographed many works including *Le Tricorne* and *El amor brujo* (both to music by de Falla) and a setting of Rodrigo's *Concierto de Aranjuez*.

Lopokova, Lydia (Lopukhova) (*b* St Petersburg, 21 Oct. 1891; *d* Seaford, 8 Jun. 1981) Russian-British dancer, sister of Andrei and Fyodor Lopukhov. She studied at the Imperial Theatre School with Fokine, making her debut when still a child and graduating in 1909 into the Mariinsky Theatre. In 1910 she joined Diaghilev's Ballets Russes and performed with that company for many seasons before its disbanding in 1929. During this period she also danced in the US, both on Broadway and in Mordkin's company, and in London with Massine, Sokolova, de Valois and Woizikovsky. A dancer of considerable charm and musicality, who displayed an infectious pleasure in performing, she was at her best in witty demi-caractère roles. She created roles in Massine's *Les Femmes de bonne humeur* and *Parade* (both 1917) and *Boutique fantasque* (1919), and was also one of the Auroras in Diaghilev's production of *The Sleeping Princess* (1921). Having settled in London with her husband, the economist John Maynard Keynes, she was a founder member of the Camargo Society creating the

Tango in Ashton's *Façade* (1931) and dancing Swanilda in the Vic-Wells Ballet's production of *Coppélia* (1933). She also worked as an actress at various times between 1910 and 1916, 1923 and 1924, and during the 1930s, performing Olivia in *Twelfth Night* (1933) and Nora in *A Doll's House* (1934). With Keynes she founded the Cambridge Arts Theatre in 1935.

Lopukhov, Fyodor (Lopokov, Fedor) (*b* St Petersburg, 20 Oct. 1886; *d* Leningrad, 28 Jan. 1973) Russian-Soviet dancer, choreographer, and teacher; brother of Lydia Lopokova. He studied at the Imperial Theatre School, graduating in 1905 into the Mariinsky Theatre, where he became one of its greatest character dancers. He transferred to the Bolshoi (1909–10) and also danced abroad, with Sedova and Legat (various tours in 1907 and 1909) and with Lopokova (1910–11), but then remained largely in Leningrad where he maintained a more-or-less close association with the Mariinsky (later GATOB, and Kirov) until 1970. He created his first ballet in 1916 and was one of the first Soviet choreographers to experiment with contemporary themes in, for example, *The Red Whirlwind* (mus. V. Deshevov, GATOB, 1924), in which he mixed classical ballet with acrobatics. In 1921 he initiated Evenings of Young Ballet with Slonimsky and was director of the Kirov (1922–30, 1944–7, and 1955–8). He was director of the Bolshoi Ballet (1926 and 1935–6) and in 1930 he founded the ballet company of Leningrad's Maly Opera House, which he directed until 1935. His other ballets include the controversial *Dance Symphony* (mus. Beethoven, 1923, performed only once), versions of Stravinsky's *Firebird* (1921), *Pulcinella* (1926), and *Renard* (1927), *The Ice Maiden* (mus. Grieg, 1927), *The Bolt* (mus. Shostakovich, 1931), and *Taras Bulba* (mus. Soloviev-Sedov, 1940), as well as *Pictures from an Exhibition* (mus. Mussorgsky, 1963, for Stanislavsky and Nemirovich-Danchenko Ballet). During his career he was also renowned for his productions of the classics for which he created several new variations in the style of Petipa, including the Lilac Fairy variation, but in his 1935 ballet *The Bright Stream* (mus. Shostakovich, Maly Theatre) he was accused by *Pravda* of formalism and fell into an official disgrace from which his career took several years to recover. He later exerted an important influence on Grigorovich's choreographic career, and was director of the choreographic faculty at Leningrad Conservatory (1962–73). He wrote several books, including *Paths of Ballet* (Berlin, 1925), *Sixty Years in Ballet* (Leningrad, 1966), and *Choreographic Confessions* (Moscow, 1972). Father of dancer Vladimir Lopukhov. His brother Andrei Lopukhov (1898–1947) was also a noted character dancer with the Mariinsky from 1916 to 1945.

Loquasto, Santo (*b* Wilkes-Barre, Pa., 26 Jul. 1944) US costume designer. He studied at the Yale School of Drama and designed for regional theatre before moving to New York in 1971. He has subsequently proved his versatility, working in film (especially with Woody Allen), theatre, and dance, and creating costumes as well as sets. He has been a long-time collaborator with Twyla Tharp, designing *Sue's Leg* (1975), *Push Comes to Shove* (1976), *The Catherine Wheel* (1981), and *Sextet* (1992). He has also worked closely with James Kudelka, designing *Alliances* (1987), *Spring Awakening* (1994), *The Nutcracker* (1995), and *Swan Lake* (1999). Other designs include Robbins's *The Four Seasons* (1979), American Ballet Theatre's *Cinderella* (1983), Morris's *Motorcade* (1990), and Paul Taylor's *Company B* (1991).

Lorca, Federico García (*b* Fuentevaqueros, 5 Jun. 1898; *d* Viznar, 19 Aug. 1936) Spanish poet and playwright. Many dance works have been inspired by his life and writings including Humphrey's *Lament for Ignacio Sánchez Mejías* (mus. N. Lloyd, 1947), *Blood Wedding* (Rodrigues, mus. Aplvor, 1953 and Gades, mus. Emilio de Diego, 1974), Reita Soffer's *Yerma* (mus. G. Crumb), Bruce's *Ancient Voice of Children* (mus. G. Crumb, also many other settings of the same score), and Bruce and L. Kemp's *Cruel Garden* (mus. C. Miranda, 1977). His 1936 play *The House of Bernarda Alba* has been most frequently used, in Ailey's *Feast of Ashes* (mus. Surinach, 1962) and MacMillan's *Las Hermanas* (mus. Martin, 1963), among others.

Loring, Eugene (orig. LeRoy Kerpestein; *b* Milwaukee, *c.*1911; *d* Kingston, NY, 30 Aug. 1982) US dancer, choreographer, and teacher. He studied dance and acting locally, then at the School of American Ballet from 1933 with Balanchine, Vilzak, Schollar, and others. He made his professional debut in 1934 with Fokine's company and joined American Ballet in 1935 where he stayed until 1938, creating roles in Balanchine's *Alma Mater* and *Card Game* (both 1935). He also danced with Ballet Caravan (1936–8) where he began to choreograph, creating works of distinctively American theme and character like his cowboy ballet *Billy the Kid* (mus. Copland, 1938). He was then soloist with Ballet Theatre (1940–1) and in 1941 formed his own company, Dance Players, for which he was choreographer and principal dancer. During the 1940s he worked on Broadway as dancer and choreographer, then moved to Los Angeles where he opened his American School of Dance in 1948 and also choreographed several films, including *Funny Face* (in collaboration with Astaire, 1956) and *Silk Stockings* (1957). He went on to choreograph other ballets including *Capital of the World* (mus. Antheil, American Ballet Theatre, 1953) and musical productions. In 1965 he became chairman of the Dance Department at the University of California.

Lorrayne, Vyvyan (*b* Pretoria, 20 Apr. 1939) S. African dancer. She studied with Salaman and Faith de Villiers, danced with Durban Civic Ballet, then studied further at the Royal Ballet School from 1956. In 1957 she joined Covent Garden Opera Ballet and then the Royal Ballet where she was appointed principal in 1967. A softly classical stylist, she created roles in several ballets including Ashton's *Monotones* (1965), *Jazz Calendar* and *Enigma Variations* (both 1968), Hynd's *Charlotte Brontë* (1974), P. Wright's *Arpège* and *El amor brujo* (both 1975), and Bintley's *Meadow of Proverbs* (1979). She retired in 1979.

Losch, Tilly (orig. Ottilia Ethel Leopoldine; *b* Vienna, 15 Nov. *c.*1904; *d* New York, 24 Dec. 1975) Austrian dancer, choreographer, actress, and painter. She studied at the Vienna Opera Ballet School and danced with the company (1921–8), creating her first major role in Kröller's *Schlagobers* (1924). During this period she also acted in plays at the Vienna Burg Theatre and choreographed and performed in Max Reinhardt's *A Midsummer Night's Dream* (Salzburg and New York, 1927). She then toured in recitals and revues before joining Les Ballets 1933, the company financed by her husband, Edward James. Here she created principal roles in Balanchine's *Errante* and *The Seven Deadly Sins*. The company disbanded after a year on her divorce from James, and she turned to film, appearing in exotic dancing acting roles. In 1940 she was guest artist with Ballet Theatre. From 1950 onwards she concentrated on painting.

Loudières, Monique (*b* Choisy le Roi, 15 Apr. 1956) French dancer. She studied at the Paris Opera Ballet School, and graduated into the company in 1972, where she was appointed étoile (1982–96). An extremely versatile dancer, she performed both the classical and modern ballerina roles and created roles in several works including Ailey's *Precipice* (1983), Nureyev's *Washington Square* (1985), and Larrieu's *Attentat poétique* (1992). After officially retiring from the stage she returned to create a role in Neumeier's *Sylvia* (1997) and to dance in *Giselle* in the 1998 homage to Yvette Chauviré.

Louis, Murray (*b* New York, 4 Nov. 1926) US dancer, choreographer, and teacher He studied with Halprin and Nikolais, performing with the latter's company between 1948 and 1969 and also teaching at the Henry Street Playhouse school where Nikolais was director. In 1953 he began choreographing for an *ad hoc* group of dancers which became the Murray Louis Dance Group

and which toured Europe for the first time in 1972. A dancer of unusual physical wit and sharp comic timing, his own choreography was often humorous in style. He went on to create over 50 works including *Calligraph for Martyrs* (1962, extended version for Berlin Opera Ballet, 1975), *Junk Dances* (1964), a three-act version of *Scheherazade* (mus. Rimsky-Korsakov plus jazz, rock, and electronic additions, 1975), *Moment* (mus. Ravel, 1975), *Five Haikus* (mus. Scriabin, 1979), *Four Brubeck Pieces* (mus. Brubeck, 1984), and *The Disenchantment of Pierrot* (mus. various, 1986). In 1989 he and Nikolais merged their two companies into Murray Louis Nikolais Dance, a company of which Louis became sole director in 1993 after Nikolais's death and for which he created *Alone* (a solo tribute to Nikolais), *Singers All* (mus. Scott Killian, 1996), and *Symphony* (mus. Nikolais, 1996), among others. In 1999 the Nikolais-Louis Dance Foundation phased out the company to focus on education although it also formed a relationship with the Ririe-Woodbury Dance Company to ensure the maintenance and performance of the Nikolais-Louis repertory. Louis has taught widely, in workshops and masterclasses, produced the film series *Dance as an Artform* in 1972, and published two books of essays, *Inside Dance* (New York, 1980) and *On Dance* (Chicago, 1992). As one of the directors of the Foundation he has also published a manual and a video series to illuminate and promote the Nikolais-Louis dance technique.

⊕ SEE WEB LINKS
• Website for the Nikolais-Louis Dance Foundation

Loup, Le Ballet in one act with choreography by Petit, libretto by Anouilh and G. Neveux, music by Dutilleux, and design by Carzou. Premiered 17 May 1953 by Ballets de Paris at Théâtre de l'Empire, Paris, with Petit, Verdy, Sombert, and Reich. It tells the story of an engaged couple who encounter a magician and his half-tamed wolf. The bride-to-be falls in love with the wolf, who in response attempts to become more human. They go into the forest together but are hunted down and killed. It was revived for Royal Danish Ballet in 1967 and for Paris Opera in 1975. Several other versions of the story have been choreographed by Walter and Keres, among others.

Louther, William (*b* New York, 22 Jan. 1942; *d* London, 7 May 1998) US dancer, choreographer, and teacher. He studied at the High School of Performing Arts and at the Juilliard School with Tudor and Graham and danced in O'Donnell's company in 1958. He subsequently performed with the companies of Ailey, Graham, and McKayle as well as in Broadway musicals and on television. A superb technician, projecting a profound sincerity, he created roles in McKayle's *District Storyville* (1959), Graham's *Circe* (1964), and *Archaic Hours* (1969), and in the revised version of Ailey's *Hermit Songs*. In 1966 he was leading dancer in the revue *Black New World*, and in 1969 joined London Contemporary Dance Theatre where he created roles in Cohan's *Stages* (1971) among others. He choreographed several works including *Vesalii Icones* (mus. Peter Maxwell Davies, 1970). Between 1972 and 1974 he was director of Batsheva Dance Company and between 1975 and 1976 director of Welsh Dance Theatre. He subsequently worked as freelance choreographer and teacher for opera and theatre as well as for dance, although his activities were curtailed by poor health.

Løvenskjold, Herman (*b* Holdenjernvärk, 30 Jul. 1815; *d* Copenhagen, 5 Dec. 1870) Norwegian-Danish composer. His most famous ballet score was for Bournonville's *La Sylphide* (1836) but he also composed the music for Bournonville's *New Penelope* (1847) and contributed to the score of his *Fantasies* (1838).

Loves of Mars and Venus Ballet d'action in six scenes with libretto and choreography by J. Weaver and music by Symonds and Firbank. Premiered 2 Mar. 1717 at Drury Lane Theatre, London, with L. Dupré, Santlow, and Weaver. It re-told the mythological story of Vulcan trapping his wife Venus and her lover Mars in his net, and employed a range of unusually naturalistic gestures and facial expressions. It was an early but sophisticated attempt to explore the dramatic possibilities of dance, and was also one of the first instances of a ballet which aimed to convey a full-length story rather than functioning as a divertissement. Extracts were reconstructed by M. Skeaping for the Royal Ballet's Ballet for All (1969).

Lubovitch, Lar (*b* Chicago, 9 Apr. 1943) US dancer and choreographer. He studied painting then turned to dance which he studied at the Juilliard School and with Sokolow, Danielian, and Graham. He made his debut in 1962 with P. Lang and also danced with the companies of Tetley and Butler as well as Manhattan Festival Ballet and Harkness Ballet (1967–9). He also worked as costume and lighting designer for Ailey and Falco and in 1968 began to choreograph, forming his own company in that year and subsequently also working as a guest choreographer for Bat-Dor Company, Gulbenkian Ballet, Dutch National Ballet, Ballet Rambert, and American Ballet Theatre. A prolific choreographer with an exuberant style of movement and a sure popular touch, his works include *Whirligogs* (mus. Berio, 1970), *Considering the Lilies* (mus.

Bach, 1972), *North Star* (mus. Glass, 1978), *Cavalcade* (mus. S. Reich, 1981), and *Othello* (mus. Goldenthal, 1997). He has created works for many other companies including New York City Ballet, Paris Opera Ballet, White Oak Dance Project, and Pacific Northwest Ballet and diversified his talents into other areas. In 1993 he choreographed a ballet for the Broadway production of *Red Shoes* which was subsequently taken into the repertory of ABT. He also choreographed the London production of *Oklahoma!* (1994), the Broadway revival of *The King and I* (1996), and the stage version of Disney's *The Hunchback of Notre Dame* (Berlin, 1999). Since the mid-1980s he has also created ice dances for skaters such as John Curry and Paul Wylie. His recent work for his company includes *My Funny Valentine* (mus. Martin Laird, 2001) which featured in Altman's film *The Company*, *Elemental Brubeck* (mus. Brubeck, 2005), and *Dvořák Serenade* (mus. Dvořák, 2007).

(( )) SEE WEB LINKS
• Website for the Lar Lubovitch company

Lucifer Modern dance in one act with choreography by Graham, music by Halim El-Dabh, set by L. Locsin, and costumes by Halston. Premiered 19 Jun. 1975 by the Martha Graham Dance Company, at Uris Theater, New York, with Nureyev and Fonteyn. The titular hero is presented as a prototype of the creative artist rather than as Satan.

Lüders, Adam (*b* Copenhagen, 16 Feb. 1950) Danish dancer. He studied at Royal Danish Ballet School and joined the company in 1968. He was then principal dancer with London Festival Ballet (1973–5) and New York City Ballet (1975–94) creating roles in Balanchine's *Davidsbündertänze* and Robbins's *In Memory of . . .* among others. Since retiring he has taught widly, including at the School of American Ballet, and staged the Balanchine repertory for the Balanchine trust.

Ludlow, Conrad (*b* Hamilton, Mont., 1935) US dancer. He studied at San Francisco Ballet School and joined the company in 1953 becoming principal in 1955. In 1957 he joined New York City Ballet where he became soloist (1961–73). He created roles in several Balanchine ballets including *Liebeslieder Walzer* and *Tchaikovsky pas de deux* (both 1960) and *Jewels* (1967). In 1973 he became artistic director of Oklahoma City Metropolitan Ballet and in 1985 became associated with the University of Utah dance department where he is now professor. He continues to teach, and to direct seasons performed by the Ballet of Utah.

Luigi (orig. Eugene Louis Facciuto; *b* Steubenville, Ohio, 20 Mar. 1925) US dancer and teacher. He studied with Bolm, Nijinska, Loring, and others and between 1949 and 1961 danced in theatres, films, night-clubs, and television productions, developing a distinctive jazz style in which the head was thrown back and the upper half of the body exaggeratedly stretched upwards. He began to teach in New York in 1955 where his classes dominated the jazz scene for the following decade.

Lukom, Yelena (*b* St Petersburg, 5 May 1891; *d* Leningrad, 27 Feb. 1968) Russian-Soviet dancer and teacher. She studied at the Imperial Theatre School, graduating in 1909 into the Mariinsky Theatre where she was ballerina (1920–41), performing a large and varied repertory of classical and contemporary roles, of which her best known was the heroine of Lopukhov's *The Red Poppy* (1929). In 1910 she also danced with Diaghilev and between 1922 and 1923 she toured Europe with her partner, Boris Sharov. Between them they developed many of the athletic lifts and balances which became a staple of the Soviet pas de deux. Between 1953 and 1965 she was teacher of the Class of Perfection and repetiteur with the Kirov. She wrote *My Work in Ballet* (Leningrad, 1940) and was made Honoured Artist of the Republic in 1925.

Lully, Jean Baptiste (orig. Giovanni Battista Lulli; *b* Florence, 29 Nov. 1632; *d* Paris, 22 Mar. 1687) Italian-French composer and dancer. He studied music as a child in Italy and came to France *c.*1644. In 1652 he was engaged at the court of Louis XIV as a violinist and dancer and performed alongside the King in several ballets, including *Ballet de la nuit* (1653), for which he also composed the music. Becoming the King's favourite, he was appointed supervisor of the royal music in 1662 and director of the Académie Royale de Musique (1672–87). He was effectively in supreme control of the Opera and was unpopular with many of his contemporaries. He composed music for many ballets and divertissements including the first significant comédie-ballet *Le Mariage forcé* (libr. Molière, chor. Beauchamps, 1664), also *Le Bourgois gentilhomme* (libr. Molière, chor. Beauchamps, 1670), *Psyché* (libr. Molière, Corneille, and Quinault, chor. Beauchamps, 1671), and *Le Triomphe de l'amour* (chor. Beauchamps and Pécourt, 1681). He was responsible for enlivening the rather slow stately dances of the ballet de cour and for introducing female dancers to the stage. He died from a gangrenous abscess on the foot, which developed after he struck himself with the long staff he used for conducting.

Lumbye, Hans Christian (*b* Copenhagen, 2 May 1810; *d* Copenhagen, 20 Mar. 1874) Danish composer who wrote the music for many Bournonville ballets including *Napoli* (1842), *Conser-*

vatory (1849), and *The Lifeguards on Amager* (1871).

Lumley, Benjamin (*b* 1811; *d* London 1875) English theatre manager. He was financier then manager (1842–58) of Her Majesty's Theatre, London, and played a key role in the presentation of Romantic ballet in England. A noted diplomat, his famous coup was successfully negotiating the order of appearance of the four ballerinas in *Pas de quatre*.

Lund, Thomas (*b* Copenhagen, 13 Sept. 1974) Danish dancer, choreographer and director. He trained at the Royal Danish Ballet School, and graduated into the company in 1993, becoming soloist in 1996 and principal in 2000. A graceful, compact, exceptionally musical dancer, he became one of the foremost Bournonville stylists of his generation. As well as dancing the Bournonville repertory Lund has also created roles in many ballets by Kylián, Martins, Ratmansky, and Lubovitch, among others. He has additionally worked as a choreographer, creating his own works and staging sections of the Bournonville repertory, and has taught both at the RDB school and abroad. In 2005 he was artistic director of the Principals and Soloists of the RDB Group and in 2007 co-author of *Danselaede of springkrafte—16 spor til dansen*, a memoir about the world of ballet. He is recipient of numerous honours and awards including the Reumert Lifetime Achievement Award, 2006.

Lunkina, Svetlana (*b* Moscow, 1979) Russian dancer. She studied at the Bolshoi Ballet school, graduating into the company in 1997 and promoted to soloist 1999 and principal 2005. A precociously gifted dancer, with a lyrical line and dramatic stage presence, she performed the title role of *Giselle* aged just 18 (coached by Maximova) and has since gone on to dance most of the classical ballerina roles in the Bolshoi's repertory, additionally performing in ballets by Petit, Fokine, Balanchine, Robbins, Ratmansky, and others. She has guested abroad, including with the touring company of *Malakhov (whom she partnered when he appeared with the Bolshoi). She appeared in the film *Saint Petersburg–Cannes Express* (2003).

Lynne, Gillian (orig. G. Pyrke; *b* Bromley, 1926) British dancer, choreographer and director. She studied at The Royal Academy of Dancing, the Cone-Ripman School, and the Arts Educational School with Volkova, Preobrajenska and others, making her debut with Ballet Guild in 1943. She danced with Sadler's Wells Ballet between 1944 and 1951 then became principal dancer at the London Palladium. She became one of the finest modern stage dancers of her generation and appeared on television and in musicals before turning to choreography. A seminal influence on British jazz dance she choreographed the hit musical *Cats* (1981) which was followed by many other productions for the commercial stage, and also by several ballets including *A Simple Man* (for Northern Ballet Theatre, mus. C. Davis, 1987), *The Brontës* (for NBT, mus. Dominic Muldowney, 1995), and *Journey* (Bolshoi Ballet, 1998). She choreographed the musical *Chitty Chitty Bang Bang* (2005).

Lyon Biennale Major international dance festival, established in 1984, hosted every two years by the French city of Lyon. Each festival focuses on a country or continent.

 SEE WEB LINKS
• Festival website

Lyon Opera Ballet Ballet company based at Lyon's Théâtre de l'Opéra. It was founded in 1969 by Louis Erlo, with 30 to 40 dancers, and under the direction of François Adret (1984–91) and Yorgos Loukos (from 1991) established its commitment to contemporary choreography. Its repertoire has included works by Petronio, Preljocaj, Childs, Mats Ek, Forsythe, Decouflé, and de Keersmaeker. Maguy *Marin was resident choreographer (1992–4), creating *Coppélia* and *Cendrillon* for the company, and Bill T. *Jones succeeded her (1994–7). The company has toured widely including to the US and Russia where in 1999 it appeared at the Bolshoi Theatre, the most radical ballet company ever to perform there.

SEE WEB LINKS
• Website for the Lyon Opera House with link to the ballet

McAllister, David (*b* Perth, Australia, 25 Nov. 1963) He trained at Australian Ballet School, graduating into the company in 1983 where he was promoted to principal in 1989. He performed both the classical and contemporary repertories, additionally guesting with the Bolshoi, Kirov, Birmingham Royal Ballet, and National Ballet of Canada. Later he became guest teacher for various institutions including the Australian Ballet School and the Royal Academy of Dance. In 2001 he was appointed artistic director of the Australian Ballet since when he has commissioned major additions to the repertory including Graeme *Murphy's *Swan Lake* (2002) and ballets by McGregor, Ratmansky, and others. He has additionally maintained the development of Australian choreographers including Stephen Baynes, Natalie Weir, and Adrian Burnett, who was appointed resident choreographer of AB in 2003.

McBride, Patricia (*b* Teaneck, NJ, 23 Aug. 1942) US dancer. She studied with Ruth Vernon and at the School of American Ballet, joining New York City Ballet in 1959, and promoted to principal in 1961. A glamorous dancer with a range embracing both romantic lyricism and vivacious display, she was one of Balanchine's favourite ballerinas and remained with NYCB for 30 years. Balanchine staged *Coppélia* for her in 1974 and also created roles for her in many other ballets: *A Midsummer Night's Dream* (1962), *Tarantella* (1964), *Harlequinade* (1965), *Don Quixote* (1965), *Brahms-Schoenberg Quartet* (1966), *Rubies* (1967), *Who Cares?* (1970), *Divertimento from Le Baiser de la fée* (1972), *Concerto No. 2* (1973), *The Steadfast Tin Soldier* (1975), *Pavane* (1975), *Union Jack* (1976), *Vienna Waltzes* (1977), and *Le Bourgeois gentilhomme* (1979). For Jerome Robbins, McBride created roles in *Dances at a Gathering* (1969), *In the Night* (1970), *The Goldberg Variations* (1971), *The Dybbuk Variations* (1974), *The Four Seasons*, and *Opus 19* (both 1979). She formed a particularly successful partnership with Edward Villella during the 1960s. In 1989 she retired from the stage and in 1996 became associate director of the N. Carolina Dance Theater, with her husband, the former dancer, Jean-Pierre *Bonnefoux as artistic director. She teaches for NCDT, and has staged several Balanchine works there.

McCabe, John (*b* Huyton, 21 Apr. 1939) British composer. He has written several ballet scores, including S. Hywel's *The Teachings of Don Juan* (Northern Dance Theatre, Manchester, 1973), Darrell's *Mary, Queen of Scots* (Scottish Ballet, Glasgow, 1976), and Bintley's *Edward II* (Stuttgart Ballet, 1995) and *Arthur* (Birmingham Royal Ballet, 2000). Several of his orchestral works, including the Second Symphony (1971) and the suite *The Chagall Windows* (1974), have additionally been used for dance.

McDonagh, Don (*b* New York, 6 Feb. 1932) US dance writer. Critic for the *New York Times* (1967–77), contributing editor of *Dance Magazine*, and author of *The Rise and Fall and Rise of Modern Dance* (New York, 1970), *Martha Graham* (New York, 1973), and *The Complete Guide to Modern Dance* (New York, 1976).

McDonald, Antony (*b* Weston-super-Mare, 11 Sept. 1950) British designer. He trained at the Central School of Speech and Drama, Manchester School of Theatre, and the Motley Theatre Course. His first design for dance was for *Something to Tell* (chor. S Davies, London Contemporary Dance Theatre, 1980) after which he created several works for Ian Spink including *There is no other Woman* (1982) and *Mercure* (Rambert, 1986), and for Richard Alston, *Dances from the Kingdom of the Pagodas* (Royal Danish Ballet, 1982), *Pulau Dewata* (Rambert Dance Company, 1989), and *Carmen* (Scottish Ballet, 2009). The majority of his dance designs have been for Ashley Page beginning with *Touch Your Coolness To My Fevered Brow* (Dutch National Ballet, 1992), followed by several works for the Royal Ballet including *Fearful Symmetries* (1994). He has also collaborated with Page on new versions of *The Nutcracker* (2003), *Cinderella* (2005), and *Sleeping Beauty* (2008) for Scottish Ballet. He has additionally designed extensively for theatre and opera.

Macdonald, Brian (*b* Montreal, 14 May 1928) Canadian dancer, choreographer, and ballet director, the first Canadian choreographer to gain international acclaim. He worked as a music critic (1949–51) while studying dance with Gerald Crevier and Elizabeth Leese in Montreal and became one of the founding members of the National Ballet of Canada (1951–3). After suffering an injury he turned to choreography, initially working in television and variety shows, then from 1958 with the Royal Winnipeg Ballet. He created many works for the company including *The Darkling* (1958), *Rose Latulippe* (the first Canadian full-length ballet, 1966), *The Shining People of Leonard Cohen* (1970), and *Ballet High* (1970). In 1964 he was appointed artistic director of the Royal Swedish Ballet, choreographing *While the Spider Slept* (1965) and *Skymning* (1966) for the company before leaving in 1966. He was then director of the Harkness Ballet (1967–8), for which he choreographed *Firebird* (1967), and of Batsheva Dance Company (1971–2), for which he choreographed *Martha's Vineyard* (1971). MacDonald also created works for other companies during this period including *Time Out of Mind* for the Joffrey (1963), *Prothalamion* for Les Grands Ballets Canadiens (1961), and *Variations on a Simple Theme (Diabelli Variations)* for the Paris Opera (1974). In 1974 he moved on to Les Grands Ballets Canadiens first as artistic director and from 1977 to 1990 as resident choreographer. Among the works he created there were *Romeo and Juliet* (1975), *Double Quartet* and *Fête Carignan* (both 1978), and *Adieu Robert Schumann* (1979). During this period he additionally created *Newcomers* (1980) for the National Ballet of Canada, a portrait of early Canadian pioneers, and *Petrushka* (1998) for the Gothenburg Ballet, updating the ballet to the ganglands of modern Russia. Other companies with Macdonald's work in their repertoire included the Berlin Opera Ballet, the Royal Danish Ballet, London Festival Ballet, and Alvin Ailey American Dance Theater. He also worked extensively as stage director for musicals, opera, and operetta, particularly at Canada's Stratford Festival where he became associate director in 1983. Among his best-known works are *The Mikado* (which toured to both New York and London in the 1980s) and *The Music Man* (1996). Between 1982 and 2002 he was director of the dance programme at the Banff Centre for the Arts, for which he staged several works and also directed the dance content of its summer festival.

MacGibbon, Ross (*b* Bromley, 29 Jan. 1955) British dancer and film-maker. He danced with the Royal Ballet from 1973 to 1986, since when he become a director, his dance films regularly seen on British television. His film of MacMillan's last ballet, *The Judas Tree*, won the 1998 International Emmy Award for Performing Arts.

McGregor, Wayne (*b* Stockport, England, 12 Mar. 1970) British choreographer and director.

He studied dance at University College Bretton Hall and the José Limon School in New York before founding his own London-based company, Random Dance in 1992. A prolific, curious-minded choreographer, he created a distinctive style of edgy, hyper-articulate dance and early on in his career began exploring developments in digital technology and science in order to find inspiration and material for his work. He was one of the first choreographers in Britain to work with animation, digital imagery, and *motion capture and in 2004 was appointed Fellow of the Neuroscience Department at Cambridge, collaborating with scientists on a study of mind-body co-ordination. He has created many works for his own company including *Sulphur 16* (1998), *Aeon* (2000), *Nemesis* (mus. Scanner 2002), *Polar Sequences* (2003), *AtaXia* (2004), *Amu* (mus. Taverner, 2005), and *Entity* (mus. Jon Hopkins and Joby Talbot, 2008). He has also created work for many other companies including Rambert (*PreSentient*, mus. Reich, 2003), English National Ballet (*2Human*, 2003), Stuttgart Ballet (*Eden/Eden*, mus. Reich, 2005), New York City Ballet (*Outlier*, 2010), Paris Opera Ballet (*Genus*, mus. Mauro Lanza, 2007) and Nederlands Dans Theater (*Renature* mus. Karen Tanaka, 2008). In 2000 he began his association with the Royal Ballet, creating *Symbiont(s)*) for the company in 2000, and going on to create *Qualia* (mus. Scanner, 2003), *Chroma* (mus. Joby Talbot and Jack White, 2006), *Infra* (mus. Max Richter, 2008), and *Limen* (mus. Kajia Saariaho, 2009). In 2006 he became resident choreographer for the company, the first modern-trained choreographer to hold that post. McGregor has also choreographed for musicals, including *Kirikou et Karaba* (mus. Yousson N'Dour, Paris 2007), for film (*Harry Potter and the Goblet of Fire*, 2004), and opera including several productions for Scottish National Opera, such as *La Boheme*, and *Dido and Aeneas* for La Scala. In 2009 he directed and choreographed a double bill of *Dido and Aeneas* and *Acis and Galatea*, working with both the Royal Ballet and Royal Opera companies.

(((⊕))) SEE WEB LINKS

• Website for Wayne McGregor/Random Dance Company

McIntyre, Trey (*b* Wichita, Kansas, 12 Nov. 1969) US choreographer. He studied at the North Carolina School of the Arts and Houston Ballet Academy before joining Houston Ballet in 1990. His interest in choreography developed as a student and he was made a choreographic apprentice in 1989, even before joining the company; he was subsequently promoted to choreographic associate (1995–2007). He created many works there including *Touched* (mus. Brubeck,

1994), *Second before the Ground* (mus. Kronos Quartet, traditional African, 1996), *Bound* (mus. Britten, 2000), *Peter Pan* (mus. Elgar, 2002), and *Touches* (mus. Brubeck, 2007) but also choreographed for other companies including American Ballet Theatre, Washington Ballet, Stuttgart Ballet, and New York City Ballet. In 2004 he formed the Trey McIntyre Project, presenting seasonal programmes of dance, and in 2008 this became full time, based in Boise, ID. McIntyre's works for this company include *Go Out* (mus. traditional bluegrass, 2006) and *The Blue Boy* (mus. Beethoven, 2007).

(⊕) SEE WEB LINKS

- Website for the Trey McIntyre project

McKayle, Donald (*b* New York, 6 Jul. 1930) US dancer, choreographer, and teacher. He studied with Graham, Shook, and Primus and began dancing in 1948. He performed with many modern dance companies, including those of Graham, Sokolow, Cunningham, and Erdman, as well as the New Dance Group. He appeared on Broadway in *House of Flowers* (1954) and *West Side Story* (1957). He choreographed the Broadway productions of *Golden Boy* (1964), *Tale of Two Cities* (1967), *Black New World* (1967), *Raisin* (1973), *Dr Jazz* (1975), and *Sophisticated Ladies* (1981). He also ran his own company (1951–69) for which he created several works exploring his own African-American background. These included *Games* (1951), a seminal work dealing with issues of racial prejudice (later taken into the repertoire of the Harkness Ballet); *Rainbow 'Round My Shoulder* (1959), a piece about Southern black chain-gangs (later taken into the Ailey repertoire); and *District Storyville*, set to New Orleans jazz (1962). He was artistic director of Inner City Repertory Dance Company (1971–4) and then resident choreographer and artistic mentor for the José Limón Dance Company, from 1995. He has also made work for the Cleveland-San Jose Ballet and San Francisco Ballet (*Gumbo Ya Ya*, 1994). McKayle, an inspirational and influential figure, has taught widely, his posts including professor in the Dance Department of University of California Irvine's School of Arts.

McKenzie, Kevin (*b* Burlington, Vt., 29 Apr. 1954) US dancer, choreographer, and ballet director. He studied at the Washington School of Ballet (1967–72) with Mary Day, and with Maggie Black in New York. He danced with the National Ballet of Washington (1972–4), with City Center Joffrey Ballet (1974–8), and with American Ballet Theatre (1979–89). He also performed as a guest artist with many companies around the world, including the Bolshoi and London Festival Ballet, and was with Nureyev and Friends in 1988. Although a talented dancer he created few roles, among them the Young Man in MacMillan's *Wild Boy* (Washington, 1981) and to some extent his career was overshadowed by Baryshnikov, who arrived at ABT at the same time. He danced most of the lead classical roles, often with van Hamel and was also acclaimed in the works of Antony Tudor. In 1990–1 he was artistic associate of Washington Ballet, and from 1984 was choreographer and associate artistic director of van Hamel's New Amsterdam Ballet for which he created several works including *Zamboria* (1984). He became artistic director of American Ballet Theatre in 1992, where he is credited with revitalizing the company. He has brought new works into the repertory by choreographers including Morris, Taylor, and Tharp, appointing Ratmansky as artistic associate in 2008 and subsequently resident choreographer. He has staged productions of the classics including *Don Quixote* (1995), *Swan Lake* (2000), and *Sleeping Beauty* (2007) and overseen the opening of the new company school.

Mackerras, (Sir) Charles (*b* Schenectady, NY, 17 Nov. 1925) Australian conductor. In his capacity as conductor of Sadler's Wells Theatre Ballet, he arranged the music for two of Cranko's most famous ballets: *Pineapple Poll* (based on Sullivan, 1951) and *The Lady and the Fool* (Verdi, 1954). He also arranged the music for Walter Gore's *Night and Silence* (Bach, 1958). A noted opera conductor, he was music director of English National Opera (1970–8). He was knighted in 1979.

MacLeary, Donald (*b* Glasgow, 22 Aug. 1937) British dancer and ballet master. He studied with Sheila Ross (1950–1) and at Sadler's Wells Ballet School, and joined Sadler's Wells Theatre Ballet in 1954. He became a principal dancer with the Royal Ballet at Covent Garden in 1959 when Beriosova requested him as her regular partner and created roles in Cranko's *The Angels* (1957), *Antigone* (1959), and *Brandenburg 2 & 4* (1966), and in MacMillan's *Solitaire* (1956), *The Burrow* (1958), *Baiser de la fée* (1960), *Diversions* (1961), *Symphony* (1963), *Images of Love* (1964), *Checkpoint* (1970), *The Poltroon* (1972), and *Elite Syncopations* (1974). He was ballet master of the Royal Ballet (1976–9) and repetiteur to principal dancers from 1984.

MacMillan, Sir Kenneth (*b* Dunfermline, 11 Dec. 1929; *d* London, 29 Oct. 1992) British dancer, choreographer, and ballet director. One of the major choreographers of the 20th century, and also one of the most innovative in British ballet. He studied with Phyllis Adams in Great Yarmouth and at the Sadler's Wells Ballet School (from 1945), joining Sadler's Wells Theatre Ballet in 1946 and Sadler's Wells Ballet (later the Royal

Ballet) in 1948. By 1952 however his dancing career was blighted by severe stage fright and he returned to SWTB in 1952, choreographing his first ballet the following year. His choreographic career with both the Royal Ballet companies went on to span almost five decades and produced some of the most important works of the latter half of the 20th century. His full-length ballets, including *Romeo and Juliet*, *Manon*, and *Mayerling*, revitalized the tradition of three-act opera house ballets, while his explorations of psychological and sexual subject-matter took ballet far out of the realm of fairy-tale. His works often dealt with violent and deviant behaviour, from *The Invitation* to *The Judas Tree* (both of which portrayed rape), while his protagonists were often outsiders and misfits, such as the dissolute Crown Prince Rudolf in *Mayerling*. MacMillan was also capable of making works of haunting beauty, such as *Gloria*, which honours the dead of the First World War, and *Song of the Earth*, and—occasionally—works of humour, like the ragtime-inspired *Elite Syncopations*. His ballets were responsible for introducing Lynn Seymour to the public; she remained his muse for many years. In 1989 he took Darcey Bussell from the corps de ballet and made her a star as the ballerina in his newly created *Prince of the Pagodas*. His relationship with the Royal Ballet was not always comfortable. After being appointed resident choreographer of the company in 1965 he moved away from it to become director of the Berlin Opera Ballet between 1966 and 1969. Although he again returned to the Royal as artistic director (1970–77) and principal choreographer (1977–92) he frequently worked away from Covent Garden. He was artistic associate for American Ballet Theatre (1984–9) and for Houston Ballet (1989–92) and he also choreographed many ballets for Stuttgart Ballet. He also worked as a theatre director; his productions including Ionesco's *The Chairs* and *The Lesson* (1982), Strindberg's *Dance of Death* (1983), and Tennessee Williams's *Kingdom of the Earth* (1984). He was knighted in 1983.

A list of his ballets includes *Somnambulism* (mus. S. Kenton, 1953), *Danses concertantes* (mus. Stravinsky, 1955), *The House of Birds* (mus. Mompou, arr. Lanchbery, 1955), *Noctambules* (mus. Searle, 1956), *Solitaire* (mus. M. Arnold, 1956), *Journey* (mus. Bartók, 1957), *Winter's Eve* (mus. Britten, 1957), *The Burrow* (mus. Martin, 1958), *Agon* (mus. Stravinsky, 1958), *Le Baiser de la fée* (mus. Stravinsky, 1960), *The Invitation* (mus. M. Seiber, 1960), *Diversions* (mus. Bliss, 1961), *The Rite of Spring* (mus. Stravinsky, 1962), *Symphony* (mus. Shostakovich, 1963), *Las Hermanas* (mus. Martin, 1963), *Images of Love* (mus. P. Tranchell, 1964), *La Création du monde* (mus. Milhaud, 1964), *Romeo and Juliet* (mus. Prokofiev, 1965), *Song of the Earth* (mus. Mahler, 1965), *Valses nobles et sentimentales* (mus. Ravel, 1966), *Concerto* (mus. Shostakovich, 1966), *Anastasia* (first version, mus. Martinů, 1967), *The Sphinx* (mus. Milhaud, 1968), *Swan Lake* (1969), *Miss Julie* (mus. Panufnik, 1970), *Checkpoint* (mus. R. Gerhard, 1970), *Anastasia* (second version, full-length, mus. Tchaikovsky and Martinů, 1971), *Side Show* (mus. Stravinsky, 1972), *Pavane* (mus. Fauré, 1973), *The Sleeping Beauty* (1973), *The Seven Deadly Sins* (mus. Weill, 1973), *Manon* (mus. Massenet, arr. Lucas, 1974), *Elite Syncopations* (mus. S. Joplin, 1974), *The Four Seasons* (mus. Verdi, 1975), *Requiem* (mus. Fauré, 1976), *My Brother, My Sisters* (mus. Schoenberg and Webern, 1978), *Mayerling* (mus. Liszt, arr. Lanchbery, 1978), *La Fin du jour* (mus. Ravel, 1979), *Gloria* (mus. Poulenc, 1980), *Isadora* (mus. R. R. Bennett, 1981), *Wild Boy* (mus. Cross, 1981), *Orpheus* (mus. Stravinsky, 1982), *Valley of Shadows* (mus. Martinů, Tchaikovsky, 1983), *Different Drummer* (mus. Webern, 1984), *The Prince of the Pagodas* (mus. Britten, 1989), *Winter Dreams* (mus. Tchaikovsky, 1991), *The Judas Tree* (mus. Elias, 1992), and *Carousel* (National Theatre production, 1992).

Madsen, Egon (*b* Ringe, 24 Aug. 1942) Danish dancer, teacher, and ballet director. Although born in Denmark he spent most of his career in Germany where he was one of the four lead dancers around whom Cranko rebuilt the Stuttgart Ballet. He studied with various teachers in Denmark before joining the Copenhagen Tivoli Theatre in 1958. In 1959 he danced with von Rosen's Scandinavian Ballet and in 1961 was invited to Stuttgart by Cranko. Appointed soloist in 1962 and then principal, he created roles in many Cranko ballets, including *Romeo and Juliet* (new version, 1962, in which he played Paris), *Jeu de cartes* (1965), *Onegin* (Lensky, 1965), *Pas de quatre*, *Nutcracker* (both 1966), *Taming of the Shrew* (1969), *Poème de l'extase*, *Brouillards* (both 1970), *Carmen* (Don José, 1971), and *Initials R.B.M.E.* (1972), in which the E referred to Egon. For MacMillan he created roles in *Song of the Earth* (1965), *The Sphinx* (1968), and *Concerto* (1973). He also created roles in Tetley's *Daphnis and Chloe* (1975) and Neumeier's *Lady of the Camellias* (1978). He was artistic director of the Frankfurt Ballet (1981–4), the Royal Swedish Ballet (1984–6), and the Teatro Comunale, Florence (1986–8). In 1990 he rejoined the Stuttgart Ballet as ballet master becoming assistant director from 1991 to 1996. In 1997 he moved to Leipzig Ballet as principal ballet master and two years later joined NDT 3 as dancer, teacher, and rehearsal director. After that group was disbanded, he continued to teach internationally and also performed in *Don Q*, a comic re-invention of the Petipa ballet, choreographed for him by Christian Spuck in 2007.

Magallanes, Nicholas (*b* Camargo, Mexico, 27 Nov. 1922; *d* North Merrick, Long Island, NY, 1 May 1977) Mexican-born, US dancer. He studied at the School of American Ballet with Balanchine and joined Ballet Caravan in 1941. He then danced with the Ballet Russe de Monte Carlo (1943–6) before becoming a permanent dancer with Ballet Society, later New York City Ballet, from 1946. For almost 30 years he was one of Balanchine's leading dancers, distinctive for his soft, poetic style. He created roles in Balanchine's *Night Shadow* (1946), *Raymonda* (1946), *Symphony in C* (new version of *Le Palais de cristal*, 1948), *Orpheus* (title role, 1948), *La Valse* (1951), *Western Symphony* (1954), *Allegro brillante* (1956), *Square Dance* (1957), *Episodes* (1959), *Liebeslieder Walzer* (1960), *A Midsummer Night's Dream* (Lysander, 1962), and *Don Quixote* (the Duke, 1965). He also created roles in Robbins's *The Guests* (1951), *The Cage* and *The Pied Piper* (both 1951), Ashton's *Illuminations* (he played the poet Arthur Rimbaud, 1950), and Butler's *The Unicorn, the Gorgon and the Manticore* (the Poet, 1957). He retired in 1973.

MaggioDanza Italian ballet company, based at the Teatro del Maggio Musicale, Florence. It dates back to a re-staging of *Excelsior* in 1967 and came to prominence in 1978 with the appointment of Eugeny Polyakov as ballet master and a series of performances featuring guests such as Fonteyn, Nureyev, Baryshnikov, and Fracci. Between 1986 and 1988 Egon Madsen was ballet master, but the return of Polykov in 1988 saw the company acquiring its current name, and an increased repertory of 19th- and 20th-century works. From 1996 to 1998 the company was directed by Karole Armitage who presented three new works including *The Predators' Ball* (1996). A series of short-term directors followed, including Davide Bombana, Elisbetta Terabust, and Giorgio Mancini who added many new works by Balanchine, Uotinen, David Parsons, Forsythe, Duato, and Childs. Mancini was succeeded in 2007 by Vladimir Derevianko as director and resident choreographer.

(((⊕))) SEE WEB LINKS
• Website for Maggio

Magic Flute, The Ballet in one act with choreography and libretto by Ivanov, music by Drigo. Premiered 22 Mar. 1893 at the Imperial Ballet School in St Petersburg. Despite its title, the ballet has nothing to do with Mozart's famous opera. It tells the light-hearted story of a country girl Lise, who is in love with the peasant boy, Luc, but is being urged by her mother to marry a wealthy Marquis. Luc, meanwhile, is given a magic flute by a hermit, and his playing forces everyone in the village into a dancing frenzy. The hermit reveals

himself to be Oberon, just in time to save Luc from being condemned to death by the irate Marquis. The ballet was created for a school performance (the cast included Mikhail Fokine as Luc) but it was taken into the Mariinsky repertoire on 23 Apr. 1893. Pavlova later performed it with her company, taking the role of Lise herself. Peter Martins staged a new version in 1981 for the School of American Ballet, and re-staged it for New York City Ballet on 21 Jan. 1982 with Darci Kistler as Lise and Martins as Luc.

Magri, Gennaro Italian choreographer and writer whose 1779 treatise, *Trattato teoretico-prattico di ballo*, is one of the leading publications about dance technique from the 18th century.

Mahler, Gustav (*b* Kalischt, 7 Jul. 1860; *d* Vienna, 18 May 1911) Austrian composer. Although he did not write specifically for ballet, his concert music has been used by many choreographers including Tudor, in *Dark Elegies* (*Kindertotenlieder*, 1937), MacMillan in *Song of the Earth* (1965), Béjart in *Le Chant du compagnon errant* (*Song of a Wayfarer*, 1971), Neumeier in *Third Symphony by Gustav Mahler* (1975), Darrell in *Five Ruckert Songs* (1978), and more recently Kim Brandstrup in *Songs of a Wayfarer* (2004).

maillot Dancers' tights. They take their name from a 19th-century costumier at the Paris Opera.

Makarova, Natalia (*b* Leningrad, 21 Nov. 1940) Russian dancer, ballet producer, and actress. One of the pre-eminent ballerinas of the 20th century. She trained at the Leningrad Ballet School (the Vaganova Institute), graduating into the Kirov in 1959 and rapidly becoming one of its leading artists. In 1970, while on tour with the company in London, she defected to the West, where she forged a stellar, international career. She was a principal dancer with American Ballet Theatre and a principal guest artist with the Royal Ballet in London, as well as appearing with numerous companies in Europe. A supremely gifted adagio dancer with a remarkably elastic technique, she was considered the foremost Odette of her day; her Giselle too was highly praised. In addition to dancing most of the classical repertory she created roles in many new ballets including Robbins's *Other Dances* (1976), Béjart's *Mephisto Waltz* (1979), the title dancing role in *Le Rossignol* for the Metropolitan Opera House in 1981 (with choreography by Ashton), MacMillan's *The Wild Boy* (1981), and Petit's *The Blue Angel* (1985). She staged a full-length version of *La Bayadère* for American Ballet Theatre in 1980, which was later taken into the repertoire of several companies including the Royal Ballet, the Royal Swedish Ballet, La Scala Ballet, Australian Ballet, and Dutch National Ballet. Her other productions include

Swan Lake for London Festival Ballet in 1984 and for Perm Ballet in 2005 (the latter taken into the repertory of the National Ballet of China), *Giselle* for Royal Swedish Ballet in 2000, and *Sleeping Beauty* for the Royal Ballet in 2003. She brought her own company to Broadway in 1980. She made her musical comedy debut in a revival of *On Your Toes* in New York in 1983 for which she won a Tony Award; the following year in London her performance, which had revealed her unexpected gift for comedy, earned an Olivier Award. In 1988 she was reunited with the Kirov when she danced with the company during its London season, partnered by Konstantin Zaklinsky in the Act II pas de deux from *Swan Lake*. In 1989 she went to Leningrad to appear with the Kirov again. She has frequently appeared on television, and conceived and presented the BBC television series *Ballerina* in 1987. In 1991 she made her debut as a dramatic actress, performing largely in Britain. She is recipient of many awards including Gold medal, Varna, 1965; Merited Artist of the RSFSR; Anna Pavlova Prize, Paris, 1970; and is author of *A Dance Autobiography* (New York, 1979).

Malakhov, Vladimir (*b* Krivoy Rog, Ukraine, 7 Jan. 1968) Russian dancer and director. He studied at the Moscow Ballet School and went on to dance with Moscow Classical Ballet, the Vienna State Opera Ballet, and the National Ballet of Canada. In 1995 he joined American Ballet Theatre as a principal, where Duato's *Without Words* was created to showcase his compelling stage presence. He also danced regularly with Stuttgart Ballet. In 1999 he made his choreographic debut with his own staging of *La Bayadère* for the Vienna State Opera and in 2002 he became artistic director of the State Opera Ballet in former East Berlin. Two years later he was appointed director of the *Berlin State Ballet, an amalgam of the three former Berlin companies. He has since brought in new dancers, as well as attracting guest ballerinas like Vishneva, and enlarged the company's repertory of both contemporary and classic works. Malakhov performs with the company while continuing to guest internationally.

(((●))) **SEE WEB LINKS**
• Website for Vladimir Malakhov

Maldoom, Royston (*b* London, 25 Mar. 1943) British choreographer and community dance pioneer. He started his dance training at the age of 20 (having been a student of agriculture) and studied at various institutions including the London School of Contemporary Dance and the Alvin Ailey School in New York. He choreographed his first work in 1975, subsequently choreographing for Dance Theatre of Harlem, Northern Ballet Theatre, and Scottish Ballet among others. In the 1980s he became involved in community projects in Scotland and helped to form the Dundee Repertory Dance Theatre (later Scottish Dance Theatre). Aspiring to high standards of dance theatre, Maldoom has worked with disadvantaged children in Ethiopia and Peru; prison inmates; and children and adults with learning difficulties. In Berlin (2003) he adapted his production of *The Rite of Spring* (1990) for a cast of 250 young people and the Berlin Philharmonic, filmed in the award-winning documentary *Rhythm Is It!*. In London in 2008 he created *Overture 2012* at the Albert Hall, with 120 young people and the London Symphony Orchestra playing Shostakovich's Tenth Symphony.

(((●))) **SEE WEB LINKS**
• Royston Maldoom official website

Maliphant, Russell (*b* Ottawa, Canada, 18 Nov. 1961) British dancer and choreographer. He studied at the Royal Ballet School and performed with Sadler's Wells Royal Ballet (1982–88) before moving into contemporary dance and working with choreographers such as Lloyd *Newson, Laurie Booth, and Michael *Clark. He founded his own company in 1996, developing a fluid, muscular style that has drawn on yoga, martial arts, and classical ballet. His works are abstract, their resonant visual imagery usually created in collaboration with his long-term lighting designer Michael *Hulls. These include *Critical Mass* (mus. Andy Cowton and Richard English, 1998), *Sheer* (mus. Sarah Sarhandi, 2001), *Broken Fall* (mus. Barry Adamson, 2003), *Push* (mus. Cowton, 2005) and *Eonnagata* (mus. several, 2009), the last three made in collaboration with the ballerina Sylvie Guillem. Maliphant's works are also in the repertories of Lyon Opera Ballet, George Piper Dances, and Batsheva, among others.

(((●))) **SEE WEB LINKS**
• Website for Russell Maliphant company

Maly Ballet *See* MIKHAILOVSKY BALLET.

Mam'zelle Angot Ballet in one act with choreography and libretto by Massine, music by Lecocq (arr. Richard Mohaupt), and designs by Mstislav Doboujinsky. Premiered 10 Oct. 1943 (as *Mademoiselle Angot*) by Ballet Theatre at the Metropolitan Opera House, New York, with Massine, Nora Kaye, André Eglevsky, and Rosella Hightower. The ballet is based on Charles Lecocq's 1872 comic opera *La Fille de Madame Angot* which portrays a group of haplessly mis-matched lovers. It was revived by Massine for Sadler's Wells Ballet in 1947, with new music arranged by Gordon Jacob and designs by André Derain, and a cast that included Fonteyn, Shearer, Grant, and Somes. Australian Ballet took it into its repertoire in 1971.

Manchester, Phyllis Winnifred (*b* London, 7 Dec. 1906; *d* Cincinnati, 18 May 1998) British dance critic and writer. She was ballet critic of *Theatre World* (1941–3), secretary to Marie Rambert (1944–6), and the author of *Vic-Wells: A Ballet Progress* (London, 1942) and *The Rose and the Star* (with Iris Morley, London, 1948). She was also co-editor (with A. Chujoy) of the *Dance Encyclopaedia*, 1967 edition. She taught dance history at the University of Cincinnati for 24 years.

Manen, Hans van (*b* Amstelveen, 11 Jul. 1932) Dutch dancer, choreographer, and ballet director. He studied with Sonia Gaskell, Françoise Adret, and Nora Kiss and danced with Gaskell's Ballet Recital (1951), Amsterdam Opera Ballet (1952–8), and Roland Petit's Ballets de Paris (1959) before becoming one of the original members of Nederlands Dans Theater in 1960. During the next ten years he was one of the company's leading choreographers, also its joint artistic director (first with Benjamin Harkavy, then with Glen Tetley). He left in 1971, firstly to pursue a freelance career and then from 1973 to 1987 to work with Dutch National Ballet as resident choreographer and ballet master. In 1988 he rejoined NDT as resident choreographer, remaining there until 2003 when he rejoined Dutch National Ballet as resident choreographer. He has created over 120 works, his style a powerful fusion of classical and modern idioms that showcases the athletic prowess of his dancers. While focusing rigorously on structure, van Manen's works often have a strong expressive subtext, evoking the complex, conflicted relationship between men and women. A list of his works for NDT includes *Symphony in Three Movements* (mus. Stravinsky, 1963), *Essay in Silence* (mus. Messiaen, 1965), *Metaphors* (mus. Daniel Lesur, 1965), *Five Sketches* (mus. Hindemith, 1966), *Solo for Voice 1* (mus. Cage, 1968), *Squares* (mus. Satie, 1969), *Situation* (sound collage, 1970), *Mutations* (with Tetley, mus. Stockhausen, 1970), *Grosse Fuge* (mus. Beethoven, 1971), *Opus Lemaître* (mus. Bach, 1972), *Septet Extra* (mus. Saint-Saëns, 1973), *Noble et sentimentale* (mus. Ravel, 1975), *Songs Without Words* (mus. Mendelssohn, 1977), *Black Cake* (mus. various composers, 1989), *Andante* (mus. Mozart, 1991), *Fantasía* (mus. Bach, 1993), *Kammerballet* (mus. several, 1995), *Zero Hour* (mus. Piazolla, 1998), and *Trilogie* (mus. several, 2000). For Dutch National Ballet he has created *Twilight* (mus. Cage, 1972), *Daphnis and Chloe, Suite No. 2* (mus. Ravel, 1972), *Adagio Hammerklavier* (mus. Beethoven, 1973), *Sacre du printemps* (mus. Stravinsky, 1974), *Ebony Concerto* (mus. Stravinsky, 1976), *Five Tangos* (mus. Piazzolla, 1977), *Live* (mus. Liszt, 1979), *Klaviervariationen I* (mus. Bach, Dallapiccola, 1980), *Bits and Pieces* (mus. Byrne, Eno, Mendelssohn, 1984), *Opening* (mus. Hindemith, 1986), *Symphonieen*

der Nederlanden (mus. Andriessen, 1987), *Three Pieces for Het* (mus. var., 1997), *Frank Bridge Variations* (mus. Britten 2005), and *Tears* (mus. Rachmaninoff 2008). He has created works for many other companies including *Four Schumann Pieces* (Royal Ballet, 1975) and the Hans van Manen Foundation has been established to ensure the survival of his extensive repertory. He is also a professional photographer and has exhibited widely. He is recipient of major honours and awards including Knight of the Order of Oranje Nassau (1992).

(((●))) SEE WEB LINKS

• Website for the Hans van Manen Foundation

manipuri A style of dance originating from the valley of Manipur in NE India. Folkloric and religious in origin, it is simple to perform and often involves the entire community. Its dramas are accompanied by dialogue and song, while its style is marked by softness and fluidity.

Manning, Frank (*b* Florida, 26 May 1914; *d* 27 Apr. 2009) US dancer, choreographer, and company director. He studied jazz dance with Whitey White in New York and during the 1930s was performer and choreographer for the company Whitey's Lindy Hoppers. The troupe toured widely and also performed in several Hollywood films, including *Hellzapoppin'* (1941). After service in the Second World War, Manning formed a short-lived company called the Congaroos but then retired from the stage. In 1988 he spearheaded the lindyhop revival after two California dancers (Erin Stephens and Stephen Mitchell) sought him out from obscurity. The lindy revival gave Manning a new career as a choreographer and among the productions on which he worked was the Broadway musical *Black and Blue* (1989), his choreography gaining a Tony Award. A much-loved, inspirational teacher he continued to conduct lindy workshops around the world until his late eighties.

Manon Ballet in three acts with choreography and libretto by MacMillan, music by Massenet (arr. Leighton Lucas), and designs by Georgiadis. Premiered 7 Mar. 1974 by the Royal Ballet at Covent Garden with Sibley, Dowell, Wall, Rencher, Mason, and Drew. The ballet is based on Abbé Prévost's *L'Histoire du Chevalier des Grieux et de Manon Lescaut* (1731), which also inspired operas by Massenet and Puccini and earlier ballets by Jean Aumer (at the Paris Opera in 1830) and Giovanni Golinelli (Vienna, 1852). The story of the ambitious and avaricious courtesan Manon provided MacMillan with one of his greatest successes, and one of the most enduring full-length ballets of the latter half of the 20th century. His treatment of Manon's doomed love for des

Grieux, which begins in Regency Paris and ends in the swamps of Louisiana, is both dramatically detailed and sensually charged and its central pas de deux revealed new physical and erotic possibilities in the language of partnering. Since its premiere it has been a constant of the Royal Ballet's repertory and has also been staged for many other companies, including the Royal Swedish Ballet, Paris Opera Ballet, the Houston Ballet, the National Ballet of Canada, American Ballet Theatre, and the Mariinsky.

Mantsoe, Vincent (full name Vincent Sekwati Koko Mantsoe; *b* Soweto, 26 Apr. 1971) S. African choreographer, dancer, and teacher. A descendant of a long line of Sangomas (traditional healers), Mantsoe participated from childhood in traditional song and dance rituals. He also taught himself to dance through youth clubs, music videos, and street dancing. In 1990 he won a scholarship to the school of Moving Into Dance Company in Johannesburg and having become a permanent member of the company developed his own 'Afro-fusion' method of performance and choreography, drawing on African and Western dance forms and Asian martial arts. Between 1997 and 2001 he was associate artistic director of Moving into Dance, after which he formed his own company. As a dancer Mantsoe has mostly performed solo, the power of his work deriving not only from his profound absorption of other dance styles but also the spirituality of his creative process, which he describes as 'borrowing' from his ancestors. His solo works include *Gula* (mus. Gabrielle Roth, 1992), *Mpheyane* (mus. James Wood and Randy Crafton, 1997), *Traduction Simultanée* (1999, in collaboration with Michel Kelemenis and Takeshi Yazaki), *Bupiro—Mukuti* (mus. Kronos Quartet and traditional, 2002), and *NDAA* (mus. various, 2003). He has also created various works for other companies including *Sasanka* (Dance Theatre of Harlem, 1997), *Majara* (Skanes Dance Theatre, Sweden, 2002) and *Skin* (ACE Company, UK, 2007). Mantsoe has taught and performed internationally and is recipient of many awards including first prize at Bagnolet 1996 and 1998, and Prix de Peuple, Montreal, 1999.

Manzotti, Luigi (*b* Milan, 2 Feb. 1835; *d* Milan, 15 Mar. 1905) Italian mime dancer and choreographer. He created his first ballet, *La morte di Masaniello*, in 1858, and built on his successes in Rome and Milan to enjoy considerable international fame. His ballets were staged around the world although by modern standards their dance content was minimal, their effects created through mime and through strikingly staged tableaux and processions.

Marceau, Marcel (*b* Strasbourg, 22 Mar. 1923; *d* Paris, 22 Sep. 2007) French mime artist. He studied with Dullin and Decroux and made his debut as Harlequin in Jean-Louis Barrault's production of *Baptiste* in 1947. That same year he formed his own company with which he then toured internationally. In 1997 he celebrated the 50th anniversary of his comic creation, Bip. Despite changes in fashion which saw mime move on from the rather naïve style he represented, Marceau remained the form's most famous practitioner. In 1971 he collaborated with the Hamburg Ballet on a version of *Candide*.

Maré, Rolf de (*b* Stockholm, 9 May 1888; *d* Barcelona, 28 Apr. 1964) Swedish art patron, impresario, and founder of the *Ballets Suédois in Paris. Although the Ballets Suédois was short-lived as a company, surviving only five years, de Maré made it an international showcase for new choreography, design, and music. Emulating Diaghilev, he encouraged collaborations with avant-garde artists, including Jean Cocteau, Bonnard, de Chirico, Léger, and the composers of Les Six. The repertoire (all of it choreographed by Jean Börlin) reflected contemporary trends in art (such as Dadaism and Surrealism) and also reflected de Maré's own interest in primitive art (he had a notable collection). When the Ballets Suédois was disbanded in 1925, he turned his attention to other projects, including the establishment of Les Archives Internationales de la Danse with Pierre Tugal in Paris in 1931. He was also responsible for organizing several choreographic competitions. In 1950, when the archive was closed, de Maré's large collection of books, magazines, and souvenir programmes chronicling dance history was divided up between the museum of the Paris Opera and the Stockholm Dance Museum.

Marguerite and Armand Ballet in one act with choreography and libretto by Ashton, music by Liszt (arr. Humphrey Searle), and designs by Cecil Beaton. Premiered 12 Mar. 1963 by the Royal Ballet at Covent Garden, with Fonteyn, Nureyev, and Somes. Based on the 1848 novel by Alexandre Dumas *fils*, *La Dame aux camélias* (which also inspired Verdi's opera *La traviata*), it tells the story of the dying Marguerite Gautier in flashback through five pas de deux. This was Ashton's last full ballet for Fonteyn. She and Nureyev performed it frequently around the world. It was revived by the Royal Ballet at Covent Garden in 2000 with Sylvie Guillem inheriting the Fonteyn role.

Mariés de la Tour Eiffel, Les Ballet in one act with choreography by Börlin, libretto by Cocteau, music by Auric, Milhaud, Tailleferre, Honegger, and Poulenc, set by Irène Lagut and costumes by J. Hugo. Premiered 18 Jun. 1921 by the Ballets Suédois at the Théâtre des Champs-Elysées in Paris with C. Ari, J. Figoni, and K. Vahlander. The ballet, a farce, is set on the first platform of the Eiffel Tower where a hunchbacked photographer tries to take pictures of a wedding party. Although L. Durey was not involved in the ballet, it is none the less considered to be a showpiece for the musical ideas of the group of composers known collectively as Les Six.

Mariinsky Ballet Russian ballet company based at the Mariinsky Theatre in St Petersburg. It dates back to court performances given by dancers trained at the Empress Anna Ivanovna's school, which evolved into a professional company, the Imperial Ballet. This was based at the Bolshoi Theatre in St Petersburg (1783–1860) and then at the Mariinsky Theatre, although the company continued to perform at the Bolshoi Theatre until 1889. It also gave smaller-scale performances at the Theatre of the Hermitage and the Theatre of Tsarskoye Selo (now the Pushkin). After the October Revolution of 1917 the theatre's name was changed to State Mariinsky Theatre, then the State Academic Theatre for Opera and Ballet (Russian abbreviation, GATOB). In 1935 it became the Leningrad Theatre for Opera and Ballet named after Kirov (the head of the Leningrad Communist Party who was assassinated in 1934), while the company itself was commonly known as the Kirov Ballet. In 1991 the theatre reverted to its original name, the Mariinsky, with the company retaining the name Kirov for foreign touring.

Originally, ballet in Russia was a foreign import. The empress's school (founded 1738) was directed by the Frenchman *Landé and early choreographers and teachers such as *Hilverding and *Angiolini brought with them European ballets and a European technical finesse. Even so, these soon became inflected with the freer style of Russian folk dance, and some early ballets were created on Russian themes, such as Angiolini's *Semira* (1772), based on a tragedy by Russian writer Sumarokov, and Valbergh's *Russia's Triumph; or, The Russians in Paris* (1814). *Didelot, who was ballet master in St Petersburg from 1801 to 1811 and again from 1816, choreographed the first ballets based on Pushkin's work and he was also responsible for widespread reforms in the school and company. Under his influence the city became one of the leading centres of ballet, producing its own star dancers. Romanticism came into vogue when Taglioni danced *La Sylphide* in St Petersburg in 1837 and many of the other great Romantic ballerinas performed there during the 1840s and 1850s. Russian ballerinas, however, proved able to compete with them, including Elena *Andreyanova who danced Giselle

in 1842, and later Marie Bogdanova. Subsequent ballet masters, *Perrot (1848–59) and *Saint-Léon (1859–69) added their own distinctive works to the repertory. But it was *Petipa who brought the St Petersburg ballet to its peak of artistic brilliance. He joined the company in 1847 as a solo dancer and was appointed chief ballet master in 1869. In a long succession of increasingly inventive and expressive works he not only extended the technical and dramatic range of the classical vocabulary but also evolved a far more sophisticated format than that of previous ballet spectacles. *The Sleeping Beauty* (1890) and *Swan Lake* (with Ivanov, 1895) were created in quasi-symphonic form comparable to the great Tchaikovsky scores to which they were set, with individual dance numbers knitted into a coherent sweep of dance and mime. Petipa's ballets were also vehicles for the increasing virtuosity of the principal dancers, trained by gifted teachers like Christian *Johansson and Enrico *Cecchetti. They included Ekaterina Vazem, Evgenia Sokolova, Pavel Gerdt, and Nicolai Legat. At the beginning of the 20th century other outstanding classical dancers emerged, including Olga Preobrajenska, Mathilda Kshessinska, and Anna Pavlova but the vitality of 19th-century choreography was exhausted. The young choreographer *Fokine was committed to replacing the old three-act ballets with dance of a new concentrated poetry or realism. But the Mariinsky Theatre was unsympathetic to his reforms and he chose to work for long periods with Diaghilev's *Ballets Russes in Europe as did many of the younger dancers, notably Vaslav *Nijinsky and Tamara *Karsavina. In 1917 the October Revolution produced a period of instability in the company and more dancers left, but during the 1920s GATOB became a platform for experimental work under the direction of *Lopukhov. He and *Balanchine (prior to the latter's 1924 departure to the West) staged Evenings of Young Ballet and many new ballets were shown. However, the company also remained committed to preserving its 19th-century traditions. During the 1930s Soviet-style ballet theatre came to prominence with many seminal works in the genre created in the company, such as Vainonen's *Flames of Paris* (1932), Zakharov's *Fountain of Bakhchisarai* (1934), and the Lavrovsky production of *Romeo and Juliet* (1940). Galina *Ulanova emerged as the company's outstanding ballerina at this time. Between 1941 and 1944 the company was evacuated to Molotov-Perm though some dancers remained in the besieged Leningrad to perform. After 1945 Moscow overtook St Petersburg as the official centre of Soviet ballet although some important works continued to be made at the Kirov, including Fenster's *Taras Bulba* (1955), Jacobson's *Spartacus* (1956), Grigorovich's *The

Stone Flower (1957) and *Legend of Love* (1961), and Belsky's *The Leningrad Symphony* (1961). With Konstantin *Sergeyev as company director and his wife Natalia *Dudinskaya as leading dancer, the classical repertory was also strictly maintained. While the Bolshoi were known for their vigorous, dramatic energy the Kirov were renowned for their purity of line, their musicality, and their adherence to classical tradition. When the company began touring to the West after 1961 dancers like Natalia Makarova, Irina Kolpakova, Rudolf Nureyev, and Yuri Soloviev impressed audiences with their refined artistry. Contact with the West, however, revealed the artistic limitations of the Kirov's repertory and many dancers chose to defect, including Nureyev, Makarova, and, later, Baryshnikov. In 1977 Oleg *Vinogradov took over direction of the company. He created many new ballets but also began to add Western works by Béjart, Balanchine, and Fokine, among others. Increased touring to the West after the late 1980s brought international fame to a new generation of Kirov dancers, notably Altynai Asylmuratova, Farukh Ruzimatov, and, later, Igor Zelensky. Vinogradov ceased to be effective director of the company in 1996 due to a series of political and financial scandals and the Kirov was then run by the director of the Mariinsky Theatre, Valery Gergiev, and by ballet director Makharbek *Vaziev (1997–2008). Reverting to its original name, the Mariinsky, the company has since attempted to sustain the traditions for which it is famous while finding a new direction for its future, enlarging its repertory with ballets by choreographers such as Balanchine, Forsythe, and Petit; with revivals of the Diaghilev repertory (including *Hodson and Archer's reconstruction of *Rite of Spring*) and with new works by, among others, Alexei Ratmansky, including his *Le Baiser de la fée* (1998) and *Pierrot Lunaire* (2008). Vaziev was succeeded by Yuri *Fateyev in 2008. The Mariinsky remains legendary for the beauty and discipline of its corps de ballet, rooted in the training which dancers receive from the company school. Based in Theatre Street (Rossi Street) the school dates back to the 1738 school founded by the Empress Anna Ivanovna. It has been successively named the Imperial Theatre School, St Petersburg, the Petrograd State Ballet School, the Leningrad Ballet School, and from 1957, the Vaganova School.

⊕ SEE WEB LINKS
• Website for the Mariinsky Ballet

Marin, Maguy (*b* Toulouse, 2 Jun. 1951) French dancer, choreographer, and company director. One of the most significant figures in the French new wave. She studied in Toulouse and Paris, performing with the Strasbourg Opera Ballet before moving to Brussels in 1970 to continue her studies at Béjart's school, Mudra. She joined his Ballet of the 20th Century (1974–7) and choreographed *Yu-ku-ri* for that company in 1976. In 1978 she won first prize at the Bagnolet choreographic competition and in the same year founded her own company, which in 1984 was renamed Compagnie Maguy Marin, resident first at Angers and from 2006 at Rillieux-la Pape. In addition to making dances for her own company, Marin has choreographed for the Paris Opera Ballet (*Jaleo*, 1983, for the experimental GRCOP, and 1988's *Leçon de ténèbres* for the main company); for Dutch National Ballet (*Groosland*, mus. Bach, 1989) and above all for Lyon Opera Ballet where she was resident choreographer between 1991 and 1994. One of her major successes there was *Cinderella* (1985), which set the familiar fairy-tale in a doll's house; this was followed by *Coppélia* (1993) which transferred the ballet to a depressed public housing estate. Marin's slant on the classical aesthetic was also evident in *Groosland* where a cast of padded 'fat' dancers satirized the sylph-like bodies of classical dancers. She also staged the Brecht/Weill *The Seven Deadly Sins* for Lyon in 1987. A list of her other works includes *Contrastes* (mus. Bartók, 1980), *May B* (mus. Schubert, Bryars, 1981, based on the writings of Samuel Beckett), *Babel Babel* (mus. Mahler, 1982), *Calambre* (mus. Rayon, 1985), *Waterzooi* (mus. Denis Mariotte, 1993), *RamDam* (mus. Mariotte, 1995), *Umwelt* (2005), and *Turba* (2007).

⊕ SEE WEB LINKS
• Website for the Marin company

Markó, Iván (*b* Balassagyarmat, 29 Mar. 1947) Hungarian dancer, choreographer, and company director. He studied at the State Ballet Institute in Budapest, graduating in 1967. He joined the Budapest Opera Ballet Company and from 1972 to 1979 danced with Béjart's Ballet of the 20th Century. In 1979 he returned to Hungary and founded the *Györ Ballet, for which he made many works. He left the company in 1991 and in 1996 founded the Budapest-based Hungarian Festival Ballet for which he continued to choreograph. He has also created work for other companies including a setting of Beethoven's 9th Symphony for the Hungarian National Ballet.

Markova, (Dame) Alicia (orig. Lillian Alicia Marks; *b* London, 1 Dec. 1910; *d* 2 Dec. 2004) British dancer, teacher, and ballet director. The first British prima ballerina and a key figure in the development of British dance. She studied with Astafieva (from 1921), Legat, Cecchetti, and Celli and as a child was nicknamed the 'Miniature Pavlova'. At the age of only 14 she was recruited by Diaghilev's Ballets Russes and danced with his company from 1925 to 1929, cast as a soloist from the start because she was too small to join the corps de ballet. She created the title role in Balanchine's *Le Chant du rossignol* in 1925. When Diaghilev died she returned to London and became key to the early development of British ballet. She danced with the Camargo Society (1931), with Ballet Rambert (1931–5), and the Vic-Wells Ballet (1932–5), years during which Ashton, Tudor, and de Valois took advantage of her strong classical technique and experience. She created roles in many of Ashton's early ballets, including *La Péri* (1931), *Façade* (1931), *Foyer de danse* (1932), *Les Rendezvous* (1933), and *Mephisto Waltz* (1934). For Tudor she created a role in *Lysistrata* (1932) and for de Valois roles in *The Wise and Foolish Virgins* (1933), *Bar aux Folies-Bergère* (1934), *The Haunted Ballroom* (1934), and *The Rake's Progress* (1935). She was the first British ballerina to dance the roles of Giselle and Odette-Odile. In 1935 she joined with Anton Dolin to form the Markova-Dolin company, a travelling ensemble which provided a vehicle for its two stars. Markova continued as its prima ballerina until 1938. She then went abroad, finding more stellar opportunities in Europe and America. For the next three years she was ballerina of the Ballet Russe de Monte Carlo where she created roles in Massine's *Seventh Symphony* (1938), *Capriccio espagnol* (1939), *Rouge et noir* (1939), and *Vienna 1814* (1940); and in Balanchine's *Jeu de cartes* (1940). From 1941 to 1945 she danced with American Ballet Theatre where in addition to performing the traditional ballerina roles she also created parts in Massine's *Aleko* (1942) and Tudor's *Romeo and Juliet* (1943, Juliet). In 1945 she re-formed the Markova-Dolin Company in the US which toured widely. In 1949 she and Dolin gave a series of gala performances of ballet in Britain, out of which grew London Festival Ballet (later *English National Ballet). She continued as prima ballerina until 1952. She guested with companies all over the world, admired for the lightness and ethereality that belied her exceptionally strong technique. Out of all her roles she was most closely associated with Giselle—many considered her reading of it to be definitive. She retired from the stage in 1962 and from 1963 to 1969 was ballet director of the Metropolitan Opera House in New York. In later years she was a coach and teacher, as well as a stager of ballets. Author of *Giselle and I* (London, 1960) and *Markova Remembers* (London, 1986). Dame of the Order of the British Empire 1963.

Markova-Dolin Ballet *See* MARKOVA, ALICIA.

Marks, Bruce (*b* New York, 31 Jan. 1937) US dancer, choreographer, and ballet director. He studied at the High School of Performing Arts, the Juilliard School, and with Tudor and Craske. He began his career in 1956 with the Metropolitan Opera Ballet, becoming a soloist in 1958. He also danced with H. Ross in Spoleto in 1959. From 1961 to 1971 he was one of the premier dancers at American Ballet Theatre. He guested with the Royal Swedish Ballet, London Festival Ballet, and the Royal Danish Ballet, joining the latter as a principal dancer (1971–6). He choreographed several ballets including *Dichterliebe* (mus. Schumann, 1972) and *Asylum* (mus. C. Ruggles, 1974). From 1976 he was artistic co-director of Ballet West in Utah and in 1985 reconstructed Bournonville's 1855 ballet *Tales of the Arabian Nights: The Story of Abdallah* for the company. He had discovered Bournonville's handwritten scenario for the forgotten ballet at Sotheby's in New York in 1971 and as well as staging it for Ballet West, he later staged it for the National Ballet of Canada (1997). In 1985 he was appointed artistic director of the Boston Ballet and during his twelve-year tenure introduced modern dance works to the repertoire, developed new choreography, and secured new premises for the company. He left Boston in 1997 but in 2006 emerged from retirement to direct Orlando Ballet, after the sudden death of Bujones.

Marseillaise, La Solo dance by Isadora Duncan. Premiered 9 Apr. 1915 at the Trocadero in Paris. She created it as an expression of French patriotism during the days of the First World War.

Marshall, Susan (*b* Pensacola, Fla., 17 Oct. 1958) US dancer and choreographer. She trained in gymnastics, then studied dance at the Juilliard School in New York (1976–8). She founded her own company in 1982 and since then has made more than 30 dance works for it. She has also choreographed for GRCOP (the experimental wing of Paris Opera Ballet), the Boston Ballet, the Frankfurt Ballet, and the Lyon Opera Ballet. A list of her works includes *Ward* (1983), *Routine and Variations* (1984), *Arms* (1984), *Opening Gambits* (1985), *Arena* (1986), *Overture* (1987), *The Aerialist* (1987), *Kiss* (1987), *Interior with Seven Figures* (1988), *In Medias Res* (1989), *Contenders* (1990), *Standing Duet* (1992), *Untitled (Detail)* (1992), *Fields of View* (1994), *Central Figure* (1994), *Spectators at an Event* (1994), *Les Enfants Terribles* (1996), a 'dance-opera spectacle' in collaboration with the composer Philip Glass, *Run Toward the Noise* (1998), *The Most Dangerous Room in the House* (1998), *The Descent Beckons* (1999), and *Cloudless* (2006). Eschewing a highly developed technical language, her work is influenced both by the contact improvisation of Steve Paxton and by the post-modernism of Trisha Brown. Her more recent work has incorporated text and video. Her first play, *Walter's Finest Hour*, premiered in New York in 1993.

(⊕) SEE WEB LINKS
• Website for the Susan Marshall company

Martin, John (*b* Louisville, Ky., 2 Jun. 1893; *d* Saratoga Springs, NY, 19 May 1985) US ballet critic and dance writer. He was a pioneer in the field of dance criticism in America, the first dance critic to be appointed by a major newspaper, in his case the *New York Times*. From that position, which he held from 1927 to 1962, he became one of the most influential champions of modern dance in America. His books include *The Modern Dance* (New York, 1933), *Introduction to the Dance* (New York, 1939), *The Dance* (New York, 1945) and *World Book of Modern Ballet* (New York, 1952).

Martinez, José Carlos (*b* Cartegena, 1969) Spanish dancer and choreographer. He studied at the Rosella Hightower Centre in Cannes, then at the Paris Opera Ballet School, entering the company in 1988 and becoming étoile in 1999. His repertory includes the 19th-century classics, notably *Swan Lake*, but he is most celebrated for his virtuosity and versatility within the 20th- and 21st-century repertories, dancing in ballets by MacMillan, Petit, Taylor, Tudor, and others and creating roles in works by Ek, Larrieu, Bart, Neumeier, and Forsythe. He choreographed his first work *Mi Favorita* in 2002 for young dancers of the Paris Opera. He is recipient of numerous prizes and awards including Gold Medal at Varna (1992).

Martins, Peter (*b* Copenhagen, 27 Oct. 1946) Danish dancer, choreographer, and ballet director. Balanchine's successor at New York City Ballet. He studied at the Royal Danish Ballet School (1953–65) and joined the Royal Danish Ballet in 1965, appointed its youngest principal in 1967. After several seasons guesting in New York, he joined New York City Ballet as a principal in 1970, and went on to forge an outstanding partnership with Suzanne *Farrell. (Upon the latter's retirement in 1988 he choreographed a work specially for her, *Sophisticated Lady* (mus. Ellington)). He created roles in many Balanchine ballets, among them *Violin Concerto* (1972), *Duo concertant* (1972), *Chaconne* (1976), *Union Jack* (1976), *Vienna Waltzes* (1977), and *Davidsbündlertänze* (1980). He also excelled in the earlier Balanchine repertoire and, with his handsome build was considered by many to be the greatest Apollo of his generation. He also created leading roles in Robbins's *In the Night* (1970), *The Goldberg Variations* (1971), and *Piano Concerto in G* (1975) and in Taras's *Daphnis and Chloe* (1975). Although Martins performed the 19th-century classics with other companies, his preference was always the

modern repertory. He retired as a dancer in 1984 but made his debut as a choreographer in 1977, with *Calcium Light Night* (mus. Ives) for his own pick-up company; in 1978 he began choreographing for New York City Ballet and has since made over 80 ballets, most of them for the company. Following Balanchine's death in 1983 he was appointed ballet master in chief of NYCB, a post he shared with Robbins. In 1990, following Robbins's departure, Martins assumed sole directorship. Some of his policies attracted criticism but he was determined to prevent the company from becoming a museum, bringing in new works to the repertory, many of them commissioned through the Diamond Project that he instituted in 1992. He was also responsible for appointing Christopher Wheeldon as the company's resident choreographer between 2001 and 2007. A list of Martins's own works includes *Eight Easy Pieces* (mus. Stravinsky, 1980), *The Magic Flute* (mus. Drigo, 1981), *A Schubertiad* (mus. Schubert, 1984), *Poulenc Sonata* (mus. Poulenc, 1985), *Eight More* (mus. Stravinsky, 1985), *Songs of Auvergne* (1986), *Ecstatic Orange* (mus. Michael Torke, 1987), *Les Gentilhommes* (mus. Handel, 1987), *Barber Violin Concerto* (mus. Barber, 1988), *Tea Rose* (mus. Gershwin, 1988), *The Chairman Dances* (mus. John Adams, 1988), *Fearful Symmetries* (mus. Adams, 1990), *Delight of the Muses* (mus. Charles Wuorinen, 1992), *Jeu de cartes* (mus. Stravinsky, 1992), *River of Light* (mus. Wuorinen, 1998), *Thou Swell* (mus. Rodgers, 2002), and the full-length *Romeo and Juliet* (2007). He also staged *The Sleeping Beauty* for New York City Ballet in 1991, trimming it to a two-act production. In 1996 he staged a new version of *Swan Lake* for the Royal Danish Ballet, which came into the repertory of NYCB in 1999. He has also choreographed for musicals, including *On Your Toes* (1982), *Song and Dance* (1985), and *Carousel* (1986). Author of the autobiography *Far from Denmark* (Boston, 1982). Knight of the Order of Dannebrog (1983). His son, Nilas Martins, joined New York City Ballet in 1986.

Martinů, Bohuslav (*b* Policka, 8 Dec. 1890; *d* Liestal, Switzerland, 28 Aug. 1959) Czech composer. He wrote the music for several ballets, including R. Remislawsky's *Istar* (Prague, 1924) and *Who Is the Mightiest in the World?* (Prague, 1972), Psota's *The Riot* (Brno, 1928), Joe Jencik's *Spalicek* (Prague, 1933), and Erick Hawkins's *The Strangler* (1948). Choreographers who have used his concert music for ballets include Tudor (*Echoing of Trumpets*, 1963), MacMillan (the one-act *Anastasia*, 1967), Tetley (*Sphinx*, 1979), Corder (*Day into Night*, 1980), Kylián (*Field Mass*, 1980), Nils Christe (*Before Nightfall*, 1991), and Christopher Hampson (*Sinfonietta Giacosa*, 2006).

Maslow, Sophie (*b* New York, 22 Mar. 1911; *d* New York, 25 Jun. 2006) US dancer, teacher, and choreographer. She studied with Blanche Talmud and Graham, eventually joining the Graham company in 1931 and dancing with her for twelve years. She appeared in some of Graham's most important works, including *American Document* and *Primitive Mysteries*. She was also a member of the politicized New Dance Group (or New Dance League), in the mid-1930s. From 1942 to 1954 she performed with Jane Dudley and William Bales in the Dudley-Maslow-Bales Trio and choreographed many works for that company, including *Folksay* (1942), which used folk-songs by Woody Guthrie and a text by Carl Sandburg to evoke life in rural America, *Champion* (1948), *The Village I Knew* (1949), based on stories by Sholom Aleichem, and *Manhattan Celebration* (1954). She formed her own company, Sophie Maslow and Company, in New York in the mid-1950s, presenting work of a distinctively populist character. In 1975 she founded the Danscompany with Joyce Trisler. She also worked with a number of other outfits, including the Batsheva Dance Company in Israel for whom she re-staged *The Village I Knew* (1950). She was a founding member of the American Dance Festival at Connecticut College in 1948. Other works include *Dust Bowl Ballads* (1941), *Raincheck* or *Rain Check* (1958), *Poem* (1963), *From the Book of Ruth* (1964), *Neither Rest Nor Harbor* (1969), *Touch the Earth* (1973), *Such Sweet Thunder* (1975), *The Decathlon Études* (1976), and *Woody Sez* (1980). She continued to teach and choreograph in New York for many decades. In 1999 she and Donald McKayle reconstructed *Champion* for the José Limón company. Maslow's ballet, based on Ring Lardner's short story about a boxer who will do anything to get to the top, had not been seen on the stage since 1950.

Mason, Monica (*b* Johannesburg, 6 Sept. 1941) South African-born British dancer. She studied with Ruth Inglestone, Nesta Brooking, and at the Royal Ballet School before joining the Royal Ballet in 1958, aged 16, where she was appointed soloist in 1963 and principal in 1968. A particular favourite of MacMillan's, she was still a member of the corps de ballet when he picked her to create the role of the Chosen Maiden in his *Rite of Spring* (1962). She also created roles in his *Manon* (1974), *Elite Syncopations* (1974), *The Four Seasons* (1975), *Rituals* (1975), and *Isadora* (1981). A strong, versatile dancer with a vibrant personality, her other repertory included *Swan Lake, Sleeping Beauty, The Firebird, Enigma Variations, Bayadère, Cinderella, Mayerling,* and *Romeo and Juliet*. She was appointed principal repetiteur of the Royal Ballet in 1984 and assistant director in 1991. In 1999 she returned to the stage to create the role of Mrs Grose in William Tuckett's *The Turn of the Screw*. She was appointed director of the Royal Ballet in 2002, and in that role has overseen the restoration of several heritage works to the repertory—including Ashton's *Sylvia*, a one-act version of MacMillan's *Isadora*, and elements of the Royal's signature 1946 staging of *Sleeping Beauty*. In 2006 she was also responsible for appointing McGregor as resident choreographer, entrusting to him the task of injecting a contemporary dynamic into the company.

masque Theatrical presentations, usually performed by members of the nobility, which were popular at the English court in the 16th and 17th centuries. They were the English equivalent of the *ballets de cour of France. Their origins were in traditional masked processions and mummings, and their subject-matter was allegorical or mythological, with music, mime, and singing featured along with the dance. The literary element was probably the most important component and among those who wrote texts for masques were Ben Jonson and John Milton. The architect Inigo Jones contributed set designs, e.g. for *Masque of Blackness* (1605) and *Masque of Beauty* (1608), both of which were conceived by Jonson. The form is rarely revived, although Leslie French staged a revival of Milton's *Comus* for International Ballet in 1946 and Helpmann produced a mimed play based on the same Milton masque for Sadler's Wells Ballet in 1942. De Valois's 1931 *Job*, a 'masque for dancing', pays homage to the form.

Massine, Léonide (orig Miassin; *b* Moscow, 8 Aug. 1895; *d* Weseke bei Borken, Germany, 15 Mar. 1979) Russian-US dancer, choreographer, ballet master, and teacher. One of the stars of Diaghilev's Ballets Russes, he became one of the most influential and controversial choreographers of the 20th century. He trained at the Bolshoi Ballet School in Moscow with Gorsky, graduating in 1912 and joining the Bolshoi Ballet. In 1914 he was recruited by Diaghilev to create the title role in Fokine's *The Legend of Joseph*. A stage performer of almost eerie glamour and expressiveness, he was suited primarily to demicaractère rather than classical roles. In 1915 he made his debut as a choreographer (with *Le Soleil de nuit*), encouraged by Diaghilev who was eager to discover a new talent following the departure of Fokine and Nijinsky. He continued his dance studies with Cecchetti and found great success as both a performer and a choreographer, often dancing the lead in his own ballets.

For Diaghilev he choreographed *Les Femmes de bonne humeur* (mus. Scarlatti, 1917), *Parade* (mus. Satie, 1917), *La Boutique fantasque* (mus. Rossini, arr. Respighi, 1919), *Le Tricorne* (mus. de

Falla, 1919), *Song of the Nightingale* (mus. Stravinsky, 1920), *Pulcinella* (mus. Stravinsky, 1920), and *Le Sacre du printemps* (mus. Stravinsky, 1920). In early 1921 he left Diaghilev, working in S. America, London, and Paris with varying combinations of dancers, including Lopokova. During this period he created several works, the best known of which, *Salade* (mus. Milhaud), *Mercure* (mus. Satie), and *Le Beau Danube* (mus. J. Strauss,) were all staged for Étienne de Beaumont's Soirées de Paris season of 1924. In 1925 he returned to the Ballets Russes as guest choreographer, where he made *Zéphire et Flore* (mus. V. Dukelsky, 1925), *Les Matelots* (mus. Auric, 1925), *Le Pas d'acier* (mus. Prokofiev, 1927), and *Ode* (mus. Nabakov, 1928). He was then in New York as solo dancer and ballet master of the Roxy Theatre in New York (1928–30), and he also revived *Sacre du printemps* with Martha Graham in the leading role in 1930 in Philadelphia. He additionally worked with Ida Rubinstein's company, for which he made *David* (mus. Sauguet, 1928) and *Amphion* (mus. Honegger, 1931). In 1932 he joined the Blum and de Basil Ballets Russes de Monte Carlo, becoming its ballet master in 1933. For them he choreographed *Jeux d'enfants* (mus. Bizet, 1932), *Choreartium* (mus. Brahms's 4th Symphony, 1933), *Les Présages* (mus. Tchaikovsky's 5th Symphony, 1933), and *Symphonie fantastique* (mus. Berlioz, 1936). When de Basil and Blum fell out, Massine went with Blum's breakaway Ballet Russe de Monte Carlo, where he was artistic director (1938–42). For this company he made *Gaîté parisienne* (mus. Offenbach–Rosenthal, 1938), *Seventh Symphony* (mus. Beethoven, 1938), *Nobilissima visione* (mus. Hindemith, 1938), *Capriccio espagnol* (with La Argentinita, mus. Rimsky-Korsakov, 1939), *Rouge et noir* (mus. Shostakovich's 1st Symphony, 1939), *Bacchanale* (mus. Wagner, 1939), and *Labyrinth* (mus. Schubert's 7th Symphony, 1941). In 1942 he joined American Ballet Theatre, making *Aleko* (mus. Tchaikovsky, 1942) and *Mademoiselle Angot* (mus. Lecocq, 1943). He also toured with his own troupe, Ballet Russe Highlights (1945–6), which premiered *Leningrad Symphony* (mus. Shostakovich) in New York in 1945.

In 1947 he returned to Europe where he choreographed for many companies, creating among others *Clock Symphony* (mus. Haydn, Sadler's Wells Ballet, 1948), *Le Peintre et son modèle* (mus. Auric, Ballets des Champs-Elysées, 1949), *Harold in Italy* (mus. Berlioz, Ballet Russe de Monte Carlo, 1954), *Donald of the Burthens* (mus. I. Whyte, Sadler's Wells Ballet, 1951), *Laudes Evangeli* (mus. Bucchi, Perugia, 1952), *Mario and the Magician* (mus. F. Mannino, La Scala, Milan, 1954), *Don Juan* (mus. Gluck, La Scala, Milan, 1959), and *Fantasmi al Grand Hotel* (mus. Chailly, La Scala, Milan, 1960). In 1960 he set up the Ballet Europeo for the Nervi Festival in Genoa and choreographed *Le Bal des voleurs* (mus. Auric, 1960) and the full-length *La commedia umana* (mus. ancient, 1960).

As a choreographer he was most popular for his comic ballets (starting with *Les Femmes de bonne humeur*) but it was his pioneering *symphonic ballets (*Choreartium*, *Présages*) that opened up new possibilities for ballet, using big concert scores that had been hitherto deemed unsuitable for dance. He travelled the world, reviving his ballets for numerous companies and became interested in a wide variety of dance styles, including that of the Native Americans. He was also involved in films, most famously acting and choreographing his own role in *The Red Shoes* (1948); he also choreographed Powell and Pressburger's *The Tales of Hoffmann* (1951). In 1923 he opened his own school in London—one of his students was Ashton. He also taught choreography at the Royal Ballet School in 1969. Author of *My Life in Ballet* (London, 1968) and the densely theoretical textbook *Massine on Choreography* (London, 1976).

Massine, Lorca (orig. Leonide Massine; *b* New York, 25 Jul. 1944) US dancer and choreographer. Son of Léonide *Massine. He studied with his father and V. Gsovsky and made his debut at the Nervi Festival in 1960. He created the role of Puck in Britten's *A Midsummer Night's Dream* at Aldeburgh in 1960. He subsequently appeared as an actor on the Paris stage, and worked as a choreographer. With his sister Tatiana he formed the European Ballet, which toured (1964–7). From 1968 to 1970 he was a soloist and choreographer with the Ballet of the 20th Century; one of his ballets was *Tenth Symphony* (mus. Mahler, 1968). From 1971 to 1973 he was a soloist at New York City Ballet, where he made *Four Last Songs* (mus. R. Strauss, 1971) and *Ode* (mus. Stravinsky, 1972). Other ballets include *Ondine* (mus. Henze, Hamburg, 1972), *Fête dansée* (mus. Theodorakis, company of A. Beranger, 1973), *Esoteric Satie* (Milan, 1978), and *Zorba* (mus. Theodorakis, Cairo, 1988). He has worked on the reconstruction and staging of his father's repertory for several companies including the Bolshoi.

Matisse, Henri (*b* Le Cateau-Cambrésis, 31 Dec. 1869; *d* Nice, 3 Nov. 1954) French painter and stage designer. He designed two ballets for Massine: *The Song of the Nightingale* (1920) and *Rouge et noir* (1939). His interest in dance can also be seen in his monumental painting *La Danse*.

Matsuyama Ballet Japanese ballet company based in Tokyo. A family-run enterprise, it was founded in 1948 by the ballerina Mikiko Matsuyama. Her husband, Masao Shimizu, was director, while she became artistic director. Today their son Tetsutaro Shimizu is director and chief choreographer, while his wife Yoko *Morishita was the company's prima ballerina. The company has always toured internationally, including to China and the US. Its early repertory featured works with strongly political themes including the 1958 revolutionary ballet *The White-Haired Girl* (which was especially popular with the Communist Chinese government) and *Gion Festival* (*Gion Matsuri*), a work choreographed by Taneo Ishida, which dealt with an uprising against the ruler of Kyoto in medieval Japan. Today the company dances a more traditional repertoire, blending 19th-century classics such as *Giselle* and *Swan Lake* with works by 20th-century choreographers such as Balanchine. Shimizu has also sought to incorporate elements of Japanese culture into the ballet, most notably in 1987 with his *Mandala*, a love story between a young Catholic girl and a young Buddhist artist, which was staged at the Edinburgh Festival in 1988. Mikiko Matsuyama retired from the stage in 1978 but continued as artistic director. The company has an associated school.

Matteo (orig. M. Marcellus Vittucci; *b* Utica, NY, 2 May 1919) US dancer, teacher, choreographer, and director. A leading authority on ethnic dance. He studied at Cornell University in New York, Ethnologic Dance Center, Springfield College, and with various ethnic dance specialists. From 1946 to 1950 he danced with the Metropolitan Opera Ballet before embarking on a career as a recitalist, and lecturer on the subject of ethnic dance. He established the Indo-American Dance Company with Carola Goya in 1967, which subsequently developed into the Indo-American Performing Arts Center of New York in 1970. After Goya's death in 1994, the renamed Foundation for Ethnic Dance lost its momentum and in 2001 was taken over by Gwendolyn Dunaif and, renamed again as Inter-Dance Foundation, moved to Brooklyn to sponsor educational and performance projects of flamenco, Korean, bharata natyam, and other ethnic forms

Matvienko, Denis (*b* Dnepropetrovsk, 23 Feb. 1979) Ukraine-Russian dancer. He studied at Kiev State Choreographic School from 1989, performing with the company in his final year (1997) as Prince Desiré in *Sleeping Beauty* and graduating into the company as a soloist. A classic Russian dancer, with a bravura jump, he has been a noted interpreter of ballets by Grigorovich. Between 2001 and 2002 he danced with the Mariinsky Ballet as first soloist, creating lead roles in Ratmansky's *Cinderella* and the company premiere of Balanchine's *Prodigal Son*. He returned

to Kiev (2003–7) as principal, danced for two years at the Mikhailovsky Ballet (2007–9) and then rejoined the Mariinsky.

He has guested with several companies including Tokyo National Theatre, Bolshoi Ballet, and Paris Opera Ballet and is recipient of numerous awards. He is married to dancer Anastasia M, and is her frequent partner.

Maximova, Ekaterina (*b* Moscow, 1 Feb. 1939; *d* Moscow, 8 Apr. 2009) Soviet dancer. She studied at the Bolshoi Ballet School, a pupil of Elisaveta Gerdt, and graduated into the company in 1958 as a soloist. She came to prominence the following year in the role of Katerina, which she created in Grigorovich's Moscow staging of *The Stone Flower*. Giselle quickly followed (with Maximova then the youngest woman to dance that role at the Bolshoi), as did Kitri. Maximova became particularly associated with the ballets of Grigorovich, creating Masha in his 1966 staging of *Nutcracker*, Phrygia in his *Spartacus* (1968), and Aurora in his *Sleeping Beauty* (1973). She also created roles in several ballets by her husband, the Bolshoi dancer Vladimir Vasiliev, both in Russia and in the West. A very versatile dancer, she had a brilliant technique and a strikingly pliable body. Although she continued to dance with the Bolshoi for 30 years (she left the company in 1989 due to political disputes), she frequently appeared as a guest artist abroad, with Béjart's Ballet of the 20th Century in 1978, Petit's Ballet du Marseilles (1987), English National Ballet (then London Festival Ballet, 1989), the Australian Ballet, and National Ballet of Canada in 1990. She also appeared in many films, including *Galatea* (1978), *Old Tango* (1979), *Gigolo and Gigoletta* (1980, directed by her husband), *La traviata* (1982, directed by Zeffirelli), *Fouetté* (1986, directed by Vasiliev), *Gappiniana* (1987), and *Volodia and Katia* (1989). In 1982 she began teaching at the Choreography Department of the Lunacharsky Theatre Technicum. She finally retired from dancing in 1994 to work as ballet mistress and repetiteur, with the Kremlin Ballet and the Bolshoi, also to aid Vasiliev in staging the classical repertory outside Russia. From 2005 she and her last stage partner, Konstantin Matveev, ran a charity to help retired stage artists. She won the Gold Medal, Varna, 1964. People's Artist, USSR. Anna Pavlova Prize, Paris 1969.

May, Pamela (orig. Doris May; *b* San Fernando, Trinidad, 30 May 1917; *d* 6 Jun. 2005) British dancer and teacher. She studied with Freda Grant in London, Olga Preobrajenska, and Lubov Egorova in Paris, and de Valois at the Sadler's Wells Ballet School from 1933. She made her debut at the Vic-Wells Ballet in 1934 and rapidly emerged, along with Fonteyn, as one of the key performers in early British ballet. She created roles in de Valois's *Checkmate* (1937), *The Prospect Before Us* (1940), *Orpheus and Eurydice* (1941), and *Don Quixote* (1950), in Ashton's *Les Patineurs* (1937), *A Wedding Bouquet* (1937), *Horoscope* (1938), *Dante Sonata* (1940), *The Wanderer* (1941), *Symphonic Variations* (1946), and *Cinderella* (1948). A dancer of enormous versatility, she started performing the classical ballerina repertory during the 1940s yet also made her mark in supporting roles like the Lilac Fairy and Myrtha. After 1952 she became a leading character artist with the company and also taught at the Royal Ballet School (1954–77).

Mayerling Ballet in three acts with prologue and epilogue, with choreography by MacMillan, libretto by Gillian Freeman, music by Liszt (arranged and orchestrated by Lanchbery), and designs by Georgiadis. Premiered 14 Feb. 1978 by the Royal Ballet at Covent Garden with Wall, Seymour, Wendy Ellis, Parkinson, Park, Connor, Somes, and Graham Fletcher. MacMillan's ballet is based on the true story of the Crown Prince Rudolf, heir to the Austro-Hungarian throne, who took part in a double suicide with his mistress at the royal hunting lodge of Mayerling in 1889. Rudolf, and the 17-year-old Baroness Mary Vetsera, are typical MacMillan protagonists: flawed characters whose amoral and uncompromising behaviour place them outside the bounds of society. Rudolf is portrayed as a depraved drug addict, riddled with venereal disease, who enters into a liaison with the reckless, ambitious young Mary. The court around them is poisoned by corruption and hypocrisy. MacMillan tells Rudolf's story through a series of pas de deux for him and the women in his life, vignettes of raw emotion that veer between extremes of desire and hate. Along with MacMillan's *Manon* and *Romeo and Juliet*, it has remained a constant of the Covent Garden repertoire.

Maywood, Augusta (*b* New York, 1825; *d* Lemberg, Austria-Hungary, now Lviv, Ukraine, 3 Nov. 1876) US dancer. The first American ballerina to achieve international fame, and one of the leading names in 19th-century Italian ballet. She studied with Paul Hazard in Philadelphia from 1836 and made her debut there in *Le Dieu et la bayadère* in 1837. The following year however she travelled to Paris where she studied with Mazilier and Coralli and appeared as a guest ballerina with the Paris Opera in *La Tarentule* (1839). She never appeared on the American stage again. She married the dancer Charles Mabille and travelled with him to Lisbon. After their divorce, she stayed in Vienna where she danced with the Kärntnertor Theatre (1845–7). In 1848 she went to La Scala, where she studied with Blasis and danced many

of the ballerina roles, including Perrot's *Faust* and Cortesi's *La silfide*. From 1850 to 1858 she toured Italy with her own company, one of the first dancers to have her own touring ensemble. She was especially admired for her dancing in *Giselle*, *Faust*, and *La Esmeralda*. She created the title role in Filippo Termanini's *Rita Gauthier* in 1856. She returned to Vienna in 1858 where she opened a school and in 1873 retired to Lake Como.

Mazilier, Joseph (orig. Giulio Mazarini; *b* Marseilles, 13 Mar. 1797 (some sources 1801); *d* Paris, 19 May 1868) French dancer, choreographer, and ballet master. Choreographer of many important ballets of the Romantic era and the first dancer to perform James in *La Sylphide*. He made his debut in Bordeaux and from 1822 appeared at the Paris Théâtre de la Porte-St-Martin, where he created roles in many ballets by Coralli. In 1830 he joined the Paris Opera, where he became a leading character dancer. He created roles in F. Taglioni's *La Sylphide* (James, 1832) and *La Fille du Danube* (1836), Coralli's *Le Diable boîteux* (1836) and *La Tarentule* (1839), and Guerra's *Les Mohicans* (1837). But although he was an important dancer, it was his career as ballet master and choreographer that was of lasting significance. From 1839 to 1851 he was ballet master of the Paris Opera, where he made more than two dozen works. He spent a year with the Imperial Theatres in St Petersburg (1851–2) but returned to the Paris Opera in 1853 as premier maître de ballet. He retired in 1860, although he came out of retirement in 1867 to revive *Le Corsaire*. A list of his works includes *La Gypsy* (mus. F. Benoist and T. Marliani, 1839), *Le Diable amoureux* (mus. Benoist and H. Réber, 1840), *Lady Henriette, ou la servante de Greenwich* (mus. Flotow, Burgmüller, and Deldevez, 1844), *Le Diable à quatre* (mus. Adam, 1845), *Paquita* (mus. Deldevez, 1846), *Griseldis, ou les cinq sens* (mus. Adam, 1848), *Vert-vert* (mus. Deldevez and J. B. Tobeque (or Tolbeque), 1851), *Jovita, ou les boucaniers* (mus. T. Labarre, 1853), *Le Corsaire* (mus. Adam, 1856), and *Marco Spada, ou la fille du bandit* (mus. Auber, 1857).

mazurka A Polish national dance for couples in 3/4 or 6/8 time. It was first recorded in the 16th century; in the late 19th century it was introduced as a ballroom dance throughout Europe. The dance features stamping of the feet and clicking of the heels. There are many famous examples of a mazurka occurring in classical ballet, including *Swan Lake* and *Coppélia*.

Mazzo, Kay (*b* Chicago, 17 Jan. 1946) US dancer. She studied with Bernardene Hayes and at the School of American Ballet (from 1959). She made her debut with Robbins's Ballets USA in 1961, appearing in his *Afternoon of a Faun* in Paris. The following year she joined New York City Ballet, becoming a soloist in 1965 and a principal in 1969. When Suzanne Farrell left NYCB in 1969, Mazzo, who bore a strong resemblance to her, inherited many of her roles. She was a dancer possessed of considerable beauty and technique, who also suggested an appealing vulnerability. She created roles in several Balanchine ballets, including *Suite No. 3* (1970), *Violin Concerto*, *Duo concertant* (both 1972), *Union Jack* (1976), *Vienna Waltzes* (1977), and *Davidsbündlertänze* (1980). She also created roles in Robbins's *Dances at a Gathering* (1969) and *In the Night* (1970). Following her retirement from the company she taught at the School of American Ballet (from 1983) becoming co-chair of the faculty in 1997.

Medea Ballet in one act with choreography and libretto by Cullberg, music by Bartók (arranged by H. Sandberg), and designs by Alvar Grandstrom. Premiered 31 Oct. 1950 at the Riksteatern, Gaevle, Sweden, with Lagerborg, Béjart, and Inga Noring. The ballet, set to music from Bartók's *Mikrokosmos*, tells of Medea's revenge against Jason, the husband who deserted her. It was revived for the Royal Swedish Ballet in 1953 and for New York City Ballet in 1958. There have been other dance treatments of the Medea story, from Noverre's *Médée et Jason* (Stuttgart, 1763) to Graham's *Cave of the Heart* (New York, 1947).

Meditation from Thaïs Pas de deux with choreography by Ashton, music by Massenet. Premiered 21 Mar. 1971 at the Gala in aid of Friends of Fatherless Families, Adelphi Theatre, London, with Sibley and Dowell. A duet evoking a dream of exotic romance, it was revived for the Royal Ballet in 1991. Pavlova had a version in her repertoire.

Meehan, John (*b* Brisbane, 1 May 1950) Australian dancer and ballet director. He studied at the Australian Ballet School and joined the Australian Ballet in 1970, where he was promoted to soloist in 1972 and principal in 1974. He created roles in Tetley's *Gemini* (1973), Helpmann's *Perisynthion* (1974), Butler's *Night Encounter* (1975), and Hynd's *Merry Widow* (1975) in which he later partnered Fonteyn. A gifted dance actor who was also a fine partner, Meehan moved to American Ballet Theatre in 1977, leaving in 1980 to work on the commercial stage and then returning in 1985. He was a guest artist with the National Ballet of Canada and New York City Ballet. Between 1989 and 1993 he was artistic director of Royal Winnipeg Ballet, after which he returned to New York to teach and in 1997 to become director of American

Ballet Theatre's junior company. In 2006 he was appointed director of the Hong Kong Ballet.

Mendelssohn-Bartholdy, Felix (*b* Hamburg, 3 Feb. 1809; *d* Leipzig, 4 Nov. 1847) German composer. Although he did not write specifically for the ballet, his incidental music to *A Midsummer Night's Dream* has inspired many choreographers, including Petipa (1876), Fokine (1906), Balanchine (1962), and—most famously—Ashton in *The Dream* (1964).

Mérante, Louis (*b* Paris, 23 Jul. (some sources say 27 Jul.) 1828; *d* Courbevoie, 17 Jul. 1887) French dancer, choreographer, and ballet master. He joined the Paris Opera in 1848, as an understudy to Lucien Petipa, and went on to become one of the finest premiers danseurs of his day and a favourite partner to several ballerinas. Between 1853 and 1866 he created roles in many ballets, including Mazilier's *Marco Spada*, L. Petipa's *Sacountala*, M. Taglioni's *Le Papillon*, and Saint-Léon's *Diavolina* and *La Source*. He was appointed ballet master in 1869 and made his first ballet, *Gretna Green* (mus. E. Guiraud), for the Paris Opera in 1873. He also choreographed Delibes's *Sylvia* (1876) and Messager's *Les Deux Pigeons* (1886). Just five years before his death he created a leading role in L. Petipa's *Namouna* (1882).

Mercure Tableaux in three scenes, with choreography and libretto by Massine, music by Satie, and designs by Picasso. Premiered 15 Jun. 1924, at the Soirées de Paris, Théâtre de la Cigale. The ballet's mythological subject matter was given a fashionably avant-garde treatment but Picasso's Cubist decor was deemed to have been more successful than the Massine choreography. Diaghilev took it into his company in 1927, although it was rarely performed.

Mercury Theatre A mid-19th-century church hall in Notting Hill Gate in W. London bought by Ashley Dukes and his wife Marie *Rambert in 1927. They converted it into a small theatre and ballet school. In 1931 the theatre opened with a performance by the Ballet Club. Early works by Tudor and Ashton were given their premieres here. It continued as a theatre until 1955.

Merry Widow, The Ballet in three acts with choreography by Hynd, scenario and staging by Helpmann, music by Lehár, arr. Lanchbery, and designs by Desmond Heeley. Premiered 13 Nov. 1975 by the Australian Ballet at the Palais in Melbourne, with M. Rowe, J. Meehan, L. Aldous, and K. Coe. The ballet, based on Lehár's 1905 operetta about the rich young widow Hanna Glawari, was later taken into the repertoires of the National Ballet of Canada and American Ballet Theatre.

Messel, Oliver (*b* Cuckfield, 13 Jan. 1905; *d* Bridgetown, Barbados, 13 Jul. 1978) British painter and stage designer. He studied art at the Slade School in London and designed for opera and ballet throughout the 1930s and 1940s, at Sadler's Wells, Covent Garden, and Glyndebourne. He designed Lichine's *Francesca da Rimini* (de Basil's Ballets Russes de Monte Carlo, 1937), Helpmann's *Comus* (Sadler's Wells Ballet, 1942), and—most importantly—the Sergeyev-Ashton-de Valois 1946 Sadler's Wells Ballet staging of *Sleeping Beauty*, which re-opened the Royal Opera House after the Second World War. His last ballet was Ashton's *Homage to the Queen* (1953). His style was spectacularly scaled but lyrical, with a strong period feel. He also worked as a designer on several films, including *The Scarlet Pimpernel* (1935), *Romeo and Juliet* (1936), *The Thief of Baghdad* (1940), *The Winslow Boy* (1948), and *Suddenly Last Summer* (1960). Author of *Stage Designs and Costumes* (London, 1934).

Messerer, Asaf (*b* Vilnius, 19 Nov. 1903; *d* Moscow, 7 Mar. 1992) Soviet dancer, ballet master, and teacher. He studied privately with Mordkin, then with Gorsky at the Bolshoi Ballet School in Moscow from 1919. He graduated in 1921, joining the Bolshoi Ballet. For the next 30 years he was one of the company's leading dancers, combining an athletic virtuosity with an exceptional dramatic range. He retired from the stage in 1954 and although he choreographed several ballets, including **Ballet Class* and the gala favourite *Spring Waters*, it was as a teacher that he made his greatest contribution. He began teaching in 1923 at the Bolshoi, directing the Class of Perfection from 1942 or 1943, and systematically introducing classical detail and complexity into the Bolshoi's distinctively broad style. His methods won international recognition and he was frequently invited to teach abroad, including a season as ballet master of the Ballet of the 20th Century (1961–2). Author of *Classes in Classical Ballet* (Moscow, 1967; English language version, New York, 1975) and *Dance, Thought and Times* (1979). Uncle of Maya Plisetskaya and the noted teacher Mikhail Messerer; brother of the Bolshoi ballerina Sulamith Messerer. Merited Artist of the USSR (1933), Stalin Prize (1941, 1947), and People's Artist of the USSR (1976).

Messiaen, Olivier (*b* Avignon, 10 Dec. 1908; *d* Paris, 28 Apr. 1992) French composer. Although he wrote no music specifically for dance, and claimed to disapprove of choreographers who used his concert music, his scores, or extracts of his scores, have been used by several choreographers among them van Dyk in *Turangalila* (Hamburg, 1960), Petit in *Turangalila* (Paris, 1968), van Manen in *Essay in Silence* (Nederlands Dans

Theater, 1965), Tetley in *Chronochromie* (Jacob's Pillow, 1967), Cranko in *Oiseaux exotiques* (Stuttgart, 1967), and Graeme Murphy in *After Venice* (Australia, 1985).

Metropolitan Ballet A short-lived London-based dance company founded by Cecilia Blatch and Leon Hepner which performed from 1947 to 1949 in Britain and abroad. Its ballet masters included Victor Gsovsky, Nicholas Beriozoff, and Celia Franca. Dancers included Svetlana Beriosova and Erik Bruhn. Its repertoire featured both classics and ballets from the Diaghilev repertoire. Choreographers included Celia Franca, Gsovsky, Andrée Howard, Frank Staff, and John Taras.

Metropolitan Opera Ballet The dance company attached to the Metropolitan Opera in New York.

Metropolitan Opera House New York's main opera house. It opened in 1883 in midtown Manhattan and closed in 1966, when it moved uptown to a new building at the Lincoln Center for the Performing Arts. American Ballet Theatre performs its New York seasons here, as do large visiting companies.

Mexico *See* BALLET FOLKLÓRICO DE MEXICO.

Meyer, Laverne (*b* Guelph, Ont., 1 Feb. 1935; *d* London, 25 Apr. 2008) Canadian dancer, choreographer, and ballet director. He studied with Graham, and at both the Rambert School and Sadler's Wells School. From 1957 to 1968 he danced with Western Theatre Ballet (now Scottish Ballet), becoming ballet master and associate artistic director in 1964. In 1969 he founded Northern Dance Theatre in Manchester (later **Northern Ballet Theatre). He resigned in 1975 and took up teaching. A list of his ballets includes *The Web* (mus. Webern, 1962), *Schubert Variations* (1972), *Cinderella* (mus. Robert Stewart, 1973), and *Aladdin* (mus. E. Tomlinson, 1974).

Meyerbeer, Giacomo (*b* Tasdorf, 5 Sept. 1791; *d* Paris, 2 May 1864) German composer. He wrote the music for Lauchery's ballet, *The Fisher and the Milkmaid* (Berlin, 1810). The music for Ashton's *Les Patineurs* (1937) derives from the ballet divertissements of his operas *Le Prophète* and *Étoile du nord*.

Mezentseva, Galina (*b* Stavropol, 8 Nov. 1952) Soviet dancer. She studied at the Leningrad Ballet School (the Vaganova), graduating into the Kirov Ballet in 1970. For twenty years she was one of the Kirov's leading dancers, especially acclaimed in *Giselle*. After leaving in 1990 she guested with Scottish Ballet and also toured America with the St Petersburg Ballet.

Miami City Ballet US dance company based in Florida. It was founded in 1986 with Edward *Villella as founding artistic director. Villella, a former New York City Ballet principal, who turned the Florida company into the foremost regional showcase for the Balanchine repertoire. He also brought in selected works by contemporary choreographers like Tharp and Taylor, as well as core 19th-century classics like *Don Quixote* and *Swan Lake*. The company's associated school was founded in 1993.

(((⊕))) SEE WEB LINKS

• Website for Miami City Ballet

Midsummer Night's Dream, A Ballet in two acts with choreography by Balanchine, music by Mendelssohn, sets and lighting by David Hays, and costumes by Barbara Karinska. Premiered 17 Jan. 1962 by New York City Ballet at City Center, New York, with Mitchell, Hayden, and Villella. The ballet, Balanchine's first original full-length work, is based on Shakespeare's play and uses Mendelssohn's incidental music. It was filmed in 1967. It was later taken into the repertoire of Pacific Northwest Ballet (1985). Other ballets on the same subject include those by Petipa (1876), Fokine (1906), Ashton (*The Dream*, 1964), Neumeier (Hamburg, 1977), Cohan (Scottish Ballet, 1993), Wheeldon (Colorado Ballet, 2000), and Bigonzetti (mus. Elvis Costello, Bologna, 2002).

Mikhailovsky Ballet Russian dance company based at the Mikhailovsky Theatre in St Petersburg. The theatre itself dates back to 1833, but was renamed in 1915 as the Maly (Small). The ballet company was formed in 1933, with F. *Lopukhov as director and made its debut on 6 Jun. with his ballet *Harlequinade*. Despite taking second place to the Kirov in St Petersburg, the Maly Ballet forged its own distinctive artistic identity, placing an emphasis on comedy and symphonic dance. One of its most controversial early productions was Lopukhov's *The Bright Stream*, a ballet set to the music of Shostakovich that proved very popular with the public but subsequently displeased the Soviet authorities who accused the ballet and its choreographer of formalism. Lopukhov had to leave Leningrad but returned during the Second World War as the Maly's temporary director. During his absence Leonid *Lavrovsky, was ballet director from 1936 to 1938, staging *Fadetta* (Delibes's *Sylvia*, 1936), *La Fille mal gardée* (1937), and Asafiev's *Prisoner of the Caucasus* (1938) for the company. Boris Fenster, one of Lopukhov's pupils, was director from 1945 to 1965 and created several works for the Maly including *An Imaginary Fiancé* (1946) and *Youth* (1949). A seminal production during this period was Gusev's reconstruction of Petipa's *Le Corsaire* which led to further revivals of ballets, like *Swan Lake* (1958) and *Giselle* (1973), which similarly attempted to restore the classics to their pre-Soviet state. Igor *Belsky, who was chief choreographer from 1962 to 1973, undertook new productions of *The Humpbacked Horse* and *Nutcracker*, as well as choreographing the first versions of Shostakovich's *Eleventh Symphony* (1966) and Tchernov's *Gadfly* (1967). Oleg *Vinogradov was chief choreographer of the Maly (1973–7) and made one of his important early ballets there, *Yaroslavna* (mus. Tishenko, 1974). While then moving on to the Kirov and being succeeded by Nikolai *Boyarchikov, Vinogradov continued to retain links with the company and his recent creations for it include *Romeo and Juliet* (2008). In 1989 the Maly Theatre was renamed the Mussorgsky Theatre of Opera and Ballet but in 2007 reverted to its original name of Mikhailovksy. The same year Farukh Ruzimatov was appointed artistic director succeeded in 2009 by Mikhail Messerer.

Milhaud, Darius (*b* Aix-en-Provence, 4 Sept. 1892; *d* Geneva, 22 Jun. 1974) French composer. He wrote many ballet scores, starting with Cocteau's *Le Bœuf sur le toit* (1920), which was originally staged as a pantomime for acrobats and clowns. For Les Ballets Suédois he wrote the music for three works by Börlin: *L'Homme et son désir* (1921), *Les Mariés de la Tour Eiffel* (with Honegger, Auric, Poulenc, and Tailleferre, 1921), and *La Création du monde* (1923). He also wrote the music for Massine's *Salade* (1924), Nijinska's *Le Train bleu* (1924), Balanchine's *Les Songes* (1933), Graham's *Imagined Wing* (1944), Page's *The Bells* (1946), Charrat's *'Adame miroir* (1948) and Petit's *La Rose des vents* (1958). Other ballets using Milhaud's music include Béjart's *Concerto pour percussion et orchestre* (1957), MacMillan's *The Sphinx* (1968), and Bintley's *Meadow of Proverbs* (1979).

Mille, Agnes de (*b* New York, 18 Sept. 1905 (some sources 1906 or 1909); *d* New York, 7 Oct. 1993) US dancer, choreographer, director, and writer. A pioneer of dance in America who helped to develop the genre of American-themed ballets and fundamentally changed the status of choreography in Broadway musicals. Born the niece of Hollywood film director Cecil B. DeMille, she was educated at the University of Southern California and studied dance with Kosloff in Los Angeles and Rambert in London (from 1932). She also studied with Tudor and Sokolova. From 1928 she toured America and Europe as a solo dancer and in 1929 made her debut as a professional choreographer, staging dances for Morley's revival of *The Black Crook*. In 1932 she moved to Europe where she toured as a solo artist before joining the Rambert company where she created roles in several Tudor ballets, including *Dark Elegies* (1937) and *Gallant Assembly* (1937). She was associated with

Tudor's first company, Dance Theatre (later becoming London Ballet), where she created the role of Venus in his *The Judgment of Paris* (1938). In 1938 she returned to America where she became resident choreographer of Ballet Theatre (later American Ballet Theatre). Her first important ballet was *Black Ritual* (using Milhaud's score for *La Création du monde*) for ABT in 1940. She also worked with the Ballet Russe de Monte Carlo (1942) and the Jooss Ballet (1942), and briefly toured with her own short-lived company, the Agnes de Mille Dance Theatre (1953–4). Her works were notable for their vivid subject matter, and their ability to marry classical and vernacular movement styles. Subsequent ballets included *Drums Sound in Hackensack* (mus. Cohen, Jooss Ballet, 1941); *Three Virgins and a Devil* (mus. Respighi, ABT, 1941); *Rodeo* (mus. Copland, Ballet Russe de Monte Carlo, 1942), in which she created the role of the Cowgirl, *Fall River Legend* (mus. Gould, ABT, 1948), about the axe-murderer Lizzie Borden, *The Harvest According* (mus. V. Thomson, ABT, 1952), *The Rib of Eve* (mus. Gould, ABT, 1956), *The Wind in the Mountains* (mus. Rosenthal, ABT, 1965), *The Four Marys* (mus. T. Rittman, ABT, 1965), *The Rehearsal* (mus. Gould, Royal Winnipeg Ballet, 1965), *A Rose for Miss Emily* (mus. Hovhaness, ABT, 1970), *Summer* (mus. Schubert, Boston Ballet, 1975), *Texas Fourth* (mus. traditional, ABT, 1976), *The Informer* (mus. Celtic, ABT 1988). She choreographed many Broadway productions, among them *Oklahoma!* (1943), which was the first musical to use dance as a means of advancing the plot and developing character, as well as being the first to require its dancers to be trained in ballet and modern dance. Subsequent Broadway productions on which she worked included *One Touch of Venus* (1943), *Bloomer Girl* (1944), *Carousel* (1945), *Brigadoon* (1947), *Gentlemen Prefer Blondes* (1949), *Paint Your Wagon* (1951), and *110 in the Shade* (1963). She also worked as a Broadway director (Cole Porter's *Out of This World*, 1950), and in film and television. She founded the Heritage Dance Theatre, based at the N. Carolina School of the Arts (1973–5). She was additionally a prolific writer whose books included *Dance to the Piper* (London, 1951, Boston, 1952), *And Promenade Home* (Boston, 1956), *To a Young Dancer* (Boston, 1962), *The Book of the Dance* (New York, 1963), *Lizzie Borden: A Dance of Death* (Boston, 1968), *Speak To Me, Dance With Me* (Boston, 1973), *Where the Wings Grow* (New York, 1978), *America Dances* (New York, 1981), *Reprieve* (1981), and *Martha, the Life and Work of Martha Graham* (New York, 1991).

Millepied, Benjamin (*b* Bordeaux, 10 Jun. 1977) French-American dancer and choreographer. He trained at the Conservatoire National in Lyon and at the School of American Ballet before joining New York City Ballet in 1995. He was promoted to principal in 2002. As well as dancing the Balanchine and Robbins repertories, he has created roles in d'Amboise's *Circle of Fifths*, Eifman's *Musagete*, Martins's *Octet*, Preljocaj's *La Stravaganza*, and Wheeldon's *Slavonic Dances*, among others. He began choreographing in 2001, and his subsequent works include *Triple Duet* (mus. Bach, 2002) for Danses Concertantes, a touring group of artists from NYCB; *Double Aria* (mus. Daniel Ott, 2005) and *Quasi Una Fantasia* (mus. Górecki, 2009) both for New York City Ballet; and *Petrushka* (2007) for Geneva Ballet.

Milloss, Aurelio (orig. A. M. de Miholy; *b* Ozora, Hungary, 12 May 1906; *d* Rome, 21 Sept. 1988) Hungarian-Italian dancer, choreographer and ballet director. He studied with Smeraldi, Nicola Guerra, Anton Romanowsky, Laban, V. Gsovsky, and Cecchetti. In 1928 he joined the Berlin State Opera, also appearing in recital performances as a solo artist and working extensively as ballet master in e.g. Hagen, Breslau, and Düsseldorf. In 1936 he moved to Budapest to become ballet master of the Hungarian State Opera House and in 1938 moved to Italy to become ballet director of the Rome Opera (1938–45, again 1966–9) and ballet director of La Scala, Milan (1946–50). He was subsequently ballet master in Cologne (1960–3), and director Vienna State Opera (1963–6 and again 1971–4). He additionally worked extensively in Italy as a visiting choreographer and also in South America and during the course of his career made more than 170 ballets, including *La follia di Orlando* (Milan, 1947), *Le Portrait de Don Quichotte* (Ballets des Champs-Elysées, 1947), and *Marsyas* (Venice, 1948). Few of his works survived in the repertoire however and Milloss is best remembered for having championed the work of many living Italian designers and composers on the ballet stage, above all for promoting dance as an art form in Italy, where it had often been viewed merely as divertissement.

mime The art of telling a story or describing an emotion without the use of words: the expression of action and feeling through gesture, movement, and facial expression. Classical ballet evolved its own specific language of mime, with a set vocabulary for familiar narrative components: the declaration of love, the desire to marry, the description of female beauty, etc. Several ballets have highly developed mime sequences, most notably *Giselle*, *Swan Lake*, and *Sleeping Beauty*. Although the use of mime was prevalent in 19th-century ballet productions, and indeed was in some cases more important than the dance, contemporary stagings have tended to strip away most of it. During the 20th century Fokine aimed to incorporate mime more organically into the flow of the dancing, and subsequent choreographers have tended to use more naturalistic body language to communicate character and action. Away from the ballet stage, mime forms the basis of much modern visual theatre, with 20th-century mime artists such as Marcel Marceau and Jacques Lecoq having revived an interest in the form and companies like Complicite taking it forward with additional theatrical elements.

Minkus, Léon (orig. Aloisius Ludwig; *b* Vienna, 23 Mar. (some sources say 28 Mar.) 1826; *d* Vienna, 7 Dec. 1917) Austrian-Russian composer. One of the most important composers in 19th-century Russian ballet; he wrote the scores for more than a dozen Petipa ballets, including *Don Quixote* and *La Bayadère*. Although he was Austrian by birth, he spent virtually all his career in Russia. He made his St Petersburg debut as first violin and conductor of a private serf orchestra belonging to Prince Nikolai Yusupov (1853–6) and was subsequently hired as violinist, then conductor at the Bolshoi Theatre in Moscow. From 1869 to 1886 he was back in St Petersburg as official ballet composer of the Mariinsky Theatre (succeeding Pugni). He worked in close association with Petipa, writing the scores for: *Don Quixote* (1869), *La Camargo* (1872), *Le Papillon* (1874), *Les Brigands* (1875), *La Bayadère* (1877), *Roxana or the Beauty from Montenegro* (1878), *The Daughter of the Snow* (1879), *Zoraya, or The Lady Moor in Spain* (1881), *Night and Day* (1883), *The Magic Pill* (1886), and *Kalkabrino* (1891). He also wrote some additional music for *Paquita* (1881). For Saint-Léon, Minkus wrote the score for *La Source* (with Delibes, 1866). His music was noted for its dance quality, even if his Austrian love of the waltz form was often inappropriate to its subject-matter (gypsies and Indian temple dancers, etc.).

minuet The name derives from the French *pas menu*, or small step. It was probably originally a peasant dance from the Poitou region of France before becoming fashionable as a court dance under Louis XIV. Its popularity among the aristocracy spread far outside France. A dance in triple time, it is both dignified and leisurely in execution, featuring many curtseys and deep bows.

Miracle in the Gorbals Ballet in one act with choreography by Helpmann, libretto by Michael Bentall, music by Bliss, and designs by Burra. Premiered 26 Oct. 1944 by Sadler's Wells Ballet at the Princess Theatre in London, with Helpmann, Clayden, Shearer, and Rassine. It tells the story of Christ's rebirth in the slums of 20th-century Glasgow, his Passion and death providing the context for a modern morality play. In the ballet, Christ was known as the Stranger and the role danced by Helpmann.

Miraculous Mandarin, The 'A pantomime in one act' with libretto by Menyhért Lengyel, music by Bartók, and direction and design by Hans Strobach. Premiered 28 Nov. 1926 at the Municipal Theatre in Cologne with Wilma Aug, and Ernst Zeiller. A melodramatic tale of three gangsters and a prostitute who steal from her clients. When she encounters a wealthy Chinese mandarin they try to rob and kill him, but discover that he cannot be killed unless the prostitute satisfies his obsessive sexual desire. The Lord Mayor of Cologne banned the original production on moral grounds and it was almost twenty years before the work gained widespread acceptance in the repertoire. Many choreographers have since been attracted to its lurid narrative, including Milloss (La Scala Milan, 1942), Harangozó (Budapest, 1945), Bolender (New York City Ballet, 1951), Rodrigues (Sadler's Wells Ballet, 1956), Erika Hanka (Vienna, 1957), Lavrovsky (Bolshoi Ballet, 1961), Flindt (Copenhagen, 1967), Petit (La Scala, Milan, 1980), Pistoni (Milan, 1986), and Ben Stevenson (Houston Ballet, 1986). It was one of the most frequently produced ballets of the 20th century.

Miró, Joán (*b* Montroig, 20 Apr. 1893; *d* Mallorca, 25 Dec. 1984) Spanish painter and designer. He did the designs for Nijinska and Balanchine's *Roméo et Juliette* (with M. Ernst, 1926) and for Massine's *Jeux d'enfants* (1932).

Miskovitch, Milorad (*b* Voljevo, 26 Mar. 1928) Yugoslavian-French dancer and teacher. He studied in Belgrade with Kirsanova, and in Paris with Kniaseff and Preobrajenska. He made his debut as a dancer at the Belgrade State Opera House in 1945. In 1947 he danced with the Ballets des Champs-Elysées, the International Ballet, and de Basil's Original Ballet Russe. He also danced with de Cuevas's Grand Ballet de Monte Carlo (1948) and Petit's Ballets de Paris (1949). After appearing with the Ballets Janine Charrat and with London Festival Ballet (1952), touring with Markova (1954) and Colette Marchand (1955), he founded his own company in 1956, Les Ballets 1956 de Miskovitch, which continued to tour for ten years. He joined Massine's Ballet Europeo in 1960 and Page's Chicago Opera Ballet in 1961. He was a frequent guest artist around Europe. He created roles in Béjart's *Haut voltage* (1956), Howard's *La Belle Dame sans merci* (1958), Massine's *Commedia umana* (1960), and Page's *Die Fledermaus* (1961). His own choreography includes Beethoven's *Creatures of Prometheus* (Genoa, 1970); in 1974 he staged *Giselle* for Carla Fracci at the Arena di Verona. President of the International Dance Council of UNESCO (1989–99).

Missa Brevis Ballet in eleven parts with choreography by Limón, music by Kodály, and designs by Ming Cho Lee. Premiered 11 Apr. 1958 by the Limón company at the Juilliard Dance Theater in New York, with Limón, Currier, and B. Jones. The ballet, set to Kodály's *Missa Brevis in tempore belli*, tells of a man's struggle for survival in the midst of chaos. It was taken into the Alvin Ailey repertoire in 1973.

Miss Julie Ballet in one act with choreography and libretto by Birgit Cullberg, music by Ture Rangström, and designs by Allan Fridericia. Premiered 1 Mar. 1950 at the Riksteatern in Västeras, Sweden, with Elsa Marianne von Rosen, Julius Mengarelli, and Cullberg. Based on Strindberg's play, the ballet is a portrait of the aristocratic Miss Julie who seduces the family butler and has to pay for her indiscretion with her life. One of Cullberg's greatest successes, it was revived for many companies, including the Royal Swedish Ballet (1950), American Ballet Theatre (1958), Royal Danish Ballet (1958), Berlin Opera Ballet (1979), Ballet of La Scala Milan (1980), Northern Ballet Theatre (1987), and Tani Ballet, Tokyo (1989). MacMillan choreographed a different ballet based on the same plot: *Fräulein Julie*, with music by Panufnik, premiered in Stuttgart in 1970 with Haydée, F. Frey, Keil, and Clauss.

Mitchell, Arthur (*b* New York, 27 Mar. 1934) US dancer, choreographer, and ballet director. He studied at the High School of the Performing Arts in New York and at the School of American Ballet. He performed on Broadway and with the Donald McKayle and John Butler modern dance troupes before joining New York City Ballet in 1955. He was one of the company's most popular soloists and was the first black dancer to reach the level of principal in an American ballet company. During his fifteen years with NYCB he created roles in many Balanchine ballets, including *Allegro brillante* (1956), *Agon* (1957), *A Midsummer Night's Dream* (Puck, 1962), *Trois valses romantiques* (1967), *Metastaseis and Pithoprakta* (1968), and *Slaughter on Tenth Avenue* (1968). He also created roles in Taras's *Ebony Concerto* (1960) and Butler's *The Unicorn, the Gorgon and the Manticore* (1957). In 1966 he became artistic director of the new National Ballet of Brazil. In 1969 he founded (with Karel Shook) the *Dance Theatre of Harlem to train black dancers in classical ballet and expand their performance opportunities. He went on to choreograph many works for the company including *Holberg Suite, Rhythmetron, Fête noire*, and *Manifestations*, and to lead it on many foreign tours. In 1996 he was awarded the US National Medal of Arts. He has remained the figurehead of the DTH organization, even when the company has had to suspend performances due to financial problems.

Mizrahi, Isaac (*b* Brooklyn, New York, 14 Oct. 1961) American designer. He trained at the Parsons School for Design where he developed his signature style, witty and clean-lined. In addition to his fashion collections he has worked extensively in theatre, his designs for dance including *Morris's *Mosaic and Untitled, Gong*, and *Joyride* (among many others), Bill T. *Jones's *Between States*, and *Tharp's *Cutting Up*.

🌐 **SEE WEB LINKS**
• Isaac Mizrahi's official website

modern dance (contemporary dance) A term widely used in America and Britain to denote theatrical dance that is not based on the academic school of classical ballet. Through early 20th-century practitioners such as Isadora *Duncan, Ruth *St Denis, Martha *Graham, and Doris *Humphrey, modern dance developed in opposition to classical ballet, rejecting the latter's structural formality and its occasionally frivolous subject matter. Modern dance pioneers eschewed the language of the *danse d'école in favour of a freer movement style—favouring bare feet over pointe shoes, for example, and a far more mobile use of the torso. Choreographers like Graham and Humphrey developed their own methods of teaching the new techniques required for their work. Early subject-matter was often political or psychological (Graham in particular was influenced by Jungian psychology). In the 1950s Cunningham took the form one step further by stripping dance of its literary and narrative context, as well as isolating it from its musical accompaniment. Subsequent generations have continued to experiment with new languages and new approaches. Modern dance choreographers in the 1960s and 1970s pared their vocabulary down to minimalist or pedestrian moves, or alternatively explored the possibilities of improvisation. Non-dance elements like text, video imagery, and art installations featured increasingly in productions. Other movement languages, such as T'ai Chi, South Asian dance, hip-hop, or capoeira were also used as sources of new inspiration, to the point where the term modern dance became extremely elastic.

A parallel development to this rapid expansion of style and aesthetic has been the softening of distinctions between ballet and modern dance. Dancers frequently take class in both techniques while modern choreographers like *Tharp, *Taylor, *Morris, and *McGregor are among many to create work for classical companies. (McGregor was appointed resident choreographer of the Royal Ballet.) Classical choreographers in turn have incorporated elements of modern dance into their work. Tetley was one of the first to be described as a 'crossover' choreographer, with ballets like *Pierrot Lunaire*.

Moiseyev, Igor (*b* Kiev, 21 Jan. 1906; *d* Moscow, 2 Nov. 2007) Soviet dancer, choreographer, and company director. Founder of the Soviet Union's first professional folk dance troupe. He studied privately with Vera Mosolova in Moscow from 1919 and at the Bolshoi Ballet School (1921–4), where he was a pupil of Alexander Gorsky. He danced with the Bolshoi from 1924 to 1939, although early on in his career he fell foul of the authorities by helping to organize a protest among young dancers against the stifling of creativity at the Bolshoi Theatre. He choreographed several works for the Bolshoi, including *The Footballer* (mus. V. Oransky, 1930), *Salammbô* (mus. A. Arends, 1932), *Three Fat Men* (mus. Oransky, 1935), and *Spartacus* (mus. Khatchaturian, 1958). In 1936 he was appointed director of the choreographic section of the Moscow Theatre for Folk Art, out of which emerged the Soviet Union's first folk dance ensemble in 1937. The group, known abroad as the Moiseyev Dance Company, travelled widely, making its Paris debut in 1955, its London debut in 1957, and its US debut in 1958. Moiseyev choreographed many productions for the company, including *Pictures from the Past, The Partisans, Tsam,* and *Regions of the World,* always aiming to set traditional folk dances within a professional theatrical context. Between 1967 and 1971 he additionally formed the Classical Ballet Company, a touring outfit which specialized in one-act ballets and divertissements.

Molière (stage name of Jean Baptiste Poquelin; *b* Paris, Jan. 1622; *d* Paris, 17 Feb. 1673) French actor, playwright, and ballet librettist. A dancer himself, Molière wrote the libretto for Beauchamps's *Les Fâcheux* (1661), which inaugurated the genre of the comédie-ballet. He collaborated with Lully on the comédie-ballets *L'Amour médecin* (1665), *Monsieur de Pourceaugnac* (1669), and *Le Bourgeois gentilhomme* (1670). He wrote the libretto for Lully's *Le Mariage forcé* (1664) and collaborated with Lully and Beauchamps on *Les Festes de l'Amour et de Bacchus* (1672). He died while performing in his own ballet, *Le Malade imaginaire*.

Momix Modern dance company founded in 1980 by Moses *Pendleton, co-founder of Pilobolus, and Alison Chase. It takes its name from a brand of cattle feed. Its members, describing themselves as 'dancer-illusionists', perform works which combine gymnastics, acrobatics, modern dance, circus, and visual theatre with imaginative lighting and props. The company frequently tours.

Monahan, James (*b* Arrah, India, 1912; *d* London, 23 Nov. 1985) British dance critic. Educated at Oxford University. He was dance critic of the *Guardian* newspaper for more than 25 years (from 1935), writing under the name of James Kennedy. He was director of the Royal Ballet School (1978–83). Author of *Fonteyn: A Study of the Ballerina in her Setting* (London, 1958) and *The Nature of Ballet* (1976).

Moncion, Francisco (*b* La Vega, Dominican Republic, 6 Jul. 1918; *d* Woodstock, NY, 1 Apr. 1995) US dancer, choreographer, and painter. He studied at the School of American Ballet (from 1938) and made his debut with the New Opera Company in 1942. He was then soloist with the Marquis de Cuevas's Ballet International, where he created the title roles in Edward Caton's *Sebastian* and Massine's *Mad Tristan* (both 1944) and in 1946 he joined Ballet Society (later New York City Ballet), where he remained for almost 40 years. He created roles in Balanchine's *Four Temperaments* (1946), *Divertimento* (1947), *Symphony in C* (1948), *Orpheus* (the Dark Angel, 1948), *Firebird* (1949), *La Valse* (1951), *Ivesiana* (1954), *Episodes* (1959), *A Midsummer Night's Dream* (1962), *Don Quixote* (1965), *Jewels* ('Emeralds', 1967). He also created roles in Ashton's *Picnic at Tintagel* (1952), and Robbins's *The Guests* (1949), *Jinx* (1949), *Age of Anxiety* (1950), *Afternoon of a Faun* (1953), and *In the Night* (1970). He also choreographed several works for NYCB, including *Pastorale* (mus. Turner, 1957) and *Les Biches* (mus. Poulenc, 1960). He retired in 1985.

Monk, Meredith (*b* New York, 20 Nov. 1942) US dancer, choreographer, composer, filmmaker, and performance artist. She made her debut as a performer in New York in 1964 after graduating from Sarah Lawrence College. Originally one of the leading voices on the American avant-garde scene, her interest in an interdisciplinary approach to performance often led her away from dance into theatre and opera. Her productions were frequently set outdoors or in novel performing spaces. *Vessel* (1971) was set in three different locations, the first part in Monk's loft, the second at the Performing Garage and the third in a car park. *Juice* (1969) started at the Guggenheim Museum and worked its way back to Monk's loft. In 1968 she formed the performance company The House; in 1978 she also launched the Meredith Monk Vocal Ensemble. She has directed many films including *Book of Days* (1989) but the focus of her work has been increasingly musical, for example the 1991 opera *Atlas*, which used almost no text, only vocal sounds.

(((🌐))) **SEE WEB LINKS**

• Website for Meredith Monk

Monnier, Mathilde (*b* Mulhouse, France, 1959) French choreographer and director. She studied with Viola Farber in France and with Cunningham in New York, where she began to choreograph. The success of *Pour Antigone* (1993), a retelling of the Greek tragedy inspired by African dance, led to her appointment the following year as director of the Centre Choregraphique National in Montpellier. The works she has created there include *Nuit* (1995), *Stop, Stop, Stop* (1997), *Signe, Signes* (2000), *Déroutes* (2002), *La Place du Singe* (with writer Christine Angot, 2005), and *Les Signes extérieurs* (with performance artist La Ribot, 2008). Monnier has also created works for other companies including *Mama Sunday Monday or Always* for Lyon Opera Ballet (1987) and *Natt and Rose* for the Royal Swedish Ballet (2001).

(((⏺))) SEE WEB LINKS
• Website for Monnier and the CCN in Montpellier

Monotones Ballet in one act with choreography and costumes by Ashton, and music by Satie. Premiered 24 Mar. 1965 by the Royal Ballet at Covent Garden with Lorrayne, Dowell, and Mead. Originally an abstract pas de trois set to Satie's *Trois gymnopédies*, it was such a success that Ashton added a second half (set to Satie's *Trois gnossiennes*) which was premiered 25 Apr. 1966 with Sibley, Georgina Parkinson, and Brian Shaw. The two parts are usually performed together as *Monotones I and II* (with *Monotones II* being the original pas de trois). *Monotones II* is for two men and one woman in white, while *Monotones I* is for one man and two women in green. The work, a fine piece of classical adagio writing, has been taken into the repertoires of the Joffrey Ballet (1974), the Australian Ballet (1975), the San Francisco Ballet (1981), and Morphoses (2008).

Montessu, Pauline (*née* Paul; *b* Marseilles, 4 Jun. 1805; *d* Amiens, 1 Aug. 1877) French dancer. She studied with her brother Antoine Paul and made her debut in Lyons in 1813. In 1820 she joined the Paris Opera where she danced Lise in the first production of *La Fille mal gardée* to use the Hérold score (1828). She also created the title role in Aumer's *Manon Lescaut* in 1830.

Monteux, Pierre (*b* Paris, 4 Apr. 1875; *d* Hancock, Me., 1 Jul. 1964) French conductor. He was chief conductor of Diaghilev's Ballets Russes from 1911 to 1914 and continued to guest with the company until 1917. Although he had no experience as a ballet conductor when he was first hired by Diaghilev, he conducted the first production of Stravinsky's *Petrushka* (1911) and went on to conduct the premieres of *Sacre du printemps* (1913) and *Le Rossignol* (1914), Ravel's

Daphnis and Chloe (1912), and Debussy's *Jeux* (1913).

Montez, Lola (orig. Marie Dolores Eliza Rosanna Gilbert; *b* Limerick, 1818; *d* New York, 16 Jan. 1861) Irish dancer. Although she made her living as a dancer, she made her reputation as an adventuress, and was a source of scandal from Europe to Australia. Her dancing credentials were based on lessons she took in Seville. From there she toured Europe as a Spanish dancer, gathering lovers in her wake. She became the mistress of Ludwig I in Munich in 1846, an affair which eventually led to the King's abdication in 1848. There were further scandals in Paris, London, and Sydney before she finally settled in New York, where she spent the rest of her life. Her colourful story has inspired several novels, plays, and films while her character has appeared in several ballets, including Massine's *Bacchanale* (1939), Caton's *Lola Montez* (1946), and J. Carter's *The Life and Death of Lola Montez* (1954).

Month in the Country, A Ballet in one act with choreography by Ashton, music by Chopin (arr. Lanchbery), and designs by Julia Trevelyan Oman. Premiered 12 Feb. 1976 by the Royal Ballet at Covent Garden, with Seymour, Dowell, Grant, Rencher, Denise Nunn, and Sleep. Ashton based his ballet on Turgenev's play and its story of the tangled relations between Natalia Petrovna, her young ward Vera, and the handsome tutor Beliaev. Ashton's ballet, which gave Lynn Seymour one of the finest roles of her career, is a subtle and moving portrait of an older woman hopelessly attracted to a younger man.

Monument for a Dead Boy Ballet in one act with choreography and libretto by van Dantzig, music by Jan Boerman, designs by van Schayk. Premiered 19 Jun. 1965, by Dutch National Ballet, at the Stadsschouwburg in Amsterdam, with van Schayk and José Lainez. Using flashback and a non-linear narrative, the ballet tells the story of a repressed homosexual boy who is ultimately destroyed by his desires. At the time the subject-matter was controversially frank: not only did it portray homosexual love on stage, it also depicted heterosexual love as brutal, even violent. This is the ballet which brought Rudi van Dantzig to international attention. It was revived for the Harkness Ballet in 1969, American Ballet Theatre in 1973, the Royal Danish Ballet, and Berlin Opera Ballet in 1976. Later interpreters of the boy included Nureyev who performed it with Dutch National Ballet in 1968.

Moon Reindeer Ballet in one act with choreography and libretto by Cullberg, music by K. Riisager, designs by P. Falk. Premiered 22 Nov. 1957 by the Royal Danish Ballet in Copenhagen with Vangsaae,

Kronstam, and Bjornsson. A Lapp girl is transformed into a white reindeer who lures young men to their deaths, until one of them breaks the spell and the girl is restored to human form. It was revived for the Royal Swedish Ballet in 1959 and for American Ballet Theatre in 1962.

Moore, Lillian (*b* Chase City, Va., 20 Sept. 1911; *d* New York, 28 Jul. 1967) US dancer, teacher, and dance writer. She studied with Balanchine, Vladimiroff, and Weidman. She joined the Metropolitan Opera Ballet at the age of 16 and performed with the American Ballet (1935–8) and with many other companies, becoming the first US dancer to perform behind the Iron Curtain when she appeared in Budapest in 1948. Following her retirement in 1954 she took up teaching and was mostly associated with Joffrey's American Ballet Center (1958–67). She became one of America's leading dance historians. Author of *Artists of the Dance* (New York, 1938), *Bournonville and Ballet Technique* (with E. Bruhn, London, 1961), and *Images of the Dance* (New York, 1965). She was also editor of *The Memoirs of Marius Petipa* (London, 1958).

Moor's Pavane, The Modern dance in one act with choreography by Limón, music by Purcell, and costumes by Pauline Lawrence. Premiered 17 Aug. 1949 by the José Limón Dance Company at Connecticut College in New London, Connecticut, with Limón, Betty Jones, Lucas Hoving, and Pauline Koner. Subtitled 'Variations on the Theme of Othello'. A highly formalized work which takes its stylistic cue from the music, it tells the Shakespearian story of Othello and Desdemona using only four dancers. Considered to be Limón's signature work, it was taken into the repertoire of many companies, including American Ballet Theatre, the Paris Opera Ballet, the Joffrey Ballet, the Royal Danish Ballet, the Royal Swedish Ballet, the National Ballet of Canada, and Phoenix.

Mordkin, Mikhail (*b* Moscow, 21 Dec. 1880; *d* Millbrook, NJ, 15 Jul. 1944) Russian-US dancer, choreographer, teacher, and ballet director. He trained at the Bolshoi Ballet School in Moscow, graduating in 1899. Upon graduation he joined the Bolshoi Ballet as a soloist, and was appointed assistant ballet master five years later. He created the role of Matoh in Gorksy's *Salammbo* (1910), the Fisherman in Gorsky's *Love is Quick* (1913), Sonnewald in Gorsky's *Schubertiana* (1913), and Petronius in Gorsky's *Eunice and Petronius* (1915). He was part of Diaghilev's 1909 Paris season before touring with Pavlova (who finally fell out with him over his demand for equal billing). By 1911 he had set up his own touring company, the All-Star Imperial Russian Ballet, which he took to America and for which he staged *Swan*

Lake. In 1912 he returned to the Bolshoi as a principal dancer (until 1918), where he created the role of Khan in Gorsky's 1914 staging of *The Humpbacked Horse*. He continued to work throughout Russia staging ballets, particularly in Tbilisi, until he left in 1924. After time spent in Lithuania, he eventually settled in America in 1924 where he became a pioneer in the development of the country's ballet culture. In 1926 he founded the Mordkin Russian Ballet, but it was not a success. When his company disbanded, he worked as a teacher and freelance choreographer for opera. In 1937 he was able to revive his company using students from his New York school, including Lucia *Chase (others included Katharine Hepburn and Judy Garland). This short-lived troupe was the precursor to Ballet Theatre (later *American Ballet Theatre), the latter having lured away Mordkin's dancers following a power struggle between himself and Richard *Pleasant in 1939. He continued to teach in New York until his death. His ballets include *The Goldfish* (mus. N. Tcherepnin, 1937), *Trepak* (mus. A. Tcherepnin, 1937), *Voices of Spring* (mus. Strauss, 1938), and *Dionysus* (mus. Glazunov, 1938). He also staged *Giselle, The Sleeping Beauty*, and *La Fille mal gardée* for the Mordkin Ballet.

Moreland, Barry (*b* Melbourne, 1943) Australian dancer and choreographer. He studied at the Australian Ballet School and joined the Australian Ballet in 1962. He continued his studies at the London School of Contemporary Dance and performed with London Contemporary Dance Theatre, for whom he made several works. From 1971 to 1975 he was resident choreographer of London Festival Ballet. In 1983 he was appointed artistic director of the West Australian Ballet in Perth, creating many works there including *Seven Deadly Sins* (1987) and *Hamlet* (1993) along with stagings of *The Nutcracker* and *A Midsummer Night's Dream*. In 1997 he left Perth to pursue an international freelance career.

A list of Moreland's other works includes *Nocturnal Dances* (mus. P. M. Davies, 1970), *Summer Games* (mus. S. Barber, 1970), *Kontakion* (medieval music, 1972), all for LCDT; *Summer Solstice* (mus. J. Field, 1972), *Dark Voyage* (mus. Satie, 1973), *In Nomine* (mus. Davies, 1973), *Prodigal Son* (mus. Scott Joplin, 1974), all for London Festival Ballet; *Sacred Space* (mus. Bach, Australian Ballet, 1974); *Journey to Avalon* (mus. P. M. Davies, London Festival Ballet, 1980).

Moreton, Ursula (*b* Southsea, 13 Mar. 1903; *d* London, 24 Jun. 1973) British dancer and teacher. She studied with Cecchetti and made her debut in the London production of *The Truth about the Russian Dancers*, a 1920 play starring Karsavina. In 1921 she appeared in the Diaghilev staging of *The Sleeping Princess* and also danced with Massine's company. Her teaching career began in 1926 when she was engaged by de Valois. In 1931 she was appointed ballet mistress of the Vic-Wells Ballet, and was assistant director of Sadler's Wells Theatre Ballet from 1946 to 1952. From 1952 to 1968 she was director of the Royal Ballet School.

Morishita, Yoko (*b* Hiroshima, 7 Dec. 1948) Japanese dancer. The first Japanese ballerina to achieve international acclaim. She studied with Michiko Suwa and Akiko Tachibana in Tokyo and later with Mikiko Matsuyama. She also studied with Igor Schwezoff in Tokyo, with Marika Besobrasova in Monaco in 1975, and with Alexandra Danilova in New York. In 1971 she joined the *Matsuyama Ballet Company in Tokyo as a principal, eventually becoming prima ballerina. She made her debut as Odette-Odile with the Matsuyama Ballet in 1975; her first Giselle followed in 1977. She appeared as a guest artist with many companies around the world, including American Ballet Theatre, the Paris Opera, the Stuttgart Ballet, also dancing with Béjart, the Margot Fonteyn World Tours (1978 and 1979), and Nureyev—dancing Kitri in his production of *Don Quixote* for the Nureyev Festival in London in 1984. She created the role of Moe in Shimizu's *Mandala* which the Matsuyama Ballet brought to the Edinburgh Festival in 1988. Gold Medal, Varna, 1974. She married the choreographer Tetsutaro Shimizu.

Morphoses Ballet company founded in 2007 by Christopher Wheeldon, and based in London (Sadler's Wells) and New York (City Center). It was created as a showcase for Wheeldon's own work but its repertory also featured significant new commissions and revivals. Wheeldon left the company in 2010.

Morrice, Norman (*b* Agua Dulce, Mexico, 10 Sept. 1931; *d* London, 11 Jan. 2008) British dancer, choreographer, and ballet director. He studied first in Mansfield, Nottinghamshire, then at the Rambert School (from 1952), and later with Graham in New York. He joined Ballet Rambert in 1953 and became a principal dancer, taking up choreography in 1958 and eventually becoming Rambert's principal choreographer in 1962. In 1966, when the company opted to focus on modern dance, he was named associate director. Under his supervision full-length classical ballets were dropped from the repertoire; new work was promoted and Tetley was invited to work with the company. Between 1970 and 1974 Morrice was promoted to full director but he then resigned the post to pursue his choreographic career, developing a contemporary idiom and subject matter in works that he created for both Rambert

and the Batsheva company in Israel. In 1977 he was appointed director of the Royal Ballet at Covent Garden, where he remained until 1986. For the Royal he staged new productions of *Swan Lake* (1979) and *Giselle* (1980). He invited Richard Alston to make his first ballet, *Midsummer*, for the Royal in 1983. From 1987 he was director of choreographic studies at the Royal Ballet School.

A list of his works includes *Two Brothers* (mus. Dohnányi, 1958), *Hazana* (mus. Surinach, 1959), *A Place in the Desert* (mus. Surinach, 1961), *Conflicts* (mus. Bloch, 1962), *The Travellers* (mus. Salzedo, 1963), *Side Show* (mus. Hindemith, 1966), *Hazard* (mus. Salzedo, 1967), *Rehearsal* (mus. Poulenc, 1968), *Them and Us* (mus. Xenakis, 1968), *Blind-Sight* (mus. Bob Downes, 1969), *The Empty Suit* (mus. Salzedo, 1970), *That is the Show* (mus. Berio, 1971), *Spindrift* (mus. J. Lewis, 1974), *Trek* (mus. Lester, 1975), *Fragments from a Distant Past* (mus. Janáček, Winnipeg Contemporary Dancers, 1976), and *Seven Songs* (Australian Dance Theatre, 1977).

Morris, Margaret (*b* London, 1891; *d* Glasgow, 29 Feb. 1980) British dancer and teacher. She studied with John d'Auban and Raymond Duncan and developed her own system of free-style movement, which she taught at her London school from 1910. She promoted her system through a performing group and through publications of the Margaret Morris Movement, which she founded in 1925. Like Laban, she also devised her own system of notation. She was responsible for starting several companies in Scotland between 1947 and 1960, but all of them were short-lived. Author of *Margaret Morris Dancing* (1925), *Notation of Movement* (1928), and *My Life in Movement* (1969).

Morris, Mark (*b* Seattle, 29 Aug. 1956) US dancer, choreographer, and company director. He studied flamenco with Verla Flowers and ballet with Perry Brunson in Seattle; also studied flamenco in Madrid. While still a teenager he joined a semi-professional Balkan dance troupe, the Koleda Folk Ensemble, whose communal style exerted a profound influence on his later choreography. From 1976 he studied ballet with Maggie Black in New York. He danced with several companies in New York, including those of Eliot Feld, Lar Lubovitch, Hannah Kahn, and Laura Dean. In 1980 he founded his own New York-based troupe, the Mark Morris Dance Group, which is today one of the world's leading contemporary dance ensembles. In 1988 it became the resident company at the Théâtre Royal de la Monnaie in Brussels, with Morris appointed the Monnaie's ballet director, a post previously held by Béjart. During the next three years, using the generous resources of Belgium's national opera

m

house, Morris produced work which confirmed his reputation; *L'Allegro, il penseroso ed il moderato* is ranked as one of the most significant modern dance works of the era. In 1991 the company returned to America. Morris has additionally worked as a guest choreographer with several ballet companies, including the Joffrey Ballet (*Esteemed Guests*, mus. C. P. E. Bach, 1986), American Ballet Theatre (*Drink to Me Only with Thine Eyes*, mus. Virgil Thomson, 1988, and *Gong*, mus. McPhee, 2001), Paris Opera Ballet (*Ein Herz*, mus. J. S. Bach, 1990), the Boston Ballet (*Mort subite*, mus. Poulenc, 1986), Les Grands Ballets Canadiens (*Paukenschlag*, mus. Haydn, 1992, and *Quincunx*, mus. Donizetti, 1995), and San Francisco Ballet (*Maelstrom*, mus. Beethoven, 1994, *Pacific*, mus. Harrison, 1995, *Sandpaper Ballet*, mus. Leroy Anderson, 1999, and *Sylvia*, mus. Delibes, 2004), among others. An intensely musical choreographer, his style has embraced a wide range, utilizing the simple everyday movements of folk dance as well as the sophisticated articulation and pointe work of classical dance. He has also made a point of treating men and women as equals in choreographic terms. His works display an affection for kitsch just as effectively as an analytic love of formal structure, while his approach can veer from the primal power of a work like *Grand Duo* to the unabashed sentimentality of a work like *New Love Song Waltzes*, from the ecstasy of *Gloria* to the irreverence of *The Hard Nut*, his 1991 Brussels staging of *The Nutcracker*. Although Morris has a particular fondness for music of the Baroque period, he is equally comfortable with both contemporary and popular music. Dancing in his own works his large and bulky frame exhibited a surprising grace, while his performance style combined innocence with sophistication. In 1990 he co-founded the *White Oak Dance Project with Baryshnikov. A list of works for his own company includes *Castor and Pollux* (mus. Partch, 1980), *Ten Suggestions* (mus. Tcherepnin, 1981), *Gloria* (mus. Vivaldi, 1981), *New Love Song Waltzes* (mus. Brahms, 1982), *Celestial Greetings* (mus. popular Thai, 1983), *Dogtown* (mus. Yoko Ono, 1983), *O Rangasayee* (mus. Tyagaraja, 1984), *Slugfest* (no music, 1984), *One Charming Night* (mus. Purcell, 1985), *Mythologies* (mus. Garfein, 1986), *Stabat Mater* (mus. Pergolesi, 1986), *Strict Songs* (mus. Harrison, 1987), *Scarlatti Solos* (mus. Scarlatti, 1987), *Offertorium* (mus. Schubert, 1988), *L'Allegro, il penseroso ed il moderato* (mus. Handel, 1988), *Dido and Aeneas* (mus. Purcell, 1989), *Love Song Waltzes* (mus. Brahms, 1989), *Wonderland* (mus. Schoenberg, 1989), *Behemoth* (no mus., 1990), *Going Away Party* (mus. Bob Wills and his Texas Playboys, 1990), *The Hard Nut* (mus. Tchaikovsky, 1991), *Beautiful Day* (mus. Georg-Melchior Hoffmann, but attrib. Bach, 1992), *Bedtime* (mus. Schubert, 1992), *Three

Preludes* (mus. Gershwin, 1992), *Grand Duo* (mus. Harrison, 1993), *Mosaic and United* (mus. Cowell, 1993), *The Office* (mus. Dvořák, 1994), *Somebody's Coming to See Me Tonight* (mus. Stephen Foster, 1995), *World Power* (mus. Harrison, 1995), *I Don't Want To Love* (mus. Monteverdi, 1996), *Rhymes With Silver* (mus. Harrison, 1997), *Dancing Honeymoon* (mus. various, 1998), *The Argument* (mus. Schumann, 1999), *V* (mus. Schumann, 2002), *Mozart Dances* (2006), a new version of *Romeo and Juliet* (2008) using Prokofiev's original score (with its happy ending), and *Empire Garden* (mus. Ives, 2009). For White Oak he choreographed *Motorcade* (mus. Saint-Saëns, 1990), *A Lake* (mus. Haydn, 1991), and *Three Russian Preludes* (mus. Shostakovich, 1995). He also worked extensively in opera, choreographing John Adams's *Nixon in China* (Houston Grand Opera, 1987) and *The Death of Klinghoffer* (Brussels, 1991) as well as choreographing and directing Rameau's *Platée* (Royal Opera, 1997), Thomson's *Four Saints in Three Acts* (English National Opera, 2000), Purcell's *King Arthur* (English National Opera, 2002), and *Orfeo ed Euridice* (Metropolitan Opera, 2007), among others. In 1997 he made his Broadway debut, directing and choreographing the Paul Simon musical *Capeman*. In 2001 his company moved to a new base in Brooklyn, NY, also launching the Mark Morris School.

He is the recipient of numerous honours and awards, including the MacArthur Foundation or 'Genius' Award, 1991.

(((⊕))) SEE WEB LINKS
• Website for the Mark Morris Dance Group

morris dance English ceremonial folk dance which first appeared in England in the 15th century. Its origins are unknown, although it may have derived from the moresca, a dance found in Burgundy in the early 1400s. Traditionally performed by men wearing bells tied to their legs, it is composed of intricate steps and is usually danced in 2/4 time, although it can also be danced in 3/4 time. The dancers may be made up to represent particular characters, such as Fool or Maid Marian, and a cardboard horse is also a regular feature. Some of the elements of morris dancing were used by Ashton in *La Fille mal gardée*.

Moscow The Russian city has been one of the world's ballet capitals for almost two centuries. It is home to the *Bolshoi Ballet, founded in the late 18th century and based at the Bolshoi Theatre. This is the city where Petipa's *Don Quixote* was first performed, also the site, in 1877, of the notorious first production of Reisinger's and Tchaikovsky's *Swan Lake*. The other major company is the *Stanislavsky Ballet which is based at Moscow's second opera house. During the 20th century, under the Communists, ballet in Moscow was well supported by the state and it was here that the heroic Soviet style flourished. In the late 1980s and early 1990s, small independent companies, such as Moscow City Ballet and Moscow Classical Ballet, began to proliferate as well as a small number of modern dance groups. Since 1969 the city has hosted an International Ballet Competition, which takes place every four years. *See also* RUSSIA.

Moscow Ballet School The school of the *Bolshoi Ballet. It was founded in 1773 by the Italian dancing master Filippo Beccari and originally took its students from the Moscow Orphanage. In 1806 the school came under control of the Russian Imperial Theatres. Teachers in the early 19th century included I. Valberkh, A. Glushkovsky, and F. Hullin-Sor. In the 1860s the school moved to a new location on Neglinnaya Street. Although standards continued to improve through the 1800s, the Moscow school was always overshadowed by its great rival in St Petersburg. In the 1930s teachers from St Petersburg began working in Moscow, among them Gerdt, Kozhukhova, and Gusev. In 1967 the school opened a new building, the largest ballet school in the world, with 20 studios and its own theatre. It is known by several other names, including the Moscow State Academy of Choreography, the Bolshoi Ballet School, the Bolshoi Academy, and the Moscow Choreographic Institute.

(🌐) SEE WEB LINKS
• Website for the Moscow Ballet School

Moscow City Ballet International touring company based in Moscow. It was founded by Victor Smirnov-Golovanov, a former dancer with the Bolshoi Ballet, in 1988 and tours with a repertoire of 19th-century Russian classics.

Motion capture Process by which the movement of dancers, as opposed to their physical appearance, is recorded and then transposed into digital imagery. These images may then be projected onto the stage and appear to merge with the live dancers, as in Cunningham's *BIPED (1999) or Wayne McGregor's *Sulphur 16* (1998).

Mottram, Simon (*b* Woodford, 3 Jul. 1937) British dancer and ballet director. He studied at the Rambert School, and danced with Ballet Rambert (1954–6), the Royal Ballet touring company (1956–60), London Festival Ballet, the Grand Ballet du Marquis de Cuevas, Western Theatre Ballet (1962–5, 1966–8), the Royal Swedish Ballet, Nederlands Dans Theater (1968–70), Northern Dance Theatre (1971–2), and New London Ballet (1973–5). He was ballet master of NDT (1975–9)

and artistic director of the Royal Swedish Ballet (1993–5).

Mounsey, Yvonne (*b* Pretoria, 1919) South African dancer. She studied with Schwezoff in London, Preobrajenska and Egorova in Paris, and at the School of American Ballet in New York. She joined Ballet Russe de Monte Carlo in 1939 and later danced with de Basil's Original Ballet Russe (1940–1). She also had a company of her own in South Africa in the late 1940s. She joined New York City Ballet in 1949 where she created roles in Robbins's *The Cage* (1951) and *The Concert* (1956), Ashton's *Picnic at Tintagel* (1952), and Balanchine's *Nutcracker* (1954). In 1958 she returned to South Africa to help launch the Johannesburg City Ballet. In the 1960s she settled in Los Angeles, founding her own school.

Moves Ballet in one act with choreography by Robbins. Premiered 3 Jul. 1959 by Ballets USA at Spoleto. Performed in silence, it was described by Robbins as 'a ballet...about relationships... between people—man and woman, one and another, the individual and the group'. It has been revived for several companies including City Center Joffrey Ballet (1969) and Nederlands Dans Theater (1973).

Movin' Out Musical directed and choreographed by Twyla Tharp and set to songs by Billy Joel. First performed on Broadway on 24 Oct. 2002 at the Richard Rodgers Theatre, where it ran for 1,303 performances. Essentially a rock ballet, it chronicled a generation of American youth affected by the Vietnam War.

Mozart Dances A triple bill choreographed by Mark Morris to piano music by Mozart. Premiered 17 Aug. 2006 by Mark Morris Dance Group at New York State Theatre, with costumes by Martin Pakledinaz and scenic design by Howard Hodgkin. The three linked works feature sixteen dancers and are called *Eleven, Double,* and *Twenty-Seven* after their scores (Piano Concerto No. 11, Sonata for Two Pianos in D, and Piano Concerto No. 27). Typically with Morris the choreography is a detailed response to the music, which carries fleeting suggestions of character and story.

Mozart, Wolfgang Amadeus (*b* Salzburg, 27 Jan. 1756; *d* Vienna, 5 Dec. 1791) Austrian composer. He wrote the music for Noverre's *Les Petits Riens* (Paris, 1778) and wrote many dances and sets of dances. His concert music has also been used by many choreographers, including Balanchine (*Symphonie Concertante*, 1945; *Divertimento No. 15*, 1956), Arpino (*Secret Places*, 1968), van Manen (*Quintet to Adante*, 1991), Kylián (*Six Dances*, 1986; *Petite Mort*, 1991), and Morris (*Mozart Dances*, 2006).

Mozartiana Ballet in one act with choreography by Balanchine, music by Tchaikovsky, and designs by Bérard. Premiered 7 Jun. 1933, by Les Ballets 1933 at the Théâtre des Champs-Elysées in Paris with Toumanova and Jasinsky. An exuberant plotless ballet set to Tchaikovsky's 4th Suite for Orchestra, it was the choreographer's first major Tchaikovsky ballet. Toumanova was 14 when he made it for her. Balanchine staged a new version for New York City Ballet in 1981, with Farrell and Ib Anderson, and new costumes by Rouben Ter-Arutunian. It was Balanchine's last major work before his death.

mudra Term denoting gesture in Hindu dancing. Béjart chose Mudra as the name for his school in Brussels.

Mukhamedov, Irek (*b* Kazan, 8 Mar. 1960) Russian dancer. He studied at the Moscow Ballet School, a pupil of Alexander Prokofiev (1970–8). Upon graduation he joined the Classical Ballet Company, the touring troupe which *Moiseyev had founded in 1967. He spent three years with the company, during which he took part in several world tours. It was with this company that he first danced Romeo, which would eventually become one of his signature roles. After winning the Grand Prix at the Moscow International Ballet Competition in 1981, he was invited to join the Bolshoi as principal. There he quickly established himself as Grigorovich's favourite, his athletic, heroic style ideally suited to the choreographer's theatrical vision. He starred in Grigorovich's *Spartacus*, *Ivan the Terrible*, and *Romeo and Juliet* and in 1984 created the role of Boris in Grigorovich's *The Golden Age*. Foreign tours with the Bolshoi earned Mukhamedov international adulation, and he was widely regarded as the most exciting male dancer of his day. In 1989 he was invited to the Paris Opera to dance the role of the Prince in Nureyev's staging of *The Sleeping Beauty*. In 1990 he left Russia to join the Royal Ballet at Covent Garden, where his roles included Solor and Romeo. He found a mentor in the choreographer Kenneth MacMillan, who helped to develop the dancer's dramatic range and refine his powerhouse style. MacMillan created *Winter Dreams* for Mukhamedov (partnering Bussell) in 1991 and *The Judas Tree* for him in 1992. In addition, Mukhamedov inherited the leading male roles in MacMillan's *Manon* (1991) and *Mayerling* (1992). A stocky and muscular dancer, he was never ideally suited to classical prince roles but he none the less distinguished himself in a wide repertoire. He created leading roles in Tharp's *Mr Worldly Wise*, Ashley Page's *Fearful Symmetries*, *now languorous, now wild*, and *Cheating, Lying, Stealing*, and in William Tuckett's *The Turn of the Screw* and *The Crucible*. With Arc Dance Company he created the title roles in *Othello* (1994) and *The Return of Don Juan* (1999). In 1998 he left the Royal Ballet, although he continued to appear as a guest artist until 2001. In 1992 he additionally founded the seasonal troupe Irek Mukhamedov and Company, which toured intermittently for several years. Since retiring from the stage he has taught internationally, joining the faculty of Elmhurst Ballet School in 2005. He has staged a new production of *Swan Lake* for the Polish National Ballet (2001) and a new version of *Spartacus* for Hong Kong Ballet (2005).

Muller, Jennifer (*b* Yonkers, NY, 16 Oct. 1944) US dancer and choreographer. She studied at the Juilliard School, and with Limón, Graham, Tudor, Craske, Horst, and Sokolow. She danced with the Limón Dance Company (1963–71) and with Louis Falco's company (1968–74). She formed her own multi-disciplinary company, Jennifer Muller and the Works, in 1974 for which she has created numerous pieces. She has also choreographed for Nederlands Dans Theater, including *An American Beauty Rose* (1974).

Munich Ballet *See* BAVARIAN STATE BALLET.

Murphy, Gillian (*b* Florence, S Carolina, 11 Apr. 1979) American dancer. She took ballet classes in Belgium, aged 3, and continued her studies at the Columbia City Ballet and North Carolina School of the Arts, under Melissa Hayden. Precociously gifted, she danced many adult roles while still a student and joined American Ballet Theatre in 1996, where she was promoted to soloist in 1999 and principal in 2002. Murphy's classical technique has been showcased in ABT's 19th-century repertory but her musical and stylistic intelligence make her versatile across a wide range, including works by Tudor, Balanchine, Graham, MacMillan, Tharp, Taylor, and Morris. She has created roles in several ballets including Elo's *Glow—Stop* and Tharp's *Rabbit and Rogue*. Murphy has guested widely including with the Mariinsky and Stiefel & Stars. She has also danced for television and was featured in the films *Center Stage* and *Center Stage 2*.

Murphy, Graeme (*b* Melbourne, 2 Nov. 1950) Australian dancer, choreographer, and company director. He studied at the Australian Ballet School (1966–8) and later at the Joffrey School in New York, dancing with Australian Ballet, Sadler's Wells Royal Ballet, and Félix Blaska's company in France. He choreographed his first work, *Ecco le diavole*, in 1971. In 1975 he returned to Australia as a freelance choreographer and the following year was appointed artistic director of the Dance Company of New South Wales, later renamed the Sydney Dance Company, where he remained until the 2006–7 season, running the company with his partner Janet Vernon. He choreographed numerous works for SDC, many of them evening-length productions, such as *Poppy* (1978, about the life of Jean Cocteau). He also choreographed for several other companies, including White Oak Dance Project (*Embodied*, 1996) and most regularly Australian Ballet, for which he created *Beyond Twelve* (1980), *Gallery* (1987), *The Nutcracker* (1992), *Swan Lake* (2003), and in association with his own company, the dance musical *Tivoli* (2001). As director of SDC he also encouraged younger Australian choreographers such as Stephen Page. A list of his own works for the company includes *Daphnis and Chloe* (1980), *After Venice* (mus. Messiaen, 1984), *Boxes* (1985), *Kraanerg* (1988), *Soft Bruising* (1990), *Piano Sonata* (1992), *Synergy with Synergy* (1992), *The Protecting Veil* (1993), *Beauty and the Beast* (1993), *Berlin* (1995), *Free Radicals* (1997), *Salome* (1998), *Air and Other Invisible Forces* (1999), *Shades of Gray* (2004), and *Grand* (2005). He also directed productions for the Australian Opera such as *Metamorphosis* (1985), *Turandot* (1990), *Salome* (1993), and *The Trojans* (1994).

Murray, Arthur and Kathryn One of America's most famous ballroom dancing couples, they helped to popularize ballroom dancing through a network of studios which provided dance instruction. Arthur Murray (*b* New York, 1895, *d* Honolulu, 1991) trained with Irene and Vernon *Castle and in the 1920s began to sell dancing lessons by post, sending out footprint diagrams that taught the steps of the popular social dances. Millions of lessons were sold through this scheme and Murray was credited with creating many of the standard steps still used today in the foxtrot and the rumba. In the 1930s he began to franchise studios of dance instruction and for the next 30 years oversaw their proliferation. He and Kathryn, who died in 1999 at the age of 92, also presented a long-running television series in the 1950s which promoted ballroom dancing. Today there are more than 200 Arthur Murray studios in the US.

musette [Fr., bagpipe] Dance performed in 2/4, 3/4, or even 6/8 time and related to the gavotte. So named because it is danced to a bass drone like a bagpipe, it was popular at the courts of Louis XIV and XV.

Mussorgsky, Modest (*b* Karevo, 21 Mar. 1839; *d* St Petersburg, 28 Mar. 1881) Russian composer. Although he wrote no ballet music, two of his concert scores have been widely choreographed: *Night on the Bare Mountain* by Gorsky (1918), Nijinska (1924), and Lichine (1943), among others, and *Pictures at an Exhibition* by Nijinska (1944), Hanka (Vienna, 1947), Lopukhov (Moscow, 1963), and Neumeier (Frankfurt, 1972).

Mutations Ballet in one act with choreography by Tetley, film choreography by van Manen, music by Stockhausen, set by Baylis, and costumes by Emmy van Leersum and Gijs Bakker. Film realization was by J. P. Vroom, lighting by J. B. Read. Premiered 3 Jul. 1970 by Nederlands Dans Theater at the Circustheater in Scheveningen, with J. Meyer, Flier, Sarstädt, Lemaitre, and A. Licher. The piece incorporated film and live dance.

My Brother, My Sisters Ballet in one act with choreography by MacMillan, music by Schoenberg and Webern, designs by Y. Sonnabend. Premiered 21 May 1978 by the Stuttgart Ballet with Cragun, Keil, Montagnon, and Reid Anderson. The ballet reveals the violent relationships between a brother and his five sisters, who live in a dangerous fantasy world. The ballet also features a mysterious figure known as He who haunts the background. MacMillan revived it for the Royal Ballet in 1980.

Mythical Hunters Ballet in one act with choreography by Tetley, music by Oedoen Partos, costumes by Anthony Binstead. Premiered 25 Nov. 1965 in Ohel-Shem by the Batsheva Dance Company. In the ballet, the hunter becomes the hunted. It was revived for Nederlands Dans Theater (1968), Stuttgart Ballet (1972), and was filmed by German television with Tetley's own company (1969).

Nabokov, Nicolas (Nicolai) (*b* Lubcha nr. Minsk, 17 Apr. 1903; *d* New York, 6 Apr. 1978) Russian-US composer. He wrote the music for Massine's ballet-oratorio *Ode* (Diaghilev's Ballets Russes, 1928), also for Massine's *Union Pacific* (Ballets Russes de Monte Carlo, 1934) and Balanchine's *Don Quixote* (1965). Author of *Old Friends and New Music* (Boston, 1951).

Nádasi, Ferenc (*b* Budapest, 16 Oct. 1893; *d* Budapest, 20 Feb. 1966) Hungarian dancer, choreographer, teacher, and ballet master. Raised as a foster child, he discovered ballet through his godmother who worked as a cleaning woman for the ballet master Jakab Holczer. Holczer adopted him as student and virtual stepson. Nádasi also studied with Henrietta Spinzi and Nicholas Guerra in Hungary and later with Cecchetti in St Petersburg. In 1910 he toured Russia with a group organized by Holczer. From 1913 to 1921 he was a dancer with the Budapest State Opera Ballet, becoming the company's first male soloist. After leaving the opera house, he embarked on more than a decade of European touring, performing classical ballet as part of a variety bill with his wife, Marcelle Vuillet-Baum. In 1936 he returned to the Budapest State Opera, becoming ballet master and eventually artistic director (1959–61). He was the first director of the Budapest State Ballet Institute (from 1950) and was responsible for training a generation of leading Hungarian dancers. He was also head of a group of teachers who produced *Method of Classic Dance* (1963), one of the standard works of classical ballet training. His works for the Hungarian State Opera Ballet include *Sylvia* (1943), *Le Spectre de la rose* (1948), and *The Birthday of the Infanta* (1959). Merited Artist of the Republic and Order of Merit, first class.

Nagrin, Daniel (*b* New York, 22 May 1917; *d* Tempe, Arizona, 29 Dec. 2008) US dancer and choreographer. He studied modern dance with Helen Tamiris, Anna Sokolow, and Martha Graham. He also studied acting. After service in the US Air Force, he danced in Broadway musicals including *Annie Get Your Gun* (1946), *Touch and Go* (1949), and *Plain and Fancy* (1954). He then became a successful solo artist, performing his own choreography, after which he collaborated with *Tamiris, (his wife until their divorce in 1964). In 1960 they formed the Tamiris-Nagrin Dance Company. Nagrin later directed the improvisational dance company Workgroup. He retired from performing in 1981 and was professor of dance at Arizona State University (1982–92). Author of *How to Dance Forever* (1988), *Dance and the Specific Image: Improvisation* (1994), and *The Six Questions: Acting Technique for Dance Performance* (1998).

Nagy, Ivan (*b* Debrecen, 28 Apr. 1943) Hungarian dancer and ballet director. He studied at the Budapest State Ballet Institute and joined the Budapest State Opera in 1960, the Washington National Ballet in 1965, and New York City Ballet in 1968. From 1968 to 1978 he was a principal dancer with American Ballet Theatre. He created leading roles in Smuin's *Gartenfest* (1968) and *Eternal Idol* (1969), in Nahat's *Brahms Quintet* (1969), and Ailey's *The River* (1970). A gifted danseur noble, and an outstanding Albrecht, he was a favourite partner of many ballerinas, including Fonteyn and Makarova. After retiring as a dancer, he served as artistic director of the Santiago Ballet (1982–9), Cincinnati Ballet, and English National Ballet (1990–3). In 1995 he returned to the Santiago Ballet as director, leaving in 2000.

Naharin, Ohad (*b* Israel, 22 Jun. 1952) Israeli dancer, choreographer, musician, and company director. He studied dance as an apprentice with the Batsheva Dance Company, and also trained in New York at the Juilliard and Graham schools. He danced with several companies, Graham, Béjart's Ballet of the 20th Century in Brussels, and Bat-Dor before forming his own small troupe in New York (from 1980) and embarking on his own choreography. He worked both in Israel and abroad before becoming artistic director of Batsheva in 1990. One of his first successes there was *Kyr*, a full-length production for which he also composed the music in collaboration with Tractor's Revenge, an Israeli rock group, and he has gone on to create numerous works for the company. His choreography is distinguished by the primal physicality of its movement style, usually in tension with a rigorous formal structure, the eclectic choice of its musical repertory, and by its occasionally surreal staging. Naharin has remained with Batsheva as artistic director (apart from a brief sabbatical) and has exerted a powerful influence on younger Israeli choreographers such as Hofesh *Shechter. Naharin's dances are in the repertoires of many companies, including Nederlands Dans Theater, Sydney Dance Company, Bavarian State Ballet, Lyon Opera Ballet, Cullberg Ballet, and Rambert Dance Company. His *Axioma 7* (mus. Bach) was created for the Geneva Ballet in 1991 and subsequently taken into the Rambert repertoire (1994). A list of works for his own company includes *Mabul* (1992), *Anaphase* (1993), *Sabotage Baby* (1997), *Zachacha* (1998), *Moshe* (1999), *Naharin's Virus* (2001), and *Bolero* (2008).

Nahat, Dennis (*b* Detroit, 20 Feb. 1946) US dancer, choreographer, and director. He studied at the Juilliard School, at the American Ballet Center, and at the School of American Ballet, making his debut with the Joffrey Ballet in 1965. Between 1968 and 1971 he was with American Ballet Theatre and from 1969 began to choreograph his own ballets including *Brahms Quintet* (1969), *Mendelssohn Symphony* (Italian Symphony, 1971), and *Some Times* (mus. Claus Ogerman, 1972). In 1976 he and Ian Horvath founded the *Cleveland Ballet where he was resident choreographer and then, from 1984, artistic director. He staged versions of *The Nutcracker*, *Romeo and Juliet*, *Giselle*, *Coppélia*, and *A Midsummer Night's Dream*, and among his original creations was *Celebrations and Ode*, set to Beethoven's 7th Symphony and the final movement of his 9th. In 1993 he and Robert Barnett, artistic director of the Atlanta Ballet, presented both companies in a version of *Swan Lake* that used Nahat's choreography. When Cleveland Ballet folded in 2000 Nahat relocated it to San José, where the company eventually became known as the Ballet San José. He has continued to create many works for it, including the full-length *Middle Kingdom—Ancient China* (2005).

Namouna Ballet in two acts with choreography by Lucien Petipa, libretto by Petipa and Charles Nuitter, music by É. Lalo, sets by Rubé, Chaperon, and J. B. Lavastre, and costumes by Eugène Lacoste. Premiered 6 Mar. 1882 at the Paris Opera with Rita Sangalli, Mérante, and Pluque. The ballet, which is set in 17th-century Corfu, tells the story of Lord Adriani who loses everything, including Namouna, his favourite slave-girl, in a bet with Count Ottavio. Peter Wright staged a new version for the Stuttgart Ballet in 1967.

Napoli, or The Fisherman and His Bride Ballet in three acts with choreography and libretto by Bournonville, music by H. S. Paulli, E. Helsted,

N. W. Gade, and H. Lumbye, and design by C. F. Christensen. Premiered 29 Mar. 1842 by the Royal Danish Ballet in Copenhagen with Bournonville, Caroline Fjeldsted, and Füssel. One of the most popular of all Danish ballets, it tells the story of Teresina, bride-to-be of the Neapolitan fisherman Gennaro, who is swept overboard in a storm, saved by the sea-sprite Golfo and spirited away to a grotto on the Island of Capri where Golfo turns her into a naiad. Gennaro tracks her down and breaks the spell and the exuberant third act celebrates their wedding. It is usually only the third act, with its lively divertissements (mainly credited to Hans Beck), which is now performed. However, the full-length ballet is still in the repertoire of the Royal Danish Ballet and was given a new staging in 2009 by Nikolaj Hubbe, with a new second act (chor. Hubbe, mus. Louise Alenius Boserup) and a 1950s' setting. Peter Schaufuss staged a full-length production for the National Ballet of Canada in 1981 and for English National Ballet in 1989. Its first full production by a British company was P. Gnatt's staging for Scottish Ballet in 1978. The Act III divertissements entered the repertoire of the Royal Ballet in 1962 staged by Bruhn, and again in 2007, staged by Kobborg, and have also been danced by American Ballet Theatre in a 1974 staging by H. Brenaa.

National Ballet of Canada Canada's leading ballet company, it was founded in Toronto in 1951 and modelled on the Sadler's Wells Ballet. Its founder director was Celia *Franca, who had been a dancer with the British company and had been recommended to the Canadians by Ninette de Valois. The classics formed its core repertory and continued to do so, from Franca's *Nutcracker* (1964) to Bruhn's controversial *Swan Lake* (1966), Cranko's *Romeo and Juliet*, and Nureyev's *Sleeping Beauty* (1972), which drew on his memories of the Kirov's staging. However it also put an emphasis on 20th-century choreography, performing ballets by Ashton, Tudor, de Valois, Howard, Cranko, and MacMillan during its early years, later adding works by Balanchine, Bruhn, Petit, Peter Wright, Nureyev, Neumeier, and Tetley. The company visited London for the first time in 1972 and went on to perform internationally. Following Franca's resignation in 1974, the company was led by Alexander Grant (1976–83) from the Royal Ballet, who introduced many Ashton ballets into the repertoire as well as commissioning early ballets from the Canadian choreographer James *Kudelka. Grant was succeeded in 1983 by Erik Bruhn, who brought modern dance influences into the company's style and continued to emphasize the creation of new work, including ballets from Tetley. Bruhn's death three years later was a significant blow to the company. Reid Anderson was director between 1989 and 1996 and was succeeded by Kudelka who staged new productions of *Nutcracker* (1995) and *Swan Lake* (1999) as well as creating many new works. The former ballerina Karen Kain replaced Kudelka in 2005, and has maintained the company's core policies, updating the repertory with work by Wheeldon, Neumeier, Davide Bombana, and others while encouraging new Canadian choreographers like Dominique Dumais.

Most of the company's dancers are trained at the National Ballet School, founded by Franca and Betty *Oliphant in 1959 and it has been home to several outstanding ballerinas, including Veronica *Tennant and Kain. From 1964 the company performed in the O'Keefe Centre (now Sony Centre) in Toronto. In 2006 it acquired a new purpose-built theatre in The Four Seasons Centre.

⊕ SEE WEB LINKS
• Website for the National Ballet of Canada

National Ballet of China Chinese national ballet company based in Beijing. Western ballet was slow to develop in China, and the emerging national ballet company was initially nurtured by Russian influences. It began as the performing group of the Beijing Dance Academy, formed in 1959 under the direction of Petr Gusev, who brought in a Russian style of schooling and staged Soviet versions of the classics such as *Swan Lake, Le Corsaire,* and *Giselle,* often with guest Russian dancers. Bai Shu-xiang was the first Chinese Swan Queen. In 1963 the company became a fully professional dance company under the direction of Dai Ailian and the following year Beryl Grey became the first English ballerina to guest with the company. However during the years of the Cultural Revolution (1966–76) the company's operations were severely restricted. Key individuals like Dai Ailian were marginalized and the repertory reduced to a skeleton of ideologically correct ballets, most typically *The *Red Detachment of Women* (1964). With its corps de ballet of rifle-wielding female soldiers—all on pointe—the work was seen as a model marriage between the political ideology and culture of contemporary China and the traditions of Western ballet. After the years of the Revolution the company was slowly opened up to outside influences, with guest appearances from Fonteyn, Nureyev, Baryshnikov, and others, and the acquisition of new repertory, including works by Balanchine and MacMillan. The company however maintained its commitment to developing a uniquely Chinese identity with ballets such as *Ode to the Yimeng Mountain, Son and Daughter of the Grassland, The Maid of the Sea, The New Year's Sacrifice,* and *Trilogy of Searching for Light.* Jiang Zuhui (one of the choreographers of *The Red Detachment of Women*)

staged several full-length ballets for the company, including *Laurencia, La Esmeralda,* and *The New Year's Sacrifice.* Under Zhao Ruheng (appointed deputy director 1993 and executive director in 1994), the company further widened its repertory. In 2001 Zhang Yimou was invited to adapt his film, *Raise the Red Lantern,* as a full-length ballet, and in 2007 dancers from the company collaborated with the UK-based choreographer Akram Khan on the dance drama *bahok.* In the same year the company acquired a new production of *Swan Lake* staged by Makarova, with Wang Qimin dancing Odette/Odile to international acclaim. Zhao retired in 2008 and was succeeded by Feng Ying. Most of the company's dancers are graduates of the Beijing Dance Academy, renowned as a centre for classical training.

⊕ SEE WEB LINKS
• Website for the Chinese National Ballet

National Ballet of Cuba Company based in Havana and founded by Alicia *Alonso and Fernando Alonso with Alberto Alonso as chief choreographer. The company gave its first performances as the Ballet Alicia Alonso in 1948 and was Cuba's first professional ballet company. It took the title Ballet de Cuba in 1955 and National Ballet of Cuba in 1959 following the revolution (which also led to its being granted a state subsidy by the Castro regime). Since then Cuban dancers have won international acclaim for their brilliant technique and appealing stage personalities. Alicia Alonso, for years the company's prima ballerina, also remained its director. The repertoire is wide, embracing the 19th-century Russian and French classics, as well as 20th-century works by Balanchine, Tudor, Robbins, Béjart, and Forsythe. Alonso herself has also contributed many ballets to the repertoire, and home-grown choreographers have made work that reflects the company's Cuban identity. The company made its US debut in 1978, and its British debut at the 1979 Edinburgh Festival. Its most successful production has been *Giselle,* staged by Alicia Alonso (who danced the title role for many years) and toured internationally. The company's official school was established in 1959 and its exceptional policies of recruitment and training have produced international stars of the calibre of *Acosta and *Carreño.

National Ballet of Mexico *See* BRAVO, GUILLERMINA.

National Ballet of Spain It was founded in 1978 when the Spanish Ministry of Culture asked Antonio *Gades to form Spain's first national dance company, Ballet Nacional Español. The following year however Victor *Ullate was invited to form the classically based Ballet Nacional

Clásico and after Gades resigned his post in 1980 (briefly succeeded by *Antonio) the two companies were jointly run by one director, María de Avila (1983–86). From 1987 they were separate again. The classical ballet company was run by Maya Plisetskaya from 1987 to 1990 but when she was replaced by Nacho *Duato in 1990 it was renamed *Compañía Nacional de Danza and assumed a more contemporary style and repertory. Ballet Nacional Español, meanwhile, had a succession of directors, most recently Elvira Andrés (appointed 2001) and has continued to focus on the traditional Spanish dance heritage, although some element of classical ballet is evident in its mix of flamenco and national styles. It maintains a policy of commissioning new work, for example Manuel Santiago's *El Estampío* (2002) and Joaquin Grito's *Tiempo* (2004).

(((⊕))) SEE WEB LINKS

• Website for information on flamenco-based dance companies in Spain

national dance *See* CHARACTER DANCE.

National Dance Company of Ghana Company founded in 1961 at the Dance Department of the University of Ghana under the direction of Albert Opoku with the aim to preserve and develop black African dance. Under the direction of F. Nii-Yartey (resident choreographer and director since 1976) it has focused primarily on traditional dance culture, as distinct from other Ghanaian companies that aim for the development of a more 21st-century aesthetic. It is now based at the National Theatre.

Nationale Ballet, Het *See* DUTCH NATIONAL BALLET.

Nault, Fernand (*b* Montreal, 27 Dec. 1921; *d* Montreal, 26 Dec. 2006) Canadian dancer, choreographer, ballet master, and teacher. He studied with various teachers including Craske, Volkova, and Preobrajenska and in 1944 joined Ballet Theatre (later American Ballet Theatre) as dancer, and eventually ballet master and co-director of the school (1958). In 1965 he moved to Les Grands Ballets Canadiens as co-artistic director and chief choreographer, and was instrumental in establishing the company's international reputation as well as maintaining its stability at home. He resigned his post as co-artistic director in 1974, while remaining as resident choreographer. His ballets include *La Fille mal gardée* (Joffrey Ballet, 1960), *Carmina Burana* (mus. Orff, Les Grands Ballets Canadiens, 1966, revived 1993), *Symphony of Psalms* (mus. Stravinsky, 1970), and *Tommy* (mus. The Who, 1970), a phenomenally successful rock ballet for Les Grands Ballets. A list of his other works for Montreal includes *Hip*

and Straight (1967), *Cérémonie* (1972), *Incohérence* (1976), *Liberté tempérée* (1976), *La Scouine* (1977), *Aurkhi* (1978), and *Les Sept Péchés capitaux* (1978). He was artistic director of Colorado Ballet (1981–2).

Neary, Patricia (*b* Miami, 27 Oct. 1942) US dancer, ballet mistress, and director. She studied with Georges Milenoff, at the National Ballet School of Canada, and at the School of American Ballet. In 1960 she joined New York City Ballet, where her exceptional height, speed and attack proved ideal for the Balanchine style. In 1962 she was appointed a soloist, but although she performed almost all the ballerina roles in the Balanchine repertoire, he created only two roles for her, in *Raymonda Variations* (1961) and *Jewels* (1967). In 1968 she left New York City Ballet, embarking on a peripatetic career in Europe as ballet mistress, director, and stager of Balanchine ballets. A tireless ambassador for the latter's work, she has mounted more than twenty of his ballets in numerous productions worldwide. She was ballet mistress of the Berlin Opera Ballet (1971–3), director of Geneva Ballet (1973–8) and Zurich Ballet (1978–85), and ballet director of La Scala in Milan (1986–7). She was also artistic director of Ballet British Columbia (1989–90), for whom she choreographed *Variations concertantes* (mus. Ginastera, 1990). Since 1988 she has worked for the Balanchine Trust.

Nebrada, Vicente (*b* Caracas, 31 Mar. 1932; *d* Caracas, 25 May 2002) Venezuelan dancer, choreographer, and ballet director. He studied in Venezuela and the US and began his stage career in 1946, performing with several companies including Ballets de Paris (1955), the Robert Joffrey Ballet from 1959, and the newly formed Harkness Ballet where he became ballet master, then resident choreographer. His ballets include *Percussions for Six* (or *Percussion for Six Men*) (1969), *Schubert Variations*, and *Gemini*. In 1977 he was appointed artistic director and resident choreographer of Ballet Internacional de Caracas, and brought many dancers from the defunct Harkness company with him. He also invited US and Canadian choreographers such as Alvin Ailey and Brian Macdonald to work with the Caracas company. In 1984 he became artistic director of the Ballet Nacional de Caracas, for whom he staged many works, including *The Firebird* (1984), *Doble Corchea*, and *Inez de Castro*, as well as productions of *Romeo and Juliet*, *Coppélia*, *Don Quixote*, *Swan Lake*, and *Cinderella*. He remained in the post until 2002, and during the 1990s he also choreographed for the newly founded Florida Ballet. His work was in the repertory of over 30 companies including American Ballet Theatre, Berlin Opera Ballet, and Australian Ballet.

n

Nederlands Dans Theater One of the most successful dance companies in the world, it was founded in 1959 by a group of breakaway dancers from Sonia Gaskell's Netherlands Ballet. They based their new company in The Hague, where it remains today, housed in superb purpose-built facilities. In 1960 Hans van *Manen became the company's co-artistic director (with Benjamin Harkarvy) and chief choreographer. From the beginning the company eschewed the classics and the hierarchy of classical ballet and built up a repertoire of new Dutch work. Much influenced by the American modern dance scene, it became the first company in Europe to give its members classes in modern dance technique. American choreographers such as Butler, Sokolow, and Tetley worked with NDT and influenced its style. Important works of the 1960s and early 1970s include Butler's *Carmina Burana*, Tetley's *Pierrot Lunaire*, *Mythical Hunters*, *Circles*, *Embrace Tiger and Return to Mountain*, van Manen's *Symphony in Three Movements*, *Five Sketches*, and *Grosse Fuge*. When Harkarvy, one of NDT's founders, resigned as co-artistic director in 1969, van Manen and Tetley assumed joint direction. Van Manen left in 1970 (although he returned in 1988 as resident choreographer) and the company's creativity suffered, but it was revitalized by the arrival in 1975 of the Czech choreographer Jiří *Kylián. As artistic director he not only rewrote the repertory in his own image, creating the majority of its works, he also led the company to international success. Kylián's numerous works for NDT included *Transfigured Night* (1975), *Symphony in D* (1976), *Symphony of Psalms* (1978), *Sinfonietta* (1978), *Glagolitic Mass* (1979), *Field Mass* (1980), *Forgotten Land* (1981), *Falling Angels* (1989), *Petite mort* (1991), *Bella Figura* (1995), and *Wings of Wax* (1997). So successful was Kylián's leadership that he was able to create two smaller offshoot companies: NDT2, for junior dancers, and NDT3, for dancers aged 40 and over (although financial issues led to the effective disbanding of the latter in 2006). In 1995 Kylián celebrated his twenty years with NDT by staging *Arcimboldo*, which brought together all three NDT companies. In 1999 he stepped down as artistic director and was succeeded by Marian Sarstädt, followed by Anders Hellström (from 2005), and Jim Vincent (from 2009). Kylián remained with NDT until 2009, however, as artistic adviser and choreographer, making several works including *Click-Pause-Silence* (2001). In 2002 he was succeeded as resident choreographer by the husband and wife partnership of Paul *Lightfoot and Sol León whose works for NDT have included *Shutters Shut* (2003) and *Postscript* (2005). Other choreographers to create recent work for the company include Jacopo Godani, Alexander Ekman, Crystal Pite, Tero *Saarinen, and *Naharin.

 SEE WEB LINKS
• Website for NDT

Negri, Cesare (*b* Milan, *c*.1536 or 1535; *d* after 1604) Italian dancer, dance master, and dance theorist. From *c*.1554 he taught in Milan with many of his students going on to become dancing masters to royal households across Europe. As a performer, he appeared in masques and royal festivities. From 1569 he also choreographed mascarades and intermedios for royal courts, elaborate allegorical works with enormous casts. He was one of the first dancing masters to write about his art. His major work was *Le gratie d'amore, di Cesare Negri Milanese, detto il Trombone*, which was published in Milan in 1602 and reissued two years later as *Nuove inventioni di balli*. It was reprinted in New York in 1969. The largest dance manual published in the 16th century, it included detailed information on technique, choreography, and historical observation.

Nemchinova, Vera (*b* Moscow, 26 Aug. 1899; *d* New York, 22 Jul. 1984) Russian dancer and teacher. She studied privately with Lydia Nelidova in Moscow from 1911 and with Elizabeth Anderson from 1914. Later she studied with both Nikolai Legat and Enrico Cecchetti. In 1915 she was recruited to join the corps de ballet of Diaghilev's company, and remained with the Ballets Russes until 1926. In 1921 she was named principal dancer and in her final years with Diaghilev she was his leading ballerina. She created roles in Massine's *Boutique fantasque* (1919), *Pulcinella* (1920), and *Les Matelots* (1925), and in Nijinska's *Les Biches* (1924), a memorable role as the girl in blue. Her career after leaving Diaghilev was peripatetic. She danced with the Cochran Revue in London, with the Mordkin Ballet on its US tour, with the Lithuanian State Opera Ballet at Kaunas (1931–5), and with Blum's Ballets de Monte Carlo (from 1936), where she created a leading role in Fokine's 1936 *L'épreuve d'amour*. She also danced with the Markova-Dolin Ballet, with de Basil's Original Ballet Russe and, after moving to New York in 1941, with Ballet Theatre. She was founder, with Anton Dolin, of the Nemchinova-Dolin Ballet in 1927, and created leading roles in Dolin's *The Nightingale and the Rose* and *Rhapsody in Blue*. She was also founder and ballerina of Ballets Russes de Vera Nemchinova (1928–30), for which Balanchine created *Aubade* (1930) with Nemchinova in the role of Diana. She toured S. America and guested in Latvia. For almost 40 years she taught in New York at her own studio.

neo-classical A style of 20th-century classical ballet exemplified by the works of *Balanchine. It draws on the advanced technique of 19th-century

Russian Imperial dance but strips it of its detailed narrative and heavy theatrical setting. What is left is the dance itself, sophisticated but sleekly modern, retaining the pointe shoe aesthetic but eschewing the well-upholstered drama and mime of the full-length story ballet.

Nerina, Nadia (orig. Nadine Judd; *b* Cape Town, 21 Oct. 1927; *d* Beaulieu-sur-Mer, 6 Nov. 2008) South African dancer. She studied in South Africa with Eileen Keegan, Dorothy McNair, and H. Grinter. In 1945 she settled in London where she studied at both the Rambert School and the Sadler's Wells Ballet School. She joined Sadler's Wells Theatre Ballet in 1946, becoming a soloist with Sadler's Wells Ballet (later the Royal Ballet) in 1947 and principal in 1952. She created leading roles in Howard's *Mardi gras* (1946), Ashton's *Cinderella* (1948), *Homage to the Queen* (1953), *Variations on a Theme by Purcell* (1955), *Birthday Offering* (1956), and *La Fille mal gardée* (Lise, 1960), in MacMillan's *Noctambules* (1956), Helpmann's *Elektra* (1963), and Darrell's *Home* (Western Theatre Ballet, 1965). She toured extensively with Alexis Rassine in the 1950s and in 1960 she appeared as a guest artist at the Bolshoi Ballet in Moscow and at the Kirov in Leningrad. A virtuoso soubrette dancer noted for her light, springy jumps, strong feet, and sunny disposition, she was a favourite of Ashton's. She retired in 1969, eventually to live in France. For many years she was patron of the London-based Cecchetti Society.

Netherlands The development of theatrical dance in the Netherlands has historically centred on Amsterdam. The first ballet performances took place there in 1642 and 1645 (*Ballet of the Five Senses*). The first Amsterdam-based choreographer of note was Pietro Nieri whose most famous ballet was *Peasant Life* (1762). In the 19th century romantic ballet became popular through the choreographer Piet Grieve, whose most important work was *The Golden Magic Rose or Harlequin Freed from Slavery* (1819). Andries Voitus van Hamme (1828–68) made 115 three-act ballets for his own company of 60 dancers; his son, Anton, was also an active choreographer (1871–87). After 1890, however, ballet declined to the status of opera divertissements and there was little local creativity. Public interest was focused on visiting stars including Fuller, Duncan, and Pavlova. In 1941 the Ballet of the Amsterdam Stadsschouwburg became influential in the renaissance of dance in the country, and after the Second World War companies like the *Scapino Ballet and the Netherlands Opera Ballet and the Ballet der Lage Landen (the latter two united in 1959 as the Amsterdam Ballet) became active. In 1954 Sonia *Gaskell established the Netherlands Ballet, which in 1961 evolved into *Dutch National Ballet, now the country's leading classical company.

Modern dance emerged after a group of breakaway dancers left Gaskell's company in 1959 to found the more contemporary based *Nederlands Dans Theater in The Hague. Under the direction of Jiří *Kylián this company came to dominate the modern dance scene in the Netherlands, however the 1970s saw a rapid increase in other activity. Introdans was founded in Arnhem in 1971 by Tom Wiggers and Hans Focking. Acquiring its current name in 1979 it built up a repertory of modern dance and contemporary ballets, nurturing Dutch choreographers but also bringing in work by outsiders such as Ek, Child, and Nils Christie. Its current director Roel Voorintholt was appointed in 2005. In 1975 Kathy Gosschalk founded Werkcentrum Dans in Rotterdam to perform both Dutch and international repertory. It changed its name to Rotterdam Dancegroup in 1988 and eventually to Dance Works. Now led by Ton Simons and associate choreographer Bruno Listopard its wide repertory includes works by Amanda Miller, De Frutos, and others and it tours widely, in the Netherlands and abroad. In 1977 Bianca van Dillen, Beppie Blenkert, and Pauline *Daniels were among the several founding members of Stichting Dansproduktie, a choreographic collective based in Amsterdam. The following year Krisztina de Châtel started her own group, which she has since merged with the Itzik Galili company. Amsterdam currently has a thriving modern dance culture, centred around the Amsterdam Theaterschool. Rotterdam Dance Academy is also one of the world's leading centres for the teaching of modern dance. Holland Dance Festival is held every year in The Hague.

Netherlands Dance Theatre See NEDERLANDS DANS THEATER.

Neumeier, John (*b* Milwaukee, 24 Feb. 1942) US dancer, choreographer, and ballet director. He studied ballet in Milwaukee, with Bentley Stone and Walter Camryn in Chicago (1957–62), with Vera Volkova in Copenhagen, and at the Royal Ballet School in London (1962–3). He also studied modern dance with Sybil Shearer in Chicago from 1957. Although he danced briefly with the Shearer company in Chicago (1960–2), he subsequently worked for most of his career in Germany. He danced with the Stuttgart Ballet (1963–9), where he began to choreograph, and was named director of the Frankfurt Ballet (1969–73) when he was only 27 years old. In 1973 he became director of the *Hamburg Ballet, a position he has held ever since. As chief choreographer, artistic director, and from 1996 'Ballettindendant' he has made Hamburg the second most important centre for ballet in Germany, after Stuttgart. In 1978 he also became director of the newly founded Hamburg Ballet School. He has created numerous ballets for Hamburg, and while remaining within the classical vocabulary has experimented with a wide range of themes and styles. He made his reputation with radical re-interpretations of pre-existent ballets, such as *Romeo and Juliet*, *The Nutcracker* (both 1971), *Baiser de la fée* (1972), and *Daphnis and Chloe* (1972), but has also tack-led musical classics, including Bach's *St Matthew Passion*, 1981, and literary texts such as *Othello* (mus. Pärt, Schnittke, Vasconcelos, and others, 1985), *Amleth* (*Hamlet*, mus. Tippett, Royal Danish Ballet, 1985), and *The Seagull* (mus. several, 2003). He has also choreographed extensively for other companies, including the Royal Winnipeg Ballet, the Royal Ballet, American Ballet Theatre, the National Ballet of Canada, the Paris Opera Ballet, the Vienna State Opera Ballet, the Royal Danish Ballet, and the Stuttgart Ballet. A list of his works includes *Separate Journeys* (mus. Bar-ber, 1968), *Rondo* (1970), *Don Juan* (mus. Gluck, 1972), *Le Sacre* (mus. Stravinsky, 1972), *Gustav Mahler's Third Symphony* (1975), *Hamlet: Con-notations* (mus. Copland, 1976), *Swan Lake* (1976), *Gustav Mahler's Fourth Symphony* (Royal Ballet, 1977), *Legend of Joseph* (mus. Strauss, Vienna, 1977), *A Midsummer Night's Dream* (mus. Mendelssohn and Ligeti, 1977), *Lady of the Camellias* (mus. Chopin, Stuttgart Ballet, 1978), *Don Quixote* (mus. 1979), *Age of Anxiety* (mus. Bernstein, 1979), *St Matthew Pas-sion* (mus. Bach, 1981), *A Streetcar Named Desire* (mus. Prokofiev and Schnittke, Stuttgart, 1983), *Sixth Symphony of Gustav Mahler* (1984), *Shall We Dance?* (mus. Gershwin, 1986), *Magnificat* (mus. Bach, 1987), *Peer Gynt* (mus. Schnittke, 1989), *Medea* (Bartók, Schnittke, Bach, Galasso, and others, 1990), *Requiem* (mus. Mozart, 1991), *A Cinderella Story* (mus. Prokofiev, 1992), *Now and Then* (mus. Ravel, National Ballet of Canada, 1992), *Serenade* (mus. Bernstein, 1993), *Zwischenräume, or Mahler's Ninth Symphony* (1994), *Ondine* (mus. Henze, 1994), *Sylvia* (Paris Opera Ballet, 1997), *Getting Closer* (American Ballet Theatre, 1999), *Death in Venice* (mus. Bach, 2003), and *The Little Mermaid* (mus. Lera Auerbach, Royal Danish Bal-let, 2005). He has also directed and choreographed opera productions, including *Orpheus and Eurydice* for Hamburg Opera. Many of his ballets have been filmed for television.

(⊕) SEE WEB LINKS
• Website for Hamburg Ballet

New Dance Modern dance in one act with choreography by Humphrey and Weidman, music by Wallingford Riegger, and costumes by Pauline Lawrence. Premiered 3 Aug. 1935, at Ben-nington School of the Dance, with Humphrey and

Weidman. According to the choreographer her-self, the piece 'represents the world as it should be, where each person has a clear and harmoni-ous relationship to his fellow beings'. It was the third part of a trilogy, including *Theater Piece* and *With My Red Fires* and was filmed in 1972.

New Dance Group A company and school founded in 1932 in New York City by six students from the Wigman School who wanted to make 'dance a viable weapon for the struggles of the working class'. It offered classes at reduced fees in an effort to spread the cause of modern dance throughout the US. By the late 1930s associated schools had been opened in several cities. Its performing group became part of the Workers Dance League (later the New Dance League) which was actively involved in left-wing politics. Choreographers involved with the company included Sophie Maslow, Jean Erdman, Charles Weidman, José Limón, William Bales, Donald McKayle, and Talley Beatty. The Dudley–Ma-slow–Bales trio helped to make the New Dance Group known across America. Jane *Dudley was the organization's first president, remaining in the post until the mid-1960s. Its activities then de-clined and the New Dance Group operating today is a different, educational body.

New Love Song Waltzes Modern dance in one act with choreography by Mark Morris, music by Brahms. Premiered 4 Nov. 1982 by the Mark Morris Dance Group at the Bessie Schönberg Theater, Dance Theater Workshop in New York. Set to the Brahms song-cycle *Neue Liebeslieder Walzer*, its subject is love in its widest and most communal sense.

New York City Ballet US ballet company based in New York. It was founded by Lincoln *Kirstein and George *Balanchine and grew out of their previous enterprises, the American Ballet, Ballet Caravan, and Ballet Society. It took its pres-ent name in 1948 upon becoming the resident ballet company of the New York City Center for Music and Drama. Its opening programme was *Concerto Barocco*, *Orpheus*, and *Symphony in C*; its first box office triumph was *Firebird*, with Maria Tallchief, who went on to become Amer-ica's first internationally famous ballerina. With Kirstein as general manager, Balanchine as artis-tic director, and Jerome *Robbins as co-director (he joined in 1949), NYCB rapidly established itself as one of the world's leading ballet compa-nies. It began touring abroad in 1950 and its brilliant and distinctive repertoire came to embody a new American style of dance: virtuosity in the strict classical tradition of Balanchine's Russian heritage married to a speedy and attack-ing dynamic more reflective of modern American life. Neo-classicism reached its apogee in the abstract works Balanchine created for NYCB as well as in the generations of dancers trained to perform them, headed by names such as Tanaquil LeClerc, Edward Villella, Arthur Mitchell, Suzanne Farrell, Merrill Ashley, and Darci Kistler. In 1964 the company moved to the New York State Theater at Lincoln Center, a 2,500-seat theatre designed to Balanchine's specifications. It is still housed there today. In 1972 the company undertook its most ambitious project, the Stravinsky Festival, for which 21 new ballets were choreographed to the composer's music. Balanchine continued to run the company (with Robbins as co-ballet master and creator of many important works) until his death in 1983, at which point Peter *Martins and Robbins took over direction. Robbins left the position shortly afterwards leaving Martins in sole charge. While continuing to maintain the Balanchine works as the company's backbone, Martins has added ballets of his own, as well as opening up the repertoire to outside choreographers such as Forsythe, Stroman, and Tharp and between 2001 and 2007 employing Christopher Wheeldon as resident choreographer. The company's associated school, the School of American Ballet, which was founded in 1933, is one of the world's leading training organizations and continues to provide NYCB with most of its dancers.

(⊕) SEE WEB LINKS

• Website for New York City Ballet

New Zealand Ballet Company *See* ROYAL NEW ZEALAND BALLET.

Nichols, Kyra (*b* Berkeley, Calif., 2 Jul. 1958) US dancer. She studied with her mother, Sally Streets, who had danced with New York City Ballet during the 1950s, then with Alan Howard, and at the School of American Ballet (from 1972). She joined New York City Ballet in 1974, becoming a principal in 1979. She spent her entire career with New York City Ballet, where she was admired as one of the most classical of the company's ballerinas. Although she danced a wide range of Balanchine roles, the choreographer created nothing for her, although he did revise his *Firebird* for her in 1980. She created roles in many Robbins ballets, including *The Four Seasons* (1979), *Rondo* (1980), *Piano Pieces* (1981), *I'm Old Fashioned* (1983), *Antique Epigraphs* (1984), and *Eight Lines* (1985). She also created roles in *Brahms/ Handel* (choreographed in 1984 by Robbins and Tharp), in several works by Martins, including *Suite from Histoire du soldat* (1981), *A Schubertiad* (1984), *Poulenc Sonata* (1985), *Tanzspiel* (1988), *Beethoven Romance* (1989), and *A Musical Offering* (1991), and in Forsythe's *Herman Schmerman* (1992). She retired from the stage in 2007.

Night Journey Modern dance in one act with choreography by Graham, music by William Schuman, and set by Noguchi. Premiered 3 May 1947 by the Martha Graham Group at Cambridge High and Latin School, Cambridge, Massachusetts, with Graham, Hawkins, and Mark Ryder. Graham's version of the Oedipus myth features Queen Jocasta as the protagonist, reviewing her life at the moment of her death.

Night Shadow (*La Somnambule*; *La sonnambula*) Ballet in one act with choreography by Balanchine, libretto and music by Vittorio Rieti (after Bellini), and designs by Dorothea Tanning. Premiered 27 Feb. 1946 by the Ballet Russe de Monte Carlo at City Center in New York with Danilova, Magallanes, Maria Tallchief, and Michel Katcharoff. A 19th century gothic romance, the ballet revolves around a poet and a sleepwalker who meet during a masked ball. Their encounter leads to jealous intrigue and the poet's eventual murder. Some of the music is taken from Bellini's opera of the same name but the plot is entirely different. The ballet was revived many times, with stagings for Grand Ballet du Marquis de Cuevas (1948), Royal Danish Ballet (1955), New York City Ballet (1960), Ballet Rambert (1961), London Festival Ballet (1967), and American Ballet Theatre (1981). One of Balanchine's few narrative ballets.

Nijinska, Bronislava (*b* Minsk, 8 Jan. 1891; *d* Pacific Palisades, Calif., 21 Feb. 1972) Russian dancer, choreographer, ballet mistress, and teacher. The daughter of Polish dancers Eleonora Bereda and Foma Nijinsky, and the younger sister of Vaslav *Nijinsky. She studied with Cecchetti and at the St Petersburg Imperial Theatre School (1900–8), graduating into the company at the Mariinsky Theatre, where she spent the next three years. In 1909 she went to Paris with Diaghilev, and again in 1910, as a member of his corps de ballet. When Nijinsky was dismissed from the Mariinsky in 1911, she resigned and joined Diaghilev's Ballets Russes as a permanent dancer. She created roles in Fokine's *Carnaval* (1910) and *Petrushka* (1911) and was one of the original Nymphs in Nijinsky's *L'Après-midi d'un faune* (1912). She returned to Russia during the First World War (after her brother had been dismissed by Diaghilev), where she danced at the Petrograd Private Opera Theatre. Influenced by radical innovations in visual art and theatre, she also choreographed her first ballets. In 1916 she moved to Kiev, where she danced at the opera house and taught (one of her students was Lifar). In 1921 she left Russia and rejoined Diaghilev to work on his London production of *The Sleeping Princess*, for which she staged several dances. Her next few years with Diaghilev gave her significant choreographic opportunities and she created *Le Renard* (mus. Stravinsky, 1922), *Les Noces* (mus. Stravinsky, 1923), *Les Biches* (mus. Poulenc, 1924), *Les Fâcheux* (mus. Auric, 1924), and *Le Train bleu* (mus. Milhaud, 1924). After a disagreement with Diaghilev, she resigned in 1925, taking a chamber group of dancers on tour in England and working as a freelance choreographer for the Paris Opera, the Buenos Aires Teatro Colón, and the Ida Rubinstein company. It was for the last that she made *Le Baiser de la fée* (mus. Stravinsky, 1928), *Bolero* (mus. Ravel, 1928), and *La Valse* (mus. Ravel, 1929). In 1932 she founded her own company, Ballets Nijinska, Théâtre de la Danse, for which she choreographed *Variations* (mus. Beethoven, 1932) and *Hamlet* (mus. Liszt, 1934), with herself in the title role. In 1935 she staged the dance sequences in Max Reinhardt's Hollywood film of *A Midsummer Night's Dream*. In 1935 she also created *Les Cent Baisers* (mus. d'Erlanger) for de Basil's Ballets Russes, the first Nijinska ballet to be shown in the US. In 1937 she served as artistic director of the short-lived *Polish Ballet for whom she made five ballets, including *Chopin Concerto*, Palester's *Le Chant de la terre*, and Kondracki's *La Légende de Cracovie*. In 1941 she opened a school in Los Angeles, which became her base, although she continued to stage ballets for companies elsewhere. Her productions included *La Fille mal gardée* (mus. Hertel, Ballet Theatre, 1940), *The Snow Maiden* (mus. Glazunov, Ballet Russe de Monte Carlo, 1942), *Brahms Variations*, and *Pictures at an Exhibition* (mus. Mussorgsky, Ballet International, 1944). After 1945 she worked as ballet mistress for the Grand Ballet du Marquis de Cuevas, for whom she mounted *The Sleeping Beauty* in 1960. Despite her substantial output of ballets, she was in danger of being forgotten as a choreographer when Ashton invited her to Covent Garden to revive *Les Biches* for the Royal Ballet in 1964 and *Les Noces* two years later. The success of these stagings confirmed Nijinska as one of the most important dancemakers of the 20th century, a radical modernist whose daring energy and wit produced some of the most distinctive and powerful ballets in the repertory. Author of *Bronislava Nijinska: Early Memoirs* (New York, 1981).

Nijinsky, clown de Dieu Ballet in two parts with choreography by Béjart, music by Pierre Henry and Tchaikovsky, costumes by Joëlle Roustan and Roger Bernard, set and lighting by R. Bernard. Premiered 8 Oct. 1971 by the Ballet of the 20th Century at Forest National in Brussels, with Donn, Bortoluzzi, Lommel, Lanner, Mejia, Van Hoecke, Farrell, Albrecht, and Ullate. Using quotations from Nijinsky's diary, the ballet presents the picture of a young man's search for truth, love, and God. There are references to

Nijinsky's four most famous roles: in *Spectre de la rose*, *Scheherazade*, *Petrushka*, and *L'Après-midi d'un faune*, characters from which appear in the ballet as companions to Nijinsky. The title is inspired by a quotation from Nijinsky's diary: 'I will introduce myself as a clown...to make myself better understood.'

Nijinsky, Vaslav (*b* Kiev, 12 Mar. 1889; *d* London, 8 Apr. 1950) Russian dancer and choreographer. The most famous dancer of Diaghilev's Ballets Russes and one of the towering figures of 20th-century ballet. He was the son of the Polish dancers Eleonora Bereda and Foma Nijinsky, and the brother of the choreographer Bronislava *Nijinska. He studied at the Imperial Theatre School in St Petersburg (1898–1907), a student of Nikolai and Sergei Legat, and joined the Mariinsky Theatre upon graduation. Immediately successful, he partnered the company's top ballerinas—Kschessinska, Preobrajenska, and Karsavina—in his first season. There he was befriended by Diaghilev, who saw in the young dancer not only a potential lover but also the potential star of his new Ballets Russes. Nijinsky confirmed Diaghilev's expectations. During the early years of the company he created roles in most of Fokine's ballets, *Cléopâtre*, *Les Sylphides*, *Scheherazade*, *Spectre de la rose*, *Narcisse*, *Petrushka*, *Le Dieu bleu*, and *Daphnis and Chloe*, and created a sensation in Europe with his virtuoso technique (he could execute entrechats huit and was even known to do an entrechat dix), his exceptional elevation, and his exotic stage charisma. His versatility was impressive: he could be savagely sexual as the Golden Slave in *Scheherazade*, or dreamily romantic as the spirit in *Spectre de la rose*. In 1911 he was forced to leave the Mariinsky following a scandal over his costume for *Giselle* (a scandal some claimed was masterminded by Diaghilev). Now free to devote his energies to Diaghilev, Nijinsky became not only the main attraction of the Ballets Russes, but also its choreographer, at Diaghilev's urging. The resulting ballets were among the most controversial in the history of ballet: *L'Après-midi d'un faune* (1912), *Jeux* (1913), and *Le Sacre du printemps* (1913). His choreography was a revolutionary break with tradition; like Fokine, his movements were moulded to reflect the different scenarios. In *L'Après-midi d'un faune*, steps were seen in profile like Greek friezes; in *Le Sacre du printemps*, the language of the body was turned in on itself, the dance was flat-footed and convulsive. The brazen modernity of his ballets, and the overt eroticism of *Faune*, provoked strong reactions from his audiences, but his notoriety was short-lived. While on tour in South America in 1913 Nijinsky married the Hungarian dancer Romola de Pulszky, an act which so infuriated Diaghilev that he immediately sacked Nijinsky. The break between the young dancer and his older impresario-lover marked the beginning of Nijinsky's mental instability. He attempted to launch a company of his own in 1914 but it failed after just two weeks at the Palace Theatre in London. When the First World War broke out he was in Budapest where he was interned as a Russian. In 1916 Diaghilev secured his release and Nijinsky joined the Ballets Russes for a North American tour, for which he choreographed *Till Eulenspiegel*. But signs of schizophrenia may already have been evident. After several subsequent tours with the Ballets Russes, Nijinsky's behaviour became extremely erratic. He moved to Switzerland in 1918 and entered a sanatorium in 1919. His last public performance was given on 19 Jan. 1919 in a St Moritz hotel ballroom; it was a solo recital called *Marriage with God*. The rest of his life was spent in and out of mental hospitals as his family travelled around Europe. He never danced again, although during his long confinement he worked on a system of dance notation. In 1947 his family moved to London, where he died of renal failure. He was buried in Montmartre cemetery. He was one of the greatest artists ballet has ever produced, a dancer of exceptional ability and vision. As a choreographer his contribution has recently been re-evaluated, with reconstructions of his lost works mounted by *Hodson and Archer, and he is now considered one of the key voices in 20th-century modernism. Herbert Ross made a film about his life in 1980, while Béjart choreographed a ballet about him (see *Nijinsky, clown de Dieu*). *The Diaries of Vaslav Nijinsky*, written over a six-week period in 1919, were first published in English in 1936 in a version heavily edited by Romola Nijinsky. In 1999 the unexpurgated version, edited by Joan Acocella, was published as *The Diary of Vaslav Nijinsky*.

Nikitina, Alice (*b* St Petersburg, *c*.1904 (some sources say 1909); *d* Monte Carlo, Jun. 1978) Russian dancer, teacher, and opera singer. She studied at the Imperial Ballet School in St Petersburg with Preobrajenska but left Russia after the October Revolution and never graduated. She made her professional debut in Ljubljana, Yugoslavia, in 1920, then performed with Boris Romanov's Romantic Ballet in Berlin (from 1921). In 1923 she joined Diaghilev's Ballets Russes, becoming a ballerina. She created roles in Massine's *Zéphyr et Flore* (Flore, 1925), Balanchine's *Apollon musagète* (Terpsichore, 1928) and *Le Bal* (The Lady, 1929). After Diaghilev's death she danced in the London Cochran revues and with Anatole Vilzak in recitals in Brussels and Paris. In 1933 she danced with Ballets Serge Lifar in London and appeared with de Basil's Ballets Russes de Monte Carlo at Covent Garden in 1937, where she created the role of the Queen in Lichine's *Le Lion amoureux*. After retiring as a dancer she turned to singing and from 1938 performed as a coloratura soprano in Italy. Eleven years later she opened a ballet school in Paris. Author of *Nikitina by Herself* (London, 1959).

Nikolais, Alwin (*b* Southington, Conn., 26 Nov. 1910; *d* New York, 8 May 1993) US dancer, choreographer, composer, designer, teacher, and director. He had an unconventional background for a dancer, working first as an organist for silent films and then as a puppet master. He studied dance with Truda Kaschmann and Hanya Holm, later with Graham, Humphrey, Weidman, and Horst. His first full-length work was *Eight Column Line* (mus. E. Křenek), which had its debut in Connecticut in 1940. He became Holm's assistant after doing his military service during the Second World War. In 1948 he was appointed director of New York's Henry Street Playhouse, a centre for experimental theatre, where he remained until 1970. It was here he met Murray Louis, who was to become a lifelong collaborator. While extensively reorganizing both the Henry Street school and the company, which later become the Nikolais Dance Theater, Nikolais developed his aesthetic of total dance theatre. This treated dance as one element in an integrated spectacle, which in itself eschewed narrative and character in the creation of spectacular stage imagery. Dancers were often unrecognizable, due to the disguising effects of costumes, props, and lighting and, as puppets of Nikolais' larger vision, they were often compared to aliens from outer space, or organisms under a microscope. Nikolais acted as his own designer and composer—most of his productions featured music written by himself—and he painted his own slide projections. One of his most important works was *Masks, Props, and Mobiles* (1953), in which the cast were concealed inside large bags, which were then stretched into different shapes by the choreography. The idea, said Nikolais, was to help the dancer 'identify with things other than himself'. He retired from performing in 1953 to devote himself to choreography, costume design, and lighting. In 1963 he was one of the first artists to use the newly invented Moog synthesizer. The Nikolais Dance Theater first toured Europe in 1965 and its 1968 Paris debut was such a success that ten years later Nikolais was invited by the French government to form the Centre National de Danse Contemporaine at Angers. He created two works for the Paris Opera Ballet: *Schema* (1980) and *Arc-en-ciel* (1987). In 1989 his American company merged with that of Murray *Louis to form Murray Louis and Nikolais Dance, an ensemble that performed both choreographers' repertories and was directed by Louis after Nikolais' death. In 1999 the company was phased out by the Nikolais-Louis Dance Foundation, in order for it to focus on educational projects based on the two men's work. However the Ririe-Woodbury Dance Company continue to perform the Nikolais-Louis repertory. A list of Nikolais' own works includes *Tensile Involvement* (1953), *Noumenon* (1953), *Kaleidoscope* (1953), *Prism* (1956), *Totem* (1959), *Allegory* (1959), *Imago* (1963), *Vaudeville of the Elements* (1965), *Sanctum* (1964), *Somniloquy* (1967), *Triptych* (1967), *Tent* (1968), *Echo* (1969), *Structures* (1970), *Scenario* (1971), *Grotto* (1973), *Tryad and Styx* (1976), *Gallery* (1978), *The Mechanical Organ* (1980), *Persons and Structures* (1984), *Video Games* (for the 1984 Olympics), *Contact* (1985), *Crucible* (1985), and *Aurora* (1992). US National Medal of Arts (1987).

Nine Sinatra Songs Ballet in one act with choreography by Tharp, costumes by Oscar de la Renta, and lighting by Jennifer Tipton. Premiered 14 Oct. 1982 by the Twyla Tharp company at the Queen Elizabeth Theatre in Vancouver. This setting of Frank Sinatra recordings features seven couples who each represent a different facet of heterosexual romance. The work is in the repertory of other companies including Pacific Northwest Ballet. It is also performed by American Ballet Theatre under the title *Sinatra Suite*, featuring only one couple.

Ninth Symphony Ballet in four movements with choreography by Béjart, music by Beethoven, lighting by T. Skelton. Premiered 28 Oct. 1964 by the Ballet of the 20th Century at the Cirque Royal, Brussels, with Höfgen, Pinet, Sifnios, Bortoluzzi, Bari, Lefèbre, and Casado. The ballet, set to Beethoven's 9th Symphony, realizes in dance the emotions evoked by the four-movement concert work. As Béjart put it, '[accompanying] the composer on his slow path, leading from anger to joy, from darkness to light.' The ballet is preceded by a prologue of texts taken from Nietzsche's *Birth of Tragedy*.

Nixon, David (b Chatham, Ontario, 20 Nov 1958) Canadian choreographer and ballet director. He trained at the school of the National Ballet of Canada and danced with the company between 1978 and 1984, rejoining it between 1989 and 1991 as principal dancer. He also spent two periods at Berlin Opera Ballet: as dancer (1985–90) then as principal dancer and ballet master (1994–96). In 1994 he additionally became artistic director of BalletMet in Columbus, Ohio, and during his six years with the company added 16 world premieres to its repertoire. In 2001 he moved to the UK to become director of Northern Ballet Theatre. He introduced several of his works to the repertory as well as creating many more including *Madame Butterfly* (orig.

version 1996; new version 2002), *Wuthering Heights* (2002), *I Got Rhythm* (2004), *Swan Lake* (2004), *A Midsummer's Night Dream* (orig. version 2000, 2004), *Dracula* (1999, new version 2005), *The Three Musketeers* (2006), *A Sleeping Beauty Tale* (2007), *The Nutcracker* (2007), and *Hamlet* (2008).

Nobili, Lila de (b Lugano, 3 Sept. 1916; d Paris, 19 Feb. 2002) Italian painter and designer. She designed several ballets, including Milloss's *Mario e il mago* (Milan, 1956), Babilée's *Sable* (Ballets Jean Babilée, Paris, 1956), Peter Wright's *Sleeping Beauty* (Royal Ballet, 1968, costumes only), and—most famously—Ashton's *Ondine* (Royal Ballet, London, 1958).

Noblet, Lise (b Paris, 24 Nov. 1801; d Paris, Sept. 1852) French dancer. She studied at the Paris Opera Ballet School and joined the Paris Opera Ballet in 1816, becoming a soloist. She was introduced to London audiences through her guest appearances at the King's Theatre (1821–4). She created roles in Aumer's new staging of Dauberval's *Le Page inconstant* (1823) and *La Fille mal gardée* (1829); in Aumer's *La Belle au bois dormant* (1829) and *Manon Lescaut* (1830). She also created roles in F. Taglioni's *La Sylphide* (Effie, 1832), *La Révolte au serail* (1833), and *La Fille du Danube* (1836).

Noces, Les Ballet in one act with choreography by Nijinska, libretto (song text) and music by Stravinsky, and designs by Goncharova. Premiered 13 Jun. 1923 by the Ballets Russes de Diaghilev at the Théâtre de la Gaîté-Lyrique in Paris, with Felia Doubrovska, Nikolai Semenov, Lubov Tchernicheva, and Leon Woizikowsky. The ballet is a rigorously unsentimental portrayal of a Russian wedding whose four scenes, 'The Blessing of the Bride', 'The Blessing of the Bridegroom', 'The Bride's Departure from her Parents' House', and 'The Wedding Feast', are more suggestive of ritual sacrifice than private joy. Although it re-creates the peasant world of Holy Russia, the ballet was, as the choreographer herself disclosed, strongly influenced by the political rise of the proletariat which she had recently witnessed in Soviet Russia as well as by new trends in Russian theatre and Constructivist art. One of Nijinska's most successful works, it was revived many times, including for de Basil's Ballets Russes (1936), Royal Ballet (1966), Stuttgart Ballet (1974), and Paris Opera (1976).

Many other choreographers have created versions of *Les Noces*, including Béjart for Ballet of the 20th Century (Salzburg in 1962), Robbins for American Ballet Theatre (1965), Lar Lubovitch for his own company (1976), Kylián for Nederlands Dans Theater (as *Svadebka* 1982), Preljocaj (1989), Bigonzetti (Aterballetto, 2002), Stijn Celis (Les

Grands Ballets Canadiens (2002), Spoerli (Zurich, 2006), Javier de Frutos as *Los Picadores* (Phoenix, 2007), and Michael Clark as *I do* (London, 2007). Nijinska's own version, however, with its eloquently muscular choreography, geometrically drilled corps de ballet and powerful designs, remains one of the undisputed masterworks of the 20th century.

Noguchi, Isamu (*b* Los Angeles, 17 Nov. 1904; *d* New York, 30 Dec. 1988) Japanese-US sculptor and set designer. He designed the sets for numerous Martha Graham works, with Graham incorporating his design elements into her choreography. They collaborated on *Frontier* (1935), *Chronicle* (1936), *El Penitente* (1940), *Appalachian Spring* (1944), *Herodiade* (1944), *Dark Meadow* (1946), *Cave of the Heart* (1946), *Errand into the Maze* (1947), *Night Journey* (1947), *Diversion of Angels* (1948), *Judith* (1950), *Seraphic Dialogue* (1955), *Embattled Garden* (1958), *Clytemnestra* (1958), *Acrobats of God* (1960), *Alcestis* (1960), *Phaedra* (1962), *Circe* (1963), and *Cortege of Eagles* (1967). He also designed Page's *The Bells* (1946), Cunningham's *The Seasons* (1947), and Balanchine's *Orpheus* (1948). Arguably the leading designer of 20th-century modern dance.

Noir et blanc See SUITE EN BLANC.

North, Robert (*b* Charleston, SC, 1 Jun. 1945) US dancer, choreographer, and company director. He studied at the Central School of Art in London in 1963 but turned to dance, studying at the Royal Ballet School (1965–7), at the London School of Contemporary Dance (1966), and subsequently with Graham and Cunningham in the US. He was a founding member of London Contemporary Dance Theatre in 1967 and while joining Graham's company briefly returned to LCDT in 1969. He choreographed his first work for London Festival Ballet Workshop in 1967 and in 1974 he created his most popular work, *Troy Game*, for LCDT; a humorous parody of masculinity, it has since entered the repertoire of many companies. In 1975 he was appointed associate choreographer of LCDT. He also worked as a guest choreographer for Ballet Rambert, Stuttgart Ballet, and the Royal Danish Ballet, among others, and choreographed for the commercial stage, including the 1975 London revue *Carte blanche* and the rock musical *Pilgrim*, seen at the Edinburgh Festival that same year. He has additionally worked in opera, film, theatre, and television. He taught contemporary dance at the Royal Ballet School (1979–81), was co-artistic director of LCDT in 1981 and from 1981 to 1986 he was artistic director of Ballet Rambert after which he was ballet director at the Teatro Regio in Turin (1990–1), artistic director of the Gothenburg Ballet in Swe-

den (1991–6), ballet director in Verona (1997–9), and artistic director of Scottish Ballet (1999–2002). Between 2002 and 2006 he worked as a freelance choreographer until being appointed artistic director of the Krefeld Mönchengladbach company in Germany. He has created over 70 works, which include *Troy Game* (mus. B. Downes, LCDT, 1974), *Still Life* (mus. Downes, LCDT, 1975), *Death and the Maiden* (mus. Schubert, LCDT, 1980), *Lonely Town, Lonely Street* (mus. Withers, Janet Smith and Dancers, 1980), *Songs and Dances* (mus. Schubert, LCDT, 1981), *Pribaoutki* (mus. Stravinsky, Rambert, 1982), *Entre dos aguas* (mus. Paco de Lucia, Rambert, 1984), *Dances to Copland* (Batsheva Dance Company, 1985), *Einsame Reise* (mus. Schubert, Stuttgart, 1985), *Elvira Madigan* (mus. several, Royal Danish Ballet, 1987), *Romeo and Juliet* (mus. Prokofiev, Geneva Ballet, 1990), *Carmina Burana* (mus. Orff, Gothenburg Ballet, 1990), *A Stranger I Came* (mus. Schubert, English National Ballet, 1992), *The Snowman* (mus. Howard Blake, 1993), *Offenbach in the Underworld* (mus. Offenbach, Stravinsky, Geneva Ballet, 1995), *Hamlet, Prince of Denmark* (mus. Shostakovich, 1997), *Carmen* (Gyor Ballet, 1997 revived Scottish Ballet, 2002), and *Bach* (Nord Rhein-Westfalen, 2005).

Northern Ballet Theatre British dance company founded in 1969 in Manchester, but now based in Leeds in Yorkshire. Originally named Northern Dance Theatre, it was started by the Canadian choreographer Laverne Meyer to tour smaller theatres with a repertoire of new choreography by Meyer and others. He resigned in 1975 and Robert de Warren took over. He made fundamental alterations to the company, by hiring more dancers, adding more full-length ballets to the repertoire (including several of his own) and emphasizing its classical basis. At this point the name was changed. In 1987 the company underwent another dramatic change when Christopher *Gable took over as artistic director. He gradually moved the repertoire away from the classics to original full-length productions, such as *A Christmas Carol*, *The Brontës*, *Dracula*, and *Hunchback of Notre Dame*, which brought dance and theatre ever closer together. Following Gable's death in 1998 the company faltered until David Nixon was appointed director in 2001. He has since maintained Gable's policies, choreographing his own narrative ballets for the company including *Hamlet* (2007) as well as commissioning new work such as Cathy Marston's *A Tale of Two Cities* (2008).

Norway Classical ballet activity in Norway dates back to the formation of the Ny Norsk Ballett in 1945 which evolved into the *Norwegian National Ballet. Modern dance did not take root until the late 1980s and 90s with the establishment of a small number of groups including Carte Blanche in Oslo (now based in Bergen) and Kreutzerkompani, in Bergen. One of the best known of these is the Jo Strømgren Kompani founded by Stromgren and Agnes Kroepelien in loose association with the Bergen International Theatre in 1998. Producing mixed-media works that incorporate dance, theatre, puppetry, and film, the company tours internationally.

Norwegian National Ballet Norway's sole classical ballet company, based in Oslo, The company's origins date from 1945 when a group called the Ny Norsk Ballett (the New Norwegian Ballet) was founded by Gerd Kjølaas and Louise Browne. In 1958 it became the nucleus of a newly formed, and publicly subsidized company based at the National Opera House in Oslo. The first production was *Coppélia*. The British dancer and teacher Joan Harris was an influential early director (1961–5). She added a corps de ballet, produced the classics, and introduced English ballets to the repertoire as well as the RAD teaching syllabus to the associated school. Other directors have included Brian Macdonald, Sonia Arova (1966–71), Anne Borg (1971–7, 1983–8), Brenda Last (1977–80), Dinna Bjørn (1990–2000) and Espen Gijane. The company made its first visit to the US in 1974. The repertoire is classically based, but each generation has added contemporary ballets from Balanchine, Tetley, Cranko, Ashton, Flindt, van Manen, and Kylián through to Ek, Forsythe, and Elo. In recent years it has encouraged young Norwegian choreographers such as Kaloyan Boyadjiev. The company adopted the name Norwegian National Ballet in 1993.

notation *See* DANCE NOTATION.

Notre-Dame de Paris Ballet in two acts with choreography and libretto by Petit, music by Maurice Jarre, sets by René Allio, and costumes by Yves St Laurent. Premiered 11 Dec. 1965 by the Paris Opera Ballet with Motte, Petit, Atanassoff, and Bonnefoux. Based on Victor Hugo's 1831 novel of the same name, Petit's ballet is centred on Quasimodo, the hunchbacked bellringer, and Petit himself danced the role at the ballet's premiere. It was his first work for the Paris Opera since leaving twenty years earlier. It was revived for the Marseilles Ballet in 1974 and for the Kirov Ballet in 1978.

Notre Faust *See* FAUST BALLETS.

Nouveau Ballet de Monte Carlo Ballet company founded in 1942, using dancers who had fled the Paris Opera Ballet in advance of German troops. Its first director was Marcel Sablon. The repertoire included Diaghilev ballets, along with new works. In 1944 it was disbanded

but was re-formed in 1946 by the impresario Eugene Grünberg. Lifar, who was artistic director, created several works for the company, including *La Péri* (mus. Dukas), *Salomé* (mus. R. Strauss), *Nautéos* (mus. J. Leleu), *Dramma per musica* (mus. Bach), and *Chota Roustaveli* (mus. Honegger). An impressive line-up of dancers included Chauviré, Charrat, Jeanmaire, Skouratoff, and Tcherina, although most of them left with Lifar when he returned to the Paris Opera in 1947. The Marquis de *Cuevas bought the company following Lifar's departure and re-named it Grand Ballet de Monte Carlo.

Noverre, Jean-Georges (*b* Paris, 29 Apr. 1727; *d* St-Germain-en-Laye, 19 Oct. 1810) French dancer, choreographer, ballet master, and dance theorist. Although his works (he choreographed more than 150) have not been performed for more than 200 years, he remains one of the most significant names in ballet history. He was a radical reformer who rejected ballet's traditional role as a decorative divertissement in opera productions and instead saw its potential for portraying real drama and character. He is generally credited with the development of the *ballet d'action and in the 20th century both Fokine and Jooss cited him as their model. Noverre studied with Marcel and Louis Dupré and made his debut at the Paris Opéra Comique in 1743. The next ten years were spent travelling as a dancer (although his was an undistinguished career) and as a ballet master in Berlin, Dresden, Strasbourg, Marseilles, and Lyon. In 1754 he returned to the Paris Opéra Comique as ballet master. There he staged the famous *Les Fêtes chinoises* (1754), *La Fontaine de Jouvence* (1754), and *Les Réjouissances flamandes* (1755). At the invitation of Garrick, who believed Noverre to be the Shakespeare of the dance, he mounted *Fêtes chinoises* at the Drury Lane Theatre in London in 1755. He remained in London for two years but was forced to keep a low profile when anti-French riots broke out. It was about this time that he wrote *Lettres sur la danse et sur les ballets*, published in Lyon and Stuttgart in 1760. It was one of the most influential books ever written about dance. It was revised in 1803 in St Petersburg and translated into English by Cyril Beaumont in London in 1930. Working in Lyon from 1757 to 1760 Noverre put his theories about the ballet d'action into practice with such works as *Les Caprices de Galathée* and *La Toilette de Vénus*. In Stuttgart, where he worked as ballet master until 1766, he created some of his most important works: *Admète et Alceste* (1761), *La Mort d'Hercule* (1762), *Psyché et l'Amour* (1762), *Médée et Jason* (1763), *Orpheus and Eurydice* (1763), *Hypermestra* (1764), *The Feast of Hymen* (1766), and *The Rape of Proserpine* (1766). From 1767 to 1774 he worked in Vienna, staging almost

50 ballets at the Burg Theatre and the Kärntnertor Theater. Among them were *Alceste* (1767), *Les Petits Riens* (mus. Aspelmayr, 1768), *Der gerächte Agamemnon* (1771), *Roger et Bradamante* (1771), *Vénus et Adonis* (1773), *Apelles et Campaspe* (1773), *Adèle de Ponthieu* (1773), and *Les Horaces et les Curiaces* (1774). From 1774 to 1776 he worked in Milan, where his public debate with Angiolini about the principles of the ballet d'action brought him to international attention. In 1776, following the intervention of his old friend Marie Antoinette, he became ballet master of the Paris Opera, where he remained until 1781. It was a period fraught with tension, thanks to the political intrigue of his rivals Gardel and Dauberval and his own much-criticized output as a choreographer, which at this time included *Annette et Lubin* (1778), *Les Petits Riens* (1778), and *Les Fêtes de Gamache* (1780). After retiring on a pension, he worked at the King's Theatre in London, forming a company that included Pierre Gardel and Antoine Bournonville, and, later, Auguste Vestris. Noverre worked on and off in London for a dozen years. Ballets of this period included *Apollo et les Muses* (1782), *Les Offrandes à l'amour* (1787), *Les Fêtes provençales* (1789), *Pas de trois et de quatre* (set to *God Save the King*) (1793), *Iphigénie en Aulide* (1793), *Adelaide ou la Bergère des Alpes* (1794). His last ballet was probably *Marriage of Peleus and Thetis*, a court spectacle devised for the wedding of the Prince and Princess of Wales in 1795. He eventually retired to St-Germain-en-Laye where he died. His *Lettres sur les art des imitateurs en général et sur la danse en particulier* was published in Paris in 1807.

Nuñez, Marianela (*b* Buenos Aires, 23 Mar. 1982) Argentinian dancer. She trained at the Teatro Colón school and joined the company at the age of 14. In 1997 she moved to London, entering the Royal Ballet School and the following year graduating into the Royal Ballet, aged just 16. An extrovert dancer with a powerful technique, she was promoted to first soloist in 2001 and principal in 2002. She has since danced all the leading roles in the classical repertoire and has created roles in several works including Baldwin's *Towards Poetry*, Bintley's *Les Saisons*, Wheeldon's *DGV*, and McGregor's *Infra*.

Nureyev, Rudolf (*b* on a train journey between Lake Baikal and Irkutsk in Siberia, 17 Mar. 1938; *d* Paris, 6 Jan. 1993) Russian dancer, choreographer, and ballet director. One of the true superstars of 20th-century dance, with a fame so international that many of those who knew nothing about dance had heard his name. His early training was in folk dance and ballet in Ufa; he began studying at the Leningrad Ballet School (the Kirov school) when he was 17. There he trained under A. Pushkin for the next three years. He joined the Kirov Ballet as a soloist in 1958 but his stay there was short-lived. On 16 June 1961, while the Kirov was on its debut visit to Paris, he was involved in a dramatic stand-off at Le Bourget Airport between his KGB minders and French police during which he appealed for political asylum. From then on his home was in the West and an exceptional career was launched. As the first dancer to defect from the Soviet Union he was an immediate celebrity, making front-page news around the world. His first performances were with the Grand Ballet du Marquis de Cuevas. At Fonteyn's invitation, he danced at a Royal Academy of Dancing gala in London, and shortly thereafter he became Fonteyn's principal partner. He was a regular guest artist with the Royal Ballet (1962–77) but made numerous appearances with companies all over the world. His stage charisma, a combination of animal grace, technical power, and sexuality, electrified audiences and inspired a new generation of male dancers. His partnership with the much-older Fonteyn was legendary: she the cool English rose, he the hot-blooded Tartar who seemed to melt her former reserve. His repertoire was enormous, including all the classics and the modern standards, and he created roles in numerous works, including Ashton's *Marguerite and Armand* (1963) and *Jazz Calendar* (1968), MacMillan's *Romeo and Juliet* (1965, inheriting the role from Christopher Gable, on whom it was made) and *Sideshow* (1972), Petit's *Paradise Lost* (1967), *L'estasi* (1968), and *Pelléas et Mélisande* (1969), van Dantzig's *The Ropes of Time* (1970), *Blown in a Gentle Wind* (1975), and *Ulysses* (1979), Béjart's *Song of a Wayfarer* (1971), Tetley's *Laborintus* (1972) and *Tristan* (1974), Graham's *Lucifer* (1975) and *The Scarlet Letter* (1975), Balanchine's *Le Bourgeois gentilhomme* (1979), Taylor's *Big Bertha* (television production, 1970), and Flindt's *The Overcoat* (1989) and *Death in Venice* (1991). He also staged works for various companies, including the Vienna State Opera Ballet, Australian Ballet, London Festival Ballet, Ballet of La Scala, Milan, National Ballet of Canada, Royal Swedish Ballet, Dutch National Ballet, and Ballet of the 20th Century, and toured extensively with several of them. He was the first major ballet star to work regularly with leading modern dance choreographers and he performed with both the Martha Graham and Paul Taylor companies. In 1989, at the age of 51, he made a historic return visit to the Kirov, performing at the Mariinsky Theatre. He appeared in many films, including *An Evening with the Royal Ballet* (1963), *Romeo and Juliet* (1966), *Le Jeune Homme et la mort* (1966), *I am a Dancer* (1972), and *Don Quixote* (1972). He played the title role in Ken Russell's 1977 film *Valentino*. He also made numerous television appearances, which additionally helped to popularize dance. He was director, principal dancer, and choreographer of *Nureyev and Friends*, which ran on Broadway (1974–5). He starred as the King of Siam in the US tour of *The King and I* in 1989. He was artistic director of the Paris Opera Ballet from 1983 to 1989. He gave the company a new profile by promoting junior dancers (including Sylvie Guillem), acquiring ballets by Cunningham, Robbins, and Paul Taylor, and commissioning original works from Maguy Marin, William Forsythe, and Karole Armitage. In the last years of his life he took up conducting. He died of an Aids-related illness at the age of 54. A list of his works as choreographer includes *Tancredi* (mus. Henze, Vienna State Opera Ballet, 1966), *Romeo and Juliet* (mus. Prokofiev, London Festival Ballet, 1977), *Manfred* (mus. Tchaikovsky, Paris Opera Ballet, 1979), *The Tempest* (mus. Tchaikovsky, Royal Ballet, 1982), *Bach Suite* (mus. Bach, Paris Opera Ballet, 1984), *Washington Square* (mus. Ives, Paris Opera Ballet, 1985), and *Cendrillon* (mus. Prokofiev, Paris Opera Ballet, 1986). His stagings of the classics include *La Bayadère* (Kingdom of the Shades scene, Royal Ballet, 1963), *Raymonda* (Royal Ballet Touring Company, 1964; American Ballet Theatre, 1975), *Swan Lake* (Vienna, 1964), *Don Quixote* (Vienna, 1966), *Sleeping Beauty* (National Ballet of Canada, 1972; London Festival Ballet, 1975), *Nutcracker* (Royal Swedish Ballet, 1967, also Royal Ballet 1968), and *La Bayadère* (mus. Minkus, Paris Opera Ballet, 1992). Author of *Nureyev, an Autobiography with Pictures* (London, 1962).

Nutcracker, The Ballet in two acts with choreography by Ivanov, libretto by Petipa, music by Tchaikovsky, and designs by M. I. Botcharov, K. Ivanov, and I. Vsevolojsky. Premiered 18 Dec. 1892 at the Mariinsky Theatre in St Petersburg with Antonietta Dell'Era (Sugar Plum Fairy), Pavel Gerdt (Prince Coqueluche), Sergei Legat (Nutcracker), and Stanislava Belinskaya (Clara). Designed to be part of a double bill with Tchaikovsky's opera *Iolanta*, it has instead become the quintessential Christmas ballet, and as such is probably the most performed ballet in the world. It is based on a story by E. T. A. Hoffmann, *Der Nussknacker und der Mäusekönig*. A young girl,

usually called Clara or Masha, is given a nutcracker doll for Christmas. She falls asleep and dreams that she saves the doll's life in a battle with the Mouse King. The nutcracker is then transformed into a handsome prince who whisks her away to the Kingdom of Sweets, where the Sugar Plum Fairy stages a grand divertissement with them as honoured guests. Originally this was to have been Petipa's ballet, but ill health forced him to bow out, leaving his assistant Ivanov to choreograph it. Little of the Ivanov choreography has survived (the grand pas de deux in Act II is his) and the ballet has been open to much re-interpretation by modern choreographers who have attempted to find psychological or sexual resonances in the tale of Clara's coming of age.

Despite its current ubiquity the ballet gained widespread popularity only after the Second World War. The first staging in London took place in 1934 when Sergeyev mounted it for Vic-Wells Ballet. W. Christensen undertook the first full-length American staging for the San Francisco Ballet in 1944. Balanchine staged it for New York City Ballet in 1954, Vainonen for the Kirov in 1934, and Grigorovich for the Bolshoi in 1966. Cranko did a *Nutcracker* for Stuttgart in 1966, Nureyev did one for the Royal Swedish Ballet in 1967, Flindt for the Royal Danish Ballet in 1971, Neumeier for Frankfurt Ballet in 1971, and Baryshnikov for American Ballet Theatre in 1976. Virtually every large-scale ballet company in the world has its own version. Two leading modern dance choreographers have staged iconoclastic versions: Mark Morris's *The Hard Nut* (Mark Morris Dance Group, Brussels, 1991) and Matthew Bourne's *Nutcracker* (Adventures in Motion Pictures, 1992).

Nyman, Michael (*b* London, 1944) British composer. In the 1980s and 1990s his music became increasingly popular with choreographers. Among the works set to his music are Ashley Page's *A Broken Set of Rules* (1984), several pieces by Shobana Jeyasingh including *Configurations* (1989) and *Exit No Exit* (2006), Christopher Bruce's *Meeting Point* (1995) and *Quicksilver* (1996), Doug Varone's *In Thine Eyes* (1996) and *Sleeping with Giants* (1999), and Wheeldon's *DGV* (2006).

Oaks, Agnes (*b* Vandra, 29 May 1970) Estonian Dancer. She trained at the schools of the Estonian State Ballet and the Bolshoi Ballet, dancing with Estonian Ballet before joining English National Ballet in 1990 with her partner (on and off stage) Thomas *Edur. An exceptionally refined classical stylist, she was most naturally suited to the 19th-century repertory. But she also danced in works by MacMillan, Corder, and Deane, while her created role in *McGregor's 2Human (2003) revealed an unexpectedly spiky, contemporary edge to her dancing. She and Edur spent a year with Birmingham Royal Ballet (1996–7) then embarked on a joint freelance career, re-establishing links with English National Ballet as principal guest artists until Oaks retired in 2009.

Obermaier, Klaus (*b* Linz, 7 Mar. 1955) Austrian composer, director, and artist. He trained in graphic design and music since when he has experimented with a series of mixed-media, interactive projects. Those for dance have offered seminal discoveries about the ways in which electronically created imagery can alter perceptions of the live body. In *Vivisector* (2002, with Chris Haring) video projections and light effects played over four dancers to create illusions of speed, altered shape, and texture. In *Le Sacre du Printemps* (2006, with Julia Mach) 3D technology created the illusion that the dancer was crossing vast stretches of space as she moved.

Obermaier's works are toured worldwide. He has additionally created video and sound installations and composed for music ensembles including the Kronos Quartet. In 1996 he was appointed visiting professor at the University IUAV, Venice, teaching new media in dance, music, and theatre.

Oboukhoff, Anatole (Obukhov) (*b* St Petersburg, 15 Jan. 1896; *d* New York, 25 Feb. 1962) Russian dancer and teacher. He studied at the Imperial Theatre School in St Petersburg and graduated into the Mariinsky Theatre in 1913 where he was promoted to premier danseur in 1917. A handsome dancer with a fine classical technique, he partnered *Pavlova on her final Russian tour in 1914. In 1920 he left the Soviet Union, dancing first with the Romanian Opera Ballet in Bucharest (1920–2) then with Boris *Romanov's Russian Romantic Ballet (1922–5). He and his wife Vera *Nemchinova danced together in the Latvian Opera Ballet in Riga (1930), at the Ballet de l'Opéra Russe à Paris (1931), at the Lithuanian Opera Ballet in Kaunas (1931–5), with de Basil's Ballets Russes (1935–6), with René Blum's Ballets de Monte Carlo (1936–7), the Markova-Dolin Ballet (1937) and de Basil's Original Ballet Russe (1930–40). From 1941 until his death he taught at the School of American Ballet in New York. In 1944 he staged the pas de deux from Petipa's *Don Quixote* for Ballet Theatre (with Toumanova and Dolin), the first time it had entered the repertoire of a Western company.

O'Brien, John (*b* Hopetown, Australia, 29 Aug. 1933) British dancer, teacher, and bookseller. He studied at the Royal Ballet School, joining Sadler's Wells Opera Ballet in 1957 and then becoming principal dancer with Ballet Rambert (1957–66). He taught at the Rambert company and abroad and in 1964 founded Ballet Bookshop (later *Dance Books) in London's Cecil Court.

Ocean Modern dance with choreography by Cunningham, music by David Tudor and Andrew Culver, costumes and lighting by Marsha Skinner. Premiered 18 May 1994 by the Merce Cunningham Dance Company at the Cirque Royal in Brussels. Performed in the round it runs 90 minutes, and uses 112 musicians who sit in a circle around the audience. It was conceived by Cunningham and Cage shortly before the latter's death, and its epic-scaled choreography is designed to have no front, back, or side perspective.

Ode Ballet-oratorio in two acts with choreography by Massine, libretto by Kochno, music by Nabokov, designs by Pavel Tchelitchev (sets and costumes) and Pierre Charbonnier (projections). Premiered 6 Jun. 1928 by the Ballets Russes de Diaghilev at the Théâtre Sarah Bernhardt in Paris, with Irina Beliankina and Serge Lifar. The ballet, based on a visionary hymn to nature by the 18th-century Russian court poet Lomonosov, made use of the latest technology, including neon lights and film projections. Despite its spectacular stage effects, *Ode* never achieved great popularity and it was dropped from the repertoire.

Odette-Odile The good and evil heroines of Swan Lake. Odette is the innocent Swan Queen, Odile the malevolent temptress who impersonates her in order to deceive Prince Siegfried. In most productions the two contrasting roles are danced by the same ballerina.

O'Donnell, May (*b* Sacramento, Calif., 1909; *d* 1 Feb. 2004) US dancer, choreographer, and teacher. She studied with Hanya Holm and danced in the Martha Graham company (1932–8, 1944–53), creating roles in Graham's *Appalachian Spring* (1944), *Herodiade* (1944), *Dark Meadow* (1946), and *Cave of the Heart* (1946). In 1939 she founded the San Francisco Dance Theatre with Gertrude Shurr and Ray Green, after which she danced with the Limón company (1941–3). From 1949 she had her own company, based in New York. She also taught at her own school and at the School of Performing Arts, as well as at London Contemporary Dance Theatre. Her works included *Suspension* (1943), *Dance Sonata No. 1* (1952), *Dance Concerto* (1954), *Dance Sonata No. 2* (1956), *Pursuit of Happiness* (1977), and *Homage to Shiva* (1980). *Suspension* was reconstructed by the Cleveland Ballet Dancing Wheels in 1999 to mark O'Donnell's 90th birthday.

Odysseus ballets The decade-long wanderings of the legendary king of Ithaca have inspired many ballets, dating as far back as Hilverding's *Ulisses und Circe* (Vienna, *c.*1740). 19th-century interpretations included G. Gioia's *Il ritorno d'Ulisse* (Naples, 1804) and Milon's *Le Retour d'Ulysse* (Paris, 1807), those of the 20th century included Hanka's *Homerische Sinfonie* (mus. T. Berger, Vienna, 1950), Gruber's *Neue Odyssee* (mus. V. Bruns, East Berlin State Opera, 1957), Murray Louis's *Odyssey* (mus. I. Fiedel, New York, 1960), and van Dantzig's *Ulysses* (mus. Haubenstock-Ramati, Vienna, 1979).

Offenbach, Jacques (*b* Cologne, 20 June 1819; *d* Paris, 5 Oct. 1880) German-French composer. He wrote the music for M. Taglioni's *Le Papillon* (Paris, 1860) but several other ballets have used his scores including Masssine's *Gaîté parisienne* (arr. M. Rosenthal, 1938), Fokine's *Bluebeard* (arr. Dorati, 1941), Tudor's *Offenbach in the Underworld* (arr. George Crumb, 1955), Cranko's *La Belle Hélène* (arr. L. Aubert, 1955), and Peter Darrell's full-length *Tales of Hoffmann* (arr. Lanchbery, 1972).

Offenbach in the Underworld Ballet in one act with choreography and libretto by Tudor, music by Offenbach (arranged by George Crumb), and designs by K. Ambrose. Premiered 17 Jan. 1955 by the National Ballet of Canada at the Palace Theatre in St Catherine's, Ontario, with Lois Smith, David Adams, and Earl Kraul. In a fashionable café in the 1870s customers flirt with each other: an operetta star, a grand duke, a starving artist, a handsome officer, and a debutante. Tudor said of this ballet: 'There isn't an ending, only a closing time.' It had earlier been staged for the Philadelphia Ballet Company in 1954, but the 1955 version for the National Ballet of Canada was considered definitive. It was revived for American Ballet Theatre in 1956 and for City Center Joffrey Ballet in 1975.

Ogden, Heather (*b* Toronto, 24 Dec. 1980) Canadian dancer. She trained at the Richmond Academy of Dance in British Columbia before joining the National Ballet of Canada in 1998, where she was promoted to principal in 2005. Noted for her musicality and on-stage glamour she dances most of the leading roles in the ballerina repertoire and in 2005 performed the role of Dulcinea in Balanchine's *Don Quixote* with the Suzanne Farrell Ballet in Edinburgh, subsequently dancing the same role in the National Ballet's company premiere of the work in 2007.

Oguike, Henri (*b* West Glamorgan, Wales, 26 Sept. 1970) British-Nigerian choreographer. He trained at the London Contemporary Dance School and in 1994 became a founder member of the Richard Alston Dance Company, dancing with the company until 1998. In 1999 he formed the Henri Oguike Dance Company, choreographing all of its repertory. His works are noted for their musical awareness and for the daring range of his physical response to his chosen scores, which run the musical spectrum from Purcell to Ali Farka Toure. In addition to choreographing for his own company, Oguike has made works for Rambert, Phoenix Dance Theatre and the Holland Dance Festival. His works include: *Front Line* (mus. Shostakovich, 2002), *Signal* (mus. Taiko, drums, and others, 2004), *Little Red* (mus. Vivaldi, 2007), and *Tread Softly* (mus. Schubert, 2009).

Ohno, Kazuo (*b* Hakodate, Hokkaido, 27 Oct. 1906; *d* 1 Jun. 2010) Japanese dancer and choreographer. He taught physical education but during the 1930s began to study dance, working with Mary Wigman's Neue Tanz and in 1949 performing his first solo recital. In the 1960s he developed the style of *butoh working in collaboration with the dancer Tatsumi Hijikata (1926–86). Many of Ohno's early creations were interpretations of Western literary texts although his most famous work, created in 1977, at the age of 71, was *Admiring La Argentina*, in which he transformed himself into the legendary Spanish dancer. During his long career he remained one of butoh's leading exponents. Other works included *My Mother* (1981), *Water Lilies* (1987), and *The Wolf* (1994). He founded his own school in 1977 and published his autobiography in Japan in 1990.

(((∙))) SEE WEB LINKS

• Website for Kazuo Ohno's school

Oiseau de feu, L' *See* FIREBIRD.

Oklahoma! Stage musical with music by Richard Rodgers, lyrics by Oscar Hammerstein II, and choreography by Agnes de Mille, first performed on Broadway in 1943. It revolutionized the American musical by fully integrating dance into the storytelling. It ran for 2,212 performances in its original New York run, while the London production at Drury Lane lasted for 1,543 performances. In 1998 it was revived by Britain's National Theatre with new choreography by Susan Stroman. It is set among cowboys and farmers in the American West.

Oliphant, Betty (*b* London, 5 Aug. 1918; *d* 12 Jul. 2004) British-Canadian dancer, teacher, and ballet mistress. She studied stage dance, and classical ballet with Karsavina and Novikov, going on to choreograph and perform in musicals on the London stage. In 1949 she opened a school in Toronto and in 1951 was appointed ballet mistress of the newly formed *National Ballet of Canada. In 1959 she became director of the National Ballet School and under her leadership this developed into one of the world's foremost training institutions. She retired in 1989. She also served as associate artistic director of the National Ballet (1969–75). She published her autobiography, *Miss O: My Life in Dance*, in 1997.

Ombre, L' Ballet in three acts with choreography and libretto by Filippo Taglioni, music by L. Wilhelm Maurer, sets by Fedorov, Serkov, Shenian, and Roller, and costumes by Mathieu. Premiered 10 Dec. 1839 at the Bolshoi Theatre in St Petersburg with M. Taglioni, and A. Guerra. The title refers to the ghost of a murdered woman who returns to dance with her grieving lover. It was revived in a two-act version at Her Majesty's Theatre in London in 1840.

Ondine Ballet in three acts with choreography and libretto by Ashton, music by Hans Werner Henze, and designs by Lila de Nobili. Premiered 27 Oct. 1958 by the Royal Ballet at Covent Garden, with Fonteyn, Somes, Farron, and A. Grant. Ashton based his libretto on the novel by Friedrich de la Motte Fouqué, which tells of a water-nymph who falls in love with a mortal, with fatal consequences

for both. Ashton's fourth three-act ballet, it was the first to have a commissioned score, composed according to the choreographer's libretto. It also marked the culmination of his creative partnership with Fonteyn; some considered it to be her greatest created role. The role of Ondine had initially been associated with Fanny Cerrito, who appeared in Perrot's 1843 version. The famous pas de l'ombre (shadow dance), in which Ondine sees her shadow for the first time, was adopted by Ashton for his version. Henze's score was later choreographed by Alan Carter for Bavarian State Opera Ballet in Munich (1959), by Tatjana Gsovsky for Berlin Ballet (1959), by Nicholas Beriozoff for Zurich State Opera Ballet (1965), and by Imre Eck for Hungarian State Opera Ballet in Budapest (1969). Earlier versions included stagings by Louis Henry (mus.Gyrowetz, Vienna, 1825), Paul Taglioni (mus. H. Schmidt, Berlin, 1836), and Jules Perrot (mus. Pugni, London, 1843), whose *Ondine, ou, La Naïade*, was later staged by Petipa for St Petersburg in 1874 as *The Naïad and the Fisherman*. In a 1903 restaging at the Mariinsky (Shiryaev after Petipa and Perrot), Pavlova danced Ondine.

Onegin Ballet in three acts with choreography and libretto by Cranko, music by Tchaikovsky (arranged by K. H. Stolze), and designs by Jürgen Rose. Premiered 13 Apr. 1965 by the Stuttgart Ballet in Stuttgart, with Barra, Haydée, Cardus, and Madsen. The ballet takes its plot from Pushkin's famous verse-novel about the humiliation and regret of love, *Eugene Onegin*. However, it does not use any of Tchaikovsky's music from his opera of the same name (the board of directors at the Stuttgart Ballet being opposed to the idea). It has been revived for many companies including Munich State Opera Ballet (1972), Royal Swedish Ballet (1976), Australian Ballet (1976), London Festival Ballet (1983), Royal Danish Ballet (1991), American Ballet Theatre (2000), Royal Ballet (2001), and Houston Ballet (2005). Eifman choreographed a version in 2009, updating its story to 1991 and the collapse of the Soviet Union.

On Your Toes American musical comedy with music by Richard Rodgers, lyrics by Lorenz Hart. Its Broadway premiere was 11 Apr. 1936 and it was the first Broadway musical to feature a classical ballet (in this case at the show's climax). Titled *Slaughter on Tenth Avenue*, it was choreographed by Balanchine and starred Tamara Geva. It was the first of four Rodgers and Hart shows choreographed by Balanchine and introduced the term choreographer to Broadway programme credits.

opera and ballet Ballet has played a role in opera since the latter's origins in the late 16th century. Festive dances were common in early operas (Monteverdi's *La favola d'Orfeo*, 1607, for example), although by the mid-18th century ballet was also used to convey drama. Act II of Handel's *Ariodante* (1735) used a danced finale to illustrate the heroine's struggle between good and evil and in Gluck's *Orfeo ed Euridice* (Vienna, 1762), the Dance of the Furies and the Dance of the Blessed Spirits were also illustrative of Orfeo's story. By the 19th century Italian opera had largely eschewed ballet, but it continued to play a major role in France, due largely to the influence of Lully and Rameau. By the mid-19th century, every French grand opera featured a formal ballet scene and non-French composers also felt obliged to incorporate them when their works were staged in France. Richard Wagner included one in his *Rienzi* (1842) and before *Tannhäuser* could open in Paris in 1861 he had to add a full-scale ballet. There are notable ballet sequences in Meyerbeer's *Robert le diable* (1831) and *Les Huguenots* (1836), in Donizetti's *La Favorite* (1840), and in Verdi's *Les Vêpres siciliennes* (1855) and *Don Carlos* (1867). Verdi added a ballet to *Il trovatore* and *Otello* for their Paris premieres. Ballet has also been prominent in Russian opera, from Glinka to Prokofiev, with major dance sequences in Mussorgsky's *Boris Godunov*, Tchaikovsky's *Eugene Onegin*, and Borodin's *Prince Igor*. In the 20th-century works such as Michael Tippett's *Midsummer Marriage* (London, 1955), Britten's *Death in Venice* (Aldeburgh Festival, 1973), and Glass's *Einstein on the Beach* (Avignon, 1976) have drawn on the long tradition of dance in opera. It has become common for choreographers such as Mark Morris, Trisha Brown, Pina Bausch, and Wayne McGregor to direct opera as well as create dances for them.

opéra-ballet A form of lyric theatre in which singing and dancing were presented as equal partners in lavish and spectacular stagings. It was popular in France in the late 17th and early 18th centuries. Early examples included Lully's *Triomphe de l'amour* (1681) and *Le Temple de la paix* (1685), with André Campra developing the form in productions such as *L'Europe galante* (Paris, 1697), *Les Fêtes vénitiennes* (Paris 1710), and *Les Amours de Vénus et de Mars* (1712). J.-P. Rameau took the opéra-ballet to its apogee with *Les Indes galantes* (1735), *Les Fêtes d'Hébé* (1739), *Le temple de la gloire* (1745), *Platée* (1745), and *La Guirlande* (Paris, 1751). In the 19th century F. Taglioni choreographed several opéra-ballets. In 1997 Mark Morris choreographed a version of *Platée* for the Royal Opera.

Orbs Modern dance in six parts with choreography by Paul Taylor, music by Beethoven, and designs by A. Katz. Premiered on 4 Jul. 1966 at the Royal Theatre in The Hague by the Paul Taylor Company, with De Jong, C. Adams, Wagoner, and Taylor. (US premiere on 8 Nov. 1966 at the Harper Theater in Chicago.) An ambitious, hour-long work addressing the theme of man's place in the universe it is set to movements from Beethoven's last three string quartets. Taylor himself danced the role of the Sun. It was his first full-length work.

Orchésographie, L' Book written by Thoinot *Arbeau, in 1588. Dealing with the history of dance and describing various dances of the time, it is the most important surviving work on 16th-century dance. It was translated into English by Cyril Beaumont (London, 1925).

Ordman, Jeannette (*b* Germiston, S. Africa, 8 Nov. 1935; *d* Tel Aviv, 7 Feb. 2007) British dancer, teacher, and ballet director. She began her career with Johannesburg Festival Ballet, and later danced with Sadler's Wells Opera Ballet in London. In 1965 she went to Israel to teach and in 1968 co-founded *Bat-Dor Dance Company (with Baroness Bethsabee de Rothschild). Despite increasing financial difficulties she served as artistic director of the company until its closure in 2001, then of its associated school.

Orff, Carl (*b* Munich, 10 Jul. 1895; *d* Munich, 29 Mar. 1982) German composer. He wrote no ballet music, although his theatre works often used an element of dance and three of his concert scores *Carmina Burana*, *Catulli Carmina*, and *Trionfo di Afrodite* have attracted many choreographers. Gsovsky choreographed the last two, in 1943 and 1953 respectively, while versions of *Carmina Burana* have been choreographed by Inge Hertling (1937), Erika Hanka (1942), Mary Wigman (1943), Heinz Rosen (1959), John Butler (1959), Fernand Nault (1962), David Bintley (1995), Damian Woetzel (1997), and S. Welch (2003), among many others.

Orlin, Robyn (*b* Johannesburg, 1955) South African dancer and choreographer. She trained at the London School of Contemporary Dance (1975–80) and during the 1980s returned to South Africa to become a member of the Federated Union of Black Artists Academy, creating a contemporary dance section for which she both choreographed and taught. In post-apartheid South Africa, Orlin became director of one of the country's leading independent dance companies, her work taking a provocative stance on issues such as HIV/AIDS, the condition of women, racial divisions, and social abuse, through a mix of dance, text, video, and striking visual imagery. Her productions include *If You Can't Change the World Change Your Curtains* (1990); the Olivier award-winning *Daddy, I've Seen This Piece Six Times Before and I Still Don't Know Why They're Hurting Each Other* (1999), and *We Must Eat Our Suckers with the Wrapper on* (2001). In 2005 she was choreographer in residence at the National Centre de Pantin, Paris and in 2007 she choreographed Handel's *L'Allegro, il penseroso ed il moderato* for Paris Opéra. She directed the short film *Hidden beauties Dirty stories* (2005). Recipient of numerous awards and honours including Knight of the French National Order of Merit (2009).

(((●))) SEE WEB LINKS
- Robyn Orlin's website

Original Ballet Russe *See* BALLETS RUSSES DE MONTE CARLO.

Orpheus 1. Ballet in one act with choreography by Balanchine, music by Stravinsky, and designs by Noguchi. Premiered 28 Apr. 1948 by Ballet Society at City Center in New York, with Nicholas Magallanes, Maria Tallchief, and Francisco Moncion. The ballet is a contemporary retelling of the Orpheus and Eurydice myth, 'the eternal domestic tragedy of an artist and his wife' according to Balanchine. Other choreographers using the same music include Milloss (Venice, 1948), Lichine (Paris, 1948), Tatjana Gsovsky (Frankfurt, 1961), Cranko (Stuttgart, 1970), van Dantzig (Amsterdam, 1974), MacMillan (London, 1982), and Tetley (Melbourne, 1987). 2. Ballet in six scenes with choreography by Forsythe, libretto by E. Bond, music by Henze, sets by Axel Manthey, and costumes by Joachim Herzog. Premiered 17 Mar. 1979 by the Stuttgart Ballet in Stuttgart, with Cragun, Keil, R. Anderson, M. Witham, and O. Neubert. A full-length ballet, it uses the story of Orpheus to show how artists have transformed the human race into a society that has no need of gods.

Elsewhere, the Orpheus myth has provided numerous choreographers with subject-matter, among them H. Schütz (Dresden, 1638), Hilverding (Vienna, 1752), Noverre (Stuttgart, 1763), Isadora Duncan (Munich, 1902), Laban (mus. Gluck, 1927), de Valois (mus. Gluck, London, 1941), Petit (Paris, 1944), Charrat (mus. R. Lupi, Venice, 1951), and Béjart (mus. P. Henry, Liège, 1958). Gluck's opera *Orpheus and Eurydice* has been choreographed and directed by several choreographers including Balanchine (at the Metropolitan Opera, 1936), Bausch (chamber version, Wuppertal, 1975), and Morris (several versions including the Metropolitan Opera 2007). Trisha Brown directed and choreographed a production of Monteverdi's *L'Orfeo* for the Monnaie, Brussels, 1998.

Orr, Terry (*b* Berkeley, Calif., 12 Mar. 1943) US dancer and company director. He studied at the San Francisco Ballet School and joined San Francisco Ballet in 1959. In 1965 he joined American Ballet Theatre where he remained for

three decades, as principal dancer (from 1972) and ballet master (from 1978). In 1997 he was appointed artistic director of Pittsburgh Ballet Theater. Married the former ABT ballerina Marianna *Tcherkassky.

Osipenko, Alla (*b* Leningrad, 16 Jun. 1932) Soviet dancer and teacher. She studied at the Leningrad Ballet School, graduating in 1950. She danced with the Kirov Ballet from 1950 to 1971, where she became prima ballerina, creating roles in Grigorovich's *The Stone Flower* (Mistress of the Copper Mountain, 1957), Belsky's *Coast of Hope* (Beloved, 1959), and Chabukiani's Kirov staging of *Othello* (Desdemona, 1960). After leaving the Kirov she joined L. Jacobson's Choreographic Miniatures company (1971–3), Leningrad Concert Organization (1973–7), and Theatre of Contemporary Ballet (directed by Boris Eifman, 1977–82), where she created the role of Nastasia in Eifman's *The Idiot*. From 1966 she also taught at the Vaganova School but after retiring from the stage she moved to N. America and Europe before returning to St Petersburg. She has also acted in several films including *The Voice* (dir. Averbach, 1981), *Sorrowful Sympathy* (dir. Alexander Sokurov, 1986), and *Russian Ark* (dir. Sokurov, 2002). Pavlova Prize (Paris, 1956). People's Artist of the Soviet Union (1960).

Osipova, Natalia (*b* Moscow, 18 May 1986) Russian dancer. She trained as a gymnast before entering the Moscow Choreographic School (Bolshoi Ballet School) in 1996, where her teachers were Marina Kotova and Marina Leonova. In 2004 she graduated into the Bolshoi, promoted to soloist and lead soloist in 2008. A technically fearless dancer with a very versatile range, she has rapidly assumed ballerina roles in the classical repertory, most notably Kitri, Medora, and the title role in *La Sylphide*, but has also excelled in 20th-century works such as Ratmansky's staging of *Flames of Paris*, and Tharp's *In the Upper Room*. In 2009 she danced a guest season with American Ballet Theatre. She is the recipient of several awards including the Golden Mask, from the Theatre Union of Russia.

(((●))) SEE WEB LINKS
- Website for Natalia Osipova

Othello Ballet in four acts with choreography and libretto by Chabukiani, music by Aleksey Machavariani, and designs by Simon Virsaladze. Premiered 29 Nov. 1957 (some sources 27 Dec. 1957) at the Paliashvili Theatre of Opera and Ballet in Tbilisi, Georgia, with Chabukiani (Othello) and Vera Zignadze (Desdemona). Chabukiani re-staged it for the Kirov in 1960 with himself in the title role and Alla Osipenko as Desdemona. Many other choreographers created versions of Shakespeare's tragedy, including Salvatore Viganò (Milan, 1818), José Limón (*The Moor's Pavane*, mus. Purcell, New London, Conn., 1949), Erica Hanka (Vienna, 1955), Serge Lifar (Monte Carlo, 1960), Jacques d'Amboise (New York, 1967), Peter Darrell (Trieste, 1971), John Butler (Ballet du Rhin, 1972), Neumeier (mus. several, Hamburg, 1985), Kim Brandstrup, (1994), and Lar Lubovitch (1997).

Other Dances Ballet in one act with choreography by Robbins, music by Chopin, and costumes by Santo Loquasto. Premiered 9 May 1976 at the Metropolitan Opera House in New York by Makarova and Baryshnikov, at a gala for Lincoln Center's Library of the Performing Arts. Danced to four mazurkas and a waltz, it is a duet that plays with the virtuosity of its two dancers. It has since been taken into the repertories of several companies including New York City Ballet, the Royal Ballet (1989), San Francisco Ballet, and Morphoses.

Overcoat, The Ballet with choreography by Flindt, music by Shostakovich. Premiered June 1989 at the Maggio Musicale in Florence. Flemming Flindt created the ballet for an ageing Nureyev, tailoring it to highlight the dancer's dramatic gifts. The ballet is based on Gogol's story.

Pacific Northwest Ballet Seattle-based ballet company founded in 1972, one of the largest regional ballet companies in America. From 1977 it was directed by Kent *Stowell and Francia *Russell who built up a broad-ranging repertoire encompassing the traditional 19th-century ballets, along with works by Stowell, Balanchine, Tudor, Tetley, Taylor, and Forsythe. In 2005 Peter *Boal was appointed artistic director, maintaining the company's former identity while introducing new works into the repertory by Morris, Tharp, Wheeldon, and others. The company performs at the Seattle Center Opera House and has an associated school.

⊕ SEE WEB LINKS
• Website of Pacific Northwest Ballet

PACT Ballet South African ballet company, formed in 1963 at the behest of the S. African government. It incorporated the old Johannesburg City Ballet, and took its name from its sponsoring body, the Performing Arts Council of the Transvaal (PACT). Its first performance featured the French ballerina Yvette *Chauviré in *Giselle*. Artistic directors included Faith de Villiers, Lorna Haupt, and Dawn *Weller. In 1981 the company moved to Pretoria, although continued to perform regular seasons in Johannesburg. In 1998 it became the State Ballet Theatre, with Weller as artistic director but was disbanded in 2000. A new company was founded in its place, South African Ballet Theatre, under the direction of Karen Beukes. Largely performing the 19th-century classics, it also presents some new work including Ed Wubbe's *Schlager* (2004) and Kenneth *Greve's *Hamlet* (2005). In 2002 it opened its associated school and in 2004 moved into its new premises in Johannesburg Civic Theatre.

⊕ SEE WEB LINKS
• Website for South African Ballet Theatre

Paeper, Veronica (*b* Port Shepstone, Natal, 9 Apr. 1944) South African dancer, choreographer, and company director. She studied with Dulcie Howes at the University of Cape Town Ballet School becoming principal dancer with three different S. African companies, CAPAB, the *PACT Ballet, and the Orange Free State Ballet. In 1972 she choreographed her first ballet, *John the Baptist* (mus. Ernest Bloch) for CAPAB Ballet, which led to her being appointed the company's resident choreographer. In 1991 she became director and in 1994 she led the company (later known as *Cape Town City Ballet) on an international tour, the first time a S. African ballet company had performed abroad. She created more than 40 ballets for it, including more than a dozen full-length works, among them *Orpheus in the Underworld* (mus. Offenbach, 1982), *A Christmas Carol* (mus. various, 1982), *Hamlet* (mus. Peter Klatzow, 1992), and *Sylvia in Hollywood* (mus. Allan Stephenson, 1993). She retired in 2005.

Paganini Ballet in one act with choreography by Fokine, libretto by Rachmaninoff and Fokine, music by Rachmaninoff, and designs by Soudeikine. Premiered 30 Jun. 1939 by Colonel de Basil's Ballets Russes at Covent Garden with Dmitri Rostov, Baronova, and Riabouchinska. Set to *Rhapsody on a Theme of Paganini*, it was created as a collaboration between composer and choreographer, portraying the tormented musical genius of Paganini. The score, minus its libretto, was also used by Lavrovsky (the Bolshoi, 1962) and by Ashton (in *Rhapsody*, 1980).

Page, Ashley (*b* Rochester, 9 Aug. 1956) British dancer and choreographer. He trained locally and at the Royal Ballet School (1968–75), dancing briefly with the Royal Ballet's Ballet for All troupe before joining the Royal Ballet in 1976. In 1984 he was promoted to principal. He danced a wide variety of roles, especially in the modern repertoire, and created roles in many ballets including Neumeier's *Beginning* (1977), MacMillan's *Gloriana* (1977), *Gloria* (1980), *Isadora* (1981), *Orpheus* (1982), *Valley of Shadows* (1983), and *The Prince of the Pagodas* (1989), Nureyev's *The Tempest* (1982), Corder's *L'Invitation au voyage* (1982), Tetley's *Dances of Albion* (1980), Alston's *Midsummer* (1983), Ashton's *Rhapsody* (1980), and Bintley's *The Sons of Horus* (1985), *The Planets* (1990), and *Cyrano* (1991). Although a powerful dancer, it was as a choreographer of one-act ballets that Page made his mark at the Royal. He began choreographing in 1982 and made his first work for the company in 1984, his style at that point based in the classical idiom but with the language pushed off its traditional axis and at times evoking dark, sexual, and psychological themes. A list of his works for the Royal includes *Waiting, Running, Running* (mus. Bartók, 1984), *A Broken Set of Rules* (mus. Nyman, 1984), *Pursuit* (mus. Colin Matthews, 1987), *Piano* (mus. Beethoven, 1989), *Bloodlines* (mus. Bruce Gilbert, 1990), *Renard* (mus. Stravinsky, 1994), the award-winning *Fearful Symmetries* (mus. John Adams, 1994), *Ebony Concerto* (mus. Stravinsky, 1995), *Sleeping with Audrey* (mus. Orlando Gough, 1996), *now languorous, now wild* ... (mus. Liszt, 1996), *Two-Part Invention* (mus. Prokofiev and Robert Moran, 1996), *Room of Cooks* (mus. Gough, 1997), *Cheating, Lying, Stealing* (mus. David Lang and Michael Gordon, 1998), and *When We Stop Talking* (mus. Gough, 1998). During this period he also choreographed for Rambert Dance Company, *Carmen Arcadiae* (mus. Birtwistle, 1986), *Soldat* (mus. Stravinsky, 1988), and *Currulao* (mus. Gough, 1990) as well as for Dance Umbrella, Dutch National Ballet, Istanbul State Ballet, and West Australian Ballet.

In 2002 he left the Royal Ballet to become artistic director of *Scottish Ballet where he was credited with revitalizing the company, although challenging its traditional audience. Re-styling it in a more contemporary mould, he brought works by Petronio, Trisha Brown, Alston, and Forsythe into the repertory. He also embarked on a project to stage his own wittily slanted versions of the classics, *Nutcracker* (2003), *Cinderella* (2005), and *Sleeping Beauty* (2007), all in close collaboration with his designer Antony *McDonald.

Page, Ruth (*b* Indianapolis, 22 Mar. 1899; *d* Chicago, 7 Apr. 1991) US dancer, choreographer and company director. She studied ballet with Bolm (from 1917) and Cecchetti (in 1920), and modern dance with Harald Kreutzberg during the 1930s, making her debut in New York in 1917. Hers was a peripatetic career. She toured South America with Pavlova (1918–19), danced in Bolm's *Birthday of the Infanta* in Chicago in 1919, and was a principal dancer with Bolm's Ballet Intime (1920–2) on its US tour, becoming a key figure in Bolm's Allied Arts Ballet in Chicago (1924–7) and creating roles in many of his ballets. She additionally danced with Irving Berlin's Music Box Revue in New York and on tour (1922–4), briefly with Diaghilev's Ballets Russes (1925), and with the Metropolitan Opera Ballet in New York (1927). She created the role of Terpsichore in Bolm's original production of Stravinsky's *Apollon musagète* (Washington, 1928). During the 1930s she continued to be an indefatigable traveller, touring America with solo recitals as well as touring with *Kreutzberg (1933–4) but was most closely associated with the city of Chicago.

She was prima ballerina and ballet mistress at Chicago Summer Opera (1929–33) and choreographed *La Guillablesse* (mus. William Grant Still, 1933), which featured Page as the only white dancer in a company of 50 black dancers led by Katherine Dunham. She was then prima ballerina and ballet mistress of the Chicago Civic Opera (1934–6, 1941–2), creating *Hear Ye! Hear Ye!* (mus. Copland, Chicago Opera Ballet, 1934); *An American Pattern* (with Bentley Stone, mus. Moross, 1937), an early feminist ballet; and *Frankie and Johnny* (with Stone, mus. Jerome Moross, 1938), based on the famous tavern ballad. In 1938 she formed the Page-Stone Ballet Company with her partner Bentley Stone, which toured extensively. She also choreographed *Revanche* (mus. Verdi) for Ballets des Champs-Elysées (1951) and *Vilia* (Lehár's *The Merry Widow*, 1953) for London Festival Ballet. In 1954 she became choreographer and director of ballet at Chicago Lyric Opera where the ballet company became known as Ruth Page's Chicago Opera Ballet and from 1966 to 1969 as Ruth Page's International Ballet). For this company she was best known for her danced versions of operas, including *Susanna and the Barber* (Rossini's *Barber of Seville*, Chicago Opera Ballet, 1956), *Camille* (Verdi's *La traviata*, 1957), *Die Fledermaus* (mus. J. Strauss, 1958), *Carmen* (staged in 1939 as *Guns and Castanets*; staged again in 1959 as *Carmen*, and in 1972 as *Carmen and José* for Dance Theatre of Harlem), and *Bullets and Bonbons* (O. Straus's *The Chocolate Soldier*, 1965). Other important works include *The Bells* (mus. Milhaud, Chicago, 1946), *Mephistophela* (mus. Berlioz, Boito, and Gounod, 1963), *Carmina Burana* (mus. Orff, 1966), and *Alice in the Garden* (mus. I. van Grove, Jacob's Pillow, 1970), which was re-staged as the full-length *Alice in Wonderland: Alice through the Looking Glass* in the 1977–8 season of the Chicago Ballet. She was founding artistic director of the short-lived Chicago Ballet (1972–8).

Page, Stephen (*b* Brisbane 1965) Australian choreographer of Aboriginal and Torres Strait Islander descent. He studied dance at the college of National Aboriginal and Islander Skills Development Association (NAISDA), graduating in 1983 and the same year joining Sydney Dance Company. Here he created the lead role in Graeme Murphy's *Late Afternoon of a Faun* as well as choreographing his own first work *Mooggrah* (1991). He additionally worked with the Aboriginal Islander Dance Theatre (performing arm of NAISDA) between 1989–9 and in 1991 joined Bangarra Dance Theatre as principal choreographer, then artistic director. His work fuses motifs from his own urban upbringing with the cultural traditions of his aboriginal inheritance. His numerous productions for Bangarra include *Praying Mantis Dreaming* (1992), *Ochres* (1995), *Fish* (1997), *Skin* (2000), *Corroboree* (2001), *Rush* (2002), *Bush* (choreographed in collaboration with Frances Rings, 2003), *Boomerang* (2005), and *Mathinna* (2008), many of them with music by his brother David Page. He has also created works for Australian Ballet, including *Alchemy* (1996), *Rites* (in collaboration with Bangarra, 1997, revised version 2006), and *Totem* (2002) as well as for Sydney Dance Company and Sydney Theatre Company. He directed the indigenous sections of the Sydney Olympic Games opening and closing ceremonies in 2000 and in 2004 directed the Adelaide Festival. He has also worked in film, theatre and opera, including directing *Orpheus and Eurydice*, Melbourne, 2007.

Palais Garnier The Paris theatre which is home to Paris Opera Ballet. It was opened in 1875 and was extensively refurbished in the 1990s. It is named after the architect who designed it.

Panov, Valery (*b* Vitebsk, 12 Mar. 1938) Russian-Israeli dancer and choreographer. He studied at the Vilnius Ballet School, Moscow Ballet School, and Leningrad Ballet School, graduating in 1957. He danced first with the Maly Ballet (1957–64), where he created roles in several ballets including Lopukhov's *Ballad of Love* (1959), and Boyarsky's *Orpheus* (title role, 1962), and *The Lady and the Hooligan* (1962). In 1964 he joined the Kirov, where he remained until 1972. There he created roles in Jacobson's *Land of Miracles* (1967), Vinogradov's *Gorianka* (1968), Sergeyev's *Hamlet* (title role, 1970), and Kasatkina's and Vasiliov's *Creation of the World* (1971). Although acclaimed as a virtuoso technician and fine dance-actor, it was for political reasons that Panov came to international attention when, in 1972, he and his wife, the Kirov ballerina Galina Ragozina, applied for an exit visa to Israel. Panov was expelled from the Kirov (along with his wife), imprisoned briefly and forbidden from taking class for two years. Many in the West appealed to the authorities on his behalf and, in 1974, the Panovs were finally allowed to leave Russia. They settled in Israel, dancing with Batsheva Dance Company and Bat-Dor Company (1974–7) while also making frequent guest appearances together abroad. Panov was also guest choreographer and principal dancer with the Berlin Opera Ballet between 1977 and 1983 where he created several ballets, including *Cinderella* (mus. Prokofiev, 1977), *Sacre du printemps* (mus. Stravinsky, 1978), *The Idiot* (mus. Shostakovich, 1979), and *War and Peace* (mus. Tchaikovsky, 1980). He additionally staged *Heart of the Mountain* (mus. Kozhlayev) for the San Francisco Ballet (1976), *Scheherazade* and *Petrushka* for Vienna State Opera Ballet (1981), *The Three Sisters* (mus. Rachmaninoff) for the Royal Swedish Ballet (1983), and *Hamlet* (mus. Shostakovich) for the Norwegian National Ballet (1984). He was then artistic director of the Royal Ballet of Flanders (1984–6), for whom he staged *Romeo and Juliet* (mus. Prokofiev, 1984) and *Moves* (mus. Glorieux, 1986). In 1988 he created *Cléopâtre* for the Istanbul Devlet Ballet, using a cast of 200. In 1991 he was appointed ballet director of the State Opera in Bonn, where he created *Dreyfus— J'accuse* (mus. Schnittke, 1994) and in 1992 he took the Bonn Ballet to Moscow. In 1993 he also opened a ballet school and company in Ashdod, Israel, where he is now settled. Author of autobiography *To Dance* (New York, 1978). Lenin Prize (1969).

pantomime [Gk., all-imitating] A term that commonly refers to theatrical shows imparting action without the use of words or song. In Britain the term more specifically refers to a form of Christmas comic entertainment, dating from the early 18th century, which uses music, dance, and mime to stage familiar fairy tales.

Papillon, Le Ballet in two acts with choreography by Marie Taglioni, libretto by de Saint-Georges, music by Offenbach, set by Martin, Despléchin, Nolau, Rubé, Cambon, and Thierry, and costumes by Albert. Premiered 26 Nov. 1860 at the Paris Opera, with Livry and Mérante. A young woman, Farfalla, is transformed into a butterfly by the wicked Fairy Hamza, and can only be reunited with her lover, the Prince Djalma, after many plot complications. It was Marie Taglioni's only ballet and Offenbach's only ballet score. Emma Livry, who triumphed in the title role, died three years after its premiere when her dress caught fire during a rehearsal, causing her to suffer terrible burns. She was just 20. Elsa-Marianne von Rosen used the Offenbach score for her ballet *Utopia*, for the Gothenburg Ballet in 1974. Pierre Lacotte staged *Le Papillon*, 'after Taglioni', for the Paris Opera in 1976. Ronald Hynd choreographed a version for Houston Ballet in 1979, which was revived for Sadler's Wells Royal Ballet in 1980.

Papillons, Les Ballet in one act with choreography by Fokine, music by Schumann (arr. Tcherepnin), set by Doboujinsky, and costumes by Bakst. Premiered 10 Mar. 1913, at the Mariinsky Theatre in St Petersburg, with Karsavina and Fokine. Pierrot encounters a group of young women in a park and imagines they are butterflies. Fokine re-staged it for Diaghilev's Ballets Russes on 16 Apr. 1914 in Monte Carlo.

Paquita Ballet in two acts with choreography by Mazilier, libretto by Paul Foucher and Mazilier, music by Edouard Deldevez, sets by Philastre, Cambon, Diéterle, Séchan, and Despléchin, and costumes by Lormier and H. de B. d'Orschwiller. Premiered 1 Apr. 1846 at the Paris Opera with

Carlotta Grisi and Lucien Petipa. Set in a Spain under Napoleonic rule, the ballet tells the story of Paquita, a Spanish gypsy, who saves the life of a French officer named Lucien. In the end, it is revealed that she is of noble birth, and she and Lucien are able to marry. Marius Petipa produced the ballet for St Petersburg in 1847 as his debut production, and in 1881 he asked Minkus to provide new music for a Pas de trois and a Grand Pas. Today, *Paquita* is best known through these two dances alone. Balanchine later staged two versions of the Pas de trois, the first for the Cuevas company in 1948 and the second for New York City Ballet in 1951. By 1910 only the third act of this expanded *Paquita* was being performed by the Kirov. In 1957 Konstantin Boyarsky revived the Grand Pas at the Maly Theatre in Leningrad and this became the standard Soviet version. In 1978 a divertissement from *Paquita* which incorporated all of Petipa's 1881 choreography and the Minkus music entered the Kirov repertoire. Elsewhere, Danilova staged a one-act version for Ballet Russe de Monte Carlo in 1949, while the Grand Pas was the first piece Nureyev danced with Fonteyn, at the RAD Gala in 1964. American Ballet Theatre and English National Ballet have the Grand Pas in their repertoires. In 2001 Lacotte staged a reconstruction of the full-length ballet for the Paris Opera Ballet.

Parade Ballet in one act with choreography by Massine, libretto by Cocteau, music by Satie, and designs by Picasso. Premiered 18 May 1917 by the Ballets Russes de Diaghilev at the Théâtre du Châtelet in Paris, with Lopokova, Massine, Woizikowsky, and Zvereff. The ballet nominally portrays a group of music hall artists performing their acts in the street in order to lure an audience inside the theatre. Its selling point however was its claim to be the world's first Cubist ballet. It was intended by Diaghilev as a complete avant-garde marriage of painting, dance, scenario, and music. Picasso's designs featured both a Cubist set and Cubist costumes, including towering 3D structures that encased the two rival managers (who introduce the artists) and a pantomime horse with an African mask. Satie's score was a collage of styles including popular tunes and extraneous noises like a typewriter and a siren and Massine's choreography made reference to classical ballet, cinema, and music hall. *Parade* was rarely performed at the time of its creation but gained an iconic status as one of the great Diaghilev experiments. It was revived for the Ballet of the 20th Century (1964), the City Center Joffrey Ballet (1973), London Festival Ballet (1974), Zurich Ballet (1981), and Bordeaux Ballet (2003).

Paradise Lost Ballet in one act with choreography by Petit, libretto by Jean Cau, music by Con-

stant, and designs by Martial Raysse. Premiered 23 Feb. 1967 by the Royal Ballet at Covent Garden, with Fonteyn and Nureyev. A modern retelling of the story of Adam and Eve. It was also staged at the Paris Opera in 1967.

Paris Opera Ballet French ballet company based in Paris, and the oldest national ballet company in the world. It has its origins in the *Académie Royale de Danse, which was founded by Louis XIV in 1661 to improve dance instruction for court entertainments, and the Académie d'Opéra (later the *Académie Royale de Musique), a performing organization founded in 1669. Pierre *Beauchamps was the first ballet master. In 1672 he and Lully inaugurated a new form of opera which included dance. The first professional ballerina was Mlle de La Fontaine (1665–1738), who danced in the premiere of *Triomphe de l'Amour* in 1681. The associated school, today known as the Paris Opera Ballet School, was opened in 1713. In the mid-18th century, the operas of Rameau demanded higher standards for the dancers, and Gluck's operas (from 1774) continued the process. A key period was the directorship of *Noverre (1776–81), who staged the first production of Mozart's *Les Petits Riens* in 1778. Noverre's successors were M. Gardel (1781–7) and Pierre Gardel (1787–1829), whose choreography included *La Marseillaise* and *Offrande à liberté*. The premiere of F. Taglioni's *La Sylphide* (which starred his daughter Marie in the title role) in 1832 was a landmark event, capitalizing on the success of the Ballet of the Nuns in Meyerbeer's 1831 opera *Robert le diable* to launch the new genre of *Romantic ballet. French Romanticism achieved its most popular classic with the premiere of Coralli and Perrot's *Giselle*, with Carlotta Grisi, in 1841. During the mid-19th century ballet masters at Paris included *Saint-Léon, *Mazilier, and L. *Petipa. Saint-Léon's *Coppélia* was premiered in 1870; it went on to become one of the most successful ballets in the Paris repertoire. At this point in the company's history male dancers had been virtually banished, with female dancers taking over male roles en travestie. The Paris Opera moved to the Palais Garnier in 1875, where it remains today. Mérante's *Sylvia* (1876), L. Petipa's *Namouna* (1882), and Mérante's *Les Deux Pigeons* (1886) were the final successes of the 19th century. By the start of the 20th century, the company was in serious decline. Despite the presence of some fine French dancers and regular guest ballerinas like Mauri and *Zambelli, the serious repertory was crowded out by opera divertissements. It was the Paris seasons of Diaghilev's Ballets Russes which revitalized the city's dance culture from 1910, followed in the 1920s by the avant-garde productions of Les Ballets Suédois and it was only when *Lifar was appointed ballet master and principal dancer of the Paris Opera in 1930 that the company began to emerge from its long stagnation. He raised technical standards, added more than 100 ballets to the repertoire, and established a more regular performing pattern. He also banished the tradition of abonnés (season ticket holders) being allowed to meet with dancers in the foyer—a practice long associated with sexual liaisons. Ballerinas like *Darsonval, Chauviré, and Schwarz were foils to Lifar's own popular performing presence. The regeneration of the company was overshadowed after the Second World War, by Lifar's temporary disgrace as a collaborator with the Nazis, and more significantly by the rise of independent companies, like those of Petit, Charrat, and Béjart, with their adventurous new work. Lifar resigned in 1958 and a succession of short-term directors followed, including George Skibine, Violette Verdy, and Rosella Hightower. Despite this instability the company produced some fine dancers, including *Thasmar, *Jude, *Platel, and *Dupond and expanded its repertory with work by Balanchine, Robbins, Béjart, Petit, Neumeier, Tetley, and others. It entered a new era with the appointment of Rudolf *Nureyev as director. Between 1983 and 1989 Nureyev brought a new dynamic to Paris, promoting young dancers like *Guillem and *Hilaire and introducing an even wider repertory with works by Forsythe, Armitage, and others. He was succeeded by Patrick *Dupond, and then by Brigitte *Lefèvre (appointed 1995) who has maintained the company's status as one of the world's major ballet institutions. Its 150 plus dancers are equally at home in the classics and in the company's modern repertory, which now also features work by Bausch, Preljocaj, McGregor, and others. Its associated school, directed by *Platel since 2004, provides most of the company's dancers, who are famous for their elegance of style and classical finish. Although the company continues to be based at the Garnier, they give occasional performances at the Bastille. Between 1970 and 1989 it had an affiliated experimental wing Groupe de Récherche Téâtrale de l'Opera de Paris (GRTOP) which ran until 1980, then Groupe de Récherche Chorégraphique de l'Opéra de Paris (GRCOP) which ran from 1981 to 1989 and presented a core repertory of new work.

(((●))) SEE WEB LINKS

• Website of the Paris Opera, with a link to the ballet company

Park, (Dame) Merle (*b* Salisbury, Rhodesia, 8 Oct. 1937) British dancer and teacher. She studied with Betty Lamb in Rhodesia, at the Elmhurst School in England (from 1951), and at the Royal Ballet School (from 1954). She joined Sadler's Wells Ballet (now the Royal Ballet) in 1954, pro-

moted to principal in 1959. A brilliant technician and a glamorous stage personality, Park danced all the ballerina roles in the classical repertoire, and was particularly acclaimed for her Aurora. She created roles in Tudor's *Shadowplay* (1967), Ashton's *Jazz Calendar* (1968) and *The Walk to the Paradise Garden* (1972), Nureyev's London *Nutcracker* (Clara, 1968), MacMillan's *Elite Syncopations* (1974), *Mayerling* (1978), *La Fin du jour* (1979), *Isadora* (title role, 1981), and Bintley's *Adieu* (1980). Director of the Royal Ballet School (1983–98). Dame Commander of the Order of the British Empire, 1986.

Parkinson, Georgina (*b* Brighton, 20 Aug. 1938; *d* New York, 18 Dec. 2009) British dancer and ballet mistress. She studied at the Sadler's Wells Ballet School and joined the Royal Ballet in 1957. She was promoted to principal in 1962 and created roles in Ashton's *Monotones I* (1966) and *Enigma Variations* (1968), among others. She left the Royal Ballet in 1978, becoming ballet mistress and character dancer with American Ballet Theatre.

Parry, Jann (*b* Salisbury, Rhodesia, 12 Feb. 1942) British dance critic. She was educated at the University of Cape Town, and at Cambridge University. Dance critic of the *Listener* (1981) and of the *Spectator* (1982), from 1983 to 2006 she was dance critic of the *Observer*. Author of *Different Drummer: The Life of Kenneth MacMillan* (2009).

Parsons, David (*b* Rockford, Ill., 29 Oct. 1959) US dancer, choreographer, and company director. He studied with various teachers and at the Ailey School (1977), dancing with Missouri Dance Theater (1972–6), Momix (1982–7) and, most importantly, with the Paul Taylor company (1978–87), where he created roles in several Taylor works. He also appeared as a guest artist with White Oak Dance Project (1992), Berlin Opera Ballet (1982), and New York City Ballet (1988–91). In 1987 he founded the Parsons Dance Company in New York for which he has since choreographed over 70 works. His choreographic style, marked by a bold athleticism, fuses both classical and contemporary idioms and Parsons has also worked as a guest choreographer for several ballet companies. A list of his works includes *Caught* (1982), *The Envelope* (1986), *Elysian Fields* (1988), *Ring Around the Rosie* (mus. Richard Peaslee, 1993), *The Almighty* (1996), *Anthem* (1998), *Instinct* (1998), *Fill the Woods With Light* (1998), *Kind of Blue* (mus. Miles Davis 2001), and *In the End* (mus. Dave Matthews Band, 2005). He has made *Walk This Way* (1986) for American Ballet Theatre, *Inner Rhythm* (1987) and *Linton* (1988) for Batsheva, *The*

p

Need (1990) for the National Ballet of Canada, *Hairy Night on Bald Mountain* (1991) for Ballet Chicago, *Touch* (1996) for New York City Ballet, *Pied Piper* (mus. Corigliano, 2001), a full-length staging for ABT, and *Shining Star* (mus. Earth Wind and Fire, 2004) for the Ailey Company.

(⊕) SEE WEB LINKS
• Website for the Parsons Dance Company

Pärt, Arvo (*b* Paide, 1935) Estonian composer. Since the 1980s his concert music has become increasingly popular with choreographers, including Dove (*Dancing on the Front Porch of Heaven*, 1992), Mats Ek (*Solo For Two*, 1996), Kylián (*Whereabouts Unknown*, 1994), van Manen (*Déjà vu*, 1995), Alston (*Unrest*, 2001), and Wheeldon (*Liturgy*, 2003; *After the Rain*, 2005; and *Elsinore*, 2008). Two of the scores most frequently used are *Tabula Rasa* (1977) and *Fratres* (1977, rev. 1991).

pas [Fr., step] The word has many meanings in classical ballet, according to which descriptive phrase is used with it. *See* PAS D'ACTION; PAS DE BASQUE; PAS DE BOURRÉE; PAS DE CHAT; PAS DE DEUX.

Pas d'acier, Le Ballet in one act with choreography by Massine, libretto and designs by G. Yakulov, and music by Prokofiev. Premiered 7 Jun. 1927 by the Ballets Russes de Diaghilev, at the Théâtre Sarah Bernhardt in Paris, with Tchernicheva, Danilova, Massine, Lifar, and Woizikowski. The ballet shows scenes of daily Soviet life and features machinery dancing in a factory. It was heavily influenced by Soviet Constructivist art.

pas d'action In classical ballet an ensemble dance composed of set elements, including entrée, adagio, variation, and coda. It includes both soloists and the corps de ballet. It often denotes a dramatic scene in ballet as for example in *La Bayadère*, when Solor is forced to dance with Gamzatti in a public display of loyalty and affection.

pas de basque In classical ballet, a complex step of three beats. It consists of transferences of weight and a change of direction. The feet remain in contact with the floor throughout.

pas de bourrée In classical ballet, it most commonly refers to a linking movement in which quick, small steps are executed close to the ground. It can travel in any direction and involves a transfer of weight. There are many varieties.

pas de chat A light, springing step which travels in a sideways direction, taking off from one foot and landing on the other. It is meant to mimic the movement of a cat.

pas de deux A dance for two, a duet. In classical ballet there are also pas de trois, pas de quatre, and pas de six, for three, four, and six dancers respectively. The classical pas de deux follows a traditional pattern: an entrée and adagio for the ballerina and her cavalier, a variation for the male dancer, a variation for the female dancer, and a final coda which reunites the partners. A classical pas de trois is usually for one male and two female dancers and follows the traditional pattern of the pas de deux.

Pas de dix Ballet in one act with choreography by Balanchine, music by Glazunov, costumes by E. Francés. Premiered 9 Nov. 1955 by New York City Ballet at City Center, New York, with Maria Tallchief and Eglevsky. A ballet for one ballerina, her partner, and a small ensemble, it is set to music from the last act of *Raymonda*.

Pas de quatre Ballet divertissement with choreography and libretto by Perrot, and music by Pugni. Premiered 12 Jul. 1845 at Her Majesty's Theatre in London, with Taglioni, Grisi, Cerrito, and Grahn. A plotless ballet in full Romantic style, it brought together the four greatest ballerinas of the day, lured into the project by the clever manager of Her Majesty's Theatre, Benjamin Lumley. Perrot tailored his choreography to suit each of the rival ballerinas in turn, playing up to their individual strengths. Evocative lithographs of the time reveal how the celebrated quartet looked as a group, but since Perrot failed to notate his choreography, attempts to re-create it have been based on pure conjecture. These have included Keith Lester for the Markova-Dolin Ballet in 1936 and Dolin for Ballet Theatre in 1941 (a staging which was later taken into the repertoire of the Kirov).

passacaglia [Sp. *pasacalle*, passing through a street] It originally described a band of musicians who marched through the street, playing marches. Later, it referred to a Spanish dance in 3/4 time which was performed at the court of Louis XIV in the ballets of Lully.

Passacaglia in C minor Modern dance in one act with choreography by Humphrey, music by Bach, set by Arch Lauterer, and costumes by P. Lawrence. Premiered 5 Aug. 1938 by the Humphrey-Weidman Dance Company at the Armory in Bennington, Vermont, with Humphrey and Weidman. A work for twelve company members and eleven apprentices, it was described by Humphrey as 'an abstraction with dramatic overtones ... inspired by the need for love, tolerance and nobility'.

passepied [Fr., pass feet] Originally a dance for sailors, it became a popular court dance during the reign of Louis XIV and featured in several ballets. A dance in 3/8 or 6/8 time, it was accompanied by singing or bagpipes.

Pastor, Krzysztof (*b* 1956, Gdansk) Polish dancer and choreographer. He trained at the Polish National Ballet School (1966–75), joining Polish Dance Theatre and then the Grand Theatre of Lodz before becoming a soloist with Lyon Opera Ballet in 1983. Between 1985 and 1995 he danced with Dutch National Ballet, performing lead roles in both the classical and modern repertories. He choreographed his first work in 1986 for a gala performance in Lodz and after several workshop pieces for Dutch National Ballet created *Shostakovich Chamber Symphony* for the main programme in 1992. From 1995 he worked as a freelance choreographer, including a season with the Washington Ballet, finally returning to DNB in 2003 as resident choreographer. Pastor's fluidly expressive and musically grounded style, a fusion of neoclassical and contemporary vocabularies, has been adapted to both narrative and non-narrative works. Those for DNB include *Do not go gentle* (mus. Stravinsky), *In Light and Shadow* (mus. Bach), and *Kurt Weill* (all 2000), *Don Giovanni* (mus. Mozart, 2005), *Crossing Paths* (2006), and *La Sylphide: Visions at Dusk* (2007). Pastor has also created works for many other companies including *Carmen Suite* (mus. Bizet, Shchedrin, 1997), *Acid City* (mus. Mindaugas Urbaitis, 2002), and *Dangerous Liaisons* (mus. Arturs Maskats, 2007) for Lithuanian National Ballet; *Firebird* (mus. Stravinsky, 1999) for West Australian Ballet; *Symphony Fantastique* (mus. Berlioz, 2007) for Australian Ballet; and *Romeo and Juliet* (mus. Prokofiev, 2008) for Scottish Ballet.

Path of Thunder, The Ballet in three acts with choreography by Konstantin Sergeyev, libretto by Slonimsky, music by Kara Karayev, and designs by V. Dorer. Premiered 31 Dec. 1957 by the Kirov Ballet in St Petersburg with Sergeyev and Dudinskaya. It was inspired by a novel by the S. African writer Peter Abrahams about the forbidden love affair between a black teacher and a white girl. The two are killed by her landowner father. It was revived for the Bolshoi Ballet in 1959. Many other versions were staged throughout the Soviet Union.

Patineurs, Les Ballet in one act with choreography by Ashton, music by Meyerbeer (arr. Lambert), and designs by William Chappell. Premiered 16 Feb. 1937 by the Vic-Wells Ballet at Sadler's Wells Theatre in London, with H. Turner, May, Brae, Mary Honer, Elizabeth Miller, Fonteyn, and Helpmann. The diversions of a party of ice skaters are presented in comic, virtuoso choreography. The music comes from Meyerbeer's opera *Le Pro-*

phète (in which there was a divertissement featuring a skater's ballet) and *L'étoile du Nord*. The ballet has also entered the repertories of Ballet Theatre (1946), Royal Winnipeg Ballet (1966), Australian Ballet (1970), and the Joffrey Ballet (1977).

Patten, Sarah van (*b* Boston, 1984) American dancer. She studied locally, and in summer school programmes at the Chautauqua Institution, School of American Ballet, and others, appearing as a child with the Boston Ballet and the Massachusetts Youth Ballet. At the age of 15 she became an apprentice with the Royal Danish Ballet, in the same year dancing Juliet in Neumeier's *Romeo and Juliet*. In 2002 she moved to San Francisco Ballet as a soloist, becoming principal in 2007. Combining technical clarity and power with a vivid dramatic talent, she has an exceptionally wide range across the classical and modern repertory and has created roles in works by Wheeldon, Morris, Tomasson, Elo, and others.

Paul, Annette av (*b* Stockholm, 1944) Swedish dancer. She studied at the Royal Swedish Ballet School, joining the Royal Swedish Ballet in 1961 and creating the role of Katerina in Grigorovich's Stockholm staging of *The Stone Flower* (1962); also roles in Tudor's *Echoing of Trumpets* (1963) and Macdonald's *While the Spider Slept* (1965). She additionally created a role in Macdonald's *Rose Latulippe*, for the Royal Winnipeg Ballet, 1966. In 1972 she moved to Les Grands Ballets Canadiens, where her husband, Brian *Macdonald, was artistic director. After retiring from the stage in 1984 she became founding artistic director of Ballet British Columbia in late 1985. She left the post in 1987 to pursue a freelance teaching career in Canada. In 2002 she was appointed director of the Dance Programme at the Banff Centre.

Paulli, Holger Simon (*b* Copenhagen, 22 Feb. 1810; *d* Copenhagen, 23 Dec. 1891) Danish conductor and composer. He wrote many ballet scores for Bournonville, including *Napoli* (with Helsted, Gade, and Lumbye, 1842), *Konservatoriet* (1849), *Kermesse in Bruges* (1851), and *Flower Festival at Genzano* (with Helsted, 1858).

pavane A formal court dance in duple time, popular in Italy, France, and Spain during the 16th and 17th centuries. Its name possibly derived from pavone (It.) or pavón (Sp.), which mean peacock, since the women sweep their trains much like a peacock sweeps its tail. The dance is sedate and dignified in style.

Pavillon d'Armide, Le Ballet in one act with choreography by Fokine, libretto and designs by Benois, and music by N. Tcherepnin. Premiered 25 Nov. 1907 at the Mariinsky Theatre in St Petersburg, with Pavlova, Gerdt, and Nijinsky. Based on a story by Gautier, the ballet tells of the Vicomte de Beaugency who seeks refuge in a mysterious pavilion during a storm. He becomes transfixed by a tapestry portraying the beautiful Armide and dreams that he falls in love with her. In the morning he returns to his senses, only to discover that he is holding Armide's scarf in his hand. Fokine originally created the work for the St Petersburg Imperial Ballet Academy graduation performance in 1907 and expanded it for the Mariinsky company. Diaghilev presented it on his first night at the Théâtre du Châtelet in Paris on 19 May 1909 (with Karalli, Nijinsky, and Mordkin), to great success. A reconstructed version was staged by *Dolgushin in 2007.

Pavlova, Anna (*b* St Petersburg, 12 Feb. 1881; *d* The Hague, 23 Jan. 1931) Russian dancer. The legendary ballerina of the 20th century. She trained at the Imperial Ballet School in St Petersburg from 1891, studying with Vazem, Gerdt, and Petipa. She graduated in 1899 and joined the Mariinsky Theatre, becoming ballerina in 1905 and prima ballerina in 1906, while still continuing her studies with Cecchetti in St Petersburg. Petipa was her champion: he cast her as Nikiya in his *La Bayadère* when she was still a coryphée in 1902. He followed that by casting her as Giselle the following year. In 1907 she created Fokine's *Dying Swan*, a brief but bewitching solo which was to become her most famous role. She created parts in Petipa's *Les Saisons* (1900), *Harlequinade* (1900), and *The Magic Mirror* (1903), Ivanov and Gerdt's *Sylvia* (1901), N. and S. Legat's *The Fairy Doll* (1903), Fokine's *The Vine* (1906), *Pavillon d'Armide* (Armide, 1907), *Chopiniana* (1907), *Eunice* (1907), and *Egyptian Nights* (1908). In 1908, dissatisfied with the limitations of her Mariinsky career, she began to tour abroad; she finally left the St Petersburg company in 1913. In 1909 she danced with Diaghilev's troupe in Paris; her final appearance with Diaghilev was in 1911 in London (she preferred the classical repertoire to Diaghilev's revolutionary modernist ballets). She danced in Berlin in 1909, New York and London in 1910. In 1911 she bought a house in London (Ivy House in Golders Green) and from there put together her own company which toured extensively in Europe, N. and S. America, and the Far East. Pavlova performed in places that had never seen ballet before and maintained her hectic touring schedule until 1929. She was the company's prima ballerina and her partners included Mordkin, Novikov, Volinine, and Vladimiroff. It was through Pavlova's exhaustive touring that classical ballet gained a new international following. Her repertoire encompassed abbreviated versions of the classics, along with ballets by Fokine and Clustine and solos she choreographed herself. She created

roles in Mordkin's *The Legend of Aziade* (1910) and *Bacchanale* (1910), Zaylich's *Amarilla* (1912), Fokine's *The Three Palms* (1913) and *Les Préludes* (1913), Clustine's *La Péri* (1917), *Noir et blanc* (1917), and *The Romances of a Mummy* (1924), and Romanov's *The Champions* (1928). Works she choreographed included *Le Papillon* (mus. Minkus, 1910), *La Rose mourante* (mus. Drigo, 1910), *Blue Danube* (mus. Strauss, 1911), *Snowflakes* (Tchaikovsky, 1911), *The Magic Flute* (mus. Drigo, 1913), *Dragonfly* (mus. Kreisler, 1915), *California Poppy* (mus. Tchaikovsky, 1916), *Christmas* (mus. Tchaikovsky, 1916), *Autumn Leaves* (mus. Chopin, 1919), and *Masquerade* (mus. Wurmser, 1926). An extraordinarily poetic dancer whose delicacy and grace transfixed audiences, she was the most famous ballerina in the world, and her performances inspired many younger dancers and choreographers (including Ashton, who saw her in Lima in 1917 while still a schoolboy). She gave her last performance in London in 1930 and died of pneumonia at the age of 50. She appeared in several films, including *The Dumb Girl of Portici*, a silent film made in Hollywood in 1915. In 1956 a film was released, entitled *The Immortal Swan*, which featured footage shot in the 1920s of Pavlova in *The Dying Swan*, *Fairy Doll*, *Oriental Dance*, *Rose mourante*, *California Poppy*, and *Colombine*. From 1912 she taught at her home in London.

Paxton, Steve (*b* Phoenix, Ariz., 21 Jan. 1939) US dancer and choreographer. Pioneer of *Contact Improvisation. He trained as a gymnast and then studied modern dance with Cunningham and Robert Dunn in New York (from 1958). He joined José Limón's company for a year (1959) and was with Cunningham's company (1961–4). He also worked with Yvonne Rainer, Robert Rauschenberg, Lucinda Childs, and Trisha Brown. He was in the first performance of Rainer's groundbreaking *Trio A* in 1966. He was one of the founder-members of the Judson Dance Theater in 1962, and a founding member of the improvisational Grand Union in 1970. Like his Judson colleagues, his choreography incorporated everyday movements: his 1967 work *Satisfyin' Lover*, for example, had performers simply walking across the floor. His 1971 work *Collaboration with Wintersoldier* had two upside-down performers watching a film made by Vietnam veterans who opposed the war. In the early 1970s his work led him to develop Contact Improvisation, a system of improvised movement based on the intimate communication and contact between two moving bodies. The technique used the free flowing weight and momentum of the performers' bodies to generate movement and was widely adapted by many choreographers of contemporary dance. During the 1980s Paxton performed less frequently, his works often solos and highly improvised. A list of his creations includes *Proxy* (1962), *Transit* (1962), *Afternoon* (1963), *Rialto* (1964), *Flat* (1964), *Jag Ville Gorna Telefonera* (1964), *Physical Things* (1966), *Backwater: Twosome* (1977), *Suspect Terrain* (with Laurie Booth, Dana Reitz, and Polly Motley; mus. Hans-Peter Kuhn, 1989), *Some English Suites* (mus. Bach, 1993), *Long and Dream* (with Trisha Brown, 1994), *Excavations Continued* (1996), and *Ash* (1997). He continues to lead workshops in Contact Improvisation.

Pécourt, Guillaume-Louis (Pécour) (*b* Paris 10 Aug. 1653; *d* Paris, 12 Apr. 1729) French dancer, choreographer, and dance master. He studied in Paris with Beauchamps and made his debut as a dancer at the Court Theatre, Tuileries, in 1671. His official debut at the Paris Opera was in 1674, probably in the opera *Cadmus et Hermione*. He became a leading dancer in the Paris Opera, while also performing frequently for the court at Saint-Germain-en-Laye and Chantilly. He created many roles in works by Lully (who composed) and Beauchamps (who choreographed), including *Le Triomphe de l'amour* (1681), *Le Temple de la paix* (1685), and *Armide* (1686). He was also dancing master to the King's pages from 1680 to 1692. In 1687 he succeeded Beauchamps as official 'composer' of the King's ballets at L'Académie Royale de Musique (as the Paris Opera was called), and continued to create new ballets until his death. He retired from dancing in 1703. He choreographed ballets in many operas, including those of Campra, Colasse or Collasse, Desmaret or Desmarets, Destouches, Bertin, and Lully. He choreographed Campra's first opéra-ballet, *L'Europe galante* (1697), his *Le Carnaval de Venise* (1699), *Hésione* (1700), *Tancrède* (1702), and *Les Fêtes vénitiennes* (1710). Several of his dances survive in Feuillet's 1700 book about notation, *Chorégraphie*, and his 1704 *Recueil de danses*; they are the most important examples of the baroque dance style. He also choreographed ballroom dances and was a leading teacher.

Peer Gynt Ballet in three acts with choreography by Orlikowsky, libretto by Eugen Wigeliew, music by Grieg, designs by Lec Bothas, and costumes by S. Schröck. Premiered 30 Oct. 1956 in Basle, with D. Christensen, M. Parnitzki, H. Sommerkamp, and Deege. The ballet is based on Ibsen's play. It was revived for London Festival Ballet in 1963. Other versions, also using Grieg's score, include G. Tregubov's (Lvov, 1955), Tomaszewski's (Cramér Ballet, 1972), and Brandstrup's (Arc Dance Company, 1991).

Pelléas et Mélisande ballets Maeterlinck's 1893 play has inspired several dance adaptations, including those by T. Gsovsky (mus. M. Bau-

mann, Berlin, 1954), Walter (mus. Schoenberg, Wuppertal, 1955), Petit (mus. Schoenberg, Royal Ballet, 1969), and Menegatti and Gai (mus. Sibelius, La Scala, 1972).

penché To bend forward. In an arabesque penché, one of the most striking poses in classical ballet, the ballerina balances on one leg on pointe, while the other leg is lifted behind the body to full height and the torso is bent towards the floor.

Pendleton, Moses (*b* Lyndonville, Vt., 28 Mar. 1949) US dancer, choreographer, and company director. Studied dance with Alison Chase. He co-founded *Pilobolus Dance Theater in 1971 (with Jonathan Wolken) in his senior year at Dartmouth College and stayed with the company as a full-time member until 1980, after which he continued to choreograph sporadically for them. In 1980 he founded *Momix Dance Theater which he continues to direct. A master of illusionist theatre both comic and fantastical, he choreographs dance sculptures that bring together acrobatics, gymnastics, mime, props, and film. He choreographed the closing ceremonies of the Lake Placid Winter Olympics in 1980; his works for other companies include *Intégrale Erik Satie* (Paris Opera Ballet 1979), a staging of the Dadaist ballet *Relâche* (Joffrey Ballet, 1980), *F.L.O.W.* (for Diana Vishneva, 2008). His works for Momix include *Passion* (1991), *Baseball* (1994), *Sputnik* (1997), *Opus Cactus* (2002), and *Lunar Sea* (2005). He has also worked extensively in television, video, and opera, including *Carmen* for Munich State Opera (1993).

Penitente, El Modern dance in one act with choreography by Graham, music by Horst, set by Arch Lauterer, and costumes by E. Gilfond. Premiered 11 Aug. 1940 by the Martha Graham company at Bennington College Theater in Bennington, Vermont, with Graham, Hawkins, and Cunningham. In a Native American community in the US Southwest, a primitive morality play is acted out by three strolling players. Graham appeared as the Virgin, Magdalen, and the Madonna, Hawkins was the Penitent, and Cunningham was Christ. In later years Pearl Lang took over Graham's part. The work was later redesigned by Noguchi and has been revived for London Contemporary Dance Theatre and White Oak Dance Project.

Penney, Jennifer (*b* Vancouver, 5 Apr. 1946) Canadian-British dancer. She studied with Gweneth Lloyd and Betty Farrally in British Columbia and at the Royal Ballet School in London (1962–3), joining the Royal Ballet in 1963, and becoming principal in 1970. She created roles in MacMillan's *Seven Deadly Sins* (1973), *Elite Syncopations* (1974), *Four Seasons* (1975), *La Fin du jour*

(1979), *Gloria* (1980), and *Orpheus* (1982), van Manen's *Four Schumann Pieces* (1975), and Neumeier's *Fourth Symphony* (1977). A dancer of exquisite physical proportions and technical fluency, she danced all the classical ballerina roles, but was most acclaimed in the modern repertoire. She was outstanding in MacMillan ballets—sensually brazen and physically fearless on stage—and when Antoinette Sibley was taken ill during the rehearsal period of *Manon*, much of the choreography was created on Penney. Dancing the role during the Royal Ballet's tour to the Soviet Union in 1987, she was hailed by *Grigorovich, as 'the best ballerina from England that I have seen since Margot Fonteyn.' She was also a gifted comedienne, her mischievous personality seen to best advantage in Robbins's *The Concert*. She retired from Covent Garden in 1988 and returned to her native British Columbia.

Pennsylvania Ballet Ballet company based in Philadelphia which was founded in 1963 by Barbara Weisberger. The early repertoire included many ballets by Balanchine, along with works by Butler, Dollar, Smuin, Moncion, Harkarvy, and van Manen. Subsequent directors have included Benjamin Harkarvy, Robert Weiss (1982–90), Christopher d'Amboise (1990–94), and Roy Kaiser. The company's current repertory includes stagings of the 19th-century classics as well as commissioned works by, among others, David Parsons, Trey McIntyre, Wheeldon, and resident choreographer Matthew Neenan.

(⊕) SEE WEB LINKS
• Website for the Pennsylvania Ballet

Percival, John (*b* Walthamstow, 16 Mar. 1927) British dance critic and writer. He was educated at Oxford University and was co-editor (with Clive Barnes) of the Oxford Ballet Club magazine *Arabesque* (1950). From 1950 he contributed to *Dance and Dancers* magazine; from 1981 he was its editor. He was dance critic of *The Times* in London from 1965 to 1994. One of Britain's most senior and influential dance critics, he was also author of *Antony Tudor* (Dance Perspectives, no. 17, 1963), *Modern Ballet* (1970, new edition, 1980), *The World of Diaghilev* (1971, new edition, 1979), *Experimental Dance* (1971), *Nureyev: Aspects of the Dancer* (1975, new edition, 1979), *The Facts about a Ballet Company* (1979), *Theatre in My Blood*, a biography of John Cranko (London, 1983), *Men Dancing* (with Alexander Bland, 1984), and *The World of Nureyev* (1996).

Peretti, Serge (*b* Venice, 28 Jan. 1910; *d* Paris, 20 Aug. 1997) Italian dancer and teacher. He studied at the Paris Opera Ballet School (from 1922) and made his debut with the Paris Opera Ballet while still a student in 1923. He was pro-

moted to premier danseur at the age of 20 and in 1931 was the first dancer to be granted the title of étoile. He created roles in Lifar's *Creatures of Prometheus* (1929), *L'Orchestre en liberté* (1931), *Bacchus et Ariane* (1931), *Jeunesse* (1933), *Salade* (1935), *Oriane et le Prince d'Amour* (1938), *Aeneas* (1938), *La Princesse au jardin* (1941), *Bolero* (1941), *Le Chevalier et la demoiselle* (1941), *Les Animaux modèles* (1942), and *Joan de Zarissa* (1942). He also created roles in most of the ballets choreographed by Léo Staats, Nicola Guerra, and Aveline. He was appointed provisional ballet master (1945–6) following Lifar's departure from the Paris Opera and choreographed *L'Appel de la montagne* (mus. Honegger, 1945). In 1946 he went on a tour of S. America with young dancers from the Opera. In 1948 he opened his own school, as well as teaching at the Paris Opera school. Among his pupils were Babilée, Petit, Golovine, Jeanmaire, and Chauviré. From 1963 to 1970 he taught at the Paris Opera.

Péri, La Ballet in two acts with choreography by Coralli, libretto by Gautier and Coralli, music by Burgmüller, sets by Séchan, Despléchin, Diéterle, Philastre, and Cambon, and costumes by Lormier and d'Orschwiller. Premiered 17 Jul. 1843 by the Paris Opera Ballet with Grisi, L. Petipa, and Coralli. An Oriental fantasy, it tells of the poet Sultan Achmet who, in an opium-induced dream, meets and falls in love with the Queen of the Fairies. Gautier and Coralli had collaborated previously on *Giselle* and were here revisiting the theme of love between a mortal and a spirit. *La Péri* proved immediately popular, with the London premiere in Sept. 1843, the St Petersburg and Vienna premieres in 1844. There have been many subsequent stagings of the story, using alternative music by Dukas: Clustine (Paris, 1912), Staats (Paris, 1921), Ashton (Ballet Club, London, 1931, Royal Ballet, 1956), Lifar (Nouveau Ballet de Monte Carlo, 1946), and Darrell (London Festival Ballet, 1973).

Perrot, Jules Joseph (*b* Lyon, 18 Aug. 1810; *d* Paramé, 24 Aug. 1892 (some sources 18 Aug. 1892)) French dancer, choreographer, and ballet master. One of the most important choreographers of the Romantic era. He studied in Lyon (from 1819), and later with Auguste Vestris. His early career as a dancer was spent in two Parisian Boulevard theatres: Théâtre de la Gaîté (1823–5) and Théâtre de la Porte-St-Martin (1826–9). In 1830 he was appointed first soloist at London's King Theatre and made his debut at the Paris Opera (in the opera *Le Rossignol* by Lebrun) the same year. There he quickly became Taglioni's favourite partner, although he left the Opera three years later, the result of a contract dispute. In later years, despite his success as a choreographer in London and St Petersburg, Paris continued to snub him: the Paris Opera produced only one of his ballets, *La Filleule des fées*. He appeared in London and Naples (1834), where he met Carlotta Grisi, who was to become his partner and lover (they had a daughter, born 1837). He performed in Munich and Vienna (1836), Milan (1838), and Lyon (1840). He created roles in Coralli's *Léocadie* (1828) and *L'Orgie* (1831), F. Taglioni's *Robert le diable* (1831), *La Révolte au sérail* (1833), *Sire Huon* (1833), and *Mazilia* (1835), Deshayes's *Zéphir berger* (1835), and in numerous ballets choreographed by himself. As a dancer he had exceptional strength and stamina, but also unusual grace. Gautier wrote that Perrot possessed 'the perfect legs of a Greek statue, somewhat feminine in their roundness'. The first major ballet he choreographed was *Le Nymphe et le papillon* for the Vienna Kärntnertor Theater in 1836. He choreographed all of Grisi's solos for *Giselle* at the Paris Opera in 1841 and partnered her as Albrecht in the ballet's London premiere in 1842. He was ballet master at Her Majesty's Theatre in London (1843–8), probably his most important years as a choreographer. He was choreographer at La Scala, Milan, in 1848 and ballet master at St Petersburg (1851–8). He also worked in Berlin, Brussels, Lyon, and Warsaw. As a choreographer, his major achievement was the integration of dance and drama, narrating stories through the dancers's steps as well as through mime. A list of his works includes *Alma ou la Fille de feu* (with Deshayes, mus. Costa, London, 1842), *L'Aurore* (mus. Pugni, 1843), *Ondine* (mus. Pugni, 1843), *La Esmeralda* (mus. Pugni, London, 1844), *Eoline ou la Dryade* (mus. Pugni, London, 1845), *Pas de quatre* (mus. Pugni, London, 1845), *Caterina ou la fille du bandit* (mus. Pugni, 1846), *Le Jugement de Pâris* (mus. Pugni, London, 1846), *Les Quatre Saisons* (mus. Pugni, 1848), *Lalla Rookh, or The Rose of Lahore* (mus. Félicien David and Pugni, 1846), *Les Eléments* (mus. Bajetti, 1847), *Faust* (mus. Penizza, Costa, and Bajetti, La Scala, Milan, 1848), *La Filleule de fées* (mus. Adam and Saint-Julien, Paris, 1849), *Le Angustie or Les Tribulations d'un maître de ballet* (mus. Pugni, St Petersburg, 1851), *La Guerre des femmes* (mus. Pugni, St Petersburg, 1852), *Gazelda ou les tziganes* (mus. Pugni, St Petersburg, 1853), *Markobomba* (mus. Pugni, St Petersburg, 1854), and *Armida* (mus. Pugni, St Petersburg, 1855). He was married to the Russian ballerina Capitoline Samovskaya.

Peter and the Wolf Ballet in one act with choreography by Bolm, music (and text) by Prokofiev, and designs by Lucinda Ballard. Premiered 13 Jan. 1940 by Ballet Theatre, in Radio City Center Theater, New York, with Loring, Dollar, V. Essen, K. Conrad, and Stroganova. The ballet follows Prokofiev's story of Peter's adventures in taming the predatory Wolf. Later versions include F. Staff's for Ballet Rambert (1940), G. Blank's

(Berlin, 1954), A. Varlamov's for the Bolshoi Ballet (1959), P. Belda's for Ballet of the 20th Century (1966), and Matthew Hart's for the Royal Ballet School (1995), later taken into the Royal Ballet repertoire.

Petipa, Lucien (*b* Marseilles, 22 Dec. 1815; *d* Versailles, 7 Jul. 1898) French dancer, choreographer and ballet master. Son of the dancer Jean Antoine Petipa, brother of Marius Petipa. He studied with his father and danced for him in Brussels and Bordeaux. In 1839 he moved to Paris, where he made his debut in 1840 partnering Elssler in *La Sylphide*. He created the role of Albrecht in *Giselle* with Grisi (1841), and was Grisi's regular partner. A fine danseur noble, he created leading roles in Coralli's *La Péri* (1843) and *Eucharis* (1844), Mazilier's *Le Diable à quatre* (1845), *Paquita* (1846), *Jovita, ou les Boucaniers* (1853), *Les Elfes* (1856), and *Marco Spada* (1857), Mabille's *Griseldis* (1849), Perrot's *La Filleule des fées* (1849), and Cerrito's *Gemma* (1854). As a choreographer, his first important ballet was *Sakountala* (mus. E. Reyer, 1858). He was ballet master of the Paris Opera (1860–8), during which time he created *Graziosa* (mus. T. Labarre, 1861) and *Le Roi d'Yvetot* (mus. T. Labarre, 1865). He also collaborated in several important opera premieres, including Rossini's *Sémiramis* (1860), Wagner's *Tannhäuser* (1861), and Verdi's *Don Carlos* (1867). He retired early from the stage, the result of injury in a hunting accident. From 1880 he was professor of pantomime at the Paris Opera.

Petipa, Maria Mariusovna (*b* St Petersburg, 29 Oct. 1857; *d* Paris, 1930) Russian dancer. Daughter of Marius Petipa. She made her debut in the title role of *The Blue Dahlia* in 1875 and became an acclaimed character dancer. Her most important created role was the Lilac Fairy in her father's *Sleeping Beauty* (1890).

Petipa, Maria Sergeyevna (*b* 1836; *d* Novocherkassk, 1882) Russian dancer. Wife of Marius Petipa, mother of Maria Mariusovna Petipa. She studied at the Imperial Theatre School in St Petersburg, graduating in 1854. That same year she married Marius Petipa and created many roles in his ballets. However, her career suffered a marked decline following her divorce in 1869. She enjoyed her greatest success as a dancer in en travestie roles.

Petipa, Marius (*b* Marseilles, 11 Mar. 1818; *d* Gurzuf, Crimea, 14 Jul. 1910) French-Russian dancer, choreographer, and ballet master. The creator of *Swan Lake* and *Sleeping Beauty*, and the most important influence on Russian ballet during the 19th century, he arguably made more impact on the history of classical ballet than any other choreographer.

He studied with his father Jean Antoine Petipa and later with A. Vestris, making his debut in Brussels in 1831 with his father's company in Pierre Gardel's *Dansomanie*. He performed with the same company in Bordeaux (from 1834) and was a principal dancer (1838) in Nantes, where he choreographed his first ballets: *Le droit du Seigneur*, *La Petite Bohémienne*, and *La Noce à Nantes*. In 1839 he toured North America with his father's company (although the tour did not go well), then danced in Paris at the Comédie-Française and in Bordeaux, dancing principal roles in *Giselle*, *La Fille mal gardée*, and *La Péri*. In Bordeaux he made several more ballets, including *La Jolie Bordelaise*, *La Vendange*, *L'Intrigue amoureuse*, and *Le Langage des fleurs*. From 1843 to 1846 he toured Spain and studied Spanish dance in Madrid with the result that the ballets he made at this time had a Spanish flavour: *Carmen et son toréro*, *La Perle de Séville*, *L'Aventure d'une fille de Madrid*, and *La Fleur de Grenade*.

It was in 1847 that Petipa made his historic move to St Petersburg, where he changed both his own fortunes and also profoundly affected the course of Russian Ballet. He was initially employed as a dancer and enjoyed success in *Giselle*, *Paquita*, *La Péri*, *Esmeralda*, and *Le Corsaire* and often partnered *Elssler. He created roles in Perrot's *The War of the Women* (1852), *Gazelda* (1853), *Marcobomba* (1854), *Armida* (1855), and *La Débutante* (1857). He was particularly admired in character roles. His early choreography in Russia included the new material he created for Act II of *Giselle* (he completely restaged the ballet in 1884) and that which he created as Perrot's assistant. It was not until 1855 that he created his first significant ballet: *The Star of Granada* (mus. various) and not until 1862 that he achieved popular success with *La Fille du Pharaon* (mus. Pugni). He was appointed ballet master the same year and in 1869 promoted to chief ballet master. He went on to choreograph about 50 ballets for the Imperial Theatres in both St Petersburg and Moscow, and it was through this repertory that the Russian Imperial ballet became pre-eminent in the latter part of the 19th century, far outstripping its European counterparts.

Stylistically Petipa brought with him a rich legacy. Schooled in the superior techniques of the French and Italian schools, fascinated by the colours and rhythms of Spanish dance, he grafted this European mix on to the grand traditions of Tsarist Russia. As he perfected his craft over his long career, Petipa not only expanded the expressive range and stylistic brilliance of the danse d'école but also refined and developed the form of classical ballet. His two Tchaikovsky productions, *Swan Lake* (created with Ivanov in 1895) and *Sleeping Beauty* (1890), are still considered the masterpieces of 19th-century classicism.

Several of his other ballets are almost as central to the canon, including *Don Quixote* (mus. Minkus, 1869, for Moscow) and *La Bayadère* (mus. Minkus, 1877). Petipa should also have choreographed *The Nutcracker*, but while he worked with Tchaikovsky on its conception, illness forced him to withdraw and he left his assistant Ivanov to choreograph it. Equally important are Petipa's restagings of the French repertoire: *Paquita* (1881), *Coppélia* (1884), *Giselle* (1884), *Esmeralda* (1886), *La Sylphide* (1892), and *Le Corsaire* (1858, 1868, and 1899) which continue to form the basis of most stagings of those ballets around the world today.

A list of his other ballets includes: *La Somnambule* (mus. Bellini, 1859), *The Blue Dahlia* (mus. Pugni, 1860), *Faust* (mus. Panica, Pugni, 1867), *King Candaule* (mus. Pugni, 1868), *La Camargo* (mus. Minkus, 1872), *Le Papillon* (mus. Minkus, 1874), *La Bayadère, Roxanna, or The Beauty of Montenegro* (mus. Minkus, 1878), *Ariadne* (mus. Gerber, 1878), *The Daughter of the Snows* (mus. Minkus, 1879), *Zoraya* (mus. Minkus, 1881), *Pygmalion* (mus. Trubetskoy, 1883), *The Tulip of Haarlem* (with Ivanov, mus. Fitinhof-Schel, 1887), *The Talisman* (mus. Drigo, 1889), *Kalkabrino* (mus. Minkus, 1891), *Cinderella* (with Cecchetti and Ivanov, mus. Fitinhof-Schel, 1893), *The Awakening of Flora* (mus. Drigo, 1894), *Bluebeard* (mus. Schenk, 1896), *Raymonda* (mus. Glazunov, 1898), *The Seasons* (mus. Glazunov, 1900), *Les Millions d'Arlequin* (mus. Drigo, 1900), and *The Magic Mirror* (mus. Koreshenko, 1903). He retired in 1903. His memoirs were published in St Petersburg in 1906; an English translation, *Russian Ballet Master: The Memoirs of Marius Petipa*, was published in London in 1958. *The Diaries of Marius Petipa* (translated by Lynn Garafola) were published in Pennington, New Jersey, in 1992.

He was brother of Lucien Petipa, husband of Maria Sergeyevna Petipa, father of Maria Mariusovna Petipa.

Petit, Roland (*b* Villemomble, 13 Jan. 1924) French dancer, choreographer, and ballet director. He studied with Lifar and at the Paris Opera Ballet School from 1934, and entered the Paris Opera Ballet in 1940. Four years later, he left to pursue an independent career as both dancer and choreographer. In 1944 he performed in the Vendredis de la Danse at the Théâtre Sarah-Bernhardt, dancing works choreographed by himself, and in 1945 he co-founded (with Boris Kochno and Christian Bérard) the *Ballets des Champs-Elysées. This featured Petit as leading dancer and chief choreographer as did the company he formed in 1948, *Ballets de Paris, after falling out with his colleagues. Petit led both companies on extensive tours, in France and abroad and it was his 1949 London staging of *Carmen* for Ballets de Paris that secured his international reputation. Ballets de Paris was eventually disbanded, but it was periodically brought back to life in order to present Petit's newest choreography. Petit's restlessness as a choreographer was evident in the many projects he undertook in film, television, and the commercial stage. From 1970 to 1975 he owned and directed the Casino de Paris, staging revues which starred his wife, Zizi Jeanmaire. For a few months in 1970 he was dance director of the Paris Opera Ballet however and in 1972 he settled into his most permanent post as director and chief choreographer of the newly founded Ballet National de Marseilles, where he remained for the next 25 years.

Petit is one of the most prolific and fashionable of 20th-century French choreographers. Stylistically his ballets were a product of his strict classical training but he was none the less a consummate showman. He aimed for glamour and drama on stage, and several of his ballets displayed an overt sexuality. His erotically charged *Carmen* (which starred himself and his wife) was considered a landmark in the liberation of French ballet as was his shockingly explicit 1946 work, *Le Jeune Homme et la mort*, in which a young man hangs himself in frustrated passion. Petit's best-known repertory consists of his single-act ballets, and while he made many full-length works at Marseilles, none of them entered the international repertoire.

After retiring from his post as director he continued to work from his own studio and school in Marseilles, and to stage his ballets for companies around the world.

A list of the numerous works he made for his own companies includes *Les Forains* (mus. Sauguet, 1945), *Le Déjeuner sur l'herbe* (mus. Lanner, Tcherepnin, 1945), *Le Jeune Homme et la mort* (mus. Bach, 1946), *Le Bal des blanchisseuses* (mus. V. Duke, 1946), *Les Demoiselles de la nuit* (mus. Françaix, 1948), *Carmen* (mus. Bizet, 1949), *La Croqueuse de diamants* (mus. Damase, 1950), *Le Loup* (mus. Dutilleux, 1953), *Deuil en 24 heures* (mus. M. Thiriet, 1953), *La Chambre* (mus. Auric, 1955), *Cyrano de Bergerac* (mus. Constant, 1959, Petit's first full-length ballet), *Les Chants de Maldoror* (mus. M. Jarre, 1962), *Pink Floyd Ballet* (mus. Pink Floyd, 1972), *La Rose malade* (mus. Mahler, 1973), *La Dame de pique* (mus. Tchaikovsky, 1978), *La Chauve-souris* (mus. J. Strauss, 1979), *Les Contes d'Hoffmann* (mus. Offenbach, 1982), and a brand new version of *Swan Lake* titled *Swan Lake and its Evil Spells* (1998). For the Paris Opera he made the full-length *Notre-Dame de Paris* (mus. M. Jarre, 1965, with himself

as Quasimodo), *Turangalila* (mus. Messiaen, 1968), *Shéhérazade* (mus. Ravel, 1974), *La Symphonie fantastique* (mus. Berlioz, 1975), *La Nuit transfigurée* (mus. Schoenberg, 1976), *Nana* (mus. Constant, 1976), *Le Fantôme de l'Opéra* (mus. Landowski, 1980), *Passacaille* (mus. Webern, 1994), *Rythme de Valses* (mus. Johann Strauss II, 1994), *Camera Obscura* (mus. Schoenberg, 1994), *Le Guépard* (The Leopard, 1994), and *Clavigo* (mus. Gabriel Yared, 1999). In 1990 he staged his own *Sleeping Beauty*, with Jeanmaire as Carabosse.

For Sadler's Wells Ballet he made *Ballabile* (mus. Chabrier, 1950); for the Royal Ballet he made *Paradise Lost* (mus. Constant, 1967, with Fonteyn and Nureyev) and *Pelléas et Mélisande* (mus. Schoenberg, 1969). For the National Ballet of Canada he created *Kraanerg* (mus. Xenakis, 1969) and for Berlin Opera Ballet he created *Blue Angel* (mus. Constant, 1985).

He provided the choreography for several Hollywood films including *Hans Christian Andersen* (1952), *Daddy Long Legs* (1955), *Glass Slipper* (1954), and *Anything Goes* (1956). The 1960 film *Black Tights* (*Les Collants noirs*) featured shortened versions of four of Petit's ballets. He was made Chevalier de la Légion d'honneur, 1974.

petits rats Affectionate term by which children of the Paris Opera Ballet School are known.

Petits Riens, Les Ballet divertissement in three scenes with choreography and libretto by Noverre, music by Mozart. Premiered 11 Jun. 1778 at the Paris Opera, with Guimard, A. Vestris, Dauberval. The original libretto is lost, although it is known that the ballet featured Cupid, a game of blind man's buff, and a trio of shepherdesses, one of whom is in male disguise. It was Mozart's only full-length score for dance, although his name did not appear on the original programme (and he was never paid for it). In 1872 Mozart's manuscript was found in the library of the Paris Opera. Since then it has been re-choreographed by Ashton (*Suites de danses*, 1927, *Nymphs and Shepherds*, Ballet Rambert, 1928, expanded as *Dances from Les Petits Riens*, 1930), de Valois (1928 and 1931), and Bintley (Royal Ballet School, 1991).

Petronio, Stephen (*b* Newark, NJ, 20 Mar. 1956) US dancer, choreographer, and company director. He began his dance studies at college in Massachusetts, and then trained with Steve Paxton. In 1979 he joined Trisha Brown's company, her first male dancer, and remained there until 1986. He also founded his own company in 1984, for which he has since choreographed many works. From 1990 to 1992 he additionally collaborated with the British choreographer Michael

Clark, co-choreographing a version of Stravinsky's *Rite of Spring* in 1991.

Petronio's own choreography bears the influence of his early training in its free flow of movement, but among its distinctive qualities are its speed and energy, its aggressive tension, and sometimes homoerotic sensibility. Many works are set to contemporary rock scores, and feature designs by contemporary artists. A list of his works includes *No. 3* (1985), *Walk-In* (1986), *Simulacrum Reels* (1987), *AnAmnesia* (1988), *Middle-Sex Gorge* (mus. Wire, 1990), *Full Half Wrong* (1992), *Lareigne* (1995), *Drawn That Way* (1996), *ReBourne* (1997), *Not Garden* (1997), *Strange Attractions* (mus. Nyman, 1999), *Strange Attractors* (mus. several 2000), *BLOOM* (mus. Rufus Wainwright, 2006), and *I Drink the Air Before Me* (mus. Nico Muhley, 2009). His works are also in the repertory of many companies, including specially commissioned works such as *Simulacrum Court* (Frankfurt Ballet, 1987), *Extravenus* (Lyon Opera Ballet, 1994), *Underland* (Sydney Dance Company, 2003), and *Ride the Beast* (Scottish Ballet, 2007).

((⊕)) SEE WEB LINKS
• Website for the Stephen Petronio company

Petrouchka *See* PETRUSHKA.

Petrov, Nicolas (*b* Novi Sad, 13 Dec. 1933) Yugoslavian dancer, choreographer, and company director. He studied at the Novi Sad Theatre Academy, at the Belgrade State Ballet Academy, and later in Paris and London. He danced with the National Popular Theatre in Novi Sad (1946–51) and the Belgrade National Popular Theatre (1951–4). In 1954 he went to France, where he danced with Charrat's company; he also danced with Massine's Ballet Europeo di Nervi. From 1967 to 1969 he was ballet master of the Pittsburgh Playhouse School of Dance; in 1969 he became founding artistic director of Pittsburgh Ballet Theater. He choreographed many ballets for the company, including the first American full-length staging of Prokofiev's *Romeo and Juliet*. He left the company in 1977.

Petrushka Ballet in one act with choreography by Fokine, libretto by Benois and Stravinsky, music by Stravinsky, and designs by Benois. Premiered 13 Jun. 1911 by the Ballets Russes de Diaghilev at Théâtre du Chatelet in Paris, with Nijinsky, Karsavina, Orloff, and Cecchetti. The story is set during Butterweek Fair in St Petersburg in 1830. In Admiralty Square three puppets in a puppet theatre come to life: Petrushka, the Ballerina, and the Moor. Petrushka falls in love with the Ballerina, but she loves the Moor, who eventually kills Petrushka in a jealous rage. It was one of the greatest successes of the Diaghilev

company and there have been many subsequent revivals including Fokine's for Ballet Theatre in 1942, Serge Lifar's and Nicholas Zvereff's staging for the Paris Opera Ballet in 1948, Beriozoff's for London Festival Ballet in 1950, Grigoriev's and Tchernicheva's for the Royal Ballet in 1957, Boyarsky's for the Maly Theatre Ballet in Leningrad in 1961, and Léonide Massine, Yurek Lazowski, and Tatiana Massine's for the Joffrey Ballet in 1970. Many other choreographers have created entirely new versions, including Jooss (Essen, 1930), T. Gsovsky (Berlin, 1946), Béjart (Brussels, 1977), Neumeier (Hamburg, 1982), Vinogradov (Scottish Ballet, 1989), Macdonald (Gothenburg Ballet, 1998), and Alston (1994).

Pharaoh's Daughter (Fr. title *La Fille du Pharaon*) Full-length ballet with choreography by Petipa, libretto by Petipa and Vernoy de Saint-Georges, music by Pugni, sets by A. Roller and G. Wagner, and costumes by Kelwer and Stolyakov. Premiered at the Bolshoi Theatre in St Petersburg, 30 Jan. 1862, with Rosati, Goltz, Petipa, and Ivanov. Set in Egypt, and inspired by the legends of Egyptian mummies, the story tells of Lord Wilson and his servant who seek refuge from a storm inside a pyramid. They smoke opium and in their dreams are visited by the resurrected vision of Aspicia, the Pharaoh's daughter, who draws them into the drama of her former life. An example of ballet *à grand spectacle*, it lasted four hours and featured a cast of 400. Petipa's first truly successful ballet, it resulted in his appointment as second ballet master in St Petersburg. Gorsky revived it for the Bolshoi in Moscow in 1905. Lacotte staged a version for the Bolshoi in 2000.

Phèdre Ballet, described as a 'tragedy in choreography', with choreography by Lifar, libretto and designs by Cocteau, and music by Auric. Premiered 14 Jun. 1950 by the Paris Opera Ballet, Paris, with Toumanova, Lifar, and Darsonval. It retells the legend of Theseus' wife, who falls violently in love with her stepson Hippolytus and commits suicide when her love is not reciprocated. Cocteau based his libretto on the version by Racine, not Euripides. There have been other ballet treatments of the Phaedra legend, including those by Angiolini (Milan, 1788 or 1789), Didelot (St Petersburg, 1825), Graham (mus. R. Starer, New York, 1962), Cullberg (for Swedish television, as *I Am Not You*, 1966), and Flindt (Dallas, 1987).

Picasso, Pablo (*b* Malaga, 25 Oct. 1881; *d* Mougins, France, 8 Apr. 1973) Spanish painter and set designer. He designed six ballets for Diaghilev's Ballets Russes, although one (Nijinska's *Trepar*) was not produced. He collaborated closely with Massine and Cocteau on *Parade* (1917), not only creating bold new Cubist designs but also influencing the ballet's scenario. He worked with Massine again on *Le Tricorne* (1919) and *Pulcinella* (1920) for Diaghilev, and also designed Massine's *Mercure* (1924), created for Comte Étienne de Beaumont's Soirées de Paris. Picasso was part of Diaghilev's circle: he sketched the dancers in rehearsal and in 1918 he married one of them, Olga Kokhlova. He also designed the drop curtain for Nijinska's Ballets Russes production of *Le Train bleu* in 1924, which was an enlargement of one of his paintings; and did the backdrop for Petit's *Le Rendezvous* in 1945. For Lifar he designed *L'Après-midi d'un faune* (1960) and *Icare* (1962).

Picnic at Tintagel Ballet in one act with choreography and libretto by Ashton, music by Bax, and designs by Beaton. Premiered 28 Feb. 1952 by New York City Ballet at City Center in New York, with Diana Adams, Moncion, and d'Amboise. Set in the Cornish castle of Tintagel in 1916 the ballet tells the story of Tristan and Isolde through the experience of a group of tourists who visit the castle and among its ancient stones find themselves swept up in the legend of the tragic lovers. The music is Bax's *The Garden of Fand*.

Pictures Modern dance in one act with choreography by Cunningham, music by David Behrman, scenery and costumes by Mark Lancaster. Premiered 6 Mar. 1984 by the Merce Cunningham Dance Company at City Center, New York. A full-company work, it proved to be one of Cunningham's most popular creations.

Pierrot Lunaire Modern dance in one act with choreography by Tetley, music by Schoenberg, and designs by Rouben Ter-Arutunian. Premiered 5 May 1962 by the Glen Tetley Company at the Fashion Institute of Technology in New York with Tetley, Linda Hodes, and Robert Powell. The story takes three characters from commedia dell'arte—Pierrot, Columbine, and Brighella—and uses them to illustrate both the vulnerability and power of innocence as Pierrot is cheated and robbed by his associates but is still able to forgive them. It was Tetley's first major work, and was revolutionary both in its fusion of contemporary and classical techniques, and in Ter-Arutunian's scaffolding set, which is an intrinsic part of the choreography. It has been revived for several companies, including Nederlands Dans Theater, (1962), Ballet Rambert (1967), Royal Danish Ballet (1968), Bavarian State Opera Ballet (1972), the Stuttgart Ballet (1975), and The Royal Ballet (2005). Prior to Tetley's successful staging, there had been earlier attempts to choreograph Schoenberg's 1912 song-cycle, which was set to 21 poems by Albert Giraud. Massine expressed an interest in 1922 but was stopped by the composer, who was not happy with the choreographer's plan to replace the vocal line with instrumentation. In 1958 Cranko's efforts to stage a production of it for the short-lived Edinburgh International Ballet were frustrated by the Schoenberg estate. Joffrey choreographed a version for his own company in 1955, although that version is now lost. In 2008 Ratmansky created a new version for Diana *Vishneva.

Pillar of Fire Ballet in one act with choreography and libretto by Tudor, music by Schoenberg, designs by Jo Mielziner. Premiered 8 Apr. 1942 by Ballet Theatre at the Metropolitan Opera House in New York, with Kaye, Chase, Annabelle Lyon, Tudor, and Laing. The music is Schoenberg's *Transfigured Night*, and the Richard Dehmel poem which inspired the score was also inspiration for Tudor's libretto. Set in small-town New England it portrays the fraught emotional situation that arises when Hagar, the ballet's sexually repressed heroine, believes the man she loves prefers her younger sister, and in despair gives herself to a sadistic stranger (the Man Opposite). She confesses her betrayal to her lover who forgives her. One of Tudor's greatest works, it was a landmark in the genre of psychological ballet. It was revived for the Royal Swedish Ballet (1962), the Vienna State Opera Ballet (1969), Australian Ballet (1969), and Birmingham Royal Ballet (1995). Kylián choreographed a different version for Nederlands Dans Theater in 1975 and Petit did his own version for the Paris Opera Ballet in 1976 using the Schoenberg score.

Pilobolus Dance Theater US modern dance company founded in 1971 by Moses *Pendleton and Jonathan Wolken, fellow students at Dartmouth College. The company took its name from a phototropic fungus found in New England and it developed a form of sculptural dance theatre combining acrobatics, gymnastics, pantomime, and modern dance with striking visual effects and optical illusions. The dancers are all involved in the creative process, sometimes collaborating with outside artists such as puppeteer Basil Twist who co-created *Darkness and Light* (2008). Over the years, members have included Lee Harris, Michael Tracy, Robby Barnett, Martha Clarke, and Alison Chase. Tracy, Barnett, and Wolken are currently its artistic directors. Pilobolus is based in Washington, Connecticut and has evolved into a tripartite organization: the Dance Theatre, which performs up to three new productions each year, the Institute which runs educational programmes, and the Creative Services which works with commercial projects such as film and advertising. In 1997 the company made its Broadway debut and it tours extensively. A list of its works includes *The Particle Zoo* (1989), *Solus* (1992), *Gnomen* (1997), and *Megawatt* (2004).

Pineapple Poll Ballet in one act with choreography and libretto by Cranko, music by Arthur Sullivan (arr. Charles Mackerras), and designs by Osbert Lancaster. Premiered 13 Mar. 1951 by Sadler's Wells Theatre Ballet, Sadler's Wells Theatre, London, with Elaine Fifield, David Poole, and David Blair. A comic ballet set on the docks of Portsmouth, it tells of the love triangle between Captain Belaye, a handsome naval officer, Poll, the pretty trinket-seller who pursues him by disguising herself as a sailor, and Jasper, the Pierrotesque character whose love for Poll is unrequited. Based on W. S. Gilbert's Bab Ballad, *The Bumboat Woman's Story*. Cranko later re-staged and revised it for the Royal Ballet in 1959 with Park, Holden, and Blair. It was also revived for Australian Ballet (1966), City Center Joffrey Ballet (1970), Stuttgart Ballet (1974), and the National Ballet of Canada.

Piper, John (*b* Epsom, 13 Dec. 1903; *d* 27 Jun. 1992) British painter and designer. He designed Ashton's *The Quest* (1943), de Valois's *Job* (1948 Covent Garden revival), and Cranko's *Sea Change* (1949), *Harlequin in April* (1951), *The Shadow* (1953), and the sets for his *Prince of the Pagodas* (1957).

piqué In classical ballet, a step which is taken directly on to pointe and without first bending the knee.

pirouette In classical ballet, a turn or series of turns travelling 360 degrees on one leg. The non-supporting leg is usually bent with the foot touching the knee of the turning leg. Multiple pirouettes are often executed by ballerinas on pointe.

Pite, Crystal (*b* Terrace, British Columbia, 15 Dec. 1970) Canadian dancer and choreographer. She trained at the Pacific Dance Centre in Victoria, British Columbia, and joined Ballet British Columbia at 17, performing with the company for eight years. In 1996 she joined Ballett Frankfurt, where under William Forsythe, she began to focus on choreography. She was resident choreographer of the Ballets Jazz de Montreal (2001–04) and founder of her own Vancouver-based company, Kidd Pivot. She has created works for Nederlands Dans Theater and Ballett Frankfurt, among others. Her works include: *Excerpts from a Future Work*, *Field: Fiction*, *Uncollected Work*, and *Lost Action*.

place, sur Remaining on the spot.

Place, The Central London home of *London Contemporary Dance School and the now-defunct *London Contemporary Dance Theatre. The Place

Theatre is London's foremost venue for small-scale independent dance.

Planets, The Several choreographers have used Holst's 1915 orchestral suite, including Kreutzberg (Berlin State Opera, 1931), Tudor (Mars, Venus, Mercury, and Neptune, Ballet Rambert, 1934), Walter (Vienna State Opera, 1961), and Bintley (Royal Ballet, 1990).

Platel, Élisabeth (*b* Paris, 10 Apr. 1959) French dancer. From 1971 she studied at the Conservatoire National Supérieur de Musique de Paris, graduating in 1975 with first prize. She then furthered her studies (1975–6) in the 'pre ballet corps' at the Paris Opera Ballet, before joining the company fully in 1976. Promoted to étoile in 1981. An outstanding ballerina, with beautiful feet and high extensions, she was the epitome of pure French classicism. As well as dancing the classical ballerina repertory she also danced in many modern works, creating roles in Childs's *Premier orage* (1984), Nureyev's *Swan Lake* (1984), van Dantzig's *Sans armes citoyens!* (1987), Neumeier's *Magnificat* (1987) and *Sylvia* (1997), and Armitage's *Les Anges ternis* (1987). She has appeared as a guest with many companies including the Royal Ballet, Royal Danish Ballet and the Bolshoi Ballet. She appeared in the 1987 BBC Television series *Ballerina* and in the 1982 French film *Le Spectre de la danse*. She retired from the Paris Opera Ballet in 1999, and became director of its school in 2004.

Pleasant, Richard (*b* Denver, Colo., 1906; *d* New York, 5 Jul. 1961) US ballet director and artists' agent. After training as an architect, he worked in Hollywood as an artists' agent. In 1937 he went to New York as manager of the newly re-established Mordkin Ballet. Two years later he founded Ballet Theatre with Lucia *Chase, a ballerina with the Mordkin company. Their new company, later *American Ballet Theatre, gave its first performance in 1940, but Pleasant resigned as director after only its second season, leaving Chase in control.

plié [Fr., bent] Bending of the knee. In classical ballet the term most commonly refers to a slow bending of both legs, knees turned out to the side at a right angle to the front of the body, heels on the floor. It is the fundamental movement of the daily ballet class, used to warm the muscles and tendons during exercises at the barre before proceeding into the centre of the studio.

Plisetskaya, Maya (*b* Moscow, 20 Nov. 1925) Russian dancer, choreographer, ballet director, and actress. Niece of both Asaf *Messerer and the Bolshoi ballerina Sulamith Messerer, and cousin of the designer Boris Messerer. She studied at the

Bolshoi Ballet School with Elisaveta Gerdt (from 1932) and later with Asaf Messerer, and after graduating in 1943 she joined the Bolshoi Ballet as a soloist. Only two years later her exceptional technique won her promotion to ballerina. She was a remarkably fluid dancer but also a very powerful one and the robust theatricality and passion she brought to her roles made her an ideal Soviet ballerina. She danced all the classical repertory, renowned especially as Odette-Odile and Kitri, and in 1962, when Galina Ulanova retired, she became prima ballerina of the Bolshoi. During her long career with the Moscow company however she was frequently in open rebellion against the policies of the management and sought new challenges abroad as an international guest artist, most notably with the Paris Opera Ballet, Ballet National de Marseilles, and Ballet of the 20th Century in Brussels. She created leading roles in Lavrovsky's *Stone Flower* (1954), Moiseyev's *Spartacus* (1958), Grigorovich's Moscow version of *The Stone Flower* (1959), Aurora in Grigorovich's staging of *The Sleeping Beauty* (1963), Grigorovich's Moscow version of *The Legend of Love* (1965), the title role in Alberto Alonso's *Carmen Suite* (1967), Petit's *La Rose malade* (Paris, 1973), Béjart's *Isadora* (Monte Carlo, 1976) and his Moscow staging of *Leda* (1979), Granero's *Maria Estuardo* (Madrid, 1988), and Lopez's *El Renedero* (Buenos Aires, 1990). She started choreographing in 1972; her first ballet was *Anna Karenina* (with N. Ryzhenko and V. Smirnov-Golovanov), set to a score by her husband, Rodion Shchedrin, and starring herself in the title role, which was staged at the Bolshoi. She also created *The Seagull* (mus. Shchedrin, Bolshoi Ballet, 1980) and *Lady with a Lapdog* (mus. Shchedrin, Bolshoi Ballet, 1985). She starred in the 1961 film of *The Humpbacked Horse*, and also appeared as a straight actress in several films, including the Soviet version of *Anna Karenina* (1968). Her own ballet of the same name was filmed in 1974. She was ballet director of the Rome Opera (1983–4), and artistic director of Ballet del Teatro Lirico Nacional in Madrid (1987–90). In 1988 an Hommage à Plisetskaya was staged in Boston. In 1996 she danced *The Dying Swan*, her signature role, at a gala in her honour in St Petersburg. Lenin Prize, 1964.

Poème de l'extase Ballet in two parts with choreography and libretto by Cranko, music by Scriabin and Fortner, and designs by Rose. Premiered 24 Mar. 1970 by the Stuttgart Ballet, with Fonteyn, Madsen, Stripling, Berg, Clauss, and Cragun. A famous stage diva is flattered by the attentions of a young man, but eventually rejects his advances, deciding that she is finished with such liaisons. The ballet was inspired by Colette's novel *La Naissance du jour* and took its visual cue from the paintings of Gustav Klimt. It was revived for Fonteyn with the Royal Ballet in 1972. Petit used the same music for his *L'estasi* (Milan, 1968) as did Ratmansky for his *Poème de l'extase* (Kirov, 1998).

pointe [Fr., point] In ballet, the term denotes dancing on the tip of the toe, in specially designed pointe *shoes whose toes have been stiffened to form a small platform on which the ballerina can balance her entire body weight. In classical ballet pirouettes are executed on pointe, as are arabesques. Pointework is traditionally restricted to female dancers, although some modern choreographers have put men 'sur les pointes' to comic effect (Bottom in Ashton's *The Dream*, for example). It is impossible to say for certain who was the first ballerina to dance on pointe, but both the French dancer Geneviève Gosselin and the Russian Avdotia Istomina are known to have danced on pointe before 1820. In the 1830s Marie Taglioni transformed pointework from a mere technical trick into the perfect vehicle for expressing the ethereality of Romantic ballet. In the early 20th century the supremacy of the pointe shoe in ballet was challenged by choreographers such as Fokine, who was one of the first to abandon it in his ballets. Demi-pointe, or half point, means balancing on the ball of the foot. It is more often used in modern dance.

Points in Space Video dance with choreography by Cunningham, direction by Elliot Caplan and Cunningham, music by Cage, sets by William Anastasi, and costumes by Dove Bradshaw. It was performed by the Merce Cunningham Dance Company and videotaped at BBC Television Centre in London in May 1986. First broadcast on BBC Television on 18 Jul. 1987. The title is taken from Albert Einstein's assertion 'There are no fixed points in space.' Cunningham made the work, for the full company, especially for the camera, taking into account the multiple points of view afforded by the medium. He later produced it for the stage at City Center, New York, 10 Mar. 1987. The Paris Opera Ballet took it into the repertoire in 1990.

Poland Ballet in Poland dates from the 16th century when it featured as a court entertainment. The first Polish company was founded in 1785, although it was short-lived, owing to the breakup of the country in 1794. Warsaw, which fell to Russia, became a centre of ballet activity. The French choreographers Louis Thierry (1818–23) and Maurice Pion (1825–43) worked here. Thierry (with Julia Mierzynska) created *Cracow Wedding* in 1823, the oldest Polish ballet still in the repertoire. F. Taglioni, who worked as director in Warsaw (1843–53), built up the repertoire and created works for the company. In the 1850s and 1860s, when Roman Turczynowicz was in charge, the company was prominent on the European dance scene and stars of the dance world, such as Grisi and Blasis, came to work in Warsaw. By the end of the 19th century, the company was heavily under the influence of the Russian ballet. Russian ballets were featured in the repertoire and Russian dancers (Pavlova and Karsavina among them) came to guest. From 1902 to 1905 Cecchetti was director of the company, and some of the dancers he taught later joined the Diaghilev company (Woizikowsky and Idzikowski). In 1920 ballet began to spread outside Warsaw, with the opening of a new centre in Poznán, attached to the Grand Theatre. Between the First and Second World Wars modern dance began to take hold, under the influence of Duncan, Jaques-Dalcroze, and Wigman, whose methods were taught in private schools. In 1937 the *Polish Ballet was founded to promote Polish ballet abroad. It was financed by the government and engaged Bronislava Nijinska as choreographer; the company toured throughout Europe but was disbanded in 1939 due to the outbreak of war. After the Second World War, which resulted in so much devastation to the companies and the theatres, ballet in the country had to rebuild, as did the Warsaw Grand Theatre which reopened in 1965. Under the current direction of Jolanta Rybarska, the ballet company performs a largely traditional repertory of 19th-century classics. Ballet in post-war Poland spread to other regional opera houses, although few survived the major restructuring following the end of Communist rule in 1989. In 1973 the independent Polish Dance Theatre was founded in Poznán by Conrad Drzewiecki with the aim of performing a more contemporary repertory. Under the current direction of Ewa Wycichowska it remains the most creatively important company in the country. While commissioning some works by outside choreographers, most of its repertory is by Polish choreographers, including Wycichowska herself and Jacek Przbylowicz. In order to expand the presence of dance in Poland, the company launched the Contemporary Dance Biennale in 1994, and in 2004 the International Festival of Dance Theatres.

SEE WEB LINKS

- Website for the Polish Dance Theatre
- Website for the Warsaw Opera with link to the ballet company

Polish Ballet Short-lived touring ballet company based in Poland in the 1930s. It was set up in 1937 to showcase Polish ballets abroad. Its first artistic director was Bronislava Nijinska, who choreographed five ballets for the company, all premiered at the 1937 Paris Exposition Internationale (at the Théâtre Mogador). In these works

Nijinska merged Polish national dance forms with classical and modernist ballet. The Polish Ballet won the Grand Prix and Nijinska won the Grand Prix for choreography. The company toured Europe, including London and Poland, under Nijinska's direction. In 1939 the Polish Ballet, directed by Nijinska's successor Woizikowsky, was disbanded at the outbreak of the Second World War.

polka Dance originating in Bohemia in the early 19th century. It is performed in quick duple time, and takes the form of step, step, step, hop. It was popular in European ballrooms and found its way onto the ballet stage in the 1840s when Maria and Eugene Coralli danced a polka at the Paris Opera.

polonaise Polish national dance executed in 3/4 time. A solemn and processional dance, it was performed when August the Strong was crowned king of Poland in 1697.

Polovtsian Dances *See* PRINCE IGOR.

Polyphonia Ballet in one act with choreography by Christopher Wheeldon and music by Gyorgy Ligeti. Premiered 4 Jan. 2001 by New York City Ballet at New York State Theater, with Wendy Whelan, Jennie Somogyi, Jennifer Tinsley, Alexandra Ansanelli, Jock Soto, Edwaard Liang, Jason Fowler, and Craig Hall. Wheeldon described his ballet, set to ten piano pieces by Ligeti, as 'romantic with comic twists'.

Ponomarev, Vladimir (*b* St Petersburg, 22 Jul. 1892; *d* Budapest, 21 Mar. 1951) Russian dancer, choreographer, and teacher. He studied at the Imperial Theatre School in St Petersburg and graduated into the Mariinsky Theatre in 1910, becoming principal in 1912. Apart from seasons with Diaghilev's Ballets Russes (1911–12) he remained at the Mariinsky (later GATOB and the Kirov) until 1951. He created the role of Prince Adam in *The Fountain of Bakhchisarai* (1934) and Montague in Lavrovsky's *Romeo and Juliet* (1940) but also worked as choreographer and director. Along with Lopukhov and Leontiev, he co-choreographed *The Red Poppy* (1929) and in 1941 he staged productions of *La Bayadère* (with Chabukiani), *Don Quixote*, and *Giselle*, Through these stagings and through his own teaching he was a major force in ensuring the survival of the 19th-century repertoire. He first began teaching in 1913 at the ballet school in St Petersburg, and over the decades his students included Gusev, K. Sergeyev, Chabukiani, Lavrovsky, and Zakharov. From 1944 to 1951 he was chief repetiteur at the Kirov, coaching dancers such as Ulanova, Grigorovich, and Jacobson. He was also assistant artistic director of the Kirov Ballet (1935–8), and acting artistic director (1941–4). He was artistic director of the Maly Theatre Ballet, Leningrad

(1938–9). He also frequently taught abroad, especially in Budapest, where he died.

Pontois, Noëlla (*b* Vendôme, 24 Dec. 1943) French dancer. She studied at the Paris Opera Ballet School and joined the Paris Opera Ballet in 1961, becoming principal in 1966 and étoile in 1968. For the next 25 years she was the company's prima ballerina. Although she created roles in a number of contemporary ballets, she was most celebrated for her interpretations of the 19th-century repertoire, to which she brought an outstanding refinement and authority, as well as a thrilling facility for balances. She created roles in Petit's *Adage et variations* (1965), *Extase* (1968), and *Mouvances* (1976), Descombey's *Jazz Suite* (1966) and *Zyklus* (1966), Flindt's *Jeux* (1973), Alonso's *Pas de quatre* (1973), Robbins's *Scherzo fantastique* (1974), Macdonald's *Diabelli Variations* (1974), and Pendleton's *Pulcinella* (Nancy, 1984). She appeared as a guest ballerina abroad, with companies such as London Festival Ballet and American Ballet Theatre. She retired from the Opera in 1983. In 1988 she began teaching at the Paris Opera Ballet School. Chevalier de la Légion d'honneur (1984).

Poole, David (*b* Cape Town, 17 Sept. 1925; *d* Cape Town, 27 Aug. 1991) South African dancer and ballet director. He trained with Dulcie Howes at the University of Cape Town Ballet School and then at Sadler's Wells Ballet School in London. In 1947 he joined Sadler's Wells Theatre Ballet, becoming a principal in 1948; in 1955 he transferred to the Sadler's Wells Ballet (later Royal Ballet) at Covent Garden. He created roles in Cranko's *Sea Change* (1949), *Beauty and the Beast* (1949), *Pineapple Poll* (1951), and *The Lady and the Fool* (1954), Rodrigues's *Blood Wedding* (1953), and MacMillan's *Danses concertantes* (1955) and *House of Birds* (1955). In 1956 he left the Royal Ballet, dancing with Ballet Rambert and Edinburgh International Ballet before returning to South Africa in 1959 to teach. In 1963 he became ballet master of CAPAB Ballet and in 1967 succeeded Dulcie Howes as artistic director; he created original works for the repertoire and added new productions of the classics, as well as raising the levels of performance and training. He retired in 1990.

Popova, Nina (*b* Novorossisk, 20 Oct. 1922) Russian-US dancer, teacher, and ballet director. She studied with T. Wassilieff, Preobrajenska, Egorova, and Vilzak and began her career dancing with Ballet de la Jeunesse in 1938. She danced with the Original Ballet Russe (1940–1), Ballet Theatre (1941–3), and Ballet Russe de Monte Carlo (1943–5). After working in American television and on Broadway, she became head of the ballet department at the New York High School of Performing Arts (1954–67). She was founder and artistic director of the Houston Ballet (1968–75).

popping One of the styles of funk street dance to come out of California in the 1970s. Its characteristic moves involve rapid and snappy flexions of the muscles, executed on the beat of the music to create a jerky 'popping' effect.

port de bras [Fr., carriage of the arms] In classical ballet there are various set positions of the arms, from en bas (in which the arms form an oval shape in front of the body about mid-thigh) to en haut (in which the arms form an oval above the head just slightly in front of the body).

Portugal As it did elsewhere in Europe, ballet in Portugal grew out of performances at court but its development was severely restricted when the decades of Spanish rule during the late 16th and early 17th century confined dance to Jesuit theatrical performances. Guest dancers from Vienna and Paris became popular in Lisbon during the 1730s and 1740s but the earthquake of 1755 curtailed theatrical life in the city for many years. In 1793 a new Royal Opera House opened with a performance of an allegorical ballet, *La Felicita lusitana*. This form was much admired in Lisbon, its storylines often based on real-life events and sometimes featuring real people on stage, such as soldiers. Later ballet trends did not meet with equal success. Romantic ballet was slow to take hold, despite seasons staged by Saint-Léon (1854–6). In the 20th century Diaghilev's debut season in Lisbon, in 1917 was disrupted by the Portuguese revolution. Dance continued to stagnate as the political situation repressed new initiatives in the arts. It was not until the Gulbenkian Foundation established its own ballet company in Lisbon in 1965 that theatrical dance became active. The company lasted until 2005 becoming increasingly contemporary in its focus and nurturing the careers of choreographers like Paulo Ribeiro and Rui *Horta. Horta himself was appointed artistic director of the smaller Lisbon Dance Theatre when it was founded in 1984. Other independent groups are active in the region including those run by Ribeiro and Olga *Roriz. The classically based Companhia Nacional de Bailado has a repertory of traditional classics plus some commissioned new work by Horta and others.

posé In ballet, stepping onto the full or half point with a straight knee. The transfer of weight can be done in any direction.

Possokhov, Yuri (*b* Lugansk, Ukraine, 1982) Ukrainian dancer and choreographer. He studied at the Moscow Ballet School and graduated into the Bolshoi Ballet in 1982, where he was eventually promoted to principal. In 1992 he moved to the Royal Danish Ballet and two years later to San Francisco Ballet. He began choreographing in 1990 and, starting with his solo for SFB principal Muriel Maffre in 1997, he has created numerous works for the company including *Magrittomania* (2000), *Damned* (2002), *Study in Motion* (mus. Alexander Scriabin, 2004), *Reflections* (mus. Mendelssohn, 2005), and *Ballet Mori* (2006). In 2003 he also collaborated with Helgi Tomasson on a new staging of *Don Quixote*. In 2006 when Possokhov retired from the stage he was made choreographer in residence at SFB. He has also made works for other companies including Oregon Ballet (*Firebird*, mus. Stravinsky, 2004 and *La Valse* mus. 2005), the Bolshoi Ballet (*Cinderella*, 2006), and Georgian State Ballet (*Sagalobeli*, 2007).

post-modern A loose term, first used by Yvonne Rainer in the early 1960s, to refer to the generation of experimental choreographers that followed on from the *modern dance period (dominated by Graham, Cunningham et al.). Initially the term was most associated with work pioneered by the *Judson Dance Theater in New York, in which choreographers like Rainer, Steve Paxton, and Trisha Brown explored the possibilities of non-theatrical dance productions, new forms of structure and pedestrian or minimalist dance vocabularies. Twyla Tharp recalled, in her autobiography *Push Comes to Shove*, 'At the Judson you could only walk and run—if you danced, you had sold out.' The term has since entered wider usage, denoting work that fuses different choreographic styles, sensibilities or aesthetic viewpoints within a single production, such as Mark Morris's *Hard Nut, or the desconstructionist approach developed by William Forsythe, in works like *Impressing the Czar.

Poulenc, Francis (*b* Paris, 7 Jan. 1899; *d* Paris, 30 Jan. 1963) French composer. He was a member of the avant-garde composers' group Les Six, who together wrote the music for Börlin's *Les Mariés de la Tour Eiffel*, a surrealist ballet performed by Les Ballets Suédois in 1921. He also wrote the music for Nijinska's *Les Biches* (1924) and *Aubade* (1929) and for Lifar's *Les Animaux modèles* (1942). Poulenc's orchestral writing has also been used for dance purposes, including his Concerto in G minor for Organ, Strings, and Timpani, which Tetley took for *Voluntaries* (1973), and his *Gloria*, which MacMillan used for his 1980 ballet of the same name.

Pourfarrokh, Ali (*b* Kermanshah, 27 Nov. 1938) Iranian dancer, ballet master, and ballet director. He studied at the Tehran Dance Academy and at the Metropolitan Opera Ballet School in New York, the School of American Ballet, and at the Graham school. He danced with American Ballet Theatre (1959–63), then with Metropolitan Opera Ballet, Harkness Ballet, Frankfurt Ballet, and Joffrey Ballet. He was associate director and ballet master of the Alvin Ailey company (1972–6), and artistic director of the Iranian National Ballet (1976–9). Artistic director of the Alberta Ballet (1988–98).

Powell, Robert (*b* Hawaii, 1941; *d* New York, 24 Oct. 1977) US dancer. He studied at the High School of Performing Arts in New York and began dancing with the Martha Graham company in 1958, eventually becoming a soloist. He created roles in Graham's *Acrobats of God* (1960), *Secular Games* (1962), *Circe* (1963), *Plain of Prayer* (1968), *A Time of Snow* (1968), and *The Archaic Hours* (1968). He also danced with Glen Tetley, creating the role of Brighella in Tetley's *Pierrot Lunaire* (1962), and with Paul Taylor, José Limón, Louis Falco, Alvin Ailey, and London Contemporary Dance Theatre, where he created a leading role in Robert Cohan's *Cell* (1969). He was also associate director of the Graham company.

Praagh, (Dame) Peggy van (*b* London, 1 Sept. 1910; *d* Melbourne, 15 Jan. 1990) British dancer, teacher, and ballet director. She studied with Aimée Phipps, Margaret Craske, Sokolova, Volkova, Karsavina, and de Mille. She made her debut dancing with Anton Dolin's company in London in 1929, performing balletic interludes in revues at the Coliseum. She danced with Ballet Rambert (1933–8) and then with Antony Tudor's London Ballet (1938). She created roles in many of Tudor's important early works: *Jardin aux lilas* (1936), *Dark Elegies* (1937), *Soirée musicale* (1938), and *Gala Performance* (1938). She was joint director, with Maude Lloyd, of the London Ballet (1939–40) then in 1941 became principal dancer with Sadler's Wells Ballet and in 1946 ballet mistress of Sadler's Wells Theatre Ballet. Between 1951 and 1955 she was assistant director of Sadler's Wells Theatre Ballet overseeing a period of exceptional creative activity. She also worked as a ballet producer for BBC Television (1949–58). In 1958 she directed the Edinburgh International Ballet; in 1959–60 she was artistic director of the Borovansky Ballet in Australia and in 1962 was invited to become the first artistic director of the newly formed Australian Ballet, where she remained until 1974 (returning for one year, 1978–9). Using the British model to build up the company's repertory and performing standards, van Praagh also ensured that it acquired a distinctive Australian identity. Between 1975 and 1982 she was also a freelance ballet producer and teacher, both at the Royal Ballet School and the Australian Ballet School, acknowledged as one of the world's leading teachers of the Cecchetti method. Author of *How I Became a Ballet Dancer* (London, 1954) and, with Peter Brinson, *The Choreographic Art* (London, 1963). DBE 1970.

Prague Ballet Company founded in the city in 1964 by the choreographers Ogoun and *Smok and the critic Vladimir Vasut. It gave its first performance on 23 Apr. 1965 at the Prague Theatre of Nusle. A chamber-sized group, it showcased contemporary Czech choreography, especially ballets by Ogoun and Smok. After a brief period of inactivity when it disbanded in 1970, it was reformed as Prague Chamber Ballet. It frequently toured abroad until it was absorbed into the newly formed ballet company at the *Prague State Opera, 2003.

Prague National Theatre Ballet Ballet company attached to the National Theatre in Prague. Founded in 1883, it remains the oldest ensemble in the Czech Republic.

Prague State Opera Ballet Company formed in 2003 when the Prague Chamber Ballet was absorbed into the ballet ensemble at the state theatre. Under the artistic direction of Pavel Dumbala the company performs the classical repertory, neo-classic works by Smok and new works by Czech choreographers such as Ján Ďurovčík and Bronislav Roznoz.

(((⊕))) SEE WEB LINKS
• Website for the Prague Opera with link to the ballet

Preljocaj, Angelin (*b* Sucy-en-Brie, 9 Jan. 1957) French dancer, choreographer, and company director. He studied modern dance with Karine Waehner and Cunningham and performed with various companies, including those of Quentin Rouiller, Viola Farber, and Dominique Bagouet (1982–4). In 1984 he founded his own group, Preljocaj Company, renamed Ballet Preljocaj in 1993, which was based first in Chateauvallon and from 1996 in Aix-en-Provence where in 2006 it acquired a purpose-built base. Preljocaj has additionally been guest choreographer with the Lyon Opera Ballet (1990) and with the Paris Opera Ballet (1994) and in 2002 created a version of *Rite of Spring* in collaboration with the Berlin Staatsoper. His choreography is noted for its strong visceral imagery and often surreal staging, and while it is rooted in the idioms of his modern dance background it has also acquired an overlay of classical detail and reference. Some of Preljocaj's most successful work has been choreographed in homage to ballet classics of the early 20th century, e.g. *Les Noces* (1989), *Parade* (Paris Opera, 1993), and *Spectre de la rose* (Paris Opera, 1993). A list of his other works includes *Black Market* (1985), *To Our Heroes* (1986), *Romeo*

and Juliet (1990, Lyon), *Bitter America* (1990), *The World Skin* (1992), *The Park* (*Le Parc*, Paris Opera Ballet, 1994), *Annunciation* (Paris Opera Ballet, 1996), *Firebird* (Munich, 1995), *Casanova* (Paris Opera, 1998), *Personne n'épouse les Méduses* (1999), *Helikopter* (2001), *Rite of Spring* (2001), *Near Life Experience* (2003), *N* (in collaboration with Granular Synthesis, 2004), *Les 4 Saisons* (in collaboration with Fabrice Hyber 2004), *Blanche Neige* (mus. Mahler, 2008), and *Siddharta* (mus. Bruno Mantovani, Paris Opera, 2010). Since 2003 his company has curated a dance festival in Aix. Chevalier of the Légion d'honneur (1998).

(((⊕))) SEE WEB LINKS
• Website for Ballet Preljocaj

premier danseur In classical ballet, a senior principal male dancer.

Preobrajenska, Olga (*b* St Petersburg, 2 Feb. 1871; *d* Saint-Mandé, France, 27 Dec. 1962) Russian-French dancer and teacher. She studied at the Imperial Theatre School in St Petersburg from 1879, where her teachers included Petipa and Ivanov. Later she trained with Cecchetti in St Petersburg. She graduated in 1889 into the Mariinsky Theatre where she was promoted to soloist (1896) and prima ballerina (1990). During her two decades at the Mariinsky she danced all the leading ballerina roles, although was particularly noted in *Coppélia, Raymonda, Sleeping Beauty, Fille mal gardée*, and *Don Quixote*. She created roles in Petipa's *Bluebeard* (1896), *Harlequinade* (1900), and *Les Saisons* (1900), in Ivanov and Gerdt's *Sylvia* (1901), N. and S. Legat's *The Fairy Doll* (1903), and in Fokine's *The Night of Terpsichore* (1908), *Egyptian Nights* (1908), and his second version of *Chopiniana* (1908). From 1895 she began to make guest appearances abroad, in Paris, London, even S. America. Short, stocky and even 'plain-looking' as one critic described her, she was also exceptionally charming on stage and was admired for her strong, precise technique and interpretative versatility. In 1914 she began teaching in St Petersburg, where her students included Danilova and Vaganova. In 1921 she left the Soviet Union and took her teaching career to Milan, London, Buenos Aires, and Berlin, before eventually settling in Paris in 1923. For almost 40 years she was one of the most famous teachers in Paris, working from her studio at the Salle Wacker, and her students included Baronova, Toumanova, and Youskevitch. She retired in 1960.

Présages, Les Ballet in four movements with choreography and libretto by Massine, music by Tchaikovsky, and designs by André Masson. Premiered 13 Apr. 1933 by Colonel de Basil's Ballets Russes, in Monte Carlo, with Verchinina, Baronova, Riabouchinska, Lichine, and Woizikowsky. The ballet is set to Tchaikovsky's 5th Symphony and portrays man's struggle with fate. The four parts are called: 'Action', 'Passion', 'Frivolity', and 'War' (or 'Fate'). It was revived by Tatiana Leskova for the Paris Opera Ballet in 1989, for the Joffrey Ballet in 1992, and for Australian Ballet in 2007. It was Massine's first symphonic ballet, part of a ground-breaking series that also included *Choreartium*, *Symphonie fantastique*, *La Septième Symphonie*, and *Rouge et noir*.

Prévost, Françoise (*b* Paris, *c.*1680 or 1681; *d* Paris, 13 Sept. 1741) French dancer. She made her official debut at the Paris Opera in 1699 in Lully's *Atys*. For three decades she was the reigning French prima ballerina and, indeed, was one of the first ballerinas in France given that women had only recently been admitted onto the stage (her predecessors were La Fontaine and Subligny). She also choreographed her own material including *Les Caractères de la danse* (mus. Rebel, 1715), in which she danced and mimed the parts of eleven different lovers, both male and female. She also taught in Paris, where her pupils included Marie Camargo and Marie Sallé, who went on to become famous rivals. She retired from the Opera in 1730.

Price family A Danish theatrical family started by an English circus rider and pantomime artist, James Price (1761–1805), who settled in Copenhagen. The family produced dancers, mime artists, actors, circus performers, and music hall artists up until the beginning of the 20th century. Juliette Price (1831–1906), his granddaughter, was a leading Danish ballerina and a great favourite of Bournonville, who often cast her in his ballets. She was also the first Danish Giselle. Her brother, Waldemar Price (1836–1908), joined the Royal Danish Ballet in 1857 and became the leading premier danseur of his day. Their cousin, Julius Price (1833–93), made his career as a dancer in Vienna, where he was the first solo dancer of the Vienna Court Opera (1855–93) and notched up almost 2,500 performances. Ellen Price (1878–1968), the great-niece of Juliette and Waldemar, was a soloist with the Royal Danish Ballet (1903–12), and created the title role in Beck's *The Little Mermaid* (1909).

prima ballerina [It., first dancer] In classical ballet, the female dancer who occupies the top position among dancers in a company. There is only one higher title, that of prima ballerina assoluta, which is very rarely given. The Royal Ballet bestowed this on Margot Fonteyn in 1979, when she was 60.

Primitive Mysteries Modern dance in three sections with choreography, libretto, and cos-

tumes by Graham, and music by Horst. Premiered 2 Feb. 1931 by the Martha Graham company at the Craig Theater in New York. Graham's first major group work, it featured twelve women and Graham herself as the central figure through whom the Christ story is re-enacted. She based her ideas for a religious ritual on the Christian Native Americans in the US Southwest. The work's three sections were 'Hymn to the Virgin', 'Crucifixus', and 'Hosannah'. One of Graham's signature works, its overt religious statement was unprecedented in modern dance at the time.

Primus, Pearl (*b* Port of Spain, Trinidad, 29 Nov. 1919; *d* New Rochelle, NY, 29 Oct. 1994) US dancer, choreographer, teacher, and anthropologist. She studied medicine and biology at Hunter College in New York and later obtained a Ph.D. in anthropology from New York University (1978). Her dance studies were undertaken via a scholarship to the New Dance Group (1941) and she gave her first solo recital in 1943, launching her own company in 1944. With her husband, Percival Borde she devoted herself to research into West Indian, African, and other native dance forms, believing in dance as a means of fostering cultural understanding. She made several trips to Africa to further her research and established the African-Caribbean-American Institute of Dance in New York in 1963. In 1978 she founded the Pearl Primus Dance Language Institute in New Rochelle. She also taught at New York's Hunter College. She choreographed *African Ceremonial* (1944) for her own company and re-staged *The Wedding* for the Alvin Ailey American Dance Theater (1974). Other works include *Fanga* (1949), inspired by a Liberian ritual dance, and *Strange Fruit* (1943), which dealt with lynching of blacks in the Deep South. She also choreographed Broadway musicals and the dances in O'Neill's play *The Emperor Jones* (1947).

Prince Igor Opera by Borodin, which includes the famous Polovtsian Dances, often performed on their own as a ballet. In the opera these dances are staged by Khan Konchak to entertain his prisoners, Prince Igor and his son Vladimir. When the opera was first produced on 4 Nov. 1890 at the Mariinsky Theatre in St Petersburg, the dances were choreographed by Ivanov, more famously Fokine re-choreographed them for Diaghilev's first Paris season in 1909. The rousing energy and scale of the choreography, rooted in Tartar folk dance, and the colourful designs of Nicholas Roerich, gave *Polovtsian Dances* an exalted place in the Diaghilev repertory. Its premiere was 19 May 1909 at the Théâtre du Châtelet, with Fedorova, Smirnova, and Bolm and Fokine's version has since been frequently revived, including Grigoriev's production for the Royal Ballet in

1965 which featured Rudolf Nureyev (himself a Tartar). Other revivals include the Royal Danish Ballet (1925), Teatro Colón, Buenos Aires (1931), Blum's Ballets de Monte Carlo (1936), Paris Opera Ballet (1949), and London Festival Ballet (1951).

Prince of the Pagodas, The Ballet in three acts with choreography and libretto by Cranko, music by Britten, sets by John Piper, and costumes by Desmond Heeley. Premiered 1 Jan. 1957 by the Royal Ballet at Covent Garden, with Beriosova, Farron, Blair, and Leslie Edwards. A fairy-tale, which has elements of both *King Lear* and *Beauty and the Beast*, it tells the story of the Emperor of the Middle Kingdom and his two rival daughters. Princess Rose, the 'good' daughter, is unfairly banished and forced to undergo a journey through air, fire, and water. In the Kingdom of the Pagodas she meets a Green Salamander who turns into a handsome prince. He helps her and her father to regain the kingdom, which has fallen into the hands of the evil sister, Princess Epine. The music, by Benjamin Britten, was the first full-length ballet score by a British composer in the 20th century. Cranko revived it for Milan (1957) and Stuttgart (1960). Vinogradov staged a new version for the Kirov as *The Enchanted Prince* (1972). In 1989 Kenneth MacMillan choreographed a new version for the Royal Ballet using the Britten score. The ballet, which featured designs by Nicholas Georgiadis, was premiered on 7 Dec. 1989 with Bussell, Cope, Dowell, and Fiona Chadwick.

Prisoner of the Caucasus, The There have been several ballets based on Pushkin's poem, including one by Didelot (mus. Cavos), which was first performed 27 Jan. 1823, at the Bolshoi Theatre in St Petersburg with Istomina and Goltz. A hundred years later it was staged by Lavrovsky (mus. Asafiev, designs Khodasevich), in a production premiered on 14 Apr. 1938 at the Maly Theatre in Leningrad. On 4 Dec. 1951 Skibine choreographed a one-act version (mus. Khachaturian from *Gayané*) for the Grand Ballet du Marquis de Cuevas at the Théâtre de l'Empire in Paris, with Skibine and Marjorie Tallchief.

Prodigal Son, The (orig. Fr. title *Le Fils prodigue*) Ballet in one act with choreography by Balanchine, libretto by Kochno, music by Prokofiev, designs by Rouault. Premiered 21 May 1929 by the Ballets Russes de Diaghilev at the Théâtre Sarah Bernhardt in Paris, with Lifar, Doubrovska, Fedorov, Woizikowsky and Dolin. A dance retelling of the biblical parable, it was the last ballet Balanchine made for the Diaghilev company. It was subsequently revived for several companies including New York City Ballet (1950, with Jerome Robbins and Maria Tallchief), the Royal Danish

Ballet (1968, with Flemming Flindt and Anna Laerkesen), the Royal Ballet (1973, with Rudolf Nureyev and Deanne Bergsma), Paris Opera (1973), American Ballet Theatre (1980, with Baryshnikov), and Les Grands Ballets Canadiens (1989). Other choreographers, including Jooss (Essen, 1931), Milloss (Düsseldorf, 1934), and Lichine (Original Ballet Russe, Sydney, 1938), have created different versions using the Prokofiev score. Barry Moreland staged a ragtime version of *The Prodigal Son*, set to music by Scott Joplin, for London Festival Ballet in 1974, and Ivo Cramér staged a folklore version of *The Prodigal Son* (mus. H. Alfvén) for the Royal Swedish Ballet in 1957.

Prokofiev, Sergei (Serge) (*b* Sontsovka, Ukraine, 5 May 1891; *d* Moscow, 5 Mar. 1953) Ukrainian-Soviet composer. Along with Stravinsky he is considered one of the most important ballet composers of the 20th century. His two best-known ballet scores are *Romeo and Juliet* (first production 1938, Brno, chor. Psota) and *Cinderella* (chor. Zahkarov, Bolshoi Ballet, Moscow, 1945) but he also composed many others. His first was *Ala and Lolly* (1914) which was commissioned by Diaghilev but not performed (it had to wait until 1927 when Terpis staged it at the Berlin State Opera). Later scores included *Chout* (Ballet Russes de Diaghilev, Paris, 1921, choreography by Slavinsky and Larionov), *Trapeze* (chor. Romanov, Russian Romantic Ballet, Berlin, 1925), *Le Pas d'acier* (Ballets Russes de Diaghilev, Paris, 1927, chor. Massine), *The Prodigal Son* (Ballets Russes de Diaghilev, Paris, 1929, chor. Balanchine), *Sur le Borsythène* (Paris Opera, 1932, chor. Lifar), and *The Stone Flower* (Bolshoi Ballet, Moscow, 1954, chor. Lavrovsky). His concert and film music has also been used by many choreographers; including Tudor in *Gala Performance* (London Ballet, 1938), Bolm and many others in *Peter and the Wolf* (Ballet Theatre, New York, 1940), MacMillan in *Triad* (Royal Ballet, 1972), Robbins in *Opus 19* (New York City Ballet, 1979), Grigorovich in *Ivan the Terrible* (Bolshoi Ballet, Moscow, 1975), Kudelka in *The Heart of the Matter* (1986) and *Désir* (1991), and Kim Brandstrup in *Rushes* (Royal Ballet, 2008).

Prokovsky, André (*b* Paris, 13 Jan. 1939; *d* 15 Aug. 2009) French dancer, choreographer, and ballet director. He studied with Lubov Egorova, Nora Kiss, Serge Peretti, and Nicholas Zvereff, making his debut in 1954 with the Comédie-Française in Molière's *Les Amants magnifiques*. He then danced with the companies of Charrat (1954), Babilée (1954), and Petit (1956) before starting a lengthy association with London Festival Ballet (1957-60, 1966-73). He additionally danced with Grand Ballet du Marquis de Cuevas

(1960–2) and New York City Ballet (1963–6). Noted for his bravura technique, he formed an acclaimed partnership with Galina Samsova while at London Festival Ballet. He created roles in Dolin's *Variations for Four* (1957), d'Amboise's *The Chase* (1963) and *Irish Fantasy* (1964), Balanchine's *Pas de deux and Divertissement* (1965) and *Brahms-Schoenberg Quartet* (1966), J. Carter's *The Unknown Island* (1969), Hynd's *Dvořák Variations* (1970), and Darrell's *Othello* (title role, 1971). In 1972 he and Samsova (then his wife) started a company which later became New London Ballet. It disbanded in 1977, although was briefly revived in 1979. For his own company he choreographed *Scarlatti and Friends* (mus. Scarlatti, 1972), *Bagatelles, Opus 126* (mus. Beethoven, 1972), *Vespri* (mus. Verdi, 1973), *Piano Quartet No. 1* (mus. Beethoven, 1974), *Folk Songs* (mus. Berio, 1974), *Elégie* (mus. Fauré, 1975), *Commedia I* (mus. R. R. Bennett, 1975), *Königsmark* (mus. Tchaikovsky, 1979). For Australian Ballet he created the full-length *Anna Karenina* (mus. Tchaikovsky, 1979) and *The Three Musketeers* (mus. Verdi, Woolfenden, 1980); for PACT Ballet *The Seven Deadly Sins* (mus. Weill, 1975); for CAPAB Ballet *Zhivago* (mus. Rimsky-Korsakov, Borodin, 1983); for London Festival Ballet *The Storm* (mus. Shostakovich, 1981), *Verdi Variations* (mus. Verdi, 1981), and *That Certain Feeling* (mus. Gershwin, 1984); for Sadler's Wells Royal Ballet *Vocalise Opus 34* (mus. Rachmaninoff, 1984); for Northern Ballet Theatre *The Nutcracker* (1981), *Brahms Love Songs* (mus. Brahms, 1983), and *Swan Lake* (1986); for London City Ballet *Romeo and Juliet* (mus. Berlioz, arr. Salzedo, 1985) and *La traviata* (mus. Verdi, arr. Woolfenden, 1989); for Pittsburgh Ballet *The Great Gatsby* (1987); for Royal Ballet of Flanders *Romeo and Juliet* (new version, 1997); and for Guangdong Ballet, *Turandot*. He was artistic director of Rome Opera Ballet (1977–8) but from 1979 he worked solely as a freelance choreographer. Later in his career a number of his works entered the repertories of the Louisville and Sarasota Ballets.

promenade In classical ballet, a slow supported turn on one foot, usually with the body held in arabesque or attitude position. The male dancer holds the hand of the ballerina (who is on pointe) and either slowly walks around her or turns her around.

Promenade Ballet in one act with choreography and libretto by de Valois, music by Haydn (arranged by E. Evans and G. Jacob), and designs by Stevenson. Premiered 25 Oct. 1943 by Sadler's Wells Ballet at the King's Theatre in Edinburgh, with G. Hamilton, P. Clayden, Fonteyn, and Paltenghi. A suite of dances linked by a single character—an elderly butterfly collector.

Prospect Before Us, The Ballet in one act with choreography and libretto by de Valois, music by William Boyce (arr. Lambert), and designs by Roger Furse. Premiered 4 Jul. 1940 by Vic-Wells Ballet, at Sadler's Wells Theatre, London, with Helpmann, C. Newman, and May. A comedy set in Georgian London, it tells of two rival theatre managers (at the King's Theatre and the Pantheon) who fight over a troupe of dancers that includes Didelot, Noverre, and Vestris. The ballet takes its title from an engraving by T. Rowlandson. It was revived by Birmingham Royal Ballet in 1998 to celebrate Dame Ninette de Valois's 100th birthday.

Pugni, Cesare (*b* Genoa, 31 May 1802; *d* St Petersburg, 26 Jan. 1870) Italian composer. It is believed he wrote more than 300 ballets, which arguably made him the most prolific ballet composer in history. He wrote his first ballet for La Scala, Milan, in 1823: *Il castello di Kenilworth* (chor. Gaetano Gioja). In 1832 he was appointed director of music at La Scala, although he left precipitately two years later (disgraced, some said, by his gambling habits). He worked in Paris for several years and in 1843 was appointed ballet composer at Her Majesty's Theatre in London where for the next seven years he worked with the choreographers Perrot, Saint-Léon, and Paul Taglioni. In 1851 he became official ballet composer in St Petersburg (probably on Perrot's recommendation). He was a hard-working journeyman composer who wrote ballet music to order, but he also had a drinking problem which left him frequently in debt. Saint-Léon records that at one point in 1869 Pugni was so impoverished that the dancers of the Imperial Ballet took up a collection to help him feed his large family. His most important collaborations were with Perrot, Saint-Léon, and Petipa. For Perrot he wrote *Ondine* (London, 1843), *La Esmeralda* (1844), *La Vivandière* (1944), *Éoline ou la dryade* (London, 1845), *Pas de quatre* (London, 1845), *Lalla Rookh, or The Rose of Lahore* (London, 1846), *Le Jugement de Pâris* (London, 1846), *Catarina ou la Fille du bandit* (London, 1846), *The Naiad and the Fisherman* (St Petersburg, 1851), *Gazelda* (St Petersburg, 1853), and *Faust* (St Petersburg, 1854). For Saint-Léon he wrote *La Fille de marbre* (Paris, 1847) and *The Humpbacked Horse* (St Petersburg, 1864). For Petipa he wrote *The Blue Dahlia* (1860), *La Fille du Pharaon* (St Petersburg, 1862), *The Beauty of Lebanon* (1863), and *Le Roi Candaule* (St Petersburg, 1868).

Puissant, Jean-Marc (*b* Grenoble, 26 Sept. 1969) French designer. He studied ballet at the Paris Opera Ballet School and Art History and Archaeology at the Sorbonne (1989–90), before performing with Birmingham Royal Ballet

(1990–94) and Stuttgart Ballet (1995–98). He then re-trained at the Motley Theatre Design course (1998–9). An elegantly original stylist, he has designed for many companies including The Royal Ballet, New York City Ballet, American Ballet Theatre, San Francisco Ballet, Nederlands Dans Theater, Dutch National Ballet, Mannheim Nationaltheater, and Rambert Dance Company. His designs for the Royal Ballet's staging of *Jewels* (2007) won an Olivier Award for best new production. He has also designed for opera and theatre.

Pulcinella Ballet in one act with choreography and libretto by Massine, music by Stravinsky, and designs by Picasso. Premiered 15 May 1920 by the Ballets Russes de Diaghilev at the Paris Opera, with Massine, Karsavina, Tchernicheva, Nemchinova, Idzikowski, Zvereff, and Cecchetti. A commedia dell'arte ballet, the libretto is based on the Neapolitan play *The Four Pulcinellas*. The unscrupulous Neapolitan lover Pulcinella is involved in a series of amorous adventures with two women, Rosetta and Prudenza, even though he has a mistress, Pimpinella. Jealous rivals appear to kill him, only to discover that his death has been a hoax. In the end, the various sets of lovers are happily reunited. Stravinsky based his score on fragments of unfinished music by the 18th-century Italian composer Pergolesi. Massine revised the ballet for a revival at La Scala, Milan, in 1971 (later revived for the City Center Joffrey Ballet in 1974). Other choreographic treatments of the ballet include those by Lopukhov (Leningrad, 1926), Jooss (Essen, 1932), Woizikowski (London, 1935), Béjart (Liège, 1957), Smuin (American Ballet Theatre, 1968), Balanchine and Robbins (New York City Ballet, 1972), Douglas Dunn (Paris Opera, 1980), Tetley (London Festival Ballet, 1984), Alston (Ballet Rambert, 1987, and Ted Brandsen (West Australia Ballet, 2001), Kim Brandstrup (Birmingham Royal Ballet, 2006), and Wheeldon (Morphoses, 2008).

Purcell, Henry (*b* London, 1659; *d* London, 21 Nov. 1695) British composer. He wrote operas, music for plays and masques, most of them choreographed by John Priest. They include *Dido and Aeneas* (1689), *The Prophetess or The History of Dioclesian* (1690), *King Arthur or The British Worthy* (1691), *The Fairy Queen* (1692), and *The Indian Queen* (1695). During the 20th and 21st centuries his music again became popular among choreographers, including Ashton, *Dances for The Fairy Queen* (Ballet Rambert, 1927), de Valois, *The Birthday of Oberon* (Vic-Wells Ballet, 1933), Tudor, *Suite of Airs* (Ballet Rambert, 1937), Helpmann, *Comus* (Sadler's Wells Ballet, 1942), and José Limón *The Moor's Pavane* (1949). A new staging of *The Fairy Queen*, with choreography by Ashton, was the first post-war opera production at Covent Garden in 1946. **Dido and Aeneas* has been an especially popular score, with many versions including Mark Morris's (Brussels, 1989), and Wayne McGregor's (Royal Ballet and Opera, 2009) among others. Morris also set *One Charming Night* (a duet in which a vampire seduces a young girl) to four songs by Purcell.

Push Modern dance work with choreography by Russell Maliphant, music by Andy Cowton, and lighting design by Michael Hulls. It was premiered on 30 Sep. 2005 at Sadler's Wells with Maliphant and Sylvie Guillem. A work characterized by hypnotic strength and beauty, it came at the start of Guillem and Maliphant's celebrated stage partnership. *Push* was also the title of the programme in which the duet appeared, and also included *Shift*, *Two*, and *Solo*, all by Maliphant. It toured widely, to international acclaim.

Push Comes To Shove Ballet in one act with choreography by Tharp, music by Haydn and Joseph Lamb (arr. David Bourne), and costumes by Santo Loquasto. Premiered 9 Jan. 1976 by American Ballet Theatre at the Uris Theater in New York, with Baryshnikov, Tcherkassky, van Hamel, Clark Tippet, and Christopher Aponte. Considered a milestone in 20th-century ballet, it married Tharp's slick modern wit and jazzy sensibility to the more rarefied sophistication of classical dance. It was made for the virtuosic talents of Mikhail Baryshnikov, who had recently defected from the Soviet Union, and it cleverly transformed him from ballet hero into bowler-hatted rogue. The score was a blend of ragtime and Haydn. It has been revived for several companies including the Paris Opera Ballet (1989), the Royal Ballet (1997), Royal Swedish Ballet (2000), and Miami City Ballet (2006).

Pushkin, Aleksandr (*b* Mikulino, 7 Sept. 1907; *d* Leningrad, 20 Mar. 1970) Soviet dancer and teacher. His early training was with Nikolai Legat. He studied at the Leningrad Ballet School, with Ponomarev and others and graduated in 1925 into the Mariinsky company, then known as GATOB, later the Kirov. He danced there until 1953, creating roles in Vainonen's *The Flames of Paris* (1932) and Zakharov's *Lost Illusions* (1936). He began teaching in 1932, and when he retired he took over the school's Class of Perfection. As a teacher he achieved legendary status, counting among his pupils at the Leningrad school Grigorovich, Nureyev, Panov, and Baryshnikov.

Pushkin ballets Works by the Russian writer Aleksandr Pushkin (1799–1837) have provided the inspiration for many ballets, especially in Russia. A list includes Glushkovsky's *Ruslan and Lyudmila* (Moscow, 1821), Didelot's *The Prisoner of the*

Caucasus (St Petersburg, 1823), Saint-Léon's *The Goldfish* (St Petersburg, 1867), F. Nijinsky's *A Victim of Jealousy* (Kiev, 1892), Lavrovsky's *The Prisoner of the Caucasus* (Leningrad, 1938), Boyarchikov's *The Queen of Spades* (1969), and Zakharov's *The Fountain of Bakhchisarai* (Leningrad, 1934), *The Aristocratic Peasant Girl* (Moscow, 1946), and *The Bronze Horseman* (Leningrad, 1949). The most famous example of a Pushkin ballet outside Russia is Cranko's *Onegin* (Stuttgart, 1965). Other Western examples include Massine's *Aleko* (New York, 1942), Skibine's *Le Prisonnier du Caucase* (Paris, 1951), Lifar's *La Dame de pique* (Monte Carlo, 1960), and Petit's *La Dame de pique* (1977).

Pygmalion ballets The story of a statue brought to life by the goddess Aphrodite has inspired a number of ballets, including those by Sallé (London, 1734), J. P. Rameau (an opera-ballet, Paris, 1748), Hilverding (St Petersburg, 1763), Angiolini (Vienna, 1776), Dauberval (London, 1784), Milon (Paris, 1800), Therese Elssler (Berlin, 1835), A. Howard (London, 1946), and V. Gsovsky (London, 1947).

quadrille A French ballroom dance for four couples which was very popular at the court of Napoleon I and which found its way into Britain in the early 19th century. The term also refers to the square formations of couples in the American Square Dance and to the position of corps de ballet dancers within the hierarchy of the Paris Opera (first and second quadrilles, two of the lowest ranks in the company).

quaternaria A 15th-century dance, very basic and consisting of just two steps which are reprised after the feet are beaten together.

Quatre Saisons, Les Ballet divertissement in one act with choreography and libretto by Perrot and music by Pugni. Premiered 13 Jun. 1848 at Her Majesty's Theatre in London, with Fanny Cerrito (Spring), Carlotta Grisi (Summer), Carolina Rosati (Autumn), and Marie Taglioni the younger (Winter). It was the fourth in the series of divertissements created by Perrot for Her Majesty's Theatre, the previous three being *Pas de quatre*, *Le Jugement de Pâris*, and *Les Éléments*. Like them, *Les Quatre Saisons* was a dancing contest between star ballerinas, whose on-stage rivalry was often matched by similar competition backstage.

Quinault, Philippe (*b* Paris, 1635; *d* Paris, 26 Nov. 1688) French poet and librettist. He was associated with the Paris Opera for 24 years. He wrote the libretto for the ballet opera *Les Fêtes de l'amour et de Bacchus* in 1672, which marked the beginning of a fourteen-year collaboration with Lully. Other ballet librettos he wrote included *Le Triomphe de l'amour* (1681) and *Le Temple de la paix* (1685).

Rábai, Miklós (*b* Békécscaba, 18 Apr. 1921; *d* Budapest, 18 Aug. 1974) Hungarian choreographer. He began collecting and arranging folk dances in 1945 and in 1949 became founding choreographer of the Hungarian State Folk Dance Ensemble, for which he produced work for the next 25 years.

Rachmaninoff, Sergei (*b* Semyonovo, Starorussky, 1 Apr. 1873; *d* Beverly Hills, Calif., 29 Mar. 1943) Russian-US composer. He wrote no ballet scores but some of his concert music has been used for dance, most frequently *Rhapsody on a Theme of Paganini*, by, among others, Fokine (Covent Garden Russian Ballet, London, 1939), Lavrovsky (Bolshoi Ballet, Moscow, 1960), and Ashton (Royal Ballet, London, 1980).

Radice, Attilia (*b* Taranto, 8 Jan. 1914; *d* Capranica, 14 Sept. 1980) Italian dancer and teacher. She studied at the La Scala Ballet School with A. Gini and Cecchetti and made her debut in the company in 1932 in Massine's *Belkis*. An elegant yet intensely expressive dancer, she was rapidly promoted to prima ballerina and in 1935 joined Rome Opera Ballet as prima ballerina assoluta. She danced there until 1957, creating roles in many works by Milloss, including *Bolero* and *The Miraculous Mandarin*, then became director of ROB's school, passing on her close knowledge of Cecchetti's method.

Radio City Music Hall New York theatre which opened as a vaudeville house but went on to present films, grand-scale musicals, dance events, ice shows, etc. It opened 27 Dec. 1932, with an auditorium seating 6,000 and one of the largest stages in the world. Martha *Graham appeared in the first night programme, and the precision dance group the *Rockettes remained one of its most popular features. It was closed for several months during 1999 for refurbishment, restoring the clean lines of its (now listed) 1930s' design.

Radunsky, Alexander (*b* Moscow, 3 Aug. 1912; *d* 27 Aug. 1982) Soviet dancer, choreographer, and teacher. Born into a family of circus clowns, his talent for mime was noted when he became a student at the Moscow Ballet School. He graduated into the Bolshoi Ballet in 1930, becoming one of its most expressive character artists. During a period when the repertoire was dominated by dramatic works his gifts were much in demand, for example as Juliet's father in Lavrovsky's *Romeo and Juliet*. He also choreographed several ballets including *The Little Stork* (chor. with Popko and Pospekhin, mus. Klebanov, 1937) and *The Little Humpbacked Horse* (mus. Shchedrin, 1960). He retired from dancing in 1962 and became chief choreographer of the Red Army Song and Dance Ensemble until 1965. He was made Merited Artist of the Russian Federation in 1958.

Rainer, Yvonne (*b* San Francisco, Calif., 24 Nov. 1934) US dancer, choreographer, and filmmaker. She studied with Graham, Cunningham, and Halprin and danced with several companies including James *Waring's. In 1962 she was a founder member of the Judson Dance Theater which gave a platform to alternative dance performances. She became an influential member of New York's *post-modern school, with its commitment to reducing dance to its basic elements and in 1965 published the notorious manifesto, which opened with the call 'NO to spectacle, no to virtuosity no to transformations and magic and make believe'. She created over 40 works, which included *Trio A* (1966), part of a longer work called *The Mind is a Muscle*, which was composed out of basic pedestrian movements like walks and somersaults, rather than technical display. In the early 1970s her works became more political, and she became increasingly interested in narrative. In 1972 she made the film *Lives of Performers* and in 1974 abandoned her career in dance to become a full-time film-maker.

RainForest Modern dance work in one act with choreography by Cunningham, music by David Tudor, and design by Andy Warhol. Premiered 9 Mar. 1968 by the Merce Cunningham Dance Company at Upton Auditorium, Buffalo, New York, with Cunningham, C. Brown, Dilley, and Solomons. Warhol's 'set' for this work is a number of helium-filled balloons that are allowed to bob freely around the stage. It was revived by Rambert Dance Company in 2010.

Rainoldi, Paolo (*b* Milan, 18 Apr. 1781 or 1784; *d* Prague, 1 Jan. 1853) Italian dancer, choreographer, and ballet master. He studied with Francesco Sedini after which he danced with F. Taglioni and S. Gallet in Vienna. He was renowned for his parody of Duport in *Flore et Zéphire*. He later taught in Prague (1840–6) and his own account of his experiences in the dancing profession is preserved in Vienna's Municipal Library.

Raise the Red Lantern Ballet in three acts with direction by Zhang Yimou, choreography by Wang Xinpeng and Wang Yuanyuan, music by Chen Qigang, designs by Zeng Li (sets) and Jérome Kaplan (costumes). Premiered by the National Ballet of China at Tianqiao Theatre, Beijing on 2 May 2001 with Zhu Yan, Zhang Jian, and Wang Qimin. Based on Zhang Yimou's 1991 film of the same title, it tells the story of a young woman in 1930s China who is forced to become the concubine of a wealthy mandarin. Meeting with her childhood lover she is spied upon by her master's first concubine. The latter's betrayal brings about a sentence of death for both women, but their shared moment of forgiveness offers an image of love and reconciliation surviving the evils of oppression. With its stylistic mix of Western dance and classical Peking opera, the ballet became one of the National Ballet of China's most popular works, nationally and internationally.

Rake's Progress, The Ballet in one act with choreography by de Valois, music and libretto by Gavin Gordon, and design by Rex Whistler. Premiered 20 May 1935 by the Vic-Wells Ballet at Sadler's Wells Theatre, London, with Gore and Markova. Its six scenes are based on the series of Hogarth paintings (hung in London's Sir John Soane's Museum) which depict the moral downfall of their feckless hero. It is regarded as one of the first 'English' ballets to be choreographed in the 20th century, not only because of the nationality of its collaborators and the source of its subject matter but because of its vividly delineated, almost literary, characterizations. It has since been revived by Sadler's Wells Ballet and the Royal Ballet; also by Munich State Opera Ballet (1956), Ballet of Flanders (1972), and Zurich Ballet (1976).

Ralov, Børge (orig. Petersen; *b* Copenhagen, 1908; *d* Copenhagen, 17 Dec. 1981) Danish dancer, teacher, and choreographer. He studied at the Royal Danish Ballet School and graduated into the Royal Danish Ballet in 1927, becoming soloist (principal) 1933, and first soloist (1942–57). He was Margot Lander's regular partner and was specially admired in *Petrushka* and *Napoli*. He

became an instructor with the RDB in 1934 and later teacher at the RDB School and also choreographed several ballets, such as *Widow in the Mirror* (mus. B. Christensen, 1934), most of which starred his wife, Kirsten Ralov.

Ralov, Kirsten (*née* Gnatt; *b* Baden, Austria, 26 Mar. 1922; *d* Copenhagen, 30 May 1999) Danish dancer and director. She studied at the Royal Danish Ballet School making her stage debut as a child in 1933 and joining the Royal Danish Ballet in 1940. A vivacious, musical dancer, she was one of the finest exponents of the Bournonville style of her era. After retiring from the stage in 1962 she travelled the world producing Bournonville ballets and was associate director of the RDB (1978–88). She also choreographed several ballets, including *The Door* (mus. Bentzon, for RDB, 1962). She was married to the dancer Borge Ralov and then to the dancer Fredbjørn Bjørnsson. In 1953 she was made Knight of Dannebrog (elevated to First Grade in 1978) and in 1981 she was accepted into the Icelandic Order of the Falcon. She wrote *The Bournonville School* (1978).

Rambert, (Dame) Marie (orig. Cyvia Rambam, then Miriam Ramberg; *b* Warsaw, 20 Feb. 1888; *d* London, 12 Jun. 1982) Polish-British dancer, teacher, and ballet director, founder of the first British ballet company. After being inspired by a performance of Isadora Duncan she began working with Raymond Duncan in Paris and taking basic ballet classes. In 1910 she studied with Jaques-Dalcroze in Geneva and worked as his assistant until 1912 when Diaghilev engaged her to assist Nijinsky and his dancers with the complex rhythms of Stravinsky's score for *Rite of Spring* (1913). She stayed with Diaghilev's Ballets Russes for a season as dancer in the corps and studying with Cecchetti, before moving to London in 1914 where she studied further with Astafieva, and gave dance recitals. In 1918 she married the dramatist Ashley Dukes and in 1920 opened her own ballet school. From this emerged the small performing group, Marie Rambert Dancers, in 1926, which became Ballet Club in 1931 and Ballet Rambert in 1935. An inspired talent spotter and legendary bully, Rambert nurtured many of Britain's most important choreographers, including Ashton, Tudor, Howard, Staff, Gore, Morrice, and Cranko. Her school also produced many renowned dancers such as Argyle, Gould, Lloyd, Franca, Gilmour, Aldous, and Turner. Though her company was often run on a shoestring its productions reflected her wit, taste, and sharp instinct for trends. She published her autobiography, *Quicksilver*, in London in 1972 and was made Chevalier de la Légion d'honneur in 1957 and DBE in 1962.

Rambert Dance Company Britain's oldest dance company, founded by Marie Rambert. It grew out of performances given by the London ballet school which she opened in 1920. From 1931 the troupe was based at London's Mercury Theatre, under the name Ballet Club; from 1935 it was known as the Ballet Rambert, giving joint performances with the London Ballet at the Arts Theatre Club (1940–1). In 1943 it was reorganized as a national touring company with public funding. Early choreographers included Frederick Ashton, who created *A Tragedy of Fashion* (1926), *Capriol Suite* (1930), and *Façade* (1931) for the company; Antony Tudor who created *Jardin aux lilas* (1936) and *Dark Elegies* (1937); Andrée Howard who created *Lady into Fox* (1939); Walter Gore who created *Simple Symphony* (1944); and Frank Staff who created *Peter and the Wolf* and *Enigma Variations* (1940). The company's leading dancers included Pearl Argyle, Diana Gould, Maude Lloyd, Hugh Laing, and Harold Turner. Alicia Markova was ballerina at the Ballet Club for four years.

After the war the company staged its first full-length classic, *Giselle* (1946), and during the 1950s, in response to changes in public taste, it was increasingly forced to tour small-scale productions of 19th-century ballets rather than new work. In 1966 under the direction of Norman *Morrice, the company abandoned its classical roots and became a small-scale modern dance troupe, eventually altering its name in 1987 to Rambert Dance Company to reflect its change of style. Since then Rambert has produced many important new choreographers and works. In the 1960s it reflected the Graham-based aesthetic of choreographers like Glen Tetley who mounted several ballets including *Ricercare* and *Pierrot Lunaire* on the company as well as making new works including *Embrace Tiger and Return to Mountain* (1968). Under the direction of Robert *North (1981–6), works by Merce Cunningham and Paul Taylor were added to the company's increasingly eclectic repertoire. Richard *Alston, resident choreographer with the company from 1984, consolidated the Cunningham influence when he became artistic director in 1986 as well as contributing many important works of his own, such as *Wildlife* (1984). Christopher *Bruce, who had been dancer and later associate choreographer with Rambert (1963–84), and whose early works for the company included *Ghost Dances* (1981), became its new artistic director in 1994, relaunching an expanded company with a repertoire of international neo-classical and modern works, such as Kylián's *Petite mort*, and his own, including *Four Seasons* (1998) and *God's Plenty* (1999). He also nurtured the choreography of company members such as Rafael Bonachela. He was succeeded by Mark *Baldwin in 2002 who has further expanded the repertory, with works by

himself, De Frutos, Armitage, André Gingras, and others; revivals of earlier works by Bruce, Davis, and others, and a partial reconstruction of Howard's *Lady into Fox*. The official school, which was founded in 1920, became the Ballet Rambert School, based at the Mercury Theatre. Rambert Academy, which was set up in conjunction with London Institute of Higher Education in 1979, merged with Rambert School in 1982.

(((●))) SEE WEB LINKS
• Rambert Dance Company website

Rameau, Jean-Philippe (*b* Dijon, baptized 25 Sept. 1683; *d* Paris, 12 Sept. 1764) French composer who wrote many opera ballets at a time when professional dancers were beginning to take over from courtly amateurs. Working in the new 'style galant' which was replacing the more formal baroque style of Lully, his music used bold harmonies, strong rhythms, and orchestral colour to animate both the choreography and the plot, and thus helped to lay the foundations of modern ballet. His works include *Les Indes galantes* (1734), *Castor et Pollux* (1737), and *Platée* (1745). Many were choreographed by Cahusac and by Sallé.

Rameau, Pierre (*b* Cirea, 1674; *d* Nanterre, 26 Jan. 1748) French dancer, ballet master, and theorist, whose books are a crucial source of our knowledge of 18th-century dance. He danced at the Lyon Opera (1703–5) and possibly at the Paris Opera (c.1710–13) and was dancing master to the pages of the Queen of Spain. He was later dancing master in the house of Louise Élisabeth de Montpensier (second dowager Queen of Spain). In 1725 he published *Le Maître à danser* in Paris which became the standard dance handbook of the age, including detailed descriptions of the floor patterns, steps, and structure of many social dances as well as their style of execution. These, invaluably, flesh out the rather basic dance notations which have survived from the period, written in the Beauchamps/Feuillet system. Six months later he published his own modification of that system in *Abrégé de la nouvelle méthode de l'art d'écrire ou de tracer toutes sortes de danses de ville*, although this book had much less public success. An English edition of *The Dancing Master* was translated and published by C. W. Beaumont (London, 1931).

Ramos, Yosvani (*b* Camaguey, Cuba, 23 Jun. 1979) Cuban dancer. He trained at the Vocational School of Arts and the National Ballet School (1994–97) in Havana and danced with Jeune Ballet de France and the Paris Opera Ballet after winning the Gold Medal at the Paris International Ballet Competition in 1998. He then joined English National Ballet in 1999, becoming principal from 2003 and performing a wide range of leading roles. He joined Australian Ballet as a principal in 2008.

Randazzo, Peter (*b* New York, 2 Jan. 1942) US-Canadian dancer, choreographer, and director. He studied at the Graham school and danced with her company from 1960 to 1967, also guesting with other companies, including Limón and American Dance Theatre. In 1967 he created his first work, for the New Dance Group of Canada, and in 1968 he co-founded, with David Earle and Patricia Beatty, the *Toronto Dance Theatre. A charismatic performer, he also created many works for the company, developing a highly physical and technically demanding style. From the late 1980s he pursued a freelance career.

Rao, Shanta (*b* Mangalore, 1930) Indian dancer. She studied kathakali with Ravunni Menon, mohini attam with Shri Pannikar, and dasi attam with Minakshisundaram Pillai. Her stylistic range and controversial dance personality helped revive interest in classical dance in her native India while her world-wide tours attracted international interest.

raqs sharqi (Eastern dance) The dominant solo dance form of Egypt. Rooted in pre-Islamic times it has always been taught within the family and performed on celebratory occasions but in the 10th- and 11th-century Islamic courts and 18th-century Ottoman courts it took on a more refined classical style. Characterized by sinuous, rhythmic hip movements and undulating arms, its debased form, belly dancing, has been popular in cabarets from the 19th century onwards. Since the mid-1970s there has been an international revival of interest in the traditional forms among both professional and amateur dancers.

Rassine, Alexis (orig. Rays; *b* Kaunas, 26 Jul. 1919; *d* Crawley, 25 Jul. 1992) Lithuanian-British dancer. He moved to Cape Town aged 10 and studied there with Helen Webb, moving to Paris aged 17 to study with Preobrajenska and others. He made his debut in the revue *Bal Tabarin*. In 1939 he moved to London where he danced with various companies including the Anglo-Polish Ballet (1940) and Sadler's Wells Ballet (1942–55). Performing as a danseur noble when most British male dancers were on war service he created roles in several works including Helpmann's *Hamlet* (1942) and *Miracle in the Gorbals* (1944), Ashton's *The Quest* (1943) and *Homage to the Queen* (1953), and de Valois's *Don Quixote* (1950). He was a frequent partner of Nerina and toured S. Africa with her in 1952 and 1955. He also danced briefly for Gore's London Ballet. In 1976 he opened his own school.

Ratmansky, Alexei (*b* St Petersburg, 27 Aug. 1968) Russian dancer, choreographer, and director. He studied at the Bolshoi Ballet School and danced in Kiev and Winnipeg before joining the Royal Danish Ballet in 1997 as soloist and promoted to principal in 2000. He began choreographing soon after graduating and one of his first ballets, *Baiser de La Fée*, was created for Kiev in 1994. He also created *Poème de l'Extase* for the Kirov in 1998. While at RDB he created a version of *The Nutcracker* (2001) which rapidly led to further commissions, including *Cinderella* for the Kirov (2002), *Firebird* for Royal Swedish Ballet (2002), and a new version of Lopukhov's *The Bright Stream* for the Bolshoi (2003). Ratmansky's choreography is rooted in the classical style but its approach to character, imagery, and narrative is distinctively contemporary. In 2004 he was appointed director of the Bolshoi and oversaw a programme of revitalization. He opened up the repertory with works by Tharp, Wheeldon, Balanchine, Possokhov, and himself and consolidated its revivals of the Soviet repertory with his own reconstructions of the *Bolt* (2005) and *Flames of Paris* (2008). An additional act of reclamation was his reconstruction of Petipa's 1899 staging of *Le Corsaire*, in 2007. He also encouraged a younger generation of dancers, including Natalia Osipova. His reforms met with some resistance, however, especially from dancers still wedded to the Bolshoi's Grigorovich legacy and in 2007 he stepped down from the post of artistic director, while retaining his position as resident choreographer. In 2009 he became resident choreographer of American Ballet Theatre, his first work for the company was *On the Dnieper* (mus. Prokofiev, 2009). He has additionally choreographed works for New York City Ballet, including *Middle Duet* (mus. Yuri Hanon, 2006), *Russian Seasons* (mus. Leonid Desyatnikov, 2006), *Concerto DSCH* (mus. Shostakovich, 2008) and *Namouna* (2010). His works for other companies include *Carnival of the Animals* (2003) for San Francisco Ballet; *Bizet Variations* (2007) for State Ballet of Georgia; a new version of *Pierrot Lunaire* (2008) for Diana *Vishneva; and a new version of *The Little Humpbacked Horse* for the Mariinsky Ballet (2009).

Rauschenberg, Robert (*b* Port Arthur, Tex., 22 Oct. 1925; *d* Florida, 12 May 2008) US painter and designer. His work in multi-media and assemblage displayed an aesthetic similar to Cunningham and he created many designs for the latter, including *Antic Meet*, *Summerspace* (both 1958), and *Winterbranch* (1964). He also worked with Paul Taylor on *Three Epitaphs* (1956) and *Tracer* (1962), among others, and with Trisha Brown on *Set and Reset* (1983) and *Astral Convertible* (1989).

Ravel, Maurice (*b* Ciboure, 7 Mar. 1875; *d* Paris, 28 Dec. 1937) French composer. He wrote several ballet scores, whose inventive orchestration, sensuous melodies, and metrical flexibility offer rich challenges to choreographers. His first was *Ma Mère l'oye* (expanded from an original piano piece) which was choreographed by Staats for the Théâtre des Arts, Paris, 1912. In the same year he completed *Daphnis and Chloe* (chor. Fokine for Diaghilev's Ballets Russes, Paris 1912). Later scores were *La Valse* (commissioned by Diaghilev in 1920, chor. Nijinska, Monte Carlo, 1929) and *Boléro* (chor. Nijinska, Rubinstein Company, Paris, 1928). He also contributed to the score *L'Éventail de Jeanne* (Paris, 1928). His lyric fantasy *L'Enfant et les sortilèges* (libr. Colette, 1925) was first choreographed by Balanchine and subsequently by Charrat (1964) and Kylián (1984), among others. Later versions of *Daphnis and Chloe* include Ashton (1951), Cranko (1962), and Tetley (1975); other versions of *La Valse* include Fokine (1935), Gsovsky (1951), Balanchine (1951), Ashton (1958), and De Frutos (2009), and other versions of *Bolero* include Fokine (1935), Lifar (1941), Béjart (1961), Lavrovsky (1964), and Ratmansky (2004). Other concert music which has been used for dance includes *Pavane pour une infante défunte* (chor. Bolm, 1928, Ashton, 1933, Lifar, 1944, R. North, 1967, Wheeldon, 1996, and Possukhov, (2002) among others); *Valses nobles et sentimentales* (chor. Ashton, 1947, MacMillan, 1966, and van Manen, 1975); the Piano Concerto in G (chor. Robbins, 1975, and MacMillan, as *Fin du jour*, 1979); and the *Introduction and Allegro for Harp* (chor. Robbins, 1975, and M. Baldwin, as *Samples*, 1995), His *Shéhérazade* is occasionally used (as distinct from the more popular Rimsky-Korsakov score). Cranko set his *Beauty and the Beast* (1949) to Ravel's *Mother Goose* suite. In 1975 New York City Ballet presented three programmes of ballets to his music in an 'Hommage à Ravel' and in Dec. 1998 Lyon Opera Ballet premiered three new works to his music, Meryl Tankard's *Bolero*, Lionel Hoche's *Origami de la chair* (*Le Tombeau de Couperin*), and Alessio Silvestrin's *Perspective depuis les ruines* (*Concerto en sol*).

Raymonda Ballet in three acts with choreography by Petipa, libretto by Petipa and Lydia Pashkova, music by Glazunov, sets by O. Allegri, K. Ivanov, and P. Lambin, and costumes by E. Ofizerova and I. Kaffi. Premiered 19 Jan. 1898 at the Mariinsky Theatre with Legnani, S. Legat, and Gerdt. The ballet is set in the time of the Crusades and tells the story of Raymonda, a beautiful noblewoman who is engaged to marry the Crusader Jean de Brienne. During her lover's absence the Saracen knight Abderakhman attempts to abduct her, but she is saved by the intervention of a protecting spirit, the White Lady, whereupon Brienne returns to slay his rival. The lovers' joyful marriage is celebrated by a lavish Hungarian divertissement. The ballet's slender storyline (which has been further whittled down over the decades) is little more than a vehicle for Petipa's choreographic invention and for the ballerina's technique (displayed in several exquisite variations). It is regarded as Petipa's last true masterpiece and has been constantly revived in Russia. It was kept unchanged in the Kirov repertoire until 1938 when Vainonen staged a new version with a revised libretto by himself and Slominsky. In 1948 Sergeyev staged a version which reverted to a close approximation of Petipa. The Bolshoi danced their first production in 1900 and in 1908 showed a brand-new version by Gorsky. Lavrovsky staged a later revival (1945) with much of Petipa's choreography restored. In the West, Petipa's ballet has appeared in many different forms. The Grand Pas hongrois (Act III) formed part of an evening of divertissements danced by Diaghilev's Ballets Russes in Paris (1909) and Pavlova presented a two-act version of the ballet staged by Ivan Clustine in New York (1914). The complete ballet was danced in Nicholas Zvereff's staging for the National Opera Ballet of Lithuania in London (1935) while the first US production was a shortened re-creation of Petipa's work by Danilova and Balanchine for the Ballet Russe de Monte Carlo (New York, 1946). Nureyev staged a complete version in 1964 for the Royal Ballet Touring Company at the Spoleto Festival although only Act III remained in the permanent repertoire. Nureyev subsequently re-staged the complete production for Australian Ballet (1965), Zurich Opera Ballet (1972), and for American Ballet Theatre (1975). Berlin Opera Ballet also staged the complete ballet in a production by T. Gsovsky (Acts I and II) and Beriozoff (Act III). Balanchine choreographed his own ballet, *Pas de dix*, to the music from the Grand Pas hongrois (1955), later developed into *Cortège hongrois* (1973), and also *Raymonda Variations* (to other extracts from Glazunov's score) in 1961.

Read, John B. British lighting designer. He has worked for many dance companies including the Royal Ballet, Birmingham Royal Ballet, Scottish Ballet, English National Ballet, Nederlands Dans Theater, Dutch National Ballet, Rambert Dance Company, and London Contemporary Dance Theatre. As lighting consultant to the Royal Ballet he has been influential in Britain in establishing lighting as an integral part of dance presentation.

Reade, Paul (*b* Lancashire, 1943; *d* 7 Jun. 1997) British composer. He studied at the Royal Academy of Music then worked as repetiteur with English National Opera. He has written the score for several ballets including Bintley's *Hobson's Choice* (1989) and *Far from the Madding Crowd* (1996).

Red Detachment of Women, The The first Chinese 'Revolutionary Model Ballet' with choreography by Li Cheng-xiang, Jiang Zu-hui, and Wung Xi-xian, music by Wu Zu-qiang and Du Ming-xin, and design by Ma Yun-hong. Premiered in Peking (now Beijing) 1 Oct. 1964 by the China Ballet Troupe (later the Central Ballet of China) with Bai Shu-xiang and Liu Qing-tang. The plot is taken from the opera of the same name and is set during the civil war of 1927–37. It tells the story of a peasant girl, Wu Qing-hua, who lives on Hainan Island in S. China and is liberated from her tyrant master by the leader of the Red Army which is stationed on the island. She joins the Red Detachment of Women and becomes a heroic fighter, finally taking over the position of commander. The ballet was choreographed just prior to the Cultural Revolution and its mix of Western ballet, folk and classical Chinese dance, and contemporary political message made it a model for the new Chinese ballet. During the Cultural Revolution it was one of the few dance works permitted on stage but it did serve to encourage a mass interest in ballet. It was filmed in 1970 and revived for the Matsuyama Ballet (Tokyo) in 1973. Performances of the entire ballet were banned in China during the backlash against the Cultural Revolution, but it regained favour in the late 1990s.

Red Flower, The *See* RED POPPY, THE.

Red Poppy, The (orig. Russ. title *Krasny mak*) Ballet in three acts with choreography by Lev Lashchilin and Tikhomirov, libretto and design by Mikhail Kurilko, and music by Reinhold Glière. Premiered 14 Jun. 1927 by the Bolshoi Ballet, Moscow, with Geltser and Tikhomirov. It is an early example of *Socialist Realism, created to fulfil State demands for populist and politically correct art. Set in China of the 1920s it tells the story of a dancer, Tao Hoa, who is exploited by a vicious manager and falls in love with the captain of a Soviet ship. She intercepts the bullet with which her manager tries to kill her lover and the red poppy which she gives to a little Chinese girl as she dies becomes a symbol of liberation—both for the Chinese people and their Soviet comrades. The ballet's attempted fusion of revolutionary good intentions, vernacular dance, and old-fashioned classical ballet prompted the critic Alexander Tcherepnin to mock 'You don't make a statue of a Red Army officer out of whipped cream'. However, it was frequently revived in the USSR (after 1957 re-named *The Red Flower*, to avoid any association with opium). New versions include Lopukhov (GATOB, 1929), Zakharov (Kirov Ballet) and Lavrovsky (Bolshoi, both 1949). A shortened

version was choreographed by Schwezoff for Ballet Russe de Monte Carlo in 1943.

Red Shoes, The Film by Michael Powell and Emeric Pressburger which created a huge popular interest in ballet around the world when it was first shown in 1948. It stars Moira Shearer (who was then dancer with the Royal Ballet) and is a dramatic portrait of the backstage life and loves of a ballet company that was roughly modelled on Diaghilev's Ballets Russes. The extended ballet sequence which forms part of the film is based on Hans Christian Andersen's tale 'The Red Shoes' and was choreographed by Robert Helpmann. The 1993 Broadway musical based on the film was a flop, although the ballet sequence, choreographed by Lar Lubovitch, was taken into the repertoire of American Ballet Theatre.

Red Whirlwind, The (orig. Russ. title *Krasny vikhr*) Ballet in two 'Processes' with choreography by Lopukhov, music by V. Deshenov, and design by K. Tshupiatov. Premiered 29 Oct. 1924 by GATOB, Leningrad, with Victor Semenov and Gerdt. Its fusion of speech, song, acrobatics, and dance was conceived as an allegory of the events of the October Revolution. It was attacked as an example of Proletkult (Proletarian Culture) and only performed twice.

Reed, Janet (*b* Tolo, Oreg., 15 Sept. 1916; *d* Seattle, 28 Feb. 2000) US dancer. She studied with W. Christensen, Balanchine, and Tudor and danced with Christensen's ballet company before joining San Francisco Opera Ballet (later San Francisco Ballet) in 1937. She was subsequently appointed principal, and danced Odile in the first American full-length production of *Swan Lake* (1940). In 1942 she performed with Eugene Loring's Dance Players and between 1943 and 1946 was ballerina with Ballet Theatre (later American Ballet Theatre), creating roles in Robbins's *Fancy Free* (1944) and *Interplay* (1945). After a brief stint on Broadway she was principal dancer with New York City Ballet from 1949 to 1960 (with periods of semi-retirement). A versatile dance actress, she created roles in Balanchine's *Bourrée fantasque* (1949) and *Western Symphony* (1954), Robbins's *Pied Piper* (1951) and *Ballade* (1952), and in the 1953 revival of Lew Christensen's *Filling Station*, among others. She was ballet mistress of NYCB (1959–64) and continued to teach after retirement.

reel Old British dance in 2/4 or 6/8 time, performed by two or more couples. It spread from Britain to many of its colonies and to parts of Scandinavia, and for a time it was the most common dance in these areas. It was first documented in the 17th century but dates back earlier.

Reich, Steve (*b* New York, 1936) US minimalist composer whose rhythmically repetitive and distinctively scored works have made him one of the most popular composers for dance in the late 20th and early 21st centuries. Among the numerous works created to his music are Laura Dean's *Drumming* (1975), de Keersmaeker's *Fase* (1982), *Rain* (2001), *Drumming—Part 1* (1997), and *Eight Lines* (2007), Eliot Feld's *Grand Canyon* (1984), Lucinda Child's *Cascade* (1984), Siobhan Davies's *Different Trains* (1990), and *Rain* (2001), McGregor's *PreSentient* (2002), J. Inger's *Phases* (2003), and *Within Now* (2004).

Reinholm, Gert (orig. Schmidt; *b* Chemnitz, 20 Dec. 1926; *d* Berlin, 15 Dec. 2005) German dancer, teacher, and director. He studied at the Berlin Staatsoper Ballet School and with T. Gsovsky, and made his debut in 1942 with the Berlin Staatsoper, becoming soloist (1946). He was principal dancer at the Buenos Aires Teatro Colón (1951–3) after which he returned to Berlin as soloist with the Municipal Opera Ballet (later Berlin Opera Ballet). In 1955 he formed the Berlin Ballet with T. Gsovsky and frequently toured with the company until the mid-1960s. A dancer of considerable sensitivity and classical style, he created roles in many ballets by Gsovsky including *Hamlet* (1953), *The Moor of Venice* (1956), and *Tristan* (1965). In 1961 he was appointed director of the newly expanded Berlin Opera Ballet bringing in many outside dancers and choreographers to broaden the company's range. He remained there as MacMillan's administrator after the latter became director in 1966 and again directed the company from 1972 to 1990. In 1967 he established his own school, the Berlin Ballet Academy where he continued to teach. He was awarded the Cross of Merit of the German Federal Republic in 1987.

Reinking, Ann (*b* Seattle, 10 Nov. 1949) US dancer, choreographer, and director. She studied ballet locally, at San Francisco Ballet School and with Joffrey, making her debut with the corps de ballet at Radio City Music Hall. She then worked as a dancer, singer, and actress on Broadway (excelling in the choreography of her mentor and partner Fosse). She appeared in the original run of *Chicago* and in television and film, including *All that Jazz* (1979). In the late 1980s she began to choreograph, starring in and choreographing the Broadway revival of *Chicago* (1996), for which she won a Tony Award for Best Choreography, and co-directing and co-choreographing *Fosse* (1999). She has also choreographed works for Joffrey Ballet of Chicago, Connecticut Ballet Theatre, Pacific Northwest Ballet, and Ballet Hispanico (*Ritmo y ruido*). In the 1990s she also became director of the Broadway

Theatre Project, training young people in musical theatre skills.

Reisinger, Julius Wenzel (*b* Prague, 14 Dec. 1828; *d* Berlin, 1892) Austrian choreographer who created the first, short-lived *Swan Lake* to Tchaikovsky's score (Moscow, 1877). His first significant professional engagement was ballet master at Leipzig (1864–72) after which he was invited to Moscow in 1871 to choreograph *Cinderella or The Magic Slipper* (mus. Wilhelm Mühldörfer). He was ballet master at the Bolshoi Theatre (1873–8) during which time he staged several ballets by P. Taglioni. After leaving he returned to Prague where he was ballet master at the National Theatre for the 1883/4 season.

Reiter-Soffer, Domy (*b* Tel Aviv, 24 Oct. 1950) Israeli dancer, choreographer, and designer. He studied with Sokolow, and others and in 1959 joined Israeli Opera Ballet. He then danced in Ireland (1962–4), moving to London in 1964 where he danced with London Dance Theatre and acted at the Royal Court, then danced with Western and Scottish Theatre Ballets (1966–70) before moving to the Irish National Ballet Company where he was artistic adviser and choreographer between 1974 and 1989. His works include *Women* (mus. Boulez, Irish National Ballet, 1974), *Equus* (mus. Wilfred Josephs, Maryland Ballet, 1980, revived Dance Theatre of Harlem, 1981, Australian Ballet, 1984, and others), *The Emperor and the Nightingale* (mus. Tang, Hong Kong Ballet, 1997), *Beauty and the Beast* (mus. Man-yee Lam, Hong Kong Ballet, 1999, revived for several companies), and *Turn of the Screw* (mus. John McCabe, Ohio Ballet, 2005). He has also directed plays, choreographed for opera and television, created the designs for numerous dance and theatre productions and exhibited widely as a painter.

Reitz, Dana (*b* Rochester, NY, 19 Oct. 1948) US dancer and choreographer. She trained in both Eastern and Western dance styles, studied with Cunningham and danced briefly with Twyla Tharp and Laura Dean. She also appeared in Robert Wilson's production of Philip Glass's opera, *Einstein on the Beach* (1976). She has since worked primarily as a solo improviser, her subtle movements playing with precise, often unexpected shifts of weight and tempo. Her style is hypnotic in flow, and wittily idiosyncratic in gesture. She has collaborated extensively with lighting designers, especially Jennifer *Tipton, for example on the duet *Necessary Weather* (1993) which she created and performed with Sara *Rudner. She has also worked closely with Baryshnikov, creating the solo *Unspoken Territory* for him in 1994 and performing the duet *Meeting Place* with him in 1996. Her recent works include *Some Chamber Pieces* (2001) and *Sea Walk* (2005).

Relâche Dadaist dance event, defined in full as an 'instantaneous ballet in two acts, a cinematographic entr'acte and a *queue de chien*', with choreography by Börlin, music by Satie, libretto and design by Picabia, and film by René Clair. Premiered 4 Dec. 1924 by Les Ballets Suédois at the Théâtre des Champs-Elysées with Bonsdorff, Börlin, and K. Smith. The title of this Dadaist ballet means 'cancelled performance', and at its premiere it achieved its desired aim—to scandalize the bourgeois press. Its cast features a fireman and nine men in their underwear, the choreography contains no recognizable classical dance; the design consists of rows of headlamps which brighten and dim, and the music features the sound of motor cars. Among the work's apparently random sequence of events is a tableau of two artists (originally Man Ray and Marcel Duchamp) playing chess, and a mock funeral (of Börlin) which turns into a chase when the hearse runs away. Between the acts Clair's film *Entr'acte* is screened—the first to be used in a ballet. It was revived by Moses Pendleton for Joffrey Ballet in 1980.

relevé [Fr., lifted] A rise from flat foot to half or full point, which may be executed smoothly or with a slight spring.

Renard, Le (orig. Russ. title *Baika*) Dance theatre work in one act with text and music by Stravinsky, choreography by Nijinska, and design by Larionov. Premiered 18 May 1922 by Diaghilev's Ballets Russes at the Paris Opera with Nijinska, Idzikowski, Javinsky, and Federov, Ansermet conducting. This farmyard fable for the stage is based on Russian tales about a fox, cock, cat, and goat. Later productions include Lifar (Ballets Russes, 1929), Balanchine (Ballet Society, 1947), Béjart (Paris Opera, 1965), Amodio (Aterballetto, 1982), and A. Page (Royal Ballet, 1994).

Renault, Michel (*b* Paris, 15 Dec. 1927; *d* Paris, 29 Jan. 1993) French dancer and teacher. He studied at the Paris Opera Ballet School and joined the Paris Opera Ballet in 1944 becoming the company's youngest ever étoile in 1946. A dancer of enormous strength, suppleness, and verve he was also an expressive dance actor. He created roles in many ballets including Balanchine's *Palais de cristal*, later *Symphony in C* (1947), Lifar's *Nautéos* (1954) and *Romeo and Juliet* (1955), and Cranko's *La Belle Hélène* (1955). In 1957 he toured Russia to great acclaim—the first major French dance personality to be invited there since Petipa. He left the Opera in 1959 and worked as a freelance choreographer for musicals, revues, and television, teaching at

the POB School (1982–90). His many awards include Chevalier de la Légion d'honneur (1975) and Prix Renaissance Descartes, Paris (1991).

Rendezvous, Le Ballet in one act with choreography by Petit, libretto by Prévost, music by J. Kosma, photos by Brassaï, and a backdrop by Picasso. Premiered in 1945 by Ballets des Champs-Elysées at Théâtre Sarah Bernhardt, Paris, with Petit and Babilée. It is a stylish evocation of Parisian street life.

Rendezvous, Les Ballet in one act with choreography by Ashton, music by Auber (from the opera *L'Enfant prodigue*, arr. Lambert), and design by Chappell. Premiered 5 Dec. 1933 by Vic-Wells Ballet at Sadler's Wells Theatre, London, with Markova, Idzikowski, de Valois, S. Judson, and Helpmann. This witty, lighthearted series of divertissements shows a group of young men and women meeting in a park and its technical brio, musicality, and above all its expression of dance for dance's sake marked a significant stage in the evolution of Ashton's personal classical style. It has undergone several revisions (the last *c.*1947) and has been revived for several companies including National Ballet of Canada (1956) and American Ballet Theatre (1980). It was filmed for the BBC in 1962 and revived by the Royal Ballet in 2000 with new designs by Antony Ward.

Rennie Harris Puremovement (RHPM) Philadelphia-based hip-hop company. It was founded in 1992 by Harris (*b* N. Philadelphia, 1963) in order to develop hip-hop as a theatrical form, communicating narratives and ideas and moving beyond the dance form's original male, competitive image. In the Bessie Award-winning *Rome and Jewels* (2000) Harris updated Shakespeare's tragedy to a scenario of inner-city gang warfare; in *Facing Mekka* (mus. Darrin M Ross, 2003) women dancers were featured strongly in the cast, with Harris's choreography deconstructing the language of hip-hop and combining it with other dance influences. Recent works include *Something to do with Love* (2006). The company tours widely in the US and Europe and also organizes an extensive network of classes and workshops.

((⊕)) SEE WEB LINKS
- Website for RHPM

renversé [Fr., overturned] A bending of the body, performed during a turning step. It creates the dizzying illusion that the dancer is momentarily off balance.

Requiem Ballet in one act with choreography by MacMillan, music by Fauré, and design by Yolanda Sonnabend. Premiered 28 Nov. 1976 by the Stuttgart Ballet with Haydée, Keil, Cragun, Madsen, and Andersen. This setting of Fauré's 1886/7 score is dedicated to the memory of Cranko and employs a large cast of dancers to explore the music's subtle delineations of sorrow. It was re-staged by MacMillan for the Royal Ballet in 1983. Russillo and Casado also choreographed Fauré's score in the same year.

Requiem Canticles Ballet in one act with choreography by Robbins, music by Stravinsky, and lighting by R. Bates. Premiered 25 Jun. 1972 by New York City Ballet at the State Theater, New York, with M. Ashley, S. Hendl, B. Wells, and R. Maiorano. This abstract setting of Stravinsky's 1966 score was later revived for the Royal Ballet (1972) and Munich State Opera Ballet (1974). Balanchine also choreographed a ballet to the same score in 1968, dedicating one performance to the memory of Martin Luther King.

Return to the Strange Land Ballet in one act with choreography and design by Kylián and music by Janáček. Premiered 17 May 1975 by Stuttgart Ballet, Stuttgart. It originated as a pas de trois, created for the Stuttgart Ballet in 1974 soon after Cranko's death. The 'Strange Land' of the title is the place we come from and to which we return after death. Its expanded version featured a lyrical series of duets and trios displaying the inventive, sculptural plastique which became Kylián's hallmark. It remains one of Kylián's most popular works and has been revived for many companies including the Royal Ballet (1984) and Joffrey Ballet.

Revelations Modern dance work in one act with choreography by Ailey, a score based on traditional black religious music (spirituals, Holy blues, etc.) arr. Howard Roberts, and design by Ves Harper. Premiered 31 Jan. 1960 by the Alvin Ailey Dance Theater at the YM-YWHA, New York. It charts man's spiritual journey from baptism through religious despair to joyous salvation in a dance language that is boldly physical and theatrical. It has become the signature work of Alvin Ailey's American Dance Theater and was performed at the company's 40th anniversary celebrations in 1998 with Judith *Jamison making her conducting debut.

révérence [Fr., curtsey] The formal bow or curtsey, performed by dancers at the end of a class or performance.

Rhapsody Ballet in one act with choreography and set by Ashton, music by Rachmaninoff, and costumes by William Chappell. Premiered 4 Aug. 1980 by the Royal Ballet at Covent Garden, London, with Baryshnikov and Collier. This setting of Rachmaninoff's *Rhapsody on a Theme of Paganini* for Piano and Orchestra was choreographed as a showcase for the virtuosity of its principal dancers and was dedicated to the Queen Mother. It was revived by the Royal in 1995 with new designs by Patrick Caulfield. Earlier ballets to the same score include Fokine's for de Basil's Ballets Russes, London (1939), and Lavrovsky's for the Bolshoi Ballet (1960).

Rhodes, Lawrence (*b* Mount Hope, W. Va., 24 Nov. 1939) US dancer and director. He studied at the Ballet Russe School and in 1958 joined Ballet Russe de Monte Carlo. Between 1960 and 1964 he danced with the Robert Joffrey Ballet where his strong technique and dramatic presence were showcased in ballets such as Arpino's *Incubus* and Macdonald's *Time Out of Mind* (1962). Between 1964 and 1970 he was principal dancer with Harkness Ballet becoming its artistic director in 1968. In 1970 he joined the Dutch National Ballet, creating the lead role in van Dantzig's *On the Way*, and in 1972 he joined the Pennsylvania Ballet where he remained until 1976, apart from a year spent with the Feld Ballet (1974–5) and extended guest appearances in Italy with Carla Fracci. In 1981 he was appointed Chairman of New York University School of Dance and in 1989 he became artistic director of Les Grands Ballets Canadiens where he opened up the repertory to new aesthetics, acquiring works by Duato, Forsythe, and Morris, and commissioning works from Canadian choreographers such as Edouard Lock and Mark Godden. He left in 1999 and in 2002 was appointed head of the Dance Division at the Juilliard School in New York.

Riabouchinska, Tatiana (*b* Moscow, 23 May 1917; *d* 24 Aug. 2000) Russian-US dancer and teacher. She studied in Paris with Volinine and Kshessinska and made her debut in the *La Chauve-Souris* revue in 1931. In 1932 she joined the Ballets Russes de Monte Carlo where she was one of its three 'baby ballerinas' and stayed with the company until 1941, creating roles in several ballets including Balanchine's *La Concurrence* (1932), Massine's *Jeux d'enfants* (1932), *Les Présages*, and *Choreartium* (1933), Lichine's *Graduation Ball* (1940), and Fokine's *Cendrillon* (1938) and *Paganini* (1939). Celebrated for her gaiety, lightness, and speed she was also capable of a touching lyricism and a rare imaginative involvement on stage. Other dancers found it difficult to recreate her roles, so intensely had she made them her own. She was guest dancer with Ballet Theatre in 1942 and then with many other companies including Ballets des Champs-Elysées and London Festival Ballet. She additionally performed in musical comedies such as *The Waltz King* (chor. Lichine, 1943), and with Lichine (whom she married in 1943) founded a dance academy in Beverly Hills in 1953 as well as several short-lived ballet companies in Los Angeles, which they ran together until his death in 1972. After retiring from the stage she turned to teaching at the dance academy in Beverly Hills founded by herself and her husband.

Ricercare Ballet in one act with choreography by Tetley, music by M. Seter, and design by Ter-Arutunian. Premiered 15 Jan. 1966 by American Ballet Theatre at New York's State Theater, with Hinkson and S. Douglas. It is a duet for a man and woman who play out their emotional and erotic tensions on and around Ter-Arutunian's large curved sculpture. It has been revived for Ballet Rambert (1967) and Royal Swedish Ballet (1970), among others.

Rich, John J. S. (*b* c.1691/2; *d* Hillingdon, 26 Nov. 1761) British mime and impresario. He was a highly successful author, producer, and actor of Harlequinades who was also responsible for bringing artists like Sallé and Noverre over to England. He inherited the patent of the Lincoln's Inn Theatre from his father in 1714 and staged his first pantomime there in 1716. In 1728 he produced Gay's highly popular *Beggar's Opera*, the money from which enabled him to build Covent Garden in 1732.

Richardson, Philip J. S. (*b* Winthorpe, 17 Mar. 1875; *d* London, 17 Feb. 1963) British writer and editor. He transformed *Dancing Times* into a major dance magazine when he became its editor in 1910, remaining there as editor and critic until 1957. During the magazine's early years he campaigned vigorously within its pages for the establishment of a national ballet. In 1920 he was co-founder of the Royal Academy of Dancing (initially called the Association of Operatic Dancing in Great Britain), and in 1930 founded the Camargo Society with Haskell. He also established the Official Board of Ballroom Dancing and the International Council of Ballroom Dancing as well as organizing many charity dance performances including the Sunshine Matinées. His written works include *A History of English Ballroom Dancing* (1948) and *Social Dances of the 19th Century* (1960).

Riegger, Wallingford (*b* Albany, Ga., 29 Apr. 1885; *d* New York, 2 Apr. 1961) US composer who wrote the music for several dance works including Humphrey's *New Dance* (1935), *Theater Piece* and *With My Red Fires* (both 1936), and Graham's *Chronicle* (1936).

Riga *See* LATVIA.

rigaudon A couple dance in lively duple time, dating from 15th-century Provence and named after a dancing master from Marseilles. It became popular at the court of Louis XIV from the 1670s and spread to most of the courts of Europe. Couples dance side by side without holding hands, executing at certain moments the distinctive, springing step, the pas de rigaudon.

Riley, Richie (*b* Jamaica, 10 Jan. 1910; *d* 8 Apr. 1997) Jamaican-British dancer and artist. He studied in Kingston then came to London for further training with Astafieva. In 1946 he founded Les Ballets Nègres, a company specializing in Afro-Caribbean dance dramas. It toured Europe with much success but disbanded in 1953 due to lack of funding. Riley went on to study art at the Slade. His life and work were reflected in the BBC documentary *Ballet Black* (1982).

Rimsky-Korsakov, Nicolai (*b* Tikhvin, 18 Mar. 1844; *d* Lubensk, 21 Jun. 1908) Russian composer. He wrote no ballet music but some of his scores have been used for dance, most famously *Scheherazade* (chor. Fokine, 1910).

Rio Grande Ballet in one act with choreography by Ashton, music by Lambert, and design by Burra. Briefly titled *A Day in a Southern Port*, it was premiered 29 Nov. 1931 by the Camargo Society at the Savoy Theatre, London, with Lopokova, Gore, Markova, and Chappell. It is set in a Southern port and its action (described by Beaumont as 'an orgy of sailors and their doxies') is loosely based on Sacheverell Sitwell's poem of the same title. It was revived for the Vic-Wells Ballet in 1935, when Fonteyn was cast as the Creole Girl, her first significant role.

Rioja, Pilar (*b* Torreón, Coahuila, 13 Sept. 1932) Spanish dancer. While living in Mexico she studied Spanish dance with her parents and ballet locally and in 1947 she began dancing on the stage and in taverns. She made her debut in Spain in 1950, then returned to Mexico City where she became a celebrated performer in clubs and theatres. She continued her training in both Mexico and Spain, becoming one of the world's pre-eminent Spanish dancers, noted for the authenticity of her flamenco style.

Rite of Spring, The (Fr. title *Le Sacre du printemps*; orig. Russ. title *Vesna svyashchennaya*) Ballet in one act with choreography by Nijinsky, music by Stravinsky, and design by Roerich. Premiered 29 May 1913 by Diaghilev's Ballets Russes at Théâtre des Champs-Elysées, Paris, with Maria Piltz, and Monteux conducting. At its controversial opening night Nijinsky's choreography was considered almost as shocking as the churning rhythms and clamorous orchestration of Stravinsky's score. The ballet depicts a primitive Russian tribe sacrificing a virgin maiden to the arrival of spring and its

r

choreography is a deliberate inversion of classicism, the dancers adopting a pigeon-toed stance, their movements heavy and constrained. Apart from the Chosen One, they move in groups, their movements uniform and ritualized. It is now regarded as a seminal moment in modernism, but it was dropped after seven performances. Many choreographers have since attempted the same score. Massine's 1920 version for Diaghilev's Ballets Russes used the original Roerich design, with Sokolova as the Chosen One. His 1930 re-staging in Philadelphia featured Graham in that role. Other versions include Wigman (Municipal Opera Berlin, 1957), Béjart (Brussels, 1959), MacMillan (Royal Ballet, London, 1962), Neumeier (Frankfurt, 1972), Tetley (Munich State Opera Ballet, 1974), van Manen (Dutch National Ballet, 1974), Bausch (Wuppertal, 1975), Graham (M. Graham Dance Company, 1984), Stanton Welch, with Stephen Page (Australian Ballet with Bangarra, 1998), Preljocaj (2001), J. Inger (*Dream Play*, Nederlands Dans Theater, 2000), Shen Wei (2003), and De Frutos (three versions including Royal New Zealand Ballet, 2005), and Michael Keegan-Dolan (English National Opera, 2009). Molissa Fenley created a solo to Stravinsky's score in 1988, as did De Frutos in his first version, *The Palace does not Forgive*, 1994: Michael Clark spliced it with rock music (including the Sex Pistols) for his work *Mmm* (1992). The score also accompanies the story of prehistoric evolution in Disney's *Fantasia*. The four-handed piano version of the music has been used by Taylor (1980), Alston (1981), and Petronio (1992). The original ballet with Nijnsky's choreography and Roerich's designs was reconstructed by Hodson and Archer for the Joffrey Ballet (1987).

Rituals Ballet in one act with choreography by MacMillan, music by Bartók, and design by Sonneband. Premiered 11 Dec. 1975 by the Royal Ballet at Covent Garden, London, with Drew, Eagling, S. Beagley, Derman, Rencher, Seymour, and Mason. This setting of Bartók's Sonata for Two Pianos and Percussion is inspired by the ritualized nature of Japanese ceremonial life.

Rivera, Chita (*b* Washington, DC, 23 Jan. 1933) US dancer, singer, and actor. She studied at the School of American Ballet and made her debut in the touring production of *Call Me Madam* in 1950. She appeared on Broadway in *Guys and Dolls* (1952) but came to fame in the created role of Anita in *West Side Story* (chor. Robbins, 1957). She went on to perform leading roles in *Sweet Charity* (1966) and *Chicago* (1975). Despite suffering major injuries in 1986 she returned to the stage to star in *Kiss of the Spider Woman* (1993) and in the Broadway revival of *Nine* (2003).

Riverdance Popular dance and music spectacle based on Irish step dance and also featuring Spanish, Russian, folk, and tap. It began as a brief entertainment to fill the interval of the 1994 Eurovision Song Contest but was then expanded, first into an hour-long video and then into a two-hour stage show, *Riverdance: The Show*. Produced by Moya Doherty, directed by John McColgan, with music by Bill Whelan, design by Mary Morrow (later by Robert Ballagh), and most of the original choreography by Michael Flatley, it was premiered 9 Feb. 1995 at The Point, Dublin, with Flatley and Jean Butler. It went on to a record-breaking London run at Labatt's Apollo, Hammersmith, and a world tour. *Riverdance: The New Show*, featuring additional material was filmed live on 11 Nov. 1996 at Radio City Music Hall, New York.

rivoltade [It., turn over] A turning step in which the dancer (usually male) gives the impression that he is jumping over his leg.

Robbins, Jerome (orig. Rabinowitz; *b* New York, 11 Oct. 1918; *d* 29 Jul. 1998) US dancer, choreographer, and director, considered by many to be the greatest American-born classical choreographer. He studied with Loring, Tudor, and others, also Spanish dance with Helene Veola, Oriental dance with Nimura, and modern dance with Alice Bentley and his sister Sonya Robbins. He additionally studied acting with Elia Kazan, making his debut as an actor in 1937 and as a dancer at the Dance Center of Felia Sorel and Gluck-Sandor. Between 1938 and 1940 he danced in Broadway musicals and in 1940 joined Ballet Theatre (later American Ballet Theatre), becoming soloist (1941–4). He created roles in several ballets including Fokine's *Bluebeard* (1941), Lichine's *Helen of Troy* (1942), and Tudor's *Romeo and Juliet* (1943). His first major choreographic work (for Ballet Theatre) was the phenomenally successful *Fancy Free* (mus. Bernstein, 1944) about three impudent sailors on shore leave which, with Bernstein, he adapted into the musical *On the Town* (1944). This work forged the style which was to characterize much of his most popular work, a fusion of classical and modern dance combined with jazz and vernacular moves, often in the creation of sharply contemporary characters. It was followed by *Interplay* (mus. Gould, 1945) and *Facsimile* (mus. Bernstein, 1946), both for Ballet Theatre, and the musicals *Billion Dollar Baby* (1946), *High Button Shoes* (1947), and *Look Ma I'm Dancing* (1948). In 1949 he joined New York City Ballet and as associate director (until 1959) created nine works for the company including *The Age of Anxiety* (mus. Bernstein, 1950), *The Cage* (mus. Stravinsky, 1951), *Afternoon of a Faun* (mus. Debussy, 1953), and *The Concert* (mus.

Chopin, 1956). His version of *Faun* is a poetic but cynical study of the ballet world as two dancers reveal how much more attracted they are by their images in the mirror than by each other. *The Concert*, one of the first of several ballets he made to Chopin's music, is a comic masterpiece which engages with the surreal fantasies of a group of people as they listen to the music and also depicts a hapless ensemble of female dancers who cannot get the hang of dancing in unison. Robbins himself danced infrequently with New York City Ballet, though he did make memorable appearances in the title roles of Balanchine's *Prodigal Son* and *Tyl Ulenspiegel* (a role he created). He continued to choreograph for musicals, including *Peter Pan* (1954), which he also adapted and directed, *West Side Story* (1957, film version 1961), which he also conceived and directed, and *Gypsy* (1959). In 1958 he formed his own company, Ballets: USA, for the Spoleto Festival; for it he choreographed *New York Export: Opus Jazz* (mus. R. Prince) and *Moves* (no mus., 1959). The company was disbanded and then re-formed for the 1961 Spoleto Festival to perform *Events* (mus. R. Prince).

During the 1960s he choreographed *Funny Girl* (1964) and *Fiddler on the Roof* (1964) as well as directing various plays including Brecht's *Mother Courage*. In 1965 he choreographed Stravinsky's *Les Noces* for ABT and in 1969 returned to NYCB as ballet master, becoming ballet master in chief (with Peter Martins) in 1983 after Balanchine's death. He choreographed many more works for the company including *Dances at a Gathering* (mus. Chopin, 1969), *The Goldberg Variations* (mus. Bach, 1971), *Watermill* (mus. Teiji Ito, 1972), *Requiem Canticles* (mus. Stravinsky, 1972), *Opus 19: The Dreamer* (mus. Prokofiev, 1979), *Glass Pieces* (mus. Glass, 1983), and *Ives Songs* (mus. Ives, 1988). Robbins's work became increasingly less reliant on narrative but embraced a wide range of styles and moods, from the tenderly romantic *Dances at a Gathering*, to the brilliant deconstruction of classical technique in *Goldberg Variations*; the use of Eastern stillness in *Watermill*, in which an older man (orig. Edward Villella) looks back over his past, and the luminous structural clarity of *Glass Pieces*. Together with the Balanchine œuvre these works defined the style of NYCB for many years, and Robbins was reluctant to allow other companies to perform his work. NYCB staged a Robbins Festival in 1990, after which he retired. His many awards included the Handel Medallion of the City of New York (1976). After his death, his personal dance archive was donated to the Dance Collection of the New York Public Library for the Performing Arts, which was renamed in his honour.

Other works include *Summer Day* (pas de deux, mus. Prokofiev, Ballet Theatre, New York, 1947),

The Guests (mus. Blitzstein, NYCB, New York, 1949), *The Pied Piper* (mus. Copland, NYCB, New York, 1951), *In the Night* (mus. Chopin, NYCB, New York, 1970), *Firebird* (with Balanchine, mus. Stravinsky, NYCB, New York, 1970), *Dumbarton Oaks* (mus. Stravinsky, NYCB, New York, 1972), *Pulcinella* (with Balanchine, mus. Stravinsky, NYCB, New York, 1972), *Requiem Canticles* (mus. Stravinsky, NYCB, New York, 1972), *Dybbuk* (later called *The Dybbuk Variations* and, after 1980, *Suite of Dances*; mus. Bernstein, NYCB, New York, 1974), *Concerto in G* (later titled *In G major*; mus. Ravel, NYCB, New York, 1975), *Other Dances* (mus. Chopin, Gala for the Library of Performing Arts, New York, 1976), *The Four Seasons* (mus. Verdi, NYCB, New York, 1979), *Piano Pieces* (mus. Tchaikovsky, NYCB, New York, 1981), *Allegro con grazia* (mus. Tchaikovsky, NYCB, New York, 1981), *Gershwin Concerto* (mus. Gershwin, NYCB, New York, 1982), *I'm Old Fashioned* (mus. Gould after Kern, NYCB, New York 1983), *Antique Epigraphs* (mus. Debussy, NYCB, New York, 1984), *Brahms/Handel* (with Twyla Tharp; mus. Brahms, NYCB, New York, 1984), *In Memory of . . .* (mus. Berg, NYCB, New York, 1985), and *West Side Story Suite* (dances from the 1957 musical, mus. Bernstein, NYCB, 1995).

Robert le diable (Eng. title *Robert the Devil*) Opera by Meyerbeer whose first staging featured F. Taglioni's 'Ballet of the Nuns', a dance which is considered to mark the beginning of the Romantic ballet movement. Premiered 21 Nov. 1831 at the Paris Opera, the role of the ghostly Abbess Helena being danced by M. Taglioni. The opera's libretto (by Scribe) tells the story of an evil man who seeks a talisman to help him win the hand of a princess. Arriving at the cloister of Sainte-Rosalie, he encounters the ghosts of nuns who have violated their vows. Their dance of wanton sensuousness shocked and enthralled the first audiences: Hans Christian Andersen recorded his own impressions of 'vaprous images' whose 'shrouds fall to the ground' so that they 'stand in all their voluptuous nakedness' and dance a 'bacchanal'.

Robinson, Bill ('Bojangles') (*b* Richmond, Va., 1878; *d* New York, 25 Nov. 1949) US tap dancer, who revolutionized the technique by dancing high up on his toes and so introducing an exceptional precision and lightness. From 1898 he danced in various venues in New York (restaurants, vaudeville theatres) as well as touring abroad. He became widely known through his appearances in the revue *Blackbird* (1928), going on to dance in leading theatres and clubs around the US. He appeared in several films and was featured in *The Hot Mikado* (1939).

Rock ballets Choreographers were quick to pick up on the rock music phenomenon which dominated youth culture from the 1960s. Some chose to reflect the lives and views of the new teenagers, such as Darrell in *Mods and Rockers* (mus. The Beatles, 1963) or Arpino in the anti-Vietnam *Trinity* (mus. Ralph Holdridge, 1970) or Nault in *Tommy* (mus. The Who, 1970). Other choreographers exploited the rhythmic drive and energy of rock music to try and re-invigorate the classical vocabulary (and attract a new young audience to ballet). It has since become commonplace for choreographers of all backgrounds to use the music of popular culture, such as *Rooster*, C. Bruce's semi-nostalgic, semi-mocking portrayal of 1960s' youth (mus. early Rolling Stones, 1991), Michael Clark's frequent use of confrontational punk music such as the Sex Pistols, and the Fall, and the Joffrey Ballet's full-length *Billboards* (1993), set to songs by the artist formerly known as Prince, which broke company box-office records.

Rockettes Female precision dance group which has appeared at New York's Radio City Music Hall since 1932. It was established by Russell Market in 1925 in Missouri, and based on the British troupe the *Tiller Girls. There are now over 175 Rockettes who are divided between individual routines, in which they step and kick in strict unison.

Rodeo Ballet in one act with choreography by de Mille, music by Copland, sets by O. Smith, and costumes by K. Love. Premiered 16 Oct. 1942 by Ballet Russe de Monte Carlo at New York's Metropolitan Opera House with de Mille, F. Franklin, Kasimir Kokitch, and Milada Mladova. It is subtitled *The Courting at Burnt Ranch* and tells the story of a cowgirl on a Texas ranch whose feminine charms are ignored by the cowboys—until she dresses up for a ball and proves that she is a real woman. It was one of the first all-American ballets, also the first to introduce square dancing to ballet, and it became de Mille's most popular work, leading to her commission to choreograph *Oklahoma!* It was revived for Ballet Theatre (1950), Joffrey Ballet (1976), and San Francisco Ballet (1989), among others.

Rodrigues, Alfred (*b* Cape Town, 18 Aug. 1921; *d* 12 Jan. 2002) British dancer and choreographer. He studied with C. Robinson in Cape Town and came to London in 1946 where he studied with Volkova and danced in the musical *Song of Norway*. A year later he joined Sadler's Wells Ballet, becoming soloist in 1949 and ballet master (1953–4). He choreographed his first ballet in 1938, going on to create, among others, *Blood Wedding* (mus. ApIvor, Sadler's Wells Theatre Ballet, 1953), *The Miraculous Mandarin* (mus. Bartók, Royal Ballet, 1956), *Romeo and Juliet* (mus. Prokofiev, La Scala, 1955), *Vivaldi Concerto* (Royal Danish Ballet, 1960), and *Le Sacre du printemps* for Warsaw Grand Opera. He also choreographed for several musicals. He married the dancer Julia Farron.

Roerich, Nicholas (*b* St Petersburg, 27 Sept. 1874; *d* Kulu, India, 13 Sept. 1947) Russian scholar, mystic, painter, and designer. He studied prehistoric culture around the world and his main association with ballet was his designs for Fokine's Polovtsian Dances from *Prince Igor* (1909) and Nijinsky's *Rite of Spring* (1913), both for Diaghilev's Ballets Russes.

Rogers, Ginger (*b* Independence, Mo., 16 Jul. 1911; *d* Rancho Mirage, Calif., 25 Apr. 1995) US dancer and actress. She was famous for her long partnership with Fred Astaire of which it was said 'he gave her class, she gave him sex appeal'. Though her technique was less brilliant than Astaire's, she was a pliant, extrovert partner who ideally complemented his personality and style. Their first film together was *Flying Down to Rio* (1933) and was followed by a string of hits including *The Gay Divorcee* (1934), *Top Hat* (1935), *Shall We Dance?* (1937), and *The Story of Vernon and Irene Castle* (1939). After the partnership split up she performed as a straight actor, though she also appeared in the musicals *Hello Dolly!* and *Mame*.

Rojo, Tamara (*b* Montreal, 17 May 1974) Spanish dancer. She studied with Ullate in Madrid, and danced with his Ballet Comunidad de Madrid (1991–6). In 1996 she came to Britain, to dance first with Scottish Ballet and in 1997 to join English National Ballet where she was rapidly promoted to principal, creating lead roles in ballets by Christopher Hampson and Derek Deane, including the latter's 1998 production of *Romeo and Juliet*. She joined the Royal Ballet in 2000 and became one of the company's leading ballerinas. Her fluidly expressive dancing, pegged to an exceptionally powerful technique, has been showcased in all the classical roles but Rojo has additionally danced the major MacMillan, Balanchine, and Ashton repertories and created roles in ballets by McGregor (*Chroma*, 2006), Brandstrup (*Rushes*, 2008, *Goldberg*, 2009) among others. She has guested worldwide, with companies including La Scala, Berlin Opera Ballet, and National Ballet of Cuba and is recipient of many awards including Critic's Circle outstanding dancer and the Spanish Gold Medal for the Arts.

Romania Ballet in Romania dates back to the founding of the Lyrical Company at Bucharest National Theatre in 1877 and the establishment of its corps de ballet in 1898. This company became state-supported in 1921 and under ballet master A. Romanowski presented stagings of the Ballets

Russes and early Soviet repertories. After the Second World War many new state-subsidized schools and companies were established, with close links to the USSR, though some native Romanian choreographers also emerged, such as Vasily Marcu. The school in Bucharest produced several major dancers, including Ileana Iliescu, Elena Dacian, and Alexa Mezincescu, but during the 1960s and again during the 1980s and 1990s the most talented, like Alina *Cojocaru, opted to make their careers abroad. The ballet company of the Bucharest National Opera, directed from 1993 by Iliescu and Mihai Babuska, then from 2009 by Gheorghe Iancu, has toured widely in Europe with a repertory of classical and contemporary works staged largely by the company's associate choreographers such as Babuska, Mezincescu, and Iancu. Other important activity has occurred within the Experimental Studios of Dance founded 1968, and the Classical and Contemporary Ballet Ensemble (orig. called Fantasio Theatre) which was founded in 1979 by Danovschi. Smaller groups, including Sergiu Anghel's contemporary Orion Ballet and more recently Marginalii and Studio DCM, have helped create a public for new and experimental work but economic and political uncertainties in Romania have made this difficult to develop. The country has a rich tradition of folk dance which is performed throughout the region, both by amateur ensembles and by the professional troupes fostered under Soviet rule after the Second World War.

(((🌐))) **SEE WEB LINKS**

- Website for the Bucharest Opera with link to the ballet
- Website for the Orion Ballet Company

Romanov, Boris (*b* St Petersburg, 22 Mar. 1891; *d* New York, 30 Jan. 1957) Russian-US dancer, choreographer, and director. He studied at St Petersburg Imperial Ballet School, graduating in 1909 into the Mariinsky Theatre where he excelled in character roles. He also danced various seasons with Diaghilev's Ballets Russes (1909–14), and choreographed *La Tragédie de Salomé* (mus. F. Schmitt, 1913) and *Le Rossignol* (mus. Stravinsky, 1914) for that company. Between 1914 and 1917 he was choreographer for the Imperial Theatres and became director of the Mariinsky Theatre in 1917. He created many opera divertissements there as well as choreographing avant-garde ballets with his wife Yelena Smirnova for the Litni Miniature Theatre. In 1921 he left Russia, founding the Russian Romantic Ballet in Berlin with Elsa Kruger. This toured Europe with a repertoire of Romanov's own works as well as a critically acclaimed staging of *Giselle*. After the company disbanded in 1926 he was choreographer at La Scala, Milan, and then ballet master of

Pavlova's company. In 1928 he became chief choreographer at the Teatro Colón, Buenos Aires, moving back to Italy in 1934 then in 1938 appointed ballet master of New York Metropolitan Opera House where he remained until 1942, returning again (1945 to 1950). He additionally worked as guest choreographer for several US ballet companies. He was much influenced by Fokine, but during his later career he abandoned the questing, modernist spirit of his earlier works for a more conventional style.

Romantic ballet A style of ballet which was extremely popular in Europe during the 1830s and 1840s, and which paralleled the vogue for exotic, escapist fantasy which dominated Romanticism in all the other arts. One of its earliest manifestations was F. Taglioni's 'Ballet of the Nuns' created for Act II of Meyerbeer's opera *Robert le diable* (1831). A major element of Romantic ballet was a fascination with the supernatural. The plots of many ballets were dominated by spirit women—sylphs, wilis, and ghosts—who enslaved the hearts and senses of mortal men and made it impossible for them to live happily in the real world. Women dancers were dressed in diaphanous white frocks with little wings at their waist, and were bathed in the mysterious poetic light created by newly developed gas lighting in theatres. They danced in a style more fluid and ethereal than 18th-century dancers and were especially prized for their *ballon as they tried to create the illusion of flight. Sometimes this was literally achieved through the use of flying harnesses and wires, but more significantly it was achieved by the new technique of dancing on pointe. Though female dancers did not yet wear the solidly blocked pointe shoes of the later 19th century—their slippers were stiffened only by lines of darning—ballerinas like M. *Taglioni succeeded, by means of considerable muscular effort and control, to rise and dance on the tips of their toes, looking to audiences as if they were hovering just above the stage. A group of St Petersburg balletomanes are said to have celebrated their devotion to Taglioni's art by cooking and eating a pair of her shoes. The great surviving works of the period are *La *Sylphide* (F. Taglioni, 1832) and *Giselle* (Perrot and Coralli, 1841). The second dominant element in Romanticism was a fascination with the exotic, which was figured through gypsy or oriental heroines and the use of folk or national dances from 'foreign' cultures (such as Spain, the Middle East, and Scotland). Such dances were considered highly expressive both of character and of exotic local colour, though in some countries, such as Italy, indigenous dances were featured in ballets whose plots reflected that region's surge of nationalist feeling. Male dancers were frequently relegated to the role of *porteur* in

Romantic ballets with much less scope for dramatic or technical display, though in Italy and in Denmark their virtuosity was still prized. The general decline of male dancing in much of Europe, however, may have influenced the short life-span of Romanticism, as ballets were so weighted towards the feminine and the febrile. Although the era saw ballet develop into a truly international art, with European ballerinas travelling to Russia and the Americas, and individual works being staged by companies around the world, it lasted only two decades. In the main European centres it then degenerated into formulaic spectacle, and fashionable audiences drifted away from ballet to opera.

Romeo and Juliet Shakespeare's tragedy has inspired dozens of choreographers since the first recorded ballet stagings by E. Luzzi (Venice, 1785) and Galeotti (mus. Claus Schall, Royal Danish Ballet, 1811). The most important 20th-century productions have been set to Prokofiev's three-act ballet score (libretto by Lavrovsky, Prokofiev, and Sergei Radlov), whose rich sonorities and narrative detail provide an unusually powerful dramatic structure. Closely following Shakespeare's plot the libretto emphasizes the clash between the two warring families and their final reconciliation over the lovers' tomb. The first choreographed version was by Psota, and was premiered 30 Dec. 1938 at Brno, Czechoslovakia, with Psota and Zora Semberová, but it was in Lavrovsky's stagings that the work achieved widespread popularity. With design by P. Williams it was premiered 11 Jan. 1940 by the Kirov, Leningrad, with Ulanova and Sergeyev, and was revived in 1946 for the Bolshoi in Moscow. Its realistic portrayal of character and emotion, its vivid contrast between the clashing swordplay of public violence and the tender pas de deux of private love, made it a landmark in Soviet ballet. When the ballet was shown in London ten years later, audiences were enthralled, and many choreographers were inspired to re-work it, though London had in fact seen Froman's *Romeo and Juliet* for the Zagreb Ballet in 1955. The most popular Western versions have been Cranko's and MacMillan's. The former was designed by Benois and premiered 26 Jul. 1958 by La Scala Ballet, in Venice, with Pistoni and Fracci. The better-known revised version, with designs by Jürgen Rose, was premiered 2 Dec. 1962 by the Stuttgart Ballet with Barra and Haydée. This has been revived by many companies, including National Ballet of Canada (1964), Australian Ballet (1974), and Paris Opera (1983). MacMillan's version, with designs by Georgiadis, was premiered 9 Feb. 1965 by the Royal Ballet, London, with Nureyev and Fonteyn. This version places a wilful, passionate Juliet at the centre of the action, battling against the violence and social restrictions which threaten her. It has been revived for Royal Swedish Ballet (1969), American Ballet Theatre (1985), and others. Frederick Ashton created a more lyrical interpretation for the Royal Danish Ballet in 1955 (before the Russian version had been seen in the West) and this was revived for London Festival Ballet in 1985; Rudi van Dantzig choreographed two versions for the Dutch National Ballet, in 1967 and 1974, and Rudolf Nureyev's was made for the London Festival Ballet in 1977; Tiit Harm choreographed a version in 1990, Preljocaj for Lyon Opera Ballet, 1991, Corder for Norwegian National Ballet, 1992, and Maillot for Les Ballets de Monte Carlo, 1998.

In 2008 Mark Morris choreographed a modern dance version of *Romeo and Juliet* for his own company that, historically, used the first version of Prokofiev's score. Written in 1935, this had been censored by the Soviet authorities due to its unacceptably modernist handling of rhythm and orchestration and its controversial adoption of a happy ending. (According to the composer 'living people dance, the dead cannot'.)

Later Soviet productions to the officially approved score include Vinogradov's (Novosibirsk, 1967) and Boyarchikov's (Perm, 1972). Other versions of the story, set to different music, include Nijinska and Balanchine's (mus. Lambert, Diaghilev's Ballets Russes, 1926); various settings of Tchaikovsky's Fantasy Overture including Bartholin's, T. Gsovsky's, and Lifar's; and various settings of Berlioz's Dramatic Symphony, including Skibine's (Grand Ballet du Cuevas, 1955), Béjart's (Ballet of the 20th Century, 1966). In 1943 Antony Tudor created a one-act version of the ballet to music by Delius which was a meditation on the story of the star-crossed lovers rather than a straightforward narrative. In 1957 Jerome Robbins choreographed the musical version *West Side Story* (mus. Bernstein) and in 2000 Rennie Harris created a hip-hop version, *Rome and Jewels*,

Ever since Galina Ulanova transfixed audiences with her poignant portrait of an adolescent girl in love the role of Juliet has been coveted by ballerinas. Famous interpretations have included Margot Fonteyn, Lynn Seymour, Carla Fracci, and Marcia Haydée.

Róna, Viktor (*b* Budapest, 17 Aug. 1936; *d* Budapest, 15 Jan. 1994) Hungarian dancer and ballet master. He studied at Budapest State Ballet Institute and in Leningrad (1959) with Pushkin. In 1950 he joined Budapest State Opera Ballet (becoming principal in 1957) where he danced all the major classical and character roles of their repertoire. An elegant technician, he was also a versatile dance actor, creating leading roles in several works including Harangozó's *The Miraculous Mandarin* (1956), Charrat's *Tu auras* *nom ... Tristan* (1963), Eck's *Ondine* (1969), and Seregi's *Sylvia* (1972). He guested widely abroad and, as an exemplary partner, danced with several leading ballerinas including Fonteyn and Samsova in 1962, Daydé in 1965, and Orosz in 1965 and 1966. He was also ballet master with Norwegian National Ballet (1974–80), Paris Opera Ballet (1980–3), and La Scala, Milan (1983–8), where he also served for a year as deputy director. He appeared as a dancer and actor in several films. He was honoured as Outstanding Artist of the Hungarian National Republic in 1975.

rond de jambe [Fr., circle of the leg] A movement in classical ballet in which one leg moves in a straight line away from the body before defining a semi-circular motion. It can be performed either on the floor (à terre) or with the leg in the air (en l'air).

Ronde, La Ballet in one act with choreography by Tetley, music by Erich Korngold, and design by John Macfarlane. Premiered 6 Nov. 1987 at the O'Keefe Centre, Toronto, by the National Ballet of Canada with Ronda Nychka, Alleyne, Glasco, Harrington, Sabina Alleman, Peter Ottmann, Kim Lightheart, Owen Montague, Kain, and Augustyn. It is based on Schnitzler's play, *Reigen* (1896–7), which satirizes the amorality of *fin de siècle* Vienna as various characters (each representing a different social rank) seduce each other in a sexual merry-go-round. Tetley's choreography mimics this concept with a series of interlocking pas de deux, graphic in their erotic content, which begin and end with a prostitute. It has been revived for several companies, including the Royal Ballet (1993).

Roof Piece Outdoor dance event choreographed by Trisha Brown during 1973 in which fifteen dancers were stationed on various rooftops in Manhattan, signalling movements to each other. The audience watched from another roof.

Rooms Modern dance work in one act with choreography by Sokolow and music by K. Hopkins. Premiered 24 Feb. 1955 at the YM-YWHA, New York, with Seckler, E. Beck, and McKayle. Sokolow's classic study of alienation is divided into nine sections which deal with a group of city dwellers, each locked in their own neurosis, and expressing their frustrations and fantasies in angularly expressive gesture. It has been revived for several companies, including Nederlands Dans Theater, Alvin Ailey Dance Theater, and the Joffrey Ballet.

Rooster Modern dance work in one act with choreography by C. Bruce, music by the Rolling Stones, and costumes by M. Bruce. Premiered 10 Oct. 1991 by Ballet de Grande Théâtre de Genève, Geneva. In this setting of early Stones' songs, the movement mimics the preening and posturing of the 1960s in a manner that is both a nostalgic recall and a mocking exposure of a past era's sexual games. It has been revived for London Contemporary Dance Theatre and Rambert Dance Company.

Roriz, Olga (*b* Viana do Castelo, 8 Aug. 1955) Portuguese choreographer. She studied at the National Theatre of San Carlos and National School of Lisbon and in 1976 became one of the leading dancers with Ballet Gulbenkian. She created her first works in the company's workshops in 1982 and went on to develop a style rooted in classical technique but also possessing the driving physicality typical of late-20th-century modern dance. Her works include *The Seven Dances of Salome* (mus. A. Emiliano, English National Ballet, 1993), one of several ballets created for an all-male cast. In 1993 she was appointed artistic director of the Lisbon Dance Company and in 1995 founded her own company with which she has developed a policy of creating dance in collaboration with a variety of artists including filmmakers, photographers and writers. Her works for the company include *Private Property* (1998), *Jump-up-and-Kiss-me* (2003), *Felicitações Madame* (trilogy, film and dance 2005–06), *Inferno* (2008).

(⊕) SEE WEB LINKS
• Website for the Olga Roriz company

Rosario (*née* Florencia Pérez Podilla; *b* Seville, 11 Nov. 1918; *d* Madrid, 24 Jan. 2000) Spanish dancer. She studied with Realito and made her debut with her cousin Antonio in 1928. They became the most renowned Spanish dance partnership of their generation and toured the world. Rosario danced briefly with Iglesias (1953–4) and performed again with Antonio during his 1964 seasons in London and New York. She also assembled various ensembles of her own with which she performed and for which she created several works including *Capriccio espagnol* (mus. Rimsky-Korsakov) and *Café de Burrero* (Andalusian folk music).

Rosas Anne Teresa de *Keersmaeker's dance company, formed in 1983 and based in Brussels. It was originally a group of four women, later expanding to include both sexes. *Rosas Danst Rosas* was also the title of the first work de Keersmaeker created for the group, which, with music by T. de Mey and P. Vermeersch, was premiered 6 May 1983 at the Kaaitheater Festival.

(⊕) SEE WEB LINKS
• Website for Rosas

Rosati, Carolina (*née* Galletti; *b* Bologna, 13 Dec., 1826; *d* Cannes, May 1905) Italian dancer. She studied with Blasis and made her debut aged 7. In 1841 she was engaged as prima ballerina at the Teatro di Apollo in Rome also performing in Trieste and Parma in 1843 and dancing with her husband Francesco Rosati at La Scala, Milan, in 1846. A plump, vivacious, and graceful dancer, she was renowned for the precision of her pointe work, also for her expressive mime. She was ballerina at Her Majesty's Theatre, London (1847–9), succeeding Grahn in Perrot's *Pas de quatre* and also creating roles in several other Perrot ballets, including *Les Quatres Saisons* (1848), as well as works by P. Taglioni, such as *Fiorita* (1848) and *La prima ballerina* (1849). She returned to London several times during the 1850s and between 1853 and 1859 also danced at the Paris Opera where she was apparently the highest paid dancer up to that time. She created roles in several Mazilier ballets including *Le Corsaire* (1856) and *Marco Spada* (1857); however, professional jealousy of her rival, Amalia Ferraris, caused her to break her contract and she left to dance at the Bolshoi Theatre, St Petersburg (1859–62), where she created leading roles in several works including Petipa's *La Fille du Pharaon* (1862) before retiring to France.

Rose, Jürgen (*b* Bernburg, 25 Aug. 1937) German theatre designer. Having been invited to design Cranko's Stuttgart production of *Romeo and Juliet* in 1962, he went on to design many other Cranko ballets including *Swan Lake* (1963), *Onegin* (1965), and the Stuttgart production of *The Merry Widow* (1971). His numerous designs for other choreographers included Tudor's *Giselle* (Berlin Opera Ballet, 1963), Franca's *Nutcracker* (National Ballet of Canada, 1964), MacMillan's *Concerto* (Berlin Opera Ballet, 1966), Neumeier's *Baiser de la fée* (Frankfurt, 1972), *Romeo and Juliet* (Royal Danish Ballet, 1974), *Sleeping Beauty* (Hamburg, 1978), and *Lady of the Camellias* (Stuttgart, 1978).

Rose Adagio The centrepiece of Petipa's *The Sleeping Beauty*, in which Princess Aurora is presented to her four suitors in Act I. With its thrilling balances and its emphasis on regally perfect presentation (Aurora has to balance unsupported on one leg and on pointe between taking each of her Princes' hands), it presents a challenge to the ballerina matched only (in theatrical lore) by the 32 fouetté turns of *Swan Lake*.

Rosen, Elsa-Marianne von (*b* Stockholm, 21 Apr. 1924) Swedish dancer, choreographer, teacher, and ballet director. She studied with various teachers and at the Royal Danish Ballet School, making her debut in independent dance

recitals. She was a soloist at the Oscarteatern, Stockholm, between 1947 and 1950 and also danced with Ballet Russe de Monte Carlo in 1948. A dancer of wide-ranging style, she was a charmingly girlish Aurora as well as an interpreter of complex psychological characters (she created the title roles in Cullberg's *Miss Julie* (1950) and *Medea* (1951). She was principal with the Royal Swedish Ballet (1951–9) where she danced some of the standard ballerina roles as well as creating roles in several ballets including Skeaping's *Cupid Out of his Humour* (1956). In 1960 she and her husband, the Danish ballet critic, designer, and director Allan Fridericia (1921–91), founded the Scandinavian Ballet which featured a number of Rosen's own ballets as well as her stagings of Bournonville works, such as *La Sylphide* (1960), which she revived for several other companies including Ballet Rambert (1960), Washington Ballet (1969), and Kirov Ballet (1975). During the 1960s she also worked around the world as a freelance ballerina, choreographer, and, with Fridericia, producer of Bournonville. Her own works from this period include *Teenagers* (mus. Bach, Scandinavian Ballet, Kalmar, 1961), *Jenny von Westphalen* (mus. Bentzon, Scandinavian Ballet, Århus, 1965), *Don Juan* (mus. Gluck, Royal Danish Ballet, Copenhagen, 1967), and *Romeo and Juliet* (mus. Prokofiev, Gothenburg Ballet, Gothenburg, 1972). She was appointed director of the Gothenburg Ballet (1970–6), and subsequently of the Malmö Ballet (1980–7), after which she continued to stage productions of the classic repertory around the world. Most have been ballets by Bournonville, including *Napoli* (Act III) for Berlin Opera Ballet (1987) and *The Lay of Thrym* for Royal Danish Ballet, Copenhagen (1990) but she has also staged productions of Galeotti's *The Whims of Cupid and the Ballet Master* and of *Swan Lake*. She opened her own school in Copenhagen where she taught. She was recipient of the Carina Ari Medal in 1962.

Rosenthal, Jean (*b* New York, 16 Mar. 1912; *d* New York, 1 May 1969) US lighting designer. A pioneer in the techniques of theatre lighting, she worked with Ballet Society and New York City Ballet (1946–57), the Martha Graham Dance Company (1958–65), and Robbins's Ballets: USA (1959–60). Her lighting designs had a choreographic quality, not only creating the impression of sculptural depth but also responding expressively to music. Robbins dedicated *Dances at a Gathering* to her memory.

Ross, Bertram (*b* Brooklyn, NY, 13 Nov. 1920; *d* 20 Apr. 2003) US dancer and teacher. He entered art school but then left to study dance with Graham, joining her company in 1953. A tall, passionate, 'granite visaged' performer, he created leading roles in many of her works including *Seraphic Dialogue* (1955), *Clytemnestra* (1958), *Acrobats of God* (1960), *Phaedra* (1962), *A Time of Snow* (1968), and *The Archaic Hours* (1969). He taught at the Graham School for many years and presented his first evening of choreography in 1965. He left Graham in 1974, after which he continued teaching and choreographing, as well as taking up a singing career.

Ross, Herbert (*b* Brooklyn, NY, 13 May 1927; *d* New York, 9 Oct. 2001) US dancer, choreographer, and director who directed the films *The Turning Point* (1977) and *Nijinsky* (1980). He started training in his mid-teens with Platova and Humphrey and danced on Broadway, creating his first dances for the New York Choreographers Workshop, including *Caprichos* (mus. Bartók, 1950). He went on to choreograph several musicals including *Wonderful Town* (1958) and *Finian's Rainbow* (1960), as well as dances for the film *Carmen Jones* (1954). He also choreographed ballets for American Ballet Theatre, including *The Maids* (mus. Milhaud, 1957), and for the Spoleto Festival of 1959 such as *Serenade for Seven Dancers* (mus. Bernstein). In 1960 he founded Ballet of Two Worlds with his wife Nora Kaye, which performed at Spoleto and toured Germany with new works including the full-length ballet *The Dybbuk* (mus. R. Starer). After the company disbanded he concentrated on musicals and films, directing over 25 of the latter.

Rossini, Gioacchino (*b* Pesaro, 29 Feb. 1792; *d* Passy, 13 Nov. 1868) Italian composer. He wrote no full-length ballet scores though his operas, such as *Moïse* (chor. Gardel, 1827) and *Guillaume Tell* (chor. Auber, 1829), featured significant ballet divertissements. Some of his arias were interpolated into 19th-century ballet scores, such as the Hérold version of *La Fille mal gardée* (1828), and many of his operatic and concert scores have been arranged for dance, including Massine's *La Boutique fantasque* (1919), Howard's *Selina* (1948), Darrell's *Cinderella* (1979), and Tharp's *Mr Worldly Wise* (Royal Ballet, 1995, a ballet loosely based on Rossini's own character). Several works have been set to Britten's two suites of Rossini melodies, *Soirées musicales* and *Matinées musicales*.

Rothschild, Bethsabee (Heb. **Batsheva**) **de** (*b* London, 1914; *d* Tel Aviv, 20 Apr. 1999) Israeli-US dance promoter and director. She studied at the Sorbonne and Columbia University and after studying dance with Graham began sponsoring her company's performances and tours. In 1958 she moved to Israel where she founded the Tel Aviv-based Batsheva Dance Company in 1964,

the Bat-Dor Dance Studios in 1967, and the Bat-Dor Dance Company in 1968.

Rowe, Danielle (*b* Shepparton, Vic., 28 Jun. 1982) Australian dancer. She studied locally and at the Australian Ballet School, graduating into the company in 2001 and promoted to principal in 2008. An incisive, dramatic dancer, she has performed both classical and contemporary repertories and has guested with Wheeldon's company Morphoses (2009). She is recipient of several awards including the Lissa Black Memorial Scholarship 2004.

Rowe, Marilyn (Marilyn Rowe Maver) (*b* Sydney, 20 Aug. 1946) Australian dancer and director. She studied at the newly founded Australian Ballet School in 1964, then joined the company, becoming principal in 1969. She danced many of the standard classical and 20th-century roles and created roles in Prokovsky's *Anna Karenina* (1974) and Hynd's *The Merry Widow* (1975), among others. In 1978 she danced with the Bolshoi in *Don Quixote* with Kelvin Coe. In 1982 she was acting director of Australian Ballet, becoming deputy director in 1983. Between 1984 and 1986, and in 1990, she was artistic director of the touring Dancers Company, attached to the AB School, where she was appointed director in 1999.

Royal Academy of Dance (RAD) (Known prior to 2001 as Royal Academy of Dancing) British dance examination board. It was founded on 31 Dec. 1920 by Philip Richardson in conjunction with an eminent group of dancers and teachers including Adeline Genée and Édouard Espinosa. It was originally known as the Association of Operatic Dancing in Great Britain and its aim was to monitor standards of classical ballet training. In 1936 it was granted its royal charter, becoming the Royal Academy of Dancing, and it developed into the world's largest examining and training body, holding examinations for all standards of ballet throughout the world. It began running a teacher-training course in 1947 and since 1954 it has also presented the annual Queen Elizabeth II Coronation Award for services to British ballet, with recipients including de Valois, Karsavina, Rambert, Dolin, Helpmann, van Praagh, Haskell, and Grey. Its first president was Genée, who was succeeded by Fonteyn (from 1954) and Antoinette Sibley (from 1991). In 1993 it forged an academic partnership with Durham University and in 1997 it was amalgamated with the Benesh Institute, allowing it to offer a wide range of diplomas and degree courses for notators and teachers.

(🌐) **SEE WEB LINKS**

• Website for the Royal Academy of Dance

Royal Ballet, The Britain's national ballet company. It grew from Ninette de *Valois's Academy of Choregraphic (*sic*) Art, founded 1926, which performed occasional ballets for opera and drama productions at London's Old Vic Theatre. In 1931 de Valois moved her school into the newly re-opened Sadler's Wells Theatre and established a small company of dancers. This gave its first performance on 5 May 1931 (at the Old Vic) showing several short de Valois ballets including *Les Petits Riens, Danse sacrée et profane, Hommage aux Belles Viennoise*, and also Dolin's *Spanish Dance*. Dolin appeared as guest artist along with de Valois, Moreton, and others. The first performance at Sadler's Wells Theatre was on 15 May 1931 and by the autumn the Vic-Wells ballet, as it had become, was giving fortnightly performances. By 1935 the company was based solely at Sadler's Wells. *Ashton joined in 1933 as choreographer and dancer (he created *Regatta* as guest choreographer in 1931) and the many works he created for the company over the next decades were—in combination with de Valois's ballets—to have a marked influence on the company's developing style, its classical purity, and expressive lyricism. Between 1932 and 1935 the company's ballerina was *Markova with *Helpmann joining in 1933. *Fonteyn performed her first important role in Ashton's *Rio Grande* in 1935 and other important dancers during the pre-war years were May, Brae, Honer, Turner, Gore, Chappell, and Somes. De Valois was committed to establishing a strong classical base to the repertoire and the company staged its first classic production in 1932, with Act II of *Swan Lake*. In 1933 Lopokova was a guest star in *Coppélia* and in 1934 full-length versions of *Swan Lake, Giselle*, and *Nutcracker* were presented in stagings by Sergeyev. Among the company's most important new works were de Valois's *The Rake's Progress* (1935) and *Checkmate* (1937) and Ashton's *Baiser de la fée* (1935), *Apparitions* (1935), and *Les Patineurs* (1937). In 1937 the company performed in Paris, its first season abroad, and in 1939 danced its first production of *The Sleeping Princess* (later called *Sleeping Beauty*), the ballet which was to become its signature work. During the war it toured widely around the country, often acccompanied only by two pianos, as well as giving London seasons in the New Theatre and Prince's Theatre. During a 1940 visit to Holland it was almost trapped there by the German invasion. Though many of its male dancers were absent on war service it continued to stage some new ballets, such as Helpmann's *Comus* (1941), *Hamlet* (1942), and *Miracle in the Gorbals* (1944). From 1941 it became generally known as Sadler's Wells Ballet. After the war it took up residence at the Royal Opera House, Covent Garden, opening with

a lavish new production of *Sleeping Beauty* on 20 Feb. 1946. This marked its coming-of-age as a world-class classical company. Internationally renowned choreographers like Massine, Balanchine, and Petit began staging works for the company, such as *Le Tricorne* (1947), *Ballet Imperial* (1950), and *Ballabile* (1950) respectively, and the company was greeted with huge acclaim when it first performed in New York in 1949. Ashton also entered the mature phase of his career, creating the luminous masterpiece *Symphonic Variations* in 1946, his first full-length ballet, *Cinderella*, in 1948, and possibly his most popular comedy ballet, *La Fille mal gardée*, in 1960. A new generation of dancers emerged including Grey, Shearer, Elvin, and Field and in 1946 the Sadler's Wells Opera Ballet was established to nurture young dancers and new choreographers.

This smaller sister company had a complicated existence. It was conceived as a touring company but was based at Sadler's Wells Theatre and changed its name to Sadler's Wells Theatre Ballet in 1947. During its first decade it gave significant opportunities to dancers such as Nerina, Beriosova, Blair, and MacLeary and choreographers such as *Cranko and *MacMillan who created their first ballets for the company: *Pineapple Poll* (Cranko, 1951) and *Danses concertantes* and *Solitaire* (MacMillan, 1955 and 1956). There was frequent exchange of dancers and repertoire between the two companies. In 1957 Sadler's Wells Theatre Ballet left its base at the Wells and was renamed the Royal Ballet Touring Company, also briefly known as the Royal Ballet Touring Section. It was under the direction of Field, with Doreen Wells as principal dancer. In 1970, during a major reconstruction of the Royal Ballet, the touring section was disbanded and briefly replaced by the Royal Ballet New Group, a small group of dancers taken from the main company, who toured small-scale experimental ballets under the direction of Peter *Wright. (This was in addition to the *Ballet for All group which had been founded in 1964 under the direction of Peter *Brinson to perform small-scale, educational tours.) In 1976 the touring company was named Sadler's Wells Royal Ballet and, still under Wright's direction, was re-established as a permanent company of about 50 dancers, based at Sadler's Wells Theatre but with extensive touring commitments. In 1990 it was re-located to the Birmingham Hippodrome where it became known as the Birmingham Royal Ballet, with David *Bintley taking over direction from Wright in 1995. In 1997 it became financially as well as administratively independent from the main company.

Both companies had received the royal charter in 1956, from which point the main company was known simply as the Royal Ballet. In 1963 de Valois resigned as director and was succeeded by Ashton with MacMillan as chief choreographer. His reign is often regarded as the company's golden age with Ashton producing ballets like *The Dream* (1964), MacMillan choreographing *Romeo and Juliet* (1965), and major revivals being added to the repertoire like Nijinska's *Les Noces* (1966) and Balanchine's *Serenade* (1964). Nureyev had joined the company as a permanent guest in 1962 and his world-famous partnership with Fonteyn headed a roster of powerful new talent, including Seymour, Sibley, Dowell, Mason, Park, Penney, Collier, Wall, and Coleman. MacMillan took over direction in 1970 with *Field and then Wright as associate directors, during which time he created several major ballets, including *Manon* (1974), as well as presenting works from an international range of choreographers, such as Tetley, Robbins, and van Manen. Norman *Morrice took over direction (1977–86), succeeded by Anthony *Dowell (1986–2001). During all these changes the company's basic commitment to the 19th-century classical repertoire remained unaltered. Under Dowell there were new productions of *Swan Lake* (1987) and *Sleeping Beauty* (1994), both with controversially untraditional designs but both with carefully authenticated choreographic texts. Dowell also acquired Makarova's full-length staging of *La Bayadère* in 1989 and Baryshnikov's full-length *Don Quixote* in 1993 and revived several Ashton ballets, including *Daphnis and Chloe* (1994), *Ondine* (1988), and *Illuminations* (1996). During the 1990s MacMillan returned to create several new works for the company, a new full-length *Prince of the Pagodas* (1989) as well as shorter works like *The Judas Tree* (1992). There were many new works commissioned from younger British choreographers such as Bintley, A. Page, and William Tuckett as well as new works by Forsythe and Tharp. With technical standards rising after a slump in the 1980s the company boasted a strong line-up of principals, headed by Bussell, with Cope, Kumakawa, Durante, and Wildor. This was bolstered by international stars Mukhamedov (who left the Bolshoi to join the company in 1990) and Guillem (who became a permanent guest in 1989). When the Opera House closed for rebuilding in July 1997 the company toured extensively both at home and abroad. Ross Stretton was director from 2001–2—a controversial period during which several new works were brought into the repertory but several dancers, including Wildor, left. Stretton was succeeded by Monica Mason in Dec. 2002, returning the company to its more traditional course but attempting to expand it with new works by Wheeldon, Brandstrup, and McGregor, who became choreographer in residence in 2006, the first modern-dance-trained choreographer to

be given that post. The company's dancers have traditionally been drawn from the associated *Royal Ballet School but in recent years the top ranks of principals have also come in from outside, including Alina Cojocaru, Tamara Rojo, Marianela Nuñez, and regular guest artist Carlos Acosta.

(((●))) SEE WEB LINKS

● Website for the Royal Opera House with link to the ballet company

Royal Ballet of Flanders, The Antwerp-based ballet company. It was formed by Jeanne Brabants who opened her own school in Antwerp in 1941 and for many years taught and choreographed for a variety of companies in Belgium and Holland, teaching also at the ballet school of Flemish Opera. It was here that the Flanders Ballet was finally established in 1969 under her direction. Funded by the state, its function was to present ballet to the Northern Flemish-speaking region of Belgium (the Ballet Royal de Wallonie serving the French-speaking area). Its repertoire was eclectic with ballets from many international choreographers as well as works by Brabants and André Leclair, the company's then resident choreographer. In 1976 it was granted the royal charter and around this time began to tour widely, visiting the US in 1978, London in 1980, and China in 1980. In 1984 Brabants was succeeded by Valery *Panov who orientated the repertoire towards full-length dramatic ballets, staging his own *Three Sisters*, *The Idiot*, *Romeo and Juliet*, and *Cinderella*. In 1987 he was succeeded by Robert *Denvers who introduced a more classical base, acquiring Nureyev's staging of *Don Quixote* and Flindt's staging of *La Sylphide* as well as several works from the Balanchine repertory. In 1999 Denvers mounted a new production of *Sleeping Beauty* but new works by Béjart and younger choreographers, such as Christopher d'Amboise, M. Wainrot, and resident choreographer Danny Rousseel, were also performed. In 2005 Denvers was succeeded by Kathryn Bennetts who, while maintaining the company's core classical identity, has brought works by Forsythe, David Dawson, and younger Belgian choreographers into the repertory. The company numbers around 50 dancers and since 1998 has had its own theatre in Antwerp, the Theater 't Eilandje.

(((●))) SEE WEB LINKS

● Website for The Royal Ballet of Flanders

Royal Ballet School, The Originating as de Valois's London Academy of Choregraphic (*sic*) Art (founded 1926), it became the Sadler's Wells School in 1931. In 1947 it moved to Baron's Court in W. London and under the direction of *Haskell it was expanded to include academic studies. In

1955 the Lower School was established at Richmond's White Lodge, for boarding- and day-pupils aged 11–16, offering secondary school education and ballet training. The Upper School moved to Covent Garden in 2003, offering full-time academic and dance studies to pupils over 16 as well as a teacher-training course. M. Wood succeeded Haskell as director in 1966 followed by J. Monahan in 1978, Merle *Park in 1983, and Gailene Stock in 1998. Students gain stage experience from annual school performances at Covent Garden as well as participation in company performances. The school provides both Royal Ballet companies with some, but not all, of their dancers.

Royal Danish Ballet Denmark's national ballet company. Records of court ballets performed at Copenhagen date back to the second half of the 16th century. During the first half of the 18th century dance became popular at the Lille Grønnengade Theatre (built 1722), and a ballet company was established at the Royal Theatre at Kongens Nytorv (opened in 1748 as a stage for music, drama, and dance). This company was directed by various French and Italian ballet masters but did not particularly flourish until *Galeotti's long reign. Between 1775 and 1811 he expanded the number of dancers as well as staging many popular ballets, although only one, *The Whims of Cupid* (1786), is still performed today. The school was founded in 1777. Antoine *Bournonville came to Copenhagen in 1816 but under his charge the ballet declined, until his son August *Bournonville took over direction of both company and school. His reign (1829–77) became a Golden Age, during which he radically overhauled the system of ballet education as well as choreographing around 50 works for the company. Several of these still survive, including *La Sylphide* (1836), *Napoli* (1842), *Konservatoriet* (1849), and *A Folk Tale* (1854). In their lively mix of classical and vernacular dance and their dramatic naturalism his works defined a new Danish idiom for ballet and in addition encouraged a new virtuosity in male dancers. His pupils Hans *Beck and Valborg *Borchsenius attempted to maintain his heritage but provided no new inspiration for the company. During the late 1920s and early 1930s both Balanchine and Fokine worked with the company but it was not until Harald *Lander took over as director (1932–51) that it regained its vigour. Lander staged many Bournonville ballets and other 19th-century classics, as well as commissioning new works by Danish choreographers and creating several of his own ballets, most notably *Études* (1948). The company became internationally renowned, revealing the riches of the hitherto little-known Bournonville repertoire on its many trips abroad. After Lander left for Paris there was a succession of directors and a period of instability followed. However, the school continued (under *Volkova) to sustain Denmark's fine dance tradition. Notable dancers during this century have included M. Lander, B. and K. Ralov, M. Vangsaae, F. Schaufuss, N. B. Larsen, T. Lander, E. Bruhn, P. Martins, P. Schaufuss, I. Andersen, A. Laerkesen, V. Flindt, J. Eliasen, Lis Jeppesen, L. Riggins, and J. Kobborg. During the 1950s and 1960s many guest choreographers, including Balanchine, Robbins, Ashton, Petit, and MacMillan, worked with the company and in 1966 *Flindt was appointed director. He worked to restore the balance between the 19th-century classics (Bournonville, Petipa, etc.) and 20th-century dance works, both established and newly created. He added several of his own works to the repertory as well as those with a modern dance element, by P. Taylor and Tetley, among others. He was succeeded by Henning *Kronstam in 1978 then by Frank *Andersen in 1985. P. *Schaufuss took over the company in 1994, also taking charge of the school and creating the full-length ballet *Hamlet*, but he left after two years to be replaced by Maina *Gielgud (1997–9), Aage *Thordal-Christensen (1991), and Frank Andersen (2002–7). New works have been brought into the repertory during this recent period from Neumeier, Brandstrup, and others as well as stagings of the non-Bournonville classics, such as Ratmansky's production of *The Nutcracker*. Leading dancers have included Kenneth Greve, Thomas Lund, Caroline Carvallo, Gudrun Bojesen, and Slija Schandorff. Nikolai Hubbe was appointed artistic director in 2007 overseeing a new production of *Giselle* the following year. The company performs at the three venues associated with the Kongelige Teater, the Old Stage, the Royal Danish Playhouse (opened in 2008), and the Opera House. Most of its dancers continue to be drawn from the associate school.

⊕ SEE WEB LINKS

- Website for the Kongelige Teater with link to the Royal Danish Ballet

Royal New Zealand Ballet New Zealand's national ballet company. Prior to its establishment there was little ballet activity. In 1953 Poul Gnatt founded the small Auckland based troupe New Zealand Ballet, which transferred to Wellington and under Gnatt's direction toured extensively for ten years. Gnatt produced many ballets from the Danish repertory but subsequent directors, including Russell Kerr (1962–1968) and Harry Haythorne (1982–1992), introduced a wider international repertory including works by New Zealand and Australian choreographers while guest stars such as Beriosova, Burr, and Comelin appeared with the company. The company presented *Swan Lake* at the 1971 Auckland Festival and also *Coppélia* in 1971 (both staged by Bryan

Ashbridge). A National School of Ballet was established in Wellington in 1967 and in 1984 the company was awarded its royal charter. In 1992 financial crisis nearly closed it down but under the direction of Ashley Killar it became notable for its original repertoire, with many new ballets created by its own choreographers such as Killar, Kerr, and Eric Langvet. Matz *Skoog was director 1996–2001 and was succeeded by Gary Harris, who has introduced a new, international generation of choreographers including Javier De *Frutos, Christopher *Hampson, and Jorma *Elo, as well as work by associate director Ou Lu. In 1998 the company acquired a permanent theatre in Wellington's Westpac St James Theatre.

(((·))) SEE WEB LINKS

• Website for Royal New Zealand Ballet

Royal Swedish Ballet Sweden's national ballet company. The first Swedish court ballet dates from 1638 and was arranged by the French ballet master Antoine de Beaulieu, but the present company dates back to 1773 when Gustav III (dubbed the 'Theatre King') founded the Swedish opera with its small ballet company of 24 dancers. Directed by Louis Gallodier, this rapidly expanded to 72 dancers, with the company's official school also being founded in 1773. With Antoine *Bournonville and Marcadet as choreographers, the company flourished but after this the nation's most important native talent, such as Didelot, M. Taglioni, and C. Johansson made their careers abroad and the company failed to build on its initial successes. During the mid-19th century it enjoyed another period of vitality under the ballet master Anders Selinder, who created ballets around folkloric material, and also with the presence of August *Bournonville who worked in Stockholm as a guest. After this the company declined again, only recovering its vitality when Mikhail Fokine and Vera Fokina worked there in 1913 and staged several of the former's ballets. Though Fokine returned several times this peak was not sustained and many of the company's best and youngest dancers left to work with the Paris-based Ballets Suédois (1920–5). Under a succession of different ballet masters the RSB increasingly lost its public to modern dance. A new generation of Swedish choreographers, such as *Cullberg and *Cramér had found their inspiration in artists like Wigman and Jooss and thus chose to establish their own small companies rather than working with RSB. However, the company regained its reputation in the 1950s with *Tudor's appointment as director (1949–50, 1962–3) followed by *Skeaping (1953–62). Both concentrated on improving the classical repertoire, with Skeaping staging *Swan Lake*, *Sleeping Beauty*, and *Coppélia* and nurturing a generation of ballerinas,

notably Elsa-Marianne von *Rosen. Many contemporary ballets, such as Cullberg's *Miss Julie* and *Medea* and Cramér's *The Prodigal Son*, were also acquired along with works by Massine, Balanchine, and Tudor who created *Echoing of Trumpets* for the company in 1963. More recently ballets by Robbins, Tetley, MacMillan, Nureyev, Cranko, and Kylián have been added to its increasingly rich repertory. Skeaping also began the reconstruction of historical ballets (beginning with the 1649 *Cupid out of his Humour* (1956)) which are performed at the 18th-century court theatre at *Drottningholm. Recent directors have included Brian Macdonald (1964–6), Bruhn (1967–71), Cramér (1975–80), Gunilla Roempke (1980–4), Simon Mottram (1993–6), F. *Andersen (1995–9), Petter *Jacobsson (1999–2002), and Madeleine Onne from 2002, and significant additions to the repertory have included MacMillan's *Mayerling*; new work by Mats Ek, Par Isberg, Per Jonsonn, and other Swedish choreographers and international repertory from Forsythe, Tharp, Duato, and others. Principal dancers have included Anneli Alhanko, Yvonne Brosset, Niklas Ek, Istvan Kisch, Kerstin Lidström, Madeleine Onne, Per Arthur Segerstrom, and Anna Valev. In 1998, as part of the company's 225th anniversary year, four reconstructed works from the Ballets Suédois repertory were staged. In 2008 Patrice Bart was commissioned to choreograph a full-length ballet in tribute to its royal founder, *Gustave III*.

Stockholm 59 Degrees North is an ensemble of soloists and principals attached to the company, performing largely contemporary work.

(((·))) SEE WEB LINKS

• Website for the Royal Swedish Ballet

Royal Winnipeg Ballet The oldest of Canada's major ballet companies. It began in 1938 as the Winnipeg Ballet Club, founded by Gweneth *Lloyd and Betty Farrally and gave its first semi-professional performances as the Winnipeg Ballet in 1939. It became fully professional in 1949 and was the first company to be granted a (British) royal charter in 1955. The company performed mostly populist works choreographed by Lloyd, such as *Shadow in the Prairie* (1952), but few of these survived a fire in 1954, and the company entered a period of some confusion until Arnold *Spohr was appointed director (1958–88). Under him, a new generation of Canadian choreographers emerged, creating works with a popular local appeal, including Brian Macdonald's *The Shining People of Leonard Cohen* (1970) and Norbert Vesak's *The Ecstasy of Rita Joe* (1971), about a Native Canadian's doomed experience of the big city. Ballets were also acquired from, among others, Neumeier, Araiz, V. Nebrada, and de Mille. In 1970 Spohr founded a school which led to significant improvements in the company's classical dancing and produced Evelyn Hart who won the Gold Medal at Varna in 1980. With a ballerina in the company he was able to stage classic ballets like *Giselle* (1982) and *Swan Lake* (1987). Spohr was succeeded by Henny Jurriëns (1988–9), John Meehan (1989–93), William Whitener (1993–5), and André Lewis (1995). The company's versatile mix has been retained with new populist works such as Jacques Lemay's *Anne of Green Gables* (1989) and Jorden Morris's *Peter Pan*, acquisitions of ballets by Balanchine, van Manen, Kylián, Tharp, and Itzik Galili, Meehan's new staging of *Sleeping Beauty* (1993), and works by emerging Canadian choreographers like Peter Quanz and the company's resident choreographer Mark Godden (appointed 1990). Its economic size (28 dancers) allows the company to tour widely both in Canada and abroad.

(((●))) **SEE WEB LINKS**
- Website for the Royal Winnipeg Ballet

Ruanne, Patricia (*b* Leeds, 3 Jun. 1945) British dancer. She studied at the Royal Ballet School and joined the Royal Ballet in 1962 where she became principal in 1969. Much of her work was with the touring company and she created roles in many works, but in 1973 she joined London Festival Ballet in order to dance classic roles, such as Aurora in Nureyev's staging of *Sleeping Beauty*. She also created several leading roles including Hynd's *The Sanguine Fan* (1976). She was ballet mistress at LFB (1983–5) then at Paris Opera (1986–96), after which she worked freelance as teacher and repetiteur. She was also acting director at La Scala (1999–2000).

Rubinstein, Ida (*b* St Petersburg (some sources say Kharkov) Oct. 1885; *d* Vence, France, 20 Sept. 1960) Russian dancer, actress, and director. Born into a wealthy family she was able to study music, dance, and acting with private teachers including Fokine who also choreographed for her the 'Dance of the Seven Veils' which she performed in her own production of *Salomé* (mus. Glazunov, 1908). Though this was privately performed it still created a scandal as Rubinstein removed most of her veils. In 1909 she joined Diaghilev's Ballets Russes where, on the strength of her personal beauty rather than her dance technique, she created the title role in Fokine's *Cléopâtre* (1909) and Zobéide in his *Scheherazade* (1910). In 1911 she left Diaghilev to form her own company for which she commissioned several lavish productions including *Le Martyre de Saint-Sébastien* (mus. Debussy, text d'Annunzio, chor. Fokine, des. Bakst, 1911). After the First World War she appeared in various plays and danced in Staat's *Istar* at the Paris Opera, 1924.

Between 1928 and 1929 she directed her own ballet company (with Nijinska as choreographer) in Paris. It was revived in 1931 and in 1934 and during its run she created leading roles in several specially commissioned works, such as Nijinska's *Bolero* (mus. Ravel) and *Le Baiser de la fée* (mus. Stravinsky), both choreographed in 1928, Massine's *David* (mus. Sauguet, 1928), *Amphion* (mus. Honegger, 1931), and *Diane de Poitiers* (libr. de Gramont, chor. Fokine, mus. Ibert, 1934). One of the few female ballet directors of her era, her commissioning record was impressive, including librettos by Valéry and Gide, and designs by Benois as well as original scores for most of her repertoire. She also possessed a fine stable of dancers including Vilzak and Schollar, Ashton, Lichine, and Krassovska. In 1935 she disbanded the company leaving several of her last commissions to the Paris Opera. Her final stage appearances were in the Claudel–Honegger play *Jeanne d'Arc au bûcher*, in Basle, 1938, and Paris, 1939. Though often dismissed as a dilettante on account of her considerable wealth, as a performer she possessed a genuinely extraordinary charisma and was one of the most powerful women in the theatre of her day.

Rudner, Sara (*b* Brooklyn, NY, 16 Feb. 1944) US dancer and choreographer. She studied with Sanasardo and performed with his company after which she worked with various groups until she became principal dancer with Tharp's company in 1966. An exceptionally intelligent dancer, combining speed, sensuousness, and vitality with a great refinement of style, she created roles in most of Tharp's work for the next twenty years. During this period she also began choreographing her own work for the Sarah Rudner Ensemble, and has continued to make work, including solos for herself, and duets, for example *Necessary Weather* (1993 with Dana Reitz). In 1999 she was appointed professor of dance at Sarah Lawrence College. She has also worked in opera, for example choreographing and performing the role of the Dancing Angel in Peter Sellars's 1992 production of Messiaen's *Francois d'Assise*.

Rudra Béjart Ballet Lausanne *See under* BÉJART.

Rumba Latin American dance in 4/4 time. Originally a courtship dance, popular in Cuba, it was introduced to the US in the 1930s. A couple dance characterized by a swaying motion of the hips.

Ruses d'amour (*The Trial of Damis*) Ballet in one act with choreography by Petipa and music by Glazunov. Premiered 29 Jan. 1900 at the Hermitage Theatre, St Petersburg, with Legnani and Gerdt. It tells the story of a duchess's daughter, Isabella, who disguises herself as a servant to test whether her fiancé, the Marquis Damis, loves her for herself rather than for her title.

Russell, Francia (*b* Los Angeles, 1938) US dancer and director. She studied with Doubrovska, Volkova, Joffrey, and Balanchine, joining New York City Ballet in 1956 where she became soloist in 1959 and ballet mistress in 1964. During the 1970s she worked as guest ballet mistress in Europe until she was appointed co-artistic director (with Kent Stowell) of the Frankfurt Ballet in 1975. In 1977 they moved to Pacific Northwest Ballet as directors (Russell also directing the company school), and until her retirement in 2004 she was responsible for staging the company's Balanchine repertory. She has additionally staged his ballets for companies throughout the world, including the Shanghai Ballet (1987) and the Kirov (1988-9), the first time Balanchine's ballets were staged in Russia.

Russia and the USSR Russian ballet has its roots in a school founded by the Empress Anna Ivanovna in 1738 for the teaching of ballet to selected servants' children. Under the direction of Jean-Baptiste *Landé, this produced a small company which during the subsequent decade performed in entertainments staged in the royal palaces of both St Petersburg and Moscow. After Landé's death ballet productions were staged by the impresario Giovanni Locatelli in an old opera house in St Petersburg, and under continuing royal patronage the art form flourished. Many guest ballet masters were invited to the city to stage their ballets, such as Hilverding and Angiolini, and though most principal dancers were foreign a new generation of Russian talent was also emerging. The young ballerina Nastasia Parfentyevna Birilova (1778-1804) was outstanding and in 1794 the first Russian ballet master Ivan *Valberkh was appointed to direct the St Petersburg School and oversee the company which now performed at the city's Bolshoi Theatre. Outside St Petersburg developments were more limited. In Moscow a dance school was attached to the city's orphanage in 1773 under the direction of the Italian ballet master Filippo Beccari and in 1776 a company of 24 dancers began giving stage performances in the Znamensky Theatre. Elsewhere, many landowners funded their own troupes of serf dancers, performing folk and ballet.

Russia finally became a major centre of ballet when *Didelot came to work in St Petersburg (1801-11 and 1816-34). During his reign he dramatically raised the standards of both the Imperial Company and its school as well as bringing important new works into the repertory. He was succeeded by Alexis Blache from France and Antoine Titus from Berlin and it was under Titus that M. Taglioni was invited to give her debut performance in St Petersburg, dancing *La Sylphide* on 6 Sept. 1837. She caused a sensation, and her continuing guest appearances over the next five years served to rekindle public enthusiasm. She also inspired a new generation of Russian dancers such as *Andreyanova, although many foreigners continued to guest in the city, e.g. Grahn in 1843 and Elssler in 1848. Between 1851 and 1859 *Perrot worked in St Petersburg, staging many of his ballets there and was succeeded by Saint-Léon (1859-69) who created his popular hit *The Humpbacked Horse* in 1864 and promoted the career of the Russian ballerina Marfa Muraieva. It was under *Petipa, however, that Russian ballet entered its golden age, developing its own distinctive style (a fusion of French elegance, Italian virtuosity, and Russian flamboyance) and its own major repertory. He had arrived in 1847 as a dancer (his father, Jean Petipa, was a teacher at the Imperial School) and after his appointment as ballet master began to create a body of about 50 ballets for the St Petersburg and Moscow companies, including *Don Quixote* (1869), *La Bayadère* (1877), *Sleeping Beauty* (1890), *Swan Lake* (1895, with Ivanov), and *Raymonda* (1898). The great Tchaikovsky ballets were commissioned by *Vsevolozhsky who was director of the Imperial Theatres from 1881 to 1899. Dancing many of the leading roles were celebrated Russian dancers such as Kshessinska and Preobrajenska who now rivalled popular guest virtuosos like Legnani and Cecchetti. At the beginning of Petipa's reign performances were given at the Bolshoi Theatre, later they alternated between there and the Mariinsky Theatre (built 1860) which from 1889 became the sole venue for grand ballet.

The successes of the St Petersburg Ballet overshadowed developments in Moscow where the Imperial company moved from the Petrovsky Theatre (under the management of Englishman Michael Maddox) to the rebuilt Bolshoi Petrovsky Theatre and thence to the replacement Bolshoi (built 1856). Its less elevated standards were typified by the failure of its own premiere of *Swan Lake* (chor. Reisinger, 1877) compared to the success of the Petipa–Ivanov version at St Petersburg. Yet it developed its own distinctive style, more theatrically colourful than the classical St Petersburg ballet, and evident in, for example, Petipa's staging of *Don Quixote* for the company in 1869. During the early 20th century *Gorsky intensified the dramatic realism of Moscow's productions, both in his revisions of Petipa's ballets and in his own works, which particularly showcased the exceptional expressive talents of *Geltser.

During this dramatic invigoration of the Moscow company the St Petersburg Ballet lost much of its own creative momentum. Petipa had been forced to retire in 1903 and though young choreographers—notably *Fokine—were eager to present their own new ballets, the conservatism of both directorate and public stifled new creativity. The extraordinary generation of dance talent that came out of the school in the first decade of the century—Pavlova, Karsavina, Nijinsky, etc.— found little to excite them in the repertoire, and not surprisingly many seized the radical opportunities offered them by Diaghilev and his Ballets Russes.

Until 1917 Russian ballet was under the Tsar's patronage but after the Revolution it was taken over by the State. Initially a new generation of choreographers, such as *Lopukhov and *Goleizovsky, pursued avant-garde principles in their vision of a new Soviet ballet but by 1932 *Socialist Realism had become established as the official style demanding realistic stagings and politically correct themes. Ballet education was centralized (and given State encouragement) under the supervision of *Vaganova whose methods became official teaching practice throughout the USSR. It was also official policy to establish an opera house—with its own ballet and opera companies—in major towns and cities throughout the Republics, such as Novosibirsk. Some were more successful than others, but none rivalled the major companies in Moscow (renamed the Bolshoi) and Leningrad (renamed GATOB, then the Kirov). During the 1930s the latter was preeminent, premiering Vainonen's *Flames of Paris* (1932), Zakharov's *Fountain of Bakhchisarai* (1934), and Lavrovsky's *Romeo and Juliet* (1940), but the Bolshoi's premiere of Zakharov's *Cinderella* (1945) marked a shift over to Moscow and the leading Soviet ballerina *Ulanova was transferred from the Kirov to the Bolshoi. However, when both companies started to tour abroad after the late 1950s Western audiences were astonished by the strength and expressiveness of their dancers, and Soviet ballet as a whole started to enjoy immense international prestige.

On these tours, however, Soviet dancers saw how varied ballet and modern dance had become in the West. Some were sufficiently frustrated by their company's artistic isolation, and lack of creative freedom that they chose to leave the USSR. Nureyev was the first famous dancer to defect, and was followed by Makarova and Baryshnikov. The West benefited greatly from the arrival of these dancers, not only their inspirational example as performers but also the traditions they brought with them. All three staged Petipa ballets which were previously little known in the West. After these defections Russian companies became much more cautious about touring, although when *Grigorovich was appointed artistic director of the Bolshoi in 1964 the company enjoyed an injection of new artistic vigour. He created a repertoire of colourful epic ballets, including *Spartacus* and *Ivan the Terrible*, which were danced by a succession of outstanding male dancers like Vasiliev, Liepa, and Mukhamedov. By the late 1980s, however, Grigorovich had ceased producing new work and the repertory had become moribund. Mukhamedov's public departure to London was one among many blows to its prestige. Under the direction of *Vinogradov the Kirov attempted to introduce new works into its repertoire, such as those of Béjart and Balanchine, but its reputation continued to rest largely on its performance of the classics and the reputation of a new generation of dancers including Asylmuratova who were still considered to embody the purity of the Kirov traditions.

During the 1980s and 1990s increasing numbers of Western companies visited Russia, including many modern dance groups such as Trisha Brown and the Rambert Dance Company, but a native Russian modern dance culture was slow to get established. Kinetic Theatre, founded by Sasha Pepelyaev in 1994, was one of the first dance groups to try to break the monopoly of the classical tradition, along with Provincial Dances, founded by Tatyana Baganova. From the late 1990s onwards more independent companies emerged including Saira Blanche, directed by Oleg Soulimenko, the Chelyabinsk Theatre of Modern Dance, the Dance Theatre Elta (from Elets), Kannon Dance Company from St Petersburg, and Nota Bene and Na.sH companies from Moscow. Several of these were featured during the First European Festival of Contemporary Dance, held in Moscow in 1999. Some of the smaller ballet companies additionally attempted to develop more contemporary repertories, including the *Stanislavsky Ballet, *Eifman's Leningrad Theatre of Contemporary Ballet, the Russian Ballet of the 21st Century, the Graphical Ballet, the Evgeny Panfilov Ballet (Perm), and St Petersburg's All-Men Ballet under Valery Mikhailovsky (a Russian version of Les Ballets Trockadero de Monte Carlo). Like the larger companies, however, their artistic aspirations were radically affected by the breakdown of the Soviet Union as state funding for the arts dramatically declined.

Funding still remains an issue for the emerging modern dance scene, but the major ballet companies have undergone significant changes during the first decade of the 21st century. Although the Bolshoi has had several changes of director, and has remained dogged by political factions, it enjoyed a period of exceptional creative activity under *Ratmansky (2004–8) who introduced many new works to the repertory as well as resurrecting or recreating some early Soviet ballets. The Kirov, reverting to its former name, the Mariinsky, also widened its scope with Gergiev as overall director of ballet and opera and *Vaziev as ballet director.

Russian Seasons Ballet in one act with choreography by Alexei Ratmansky and music by Leonid Desyatnikov. Premiered 8 Jun., 2006, by New York City Ballet at New York State Theater, with Jenifer (*sic*) Ringer, Sofiane Sylve, Wendy Whelan, and Albert Evans. The ballet evokes the music's changing moods and is inspired by Russian folk dance and imagery.

Ruzimatov, Farukh (*b* Tashkent, 26 June 1963) Russian-Uzbek dancer. He studied at the Leningrad (Vaganova) Ballet School under Gennady Selyutsky and in 1981 graduated into the Kirov Ballet where he rapidly became a soloist. A powerful but unusually fluid dancer with a flamboyantly arched line, he performed his first principal role in 1984 as Basil in *Don Quixote*, going on to create roles in new ballets as well as the role of Ali in Vinogradov's new production of *Le Corsaire* (1987). In 1990 he was a guest principal with American Ballet Theatre and between 2007 and 2009 was artistic director of the Mikhailovsky (formerly Màly) Ballet in St Petersburg. He is the recipient of numerous awards including Honoured Artist of Russia 2000.

Ryom, Heidi (*b* Copenhagen, 26 Aug. 1955) Danish dancer. She studied at the Royal Danish Ballet School graduating into the company in 1974 where she became solo dancer (principal) in 1982. Initially regarded as a soubrette, with her petite build and speed, she matured into a poetically expressive performer, dancing most of the principal roles in the Bournonville repertoire as well as modern works by, among others, Ailey, Balanchine, and Béjart, and creating a role in Neumeier's *Birthday Dances* (1990). In 1988 she formed a partnership with Julio Bocca and they guested together around the world. She retired in 1997.

r

Saarinen, Tero (*b* 4 Sept. 1964) Finnish chore-ographer. He trained at the Finnish National Opera Ballet School and entered the company in 1985. Rising to the rank of soloist he nonetheless left the company in 1992, moving to Japan where he spent a year studying butoh, kabuki, and mar-tial arts. In 1996 he founded his own company in Helsinki, eventually resident at the city's Alexander Theatre, for which he subsequently created nu-merous works, including *Borrowed Light* (2004) and *Next of Kin* (mus. Jarmo Saari, 2008). His style, which reflects the different idioms of his training, is intensely imagistic, often dealing with interior, visionary states. He has also created works for other companies including Nederlands Dans Theater (*Frail Line*, 2006 and *Scheme of Things*, 2009), Batsheva Dance Company, Finnish National Ballet, and Lyon Opera Ballet.

((●)) SEE WEB LINKS

• Website for the Saarinen company

Sachs, Curt (*b* Berlin, 29 Jun. 1881; *d* New York, 5 Feb. 1959) German-US musicologist and author of the classic *World History of the Dance* (1937), first published in German as *Eine Weltgeschichte des Tanzes* (Berlin, 1933).

Sacre du printemps, Le *See* RITE OF SPRING, THE.

Saddler, Donald (*b* Van Nuys, Calif., 24 Jun. 1920) US dancer and choreographer. He studied with Maracci, Dolin, and Tudor and danced with Ballet Theatre (1939–43 and 1946–7). He is best known for choreographing musicals, such as Bernstein's *Wonderful Town* (1953) and *No, No, Nanette* (1971), but was also assistant and later associate director of the Harkness Ballet (1964–9). In 2001 he returned to the stage in the revival of *Follies*, the musical.

Sadler's Wells North London theatre. It dates back to Dick Sadler's musick house in the 1680s, but its significance for dance dates back to the theatre, financed by Lilian Baylis, that opened in 1931, primarily as a venue for dance and opera. It was the birthplace of the Royal Ballet and English National Opera, and many important British ballets had their premieres there. In 1998 it was replaced by a new building, which has since be-come the pre-eminent venue for contemporary dance in the UK. As both a production and receiv-ing house the theatre presents a wide range of British and international dance, and has several leading choreographers and performers as asso-ciate artists. It hosts the annual hip-hop festival, Breakin' Convention.

See SPALDING, ALISTAIR.

Sadler's Wells Ballet and Sadler's Wells Theatre Ballet *See* ROYAL BALLET.

Sadler's Wells Royal Ballet *See* BIRMING-HAM ROYAL BALLET.

St Denis, Ruth (originally Ruth Dennis; *b* Som-erville, NJ, 20 Jan. 1879; *d* Hollywood, Calif., 21 Jul. 1968) US dancer, teacher, and choreographer who is considered one of the pioneering influences in American modern dance. She began her dance career in the music hall, having studied mime, social dance, and recitation with her mother, but was inspired to create her own oriental-style dance productions in 1904 after seeing a cigarette adver-tisement depicting the Egyptian goddess Isis. The ethnic authenticity of these works was always du-bious; her first 'Hindu 'ballet, *Radha* (1906), was set to music from Delibes's *Lakmé*, and her style mixed 'exotic' elements, such as snaking arm movements and mobile hips, with popular dance steps and gymnastics. She was very successful in both the US and Europe, where she toured for three years and in 1909 she created *Egypta* for a major US tour and the Japanese ballet *O-Mika* (1913). Despite her commercial appeal, St Denis aspired to a profound moral seriousness in her work. She once described herself as a 'rhythmic and impersonal instrument of spiritual revelation', and many of her works centred on the drama of spiritual awakening or the beauty of the inner life. Her choreography was also an attempt to make an exact translation of music into dance. She was never less than an extremely adroit entertainer, however, using drapes, jewellery, and lighting to create gorgeously memorable stage pictures as well as to flatter her own highly flexible body. In 1914 Ted *Shawn became her partner and in 1915 they set up the Denishawn Dance School in Los

Angeles where they trained dancers for their company. Humphrey, Weidman, and Graham all began their careers at Denishawn. Major productions included *A Dance Pageant of Egypt, Greece and India* (mus. W. Myrowitz, Horst, and A. Nevins, 1916) and their 1918 staging of Gluck's *Orpheus and Eurydice*. Denishawn was disbanded after her separation from Shawn in 1931 but she went on to found the Society of Spiritual Arts and the New York School of Natya with La Meri in 1938. She continued giving recitals and demonstration performances until she was 87. In 1932 she published a volume of poetry, *Lotus Light*, and in 1939 her autobiography, *An Unfinished Life*. There are several films about her work, including *Ruth St Denis and Ted Shawn* (NBC, 1958) and the 1941 film *Radha*, which was edited in 1973. There has been much recent interest in reconstructing her dances.

Saint-Léon, Arthur (*b* Paris, 17 Sept. 1821; *d* Paris, 2 Sept. 1870) French dancer, choreographer, ballet master, and teacher. He studied with his father, a ballet master, in Tuscany and Stuttgart and made his stage debut as a violinist in 1834 and as a dancer in Munich in 1835. He subsequently danced all around Europe, including Milan (1842) and London (various seasons, 1843–8). In Rome (1843) he choreographed his first ballet, *Vivandiera ed il postiglione* (mus. E. Rolland), which starred Cerrito. He married her in 1845 and they toured extensively together. In 1847 he created *La Fille de marbre* (mus. Pugni, after Costa) for her debut at Paris Opera and after its success he remained in Paris becoming teacher of the Class of Perfection and choreographer in 1851 and also mounting many ballets and divertissements including *La Violon du diable* (mus. Pugni, 1849) in which he himself played the violin. He separated from Cerrito in 1851 and left the Opera a year later. He worked as choreographer in Paris (Théâtre Lyrique) and Lisbon and in 1859 became Perrot's successor as ballet master of the St Petersburg Imperial Theatres where he staged many of his earlier works and created several new ones, including *The Humpbacked Horse* (mus. Pugni, 1864). Between 1863 and 1870 he also worked as ballet master at Paris Opera where he revived *La Fille mal gardée* in 1866 and in the same year choreographed *La Source* (mus. Delibes and Minkus). In 1869 he left Russia for good and in 1870 choreographed his last and most successful ballet, *Coppélia* (mus. Delibes).

He was acclaimed as a prodigiously talented dancer, with unusually high elevation and control though he was sometimes criticized for indulging in gratuitously acrobatic display. He was also considered a virtuoso on the violin and composed over 70 pieces of music, including scores for his own ballets, such as *Saltarello* (Lisbon, 1855). His choreography reflected his accomplishment in both fields. Though some of the librettos he used were thin or derivative, the ballets themselves featured brilliantly crafted, musical choreography, usually with passages of folk and national dance colourfully adapted for ballet. He also invented his own pin-figure system of dance notation which he published in 1852 as *La Sténochorégraphie ou Art d'écrire promptement la danse*. This was part of his endeavour to strengthen dance training, improve performance standards, and so halt the decline in ballet's popularity. The exercises and sequences he recorded give a clear indication of the advanced point to which dance technique had developed by the mid-19th century, though, ironically, he recorded none of his own major works for posterity.

St Petersburg *See also* KIROV; RUSSIA. The birthplace of Russian ballet. The Empress Anna Ivanovna founded a school in 1738 under the direction of *Landé and from this developed the Imperial company which performed in St Petersburg and also Moscow. After Landé's death in 1748, ballets were staged by G. Locatelli in an old opera house near the Summer Garden in St Petersburg and the company grew in strength under the influence of visiting ballet masters like Hilverding and Angiolini as well as native ballet masters like *Valberkh. Under *Didelot (1801–11 and 1816–34) it achieved impressive standards, giving its performances at the Bolshoi Theatre, while the city itself became a leading centre of Romantic ballet. Many ballerinas visited, including Taglioni (first perf. 1837), Grahn (first perf. 1834), and Elssler (first perf. 1848). Perrot was ballet master with the company (1851–8), followed by Saint-Léon (1859–69). In 1860 the Mariinsky Theatre was built in the city and performances alternated between it and the Bolshoi until 1889 when the former became the sole stage for grand ballet. Under *Petipa (ballet master 1862–1903) the Imperial Ballet at St Petersburg reached a magnificent peak, with a succession of spectacular works, including *La Bayadère* (1877), *Sleeping Beauty* (1890), and *Swan Lake* (1895), and a generation of virtuoso ballerinas, such as Kshessinska and Preobrajenska, who had been inspired by guest stars like Legnani and Zucchi. After Petipa was forced to retire, the next generation, including Pavlova, Karsavina, and Nijinsky, were left with few new challenges. The reforming vision of *Fokine was spurned by the conservative theatre management and much of the new talent left to join Diaghilev. After the 1917 revolution, choreographers like *Lopukhov and *Goleizovsky experimented with new forms and ideas and in 1932 *Socialist Realism was introduced as the new mould for Soviet ballet. However, the classics did remain in the repertory of the Mariinsky company (renamed the Kirov) and rigorous training under *Vaganova ensured that high standards remained. A succession of major new ballets, including Zakharov's *Fountain of Bakhchisarai* (1932) and Lavrovsky's *Romeo and Juliet* (1940), maintained Leningrad's dominance but in 1945 there was a shift of emphasis to Moscow, marked by the country's most renowned ballerina, Ulanova, being transferred to the Bolshoi. During the 1960s and 1970s dissatisfaction with the Kirov's rigid artistic and political policies caused a number of famous defections by leading dancers, including Nureyev, Makarova, and Baryshnikov. Under the direction of *Vinogradov some Western ballets were acquired, by Petit, Balanchine, and Béjart, among others, but although the new political climate of the 1990s freed the company to experiment with Western influences it also created financial problems. Cuts in state funding meant that the Kirov had to undertake extensive foreign touring to remain solvent, and there was little money to fund new productions. After Vinogradov's departure in 1996, the company was run by Vasiev, then Yuri Fateyev, also Valery Gergiev, the overall director of the Kirov Theatre, which around this time reverted to its original name, the Mariinsky. New ballets were slowly but steadily added to the repertory, as well as revivals of early classics from Diaghilev's Ballets Russes, such as *Rite of Spring*.

The city's second classical troupe, the Maly Theatre of Opera and Ballet, was founded in 1915, and gave its first full ballet performance in 1933, with Lopukhov's *Harlequinade*. It subsequently became a centre for new choreography with works by *Fenster, *Belsky, *Boyarchikov, and Vinogradov but during the 1990s it, too, had to sacrifice some new creation to the financial requirement of foreign touring. In 2007 it moved towards a re-vitalization with the appointment of *Ruzimatov as director and the subsequent appointment of Michael Messerer as ballet master. The company also reverted to its original name, *Mikhailovsky Ballet.

In 1977 an additional focus for new work was established with the founding of the Leningrad Theatre of Contemporary Ballet, under the direction of choreographer *Eifman. Though he developed his own style of modern ballet, there was little development of Western-influenced modern dance, largely because of the financial and political problems of establishing small independent groups. Rare exceptions during the last two decades have included the All-Men Ballet, Kannon Dance, Kinetic Dance, and Modern Dance theatre. The city has begun hosting a regular festival that embraces modern and classical dance.

Saisons, Les (orig. Russ. title *Vremena goda*) Ballet in one act, with choreography by Petipa, music by Glazunov, and design by P. Lambin and I. Ponomariov. Premiered 20 Feb. 1900 at St Petersburg's Hermitage Theatre, with Pavlova, Preobrajenska, Kshessinska, and Legat. It is essentially a grand divertissement, which depicts each of the four seasons and concludes with an apotheosis of the stars. Later versions include Legat (1907), A. Varlamov (Bolshoi Ballet, 1959), and Cranko (Stuttgart, 1962). Pavlova's company often danced the Bacchanale section and Ashton used part of the music for his *Birthday Offering* (1956). *See also* FOUR SEASONS, THE.

Sakuma, Nao (*b* Fukuoka, 6 Feb. 1976) Japanese dancer. She trained at the Michiko Komori Ballet School and Royal Ballet School, joining Birmingham Royal Ballet in 1995 and promoted to principal in 2002. A formidable technician she has danced lead roles in BRB's classical repertory (often partnered by Chi Cao) as well as works by Ashton, MacMillan, Bintley, and Tharp.

She has created roles in Bintley's *The Seasons* (2001) and *Concert Fantasy* (2002).

Salade Avant-garde commedia dell'arte ballet in one act with choreography by Massine, text by Albert Flamand, music by Milhaud, and design by Braque. Premiered 17 May 1924 at Comte Étienne de Beaumont's Soirées de Paris, Théâtre de la Cigale, Paris, with Massine and Eleanora Manna. Later versions include Lifar (Paris Opera, 1935), Darrell (Western Theatre Ballet, 1961), and Milloss (Vienna State Opera, 1963).

Salammbô Ballet in five acts with choreography and libretto by Gorsky, music by A. Arends, and design by K. Korovin. Premiered 10 Oct. 1910 by the Bolshoi Theatre, Moscow, with Geltser and Mordkin. It is based on Flaubert's novel of the same name and tells the story of Matoh's love for Salammbô, the princess of Carthage who is sacrificing herself to save her city. This was one of Gorsky's most seminal attempts at dramatic realism.

Sallé, Marie (*b* 1707; *d* Paris 27 Jul. 1756) French dancer and choreographer who was considered one of the most expressive performers of her time. She was born into a family of travelling actors and from an early age was taught the art of dramatization in dance. Aged 9 she appeared with her brother in London in the pantomimes of John Rich (giving 100 performances between 1716 and 1717) and two years later made her debut in Paris, performing regularly at the Foire Saint-Laurent and Foire Saint-Germain. She studied in Paris with Prévost (herself a gifted dance actress) and when she made her debut at the Paris Opera in 1727 she was rapidly established as a rival to Camargo, her own delicate grace and expressive mime contrasting with the latter's technical brilliance. She continued to dance regularly in London, where in 1734 she created a sensation with her first choreographed ballet, *Pygmalion* (premiered 14 Feb.). This may have been influenced by the work of John Weaver and by the art of dance-actress Hester Santlow, and was also a forerunner of Noverre's ballet d'action. Sallé herself performed Galatea, the statue who comes to life in answer to its maker's prayers, and impressed audiences not only with the eloquence of her dancing but also with her dress. In keeping with her subject she abandoned the ballerina's standard costume of voluminous skirts and panniers and appeared instead with her hair loose, wearing nothing but sandals and a simple muslin tunic. While still in London she worked with Handel who composed for her the ballet music *Terpsichore* as prologue to his opera *Il Pastor Fido* (1734) and divertissements in his operas *Oreste* (1734), *Ariodante*, and *Alcina* (both 1735). In the suite of dances which she created for the latter she appeared as Cupid, in male dress. The audience booed and she never danced in a London theatre again. In Paris she was very successful in Molière and Lully's comédie-ballets and also worked closely with Rameau. She choreographed and danced roles in several of his works, such as *Les Indes galantes* (1735), *Castor et Pollux* (1737), and *Dardanus* (1739). But Paris was not so receptive to Sallé's choreography and, chafing under the conventions of the Opéra's regime, she retired in 1740. After five years' seclusion she returned to choreograph several more dances including those for Rameau's *Platée* (1745) and to make successful appearances at court, dancing her last performance in 1753 at Fontainebleau. During her career she was partnered by many great dancers including Louis Dupré and Gaetano Vestris; her portrait was painted by Nicolas Lancret and Maurice-Quentin de la Tour, and Voltaire, Pope and Gay all wrote poems about her. *Noverre, whose own reforming attempts at realism were partly inspired by her, said 'she replaced showiness by simple, touching graces; free from affectation, her features were refined, expressive and intelligent. It was not by means of leaps and jumps that she stirred the heart.'

Salome Ballet in two acts with choreography and libretto by Flindt, music by P. M. Davies, and design by Daydé. Premiered 10 Nov. 1978 at Circus Theatre, Copenhagen, with a specially assembled company including F. and V. Flindt, Eliasen, and L. Rhodes. It is based on the biblical story in which King Herod's daughter asks for the head of John the Baptist as reward for her dancing, but concludes with an apotheosis in which the heroine and John meet as lovers in an afterlife. Other versions of the story include Fuller (mus. F. Schmitt, Paris, 1907), Gorsky (mus. R. Strauss, Moscow, 1921), Lifar (mus. R. Strauss, Monte Carlo, 1946), Cullberg (mus. H. Rosenberg, Stockholm, 1964),

Darrell (mus. Hindemith, Scottish Theatre Ballet, 1970), L. Kemp (mus. various, New York, 1975), M. Morris (mus. R. Strauss, Seattle, 1986, performed by the singer Josephine Barstow), and G. Murphy (mus. various, Sydney Dance Company, 1999). Many artists have choreographed Salomé's 'Dance of the Seven Veils' for productions of the Strauss opera, including Doug Varone, Metropolitan Opera (2004).

Salsa Latin American dance in 4/4 time, which is performed to salsa music. Literally meaning sauce (with spicy connotations), salsa is a fusion of Caribbean and European elements. The term itself is a recent creation, coined in the 1960s to market a range of Latin music, but the origins of salsa go back to much older and diverse forms, one of which is son, from Cuba. Usually a couple dance, characterized by rhythmic footwork, fluid turns, and quick changes of balance, it can also be danced as a solo, line, or circle dance. It achieved international popularity in the 1980s and has continued to evolve, styled with elements from other dances, including hip-hop, jazz, and flamenco.

saltarello A lively jumping dance in 3/4 or 6/8 time, quite similar to the tarantella which dates back to 14th-century Rome. It features in Perrot's *Caterina ou la fille du bandit* (1846).

Salzedo, Leonard (*b* London, 24 Sept. 1921; *d* Leighton Buzzard, 6 May 2000) British violinist, composer, and conductor. He was music director of Ballet Rambert (1966–72), principal conductor of Scottish Theatre Ballet (1972–4), and conductor of New London Ballet in 1974. He composed the scores for eight ballets, including Howard's *The Fugitive* (1944) and *Mardi Gras* (1946), J. Carter's *The Witch Boy* (1956), and Morrice's *Hazard* (1967).

samba Generic form of Brazilian music and dance, including group, couple, and solo dances in 2/4 time with a syncopated accompaniment.

Samsova, Galina (orig. Samtsova; *b* Stalingrad, 17 Mar. 1937) Soviet-Canadian dancer and ballet director. She studied at the Kiev Ballet School and in 1956 graduated into the Kiev Ballet where she became a soloist. In 1960 she married the Canadian Alexander Ursuliak and moved to Canada where she joined the National Ballet of Canada in 1961. She was soon appointed principal and in 1963 she created the title role in Orlikowsky's *Cinderella* at the Paris International Festival of Dance where she won a gold medal. From 1964 to 1973 she was ballerina with London Festival Ballet. Though she shone in virtuoso roles like the pas de deux from *Le Corsaire*, she was essentially a lyrical, romantic ballerina, and a renowned Giselle. Her combined dramatic and technical gifts made her popular with choreographers and she created roles in many ballets, including Hynd's *Dvořák Variations* (1970) and *Valses nobles et sentimentales* (1975); Darrell's *Othello* (1971), *La Péri* (1971), and *Chéri* (1980), and Prokovsky's *Vespri* (1973) and *The Seven Deadly Sins* (1975). She married Prokovsky in 1972 (they divorced in 1981) and a year later founded the New London Ballet with him, with which she toured extensively until 1977. She performed as an international guest artist (1977–9) and was then principal dancer and teacher with Sadler's Wells Royal Ballet (1979–90), where she staged the Grand Pas from *Paquita* (1980) and also assisted Peter Wright on his 1981 production of *Swan Lake*. In 1990 she was appointed guest artistic director of Scottish Ballet, becoming artistic director (1991–7) and staging *Raymonda* Act III (1990) and *Swan Lake* (1995). She continues to coach, and to stage productions of the classics.

Sanasardo, Paul (*b* Chicago, 15 Sept. 1928) US dancer, teacher, and choreographer. He studied with Tudor, Graham, and others, making his debut with the Erika Thimey Dance Theater in 1952. He performed with Sokolow in 1955, creating a role in *Rooms*, and with P. Lang in 1957 and 1964. He also appeared on Broadway. In 1957 he founded the Paul Sanasardo-Donya Feuer Dance Company and a year later his own school, the Studio for Dance (later named Modern Dance Artists Inc.). He choreographed many works, including *Cyclometry* (1971). He was also artistic director of Batsheva Dance Company (1977–81). After disbanding his company in 1986 he continued to teach and choreograph, including *The Seven Last Words* (mus. Kancheli, 1994). His works have remained in the repertory of several companies, including Ailey's.

Sand, Inge (orig. Inge Sand Sørtensen; *b* Copenhagen, 6 Jul. 1928; *d* Copenhagen, 9 Feb. 1974) Danish dancer, choreographer, and ballet director who helped to bring the Bournonville style to international prominence. She studied at the Royal Danish Ballet School and joined the Royal Danish Ballet in 1947 where she was appointed soloist (i.e. principal) in 1950. She was essentially a soubrette—her finest role was Swanilda—and her dancing was admired for its lightness and wit although she brought a dramatic intensity to works such as Béjart's *Sonate à trois* (1965). From 1951 to 1952 she was an international guest artist, appearing, for example, with Original Ballet Russe, and during the 1950s and 1960s she directed touring ensembles of RDB dancers which brought the then little-known Bournonville technique and Danish dance to a worldwide audience. In 1965 she directed a season of new choreography at Copenhagen's New Theatre and in 1966 was appointed assistant director (to Flindt) of RDB.

From 1971 until her death she was manager of the company's tours.

San Diego Ballet Company Classical company founded in 1961 by Richard Carter. A small concert ensemble, it originally worked in close collaboration with San Francisco Ballet. Its directors included Sonia Arova and Thor Sutowski from 1971, the former staging several classics for the company, the latter creating new works. The company expanded to about 40 dancers but was disbanded in 1980. In 1984 it was temporarily revived and then merged with Hartford Ballet.

San Francisco Ballet US ballet company. It was founded in 1933 as San Francisco Opera Ballet, together with an affiliated school, and at first performed primarily in opera, its few ballet productions choreographed by its ballet master, *Bolm. When Serge Oukrainsky succeeded Bolm in 1937 the company became more independent and after its premier danseur Willam *Christensen took over direction a year later it began to present full-length classics. Christensen choreographed the first US full-length production of *Coppélia* in 1939, followed by its first complete *Swan Lake* (1940) and *Nutcracker* (1944). Harold Christensen joined the company as dancer and director of the school and in 1942 the two brothers bought both school and company from the Opera board, renaming them San Francisco Ballet and San Francisco Ballet School. In 1951 the third brother, Lew *Christensen, joined as co-director, becoming sole director of the company in 1952. He established links with New York City Ballet and acquired many Balanchine works. The company began foreign touring in 1957 (making its British debut in Edinburgh, 1981) but during the 1960s it was weakened by the departure of many dancers to New York. In 1973 Michael *Smuin joined as co-director. He brought a new theatrical style to the repertory, including his own versions of *Cinderella*, *The Tempest*, and *Romeo and Juliet*. He was sole director in 1984 but was then succeeded by Helgi *Tomasson who reinvigorated the company's classical base and re-established its international reputation. He expanded the number of dancers, acquired new Balanchine works, re-staged some of the classics, and added new works by himself, Morris, Bintley, Kudelka, Forsythe, Taylor, Possokhov, Wheeldon, and others to the repertory. Its dancers, many of them trained at the school, are renowned for their versatility in both classical and contemporary idioms, with recent ballerinas including Tina LeBlanc, Yuan Yuan Tan, and Sofiane Sylve.

(((●))) **SEE WEB LINKS**

• Website for San Francisco Ballet

Sangalli, Rita (*b* Milan, 1850; *d* Carpesino d'Arcellasco, 3 Nov. 1909) Italian dancer. She made her debut in 1865 at La Scala in P. Taglioni's *Flik and Flok* and toured widely in Italy, Austria, and England. In 1866 she went to America, making her debut in the New York production of *The Black Crook*. Later, at the Paris Opera, she created the ballerina roles in Mérante's *Sylvia* (1876) and *Yedda* (1879). She was considered one of the beauties of her time. In 1875 she wrote the preface for a book about dance technique, *Terpsichore*.

Sanguine Fan, The Ballet score in one act composed by Elgar in 1917. It was originally produced as a mime play at London's Chelsea Palace in aid of war charities and the first ballet production under the title *L'Éventail* was choreographed by Hynd in 1976. With design by Docherty it was premiered 6 Jul. by London Festival Ballet at Théâtre de l'Opéra de Monte Carlo with P. Clark, von Loggenburg, Asensio, and Ruanne. A comedy of manners, whose plot centres on a lost fan. The English title was restored for later performances.

Sankai Juku (Studio of the Mountain and Sea) Japanese butoh company, founded by Ushio *Amagatsu in 1975. It began as a series of workshops and gave its first full-scale performance in 1978 with *Kinkan Shonen* or *The Kumquat Seed*. Though its productions bear some hallmarks of classic butoh (near-naked bodies daubed with white rice flour, slow movements which evoke extreme spiritual and physical states), it is less confrontational than original butoh works and more focused on the creation of spectacular imagery. State-of-the-art lighting and stage machinery combine to create zen-like stage pictures, such as a constant trickle of sand from ceiling to floor that marks the stream of time passing, while jazz or rock music accompanies the often risk-taking stunts of the five male dancers. Its productions include *Unetsu* (*The Egg Stands out of Curiosity*) (1987), *Hibki* (1998), and *Toki* (2007). It is nominally based in Japan but tours internationally.

(((⊕))) SEE WEB LINKS
• Website for Sankai Juku

Sankovskaya, Ekaterina (*b* Moscow, 1816; *d* Moscow, 28 Aug. 1878) Russian dancer who became the most admired ballerina in Moscow of her time. She studied at the Moscow Bolshoi Ballet School and graduated in 1836, going on to dance the title role in the Moscow premiere of *La Sylphide* on the same day that Taglioni danced the role for the first time in St Petersburg (6 Sept. 1837). She was renowned for her impassioned performances of tragic roles such as Giselle and Esmeralda. After retiring in 1854 she taught ballroom

dance in private houses. One of her pupils was the theatre director Stanislavsky.

Sansom, Bruce (*b* Berkshire, 8 Sept. 1963) British dancer. He studied at the Royal Ballet School and joined the company in 1982 where he was promoted principal (1987). A lyrical dancer with a classical purity of line, he was compared to Dowell and danced several of the latter's roles in *The Dream* and *Manon*, among others. He also danced the standard classic roles and his created roles included Bintley's *Galanteries* (1986) and *Cyrano* (1991), MacMillan's *Prince of the Pagodas* (1989), A. Page's *Pursuit* (1987), and Tuckett's *Turn of the Screw* (1999). He retired from the stage in 2002 and in 2005 was appointed director of the Central School of Ballet, then in 2009 ballet master and assistant director at San Francisco Ballet.

Santiago Ballet (Ballet de Santiago) Chilean ballet company founded by Vadim Sulima and Nina Gritsova, and originating in the ballet school founded in 1949. In 1960 both school and company were reorganized by Ottavio *Cintolesi to focus on a more contemporary repertory and renamed, temporarily, Ballet Arte Moderno. After a decade its creativity stagnated and Ivan Nagy was brought in to reform the company as a classical troupe, under its present name. Under Nagy's direction (1982–9) its standards were raised to a high international level and its repertory balanced between classical ballets and new works by Chilean choreographers such as Hilda Riveros. Nagy additionally brought in guest dancers and choreographers, including Bocca, Stevenson, and Hynde, and the company made its North American debut in 1986. Between 1989 and 1993 the company lost some momentum but the arrival of Marcia Haydée had a galvanizing effect. Setting up an exchange policy between Santiago and Stuttgart (where she was also director), dancers and repertory were moved between the two companies, with Santiago gaining ballets by MacMillan, Béjart, and Cranko. In 1995 Nagy returned as artistic director of the company, to be succeeded yet again by Haydée who has subsequently overseen a further expansion of the repertory, including a version of *Carmen* by herself and Ismael Ivo. *See also* CHILE.

Santlow, Hestor (*b* c.1690; *d* 15, 21, or 31 Jan. 1773) British dancer and actress. She gave her debut performance as a dancer in London's Drury Lane Theatre in 1706 and as an actress in Congreve's *Love for Love* in the same theatre in 1709 and went on to become the leading interpreter of Weaver's seminal dramatic ballets. She created the roles of Venus in *Loves of Mars and Venus* (1717) and Helen in *The Judgement of Paris* (1733), enthralling the public with the eloquent realism of her performances. She also appeared in the ballets and masques of John Thurmond. Her dancing was praised by James Thomson for its 'melting lascivious motions, airs and postures'.

Sappington, Margot (*b* Baytown, Tex., 30 Jul. 1947) US dancer and choreographer. She studied with Matt Mattox, and at the American Ballet Centre and danced in musicals. As a choreographer she is best known for *Oh Calcutta!* (1969) and the 'Slide' section in *Billboards* (mus. Prince, Joffrey Ballet, 1993).

sarabande Dance in triple time with the accent on the second beat. Originally a somewhat erotic dance with a Spanish influence, it was danced in both S. America and Spain during the 16th century. It developed a more dignified form when it became popular in Europe during the 17th and 18th centuries.

Sarabhai, Mrinalini (*b* Chennai, 11 May 1918) Indian dancer. She trained in kathakali, Greek and Javanese dance, and Russian ballet and made her debut in Madras in 1939. She subsequently performed world-wide with Ram Gopal and with her own company and in 1949 formed the Darpana Academy of Dance and Drama in Ahmadabad, her daughter Mallika Sarabhai becoming co-director in 1989 and widening its scope to include film and media studies. In 1955 she was also appointed director of the Sangit Natak Academy. She is author of *This Alone is True* (1952) and *Creations* (1986).

Sarafanov, Leonid (*b* Kiev, Jun. 1982) Ukrainian-Russian dancer. He trained at Kiev State Ballet school and graduated into the National Ballet of Ukraine in 2000 as a soloist, moving to the Mariinsky in 2002. A dancer of extrovert virtuosity, his major roles have included James in *La Sylphide* and lead roles in Balanchine's 'Rubies' and Forsythe's *Vertiginous Thrill of Exactitude*. He has guested with La Scala Ballet, Milan and is recipient of several awards.

Sarasota Ballet US ballet company founded in 1987 in Florida by Jean Weidner as a presenting organization and in 1990 expanded into a full-scale resident company under the direction of Eddie Toussaint. In 1994 Robert de Warren succeeded as artistic director, followed by Ian Webb in 2007.

Webb has introduced works by MacMillan, Ashton, van Manen, Balanchine, Matthew Bourne, and others into the repertory, and commissioned *The Trilogy* (mus. Mozart, 2009) from Dominic Walsh, performed in collaboration with the Dominic Walsh Dance Theater.

Sardanapal Ballet in four acts with choreography by P. Taglioni and music by Paul Hertel.

Premiered 24 Apr. 1865 at the Berlin Royal Opera House. Its plot is a colourful telling of the life of the famous king of Assyria and the ballet was so popular that it was selected as the opening production of the newly built Vienna Court Opera in 1869.

Sasha Waltz and Guests German dance-theatre company. It was founded in 1993 by Sasha Waltz (*b* Karlsruhe, 8 Mar. 1963) in collaboration with Jochen Sandig, a year after Waltz became artist in residence at Kunstlerhaus Bethanian. Waltz trained with a student of Wigman, then in New York (1986–7) danced with Yoshiko Chuma's School of Hard Knocks and others. Her new ensemble resulted from a period of collaboration between dancers, musicians, and visual artists and in the first three years she and Sandig produced the multi-media piece *Travelogue-Trilogy*. In 1996 they founded the Sophiensaele as a centre for experimental theatre and dance, their works including *Zweiland* (1997). In 1999 Waltz and Sandig became directors of the Schaubühne in Berlin, creating *Kürper* (2000) and *noBody* (2002), among others. In 2005 the company reverted to independent status, with a permanent ensemble of performers and a wide group of associate artists. Recent works include *Dido and Aeneas* (2005), a staging of Purcell's opera that featured dancers in a water tank.

(⊕) SEE WEB LINKS
• Website for Sasha Waltz and Guests

Satie, Erik Alfred Leslie (*b* Honfleur, 17 May 1866; *d* Paris, 1 Jul. 1925) French composer whose melodic simplicity and witty experimentation with popular song and dance forms made him one of the seminal influences in 20th-century music. He wrote scores for several ballets including Massine's *Parade* (Diaghilev's Ballets Russes, 1917) and *Mercure* (de Beaumont's Soirées de Paris, 1924) and Börlin's Dadaist ballet *Relâche* (Les Ballets Suédois, 1924). During the latter Satie rode around the stage in a tiny car, lifting his hat to the audience. The serene and limpid *Trois gymnopédies* has been used by many choreographers, often in the orchestral arrangement by Debussy and Roland-Manuel, for example by Ashton in *Monotones* (1965) with the later addition of *Trois gnossiennes* (1966), and van Manen in *Squares* (1969). Satie's music has been used by Cunningham several times, in *Idyllic Song* (1944), *Septet* (1953), and *Nocturnes* (1956), for example, and by Mark Morris in *Bijoux* (1983), *The Death of Socrates* (1983), and *Pas de poisson* (1986).

Sauguet, Henri (orig. Jean-Pierre Poupard; *b* Bordeaux, 18 May 1901; *d* Paris, 22 Jun. 1989) French composer who wrote the scores for over two dozen ballets, including Balanchine's *La*

Chatte (1927), Lifar's *La Nuit* (1930), Petit's *Paul et Virginie* (1943) and *Les Forains* (1945), and Taras's *Cordelia* (1952). Although Sauget lacked the experimental vigour of some of his modernist contemporaries, his ability to evoke character and atmosphere in his score, and his expressive, danceable melodies were much admired.

saut [Fr., leap] A jump that takes off from two feet and lands in the same position.

Savignano, Luciana (*b* Milan, 30 Nov. 1943) Italian dancer. She trained at the ballet school of La Scala and joined the company in 1961, creating works in several ballets by Pistoni, including *The Miraculous Mandarin* (1968). Her exotic, somewhat mysterious qualities were captured in the solo 'La Luna' which Béjart created for her in the ballet *Héliogabale ou l'anarchiste couronné* in 1976. During the 1980s she gave a series of solo recitals, performing pieces by Petit and Béjart, among others, and also appearing as guest star with La Scala and principal with the ballet company at the Teatro Nuovo Torino.

Scala Ballet, La Italian ballet company which was established as the official dancing company of the Teatro alla Scala in Milan when it opened in 1778. *Angiolini created many ballets for it but it reached its peak of activity during the first half of the 19th century when it became one of the great centres for Romantic ballet. Many of Europe's leading ballerinas appeared as guest artists including Cerrito, Elssler, Taglioni, and Grisi, and most of the important works of the repertoire were staged there, either in their original or in re-worked versions. Salvatore *Vigano staged many of his own ballets at La Scala including his 1813 re-working of *Creatures of Prometheus* and his 1818 *Othello*. Antonio Cortesi staged his version of *La Sylphide* in 1841 with Cerrito, and a *Giselle* in 1843 with new music by Bajetti. *Perrot produced and danced in his own *Esmeralda* with Elssler. The school at La Scala, originally called the Imperial Academy of Dance, was founded in 1813 and after *Blasis was appointed director in 1837 became one of the most important training centres in Europe, its pupils including Cerrito and Legnani. But during the second half of the century ballet declined into formulaic spectacle and La Scala's repertoire was dominated by the large theatrical works of *Manzotti, such as *Excelsior* (1881) and *Amor* (1886). Opera, particularly the works of Verdi, took precedence over ballet at the theatre and several of the great Italian ballerinas, like Legnani and Zucchi, left to advance their careers in Russia. In 1925 *Cecchetti was brought in to try to improve ballet's status at the theatre but failed, and when Diaghilev's company visited the theatre in 1927 it had little success. Since then there has been a succession of short-term ballet masters, such as Aurelio *Milloss, whose attempts to revive the company's status and build a solid repertoire have never had more than temporary effect due to the continuing dominance of opera. Carla *Fracci, a pupil of the school, did bring some renown to the Scala Ballet after her much-admired performance in H. Lander's *La Sylphide* in 1962, and in 1966 Nureyev staged his first production of *The Sleeping Beauty* for the company with himself and Fracci in the leading roles. She led the company for many years and during the late 1960s and 1970s Nureyev continued to make regular guest appearances, also partnering Liliana Cosi who left the company in the early 1970s due to the limited opportunities it offered her. The company's 20th-century repertory was expanded with works by Cranko, Balanchine, P. Taylor, de Warren, B. Stevenson, Cullberg, and Massimo Moricone, although it did not establish a distinctive identity. Subsequent directors included Robert de *Warren, Elisabetta *Terabust, and Giuseppe Carbonne, with Fracci briefly occupying the post in 2000. Several internationally ranked dancers were produced during this era, among them Roberto Bolle, Massimo Murru, and Alessandra Ferri (the latter made prima ballerina assoluta in 1992), however due to the company's relatively constricted performing schedule and limited repertory these dancers worked extensively abroad. In 2002 Frédéric Olivieri was appointed director, acquiring works by Neumeier and Preljocaj among others and showcasing a new generation of Italian-schooled dancers, including Marta Romagna and Mick Zeni. Olivieri left in 2007, however, to be replaced by Terabust, then by M. *Vaziev in 2009, and the ballet still struggles to assert its status against the competition of the opera. In 1999 the company offices and school moved into new premises, on Via Campo Lodigiano, the latter under the direction of Frédéric Olivieri.

(🌐) SEE WEB LINKS

• Website for La Scala with a link to the ballet

Scandinavian Ballet, The Ballet company formed by E. M. von *Rosen and her husband A. Fridericia. It was funded by both Sweden and Denmark, and opened in Vaxjö, Sweden, in Feb. 1960, touring Scandinavia and Germany until it folded in late 1961. Its repertory featured some Bournonville ballets and works by Rosen and Cramér.

Scanner (*b* Robin Rimbaud; London, 6 May 1964) British composer and writer. His professional name originated from his use of mobile phone and police scanners in live performance. He began creating electronic sound scores in the early 1980s under the name Dau Al Set and The Rimbaud Brothers and has since produced his music in many forms including CDs, sound installations, film scores, and collaborations with classical musicians. He has also worked extensively in dance, creating the music for McGregor's *Nemesis* (2002), *Detritus* (2003), *Qualia* (2004), and *Kirikou & Karaba* (2007); provided the accompanying sound for one of Cunningham's Events at London's Barbican; and contributed to the score for Shobana Jeyasingh's *Faultline* (2006).

SEE WEB LINKS
• Official website for Scanner

Scapino Ballet The Netherlands' oldest ballet company, founded in 1945 in Amsterdam by Hans (Johanna) *Snoek to provide performances for children. Although it still tours schools and youth centres, the company now also performs a wide-ranging adult repertoire. Snoek retired in 1970 and in 1988 the company moved from its Amsterdam base to Rotterdam. When Ed Wubbe was appointed director in 1992 the company was renamed Scapino Rotterdam, and a more abrasive edge introduced to the repertory with works like *Kathleen* (1992), a *West Side Story* of the 1990s, and Wubbe's version of *Le Sacre du printemps* (1996). Wubbe continues to create works for the company alongside resident choreographers, Marco Goecke and Georg Reischl. Some of the repertory is also commissioned from guest choreographers such as André Gingras.

SEE WEB LINKS
• Website for Scapino Ballet

Scarlatti, Domenico (*b* Naples, 26 Oct. 1685; *d* Madrid, 23 July 1757) Italian composer. He wrote no ballet scores but his music has often been used for dance, including Massine for *Les Femmes de bonne humeur* (arr. Tommasini, 1917), Cranko for *The Taming of the Shrew* (arr. Stolze, 1969), Prokovsky for *Scarlatti and Friends* (1973), P. Martins for *S* (1979), Mark Morris for *Lies* (performed under various alternative titles, 1987), and S. Davies for *The Art of Touch* (with additional mus. Matteo Fargion, 1995).

Scènes de ballet Ballet in one act choreographed to Stravinsky's score of the same title. The definitive version was choreographed by Ashton with designs by A. Beaurepaire and was premiered 11 Feb. 1948 by Sadler's Wells Ballet at the Royal Opera House, London, with Fonteyn and Somes. Ashton described his ballet as 'just an exercise in pure dancing'; in fact it is one of his finest works, the complex geometries of its choreography wittily evoking the grandeur of 19th-century classicism. Stravinsky's score was originally composed for a divertissement in Billy Rose's revue *The Seven*

Lively Arts, and he himself specified that it should have a cast of two soloists and a corps of four men and twelve women. Dolin choreographed and danced in it (with Markova) at its first performance, 7 Dec. 1944, at the Ziegfeld Theater, New York. This production did not use the entire score; Ashton's was the first to do so. Later versions include G. Blank (Berlin Opera Ballet, 1952), Cranko (Stuttgart Ballet, 1962), and Taras (New York City Ballet, 1972). The Ashton version has been revived by Berlin Opera Ballet (1968) and Dutch National Ballet (1992), among others.

Schall, Claus (*b* Copenhagen, 28 Apr. 1757; *d* Copenhagen, 9 Aug. 1835) Danish composer, dancer, and violinist. He became a dancer with the Royal Danish Ballet in 1772, and in 1775 conductor of ballet music and repetiteur. In 1795 he was made composer for the ballet and in 1818 music director of the Opera. He composed many ballet scores, mostly for Galeotti, including *Laurette* (1785), *Lagetha* (1801), *Romeo and Juliet* (1811), and *Macbeth* (1816).

Schandorff, Silja (*b* 10 Feb. 1969) Danish dancer. She studied at the Royal Danish Ballet School and became an apprentice with the company in 1985, full company member in 1987, and principal dancer in 1992. Her wide repertory has included the standard classical and Bournonville roles, the Balanchine and Forsythe repertories, as well as new works by Flindt, Ib Andersen, and Anna Laerkesen, among others.

Schanne, Margrethe (*b* Copenhagen, 21 Nov. 1921) Danish dancer who became the foremost interpreter of the Romantic repertoire of her time. She studied at the Royal Danish Ballet School with H. Lander and later in London and Paris with Kniaseff and Egorova. She danced with RDB from 1940 to 1966, becoming soloist (principal) in 1943 and was much admired for the evanescent quality she brought to *La Sylphide* (a ballet she danced over 100 times) and for her poetic interpretation of Giselle. She guested with Petit's Ballets des Champs-Elysées in 1947 and Grand Ballet du Marquis de Cuevas in 1956, and during the 1950s and 1960s she toured extensively in the US, S. Africa, and Europe. In 1966 she left the stage to become a teacher of dance and physical education until she retired in 1986. She was made a Knight of Dannebrog in 1953 and in 1957 became the first Danish dancer to appear on a postage stamp.

Schaufuss, Frank (*b* Copenhagen, 13 Dec. 1921; *d* Copenhagen, 10 Oct. 1997) Danish dancer, choreographer, and teacher. He studied at the Royal Danish Ballet School and with Bartholin and after dancing with the N. B. Larsen Ballet he entered the Royal Danish Ballet in 1941

S

where he remained until 1970. He was appointed soloist (principal) in 1949, performing a wide range of roles including Mercutio in Ashton's *Romeo and Juliet* (1955), and was ballet master (1956–8). He also guested abroad, with, for example, the de Cuevas Ballet and National Ballet of Canada. After retiring he founded the Danish Ballet Academy with his wife, Mona Vangsaae, in 1970. From this emerged the Danish Ballet Theatre which he directed until it closed in 1974. He and Vangsaae were the parents of Peter Schaufuss. His last stage appearances in England were as Escalus in his son's 1985 revival of Ashton's *Romeo and Juliet*.

Schaufuss, Peter (*b* Copenhagen, 26 Apr. 1949) Danish dancer, choreographer, and director. Son of Frank Schaufuss and Mona Vangsaae; studied at the Royal Danish Ballet School with S. Williams and H. Brenaa and joined the RDB in 1965. Partly because of his family connections with the company, he chose to establish himself as an international performer, dancing with National Ballet of Canada (1967–8 and 1977–83), London Festival Ballet (1970–4), and New York City Ballet (1974–7) as well as making numerous guest appearances. He was an ardent partner with a powerful virtuoso technique which allowed him to encompass the demands of the Bournonville and Petipa repertoires as well as Balanchine and Petit. From 1984 to 1990 he was artistic director of London Festival Ballet, during which time it became English National Ballet. He introduced radical new works into the repertoire (including a ballet by Michael Clark) as well as staging productions of Bournonville's *La Sylphide* (1979) and *Napoli* (1989), and a new version of *The Nutcracker* (1986) which emphasized connections between the Hoffmann tale and Tchaikovsky's personal life. He also oversaw the reconstruction of Ashton's *Romeo and Juliet*. In 1990 he was appointed director of the Berlin Opera Ballet where he continued to commission experimental work, by Bill T. Jones and Stephen Petronio, among others, and staged new productions of *Giselle* (1991), *Swan Lake* and *Sleeping Beauty* (both 1992). In 1994 he was appointed director of the Royal Danish Ballet for which he choreographed a new production of *Hamlet* (1996). In 1997 he founded the Peter Schaufuss Ballet, based in the theatre of Holstebro, Denmark, for which he radically re-choreographed the three Tchaikovsky classics and also created populist works such as *The King* (mus. Wagner and Elvis Presley, 1999) and *Divas* (songs by Piaf, Garland, and Dietrich, 2006).

⊕ SEE WEB LINKS
● Website for the Peter Schaufuss company

Schayk, Toer van (*b* Amsterdam, 28 Sept. 1936) Dutch dancer, choreographer, and stage designer. He studied with Gaskell and danced with her company (1955–9) before working as a painter and sculptor. He returned to dance in 1965 to perform the lead in van Dantzig's *Monument for a Dead Boy* for Dutch National Ballet, a role created to exploit his unusually direct, expressive talent. He also designed the set and costumes for the ballet and went on to design and dance in many other van Dantzig works. He choreographed his own first work for DNB in 1971, *Past Imperfect*, set to music by Ligeti and this led to his appointment as the company's resident choreographer. His subsequent works tended to deal with political and moral issues though with a vein of ironic humour, while his movement language had a distinctively angular sculptural quality as seen in *Still Life with White Square* (mus. Schoenberg, 1992). He also reworked two Nijinsky ballets, *Jeux* (1977) and *Faun* (1978). Several of his works were mounted on other companies, including *Seventh Symphony* (1986, revived Royal Winnipeg Ballet, 1997). He left DNB in 1991, and while continuing to create work for the company his commitment to ballet waned. Since 2001 he has focused exclusively on painting and sculpture.

Scheherazade (*Schéhérazade*) Ballet in one act with choreography by Fokine, libretto by Benois, music by Rimsky-Korsakov (the symphonic suite *Scheherazade* minus its 3rd part), and design by Bakst. Premiered 4 Jun. 1910 by Diaghilev's Ballets Russes at Paris Opera, with Ida Rubinstein, Cecchetti, and Nijinsky. It is based on the first story from *A Thousand and One Nights* in which the women of the Shah's harem persuade the Chief Eunuch to admit the male slaves to their quarters while their master is absent. In the orgy that follows the Shah returns to discover his favourite concubine Zobeide consorting with the beautiful Golden Slave. The latter is killed and Zobeide is forced to stab herself. Bakst's designs with their revealing oriental costumes and voluptuous palette of colours were considered almost as daring as the graphic eroticism of the dancing and mime. It has been revived by many companies including London Festival Ballet in Beriozoff's 1952 staging, and the Kirov in A. Liepa and I. Fokine's 1993 staging, although its exoticism and sexuality seem, inevitably, rather tame to modern audiences. Other new versions include V. Panov's for Vienna State Opera Ballet (1981). Ravel also composed a *Shéhérazade* which has been choreographed by, among others, G. Murphy (Sydney Dance Company, 1979) and Petit (1974).

Schilling, Tom (*b* Esperstedt, 23 Jan. 1928) German dancer, choreographer, and dance director. He studied at Dessau Opera Ballet School and later with Hoyer (while he was dancing in Dresden in 1945) and with Wigman (while he was with Leipzig Ballet, 1946–52). In 1953 he became ballet master at the German National Theatre in Weimar, where he created his first works. In 1956 he was appointed director of Dresden Ballet where he remained until 1964, becoming artistic director of the ballet at Komische Oper in E. Berlin from 1965. He choreographed the first German production of Asafiev's *Fountain of Bakhchisarai* (Weimar, 1959), and his large output also included *Abraxas* (1957), *Cinderella* (mus. Prokofiev, 1968), *Romeo and Juliet* (mus. Prokofiev, 1972), *Ondine* (mus. Henze, 1970), *La Mer* (mus. Debussy, 1968), and *A New Midsummer Night's Dream* (mus. Katzer, 1981), all for E. Berlin. His works typically relocated the language and scenarios of classical ballet into contemporary settings. He was also a guest choreographer for Western companies including Grand Ballet Classique de France, Norwegian National Ballet, and Vienna State Opera Ballet.

Schlemmer, Oskar (*b* Stuttgart, 4 Sept. 1888; *d* Baden-Baden, 13 Apr. 1943) German choreographer and designer who pioneered the concept of abstract dance in Central Europe. In 1921 he joined the faculty of Weimar's Bauhaus school where he developed his *Triadic Ballet* (Stuttgart, 1922). In a work which aimed to explore the relationship between figure, movement, and space, uncluttered by character or plot, he disguised the dancers' humanity by using repetitive, mechanical movements and costumes which resembled models or abstract sculptures. Between 1925 and 1929 he directed the Theatre Workshop of the Bauhaus in Dessau, creating more of his 'architectonic dances', such as *Space Dance*, *Hoop Dance*, and *Gesture Dance*. He also designed dance productions for other companies including Dresden and Breslau. Since 1982 his Bauhaus Dances have been researched and re-created by New York dancer and movement therapist Debra McCall.

Schneitzhoeffer, Jean (*b* Toulouse, *c*.13 Oct. 1785; *d* Paris, 4 Oct. 1852) French composer. He was chorus master at the Paris Opera (1823–40) and he wrote the scores for several ballets, most famously *La Sylphide* (1832).

Schoenberg, Arnold (*b* Vienna, 13 Sept. 1874; *d* Los Angeles, 13 Jul. 1951) Austrian composer. He wrote only one ballet score, 'The Dance Around the Golden Calf' which features in his opera *Moses and Aaron*, but much of his concert music has been adapted for dance. *Transfigured Night* has been used by several choreographers including Tudor (in *Pillar of Fire*, New York, 1942), Kylián (The Hague, 1975), Petit (Paris,

1976), and de Keersmaeker (Rotterdam, 1997); *Pelléas and Mélisande* has been used by Petit (Royal Ballet, 1969); and *Pierrot lunaire* by Tetley (New York, 1962) and Joffrey (New York, 1965). Balanchine used Schoenberg's orchestration of Brahms's Piano Quartet in his *Brahms–Schoenberg Quartet* (1966) and Morris used Schoenberg's *Accompaniment Music for a Motion Picture*, Op. 34, and *Five Orchestral Pieces*, Op. 16, for *Wonderland* (Brussels, 1989).

Schollar, Ludmila (Shollar) (*b* St Petersburg, 15 Mar. 1888; *d* San Francisco, 10 Jul. 1978) Russian-US dancer and teacher. She studied at the Imperial Ballet School with Fokine and graduated into the Mariinsky in 1906 where she danced until 1914. In 1909 her delicate beauty and musical technique brought her to the attention of Diaghilev and she danced several seasons with his company until 1914. She created the roles of Estrella in Fokine's *Carnaval* (1910), Street Dancer in his *Petrushka* (1911), and Papillon in his *Les Papillons* (1914), as well as one of the women tennis players in Nijinsky's *Jeux* (1913). During the war she nursed with the Red Cross then in 1917 returned to Russia where she again danced at the Mariinsky. In 1921 she married dancer Anatole Vilzak and they both returned to Diaghilev's company (1921–5). She was dismissed for sympathizing with striking dancers, and she and Vilzak went to dance at the Teatro Colón, Buenos Aires (1926–7). She subsequently danced in the companies of Rubinstein and Nijinska and also in the Karsavina-Vilzak Company. In 1936 she and Vilzak settled in America and between 1940 and 1946 ran their own ballet school in New York. She also taught at the School of American Ballet from 1936, Ballet Theatre School (1951–3), Washington School of Ballet (1963–5), and at the San Francisco Ballet School from 1965.

Scholz, Uwe (*b* Darmstadt, 1958; *d* Berlin, 21 Nov. 2004) German dancer, choreographer, and director. He studied at the Stuttgart School and briefly at the School of American Ballet before returning to dance in the Stuttgart Ballet. He began choreographing in the 1980s, including *The Creation* (mus. Haydn, 1984), and after directing the Zurich Ballet (1986–91) he was appointed artistic director of Leipzig Ballet. He was a prolific choreographer, and his works entered the repertory of many companies, including Stuttgart, Leipzig, Zurich, Royal Winnipeg Ballet, La Scala, and Nederlands Dans Theater. He took his inspiration from a wide range of music, e.g *Amerika* (mus. various US composers, 1994) and Mozart's 'Great' Mass, K. 427 (1998).

Schönberg, Bessie (*b* Hanover, 27 Dec. 1906; *d* New York, 14 May 1997) German-US dancer and teacher. She studied eurythmics in Dresden, modern dance with Martha Hill in Oregon, and with Graham in New York. She danced with Graham's company (1929–32) but was forced to retire from the stage because of a knee injury. From 1933 she became one of the US's most celebrated teachers of modern dance composition, and in 1984 Dance Theater Workshop named its annual New York Dance and Performance Awards, the Bessies, after her.

Schooling, Elizabeth (*b* London, 27 Apr. 1915; *d* 22 Jun. 1998) British dancer and teacher. She studied with Rambert and joined her company in 1930 where she remained, apart from a few brief absences, until 1948. A versatile dancer, she created roles in many works by Ashton, Tudor, Gore, Howard, and Staff (her first husband). She also danced in Nijinsky's *L'Après-midi d'un faune*, a ballet which she staged for many companies including Paris Opera. After retiring from the stage she taught at her own school in Devon.

School of American Ballet The official school of New York City Ballet. It was founded in Hartford in 1933 by Balanchine, Kirstein, Dimitriev, and Warburg and in 1934 moved to New York. It is now housed in the Juilliard School building of Lincoln Center. Under the artistic direction of Peter Martins, its graduates continue to provide NYCB with the majority of its dancers, and many return to teach in the school. Past members of the faculty have included Danilova, Doubrovska, Eglevsky, and S. Williams.

(((⊕))) SEE WEB LINKS

• Website for the School of American Ballet

schottische A German couple dance in 2/4 time that became very popular during the mid-19th century.

Schubert, Franz (*b* Liechtenthal, 31 Jan. 1797; *d* Vienna, 19 Nov. 1828) Austrian composer. He wrote no ballet scores but his concert music has often been used for dance. *Rosamunde* has been used by, among others, Leontiev (Vienna State Opera, 1928), Adama (Hanover, 1968), and Catá (Geneva, 1968); *The Unfinished Symphony* by Isadora Duncan (Paris, 1927); *The Wanderer Fantasy* by Balanchine (in *Errante*, Les Ballets 1933) and by Ashton (in *The Wanderer*, Sadler's Wells Ballet, 1941); *Death and the Maiden* by A. Howard (1st movement only; Ballet Rambert, 1937), by R. North (Ballet Rambert, 1984), and Marin (*May B*, Angers, 1991); 7th Symphony by Massine (in *Labyrinth*, Ballet Russe de Monte Carlo, 1941); 2nd Symphony by H. Lander (in *Printemps à Vienne*, Paris, 1954); the Trio in B major by van Manen (in *Grand Trio*, Vienna, 1978); *Winterreise* by T Brown (2002) and Emanuel Gat (in *Winter Journey*, 2004); the songs

Wiegenlied, Ständchen, and *Erlkönig* by Mark Morris in *Bedtime* (1992); and the Piano Trio in E flat by Morris in *Rock of Ages* (2005). Kudelka used an arrangement of his music in *Mixed Program* (Toronto, 1991).

Schuman, William (*b* New York, 4 Aug. 1910; *d* New York, 15 Feb. 1992) US composer. He was president of the Juilliard School (1945–62) and invited Martha Hill to head a radical new dance department there; from 1962 to 1968 he was president of the Lincoln Center. He wrote the scores for Tudor's *Undertow* (1945) and for Graham's *Night Journey* (1947), *Voyage* and *Judith* (both 1950), and *Witch of Endor* (1965).

Schumann, Robert (*b* Zwickau, 8 Jun. 1810; *d* Endenich, 29 Jul. 1856) German composer. He wrote no ballet scores but his concert music has frequently been used for dance. Arrangements of various scores were used by Fokine (in *Le Carnaval*, Berlin, 1910), and in *Les Papillons* (St Petersburg, 1913); the Piano Concerto in A minor by Nijinska (in *Schumann Concerto*, New York, 1951); *Dichterliebe* by Marks (Copenhagen, 1973); the String Quartet No. 3 by van Manen (in *Four Schumann Pieces*, Royal Ballet, 1975); *Davidsbündlertänze* by Balanchine (New York City Ballet, 1980); and *Fünf Stücke im Volkston* by Morris in *The Argument* (1999); and the Piano Quintet in E flat by Morris in *V* (2001). His music has also been used by Kudelka in *Dreams of Harmony* (San Francisco Ballet, 1987) and *Divertissement Schumann* (Les Grands Ballets Canadiens, 1989).

Schwarz, Solange (*b* Paris, 12 Nov. 1910) French dancer; daughter of the famous Paris ballet teacher Jean Schwarz. She studied at the Paris Opera Ballet School and joined the company in 1930. In 1932 she was made étoile of the Opéra Comique and after returning to the Opera in 1937 she was promoted étoile in 1940. With her petite, blonde looks, and technical precision she became a favourite Swanilda, the role which she danced for her farewell performance at the Opera in 1957. She also created roles in several ballets by Lifar (who was her frequent partner), such as *Entre deux rondes* (1940) in which she took the role of Degas's little dancer, *Le Chevalier et la damoiselle* (1941), and *Sylvia* (1941). After the war she and Lifar left the Opera. She was ballerina with Ballets des Champs-Elysées; returned to the Opéra Comique (1949–51), then guested with Grand Ballet du Marquis de Cuevas and Bejart's Ballet de l'Étoile de Paris. After retiring in 1957 she taught at the Paris Conservatoire for twenty years.

Schwezoff, Igor (*b* St Petersburg, 1904; *d* New York, 28 Oct. 1982) Soviet-US dancer, choreographer, and teacher. He started training aged 16 and entered the Leningrad Ballet School at 20.

S

During his studies he also performed with a provincial touring operetta company, useful experience for his exceptionally peripatetic career. He toured the Ukraine (1926–8) as a dancer with the New Academic Theatre, and in 1928 was appointed first dancer and choreographer of the Kiev opera house. He additionally danced with the Propaganda Studio Opera which brought Socialist art to the provinces. In 1930 he left to dance in revues in China then moved to Buenos Aires where he was principal dancer at the Teatro Colón, under the direction of Nijinska. With her he moved to Paris and then to the Netherlands, where he opened a school in The Hague which evolved into his own company, Ballet Igor Schwezoff (1934–6). He danced and choreographed in Monte Carlo (1936–7) then opened a school in London, after which he was a soloist with de Basil's Original Ballet Russe (1939–41). In 1941 he moved to New York where he became choreographer of the New Opera Company. After military service he divided his time between New York and Rio de Janeiro, where he was director, dancer, and choreographer of Teatro Municipal and where he choreographed his ballet *Concertanto dansante* (mus. Saint-Saëns, 1945). In New York in 1943 he staged the first US production of *The Red Poppy* (1927) for the Ballet Russe de Monte Carlo. In 1946 he was choreographer for New York City Center Opera, and in 1947 became founder director of Ballet da Juventude in Rio de Janeiro. He opened a school in New York in 1949 and a company in 1953. He taught at the Ballet Theatre School in New York (1956–62) and then with many other institutions. He published his autobiography, *Borzoi*, in 1935.

Scotch Symphony Ballet in one act with choreography by Balanchine, music by Mendelssohn, set by H. Armistead, and costumes by Karinska and D. Ffolkes. Premiered 11 Nov. 1952 by New York City Ballet at City Center, New York, with Maria Tallchief, Eglevsky, Wilde, Hobi, and Maule. In this setting of Mendelssohn's A minor Symphony (minus the 1st movement) classical dance is infused with a Romantic Scottish atmosphere, particularly in the second of its three movements which makes reference to *La Sylphide*. It has been revived for Munich State Opera Ballet (1964), the Kirov (1989), and others.

Scottish Ballet Scotland's national ballet company. It was originally founded in 1957 as the Western Theatre Ballet by Peter *Darrell and Elizabeth *West. It operated from Bristol (it was the first regionally based British ballet company) but toured extensively, aiming to create new audiences by focusing on the dramatic elements of ballet. Darrell, who gradually became its chief choreographer (and sole director after West's

death in 1962), experimented with a wide range of sometimes controversial material—domestic drama, homosexuality, murder—often collaborating with playwrights and theatre producers. His early works included *The Prisoners* (1957), *Mods and Rockers* (1963) which was the first Beatles ballet, and also Britain's first full-length ballet with a contemporary setting, *Sun into Darkness* (1966). Also in the repertoire were other dramatic works like Béjart's *Sonate à trois* and MacMillan's *Las Hermanas*. Surviving near-bankruptcy in its early years, the company gained an international profile at various festivals during the 1960s and in 1969 was invited by the Scottish Arts Council to form the basis of a national ballet company for Scotland. Renamed Scottish Theatre Ballet, it attempted to marry its commitment to experimental work with the need to incorporate popular classics into the repertoire, though it inevitably became less pioneering in style. In 1972 it was renamed Scottish Ballet (with its official school, the Dance School of Scotland, also based in Glasgow). Darrell himself choreographed several full-length populist works for the company, including *Beauty and the Beast* (1969), *Tales of Hoffmann* (1972), *Mary Queen of Scots* (1976), and *Cinderella* (1979). He remained artistic director until his death in 1987, after which there was a series of temporary replacements until Galina *Samsova took on the post in 1991. She increased the emphasis on classics in the repertoire, including her own new production of *Swan Lake* (1995), and introduced ballets by Balanchine, Robert Cohan, and Mark Baldwin, among others. Samsova resigned in 1997 and after Robert *North's brief period as her successor (1999–2002) the company underwent a complete change of style with the appointment of Ashley *Page. As artistic director and choreographer his policy has been to expand the company's range by importing both contemporary dance repertory and contemporary dancers. With this dual focus Scottish Ballet performs works by Balanchine, Forsythe, Petronio, Krzysztof Pastor, and Page himself, including radically updated versions of the classics.

((⊕)) SEE WEB LINKS
- Website for Scottish Ballet

Scottish Dance Theatre Contemporary dance company founded in 1986, originally known as Dundee Rep Dance Company. Under the direction of Janet Smith, who took over in 1997, the company pursues an adventurous commissioning policy with new works by Rui Horta, Willi Dorner, Hofesh Shechter among others, and an active international touring schedule.

((⊕)) SEE WEB LINKS
- Company website for SDT

Scriabin, Alexander (*b* Moscow, 6 Jan. 1872; *d* Moscow, 27 Apr. 1915) Russian composer. He wrote no ballet scores but some of his concert music has been used for dance particularly his *Poème de l'extase* which has been used by Sokolow (New York, 1956), Petit (Milan, 1968), Cranko (Stuttgart, 1970), Beatty (Stockholm, 1972), and others. Other ballets created to his music include Neumeier's *Dämmern* (Frankfurt, 1972) and R. North's *Scriabin Preludes and Studies* (London Contemporary Dance Theatre, 1978).

Second Stride British modern dance company. It was formed in 1982 by choreographers Richard *Alston, Ian *Spink, and Siobhan *Davies. Each had initially run their own company, Richard Alston and Dancers (1977–80), the Ian Spink Group (1978–81), and Siobhan Davies and Dancers (1981), and the combined ensemble was initially intended to last only one season (the name referred to Alston's first, seminal group Strider (1972–6)). Its first programme included Alston's *Doublework* (1978, revived 1982), Davies's *Plain Song* (1981), and Spink's *Canta* (1981) and was so well received that the company continued. Alston withdrew after a second season, followed by Davies in 1986. From 1988 Second Stride moved towards multi-disciplinary work such as *Heaven Ablaze in his Breast*, a dance-opera based on Hoffmann's tale *The Sandman* with choreography by Spink, design by Antony *McDonald, and music by composer Judith Weir (1990). The company was disbanded in 1997.

seguidillas One of the oldest Spanish dances. In triple time, it is characterized by lively footwork contrasting with a more restrained use of the upper body and the dramatic use of stillness between sections. There are different variants, including the seguidillas sevillanas (dubbed 'the mother of Spanish dance') and the slightly more stately seguidillas machegas originating in La Mancha.

Self, Jim (*b* Greenville, Ala., 6 Mar. 1954) US dancer and choreographer. He studied at the Merce Cunningham Studio and with Maggie Black, performing with several companies including Cunningham's (1976–9) and his own Self Performing Arts Company (1975–6), and Jim Self and Dancers (1980–8). He also choreographed and performed in Robert Wilson's *The CIVIL WarS* (1980–4). His movement style is partially influenced by Cunningham but his work is often categorized as performance art, due to its reliance on theatrical and visual elements. He has taught widely and in 1996 was appointed dance lecturer at Cornell University.

Semenyaka, Ludmila (orig. Lyudmila; *b* Leningrad, 16 Jan. 1952) Soviet dancer. She trained at the Leningrad Ballet School with Belikova and danced with the Kirov (1970–2) before moving to the Bolshoi as a principal dancer. Here, under the tutelage of Ulanova, her technical brilliance acquired a new lyricism and dramatic subtlety which equipped her both for the 19th-century classics (especially *Raymonda*, *Swan Lake*, and *Sleeping Beauty*) and for the more expansive Grigorovich roles like Phrygia in *Spartacus*. Between 1979 and 1986 Bolshoi tours of Britain and America were halted by defections from the company but when the company again travelled to the West Semenyaka rapidly acquired an international reputation. After 1991 she guested abroad, including performances with Moscow City Ballet on its British tour, Scottish Ballet, and English National Ballet, and also with her own concert group in Japan (1991). After retiring from the stage she became repetiteur at the Bolshoi. She was made Honoured Artist of the Russian Federation in 1976.

Semionova, Marina (orig. Semyonova; *b* St Petersburg, 12 Jun. 1908; *d* St Petersburg, 9 June 2010) Russian dancer. She studied under Vaganova (the latter's first great pupil) at the Petrograd (later Leningrad) Ballet School (1919–25) and graduated into GATOB (later Kirov) before moving to the Bolshoi in 1930 as prima ballerina. In both companies she was renowned for her virtuosity and regal bearing. She also guested with the Kirov and in Paris (1935) where she performed *Giselle* with Lifar. She created or danced the leading roles in many new ballets by Zakharov (*The Prisoner of the Caucasus*, 1938, and *Taras Bulba*, 1941) and Vainonen (*Flames of Paris*, Moscow version, 1933), as well as excelling in classic roles like Nikiya in *Bayadère* and Odette-Odile in *Swan Lake*. Her career as well as her personal life suffered when her second husband was detained in 1936 during a Stalin purge but she continued to dance and teach with the Bolshoi until 1952. In 1953 she was appointed teacher at the Moscow Ballet School and repetiteur at the Bolshoi, continuing in that role for over four decades. Her pupils included Plisetskaya and Bessmertnova. She was married to dancer and teacher Victor Semonov and made People's Artist of the USSR, 1975.

Semionova, Polina (*b* Moscow, 1984) Russian dancer. She trained at the Moscow State Choreographic School, winning several awards, including first prize at the Vaganova Competition, before graduating in 2002. She joined the Berlin Staatsoper Ballet as principal the same year, and became the regular partner of Vladimir Malakhov. A tall, technically powerful dancer with a distinctively lush line, she has additionally guested with

S

other companies, including English National Ballet, Paris Opera, American Ballet Theatre, the Mariinsky, and National Ballet of Canada.

Septet Modern dance work in one act with choreography by Cunningham, music by Satie, and design by R. Charlip. Premiered by the Merce Cunningham Dance Company at Black Mountain College, N. Carolina, on 22 Aug. 1953, with Cunningham, C. Brown, Farber, Melsher, Charlip, P. Taylor, and Dencks. This alternately grave and witty setting of Satie's *Trois morceaux en forme de poire* is one of Cunningham's rare surviving settings of a pre-existent score. Created in seven movements it is now performed by a cast of six (rather than the original seven). It has been revived for Rambert Dance Company (Glasgow, 1987), Pacific Northwest Ballet (Seattle, 1989), White Oak Dance Project (Fort Lauderdale, 1996), and others.

Seraphic Dialogue Modern dance work in one act with choreography by Graham, music by Dello Joio, set by Noguchi, costumes by Graham, and lighting by Rosenthal. Premiered 8 May 1955 by the Martha Graham Dance Company at the ANTA Theater, New York, with Margolies, Birch, Hinkson, Turney, and Ross. A dance portrait of Joan of Arc. It was originally choreographed as a solo (same music, 1950) under the title *Triumph of St Joan*. In the revised version Joan looks back over her life in a series of danced dialogues with her guiding spirit, St Michael, and with three figures who represent different aspects of her nature—maid, warrior, and martyr. At the work's close the transfigured Joan finally takes her place among the saints.

Seregi, László (*b* Budapest, 12 Dec. 1929) Hungarian dancer and choreographer. He studied dance while a member of the Hungarian Army Ensemble, also with Nádasi and Harangozó, and in 1957 the Hungarian State Opera Ballet as character dancer. In 1965 he began choreographing for opera and in 1968 created his version of *Spartacus* (mus. Khachaturian) which was considered seminal in the way it combined Soviet and Hungarian traditions. In 1970 he choreographed three works to Bartók's music: *The Miraculous Mandarin*, *The Wooden Prince*, and dances for the opera *Duke Bluebeard's Castle*. The first, in a new 1981 version, became the trademark ballet of the Hungarian State Ballet. His works were driven by powerful drama and characterization, some like his 1975 ballet *The Cedar Tree* (mus. Hidas) were profoundly Hungarian in character. But his 1972 version of *Sylvia* (mus. Delibes) was a more light-hearted mix of folk, classical Greek culture, and neo-classical dance and later works like *On the Town* and *Serenade*, both made in 1977 to music

by Bernstein, reflected more Western influences. In 1974 he was appointed chief choreographer for Hungarian State Opera Ballet and between 1977 and 1984 he directed the Budapest State Opera Ballet. In 1994 he choreographed *The Taming of the Shrew* (mus. K. Goldmark). His work did not become widely known in the West, even though he choreographed and staged ballets in W. Germany, Zurich, and Vienna, and Australian Ballet revived his *Spartacus* in 1994. In his own country he has a considerable reputation.

Serenade Ballet in one act with choreography by Balanchine and music by Tchaikovsky. Premiered 10 Jun. 1934 by students of the School of American Ballet in a private performance at Felix M. Warburg's estate, White Plains, New York; given its first public performance 8 Dec. 1934, Avery Memorial Theater, Hartford, Connecticut, and its first professional performance, with scenery by Gaston Longchamp and costumes by Jean Lurcat, on 1 Mar. 1935 by American Ballet at Adelphi Theater, New York. This setting of Tchaikovsky's Serenade in C major for String Orchestra (with the 3rd and 4th movements of the score interchanged) is probably the most popular and widely performed of all Balanchine's works. It is essentially a plotless ballet, though romantic images are suggested in its final movement, which evoke earlier ballets such as *Swan Lake* and *Giselle*. Its pure dance sections are largely performed by women, reflecting the gender balance of students for whom it was first choreographed, and two moments—when a woman arrives late to take her place amongst the rows of dancers, and when another woman falls to the floor—were famously incorporated from real events which occurred during rehearsal. After 1936 the work was performed without scenery and new costumes were designed for later productions such as those by Karinska, 1964. It has been revived for many companies, including Ballet Russe de Monte Carlo (1940), Paris Opera Ballet (1947), San Francisco Ballet (1952), Royal Danish Ballet (1957), La Scala (1960), Royal Ballet (1964), Australian Ballet (1970), Berlin Opera Ballet (1970), Hungarian State Opera Ballet (1977), Dance Theatre of Harlem (1979), Matsuyama Ballet (1982), the Kirov (1998), and the Bolshoi (2007).

Sergeyev, Konstantin (*b* St Petersburg, 5 Mar. 1910; *d* St Petersburg, 1 Apr. 1992) Soviet dancer and choreographer. He took evening classes at the Leningrad Ballet School and danced with the Joseph Kschessinsky company (1928–9) before returning full-time to the LBS. In 1930 he joined GATOB (later Kirov Ballet) where he remained until 1961. Dubbed as a 'poet of dance', his lyric, Romantic style was showcased in all the major classic roles in which he regularly partnered Ulanova or his second wife Dudinskaya. He was also considered the definitive Kirov Romeo, creating the role in Lavrovsky's 1940 ballet opposite Ulanova, and he created roles in many other new ballets including Vatslav in Zakharov's *The Fountain of Bakhchisarai* (1934), Armen in Anisimova's *Gayané* (1942), and Andrei in Fenster's *Taras Bulba* (1955). In 1946 he choreographed the first Leningrad production of Prokofiev's *Cinderella*, casting himself as the Prince, and he created several other original ballets including *Path of Thunder* (mus. Karayev, 1957) and *Hamlet* (mus. Chervinsky, 1970). He also staged many productions of the classics including *Raymonda* (1948), *Swan Lake* (1950), and *Sleeping Beauty* (1952), all for the Kirov. He was artistic director of the Leningrad Ballet School (1938–40 and 1973–82) and was also artistic director of the Kirov (1951–6 and 1960–70), leading the company on its first Western tours. His career was not without political complications but he is widely credited with having preserved the Kirov's classical heritage. Among his many honours were People's Artist of the USSR, 1957, and Honorary Award, Academy of Dance, Paris, 1965.

Sergeyev, Nicholas (*b* St Petersburg, 27 Sept. 1876; *d* Nice, 24 Jun. 1951) Russian dancer, teacher, ballet master, and director. He studied at the Imperial Theatre School, St Petersburg, and graduated into the Mariinsky Theatre in 1894, becoming a soloist in 1904. In 1903 he became the company's regisseur in charge of notation and in 1914 its regisseur general. During this time he recorded 21 ballets in the Stepanov notation (in varying degrees of completeness) and when he left Russia after the October Revolution he took his scores with him. From these he mounted the productions of the standard classics in the West which in turn formed the basis of most subsequent Western productions, including *The Sleeping Princess* (*Sleeping Beauty*) for Diaghilev (1921), *Giselle* for Spessivtseva at Paris Opera (1924), for London's Camargo Society (1932), for Markova-Dolin Ballet (1935), and for Vic-Wells Ballet (1934), *Coppélia* for Vic-Wells Ballet (1933) and Ballet Russe de Monte Carlo (1938), *Nutcracker* and *Swan Lake* for Vic-Wells Ballet (1934), and *Sleeping Beauty* for Vic-Wells Ballet (1939). (The historical accuracy of his stagings was recognized when the Royal Ballet took this last production to Leningrad in 1961 and it was compared with older Kirov stagings.) He worked as a ballet master in Riga (1922–4) and also for Pavlova's company and for Opera Privé de Paris (1927–9). In 1934 he founded and directed his own Sergeyev Russian Ballet (performing in the UK) and was chief regisseur for Inglesby's Inter-

national Ballet (1941–8). The Stepanov scores are now in the Harvard Theater Collection.

Servant of Two Masters (orig. Czech title *Sluha dvou pánu*) Ballet in three acts with choreography by Němeček, libretto by J. Rey, music by J. Burghauser, and design by V. Heller. Premiered 9 May 1958, Tyl Theatre, Prague, with Kůra. Based on Goldoni's comedy, it became one of the most popular ballets in the Czech repertoire, also appearing in different versions throughout the Eastern Bloc. Fenster also used Goldoni's play as a basis for *The False Bridegroom* (mus. Chulaki, Maly Theatre, Leningrad, 1946).

Set and Reset Modern dance work in one act with choreography by Trisha Brown, music by Laurie Anderson, and costumes and film projections by Rauschenberg. Premiered 1983 by Trisha Brown Dance Company. It became one of Brown's most popular works with densely counterpointed dance and images of lively visual wit.

Setterfield, Valda (*b* Margate, 17 Sept. 1934) British dancer She studied with Rambert and A. de Vos, and danced briefly with Ballet Rambert before touring Italy in a revue during 1956. In 1958 she moved to America where she danced with Waring (1958–60), Cunningham (1960–1 and 1965–74), Rainer (1971–2), and Grand Union (1976). Married to David *Gordon, she has danced with him in many of his works.

Seven Deadly Sins, The (orig. Ger. title *Die sieben Todsünden der Kleinburger*; title of 1st Fr. production *Les Sept Péchés capitaux*) Ballet with songs in seven scenes with prologue and epilogue, choreography by Balanchine, text by Berthold Brecht, music by Kurt Weill, and design by C. Neher. Premiered 7 Jun. 1933 by Les Ballets 1933, Théâtre des Champs-Elysées, Paris, with Lenya (singing) and Losch. The heroine, Anna, is played by a singer and a dancer, the former narrating Anna's story as she travels around America in search of money to build a home for her family. In each of seven cities she experiences one of the seven sins. It was revived for New York City Ballet in 1958 with new choreography by Balanchine and design by Ter-Arutunian, with Lenya and Kent. There have been many other versions, including those of H. Lander (Copenhagen, 1936), Béjart (Brussels, 1961), MacMillan (Edinburgh Festival, 1961 and Royal Ballet, 1973), Prokovsky (PACT Ballet, 1975), Bausch (Wuppertal, 1976), Marin (Lyon Opera Ballet, 1987), and Tuckett (Royal Ballet, 2007).

Seventh Symphony Ballet in one act with choreography by Massine, music by Beethoven, and design by Bérard. Premiered 5 May 1938 by Ballet Russe de Monte Carlo, Monte Carlo, with

Markova, Theilade, Franklin, and Youskevitch. It is set to Beethoven's 7th Symphony and was one of Massine's most influential symphonic ballets. Though essentially plotless, its underlying theme is the creation and destruction of the Earth and its four movements are entitled: 'The Creation', 'The Earth', 'The Sky', and 'Bacchanale'. Isadora Duncan also created a work to this score in New York, 1908.

Seymour, Lynn (orig. Springbett; *b* Wainwright, Alta., 8 Mar. 1939) Canadian dancer and choreographer. She studied in Vancouver and then at Sadler's Wells School. In 1956 she joined Covent Garden Opera Ballet, then moved to the Touring Royal Ballet in 1957, and a year later to the Royal Ballet as a soloist, becoming principal in 1959. Her first created role was the Adolescent in MacMillan's *The Burrow* (1958), the first of many ballets on which she worked with the choreographer and which showcased her softly lyrical technique and unusual dramatic intensity. Further roles she created with MacMillan included the Girl in *Invitation* (1960), the Fiancée in *Baiser de la fée* (1960), Juliet in *Romeo and Juliet* (1965, though Fonteyn danced the role at the ballet's premiere), Anna Andersen in the one-act version of *Anastasia* (1967) and later the Grand Duchess Anastasia in the three-act version (1971), and Mary Vetsera in *Mayerling* (1978). These works established her as the leading dance-actress of her generation, projecting a raw immediacy of emotion that had not previously been associated with ballet. However she also danced the classic repertory, including Odette-Odile (1958), Giselle and Aurora (both 1960), and created roles in Ashton ballets including the Young Girl in *Two Pigeons* (1961) and Natalia Petrovna in *A Month in the Country* (1976). She was prima ballerina at Berlin Opera Ballet (1966–9) under MacMillan's direction, after which she guested with various companies including London Festival Ballet, National Ballet of Canada, Alvin Ailey American Dance Theater, London Contemporary Dance Theatre, and American Ballet Theatre. In 1971 she returned to the Royal Ballet as principal guest ballerina (until 1978) and created her first ballet for the Royal Ballet Choreographic Group in 1973, *Night Ride* (mus Finnissy). Her other works included *Gladly, Sadly, Badly, Madly* for LCDT (mus. Davis, 1975), *Wolfie* for Rambert Dance Company (mus. Mozart, 1987), and *Bastet* for Sadler's Wells Royal Ballet (mus. Berkeley, 1988). She was artistic director of Munich State Opera Ballet (1978–80), then rejoined the Royal briefly as a dancer in 1981, and subsequently as guest coach. She also danced with Northern Ballet Theatre in Lynne's *A Simple Man* (1987), with Second Stride in *Escape at Sea* (1993), and with Adventures in Motion Pictures in M. Bourne's *Swan Lake* (1996) and *Cinderella* (1997), in which she created the role of the Stepmother.

Shabelevsky, Yurek (*b* Warsaw, 1911) Polish-US dancer and director. He studied at Warsaw Opera Ballet School and with Nijinska, joining Ida Rubinstein's company in Paris in 1928. A glamorous dancer with a versatile instinct for different styles, he danced with many companies including Spessivtseva's (1930), with which he created the leading role in Nijinska's *Paysage enfantin*; de Basil's Ballets Russes de Monte Carlo (1932–9), with which he created roles in many ballets by Balanchine, Massine, and Nijinska; with Ballet Theatre (1940); and with Teatro Colón (various seasons, 1937–47). He was guest artist at La Scala, Milan (1949–50), and directed his own touring groups in the US and S. America from the 1940s.

Shadowplay Ballet in one act with choreography and libretto by Tudor, music by Charles Koechlin, and design by Michael Annals. Premiered 25 Jan. 1967 by the Royal Ballet at Covent Garden, London, with Dowell, Rencher, and Park. It was Tudor's only created work for the Royal's main company and he referred to it as a 'Buddhist ballet in disguise'. Its allegorical plot tells the story of a wild boy who is confronted by various animal creatures and deities with whom he has to grapple before reaching adult knowledge. Koechlin's score, *Les Bandar-Log* (interpolated with an excerpt from *La Course de printemps*), was partly inspired by Kipling's *The Jungle Book*, as was Tudor's choreography which mixed suggestions of animal movements with elements from Cambodian and Hindu dance. It was revived for American Ballet Theatre in 1975 with Baryshnikov, Kirkland, and Jonas Käge.

Shakers, The Modern dance work in one act with choreography by Humphrey and music and costumes by Pauline Lawrence. Premiered 12 Nov. 1930 by the Humphrey Weidman Company at Hunter College, New York. It was originally titled *Dance of the Chosen*, and portrays a religious meeting held by the Shakers during the early pioneer period of American history. Its first professional performance was 1 Feb. 1931 at the Craig Theater, New York, and it has been revived several times, by Welsh Dance Theatre (1975) and others. The Shakers were a unique Christian sect who valued dance and song as part of their religious ritual. Shaker dance dates back to early converts who were known to break into ecstatic trembling movements. After a time such movements were deliberately performed and eventually choreographed into formal dances.

Shakespeare ballets (*See also under individual titles of plays.*) The plays of Shakespeare

(1564–1616) have proved a rich source of character and plot for choreographers. Versions of *The Taming of the Shrew* include Béjart (mus. D. Scarlatti, Paris, 1954), Cranko (mus. D. Scarlatti, arr. Stolze, Stuttgart, 1969), and L. Falco in *Kate's Rag* (1980); versions of *Romeo and Juliet* include Eusebio Luzzi (Venice, 1785), Galeotti (mus. C. Schall, Copenhagen, 1811), Nijinska (mus. Lambert, Monte Carlo, 1926), Bartholin (mus. Tchaikovsky, Paris, 1937), Psota (mus. Prokofiev, Brno, 1938), with versions of Prokofiev's score including Lavrovsky (Leningrad, 1940), Ashton (Copenhagen, 1955), Lifar (Paris, 1955), Cranko (Stuttgart, 1962), MacMillan (London, 1965), van Dantzig (Amsterdam, 1967), Neumeier (Frankfurt, 1971), Smuin (San Francisco, 1976), Vinogradov (Maly Theatre, Leningrad, 1976), Nureyev (London Festival Ballet, 1977), Grigorovich (Moscow, 1979), and Morris (New York, 2008), with Preljocaj (Lyon, 1990) and Krsysztoff Pastor (Scotland, 2008), both creating versions to contemporary arrangements of Prokofiev; later versions of *R and J* set to other scores include T. Gsovsky (mus. L. Spies, Leipzig, 1942), Tudor (mus. Delius, New York, 1943), Skibine (mus. Berlioz, Paris, 1955); versions of *A Midsummer Night's Dream* include M. Petipa (mus. Mendelssohn, St Petersburg, 1877), Balanchine (New York, 1962), Ashton (*The Dream*, London, 1964), Neumeier (mus. Ligeti and Mendelssohn, Hamburg, 1977), Bigonzetti (mus. Elvis Costello, 2000), Wheeldon (Colorado Ballet 2000); versions of *Twelfth Night* include Tudor (in *Cross-Gartered*, mus. Frescobaldi, London, 1937) and Howard (mus. Grieg, Liverpool, 1942); versions of *Hamlet* include Francesco Clerico (mus. by himself, Venice, 1788), L. Henry (mus. W. R. Gallenberg, Paris, 1816), Nijinska (mus. Liszt, Paris, 1934), Helpmann (mus. Tchaikovsky, London, 1942), V. Gsovsky (mus. Blacher, Munich, 1950), Sergeyev (mus. Chervinsky, Leningrad, 1970), Neumeier (in *Hamlet: Connotations*, mus. Copland, American Ballet Theatre, New York, 1976), MacMillan (in *Sea of Troubles*, mus. Martinů and Webern, London, 1985), Paeper (mus. Klatzow, Cape Town, 1992), P. Schaufuss (mus. Black Sun and R. Langgaard, Elsinore, 1996), Wheeldon (*Elsinore* mus. Pärt 2008); versions of *The Merry Wives of Windsor* by Bourmeister and I. Kurilov (mus. V. Oransky, Moscow, 1942); versions of *Much Ado About Nothing* by V. Boccadoro (mus. T. Khrennikov, Moscow, 1976); versions of *Othello* by S. Viganò (mus. various, Milan, 1818), and Lubovitch for San Francisco Ballet and American Ballet Theatre (1998), Limón in *The Moor's Pavane* (mus. Purcell, New London, Conn., 1949), Chabukiani (mus. V. Machavariani, Tblisi, 1957), Němeček (mus. J. Hanuš, Prague, 1959), Lifar in *Le Maure de Venise* (mus. Thiriet, Amsterdam, 1960), Darrell (mus. Liszt, Trieste, 1971),

Brandstrup (mus. I. Dearden, London, 1994); versions of *Macbeth* by Le Picq (mus. Locke, arr. Barthelémon, London, 1785), Galeotti (mus. Schall, Copenhagen, 1816), H. Henry (mus. Pugni, Milan, 1830), and Pistoni (mus. R. Strauss, Milan, 1969); versions of *Antony and Cleopatra* by Noverre (Stuttgart or Ludwigsburg, after 1761), Aumer (mus. Kreutzer, Paris, 1808), and dell'Ara (mus. Prokofiev, Milan, 1971); versions of *Coriolanus* by S. Viganò (mus. Weigl, Milan, 1804); versions of *The Tempest* by Coralli (mus. Schneitzhoeffer, Paris, 1834), F. Taglioni (in *Miranda*, London, 1838), Howard (mus. Tippett, London, 1964), Eck (mus. Sibelius, Helsinki, 1974), Tetley (mus. Nordheim, Ballet Rambert, 1979), Smuin (mus. Chihara after Purcell, San Francisco, 1981), and Nureyev (mus. Tchaikovsky, London, 1982). Other ballets based on Shakespearian material include Lacotte's *Such Sweet Thunder* (mus. Ellington, Berlin, 1959, also Bintley's *The Shakespeare Suite*, Birmingham, 1999, set to the same music) and MacMillan's *Images of Love* (mus. P. Tranchell, London, 1964).

Shankar, Uday (*b* Udaipur, 8 Dec. 1900; *d* Calcutta, 26 Sept. 1977) Indian dancer and choreographer who pioneered the serious understanding of Indian dance in the West. He studied dance at the J.J. School of Arts in Bombay, and in 1920 went to London to study painting at the Royal College. He also performed in programmes of Indian dance and music, produced by his father and was recommended to Pavlova to assist her in the staging of two Indian ballets, *Hindu Wedding* and *Radha Krishna* (1923). He partnered her in London and the US but then went on to tour internationally as a soloist and later with his own company. In 1938 he established a dance school in Almora, India, where he helped encourage the revival of dance as a creative art. It closed in 1942 and he toured with various companies of his own, also setting up another school in Calcutta. He continued performing until the early 1960s.

Shaw, Brian (orig. Earnshaw; *b* Huddersfield, 28 Jun. 1928; *d* London, 2 Apr. 1992) British dancer and teacher. He studied at the Sadler's Wells School and joined Sadler's Wells Ballet in 1944, becoming soloist and principal. He was one of the finest classical male dancers of his generation, creating roles in Ashton's *Symphonic Variations* (1946), *Ondine* (1958), and *Monotones* (1966). He also created roles in Cranko's *Prince of the Pagodas* (1957) and MacMillan's *Noctambules* (1956). He was an outstandingly virtuoso Blue Bird in *Sleeping Beauty*. He became a principal teacher with the company in 1972 and received the Queen Elizabeth II Coronation Award in 1975.

Shawn, Ted (*b* Kansas City, 21 Oct. 1891; *d* Orlando, Fla., 9 Jan. 1972) US dancer, teacher, and choreographer. He began studying ballet in Denver in order to recover from illness and made his first public appearance as a dancer there in 1911. He opened a dance school in Los Angeles where he appeared in an early dance film, *Dance of the Ages*. During 1914 he toured with a small company and in New York he met and married Ruth *St Denis. They toured together as partners, then in 1915 founded *Denishawn. Both as a school and a company this was seminal in the development of American modern dance. The company toured widely until it was disbanded in 1931 after his separation from St Denis. He formed his own Company of Male Dancers in 1933, partly with the aim of countering popular prejudice against men dancing. His choreography drew on folk, aboriginal, and popular American material. In 1933 he also bought a farm in Massachusetts called *Jacob's Pillow which he turned into a dance studio. After disbanding his company in 1940 he became director of the Jacob's Pillow Dance Festival and summer school which was to become the most important American dance festival, offering teaching courses and performances in many aspects of dance. He continued to perform until he was over 70. He was a prolific choreographer, creating around 190 works for Denishawn which included many solos and duets for himself and St Denis, as well as group works such as *Prometheus Bound* (mus. Scriabin, 1929). He also choreographed over 50 works for his own male company, including *Kinetic Molpai* (1935). He wrote many books including *Ruth St Denis: Pioneer and Prophet* (1920), *Gods Who Dance* (1929), *Every Little Movement* (1954), and also his autobiography (with Gray Poole), *One Thousand and One Night Stands* (1960).

Shearer, Moira (orig. Shearer-King; *b* Dunfermline, 17 Jan. 1926; *d* Oxford, 31 Jan. 2006) British dancer and actor who became world famous after starring in Powell and Pressburger's film *The Red Shoes*. She began her training in N. Rhodesia and in England studied with Flora Fairbairn, then at the Legat School and Sadler's Wells Ballet School. She made her debut with International Ballet in 1941 then joined Sadler's Wells Ballet in the same year, becoming ballerina from 1944 to 1952. She created roles in several Ashton ballets including *The Quest* (1943), *Symphonic Variations* (1946), and *Cinderella* (1948) as well as in Helpmann's *Miracle in the Gorbals* (1944) and Massine's *The Clock Symphony* (1948). The polished brilliance of her style set her apart from the lyricism of her British contemporaries (when Balanchine mounted *Ballet Imperial* on Sadler's Wells Ballet in 1950 he preferred her to Fonteyn) and this may have hindered her career.

But her stage career was also disrupted by her popular success at the age of 22 in *The Red Shoes* (1948), which was followed by other films including *Tales of Hoffmann* (1951), *The Man Who Loved Redheads* (1955), and *Black Tights* (1960). She guested with Ballets de Paris in 1950, with Sadler's Wells Ballet from 1952, and with London Festival Ballet in 1954 but increasingly concentrated on acting, for example playing Titania in *A Midsummer Night's Dream* (Edinburgh Festival, 1954). She married author and broadcaster Ludovic Kennedy.

Shechter, Hofesh (*b* Jerusalem, 1975) Israeli dancer, choreographer, and composer. He trained at the Jerusalem Academy for Dance and Music, moving to Tel Aviv to join Batsheva Dance Company, where he created roles in works by Naharin and Vandekeybus while additionally studying percussion. In 2002 he moved to London to perform with Jasmin Vardimon's company, creating his first work *Fragments* in 2003 for which he also composed the music. In 2004 he created *Cult*, a sextet that revealed his trademark combination of philosophical enquiry and viscerally expressive choreography. In 2007 he was commissioned to expand a single work, *In Your Rooms*, through three different London performance venues: The Place, Southbank Centre, and Sadler's Wells. His 2009 work *The Art of Not Looking Back* was created for an all-female cast. Shechter has additionally created work for several companies including Scottish Dance Theatre, Candoco, and Bern Ballet. He has also choreographed for theatre and for the television series *Skins* (2008).

(()) SEE WEB LINKS
- Website for the Hofesh Shechter company

Shéhérazade *See* SCHEHERAZADE.

Shelest, Alla (*b* Smolensk, 29 Feb. 1919; *d* St Petersburg, 7 Dec. 1998) Russian dancer and teacher. She studied at the Leningrad Ballet School with E. Gerdt and Vaganova and graduated in 1937 into the Kirov Ballet where she danced until 1963. Her technique was characterized by a huge jump, lyrical fluency, and a classical purity of style. These qualities, combined with the boldness of her dramatic interpretations, made her one of the company's most popular ballerinas. Ulanova wrote of her: 'She is a tragic and inspired ballerina. You can always recognise [her] by the perfection of the sketch, by the emotion and by the dancer's self-abandon.' She performed many of the standard ballerina roles, famed especially for her portrayal of Nikiya in *La Bayadère*, and created the role of Aegina in Jacobson's *Spartacus* (1956) and Zarema in *Fountain of Bakhchisarai*. She was married for a time to Grigorovich. She performed in several ballet films and television programmes, and was artistic director of the Kuibyshev Ballet (1970–3) and ballet mistress of the Kirov (1977–9). She was made People's Artist of the Russian Federation in 1957.

Shen Wei Dance Arts New York-based dance company founded in 2000 and named after the Chinese-born choreographer and visual artist Shen Wei. His work is devoted to the fusion of dance, theatre, Chinese opera, painting, and sculpture. Shen Wei was a founding member of the Guangdong Modern Dance Company (1991–94) in China before moving to New York City. His repertory includes *The Rite of Spring* (2003) and *Connect Transfer* (2005), the latter culminating in the dancers creating a painting by using their limbs to produce brushstrokes on a canvas that covers the stage.

SEE WEB LINKS
• SWDA website

Shklyarov, Vladimir (*b* St Petersburg (Leningrad), 1985) He studied at the Vaganova Academy and graduated into the Mariinsky Ballet in 2003, promoted to first soloist in 2007. A dancer of engaging classical style and depth of expression he has excelled as Romeo and James (*La Sylphide*) as well as the more modern repertory. He created lead roles in revivals of *Le Reveil de Flore* (1894 production, Vikharev, 2007), Fokine's *Carnaval* (revival of the 1910 production, choreography staged by Sergei Vikharev, 2008). Recipient of numerous awards including Vaganova and Moscow competitions.

shoes The shoes worn by dancers have played a crucial role in the development of style and technique. During the 18th century light, heeled shoes showed off the dancers' feet and ankles and focused attention on the brilliant footwork of the period, particularly enhancing stamping steps. They did not, though, have the suppleness necessary for the preparations and landings of very high jumps, nor did they allow the dancers to skim the floor at speed or dance on pointe. By the early 19th century women dancers began to wear the new thin, heelless, satin ballet slipper, tied with ribbons around the ankle and stiffened at the toe by rows of darning. These allowed ballerinas to stand, very briefly, on their toes, which were protected by cotton wadding. This new feat ushered in a new dance vocabulary of hovering balances and quick, light bourrées, as well as a new image of the ballerina as gravity-defying sylph. Low-heeled slippers were also worn by women, and both sexes wore a wide variety of other footwear as determined by the nature of their role; for example, boots, sometimes with spurs, were worn by both sexes in Polish roles, low-heeled shoes with bows were worn by male courtiers, and sandals were sometimes worn by gypsy characters. The boxed-toe shoe (stiffened through layers of shellac and wadding around the toe area and with a strong, springy inner shank to support the arch) began to be developed in the latter half of the 19th century and paved the way for another quantum leap in female technique. It made possible a range of bravura effects which we now regard as standard, including multiple pirouettes and hopping on pointe. It also changed the nature of the pas de deux, since ballerinas could sustain extended balances during which their partners could angle them through the numerous flattering positions.

When Isadora *Duncan and Martha *Graham chose to perform barefoot at the end of the 19th century and beginning of the 20th, this not only changed the appearance of dance but was also a powerful statement of their artistic philosophies. Now that they no longer had a thin-soled ballet slipper to create a slippery divide between them and the floor, or pointe shoes on which to perch, Duncan and Graham presented themselves as women of the earth, acknowledging gravity rather than floating away from it. The naked traction of their feet against the floor gave their dancing a more vigorous, sensuous, and emphatic rhythm and provided the leverage necessary for some of Graham's most vertiginous backward falls.

Some later choreographers returned to shoes, but these fulfilled very different functions from the classical ballet slipper. Trainers were favoured by the 1960s' avant-garde who were creating minimalist, anti-virtuoso dance. These shoes were designed by sports manufacturers for speed, comfort, and cushioning, and on the feet of dancers they not only carried no suggestion of art or glamour but also implied that dance was a kind of task to be performed in the most practical and sensible way. In the 1980s choreographers temporarily lighted on another item of street fashion, the Doc Marten shoe whose blunt, rubber-soled heft was closely linked with the crashing momentum, violence, and risk taking that characterized that decade's New Dance.

Tap shoes have thin metal plates, usually made of aluminium, screwed onto the sole and heel, allowing dancers to create percussive effects as they move.

Shostakovich, Dmitri (*b* St Petersburg, 25 Sept. 1906; *d* Moscow, 9 Aug. 1975) Soviet composer. He wrote three ballet scores: *The Golden Age* (chor. Kaplan, Vainonen, Tchesnakov, and Jacobson, 1930), *The Bolt* (chor. Lopukhov, 1931), and *The Bright Stream* (chor. Lopukhov, 1935). These were seminal in their treatment of contemporary subject-matter but at the time were criticized by the Soviet authorities for their 'incorrect' representation of class issues and, in the case of *Bright Stream*, inappropriate use of classical forms. Much of Shostakovich's concert music has also been adapted for dance, including the 7th Symphony (chor. Massine in *Leningrad Symphony*, New York, 1945, and by Belsky, Leningrad, 1961); the 10th Symphony (chor. Maldoom, in *Overture 2012*, London, 2008), 1st Piano Concerto (chor. Cranko in *The Catalyst*, Stuttgart, 1961 and Wheeldon in *Mercurial Manoeuvres*, New York, 2000); the 2nd Piano Concerto (chor. MacMillan in *Concerto*, W. Berlin, 1966, and by Mitchell in *Fête noire*, New York, 1971); the Cello Sonata in D minor (chor. Morris, in *Vestige*, minus the 1st movement, Spokane, 1984); various pieces in Béjart's *Trois études pour Alexandre* (Paris, 1987), the 3rd String Quartet (chor. Alston, *Tremor*, London 2001), and the 9th String Quartet (chor. Henri Oguike, *Front Line*, 2002).

Shuraleh Ballet in three acts with choreography by Jacobson, libretto by Jacobson and A. Faysi, music by Farid Yarullin, and design by P. Speransky. First staged for the Kazan Theatre for Opera and Ballet in 1945; the definitive version, briefly titled *Ali-Batyr* and with revised instrumentation by V. Vlasov and V. Fereh, and design by L. Milchin and I. Vano, was premiered 28 May 1950 by the Kirov, Leningrad, with Shelest, Dudinskaya, Zubkovsky, Sergeyev, Makarov, Belsky, and Gerbeck. It was a uniquely Tartar-based work, using Tartar folk tales and mixing classical vocabulary with Tartar national dance, and it was seminal in the development of Soviet ballet in its close integration of dance and mime. The title refers to a malicious wood-sprite of Tartar lore, and the ballet tells the story of a maiden Suimbike who has been turned into a bird but falls in love with a hunter, Ali-Batyr. The sprite Shuraleh vindictively tries to keep them apart but in the end, by risking death together, the couple break the spell which has been cast on Suimbike and she is able to return Ali-Batyr's love as a woman. Under its original title it was revived for many companies in Eastern Europe.

Sibelius, Jean (*b* Hämeenlinna, 8 Dec. 1865; *d* Jarvenpaa, 21 Sept. 1957) Finnish composer. He wrote the music for the ballet *Scaramouche* in 1913, which was premiered in Copenhagen, 1922, with choreography by E. Walbom. Much of his other theatre and concert music has also been adapted for dance, including selected piano pieces (chor. Ashton in *Lady of Shalott*, London, 1931), *Perisynthion* (chor. Helpmann, Sydney, 1974), *The Tempest* (chor. Eck, Helsinki, 1974), *Swan of Tuonela* (numerous versions including Dolin, Ulbrich, and Bintley), and *Tapiola* (chor. Montagnon in *Sleepwalkers*, Stuttgart, 1979).

Sibley, (Dame) Antoinette (orig. A. S. Corbett; *b* Bromley, 27 Feb. 1939) British dancer. She studied at the Cone-Ripman School and Sadler's Wells School and joined Sadler's Wells Ballet in 1956 (just before it became the Royal Ballet). She was promoted to soloist in 1959 and principal in 1960. She danced her first Odette-Odile aged 20 with only two weeks' notice and from then on danced all the standard ballerina roles. The elegant clarity of her technique, coupled with her innate musicality, made her the natural successor to Fonteyn in ballets like *The Sleeping Beauty*, but her more individual dramatic qualities were brought out in created roles such as Titania in Ashton's *The Dream* (1964) and in the title role of MacMillan's *Manon* (which she created only part of, due to injury, prior to premiering the part in 1974). In these ballets she danced with Dowell, with whom she developed an internationally celebrated partnership. She also created roles in MacMillan's *Anastasia* (1971 version) and *Triad* (1972), among others, and in Ashton's *Monotones* (1966), *Jazz Calendar* and *Enigma Variations* (both 1968), and *Meditation from Thaïs* (1971). In 1979 she retired but returned to the stage in 1981 and continued dancing occasional guest performances until 1989. In the same year she was appointed vice-president of the Royal Academy of Dancing, becoming president in 1991. She has regularly returned to the Royal to coach her former repertory. She was married to Michael Somes (1964–9). Awarded the title Dame Commander of the British Empire in 1996.

Siegel, Marcia B. (*b* New York, 17 Sept. 1932) US dance writer. She was educated at Connecticut College and has been the long-standing dance critic of the *Hudson Review*, and of the *Boston Phoenix* since 1996. She founded *Dance Scope* (1964–6) and has contributed to many publications. She is author of *At the Vanishing Point* (New York, 1972), *Watching the Dance Go By* (Boston, 1977), *The Shapes of Change* (Boston, 1979, repr. California), *Days on Earth—the Dance of Doris Humphrey* (Yale, 1987, repr. Duke Univ. Press), and *The Tail of the Dragon: New Dance 1976–1982* (Duke Univ. Press, 1991), and *Howling Near Heaven* (St Martins Press, 2006). She taught on the faculty of Performing Arts at New York University from 1983 to 1999 and has lectured internationally on dance history and criticism.

Simone, Kirsten (*b* Copenhagen, 1 Jul. 1934) Danish dancer and teacher. She studied at Royal Danish Ballet School with Volkova and joined the Royal Danish Ballet in 1952. She was promoted to soloist (principal) in 1956 and 1st soloist in 1966. A dancer with an unusually clean and powerful classical technique, she was initially considered somewhat cool in performance, but subsequently developed into a fine mime and character dancer. She danced all the standard ballerina roles

(Petipa and Bournonville) as well as the 20th-century repertory (Ashton, Balanchine, MacMillan, Petit, etc.), and created roles in Flindt's *The Three Musketeers* (1966), von Rosen's *Don Juan* (1967), and H. Lander's *Fête polonaise* (1970 version). She guested with several companies, including American Ballet Theatre and London Festival Ballet. After retiring from ballerina roles she continued to perform with RDB as a character artist and to teach at the school.

Sinfonietta Ballet in one act with choreography by Kylián, music by Janáček, and design by Walter Nobbe. Premiered 9 Jun. 1978 by Nederlands Dans Theater at Spoleto Festival, Charleston, S. Carolina. It is set to Janáček's 1926 score of the same title and the exuberant physicality of the choreography reflects the composer's stated desire to express 'the contemporary free man, his spiritual beauty and joy, his strength, courage and determination'. It has become one of NDT's signature pieces and has been revived for many other companies including Paris Opera (1989), American Ballet Theatre (1991), Houston Ballet (1995), and Royal Ballet (2003). P. Smok has also choreographed a ballet to the same score (Basle, 1971).

Also the title of Ashton's one-act ballet to M. Williamson's score, premiered by Touring Royal Ballet at Stratford-upon-Avon, 10 Feb. 1967, and revived for Sadler's Wells Royal Ballet, 1981.

Singapore Traditional dance culture retained a powerful hold in Singapore and it did not significantly open up to Western influences before the mid-20th century. In 1950 the Goh sisters founded the Singapore Academy for the teaching of ballet and in 1988 the city founded its first professional classical company, Singapore Dance Theatre. This was dedicated to Singapore-born choreographer Choo-San *Goh, who developed an international reputation before his premature death, and SDT continues to perform many of his ballets as well as a selection of the 19th-century classics and works by Balanchine Kylián, Duato, and G. Murphy among others. It also showcases new Asian choreographers such as Jeffrey Tan and Kuik Swee Boon. In the mid-1990s modern dance became active with the founding of Arts Fission, a company dedicated to merging the cultures of Western contemporary choreography and Asian dance. Several other companies have followed, including Odyssey Dance Theatre, founded by Danny Tan in 1999, and the multi-disciplinary ECNAD (founded as Dance Dimension) in 1996. Singapore also runs a biennial arts festival which programmes some modern and classical dance.

((⊕)) SEE WEB LINKS

• Website for the Singapore Dance Theatre

Singin' in the Rain Film directed by Kelly and Donen (1952) which features Kelly's famous tap sequence along a rain-drenched street.

Sirènes, Les Ballet in one act with choreography by Ashton, music by Lord Berners, and design by Beaton. Premiered 12 Nov. 1946 by Sadler's Wells Ballet at Covent Garden, London with Fonteyn, Helpmann, and Ashton. It is loosely based on Ouida's novel *Moths* and is set in 1904 on the beach at Trouville at the height of the Season, where its cast of eccentric characters feign social bonhomie to mask their private desolation.

sissonne [from the Fr. ciseaux] A scissor-like movement where the dancer jumps from both feet onto one.

Sizova, Alla (*b* Moscow, 22 Sept. 1939) Soviet dancer. She studied at the Leningrad Ballet School and graduated to the Kirov Ballet in 1958 where she danced until 1988. Her high leaps earned her the nickname 'flying Sizova' and the classical elegance of her style made her a natural Aurora which she danced in Sergeyev's 1964 film of *The Sleeping Beauty*. Though slightly overshadowed by ballerinas like Kolpakova she was one of the company's most popular ballerinas and created roles in Belsky's *Leningrad Symphony* (1961) and Sergeyev's *Hamlet* (1971). She was also Nureyev's preferred partner before he defected. After retiring she taught at the Leningrad (Vaganova) Ballet School. She was made People's Artist of the USSR in 1983.

Skating Rink Ballet in one act with choreography by Börlin, music by Honegger, and design by Léger. Premiered 20 Jan. 1922 by Ballets Suédois at Théâtre des Champs-Elysées, Paris, with Figoni, K. Smith, and Börlin. Dominated by Léger's monumental Cubist designs it portrays skaters as grotesque caricatures of urban people. It was staged by Hodson for Zurich Ballet in 1996 and Royal Swedish Ballet (1998).

Skeaping, Mary (*b* Woodford, 15 Dec. 1902; *d* London, 9 Feb. 1984) British dancer, choreographer, ballet director, and international authority on early ballets. She studied with some of the great teachers of the period, including Massine, Astafieva, Egorova, and Craske and danced with Pavlova's company (1925 and 1930–1) and with the Nemchinova-Dolin company (*c*.1927–30). She also appeared in cabaret, music hall, and experimental theatre productions as well as dancing occasionally for Ballet Club. Between 1948 and 1951 she was ballet mistress of Sadler's Wells Ballet and she directed the first live full-length classic for the BBC, *Sleeping Beauty* (1951). She worked as guest ballet mistress and producer of ballets for various companies in Cuba and

S

Canada (1952–4), after which she was appointed director of the Royal Swedish Ballet (1953–62) where she not only produced the standard 19th-century classics but revived historic Swedish court ballets (often in collaboration with Ivo Cramér), including *Cupid Out of his Humour* (mus. Purcell, Drottningholm Court Theatre, 1956). She became an authority on the 17th-century ballet de cour and published many articles. She mounted several early ballets for the Royal Ballet's Ballet for All group and after researching into the 1841 *Giselle* she mounted a production for London Festival Ballet (1971) which was widely praised for capturing the original's Romantic style and content. She was also a freelance producer of the classics in Finland and the USA. She was awarded the King's Own Medal, Sweden, in 1980.

Skibine, George (orig. Yuril Borisovich Skibin; *b* Yasnaya Poliana, Ukraine, 20 Jan. 1920; *d* Dallas, Tex., 14 Jun. 1981) Russian-US dancer, choreographer, and ballet director. The son of Boris Skibine, a dancer with Diaghilev's company, he studied with various teachers including Preobrajenska, Sedova, and Volinine. He made his debut as a can-can dancer at the Bal Tabarin night-club and as a classical dancer with Ballet de la Jeunesse in 1937. Throughout his career his romantic good looks and elegant style made him popular in roles such as Romeo and the Poet in *Les Sylphides*, as well as in the 19th-century classics, though he also created roles in many new works. As a young dancer he performed with several companies: (Denham's) Ballet Russe de Monte Carlo (1938–9), de Basil's Ballets Russes (1939–41), and American Ballet Theatre (1941–2), where he created the role of the Hermit in Massine's *Aleko*, partnering Markova. After military service he danced with the Markova-Dolin Ballet (1946) and Original Ballet Russe (1947), then from 1947 to 1956 he danced with Grand Ballet du Marquis de Cuevas becoming étoile in 1959. Here he choreographed his first ballet, *Tragédie à Vérone* (mus. Tchaikovsky, 1950). His later works include *Romeo and Juliet* (mus. Berlioz, Grand Ballet du Marquis de Cuevas, 1955), *Daphnis and Chloe* (mus. Ravel, Paris Opera, 1959), *The Firebird* (mus. Stravinsky, for French television, 1967, and for Dallas Civic Ballet, 1968), and *Gloria* (mus. Poulenc, Dallas Civic Ballet, 1974). After a brief period partnering his wife, Marjorie Tallchief, with Ruth Page's Chicago Ballet (1956–7 and again in 1959), he and Tallchief joined Paris Opera as danseurs étoiles. He was also choreographer there and ballet master between 1958 and 1962. In 1964 he became artistic director and choreographer of Harkness Ballet; from 1967 he worked as freelance choreographer in the US and Europe; and from 1969 he was artistic director of

Dallas Civic Ballet and its school. He was made Chevalier de l'Ordre des Arts et Lettres in 1967.

Skoog, Matz (*b* Stockholm, 10 Apr. 1957) Swedish dancer and director. He studied at the Royal Swedish Ballet School and later in Leningrad (1978) and danced with the Royal Swedish Ballet as apprentice (1973–5) then as full company member (1975–9). In 1979 he moved to London Festival Ballet where he was promoted to principal in 1981. He remained there until 1989 (apart from a season with Nederlands Dans Theater, 1982–3) and danced leading roles in the classics as well as the 20th-century repertory creating roles in Tetley's *Pulcinella* (1984), C. Bruce's *Swansong* (1987), and others. He then worked as a freelance dancer and producer, for example staging *La Sylphide* in Rome (1991), after which he was ballet master at London City Ballet (1991–3), assistant artistic director at Aterballetto (1993–4), dancer and teacher with Rambert Dance Company (1994), and was also guest teacher with many companies. In 1996 he was appointed artistic director of Royal New Zealand Ballet, where he was responsible for expanding the repertory with a more international range of work. Between 2001 and 2005 he was then artistic director of English National Ballet (2001–05) where he attempted, conversely, to encourage British choreographers, for example Christopher Hampson and Michael Corder. He has since returned to teach at the Royal New Zealand Ballet and its school.

Skouratoff, Vladimir (*b* Paris, 12 Mar. 1925) French dancer and teacher. He studied in wartime Paris with Preobrajenska, Volinine, and Kniaseff and began performing in the corps at the Lido, Paris, also appearing with Janine Charrat in recitals and with Jeanmaire in Lifar ballets. During the following decade he danced with a succession of companies: Nouveaux Ballets de Monte Carlo (1946) Original Ballet Russe (1947), Ballets de Paris (1948). Ballets des Champs-Elysées (1951), and finally Grand Ballet du Marquis de Cuevas (1952–7). In 1958 he turned freelance, partnering T. Lander in the musical *Le Rendezvous manqué* (written by Françoise Sagan, chor. John Taras, for Opera de Monte Carlo), and guesting with various companies including London Festival Ballet (1959) and Scandinavian Ballet (1960). He never ranked highly as a pure classical dancer, but excelled in both character roles and the modern repertory, creating roles in many ballets including Lifar's *Dramma per musica* and *Chota Roustaveli* (both 1946) and Skibine's *Idylle* (1954). He was ballet master with Strasbourg Opera, then with Bordeaux Opera (1970–90).

Slaughter on Tenth Avenue Ballet from the musical comedy *On Your Toes*. With choreography by Balanchine, music by R. Rodgers, set by Joe Mielzner, and costumes by Sharaff it was premiered 11 Apr. 1936 at Imperial Theatre, New York, with Bolger, Geva, and G. Church. The hero is an American dancer with a Russian ballet company who finds himself dancing for his life as gangsters pursue him. It was produced as a separate ballet 2 May 1968 by New York City Ballet, State Theater, New York, with Farrell and Mitchell and has been revived by Birmingham Royal Ballet (Birmingham, 1999) and others.

Slavenska, Mia (orig. Corak; *b* Slavonski-Brod, 20 Feb. 1914; *d* 5 Oct. 2002) Yugoslavian-US dancer, teacher, choreographer, and ballet director. She studied at the National Ballet Theatre School in Zagreb with Josephine Weiss and Margarita Froman, took further ballet studies with Leo Dubois in Vienna, and modern dance with Gertrud Kraus, then went to Paris where she studied with Egorova, Kshessinska, and Preobrajenska, later studying with Vincenzo Celli in New York. She had made her stage debut as a child prodigy in 1922 and became renowned for her virtuoso terre-à-terre technique. In 1930 she joined Zagreb Opera Ballet as a soloist, becoming prima ballerina (1934–5), then danced in London and Paris before becoming principal with (Denham's) Ballet Russe de Monte Carlo (1938–42, later returning as guest artist for various seasons, 1948–56). Between 1944 and 1945 she directed her own touring group, which toured N. and S. America for various seasons between 1947 and 1952. In 1952 she co-founded the Slavenska-Franklin Ballet which toured N. America and abroad for three years. She choreographed several works for these companies including *Trilogy* (mus. Chopin, Slavenska Thimar and Company, 1945) and also created the role of Blanche in Bettis's *A Streetcar Named Desire* (with Slavenska-Franklin Ballet, 1952). She continued to guest with many companies including London Festival Ballet and Ballet Theatre (both 1951) and Metropolitan Opera Ballet, New York (1954–5). She was ballerina and guest director with Louisville Ballet (1956–8) and director of Fort Worth Civic Ballet (1958–60). She taught at her own studio in Hollywood (1946–7) and subsequently at several other institutions including Univ. of California at Los Angeles. She starred in Benoit-Levy's film, *La Mort du cygne* (1938).

Sleep, Wayne (*b* Plymouth, 17 Jul. 1948) British dancer. He studied at the Royal Ballet School and joined the Royal Ballet in 1966, becoming soloist (1970) and principal dancer (1973–83). Though too short for the standard Prince roles, his virtuoso technique made him outstanding in demi-caractère roles like Puck in *The Dream*. He created roles in Ashton's *Jazz Calendar*, *Enigma*

Variations (both 1968), and *A Month in the Country* (1976), also in MacMillan's *Anastasia* (1971 version), *Elite Syncopations*, *Manon* (both 1974), and *The Four Seasons* (1975). He formed his own dance group, Dash, in 1980 which also toured under the names The Hot Shoe Show and Bits and Pieces as well as developing a successful freelance career in film, theatre, and opera, creating a role in the Lloyd Webber musical *Cats* and acting with the Royal Shakespeare Company. He choreographed his first work, *David and Goliath*, for London Contemporary Dance Theatre in 1975 (with Robert North, mus. C. Davis, London), *Savoy Suite* for English National Ballet (mus. Gilbert and Sullivan, arr. C. Davis, 1993), and many works for his own company. In 2003 he returned to the Royal to guest as the little Ugly Sister in Ashton's *Cinderella*.

Sleeping Beauty, The (Fr. title *La Belle au bois dormant*; Russ. title *Spyashchaya krasavitsa*) Ballet in prologue and three acts with choreography by Petipa, libretto by Petipa and Ivan Vsevolozhsky, music by Tchaikovsky, and design by Vsevolozhsky (costumes) and Ivan Andreyev, Mikhail Botcharov, Konstantin Ivanov, Heinrich Levogt, and Matvei Shishkov (sets). Premiered 15 Jan. (public dress rehearsal), 16 Jan. (first perf.) 1890 at the Mariinsky Theatre, St Petersburg, with Brianza as Aurora, Gerdt as Prince Désiré, Maria Petipa as the Lilac Fairy, and Cecchetti as Carabosse and the Blue Bird. It is widely considered to be a summation of 19th-century classicism, with its exemplary collaboration between composer and choreographer. The libretto is based on Perrault's fairy-tale, but Petipa did much more than tell the story of Aurora's 100-year sleep and magical awakening. Rather, he created a homage to 17th- and 18th-century French ballet. The choreography makes detailed reference to court ballets in its use of period dances and processionals and the costumes were designed in Louis XIV style. (It was reputed to be the most expensive ballet produced at the Russian Imperial Theatres.) At the same time, the ballet features Petipa's own brilliant syntheses of contemporary French, Italian, and Russian styles in passages of technically complex and stylistically varied dance. His variations for the fairies in the Prologue and for the fairy-tale characters in Act III vividly display their different virtues, while the choreography for Aurora shows her developing from a young girl in Act I (where she has to perform the notoriously testing balances of the *Rose Adagio), to an ethereal spirit in the Vision Scene of Act II, to a radiant bride in Act III.

The ballet made a profound impression on younger artists such as *Benois because of its unusually harmonious accord between dance, music, and design (in the 19th century it was rare to aim for an overall consistency of style and period in ballet productions). It certainly encouraged *Diaghilev to stage his own production for the Ballets Russes in 1921, which was so lavish that it nearly bankrupted his company. He salvaged a shortened version, based largely on the final act, called *Le Mariage de la belle au bois dormant* which was staged in Paris in 1922. Other productions of the ballet had been staged in the West including Savocco's staging at La Scala in 1896 and Clustine's 48-minute version which Pavlova danced in New York in 1916, but it was Diaghilev's which inspired de Valois to revive the ballet for Vic-Wells Ballet in 1939. This was staged by *Sergeyev who also mounted the more lavish and famous production of 1946 which the company danced when they moved to Covent Garden after the war, and also at their first New York season at the Met. With its luminous, spacious designs by Oliver Messel, this production stayed in the repertoire for eighteen years and formed the basis of later productions at the Royal Ballet: Peter Wright's (1968, with additional choreography by Ashton), MacMillan's (1973 and 1977, with additional choreography by Ashton and de Valois), and Anthony Dowell's (1994, excising most later additions in an attempt to revert to the original choreographic text). It was also reconstructed by Monica Mason and Christopher Newton in 2006, using many of Messel's original designs. This 1946 production also became a model for others outside Britain, including MacMillan (Berlin Opera Ballet, 1977) and Nureyev (La Scala, 1966, revived National Ballet of Canada, 1972, and London Festival Ballet, 1975). In June 1999 Makharbek Vaziev oversaw a historic production for the Kirov, which was based on the 1890 staging and designs, and which was claimed to be the most authentic in the repertory. Other productions have included Nijinska–Helpmann (Grand Ballet du Marquis de Cuevas, 1960), Grigorovich (Bolshoi Ballet, 1973), Helpmann (Australian Ballet, 1973), Alicia Alonso (Paris Opera Ballet, 1974), Mary Skeaping (American Ballet Theatre, 1976), and Peter Martins (New York City Ballet, 1991). Béjart's *Ni fleurs, ni couronnes*, based on images from Petipa's choreography, was created for Ballet of the 20th Century (Grenoble, 1968), and a chamber ballet version by H. W. Henze was produced by A. Bortoluzzi (Essen, 1951). Other versions of the story include Aumer's *La Belle au bois dormant* (mus. Hérold, Paris, 1829), Laban's *Dornröschen* (mus. J. Strauss, Berlin Staatsoper, 1934), and Ek's *Sleeping Beauty* (Hamburg, 1996). There are various films of the ballet including K. Sergeyev's, Leningrad, 1965, and the BBC's film of the Royal Ballet's production (1994).

Sleeping Princess, The The title of Diaghilev's production of *The Sleeping Beauty* when it was first danced in London in 1921, also of the 1939 Vic-Wells production.

Slingsby, Simon Eighteenth-century British dancer, about whom little is known except that he may have been the first British dancer to have had a career at the Paris Opera, where he danced during the 1790s. He also performed with Baccelli and A. Vestris during the 1780s at London's King's Theatre.

Slonimsky, Yuri (*b* St Petersburg, 12 Mar. 1902; *d* Moscow, 23 Apr. 1978) Soviet dance writer and librettist. He took private dance lessons in 1918, and began writing dance criticism in 1919. In 1921 he was a founder member of the Young Ballet group (with Balanchine and others). During the 1920s, 1930s, and 1940s he lectured on ballet history in Moscow and Leningrad and in 1937 he worked with Lopukhov in organizing a new choreography department at the Leningrad Ballet School. As a critic he brought a pioneeringly analytic approach to Soviet ballet. He wrote many books of history and criticism, including *Didelot* (1958) and *In Honour of Dance* (Moscow, 1968), as well as several ballet librettos, including Sergeyev's *Path of Thunder* (1957) and Belsky's *Coast of Hope* (1959).

Slovak National Theatre Ballet The company dates back to the opening of the Slovak National Theatre in Bratislava in 1920, and its debut performance of *Coppélia*, choreographed by Czech choreographer Václav Kalina. Under the direction of Stanislav Remar (1948–55) many Soviet dance-dramas were staged in this theatre as well as some national Slovak ballets. Karol Tóth was director from 1961 and, after a period of decline in the 1970s, the company regained its vigour and a newly varied repertory of 19th- and 20th-century ballets under Boris Slovak and Toth (returning as director in 1980). Emil Bartko took over in 1990 and encouraged work by younger choreographers, including Libor Vaculík and Ondrej Soth. Mário Radačovský became director in 2005, bringing several of his own works into the repertory, including WARHOL (2006). In 2007 the company acquired a second theatre in the newly built New National Theatre.

(((⊕))) SEE WEB LINKS
* Website for the Slovak National Theatre Ballet

Smith, George Washington (*b* Philadelphia, *c.*1820; *d* Philadelphia, 18 Feb. 1899) US dancer, ballet master, and teacher who helped establish ballet as a popular dance form in the US. He began his career as a clog dancer but also studied ballet, and during Elssler's American tour of 1840–2 he joined her company as a member of the corps and studied with her then partner,

James Sylvain. He went on to partner most of the leading European and American ballerinas who appeared in the US. He was America's first Albrecht, partnering Mary Ann Lee (Boston, 1846), and he was appointed principal dancer and ballet master at the New York Bowery Theater in 1847 and at Brougham's Lyceum Theatre in 1850, during which time he staged and danced in several Romantic ballets including *Giselle* (after Coralli, Perrot, 1847). He toured the US with Lola Montez (1851–2) and in 1859 was principal dancer with the Ronzani Ballet (the first Italian company to tour the US; one of their dancers was Cecchetti). He continued to perform numerous Harlequinade roles, and staged numerous divertissements and circus ballets. He taught a variety of dance forms throughout his career and opened a school in Philadelphia in 1881 where he taught until his death. His son, Joseph Smith, became a well-known choreographer of musicals.

Smith, Oliver (*b* Waupawn, Wis., 13 Feb. 1918; *d* 23 Jan. 1994) US designer and director. He became co-director (with Lucia Chase) of American Ballet Theatre in 1945 and continued there until 1980, returning in 1990. During much of this time he was American Ballet Theatre's resident designer, designing over 30 works for it (and other companies), including de Mille's *Rodeo* (1942) and *Fall River Legend* (1948), Robbins's *Fancy Free* (1944), David Blair's productions of *Swan Lake* (1967) and *Giselle* (1968), and Tetley's *Contredances* (1979). He also designed many Broadway shows, including *West Side Story* (chor. Robbins, 1957), and several films, including *Oklahoma!* (dir. Zinnemann, 1955), *Guys and Dolls* (dir. Mankiewicz, 1955), and *Porgy and Bess* (dir. Preminger, 1959). He was awarded the Handel Medallion (New York, 1975).

Smok, Pavel (*b* Levoča, 22 Oct. 1927) Czech dancer, choreographer, and ballet director. He began his training late, graduating from Prague State Conservatory aged 26. He danced with the Army Ensemble (1952–5) and in Pilsen (1955–8) but injury forced him to retire from the stage. He was ballet master in Usti and Labem (1958–60) and in Ostrava (1960–4) then in 1964 he co-founded Prague Ballet with Lubos Ogoun. He remained there as ballet master until 1970, after which he was director of Basle Ballet (1970–3). Between 1973 and 1975 he worked as a freelance choreographer until forming the Chamber Ballet Prague in 1975. His ballets for that company such as *Intimate Letters* (mus. Janáček, 1969), *Sinfonietta* (mus. Janáček, 1971), and *Stabat Mater* (mus. Dvořák, 1995), frequently used Czech and Slovak scores, the tense angular style of his early ballets softening into a more rounded lyricism in the later

works. In 1990 he was appointed professor in the music faculty of the Prague Academy of Arts.

Smuin, Michael (*b* Missoula, Mont., 13 Oct. 1938; *d* San Francisco. Calif., 23 Apr. 2007) US dancer and choreographer. He studied with the Christensen brothers in Utah and at San Francisco Ballet School, dancing first with University of Utah Ballet (1955–7) then with San Francisco Ballet (1957–62). Between 1962 and 1967 he worked as a freelance dancer and choreographer after which he moved to American Ballet Theatre as principal dancer and choreographer (1969–73). He was then appointed co-director (with Lew Christensen) of San Francisco Ballet, becoming the company's sole director (1984). His many ballets for that company included *Pulcinella Variations* (mus. Stravinsky, 1968), *Romeo and Juliet* (mus. Prokofiev, 1976), and *The Tempest* (mus. P. Chihara, 1980), and demonstrated his commitment to accessible, highly charged dance theatre. He also worked extensively on Broadway, for example choreographing and directing *Sophisticated Ladies* (mus. Ellington, 1981). In 1991 he founded his own company, Smuin Ballet for which he created around 40 ballets, including *Pinocchio* (1999). After his sudden death from a heart attack, the company remained active, maintaining the Smuin repertory and commissioning new works.

(((●))) **SEE WEB LINKS**
• Website for the Smuin Ballet

Snoek, Hans (orig. Johanna Snoek; *b* Geertruidenberg, 29 Dec. 1910; *d* 2001) Dutch dancer, choreographer, and ballet director. She studied with Jooss and Leeder and during the war (illegally) opened her own school in Amsterdam, staging 'underground' performances in aid of artists working in the resistance movement. In 1945 she founded the *Scapino Ballet to present dance for children, for which she choreographed many ballets, and she was a pioneer in Dutch dance education. She was made Officer of the Order of Oranje Nassau in 1960 and retired from Scapino in 1970.

Snow Maiden, The Ballet in three acts with libretto and choreography by Bourmeister, music by Tchaikovsky, and design by Yuri Pimenov and Gennadi Epishin. Premiered 17 Jul. 1961 by London Festival Ballet at Royal Festival Hall, London, with B. Wright, Burr, and Briansky. It is set to Tchaikovsky's incidental music for Ostrovsky's fairy-tale play *Snegurochka* (as well as the first two movements of his 1st Symphony) and follows Ostrovsky's poignant story of a snow maiden who visits a human village and falls in love for the first time with the youth Mizgir, but is melted away when the spring sun shines on her. It was revived for the Stanislavsky and Nemirovich-Danchenko

S

Lyric Theatre (Moscow, 1963). Other ballets using the same subject are by Nijinska (mus. Glazunov, Ballet Russe de Monte Carlo, 1942), Varkovitsky (mus. Tchaikovsky, Bolshoi Ballet School, 1946), and Ben Stevenson (mus. Tchaikovsky, arr. Lanchbery, Houston Ballet and American Ballet Theatre, 1998).

Sobeka The pen-name used by *Kochno for several of the librettos he wrote for Diaghilev.

Socialist Realism Under Stalin, dance in the Soviet Union was expected to conform to Party doctrine. Ideally, choreographers were meant to portray contemporary life in a realistic style while at the same time glorifying the workers' revolution and denouncing the bourgeoisie. Not all artists toed the official line, some finding subtle ways of introducing irony into their work, but the plots of many ballets created between the late 1920s and 1950s show remarkable political correctness. One of the earliest examples was Lashchilin and Tikhomirov's The *Red Poppy; another notable instance was Belsky's *Coast of Hope* (mus. A. Petrov, Kirov, Leningrad, 1959). This ballet is set in two contrasting fishing villages, one on the Soviet side of the sea, whose citizens are happy and loyal, and one on the other side where life is unhappy and repressive. A Soviet fisherman is shipwrecked on the other shore and its people take him prisoner in order to convert him to their ways. He remains faithful to his own comrades, though, and one day the walls of his prison magically burst open and he finds himself back home. Some of the most apparently correct librettos, such as Lopukhov's The *Bright Stream*, did not always find approval, though. While this ballet showed Socialist morals triumphing over regressive behaviour, its use of classical dance to portray the lives of ordinary people was considered unacceptable as was Lopukhov's use of Shostakovich's score and he was dismissed from his post as ballet chief of the Maly Theatre.

soft shoe dance A close relative of tap dance, but performed in soft-soled shoes with no metal taps.

Soirées de Paris, Les A season of ballet performances organized at Paris's Théâtre de la Cigale by Comte Étienne de Beaumont, 17 May to 30 Jun. 1924. Its premieres included *Mercure* (mus. Satie, des. Picasso), *Salade* (mus. Milhaud, des. Braque), and *Le Beau Danube* (mus. J. Strauss, arr. Desormière, des. V. Polunin), all choreographed by Massine. The season also featured Cocteau's production of *Romeo and Juliet* (des. J. Hugo).

Soirées musicales A suite of Rossini melodies arranged by Britten (1936), which has often been used for dance. The first version was choreographed by Tudor and premiered 26 Nov. 1938 for a Cecchetti Society matinée at Palladium Theatre, London, with Larsen, Lloyd, Laing, Tudor, and van Praagh. Later versions include Zolov (Metropolitan Opera House, 1955) and Cranko (in *Bouquet garni*, Stuttgart, 1965).

Sokolova, Evgenia (*b* St Petersburg, 1 Dec. 1850; *d* Leningrad, 2 Aug. 1925) Russian dancer and teacher. She studied at the Imperial Theatre School, St Petersburg, making her unofficial debut while still a student in 1862 and in 1869 graduated into the St Petersburg Bolshoi Theatre as a premiere danseuse. A lyrical, expressive dancer she was often overshadowed by the technical brilliance of her contemporary, Ekaterina Vazem, who was preferred by Petipa, but she did create several roles in the latter's works including the title role of *Mlada* (1879) and Galatea in his *Pygmalion* (1883), as well as dancing the lead in many ballets. She retired from the stage in 1886 and became a teacher at the Mariinsky Theatre. Among her pupils were Pavlova, Karsavina, Egorova, Spessivtseva, and Trefilova.

Sokolova, Lydia (orig. Hilda Munnings; *b* Wanstead, 4 Mar. 1896; *d* Sevenoaks, 5 Feb. 1974) British dancer. She studied at Stedman's Academy, London, and with Pavlova, Mordkin, Clustine, and, later, Cecchetti. She toured with Mordkin's company in 1911 and danced with Diaghilev's Ballets Russes (1913–22 and 1923–9). She was among the first English dancers to perform for Diaghilev and it was he who chose her Russian name. Between 1922 and 1923 she danced with Massine's company and with her husband, Nicholas Kremnev, in music halls. She was a lively and dramatic dancer rather than a classical technician and created roles in many Massine ballets, including *Boutique fantasque* (1919), *Le Chant du rossignol*, and *Sacre du printemps* (both 1920). The Miller's Wife in *Le Tricorne* (1919) was also choreographed on her though Karsavina performed it at the premiere. She also created roles in Nijinsky's *Tyl Eulenspiegel* (1916), Nijinska's *Les Biches* and *Le Train bleu* (both 1924), *Romeo and Juliet* (1926), and Balanchine's *Le Bal* (1929). After Diaghilev's company disbanded she danced with Woizikowsky's company in London in 1935 and Lydia Kyasht's Ballet de la Jeunesse Anglaise in 1939. She returned to the stage to perform in Massine's revival of The *Good-Humoured Ladies* for the Royal Ballet in 1962. Her memoirs, *Dancing for Diaghilev*, were edited by Richard Buckle (London, 1960).

S

Sokolow, Anna (*b* Hartford, Conn., 9 Feb. 1910; *d* New York, 29 Mar. 2000) US dancer, choreographer, and teacher. She studied with various teachers including Graham and Horst and at the New York Metropolitan Opera Ballet School, leaving home at 15 to join Graham's company with which she danced until 1938. In 1934 she formed the first of several temporary companies which performed until the late 1960s. From the beginning her work dealt with social issues, for instance in *Slaughter of the Innocents* (mus. Alex North, 1934), and throughout her career she remained uncompromising both in her choice of subject-matter, such as the Spanish Civil War and the Holocaust, and in the bleak realism of her handling of themes such as urban alienation. In 1939 she began working as a choreographer and teacher in Mexico City where she founded the first Mexican modern dance company, La Paloma Azul. She frequently returned there and created some of her most important works, including *Lyric Suite* (mus. Berg, 1953) and *Dreams* (mus. Bach and Webern, 1961). She stopped dancing in 1954 but continued choreographing, mostly for her own company in the US, including *Rooms* (mus. Hopkins, 1955) and *Steps of Silence* (mus. Vieru, 1968). She also worked in opera and musicals, choreographing *Candide* (1956) and the off-Broadway production of *Hair*—she is credited with much of its staging though her name was excised from the credits. She occasionally choreographed for other dance companies including Nederlands Dans Theater (*The Seven Deadly Sins*, mus. Weill, 1967), Ballet Rambert (*Deserts*, mus. Varèse, 1967), and Batsheva Dance Company (*In memoriam No. 52436*, mus. Baird, 1973). For many years she taught at the Juilliard.

Soldier's Tale, The (Fr. title *L'Histoire du soldat*) Dance theatre score, composed by Stravinsky and with a libretto by C. F. Ramuz. Its first production was staged with a combination of dance, mime, and spoken word and, with design by R. Auberjonois, was premiered 28 Sept. 1918 in Lausanne with Ansermet conducting and performers G. Rosset, J. Vilard-Gilles, and G. and L. Pitoëff. It tells the story of a soldier's battle of wits with the Devil. Later productions include Rennert and Helpmann (Edinburgh Festival, 1954), Babilée (Spoleto, 1967), and William Tuckett (London, 2004). Pure dance versions set to the concert suite include Cranko (Cape Town, 1942), Feld (American Ballet Theatre, 1971), P. Martins (New York City Ballet, 1981), A. Page (*Soldat* for Rambert Dance Company, 1988), and Javier De Frutos (*The Fortune Biscuit*, Rotterdam Dansgroep, 1998).

Solitaire Ballet in one act with choreography by MacMillan, music by Arnold, and design by D. Heeley. Premiered 7 Jun. 1956 by Sadler's Wells Theatre Ballet at Sadler's Wells Theatre with M. Hill, S. Neil, Annette Page, M. Boulton, and D. Britton. This setting of Arnold's two Suites of English Dances portrays a young woman who attempts to join in the activities of her friends but always ends up alone. MacMillan described it as 'A kind of game for one'. It has been revived for Stuttgart Ballet and Royal Danish Ballet (1961), Berlin Opera Berlin (1967), and London City Ballet (1996).

solo-dancer Traditional term given to the highest rank in the Royal Danish Ballet, equivalent to étoile or principal in other companies, though for international purposes the company has now standardized its terminology. Occasionally, dancers were given the title of first solo-dancer (e.g. K. Simone) but Margot Lander was the only one to have been granted the rank of prima ballerina.

Solomons, Gus, jun. (*b* Boston, 27 Aug. 1940) US dancer, choreographer, and writer. He studied at the Martha Graham School and performed with the companies of Donald McKayle (1961–4), Graham (1964–5), and Cunningham (1965–8) before founding his own company in 1969. He choreographed many works for it, which frequently incorporated chance procedures and improvisation with set choreography. In 1998 he founded Paradigm, a company for senior dancers. He also teaches widely and reviews for various publications, including *Village Voice* and *Dance Magazine*.

Soloviev, Yuri (*b* Leningrad, 10 Aug. 1940; *d* nr. Leningrad, 12 Jan. 1977) Soviet dancer. He studied at the Leningrad Choreographic School and graduated into the Kirov in 1958 where he became one of its most virtuoso principals. His pure technique and extraordinary elevation were shown off to an exceptional degree in the role of the Blue Bird, but he also danced the standard danseur noble roles including the Prince in the Kirov's 1965 film of *Sleeping Beauty*. He created roles in several ballets, including Belsky's *Leningrad Symphony* (1961), Sergeyev's *The Distant Planet* (1963), Jacobson's *Land of Miracles* (1967), and the title role in Belsky's *Icarus* (1974). He was made People's Artist of the USSR in 1973. His death was apparently by suicide, and was possibly prompted by despair at being trapped in the stagnant political and artistic climate of his era (the same frustration which impelled other contemporaries, such as Nureyev, to defect).

Somes, Michael (*b* Horsley, 28 Sept. 1917; *d* 19 Nov. 1994) British dancer and ballet director. He studied with Espinosa and Bedells and in 1934 won the first male scholarship to Sadler's Wells School. In 1936 he joined Vic-Wells Ballet becoming principal in 1938. His career was disrupted by war service and injury, and this prevented him from realizing his early technical potential. But when Helpmann retired in 1949 he became the company's leading male dancer and also Fonteyn's partner. His commanding stage presence, coupled with his quiet strength and lyricism, made him an important role model for younger male dancers. He danced leading roles in all the classics and created roles in many ballets including Ashton's *The Wanderer* (1941), *Symphonic Variations* (1946), *Scènes de Ballet* and *Cinderella* (both 1948), *Sylvia* (1952), *Homage to the Queen* (1953), *Birthday Offering* (1956), and *Ondine* (1958); also in Massine's *Clock Symphony* (1948) and Cranko's *Antigone* (1959). He retired from dancing in 1961 though he continued to perform mime roles, creating Capulet in MacMillan's *Romeo and Juliet* (1965) and the title role in Layton's *O.W.* (1972). He was assistant director of Royal Ballet (1963–70) and principal repetiteur and teacher until 1984, particularly responsible for revivals of Ballets Russes works and the Ashton repertoire. He was married to the dancers Deirdre Dixon, Antoinette Sibley, and Wendy Ellis.

Somnambule ou l'Arrivée d'un nouveau Seigneur, La

Ballet in three acts with choreography by Aumer, music by Hérold, and sets by Ciceri. Premiered 19 Sept. 1827 at Paris Opera. Its sleepwalking heroine, Thérèse, causes an inadvertent scandal by wandering, unconscious, into the bedroom of the lord of the manor. Her fiancé Edmond breaks off their engagement, but then fortuitously discovers the truth of her condition. It inspired Bellini to write his opera *La sonnambula*. For Balanchine's ballet *La Somnambule, see* NIGHT SHADOW.

Somova, Alina (*b* St Petersburg, 1986) She trained at the Vaganova Academy and graduated into the Mariinsky Ballet in 2003, where she became principal in 2008. A dancer of exceptionally long, flexible limbs, her extreme athleticism made her initial promotion controversial, although her interpretations have subsequently matured in expression and style. She is particularly associated with the Balanchine repertory and has guested with several companies, including Tokyo National Theatre and Vienna State Opera Ballet. She won the Vaganova competition in 2002.

Song of a Wayfarer (orig. Fr. title *Chant du compagnon errant*) Ballet in one act with choreography by Béjart and music by Mahler. Premiered 11 Mar. 1971 by the Ballet of the 20th Century at Forest National, Brussels, with Paolo Bortoluzzi and Nureyev. This frequently performed duet is set to Mahler's song-cycle *Lieder eines fahrenden Gesellen* and portrays a romantic youth who rages in despair but is soothed by the

dark figure of Fate. It has been revived for many different pairs of dancers.

Song of the Earth (orig. Ger. title *Das Lied von der Erde*) Ballet in one act with choreography by MacMillan and music by Mahler. Premiered 7 Nov. 1965 by the Stuttgart Ballet, Stuttgart, with Madsen, Haydée, and Barra. It is set to Mahler's song-cycle of the same title, but its six episodes are atmospheric rather than literal interpretations of the text (German translations of 8th-century poets of the T'ang Dynasty). They are linked by archetypal figures of a man, a woman, and Death. MacMillan had originally wanted to choreograph the work for the Royal Ballet but had been told Mahler's score was inappropriate for dance. He therefore took the idea to Cranko and the Stuttgart production proved so successful that it was revived by the Royal Ballet six months later, with designs by Georgiadis, and later by Paris Opera (1978), Australian Ballet (1987), and National Ballet of Canada (1988) among others. Earlier settings of the same score were Tudor (*Shadow of the Wind*, American Ballet Theatre, 1948) and Koner (last movement only, *Farewell*, 1962).

Song of the Nightingale *See* CHANT DU ROSSIGNOL, LE.

Sorcerer's Apprentice, The (orig. Fr. title *L'Apprenti sorcier*) Dukas's 1897 score, *Scherzo d'après une ballade de Goethe*, has inspired ballets by several choreographers including Fokine (Mariinsky Theatre, Petrograd, 1916) and H. Lander (Royal Danish Ballet, Copenhagen, 1940).

Sorley Walker, Kathrine (*b* Aberdeen) British dance writer. She was critic for *Playgoer* (1951–6), for the *Daily Telegraph* (1962–95), and contributed to many publications including *Dancing Times* and *Encylopaedia Britannica*. She edited the collected criticism of A. V. Coton and is author of several books, including *Robert Helpmann* (Rockliff, 1957), *Eyes on the Ballet* (London, 1963), and *Ninette de Valois* (London, 1987).

Sorokina, Nina (*b* 13 May 1942) Soviet dancer. She studied at the Bolshoi School, and graduated into the company in 1961 where she became one of its most celebrated ballerinas. She created roles in Vasiliev's *The Geologists* (1964); Vinogradov's *Asel* (1967), and Vasiliev's *Icarus* (1971).

Sorrell, Walter (*b* Vienna, 2 May 1905) Austrian-US dance writer. He studied at the Universities of Vienna and Columbia and contributed to *Dance Magazine*, *Ballet Today*, and *Dance News* as well as being contributing editor of *Dance Scope*. He lectured at Barnard College and has written several books, including *The Dancer's Image* (New York, 1971), *The Mary Wigman Book*

(Middletown, 1975), and *Dance in its Time* (New York, 1981). He was author-editor of *The Dance has Many Faces* (New York, 1951).

Soto, Jock (*b* New Mexico, 1965) US dancer. He studied ballet in Phoenix, and at the School of American Ballet, joining New York City Ballet in 1981 aged 16, and becoming principal in 1985. A dancer of exceptional musicality and an instinctive partner, he danced leading roles in many Balanchine and Robbins ballets, and also created roles in works by Martins, such as *Fearful Symmetries*, *A Schubertiad*, and *Songs of the Auvergne*; by Dean, Weiss, Bonnefoux, and Tanner in the 1988 American Music Festival, and also by Taylor-Corbett, Woetzel, O'Day, Mahdaviani. He danced regularly with Wendy Whelan and their partnership was showcased in many works by Wheeldon, including *Polyphonia* (2001) and *After the Rain* (2005). He made many television appearances as a dancer, also as a celebrity chef. In 2005 he retired from the stage but continued to teach at the School of American Ballet.

soubresaut [Fr., sudden leap] A jump both taking off from and landing in fifth position with the legs tightly crossed and feet pointed in the air.

Soubrette In classical ballet, a lighthearted or comedic female character often flirtatious or mischievous in nature. Examples include Lise in *La Fille mal gardée* and Swanilda in *Coppélia*.

Source, La Ballet in three acts with choreography by Saint-Léon, libretto by Saint-Léon and Charles Nuitter, music by Minkus (1st and 4th scene) and Delibes (2nd and 3rd scene), sets by E. Desplechin, J.-B. Lavastre, A. Rubé, and Chapérone, and costumes by P. Loumier and Albert. Premiered 12 Nov. 1866 at the Paris Opera with Salvioni as Naila (replacing the injured Grantzow on whom the role had been conceived), Fiocre, and Mérante. It was created in an attempt to revive the public's flagging interest in ballet and combined spectacular stage effects with virtuoso dancing and a populist score. It tells the story of Naila, Spirit of the Spring, who is protected by the hunter Djemil from a gypsy who is threatening to poison her water. In return she helps Djemil to win his beloved Nouredda. Though the ballet made little lasting impact, it established a creative relationship between Nuitter, Saint-Léon, and Delibes which achieved much greater success in *Coppélia*. Saint-Léon choreographed a new version of the ballet as *Le Lys* for St Petersburg in 1869 and re-staged it as *Naila* for the Vienna Court Opera in 1878. Other productions include A. Koppini (staged after Saint-Léon as *Ruchei*, St Petersburg, 1902) and Vaganova and Ponomarev (staged after Saint-Léon as *Naila*, Leningrad, 1925). Staats choreographed a new version as *Soir de fête* using H. Busser's arrangement of the score (Paris Opera, 1925), and pas de deux versions were choreographed by Cranko (Stuttgart Ballet, 1964) and Balanchine (New York City Ballet, 1968, re-staged with additional ensemble in 1969).

Souritz, Elizabeth (*b* Berlin, 25 Feb. 1923) Russian dance writer. She studied at the Moscow Theatre Institute and worked in the Moscow Theatre museum and Theatre library and from 1964 in the Institute for Studies in the Arts. As a specialist in dance activity in Moscow in the late 19th and early 20th centuries, and the careers of émigré Russian dancers she has contributed to several reference books and is author of numerous articles, including 'Moscow's Island of Dance (1934–41)' in *Dance Chronicle* (1994). She is also author of *Soviet Choreographers in the 1920s* (1990).

soutenu [Fr., sustained] A very controlled, drawn-out execution of a movement.

South Africa Black South Africa has always had rich indigenous dance traditions, but the European settlers who came to the area were slow to establish their own. In Cape Town during the 19th century ballet masters and their pupils put on amateur productions which imitated the fashions of Europe, but no professional companies were established. In 1926 the Cape Town Dance Teachers Association was formed and Édouard Espinosa visited as its first examiner. In 1934 Dulcie *Howes (returning from touring with Pavlova) started up the University of Cape Town School of Ballet and later the University of Cape Town Ballet company. In Johannesburg the Dancing Teachers Association, established in 1923, staged some performances and in the early 1940s other companies were formed including the Johannesburg Festival Ballet and the Pretoria Ballet Club. In 1947 Faith de Villiers and Joyce van Greems started a professional company, Ballet Theatre, which collaborated with UCT Ballet for its first programme. Frank *Staff founded the South African Ballet company, producing fifteen ballets for them between 1955 and 1958, but like other companies it was short-lived because it had no financial backing from the state. In 1960 de Villiers founded the Johannesburg City Ballet which was to form the nucleus for the *PACT Ballet which emerged in 1963 after the government began to subsidize the performing arts (in 1981 it was relocated to Pretoria). Other professional companies to emerge were CAPAB Ballet and NAPAC (Natal Performing Arts Council; 1964–78). South Africa finally had an opportunity to hold on to its talented dancers and choreographers who, prior to 1963, had always left to work abroad (Maude

Lloyd, Howes, Nadia Nerina, Maryon Lane, Frank Staff, John Cranko, Monica Mason, Deanne Bergsma, and Vyvyan Lorrayne). However, during the worst era of apartheid, ballet in South Africa developed largely in isolation from the rest of the world, as international sanctions blocked the free exchange of dancers and companies. One exception was Ballet International, founded in 1976 with backing from the Performing Arts Council of the Orange Free State (PACOFS). Based in Britain and under the artistic direction of Larry Long it gave performances in South Africa of full-length classics staged by Ben Stevenson and some modern works. Its first performance was at the Oppenheimer Theatre, Welkom, Transvaal, and among its guest dancers were Samsova and Nagy. Apart from this venture there was little modern dance activity until the formation of the Jazzart Dance company in 1982. Emerging from a jazz and modern dance studio in Cape Town it developed a fusion of African and Western contemporary dance idioms.

Under apartheid black and white dance had otherwise remained strictly segregated but in the new S. Africa of the 1990s links were forged between them, and the liberalized atmosphere saw a large expansion of activity. Several new companies emerged such as Soweto Dance Theatre, which originated from a break-dance troupe; Bop dance company based in Bobothuthaswan and performing work by local choreographers; and PACT Dance Company which became South Africa's first fully state-funded modern dance company. Vita Life Dance Umbrella (founded 1988) became S. Africa's most important platform for modern dance and regularly boasted seasons of new works; the Dance Factory in Johannesburg (founded 1990) became a major presenter and training facility for modern dance; and Dance Alliance (founded in Johannesburg in the early 1990s) emerged as an important lobbying organization. Other artists to emerge during the 1990s included Robyn *Orlin, whose dance-theatre works presented a satirical slant on the politics and culture of the new S. Africa and Vincent *Mantsoe, Nelisiwe Xaba, and Gregory Maqoma, who founded the Johannesburg-based Vuyani Dance Theatre Project in 1999. However in the middle of this expansion, changes in funding structures also generated a climate of acute uncertainty. Bop dance company was disbanded in 1995 (though its director, David Krugel, subsequently founded the Batho Dance Company). PACT Dance Company and PACT Ballet lost their full state subsidy in 1997 and, while reforming as State Theatre Ballet and State Theatre Dance Company respectively, were both disbanded in 2000, as being too cost-intensive and, in the case of the classical company, too Eurocentric. However the new South African Ballet Theatre was founded in the latter's place, under

the direction of Karen Beukes and with a repertory of 19th-century classics and some new work. In 2002 it opened its associated school and in 2004 moved into its new premises in Johannesburg Civic Theatre. The country's other main classical company CAPAB Ballet also lost its state subsidy in 1997 but with drastically reduced numbers was able to continue as *Cape Town City Ballet. NAPAC Ballet was scaled down to become the Durban-based Playhouse Dance Theatre and reformed once again as the Fantastic Flying Fish Dance Company. Significant work is being done within education and community, including the ZAMA dance school in Gugulethu, Western Cape, that teaches a mix of classical and contemporary forms, Dare 2 Dance company, and Flatfoot dance company, both in Durban.

South Asia The classical dance forms of South Asia, or the Indian sub-continent, evolved as vehicles for portraying the characters and stories of the gods. Shiva is known as the Lord of the Dance and according to Hindu legend created heaven and earth when he performed his Dance of Creation. Bharata's treatise the *Natya Shastra* was written c.200BC–AD300 and its guidelines on dance, drama, and music acquired the status of holy writ. The main dance forms are *bharata natyam from S. India, *kathakali from S.W. India, manipuri from N.E. India, kuchipudi from S.E. India, odissi from Orissa, and *kathak from N. India. These also had a formative influence on the dances of S.E. Asia. Under colonial rule these ancient dance forms were frequently degraded but the 20th century saw a major renaissance of standards in both teaching and performance. Pavlova learnt Indian dance from Uday *Shankar and performed the duet *Radha and Krishna* with him in 1923, but the most influential performer in the West for many years was Ram *Gopal. On his many tours from the late 1930s through to the 1970s he initiated a new international audience into the aesthetic of Indian dance and also performed with Markova. Today classical Indian dance is taught and performed in many countries and a new generation of artists has begun to evolve contemporary versions of classical forms. British-based choreographers like Shobana *Jeyasingh and Akram *Khan have brought aspects of Western modern dance to their choreographic idiom while Indian-based *Chandralekha turned to martial arts and yoga for new influences. Among younger choreographers based in India there is wide experimentation with new music, a marked modernization of costume and stage manner, and a tendency to work with ensembles rather than soloists. At the Keralan-based Samudra Centre for Performing Arts, choreographers work within a fusion of classical Indian and contemporary Western forms, eschewing traditional narrative.

Other centres of experimentation include the Darpana Academy supporting work by Mallika Sarabhai, and the Attakkalari Centre for Movement Arts in Bangalore, an umbrella organization for dancers and choreographers founded in 1992 by Jayachandran Palazhy. The commercial Indian film industry has exerted a strong influence on popular dance. While earlier films featured choreography modelled on classical Indian styles, more recent films have developed styles influenced by MTV, street dance, and stage musicals.

(SEE WEB LINKS)
• Website for the Attakkalari Centre

South Korea *See* KOREA.

Soviet Realism *See* SOCIALIST REALISM.

Soviet Union *See* RUSSIA.

Spain Spanish dance tended to adhere to its own traditions during the 19th and much of the 20th century, rather than slavishly following the ballet trends set by the rest of Europe. The dominant dance form was escuela bolera which dated from the early 19th century and fused Spanish dance forms like the *bolero and the *cachucha with elements from French ballet. During the second half of the 19th century *flamenco began to change from an intimate social dance to a professional artform with the establishment of performances in clubs and bars. Some foreign ballet was presented in major theatres and the Teatro del Liceu in Barcelona and the Teatro Real in Madrid had corps de ballet, while the Real ran its own ballet school. Few permanent professional companies were founded during this period but several individual performers emerged as stars on the international scene. One of the most famous was Buenos Aires-born Antonia Mercé who called herself La *Argentina. She trained as a classical dancer and became prima ballerina of the Royal Opera Theatre, Real Madrid, in 1899 at the age of 11. At 14 she gave up classical dance and studied traditional Spanish dance with her mother, after which she began touring the world as a concert artist, displaying an extraordinary castanet technique, and using largely Spanish music. In 1928 she formed her own company and choreographed several ballets on Spanish themes. European and American audiences at this time were fascinated by Spanish dance and culture. Massine's popular *Le Tricorne* (1919), with its flamenco-inspired choreography and music by de Falla, was widely performed and the Ballet de Madrid, founded in 1927 by Encarnacion López Julvez (who called herself La *Argentinita in homage to Mercé) with Federico García Lorca, scored a huge success in New York during 1928. In 1933 La Argentinita attempted the first large-scale theatri-

cal presentation of authentic flamenco in *Las calles de Cadiz* and in 1939 she collaborated with Massine on *Capriccio espagnol*. Her sister, Pilar *López danced in her company and after the latter's death in 1946 López created her own company, Ballet Espagnol, with José *Greco. She trained a new generation of male dancers who in turn left to form their own companies. José Greco launched a company in America with his wife Nila Amparo which toured widely and also established a Foundation of Spanish Dance in America. Antonio *Gades, who also danced with López, trained in both Spanish and classical dance and collaborated with Dolin in creating *Bolero* for Rome Opera. In 1964 he set up his own company which blended Spanish idioms with modern and classical dance.

Other international stars were gypsy-born Carmen *Amaya who toured the world with a company drawn from her relatives between the late 1920s and 1940s, and the two cousins *Antonio and Rosario who also danced at the Edinburgh Festival in 1950. In 1953 Antonio formed his own Spanish ballet company, Antonio and the Ballets de Madrid. More recently Cristina *Hoyos, originally a dancer with Gades, has formed her own renowned flamenco company, which along with the government-sponsored Cumbre Flamenco has generated a new international vogue for gypsy-style flamenco. Joaquín Cortés has drawn new audiences with his fusion of flamenco and rock, as has Sara *Baras with her contemporary virtuoso style. The first government-sponsored Spanish company to operate on a permanent basis was the National Dance Company of Spain (replacing the Ballet Antología Española), founded in 1978, under Gades, for the performance of Spanish dance, and now known as the *National Ballet of Spain. There have been recent attempts to establish a classical dance culture in Spain but they have been slow to take off. Ballet Clásico was founded in 1979, becoming Ballet Lírico Nacional, but under the direction of Nacho *Duato since 1990 the repertory became exclusively contemporary and was renamed *Compañia Nacional de Danza. The chamber ensemble Ballet de Zaragoza performed some classics, such as *The Nutcracker* and *Coppélia*, alongside 20th-century ballets but was closed in 2005 and the major classical company of any significance remains Ballet *Ullate. Formed in 1988 by the teacher and choreographer Victor Ullate this became funded by Madrid when it moved into the city's newly rebuilt Opera House in 1996, It was officially renamed Ballet de la Comunidad de Madrid, although is popularly still known as the Victor Ullate Ballet. It performs a repertory of neo-classical works, many of them choreographed by Ullate (now General Director of the company) and his current artistic director

S

Eduardo Lao. Ullate's other major contribution to ballet in Spain has been his school, which he opened in Madrid in 1983. Gaining an international reputation for its training, this school has produced some exceptional Spanish dancers, including Angel *Corella, who now directs his own company in Spain, and Tamara *Rojo, though most have made their careers elsewhere. The country's most energetic area of growth has been in modern dance as a new generation of choreographers have looked outside Spain. Companies like Danat Danza, Mal Pelo, Lanonima Impérial, Cia. Vicente Saez, and Cia. Cesc Gelabert have all gained international reputations.

Spalding, Alistair (*b* Bedfordshire, 25 Aug. 1957) Producer and theatre director. He had no formal training in the arts but in 1988 was appointed programmer of arts events at the Hawth, Crawley. In 1994 he was appointed head of dance and performance at London's Southbank Centre then in 2000 moved to Sadler's Wells, initially as director of programming, and from 2004 as CEO and artistic director. He has developed Sadler's Wells into a leading international dance venue and a major co-producer of new work. Associate artists of the theatre include Matthew Bourne, Sylvie Guillem, Akram Khan, Russell Maliphant, Wayne McGregor, and BalletBoyz (Michael Nunn and William Trevitt).

Spalding was made Chevalier des Artes et Lettres in 2005. *See also* SADLER'S WELLS.

Spartacus (orig. Russ. title *Spartak*) Ballet in four acts with libretto by Nikolai Volkov and music by Khachaturian. The ballet tells the story of the slave-leader Spartacus who incites his fellow slaves to revolt against their Roman oppressors. It is now one of the world's most popular modern ballets, although it was not initially a success. Jacobson's version, premiered 27 Dec. 1956 by the Kirov, Leningrad, with designs by V. Khodasevich, failed to please the public. Moiseyev's 1958 version for the Bolshoi was given only nine performances. The definitive version was choreographed by Grigorovich, with design by Simon Virsaladze, and was premiered 9 Apr. 1968 by the Bolshoi. Vasiliev danced the ardent, idealistic Spartacus and Maximova his virtuous wife Phrygia, M. Liepa was the cruel and narcissistic Roman general Crassus, and Timofeyeva the sensual, whoring Aegina. The ballet's combination of power choreography and sharply delineated characters created a sensation when it was first performed in the West (London, 1969). Several other versions have been mounted including László Seregi's for Budapest (1968).

Speaking in Tongues Modern dance in one act with choreography by Paul Taylor, music by Matthew Patton, design by Santo Loquasto, and lighting by Tipton. Premiered 1988 by the Paul Taylor Dance Company. One of Taylor's most darkly dramatic works, it portrays the emotional and spiritual conflicts within a group of fundamentalist Christians, under the warped, charismatic leadership of their preacher, designated simply as a Man of the Cloth. It was later filmed for television and won an Emmy Award.

Spectre de la rose, Le Ballet in one act with choreography by Fokine, libretto by J.-L. Vaudoyer, music by Weber, and design by Bakst. Premiered 19 Apr. 1911 by Diaghilev's Ballets Russes at Théâtre de Monte Carlo with Karsavina and Nijinsky. It is set to Weber's *Invitation to the Dance* (orch. Berlioz), and its libretto, based on lines from a poem by Gautier, portrays a young girl who returns from a ball with a rose and, on falling asleep, dreams that the spirit of the rose is dancing with her. In the ballet, the spirit disappears with a spectacular leap through her window and she awakes. Its atmosphere was defined by its original dancers—Karsavina tenderly lyrical as the Young Girl, Nijinsky showcasing his extraordinary jump as the Spirit of the Rose—and few dancers have been able to re-create their impact. The ballet has, however, been frequently revived, by, among others, American Ballet Theatre (1941), Sadler's Wells Ballet (1944, with designs by Rex Whistler), London Festival Ballet (1950 and 1962), Bolshoi Ballet (1967), Joffrey Ballet (1979), and Kirov Ballet (London, 1997). New versions include John Neumeier (Hamburg Ballet, 1986), Angelin Preljocaj (Compagnie Preljocaj, 1993), and Elo (Alberta Ballet, 2002).

Spessivtseva, Olga (Spessiva; Spessivtzeva) (*b* Rostov, 18 Jul. 1895; *d* Tolstoy Farm, NY, 16 Sept. 1991) Russian dancer, widely considered one of the greatest classical ballerinas in history. She studied at the Imperial Theatre School, St Petersburg, graduating in 1913 to join the Mariinsky Theatre. She soon became one of the most admired dancers in the company, promoted to soloist (1916) and ballerina (1918). During 1916 and 1917 she was in the US with Diaghilev's Ballets Russes and also guested in their London production of *The Sleeping Princess* (1921–2). Similar in type to Pavlova, she was regarded by many as the greater artist with her slender limbs, her air of spiritual purity, and her fine classical technique. Her most famous role was Giselle, though she performed all the other standard ballerina roles as well. She left Russia for the last time in 1924 to become étoile at the Paris Opera where she remained until 1932, creating roles in Nijinska's *Les Rencontres* (1925), Lifar's

Creatures of Prometheus (1929), and *Bacchus and Ariadne* (1931). She also appeared with Diaghilev in 1927 and 1929, creating the title role in Balanchine's *La Chatte* (1927), though it was danced by Nikitina at the premiere. In 1931 she danced at the Teatro Colón in Buenos Aires (she had visited previously in 1923) and in 1932 she danced Giselle for the Camargo Society in London. In 1934 she was ballerina of the Victor Dandré and Alexander Levitov Ballet, touring Australia, and in 1935 she danced in Fokine's ballets at Paris's Opéra Comique. She gave her farewell performance at the Teatro Colón in 1939 and in the same year moved to the US, where she became adviser to Ballet Theatre. She was already showing signs of depression and in 1943 suffered a nervous breakdown. She remained in a mental hospital until 1963 when friends, including Dolin, Doubrovska, and Dale Fern, got her settled into the Tolstoy Farm, a Russian settlement in Rockland County, New York, maintained by the Tolstoy Foundation. Eifman based his ballet *Red Giselle* (1997) around her.

Spink, Ian (*b* Melbourne, 8 Oct. 1947) Australian-British dancer, choreographer, and director. He studied at the Australian Ballet School and briefly with Cunningham, and danced with Australian Ballet (1969–74), Australian Dance Theatre (1973), Dance Company of New South Wales (now Sydney Dance Company, 1975–7), Richard Alston and Dancers (1978–9), and Basic Space Dance Theatre (1978–9). He created his first work in 1971 for the Australian Ballet Workshop and subsequently choreographed for various companies, forming his own group in the UK in 1978. He became co-artistic director of *Second Stride in 1982 (sole director in 1988), his experimental, densely allusive style of dance theatre frequently made in close collaboration with his composers and designers, including *Bosendorfer Waltzes* (mus. Orlando Gough, des. Antony McDonald, 1986). After the company disbanded he worked freelance as a choreographer and director. His recent works include a re-interpretatioin of Ashton's *A *Tragedy of Fashion* (mus. Elena Kats-Chernin, Rambert, 2004) and a new version of *Petrushka* (Scottish Ballet 2009), He has also directed operas and plays, including Judith Weir's *The Vanishing Bridegroom* (1990).

Spira, Phyllis (*b* Johannesburg, 18 Oct. 1943; *d* Cape Town, 11 Mar. 2008) South African dancer. She studied in Johannesburg and in 1959 attended London's Royal Ballet School. In 1960 she joined the Royal Ballet touring company, becoming soloist (1961–5), though returning to S. Africa as principal dancer of PACT Ballet (1963–4). In 1965 she returned again, as ballerina with CAPAB. She then toured with National Ballet

of Canada (1967–8) and in 1968 returned to CAPAB as guest artist, then ballerina.

Spoerli, Heinz (*b* Basel, 8 July 1941) Swiss dancer, choreographer, and ballet master. He studied with Walter Kleiber in Basel then at the School of American Ballet, American Ballet Center, and London Dance Centre. He was a soloist with Basel Ballet (1960–3), then danced with Cologne Ballet (1963–6), Royal Winnipeg Ballet (1966–7), and Les Grands Ballets Canadiens (1967–71). In 1971 he became choreographer and soloist with Geneva Ballet where he created his first work, *Le Chemin* (mus. Gaudibert, 1971), after which he was ballet director with Basel Ballet (1973–91). Here, he raised the company's technical standards, introducing works from many choreographers, such as Balanchine, Béjart, Taylor, and Cranko. He also choreographed over 80 works including *Petrushka* (mus. Stravinsky 1974), *A Midsummer Night's Dream* (mus. Mendelssohn, 1976), *Romeo and Juliet* (mus. Prokofiev, 1977), and *Stabat Mater* (mus. Pärt, 1987). His style is neo-classical but his dramatic, full-length ballets feature distinctive characterization and humour. His version of *La Fille mal gardée*, created for the Paris Opera in 1981, is widely considered to be the most successful since Ashton's. He has created works for many other companies, including Berlin Opera Ballet and Stuttgart Ballet, as well as choreographing for television and film. In 1991 he was appointed artistic director and choreographer of the German Opera on the Rhine, Düsseldorf, where he raised technical standards and built up audiences with a neo-classical repertoire that includes his own works plus those of choreographers like Balanchine and van Manen. Between 1996 and 2010 he returned to direct the Zurich Ballet where he introduced works by choreographers like van Manen and Forsythe as well as creating numerous ballets, including his fourth version of *A Midsummer Night's Dream*, and versions of *Cinderella* (mus. Prokofiev, 2000), *Daphnis and Chloe* (2004), *Les Noces* (2006), and *Don Quixote* (2006). He has worked as guest choreographer and teacher all around the world.

(⊕) SEE WEB LINKS

• Website for Heinz Spoerli

Spohr, Arnold (*b* Rhein, Sask., 26 Dec. 1927; *d* Winnipeg, 12 Apr. 2010) Canadian dancer, choreographer, and director. He studied in London, New York, Hollywood, and Leningrad with various teachers including Pushkin and Volkova. He joined Winnipeg Ballet in 1945, becoming principal (1947–54). He then worked with Canadian television and partnered Markova in the London production of *Where the Rainbow Ends* (1956–7). In 1958 he was appointed director of Royal Winnipeg Ballet, and successfully established the company's international reputation until retiring in 1988. He retained an advisory position as the company's artistic director emeritus and was additionally co-director of the Toronto-based company Ballet Jorgen. He also choreographed several ballets and performed as a professional pianist.

sport The physical language and energy of the sporting world have inspired several choreographers. It is frequently claimed that the sportiness of American culture influenced Balanchine as he was evolving his own athletic version of 20th-century classicism. Early ballets tackling the subject were Katti Lanner's *Sports of England* (1887) and Nijinsky's *Jeux* (1913). In the latter, the three dancers are dressed in approximations of Edwardian tennis dress, and stylized versions of sporting gestures (leaps and arm swings) are performed. (Nijinsky, however, possessed only a hazy idea of the game; the first version of the tennis ball which appeared in rehearsals was the size of a football.) Tennis also inspired Schilling whose 1971 ballet *Match* is a pas de deux in the form of a tennis match. A football player stars in Kurdyumov's three-act ballet *The Footballer* (Bolshoi, 1930), though the plot is more concerned with class satire than sport, and Moiseyev choreographed the comic ballet *Football* in 1948. Jo Strømgren choreographed his award-winning *Dance Tribute to the Art of Football* (1998) in collaboration with his home team, Brann, portraying the rituals of football from training ground to locker room. In Arpino's *Olympics* (1966) the choreography is based on various all-male events (wrestling, running, jumping, etc.) and features a linking figure who runs through the ballet holding a torch. MacMillan's 1969 ballet *Olympiad* was also inspired by athletics. The conventions of wrestling are deconstructed in Mark Morris's *Championship Wrestling* (1984), while the dancers in Darshan Singh Bhuller's *Heart of Chaos* (1993) were given boxing lessons in order to master authentic boxing moves.

spotting A means of avoiding giddiness while turning. Dancers fix their eyes on a chosen spot in the studio or theatre and during a sequence of one or more turns aim to keep focusing on it until the last possible moment, when they rapidly whip their heads around to 'spot' it again.

Spring Waters Pas de deux with choreography by A. Messerer and music by Rachmaninoff. Premiered in 1953 at the Bolshoi School's annual performance, the Bolshoi Theatre, with Natalia Filippova and Evgeny Kuzmin. This setting of Rachmaninoff's *Spring Waters* Op. 14 No. 11, is roughly two minutes in length and is one of the shortest but most concentrated pieces in the ballet repertory. It was created to showcase the virtuoso partnerwork of the Soviet school and has become a favourite gala divertissement both in Russia and abroad.

Spuck, Christian (*b* Marburg, 28 Sep. 1969) German dancer, choreographer and director. He trained at the John Cranko School, graduating in 1993 and performing first in Brussels (Needcompany and Rosas), then from 1995 with Stuttgart Ballet. He created his first work in 1996 for the Noverre Society but two years later had his first commission for Stuttgart Ballet and in 2001 was appointed the company's choreographer in residence. His style fused a sharp neo-classical aesthetic with a post-modern theatricality, as in his first full-length ballet *Lulu: A Monster Tragedy* (mus. Shostakovitch, Berg, and Schöenberg) which he created for Stuttgart in 2001. Other works in a similar vein have included *The Children* (based on Edward Bond's Play, Aalto Ballet Essen, 2004), *The Return of Ulysses* (The Royal Ballet of Flanders, mus. Purcell and others, 2006), and *Der Sandmann* (mus. Schumann and Martin Donner, 2006) and *Don Q* (mus. Martin Donner, 2007) both for Stuttgart.

He has gained an international reputation, additionally choreographing for Aterballetto (*Morphing*, 1999), New York City Ballet (*Adagio for 6 Dancers*, mus. Mozart, 2000) and The Royal Swedish Ballet (*Le tableau perdu*, mus. Mendelssohn, 2007), also for Hubbard Street Dance 2 (Chicago) where he took up a second resident choreographer post in 2006. In 2010 he was appointed artistic director of Zurich Ballet.

(⊕) SEE WEB LINKS
• Personal website for C. Spuck

square dance American couple dance in which the dancers are positioned in a square formation, though some regional variants include line formations and circles. At a square dance event, the various moves are called out by a caller.

Square Dance Ballet in one act with choreography by Balanchine and music by Corelli and Vivaldi. Premiered 21 Nov. 1957 by New York City Ballet with P. Wilde and Magallanes, and Elisha C. Keeler (caller). Balanchine's classical version of a square dance is choreographed for one leading couple and six other couples. Its sophisticated and elegant classical vocabulary makes witty reference to American folk and social dance, even while being set to the baroque music of Vivaldi (Concerti Grossi, Op. 3, Nos. 10 and 12, 1st movement only) and Corelli's *Sarabande, Giga*, and *Bandineri*. A revised version was premiered by the same company, with Mazzo and Cook in 1976. It has been revived for several companies including Joffrey Ballet (1971), Pacific Northwest Ballet (1981), English National Ballet (1994), and San Francisco Ballet (2004).

Staats, Léo (*b* Paris, 26 Nov. 1877; *d* Paris, 20 Feb. 1952) French dancer, choreographer, ballet master, and teacher. He studied at the Paris Opera Ballet School under Mérante, and made his debut with the company aged 10. In 1893 he joined the company, dancing principal roles, and was appointed premier danseur (1898–1909), partnering Zambelli. He was ballet master between 1908 and 1909 and again between 1919 and 1926, leaving the Opera between 1910 and 1914 to become artistic director of Théâtre des Arts where he choreographed *Le Festin de l'araignée* (mus. Albert Roussel, 1913). Among his many ballets for the Paris Opera were *Cydalise et le chèvre-pied* (mus. Pierné, 1923) and *Soir de fête* (mus. Delibes, arr. H. Busser, 1925). The latter is often regarded as a precursor of Balanchine's plotless ballets. He also revived works by other choreographers, including *Sylvia* (after Mérante, 1919) and *La Péri* (after Coralli, 1931), and created numbers for music hall and revue. In 1926 he invented the *Defilé du corps de ballet* which is still part of company tradition. He opened his own school where he taught until his death.

Staatsoper Berlin *See* GERMAN STATE OPERA BALLET; BERLIN STATE BALLET.

Stabat Mater Many composers have composed settings of this devotional text including Pergolesi, Vivaldi, and Rossini. Dance versions include R. Cohan's (mus. Vivaldi, 1975), Mark Morris (mus. Pergolesi, 1986), P. Martins (Pergolesi, 1998), and Smuin (Dvořák, 2002).

Staff, Frank (*b* Kimberley, 15 Jun. 1918; *d* Bloemfontein, 10 May, 1971) South African dancer and choreographer. He studied with Helen Webb and Maude Lloyd in Cape Town before going to London where he studied with Rambert and Tudor. Between 1933 and 1945 he danced with Ballet Club (later Ballet Rambert) as well as with Vic-Wells Ballet (1934–5 and 1938–9), and he created roles in several ballets by Howard, Ashton, and de Valois, including Cupid in Ashton's *Cupid and Psyche* (1939). He also danced with London Ballet in 1940, creating Julien in Howard's *La Fête étrange* (1940) and appeared in Herbert Farjeon's revue *Spread it Around* (chor. Walter Gore, 1936). He began choreographing in 1938, displaying a facility for witty invention, and his works include *Peter and the Wolf* (mus. Prokofiev, 1940) and *Enigma Variations* (mus. Elgar, 1940), both for Ballet Rambert. After military service he became an international freelance choreographer,

returning to S. Africa in 1953 where he became founder and director of S. African Ballet (1955–8). He was then choreographer with UCT/CAPAB Ballet, Cape Town (1963–4), choreographer for PACT Ballet, Johannesburg (1965–8), and director of Performing Arts Council Orange Free State Ballet (1969–71). His later works included *Romeo and Juliet* (mus. Prokofiev, 1964), *Raka*, a three-act ballet on S. African themes (mus. G. Newcater, 1967), and *Soirée* (mus. Rossini, Britten, 1968). He was married four times, his last wife being dancer Veronica *Paeper.

Stages Multi-media work with choreography by Robert Cohan, music by Arne Nordheim and Bob Downes (2nd stage), film sequences and projections by A. McCall, lighting by J. B. Read, and scenery by Peter Farmer. Premiered 22 Apr. 1971 by London Contemporary Dance Theatre at The Place Theatre, London, with Louther, Lapzeson, and North. The audience sat on the stage while the dancers occupied the area normally taken up by the seating. The action presented a mythic world in which a space age protagonist questioned his perceptions and beliefs. As one of LCDT's most popular works, it helped establish a British audience for modern dance.

Stanislavsky and Nemirovich-Danchenko Music Theatre Ballet (Stanislavsky Ballet) The ballet company of Moscow's second opera house which evolved from the Arts Ballet, founded by V. Krieger in 1929, and which was inspired by Stanislavsky's principles of theatrical realism. Under Krieger and Bourmeister (respectively director and chief choreographer, 1930–71), the company performed ballets which made a feature of dramatic realism and emotional truth. Its first production was *The Rivals* (a version of *La Fille mal gardée*, chor. N. Kholfin and P. Markov, 1933) and other ballets included *Lola* (chor. Bourmeister, mus. Vasilenko, 1943), *Coast of Happiness* (chor. Bourmeister, mus. A. Spadavecchia, 1948), *Swan Lake* (chor. Bourmeister, 1953), *Pictures from an Exhibition* (chor. Lopukhov, mus. Mussorgsky, 1963), Dmitri Briantzev's new version of *Le Corsaire* (mus. Adam, 1989), and Vasiliev's *Romeo and Juliet* (mus. Prokofiev, 1991). Its first appearance in the West was in Paris, 1956, and it gave its New York debut in 1998. Dmitri Briantzev was appointed director in 1985.

Stars and Stripes Ballet in one act with choreography by Balanchine, music by Sousa (arr. H. Kay), set by David Hays, and costumes by Karinska. Premiered 17 Jan. 1958 by New York City Ballet at City Center, New York, with Kent, D. Adams, Hayden, Barnett, and d'Amboise. This setting of Sousa's marches was described by the choreographer as a 'balletic parade, led by four "regiments"'. La Fosse choreographed a parody (*Stars & Stripes Forever*) for Les Ballets Trockaderos de Monte Carlo, 1996.

Starzer, Joseph (*b* Vienna, 1726; *d* Vienna, 22 Apr. 1787) Austrian composer who wrote the music for many Noverre ballets, including *Diana and Endymion* (1770) and *The Horatians and the Curatians* (1774), as well as some ballets for Angiolini.

State Ballet of Georgia Company based at the State Opera and Ballet Theatre in Tbilisi. After the theatre was built in 1852, there were ballet performances in opera as well as a programme of visiting dance companies and stars, including Pavlova and Kshessinska. In 1935 a resident dance company was set up by the Kirov dancer V. *Chabukiani and others, with Chabukiani becoming sole artistic director in 1941. He choreographed several major works for the company including *Othello* (1957) and *Hamlet* (1971). He remained director until 1973 when he was succeeded by George Aleksidze who created more than 40 works for the company during his 30-year directorship. In 2004 Nina Ananiashvili was invited by the Georgian government to take over the company. As well as giving a significant number of performances as the company's leading ballerina she substantially enriched the repertory, with stagings of the 19th-century classics by Alexei Fadeyechev, revivals of Balanchine and Ashton, and new commissions from Ratmansky, Possokhov, S. Welch, and others. The company tours internationally.

Stepanov, Vladimir (*b* 29 Jun. 1866; *d* St Petersburg, 28 Jan. 1896) Russian dancer, teacher, and inventor of dance notation system. He studied anatomy at St Petersburg University while dancing with the Mariinsky and as a result developed his notations system based on the principles of musical notation which he published as *Alphabet des mouvements du corps humain* in Paris in 1892. (This was not geared specifically to ballet, though it was used for that purpose.) His system was not published in Russia until after his death and though it was never very widely adopted it was used to notate the Mariinsky classics in St Petersburg. Sergeyev took these notations with him to the West and used them as the basis from which to mount productions of *Swan Lake*, *Sleeping Beauty*, etc. in England and in France.

step dancing Traditional solo dance performed in a variety of styles in the British Isles, Nova Scotia, and the US. All forms are characterized by deft, complicated footwork usually performed in a tightly restricted floor area. Many forms are percussive, the sound being produced by a range of hard shoes, such as wooden clogs, or shoes with hard leather soles or metal taps. In Ireland and parts of the US it has become a competition form, characterized by complex footwork and flamboyant aerial manœuvres, performed with a rigid torso. The show *Riverdance* brought Irish step dance to a world-wide audience.

Stevenson, Ben (*b* Southsea, 4 Apr. 1937) British dancer, choreographer, teacher, and director. He studied at Arts Educational School and in 1953 joined the Theatre Arts Ballet. In 1956 he danced with Sadler's Wells Opera Ballet, then with Sadler's Wells Ballet (1957–9). In 1959 he joined London Festival Ballet as soloist, after which he danced in theatre and television, returning to LFB as principal and ballet master and mounting *Sleeping Beauty* in 1967 with Beryl Grey. In 1969 he moved to America as Director of Harkness Youth Company for which he choreographed *Bartók Concerto*. He was then assistant director and subsequently artistic director of R. Page's Chicago Ballet (1971–5) and artistic director of *Houston Ballet from 1976 to 2004. He had a significant impact on the company, opening up the repertory to many new choreographers and consolidating public interest in ballet as an art form. As well as creating many new works for Houston he also produced many popular versions of the standard classics, including *Nutcracker* (1991) and *Cinderella* (1992) for English National Ballet. In 1998 he created *The Snow Maiden* (mus. Tchaikovsky) for both American Ballet Theatre and Houston Ballet.

Stevenson, Hugh (*b* 1910; *d* London, 16 Dec. 1946) British designer who worked on Tudor's early ballets, such as *Jardin aux lilas* (1936) and *Soirée musicale* (1938), as well as several other important British productions including de Valois's *The Gods Go a-Begging* (1936), Cranko's *Pastorale* (1950), and *Swan Lake* for Vic-Wells Ballet (1934).

Stewart, Garry (*b* Gunnedah, Australia, 19 May 1962) Australian dancer, choreographer, and director. He trained at the Sydney City Ballet Academy (1983) and at the Australian Ballet School (1984–5) dancing with several companies including Australian Dance Theatre and Queensland Ballet. He choreographed his first work in 1985 for the Australian Ballet School and during the 1990s worked as a freelance choreographer, creating works for Sydney Dance Company among others. In 1997 Stewart founded the dance company Thwack for which he created *Plastic Space* and in 1999 was appointed artistic director of *Australian Dance Theatre. His works for the company reflect his driving physical style, his preference for collaboration with artists from other disciplines and occasionally confrontational choice of subject matter. They include *Birdbrain* (2001), a deconstruction of *Swan Lake*, *The Age of Unbeauty* (2002), *HELD* (2004), a collaboration with celebrated dance photographer Lois Greenfield, and *G* (2008), a deconstruction of *Giselle*. In 2006 he collaborated with director Nigel Jamieson on *Honour Bound* (2006), a mixed-media work about prisoners held in Guantanamo Bay. He has also created works for other companies including *Infinity* (Rambert Dance Company, 2007) and *The Centre and its Opposite* (Birmingham Royal Ballet, 2009).

Stiefel, Ethan (*b* Tyrone, Pa., 13 Feb. 1973) US dancer. He trained locally in Wisconsin, then at Milwaukee Ballet School and Pennsylvania Youth Ballet before moving to New York where he studied at American Ballet Theatre's school and at the School of American Ballet. A precocious talent, he joined New York City Ballet aged 16 and after a season with Zurich Ballet (1992) returned as soloist, becoming principal in 1995. He danced leading roles in a wide range of Robbins and Balanchine ballets and created roles in several works including Martins's *Fearful Symmetries* (1990) and *Sleeping Beauty* (1991). In 1997 he joined American Ballet Theatre as principal, dancing many classical roles and creating roles in Tharp's *Known by Heart* (1998), among others. In 2000 he starred in the film *Center Stage* (dir. Nicholas Hytner), also its sequel, *Center Stage 2* (2008). In 2007 he was guest principal with Australian Ballet and the same year was appointed Dean of the School of Dance at the North Carolina School of the Arts.

Still/Here Dance theatre work in two acts with choreography by Bill T. Jones, music by Kenneth Frazelle and Vernon Reid, visual concept by Gretchen Bender, costumes by Liz Prince, and lighting by Robert Wierzel. Premiered 14 Sept. 1994 at TNP Villeurbanne, Lyon, by Bill. T. Jones/Arnie Zane and Dancers. It explores the experience of being sentenced to an early death using material gleaned from workshops with terminally ill patients. The patients' words and gestures are woven into both the songs and the movement and they also feature in videos projected on stage. The work became the subject of considerable controversy when critic Arlene Croce claimed in her article 'A Critic at Bay: Discussing the Undiscussable' (*New Yorker*, 26 Dec. 1994–2 Jan. 1995) that the work constituted a piece of 'victim art' and that it was inherently un-reviewable due to the raw emotional nature of its material.

Stimmung Ballet in one act with choreography by Béjart, music by Stockhausen, set by R. Gernard, and costumes by J. Roustan. Premiered 19 Dec. 1972 by the Ballet of the 20th Century at the

Free University, Brussels. It aims to create a dance equivalent of the music's hypnotic spacious quality, using slow motion gesture and some free improvisation around the choreographed material.

Stockhausen, Karlheinz (*b* Mödrath, 22 Aug. 1928; *d* Kürten, 5 Dec. 2007) German composer. He wrote no dance scores but his music was ideally suited to the experimental zeitgeist of the 1960s and 1970s, for example *Gesang der Jünglinge* and a section of *Kontakte* chor. Tetley in *Ziggurat*, Ballet Rambert, 1967), two pieces from *Aus den sieben Tagen* (chor. Tetley in *Field Figures*, Royal Ballet, 1970), *Mixtur* and *Telemusic* (chor. Tetley and van Manen in *Mutations*, Nederlands Dans Theater, 1970), *Hymnen* (chor. Desombey, Garnier, and others, Amiens, 1970), and *Stimmung* (chor. Béjart, Ballet of the 20th Century, 1972). K. Stuyf used his music in *Reflections on Pale Silence* (Foundation Contemporary Dance, 1964), as did Manfred Taubert in *Electra* (Brunswick, 1972). More recent works made to his music include Preljocaj's *Helikopter* (2001).

Stone Flower, The (orig. Russ. title *Kamenni tsvetok*) Ballet in three acts with choreography by Lavrovksy, libretto by Lavrovsky and Mira Mendelson-Prokofieva, music by Prokofiev, and design by T. Starzhensky. Premiered 12 Feb. 1954 at the Bolshoi Theatre, Moscow, with Ulanova, Plisetskaya, and Preobrajenska. The definitive version was choreographed by Grigorovich and designed by Simon Virsaladze and was premiered 25 Apr. 1957 by the Kirov, Leningrad, with Kolpakova, Osipenko, and Gribov. It is set to Prokofiev's last ballet score and its plot, based on fairy-tales collected from the Urals, is an allegory of the artist's impulse to create. The story focuses on Danila, a stone-worker, who dreams of creating a beautiful vase. The Mistress of the Copper Mountain leads him to her subterranean kingdom where she commands him to work until he is master of his art. As he labours, his beloved, Katerina, is threatened by the aggressive attentions of the stone-workers' steward, Severyan. She goes in search of Danila, pursued by Severyan who is swallowed up by the Earth. Meanwhile, the Mistress of the Copper Mountain has fallen in love with Danila and is unwilling for him to return to the human world with the newly discovered secret of his art (symbolized by a Stone Flower). Katerina, however, begs successfully for his release. Lavrovsky's original production was not a success, as it was considered to be over-burdened with mime scenes. In Grigorovich's version the dramatic integration of choreography and design was hailed as a landmark in Soviet choreography and it was revived for the Bolshoi in 1959 with Maximova and Vasiliev, and for the Royal Swedish

Ballet in 1962. Other versions include Erich Walter's for German Opera on the Rhine (Düsseldorf, 1976). Prokofiev's score was used by Michael Corder for *The Snow Queen* (English National Ballet, 2007).

Stowell, Kent (*b* Idaho, 1939) US dancer, choreographer, and director. He studied with Willam Christensen and at the University of Utah, performing first with San Francisco Ballet and then New York City Ballet (1962–70). In 1970 he joined Munich Opera Ballet as dancer and choreographer, then in 1973 moved to Frankfurt Ballet as ballet master and choreographer, becoming co-artistic director in 1975. Between 1977 and 2005 he was choreographer and co-artistic director of Pacific Northwest Ballet. He created many works for the company including *Orpheus Portrait*, *Carmina Burana* (mus. Orff), and *Quaternary* (mus. Rachmaninoff) and mounted productions of several classics including *Nutcracker* and *Swan Lake*. He is married to Francia *Russell.

Strauss, Johann II (*b* Vienna, 25 Oct. 1825; *d* Vienna, 3 Jun. 1899) Austrian composer. He wrote only one ballet score, *Cinderella*, which was discovered after his death and has been used by E. Graeb (Berlin, 1901) and R. de Warren (Manchester, 1979). Many ballets have been set to arrangements of his other music, including Massine's *Le Beau Danube* (1924), Lichine's *Graduation Ball* (1940), Bourmeister's *Straussiana* (1941), Balanchine's *Vienna Waltzes* (with additional music by Lehár and R. Strauss, New York, 1977), J. Burrows's *Stoics* (London, 1991), Naharin's *Perpetuum* (Geneva, 1992) and De Frutos's *Jota Dolce* (Barcelona, 1993). The German Wiesenthal sisters were well-known interpreters of his waltzes.

Strauss, Richard (*b* Munich, 11 Jun. 1864; *d* Garmisch, 8 Sept. 1949) German composer. He wrote the music for *The Legend of Joseph* (chor. Fokine, Diaghilev's Ballets Russes, Paris, 1914) and *Schlagobers* (chor. Kröller, Vienna State Opera, 1924). In 1923 Kröller also choreographed a work to his *Couperin Dance Suite*, a score that was later extended for the ballet *Verklungene Feste* (chor. Mlakers, Munich State Opera Ballet, 1941). Several of his other scores have also been used for dance, including *Tyl Eulenspiegel* (chor. Nijinsky, Diaghilev's Ballets Russes, New York, 1916; chor. Babilée, 1949, and chor. Balanchine, 1951), extracts from *Salome* (chor. Gorsky in *Salome's Dance*, Bolshoi, Moscow, 1921; for other versions see SALOME), *Le Bourgeois gentilhomme* (chor. Balanchine, Ballets Russes de Monte Carlo, 1932, and chor. Tudor in *Knight Errant*, Royal Ballet, 1968), *Death and Transfiguration* (chor. Milloss, Augsburg, 1934, and chor. van Dantzig in *Blown in a Gentle Wind*, Dutch National Ballet, 1975), *Burlesque for Piano* (chor. Tudor in *Dim Lustre*, Ballet Theatre, 1943), and *Four Last Songs* (many versions, including Macdonald, Royal Swedish Ballet, 1966; van Dantzig, Dutch National Ballet, 1977; Béjart, in *Serait-ce la mort?*, Marseilles, 1970); and Stevenson (Houston Ballet, 1999).

Stravinsky, Igor (*b* Oranienbaum, 17 Jun. 1882; *d* New York, 6 Apr. 1971) Russian-French-US composer, one of the greatest and most prolific composers for dance in the 20th century. His first ballet score, *The *Firebird*, commissioned by Diaghilev and choreographed by Fokine in 1910, already displayed the rhythmic invention and brilliant variations of timbre and colour that were to make much of his music so atmospheric and danceable. In *Petrushka* (chor. Fokine, 1911) he developed a distinctive Russian sound using folk themes woven into the music's fabric, and in *Rite of Spring* (chor. Nijinsky, 1913) he created a radical sound of clashing tonalities and violently irregular rhythms that, together with the primitivist choreography, generated a storm of controversy on the opening night. The score was subsequently used by Massine in 1920 and by many other choreographers and is now a classic of the concert hall repertory. Other commissions from Diaghilev included *Pulcinella* (chor. Massine 1920) and *Les Noces* (chor. Nijinska, 1923), and later scores written specially for dance included *Le Baiser de la fée* (chor. Nijinska, Ida Rubinstein's Company, Paris, 1928), *Perséphone* (chor. Joos, Ida Rubinstein's Company, Paris, 1934), and *Scènes de Ballet* (chor. Dolin for *Seven Lively Arts* revue, Ziegfeld Theater, New York, 1948). It is, though, with Balanchine that Stravinsky's music has become most closely associated. *Apollon musagète* was first used by Bolm in Washington in 1928, but when Balanchine came to choreograph his own version later that year he claimed it as a personal turning point, Stravinsky's austere neo-classicism inspiring a luminous clarity in his own invention. Stravinsky composed only four ballet scores for Balanchine—*Jeu de cartes* (American Ballet, New York, 1937), *Circus Polka*, a ballet for elephants (Barnum and Bailey Circus, New York, 1942), *Orpheus* (Ballet Society, New York, 1948), and *Agon* (New York City Ballet, 1957)—but the latter used many of the concert works for his ballets, including *Danses concertantes* (1944), *Jewels* ('Rubies' section, set to Capriccio for Piano and Orchestra, 1967), *Duo Concertant* (1972), and *Symphony in Three Movements* (1972).

The rhythmic wit and drive of Stravinsky's music, coupled with its frequent incorporation of dance forms and popular themes, have made it popular with many other choreographers, including Béjart, MacMillan, Robbins, and A. Page. Among the concert pieces used for dance are the Concerto in D (chor. Hoyer, Hamburg, 1950; chor.

Robbins in *The Cage*, New York City Ballet, 1951; chor. van Manen in *Tilt*, Nederlands Dans Theater, 1972); *Ebony Concerto* (chor. Taras, New York City Ballet, 1960; chor. Cranko, Munich State Opera, 1970; chor. van Manen, Dutch National Ballet, 1976; chor. Woitzel, NYCB, 1994; chor. A. Page, Royal Ballet, 1995), the Concerto for Piano and Brass Instruments (chor. Taras in *Arcade*, New York City Ballet, 1963; chor. Robbins in *Dumbarton Oaks*, NYCB, 1972), and Serenade in A (chor. Morris in *Candleflowerdance* 2005). On 25 Jun. 1972 NYCB began a week-long Stravinsky Festival featuring 31 ballets to his music, 21 of them new creations. A second festival was held in 1982. Stravinsky's published writings include *Chronicle of My Life* (London, 1936), *Conversations with Igor Stravinsky* (with Robert Craft, New York, 1959), *Dialogues and a Diary* (with Robert Craft, New York, 1963 and London, 1968), and *Themes and Episodes* (with Robert Craft, New York, 1966).

(((●))) SEE WEB LINKS

• Comprehensive website chronicling dance works created to Stravinsky scores

Streb, Elizabeth (*b* Rochester, NY, 23 Feb. 1950) US dancer, choreographer, and director. She studied at the State University of New York and with various teachers, including Cunningham. She made her debut with Margaret Jenkins's company (1972–4), then moved to New York where she began to choreograph and perform her distinctively acrobatic, risk-taking works, such as *Fall Line* (1981), a duet in which she and her partner performed on a platform angled at 35 degrees, and *Little Ease* (1985) in which she attempted to dance in a small, cramped box. In 1985 she formed her own company, choreographing for larger numbers and using sophisticated equipment like flying harnesses, trampolines, walls, and platforms to facilitate more strenuous and daring moves. The titles of her works frequently indicate the nature of the action: *Impact* (1991), *Up* (1995), *Streb vs Gravity* (2006). Her early works were performed in silence, except for the amplified sound of the dancers, but more recently Streb has worked with music.

(((●))) SEE WEB LINKS

• Website for the Streb company

Streetcar Named Desire, A Ballet in one act with choreography by Bettis, music by Alex North (arr. Rayburn Wright), and costumes by Saul Bolasni. Premiered 9 Oct. 1952 by the Slavenska-Franklin Ballet at Her Majesty's Theatre, Montreal, with Slavenska and Franklin. It is based on Tennessee Williams's 1947 play and has been revived for American Ballet Theatre (1954), Washington National Ballet (1974), and Dance Theatre of Harlem (1982).

Stretton, Ross (*b* Canberra, 6 Jun. 1952; *d* Melbourne, 16 Jun. 2005) Australian dancer and director. He studied at the Australian Ballet School and graduated into the company, where he became principal. In 1979 he moved to America where he joined the Joffrey Ballet and then American Ballet Theatre in 1981. He retired in 1990 to become assistant to the directors, company regisseur, and then assistant director (from 1992). In 1997 he was appointed director of Australian Ballet and between 2001 and 2002 he was director of the Royal Ballet.

Strider Modern dance group founded by Richard *Alston in 1972. Featuring choreography by himself, Jacky Lansley, Sally Potter, and others, it was one of the first small-scale independent dance groups in the UK and had a seminal influence on the development of modern dance. It folded in 1975 and was a forerunner to *Second Stride.

Stroman, Susan (*b* Delaware, 17 Oct. 1954) US choreographer. She was active during the 1980s, choreographing for various regional productions, but it was with the off-Broadway show *And the World Goes Round* (1991), which she co-conceived and choreographed, that she was acknowledged as a leading talent in musical theatre. She has since received numerous awards for her choreography, including *Crazy for You* (Broadway, 1992), *Show Boat* (Broadway, 1994), *Steel Pier* (Broadway, 1997), and *Oklahoma!* (London, 1998). She has also choreographed works for the Graham company, *But Not For Me* (mus. Gershwin, 1998), for New York City Ballet, *Blossom Got Kissed*, the final section of *Duke!* (mus. Ellington, 1999), and *Double Feature* (mus. various, 2004), and Pacific Northwest Ballet, *Take Five…More or Less* (mus. Brubeck, 2008). In 1999 she choreographed, directed, and co-created (with author John Weidman) the acclaimed dance theatre work *Contact* (mus. various, Lincoln Center, New York) and in 2001 directed and choreographed the multi-award winning musical *The Producers*.

Struchkova, Raissa (*b* Moscow, 5 Oct. 1925; *d* Moscow, 2 May 2005) Russian dancer. She studied at the Moscow Ballet School with E. Gerdt from whom she acquired a classical technique which was unusually pure for Moscow dancers of that time. She made her debut while still a student, in *The Little Stork* (1937), creating the title role, and in 1944 graduated into the company where she danced until 1978. Her light, lyrical style equipped her for the standard ballerina repertory though she was also noted for her distinctive dramatic interpretations of contemporary

S

roles including Cinderella, which she danced in the 1961 Bolshoi film, and Parasha in Zakharov's *The Bronze Horseman*. She created roles in *Song of the Woods* (1961) and *Lieutenant Kije* (1963)—both by Tarasova and her husband Lapauri, with whom she also famously danced in display pieces like *Spring Waters*. In 1967 she became a teacher of the choreographer's faculty at GITIS (State Institute of Theatrical Art) and in 1981 she became writer and editor of the ballet magazine *Sovetsky Ballet*. She staged a production of *Swan Lake* for English National Ballet in 1993. She was made People's Artist of the USSR in 1959.

Studio Wacker The Paris studio at 69 Rue de Douai where Preobrajenska, Rousanne, V. Gsovsky, and others taught for many years and which served as an unofficial networking centre for the international dance community until it was demolished in 1974.

Stukolkin, Timofei (*b* 6 May 1829; *d* St Petersburg, 1894) Russian dancer who was considered one of the greatest character dancers of the Mariinsky Theatre during his time there (1848–94). He created the roles of Catalabutte in *Sleeping Beauty* (1890) and Drosselmeyer in *Nutcracker* (1892).

Sturman, Marjorie (*b* London, 1902) British teacher and director. She studied with Ray Espinosa in Johannesburg and with E. Espinosa and Volkova in London. In 1922 she began her teaching career in Pretoria and went on to open a school in Johannesburg in 1934. She formed Pretoria Ballet Club in 1943 and co-founded Festival Ballet Society in 1944, from which PACT Ballet developed.

Stuttgart Ballet, The Germany's leading classical ballet company, based in Stuttgart. The city has a long history of ballet that dates back to court ballets performed there in 1609, and the flourishing period (1684–1709) when Jacques Courcelles was court ballet master. It came to international prominence when *Noverre became ballet master of the Württemburg Court (1759–67). During his tenure he pioneered the *ballet d'action and choreographed many works, including *Rinaldo und Armida* and *Medea und Jason*. He enlarged the company and attracted many guest artists, including G. Vestris, Dauberval, and Heinel. The Duke of Württemburg supported a school between 1771 and 1794. In 1824 F. Taglioni became ballet master (remaining until 1828) and his highly successful ballet *Jocko, or the Brazilian Ape* was premiered in 1826 with Marie Taglioni in the leading role. After this, ballet productions were largely subsumed into opera, though foreign companies continued to visit. In 1922 Schlemmer's *Triadic Ballet* had its first complete performance in the city's Landes Theater

and between 1927 and 1939 Lina Gerza was an active choreographer and director of what was then known as the Ballet of the Württemberg State Theatre. She was succeeded there by six more ballet directors but in 1957 the company appointed *Beriozoff who renewed public interest in classical ballet with his stagings of the 19th-century classics such as *Sleeping Beauty* (1957) and *Swan Lake* (1960) and the Fokine repertoire. He brought in international guest artists like Chauviré, Marjorie Tallchief, and his daughter Svetlana Beriosova, and in 1960 invited *Cranko to come and create his *Prince of the Pagodas*. In 1961 Cranko took over direction of what had become known as the Stuttgart Ballet, turning it into one of the world's leading companies. Under his care Marcia *Haydée developed into a great dramatic ballerina, in partnership with Richard *Cragun, and Cranko's concern to raise technical standards produced many other fine principals, including Keil and Hanke. (Stuttgart Ballet School, founded in 1958, was made residential in 1971 under his direction and renamed the John Cranko School in 1974.) Cranko choreographed many works for the company including *Romeo and Juliet* (1962), *Onegin* (1965), and *The Taming of the Shrew* (1969), and he also brought in works by MacMillan, P. Wright, and others. The repertoire's strong dramatic bias developed dancers less famous for their uniformity of style than for their acting ability, personality, and adaptability to both classic and contemporary roles. As foreign tours became more extensive (New York, 1969, Russia, 1971), a second company, the Noverre Ballet, was formed to perform in opera productions and give its own chamber performances, but it was re-absorbed into the main company in 1973. The Noverre Society, formed in Stuttgart in 1958, developed into an important platform for new choreographers during this period with Kylián, Neumeier, and more latterly *Forsythe showing their first works there. After Cranko's death in 1973, Tetley became director but though he created three works for the company, including *Voluntaries*, his style was not liked and Haydée took over in 1976. She continued there for nineteen years, maintaining the Cranko inheritance and acquiring a repertory of new work from Béjart, van Manen, and others. However, she came under increasing criticism for her frequent absences while running her other company in Santiago de Chile. With less new work coming into the repertory and the younger dancers receiving insufficient nurturing, the Stuttgart declined from its golden age of the 1960s and 1970s. In 1996 Reid *Anderson was appointed director and made significant moves to revitalize the company. While maintaining the Cranko heritage, he also widened the repertory with work by Bigonzetti, Forsythe, McGregor, and others, and additionally encouraged new choreography from within the company, appointing two choreographers in residence, Christian *Spuck and Marco Goeck. He also nurtured a new generation of dancers, including Alicia Amatriain, Sue Jin Kang, Katje Wünze, Filip Barankievicz, and Friedemann *Vogel.

(⊕) SEE WEB LINKS
• Website for the Stuttgart Theatre with link to the ballet company

Subligny, Marie-Thérèse (*b* Paris, Jul. 1666; *d* possibly 1735) French dancer. She appeared in the last court ballets given by Louis XIV and was premiere danseuse at Paris Opera (1690–1705), appearing in the opera ballets of Lully and Campra. This was at a time when women were just beginning to enter the dance profession and when she performed in London in 1699 she was the first professional ballerina ever seen by English audiences, performing with Claude Ballon.

Suite en blanc Ballet in one act with choreograhy by Lifar, music by Lalo, and design by Dignimont. Premiered by Paris Opera Ballet, 19 Jun. 1943 at Zurich, with Schwarz, Chauviré, Darsonal, and Lifar. It is set to Lalo's Suite from *Namouna* and is one of Lifar's rare plotless ballets, designed to display the elegance and virtuosity of its dancers. Its title was taken from the white costumes worn by the original cast, although in subsequent revivals the men wore black tights (Nouveau Ballet de Monte Carlo, 1946) and black boleros (London Festival Ballet, 1966) and the title had to be changed to *Noir et blanc*. Australian Ballet revived it under its original title in 1981.

Summers, Elaine (*b* Perth, Australia, 20 Feb. 1925) US dancer, choreographer, and film-maker. She studied with Graham, Cunningham, and others and was one of the original members of the New York Judson Church dance collective. One of the first choreographers to explore the use of multi-media in dance, she created the show *Fantastic Garden* in 1964. She subsequently became director of the Experimental Intermedia Foundation, then co-director of the Sarasota Visual Arts Center.

Summerspace Modern dance work in one act with choreography by Cunningham, music by Morton Feldman, and design by Rauschenberg. Premiered 17 Aug. 1958 by the Merce Cunningham Dance Company at Connecticut College, New London, Connecticut, with Cunningham, Brown, Farber, and Charlip. It is choreographed for six dancers and deals with changing tempos, the dancers performing jumps at contrasting speeds in an airy space created by the pointillist effect of costumes and backdrop. It was Cunningham's first work to enter the repertoire of classical ballet companies. In the New York City Ballet

revival (1966) the dancers wore shoes and danced on pointe. Other companies to dance it include Cullberg Ballet (1967) and Boston Ballet (1974).

Sunshine Matinées Annual dance performances established in London in 1919 by P. J. S. Richardson and D. Claremont (from the Sunshine Home for Blind Babies) which at the time formed a significant showcase for English dancing. The first took place at the London Queen's Theatre and the series ended in 1930 when the Camargo Society took over its function. During that time it featured dancers such as Wigman, Trefilova, Dolin, Bedells, de Valois, and Astafieva.

Surinach, Carlos (*b* Barcelona, 14 Mar. 1915; *d* Connecticut, 12 Nov. 1997) Spanish-US composer who wrote several dance scores including Graham's *Embattled Garden* (1958) and *Acrobats of God* (1960). His concert music was also used for dance, for example in Ailey's *Feast of Ashes* (1962) and P. Taylor's *Agathe's Tale* (1967).

Swan Lake (Fr. title *Lac des cygnes*; Russ. title *Lebedinoe ozero*) Ballet in four acts, arguably the most famous, and certainly one of the most frequently performed works in the international repertory. The first production was choreographed by V. Reisinger, with libretto by V. P. Begitchev and Vasily Geltser, music by Tchaikovsky, and design by H. Shangin, K. Valts, and H. Groppius (sets) and H. Simone and Vormenko (costumes). It was premiered 4 Mar. 1877 at the Bolshoi Theatre, Moscow, with P. Karpakova, but neither the ballet nor its ballerina were well received. Joseph Hansen's revised versions of 1880 and 1882 continued in the Bolshoi repertory for over 40 performances but Petipa and Ivanov's production for the Mariinsky Theatre, St Petersburg, became the definitive version. Ivanov originally choreographed Act II for a Tchaikovsky Memorial Matinée, 1 Mar. 1894, with Legnani and P. Gerdt. The full ballet, with Acts I and III choreographed by Petipa and Acts II and IV by *Ivanov and with designs by M. I. Bocharov and H. Levogt, was performed 27 Jan. 1895, again with Legnani and Gerdt. Some major changes were made in the order of Tchaikovsky's score.

The ballet's libretto is based on German folk tale elements and tells the story of the Princess Odette who is turned into a swan by the magician Rothbart. She and her companions can only be restored to human form if a man swears true love for her. One night she is met by Prince Siegfried hunting by the lake—she tells him her story; he falls in love and vows to rescue her. Back at his castle, Siegfried attends a ball where he is expected to choose his future bride. Rothbart appears with his daughter Odile who is disguised as a black swan and appears to be identical to Odette (in most productions the roles of Odette and

Odile are danced by the same ballerina). Though her dancing is much harder and flashier than Odette's she ruthlessly imitates the latter's characteristic motifs, such as her fluttering arm movements. Siegfried is dazzled by Odile's trickery and begs to marry her. Once his vow to Odette is broken Rothbart and his daughter triumphantly reveal their true identity. Heartbroken, Siegfried races back to the lake to console Odette. In some versions he fights with Rothbart, overcomes him and the spell is broken. In others he and Odette plunge into the lake together, and in a final apotheosis are shown to find perfect love and happiness after death. The enduring success of the ballet owes much to the music's dramatic variety and exquisite lyricism. The extreme challenge between the romantic purity of Odette and the seductive virtuosity of Odile make this dual role one of the greatest challenges in the ballerina's repertory.

The Petipa–Ivanov production has formed the basis of most subsequent stagings around the world. The first London production was a two-act version, shown at the Hippodrome in 1910 (with Preobrajenska), and Diaghilev's company also toured a two-act version in 1911, staged and revised by Fokine. In New York an abridged version was first produced by Mordkin in 1911, but the complete ballet was not seen in the West until 1934 when Nicolai Sergeyev staged it for the Vic-Wells Ballet. This itself formed the basis for many subsequent versions outside Russia (see below). Performances of the ballet in Leningrad were disrupted during the revolution and First World War but Vaganova staged an important production for the Kirov in 1933. Lopukhov's 1945 staging for the Kirov later became the basis for an important version by Bourmeister in 1953 (for the Stanislavsky and Nemirovich-Danchenko Theatre) which restored Tchaikovsky's music to its original order. At the Bolshoi in Moscow, performances were more continuous. Gorsky mounted a version in 1901, which was to be the basis for most later productions.

Outside Russia there were countless new productions during the 20th century, including Balanchine's extended version of Act II for New York City Ballet, 1951, Cranko's for Stuttgart Ballet, 1963, Ashton's for the Royal Ballet, 1963, Nureyev's for the Vienna State Opera Ballet, 1964, Erik Bruhn's for National Ballet of Canada, 1966, Yuri Grigorovich's for Bolshoi Ballet, 1969, Dowell's for the Royal Ballet, 1987, Tomasson's for San Francisco Ballet, 1988, Peter Martins's for Royal Danish Ballet, 1996, and Peter Schaufuss's for Berlin Opera Ballet, 1992. Most versions retain the core of what is considered the original Petipa-Ivanov text, though with some new choreography added. Over the years some additions have become regarded as standard, such as the Prince's

solo just before he meets Odette, and Rothbart and Odile's fantastical entrance in Act III. In some productions the story has been presented from a new perspective. Bruhn's 1966 version portrayed Rothbart as a woman, implying that Siegfried suffers from an oedipal complex, while Christopher Gable's for Northern Ballet Theatre in 1992 presented Rothbart as a fascist dictator. Wheeldon's 2006 production for Pennsylvania Ballet retold the story as the fantasy of a romantic young ballet dancer.

There are a few productions which retain little or none of the original choreography. Neumeier's *Illusions—Like Swan Lake* (chor. for Hamburg Ballet, 1976) recasts Siegfried as the mad King Ludwig of Bavaria. Mats Ek's, for Cullberg Ballet (1987), pivots around the Prince's oedipal relationship with his mother; and Matthew Bourne's for Adventures in Motion Pictures (1995) presents Odette as a male swan and Odile as a glamorous stud. Both characters function as seductive alter egos for Siegfried in a version that puts the Prince and his search for love and identity at the centre of the plot and re-casts the traditional female swan choreography into dance that is raw, powerful, and very male.

Swan of Tuonela Sibelius's Legend for Orchestra has been used by several choreographers including A. Saxelin (Helsinki, 1948), W. Ulbrich (Leipzig, 1958), Dolin (Guatemala, 1965), Bintley (Sadler's Wells Royal Ballet, 1982), and Ek (pas de deux for Finnish National Ballet, 1998).

Swansong Ballet in one act with choreography and design by C. Bruce and music by Phillip Chambon. Premiered Nov. 1987 by London Festival Ballet in Bilbao with Koen Onzia, Matz Skoog, and Kevin Richmond. A stark male trio evoking the psychological and physical torture experienced by political prisoners. It has been revived by Houston Ballet (1991) and Rambert Dance Company (2007).

Sweden Ballet came to Sweden in the 17th century when Antoine de Beaulieu staged court ballets in the French style. These were particularly brilliant during Queen Christina's reign. The first professional troupe and ballet school were founded by King Gustav III in 1773 at the Royal Opera and Louis Gallodier was the ballet master. Antoine *Bournonville joined the company in 1781 bringing with him the new style of *ballet d'action, and in the early 19th century many foreign artists performed with it. F. Taglioni was premier danseur (1803–4) and also ballet master in 1818. Marie, his daughter, was born in Stockholm and danced in the city in 1841 with the Swedish dancer C. Johansson just before he left to pursue his career in St Petersburg. Several ballets by August *Bournonville were staged for the Royal Swedish Ballet, and Anders Selinder, its first Swedish ballet master, created many folk ballets for its repertoire. Towards the end of the 19th century ballet went into a decline though public interest was revived by performances by Isadora Duncan (1906) and Pavlova (1908) in Stockholm. *Fokine worked with the RSB (1913–14) staging *Carnaval, Les Sylphides*, etc. and dancing leading roles with V. Fokina, but war interrupted plans for his appointment as ballet master. In 1920 Rolf de Maré founded Les *Ballets Suédois in Paris taking some of the best dancers from RSB with him, and the ballet company became largely subsumed into opera productions. Some dance activity persisted elsewhere, such as the Gothenburg Opera Ballet (see below), which staged some extracts of the classics, the company of Birgit *Cullberg (founded 1939), and the Svensk Dansteatre which Cullberg later co-founded with Ivo *Cramér. However, in 1949 the Royal Theatre engaged Tudor to overhaul the ballet. He staged *Giselle* and several of his own works including *Jardin aux lilas* and *Gala Performance*. In 1953 *Skeaping took over adding other standard classics like *Swan Lake* and *Sleeping Beauty* and also new works by Swedish choreographers like Cullberg, *Åkesson and Cramér. The RSB began to acquire an international reputation with dancers like von Rosen and Andersen. A succession of directors followed including Tudor (1961 and 1963) who choreographed *Echoing of Trumpets* (1963) for the company, Bruhn (1967–72) who introduced works by Robbins, Tetley, MacMillan, and others, and Cramér (1975–80). Under the direction of Frank *Andersen (1995–9) the company ran an ambitious programme of works to celebrate its 225th anniversary, including a revival of MacMillan's *Mayerling*, the reconstruction of four works from Les Ballets Suédois's repertory, and Neumeier's *Peer Gynt*. Andersen was succeeded by Petter *Jacobsson (1999–2002), and Madeleine Onne from 2002, and new additions to the repertory included works by Ek, Par Isberg, Per Jonsonn, and other Swedish choreographers as well as international repertory from Forsythe, Tharp, Duato, and others. In 2008 Patrice Bart was commissioned to choreograph a full-length ballet in tribute to its royal founder, *Gustave III*. Stockholm 59 Degrees North is an ensemble of soloists and principals attached to the company, performing largely contemporary work.

In Gothenburg the Stora Theatre became a full-time opera house in 1920 with a ballet company attached. At first it performed largely in opera productions but after 1967 directors C. Borg, von *Rosen, and U. *Gadd succeeded in raising both artistic and innovative standards. In 1988 the new director, Juhani Terasvuori, shifted the emphasis more towards the 19th-century classics, but when Robert North was director (1991–5) he restored a more contemporary focus, introducing several of his own works into the repertory. Gadd was re-appointed director 1995–9. The company's repertory is currently dominated by modern work and contemporary ballets, by Forsythe, Kylián, Tankard, and some Swedish choreographers. Its director Johannes Öhman was appointed 2007. The Opera House also showcases guest dance companies and Gothenburg city additionally hosts an annual dance and theatre festival. The 1960s was generally a fruitful period for dance in Sweden, with many new companies emerging. The Scandinavian Ballet, founded by von Rosen, and A. Fridericia, presented a Swedish-Danish repertoire of works by Bournonville, van Rosen, and Cramér, and Cullberg became director of the state-subsidized *Cullberg Ballet which presented her own works. She was succeeded by her son Mats *Ek, whose own work dominated the repertory, and briefly by C. Carlson and Anna Grip who added new works by Johan Inger, Stijin Celis, and others. In 1968 Cramér founded Cramérballetten in Stockholm to present his own ballets. The ballet company attached to the Stadsteatern at Malmö until 1994 performed a repertory of largely neo-classical works and has since relocated to the town of Lund. Since the 1980s a small but vigorous independent dance scene has also developed, with companies like Efva Lilja Danceproduction, Rubicon, and the Modern Dance Theatre presenting regular dance performances in Stockholm, also Skånesdansteater based in Malmö from 1995, which presents an international range of work by Vincent Mantsoe, Jo Strøomgren and others.

(⊕) **SEE WEB LINKS**
- Link to Gothenburg Opera Ballet
- Website for Cullberg Ballet
- Website for Skånes Dansteater

Swinson, Cyril (*b* London, 1910; *d* St Albans, 3 Jan. 1963) British publisher and writer. As a director of A. & C. Black, London, he facilitated the publication of many important dance books in England and America. He was also associate editor of *Ballet Annual* for seventeen years, and author, sometimes under the pen-names of Joseph Sandon or Hugh Fisher, of several books, including *The Sadler's Wells Theatre Ballet* (London, 1956).

Switzerland There is no national Swiss ballet but companies are attached to opera houses in Zurich, Berne, Basel, St Gall, Lucerne, and Geneva. In Zurich, ballet was subservient to opera, for much of this century, though during the 1930s Mlakar bolstered its image with the success of his own original ballets. It was only when *Beriozoff was appointed ballet master in 1964 that a regular repertory was established, with stagings of the classics, works from the Fokine repertoire, and some of his own ballets. After he left in 1971 he was followed by a succession of short-lived ballet directors including G. Cauley (1973–5) and H. Meister and J. Burth (1975–8). Stability returned with the appointment of P. *Neary (1978–85) who revived many Balanchine works. She was succeeded by Uwe *Scholz and then Bernd Bienert who brought in many experimental works by Amanda Miller, M. *Ek, and himself. In 1996 Heinz *Spoerli was appointed director. In Geneva public interest in dance was galvanized at the beginning of the century through performances by Isadora Duncan and pupils of Jaques-Dalcroze but regular ballet performances only started with the opening of the rebuilt Grand Theatre and its associate company, directed by J. *Charrat (1962–4), A. Catá (1969–73) who established a Balanchine repertory, P. Neary (1973–8), who continued the emphasis on Balanchine, Araiz (1980–8), Gradimir Pankov (1988–96), François Passard and Giorgio Mancini (1996–2003), and finally by Philippe Cohen, the last three introducing works by younger choreographers such as A. Miller, Naharin, and Cherkaoui into the repertory. At Basel, ballet became a major force within its Municipal Theatre when V. Orlikovsky was ballet director (1955–67). He staged many of the standard classics and ballets from the Soviet repertory including the first W. European production of *The Stone Flower* (1962). Standards declined after he left, but they began an upturn under the direction of P. *Smok (1970–3) which was furthered by Spoerli (1973–92). Under his direction Basel became an international centre for dance, with a repertory composed of both classical and contemporary works, many by himself. He was succeeded by Youri Vámos and in 1996 the company was disbanded and replaced by a Tanztheater directed by Joachim Schlömer. In Windisch, Jean Deroc founded the Swiss Chamber Ballet in 1968. Ballet activity is also focused on Lausanne where the international Prix de Lausanne was founded for students aged 16–19 (*see* COMPETITIONS). The city is also home to Béjart's company which was renamed Béjart-Ballet Lausanne when it moved there in 1987.

Modern dance was established in the country when *Laban set up his 'Dance Farm' near Locarno and later his school in Zurich. This was one of the focal points of Central European modern dance just prior to, and during, the First World War. Dancer Charlotte Bara built herself the Teatro San Martino at Ascona and staged modern dance performances there for many years. There was also strong interest in modern dance in Basel when R. Chladek and H. Rosen performed regularly at the Municipal Theatre during the late 1920s and 1930s. Since the 1980s a small number of independent modern dance companies have emerged, despite the shortage of subsidy, such as Compagnie Philippe Saire, which is based in

Morges and has established a high international reputation, Cathy Sharp Ensemble, based in Basel since 1991, and the multi-disciplinary company Avant-Scene, based in Lausanne since 1991. Since Cathy Marston took over Bern Ballet in 2007, it too has focused on a contemporary repertory, much of it choreographed by herself.

⊕ SEE WEB LINKS
• Website for Geneva Ballet

Swope, Martha (*b* c.1933) US photographer who has been official photographer of New York City Ballet, Martha Graham Dance Company, and Dance Theatre of Harlem. Some of her portraits have become iconic images of 20th-century dance. She is co-author of *Martha Graham* (with L. Leatherman; New York, 1967) and *New York City Ballet* (with L. Kirstein; New York, 1973).

Sydney Dance Company Australian modern dance company. It was founded by S. Musitz in 1965 as an education group and re-formed as the Dance Company of New South Wales in 1971. Jaap *Flier was artistic director 1975–6 and introduced works by himself, Tetley, Sokolow, and others into the repertory. In 1976 G. *Murphy took over, running the company with his partner Janet Vernon and creating numerous works for it, including *Synergy with Synergy* (1992), created with the percussion group Synergy, *The Protecting Veil* (mus. J. Tavener, 1993), the dance theatre piece *Free Radicals* (mus. M. Askill, 1997), *Salome* (mus. various, 1998), *Ellipse* (mus. Matthew Hindson, 2003), *Shades of Gray* (2004), and *Grand* (2005). Other guest choreographers showcased within SDC's repertory were Stephen Page and Stephen Petronio. Murphy retired in 2007 and Noel Staunton ran the company as Executive Director until Rafael *Bonachela was appointed director in 2008. The company's home performance base moved to Sydney Opera House in 1977 where it has since performed twice a year. It also undertakes frequent international tours—its European debut was in 1980 and its New York debut in 1981.

⊕ SEE WEB LINKS
• Website for the Sydney Dance Company

Sylphide, La Ballet in two acts with choreography by F. Taglioni, libretto by A. Nourrit, music by Schneitzhoeffer, sets by P. L. C. Ciceri, and costumes by E. Lami. Premiered 12 Mar. 1832 at the Paris Opera with M. Taglioni, Noblet, Mazilier, and Elie. It was the first fully fledged Romantic ballet. Based on Charles Nodier's *Trilby, ou le Lutin d'Argail* (1822), its plot and atmosphere were also inspired by the supernatural 'Ballet of the Nuns' which had appeared in Meyerbeer's opera *Robert le diable* (1831). It tells the story of a young Scottish farmer, James, who is visited by the Sylphide on the eve of his wedding to Effie. She entices him away to the woods, where, enchanted by her, he wishes to keep her for ever. The evil witch Madge gives him a magic shawl to put around her shoulders but when he does so the Sylphide's wings fall off and she dies. As in so many Romantic ballets, the hero haplessly pursues an otherworldly beauty and in doing so destroys his chances of happiness in the real world. In the final scene, as James stands alone and distraught, Effie passes by on her way to marry her other suitor, Gurn. The ballet introduced many of the elements that dominated the Romantic movement—female dancers as supernatural beings dressed in white tulle, an intensely poetic atmosphere (created by the recently installed gas lamps at the Opera), and at the centre Taglioni herself, with her famously light jump and graceful facility in dancing on pointe. The ballet was performed all around the world, premiering in London and Berlin in 1832, New York and St Petersburg in 1835, and Vienna in 1836. An earlier version had been choreographed by L. Henry in Milan (1828) as *La silfide*, and Bournonville staged his own new version with music by Løvenskjold in Copenhagen 28 Nov. 1836 with himself and Grahn in the leading roles. This production is still in the repertoire of the Royal Danish Ballet and has been revived many times, including by von Rosen (Ballet Rambert, 1960), Bruhn (National Ballet of Canada, 1964), Lander (American Ballet Theatre, 1964), Brenaa (Scottish Ballet, 1973), P. Schaufuss (English National Ballet, 1979), D. Bjørn (Royal Danish Ballet, 2000 and Dutch National Ballet, 2001), and Kobborg (Royal Ballet, 2005, also Zurich Ballet and Kobayashi Ballet Tokyo). Productions using the Schneitzhoeffer score have been staged by V. Gsovsky (Ballets des Champs-Elysées, 1946), Adama (a version which also goes back to the original sources, Bremen, 1964), and Lacotte (Paris Opera, 1972).

Sylphides, Les (orig. Russ. title *Chopiniana*) Ballet in one act with choreography by Fokine and music by Chopin. The original version was premiered 23 Feb. 1907 at the Mariinsky Theatre, St Petersburg, with Pavlova, Fokina, and Oboukhoff. It was set to five piano pieces orchestrated by Glazunov and unlike the final version was Polish rather than Romantic in character. The opening Polonaise in A major (Op. 40, No. 1) was set in a ballroom; the Nocturne in A flat (Op. 32, No. 2) represented Chopin, dreaming feverishly in Majorca; the Mazurka in C sharp minor (Op. 50, No. 3) depicted a Polish wedding; the Valse in C sharp minor (Op. 64, No. 2) was a pas de deux in which the ballerina wore Romantic ballet dress; and the final Tarantella in A flat major (Op. 43) represented a Neapolitan folk scene. A year later

Fokine revised the ballet, taking the Romantic pas de deux as his inspiration. Some extra Chopin pieces (orch. Maurice Keller) were added to the score and the ballet became a plotless work in which a poet dances with a group of sylphides, the choreography recreating the soft lines and lilting *ballon* of the Romantic style. This version was premiered 21 Mar. 1908 at the Mariinsky Theatre, St Petersburg, with Preobrajenska, Pavlova, Karsavina, and Nijinsky. The third version, which is the one seen today, was created for Paris. Diaghilev, initially against Fokine's wishes, retitled it *Les Sylphides* and added new designs by Benois which placed the sylphides in the setting of a ruined monastery. It was premiered 2 Jun. 1909 by Diaghilev's Ballets Russes at Théâtre du Chatelet with Pavlova, Karsavina, Baldina, and Nijinsky. It opens with the Polonaise in A major (although in Western performances this tends to be replaced by the Prelude in A major (Op. 28, No. 7), and is followed by the Nocturne in A flat major (Op. 33, No. 2) which is danced by three female soloists, one male soloist, and the corps. After this comes the Valse in G flat major (Op. 70, No. 1) danced by the first female soloist; the Mazurka in D major (Op. 32, No. 2), usually danced by the ballerina; the Mazurka in C major (Op. 67, No. 3), danced by the poet; the repeated Prelude in A major (Op. 28, No. 7) danced by the second female soloist; the Valse in C sharp minor (Op. 64, No. 2), which is the pas de deux for the poet and ballerina in the original version; and finally the Grande Valse in E flat major (Op. 18) for the whole ensemble. For a later production Fokine choreographed the Mazurka in C major (Op. 33, No. 3) as an alternative variation for the poet, which is still danced by the Kirov. Fokine revived the work for many companies around the world including Ballet Theatre (1940). The Royal Ballet's production goes back to Markova's staging for the Vic-Wells Ballet (1932). Fokine wrote about its creation in *Memoirs of a Ballet Master* (Boston, 1961).

Sylvia, ou La Nymphe de Diane Ballet in three acts with choreography by Mérante, libretto by Jules Barbier and Baron de Reinach, music by Delibes, sets by Chéret, Rubé, and Chaperon, and costumes by E. Lacoste. Premiered 14 Jun. 1876 at the Paris Opera with Mérante and Sangalli. Delibes's score is considered to be one of the masterpieces of the ballet repertoire with its vividly descriptive orchestration and exquisite melodies, but the ballet's success has been compromised by its contrived and flimsy libretto (written after Tasso's pastoral *Aminta*). It tells the story of the shepherd Aminta who falls in love with Sylvia, a nymph of Diana. She rejects him but, undaunted, he pursues her and attempts to rescue her when she is captured by the huntsman, Orion. Sylvia's escape is finally facilitated by

Eros rather than Aminta as the former has been keeping a benign watch over the lovers' fate. But even so, Sylvia decides she loves Aminta and confesses this to Diana. At first the goddess forbids the match but, after the intervention of Eros, she blesses their union.

Though Mérante's version was short-lived, Staats subsequently used it as a basis for his revival at Paris Opera in 1919. Many other choreographers have also been drawn to Delibes's score including Ivanov, for Mariinsky Theatre in 1901; Lifar for Paris Opera in 1941 (revived by Lycette Darsonval in 1979); and Balanchine, whose Act III pas de deux for New York City Ballet was first danced by Maria Tallchief and Magallanes in 1950. Ashton choreographed a complete new version for Sadler's Wells Ballet (premiered 3 Sept. 1952 at the Royal Opera House) with Fonteyn and Somes. The libretto was revised but despite praise for the music and for the writing of Fonteyn's role, in 1967 Ashton chose to compress the ballet to a single act and it was subsequently dropped from the repertory until 2004 when the original work was successfully revived for Covent Garden. Bintley's version for Birmingham Royal Ballet (1993) was also problematic. While the choreography for Sylvia (M. Yoshida) and Aminta (J. Cipolla) was considered lyrically inventive and the designs by Sue Blane added a contemporary twist (Eros drove a large limousine through the leafy archaic setting), these did not successfully conceal the cracks in the old plot, which remained even in Bintley's more successful second version for BRB, created in 2009. Other new versions include Neumeier's (1997) for Paris Opera, which updated the ballet to a contemporary, minimalist setting, and Mark Morris's (2004) for San Francisco Ballet.

symphonic ballets The term used to describe several ballets choreographed by Massine during the 1930s which were settings of entire symphonies, including *Les Présages* (Tchaikovsky's 5th, 1933); *Choreartium* (Brahms's 4th, 1933), and *Symphonie fantastique* (Berlioz, 1936). Massine claimed to express the form and content of the music through pure dance, though some dramatic elements of character and symbolism were also conveyed. His use of symphonic scores outraged members of the music establishment who argued that they had not been written for dance, even though Massine was not the first choreographer to use symphonic music. Duncan had performed to Beethoven's 7th in New York, 1908; Gorsky had choreographed Glazunov's 5th, Moscow, 1915; and Lopukhov had set Beethoven's 4th in *Dance Symphony*, 1923. The term has dropped out of use and many choreographers use symphonies with impunity, such as Béjart's setting of Beethoven's 9th and Tharp's of Beethoven's 7th.

Symphonic Variations Ballet in one act with choreography by Ashton, music by Franck, and design by Fedorovitch. Premiered 24 Apr. 1946 by Sadler's Wells Ballet at Covent Garden, London, with Fonteyn, May, Shearer, Somes, Shaw, and Henry Danton. It is set to Franck's score of the same title. The horrors of the Second World War and the death of his mother had inspired Ashton to undertake a study of mysticism during the 1940s and though this ballet has no plot its defining atmosphere is one of transcendence and calm. It was also the first work he choreographed for the Royal Opera House stage (after the company moved there from the smaller Sadler's Wells) and he exploited its scale in choreography of a profoundly spacious quality. Its six dancers seem to move on the ebb and flow of Franck's music, and though the choreography is pared to essentials it requires precise musicality and transparently pure technique. The ballet has since been revived by Dutch National Ballet (1979) and American Ballet Theatre (1992).

Symphonie fantastique Ballet in one act with choreography by Massine, music by Berlioz, and design by Bérard. Premiered 24 Jul. 1936 by Ballets Russes de Monte Carlo at Covent Garden, London, with Massine and Toumanova. This symphonic ballet follows closely both the music and libretto of Berlioz's score. It shows a young musician who, in a series of opium-induced dreams, pursues his unattainable Beloved or *idée fixe* through a ballroom, an idyllic landscape, a prison, and a witches' sabbath where she appears hideously transformed. Each of its five scenes is choreographed in a very distinct style. It has been revived by several companies, such as Paris Opera (1957), sometimes as *Episode in the Life of an Artist*. Petit choreographed a new version for Paris Opera in 1975.

Symphonie pour un homme seul (Eng. title *Symphony for a Lonely Man*) Ballet in one act with choreography by Béjart and music by P. Henry and P. Schaeffer. Premiered 26 Jul. 1955 by Ballet de l'Etoile, Paris, with Béjart and Seigneuret. It was Béjart's first success and explores the dilemma of modern man, trapped between his instincts and modern technology. It has been revived for his various companies and for Cologne Ballet (1963).

Symphony in C (orig. *Le Palais de cristal*) Ballet in one act with choreography by Balanchine, music by Bizet, and design by L. Fini. Premiered 28 Jul. 1947 by Paris Opera with Darsonval, Toumanova, Bardin, Kalioujny, Ritz, Renault, and Bozzoni. It was created as a showcase for the talent of the whole company. A different 'team' of dancers (corps, two demi-soloist couples, and a principal couple) dance each of the first three movements, with a fourth 'team' initiating the final movement before being joined by the whole cast on stage. Balanchine re-staged it a year later for New York City Ballet as *Symphony in C* and it has subsequently been revived for companies all round the world, including Royal Danish Ballet (1953), Dutch National Ballet (1962), Berlin Opera Ballet (1969), Stuttgart Ballet (1976), Royal Ballet (1991), and the Kirov in 1996.

Symphony in Three Movements Ballet in one act with choreography by Balanchine and music by Stravinsky. Premiered 18 Jun. 1972 by New York City Ballet at State Theater, New York, with Leland, Villella, and Tomasson. This plotless setting of Stravinsky's 1945 score contains some of Balanchine's fleetest and most densely patterned dance. Van Manen choreographed a work to the same music for Nederlands Dans Theater (1963).

Symphony of Psalms (orig. *Psalmensymfonie*) Ballet in one act with choreography by Kylián, music by Stravinsky, set by W. Katz, and costumes by J. Stokvis. Premiered 24 Nov. 1978 by Netherlands Dance Theatre at Circustheater, Scheveningen. In this celebrated setting of Stravinsky's 1930 score, the sixteen dancers frequently appear to move as a single unit through the surging patterns of the choreography, giving powerful physical expression to emotions of both ecstasy and sorrow. Sparemblek used the same score in a version for Gulbenkian Ballet (1972).

Szeged Contemporary Ballet Hungarian modern dance company. It took its present name in 1993 but dates back to ballet performances staged in the city by Károly Zsedényi during the 1940s. A full-time company was formed at the Szeged National Theatre in which Zoltán *Imre came to prominence as dancer and choreographer. Economic problems caused its decline but it was relaunched in 1987 as Szeged Ballet by Roland Boker under the guidance of Imre, performing modern dance works and contemporary ballets. In 1993 András Patki and Tamás Juronics were appointed directors. Renamed Szeged Contemporary Ballet and oriented towards contemporary dance theatre, the company performs a wide repertory of Hungarian and international work, including modern versions of *Carmina Burana* and *The Miraculous Mandarin*.

S

Taglioni Famous Italian family of dancers and choreographers. *See* TAGLIONI, FILIPPO; TAGLIONI, MARIE; TAGLIONI, MARIE THE YOUNGER; TAGLIONI, PAUL; TAGLIONI, SALVATORE.

Taglioni, Filippo (*b* Milan, 5 Nov. 1777; *d* Como, 11 Feb. 1871 (some sources 11 Sept. 1871)) Italian dancer and choreographer, and creator of the seminal Romantic ballet *La *Sylphide*. The son of Carlo T. and the father of Marie T. and Paul T. He made his debut in 1794 as a child dancing female roles in Pisa. After performing around Italy he moved to Paris in 1799 where he studied with Coulon and danced at the Paris Opera, then in 1802 he left the Opera to work as principal dancer and ballet master in Stockholm. From then on he travelled throughout Europe, working in Vienna (where he made his choreographic debut in 1805), Munich, Milan, Turin, Stuttgart, Paris, Berlin, St Petersburg, and Warsaw before retiring to Como. As a choreographer his style emphasized ballon, graceful deportment, and quick light footwork, his subject-matter tended towards the mystical. His most important work probably took place in Paris, where he choreographed the first productions of the operas *Le Dieu et la bayadère* (1830), *Robert le diable* (1831), *Gustave III* (1833), and *Les Huguenots* (1836), and the ballets *La Sylphide* (mus. Schneitzhoeffer, 1832), *Nathalie; ou, La Laitière suisse* (mus. Gyrowetz, Carafa, 1832), *Brézilia; ou, La Tribu des femmes* (mus. von Gallenberg, 1835), and *La Fille du Danube* (mus. Adam, 1836). With his daughter Marie as ballerina he was visiting ballet master to the Imperial Theatres, St Petersburg (1837–42). For St Petersburg he made *Miranda* (mus. Auber and Rossini, 1838), *La Gitana* (mus. Schmidt and Aumer, 1838), *L'Ombre* (mus. Maurer, 1839), *L'Écumeur de mer* (mus. Adam, 1840), and *Aglaë, ou L'Élève d'amour* (mus. Keller, 1841). For Stuttgart he made **Danina, or Jocko the Brazilian Ape* (1826). Much of his energy was devoted to furthering his daughter's career. For her debut in Vienna he created *La Réception d'une jeune nymphe à la cour de Terpsichore* (1822) and it was his *La Sylphide* which launched Marie as the foremost Romantic ballerina of her day.

Taglioni, Marie (*b* Stockholm, 23 Apr. 1804; *d* Marseilles, 22 Apr. 1884) Swedish-Italian dancer. One of the greatest names in the history of ballet and the most famous dancer of the Romantic era, she was the first Sylphide. Daughter of Filippo T. and sister of Paul T. She studied with her father in Vienna and Kassel and with Coulon in Paris. She made her debut on 10 June 1822 at the Hoftheater in Vienna, dancing in her father's divertissement *La Réception d'une jeune nymphe à la cour de Terpsichore*. After performing in Munich and Stuttgart, where she created the title role in her father's *Danina* (1826), she made her Paris debut in 1827 dancing a variation inserted into the ballet *Le Sicilien*. She was a star of the Paris Opera for the next ten years, adored by the public and made even more famous by her high-profile rivalry with Fanny *Elssler. In London her fans included the young princess who would become Queen Victoria. The product of her father's aesthetic ideals, she became the most ethereal dancer of the Romantic era, the embodiment of an elusive spirituality and grace. It was she who transformed dancing on pointe from a technical novelty into poetic expression. She was also an outstanding character dancer, admired, for instance, for her gypsy dancing in the title role of *La Gitana*. Among her major creations in Paris were leading roles in Aumer's *La Belle au bois dormant* (1829) and in her father's *La Sylphide* (1832), *Nathalie; ou, La Laitière suisse* (1832), *La Révolte au sérail* (1833), *Brézilia* (1835), and *La Fille du Danube* (1836), along with dancing roles in the operas *Le Dieu et la bayadère* (1830) and *Robert le diable* (1831). In 1832 she married Comte Gilbert de Voisins in London, but they separated three years later. From 1837 to 1842 she was fêted in St Petersburg, as the city's star ballerina, and she danced to great acclaim all over Europe, including her native Stockholm. In St Petersburg she created roles in her father's *Miranda* (1838), *La Gitana* (1838), *L'Ombre* (1839), *L'Écumeur de mer* (1840), *Aglaë, ou L'Élève d'amour* (1841), and *Gerta, Queen of the Elfrides* (1842); in Milan she created the title role in her father's staging of *La Péri* (1843), while at Her Majesty's Theatre in London she created roles in Perrot's *Pas de quatre* and *Le Jugement de Pâris*

(1846). She gave her farewell performance in 1847, retiring to Lake Como, but by 1858 she was back in Paris (forced back to work, said some, by her father's profligate handling of her finances). In 1860 she choreographed her only ballet, *Le Papillon* (mus. Offenbach), in Paris for her protégé, the tragically short-lived Emma *Livry. She was Inspectrice de la Danse at the Paris Opera (1859–70) and initiated the system of examinations at the Opera. In the war of 1870–1 she lost her entire fortune and was forced to make a living by teaching ballroom dancing in London. She died in Marseilles where she had been living with her son since 1880.

Taglioni, Marie, the younger (*b* Berlin, 27 Oct. 1833 (some sources say 1830); *d* Neu-Aigen, nr. Vienna, 27 Aug. 1891 (some sources say 27 Apr. 1891)) German dancer. Daughter of Paul T., granddaughter of Filippo T., and niece of the more famous Marie T., with whom she is sometimes confused. She studied with her father and made her debut in his *Coralia* at Her Majesty's Theatre in London in 1847. Subsequent roles included his *Théa ou La Fée aux fleurs* (1847) and Perrot's *Les Quatre Saisons* (1848). From 1853 to 1856 she danced in Vienna; and she was prima ballerina of the Berlin Court Opera until 1866 when she married Prince Joseph Windisch-Grätz. She created roles in her father's *Flick und Flocks Abenteuer* (1858), *Des Malers Traumbild* (1859), and *Sardanapal* (1865). Johann Strauss wrote the Taglioni-Polka for her.

Taglioni, Paul (*b* Vienna, 12 Jan. 1808 (some sources say 12 Jan. 1800); *d* Berlin, 6 Jan. 1884 (some sources say 1888)) German dancer and ballet master. Son of Filippo T., brother of Marie T., and father of Marie T. the younger. He studied with his father and with Coulon in Paris. He made his debut in Stuttgart in the 1820s, dancing the pas de deux *Zémire et Azor* with his older sister. For several years he was Marie's partner, appearing with her in Vienna, Munich, Paris, and Berlin. In 1829 he married the ballerina Anna Galster in Berlin, where he eventually settled. In 1839 the two of them toured America. He choreographed his first major ballets in Berlin: *Amors Triumph* (mus. H. Schmidt, 1835) and *Der arme Fischer* (mus. H. Schmidt, 1836) but additionally worked as guest choreographer and dancer in Vienna (where he had a long association from 1853 to 1874), Naples (1853–6), and Milan (1861–2). He was ballet master of the Berlin Court Opera (1856–83) and ballet master of Her Majesty's Theatre in London (1847–51, 1856, and 1857). He choreographed about 40 ballets including *Undine, die Wassernymphe* (mus. Schmidt, Berlin, 1836), which was revised as *Coralia* for London in 1847, *Don Quixote* (mus. Gährich, Berlin,

1839), *Théa ou La Fée aux fleurs* (mus. Pugni, London, 1847), *Fiorita et la reine des Elfrides* (mus. Pugni, London, 1848), *Electra* (mus. Pugni, London, 1849, notable for its then revolutionary use of electric lighting), *Les Plaisirs de l'hiver* (mus. Pugni, London, 1849), *Les Métamorphoses* (mus. Pugni, London, 1850), *Santanella* (mus. Hertel, Berlin, 1852); *Flick und Flocks Abenteuer* (mus. Hertel, Berlin, 1858), *La Fille mal gardée* (after Dauberval, new music by Hertel, Berlin, 1864), *Sardanapal* (mus. Hertel, Berlin, 1865), *Fantasca* (mus. Hertel, Berlin, 1869), and *Militaria* (mus. Hertel, Berlin, 1872). His daughter, Marie the younger, starred in most of his ballets until her retirement in 1866.

Taglioni, Salvatore (*b* Palermo, 1789; *d* Naples 1868) Italian dancer, teacher, and choreographer. Brother of Filippo T., father of Luisa T. (1823–93), a ballerina at the Paris Opera, and Fernando T. (1810–74?), a composer. He studied in Paris with Coulon and from about 1806 danced in Lyons and Bordeaux. He then returned to Italy where with Louis Henry he established a ballet school in Naples in 1812, attached to the opera house of Teatro San Carlo. He was ballet master in Naples and had a flourishing company based at the opera house, but he also worked as a choreographer in Milan, Turin, and Florence, often casting himself and his wife, Adélaide Perraud, in his ballets. He is credited with choreographing more than 200 ballets, among them *Romanow* (1832), which used horses on stage, *I promessi sposi* (1836), and *Faust* (1838). Most were based on historical or literary subjects.

T'ai Chi A form of Chinese martial arts which is characterized by the serenity of its inner focus, and the grace and liquidity of its slowly unfolding movement. It has influenced many choreographers, including Glen Tetley, whose *Embrace Tiger and Return to Mountain* (1968) was directly inspired by T'ai Chi.

Tait, Marion (*b* London, 7 Oct. 1950) British dancer and ballet mistress. She studied at the Royal Ballet School, graduating in 1968 into the Royal's touring company. She was promoted to principal in 1974 and remained with the company, then called Sadler's Wells Royal Ballet, later Birmingham Royal Ballet, until she retired from the stage in 1995. She created roles in Christopher Bruce's *Unfamiliar Playground* (1974), J. Carter's *Shukumei* (1975), D. Morse's *Pandora* (1976), Bintley's *Meadow of Proverbs* (1979), *Punch and the Street Party* (1979) and *Night Moves* (1981), MacMillan's *Playground* (1979), and Corder's *Day into Night* (1980). An intensely dramatic dancer, who nonetheless had a flair for comedy, she was outstanding in the MacMillan and Tudor repertories. After retiring from the stage she became ballet mistress of Birmingham Royal Ballet and continued to perform occasional character roles with the company.

Takei, Kei (*b* Tokyo, 30 Dec. 1946) Japanese-US dancer, choreographer, company director, and teacher. She studied at various schools in Japan, then on the recommendation of Anna Sokolow moved to New York to study at the Juilliard School of Music (1967–9) and additionally train with Nikolais, Cunningham, and Trisha Brown. She founded her own company, Moving Earth, in 1969 and with it presented the first part of *Light*, a dance-cycle that subsequently expanded over the next three decades into a work of over 30 sections. Inspired by Japanese butoh and Western contemporary dance, *Light* is considered a single theatrical entity, even though it is far too long to be performed all at once. Moving Earth is now based in both Japan and New York and is run by Kei Takei and her partner and co-choreographer Lazuro Brezer.

(((●))) SEE WEB LINKS

• Website for Moving Earth

Talbot, Joby (*b* London, 25 Aug. 1971) British composer. He trained with Brian Elias and at the Guildhall School of Music and Drama (1994–5) and received his first major commission, from the BBC Philharmonic, for his score *Luminescence* (1997). His scores have been written for film and television as well as for concert hall, and his compositions for dance have included *Chroma* (2006, including music by Jack White) and *Genus* (2007) both for McGregor, and *Eau* (2008) for Carolyn Carlson. Wheeldon's *Fool's Paradise* (2008) uses music from Talbot's film score *Dying Swan*.

(((●))) SEE WEB LINKS

• Official website for Joby Talbot

Tales of Beatrix Potter Originally a 1971 ballet film directed by Reginald Mills with choreography by Ashton, music by Lanchbery, designs by Christine Edzard and masks by R. Doboujinsky. Based on the famous children's stories, its cast of animal characters—Mrs Tiggy-Winkle, Peter Rabbit, Jemima Puddle-Duck, et al—were danced by members of the Royal Ballet, including Ashton, A. Grant, K. Martin, Mead, Last, Coleman, Sleep, Collier, and L. Edwards. In 1992 Ashton's choreography was staged by Anthony Dowell for Covent Garden.

Tales of Hoffmann Ballet in three acts with choreography and libretto by Peter Darrell, music by Offenbach (arr. Lanchbery), and designs by Alistair Livingstone. Premiered 6 Apr. 1972 by Scottish Theatre Ballet at the King's Theatre in Edinburgh, with Cazalet, Aitken, Hilary Debden, Marian St Claire, and E. McDonald. Based on Offenbach's opera, the ballet departs from its source by placing the Antonia act in the middle (between those of Olympia and Giulietta) and making Antonia a would-be ballerina rather than a singer. It was revived for American Ballet Theatre (des. P. Docherty) in 1973, a staging that had one ballerina dancing all three heroines. In 1961 Béjart choreographed a dance production of the opera at the Monnaie Theatre in Brussels. Massine provided the choreography for Powell and Pressburger's 1951 film of the opera.

Tallchief, Maria (orig. Elizabeth Marie Tall Chief; *b* Fairfax, Okla., 24 Jan. 1925) US dancer, teacher, and ballet director. Sister of Marjorie Tallchief. The daughter of a Native American father (a chief of the Osage tribe) and a Scottish-Irish mother. She studied in Los Angeles with Bronislava Nijinska then later at the School of American Ballet, joining Serge Denham's Ballet Russe de Monte Carlo in 1942, where she became a soloist and created roles in Balanchine's *Danses concertantes* (1944), *Le Bourgeois gentilhomme* (1944), and *Night Shadow* (1946). In the summer of 1947 she joined Balanchine as a guest at the Paris Opera Ballet dancing in his *Serenade*, *Apollon musagète*, and *Baiser de la fée*. She then went with him to Ballet Society in New York and went on to become the leading ballerina of New York City Ballet. From 1946 to 1951 she was married to Balanchine, but she was his muse for a much longer period, creating roles in over 25 of his ballets during the next two decades and dancing lead roles in many more. She was one of the first virtuosic American ballerinas, and one of the first to achieve widespread popularity. Her performance in the technically flamboyant title role of Balanchine's *Firebird* made a particular impact and it became her signature piece. The list of her created roles for Balanchine includes *Symphonie concertante* (1947), *Symphony in C* (new staging, 1948), *Orpheus* (1948), *Firebird* (1949), *Bourée fantasque* (1949), *Sylvia Pas de deux* (1950), *Jones Beach* (1950), *Swan Lake* (Odette, 1951 one-act staging), *Caracole* (1952), *Scotch Symphony* (1952), *Nutcracker* (1954), *Pas de dix* (1955), *Allegro brillante* (1956), and *Gounod Symphony* (1958). She also created leading roles in Robbins's *The Guests* (1949) and Bolender's *The Filly* (1953). She additionally guested with American Ballet Theatre (1949, 1960–2), where she danced the Tudor and Cullberg repertoire, Ballet Russe de Monte Carlo (1955), and the Hamburg Ballet (1965), where she created the title role in van Dyk's *Cinderella*; her occasional film appearances included the 1952 Hollywood movie *The Million Dollar Mermaid*. (Her guest performances with Ballet Russe de Monte Carlo reportedly made her the highest paid ballerina in the world).

Tallchief left New York City Ballet in 1966 after which she became artistic director of the Chicago Lyric Opera Ballet from 1975 to 1981, and from 1981 to 1987 was founding artistic director of Chicago City Ballet. After that company folded she was artistic adviser to Chicago Festival Ballet, also a coach for the Balanchine foundation. Her autobiography, *Maria Tallchief: America's Prima Ballerina*, was published in 1997.

Tallchief, Marjorie (*b* Denver, Colo., 19 Oct. 1927) US dancer. Younger sister of Maria Tallchief. She studied with Nijinska and Lichine in Los Angeles and later with Preobrajenska in Paris, making her debut with Ballet Theatre in 1944. She danced with that company for two years then joined de Basil's Original Ballet Russe from 1946 to 1947. Although overshadowed by her more famous sister in America, she achieved great success in Europe. In 1947 she married the dancer and choreographer George *Skibine and with him joined the European-based Grand Ballet du Marquis de Cuevas. Until 1957 she was one of that company's leading ballerinas, excelling in works such as Lifar's *Noir et blanc*, Nijinska's *Les Biches*, and Fokine's *Les Sylphides*. She was initially celebrated for her strength and technical virtuosity although in later years her dancing developed more lyrical qualities. While with the de Cuevas company she created roles in Skibine's *Annabel Lee* and *Le Prisonnier du Caucase* (1951), *L'Ange gris* (1953), *Idylle* (1954), and *Romeo and Juliet* (1955), and in Balanchine's *Pas de trois classique* (1948). From 1957 to 1962 she was premiere danseuse étoile at the Paris Opera, the first American to hold that title, and created roles in Skibine's *Concerto* (1958), *Conte Cruel* (1959), and *Pastorale* (1961). She additionally appeared as a guest ballerina with Ruth Page's Chicago Opera Ballet, first in 1956 then in 1958 when she created the ballerina role in Page's *Camille*. She also danced with the Harkness Ballet (1964–6), where she created a principal role in Bruhn's *Scottish Fantasy* (1965) and the title role in Ailey's *Ariadne* (1965). She was associate director of the Dallas Ballet (1967–81) and director of the ballet school of the Chicago City Ballet (1981–7). She later taught in Florida.

tambourin A lively Provençal dance in 2/4 time accompanied by a tambourine or tabor. It was at its most popular in the 18th century, when J. P. Rameau composed many examples of it.

Taming of the Shrew, The Ballet in two acts with choreography and libretto by Cranko, music by Kurt-Heinz Stolze after Scarlatti, and designs by Elisabeth Dalton. Premiered 16 Mar. 1969, by the Stuttgart Ballet at the Württembergische Staatstheater in Stuttgart, with Haydée, Cragun, Madsen, Neumeier, and Clauss. Its portrait of the warring couple Petruchio and Katherine is closely based on Shakespeare's comedy. It was revived for Bavarian State Opera Ballet (1976), the Royal Ballet (1977), Sadler's Wells Royal Ballet (1980), Joffrey Ballet (1981), Australian Ballet (1986), Rome Opera Ballet (1989), English National Ballet (1991), and National Ballet of Canada (1992). A previous version was choreographed by Béjart (mus. Alwyn–Scarlatti) for the Ballets des Étoiles de Paris in 1954, while Louis Falco staged it as *Kate's Rag* in 1980. Petruchio and Katherine also feature in Bintley's *Shakespeare Suite* (1999).

Tamiris, Helen (orig. Helen Becker; *b* New York, 24 Apr. 1905 (some sources 23 Apr. 1903); *d* New York, 4 Aug. 1966) US dancer, choreographer, company director, and teacher. She studied with I. Lewinson, Fokine, and Galli and performed with the Metropolitan Opera Ballet, as well as in nightclubs and revues. In 1927 she began to re-invent herself as a modern dance soloist, and during the next two years gave recitals in America and Europe, creating and performing 27 different dances. From 1930 onwards she began to choreograph for her own group, her work eloquently addressing social and political issues. Her works include *Walt Whitman Suite* (1934), *Cycle of Unrest* (1935), *Salut au monde* (1936, a study of the struggle for racial equality), and *How Long, Brethren?* (1937). Ironically, this last, which was based on African-American songs of protest, was performed by an all-white company of women. From 1945 to 1957 Tamiris worked on Broadway where she choreographed many musicals, including *Up in Central Park* (1945), *Show Boat* (1946), *Annie, Get Your Gun* (1946), *Touch and Go* (1949) for which she won a Tony Award, *Fanny* (1954), and *Plain and Fancy* (1955). With her husband Daniel *Nagrin she directed the Tamiris-Nagrin Dance Company (1960–3). She also taught stage movement for actors for many years.

Tan, Yuan Yuan (*b* Shanghai, 1976) Chinese dancer. She studied at the Shanghai Ballet School and the John Cranko School in Stuttgart, joining San Francisco Ballet in 1995 and promoted to principal in 1997. A delicately built dancer possessing a steely technical clarity she performs most of the classical repertory but has also created roles in works by Possokhov, Wheeldon, Tomasson, and S. Welch. She additionally guests with Hong Kong Ballet, and is celebrated in China as that country's leading native ballerina.

tango South American dance in slow 2/4 time which is characterized by sensual partnering and fast interlocking footwork, It was based on dances brought to Argentina by African slaves and was originally performed in the slums of Buenos Aires in the 1860s. It was also closely linked to tango music and song. In the 1920s however the tango became popular worldwide as a form of ballroom dancing. In the 1930s and 1940s it was further popularized by Hollywood in such films as *Flying Down to Rio* (1933) and *Down Argentine Way* (1940). It went into decline in the mid-20th century but enjoyed a massive revival in the 1980s. The theatrically staged show *Tango Argentino* opened in Paris in 1983 and subsequently became a major hit on Broadway and in London's West End. Numerous shows followed in its wake, in which the improvised, dance hall idiom of tango gave way to choreographed and often highly stylized performances, with professionally trained dancers and, sometimes, orchestral accompaniment. Several choreographers have used the tango in their ballets, including Ashton in *Façade*, Bolender in *Souvenirs*, Flindt in *Tango Chicane*, van Manen in *5 Tangos*, and Araiz in his full-length *Tango*.

Tankard, Meryl (*b* Darwin, 8 Sept. 1955) Australian dancer, choreographer, and company director. She studied dance at the Australian Ballet School and joined the Australian Ballet in 1974. She danced with the company for three years and also made her first ballet, *Birds Behind Bars* (1977), part of a tribute programme to Dame Peggy van Praagh. In 1977 she joined Pina Bausch's Tanztheater Wuppertal and for the next six years was a leading soloist, featuring in important Bausch creations such as *Le Sacre du printemps* and *Bluebeard*. While in Germany she co-wrote and starred in an experimental film, *Sydney on the Wupper*, which was awarded a gold medal at the Berlin Film Festival in 1983. In 1984 she returned to Australia as a freelance choreographer and performer, while continuing to appear as a guest artist with Bausch's company on its international tours (1984–8). She was director of her own company in Canberra (1989–92) then director (1993–9) of *Australian Dance Theatre, which was renamed the Meryl Tankard Australian Dance Theatre during her directorship. As a choreographer she has been greatly influenced by Bausch's brand of image-based dance theatre. Her works include *Echo Point* (1984), *Travelling Light* (1986), *Two Feet* (1988), *Furioso* (1993), *Songs with Mara* (1993), *Banshee* (1989), *Nuti* (1990), *Aurora* (1994), a post-modern version of *The Sleeping Beauty*, *Possessed* (1995), *Rasa* (1996), and *Inuk* (1997). She also choreographed *Death in Venice* (1989) and *Orphée et Eurydice* (1993) for the Australian Opera; *The Deep End* (a work set in and around a swimming pool, 1997) and *Wild Swans* (mus. Elena Kats-Chernin, 2003) for the Australian Ballet; @*North* (2004) for Berlin

Opera Ballet, and *Inuk2* (2008) for Sydney Dance Company.

((( )))) SEE WEB LINKS

• Official website for Meryl Tankard

tanztheater [Ger., dancetheatre] A form of dance that emphasizes the theatrical staging of the work as much as the choreography and that takes its material from real-life issues and emotions. The leading exponent of tanztheater was Pina *Bausch.

tap dancing An American dance form characterized by rapid foot-tapping movement. The dancer wears shoes with metal cleats (plates) so that when the toe or heel is tapped on the floor it makes a distinctive percussive sound. Tap routines encompass complex rhythmical patterns and syncopated phrasing, and can be performed to a wide variety of musical styles, but most especially jazz. A cultural product of the slave trade, tap dancing was derived from Irish jigs and Lancashire clog dancing but was heavily influenced by the musicality of African tribal dances. Although the fusion of West African and British Isles traditions began in the mid-17th century, tap dancing did not become truly popular as a form of stage entertainment in America until the mid-19th century, first through variety shows (the minstrel shows, in which white men blackened their faces to perform the dance and music of black slaves) and then through early Hollywood musicals. At the turn of the century tap dancing absorbed elements from social dances (like the cakewalk strut or the camel walk), and by the 1920s it had absorbed the new jazz rhythms and found a home on Broadway, where the tap dancing chorus line was born. The term tap dancing came into widespread usage in the early 20th century. Two of its foremost exponents, the Nicholas Brothers, were instrumental in bringing tap to a white audience through their performances at The Cotton Club in New York, and subsequently in Hollywood films and on Broadway in the 1930s and 1940s. In the 1930s Fred Astaire added a new sophistication and elegance to the form with his ballroom-influenced style of tap, showcased in such films as *The Gay Divorcee* (1934) and *Top Hat* (1935). Other famous tap dancers of the mid-20th century included William Henry Lane, Bill ('Bojangles') Robinson, John W. Bubbles, Ruby Keeler, Ginger Rogers, Eleanor Powell, Ray Bolger, Ann Miller, Donald O'Connor, Paul Draper, and Gene Kelly, whose film *Singin' in the Rain* (1951) contains one of the most famous tap dances ever committed to celluloid. By the 1950s jazz and ballet had largely replaced tap on Broadway, although the 1970s and the 1990s both saw a revival of interest in tap dancing through musicals such as *No, No, Nanette* (1971), *Jelly's Last Jam* (1991), and *Bring in 'da Noise, Bring in 'da Funk* (1996), the latter staged by George Wolfe and choreographed by Savion *Glover, who welded the traditions of tap to the heavy bass beat of contemporary African-American music. The brand of rhythm tap favoured by Glover—which focuses on the acoustic detail of the footwork rather than the elegant carriage and arm movements favoured by Astaire—also dominated *Tap Dogs*, the all-male tap show that toured internationally after its 1995 Sydney premiere.

Tap Dogs Australian tap dance show. With choreography by Dein Perry, music by Andrew Wilkie and direction and design by Nigel Triffitt, it was premiered Jan. 1995 at the Sydney Theatre Festival by Dein Perry, Drew Kaluski, and others. Perry's 80-minute production created a new macho image for tap dance, with six male dancers dressed in builders' gear and customized 'Blundstone' boots, performing on a set designed like a construction site. The work has toured internationally and featured in the opening ceremony of the 2000 Sydney Olympics. Perry directed a film *Bootmen* (2000) based on the production, and created variations of the original concept including *Tap Dogs Rebooted* which featured some women dancers.

tarantella An Italian folk dance executed in accelerating 3/8 or 6/8 time. It is usually danced by couples and takes its name from the Italian city of Taranto whose 14th-century inhabitants, according to legend, would cure themselves from the bite of a tarantula spider by dancing vigorously and sweating the spider's poison out of their systems. There have been ballets based on the tarantella, including Coralli's *La Tarentule* (1839) and Milloss's *La Tarantola* (1942), while the third act of *Swan Lake* contains ballet's most famous example of the tarantella. The tarantella was one of Fanny Elssler's most popular show pieces.

Taras, John (*b* New York, 18 Apr. 1919; *d* 2 Apr. 2004) US dancer, choreographer, and ballet master. He began dancing as a child in a Ukrainian folk dance ensemble in New York and took up ballet in 1936 in his late teens. He studied with Fokine, then with Vilzak, Schollar, Anderson-Ivantzova, and at the School of American Ballet before performing with Ballet Caravan (1940), Catherine Littlefield's Philadelphia Ballet (1939–41), and Ballet Theatre (1942–6), where he was soloist, choreographer, and ballet master. He left Ballet Theatre in order to pursue a career as a choreographer and worked with many companies in that capacity, including the Markova-Dolin Ballet in Chicago (1946), de Basil's Original Ballet Russe

(1946), Ballet Society (1947), Metropolitan Ballet (1948), San Francisco Ballet (1948), and Les Ballets des Champs-Elysées (1949). From 1948 to 1953 he was principal choreographer and ballet master with the Grand Ballet du Marquis de Cuevas. From 1959 he was ballet master of New York City Ballet, and his association with the company continued until Balanchine's death in 1983. During this period he additionally worked as ballet master of the Paris Opera (1969–70) and ballet director at the Berlin Opera Ballet (1971–2). Following his departure from New York City Ballet, he became associate director of American Ballet Theatre in 1984. He later staged Balanchine's ballets for companies around the world. A list of his own ballets includes *Graziana* (mus. Mozart, Ballet Theatre, 1945), *Camille* (mus. Schubert, arr. Rieti, Original Ballet Russe, 1946), *The Minotaur* (mus. E. Carter, Ballet Society, 1947), *Designs with Strings* (also *Design for Strings*, mus. Tchaikovsky, Metropolitan Ballet, 1948), *Piège de lumière* (mus. J. M. Damase, de Cuevas, 1952), *Le Fôret romantique* (mus. Glazunov, Monte Carlo Opera, 1957), *Ebony Concerto* (mus. Stravinsky, New York City Ballet, 1960), *Arcade* (mus. Stravinsky, New York City Ballet, 1963), *Jeux* (mus. Debussy, New York City Ballet, 1966), *Concerto for Piano and Winds* (mus. Stravinsky, New York City Ballet, 1972), *Le Sacre du printemps* (mus. Stravinsky, La Scala, Milan, 1972 or 1973), *Daphnis and Chloe* (mus. Ravel, New York City Ballet, 1975), *Souvenir de Florence* (mus. Tchaikovsky, New York City Ballet, 1981), *Firebird* (mus. Stravinsky, Dance Theatre of Harlem, 1982), *Francesca da Rimini* (mus. Tchaikovsky, American Ballet Theatre, Miami, 1986), and *Trio* (mus. Tchaikovsky, Pittsburgh Ballet, 1991).

Taras Bulba Ballet in three acts with choreography by Lopukhov, libretto by Semyon Kaplan, music by Soloviev-Sedoy, and designs by Vadim Rindin. Premiered 12 Dec. 1940 by the Kirov Ballet at the Kirov (Mariinsky) Theatre in Leningrad, with Dudinskaya and Chabukiani. Based on Gogol's short story, the ballet tells of the struggle for freedom by the 16th-century Cossack general Taras and the Ukrainians against Polish aggressors. Andriy, the general's second son, falls in love with a Polish girl, Pannochka, and joins the enemy. Taras is then forced to kill him and watch in horror as his other son, Ostap, is executed. Subsequent versions were staged by Zakharov at the Bolshoi Ballet (1941) and Fenster at the Kirov (1955).

Tarentule, La Ballet in two acts with choreography by Coralli, libretto by Scribe, music by Casimir Gide, sets by Séchan, Diéterle, Feuchères, and Despléchin, and costumes by Lormier. Premiered 24 Jun. 1839 at the Paris Opera, with Elssler and Mazilier. In the ballet, Luigi is bitten by a tarantula and can be healed by Dr Omeopatica only if he agrees to hand over his lover Lauretta to the lecherous doctor. Lauretta agrees to this, but in secret plots against the doctor. In the end the lovers are reunited and Dr Omeopatica is returned to his wife. It was one of the few comic ballets produced at the Paris Opera during the Romantic period and it helped to popularize the tarantella.

Taylor, Paul (*b* Edgewood, Pa., 29 Jul. 1930) US dancer, choreographer, and company director. Having trained extensively as a swimmer, he took up dance while at Syracuse University (where he was studying art). In 1952 he moved to New York and studied modern dance with Graham, Humphrey, Limón, and Cunningham, and ballet with Tudor and Craske. He performed with Cunningham (1954), Lang (1955) and with the Martha Graham Dance Company (1955–62). Here he created the role of Aegisthus in *Clytemnestra* (1958), the Stranger in *Embattled Garden* (1958), a leading role in *Alcestis* (1960), *Acrobats of God* (1960), and a role in *Episodes* (1959), the joint Graham–Balanchine work in which Balanchine choreographed a solo for Taylor. He founded his own company in 1954, only a year after making his first piece. He collaborated with the painter Robert Rauschenberg and, like him, worked as a window dresser at Tiffany's, the New York jewellers, in order to finance his early works. Their first collaboration was *Jack and the Beanstalk* (1954); Rauschenberg then designed all of Taylor's works in the 1950s, including *Three Epitaphs* (1956) and *Seven New Dances* (1957). With his company he travelled the world and consolidated his position as one of the most eclectic and popular masters of American modern dance, his works encompassing a range of influences, from dance, theatre, and the wider culture; his expansive, athletic style of movement proving unusually accessible. Some of Taylor's early work belied his later appeal: *Duet* (1957), premiered in the *Seven New Dances* evening, featured him and his pianist performing neither music nor movement for the duration of the piece (which was set to John Cage's 'non-score'). The critic Louis Horst responded by leaving his review space in *Dance Observer* a blank. Later works however combined Taylor's experimental approach with a sure populist touch. In *Esplanade* (1975) he used a movement vocabulary that consisted of little more than walking, running, jumping, and falling, but still created an effect of infectious, exuberant power. In *The Rehearsal* (1980) he reworked Nijinsky's *The Rite of Spring*, into a tale of gangsters and kidnapping. In *Company B* (1991) Taylor explored the power of nostalgia and popular music, using

songs by the Andrews Sisters to evoke the era of the Second World War.

Taylor's choreography divides roughly into three styles, the lyrical, the comic, and the darkly psychological. Several of his more buoyant and fluidly phrased works have been taken into the repertoires of classical companies, including the Royal Danish Ballet, American Ballet Theatre, Joffrey Ballet, Paris Opera Ballet, Les Grands Ballets Canadiens, and San Francisco Ballet. *Aureole*, *Airs*, and *Arden Court* have proved among the most internationally popular. Taylor retired from dancing in 1974 but continued to choreograph for his company. (The commissions he accepted from other companies were also created for, and with, his own dancers.)

A list of his works includes *3 Epitaphs* (mus. Laneville-Johnson Union Brass Band, 1956), *Seven New Dances* (mus. Cage and various sounds, 1957), *Images and Reflections* (mus. Feldman, 1958), *Meridian* (mus. Boulez, later Feldman, 1960), *Fibers* (mus. Schoenberg, 1960), *Insects and Heroes* (mus. John Herbert McDowell, 1961), *Junction* (mus. Bach, 1961), *Tracer* (mus. James Tenny, 1962), *Piece Period* (mus. various, 1962), *Aureole* (mus. Handel, 1962), *Poetry in Motion* (mus. L. Mozart, 1963), *Scudorama* (mus. Clarence Jackson, 1963), *Party Mix* (mus. Haieff, 1963), *Duet* (mus. Haydn, 1964), *Post Meridian* (mus. E. Lohoeffer de Boeck, 1965), *From Sea to Shining Sea* (mus. McDowell, 1965), *Orbs* (mus. Beethoven, 1966), *Agathe's Tale* (mus. Surinach, 1967), *Lento* (mus. Haydn, 1967), *Public Domain* (mus. collage McDowell, 1968), *Churchyard* (mus. Cosmos Savage, 1969), *Private Domain* (mus. Xenakis, 1969), *Foreign Exchange* (mus. Morton Subotnick, 1970), *Big Bertha* (mus. Band Machines from the St Louis Melody Museum, 1970), *The Book of Beasts* (mus. various, 1971), *Guests of May* (mus. Debussy, 1972), *American Genesis* (mus. vars., 1973), *Sports and Follies* (mus. Satie, 1974), *Esplanade* (mus. Bach, 1975), *Runes* (mus. Gerald Busby, 1975), *Cloven Kingdom* (mus. Corelli, Cowell, 1976), *Polaris* (mus. Donald York, 1976), *Images* (mus. Debussy, 1977), *Dust* (mus. Poulenc, 1977), *Aphrodisiamania* (mus. various, 1977), *Airs* (mus. Handel, 1978), *Diggity* (mus. D. York, 1978), *Nightshade* (mus. Scriabin, 1979), *The Rehearsal* (mus. Stravinsky's *Rite of Spring*, 1980), *Arden Court* (mus. William Boyce, 1981), *House of Cards* (mus. Milhaud, 1981), *Lost, Found and Lost* (mus. 'wallpaper' muzak, 1982), *Mercuric Tidings* (mus. Schubert, 1982), *Musette* (mus. Handel, 1983), *Sunset* (mus. Elgar, 1983), *Byzantium* (mus. Varèse, 1984), *Last Look* (mus. York, 1985), *Musical Offering* (mus. Bach, 1986), *Kith and Kin* (mus. Mozart, 1987), *Syzygy* (mus. York, 1987), *Brandenburgs* (mus. Bach, 1988), *Counterswarm* (mus. Ligeti, 1988), *Danbury Mix* (mus. Ives, 1988), *Speaking in Tongues* (mus. Matthew Patton, 1988), *Minikin Fair* (mus. various, 1989), *The Sorcerer's Sofa* (mus. Dukas, 1990), *Of Bright and Blue Birds and the Gala Sun* (mus. Donald York, 1990), *Fact and Fancy* (mus. New Orleans jazz and reggae, 1991), *Company B* (mus. The Andrews Sisters, 1991), *Oz* (mus. Wayne Horvitz, 1992), *Spindrift* (mus. Schoenberg, 1993), *Field of Grass* (mus. Harry Nilsson, 1993), *Funny Papers* (1994), *Moonbine* (mus. Debussy, 1994), *Offenbach Overtures* (1995), *Prime Numbers* (mus. David Israel, 1996), *Eventide* (mus. Ralph Vaughan Williams, 1996), *Piazzolla Caldera* (mus. Astor Piazzolla, 1997), *The Word* (mus. David Israel, 1998), *Oh, You Kid!* (mus. ragtime, 1999), *Cascade* (mus. Bach, 1999), *Black Tuesday* (2001), *Promethean Fire* (mus. Bach, 2002), *Banquet of Vultures* (mus. Morton Feldman, 2005), and *Lines of Loss* (mus. several, 2007). Emmy Award (for television production of *Speaking in Tongues*), 1991. Subject of the 1999 film documentary *Dancemaker*. Kennedy Center Award, Washington, DC, 1992. Author of autobiography *Private Domain* (New York, 1987).

(((⊕))) SEE WEB LINKS

• Website for Paul Taylor company

Tchaikovsky, Pyotr (*b* Votkinsk, 7 May 1840; *d* St Petersburg, 6 Nov. 1893) Russian composer. The most significant ballet composer of the 19th century, he wrote the music for *Swan Lake* (staged Moscow 1877, restaged St Petersburg 1895), *The Sleeping Beauty* (St Petersburg 1890), and *The Nutcracker* (St Petersburg, 1892). The emotional depth and compositional sophistication of these scores raised the standard of ballet music and they remain among the best known and loved of all ballet music. His concert music has also been extensively used and among the major works choreographed to Tchaikovsky scores are *Autumn Song* (Nijinska, 1915), *Eros*, *Francesca da Rimini*, *Prelude*, *Romance* (all Fokine, 1915), *Andantino* (Fokine, 1916), *The Seasons* (Lavrovsky, 1928), *Mozartiana* (Balanchine, 1933), *Les Présages* (Massine, 1933), *Serenade* (Balanchine, 1934), *Kittens* (Jacobson, 1936), *Romeo and Juliet* (Bartholin, 1937), *Francesca da Rimini* (Lichine, 1937, Lifar, 1958), *Meditations* (Jacobson, 1938), *Romeo and Juliet* (W. Christensen, 1938, also Lifar, 1942, Jacobson, 1944, Skibine, 1950), *Ballet Imperial* (Balanchine, 1941), *Aleko* (Massine, 1942), *Hamlet* (Helpmann, 1942), *Ancient Russia* (Nijinska, 1943), *Tchaikovsky Waltz* (Taras, 1946), *Theme and Variations* (Balanchine, 1947), *Designs with Strings* (Taras, 1948), *Waltz* (Jacobson, 1948), *Tragédie à Verone* (Skibine, 1950), *Les Oiseaux d'or* (Lichine, 1954), *Eugene Onegin* (V. Gsovsky, 1954), *Allegro Brillante* (Balanchine, 1956), *L'Amour et son destin* (Lifar, 1957), *Beauty and the Beast* (L. Christensen,

1958), *Pas de deux* (Balanchine, 1960), *La Dame de pique* (Lifar, 1960, also Petit, 1978), *Snow Maiden* (Bourmeister, 1961), *Mirror Walkers* (P. Wright, 1963), *Onegin* (Cranko, 1965), *Jewels* (Balanchine, 1967, 'Diamonds' section), *Ni fleurs ni couronnes* (Béjart, 1968), *Suite No. 3* (Balanchine, 1970), *Anastasia* (MacMillan, 1971), *Nijinsky, clown de Dieu* (Béjart, 1971), *Reflections* (Arpino, 1971), *War and Peace* (Panov, 1980), *Souvenir de Florence* (Taras, 1981), *Capriccio italien* (Martins, 1981), *Symphony No. 1* (Martins, 1981), *Andantino* (Robbins, 1981), *Piano Pieces* (Robbins, 1981), *The Tempest* (Nureyev, 1982), *Family Portraits* (Cullberg, 1985), *Le Chat botté* (Petit, 1985), *Battleship Potemkin* (Vinogradov, 1986), and *Winter Dreams* (MacMillan, 1991).

Tchelitchev, Pavel (*b* Moscow, 21 Sept. 1898; *d* Rome (or Frascati), Italy, 31 Jul. 1957) Russian-US painter and designer. He worked as a stage designer in Paris, New York, London, and Monte Carlo from 1923 and settled in America in 1934. Ballets he designed include *Ode* (Massine, Ballets Russes de Diaghilev, 1928), *L'Errante* (Balanchine, Les Ballets 1933, Paris), *Orpheus and Eurydice* (Balanchine, Metropolitan Opera House, 1936), *Nobilissima visione* (Massine, Ballet Russe de Monte Carlo, London, 1938), *Balustrade* (Balanchine, Original Ballet Russe, New York, 1941), and *Apollon musagète* (Balanchine, new production Teatro Colón, Buenos Aires, 1942). With *Ode*, he became the first designer to use film projections in a ballet.

Tcherepnin, Nicolai (*b* St Petersburg, 15 May 1873; *d* Issy-les-Moulineaux, 26 Jun. 1945) Russian composer. He was conductor of the Ballets Russes de Diaghilev from 1909 to 1914 and wrote the music for several ballets, including Fokine's *Le Pavillon d'Armide* (St Petersburg, 1907), *Cléopâtre* (Diaghilev, 1909), and *Narcisse* (Diaghilev, 1912). For Pavlova he wrote *Dionysus* (1922), *Russian Fairy Tale* (1923), and *The Romance of a Mummy* (1924), while Mordkin used his music for his ballet *The Goldfish* (1937). He was the father of Alexander Tcherepnin (*b* 1899; *d* 1977), who wrote the music for Petit's *Déjeuner sur l'herbe* (1945), Lifar's *Chota Roustaveli* (1946), and Charrat's *La Femme et son ombre* (1948).

Tcherina, Ludmila (orig. Monika (Monique) Tchemerzina; *b* Paris, 10 Oct. 1924; *d* Paris, 21 Mar. 2004) French dancer, actor, and painter. She studied with Blanche d'Alessandri, Preobrajenska, and Clustine making her debut at the Opéra de Marseilles at the age of 16 and then dancing with the Ballets de Monte Carlo, where she was spotted by Lifar. He invited her to Paris where she created the role of Juliet in his *Romeo and Juliet* at the Salle Pleyel in 1942. She was a principal dancer with the Ballets des Champs-Elysées (1945) and performed in dance concerts in Paris with her husband Edmond Audran (who was killed in a car accident in 1951). She additionally danced with the Ballets de Paris and the Nouveaux Ballets de Monte Carlo (directed by Lifar). Among the other ballets in which she created roles were Lifar's *Mephisto Waltz* (1945) and *Le Martyre de Saint-Sébastien* (title role, 1957) and Béjart's *Gala* (Venice, 1961). She appeared frequently as a guest ballerina, at the Paris Opera, the Bolshoi, and the Kirov in Russia, and the Metropolitan Opera in New York, where she was principal dancer in Joseph Lazzini's production of *The Miraculous Mandarin* (1967), later filmed and televised. She briefly directed her own company between 1958 and 1959, which performed at the Théâtre Sarah Bernhardt. She also acted in several films including *Les Rendezvous*, *The Red Shoes* (1948), and *Tales of Hoffmann* (1951), for which she won an Academy Award in 1952. As a painter she exhibited in Paris. She also wrote two novels about dance: *L'Amour au miroir* (1983) and *La Femme à l'envers* (1986).

Tcherkassky, Marianna (*b* Glen Cove, NY, 28 Oct. 1952) US dancer. She studied at the Washington School of Ballet and at the School of American Ballet from 1967, making her debut with the André Eglevsky Ballet in 1968 before joining American Ballet Theatre in 1970. An exceptionally lyrical dancer she was promoted to principal in 1976 and created roles in many ballets including Tudor's *The Leaves are Fading* (1975), Tharp's *Push Comes to Shove* (1976), Baryshnikov's *The Nutcracker* (Clara, 1976), Choo-San Goh's *Configurations* (1981), and Bujones's *Grand pas romantique* (1985). She was also acclaimed for her performances in the 19th-century repertoire. In 1997, following her retirement from ABT, she became ballet mistress at Pittsburgh Ballet Theater where her husband Terry *Orr was artistic director.

Tchernicheva, Lubov (*b* St Petersburg, 17 Sept. 1890; *d* Richmond, Surrey, 1 Mar. 1976) Russian-British dancer, teacher and ballet mistress. She studied at the Imperial Theatre School in St Petersburg with Fokine; later with Cecchetti. Upon graduation in 1908, she joined the Mariinsky Theatre where she married the ballet regisseur Grigoriev in 1909. Together they went to the Diaghilev company in 1911. She became a principal dancer with Diaghilev and stayed with the company until it folded in 1929, one of its finest character dancers. She created roles in many ballets, among them Massine's *The Good-Humoured Ladies* (1917), *La Boutique fantasque* (1919), *Pulcinella* (1920), *Zéphire et Flore* (1925), and *Le Pas d'acier* (1927), Nijinska's *Les Noces* (1923) and *Les Fâcheux* (1924), and Balanchine's *Jack-in-the-Box*

(1926), *The Triumph of Neptune* (1926), *Apollon musagète* (Calliope, 1928), and *The Gods Go a-Begging* (1928). She also danced the Fokine repertory including the roles of Zobeide, Thamar, and Cleopatra. In 1926 she was appointed ballet mistress to the Diaghilev company. In 1932 she and her husband joined de Basil's Ballets Russes de Monte Carlo, where she worked as ballet mistress, remaining with the company (later the Original Ballet Russe) until de Basil's enterprise finally folded in 1952. She came out of retirement to create the title role in Lichine's *Francesca da Rimini* (1937). In 1952 she settled in England. Thereafter she and her husband staged productions of the Diaghilev repertoire, including *Firebird* for Sadler's Wells Ballet in 1954 and *Petrushka* for the Royal Ballet in 1957. She worked as a teacher for both Sadler's Wells Ballet and London Festival Ballet. She made her last stage appearance in 1957 as Juliet's mother in Cranko's *Romeo and Juliet*.

television In Britain dance was first broadcast on television in 1936 when the BBC presented a programme of nine pieces danced by members of Ballet *Rambert. Later that year de Valois's *Job* was televised. Tudor's *Fugue for Four Cameras*, created as a solo for Maude Lloyd in 1937, was one of the earliest examples of dance made especially for television. After the Second World War the BBC continued to televise dance; in 1952 a full-length *Sleeping Beauty* directed by Mary Skeaping was broadcast. In 1957 the producer Margaret *Dale (herself a former dancer with Sadler's Wells Ballet) televised a series of classical ballets that had been condensed and specially adapted for the camera. These were performed in the television studio but in the late 1960s technical developments made it possible to relay live stage performances on television, a significant example being the Bolshoi Ballet's *Romeo and Juliet*, that was filmed for international television to celebrate the company's 200th anniversary. In other parts of Europe there was particular interest in the creation or adaptation of ballets especially for television. In Sweden Birgit Cullberg was very active in this area. She created a revised version of *Miss Julie* to suit the camera, and with the introduction of colour television, choreographed *Red Wine in Green Glasses* (1971), a pas de deux in which the performers danced inside the paintings of Watteau, Fragonard, and Bruegel. In Denmark, Flemming Flindt also choreographed many television ballets, including *The *Lesson* (1963), *The Young Man Must Marry* (1968), and *Felix Luna* (1973).

In Canada, the animator Norman McLaren played a pioneering role in creating new televisual possibilities for choreography, his 1967 film *Pas de Deux* using an optical printer to duplicate the dancers and create a stroboscopic effect. In the US commercial television began transmitting dance programmes in the 1940s, showcasing the work of Erick Hawkins, Eugene Loring, Agnes de Mille, and Ruth Page among others. By 1946 Pauline Koner and Kitty Doner were presenting a weekly programme that experimented with choreography made for television. In 1949 the CBS series *Through the Crystal Ball* offered an original ballet choreographed for television every week; it included Balanchine's *Cinderella*, Helen Tamiris's *Ali Baba*, and Todd Bolender's *The Wild West*. In 1950 American Ballet Theatre's *Giselle* was televised (starring Nora Kaye and Igor Youskevitch); in 1955 NBC presented the Royal Ballet dancing *The Sleeping Beauty*, which was watched by 30 million Americans, and in 1957 the Royal Ballet were again filmed, dancing Ashton's *Cinderella*. Less successful was the 1962 CBS broadcast of Stravinsky and Balanchine's *The Flood*, which suffered from technical problems. In the mid-1960s *USA: Dance* offered videotaped dance performances of works by Anna Sokolow and Balanchine but it was not until the 1976 launch of *Dance in America* on PBS, that a truly first-class showcase existed on television for America's leading dance companies. Important stage productions were brought to a mass audience in the 1970s and 1980s, and important choreographers such as Robbins, Graham, Taylor, and Balanchine were featured. Series such as *Live from Lincoln Center* and *In Performance at Wolf Trap* telecast live events into American living rooms. *Alive from Off Center*, from KTCA in Minneapolis, highlighted experimental dance on video.

In America as in Europe this led to a new wave of television dance in which choreographers exploited the increasingly wide-ranging technological possibilities of the medium. Cunningham led the field in this—his *Points in Space* (dir. F. Caplan, 1986) was specifically choreographed to exploit the multiple points of view afforded by different cameras. The work was later adapted for the stage.

The 1980 and 1990s were a golden era for dance on television. In Britain, BBC2's *Dance for the Camera* series and Channel 4 were prime outlets for new dance on television. European channels like Arte (based in France and Germany) were also major showcases for television dance. Highlights from this period included Cunningham's *Channels/Inserts* (dir. Charles Atlas, 1982), Tharp's *Catherine Wheel* (stage version, 1981, television version, 1983), and DV8's *Strange Fish* (stage version 1992, television version dir. D. Hinton, 1993). The amount of work being made or adapted for the camera became so significant that television dance was established as a distinct genre with its own awards, e.g. IMZ Dance Screen. In the 21st century the experimental momentum has slowed, partly due to commercial constraints on broadcasters, but partly due to the fact that a new generation of choreographers have switched their focus away from television to the internet and to various forms of interactive technology.
See also under FILM.

Tempest, The Ballet in two parts with choreography by Tetley, music by Arne Nordheim, and designs by Baylis. Premiered 3 May 1979 by Ballet Rambert at Schwetzingen, with Christopher Bruce, L. Burge, Gianfranco Paluzi, Thomas Yang, and Mark Wraith. Based on Shakespeare's play, the ballet is, according to Tetley, 'about voyage and loss, and regaining that which is lost'. It was revived for the Norwegian Ballet in 1980. Other *Tempest* ballets include Nureyev's (London 1982). *See also* SHAKESPEARE.

tendu In classical ballet, a movement which is stretched or held.

Tennant, Veronica (*b* London, 15 Jan. 1947) British-born Canadian dancer. She studied at the Cone-Ripman School in London (1952–5) and at the National Ballet School of Canada (with Betty Oliphant, from 1956), joining the National Ballet of Canada in 1965 where she was immediately given the rank of principal as well as the role of Juliet in Cranko's *Romeo and Juliet*. While lacking an ideal classical physique, Tennant possessed an exceptional dramatic quality and she was rapidly established as the company's lead ballerina, making her debuts as Kitri, Odette-Odile, and Cinderella between 1965 and 1969. She was also the National's first internationally ranked ballerina, touring extensively with the company and leading it during the company's London debut (1972) and its Metropolitan Opera debut (1973). Her partners included Nureyev and Dowell, and she was the first ballerina to partner Baryshnikov following his defection in Toronto in 1974, dancing in a CBC-TV production of Bruhn's *La Sylphide*. She additionally guested with companies throughout North America and made numerous appearances on Canadian television, including in *Romeo and Juliet* (1965), the Emmy Award-winning *Cinderella* (CBC, 1967), and the Emmy Award-winning *Sleeping Beauty* (CBC/PBS 1972). During her 25 years with the National she danced all the major ballerina repertory and created roles in Petit's *Kraanerg* (1969), Kudelka's *Apples* (1974), *The Party* (1976), *Washington Square* (1978), *All Night Wonder* (1981), and *Hedda* (1982), Swanilda in Bruhn's new staging of *Coppélia* (1975), in Vesak's *Whispers and Darkness* (1975), Ditchburn's *Mad Shadows* (1979), Macdonald's *Newcomers* (1980), Patsalas's *Paranda Criolla* (1980), *Liebestod* (1982), and *Canciones*

(1983), Nebrada's *Portrait of Love and Death* (1982), David Allan's *Etc!* (1985), *Villanella* (1986), *Capriccio* (1986), *Masada* (1987), and *Botticelli Pictures* (1988). Two documentaries were made about her: *Veronica Tennant: A Dancer of Distinction* (CBC, 1983) and *Veronica: Completing the Circle* (CBC, 1989). She retired from the stage in 1989; her farewell performance was as Juliet, the role which had brought her to stardom 24 years earlier. Following her retirement, she pursued a career as an actress, television presenter, producer, and director. Officer of the Order of Canada 1975.

Terabust, Elisabetta (*b* Varese, 5 Aug. 1946) Italian dancer and company director. She studied at the Rome Opera Ballet School and joined the Rome Opera Ballet in 1964. She became a principal in 1966, having danced her first Giselle in 1965, and remained with the company until 1974, creating roles in Milloss's *Jeux* (1967) and *La pazzia senile* (1969). From 1974 to 1977 she was a principal with Ballet National de Marseilles, where she created the role of Marie in Petit's new *Nutcracker* (1976) as well as performing in revivals of his *Carmen* and *Notre-Dame de Paris*. In 1973 she embarked on a long association with London Festival Ballet, dancing with the company as both permanent member and guest artist. While there she created roles in Hynd's *La Chatte* (1978), Moreland's *Fantaisie* (1978), and Tetley's *Pulcinella* (1984) and danced the title role in Peter Schaufuss's revival of *La Sylphide* (1978). She additionally appeared as a guest artist with La Scala, Milan, the National Ballet of Canada, and Aterballetto. For this last she created roles in MacMillan's *Verdi Variations* (1982) and Amodio's *Afternoon of a Faun* (1983). From 1990 she was artistic director of the Rome Opera Ballet and it was there in 1992 that she created the role of Elisabeth, Empress of Austria, in Petit's *La Valse triste*. In 1993 she was appointed artistic director of La Scala Ballet, remaining in that post until 1996 and then returning to it from 2007 to 2008. She also appeared frequently on television in Italy and featured in the 1983 BBC programme *Dancer*.

Ter-Arutunian, Rouben (*b* Tbilisi, Georgia, 24 Jul. 1920; *d* New York, 17 Oct. 1992) Armenian-US stage designer. He studied in Berlin, Vienna, and Paris before emigrating to the US in 1951. He designed many ballets for Balanchine, among them *The Seven Deadly Sins* (1958 staging), *Ballet Imperial* (1964 staging), *Nutcracker* (1964), *Harlequinade* (1965), *Coppélia* (1974), *Union Jack* (1976), *Vienna Waltzes* (1977), and *Davidsbündlertänze* (1980). He also worked frequently with Tetley, designing his *Pierrot lunaire* (1962), *Sargasso* (1964), *Field Mass* (1965), *Ricercare* (1966), *Chronochromie* (1971 Hamburg staging), *Laborintus*

(1972), and *Voluntaries* (1973). He also designed Graham's *Visionary Recital* (1961), Macdonald's *Time Out of Mind* (1963), and Butler's *Villon* (1969). In all, he designed more than three dozen ballets. Other choreographers he worked with included Robbins, Taras, Ailey, Feld, and Arpino.

Terpsichore One of the nine Muses of Greek mythology, she later came to be associated with lyric poetry and dance. Terpsichore, the daughter of Zeus and Mnemosyne, is symbolized by the lyre. Her most famous appearance in ballet is in Balanchine's *Apollo*.

terre à terre In ballet, a movement in which the feet barely leave the ground. It is also sometimes used to describe a dancer who lacks elevation and has a more earthbound quality to his or her dancing.

Terry, Walter (*b* New York, 14 May 1913; *d* New York, 4 Oct. 1982) US dance critic and writer. He studied dance at the University of N. Carolina, and additionally with Markova, Dolin, Vilzak, Joffrey, Shawn, Graham, Humphrey, and Limón, becoming one of the first American critics to write with authority on both modern and classical dance. He was dance critic of the *Boston Herald* (1936–9), *New York Herald Tribune* (1939–42 and 1945–66), and *Saturday Review* (1967–82), lectured widely and was also artistic director of Jacob's Pillow Festival 1973. He wrote 22 books on dance, including *Star Performance* (1954), *Ballet* (1958), *The Dance in America* (1968), *The Ballet Companion* (1968), *Isadora Duncan: Her Life, Her Art, Her Legacy* (1963), *Miss Ruth—The More Living Life of Ruth St Denis* (1969), *Ted Shawn—Father of American Dance* (1976), *I Was There* (1978), *Great Male Dancers of the Ballet* (1978), and *The King's Balletmaster* (1980). He also lectured on dance. Knight of the Order of Dannebrog (1976).

Teshigawara, Saburo (*b* Tokyo, 15 Sept. 1953) Japanese modern dancer, choreographer, and director. He studied sculpture before beginning ballet training with Saiga Toshiko. From 1981 he gave solo recitals and from 1985 he worked with his own group, Company KARAS. Its first production, *The Pale Boy*, was performed as part of the Tokyo Scene Dance Series of 1986 and the same year he came to international attention when *The Point of the Wind* won the silver prize at the *Bagnolet choreography competition. His works (designed by himself) often resemble art installations in their striking and symbolic use of props. *Bones in Pages* (1991, new version 2003) featured a set made of 1,000 books, 1,000 shoes, and sections of furniture stuck into Perspex screens. In contrast to their meticulous staging the choreography in these works often veers

manically between extremes of energy and stillness. A list of Teshigawara's works for his own
company includes *The Arm of the Blue Sky*
(1987), *The Moon is Quicksilver* (1987), *A Thought
in the Night* (1988), *Dah-Dah-Sko-Dah-Dah*
(1991), *Noiject* (1992), accompanied by a sound
score of shockingly high volume, *I Was Real-
Documents* (1996), *Petrouchka* (1997), *Triad*
(1999), *Luminous* (2001), *Green* (2003), and
Glass Tooth (2006). He has additionally made
work for several other companies including
Frankfurt Ballet (*White Clouds under the Heels,
Part 1*, 1994, and *Part 2*, 1995), Geneva Ballet
(*Para-dice*, 2002), and Paris Opera (*Air* 2003). In
addition to his stage work he has also created
art installations and directed films including
Keshioko (1993). His book *Hone to Kuki* (*Bones
and Air*) was published in 1994.

(((•))) SEE WEB LINKS
• Website for KARAS

Tetley, Glen (*b* Cleveland, 3 Feb. 1926; *d* Palm
Beach, 26 Jan. 2007) US dancer, choreographer,
and director. He began his dance training while a
medical student at New York University (1946–8)
studying part time with Holm, Graham, Craske,
Tudor, and at the School of American Ballet. He
performed as an apprentice dancer with Holm's
company between 1946 and 1951, also appearing
in Holm's Broadway production of *Kiss Me, Kate*
in 1948. He then danced with New York City
Opera (1952–4) and John Butler's company
(1953–5), performing in the premiere of Gian-
Carlo Menotti's *Amahl and the Night Visitors*
(NBC Television, 1951), which was choreographed by Butler. Between 1956 and 1957 he
was with the newly formed Joffrey Ballet, then
spent two years dancing with Martha Graham
creating the role of the Stranger in *Embattled
Garden* and Apollo in *Clytemnestra* (both 1958).
He returned to Broadway to dance in Holm's *Juno*
(1959) then joined American Ballet Theatre
(1960–1), and Robbins's *Ballets: USA* (1961). Having fallen out with Robbins he created his own
company, in 1962.

Tetley had begun choreographing in the 1940s
but it was with his own company that he established his reputation and his distinctive style—a
then revolutionary fusion of classical and modern
idioms. His breakthrough work was **Pierrot
Lunaire* (mus. Schoenberg, 1962, which featured
himself in the title role). The success of this work
led to an invitation from Nederlands Dans Theater in 1964 to work with the company as dancer
and choreographer, and eventually as co-director
(with van Manen, 1969–71). In 1967 he also
formed an association with Ballet Rambert, becoming central to that company's transition from
ballet company to modern dance troupe and

creating among other works the T'ai Chi-inspired
Embrace Tiger and Return to Mountain (1968).
During the late 1960s and early 1970s Tetley was
considered a revolutionary, bringing the music of
Berio and Stockhausen and the language of modern dance into the repertories of companies like
The Royal Ballet. From the mid-1970s, however,
his work became more lyrical and more classical
in its focus. In 1974 he took over the artistic direction of the Stuttgart Ballet, where he remained for
two years, adding ten of his works to the repertoire. From 1987 to 1989 he was artistic associate
of the National Ballet of Canada.

Tetley was a prolific choreographer, his works
entering the repertories of numerous companies,
both classical and modern. A list of his creations
includes *Mountain Way Chant* (mus. Chavez,
Alvin Ailey American Dance Theater, 1959), *Pierrot lunaire* (mus. Schoenberg, Glen Tetley company, 1962), *The Anatomy Lesson* (mus. M.
Landowski, Nederlands Dans Theater (NDT),
1964), *Sargasso* (mus. Krenek, NDT, 1964), *Field
Mass* (mus. Martinů, NDT, 1965), *Mythical Hunters* (mus. O. Partos-Hezionot, Batsheva Dance
Company, 1965), *Ricercare* (mus. M. Seter, American Ballet Theatre, 1966), *Chronochromie* (mus.
Messiaen, Glen Tetley company, 1966), *Psalms*
(mus. Partos-Tehilim, Batsheva Dance Company,
1966), *Freefall* (mus. M. Schubel, University of
Utah Repertory Dance Theatre, 1967), *The Seven
Deadly Sins* (mus. Weill, Glen Tetley company,
1967), *Ziggurat* (mus. Stockhausen, Ballet Ram-
bert, 1967), *Circles* (mus. Berio, NDT, 1968), *Em-
brace Tiger and Return to Mountain* (mus.
Subotnick, Ballet Rambert, 1968), *Arena* (mus.
Subotnick, NDT, 1969), *Field Figures* (mus. Stock-
hausen, Royal Ballet, 1970), *Imaginary Film* (mus.
Schoenberg, NDT, 1970), *Mutations* (with van
Manen, mus. Stockhausen, NDT, 1970), *Rag
Dances* (mus. A. Hymas, Ballet Rambert, 1971),
Threshold (mus. Berg, Hamburg State Opera,
1972), *Laborintus* (mus. Berio, Royal Ballet,
1972), *Small Parades* (mus. Varèse, NDT, 1972),
Gemini (mus. Henze, Australian Ballet, 1973), *Vo-
luntaries* (mus. Poulenc, Stuttgart Ballet, 1973), *Le
Sacre du printemps* (mus. Stravinsky, Munich Bal-
let, 1973), *Tristan* (mus. Henze, Paris Opera,
1975), *Daphnis and Chloe* (mus. Ravel, Stuttgart
Ballet, 1975), *Greening* (mus. A. Nordheim, Stutt-
gart Ballet, 1975), *Sphinx* (mus. Martinů, American
Ballet Theatre, 1977), *Contredances* (mus. Webern,
American Ballet Theatre, 1979), *The Tempest* (mus.
Nordheim, Ballet Rambert, 1979), *Dances of Albion*
(mus. Britten, Royal Ballet, 1980), *Summer's End*
(mus. Dutilleux, NDT, 1980), *The Firebird* (mus.
Stravinsky, Royal Danish Ballet, 1981), *Murderer,
Hope of Women* (mus. percussion arranged by
Tyrrell, Ballet Rambert, 1983), *Pulcinella* (mus.
Stravinsky, London Festival Ballet, 1984), *Revela-
tion and Fall* (mus. Maxwell, Australian Dance

Theatre, 1984), *Dream Walk of the Shaman* (mus. Krenek, Aterballeto, 1985), *Alice* (mus. Del Tredici, National Ballet of Canada, 1986), *Orpheus* (mus. Stravinsky, Australian Ballet, 1987), *La Ronde* (mus. Korngold, National Ballet of Canada, 1987), *Tagore* (mus. Zemlinsky, National Ballet of Canada, 1989), *Amores* (mus. Torke, Royal Ballet, 1997), and *Lux in Tenebris* (mus. Sofia Gubaidulina, Houston Ballet, 1999).

Texas Ballet Theatre US ballet company. It was founded in 1957 as an educational organization called the Dallas Civic Ballet, but in 1969 expanded its professional scope with the appointment of G. *Skibine and Marjorie *Tallchief as director and associate director respectively. The company's associated school was opened in 1971 and the repertoire grew to include many Skibine ballets as well as works by Balanchine and Taras. After Skibine's death, F. *Flindt was appointed artistic director (1981–9). The company was then dissolved and in 1993 the Fort Worth Ballet was renamed Fort Worth-Dallas Ballet, incorporating works by S. Welch and Kevin O'Day into its repertory. In 2003 it was constituted again, as Texas Ballet Theatre, under the direction of Ben *Stevenson who brought several of his own productions into the repertory.

Thaïs pas de deux See MEDITATION FROM THAÏS.

Tharp, Twyla (*b* Portland, Ind., 1 Jul. 1941) US dancer, choreographer, and company director. She grew up in California, studying ballet with Beatrice Collenette (once a member of Pavlova's company), baton-twirling, and Hawaiian tap. She moved to New York to study art history at Barnard College, and there studied ballet with Igor Schwezoff, Richard Thomas, and Margaret Craske, modern dance with Graham, Nikolais, Cunningham, and Taylor, and jazz with Matt Mattox. From 1963 to 1964 she danced with Paul Taylor, but in 1965 formed a company to present her own work. Her first dance concert was at Hunter College on 29 Apr. 1965, a performance of the seven-minute long *Tank Dive*, choreographed for herself and four non-dancers. Initially Tharp was part of New York's avant-garde, her choreography performed without music and often set in unusual spaces (out of doors, in art galleries and gymnasiums). One of her first creations, *Re-Moves*, performed at the Judson Memorial Church, ended with the dancers inside a giant box, invisible to the audience. Then in 1970 Tharp set her first choreography to music and her work steadily became more mainstream, incorporating elements of popular culture, mixing different

dance idioms. In 1973 her first commissioned work for Robert Joffrey *Deuce Coupe* was a turning point in her career. Set to songs by the Beach Boys, it redefined Tharp as one of America's wittiest, most entertaining and versatile choreographers. Her loose-limbed, jazz-influenced style gave the classically trained dancers of Joffrey a new performing attitude, and Tharp repeated this success with *Push Comes to Shove* (1976). This was for American Ballet Theatre and was a tailor-made showcase for Baryshnikov, redefining ballet's supreme classicist as a roguish bowler-hatted womanizer. It was one of the biggest successes in ABT's history. Later, Tharp brought together her own dancers and those of ABT for *In the Upper Room*, a work whose exhilarating speed and aggressive physicality brought a new public to dance. From 1988 to 1990 she was artistic associate at American Ballet Theatre. She also worked with the Paris Opera Ballet, and for the Royal Ballet created *Mr Worldly Wise*, a full-length 'themed' ballet, loosely based on the life of Rossini.

Despite her early rigorous experiments Tharp also began to work extensively in commercial theatre. She has created five full-length dance shows on Broadway: *When We Were Very Young* (mus. John Simon, 1980), *The Catherine Wheel* (mus. David Byrne, 1981), the Tony Award-winning *Movin' Out* (mus. Billy Joel, 2002), *The Times They Are A-Changin'* (mus. Bob Dylan, 2006), and *Come Fly Away* (mus. Sinatra songs, 2010). In addition she has choreographed and directed the Broadway musical *Singin' in the Rain* (1985) and choreographed for the films *Hair* (1979), *Ragtime* (1981), *Amadeus* (1984), and *White Nights* (1985).

A list of her works includes *Tank Dive* (1965), *Re-Moves* (1966), *After Suite* (1969), *Medley* (1969), *Group Activities* (1969), *Dancing in the Streets of London and Paris, Continued in Stockholm and Sometimes Madrid* (1969), *The Fugue* (1970), *The One Hundreds* (1970), *Eight Jelly Rolls* (mus. Jelly Roll Morton, 1971), *The Bix Pieces* (mus. Bix Beiderbecke, 1971), *The Raggedy Dances* (mus. Scott Joplin, Mozart, 1972), *Deuce Coupe* (mus. Beach Boys, Joffrey Ballet, 1973), *As Time Goes By* (mus. Haydn, Joffrey Ballet, 1973), *In the Beginnings* (mus. Moss, 1974), *Sue's Leg* (mus. Fats Waller, 1975), *Ocean's Motion* (mus. Chuck Berry, 1975), *Push Comes to Shove* (mus. Haydn and Joseph Lamb, American Ballet Theatre, 1976), *Give and Take* (mus. various, 1976), *Once More, Frank* (mus. recordings by Frank Sinatra, 1976), *Happily Ever After* (mus. traditional American country music, Joffrey Ballet, 1976), *After All* (mus. Albinoni, for ice skater John Curry, 1976), *Mud* (mus. Mozart, 1977), *Baker's Dozen* (mus. Willie 'the Lion' Smith, 1979),

Brahms' Paganini (mus. Brahms, 1980), *Short Stories* (mus. Supertramp, Bruce Springsteen, 1980), *Third Suite* (mus. Bach, 1980), *Nine Sinatra Songs* (mus. recordings by Frank Sinatra, 1982), *Bad Smells* (mus. Glenn Branca, 1982), *Telemann* (mus. Telemann, 1983), *The Golden Section* (mus. David Byrne, 1983), *Bach Partita* (mus. Bach, American Ballet Theatre, 1983), *Brahms/Handel* (with Robbins, mus. Brahms, New York City Ballet, 1984), *Sinatra Suite* (mus. recordings by Frank Sinatra, American Ballet Theatre, 1984), *The Little Ballet* (mus. Glazunov, American Ballet Theatre, 1984), *In the Upper Room* (mus. Glass, 1986), *Quartet* (mus. Terry Riley, American Ballet Theatre, 1989), *Bum's Rush* (mus. Dick Hyman, American Ballet Theatre, 1989), *Rules of the Game* (mus. Bach, Paris Opera Ballet, 1989), *Brief Fling* (mus. Colombier, Grainger, American Ballet Theatre, 1990), *Grand Pas: Rhythm of the Saints* (mus. Paul Simon, Paris Opera Ballet, 1991), *The Men's Piece* (1991), *Octet* (mus. Edgar Meyer, 1991), *Sextet* (mus. Bob Telson, Peter Melnick, 1992), *Demeter and Persephone* (mus. various, klezmer, Martha Graham company, 1993), *Pergolesi* (mus. Pergolesi, White Oak Dance Project, 1993), *Waterbaby Bagatelles* (mus. various, Boston Ballet, 1994), *How Near Heaven* (mus. Britten, American Ballet Theatre, 1995), *Americans We* (mus. Donald Hunsberger, ABT, 1995), *Jump Start* (mus. Wynton Marsalis, ABT, 1995), *Mr Worldly Wise* (mus. Rossini, Royal Ballet, 1995), *Sweet Fields* (mus. William Billings, 1996), *Heroes* (mus. Glass, 1996), *66* (mus. various, 1996), *The Storyteller* (mus. Kiyong Kim, Australian Ballet, 1997), *Roy's Joys* (mus. Roy Eldridge, 1997), *Known By Heart* (mus. Mozart, Donald Knaack, Steve Reich, ABT, 1998), *Diabelli Variations* (mus. Beethoven, 1999), *Grosse Sonate* (mus. Beethoven, 1999), *The Beethoven Seventh* (mus. Beethoven, New York City Ballet, 2000), *Surfer at the River Styx* (mus. Donald Knaack, 2000), *Rabbit and Rogue* (mus. Danny Elfman, ABT, 2008). Author of autobiography *Push Comes to Shove* (New York, 1992).

(((⊕))) **SEE WEB LINKS**
• Twyla Tharp website

Theater Piece Modern dance in eight parts with choreography by Humphrey, music by W. Riegger, and costumes by P. Lawrence. Premiered 19 Jan. 1936 by the Humphrey-Weidman Company, at the Guild Theater, New York. A group work for nineteen dancers, it depicts the world as a grim and dehumanizing place. Humphrey danced the role of the rebellious outsider. *Theater Piece* was part of a trilogy, with *New Dance* and *With My Red Fires*.

Theme and Variations Ballet in one act with choreography by Balanchine, music by

Tchaikovsky, designs by Woodman Thompson. Premiered 26 Nov. 1947 by Ballet Theatre in New York, with Alonso and Youskevitch. A plotless ballet set in a chandeliered ballroom, it is Balanchine's homage to the Imperial Russian ballet tradition within which he trained and in particular to Petipa's *The Sleeping Beauty*. It is set to the final movement of Tchaikovsky's Suite for Orchestra No. 3. It has been taken into the repertories of many companies including New York City Ballet, Les Grands Ballets Canadiens, Dutch National Ballet, Sadler's Wells Royal Ballet, the Kirov Ballet, San Francisco Ballet, the Royal Ballet, and the Royal Danish Ballet. In 1970 Balanchine choreographed the first three movements of Tchaikovsky's suite. The complete ballet is called *Suite No. 3*.

Théodore, Mlle (orig. Marie-Madeleine de Crépé or Crespé; *b* Paris, 6 Oct. 1760; *d* Audenge, 9 Sept. 1796) French dancer. She studied with Jean-Barthélemy Lany in Paris and made her debut at the Paris Opera in 1777, where she excelled in ballets by Noverre and Gardel. She was eager to guest abroad however, dancing in Brussels and in London (1781–4, King's Theatre), and in 1783 she was imprisoned for eighteen days for allegedly breaking her contract with the Paris Opera. That same year she left Paris, along with her husband, the choreographer *Dauberval and the two of them ended up in the Grand Theatre in Bordeaux, where he as ballet master and she as principal dancer (1785–90). It was there that she created the role of Lise in the first production of Dauberval's *La Fille mal gardée* (1789). She later returned to London (1791–2) to dance at the Pantheon and Haymarket Theatres. It is said she was once involved in a duel with Mlle Beaumesnil of the Paris Opera; apparently it came to nothing when both their pistols misfired.

There is a Time Modern dance in one act with choreography by Limón, music by Dello Joio, and costumes by P. Lawrence. Premiered 20 Apr. 1956 by the José Limón Dance Company at the Juilliard Concert Hall, New York, with Limón, Koner, Currier, B. Jones, L. Nielsen, and Hoving. The ballet is based on the passage from Ecclesiastes: 'To everything there is a season, and a time to every purpose under the heaven.'

Thesmar, Ghislaine (*b* Peking, 1943) French dancer. She studied at the Paris Conservatoire and made her debut with the Grand Ballet du Marquis de Cuevas in 1961. She danced with Pierre Lacotte's company, Ballet National des Jeunesses Musicales de France, and married him in 1968. She also danced with Ballet Rambert, Petit's company, Les Grands Ballets Canadiens, and from 1972 to 1985 was an étoile at the Paris

Opera Ballet. She created roles in Petit's *Formes* (1967), *Shéhérazade* (1974), and *La Nuit transfigurée* (1976), Nault's *Catulli Carmina* (1969) and *Pas Rompu* (1969), and created the title role in Lacotte's television production of *La Sylphide* in 1971. She appeared as a guest artist with New York City Ballet in 1976. From 1986 to 1988 she and Lacotte were joint artistic directors of the Ballets de Monte Carlo. She then taught at the Paris Opera Ballet.

Thordal-Christensen, Aage (*b* Frederiksberg, 30 Oct. 1965) Danish dancer, choreographer, and ballet director. He trained at the Ballet School of the Royal Theatre, Copenhagen (1972–82); later studied at the School of American Ballet in New York and at the National Ballet School in Toronto. He joined the Royal Danish Ballet in 1984 but left for America the following year. He was a dancer with Pacific Northwest Ballet for six years (1986–92), becoming a principal in 1989. In 1992 he returned to the Royal Danish Ballet as a soloist, where he danced a wide range of roles in both the traditional and modern repertoire. He made his debut as a choreographer in Copenhagen in 1994 with *Behind the Curtain* (mus. Kim Helweg) and followed that with *Room 7* (mus. Luigi Ceccarelli, 1994), *Something Like That* (mus. Helweg, 1995), and *Shaken* (mus. Ben Horn, 2002). Between 1999 and 2002, he was artistic director of the Royal Danish Ballet, the youngest in the company's history, and during that time commissioned several new works by Martins, Ratmansky, Lila York, and others, as well as overseeing the company's restructuring. In 2006 he became founding artistic director of Los Angeles Ballet, with his wife Colleen Neary, and has created several works for the company including a new version of *Nutcracker* (2007).

(((⊕))) SEE WEB LINKS
• Website for Los Angeles Ballet

Three-Cornered Hat, The (*La Tricorne*) Ballet in one act with choreography by Massine, libretto by Martinez Sierra, music by de Falla, and designs by Picasso. Premiered 22 Jul. 1919 by the Ballets Russes de Diaghilev at the Alhambra Theatre, London, with Massine, Karsavina, Woizikowsky and Idzikowski. Based on a comic story by Pedro Antonio de Alarcón (*El sombrero de tres picos*, 1874), it tells how the neglected wife of a miller attempts to teach her husband a lesson by pursuing an ageing Corregidor, who turns out to be less feeble than he seems. Massine's choreography was strongly influenced by the folk dances of Spain. The ballet is widely regarded as one of the most successful collaborations between choreographer, composer, and designer in the 20th century. Massine revived it for Ballet Theatre

(1943), Sadler's Wells Ballet (1947), Royal Swedish Ballet (1956), City Center Joffrey Ballet (1969), and London Festival Ballet (1973).

3 Epitaphs Modern dance in one act with choreography by Paul Taylor, music early New Orleans jazz recorded by the Laneville-Johnson Union Brass Band, costumes by Rauschenberg. Premiered 27 Mar. 1956 by the Paul Taylor Dance Company at the Master Institute of United Artists, New York, part of the Dance Associates concerts. The dancers, their faces completely hidden, are dressed head to toe in black costumes with tiny mirrors that mark out their eyes and their hands. It was later reworked as *Four Epitaphs*. It is Taylor's oldest surviving work.

Three Virgins and a Devil Ballet in one act with choreography by de Mille, libretto by Ramon Reed, music by Respighi, set by Arne Lundborg, and costumes by Motley. Premiered 11 Feb. 1941 by Ballet Theatre at the Majestic Theatre in New York, with de Mille, Chase, Lyon, Loring, and Robbins. The Devil lures the three Virgins into Hell.

Tikhomirov, Vassily (*b* Moscow, 29 Mar. 1876; *d* Moscow, 20 Jun. 1956) Russian dancer, choreographer, and teacher. He studied at the Moscow Theatre School from 1886 and after graduating in 1891 was sent to the St Petersburg Theatre School to join Pavel Gerdt's *Class of Perfection*. After two years he returned to dance in the Bolshoi Ballet where from 1899 he was its leading premier danseur. He created roles in Gorsky's *Don Quixote* (1900), *The Goldfish* (1903), *The Magic Mirror* (1905), *Pharaoh's Daughter* (1905), *Salammbô* (1911), *Dance Dream* (1911), *Le Corsaire* (1912, starred as Conrad). In 1911 he was leading dancer at the Alhambra Theatre in London, and he was Pavlova's partner during her 1913 world tour. He danced frequently with Ekaterina *Geltser (later his first wife) notably in his own ballets, *The Red Poppy* and *Esmeralda*. He started to teach at the Moscow school in 1896, a distinguished career that saw him guiding the careers of Volinine and Messerer, among others; from 1917 he was head of the school. He was a traditionalist and a conservative, and following the 1917 Revolution he worked to preserve the classics in the grand manner of Petipa, campaigning in opposition to Gorsky, who had been aiming to inject a more contemporary dramatic relevance. Tikhomirov succeeded Gorsky as chief ballet master of the Bolshoi Ballet (1925–30), and mounted several productions of the classics, as well as creating a new production of *La Esmeralda* (1926). To conform to Soviet cultural policy he also choreographed (with Lashchilin) *The Red Poppy* in 1927, attempting to marry an ideologically correct story (the struggle of the Chinese against their English colonial masters) to the conventions of 19th-century Imperial Russian ballet (variations, pas de deux, a grand pas). *The Red Poppy* was a popular success, especially for Geltser, who danced its heroine, although Tikhomirov's choreography for the second act was judged by the critics to be archaic. He retired from teaching in 1937.

Tiller Girls Troupes of English dancing girls founded in 1901 by John Tiller (*c*.1851–1925). The first of the modern precision dance groups, they were trained in London by Mrs John Tiller and appeared in music halls and variety shows. They were the model for the famous US troupe the *Rockettes.

Till Eulenspiegel (*Tyl Ulenspiegel*) Several ballets have been inspired by Richard Strauss's 1895 tone-poem among them Nijinsky's version for Diaghilev's Ballets Russes (New York, 1916), Babilée's for the Ballets des Champs-Elysées (Paris, 1949), and Balanchine's for New York City Ballet (New York, 1951).

Timofeyeva, Nina (*b* Leningrad, 11 Jun. 1935) Soviet dancer. She studied at the Leningrad Ballet School (the Vaganova Academy), graduating in 1953 and joining the Kirov. In 1956, however, she was invited to join the Bolshoi Ballet as a soloist. She went on to become one of the Bolshoi's leading ballerinas and stayed with the company until she retired in 1988. She created a total of 50 roles, including in Lavrovsky's *Night City* (1961), the title role in Vinogradov's *Asel* (1967), Aegina in Grigorovich's *Spartacus* (1968), and Lady Macbeth in Vasiliev's *Macbeth* (1980). She also appeared in fifteen films, including *Fedra and the Twilight Nights* (1971), *Raymonda* (1974), and *The Three Cards* (1983). She later settled in Israel, and taught at the Jerusalem Academy of Dance and Music. She married the conductor Gennadi Rozhdestvensky. People's Artist USSR (1969).

Tippet, Clark (*b* Parsons, Kan., 5 Oct. 1954; *d* Parsons, Kan., 28 Jan. 1992) US dancer and choreographer. He studied in New York at Thalia Mara's National Academy of Ballet and briefly at the American Ballet Theatre School. He joined American Ballet Theatre in 1972, becoming a principal in 1976 and creating a role in Tharp's *Push Comes to Shove* (1976). He appeared in the Hollywood film *The Turning Point* (1977). In 1979 he left ABT to join the Cleveland Ballet and to dance in Australia and Israel. Returning to ABT he choreographed his first ballet in 1986 which was followed by *Bruch Violin Concerto No. 1* (1988) and several works for Pacific Northwest

Ballet. He died prematurely from an Aids-related illness.

Tipton, Jennifer (*b* Columbus, Ohio, 11 Sept. 1937) US lighting designer. She studied dance with Graham and Limón, and stage lighting with Thomas Skelton (1963), becoming his assistant. She became resident lighting designer of the Paul Taylor Dance Company in 1966 and has subsequently lit most of his repertory. Since 1965 she has also been a close associate collaborator of Twyla Tharp, lighting many of her ballets, including *In the Upper Room*. Tipton has also worked with many other companies including the Joffrey Ballet, the Feld Ballet, the Limón Dance Company, American Ballet Theatre, the National Ballet of Canada, and the Royal Ballet. In 1987 she began to work with the choreographer Dana Reitz; in 1993 they joined forces with Sara Rudner on the revolutionary *Necessary Weather*, a work that featured lighting as a full partner to the choreography. She has worked extensively in theatre as a lighting designer and made her directorial debut in 1991 with a production of *The Tempest* in Minneapolis. In 2008 she created her first non-theatrical lighting installation at the Rensselaer Polytechnic, Troy. Since 1981 she has taught lighting design at the Yale University School of Drama. She has received numerous awards, including a Tony Award for the musical *Jerome Robbins' Broadway* (1989) and a MacArthur 'Genius' Award (2008).

Tivoli Pantomime Theatre A theatre situated in Copenhagen's Tivoli Gardens, opened in 1874; built by Vilhelm Dahlerup and Ove Petersen (who also designed the Royal Theatre in Copenhagen). Traditional pantomimes based on the Italian commedia dell'arte are performed there in the summer months, along with small-scale ballets.

Tobias, Tobi (*b* New York, 12 Sept. 1938) US dance critic and writer. She studied at Barnard College and New York University beginning her long association with *Dance Magazine* in 1971, and becoming senior editor from 1983 to 1998. She was additionally dance critic of *Soho News* (1979–81) and *New York Magazine* (1980–2002) and consultant and writer to the *Dance in America* television series (1976–90). She taught dance criticism at Barnard College (1977–92) and, as a leading authority on the Danish ballet, initiated *An Oral History of the Royal Danish Ballet and Its Bournonville Tradition*. She has also written books for children while her books on dance include *Maria Tallchief* (1970) and *Arthur Mitchell* (1975).

Tokyo Ballet, The Ballet company based in Tokyo which grew out of the city's first classical ballet school, the Tokyo Ballet Gakko, founded by Koichi Hayashi in 1960 and based on the Soviet model. When the company first performed it was known as the Tchaikovsky Memorial Ballet. In 1964, after going bankrupt, the school and company were reorganized by the impresario Tadatsugu Sasaki, who greatly expanded their activities. The company made its first visit to Western Europe in 1970, and performed an extensive European tour five years later, the first Japanese ballet company to do so. Alongside its repertoire of standard ballet classics, the company has acquired modern works by Western choreographers, including Petit, Kylián, Neumeier, and Béjart, who for several years was artistic adviser to the company. Russian and European stars have frequently appeared as guest artists, including *Guillem who in 2008 danced a Béjart tribute programme with Tokyo Ballet dancers. The company continues to tour internationally, although in its home city it is under competition from the New National Theatre Ballet founded in 1997.

Tomasson, Helgi (*b* Reykjavik, 8 Oct. 1942) Icelandic-US dancer, choreographer, and company director. He studied with Sigridur Arman, Erik Bidsted, Volkova, at the School of American Ballet in New York, and with Stanley Williams. He made his debut with the Tivoli Ballet in Copenhagen in 1958; joined the Joffrey Ballet in 1962 and the Harkness Ballet in 1964. He created roles in Joffrey's *Gamelan* (1963), Walker's *Night Song* (1967), Butler's *A Season in Hell* (1967), Neumeier's *Stages and Reflections* (1968), and Harkarvy's *La Favorita* (1969). In 1970 he joined New York City Ballet as a principal dancer, where he remained for fifteen years, acclaimed as one of the most elegant and technically accomplished classical male dancers in America. At NYCB he created roles in Robbins's *The Goldberg Variations* (1971), *Dybbuk Variations* (1974), and *Introduction and Allegro for Harp* (1975), in Balanchine's *Symphony in Three Movements* (1972), *Divertimento from Le Baiser de la fée* (1972), *Coppélia* (1974), *Union Jack* (1976), and *Vienna Waltzes* (1977) and in Martins's *The Magic Flute* (1982). He started choreographing in 1982 and retired from dancing in 1985 when he became artistic director of San Francisco Ballet. For San Francisco he has made many one-act ballets, including *Handel—A Celebration* (mus. Handel, 1989), *Meistens Mozart* (mus. Mozart, 1991), *Nanna's Lied* (mus. Weill and Hollander, 1993), *Sonata* (mus. Rachmaninoff, 1995), *Twilight* (mus. Mendelssohn, 1998), *Bartók Divertimento* (mus. Bartók, 2002), *Con Brio, 7 for Eight* (mus. Bach, 2004), and *On Common Ground* (mus. Ned Rorem, 2007). He has also staged productions of *Romeo and Juliet*, *Swan Lake*, *The Sleeping Beauty*, *Giselle*, and *Nutcracker*. His most significant contribution to SFB however has been its revitalization to a world class company—achieved through his innovative commissioning of works by Morris, Wheeldon, and others, his nurturing of the dancers and his expansion of a serious audience for ballet.

tombé [Fr., fallen] In ballet a movement which involves falling from one leg onto the other, or from two legs onto one, and landing with a bent knee.

Toronto Dance Theatre Toronto-based Canadian modern dance company founded in 1968 by Patricia *Beatty, David Earle, and Peter Randazzo. The repertoire, heavily influenced by Graham, was made up of works by all three choreographer-directors until Christopher *House joined as resident choreographer in 1981. Earle assumed sole artistic direction in 1987 and was succeeded by House in 1994, since when the latter has created most of the company's repertory including *Nest* (2000), *Sly Verb* (2003), and *Timecode Break* (2006). The company has had a major influence on the development of modern dance in Canada with some of its former dancers, such as Peggy Baker and Robert Desrosiers, going on to run companies of their own. It also has an associate school.

(⊕) SEE WEB LINKS

• Website for Toronto Dance Theatre

Torvill and Dean Jayne Torvill (*b* Nottingham, 7 Oct. 1957) and Christopher *Dean (*b* Nottingham, 27 Jul. 1958), British ice dancers and Olympic gold medallists. As a partnership they revolutionized ice dancing, bringing it closer to dance and in doing so raising questions about its viability as a sport. At the 1984 Olympic Games, where they won a Gold Medal, their free dance to Ravel's *Bolero* earned a perfect score and captured an international audience, establishing Torvill and Dean as the most famous ice dancers in history. Dean's artistic choreography widened the horizons for competitive ice dancing and he was even commissioned to make a work for English National Ballet. As professional skaters they mounted large-scale ice dancing shows and appeared in several television specials. They performed routines based on the musicals *Mack and Mabel* and *Barnum*, as well as tributes to 'Fred and Ginger' and John Lennon.

Toumanova, Tamara (*b* Tyumen, Siberia, 2 Mar. 1919; *d* Santa Monica, Calif., 29 May 1996) Russian-US dancer. An exceptionally glamorous international ballerina, she was exotic from birth, born on a train near Shanghai as her parents were leaving Russia after the Revolution. Her earliest dance classes were in China but when she was 5 the family moved to Paris, where she studied with Preobrajenska; later she trained with Balanchine and Nijinska. She made her debut as a child prodigy in the 1929 Paris Opera production of *L'Éventail de Jeanne*, in which she danced a leading role. She was then one of the trio of 'baby ballerinas' (along with Baronova and Riabouchinska) who were hired by Balanchine to generate publicity for René Blum and de Basil's new Ballets Russes de Monte Carlo in 1932. Only 13 at the time of her first performance, she went on to create roles in Balanchine's *Cotillon*, *La Concurrence*, and *Le Bourgeois gentilhomme* (1932) and in Massine's *Jeux d'enfants* (all 1932). For much of her career she remained closely associated with Balanchine: she joined his Les Ballets 1933 and created roles in his *Les Songes*, *Mozartiana*, and *Fastes*. She then returned to de Basil's Ballets Russes de Monte Carlo, where she stayed until 1937, creating roles in Massine's *Choreartium* (1933), *Union Pacific* (1934), *Jardin public* (1935), and *Symphonie fantastique* (1936). In 1938 she danced with the new Ballet Russe de Monte Carlo, which had Massine as its artistic director, and during its London season danced her first Giselle. During the war years she was firstly with de Basil's Original Ballet Russe (1939–41), creating a ballerina role in Balanchine's *Balustrade* (1941); then with Denham's Ballet Russe de Monte Carlo (1941–2) creating roles in Massine's *Labyrinth* (1941) and *Saratoga* (1941); and finally with Ballet Theatre (1944–5), where she created roles in Massine's *Moonlight Sonata* (1944) and Nijinska's *Harvest Time* (1945). A sought-after guest artist, she subsequently worked as a freelance ballerina with companies in Europe and America, creating roles in Balanchine's *Le Palais de cristal* (Paris Opera, 1947), Lifar's *Phèdre* (title role, Paris Opera, 1950), *L'Inconnue* (Paris, 1950), and *La Pierre enchantée* (Paris, 1950), Wallmann's *La vita dell'uomo* (La Scala, Milan, 1951), Dolin's *Rêve* (London Festival Ballet, 1952), Charrat's *The Seven Deadly Sins* (Milan, 1956), and Taras's *Le Fanfare pour le Prince* (Monte Carlo, 1956). She also gave concert performances, appearing mainly with Vladimir Oukhtomsky as her partner. She appeared in many Hollywood films, including *Days of Glory* (1944, produced by her husband, Casey Robinson), *Tonight We Sing* (1953), *Deep in My Heart* (1954), *Invitation to the Dance* (1956), Hitchcock's *Torn Curtain* (1966), and Wilder's *The Private Life of Sherlock Holmes* (1970). She also appeared on stage, in the Broadway production of the musical *Stars in Your Eyes* (1939). A dancer of great beauty and virtuosity, she was admired for both her tragic and comedic interpretative skills.

tour en l'air [Fr., turn in the air] In ballet a movement which involves the dancer turning

while at the same time jumping straight up into the air. There are multiple tours en l'air, mostly performed by the male dancer.

Tragedy of Fashion, A, or The Scarlet Scissors Ballet in one act with choreography by Ashton, libretto by Ashley Dukes, music by Eugene Goossens (arr. Ernest Irving), and designs by Fedorovitch. Premiered 15 Jun. 1926 in the revue *Riverside Nights* at the Lyric Theatre in Hammersmith, London, with Ashton and Rambert. The ballets tells of a couturier who is so dejected when his dress is rejected by a wealthy customer that he commits suicide by stabbing himself with his dressmaker's shears. It was Ashton's first ballet and was produced by Rambert and her company. In 2004 Ian Spink created a revisionist homage.

Train bleu, Le Ballet in one act with choreography by Nijinska, libretto by Cocteau, music by Milhaud, curtain by Picasso, set by Henri Laurens, and costumes by Chanel. Premiered 20 Jun. 1924, by the Ballets Russes de Diaghilev at the Théâtre de Champs-Elysées, Paris, with Nijinska, Sokolova, Dolin, and Woizikowsky. A ballet with a sporting theme, it features a group of the rich and fashionable disporting themselves on the Mediterranean coast. Cocteau's scenario was influenced by the Olympic Games, silent films, and jazz music, while Nijinska's choreography had a strong gymnastic element to it. Nijinska danced the role of the Champion Tennis Player, Woizikowsky the golfer, and Dolin (an accomplished athlete) was the swimming champion. The Train Bleu itself, an express train between Paris and the Côte d'Azur, does not appear in the ballet. The ballet's first complete revival was at the Oakland Ballet in 1989; it was restaged at the Paris Opera in 1992.

Transfigured Night (orig. Ger. title *Verklärte Nacht*) A String Sextet by Schoenberg, written in 1899, it has inspired several ballets, among them Tudor's *Pillar of Fire* (Ballet Theatre, New York, 1942), Kylián's *Transfigured Night* (Nederlands Dans Theater, 1975), and Petit's *La Nuit transfigurée* (Paris Opera, 1976). It has also been used in the scores of Graeme Murphy's *Shades of Gray* (2004) and de Keersmaeker's *Woud* (1995).

travestie, en Originally used to describe the practice of a man playing a woman's role on stage (and hence wearing female attire). The need for cross-dressing arose because women in ancient Greece were not allowed to appear on stage and female roles had to be performed by men. In W. Europe the early Christian Church also prohibited women from acting on stage and in Shakespeare's day men routinely played the women's parts. It was not until the 17th century (a century later in Italy) that women were generally allowed to perform in public. Today, the practice of en travestie on the ballet stage is usually associated mainly with burlesque and parody. The term can also be used to describe a woman playing a man's role (and hence wearing male attire). Famous examples of female impersonation in classical ballet today include the Widow Simone in Ashton's *La Fille mal gardée*, Carabosse in *The Sleeping Beauty*, and the witch Madge in Bournonville's *La Sylphide*. Les *Ballets Trockadero, founded in New York in 1974, is an all-male troupe of dancers who perform the standards of the classical ballet repertoire en travestie.

Trefilova, Vera (*b* St Petersburg (or Vladikavkaz), 8 Oct. 1875; *d* Paris, 11 Jul. 1943) Russian dancer and teacher. She studied at the Imperial Theatre School in St Petersburg with Ekaterina Vazem and later with Eugenia Sokolova, Nikolai Legat, and Enrico Cecchetti. She graduated into the ballet company at the Mariinsky Theatre in 1894 and was promoted to soloist in 1901. She created roles in Ivanov's *Acis and Galatea* (1896), N. and S. Legat's *The Fairy Doll* (1903), N. Legat's *The Blood-Red Flower* (1907), and Fokine's *The Night of Terpsichore* (1907). In 1906 she was promoted to principal but only four years later she resigned, either out of disaffection with her repertory (she was not a fan of Fokine's innovations) or because she fell victim to a campaign against her led by Kschessinska, the Mariinsky's reigning ballerina. In 1915 she made her debut as an actress at the Mikhailovsky Theatre in St Petersburg. In 1917 she left Russia and opened a ballet school in Paris but returned to the stage to dance Aurora in Diaghilev's 1921 London production of *The Sleeping Princess*. In 1924, almost 50 years old, she danced Odette-Odile for Diaghilev's Ballets Russes in Monte Carlo, still amazing audiences with her fouetté turns. She gave her final performance at His Majesty's Theatre in London in 1926. She was described as a ballerina of great expressive power, and the finest Aurora since Carlotta Brianza, who created the role. She was married to the dance critic Valerian Svetlov, who wrote *Contemporary Ballet* (St Petersburg, 1911), a standard reference work.

Trend Modern dance in six parts with choreography and libretto by Hanya Holm, music by Wallingford Riegger and Edgard Varèse, set by Arch Lauterer, and costumes by Betty Joiner. Premiered 13 Aug. 1937 by the Hanya Holm Company at Bennington College for Women in Vermont. Holm's signature work, it is an ambitious 55-minute dance for an all-female cast which deals with the theme of the destruction of society through its own decadence.

trepak A bravura Ukrainian folk dance in 2/4 time performed exclusively by men. It features deep squats and split leaps and appears, most famously, in the second act of *The Nutcracker*.

Triadic Ballet Modern dance by Oskar *Schlemmer. Premiered 30 Sept. 1922 at the Landes Theater in Stuttgart, with Schlemmer, Albert Burger, and Elsa Hötzel. Schlemmer, one of the pioneers of the Bauhaus movement, used the piece to explore the relationship between the moving body and abstract space. It was prefigured by earlier productions in 1911 and 1916. The work was in three sections, colour-coded yellow, pink, and black to reflect a different mood. It was further subdivided into twelve dances performed by three people (two men, one woman) who between them wore eighteen costumes. These dominated, and in some cases dramatically altered the body shapes of the dancers. Shaped in spirals, triangles, and cones, they were constructed out of padded cloth and papier-maché, and coated with metallic paint. The choreography was simple, consisting mainly of repetitive movements. For subsequent performances Hindemith composed music for a mechanical organ. In 1970 Margarethe Hasting reconstructed *Triadic Ballet* for German television.

Tricorne, Le See THREE-CORNERED HAT, THE.

Trinity Ballet in one act with choreography by Gerald Arpino, music by Alan Raph and Lee Holdridge. Premiered 9 Oct. 1970 by the City Center Joffrey Ballet at City Center in New York. One of the first ballets to reflect the radical youth culture of 1960s America, it espoused the cause of peace and love and featured a live rock band in the orchestra pit. For many years it was the Joffrey's signature piece. When it was performed in Moscow in 1974 it reportedly generated 42 curtain calls on closing night.

Triomphe de l'amour, Le Ballet de cour in twenty entrées with text by I. de Benserade and P. Quinault, music by Lully, production and choreography by Beauchamps and Pécour, and designs by J. Bérain. Premiered 21 Jan. 1681 at the Château de Saint-Germain-en-Laye, with Beauchamps as Mars and Pécour in various entrées. The ladies and gentlemen of the court provided the rest of the cast in this baroque extravaganza. The work's finale celebrated Love as the ruler of both gods and men. Four months after its premiere, a performance (at the Paris Palais Royal) featured the first appearance of a professional ballerina, Mlle Lafontaine. Harald Lander staged a new version for the Royal Danish Ballet in 1962.

Tristan ballets The legend of Tristan and Isolde has provided the subject for several ballets, including Massine's *Mad Tristan* (mus. Wagner, Ballet International, 1944), Ashton's *Picnic at Tintagel* (mus. Bax, New York City Ballet, 1952), Charrat's *Tu auras nom...Tristan* (mus. Jef Maes, Geneva, 1963), T. Gsovsky's *Tristan* (mus. Blacher, German Opera Berlin, 1965); Béjart's *Les Vainqueurs* (mus. Tibetan music and Wagner, Brussels, 1969), Tetley's *Tristan* (mus. Henze, Paris Opera, 1974), which starred Nureyev and Carlson, and K. Pastor's *Tristan* (mus. Wagner, arr. Henk de Vlieger, Royal Swedish Ballet, 2006).

Triumph of Death, The Television ballet choreographed by Flindt, with music by Thomas Koppel, sets by Poul Arnt Thomsen, and costumes by Soren Breum. Premiered by Danish television on 23 May 1971 with Flindt, F. Schaufuss, Eliasen, and Vivi Flindt. It is based on Ionesco's *Jeu de massacre*, and is a strident attack on capitalist ideology. In the famous nude scene, the choreographer himself appeared with his body sprayed with pink disinfectant. The piece was first performed on the stage on 19 Feb. 1972 by the Royal Danish Ballet in Copenhagen.

Troy Game Modern dance work in one act with choreography by Robert North, music by Bob Downes and Batucada (Brazilian), and costumes by Peter Farmer. Premiered 3 Oct. 1974 by London Contemporary Dance Theatre at the Royal Court Theatre in Liverpool. A comic, bravura work for men, it parodies extremes of muscle-bound machismo. It has been revived for several companies including Dance Theatre of Harlem, the Royal Ballet, Scottish Ballet, Tulsa Ballet, and Sarasota Ballet.

Tryst One-act ballet with choreography by Christopher Wheeldon, music by James MacMillan, and designs by Jean-Marc Puissant. Premiered 18 May 2002 by the Royal Ballet at Covent Garden with Darcey Bussell and Jonathan Cope. The complex partnerwork of its central duet evokes a dark dance of courtship, chiming with the recurrent imagery of secrets and shadows in Wheeldon's work.

Tsao, Willy (*b* Hong Kong, 7 Oct. 1955) Chinese dancer, choreographer, and director, widely regarded as the father of Chinese modern dance. He trained at the Pacific Lutheran University, Washington, between 1973 and 1997, returning to graduate from the University of Hong Kong in 1979 and in the same year to found the City Contemporary Dance Company. This has since become that region's major promoter of modern dance, featuring an extensive repertory of works, the majority created by Chinese choreographers including Tsao himself. The company has also toured internationally.

In 1984 Tsao was additionally appointed artistic associate of Vancouver's Goh Ballet. In 1986 he was invited to extend his pioneering work in Chinese dance to the mainland, teaching modern dance at the Beijing Dance Academy and the following year at the Guangdong Dance School. In 1992 he became founding artistic director of the Guangdong Modern Dance Company and remained with the company until 1998. In 1999 he became artistic director of Beijing Modern Dance Company, founding the new Beijing LDTX Modern Dance Company in 2005, having also returned to his post as director of Guangdong MDC in 2004.

A list of his works includes *Wanderings in the Realm of Lightness* (mus. Wong Sun-keung, 1989), *China Wind—China Fire* (mus. various, 1995), *Sexing Three Millennia* (Wong, 1998), *365 Ways of Doing and Undoing Orientalism* (mus. Peter Stuart, 2002), *The Conqueror* (mus. Chan Hing-yan, 2005), and *Warrior Landing* (mus. Chan, 2007).

(⊕) SEE WEB LINKS

• Website for City Contemporary Dance Company (CCDC)

Tsiskaridze, Nikolai (*b* Tbilisi, 31 Dec. 1973) Georgian dancer. He trained at the Tbilisi Ballet School and the Moscow Ballet School, graduating into the Bolshoi Ballet in 1992, where he rapidly came to prominence for his flamboyant interpretations of the classical repertoire. In 2001 he became the youngest person to be named a People's Artist of Russia. A frequent international guest artist.

Tuckett, William (*b* Birmingham, 3 Feb. 1969) British dancer, choreographer, and theatre director. He trained locally and at the Royal Ballet School in 1986; graduating into Sadler's Wells Royal Ballet (now Birmingham Royal Ballet) in 1988. Two years later he moved to the Royal Ballet where he was promoted to soloist in 1998 and principal character artist in 2002. He danced a wide range of solo and character roles but increasingly focused on his choreography. He created his first works as a student, including *On Classicism* (1987) for the Royal Ballet School and went on to produce numerous works for the two Royal companies. For Birmingham his works included *Those Unheard* (mus. Britten, 1989) and for the Royal *The Turn of the Screw* (mus. Panufnik, 1999), *Mr-Bear-Squash-You-All-Flat* (a tribute to Constant Lambert, 2001), and *The Seven Deadly Sins* (mus. Weill, 2007).

He has also choreographed for other companies including Rambert Dance Company, National Ballet of China, and English National Ballet (*The Canterville Ghost*, 2006), as well as for opera, television and film.

Tuckett's work has always tended towards narrative, his style blending contemporary and classical vocabularies; but after 2000 it widened to embrace more overtly theatrical conventions. Works like *Wind in the Willows* (2002), *The Soldier's Tale* (2003), and *The Thief of Baghdad* (2008)—all for the Royal Opera House's Linbury Theatre—incorporated puppetry, props, and spoken text. Tuckett has also worked as a theatre director, directing the Sondheim musical *Into the Woods* and a stage adaptation of the novel *Marianne Dreams* (both London, 2007).

Tudor, Antony (orig. William John Cook; *b* London, 4 Apr. 1908; *d* New York, 19 Apr. 1987) British dancer, choreographer, and teacher. He began his training with Marie Rambert in 1928, and later studied with Pearl Argyle, Harold Turner, and Margaret Craske. In 1930 he joined Rambert's company as a dancer, and also as her assistant. He immediately began choreographing ballets, and his early works (all of which he starred in) included *Cross-Garter'd* (mus. Frescobaldi, 1931), *Lysistrata* (mus. Prokofiev, 1932), *Adam and Eve* (mus. Lambert, Camargo Society, 1932), *The Planets* (mus. Holst, 1934), and *The Descent of Hebe* (mus. Bloch, 1935). It was with his subsequent ballets *Jardin aux lilas* (*Lilac Garden*, mus. Chausson, 1936) and *Dark Elegies* (mus. Mahler, 1937) that Tudor began to reveal his distinctive genius for choreographing psychological depths of character combining classical dance language and expressive gesture. In 1937 he left Rambert's company and with de Mille established Dance Theatre, with Hugh Laing as principal dancer, but the company was disbanded after one week in Oxford. He choreographed *The Judgment of Paris* (mus. Weill) in 1938 for an *ad hoc* company at the Westminster Theatre in London. Later that year he formed the *London Ballet with Laing, Maude Lloyd, and Peggy van Praagh as its stars; for this troupe he created *Soirée musicale* (mus. Rossini and Britten) and *Gala Performance* (mus. Prokofiev). In 1939 he and Laing moved to New York, where he became choreographer for Ballet Theatre, as well as dancing with the newly formed company. For Ballet Theatre he created *Goya Pastoral* (mus. Granados, 1940), *Pillar of Fire* (mus. Schoenberg, 1942), *The Tragedy of Romeo and Juliet* (mus. Delius, 1943), *Dim Lustre* (mus. R. Strauss, 1943), *Undertow* (mus. W. Schuman, 1945), and *Shadow of the Wind* (mus. Mahler, 1948). He worked for the Royal Swedish Ballet (1949–50), and New York City Ballet (1951–2), for whom he made *Lady of the Camellias* (mus. Verdi, 1951) and *La Gloire* (mus. Beethoven, 1952). In 1950 he left Ballet Theatre and was appointed director of the Metropolitan Opera Ballet School; later (1957–63) he

was ballet director of the Juilliard School. He made *Offenbach in the Underworld* for the Philadelphia Ballet Company (1954); and *Echoing of Trumpets* (mus. Martinů, 1963) for the Royal Swedish Ballet, where he briefly served as artistic director. As a freelance choreographer he made *Shadowplay* (mus. Koechlin, 1967) for the Royal Ballet, a company which had neglected him for decades, and *Knight Errant* (mus. R. Strauss, 1968) for the Royal Ballet Touring Company; and *The Divine Horsemen* (mus. Egk, 1969) for the Australian Ballet. He joined American Ballet Theatre as associate director in 1974, and choreographed *The Leaves Are Fading* (mus. Dvořák, 1975) and *The Tiller in the Fields* (mus. Dvořák, 1978), both of them made for Gelsey Kirkland. Although not especially prolific, Tudor was one of the great choreographers of the 20th century, admired by Ashton for the 'depth charge' of his character portrayals. He was an astute observer of human nature and behaviour, and was able to transmit a wealth of psychological detail—especially sorrow and yearning—with a single step or gesture. He was one of the first choreographers to concentrate on the emotional anguish of ordinary men and women, exploring the darkness of their interior lives with extraordinary grace and sympathy.

Tulip of Haarlem, The Ballet in three acts with choreography by Ivanov, music by Baron Fitingoff-Shell (or Baron Boris Shel). Premiered 4 Oct. 1887 at the Mariinsky Theatre in St Petersburg, with Emma Bessone, Legat, and P. Gerdt. Emma, a Dutch peasant girl, is turned into a tulip; a kiss from her sweetheart Peter returns her to human form. It was Ivanov's first original full-length ballet.

Tune, Tommy (*b* Wichita Falls, Tex., 28 Feb. 1939) US dancer, director, and choreographer. He studied ballet with Camille Hill, Emma Mae Horn, and Shirley Dodge but at six ft. six in. he became too tall for a classical dancer and focused on the theatre instead. He performed in Broadway musicals, including *Baker Street* (1965), *A Joyful Noise* (1966), *How Now Dow Jones?* (1967), and *Seesaw* (1973), for which he won his first Tony Award. He revealed his skill as a tap dancer in such films as *Hello, Dolly!* (1969) and *The Boy Friend* (1971). He made his New York directing debut in 1976 with *The Club*. His subsequent production, *The Best Little Whorehouse in Texas*, which he co-directed and co-choreographed, won him a 1978 Tony Award as Best Director of a Musical. He won additional Tonys in 1980 for direction and choreography on *A Day in Hollywood/A Night in the Ukraine*. Other successes followed, including Caryl Churchill's non-musical *Cloud 9* (1981) and *Nine* (1981), a musical based on Fellini's film *8½*; both productions earned him further directing awards. In 1983 he starred in, directed, and co-choreographed (with Thomie Walsh) *My One and Only*, in which he and Twiggy donned top hats to sing and dance to a selection of George Gershwin show tunes. This resulted in another Tony award, this time for Best Actor in a Musical. After two attempts at *Stepping Out* (1983 and 1987), Tune staged the darker *Grand Hotel* (1989) and *The Will Rogers Follies* (1991), winning Tonys for both shows. In all, he has won nine Tony Awards. He published his autobiography, *Footnotes: A Memoir*, in 1997.

Turkey Before the Second World War, theatrical dance in Turkey was restricted to appearances by foreign dance companies. Following a visit by Ninette de Valois, a national ballet school was set up in Istanbul in 1948, with Joy Newton as director. In 1950 it was moved to the Ankara State Conservatory. In 1960 the company, Turkish State Ballet staged its first professional performance; Robert Harrold's production of Manuel de Falla's *El amor brujo* featured an all-Turkish cast. Lorna Mossford staged the first production of *The Sleeping Beauty* in Turkey in 1963. De Valois contributed several works to the repertoire in the 1960s, including *Cesmebast* (*At the Fountain*), which used a score by the Turkish composer Ferit Tuzun, and *Sinfonietta*, with music by Nevit Kodali. Richard Glasstone (director 1965–9) staged *Sylvia* and *Prince of the Pagodas*, as well as *Hancerli Hanim* (*The Lady with the Dagger*), which took as its theme a famous tale of love, jealousy, and murder in 17th-century Istanbul. In 1968 the company performed the first ballet by a native choreographer, Sait Sokmen. The ballet, called *Cark* (*The Wheel*), was an abstract work set to Ravel's String Quartet. It helped to pave the way for other Turkish choreographers such as Mehmet Balkan. In 1970 a second company was founded, called the Istanbul State Ballet. There has been only sporadic modern dance activity in Turkey due to lack of funding. The sole state-supported company has been the Ankara-based Modern Dance Turkey, which was founded in 1993 by Turkish-born Beyhan Murphy, a graduate of London Contemporary Dance Theatre. With about 18 dancers, a repertory of works by Murphy herself, Turkish choreographers, and British choreographers like Ashley Page, Mark Baldwin, and Richard Alston, the company achieved both international and local success. There is little independent modern dance activity, although in Istanbul the Ceti studio run by Mustafa Kaplan offers a base for freelance choreographers and dancers, and a performance space for small-scale work. In 2008 Istanbul hosted its first international ballet competition.

Turner, Harold (*b* Manchester, 2 Dec. 1909; *d* London, 2 Jul. 1962) British dancer and teacher; one of the key figures in early British ballet. He studied with Alfred Haines in Manchester and performed in his company; further studies with Rambert in London from 1927. He danced with Dolin and Karsavina's companies (partnering Karsavina when he was just 20) and with Rambert's Ballet Club (1928–32). He created roles in Ashton's *Nymphs and Shepherds* (1928) and *Capriol Suite* (1930); in de Valois's *Suite of Dances* (1930) and *Cephalus and Procris* (1931); and in Salaman's *Le Rugby* (1930). In 1935 he joined Vic-Wells Ballet, becoming one of its principal dancers and remaining with the company (with two interruptions) until 1951. From 1941 to 1942 he danced with Mona Inglesby's International Ballet; he also served with the Royal Air Force during the Second World War. He created roles in de Valois's *The Rake's Progress* (1935), *Checkmate* (1937), *The Emperor's New Clothes* (1938), and *Don Quixote* (1950); and in Ashton's *Le Baiser de la fée* (1935), *Apparitions* (1936), *A Wedding Bouquet* (1937), and *Les Patineurs* (1937). After returning to Sadler's Wells in 1945, he starred in Massine's ballets, *La Boutique fantasque* and *The Three-Cornered Hat* (*Le Tricorne*). He also created a role in Massine's *Clock Symphony* (1948). An outstanding virtuoso dancer (who inspired Ashton to create the Blue Boy in *Les Patineurs*), he transformed himself in maturity into a fine character actor. After retirement, he taught at Sadler's Wells Ballet School and worked as ballet master of the Covent Garden Opera Ballet, as well as appearing as a guest artist with Sadler's Wells Ballet. He died during rehearsals for a 1962 Sadler's Wells revival of Massine's *The Good-Humoured Ladies*, in which he was to appear as the Marquis di Luca.

Turning Point, The A 1977 Hollywood film (made by Twentieth-Century Fox) about an ageing ballerina (Anne Bancroft) and her former colleague (Shirley MacLaine), who has abandoned her career to raise a family. The plot revolves around the latter's daughter (real-life ballerina Leslie *Browne) who seeks to pursue the career her mother never had. The film portrays the daily life of a major ballet company (American Ballet Theatre) and its cast also features Mikhail Baryshnikov, Antoinette Sibley, and Alexandra Danilova. There is additional performance footage of Fernando Bujones, Richard Cragun, Suzanne Farrell, Marcia Haydée, and Peter Martins. The script was written by Arthur Laurents; direction was by the former dancer and choreographer Herbert Ross, whose wife, the former ballerina Nora Kaye, assisted him.

turnout A fundamental requirement of all classical ballet, which involves rotating the legs and feet outwards from the hips so that the feet point sideways while the hips remain facing forward. Turnout was declared an essential element for dance by Blasis in 1820, although it had been around for more than 200 years before his pronouncement. The use of turnout was documented in Feuillet's *Chorégraphie* (1700), which codified the five positions of the feet. The idea of turnout is to give the lower body greater freedom of movement in every direction. Turnout depends on flexibility in the hip socket, which is developed over many years of careful ballet training.

tutu The standard bodice and skirt worn by female ballet dancers. It is usually made from layers of tarlatan, muslin, silk, tulle, gauze, or nylon. It first came into prominence in the 1830s when Taglioni wore a Romantic tutu for her performance in *La Sylphide*. This early form of the tutu extended down the leg towards the ankle. In the late 19th century, Classical ballet shortened the tutu to above the knee, to allow greater virtuosity of movement in the lower body and to show off the ballerina's legs. Modern tutus are frequently hip length and stand out stiffly from the hips.

Twilight Ballet in one act with choreography by van Manen, music by Cage, and designs by Vroom. Premiered 20 Jun. 1972 by the Dutch National Ballet at Stadsschouwburg in Amsterdam with Radius and Ebbelaar. The ballet is set to Cage's *Perilous Night* and portrays a man and a woman engaged in an aggressively confrontational relationship. It was revived for the Royal Ballet in 1973.

Two Pigeons, The Ballet in two acts with choreography and libretto by Ashton, music by André Messager, arranged by John Lanchbery, and designs by Jacques Dupont. Premiered 14 Feb. 1961, by the Royal Ballet Touring Company at the Royal Opera House in London, with Seymour, Gable, and Anderton. Loosely based on La Fontaine's fable, Ashton's ballet transposes the story to Bohemian Paris in the late 19th century. A young painter, bored with his domestic life, flirts with a gypsy girl but is finally reconciled with his forgiving fiancée. The ballet's lightly comic demeanour hides a deeper, more serious statement about the loss of innocence in love. One of the ballet's many charms is its use of two live pigeons to represent the lovers. It was restaged for the Royal Ballet in 1962 (with Seymour and Gable). It has also been revived for CAPAB Ballet (1968), Australian Ballet (1975), National Ballet of Canada (1979), Teatro Regio Ballet (1992), and Sarasota Ballet (2007). *Les Deux Pigeons*, the original production of the Messager score, with choreography by Louis Mérante, was premiered at the Paris Opera on 18 Oct. 1886 with Rosita Mauri and Marie Sanlaville. The hero was danced en travestie.

Ulanova, Galina (*b* St Petersburg, 8 Jan. 1910; *d* Moscow, 21 Mar. 1998) Soviet dancer and teacher. One of the definitive Russian ballerinas of the 20th century. She was the daughter of the regisseur Serge Ulanov and the dancer Maria Romanova and trained with her mother (from 1919) before entering the St Petersburg Ballet School (Petrograd Choreographic Institute) where she studied with Vaganova. In 1928 she graduated into the Mariinsky Ballet (then called the GATOB, later the Kirov) where she was rapidly promoted to ballerina, her exceptional gifts—especially her poetic sensitivity to music and character—showcased in her early interpretations of *Swan Lake, Sleeping Beauty*, and *Giselle*. It was in the new Soviet ballets however that she made her greatest impact. She created the role of Maria in Zakharov's *The Fountain of Bakhchisarai* (1934) and Coralie in his *Lost Illusions* (1936), Masha in Vainonen's *The Nutcracker* (1934) and—most significantly—Juliet in Lavrovsky's *Romeo and Juliet* (1940). During the Second World War she was evacuated to Perm with the Kirov Ballet (1941–2) and to Alma-Ata (1942–3) then in 1944 she joined the Bolshoi Ballet in Moscow where she remained until the end of her career. She created Tao-Hoa in Lavrovsky's new version of *The Red Poppy* (1949) and Katerina in his *The Stone Flower* (1954). It is said that Prokofiev was inspired by her when he wrote the scores for *Romeo and Juliet* and *The Stone Flower*.

Ulanova made her first appearance in the West in 1945, with a trip to Vienna, and was the Bolshoi's leading ballerina when the company visited London in 1956 and New York in 1959. The response from Western critics was rapturous; the intensity of her performances, even as she approached 50, confirmed her reputation as one of the world's leading ballerinas. She gave her farewell performance in 1962 but continued to work with the Bolshoi as ballet mistress and coach. Her pupils included Nina Timofeyeva, Ekaterina Maximova, Ludmila Semenyaka, and Nina Semizorova. Regarded as the embodiment of Soviet ballet in the middle of the 20th century, her unique stage presence was successfully captured in several films, among them *Stars of the Ballet* (1946), *Ballerina* (1947), *Trio Ballet* (1953), *Romeo and Juliet* (1954), and *The Bolshoi Ballet* (British film, 1957). She was chairman of the jury at the Varna international ballet competitions from 1964 to 1972. People's Artist of the USSR (1951). Lenin Prize (1957).

Ullate, Victor (*b* Saragossa, 9 May 1947) Spanish dancer, choreographer, and ballet director. He studied with María de Avila and Rosella Hightower before joining Antonio's company in 1962, moving on to Béjart's Ballet of the 20th Century in 1965. During his fourteen years with the company he created roles in several Béjart ballets including *Offrande chorégraphique* (1970), *Nijinsky, clown de Dieu* (1971), and *I trionfi di Petrarca* (1974). In 1979 he moved back to Spain, invited by the Spanish Ministry of Culture to form the Ballet Nacional Clásico. Four years later he founded his own school in Madrid and in 1988 formed his own Madrid-based ballet company, Ballet de Victor Ullate. This acquired significant state support in 1997 when it was invited to become resident at the newly rebuilt Opera House in Madrid, and was officially renamed Ballet de la Comunidad de Madrid. It performs a repertory of neoclassical works by Balanchine, van Manen, Forsythe, and others as well as by the company's current director Eduardo Lao and by Ullate himself (including *Jaleos*, 1996, *La Inteligencia de Las Flores*, 2001, and *El sur*, 2005). Ullate has also staged productions of *Les Sylphides, Giselle*, and *Don Quixote*. Beyond his company Ullate's prime importance lies in his school (also his foundation for professional dancers, set up in 2000) which has acquired an international reputation for the quality of its training, and has ranked among its students dancers of the calibre of Angel *Corella and Tamara *Rojo.

Ullmann, Lisa (*b* Berlin, 17 Jun. 1907; *d* Chertsey, 25 Jan. 1985) German-British dance and movement teacher. She studied dance at the Berlin Laban School, graduating in 1929. She taught in Nuremberg and at the Essen Folkwang School, where she worked for Kurt Jooss. In 1933, to escape Nazi persecution, she went to England with Jooss and his company. She taught at Dartington Hall until 1940, lectured and choreographed, and for twenty years (1938–58) was Laban's main collaborator. She was co-founder of the Laban Art of Movement Guild in 1945 and the Art of Movement Studio in Manchester in 1946. She was responsible for revising several books written by Laban, and catalogued the Laban Archives.

Ulrich, Jochen (*b* Osterode, 3 Aug. 1944) German dancer, choreographer, and company director. He studied at the Cologne Institute of Theatre Dance (1964–7) and joined the Cologne Opera Ballet in 1967, becoming a leading soloist and choreographer. His work combined classical and modern dance elements and in 1971, when the company assumed a more contemporary focus and was renamed Dance Forum of the Cologne State Opera, Ulrich was appointed one of its three artistic directors, becoming sole director and chief choreographer in 1987. He and the company played a significant role in establishing Germany's post-war modern dance scene, staging works by choreographers like Bruce, van Manen, and Tetley as well as a large repertory of works by Ulrich himself, many full length. In 1997, two years after the Cologne Dance Forum became independent from the opera house, the company folded. Since then Ulrich has worked as a freelance choreographer, creating several works for Iceland Dance Theatre and also directing Tanztheater of the Tiroler in Innsbruck. A list of his works includes *Lewis C.* (mus. Ivo Malec, 1970), *The Miraculous Mandarin* (mus. Bartók, 1980), *American Landscapes* (mus. Gershwin and Ives, 1983), *Lyric Suite* (mus. Berg, 1984), *Neue und Curieuse Theatralische Tantz-Schul* (mus. Mauricio Kagel, 1988), *Lulu* (mus. Nino Rota, 1990), *Graf Dracula* (mus. Samuelina Tahija, 1991), *Carmen* (mus. Egberto Gismondi, 1993), *Peer Gynt* (mus. Sibelius and Górecki, 1994), *Goya* (mus. Bo Spaenc, 1995), *Get Up Early* (mus. Joachim Kühn, 1996), *Ein* (1999), and *Diaghilev, the legends* (2000), both for Iceland Dance Theatre. He also choreographed extensively for theatre and musicals, including a production of *Chicago* at Reykjavik City Theatre.

Undertow Ballet in one act with prologue and epilogue, with choreography and libretto by Tudor, music by William Schuman, and designs by Raymond Breinin. Premiered 10 Apr. 1945 by Ballet Theatre at the Metropolitan Opera House, New York, with Hugh Laing, Diana Adams, Alicia Alonso, John Kriza, Lucia Chase, Patricia Barker. The ballet portrays the psyche of a disturbed young man who murders a prostitute (by choking her to death) during sex. All the characters in the ballet, with the exception of the young man (known as the Transgressor), have names taken from Greek and Roman mythology.

unitard All-in-one leotard and tights.

United Kingdom *See* GREAT BRITAIN.

United States, The In the 18th and 19th centuries ballet was imported to America by European artists and companies. The earliest recorded ballet performance took place in 1735, when America was still a British colony: the English dancer Henry Holt appeared in *The Adventures of Harlequin and Scaramouche* and *The Burgo'-master Trick'd* in Charleston, S. Carolina. In 1792 the Frenchman Alexandre Placide presented an entire season of ballet in New York, offering *The Bird Catcher*, *The Return of the Labourers*, and *The Philosophers, or the Merry Girl*. America's first professional dancer was said to be John *Durang (1768–1822), who was a member of Placide's company. Mme Placide (in reality Suzanne Vaillande) later settled in New Orleans where she became prima ballerina and staged several original ballets—she was in effect America's first woman choreographer. Placide, meanwhile, opted to stay in Charleston, where he continued to stage ballets until he died in 1812. In those days most ballets were derived from the Paris Opera model of *Noverre, *Dauberval, and *Gardel. The first truly American production was *La Forêt noire*, staged in 1794 for Anna Gardie in Philadelphia. Philadelphia was an important early centre of dance—the Englishman James Byrne enjoyed great success there when he brought his Harlequin pantomimes at the turn of the century. Also important was Charleston where the French choreographer Jean Baptiste Francisqui presented 34 ballets during the 1794–5 season. (Francisqui, along with Durang and Gardie, later went to New York where they danced in *Pygmalion*, *The Milkmaid, or The Death of the Bear*, and *The American Heroine* (a 'grand historic and military pantomime').

In the 1820s a number of French artists toured America, accustoming audiences to a much more virtuosic style of classical dance and during the following decades ballet activity expanded. The US saw *La Sylphide* for the first time in 1835 and *Giselle* (in Boston) in 1846. Elssler's US tours (1840–2) were very popular; the Cecchetti family (including Enrico) also toured the US in 1857; and the Ravel family spent more than 30 years on the road in America, with a repertoire of original ballets, pantomimes, and circus acts. In 1837 Mary Ann Lee and Augusta *Maywood, two of America's first native ballerinas, gave their professional debuts in Philadelphia. In 1883 the Metropolitan Opera House opened in New York, although at that point dance played only a small role in its productions. *Coppélia* and *Sylvia* were introduced to America through Theodore Thomas's American Opera Company.

Ballet did not yet develop as an American dance form however and was far outstripped by developments in popular dance. *The *Black Crook,* a theatrical extravaganza which opened in 1866 in New York was historically successful, running for more than a year before being re-incarnated in revivals and touring productions which continued until 1903. Through it, thousands of Americans were introduced to dance.

The 19th century also saw the development of the first truly American theatrical dance form, *tap, a fusion of West African rhythms and European hard-shoe step dances. By the early 20th century, popular dances like skirt dances, clog dances, and hula dances were an essential ingredient in vaudeville programmes, revues, and musical comedies.

At the beginning of the 20th century most ballet performances were still provided by foreign artists such as *Pavlova, *Genée, *Mordkin, and *Diaghilev's Ballets Russes. This changed in the 1930s. The School of American Ballet was founded in 1933, and two years later *Kirstein and *Balanchine formed their first company (the American Ballet, which was resident at the Metropolitan Opera House for two years). In 1940 Ballet Theatre (later *American Ballet Theatre) was founded. Outside of New York other companies were springing up, among them the *Atlanta Ballet, founded in 1929, *San Francisco Ballet (founded in 1933), *Littlefield's company in Philadelphia (1935–41), and *Page and Stone's (founded 1938) in Chicago.

As classical ballet developed into an indigenous form modern dance in America was more rapidly established. The recitals of *Duncan and *St Denis in the early years of the 20th century paved the way for *Graham, *Humphrey, and *Weidman whose distinctive dance idioms were all forged during the late 1920s and 1930s. Graham's highly structured system of dance training was particularly significant, exerting a global influence as well as fostering new companies and choreographers in America. During this period, show dancing flourished on Broadway, absorbing the rhythms of the jazz age and defining a new theatrical style; dance also flourished in Hollywood with Busby *Berkeley's dazzling ensemble choreography created especially for the camera and Fred Astaire and Ginger Rogers becoming household names.

After the Second World War dance activity in America grew exponentially. New York City Ballet was founded in 1948, *Joffrey formed his first company in 1954, and regional ballet companies thrived. A new generation of modern dance choreographers, including *Cunningham, *Taylor, *Limón, and *Ailey, set up companies to showcase their individual dance aesthetics. The range of modern dance proliferated further in the 1960s with a growth in the independent dance sector.

During this highly experimental period choreographers like Tharp, Trisha *Brown, *Childs, and *Paxton all began working, challenging pre-existing notions of dance and dance practice. As these choreographers entered the mainstream other choreographers emerged, with *Morris, *Petronio, *Varone, and many others forming their own successful companies. A wide network of performance venues, both classical and modern, plus numerous studios allowed New York to remain the epicentre of American dance activity for several decades. However in other parts of the US, companies like *Miami City Ballet and *Pacific Northwest Ballet both gained significant reputations as did San Francisco Ballet under *Tomasson. A modern dance scene also developed on the West coast, around choreographers like Margaret *Jenkins. The region was also home to some of the first professional *hip-hop troupes, like the *Electric Boogaloos.

At the beginning of the 21st century dance remains a core element of American culture, but constraints in public funding and rising living costs—above all in New York—have made it difficult for younger dancers and choreographers to start careers. Established companies like those of Morris and Ailey have been able to expand into purpose-built bases, but these have all depended on private patronage, a resource not available to less well-known artists.

Un jour ou deux Modern dance in one act with choreography by Cunningham, music by Cage, and designs by Jasper Johns. Premiered 6 Nov. 1973 by the Paris Opera Ballet, with Piollet, Denard, Guizerix, and Ariel. It had a cast of 26 dancers and lasted more than 90 minutes without an intermission.

Urban Bush Women All-female black dance company founded by Jawole Willa Jo *Zollar in New York in 1984. Zollar's politically outspoken choreography draws on the folk traditions of the African diaspora as well as on the music and dance of modern American black culture. The company's productions tackle tough subject-matter, including racism, abortion, and the disenfranchisement of black American women. A list of its works includes *Anarchy, Wild Women, and Dinah* (1986), *Heat* (1988), *Praise House* (1990), and *Bones and Ash: A Gilda Story* (mus. Toshi Reagon, 1995), and the Bessie Award-winning *Walking with Pearl... Southern Diaries* (2005), based on the life of Pearl Primus.

(((●))) SEE WEB LINKS
• Website for Urban Bush Women

USSR *See* RUSSIA AND THE USSR.

Uthoff, Ernst (*b* Duisburg, 28 Dec. 1904; *d* Santiago de Chile, 19 Feb. 1993) German-Chilean dancer, choreographer, teacher, and director. He studied with Laban, Jooss, and Leeder and joined the Folkwang Ballet in 1927. He created the role of Standard Bearer in Jooss's *The Green Table* (1932) and the Libertine in his *Big City*. Along with the other members of the Jooss company, he fled Nazi rule in the mid-1930s and settled in England. However in 1941, following the Ballets Jooss 1940 tour to South America, he settled in Santiago with his wife Lola Botka. Together they opened a dance school at the University of Chile, out of which was born the Chilean National Ballet (Ballet Nacional Chileno). He choreographed many dance-theatre works for the company and retired in 1965 after 24 years as director. A list of his ballets includes *Drosselbart, Don Juan, Petrushka, The Prodigal Son, Alotria*, and *Carmina Burana*, his greatest success. His son Michael, a dancer and choreographer, worked in America directing the Hartford Ballet and Ballet Arizona.

Vaganova, Agrippina (*b* St Petersburg, 26 Jun. 1879; *d* St Petersburg, 5 Nov. 1951) Soviet dancer, teacher, and director. She trained at the Imperial Theatre School in St Petersburg, a student of Ivanov, Vazem, Pavel Gerdt, and Nikolai Legat, and later studied with Preobrajenska. She graduated in 1897 into the Mariinsky Theatre, but despite her powerful technical skills was not promoted to ballerina until 1915, a year before she retired. Her career had not been helped by the fact that she was dancing at the same time as Pavlova, Karsavina, Preobrajenska, and Kschessinska, and lacked their political influence—the critic Valerian Svetlov once described her as 'the queen of variations'. Disillusioned with her stage career, Vaganova none the less achieved lasting fame as one of the most important teachers in the history of ballet. She began teaching at a private ballet school in St Petersburg, the School of Russian Ballet run by Akim *Volynsky, in 1917. In 1920 she transferred to the Imperial Theatre School (by now renamed the Leningrad Ballet School) where she remained until her death in 1951. Her students included Semonova, Ulanova, Dudinskaya, Moiseyeva, Kolpakova, and Volkova. One of her early choreographic works, *The Visions of a Poet* (1927), was made for the school's theatre. A woman of great analytical power, she developed her own system of teaching which still carries her name. It gave birth to the new Soviet style and today is used as the basis of ballet training both in Russia and in the West. She published the details of her system in *Fundamentals of the Classic Dance* in Leningrad in 1934 (English translation by Anatole Chujoy, New York, 1937). From 1917 to 1951 she taught and coached at the Kirov; from 1931 to 1937 she was artistic director of the Kirov Ballet. She encouraged the first productions of Vainonen's *Flames of Paris* (1932) and Zakharov's *Fountain of Bakhchisarai* (1934), and herself staged new productions of *Swan Lake* (1933) and *La Esmeralda* (1935). In 1957 the St Petersburg ballet school was renamed the Vaganova Institute in her honour.

Vainonen, Vassily (*b* St Petersburg, 21 Feb. 1901; *d* Moscow, 23 Mar. 1964) Soviet dancer, librettist, and choreographer. He studied at the Imperial Ballet School in St Petersburg, with Leontiev, Shiryaev, and Ponomarev, and graduated in 1919. He joined the Kirov Ballet (then known as the GATOB) and won acclaim as a character dancer, continuing to perform until 1938. As a choreographer, starting out in the 1920s, one of his first works was *Moszkovsky Waltz*, created for the Evenings of Young Ballet; his early work reflected the influence of Isadora Duncan and Fokine. From 1930 to 1938 he was a choreographer with the Kirov. His first important production was the full-length *The Golden Age* (mus. Shostakovich, Kirov, 1930), which incorporated a revolutionary acrobatic element into its choreography as well as the visual influences of cinema and Russian propaganda posters. His next work was *Flames of Paris* (mus. Asafiev, 1932), a heroic ballet based on the French Revolution that was a notable success for both him and the Kirov. His staging of *Nutcracker* (1934), was equally successful, remaining in the Kirov's repertoire for decades. Vainonen was additionally ballet master and choreographer of the Bolshoi Ballet in Moscow (1946–50, 1954–8). A list of his ballets includes *Partisan Days* (mus. Asafiev, Kirov, 1936), *Mirandolina* (mus. Sergei Vasilenko, Bolshoi Ballet, Moscow, 1949), *The Coast of Happiness* (mus. Antonio Spadavecchia, Novosibirsk, 1952), and *Gayané* (mus. Khachaturian, Bolshoi Ballet, Moscow, 1957).

Valberkh, Ivan (Valberg) (*b* Moscow, 14 Jul. 1766; *d* St Petersburg, 26 Jul. 1819) Russian dancer, choreographer, teacher, and ballet master. He trained at the St Petersburg Ballet School with Angiolini and Canziani, and graduated in 1786, becoming premier danseur at the Bolshoi Theatre in St Petersburg the same year and later ballet inspector of the company, from 1794. He made his choreographic debut in 1795 with *A Happy Repentance*, and went on to choreograph more than 36 ballets and divertissements, many of them with moral and patriotic themes (especially during the Napoleonic wars). He worked with Charles Didelot at the Bolshoi Theatre in St Petersburg (from 1801) and succeeded Didelot as ballet master when the Frenchman left in 1811. He taught at the Bolshoi Theatre in St Petersburg (from 1794) and at the Bolshoi Theatre in Moscow (1808). A list of his ballets includes *The New Werther* (mus. Serge Titov, 1799), *Blanca, or,*

A Marriage of Revenge (mus. Titov, 1803), *The Count Castelli, or A Murderous Brother* (mus. various, 1804), *Orpheus and Eurydice* (mus. Gluck, 1808), *Romeo and Juliet* (tragic ballet with choruses, 1809), *The New Heroine, or The Cossack Woman* (1811), *The People's Volunteer Corps, or Love for the Motherland* (mus. Catarino Cavos, 1812), *Russians in Germany, or What Comes of Love for the Motherland* (mus. Cavos, 1813), *Cossack in London* (1813), *Festival in the Allied Armies' Camp at Montmartre* (1813), *The American Heroine, or Perfidy Punished* (1814), and *Russian Victory, or The Russians in Paris* (1814). He was Russia's first native-born ballet master and choreographer.

Valdés, Viengsay (*b* Havana, 1977) Cuban dancer. She trained in gymnastics, beginning her ballet training, aged 9, at the Alejo Carpentier Provincial Ballet School, then at the Escuela Nacional de Arte (ENA). In 1994 she joined the National Ballet of Cuba, aged 17, where she was promoted to principal in 1995, premier dancer in 2001, and prima ballerina (2003).

A dancer of exceptional technical skills, especially in pirouettes and adage, she has toured widely with the company and has appeared in major galas, with the Danish Royal Ballet among others. She has been most frequently partnered by Joel Carreño but also by Carlos Acosta, Jose Manuel Carreño, and Giuseppe Picone. In 2007, Valdés collaborated with British director Sebastian Doggart on the mixed-media performance *Balance of Ice*.

Valois, (Dame) Ninette de (orig. Edris Stannus; *b* Baltiboys, Ireland, 6 Jun. 1898; *d* London, 8 Mar. 2001) Irish-born British dancer, choreographer, teacher, and ballet director. Founder of the *Royal Ballet and one of the pioneering figures in 20th-century dance. She studied with Lila Field, Édouard Espinosa and Cecchetti in London, later with Nikolai Legat, and made her professional debut in 1914, dancing in *Jack and the Beanstalk*, a pantomime at the Lyceum Theatre in London. Revues and pantomimes provided her early employment; then in 1919 she appeared in the Covent Garden Opera season and in 1922 appeared as a principal dancer with the Massine-Lopokova company in their London season. She joined *Diaghilev's Ballets Russes in 1923 and stayed with the company until 1925, returning as a guest artist the following year. With Diaghilev she created roles in Nijinska's *Les Biches*, *Les Fâcheux*, and *Le Train bleu* and in Balanchine's *Le Rossignol*. She also danced with Anton *Dolin's company (1926) and with the Covent Garden Opera (1928). In 1926 she opened her own school in London, the Academy of Choregraphic (*sic*) Art, and began her association with Lilian *Baylis at the Old Vic, a

relationship that provided the foundation for what would become the Royal Ballet. De Valois gave movement classes to the actors at Baylis's theatre and her dancers appeared in the opera productions. She also worked as a dancer and choreographer for the Abbey Theatre in Dublin (where she collaborated with W. B. Yeats) and the Festival Theatre in Cambridge. She made her first ballet at the Old Vic, *Les Petits Riens*, in 1928. In 1931 she closed her school and moved over to the official school linked to the newly re-opened *Sadler's Wells Theatre; it eventually became the Royal Ballet School. She now had a company based at the Wells, the Vic-Wells Ballet, which gave regular performances. It later became the *Sadler's Wells Ballet which, in 1946, moved to the Royal Opera House. In 1956 the company became the Royal Ballet. She also founded a second company in 1946, first called the Sadler's Wells Opera Ballet, then Sadler's Wells Theatre Ballet, Sadler's Wells Royal Ballet and, in 1990, Birmingham Royal Ballet. She continued to dance until 1937, and created roles in Ashton's *Regatta* (1931), *Les Rendezvous* (1933), and *A Wedding Bouquet* (1937) but during the 1930s her energies were increasingly focused on choreography, as she created works for the Camargo Society, Ballet Club (later Ballet Rambert), as well as for own company. Influenced by European modern dance as well as by her classical training, ballets like *The Rake's Progress*, *Checkmate*, and *The Prospect Before Us* revealed de Valois's distinctive, and economical gift for storytelling and character portrayal. During the 1930s she also staged the Petipa-Ivanov classics for her company, thus helping to bring the Russian ballet heritage to the West. Under her direction, both the Royal Ballet and the Royal Ballet School became internationally recognized as leading dance institutions. She was artistic director of the Royal Ballet until she retired in 1963, although she continued to work at the Royal Ballet School. She was founder and director of the Turkish School of Ballet in Ankara (1948) and the Turkish State Ballet (1956). A list of her ballets includes *Danse sacrée et danse profane* (mus. Debussy, Camargo Society, 1930), *La Création du monde* (mus. Milhaud, Camargo Society, 1931), *Job* (mus. Vaughan Williams, Camargo Society, 1931), *The Jackdaw and the Pigeons* (mus. Bradford, Vic-Wells, 1931), *Narcissus and Echo* (mus. Bliss, Vic-Wells, 1932), *The Origin of Design* (mus. Handel, arr. Beecham, Camargo Society, 1932), *The Wise and Foolish Virgins* (mus. Atterberg, Vic-Wells, 1933), *Bar aux Folies-Bergère* (mus. Chabrier, Ballet Rambert, 1934), *The Haunted Ballroom* (mus. G. Toye, Vic-Wells, 1934), *La Jarre* (mus. Casella, Vic-Wells, 1934), *The Rake's Progress* (mus. G. Gordon, Vic-Wells, 1935), *The Gods Go a-Begging* (mus. Handel, arr. Beecham, Vic-Wells, 1936),

Barabau (mus. Rieti, Vic-Wells, 1936), *Prometheus* (mus. Beethoven, Vic-Wells, 1936), *Checkmate* (mus. Bliss, Vic-Wells, 1937), *Le Roi nu* (mus. Françaix, Vic-Wells, 1938), *The Prospect Before Us* (mus. Boyce, arr. Lambert, Vic-Wells, 1940), *Orpheus and Eurydice* (mus. Gluck, Sadler's Wells Ballet, 1941), *Promenade* (mus. Haydn, arr. Evans, Jacob, Sadler's Wells Ballet, 1943), *Don Quixote* (mus. R. Gerhard, Sadler's Wells Ballet, 1950), *At the Fountainhead* (mus. Tuzun, Turkish State Ballet, 1964), *Sinfonietta* (mus. Kodalli, Turkish State Ballet, 1966), and *The Wedding of Harlequin* (with Ashton, Ballet for All, 1973). Author of *Invitation to the Ballet* (1937), *Come Dance With Me* (1957), and *Step by Step* (1977). Dame Commander of the Order of the British Empire 1951. Chevalier de la Légion d'honneur, 1950. Erasmus Prize, 1974. Companion of Honour, 1983. Order of Merit, 1992.

Valse, La Ballet in one act with choreography by Nijinska, music by Ravel, and designs by Benois. Premiered 12 Jan. 1929 by the Ida Rubinstein Company in Monte Carlo, with Rubinstein and Vilzak. An abstract ballet, set in a ballroom, it was described by Ravel as 'a kind of apotheosis of the Viennese waltz'. The score had initially been commissioned by Diaghilev but was rejected by him. It subsequently inspired many choreographers, however, including Fokine, H. Lander, Massine, Charrat, and De Frutos. The two most famous versions are by Balanchine and Ashton. Balanchine's version (costumes by Karinska, lighting by Rosenthal) was premiered 20 Feb. 1951 by New York City Ballet at City Center in New York, with LeClercq, Magallanes, and Moncion. Balanchine coupled the score with Ravel's earlier *Valses nobles et sentimentales*. Ashton's version (des. André Levasseur) was first performed by the La Scala Ballet in Milan, 31 Jan. 1958, and revived for the Royal Ballet on 10 Mar. 1959.

Valses nobles et sentimentales Ravel's eight short waltzes for piano has been used by several choreographers, among them Clustine (Paris, 1912), Lifar (Paris Opera, 1938), Ashton (Sadler's Wells Ballet, London, 1947), and MacMillan (German Opera, Berlin, 1966). Balanchine used them as the introduction to his version of *La Valse* (New York City Ballet, New York, 1951).

van Names preceded by 'van' are listed under the family name. *See* DANTZIG; HAMEL; MANEN; PRAAGH; SCHAYK.

Vandekeybus, Wim (*b* Herentals, Flanders, 1964) Belgian dancer, choreographer, filmmaker, and company director. He studied psychology at the University of Leuven, before turning to theatre and film. He worked for two years with the theatre director Jan Fabre (with whom he would later collaborate on *Body, Body on the Wall*, 1997) and in 1985 founded his own company, Ultima Vez. Two years later he premiered *What the Body Does Not Remember* (mus. Thierry de Mey and Peter Vermeersch). The work's raw athleticism, its high impact partnering and apparent risk-taking (the dancers hurled bricks) established Vandekeybus at the forefront of a new genre of extreme dance theatre. His subsequent works have tended to use an equally visceral dance language and have often incorporated film and text to explore intense emotional themes, including blindness (*Her Body Doesn't Fit Her Soul*, 1993), death (*In As Much As Life Is Borrowed*, 2000), and eroticism (*Blush*, 2002, filmed 2003). Vandekeybus was artist in residence at the Royal Flemish Theatre in Brussels (1993–99) and Ultima Vez were company in residence at the Teatro Comunale di Ferrara (2000–2). For Batsheva Dance Company he choreographed *Exhaustion from Dreamt Love* (1996). Other works for his own company include *Les Porteuses de mauvaises nouvelles* (1989), *Immer das Selbe gelogen* (1991), *Mountains Made of Barking* (1994), *Bereft of a Blissful Union* (1996), *7 for a Secret Never to be Told* (1997), *In Spite of Wishing and Wanting* (1999), and *Sonic Boom* (2003, in collaboration with the Dutch theatre group Toneelgroep Amsterdam). Since 2002 he has additionally worked on children's projects including *Bet Noir*, an adaptation of the Oedipus myth.

(((●))) **SEE WEB LINKS**
● Website for Ultima Vez

Vangsaae, Mona (*b* Copenhagen, 29 Apr. 1920; *d* Copenhagen, 17 May 1983) Danish dancer and teacher. She studied at the Royal Danish Ballet School with Harald Lander, later in Paris and London, and in 1938 joined the Royal Danish Ballet. In 1942 she was promoted to soloist (principal) and created roles in many ballets including Juliet in Ashton's *Romeo and Juliet* (1955) and the title role in Cullberg's *Moon Reindeer* (1957). She retired from the stage in 1962 and was co-director (with her former husband Frank *Schaufuss) of the Danish Ballet Academy and its associated performing group Danish Ballet Theatre until it was disbanded in 1974. She also choreographed two works, both in 1958: *Spectrum* (mus. Scriabin, Royal Danish Ballet) and *A Note Page* (mus. Mozart, Charlottenborg), as well as staging Bournonville's *Conservatoire* for London Festival Ballet (1973) and Bournonville's *La Sylphide* for the Stuttgart Ballet (1982). She additionally worked as a guest teacher, including the Royal Ballet School (1982–3). Mother of the dancer Peter *Schaufuss.

variation In classical ballet, a solo dance performed by both male and female dancers usually within a structured dance such as a pas de deux. It is designed to showcase a dancer's individual virtuosity.

Variations Ballet in three parts with choreography by Balanchine, music by Stravinsky, and lighting by R. Bates. Premiered 31 Mar. 1966 by New York City Ballet, at the State Theater in New York, with Farrell. A plotless work set to Stravinsky's *Variations for Orchestra*, which is played three times for three different groups of dancers, the first comprising twelve women, the second six men, and the third one ballerina.

Variations for Four Divertissement with choreography by Dolin, music by Marguerite Keogh, and costumes by Tom Lingwood. Premiered 5 Sept. 1957 by London Festival Ballet at the Royal Festival Hall, London, with Gilpin, Flindt, Godfrey, and Prokovsky. A virtuoso display piece for a quartet of male dancers.

Varna, International Ballet Competition
See COMPETITIONS.

Varone, Doug (*b* Syosset, NY, 5 Nov. 1956) US dancer, choreographer, and director. He studied tap dancing as a child, modern dance at the State University of New York at Purchase, and ballet with Maggie Black and Zena Rommett. He danced with José Limón's company (1978–9) and with Lar Lubovitch (1979–86) before founding his own company, Doug Varone and Dancers, in 1986. He choreographed his first piece, *Mendet*, in 1978 and as well as creating the repertory for his own company he has also made work for many others including the Limón company, Rambert Dance Company, Batsheva, and Colorado Ballet. A list of his works includes *Cantata 78* (mus. Bach, 1987), *Rise* (mus. John Adams, 1993), *Possession* (mus. Philip Glass, 1995), *In Thine Eyes* (mus. Michael Nyman, 1996), *Sleeping With Giants* (mus. Nyman, 1999), *Tomorrow* (mus. Hahn, 2000), *Short Story* (mus. Rachmaninoff, Limón company 2001, Varone company, 2002), *Castles* (mus. Prokofiev, 2004), *Boats Leaving* (mus. Pärt, 2006), and *Lux* (mus. Glass 2006). In 1997 he made his Broadway debut with the musical *Triumph of Love*. He has also worked extensively in opera, choreographing and staging the US premiere of George Antheil's *Transatlantic*, for the Minnesota Opera (1998); choreographing various productions for the Metropolitan Opera, including *Les Troyens* and *Salome*; directing and choreographing *Orfée et Euridice* for Opera Colorado; and *Joseph Merrick: Elephant Man* and Gounod's *Faust* for Minnesota Opera, among others.

(⊕) SEE WEB LINKS
• Website for Doug Varone and Dancers

Vasiliev, Ivan (*b* Vladivostok, 1989) Russian dancer. He trained at the Belorussian Ballet School from the age of 10, performing lead roles with the Ballet Theatre of Belarus while still a student and graduating into the company as a principal in 2006. The same year he moved to the Bolshoi Ballet. A compact dancer and fearless athlete, admired for his superbly controlled pirouettes and bravura elevation, Vasiliev's technique has so far been showcased in roles such as Basil (*Don Quixote*) and Ali (*Le Corsaire*). In 2008 he made his debut as Spartacus, the youngest dancer to take that role in the Bolshoi's history. He has also danced in the works of Wheeldon and Ratmansky, dancing the role of Philippe in the latter's production of *Flames of Paris*. He is recipient of numerous prizes and awards, including first prize in Moscow 2005.

Vasiliev, Vladimir (*b* Moscow, 18 Apr. 1940) Russian dancer, choreographer, and company director. He studied at the Moscow Ballet School, a student of Mikhail Gabovich, and graduated into the Bolshoi Ballet in 1958. He was quickly promoted to principal dancer and for the next twenty years was the Bolshoi's leading male star. Heroic and dynamic, possessing a then unparalleled virtuoso technique, he came to embody the image of the post-war Bolshoi male dancer. His dramatic athleticism was showcased most famously in *Spartacus*, but was also acclaimed for the romantic intensity with which he interpreted Albrecht. He created leading roles in Radunsky's new staging of *The Humpbacked Horse* (1960), Tarasova and Lapauri's *Song of the Forests* (1961), Lavrovsky's *Pages of (from) a Life* (1961), Goleizovsky's *Leili and Medzhnun* (1964), Grigorovich's *Nutcracker* (1966), *Spartacus* (1968), *Sleeping Beauty* (1973), and *Angara* (1976), and Béjart's *Petrushka* (1977). He also created the leading roles in several of his own ballets including *Icarus* (Bolshoi 1971), *Macbeth* (Bolshoi 1980), and *Anyuta* (Naples, 1986). He often danced abroad as a guest artist, in concert tours with his wife, the ballerina Ekaterina *Maximova, and also with Béjart's Ballet of the 20th Century, the Ballet de Marseilles, and American Ballet Theatre. The couple performed more frequently in the West after their open criticicism of Grigorovich's directorship of the Bolshoi and from the late 1980s they were effectively banished from the Bolshoi's stage. During the 1980s Vasiliev additionally worked as a guest choreographer in Berlin, Budapest, Naples, and Riga. From 1990 he was a member of the board of directors of the Ballet Theatre of the Kremlin Palace of Congress, for whom he made several ballets, including *Cinderella* (1991). He was artistic director of the Rome Opera Ballet (1993–5). In 1995 he returned to the Bolshoi to assume direction of the theatre's opera and ballet companies. During the following five years he

opened up the ballet's repertoire to outside choreographers, and encouraged young choreographers at home. He also staged new productions
of the classics, including *Giselle* and a much-criticized *Swan Lake*, and choreographed *Balda*
(mus. Shostakovich, 1999). In 2000 he was replaced, since when he has worked as a freelance
choreographer, staging his ballets worldwide including Argentina, Brazil, Tokyo, Europe, and
Russia, choreographing Zeffirelli's production of
Aida (Verona, 2002), a new *Cinderella* for the State
Ballet Theatre of Russia (2006), and *Lungo Viaggio
della Notte di Natale* (mus. Tchaikovsky, Rome
Opera). A list of his other ballets includes *Icarus*
(mus. S. Slonimsky, 1971), *These Charming Sounds*
(mus. Rameau, Mozart, and others, 1978), *Macbeth*
(mus. K. Molchanov, 1980), *Juno and Avos* (mus.
Rybnikov, 1981), *Anyuta* (mus. Gavrillyn, 1986), and
Romeo and Juliet (mus. Prokofiev, 1990). He has
appeared in many films including *The Humpbacked
Horse* (1961), *Secret of Success* (1967), *Narcissus*
(1971), *Duet* (also directed, 1972), *Spartacus*
(1976), *Gigolo and Gigoletta* (also directed, 1980),
The World of Ulanova (also directed, 1981), *These
Charming Sounds* (also directed, 1981), *La traviata*
(dir. Zeffirelli, 1982), *Anyuta* (also directed, 1982), *I
Want to Dance: Fragments of a Biography* (also
directed, 1985), and *Fouetté* (also directed, 1986).
He also directed... *And there remains, as always,
something else* (1990). He lectures widely and has
served on many competition juries. Gold medal
Varna (1964); Nijinsky Prize (Paris, 1964); Lenin
Prize (1970).

Vaughan, David (*b* London, 17 May 1924)
British dancer, administrator, archivist, and writer. He studied dance with Rambert and Audrey de
Vos in London and at the School of American
Ballet in New York, and with Tudor and Cunningham. He settled in the US in 1950 and was co-
founder with James Waring of Dance Associates
in 1951. He danced with the companies of Shirley
Broughton, Louis Johnson, Katherine Litz, Paul
Taylor, and Waring. He was associated with Cunningham for more than 30 years, as administrator
of the Cunningham Studio, as company tour
manager, and from 1976 as archivist of the Cunningham Dance Foundation. Author of *The Royal
Ballet at Covent Garden* (1975), *Frederick Ashton
and his Ballets* (London, 1977), and *Merce Cunningham: Fifty Years* (New York, 1997); co-author
(with Mary Clarke) of *The Encyclopedia of Dance
and Ballet* (London, 1977).

Vazem, Ekaterina (*b* Moscow, 25 Jan. 1848; *d*
Leningrad, 14 Dec. 1937) Russian dancer and
teacher. She studied at the Imperial Theatre
School in St Petersburg with Ivanov, graduating
in 1867. From 1867 until 1884 she was a leading
dancer at the St Petersburg Bolshoi Theatre, and
she was one of the first Russians to rival the
technically superior Italian ballerinas of the day.
She was Petipa's favourite Russian ballerina and it
was she who provided the inspiration for Nikiya
in his *La Bayadère*. Among the ballets he made for
her were *Le Papillon* (1874), *The Bandits* (1875),
La Bayadère (1877), *The Daughter of the Snows*
(1879), *Zoraya* (1881), *Night and Day* (1883), and
the Grand Pas in his re-staging of *Paquita* (1881).
She appeared as a guest artist in America and
visited the Paris Opera School in 1880. She retired
in 1884, but continued to teach at the Imperial
Theatre School (1886–96) where her students
included Pavlova and Vaganova. She then taught
privately for many years. Author of *Memoirs of
a Ballerina of the St Petersburg Bolshoi Theatre*
(Leningrad, 1937).

Vaziev, Makharbek (*b* Alagir, 16 Jun. 1961)
Russian dancer and company director. He trained
at the Vaganova Ballet Academy and joined the
Kirov Ballet in 1979. His repertoire included the
leading male roles in *Swan Lake, Don Quixote, La
Sylphide, Giselle, La Bayadère*, and *The Sleeping
Beauty*, as well as dancing Ali in *Le Corsaire*
and the slave in *Scheherazade*. In 1997 he was
appointed to succeed *Vinogradov as director of
the Kirov (later Mariinsky), reportedly the youngest director in the company's history. Since
taking over, he promoted a new generation of
younger dancers, among them *Lopatkina and
*Vishneva and opened up the repertory to West-
ern ballets, including Forsythe, Balanchine, and
the Diaghilev repertory. One of his major achievements was the four-hour reconstruction of Petipa's 1890 production of *The Sleeping Beauty*,
complete with reproductions of the original sets
and costumes. He left the Mariinsky in 2008 and
in 2009 became artistic director of La Scala Ballet.

Vecheslova, Tatyana (*b* St Petersburg,
25 Feb. 1910; *d* St Petersburg, 11 Jul. 1991) Russian dancer, teacher, and ballet mistress. She
studied at the St Petersburg (Leningrad) Ballet
School, a pupil of Maria Romanova and Vaganova. Upon graduation in 1928 she joined the
GATOB (later the Kirov) where she became a
leading ballerina. She created the title role in
Vaganova's new staging of *Esmeralda* (1935), the
role of Florine in Zakharov's *Lost Illusions*, the
title role in Bourmeister's *Tatyana* (1947), and
roles in Chabukiani's *Heart of the Hills* (1938)
and *Laurencia* (1939). She was the first Soviet
ballerina to tour abroad when she and Chabukiani went to the US in 1934. She retired from
the stage in 1953. She taught (1950–70) at the
Leningrad Ballet School, which she also directed
(1952–4). She was rehearsal director of the Kirov
Ballet (1954–71). She also wrote several books

about dance, including *I am a Dancer* (1964) and *Of the Things I Value Most* (Leningrad, 1984).

Ventana, La Ballet in one act with choreography and libretto by Bournonville, music by Christian Lumbye and Wilhelm Christian Holm. Premiered 19 Jun. 1854 by the Price family at the Casino Theatre in Copenhagen. The ballet, about a young Spanish woman dreaming of the handsome man she has just met, features a scene in which the ballerina apparently dances with her image in a mirror but is actually dancing in unison with another ballerina. Bournonville created the ballet for Juliette Price, a member of the famous English circus family, whom he idolized. He revised *La Ventana* for the ballet's premiere at the Royal Danish Ballet (Royal Theatre, Copenhagen) in 1856. For the latter staging, he added a seguidilla, which he had borrowed from Paul Taglioni and a pas de trois. *La Ventana* was revived by Frank Schaufuss and Hans Brenaa for the Royal Danish Ballet in 1941 and has been revived for various companies abroad, including the Bolshoi Ballet. Erik Bruhn staged the pas de trois from *La Ventana* for American Ballet Theatre in New York in 1975 for himself, Cynthia Gregory, and Nureyev. Revived for Western Theatre Ballet (Sadler's Wells, 1968), Scottish Theatre Ballet (1969–71), and Irish Ballet (Cork, 1977).

Verchinina, Nina (*b* Moscow, 1912; *d* Rio de Janeiro, 16 Dec. 1995) Russian-Brazilian dancer, teacher, and choreographer. She was born in Russia, raised in Shanghai and studied ballet with Preobrajenska and Nijinska, later modern dance with Laban in Germany. From 1929 she danced with Ida Rubinstein's company, moving on to de Basil and Blum's Ballets Russes de Monte Carlo in 1933, where she created roles in Massine's *Les Présages* and *Choreartium* (1933), and *Symphonie fantastique* (1936). She stayed with de Basil following his break with Blum, dancing with his Original Ballet Russe from 1939. She first began to choreograph in 1937 and was invited to work with the San Francisco Ballet (1937–8) and the Ballet Opera of Havana (1942–5). In 1949 she founded her own company in Madrid, for whom she made *The Quest* and *Valse Triste*. In the 1950s she moved to South America, working firstly in Argentina then in Brazil where she was choreographer at the Rio de Janeiro City Theatre. Her works there included *Tahina Can* (mus. Villa-Lobos) and *Zuimaaluti* (mus. Claudio Santoro). She gave up choreography in the 1960s to devote herself to teaching. With her emphasis on expressionist dance theatre, she was a major influence in the development of modern dance in Brazil.

Verdi, Giuseppe (*b* Le Roncole, 10 Oct. 1813; *d* Milan, 27 Jan. 1901) Italian composer. He wrote

no full ballet scores although several of his operas contain ballet sequences, especially those he revised for Paris. These include *Jérusalem* (or *I lombardi*, Paris, 1847), *Les Vêpres siciliennes* (Paris, 1855), *Il trovatore* (Paris, 1857), *Macbeth* (Paris, 1865), *Don Carlos* (Paris, 1867), *Aida* (Cairo, 1871), and *Otello* (Paris, 1894). Peter Anastos choreographed the mock Verdi ballet *La Troviatara* for Les Ballets Trockadero de Monte Carlo. The *Four Seasons* ballet from *Vêpres siciliennes* is often performed as a separate ballet; versions include those by MacMillan (Royal Ballet, 1975) and Robbins (New York City Ballet, 1979). His operas have inspired several ballet adaptations, including Filippo Termanini's *Rita Gauthier* (*La traviata*, Turin, 1857) and Page's *Revanche* (*Il trovatore*, 1951) and *Camille* (*La traviata*, 1957). Ballets using Verdi's music include Cranko's *The Lady and the Fool* (arr. Mackerras, Sadler's Wells Theatre Ballet, 1954) and Prokovsky's *The Three Musketeers* (arr. G. Woolfenden, Australian Ballet, 1980).

Verdon, Gwen (*b* Culver City, Calif., 13 Jan. 1925; *d* 18 Oct. 2000) US dancer, singer, actress, and choreographer. She studied ballet, Spanish dance, and East Indian dance (with La Meri) before appearing with Jack Cole's jazz troupe on Broadway. Her first major success was in Cole Porter's *Can-Can*, 1953, which won her the first of her four Tony Awards. Later starring roles were in the musicals *Damn Yankees* (1955), *New Girl in Town* (1957), *Redhead* (1959), *Sweet Charity* (title role, 1966), and *Chicago* (1975). She also appeared in many Hollywood films, and the big-screen version of *Damn Yankees* (1958), in which she reprised her stage role as the 172-year-old witch Lola. She was married to the choreographer and director Bob *Fosse, with whom she often worked. In the 1990s she was involved in reviving and staging her husband's choreography and acted as artistic adviser to the 1999 Broadway show *Fosse: A Celebration in Song and Dance*.

Verdy, Violette (orig. Nelly Guillerm; *b* Pont-l'Abbé, 1 Dec. 1933) French dancer and ballet director. She studied with Rousanne Sarkissian and Victor Gsovsky in Paris and made her debut in 1945 with the Ballets des Champs-Elysées, with whom she danced for several years, graduating from children's roles into soloist's roles. Her early career was marked by a restless energy. In 1950 she joined Petit's Ballets de Paris (and rejoined 1953–4); after which she danced with the company of Maggio Musicale Fiorentino (later *Maggio-Danza) in 1951, Chauviré's Ballet de Marigny (1952), London Festival Ballet (1954), La Scala, Milan (1955), Ballet Rambert (1957, where she danced her first Giselle), and American Ballet Theatre (1957–8), for whom she created the title role in ABT's production of Cullberg's *Miss Julie*. In 1958, with the temporary closure of ABT, she moved to New York City Ballet, the company which was to be her home until she retired from the stage in 1976. A sparkling, vivacious ballerina, she inspired Balanchine to create many roles for her, most notably in *Tchaikovsky Pas de deux* and the 'Emeralds' section of *Jewels*. Her partnership with Edward Villella in the Balanchine repertoire was widely acclaimed. She also appeared as a guest artist with other companies, performing the 19th-century repertoire; she danced her first Aurora in 1964 with the Royal Ballet. In 1976, three years after her third foot operation, she retired from New York City Ballet to become the first woman to direct the Paris Opera Ballet (1977-80). After leaving Paris, she became associate director of the Boston Ballet (1980-4). From 1984 she worked as a teaching associate with New York City Ballet and in 1996 was appointed professor of dance at Indiana University. She also worked as a guest teacher, coaching her former repertory.

A list of her created roles includes Petit's *Le Loup* (1953), Rodrigues's *Romeo and Juliet* (Verona, 1955) and *Cinderella* (Milan, 1955), Howard's *Conte fantastique* (London, 1957), Balanchine's *Episodes* (1959), *Tchaikovsky Pas de deux* (1960), *Figure in the Carpet* (1960), *Liebeslieder Walzer* (1960), *Electronics* (1961), *A Midsummer Night's Dream* (1962), *Jewels* (1967), *La Source* (1968), and *Sonatine* (1975), Robbins's *Dances at a Gathering* (1969), *In the Night* (1970), and *A Beethoven Pas de deux* (1973), and Balanchine and Robbins's *Pulcinella* (1972). She also worked as an actress, appearing with Madeleine Renaud and Jean-Louis Barrault's company; and in films, including *Ballerina* (in America, *Dream Ballerina*, 1950, directed by Berger) and *The Glass Slipper* (directed by Walters, with choreography by Petit, 1954). Author of *Giselle* (New York, 1970) and *Giselle: A Role for a Lifetime* (New York, 1977).

Vesak, Norbert (*b* Vancouver, 22 Oct. 1936; *d* Charlotte, NC, 2 Oct. 1990) Canadian dancer and choreographer. He studied with Cunningham, Craske, La Meri, Volkova, G. Holder, and Pauline Koner and after dancing with various Canadian companies embarked on his choreographic career. Among his best-known works were *The Ecstasy of Rita Joe* (mus. Mortifee, 1971), which highlighted the plight of North American Natives in a brutal white society, and *What to Do till the Messiah Cometh* (mus. Chilliwack, Werren, and Syrinx, 1972), an early rock ballet which featured the famous 'Belong' pas de deux—both for the Royal Winnipeg Ballet. He also choreographed for the National Ballet of Canada, and was director (1976–80) and subsequently guest choreographer with the Metropolitan Opera Ballet in New York.

Vestris A famous Italian-French family of dancers and actors who were influential in the 18th and 19th centuries. *See* VESTRIS, AUGUSTE; VESTRIS, GAETANO; VESTRIS, TERESA.

Vestris, Auguste (orig. Marie-Jean Augustin Vestris, *b* Paris, 27 Mar. 1760; *d* Paris, 5 Dec. 1842) French dancer and teacher. Illegitimate son of Gaetano Vestris and the dancer Marie Allard. He studied with his father and made his debut in the divertissement *La Cinquantaine* in 1772, at the age of 12. His first major success was dancing Amor in his father's ballet *Endymion* the following year. In 1776 he was appointed a soloist at the Paris Opera; in 1778 he became premier danseur and in 1780 premier sujet de la danse. He danced in the first production of Noverre's *Les Petits Riens* (1778) and in Gluck's *Alceste* (1778). During the 1780s he and his father made frequent appearances at the King's Theatre, London, where their popularity was such that Parliament stopped sitting in order to see them dance. In London and Paris, he created many roles in ballets by his father, as well as by Dauberval, Gardel, and Noverre. A short dancer, he possessed an extraordinary elevation and technical virtuosity that made him the most famous dancer in Europe. His rapid beats and multiple pirouettes were considered superhuman and they inspired improvements in technique throughout the dance world. In 1807, it is said, Napoleon refused to allow the dancer to leave Paris, saying: 'Foreigners must come to Paris to see Vestris dance.' By 1803, however, he had to contend with a rival: Louis-Antoine Duport, a 22-year-old whose challenge to the older Vestris was the subject of much gossip. Vestris retired from the Paris Opera in 1816. In 1819 he was imprisoned for debt, although his financial situation subsequently improved. He was also one of the leading teachers of the day, counting among his pupils Didelot, Perrot, Elssler, Bournonville, and Marie Taglioni, with whom he performed a minuet at the Paris Opera in 1835, when he was 75. He choreographed several unremarkable ballets, all for the King's Theatre in London: *The Nymphs of Diana* (1781), *Le Premier Navigateur* (1786), dances in Grétry's opera *L'Épreuve villageoise* (1786), and *Les Folies d'Espagne* (1791).

Vestris, Gaetano (orig. Gaetano Apolline Baldassare Vestris, *b* Florence, 18 Apr. 1728 (or 1729); *d* Paris, 23 (or 27) Sept. 1808) Italian dancer and choreographer. Father of Auguste Vestris. He studied in opera houses in Italy and Germany and with Louis Dupré in Paris. After dancing at various opera houses in Italy, he made his debut at the Paris Opera in 1748 and was appointed premier danseur in 1751. He performed in works by Rameau and Lully, and danced in court spectacles with his sister Teresa and his brother Angiolo (1730–1809). In 1754, however, he ran foul of the ballet master Lany whom he challenged to a duel on behalf of Teresa. The duel never took place, but Vestris was briefly imprisoned. Once released, he worked in Berlin and Turin, where he was ballet master for a short time. Returning to the Paris Opera in 1755 he continued to enjoy enormous popularity for more than thirty years, dancing leading roles in more than 70 ballets and operas. From 1761, on leave from the Paris Opera, he also danced with Noverre in Stuttgart, the latter exercising a great influence over Vestris's style. He created leading roles in Noverre's *Admète et Alceste* (1761), *La Mort d'Hercule* (1762), *Médée et Jason* (1763), and *Orpheus and Eurydice* (1763). In 1761 he was appointed co-choreographer (with Dauberval) of the Paris Opera and in 1770 he succeeded Lany as chief choreographer, a post he held until 1776 when Noverre succeeded him. As chief choreographer, he introduced the *ballet d'action to the Paris Opera. In 1781 he danced with his son Auguste at the King's Theatre in London, a venue he returned to over the years. Their appearance there caused such a sensation that Parliament suspended its sitting to see them dance. He continued to perform at the Paris Opera until 1782, although he devoted much of his time to running the Paris Opera Ballet School and furthering the career of his son Auguste. Tall, long-legged, noble, and very dignified (in contrast to his small and athletically virtuosic son), he was considered a modernist and was one of the first dancers ever to appear on stage without a mask. He was also vain, once declaring that there were only three great men in Europe: Frederick the Great of Prussia, Voltaire, and himself. Still, there were those who would agree with him: he was often referred to as 'Le Dieu de la danse'—the god of dance.

Vestris, Teresa (Thérèse) (*b* Florence, 1726; *d* Paris, 18 Jan. 1808) Italian dancer. Sister of Angiolo and Gaetano Vestris. She studied in Naples and made her debut in Palermo. While performing in Vienna she became the mistress of Prince Esterhazy, a liaison which prompted a jealous Empress Maria Theresa to order the dancer's immediate transfer to Dresden. From there she went to Florence before settling in Paris in 1746. Socially well-connected, she was able to secure positions at the Paris Opera for her brothers Angiolo and Gaetano; in 1751 she made her debut at the Paris Opera. Frequently embroiled in intrigues and plots, she left the Paris Opera in 1754 with her brothers and went to Berlin. However, a year later she was back. Dubbed 'the Italian Beauty', Vestris often danced with her brother Gaetano and was particularly acclaimed in Lully's *Alceste* and *Amadis*. She continued as a soloist until 1766.

Vic-Wells Ballet, The *See* ROYAL BALLET, THE.

Vienna *See* AUSTRIA.

Vienna Children's Ballet In the early 1800s Friedrich Horschelt's Children's Ballet was a very popular enterprise. It adapted existing full-length ballets, such as Louis-Antoine Duport's *Aschenbrödel* (*Cinderella*), to allow all the adult roles to be danced by children. However, an investigation by the Viennese Police in 1818 found that the boys and girls, who ranged in age from 8 to 19, were in danger of having their morals corrupted by being in Horschelt's company. This finding prompted the Empress Caroline Augusta to order the disbanding of the company, and by 1822 Horschelt had left Vienna to accept a post in Munich. In 1841 children's ballet in Vienna was revived when Josefine Maudry Weiss started an all-girls' company at the Theater in der Josefstadt. This troupe, known as the Danseuses Viennoises, toured not only Austria, but Germany, Italy, London (1845, 1846, and 1849), and Canada and the US (1846 and 1847) with great success. The company was disbanded in 1852 after the sudden death of Weiss.

Vienna State Opera Ballet Austrian ballet company based at the Vienna Staatsoper. The first ballet production at the new Opera House on the Ring, which opened in 1869, was a revival of P. Taglioni's *Sardanapal*. The German dancer Karl Telle, who ran the ballet company until 1890, staged productions of *Coppélia* (1876) and *Sylvia* (1877). His successor, Josef Hassreiter, staged nearly 50 ballets during his reign, which continued until 1920. Heinrich Kroller (1922–8) offered ballets to music by Richard Strauss. Margaretha Wallmann directed the State Opera Ballet and its school (1934–9). During the Second World War the theatre's stage and auditorium were gutted by bombs and the Staatsoper was rebuilt, opening again in 1955. Erika *Hanka, who ran the company for more than fifteen years until her death in 1958, made about 50 ballets, including *Der Mohr von Venedig* (*The Moor of Venice*), which was premiered on 29 Nov. 1955 to celebrate the first evening of dance in the reopened Staatsoper. Hanka brought current ideas in European modern dance into the repertoire, although she was also responsible for introducing the classics to the new theatre. After Hanka's death the company underwent a period of instability. Key productions in the 1960s and 1970s included Nureyev's stagings of *Swan Lake* (1964, revived 1996) and *Don Quixote* (1966), and Grigorovich's *Nutcracker* (1973). Russian guest artists frequently performed with the company; and the Russian ballet mistress Elena Tchernichova did much to improve technical standards when she directed the company (1991–3). Gerhard Brunner, artistic director from 1976 to 1980, commissioned new ballets from Neumeier (*Josephslegende*, 1977), van Manen (*Grand Trio*, 1978), van Dantzig (*Ulysses*, 1979), and Jochen Ulrich (*Tantz-Schul*, 1988). In 1995 Renato Zanella was appointed director commissioning Vladimir Malakhov to stage *La Bayadère* for the company in 1999. Gyula *Harangozó (jun.) was appointed director in 2005, however the company's development continued to be hampered by the dominance of opera productions within the theatre and its repertory remained a conservative mix of 19th-century classics and key MacMillan and Cranko works (e.g. *Mayerling* and *Onegin*). In 2010 Harangozó was succeeded by Manuel Legris.

(((∰))) SEE WEB LINKS

• Website for Vienna State Opera with link to the ballet

Vienna Waltzes Ballet in one act with choreography by Balanchine, music by Johann Strauss II, Franz Lehár, and Richard Strauss, sets by Ter-Arutunian, and costumes by Karinska. Premiered 15 Jun. 1977 (gala preview) and 23 Jun. 1977 by New York City Ballet, at the State Theater, New York, with von Aroldingen and Lavery, McBride and Tomasson, Leland and Cook, Mazzo and Martins, Farrell and Donn. A suite of waltzes inspired by nostalgia for 19th-century Vienna, the ballet is set to *Tales from the Vienna Woods*, *Voices of Spring*, *Explosion Polka*, *Gold and Silver Waltz*, and the waltzes from *Der Rosenkavalier*. The sets move from the Vienna Woods to an art nouveau café and a mirrored ballroom.

Viganò, Salvatore (*b* Naples, 25 Mar. 1769; *d* Milan, 10 Aug. 1821) Italian dancer and choreographer. Son of the dancer and choreographer Onorato Viganò and the ballerina Maria Boccherini, he studied composition with his uncle, the composer Luigi Boccherini. He later studied dance with Jean Dauberval. He made his debut in 1783 dancing female roles. He danced in Rome (1786) and Venice (1788), and in 1789 appeared in the coronation festivities of the Spanish king, Charles IV. It was in Spain that he met Dauberval, whom he followed to Bordeaux and then to London (1791). In 1789 he married the Spanish dancer Maria Medina and with her made frequent tours of Europe, especially Venice, Vienna, Paris, Prague, Dresden, Berlin, and Hamburg, until their separation ten years later. He choreographed his first ballet in Venice in 1791: *Raoul Signor de Crequi* or *Raul Signore di Crequi*, for which he also composed the music (as he frequently did). From 1799 to 1803 he worked in Vienna, then in Italy where he choreographed Shakespeare's *Coriolanus* for Milan. From 1811 (some sources say

1813) until his death in 1821 he was ballet master at La Scala, Milan, where his most important ballets were made. Among his most notable achievements as a choreographer was the seamless incorporation of pantomime into the dance material, also the striking impact of his tableaux. He had lavish tastes, especially in costume: one ballet at La Scala was said to feature 1,085 dresses. A list of his ballets includes *Die Tochter der Luft, oder: Die Erhöhung der Semiramis* (Vienna, 1793), *Richard Löwenherz, König von England* (mus. Weigl, Vienna, 1795), *Das gefundene Veilchen* (Vienna, 1795), *Clothilde, Herzogin von Salerno* (after Gozzi, Vienna, 1799), *The Creatures of Prometheus* (mus. Beethoven, Vienna, 1801), *I giuochi istmici* (mus. Weigl, Vienna, 1803), *Cajo Marzio Coriolano* (mus. Weigl, Milan, 1804), *Gli Strelizzi* (Venice, 1809), *Prometeo* (mus. Beethoven, Milan, 1813), *Gli Ussiti sotto a Naumburgo* (Milan, 1814), *Numa Pompilio* (Milan, 1815), *Mirra; o sia, La Vendetta di Venere* (Milan, 1817), *Psammi, re d'Egitto* (Milan, 1817), *Otello* (mus. various, Milan, 1818), *La vestale* (Milan, 1818), *I titani* (mus. Ayblinger, Milan, 1819), *Alessandro nell'Indie* (mus. Ayblinger, Milan, 1820), *Giovanna d'Arco* (mus. Ayblinger, Milan, 1820), and *Didone* (mus. Ayblinger, Milan, 1821).

Villella, Edward (*b* Bayside, NY, 1 Oct. 1936) US dancer and ballet director. He studied at the School of American Ballet from 1946 as a scholarship student and at the High School of Performing Arts. His training was interrupted when, at his parents' urging, he attended New York State Maritime College in Fort Schuyler (1951–5), but he returned to the School of American Ballet in 1956. He joined New York City Ballet in 1957, becoming soloist in 1958 and principal in 1960. Throughout his twenty years with the company he was one of its leading male dancers, also one of America's first male ballet stars. An athletic, virile dancer of compact build, he possessed unusual power, speed, and elevation. He partnered several ballerinas, most notably Patricia McBride, and created roles in many Balanchine ballets, *Electronics* (1961), *A Midsummer Night's Dream* (1962), *Bugaku* (1963), *Tarantella* (1964), *Harlequinade* (1965), *Brahms-Schoenberg Quartet* (1966), *Jewels* (1967), *Suite No. 3* (1970), *Symphony in Three Movements* (1972), and *Scheherazade* (1975); also in Robbins's *Dances at a Gathering* (1969), *Watermill* (1972); and in Balanchine and Robbins's *Pulcinella* (1972). Balanchine also revived *Prodigal Son* for Villella, which became one of his most celebrated roles. He additionally danced in musicals, including *Brigadoon* (1962) at the City Center of Music and Drama in New York. In 1966 he choreographed his first major ballet, *Narkissos* (mus. R. Prince) and two years later was the subject of the NBC-TV documentary *Man Who*

V

Dances; in the 1970s he worked as a producer and director on the PBS series, *Dance in America*. After leaving New York City Ballet in 1979 he was artistic co-ordinator of the Eglevsky Ballet (1979–4) then director of Ballet Oklahoma (1984–6). In 1986 he became founding director of *Miami City Ballet, which he built into one of America's most successful regional companies known particularly for its Balanchine repertory. He has choreographed occasional works for MCB, including the four-part *Neighbourhood Ballroom* (mus. several, 2003). He published (with Larry Kaplan) his autobiography, *Prodigal Son*, in New York in 1992.

Vilzak, Anatole (*b* Vilnius, Lithuania, 29 Aug. 1896 (some sources say St Petersburg, 31 Aug. 1896); *d* San Francisco, 15 Aug. 1998) Russian-US dancer and teacher. He studied at the Imperial Theatre School in St Petersburg, graduating in 1915 into the Mariinsky Theatre and becoming a principal in 1917. In 1921 he and his wife, the ballerina Ludmila *Schollar, left Russia and joined Diaghilev's Ballets Russes, where Vilzak danced the role of Prince Charming in Diaghilev's 1921 production of *The Sleeping Princess* and created roles in Nijinska's *Les Biches* (1924) and *Les Fâcheux* (1924). He was the Ballets Russes leading danseur noble, and also in 1923 staged *Swan Lake* (with Schollar) for the company. In 1925, however, he was dismissed by Diaghilev for supporting the dancers' attempts to gain better working conditions. He subsequently danced for Bronislava Nijinska at the Teatro Colón in Buenos Aires (1926) and joined Ida Rubinstein's company, where he was premier danseur, dancing in the first productions of Nijinska's *Les Noces de Psyché et de l'Amour*, *La Bien-aimée*, *Baiser de la fée*, and *Bolero* (all 1928) and *La Valse* (1929), Jooss's *Persephone* (1934), and Fokine's *Diane de Poitiers*. He was then ballet master and principal dancer at the State Opera in Riga (1932–4) and in 1932 performed with Théâtre de la Danse Nijinska, creating roles in her *Les Comédiens jaloux* and *Variations*. In 1935 he joined the Ballets Russes de Paris and in 1936 René Blum's Ballet Russe de Monte Carlo, where he created the title role in Fokine's *Don Juan*. He danced in America with Balanchine's American Ballet at the Metropolitan Opera House in New York (1936–7) and in 1940 he began his teaching career in America at the School of American Ballet. He later taught at his own Vilzak-Schollar School in New York (1940–6), the Ballet Russe de Monte Carlo School in New York (1949–51), the American Ballet Theatre School (1951–63), Washington School of Ballet (1963–5), and the San Francisco Ballet School (1965–86). He became one of the most important teachers of the Russian style in America.

Vinogradov, Oleg (*b* Leningrad, 1 Aug. 1937) Soviet dancer, choreographer, and ballet director. He studied at the Leningrad Ballet School, a student of Aleksandr Pushkin, graduating in 1958. He joined the Novosibirsk company (1958–65) as a character dancer, and there began his career as a choreographer, making ballets for opera productions, as well as acting as assistant ballet master to Petr Gusev. His first important ballet stagings were Prokofiev's *Cinderella* (1964) and *Romeo and Juliet* (1965), fresh and radical productions which brought him much attention throughout Russia. In 1967 the Bolshoi Ballet invited him to stage *Asel* (mus. V. Vlasov) and in 1968 the Kirov asked him to stage *Goryanka* (*Mountain Girl*, mus. M. Kashlaiev). From 1968 to 1972 he was a choreographer with the Kirov and from 1973 to 1977 he was artistic director and chief choreographer of the Maly Theatre Ballet in Leningrad, where he helped to restore the theatre's reputation for innovation. In 1977 he returned to the Kirov as artistic director and chief ballet master, where his first act was to fire more than half of the dancers, most of whom were of pensionable age. During the following two decades he did much else to re-invigorate the company, bringing in younger dancers, broadening the repertoire, and opening it up to foreign choreographers like Petit, Béjart, and Balanchine. He also imposed a stricter sense of style, both in the appearance of the dancers and their technique. The company toured abroad frequently, but as it began to spend less and less time in its home theatre, critics complained that its productions were becoming stale. In 1997 Vinogradov's directorship ended when Kirov Opera director Valery Gergiev took over the ballet company as well. In 1998 Vinogradov became director of the Universal Ballet in Seoul and its associate Ballet Academy in Washington, where he staged many of his former ballets and productions of the classics. He also worked freelance, including staging *La Fille mal gardée* for the Stanislavsky Ballet. In 2008 he left the Seoul company and became associate choreographer for the Mikhailovsky Ballet. A list of his other works includes *Alexander Nevsky* (mus. Prokofiev, Kirov, 1969), *La Fille mal gardée* (mus. Hérold, Maly Theatre Ballet, 1971), *The Enchanted Prince, or Prince of the Pagodas* (mus. Britten, Kirov, 1972), *Yaroslavna* (mus. B. Tishenko, Maly Theatre Ballet, 1974), *The Fairy of the Rond Mountains* (mus. Grieg, Kirov, 1980), *The Government Inspector* (mus. A. Tchaikovsky, 1980), *Testaments of Past Times* (mus. various, Kirov, 1983), *The Knight in Tigerskin* (mus. Machavarian, Kirov, 1985), *Battleship Potemkin* (mus. Tchaikovsky, Kirov, 1986), *Petrushka* (mus. Stravinsky, Scottish Ballet, 1989), *Adagio* (mus. S. Barber, Kirov, 1991).

Violin Concerto Ballet in one act with choreography by Balanchine, music by Stravinsky, and lighting by R. Bates. Premiered 18 Jun. 1972 by New York City Ballet at the State Theater in New York, with von Aroldingen, Mazzo, Bonnefoux, and Martins. A plotless ballet for two couples and a corps de ballet of sixteen, it was made for New York City Ballet's Stravinsky Festival. It features two strongly contrasting pas de deux. The work, later renamed *Stravinsky Violin Concerto*, has been revived for many other companies, including the Paris Opera Ballet (1989), the Royal Ballet (1990), San Francisco Ballet (1995), and Birmingham Royal Ballet (2007). Balanchine used the same music for his 1941 ballet, *Balustrade*.

Violon du Diable, Le Ballet in two acts with choreography and libretto by Saint-Léon, music by Pugni, sets by Despléchin and Thierry, and costumes by Lormier. Premiered 19 Jan. 1849 at the Paris Opera, with Cerrito and Saint-Léon. The ballet is a retelling of the Faustian legend, in which a young violinist Urbain allows the Satanic Doctor Matheus to bewitch his violin so that its beautiful sound will win the heart of his beloved, Hélène. When Matheus comes to claim the violinist's soul, he resists and the ballet ends happily with Urbain delivered from evil and the lovers united. At the ballet's premiere Saint-Léon played the violin as well as dancing the role of Urbain.

Virsaladze, Simon (*b* Tbilisi, 24 Jan. 1909; *d* Tbilisi, 9 Feb. 1989) Soviet ballet designer. As a child he studied both ballet and art, and although he went on to design for plays, operas, and films it was as a ballet designer that he made his name. He was chief designer for the Paliashvili Theatre for Opera and Ballet in Tbilisi (1932–6) and designed Chabukiani's *The Heart of the Hills* (1938) for the Kirov in Leningrad, where he eventually became chief designer (1945–62). He also designed for the Maly Theatre Ballet and the Novosibirsk Theatre. He was chief designer of the Bolshoi Ballet in Moscow from 1964 until his death. He collaborated with Chabukiani on many productions in Tbilisi, but he was best known internationally as Grigorovich's designer, having collaborated on all of his major ballets: *The Stone Flower* (1957), *Legend of Love* (1961), *Sleeping Beauty* (1965 and 1973), *Nutcracker* (1966), *Spartacus* (1968), *Swan Lake* (1969), *Ivan the Terrible* (1975), *Angara* (1976), *Romeo and Juliet* (1979), *The Golden Age* (1982), and *Raymonda* (1984). He also designed Sergeyev's *Raymonda* (Kirov, 1948), *Swan Lake* (Kirov, 1950), and *The Sleeping Beauty* (Kirov, 1952) and Vainonen's *The Nutcracker* (Kirov, 1954).

Vishneva, Diana (*b* St Petersburg, 13 Jul. 1976) Russian dancer. She trained at the Vaganova Ballet Academy with Ludmila Kovaleva and graduated in 1995. She joined the Kirov Ballet that same year and was promoted to principal in 1996. She danced the classical ballerina roles but the distinctive boldness of her attack was best showcased in the modern repertory, as she became one of the first generation of Kirov dancers to perform Balanchine, MacMillan, and Forsythe. In 2002 she created the title role in Ratmansky's *Cinderella*. Restless to expand her repertory she went on to guest with many companies, including La Scala, Berlin Staatsoper, Paris Opera, and American Ballet Theatre, becoming guest principal with ABT in 2003. In 2008 she also formed a temporary ensemble, Beauty in Motion, for which she commissioned three works, Ratmansky's *Pierrot Lunaire*, Dwight Rhoden's *Three Point Turn*, and Moses Pendleton's *F.L.O.W.*

Vivandière, La Ballet in one act with choreography and libretto by Saint-Léon and Cerrito, music by Pugni, and designs by Despléchin, Séchan and Diéterle. Premiered 23 May 1844 at Her Majesty's Theatre in London with Cerrito and Saint-Léon. The ballet, set in a village in Hungary, features the lovers Kathi and Hans, who have to overcome the jealous machinations of the Burgomaster and the Baron, both of whom have their eye on Kathi. The ballet introduced the Redowa, or 'Original Polka of Bohemia', to London. *La Vivandière* was later staged for the Paris Opera (1848), the Bolshoi Theatre in St Petersburg (re-staged Jules Perrot, 1855), and the Bolshoi Theatre in St Petersburg (re-staged Petipa, 1881). In 1979 the Kirov Ballet performed a reconstruction of the Pas de six by Pierre Lacotte after Saint-Léon. In 1982 Sadler's Wells Royal Ballet performed the Pas de six in a reconstruction by Ann Hutchinson Guest. Saint-Léon and Cerrito staged an earlier version in 1843 in Rome with music by Enrico Roland.

Vladimiroff, Pierre (Vladimirov) (orig. Piotr; *b* St Petersburg, 13 Feb. 1893; *d* New York, 25 Nov. 1970) Russian-US dancer and teacher. He studied at the Imperial Theatre School in St Petersburg, a student of Sergei Legat and Mikhail Fokine and in 1911 graduated into the Mariinsky company where he danced until 1918. He was promoted to principal in 1915, inheriting some of Nijinsky's former roles (he was a similarly virtuoso and athletic dancer) and also creating roles in Fokine's *Francesca da Rimini* and *Eros* (both 1915). He left revolutionary Russia in 1920, literally skiing his way to freedom with his wife, the ballerina Felia *Doubrovska. In the West he joined Diaghilev's Ballets Russes, with whom he had guested in 1912 and 1914. In 1921 he danced the role of the Prince in Diaghilev's London production of *The Sleeping Princess*. From

1922 he toured independently with Doubrovska, and later toured with Karsavina (1924), with the Mordkin Ballet (1925–7), and with Pavlova's company (1928–31), touring worldwide as her favoured partner (including India, Egypt, and S. America). He eventually settled in New York, where he taught at the School of American Ballet (1934–67) and became one of the most influential Russian teachers in the US, his students including Todd Bolender, Willam Christensen, William Dollar, Tanaquil LeClercq, and Maria Tallchief.

Vladimirov, Yuri (*b* Kosterovo, 1 Jan. 1942) Soviet dancer. He studied at the Bolshoi Ballet School, graduating in 1962. He joined the Bolshoi Ballet and became one of the company's leading soloists, a dancer noted for his daring and roughly hewn bravura. He created major roles in Kasatkina–Vasiliov's *Heroic Poem* (1964) and *Sacre du printemps* (1965), in Vasiliev's *Icarus*, and the title role in Grigorovich's *Ivan the Terrible* (1975), also appearing in the film of *Ivan the Terrible*. Gold medal (Varna, 1966; Moscow, 1969). He retired from dancing in the 1990s but has continued to coach for the company.

Vogel, Friedmann (*b* Stuttgart, 1981) German dancer. He trained at the John Cranko Ballet School, then at the Princess Grace Academy, Monte Carlo, before joining Stuttgart Ballet in 1998, where he was promoted to first soloist (principal) in 2002. A lyrical stylist, unusually supple for a male dancer, he has danced both classical and contemporary repertories, including ballets by Forsythe. He has also guested with several companies, including English National Ballet. He is recipient of numerous awards including the Erik Bruhn Prize (2002).

Volinine, Alexandre (orig. Aleksandr Volinin; *b* Moscow, 16 Sept. 1882; *d* Paris, 3 Jul. 1955) Russian-French dancer and teacher. He studied at the Bolshoi Ballet School, with Tikhomirov and Gorsky, graduating into the Bolshoi Ballet in 1901 and promoted to principal in 1903. He created roles in Gorsky's *Robert and Bertram* (1906) and *Nur and Anitra* (1907), and danced all the leading male roles in the classical repertoire, unusual among Bolshoi dancers in combining strength with elegance. In 1910 he left the Bolshoi, dancing first with Diaghilev's Ballets Russes in Paris, when he created a principal role in Fokine's *Les Orientales*, and then touring with Lydia Lopokova (1910–11) in America, also appearing with her in Gertrude Hoffmann's Ballets Russes at the Winter Garden Theater in New York (1911). He then joined Mordkin's All-Star Imperial Russian Ballet (1911–12), after which he partnered Adeline Genée on tour to America, Australia, and New Zealand (1912–13); then partnered Lydia Kyasht

at the Empire Theatre in London in 1913. From 1914 to 1925 he partnered Pavlova on various world tours, creating the role of the Young Poet in her *Autumn Leaves* (1919). In 1926, having retired from the stage, he opened a school in Paris, where his students famously included Babilée, Eglevsky, Jeanmaire, and Lichine. In 1946 he staged *Giselle* for the Royal Danish Ballet.

Volkova, Vera (*b* St Petersburg, 7 Jun. 1904; *d* Copenhagen, 5 May 1975) Russian dancer and teacher. A late starter to ballet training, she studied with Vaganova and Maria Romanova (Galina Ulanova's mother) at Volynsky's private Russian Choreographic School (1920–5). She danced with the GATOB (later the Kirov) from 1925 to 1929 and then toured Japan and China with a small ensemble. In 1929, hoping to join Diaghilev's Ballets Russes, she defected in Shanghai, but upon hearing of Diaghilev's death she opted to remain in China. There she danced with Georgi Goncharov's Russian ballet company and taught in his school. In 1932 she founded her own school in Hong Kong. In 1936 she and her husband, the architect Hugh Finch Williams, moved to London where she opened another ballet school and taught at the Sadler's Wells Ballet and its school (1943–50). She eventually became the leading Western authority on the Vaganova teaching method and her teaching had a significant influence on a generation of British dancers, including Fonteyn. In 1950 she went to La Scala, Milan, as teacher and artistic adviser, and the following year went to Copenhagen, where she became a permanent teacher and artistic adviser to the Royal Danish Ballet (1952–75), doing much to improve standards and restore the company's international reputation. Among her students in Copenhagen were Erik Bruhn, Peter Martins, and Peter Schaufuss. She also worked as a guest teacher for various companies, including Kurt Jooss's Folkwang Ballet, New York City Ballet, and the Harkness Ballet. Knight of Order of Dannebrog (1956).

volta [It. and Fr., turn] A fast dance for couples performed in simple triple time, it is related to the Italian *galliard. It features quick, leaping turns during which the woman is lifted by her male partner. A lusty dance, considered by some to be immoral, it was a favourite of Queen Elizabeth I. In Britten's opera *Gloriana* the volta is danced by Elizabeth I and her court.

Voluntaries Ballet in one act with choreography by Tetley, music by Poulenc, and designs by Ter-Arutunian. Premiered 22 Dec. 1973 by the Stuttgart Ballet at the Württembergische Staatstheater in Stuttgart, with Haydée, Cragun, Keil, R. Anderson, and Stripling. The ballet, created as a memorial to the choreographer John Cranko, who had died suddenly earlier in the year, is set to Poulenc's Concerto in G minor for Organ, Strings, and Timpani. According to Tetley, 'Voluntaries—by musical definition—are free-ranging organ improvisations, often played before, during and after religious service. The Latin root of the word can also connote flight or desire, and the ballet is conceived as a series of linked voluntaries.' It was revived for the Royal Ballet (1976), American Ballet Theatre (1977), Royal Danish Ballet (1978), Paris Opera Ballet (1982), Australian Ballet (1984), the National Ballet of Canada (1988), and English National Ballet (2000).

Volynsky, Akim (*b* Zhitomir, 11 Apr. 1865; *d* Leningrad, 6 Jul. 1926) Russian dance critic, art historian, and ballet school director. One of the most influential ballet critics in St Petersburg in his day and an outspoken critic of Fokine, whom he blamed for leading ballet away from its true course. Author of *Problems of Russian Ballet* (1923) and *The Book of Exultation: A Primer in the Classical Dance* (1926). He founded the private Russian Choreographic School, where Vaganova had her first teaching job.

von Aroldingen, Karin *See* AROLDINGEN, KARIN VON.

von Rosen, Elsa-Marianne *See* ROSEN, ELSA-MARIANNE VON.

Vsevolozhsky, Ivan (*b* 1835; *d* 1909) Russian diplomat, theatre director, and designer. He was director of the Russian Imperial Theatres from 1881 to 1899 and was responsible for commissioning Tchaikovsky's scores for *The Sleeping Beauty* and *The Nutcracker*, as well as many Petipa ballets. He also designed the costumes for about 25 ballets, including *The Sleeping Beauty*, *Nutcracker*, and *Raymonda*. After he left the Imperial Theatres he was appointed Director of the Imperial Hermitage, a post he held until his death.

Vyroubova, Nina (*b* Gurzof, Crimea, 4 Jun. 1921; *d* Paris, 24 Jun. 2007) Russian-French dancer and teacher. As a child she emigrated to Paris with her grandmother and widowed mother. She was inspired to dance after seeing Pavlova perform at the Théâtre des Champs-Elysées in 1931 and went on to study with her mother and with Trefilova, Preobrajenska, Egorova, and later Victor Gsovsky and Serge Lifar. She made her debut as Swanilda in Caen in 1937, going on to dance with the Ballets Polonais (1939), the Ballet Russe de Paris (1940), and then perform solo recitals (1941-4). She frequently appeared in the famous Vendredis de la Danse at the Sarah Bernhardt Theatre where she met Petit. In 1945 she danced in his *Les Forains*, and joined his newly formed Ballets des Champs-Elysées. A lyrical dancer, noted for her sensitivity and romantic expressiveness, she danced the title role in Victor Gsovsky's *La Sylphide* for the company. In 1949 she appeared with Petit's Ballets de Paris in London before Serge Lifar invited her to join the Paris Opera Ballet as an étoile. She performed with the Opera from 1949 until 1956, when she left to join the Grand Ballet du Marquis de Cuevas (1957-62). After the de Cuevas company folded, she appeared as a guest ballerina with many companies. She created roles in Petit's *Ballet blanc* (1944), *Le Rossignol et la rose* (1944), *Un American à Paris* (1944), *Les Forains* (1945), *Treize danses* (1947), and *L'œuf à la coque* (1949); in V. Gsovsky's *La Sylphide* (1946); in Lifar's *Blanche-neige* (1951), *Fourberies* (1952), *Variations* (1953), *The Firebird* (title role, 1954), *Les Noces fantastiques* (1955), *Apollon musagète* (1956), and *L'Amour et son destin* (1957); in Golovine's *La Mort de Narcisse* (1958); and in van Dyk's *Abraxas* (1965). She appeared in the films *Le Calvaire de Cimiez* (1932), *Le Spectre de la danse* (chor. Lifar, 1960), and *L'Adage* (1965). She taught privately at her own studio in Paris and at the Troyes Conservatoire (1983-8).

V

Wagner, Richard (*b* Leipzig, 22 May 1813; *d* Venice, 13 Feb. 1883) German composer. He wrote no ballet scores but his music (usually in extracted form) has been used for dance: *Tannhäuser* has been choreographed by Massine in *Bacchanale*, New York, 1939, also by Béjart in *Bacchanale de Tannhäuser* (a dance initially performed within the opera at Bayreuth, 1961, then as a separate ballet, Brussels, 1963); *Tristan and Isolde* by Massine in *Mad Tristan*, New York, 1944, by H. Ross in *Tristan*, New York, 1955, and K Pastor in *Tristan*, Royal Swedish Ballet, 2006 among others; *Siegfried Idyll* by Sparemblek, (Brussels, 1965) and *Wesendonck Lieder* by Joffrey in *Remembrances*, New York, 1973, Spoerli in *Dreams*, Stuttgart, 1980, and Stevenson in *Five Poems*, Houston, 2001). Extracts from the *Ring Cycle* have been used by several choreographers, among them Béjart in *Ring around the Ring* (Berlin, 1990), M. Lavrovsky in *More Powerful Than Gold and Death* (Moscow, 1996), and P. Schaufuss in *The King* (Holstebro, 1999, in combination with songs by Elvis Presley).

Wagoner, Dan (*b* Springfield, W. Va., 31 Jul. 1932) US dancer and choreographer. He came to professional dance late, studying with Ethel Butler and Graham and making his debut in Graham's company in 1958 where he stayed until 1962. He also danced a season with Cunningham (1959–60) before becoming a full-time member of Paul Taylor's company in 1962, where he created roles in *Aureole* (1962), *Orbs* (1966), and other works. He choreographed his first work in 1968, and in 1969 formed his own company, which toured the US, S. America, and the UK. His works, choreographed for Ballet Rambert and London Contemporary Dance Theatre as well as for his own company, frequently employed American vernacular music and themes. They included *Flee as a Bird* (mus. trad. jazz and ragtime, 1985), *An Occasion for Some Revolutionary Gestures* (mus. M. Sahl, 1985), and *White Heat* (mus. Bartók, 1990). He was also artistic director of LCDT (1988–91). In 1994 financial problems forced the closure of his own company and he continued as a freelance choreographer and teacher, eventually joining the faculty of the University of Wisconsin-Madison and Connecticut College in 1999.

Wakevich, Georges (Wakevitch) (*b* Odessa, 18 Aug. 1907; *d* Paris, 11 Feb. 1984) Russian-French designer. He created the designs for many ballets, including Petit's *Le Jeune Homme et la mort* (Ballets des Champs-Elysées, 1946), Dollar's *The Combat* (American Ballet Theatre, 1953), Lifar's *Firebird* (Paris Opera, 1954) and *L'Amour et son destin* (Grand Ballet du Marquis de Cuevas, 1957), Hanka's *Moor of Venice* (Vienna State Opera, 1955), and Taras's *Petrushka* (Berlin Opera Ballet, 1971).

Walkaround Time Modern dance work in one act with choreography by Cunningham, music by David Behrman, and design by Jasper Johns. Premiered 10 Mar. 1968 by Merce Cunningham Dance Company at State University, Buffalo, New York, with Cunningham, Brown, B. Lloyd, Neels, Setterfield, Harper, Reid, Solomons, and Slayton. Various elements of the work were conceived as a homage to Marcel Duchamp: Johns's set consisted of seven vinyl boxes with images from Duchamp transcribed onto them, the improvisatory section which divided the two parts of the dance was a reference to *Relâche*, and the title of Behrman's score ('... *for nearly an hour*') refers to the Duchamp painting titled *To Be Looked at with One Eye, Close to, for Almost an Hour*.

Walker, David (*b* Calcutta, 18 Jul. 1934; *d* Herefordshire, 27 Dec. 2008) British designer. He studied at the Central School of Arts and Crafts and began his career with Joan Littlewood at Theatre Workshop. A designer capable of great romantic charm and delicacy he created costumes for many ballet and opera companies, including Royal Ballet, English National Ballet, Joffrey Ballet, Stuttgart Ballet, Berlin Opera Ballet, and Houston Ballet. His set and costume designs include Ashton's *The Dream* (1964) and *Cinderella* (1965 revival), both for the Royal Ballet, *The Nutcracker* (Boston Ballet, 1979, 1995, and 2003) and Corder's *Cinderella* (1996, English National Ballet and also Boston Ballet).

Walking on the Walls Trisha Brown's 1971 'equipment piece' in which performers were rigged into harnesses and traversed the walls of the Whitney Museum, New York. A documentary film record is in the New York Public Library Archives.

Wall, David (*b* Chiswick, 15 Mar. 1946) British dancer. He studied in Windsor and at Royal Ballet School, joining the Royal Ballet Touring Company in 1963, becoming soloist in 1964 and principal in 1966 and joining the main company in 1970 as a principal. A strong technician with an equal talent for romantic and comedy roles he was especially outstanding as Lescaut in MacMillan's *Manon* which he created in 1974. Other created roles were in Ashton's *Sinfonietta* (1967), MacMillan's *Anastasia* (1971 version), *Elite Syncopations* (1974), and *Mayerling* (1978), Nureyev's *Tempest* (1982), and Tudor's *Knight Errant* (1971, although injury prevented him from dancing the first night). He frequently partnered Fonteyn. After retiring in 1984 he was associate director of the Royal Academy of Dancing (1984–7) and then director (1987–91). Between 1995 and 2007 he was ballet master with English National Ballet.

Wallis, Lynne (*b* Windsor, 11 Dec. 1946) British dancer and director. She studied at the Royal Ballet School and graduated into the Royal Ballet Touring Company. In 1969 she became ballet mistress at the RB Upper School and in 1981 deputy ballet principal of the RB School. She then worked as ballet mistress and staged the classical repertory for companies all around the world, additionally becoming artistic co-ordinator of National Ballet of Canada in 1984 and co-artistic director of that company (with Valerie Wilder) between 1987 and 1989. In 1990 she became deputy artistic director of English National Ballet, and in 1994 artistic director of the Royal Academy of Dancing.

Wallmann, Margarete (Margarita) (*b* Vienna, 22 Jul. 1904; *d* Monte Carlo, 2 May 1992) Austrian dancer and choreographer. She studied at the schools of the Berlin State Opera and Munich State Opera, and in 1923 began studying with Wigman in Dresden. In 1929 she took over the Berlin branch of Wigman's school, and a year later, she and her company, the Tanzer-Kollectiv, performed with Ted Shawn in Munich. She became a leading exponent of expressionist dance and choreographed for many opera productions particularly at the Salzburg Festival. In 1934 she became ballet director of the Vienna State Opera and its school, and during the 1930s also choreographed for Hollywood and La Scala. Between 1938 and 1948 she worked at the Teatro Colón, where she staged productions of *Die Josephslegende* and *Don Juan*. After 1949 she worked mainly in Italy and New York, producing opera.

Walpurgis Night Ballet divertissement, choreographed by Henri Justament for the last act of Gounod's opera *Faust*. Premiered 3 Mar. 1869 at Paris Opera. It is often performed as a separate ballet, as in Lavrovsky's version for the Bolshoi Ballet (Moscow 1941) or Balanchine's version, originally choreographed for Paris Opera's production of the *Faust* opera, 1975, and then danced alone by New York City Ballet in 1980.

Walsh, Christine (*b* Sydney, 22 Mar. 1954) Australian dancer. She studied at the Australian Ballet School and with M. Besobrasova in Monte Carlo, joining Australian Ballet in 1972 and becoming soloist (1975) and principal (1978). She remained with the company until 1989 apart from two seasons with Petit's Ballet National de Marseilles (1977–8 and 1980–1), and other international guest engagements. Her personality and dramatic intelligence made her renowned in a variety of roles from the classics through to the modern repertory of Kylián, Béjart, etc. She created roles in Murphy's *Tekton* (1978) and *Beyond Twelve* (1987) and Tetley's *Orpheus* (1987), among others. After retiring she worked as a producer and teacher in her own school.

Walter, Erich (*b* Fürth, 30 Dec. 1927; *d* Herdecke, 23 Nov. 1983) German dancer, choreographer and director. He studied with Olympiada Alperova in Nuremberg and danced with Nuremberg Opera Ballet (1946–50), Göttingen Ballet (1950–1), and Wiesbaden Ballet (1951–3). In 1953 he was appointed ballet master at Wuppertal where, in collaboration with designer Heinrich Wendel, he built up a repertoire of neo-classical ballets that established Wuppertal as one of Germany's leading companies. These included *Pelléas and Mélisande* (mus. Schoenberg, 1955), *Jeux* (mus. Debussy, 1958), *Romeo and Juliet* (mus. Berlioz, 1959), and *Ondine* (mus. Henze, 1962). In 1964 he became ballet director at Düsseldorf's German Opera on the Rhine, building up such a successful ballet company that a second had to be formed in 1970 to perform in opera productions. He also worked as guest choreographer for other companies, including Berlin Opera Ballet, and La Scala, Milan. His later ballets included *String Quartet no. 1* (mus. Janáček, 1966), *Dance Around the Golden Calf* (staged in Schoenberg's opera *Moses and Aaron*, 1968), and *Le Sacre du printemps* (Stravinsky, 1970), as well as stagings of several classics.

waltz [Ger. *Walzer*; Fr. *valse*] A German-Austrian turning dance in 3/4 or 3/8 time whose origins are not clear, though it bears similarities to the volta, the weller, and the ländler. The last was danced in Austria and Bavaria for centuries and was also called the deutsch. The name waltz appeared in the late 18th century and the dance itself gained widespread popularity through the ballroom waltz music of Lanner and the Strausses. Some authorities tried to ban it on account of the daringly close embrace required between male and female dancers. Its first stage appearance was in Vicente Martín y Soler's opera *La cosa rara* (Vienna, 1786) and its first ballet showing was in Gardel's *La Dansomanie* (Paris, 1800). It features prominently in *Swan Lake*, *Sleeping Beauty*, and *The Nutcracker*, while individual works have been choreographed in celebration of its music and its romantic associations, including Nijinska's *La Valse* (mus. Ravel, Monte Carlo, 1929, also several later versions including one by Ashton, 1958), Balanchine's *Liebeslieder Walzer* (mus. Brahms, New York, 1960), and his *Vienna Waltzes* (mus. J. Strauss II, Lehár, and R. Strauss, New York, 1977); also Mark Morris's *New Love Song Waltzes* (mus. Brahms, New York, 1982).

Wanderer, The Ballet in one act with libretto and choreography by Ashton, music by Schubert, and design by Graham Sutherland. Premiered 27 Jan. 1941 by Sadler's Wells Ballet at New Theatre, London, with Helpmann and Fonteyn. Set to Schubert's *Wanderer Fantasie*, it portrays a man recalling significant moments from his life. Balanchine used the same music (arr. Liszt) for his ballet *Errante* (Paris, 1933).

Wang Qimin (*b* Chengdu, Sichuan Province, 1981) Chinese dancer. She studied at the Beijing Dance Academy from the age of 10, and in 1998 graduated into the National Ballet of China. A dancer of delicately expressive style but capable, too, of an exceptional grandeur of scale, she was rapidly promoted to principal, performing the company's Western and Chinese repertories. She has guested with Hong Kong Ballet and with Roland Petit's international touring company (2006) and is recipient of several awards, including Special Prize at the Paris International Ballet Competition (1998).

Waring, James (*b* Alameda, Calif., 1 Nov. 1922; *d* New York, 2 Dec. 1975) US dancer, choreographer, and teacher. He studied in San Francisco, at the School of American Ballet, and with Vilzak, Tudor, Cunningham, Halprin, and Horst. He created his first work in 1946 at the Halprin-Lathrop Studio Theater, San Francisco, and in 1951 was co-founder of the choreographers' co-operative, Dance Associates, in New York. From 1954 to 1969 he presented annual concerts with his own company. Considered one of dance's great eccentrics, his style was characterized by its wit, musicality, and fantasy. He created over 135 works both for his own and other companies,

including Nederlands Dans Theater, among them *Dances before the Wall* (mus. several, 1958), *Variations on a Landscape* (mus. Schoenberg, 1971), and *Sinfonia semplice* (mus. Mozart, 1975). He was artistic director of New England Dinosaur (1974-5).

Warren, Robert de (*b* Montevideo, 1933) British dancer, choreographer, and director. He studied at the Sadler's Wells School before joining National Ballet of Uruguay in 1954, and subsequently dancing with Covent Garden Opera Ballet (1958-60), Stuttgart Ballet (1960-2), and Frankfurt Ballet (1962-4). In 1968 he was appointed director of the National Ballet of Iran (until 1970) and in 1971 formed the Mahalli folk dance troupe, choreographing the full-length ballet *Simorgh* (mus. Tjeknavorian, 1975). He was then artistic director of Northern Ballet Theatre (1976-87), for which he choreographed several ballets, including *Romeo and Juliet... Tragic Memories* (mus. Tchaikovsky, 1978), *Cinderella* (mus. J. Strauss, 1979), and *A Midsummer Night's Dream* (mus. Mendelssohn, arr. Salzedo, 1981). He was artistic director of La Scala (until 1992) and between 1994 and 2007 was artistic director of Sarasota Ballet, creating many works including *Eva Peron: A Dance Portrait* (1997) and a new staging of *Swan Lake* (1999).

Warsaw Ballet Polish ballet company. It was founded in 1818 at Warsaw's National Theatre under the direction of L. Thierry and in 1833 moved into the newly built Great Theatre. Maurice Pion was director (1826-43), followed by F. Taglioni (1843-53), and Roman Turczynowicz (1853-66), and during this period it was an important centre of Romantic ballet. With the general decline of ballet in Europe artistic standards fell, although under the direction of Piotr Zajlich (1917-34) the company was rejuvenated with a repertory that included the 19th-century classics, various Ballets Russes works, and some nationally inspired ballets. The theatre was destroyed during the Second World War and the company worked in temporary quarters. In 1965 it moved back to the rebuilt theatre, presenting a largely 20th-century repertory. Economic conditions in Poland made its continuing survival difficult and under the current direction of Jolanta Rybarska, it has reverted to a largely traditional repertory of 19th-century classics.

(∰) SEE WEB LINKS

• Website for the Warsaw Opera with link to the ballet company

Washington, Shelley (*b* Washington, DC, 3 Nov. 1954) US dancer. She studied at the Interlochen Arts Academy and at the Juilliard School and performed with the Martha Graham company

(1974–5). In 1975 she joined Tharp's company as a dancer and in 1988 was also appointed soloist with American Ballet Theatre in association with Tharp. She retired from the stage in 1991 since when she has staged many of Tharp's works, for the Royal Ballet, Australian Ballet, Dutch National Ballet, Birmingham Royal Ballet, and Rambert Dance Company, among others.

Washington Ballet US ballet company. It dates back to a school opened by Lisa Gardiner in Washington in 1922 which incorporated a small company called Washington Ballet. A second school was founded in 1944 by Gardiner and Mary Day, which in 1946 started to run its own performing ensemble and became known as Washington Ballet in 1956. Frederic Franklin was co-artistic director with Day until 1961, when the company ceased operation. Day re-established it in 1974 and in 1976 appointed Choo-San Goh as resident choreographer. After his death in 1987 Goh's works continued to dominate the repertoire, alongside ballets by Balanchine and others. In 1992 Elvi Moore joined Day as co-director, and both were succeeded in 1999 by Septime Webre. Under his direction the company has acquired a number of contemporary ballets, by Morris, Wheeldon, Tharp, Duato, and others, as well as populist works by himself, including *Rocketman* (mus. Elton John 2009).

⊕ SEE WEB LINKS

• Website for Washington Ballet

Watermill Ballet in one act with choreography by Robbins, music by Teiji Ito, set design by Robbins and David Reppa, and costumes by P. Zipprodt. Premiered 3 Feb. 1972 by New York City Ballet, at State Theater, New York, with Villella. The choreography is influenced by Japanese noh theatre and portrays a man looking back over his life.

Waterproof Dance event, for Olympic-sized swimming pools, created by Daniel Larrieu, with a sound score by J.-J. Palix (including music by Mahler), lighting by F. Michel, costumes by R. Fléa, and video by L. Riolon. Premiered in 1986 by Astrakan Dance Company at the Jean Bouin municipal pool, Angers. The dancers wear black swimsuits and goggles and perform on, under, and out of the water while video screens project the choreography filmed from underwater cameras. It continues to be staged at many pools around the world and was filmed for British television (Channel 4).

Water Study Modern dance work in one act with choreography by Humphrey, no music, and design by P. Lawrence. Premiered 28 Oct. 1928 by the Humphrey-Weidman Group at Civic Repertory Theater, New York. The sixteen dancers create images of the energy and movement of water.

Watson, Edward (*b* London, 21 May, 1976) British dancer. He trained at the Royal Ballet School and graduated into the company in 1994, where he was promoted to principal in 2005. An exceptionally supple, articulate dancer, he has performed most of the classical and heritage repertory but is most noted for performances in new works. He has created roles in Ashley Page's *Sleeping with Audrey*; *Two Part Invention*; *Cheating, Lying, Stealing*; *Hidden Variables*; and *This House Will Burn*, among others; in Wayne McGregor's *Symbiont(s)*, *Chroma, Qualia, Infra*, and *Acis and Galatea*; in Will Tuckett's *The Seven Deadly Sins*; and in Wheeldon's *Tryst, DGV*, and *Electric Counterpoint*.

Watts, Heather (*b* Long Beach, Calif., 27 Sept. 1953) US dancer. She studied in California and at the School of American Ballet with S. Williams, Eglevsky, and Danilova and joined New York City Ballet in 1970, where she was promoted to soloist (1978) and principal in 1979. A dancer gifted with unusual elevation and dramatic intensity she projected a challenging independence on stage. She performed a wide range of works and created roles in, among others, Balanchine's *Walpurgisnacht Ballet* (1980) and *Davidsbündlertänze* (1980), Robbins's *Four Seasons* (1979), *Piano Pieces* (1981), *Four Chamber Works* (1982), and *Tango* (1983), and Martins's *Calcium Light Night* (1977) and *Fearful Symmetries* (1990). After retiring from the stage in 1995 she taught ballet and dance history at Harvard.

Weaver, John (*b* Shrewsbury, baptismal date 21 Jul. 1673; *d* Shrewsbury, 24 Sept. 1760) British dancer, choreographer, teacher, and dance theorist, regarded as the father of British pantomime and a pioneer of the *ballet d'action. The son of a dancing master, he himself was apprenticed to a dancing master in Shrewsbury, probably Edward Dyer, and became a dancing master in Shrewsbury from 1695. From 1700 to 1736 he danced in the London theatres of Drury Lane, Lincoln's Inn Fields, and York Buildings, performing mostly comic and character roles, and he choreographed his first work *The Tavern Bilkers* (1702/3) at Drury Lane. His seminal work was *The Loves of Mars and Venus* (mus. Symonds, 1717), in which he attempted to fuse dance and mime into a coherent narrative, rather than presenting ballets as decorative divertissements. He continued his narrative experiment with *Orpheus and Eurydice* (1718) and *The Judgement of Paris* (after the masque by Congreve, mus. Seedo, 1733). He wrote his own libretti and in addition notated many court dances, translated Feuillet's *Chorégraphie* (pub. as

W

Orchesography, 1706), and was author of, among other works, *An Essay towards a History of Dancing* (1712), *Anatomical and Mechanical Lectures upon Dancing* (1721), and *The History of Mimes and Pantomimes* (1728).

Weber, Carl Maria von (*b* Eutin, 18 Dec. 1786; *d* London, 5 Jun. 1826) German composer. He wrote no ballet scores but composed many polkas, waltzes, and polonaises and some of his concert music has been used for dance, including *Invitation to the Dance* (orch. Berlioz, chor. Fokine, in *Spectre de la rose,* 1911) and *Konzertstück* (chor. van Dyk, 1965, and K. Stowell, 1972).

Webern, Anton von (*b* Vienna, 3 Dec. 1883; *d* Mittersill, 15 Sept. 1945) Austrian composer. He wrote no ballet scores but his concert music has frequently been used for dance, most notably in Graham and Balanchine's *Episodes* (Martha Graham Dance Company and New York City Ballet, 1959) where Graham used the Passacaglia, Op. 1, and Six Pieces for Orchestra, and Balanchine used the Sinfonie, Op. 21, Five Pieces for Orchestra, Op. 6, Concerto for Orchestra, Op. 24, Variations for Orchestra, Op. 30, and the Ricercare from Bach's *Musical Offering.* Other Webern music which has been used for dance includes Pieces for Orchestra, Op. 6 and 10 (chor. Béjart in *Temps,* 1960, and MacMillan in *My Brother, My Sisters,* 1978), Passacaglia, Op. 1 (chor. Cranko, *Opus 1,* 1965), six Bagatelles, Op. 9, and String Quartet, Op. 5 (chor. van Dantzig in *Moments,* 1968), Four Pieces for Violin and Piano, Op. 7, String Quartet, Op. 28, and Five movements for String Quartet, Op. 5 (chor. Trisha Brown in *Twelve Ton Roses,* 1996) and various excerpted pieces (chor. Kylián in *No More Play,* 1988 and *Sweet Dreams,* 1990, also chor. de Keersmaeker in *Zeitung,* 2008).

Webster, Clara Vestris (*b* Bath, 1821; *d* London, 17 Dec. 1844) British dancer. She studied in Bath with her father Benjamin Webster (who had himself studied with Vestris, hence her middle name) and in 1830 made her debut at the Theatre Royal, Bath, in a pas de deux with her brother, Arthur Webster. In 1836 she went to London where she danced at the Haymarket and subsequently went on to dance in Dublin, Liverpool, and Manchester. She was one of the first British dancers to perform the cachucha and the tyrolienne (which she danced with her brother) and might have become an outstanding Romantic ballerina had she not died after her costume caught fire during a performance of *The Revolt of the Harem* at Drury Lane Theatre.

Wedding Bouquet, A Ballet in one act with choreography by Ashton, libretto, music, and design by Lord Berners. Premiered 27 Apr. 1937 by Vic-Wells Ballet at Sadler's Wells Theatre, London, with Honer, Helpmann, de Valois, and Fonteyn. This comic ballet is based on and accompanied by text from Gertrude Stein's play *They Must be Wedded To Their Wife.* It is set at a French provincial wedding and portrays the various eccentricities of the guests, who include several of the groom's former mistresses. Stein's text was originally sung by a chorus but subsequently it has been spoken by a narrator seated at a table on the stage. The ballet has been revived by Royal Ballet Touring Company (1974) and Joffrey Ballet (1979).

Weidman, Charles (*b* Lincoln, Nebr., 22 Jul. 1901; *d* New York, 16 Jul. 1975) US dancer, choreographer, and teacher. He studied with E. Frampton, T. Koslov, and at Denishawn and after dancing in Shawn's Broadway show, *Xochitl,* and briefly with Graham in 1921, he joined Denishawn. He toured widely with the company until 1927 when he and Humphrey left to form their own school and company which lasted until 1945. The works he choreographed for this, such as *And Daddy Was a Fireman Too* (1943) often dealt with American social themes and featured his distinctive satirical wit. He also collaborated with Humphrey on several works, including *New Dance* (1935), and choreographed for Broadway. In 1945 he founded his own school and in 1948 his own company for which he choreographed many more works, including *A House Divided* (about Lincoln, 1945), *Fables for Our Time* (after Thurber, 1947), and *Is Sex Necessary?* (1959). He later choreographed for New York City Opera and for various drama productions as well as teaching in New York and California. In 1960 he founded the Expression of Two Arts Theater in New York with the sculptor Mikhail Santaro where he taught and gave regular concerts until his death. Limón and Bob Fosse were among his pupils.

Weidt, Jean (*b* Hamburg, 7 Oct. 1904; *d* Berlin, 29 Aug. 1988) German dancer and choreographer. He studied with Leeder and Olga Brandt-Knaack, giving his first solo concert in Hamburg in 1925, which included the first version of his signature piece, *The Worker.* In the same year he formed his own company, moving with it to Berlin in 1929 where it became known as the Red Dancers. The political content of his works intensified with the rise of fascism and he was briefly arrested in 1933. He subsequently lived and worked in Moscow, Prague, and Paris, continuing to choreograph work with intense political and humanitarian concerns, such as *The Cell* (1947). From 1948 to 1950 he directed the Dramatic Ballet at the Volksbühne in E. Berlin, then worked at opera houses in Schwerin and Karl-Marx-Stadt and at Berlin's Komische Oper (1958–66 and 1978–80).

W

Weir, Natalie (*b* Townsville, Far North Queensland, 1967) Australian dancer and choreographer. She studied locally and at the Kelvin Grove College, Brisbane, becoming a founder member of Expressions Dance Company in 1984. She created her first work *The Players* for that company, and in 1994 was appointed resident choreographer of Queensland Ballet, moving to Australian Ballet as resident choreographer in 2000. A prolific choreographer, her works draw on both modern and classical dance vocabularies and include *Mirror, Mirror* (2000) and *Carmina Burana* (Orff, 2001), both for Australian Ballet, *Steppenwolf* (2001) and *The Host* (mus. Elgar, 2004) for Houston, *Harmonium* (Adams, 2003) for American Ballet Theatre, *Turandot* (mus. Puccini, 2003) for Hong Kong Ballet, as well as *Lacrimosa* (mus. Mozart, 2009) for the West Australian Ballet. In 2009 she was appointed artistic director of the first company she worked with, Expressions.

Weiss, Josephine (*b* 1805; *d* Vienna, 18 Dec. 1852) Austrian dancer and ballet mistress. She was soloist at the Kärntnertor Theater, Vienna (1820–6) then ballet mistress at the Josephsstädter Theater where she formed Les Danseuses Viennoises (*see* VIENNA CHILDREN'S BALLET) and, after 1845 toured widely with them.

Welch, Damien (*b* Melbourne, 29 Oct. 1972) Australian dancer. He studied at the school of his parents, Marilyn Jones and Garth Welch, then at the Australian Ballet School, graduating into the Australian Ballet in 1992. He was promoted to principal in 1998, dancing the classical and contemporary repertoires. Between 2000 and 2002 he danced with Nederlands Dans Theater and he has additionally guested with National Ballet of Canada (2000) and Houston Ballet (2003 and 2006). He is the brother of Stanton W.

Welch, Garth (*b* Brisbane, 14 Apr. 1936) Australian dancer, choreographer, and director. He studied ballet with V. Gsovsky, van Praagh, and others and later modern dance with Graham (1966–7), making his debut in the musical *Call me Madam* in 1953. He then danced with Borovansky Ballet (1954–58 and 1960–1), Western Theatre Ballet (1958–60), and Grand Ballet du Marquis de Cuevas (1961–2) before joining Australian Ballet in 1962, where he remained as principal until 1973, performing modern and classical roles. An unusually dramatic dancer, he was outstanding as both Albrecht and Hilarion in *Giselle* and he continued to dance character roles after officially retiring from the company, including von Aschenbach, which he created in Murphy's *After Venice* (1984). In 1964 he choreographed his first ballet, *Variations on a Theme* (mus. Arensky, Australian Ballet) which was followed by *Othello* (mus. Jerry

Goldsmith, Australian Ballet School, 1968, revived Australian Ballet, 1970), *Images* (mus. Rachmaninoff, Ballet Victoria, 1974), *The Tempest* (1983), and *Voyage Within* (mus. G. Koehne, 1989, both for West Australian Ballet), among others. He was assistant artistic director of Ballet Victoria (1974–6) then associate, becoming artistic director of West Australian Ballet (1979–82). He has since taught at various institutions including his own school (1983–8). He was married to dancer Marilyn Jones and his sons are Stanton and Damien W. He was awarded Order of Australia in 1981.

Welch, Stanton (*b* Melbourne, 15 Oct. 1969) Australian dancer, choreographer, and director. He started studying at 17 but a year later won a scholarship to San Francisco Ballet School, also performing small roles with the company. In 1989 he joined Australian Ballet and in 1990 created his first work for the company, *The Three of Us*, followed by *Of Blessed Memory* (mus. Canteloube, 1991), *Divergence* (1994), and others. He was appointed resident choreographer of Australian Ballet in 1995 and went on to make many works for the company, including *Madam Butterfly* (mus. Puccini, arr. Lanchbery, 1995), *Corroboree* (mus. John Antill, 1995), *Cinderella* (1997), *Velocity* (mus. Torke, 2003), and a new staging of *Sleeping Beauty* (2005). His classically based style reflects the influence of modern choreographers like Graham and Limón in its weight and fluency, but also tends towards a more fractured edginess and while working at Australian Ballet Welch became one of the most internationally sought-after choreographers of his generation, making *Powder* (mus. Mozart, 1998) for Birmingham Royal Ballet, *Indigo* (mus. Vivaldi, 1999), and *Bruiser* (mus. Graeme Koehne, 2000) for Houston Ballet, *Clear* (mus. George Harrison, 2000) for American Ballet Theatre, as well as works for San Francisco Ballet, Royal Danish Ballet, Atlanta Ballet, and Moscow Dance Theatre. In 2003, after a brief period as associate choreographer with BalletMett, he was appointed director of Houston Ballet. He has created numerous works for the company, including *Tales of Texas* (mus. several) and *Bolero* (mus. Ravel) both 2004, *Nosostros* (mus. Rachmaninoff, 2005), *Brigade* (2006), *Swan Lake* (2006), *The Four Seasons* (mus. Vivaldi, 2007), *A Doll's House* (mus. István Márta, 2008), and *Marie* (mus. several, 2009) as well as bringing works by Wheeldon, van Manen, Forsythe, Robbins and others into the repertory. A list of his other created works includes *Tu Tu* (mus. Ravel, 2003), *Falling* (mus. Mozart, 2005), *Naked* (mus. Poulenc, 2008), all for San Francisco Ballet; *Carmina Burana* (American Ballet Theatre, 2003). He has additionally staged works for Colorado Ballet, Cincinnati Ballet, Royal New Zealand Ballet, and Tulsa Ballet among others.

Weller, Dawn (*b* Durban, 16 Dec. 1947) South African ballet dancer and director. She studied locally with Iris Manning and Arlene Speark and in 1964 joined Natal Performing Arts Council Ballet, then PACT Ballet in 1965 where she was appointed principal in 1968. A musical and dramatic dancer, she was highly acclaimed in Prokovsky's *Anna Karenina* (1980). In 1983 she was appointed artistic director of PACT and in 1986 she was made prima ballerina, but in 1987 injury forced her to retire from the stage. In 1994 she took over direction of PACT Ballet School, retaining direction of the company which became State Theatre Ballet in 1997. In 1996 she staged a full-length version of *La Bayadère* there, which has since been taken into the repertories of several companies. After the company was disbanded in 2000 she moved to Australia and in 2002 was appointed director of dance at Queensland University.

Wells, Bruce (*b* Tacoma, Wash., 17 Jan. 1950) US dancer and choreographer. He studied at the School of American Ballet, joining New York City Ballet in 1967 and becoming soloist in 1970. In 1975 he became resident choreographer at Connecticut Ballet where his ballets included *Coppélia* (1977) and *Beauty and the Beast* (mus. Debussy, 1979). In 1979 he moved to Boston Ballet as resident choreographer, principal dancer, and teacher. He choreographed many ballets, such as *La Fille mal gardée* (1990), and became associate artistic director. During the mid-1990s he was resident choreographer for Pittsburgh Ballet Theater. He has also choreographed for other companies, including *Hunchback of Notre Dame* (mus. Bartók, 1981) for Australian Ballet.

Wells, Doreen (*b* Walthamstow, 25 Jun. 1937) British dancer. She studied at the Bush-Davies School and Sadler's Wells School, joining Sadler's Wells Theatre Ballet in 1955 and Sadler's Wells Ballet (becoming Royal Ballet) in 1956, where she became soloist. From 1960 to 1974 she was ballerina of Touring Royal Ballet (while still dancing with the main company). An elegant dancer with a pure classical line, she created the title role in Nureyev's production of *Raymonda* (Spoleto, 1964) and also roles in, among others, Ashton's *The Creatures of Prometheus* (1970). After retiring she made occasional guest appearances in musicals and with London City Ballet. She became Marchioness of Londonderry on her marriage in 1972.

West, Elizabeth (*b* Alassio, 1927; *d* nr. Matterhorn, 28 Sept. 1962) British dancer, choreographer, and director. She studied with E. Espinosa and at Bristol Old Vic Theatre School. From 1946 she worked at the Bristol Old Vic, choreographing occasionally there and at the Shakespeare Festival in Stratford-upon-Avon. In 1957 she founded Western Theatre Ballet (now Scottish Ballet) with Darrell. As well as choreographing Stravinsky's *Pulcinella* and Prokofiev's *Peter and the Wolf* (both 1957) for the company she was the visionary driving force behind it. She died in a climbing accident.

Western Symphony Ballet in one act with choreography by Balanchine, music by H. Kay, set by John Boyt, and costumes by Karinska (although danced in practice clothes at its premiere). Premiered 7 Sept. 1954 by New York City Ballet at City Center, New York, with D. Adams, Bliss, Reed, Magallanes, P. Wilde, LeClercq, and d'Amboise. It evokes the atmosphere and dance vernacular of the American West within the frame of classical ballet. It is now in the repertory of many companies, including Houston Ballet, San Francisco Ballet, Pacific Northwest Ballet, Miami City Ballet, Colorado Ballet, and Birmingham Royal Ballet.

Western Theatre Ballet *See* SCOTTISH BALLET.

West Side Story Musical, produced and choreographed by Jerome Robbins, with libretto by A. Laurents, music by Bernstein, sets by Oliver Smith, and costumes by Irene Sharaff. Premiered 26 Sept. 1957 at Winter Garden Theater, New York. This updating of Shakespeare's *Romeo and Juliet* to a story of modern gang warfare in New York was a huge popular and critical success and was staged all around the world. A film version was produced in 1961 and in 1995 Robbins produced a suite of dances, *West Side Story Suite*, for New York City Ballet. Neumeier produced and choreographed a version for Hamburg State Opera in 1978.

Wheater, Ashley (*b* Biggar, Scotland, 16 Aug. 1959) British dancer and director. He studied at the Royal Ballet School and in 1973, while still a student, created the role of the Polish Child in Ashton's choreography for the Britten opera, *Death in Venice*. He graduated into the Royal Ballet in 1978, subsequently dancing with London Festival Ballet (1979), Australian Ballet (1982–85), Joffrey Ballet (1985–89), and San Francisco Ballet (from 1989). Here he danced most of the classical and contemporary repertories as well as creating roles in works by Tomasson, Kudelka, Bintley, and Morris. In 1996 an injury curtailed his stage career and while he continued to perform character roles he was appointed ballet master and then in 2002 assistant artistic director of SFB. He became artistic director of the Joffrey Ballet in 2007.

W

Wheeldon, Christopher (*b* Somerset, 22 Mar. 1973) British dancer and choreographer. He studied locally and at the Royal Ballet School, and graduated into the company in 1991. In 1993 he moved to New York City Ballet, where he created roles in several ballets, including Martins's *Symphonic Dreams* and Robbins's *West Side Story Suite* and *Brandenburg*, and was appointed soloist in 1999. He began choreographing as a student (he won the gold medal at Lausanne in a solo created by himself) and made ballets for several student performances and workshops before choreographing his early professional works. These included *Pavane pour une infante défunte* (mus. Ravel, 1996) for the Royal Ballet; *Slavonic Dances* (1997) and *Mercurial Manoeuvres* (2000) for New York City Ballet; and *Firebird* (1997) and *Corybantic Ecstasies* (1999) both Boston Ballet. He was briefly appointed principal guest choreographer at Boston before being appointed resident choreographer at NYCB in 2001. He went on to create many works for NYCB, his style a fusion of American neo-classicism and the more dramatic, lyrical influences of his Royal Ballet background. His works for the company included *Polyphonia* (mus. Ligeti, 2001), *Morphoses* (mus. Ligeti 2002), *Carousel* (mus. Rodgers, 2002), *Liturgy* (mus. Pärt, 2003), *Shambards* (mus. James MacMillan, 2004), *An American in Paris* (mus. Gershwin, 2005), *After the Rain* (mus. Pärt, 2005), *Klavier* (mus. Beethoven, 2006), *Evenfall* (Bartók, 2006), and *The Nightingale and the Rose* (mus. Bright Sheng, 2007). Many of these works featured the partnership of Wendy Whelan and Jock Soto, and revealed Wheeldon's distinctively inventive and expressive handling of the pas de deux form. During this period he was additionally commissioned to create work by many of the major international companies, arguably making him the most successful classical choreographer of his generation. His works for San Francisco Ballet included *Sea Pictures* (mus. Elgar, 2000), *Continuum* (mus. Ligeti, 2002), *Rush* (mus. Martinu, 2003), *Quaternary* (mus. several, 2005), and *Within the Golden Hour* (mus. Ezio Bosso 2008); for the Royal Ballet, *Tryst* (mus. James MacMillan, 2002), Fire Section of *Homage to the Queen* (mus. Arnold, 2006), *DGV* (mus. Nyman, 2006), and *Electric Counterpoint* (mus. Reich, 2008); for Colorado Ballet, *A Midsummer Night's Dream* (2000); for Pennsylvania Ballet, *Swan Lake* (2004); and for the Bolshoi Ballet, *Elsinore* (mus. Pärt, 2007). Among the other companies who performed his work are George Piper Dances, Norwegian Ballet, Houston Ballet, Miami City Ballet, and Pacific Northwest Ballet.

He left his post at NYCB in 2008 having launched his own company, and Morphoses, in 2007. The company had bases in both New York and London,

and performed a selection of 20th-century ballets by Ashton, Robbins, Balanchine, and Forsythe, among others, newly commissioned work, and ballets by Wheeldon himself including *Fool's Paradise* (mus. Joby Talbot, 2007), *Commedia* (mus. Stravinsky, 2008), and *Rhapsody Fantaisie* (mus. Rachmaninoff, 2009). In 2010 Wheeldon left Morphoses to pursue his freelance career.

Wheeldon has also choreographed for film, opera, and musicals, including Nicholas Hytner's *The Sweet Smell of Success* (2002). He is recipient of numerous awards, including the Critics Circle Dance Award for best classical choreography.

((⊕)) SEE WEB LINKS
• Website for Morphoses

Whelan, Wendy (*b* Louisville, Ky., 1967) US dancer. She studied ballet locally, at Louisville Ballet Academy, and the School of American Ballet before becoming an apprentice with New York City Ballet in 1984 and a full member in 1986. She was promoted to principal in 1991. An exceptionally lean and supple dancer with a fearless athleticism and musicality she performed leading roles in most of the Balanchine and Robbins repertories and created roles in many works, including Martins's *Adams Violin Concerto*, *Ash*, *Concerti Armonici*, *Jazz*, *Les Petits Riens*, and *Reliquary*; Robbins's *Brandenburg*; and Ratmansky's *Russian Seasons*; also in works by Dove, O'Day, C. d'Amboise, and La Fosse. She formed a celebrated partnership with Jock Soto, and with him was particularly associated with the ballets of *Wheeldon, creating roles in *Polyphonia*, *Morphoses*, *Liturgy*, *After the Rain*, and *Klavier*, among others. She also made many guest appearances with Wheeldon's company Morphoses.

Whims of Cupid and the Ballet Master, The (orig. Dan. title *Amors og Balletmesterens Luner*) Ballet in one act with libretto and choreography by Galeotti and music by Jens Lolle. Premiered 31 Oct. 1786 by the Royal Danish Ballet, Copenhagen. This comic work is the oldest ballet to survive with its original choreography and is still in RDB's repertory. It portrays several couples of different nationalities who come to pay tribute to Cupid but who are then blindfolded by the god (played by a child) and re-paired, with comic results. It has been revived by Paris Opera (1952) and Netherlands Ballet (1957).

White-Haired Girl, The Ballet in eight acts with choreography and libretto by Hu Rongrong, Fu Aidi, Cheng Laihui, and Lin Yangyang, music by Yan Dinxian, and design by Du Shixiang and Zhu Shichang. Premiered May 1965 at Shanghai School of Dancing with Cai Kuoying, Long Guiming, and

Ga Xiamei. It is based on a 1945 Chinese opera which tells the story of a young girl who suffers at the hands of her oppressive landlord until rescued by the Red Army. Originally only half an hour long it was later extended to its full eight acts, and the title role became so strenuous it had to be performed by several ballerinas during the course of one performance. It was filmed by Shanghai Film Studio in 1972.

White Oak Dance Project, The Dance company founded in 1990 by Mikhail *Baryshnikov in collaboration with Mark Morris. Led by Baryshnikov it drew on a pool of mature, independent dancers from a wide range of backgrounds, including Jamie Bishton (ex-Tharp company), Rob Besserer (ex-Morris company), and Patricia Lent (ex-Cunningham company). During its first year it performed only Morris's choreography, but then added new works by Taylor, Tharp, Robbins, Lubovitch, Reitz, G. Murphy, and others, and revived works by Graham, Holm, Dudley, M. Monk, Limón, and Cunningham, among others. With a base at the White Oak Plantation wild life reserve, it toured internationally and in the US. It closed in 2002 to allow the Baryshnikov Foundation to focus its resources on the founding of a New York-based arts centre in 2005.

Who Cares? Ballet in one act with choreography by Balanchine, music by Gershwin, lighting by R. Bates, and costumes by Karinska. Premiered 5 Feb. 1970 by New York City Ballet at State Theater, New York, with von Aroldingen, McBride, Marnee Morris, and d'Amboise. A suite of dances to melodies like 'Fascinatin' Rhythm' and 'The Man I Love' (all arr. H. Kay), it presents classical dance in the style of a Gershwin musical. It is in the repertory of several companies, including English National Ballet, Los Angeles Ballet, and North Carolina Dance Theatre.

Wiesenthal, Grete (*b* Vienna, 9 Dec. 1885; *d* Vienna, 22 Jun. 1970) Austrian dancer and choreographer. She and her sister Elsa (1887–1967) were both dancers with the Vienna Court Opera Ballet but she left in 1904 to choreograph and perform her own work, which was accompanied primarily by waltz music (Chopin and J. Strauss). She proved so popular that her sisters Elsa and Berta joined her in works that communicated a (then) revolutionarily ecstatic response to waltz rhythms. The sisters moved to Berlin where they performed together until 1910, after which Grete worked independently, choreographing and performing in vaudeville, film, and opera around Europe and the US. The Grete Wiesenthal Dance group (1945–56) toured the world and two of its members subsequently staged her dances for the Vienna State Opera Ballet.

Wigman, Mary (orig. Marie Wiegmann; *b* Hanover, 13 Nov. 1886; *d* Berlin, 18 Sept. 1973) German dancer, choreographer, teacher, and leading pioneer of European modern dance. In 1911 she began studying with Dalcroze in Hellerau/Dresden and then from 1913 with Laban in Munich and Zurich, becoming his assistant. She gave her first solo recital in 1914 in the earliest version of her famous solo *Witch Dance*, whose distorted body shapes and dramatic intensity prefigured the spare expressionism of her mature and extremely influential style. She worked largely without music and her dances had no plot. Further recitals in Zurich and Hamburg (1919) established her reputation and in 1920 she opened her own school in Dresden which became the centre of German modern dance. Holm, Georgi, and Palucca were among her pupils and also appeared in her performing group. She choreographed many solos and group dances and toured widely, making her London debut in 1928. Branches of her school were established throughout Germany, and the one in the US, under Holm's direction, numbered almost 2,000 pupils. She was condemned by the Nazis, who closed her school, and she gave up performing in 1942. After the war she opened a school in Leipzig and in 1949 moved to W. Berlin where her school again became a focus of European modern dance activity. She also began choreographing for several German opera houses, including Gluck's *Orpheus and Euridice* (fully choreographed, Leipzig, 1947, and later for Berlin Opera Ballet, 1961), Stravinsky's *Sacre du printemps* (Municipal Opera, Berlin, 1957), and Gluck's *Alcestis* (Mannheim, 1958). She was author of *Deutsche Tanzkunst* (Dresden, 1935), *Die Sprache des Tanzes* (Stuttgart, 1963, American trans. *The Language of the Dance*, Middletown, Conn., 1966), and the posthumous *Mary Wigman Book* (ed. W. Sorrell, Middletown, Conn., 1973).

Wilde, Patricia (*b* Ottawa, 16 Jul. 1928) Canadian-US dancer, teacher, and director. She studied with G. Osborn, C. and D. Littlefield, at the School of American Ballet, and later with Preobrajenska. She danced with American Concert Ballet (1943–4), then with Ballet International (1944–5), Ballet Russe de Monte Carlo (1945–9), and with Petit's Ballets de Paris, and Metropolitan Ballet, England (1949–50). In 1950 she became principal with New York City Ballet, where, as a dancer of exceptional speed, clarity, and power, she created roles in many Balanchine works, including *La Valse* (1951), *Caracole* and *Scotch Symphony* (both 1952), *Western Symphony* and *Ivesiana* (both 1954), *Divertimento no. 15* (1956), *Square Dance* (1957), and *Raymonda Variations* (1961), also Robbins's *Quartet* (1954). She left in 1965 to become director of Harkness Ballet

School (until 1967). She then taught for various companies and was director of American Ballet Theatre School (1977–82), until becoming artistic director of Pittsburgh Ballet Theater in 1982 where she remained until 1997, bringing works by Balanchine into the repertory.

Wilde ballets Ballets based on Oscar Wilde's writings include Bolm's *Birthday of the Infanta* (mus. J. A. Carpenter, Chicago, 1919), Dolin's *The Nightingale and the Rose* (mus. H. Frazer-Simson, Nemchinova-Dolin Ballet, London, 1927), Wheeldon's *Nightingale and the Rose* (mus. Bright Sheng, 2007, New York City Ballet), Etchévery's *Ballade de geôle de Reading* (mus. Ibert, Opéra Comique, Paris, 1947), and several versions of *The Picture of Dorian Gray*, for example Orlikowsky (mus. M. Lang, Basle, 1966), D. Deane (mus. Carl Davis, 1987, Sadler's Wells Royal Ballet), Robert Hill (mus. Chausson, 2003, American Ballet Theatre) and Matthew Bourne (mus. Terry Davies, 2008). A version by Layton was titled *Double Exposure* (mus. Scriabin and H. Pousseur, City Center Joffrey Ballet, New York, 1972). Layton additionally choreographed a ballet based on Wilde's life: *Oscar Wilde* (mus. Walton, Royal Ballet, London, 1972). For ballets based on the play *Salome, see* SALOME.

Wildor, Sarah (*b* Eastwood, 29 Jan. 1972) British dancer. She studied at the Royal Ballet School and graduated into the company in 1991 where she was promoted first soloist in 1995 and was principal from 1999–2001 after which she became freelance. A dancer of outstanding musicality, she performed classical roles with individuality but was most renowned for the originality and intensity of her dramatic interpretation in roles such as Manon. She created roles in Tharp's *Mr Worldly Wise* (1995), in M. Bourne's *Cinderella* (1997), and Adam Cooper's *Dangerous Liaisons* (2005), among others, and appeared in the London production of Stroman's *Contact*. She has also worked as an actor. She is married to Adam *Cooper.

Wiley, Roland John (*b* California, 27 Jan. 1942) US musicologist and writer. His closely researched study *Tchaikovky's Ballets* (New York, 1985) has shed important light on the history and construction of *The Nutcracker*, *Sleeping Beauty*, and *Swan Lake*, as well as on the state of ballet in Petipa's time. It has influenced several stagings of the classics including P. Schaufuss's *Nutcracker* (London Festival Ballet, 1986) and A. Dowell's *Swan Lake* (Royal Ballet, 1986). His subsequent publications include *A Century of Russian Ballet* (1990) and *The Life and Ballets of Lev Ivanov* (1997).

Williams, Dudley (*b* New York, Aug. 1938) US dancer. He studied tap and ballet locally, after which he attended the High School of Performing Arts, and studied ballet with Tudor and others and modern dance with May O'Donnell. He joined her company in 1958 then danced with McKayle (1960), Graham (1962–6), and Ailey from 1964. A dancer who combined exceptional dramatic fervour with technical control, he created roles in many of Ailey's works including the solo *Love Songs* (1972), and continued to perform with the company until 2005. He then joined Paradigm, Gus Solomons jun.'s company for senior dancers.

Williams, Ellen Virginia (E. Virginia Williams) (Salem, Mass., 12 Mar. 1914; *d* Boston, 8 May 1984) US teacher, choreographer, and director who played a pioneering role in the development of American ballet. She studied with M. Winslow (of Denishawn) and Balanchine, among others, becoming dancer with San Carlo Opera. She began teaching at the age of 16 and established numerous schools including the E. Virginia Williams School of Ballet in Boston (1940). In 1958 she was founder and artistic director of New England Civic Ballet from which developed the professional Boston Ballet in 1964. As director of the company (until 1980) she brought in many guest stars, including Fonteyn, Nureyev, and Makarova, and pursued the then-controversial policy of commissioning work from modern dance choreographers. She was co-director of the company with V. Verdy (1980–3) and then artistic adviser (1983–4). She was also adviser to the Lyric Opera of Chicago (1971–3). She choreographed several works for Joffrey, Boston, and Pennsylvania Ballets, among others.

Williams, Peter (*b* Burton Joyce, 12 Jun. 1914; *d* Cornwall, 10 Aug. 1995) British dance writer and adviser. He was educated at the London Central School of Art and Design and in 1949 was assistant editor of Buckle's magazine, *Dance*. In 1950 he founded *Dance and Dancers* which he edited until 1980. He was also dance critic of the *Daily Mail* (1950–3), chairman of the Arts Council Dance Advisory Committee (1973–80), and founder-chairman of the Dancers Resettlement Fund from 1975. He occasionally designed for ballet, such as Howard's *Selina* whose libretto he also wrote (Sadler's Wells Theatre Ballet, 1948). He taught dance design at the Slade and was author of *Masterpieces of Ballet Design* (1981). The Peter Williams Design for Dance Project was founded in his memory.

Williams, Stanley (*b* Chappel, 1925; *d* New York, 21 Oct. 1997) British-Danish dancer and teacher. He grew up in Copenhagen where he studied at the Royal Danish Ballet School and graduated into the company. A gifted mime and

exponent of the Bournonville style he was promoted soloist (principal) in 1949 and became a
teacher at the school in 1950. After leaving in 1963
he joined the School of American Ballet (1964)
where he was one of its most respected teachers.

Williams-Yarborough, Lavinia (*b* Philadelphia, Pa., 2 Jul. 1926; *d* Haiti, 19 Jul. 1989) US
dancer and teacher. She studied with Sokolow,
Lisan Kay, and at the Graham school and danced
with Eugene von Grona's Negro Ballet (1937–9).
In 1940 she danced with Ballet Theatre in de
Mille's *Obeah* as well as appearing in musicals
and films. In 1953 she went to Haiti where she
remained until 1980, helping to found various
institutions including the National School of
Dance and the National Dance Troupe of Jamaica, as well as the Haitian Institute of Folklore
and Classic Dance. She taught and choreographed widely in the W. Indies and Europe,
returning to the US in 1980 where she taught at
Ailey's school and her own Brooklyn-based
school (1983). She returned to Haiti in the mid-
1980s. She was the mother of the dancer Sarah
Yarborough.

Wilson, Robert (*b* Waco, Tex., 4 Oct. 1941) US
artist and director. His works range from art installations to theatre events, in which music, text,
dance, and the visual arts are combined to often
hallucinatory effect. His most frequent dance collaborators have been Andy de Groat and L. Childs
who was the dancer in his production of P. Glass's
opera *Einstein on the Beach* (Avignon, 1976) and
in *La Maladie de la mort* (1993). His first production was *Dance Event* at the 1965 New York
World's Fair and others include *The Life and
Times of Sigmund Freud* (New York, 1969), *The
CIVIL WarS* (*sic*), a fourteen-hour extravaganza
which was created over four years and was to
have been premiered at the Los Angeles Olympic
Arts Festival in 1984, but proved too unwieldy, *O
Corvo Branco* (1998), *POEtry* (2000), and *Fables*
(2005). He also works as a film-maker, painter,
and workshop director and was invited by Nureyev to stage *Le Martyre de Saint-Sébastien* (mus.
Debussy) for the Paris Opera Ballet in 1988.

Wilson, Sallie (*b* Fort Worth, Tex., 18 Apr.
1932; *d* New York, 27 Apr. 2008) US dancer. She
studied with Craske, Tudor, and others and in
1949 joined Ballet Theatre. After a period with
Metropolitan Opera Ballet (1950–5) she returned
to American Ballet Theatre, becoming soloist in
1957 and ballerina in 1961. She stayed with the
company until 1980 except for a period with New
York City Ballet (1958–60), and was considered
one of their greatest dance actresses, performing
in many Tudor works. She created the role of
Queen Elizabeth in Graham's section of *Episodes*

(1959) as well as roles in Robbins's *Les Noces*
(1965), among others. After retiring from the
stage she worked as guest teacher and producer,
reviving Tudor ballets for companies all round the
world and also choreographing several works of
her own, including *The Idol* (Fort Worth Ballet,
1983).

Winter, Ethel (*b* Wrentham, Mass., 18 Jun.
1924) US dancer, choreographer, and teacher.
She studied at Bennington College and with Graham, joining her company in 1946. Here she
danced many leading roles, and was the first
dancer Graham chose to take over her roles including those in *Herodiade* and *Frontier*. Winter
also danced with other companies, including her
own, and created roles in Sokolow's *Lyric Suite*
and Maslow's *The Dybbuk* (1964), among others.
As a choreographer she worked with Batsheva
Dance Company and Repertory Dance Theater
of Utah. She taught at the Graham company and
school until 1993 and additionally at the Juilliard
School from 1953–2003, directing its dance department for several years.

Winterbranch Modern dance work in one act
with choreography by Cunningham, music by La-
Monte Young, and design by Rauschenberg. Premiered 21 Mar. 1964 by the Cunningham Dance
Company at Wadsworth Atheneum, Hartford,
Connecticut, with Cunningham, Brown, Farber,
B. Lloyd, W. Davies, and Paxton. It was conceived
as a plotless work although its abrasive music and
glaring lighting design suggest images of violence
and destruction. The New York premiere was
4 Mar. 1965 at New York State Theater, and it
was revived for Boston Ballet in 1974.

Witch Boy, The Ballet in one act with libretto
and choreography by J. Carter, music by Salzedo,
and design by N. McDowell. Premiered 24 May
1956 by Ballet der Lage Landen, Amsterdam, with
McDowell, A. Bayley, and Carter. It is based on
the 'Ballad of Barbara Allan' and tells the story of a
love affair between a girl and a witch boy who is
murdered by villagers suspicious of his strange-
ness. The boy is reborn, however, suggesting that
the situation will endlessly repeat itself through
time. It was revived for several companies, including London Festival Ballet and Buenos Aires.

With My Red Fires Modern dance work in one
act, which constitutes the middle piece in Humphrey's dance trilogy (parts 1 and 3 being *Theater
Piece* and *New Dance*). With music by W. Riegger
and design by P. Lawrence. Premiered 13 Aug.
1936 by the Humphrey-Weidman Company at
Bennington College. The title is taken from Blake's
poem *Jerusalem, II* and its two sections, subtitled
'Ritual' and 'Drama', portray a pair of lovers

affirming their love against the oppressive rule of a Matriarch. It was filmed in 1972.

Woetzel, Damian (*b* Boston, 17 May 1967) US dancer, choreographer, teacher, and director. He studied locally and at the Boston Ballet School. He then danced for a year with Los Angeles Ballet (1983–4), spending a further six months training at the School of American Ballet before joining New York City Ballet in 1985, where he was promoted principal in 1989 and remained until 2008. He danced over 50 leading roles during this period and created roles in several works, including Robbins's *Ives Songs* and *Quiet City*, Martins's *Les Gentilhommes*, *A Musical Offering*, and *Sleeping Beauty*, Wheeldon's *Carousel* and *American in Paris*, among others, and works by Tharp, Taylor-Corbett, Tanner, and O'Day. He has also choreographed several works, including *Ebony Concerto* (mus. Stravinsky, NYCB, 1994), *Glazunov pas de deux* (NYCB, 1994), and a version of *An American in Paris* (mus. Gershwin, Gershwin Centennial Gala, 1998). In 1994 he became director of the ballet programme at New York State Summer School as well as guest teacher at the School of American Ballet, and in 2007 became director of the Vail International Dance Festival.

Woizikowsky, Léon (Woizikowski) (orig. Wójcikowski; *b* Warsaw, 20 Feb. 1899; *d* Warsaw, 23 Feb. 1974) Polish dancer, ballet master, and teacher. He studied at Imperial Theatre School, Warsaw, and with Cecchetti, joining Diaghilev's Ballets Russes (1915–29). A dancer of unusual suppleness, vitality, and wit, he became the company's leading character dancer creating roles in, among others, Massine's *Las Meninas* (1916), *Les Femmes de bonne humeur*, and *Parade* (1917), *La Boutique fantasque* and *Le Tricorne* (both 1919), *Les Matelots* (1925), and *Le Pas d'acier* (1927); Nijinska's *Les Noces* (1923), *Les Biches* and *Le Train bleu* (both 1924); and Balanchine's *The Gods Go a-Begging* (1928), *Le Bal*, and *Prodigal Son* (1929). He also danced in many Fokine ballets, including *L'Après-midi d'un faune* which he later staged and danced for Ballet Rambert in 1931. After Diaghilev's Ballets Russes disbanded he performed with Pavlova's company (1929–30), Ballet Club, later Rambert (1930–1), Ballets Russes de Monte Carlo (1932–4), and de Basil's Ballets Russes de Monte Carlo (1936–45). He was also director of his own company, Les Ballets de Léon Woizikowsky which toured Europe (1935–6) and for which he also choreographed several ballets, also of Ballets Russes de Léon Woizikowsky which toured Australia (1936–7), and Europe (1937–8). In 1938 he was dancer and ballet master with the Polish Ballet for its European and American tour. After 1945 he returned to Warsaw where he taught at Opera Ballet School and choreographed for the Polish Opera Ballet. After 1958 he worked mainly in the West, staging *Petrushka* and *Scheherazade* for London Festival Ballet in 1958 and 1960. He also danced with Massine's company (1960), was ballet master with London Festival Ballet (1961), and worked in Cologne, Bonn, and Antwerp teaching and staging the Diaghilev repertory.

Wooden Prince, The (orig. Hung. title *A Fából Faragott Királyfi*; also known as *The Woodcut Prince*) Ballet in one act with choreography by Ottó Zobisch and Ede Brada, libretto by Béla Balász, music by Bartók, and design by Count Bánffy. Premiered 12 May 1917, Budapest, with Anna Palley (en travestie as the Prince), Emilia Nirschy, Brada, and Boriska Hormat. Its tells the story of a prince who tries to woo a princess by carving her a wooden prince. She falls in love with the toy instead and only when she tires of it does she seek in earnest to win the affections of the real man. Other versions include Harangozó (Budapest, 1939), Milloss (Venice, 1950), Walter (Wuppertal, 1962), Seregi (Budapest, 1970, also for Hungarian television), and Cauley (London Festival Ballet, 1981).

Woolliams, Anne (*b* Folkestone, 3 Aug. 1926; *d* Canterbury, 8 Jul. 1999) British dancer and teacher. She studied with J. Espinosa and Volkova and danced with, among others, Kyasht Ballet, Russian Opera Ballet, and in the film *The Red Shoes*. She taught at Essen Folkwang School (1958–63), was character artist, ballet mistress, and then assistant director at Stuttgart Ballet (1963–75) and also director of Cranko Ballet school, which she co-founded with Cranko in 1964. In 1976 she became artistic director of Australian Ballet (1976–8) where she staged a new version of *Swan Lake* (1977). She was appointed Dean of Dance at Victoria College of Arts, Melbourne. In 1988 she returned to Europe and established the Schweizerische Ballettberufsschule in Zurich, then in 1993 became artistic director of the Vienna State Opera Ballet, finally retiring to Canterbury.

Wright, Douglas (*b* Tuakau, S. Auckland, 1956) New Zealand dancer and choreographer. He trained in dance and gymnastics and in 1980 joined Limbs Dance Company for which he choreographed several works. Between 1983 and 1987 he danced with P. Taylor's company and in 1988 with DV8. In 1984 he formed his own company in New York, moving with it to New Zealand in 1989. He has choreographed many works for this, including *Gloria* (mus. Vivaldi, 1990), *Forever* (mus. various, 1993), *Inland* (2002), and *Black Milk* (2006). He has also created works for Australian Dance Theatre, Royal New Zealand Ballet, and others.

W

Wright, (Sir) Peter (*b* London, 25 Nov. 1926) British dancer, choreographer, and director. He studied with Jooss, Volkova, and van Praagh and danced with Ballets Jooss (1945–7 and 1951–2), Metropolitan Ballet (1947–9), St James' Ballet (1948), and Sadler's Wells Theatre Ballet (1949–51 and 1952–5) where he also became assistant ballet master. He taught at the Royal Ballet School (1957–9), and was ballet master at Stuttgart Ballet (1961–7) where he choreographed several works and staged *Giselle* in 1965. During this period (1963–5) he also worked at the BBC as ballet master and choreographer for television productions, creating *Peter and the Wolf* (mus. Prokofiev, 1965), and others. He subsequently worked as freelance choreographer and ballet master for such companies as Cologne and Western Theatre Ballet until 1970 when he was appointed associate director of Royal Ballet, becoming director of the Royal Ballet Touring Company in 1975 (renamed Sadler's Wells Royal Ballet and subsequently Birmingham Royal Ballet). He created his first ballet in 1957, *A Blue Rose* (mus. Barber, for Royal Ballet Touring Company) and later works included *The Mirror Walkers* (mus. Tchaikovsky, 1962, for Stuttgart Ballet), *Arpège* (mus. Boieldieu, 1974), and *Summertide* (mus. Mendelssohn, 1976, both for Royal Ballet Touring Company). However, it was his detailed, dramatically acute stagings of the classics that brought him greatest acclaim, including *Swan Lake, Giselle, The Sleeping Beauty*, and *The Nutcracker*. As a director he was also a major force in British ballet, tranforming the Royal's second company into a significant classical company, with a fine ensemble of dancers and a distinctive repertory that spanned the standard classics, revivals of major 20th-century works such as Massine's *Choreartium* and Jooss's *The Green Table*, and new works by company members like *Bintley. He oversaw the company's historic re-location to Birmingham in 1990 before retiring in 1995. He was knighted in 1993.

Wuppertal Dance Theatre (Tanztheater Wuppertal) The dance company of Pina *Bausch. It was established in Wuppertal in 1973 at the city's invitation after the success of Bausch's highly individual opera stagings for Wuppertal Opera House. Following the death of Bausch in 2009 the company continued to perform her work internationally.

(())) SEE WEB LINKS

• Website for Tanztheater Wuppertal

Wu Xiao-bang (*b* Jiangsu, 18 Dec. 1906; *d* Beijing, 8 Jul. 1995) Chinese dancer, choreographer and teacher, considered the father of Chinese modern dance. He studied ballet and modern dance and in 1931 opened a dance studio in Shanghai with the intention of bringing Western ballet to China. This met with no success and he went on to develop his own New Chinese Dance style, influenced by German expressionism and Duncan—his bare feet causing outrage among traditionalists. His many works during the 1930s were political attacks on the invading Japanese, but in 1949 he began to create more utopian works using traditional Chinese music to accompany his still experimental dance style. In 1960 he was forced to stop performing and teaching and for eighteen years remained inactive, but subsequently continued his activities as a committed dance educator.

W

Yakobson, Leonid *See* JACOBSON, LEONID.

Yanowsky, Zenaida (b Lyon, 23 Dec, 1974) Spanish dancer. She grew up in Madrid and Las Palmas and trained at her parents' school. In 1993 she joined the Paris Opera Ballet, dancing Kitri in *Don Quixote* before moving to the Royal Ballet in 1994, where she was promoted to principal in 2001. An exceptionally expressive, intelligent dancer, she has performed leading roles across the repertory and also created roles in many ballets, including Tharp's *Mr Worldly Wise*; Tuckett's *The Turn of the Screw*, *The Crucible*, *Proverb* and *The Seven Deadly Sins*; Wheeldon's *Electric Counterpoint*; Christopher Bruce's *Three Songs—Two Voices*; and Kim Brandstrup's *Two Footnotes to Ashton*.

Yerbabuena, Eva La (orig. Eva María Garrido García; b Frankfurt 1970) Spanish dancer and choreographer. She grew up in Granada, and from the age of 11 began to study dance locally. Her training expanded to include drama studies in Seville (1983) and choreography in Havana (1984) before she made her debut in the company of Rafael Aguilar (1985). For the next 12 years she collaborated and performed with a variety of flamenco artists, including Javier Latorre, Manolete and Merche Esmeralda and in 1997 created her own full-length work *The Claw and the Angel*. The production not only showcased her exceptionally expressive and articulate dancing but also her interest in forging a new dance theatre language for flamenco. The following year she formed her own company, with her husband Paco Jarana as music director, and her subsequent productions have included *5 Women 5* (2000), *Four Voices* (2004), *The Spindle of Memory* (2006), *Signs and Wonders* (2007), and *Rain* (2009). Her company tours internationally. In 1997 she was featured in the Mike Figgis documentary *Flamenco Women* and also appeared in his 2002 film *Hotel*. She is recipient of numerous awards.

⊕ SEE WEB LINKS
- Personal and company website for Yerbabuena

Yermolayev, Alexei (Aleksei) (b St Petersburg, 23 Feb. 1910; d Moscow, 12 Dec. 1975) Soviet dancer, choreographer, and teacher. He studied at the Leningrad Ballet School with Vladimir Ponomarev, graduating in 1926 after just five years. He joined GATOB (later the Kirov) as a soloist where his exceptional virtuosity did much to expand the boundaries of male technique. He particularly excelled in the modern repertory, creating roles in Lopukhov's *The Ice Maiden* (1927) and in Lopukhov, Ponomarev, and Leontiev's *The Red Poppy* (1929). In 1930 he moved to the Bolshoi Ballet as principal, creating lead roles in Vainonen's Moscow version of *The Flames of Paris* (1933), *Mirandolina* (1949), also Tybalt in Lavrovsky's Moscow version of *Romeo and Juliet* (1946), Severyan in Lavrovsky's *The Stone Flower* (1954), and Yevgeny in Zakharov's *The Bronze Horseman* (1949). He danced the role of Tybalt in the Soviet film of *Romeo and Juliet* (1954). He retired from dancing in 1958 but from 1960 until his death he remained at the Bolshoi as teacher and coach. From 1968 to 1972 he was also artistic director of its school. He made his first major ballet in 1939, *Nightingale* (with Lopukhov, mus. M. Kroshner), for the Byelorussian Theatre of Opera and Ballet in Minsk, where he also made his last ballet, *Burning Hearts* or *Fiery Hearts* (mus. V. Zolotarev), in 1955.

YMHA The Young Men's (and Young Women's) Hebrew Association. Situated on East 92nd Street in New York, it has since 1937 been the site of many important dance recitals. It is widely known as the 92nd Street Y.

York, Lila (b Syracuse, NY, 29 Nov. 1948) US dancer and choreographer. She trained in ballet as well as studying modern dance with Paul Sanasardo and at the Graham school, joining Paul Taylor's company in 1973. Here she created roles in many of Taylor's works, including *Cloven Kingdom*, *Esplanade*, *Mercuric Tidings*, *Sunset*, *Byzantium*, and *Lost, Found and Lost*. After leaving Taylor in 1985 she collaborated with Martha Clarke on *Vienna: Lusthaus* and appeared in her *The Garden of Earthly Delights*. From the mid-1980s she staged Taylor's works for other companies as well as working as a freelance choreographer, making *Celts* (1996) and *Ode to Joy* (1998) for Boston Ballet, *El Grito* (1997) for San

Francisco Ballet, *Psalms* (1992) for Pacific Northwest Ballet, *Sanctum* (1997) for Birmingham Royal Ballet, and *Rules of the Game* (1999) for Houston Ballet. Her 1995 ballet *Rapture*, which was originally made for the Juilliard Dance Ensemble, has entered the repertoire of several companies, including Pacific Northwest Ballet, Houston Ballet, Cincinnati Ballet, Atlanta Ballet, and Scottish Ballet. From 1989 to 1994 she was director of Pacific Northwest Ballet Offstage, a showcase for new choreography in Seattle.

Yoshida, Miyako (*b* Tokyo, 28 Oct. 1965) Japanese-British dancer. She trained in Tokyo and joined Britain's Royal Ballet School in 1983 after winning the Prix de Lausanne. In 1984 she joined Sadler's Wells Royal Ballet (later Birmingham Royal Ballet) where she was promoted to principal in 1988. In 1995 she joined the Royal Ballet at Covent Garden where her outstanding classical technique and musicality were primarily showcased in the 19th-century repertory. She also danced in works by Ashton, Bintley, and MacMillan and created roles in Wheeldon's *A Royal Ballet* (1998) and Corder's *Masquerade* (1999). In 2006 she joined Kumakawa's K Ballet in Japan while continuing to dance with the Royal. She gave her last performance at Covent Garden in 2010.

Youskevitch, Igor (*b* Piriatin or Pieyatin, Ukraine, 13 Mar. 1912; *d* New York, 13 Jun. 1994) Russian-US dancer and teacher. He left Russia aged 8 and was brought up in Belgrade where he studied engineering and additionally trained as a gymnast. In 1932 he competed in the Olympic Games and also began studying ballet with Xenia Grunt, who chose him as her stage partner. Further studies were with Preobrajenska in Paris and Anatole Vilzak and Alexandra Fedorova in New York. He made his debut as a professional dancer in 1934, dancing with the Ballets Russes de Paris, then with Woizikowsky's company (1935–6) and de Basil's Ballets Russes Australian tour (1936–7) and European tour (1937–8). From 1938 to 1944 he was a principal dancer with Serge Denham's Ballet Russe de Monte Carlo, where he created roles in Massine's *Gaîté parisienne* (1938), *Seventh Symphony* (1938), *Bogatyri* (1938), *Rouge et noir* (1939), *Vienna 1814* (1940), and *The New Yorker* (1940), in Nijinska's *The Snow Maiden* (1942), and *Ancient Russia* (1943), and Igor Schwezoff's *The Red Poppy* (1943). After war service with the US Navy, he danced with Massine's Ballet Russe Highlights in 1946 before joining (American) Ballet Theatre, the company that was his home for the next nine years. At ABT he created roles in Balanchine's *Theme and Variations* (1947), Tudor's *Shadow of the Wind* (1948), and Nijinska's *Schumann Concerto*

(1951). A distinguished and elegant stylist, with a romantic stage presence, he excelled in the 19th-century classics, especially renowned as Albrecht in *Giselle*. He made frequent guest appearances with Alicia Alonso, performing with her company in Cuba (later the National Ballet of Cuba) from its beginning in 1948 until 1960, and creating the role of Romeo in Albert Alonso's 1956 staging of *Romeo and Juliet* in Havana. From 1955 to 1957 he returned to the Ballet Russe de Monte Carlo as principal dancer and artistic adviser. He retired from the stage in 1962. With his wife, the dancer Anna Scarpova, he ran a school in Long Island, New York (1962–80), which also served as the base for his touring company, Ballet Romantique. From 1983 until his death he was artistic director of the New York International Ballet Competition. He appeared in Gene Kelly's 1956 film *Invitation to the Dance*. He was one of the most significant male dancers of 20th-century American ballet, and provided inspiration to many who followed including Erik Bruhn.

Yugoslavia The diverse cultural groups that made up the former Federal Republic of Yugoslavia developed their own traditional dance forms for many centuries before Yugoslavia was created in 1918. Western theatrical dance first became popular in the region in the late 19th century through visits from foreign artists like Pietro Coronelli's company (1876)—the first full ballet troupe to perform there. In 1894 a native ballet company was briefly established at the Croatian National Theatre in Zagreb, under the management of Stjepan Miletic. Early productions included *Coppélia* and *Giselle* and one of the first choreographers was the Budapest-born Erna Grondona. Following Miletic's departure at the turn of the century, however, classical dance was more or less abandoned until the 1920s when Russian dancers (such as Margarita Froman in Zagreb and Jelena Poljakova in Belgrade) helped to revitalize it, bringing the Russian repertoire to Yugoslav audiences and encouraging the development of native choreographers and the creation of ballets with native themes. *Froman staged the first Yugoslav ballet, *The Gingerbread Heart* (mus. Kresimir Baranovic), in Zagreb in 1924. From 1921 Belgrade had a ballet company attached to its opera house, and shortly thereafter a ballet school. However, many Yugoslavian dancers chose to make their careers abroad where the opportunities were greater. It was only after the Second World War, with the introduction of state funding, that a truly Yugoslav style emerged. Ballet companies were established around the country and full-length contemporary ballets added to the repertoire by choreographers such as Froman, the husband-and-wife-team of Pia and Pino Mlakar, Franjo Horvat, and Dimitrije Parlic.

y

The first major production after the war was Froman's *The Legend of Ochrid* (mus. Stevan Hristíc), staged in Belgrade in 1947. Based on a Macedonian folk tale, it became the most famous Yugoslavian ballet. Modern dance, meanwhile, began to make an impact during the 1930s, largely influenced by Rudolf Laban and students from his Berlin school. Ana Maletic was one of the pioneers of modern dance in Yugoslavia; in 1955 a state school, the Zagreb School for Rhythmics and Dance, was established due to her initiatives. Her daughter, Vera Maletic, opened the Studio of Contemporary Dance in Zagreb in 1962. In Yugoslavia, as elsewhere, the 1960s saw an explosion of experimental dance and a growth in the number of small modern dance companies. Following the breakup of Yugoslavia, the National Theatre in Belgrade has maintained its ballet company under the direction of Konstantin Kostjukov, performing a repertory of largely Yugoslav/Serbian work. Belgrade also hosts an international dance festival. The Serbian National Theatre in Novi Sad additionally has a ballet company directed by Ratislav Vaga, which performs a repertory dominated by the 19th-century classics.

Yuriko (orig. Yuriko Kikuchi; *b* San Jose, Calif., 2 Feb. 1920) US dancer, teacher, and choreographer. She grew up in Japan where she danced with the Konami Ishii Dance Company of Tokyo (1930–7) then moved back to the US where she became a member of the Dorothy S. Lyndall Junior Dance Group in Los Angeles (1937–41). After being interned in Arizona during the Second World War, she moved to New York to study with Martha Graham and from 1944 to 1967 was a member of Graham's company, thereafter appearing with it as guest artist. She created roles in *Canticle for Innocent Comedians* (1952), *Clytemnestra* (1958), and *Embattled Garden* (1958) and inherited many of Graham's own roles. From 1968 she had her own company, for which she choreographed many works. She also danced on Broadway as Eliza in Jerome Robbins's choreography for *The King and I* (1951–4) and in the film version (1956). She later returned to the Graham company to teach and assist in revivals of Graham's works; from 1991 to 1994 she was associate artistic director of the Graham company.

Zakharov, Rostislav (*b* Astrakhan, 7 Sept. 1907; *d* Moscow, 14 Jan. 1984) Soviet dancer, choreographer, ballet director, and teacher. He studied at the Petrograd State Ballet School (later the Leningrad Ballet School) with Pono-marev, and graduated in 1926. He joined the Kharkov Ballet, then the Kiev Ballet (1926–8) be-fore furthering his studies at the Leningrad Insti-tute of Theatrical Art, where he studied directing with Vladimir Soloviev, graduating in 1932. His first choreography was created for students at the School for Circus and Variety Actors, but in 1934 he was invited to join GATOB (later the Kirov) as dancer and choreographer. Here he choreo-graphed *The Fountain of Bakhchisarai* (mus. Asafiev, 1934), which became one of the most important ballets in the Kirov's repertoire and was subsequently staged by virtually every ballet company in the former Soviet Union. Its success was due in part to Zakharov's application of Sta-nislavsky's ideas about theatre to ballet, as well as to the power of its literary source (Pushkin's nar-rative poem). His subsequent work, *Lost Illusions* (mus. Asafiev, 1935), based on Balzac, was less acclaimed however. In 1938 he moved to the Bolshoi as choreographer and opera director, cre-ating *The Prisoner of the Caucasus* (mus. Asafiev, 1938), based on Pushkin, *Don Quixote* (mus. Minkus, 1940), *Taras Bulba* (mus. Soloviev-Sedoy, 1941), based on Gogol, *Cinderella* (mus. Prokofiev, 1945), and *Mistress into Maid* (mus. Asafiev, 1946), again based on Pushkin. For the Kirov, he additionally choreographed *The Daugh-ter of the People* (mus. Kreyn, 1947) and *The Bronze Horseman* (mus. Glière, 1949). His influ-ence, as a pioneer of new Soviet ballet, and espe-cially the genre of 'dram-ballet', was long-lasting although his critics complained about the lack of genuinely inventive dance in his productions. Za-kharov retaliated in print, frequently attacking young choreographers such as *Grigorovich and *Belsky, however his last ballet, *Into the Port Came Russia* (mus. Soloviev-Sedoy, 1964, the Kirov), was considered a total failure. He remained at the Bolshoi until 1958 and was addi-tionally artistic director of the Moscow Choreo-graphic School (1945–7) and head of the choreography department at the State Institute for Theatrical Art (the Lunacharsky Institute) in Moscow from 1946 until his death. Author of *The Art of the Choreographer* (Moscow, 1954), *Conver-sations on Dance* (Moscow, 1963), *The Choreogra-pher's Work with Dancers* (Moscow, 1967), *Notes of a Choreographer* (Moscow, 1976), and *On Dancing* (Moscow, 1977).

Zakharova, Svetlana (*b* Lutsk, Ukraine, 10 Jun. 1979) Russian-Ukranian dancer. She stud-ied dance, mostly folk, from the age of 6, then from 1989 to 1995 trained at the Kiev Choreo-graphic School, spending a final year at the Vaga-nova Academy. She possessed an exceptionally precocious talent, and while still a student danced several adult roles with the Mariinsky (then Kirov) including Queen of the Dryads in *Don Quixote*. Graduating into the company in 1996 she was promoted to principal the following year, coached primarily by Olga Moiseyeva. A tall and supple dancer—in the modern Russian mould—she danced most of the 19th-century ballerina roles, as well as 20th-century works by Balanchine, MacMillan, and others. In 2003 she moved to the Bolshoi and under the coaching of Semenyaka her dancing acquired a greater fluency and dra-matic range. She has subsequently created roles in several works, including the title role of Posso-khov's *Cinderella* (2006) and Medora in Ratmans-ky's staging of *Le Corsaire* (2007). She has also guested with many companies including American Ballet Theatre, Paris Opera Ballet, La Scala, Milan, and New National Theatre Ballet in Tokyo. She is recipient of numerous awards and titles including Golden Mask Award, Honoured Artist of Russia (2005), and People's Artist of Russia (2008).

(((●))) **SEE WEB LINKS**
- Official website for Svetlana Zakharova

Zaklinsky, Konstantin (*b* Leningrad, 28 May 1955) Russian dancer. He studied at the Lenin-grad Ballet School (Vaganova) with Abdurakh-man Kumysnikov, and graduated into the Kirov Ballet, in 1974. In 1980 he was promoted to prin-cipal, an outstanding danseur noble who excelled in the 19th-century classics although he also dis-played a flair for comedy. When Natalia Makarova danced her televised reunion with the Kirov Ballet in London in 1988, she chose Zaklinsky as her partner. He created roles in Vinogradov's *The Fairy of the Rond Mountains* (1980) and *The Knight in Tigerskin* (1985). He frequently appeared as an international guest artist, including with the Royal Ballet in London (1989–90). He retired from dancing in the late 1990s and now teaches. He appeared in a number of films, including *Tristan and Isolde* (1976), *Fouetté* (1986), and *Chapliniana* (1988). Gold medal Tokyo, 1984. He married the Kirov ballerina Altynai *Asylmuratova.

Zambelli, Carlotta (*b* Milan, 4 Nov. 1875; *d* Milan, 28 Jan. 1968) Italian dancer and teacher. She studied at the La Scala Ballet School, a pupil of Adelaide Viganò and Cesare Coppini, from 1884; further studies at the Paris Opera Ballet School with Rosita Mauri. She made her debut at the Paris Opera in 1894 and was promoted to étoile in 1898. She caused a sensation in 1896 when she executed fifteen fouetté turns—never seen before in Paris—in a divertissement from the opera *La Favorita*. She was the reigning ballerina of the Paris Opera from 1898 to her retirement in 1930. She created leading roles in Staats's *Namouna* (1908), *Javotte* (1909), *España* (1911), *Sylvia* (1919), *Taglioni chez Musette* (1920), and *Cydalise et le chèvre-pied* (1923), and in Nijinska's *Impressions de music-hall* (1927). She was a guest ballerina with the Mariinsky Theatre in St Petersburg in 1901, where she danced *Coppélia, Paquita,* and her first Giselle. She toured extensively, performing for the troops in the First World War. Following her retirement from the stage she became a senior teacher at the Paris Opera Ballet School, where she remained until 1955.

Zane, Arnie (*b* New York, 26 Sept. 1947; *d* New York, 30 Mar. 1988) US dancer and choreographer. He was a photographer when he met Bill T. *Jones and with him formed the American Dance Asylum, a collective based in Binghamton, New York (1974–6). In 1982, after touring as a duo, they formed the company Bill T. Jones/Arnie Zane and Dancers. Zane's stage partnership with Jones relied for effect on their striking physical contrast: Zane was short and white, and moved with an agitated energy; Jones was tall and black, and moved with a generous grace. Their duets, influenced by Jones's studies of Contact Improvisation, were athletic and to some extent autobiographical (they were partners off stage as well), and their work explored a wide range of issues, including racism, sexism, and religion. Among their creations were *Monkey Run Road, Blauvelt Mountain* (both 1979), *Valley Cottage* (1980), and *Secret Pastures* (1984). Zane and Jones also collaborated on *Ritual Ruckus* (*How to Walk an Elephant*) for the Ailey company in 1985. Following Zane's

premature death from an Aids-related illness, Jones continued to run their company.

Zelensky, Igor (*b* Labinsk, Krasnodar, 13 Jul. 1969) Russian dancer. He studied at the Tbilisi Ballet School with Chabukiani and then at the Vaganova Academy (the St Petersburg Ballet School) with Gennady Seliutsky. He joined the Kirov (Mariinsky) Ballet in 1988, and was promoted to principal in 1991. One of the newer breed of Russian male dancers, he combined a powerful classical technique with a curiosity for the 20th-century Western repertory. He developed his stylistic versatility through early guest seasons with the Berlin Opera Ballet (1990–1) and New York City Ballet (1992–7), where he performed more than 25 works by Balanchine, Robbins, and Martins. From 1996 he widened his repertory further partnering Darcey Bussell at the Royal Ballet in MacMillan ballets, and appearing as principal guest dancer at La Scala from 1999 and at Bayerisches Staatsballett (Bavarian State Ballet) from 2000. In 2001 he suffered a severe injury but returned to the stage to continue dancing with the Mariinsky, Royal Ballet, and NYCB, as well as heading his own small ensemble. In 2006 he was appointed director of the Novosibirsk State Ballet, for which he has subsequently staged *La Bayadère*. He is recipient of numerous prizes including the Gold Medal and the Grand Prix at the Paris International Competition, 1990.

Zero Degrees Dance-theatre production choreographed by Akram Khan and Sidi Larbi Cherkaoui, with music by Nitin Sawhney and designs by Antony Gormley. Premiered 8 Jul. 2005 at Sadler's Wells. The piece, a danced and spoken conversation between Khan and Cherkaoui, explores the borders that lie between countries, cultures, life, and death.

Zhao, Ruheng (*b* Feb. 1944) Chinese dancer and director. She trained at the Beijing Dance Academy from 1955 and danced with the National Ballet of China from 1960, a year prior to her formal graduation. She was rapidly promoted to principal roles but in 1972 was injured and forced to retire from the stage. During the next two decades she studied languages but also continued working with NBC fostering its education and cultural exchanges. In 1993 she was appointed deputy director, and director the following year, since when she created a modern identity for the company—revitalizing its classical repertory, for example with a staging of *Swan Lake* by Makarova; commissioning Chinese works such as *Raise The Red Lantern*; and initiating collaborations, for example with Akram Khan on *bahok* (2008). Her interest in expanding the Chinese dance scene expanded when she additionally took over artistic

Z

direction of the Tianqiao Theatre and introduced seasons of Western companies such as Pina Bausch. She retired at the end of 2008.

Zhdanov, Yuri (*b* Moscow, 29 Nov. 1925; *d* Moscow, 9 Apr. 1986) Soviet dancer and ballet director. He studied at the Bolshoi Ballet School, graduating in 1944 into the Bolshoi Ballet. He was promoted to principal in 1951 and was Ulanova's regular partner, starring with her in the Bolshoi Ballet film of Lavrovsky's *Romeo and Juliet* (1954). He also partnered Struchkova and Plisetskaya. He danced with the Bolshoi for 25 years and was then director of the State Ensemble of Classical Ballet in Moscow (1972–6), for which he choreographed *Francesca da Rimini* (mus. Tchaikovsky), among other works. He toured widely with his company to Europe. He was also a noted painter.

Ziggurat Modern dance in one act with choreography by Tetley, music by Stockhausen, designs by Baylis, and projections by Alan Cunliffe. Premiered 20 Nov. 1967 by the Ballet Rambert at the Cochrane Theatre in London with Chesworth, Curtis, Smith, Taylor, and Craig. Tetley's first created work for Rambert, it was inspired by the ancient Assyrian temple, and its rich associations with myth and religion.

Zollar, Jawole Willa Jo (*b* Kansas City, Mo., 21 Dec. 1950) US dancer, choreographer, and company director. She studied with Katherine Dunham, and gained a BA in dance from the University of Missouri at Kansas City as well as a Master of Fine Arts from Florida State University. In 1980 she moved to New York where she studied and performed with Dianne McIntyre (1980–3) before forming her company *Urban Bush Women in 1984. Its repertory of full-length dance theatre works, mostly by Zollar herself, have explored a range of issues affecting African-American women and include *Anarchy, Wild Women, and Dinah* (1986), *Heat* (1988), *Song of Lawino* (1988), *Praise House* (1990), *Batty Moves* (1995), *Bones and Ash: A Gilda Story* (1995), *Self Portrait* (1997), and the Bessie Award-winning *Walking with Pearl... Southern Diaries* (2005), based on the life of Pearl Primus.

Zorina, Vera (orig. Eva Brigitta Hartwig; *b* Berlin, 2 Jan. 1917; *d* 9 Apr. 2003) German-US dancer and actress. She studied dance with Tatiana and Victor Gsovsky in Berlin, making her stage debut at the age of 13 as a fairy in Max Reinhardt's production of *A Midsummer Night's Dream* (1930). She went to London in 1933 where she studied with Nikolai Legat and Marie Rambert. That same year she partnered Anton Dolin in the West End staging of *Ballerina*, a play by Lady Eleanor Smith with ballet interludes choreographed by Dolin. This led to an invitation to

join de Basil's Ballets Russes de Monte Carlo (1934–6), which is where Zorina acquired her stage name. In 1937 her performance as the temperamental Russian ballerina in the London staging of *On Your Toes*, brought her to the attention of US film and theatre producers. In 1938 she made her debut on Broadway dancing in *I Married an Angel* (1938) and *Louisiana Purchase* (1940), both of which were choreographed by Balanchine. She also signed a seven-year contract with Metro-Goldwyn-Mayer, which led to her performing in a string of film musicals, including *The Goldwyn Follies* (1938), *On Your Toes* (1939), *I Was an Adventuress* (1940), *Louisiana Purchase* (1941), *Star Spangled Rhythm* (1942), *Follow the Boys* (1944), and *Lover Come Back* (1946). During this period (1938–46) she was married to Balanchine who choreographed much of her dance material, and her extensive appearances did much to popularize ballet in the US. After her Hollywood contract expired, Zorina returned to the ballet stage, as a guest artist with Ballet Theatre (1943), but did not have much success. She did however make a new career as a narrator-performer of dramatic oratorios, including Honegger's *Joan of Arc at the Stake* (1948), Stravinsky's *Persephone* (1955), and Debussy's *Le Martyre de Saint-Sébastien*. She later worked as an opera director for the Santa Fe Opera, the New York City Opera, and the Norwegian Opera. She published her autobiography, *Zorina*, in New York in 1986.

Zucchi, Virginia (*b* Parma, 10 Feb. 1849; *d* Nice, 9 Oct. 1930) Italian dancer and teacher. She studied with Blasis and Lepri in Milan, making her debut in Varese in 1864. She danced throughout Italy and at La Scala (1874–6, 1882–3); also at the Berlin Opera (1876–8), the Royal Italian Opera at Covent Garden (1878), and Paris (1883). In 1885 she was invited to St Petersburg to appear at the relatively minor theatre, Kin Grust, and was so successful that she was transferred to the city's Mariinsky and Bolshoi theatres (1885–8). Russian audiences flocked to see her Italian-style virtuosity and although not a personal favourite of Petipa's, Zucchi was acclaimed for her performances in his ballets, including *La Fille mal gardée*, *La Fille du Pharaon*, *Esmeralda*, *Paquita*, and *Coppélia*. Her popularity helped to revitalize the public's interest in the ballet and she also helped in coaching students at the Imperial Ballet School. She danced in Moscow (1888) with her own company, and again in St Petersburg (1889 and 1892) but was otherwise in Europe, performing in Nice (1889, 1890) and at the Bayreuth Festival, where she produced the Venusberg scene in Wagner's *Tannhäuser* (1891). She made her debut at the Paris Opera in 1895 and performed for the last time in Milan in 1898. After retirement she opened a school in Monte Carlo.

Zurich Ballet The ballet company of the Zurich Opera House, like many similar institutions in Europe, has been historically constrained by the demands of opera productions. Comparatively few ballets were staged in Zurich during the 19th century and even after the new municipal theatre was opened in 1891 the repertory remained small, with just one ballet *Die Josephslegende* gaining significant success. In the 1930s Pino and Pia Mlakar, both former students of Rudolf *Laban, worked as ballet directors and expanded the repertory, with new works including *The Devil in the Village* (1935) and *The Ballad of Medieval Love* (1937), both with music by the Yugoslav composer Fran Lhotka. During the Second World War ballet activity virtually ceased and it was only with the appointment of Nicholas *Beriozoff as director in 1964 that the form was significantly re-invigorated. Beriozoff built up a repertory of 19th-century classics, with new works by himself and this momentum was sustained after his departure in 1971, by the management's invitation to *Nureyev to stage a new production of *Raymonda*. A succession of short-lived directorships however stalled the company's revival, until Patricia *Neary succeeded to the post in 1978. A former dancer with New York City Ballet, she added Balanchine works to the repertoire, along with Heinz Spoerli's celebrated production of *Giselle* (1980). She also oversaw a marked improvement in technical standards before leaving in 1985. Under the direction of Bernd Roger Bienert, the Zurich Ballet again came to prominence with the acquisition of *Hodson and Archer's reconstructions of Nijinsky's *Rite of Spring* and Jean Börlin's *Skating Rink*. However the company's most sustained period of growth in recent years was under Heinz *Spoerli. Appointed in 1996, Spoerli oversaw a major improvement in standards, in part through the restructuring of Zurich's associate ballet school and the formation of a junior ballet troupe to feed into the main company. He maintained the core classical repertory, with new productions including *La Sylphide*, and also acquired contemporary ballets from Kylián, van Manen, Forsythe, and others as well as choreographing many of his own including *Goldberg Variations*, *A Midsummer Night's Dream*, and *In Den Winden Im Nichts* (*Winds in the Void*, mus. Bach). In 2010 he was succeeded by Christian *Spuck. The company tours internationally.

(⊕) SEE WEB LINKS

• Website for Zurich Opera House with link to the ballet

Zvereff, Nicholas (*b* Moscow, 1888; *d* St Raphael, Jun. 1965) Russian-French dancer, ballet master, and teacher. He danced with Diaghilev's Ballets Russes (1912–26), appearing mostly in character roles. With his wife, the ballerina Vera *Nemchinova (they later divorced), he toured internationally. He was ballet director of the Kaunas Opera House (1930–6); soloist and ballet master of Blum's Ballets de Monte Carlo (1936–45); he reorganized the ballet company at the Théâtre de la Monnaie in Brussels (1952); and was ballet master of the Teatro Colón in Buenos Aires (1957–60). He had his own dance studio in Paris (1946–52). He also staged revivals of the Diaghilev repertoire at the Paris Opera Ballet and at La Scala, Milan.

Selected Bibliography and Further Reading

The following reference books have either proved invaluable in the writing of this dictionary or are recommended by the authors. An additional list includes key periodicals, magazines and websites that have not been included at the end of individual entries.

Anderson, Jack, *Dance* (New York: Newsweek, 1974).

——*The World of Modern Dance: Art without Boundaries* (Iowa City: University of Iowa Press, 1997).

Anderson, Zoe, *The Royal Ballet:75 Years* (London: Faber and Faber, 2006).

Au, Susan, *Ballet and Modern Dance* (London: Thames and Hudson, 1988).

Balanchine, George, and Mason, Francis, *Balanchine's Festival of Ballet*, i and ii (London: W. H. Allen, 1978); originally published as *Balanchine's Complete Stories of the Great Ballets* (Garden City, NY: Doubleday, 1954).

Banes, Sally, *Terpsichore in Sneakers: Post-Modern Dance* (Middletown, Conn.: Wesleyan University Press, 1987).

——*Dancing Women: Female Bodies on Stage* (London: Routledge, 1998).

Beaumont, Cyril W., *Complete Book of Ballets* (London: Putnam, 1951); *Supplement to Complete Book of Ballets* (London: Putnam, 1952).

Bland, Alexander, *The Royal Ballet: The First Fifty Years* (Garden City, NY: Doubleday, 1981).

Bremser, Martha, *Fifty Contemporary Choreographers* (London: Routledge, 1999).

Chazin-Bennahum, Judith, *The Ballets of Antony Tudor* (New York: Oxford University Press, 1994).

Chujoy, Anatole, and Manchester, P. W., *The Dance Encyclopedia* (New York: Simon and Schuster, 1967).

Clarke, Mary, *Dancers of Mercury: The Story of Ballet Rambert* (London: Adam and Charles Black, 1962).

——and Crisp, Clement, *London Contemporary Dance Theatre: The First 21 Years* (London: Dance Books, 1989).

——*Ballet: An Illustrated History* (London: Hamish Hamilton, 1992).

——and Vaughan, David, *The Encyclopedia of Dance and Ballet* (London: Pitman, 1977).

Copeland, Roger, and Cohen, Marshall, *What is Dance? Readings in Theory and Criticism* (New York: Oxford University Press, 1983).

Croce, Arlene, *Afterimages* (New York: Alfred A. Knopf, 1977).

——*Going to the Dance* (New York: Alfred A. Knopf, 1982).

——*Sight Lines* (New York: Alfred A. Knopf, 1987).

Denby, Edwin, *Dance Writings* (London: Dance Books, 1986).

Garafola, Lynn, *Diaghilev's Ballets Russes* (New York: Oxford University Press, 1989).

——(ed.), *Rethinking the Sylph: New Perspectives on the Romantic Ballet* (Middletown, Conn.: Wesleyan University Press, 1997).

Greskovic, Robert, *Ballet: A Complete Guide* (London: Robert Hale, 2000); first published in the USA in 1998 as *Ballet 101*.

Guest, Ivor, *The Romantic Ballet in Paris* (London: Sir Isaac Pitman and Sons, 1966).

——*The Ballet of the Second Empire* (Middletown, Conn.: Wesleyan University Press, 1974).

Guillot, Genevieve, and Prudhommeau, Germaine, *The Book of Ballet* (Englewood Cliffs, NJ: Prentice-Hall, 1976).

Häger, Bengt, *Ballets Suédois* (London: Thames and Hudson, 1990).

International Dictionary of Ballet, i and ii, ed. Martha Bremser (London: St James Press, 1993).

International Dictionary of Modern Dance, ed. Taryn Benbow-Pfalzgraf (Detroit: St James Press, 1998).

International Encyclopedia of Dance, founding editor Selma Jeanne Cohen (6 vols.; New York: Oxford University Press, 1998).

Jordan, Stephanie, *Striding Out* (London: Dance Books, 1992).

——*Moving Music* (London: Dance Books, 2000).

Jowitt, Deborah, *Time and the Dancing Image* (New York: William Morrow, 1988).

Jürgensen, Knud Arne, *The Bournonville Tradition: The First Fifty Years, 1829-1879* (2 vols.; London: Dance Books, 1997).

Kendall, Elizabeth, *Where She Danced* (New York: Knopf, 1979).

Kennedy, Michael, *Oxford Concise Dictionary of Music* (Oxford: Oxford University Press, 1996).

Kirstein, Lincoln, *Thirty Years: The New York City Ballet* (London: Adam and Charles Black, 1979).

——*Four Centuries of Ballet: Fifty Masterworks* (New York: Dover Publications, 1984).

Kochno, Boris, *Diaghilev and the Ballets Russes*, trans. from the French by Adrienne Foulke (New York: Harper and Row, 1970).

Koegler, Horst, *The Concise Oxford Dictionary of Ballet* (Oxford: Oxford University Press, 1987).

McDonagh, Don, *The Rise and Fall and Rise of Modern Dance* (New York: Outerbridge and Dienstfrey, 1970).

Macdonald, Nesta, *Diaghilev Observed: By Critics in England and the United States, 1911-1929* (London: Dance Books, 1975).

Mackrell, Judith, *Reading Dance* (London: Michael Joseph, 1997).

Newman, Barbara, *Striking a Balance* (New York: Limelight Editions, 1992).

Reynolds, Nancy, *Repertory in Review: 40 Years of the New York City Ballet* (New York: Dial Press, 1977).

——and Reimer-Torn, Susan, *In Performance: A Companion to the Classics of Dance* (New York: Harmony Books, 1980); republished as *Dance Classics: A Viewer's Guide to the Best-Loved Ballets and Modern Dances* (Pennington, NJ: A Cappella Books, 1991).

—— and McCormick, Malcolm, *No Fixed Points: Dance in the Twentieth Century* (Yale University Press, 2003).

Robertson, Allen, and Hutera, Donald, *The Dance Handbook* (Harlow, Essex: Longman, 1988).

Scholl, Tim, *Sleeping Beauty: A Legend in Progress* (Yale University Press, 2004).

Siegel, Marcia B., *The Shapes of Change: Images of American Dance* (Boston: Houghton Mifflin, 1979).

Souritz, Elizabeth, *Soviet Choreographers in the 1920s* (London: Dance Books, 1990).

Vaganova, Agrippina, *Basic Principles of Classical Ballet* (London: Adam and Charles Black, 1948).

Vaughan, David, *Merce Cunningham: Fifty Years* (New York: Aperture, 1997).

——*Frederick Ashton and his Ballets* (London: Dance Books, 1999).

Volynsky, A. *Ballet's Magic Kingdom: Selected Writings on Dance in Russia, 1911-1925* (Yale University Press, 2009).

Wigman, Mary, *The Mary Wigman Book*, ed. and trans. Walter Sorrell (Middletown, Conn.: Wesleyan University Press, 1975).

Wiley, Roland John, *Tchaikovsky's Ballets* (New York: Oxford University Press, 1985).

——*A Century of Russian Ballet* (New York: Oxford University Press, 1990).

——*The Life and Ballets of Lev Ivanov* (New York: Oxford University Press, 1997).

Wilson, G. B. L., *A Dictionary of Ballet* (London: Adam and Charles Black, 1974).

Woodall, James, *In Search of the Firedance: Spain through Flamenco* (London: Sinclair-Stevenson, 1992).

Woodcock, Sarah C., *The Sadler's Wells Royal Ballet, Now the Birmingham Royal Ballet* (London: Sinclair-Stevenson, 1991).

Periodicals
Ballet Review, New York
Ballett International/Tanz Aktuell, Seelze, Germany
Dance Chronicle, New York
Dance Europe, London
Dance Magazine, New York
Dance Theatre Journal, London
Dancing Times, The, London

Biographies and Autobiographies (also see published works listed within individual entries)
The following is a selected list of recently published and/or readily available works of biography and autobiography, concentrating on those we consider most useful as factual sources.

Abeele, Maarten Vanden, *Pina Bausch* (Edition Plume, 1996).

Acocella, Joan, *Mark Morris* (New York: Farrar Straus Giroux, 1993).

Ailey, Alvin, *Revelations: The Autobiography of Alvin Ailey*, with A. Peter Bailey (New York: Birch Lane Press, 1995).

Ashley, Merrill, *Dancing for Balanchine* (New York: Dutton, 1984).

Buckle, Richard, *Nijinsky* (London: Weidenfeld and Nicolson, 1971).

——*Diaghilev* (London: Weidenfeld and Nicolson, 1979).

——*George Balanchine: Ballet Master*, in collaboration with John Taras (London: Hamish Hamilton, 1988).

Cohen, Selma Jeanne, *Doris Humphrey: An Artist First* (Middletown, Conn.: Wesleyan University Press, 1972).

Daneman, Meredith, *Margot Fonteyn* (London: Viking, 2004).

Danilova, Alexandra, *Choura* (London: Dance Books, 1987).

Duncan, Isadora, *My Life* (New York: Theatre Arts Books, 1928, repr. 1955).

Farrell, Suzanne, *Holding on to the Air* (New York: Summit Books, 1990).

Fokine, Mikhail, *Memoirs of a Ballet Master*, trans. Vitale Fokine, ed. Anatole Chujoy

(London: Constable and Company, 1961).

Fonteyn, Margot, *Autobiography* (New York: Warner Books, 1977).

García-Márquez, Vicente, *Massine: A Biography* (London: Nick Hern Books, 1996).

Graham, Martha, *Blood Memory* (New York: Doubleday, 1991).

Guest, Ivor, *Jules Perrot: Master of the Romantic Ballet* (New York: Dance Horizons, 1984).

Jowitt, Deborah, *Jerome Robbins: His Life, His Theatre, His Dance* (Simon and Schuster, 2004).

Karsavina, Tamara, *Theatre Street* (London: Constable and Company, 1948).

Kavanagh, Julie, *Secret Muses: The Life of Frederick Ashton* (London: Faber and Faber, 1996).

——*Rudolf Nureyev: The Life* (London: Fig Tree/Penguin, 2007).

Laban, Rudolf, *A Life for Dance*, trans. Lisa Ullmann (New York: Theatre Arts Books, 1975).

Leonard, Maurice, *Markova the Legend* (London: Hodder and Stoughton, 1995).

Lifar, Serge, *Ma vie*, trans. James Holman Mason (London: Hutchinson, 1970).

Limón, José, *José Limón: An Unfinished Memoir*, ed. Lynn Garafola (Middletown, Conn.: Wesleyan University Press, 1998).

Mackrell, Judith, *Bloomsbury Ballerina: A Life of Lydia Lopokova* (London: Weidenfeld and Nicolson, 2008).

Mannoni, G., *Maurice Béjart* (Paris, 1991).

Mille, Agnes de, *Dance to the Piper* (Boston: Little, Brown, 1952).

——*And Promenade Home* (Boston: Little, Brown, 1958).

——*The Life and Work of Martha Graham* (London: Hutchinson, 1992).

Money, Keith, *Anna Pavlova: Her Life and her Art* (London: Collins, 1982).

Newman, Barbara, *Antoinette Sibley: Reflections of a Ballerina* (London: Hutchinson, 1986).

Nijinska, Bronislava, *Early Memoirs*, trans. and ed. Irina Nijinska and Jean Rawlinson (New York: Holt, Rinehart

and Winston, 1981; Durham, NC: Duke
University Press, 1992).

Parry, Jan, *Different Drummer: The Life of
Kenneth MacMillan* (London: Faber and
Faber, 2009).

Percival, John, *Theatre in my Blood: A
Biography of John Cranko* (London:
Herbert Press, 1983).

Perlmutter, Donna, *Shadowplay: The Life of
Antony Tudor* (New York: Viking, 1991).

Rambert, Marie, *Quicksilver* (London:
Macmillan, 1972; repr. 1983).

St Denis, Ruth, *An Unfinished Life* (New
York and London: Harper and Bros.,
1939; repr. Brooklyn: Dance Horizons,
1979).

Scheijen, Sjeng, *Diaghilev: A Life* (London:
Profile Books 2009).

Shawn, Ted, *One Thousand and One Night
Stands*, with Gray Poole (New York:
Doubleday, 1960; repr. New York:
DaCapo Press, 1979).

Shelton, Suzanne, *Divine Dance: A
Biography of Ruth St Denis* (Garden City,
NY: Doubleday, 1981).

Smakov, Gennady, *The Great Russian
Dancers* (New York, 1984).

Solway, Diane, *Nureyev: His Life* (London:
Weidenfeld and Nicolson, 1998).

Sorley Walker, Kathrine, *Ninette de Valois:
Idealist without Illusions* (London: Dance
Books, 1998).

Taylor, Jeffery, *Irek Mukhamedov: The
Authorized Biography* (London: Fourth
Estate, 1994).

Taylor, Paul, *Private Domain* (New York:
Alfred A. Knopf, 1987).

Tharp, Twyla, *Push Comes to Shove* (New
York: Bantam Books, 1992).

Valois, Ninette de, *Come Dance with Me*
(London: Hamish Hamilton, 1957; repr.
Dublin: Lilliput Press, 1992).

Zola, Meguido, *Karen Kain: Born to Dance*
(Danbury, 1983).

Websites

(⊕) **SEE WEB LINKS**

This is a selection of the many sites currently
in operation. Due to the nature of the sites,
accuracy cannot be guaranteed but all offer useful
links.

Ballet.co
Online UK magazine features links to reviews
and interviews, with items on ballet history and
professional blogs

Ballet Talk!
Online discussion group with useful emphasis on
shared information

Critical Dance
Online magazine and discussion forum

Culturekiosque: Dance
Online European dance magazine

Cyberdance
Carries links to many international companies
and their websites

Dance Current
Online Canadian dance magazine

Dance Insider
Useful source for US dance reviews

Dance Magazine
Online version of the print magazine

Oxford Paperback Reference

The Oxford Dictionary of Dance
Debra Craine and Judith Mackrell

Over 2,500 entries on everything from hip-hop to classical ballet,
covering dancers, dance styles, choreographers and composers,
techniques, companies, and productions.

'A must-have volume ... impressively thorough'

Margaret Reynolds, *The Times*

The Oxford Guide to Plays
Michael Patterson

Covers 1,000 of the most important, best-known, and most popular
plays of world theatre.

'Superb synopses ... Superbly formatted ...
Fascinating and accessible style'

THES

The Concise Oxford Dictionary of Music
Michael Kennedy and Joyce Kennedy

The most comprehensive, authoritative, and up-to-date dictionary of
music available in paperback.

'clearly the best around ... the dictionary that everyone should have'

Literary Review

Oxford Paperback Reference

The Oxford Dictionary of Art & Artists
Ian Chilvers

Based on the highly praised *Oxford Dictionary of Art*, over 2,500 up-to-date entries on painting, sculpture, and the graphic arts.

'the best and most inclusive single volume available, immensely useful and very well written'

Marina Vaizey, *Sunday Times*

The Concise Oxford Dictionary of Art Terms
Michael Clarke

Written by the Director of the National Gallery of Scotland, over 1,800 terms cover periods, styles, materials, techniques, and foreign terms.

A Dictionary of Architecture and Landscape Architecture
James Stevens Curl

Over 6,000 entries and 250 illustrations cover all periods of Western architectural history.

'splendid ... you can't have a more concise, entertaining, and informative guide to the words of architecture.'

Architectural Review

'excellent, and amazing value for money ... by far the best thing of its kind.'

Professor David Walker

OXFORD